SIXTEENTH EDITION

The Kovels' Antiques & Collectibles Price List

A guide to the 1983–1984 market for professionals, dealers, and collectors

Ralph & Terry Kovel

Illustrated

CROWN PUBLISHERS, INC.
New York

*To Alberto—welcome to the family—and of course
to Lee and Kim*

Books by Ralph and Terry Kovel

Dictionary of Marks—Pottery and Porcelain
A Directory of American Silver, Pewter and Silver Plate
American Country Furniture 1780–1875
The Kovels' Antiques & Collectibles Price List
The Kovels' Bottle Price List
The Kovels' Collector's Guide to American Art Pottery
Kovels' Organizer for Collectors
The Kovels' Price Guide for Collector Plates, Figurines,
    Paperweights, and Other Limited Editions
The Kovels' Illustrated Price Guide to Royal Doulton
The Kovels' Illustrated Price Guide to Depression Glass
    and American Dinnerware
Kovels' Know Your Antiques
Kovels' Know Your Collectibles
The Kovels' Book of Antique Labels
The Kovels' Collectors' Source Book

Inquiries should be addressed to Crown Publishers, Inc., One Park
Avenue, New York, New York 10016

Printed in the United States of America

Published simultaneously in Canada by General Publishing Company
Limited

Library of Congress Catalog Card Number: 72-84290

ISBN: 0-517-55028-8

10 9 8 7 6 5 4 3 2 1

Introduction

Inflation is down, the economy is improving, and the antiques market is enjoying new interest and added buyers. The major auction galleries in the large cities seem to have solved many of the reorganization and expansion problems that plagued them through 1982, and sales are brisk. Once again, the old rule seems true—the top-quality items in evey field of collecting bring top prices and sell quickly. Silver has come back up in price, Oriental rugs are still less than the peak prices they brought a few years ago, but Chinese rugs are becoming good sellers. Carnival glass is down slightly, but Heisey, Cambridge, Fenton, and the other hand-finished Depression-era glasswares are rising in value. Toys, especially dolls, continue to be setting price records.

Specialized shows seem to be helping the collector find the desired rarities in limited fields of collecting. Doll and toy shows, glass shows, paper and advertising shows, comic book and sports memorabilia shows can be found nationwide.

Record prices are always of interest. Top price for the decorative arts this year was $3,041,000 for a royal suit of armor. Furniture records include $121,000 for an American federal satinwood tambour lady's desk, $385,000 for a Chippendale mahogany blockfront carved desk, $286,000 for a Chippendale mahogany circular card table, and $275,000 for a Chippendale carved mahogany hairy-paw foot side chair. A Duncan Phyfe sofa sold for $66,000, a Salem four-poster bed for $44,000, and a Greene and Greene vitrine for $39,500. Glass records included a Columbia-eagle flask in cobalt blue for $32,000, a Tiffany stained-glass window for $99,000, and a Frank Lloyd Wright stained-glass door for $110,000. A silver castor by John Coney sold for $55,000. Less decorative, but equally interesting, items brought record prices. A Sebastian Miniature group of the Nativity sold for $3,800, a Millard Fillmore printed check brought $2,860, a ship's journal from the whaleship *Susan* sold for $82,000, a tinware lantern for $990, and an Imperial Chinese robe for $14,300. Toy records include $38,000 for an A. Marque doll, $1,800 for Amos 'n Andy toys, and $850 for a Buck Rogers' twenty-fifth-century rocket ship by Marx.

The prices listed in the remainder of this book are reports of the more general antiques market. All the record prices we have mentioned were set at auction. The other pieces that are listed in this book are *retail prices* asked when the items were offered in shops, sales, antiques shows, flea markets, or mail-order listings. They represent the *actual asking price* of the item, although it is possible that the buyer negotiated the final price to a slightly lower figure. *None of these prices is an estimate.* If a range of price is given, it is because we have found at least two of the identical items offered for sale at different places. The computer records the various prices and prints the high and low figures. It does not estimate. The range may represent two sales or as many as eight sales. Note that price ranges are only found in categories like "pressed glass," where the identical item can be accurately identified.

If you are selling your antiques and collectibles, do not expect to get the retail value unless you are a dealer. Wholesale prices for antiques can be from 20 to 50 percent less than retail. Remember that the antiques dealer, like any store owner, must make a profit or go out of business.

The High Museum of Art
1280 Peachtree Street, NE
Atlanta, Georgia 30309
(404) 892-3600

In the fall of 1983 the High Museum of Art in Atlanta, Georgia, opened a new facility, which included in the exhibits the Virginia Carroll Crawford Collection of American Decorative Arts, 1825–1917. The High Museum has had a small collection of eighteenth-century American furniture and regional Southern furniture. Some European ceramics were also exhibited. It was decided in 1978 that American decorative arts should be added. One hundred and forty objects can be seen. They range from woodwork, metalwork, glass, and ceramics to textiles. Pieces were selected for their high quality and positive documentation of the craftsmen or firms. Most of the pieces date from the last half of the nineteenth century, including pieces made by John Henry Belter, Alexander Roux, Samuel Kirk, Tiffany and Company, and Herter Brothers. The wide range of decorative styles range from the classical look of the 1830s to the Rococo Revival Victorian and the Arts and Crafts work of the twentieth century.

The museum is located near downtown Atlanta on the new MARTA rapid rail system. It is open Tuesday through Saturday, 10:00 A.M. to 5:00 P.M. and Sunday, noon to 5:00 P.M. The general admission is $2.00; students and senior citizens, $1.00; children under 12, 50¢. There are restaurants and hotels nearby. Ample parking is available in the underground Arts Center lot behind the museum.

The American decorative arts in the collection are of interest to the serious student of antiques as well as the casual collector who wants to learn more about the best that was available. The Virginia Carroll Crawford Collection has been assembled since 1979. It is further proof that museum-quality pieces of American decorative arts are still available.

How to Use This Book

There are just a few simple rules to follow in using this book. Each listing is arranged in the following manner: CATEGORY (such as pressed glass, silver, or furniture); OBJECT (such as vase, spoon, table); DESCRIPTION (which includes as much information as possible about size, age, color, and pattern). Glass is the only exception to this rule, and it is listed CATEGORY, PATTERN, OBJECT, DESCRIPTION. All items are presumed to be in good condition, undamaged, unless otherwise noted.

Several special categories were formed to make a more sensible listing of items possible. "Kitchen" and "tool" include special equipment. Since it would be unreasonable to expect the casual collector to know the proper name for each variety of tool, such as an "adze" or a "trephine," we have lumped them together in the special categories. Other special categories are "commemorative," "store," "nautical," and "railroad." The index can help you locate items in these sections.

This book has several idiosyncrasies of style that must be noted before it can be used properly. The final prices are compiled by a computer, and the machine has dictated several strange rules. Everything in the book is listed alphabetically according to the IBM alphabetizing system. This means that words such as "mt." are alphabetized as "M-T," not as "M-O-U-N-T." Another peculiarity of the machine alphabetizing is that all numerals come after all letters, thus 2 comes after z. A quick glance at a listing will make this clear, as the alphabetizing is consistent throughout the book. We have not listed any pieces priced over $9,999.

We have made several editorial decisions that affect the use of the book. A bowl is a bowl and not a dish unless it is a special type of dish, such as a pickle dish. A butter dish is a "butter" and a celery dish is a "celery." A salt dish is called a "salt" to differentiate it from a saltshaker. A toothpick holder is called a "toothpick." It is always a "sugar and creamer," never a "creamer and sugar." Where one dimension is given, it is the height of the piece, or if the object is round, the dimension is the diameter. Height of a picture is listed before width. Glass is clear unless a color is indicated.

This book does not include price listings of fine art paintings, books, comic books, stamps, coins, and a few other categories that are covered in specialized books. Prices for collectors' editions, bottles, Royal Doulton, Depression glass, and American dinnerware are included although they are more completely reported in *The Kovels' Price Guide for Collector Plates, Figurines, Paperweights, and Other Limited Editions; The Kovels' Bottle Price List; The Kovels' Illustrated Price Guide to Royal Doulton;* and *The Kovels' Illustrated Price Guide to Depression Glass and American Dinnerware.*

Several categories such as "milk glass" and "bottles" include special reference numbers. These numbers refer the reader to the most widely known books about the category. When these numbers appear, the name of the special book is given in the paragraph heading. All these numbers take the form "B-22," "McK-G-11," and so forth. The letter is the author's initial; the number refers to a picture in the author's book.

All black-and-white pictures in *The Kovels' Antiques & Collectibles Price List* are of antiques sold during the past year. The prices are as reported by the seller. Each piece pictured is listed with the word "Illus" as part of the description. Pictures are placed as close to the price listing as is possible.

All of the color pictures are from the newly opened wing of the High Museum of Art, Atlanta, Georgia. Because these pieces are part of a museum collection and are not offered for sale in the open market, no prices are given.

There have been many misinformed comments about how this book is written. We *do* use the computer. It alphabetizes, ranges prices, sets the type, and does many other time-consuming jobs. Because of the computer, the book can be produced faster than a price book printed by conventional methods. The last entries in the book are added in June; the book is available in October at bookstores. This is about six months faster than would be possible any other way. But it is human help that finds the prices and checks the accuracy. We read everything in each book at least twice, sometimes more. We edit from 100,000 entries (prices recorded in all parts of the country) to the 45,000 entries found in this book. We remove incorrect data, correct the spelling, write the category headings, and decide on the new categories to be included. We sometimes make errors. Collector-specialists often make suggestions for changes in the way various categories are listed to make them more useful to the collector. This type of suggestion is always welcome. For example, this year for the first time, Hummel figurines are listed by number instead of alphabetically. We *do not* ask dealers or collectors to price items for the book.

We have tried to make the entries in this book as easy to find as possible. Every entry is listed alphabetically and there is also a full index. One problem we cannot solve is that of language. Several antiques terms have two meanings such as "Sheffield," "Salopian," and "snow baby." Be sure to read the paragraph headings to know the meaning we used. All the category headings are based on the language of the average person at an average show, and we use terms like "mud figures" even if that is not technically correct.

All prices included in this book are reports, not estimates. This means that somewhere in the United States, between June 1982 and June 1983, the antiques described were offered for sale at the prices we have listed. A few prices are from auctions, but most are from shops and shows. The prices have been taken from sales in all parts of the country, and variations may be caused by geographic differences in pricing. Every price has been checked for accuracy, but we cannot be responsible for any errors that may have occurred. We welcome any suggestions for future editions of this book but cannot answer letters asking for advice or appraisals.

Ralph M. Kovel,
American Society of Appraisers, Senior Member
International Society of Appraisers

Terry H. Kovel,
American Society of Appraisers, Senior Member
International Society of Appraisers

Update for Prices Available

Each year *The Kovels' Antiques & Collectibles Price List* is completely rewritten. Every entry is new because of the rapidly changing antiques market. The only way so complete a revision can be accomplished is by using a computer, making it possible to publish the bound book a few months after the last price is received.

Yet many price changes occur between editions of *The Kovels' Antiques & Collectibles Price List*. Important sales produce new record prices each day. Inflation, the changing price of silver and gold, and the international demand for some types of antiques influence sales in the United States.

You can keep up with developments from month to month. *Kovels on Antiques & Collectibles* is a nationally distributed, illustrated newsletter, published monthly. It covers prices, how to buy or sell, special interest antiques, refinishing and first aid for your possessions, marks, book reviews, and other pertinent antiques news.

Information about the newsletter is available from the authors at P.O. Box 22200-K, Beachwood, Ohio 44122.

Picture Acknowledgments

Auctions by Theriault; Richard Bourne; Bowers & Ruddy Galleries, Inc.; Charlton Gallery; Christie's; William Doyle Galleries, Inc.; Richard and Eileen Dubrow; DuMouchelle Art Galleries; Robert C. Eldred Co., Inc.; Garth's Auctions, Inc.; Gene Harris Antique Auction Center, Inc.; Willis Henry Auctions; Hesse Galleries; Hollander Gallery; Hutchens & Caldwell; James D. Julia; Kurt Krueger; Mapes Gallery; Morton's Auction Exchange; Numismatic and Antiquarian Service Corporation of America; Phillip's; Lloyd Ralston; Bob, Chuck, & Rich Roan, Inc.; Robert W. Skinner, Inc.; R. M. Smythe & Co.; Sotheby's; Adam A. Weschler & Son; Weiss Auctioneers; Richard W. Withington, Inc.; Wolf's Shaker Gallery; Woody Auction Co. All photographs in the color inserts have been provided by the High Museum of Art, Atlanta, Georgia.

Almaric Walter made pate-de-verre glass under contract at the Daum glassworks from 1908 to 1914. He started his own firm in Nancy, France, in 1919. Pieces made before 1914 are signed "Daum, Nancy" with a cross. After 1919 the signature is "A. Walter Nancy."

A.WALTER, Figurine, Climbing Moth, Pate De Verre, Signed, 4 X 3 1/2 In.Wide 1750.00
Figurine, Loie Fuller, Pate De Verre, Signed, 11 1/2 In. 3950.00

ABC plates, or children's alphabet plates, were popular from 1780 to 1860. The letters on the plate were meant as teaching aids for children learning to read. The plates were made of pottery, porcelain, metal, or glass.

ABC, Bowl, Baby Bunting, Poem, Child & Dog 50.00
Bowl, Feeding, Girl, Green Dress, Clown Doll, Boy, Dog, Marked, 7 In. 35.00
Jug, Animals With Letters, Child's, White 25.00
Plate, Archery, Glass 90.00
Plate, Archery, Staffordshire, 5 1/4 In. 85.00
Plate, Baby Bunting & Pigs, K.T.K. 45.00
Plate, Baseball Caught On Fly, Glass 90.00
Plate, Behold Him Rising From The Grave, Glass 85.00
Plate, Boy & Girl Rolling Hoops, Tin, 3 In. 150.00
Plate, Bulldog In Green, My Face Is My Fortune, Staffordshire, 7 1/4 In. 45.00
Plate, Catch It Carlo, Glass 75.00
Plate, Chickens, Gold Trim, 7 In. 40.00
Plate, Children, Beehive & Verse, Staffordshire, 7 In. 35.00
Plate, Christmas Eve, Santa On Chimney, 6 In. 65.00
Plate, Clock Center, Glass, 6 In. 35.00
Plate, Crusoe Finding The Footprints 85.00
Plate, Desert Scene, 2 Riders, Horses, Staffordshire, 7 In. 45.00
Plate, Donkey & Foal, Glass 65.00
Plate, Electrical Building, Columbian Exposition, 7 1/4 In. 59.00
Plate, Emma, Intaglio Center, ABC's Around Rim, Vaseline Glass 85.00
Plate, Feeding, Boys Playing Leapfrog, 1905 Stamp 37.00
Plate, Fishing Elephant, Glass 70.00
Plate, Girl In Center, Higbee 52.00
Plate, Hare Coursing, Brown Transfer, 8 1/2 In. 95.00
Plate, Hens, Rooster 35.00
Plate, Hi-Diddle-Diddle, Tin .... 15.00 To 50.00
Plate, Kitten 65.00
Plate, Little Boys At Marbles Play, Glass 65.00
Plate, Little May Children's Tea Set, Glass, 21 Piece 195.00
Plate, N On Front, Ironstone, 6 In. 35.00
Plate, Nations Of The World, Venetian, Ceramic, 7 1/4 In. 28.00
Plate, New Pony, Glass 65.00
Plate, Organ Grinder With Children, Stippled Ground, 7 1/2 In. 72.00
Plate, Parrot, Children, Dog, & Pretty Poll Verse, 5 3/8 In. 58.00
Plate, Raised ABC Border, Transfer Center, C.1845 .... 72.00
Plate, Red Riding Hood, Wolf Center, ABC Edge, 6 In. 27.50
Plate, Scene Of Leaping Lamb, Embossed Alphabet Border, 8 1/2 In. 22.00
Plate, Sign Language Border, Aynsley 35.00
Plate, Silks & Satins, Glass 80.00
Plate, Sioux Indian Chief 65.00
Plate, The Drive, Glass 65.00
Plate, The Walk, Glass 65.00
Plate, Tired Of Play, Glass 75.00
Plate, Village Blacksmith, Glass 65.00
Plate, Village Scene At Ferry Dock, C.1890, 7 1/2 In. 35.00
Plate, Who Killed Cock Robin, 7 3/4 In. 37.00
Plate, Who Killed Cock Robin, 8 In. 69.00
Plate, Wild Bear With Cubs, Polychrome, English, 7 1/2 In. 65.00
Plate, 3 Carts, In Dresses & Suits, Teaching School, Germany, 7 In. 40.00
Plate, 3 Children, Watching Beehive, Verses, 6 1/4 In. 85.00
Tea Set, Little May, 21 Piece 195.00
Tea Set, Nursery Rhyme Characters On Plates, Child's, 6 Piece 135.00

Abingdon Pottery was established in 1934 by Raymond E. Bidwell as the Abingdon Sanitary Manufacturing Company. The company made art pottery. The factory ceased production in 1950.

ABINGDON, Basket, White Star 10.00
  Bookends, Dolphin, Green 27.50
  Bookends, Horsehead, Pink 22.50
  Bowl, Console, Impressed Mark, Oval, 14 1/2 In. 14.00
  Bowl, Console, Salmon, Flowers, Gold Trim, 15 X 5 1/2 In. 35.00
  Bowl, Hibiscus Pattern, Cameo Pink 30.00
  Bowl, Scalloped, Acanthus Handles, Oval, Blue, 14 In. 14.00
  Box, Cigarette, Elephant, No.60, ... 45.00
  Candleholder, Scroll, Blue, Pair 10.00
  Candlestick, Beige, Gold Trim 10.00
  Candlestick, Pink, Double, 5 In. 7.00
  Console Set, Scroll Bowl, Candleholders, Pink 20.00
  Cookie Jar, Money Bag 35.00
  Cookie Jar, Pineapple 22.00
  Cookie Jar, Schoolgirl's Face, Glasses & Pigtails 18.00
  Cornucopia, Double, Pink 8.00
  Planter, Shell Shape, High Gloss, Beige, 11 1/2 In. 12.00
  Planter, White, Scalloped, 10 3/4 In. 6.00
  Vase, Deer & Woods, Side Handles, Green, 9 3/4 In. 30.00
  Vase, Double, Cornucopia, Rose, 5 1/2 X 11 In. 14.00
  Vase, Flesh Orange, 4 In. 6.00
  Vase, Silver Deposit Deer & Woods, Side Handles, 9 3/4 In. 30.00
  Vase, Turned-In Rim, Footed, Gold Sticker, Marked, 9 In. 20.00
  Vase, Yellow, Slant Top, Scalloped Rim, Footed, 10 3/4 In. 8.00
  Vase, 2 Shells, Blue, 7 In. 10.00

ADAMS
ENGLAND

Adams china was made by William Adams and Sons of Staffordshire, England. The firm was founded in 1769 and is still working.

  ADAMS, see also Flow Blue

ADAMS, Bowl, Pedestal, Underplate, Yellow, Blue, Green, White 40.00
  Bowl, Yellow, Blue, Green, White, Octagon 65.00
  Plate, Sweet China Oranges, Green, 8 In. 40.00
  Vase, Cries Of London, Lady With Donkey, 10 In. 88.00
  ADVERTISING, see Store

Agata glass was made by Joseph Locke of the New England Glass Company of Cambridge, Massachusetts, after 1885. A metallic stain was applied to New England Peachblow and the mottled design characteristic of agata appeared.

AGATA, Cruet 800.00
  Tumbler, New England 945.00
  Tumbler, Wild Rose 385.00

Akro agate glass was made in Clarksburg, West Virginia, from 1932 to 1951. Before that time the firm made children's glass marbles. Most of the glass is marked with a crow flying through the letter A.

AKRO AGATE, Ashtray, Standing, Lighter, 22 In. 48.00
  Ashtray, Swirl Shell, Orange 3.00
  Box, Marbles, Tin, Children & Marbles, 4 X 8 In. 30.00
  Box, Partitioned, Marble Bag With 100 Marbles, 13 X 8 In. 75.00
  Cup, Child's, Green, Signed 10.00
  Game, Chinese Checkers, Marbles, Original Box 16.00
  Jar, Powder, Orange 10.00

Lamp, Custard With Caramel Swirl, Shade, Pair 150.00
Lemonade Set, Child's, Green, 7 Piece 55.00
Luncheon Set, Child's, Chiquita Pattern, Green & White, 17 Piece 62.50
Planter, Daffodils, Orange & White 12.00
Planter, Ribbed, Green & White Swirls, 6 X 3 1/4 X 2 1/2 In. 12.00
Plate & Saucer, Dragon Design, Green, 3 In. 7.00
Plate, White, 3 In., Set Of 4 .... 5.50
Tea Set, American Maid Pattern, Open Handles, Boxed, 11 Piece 150.00
Tea Set, Child's, Concentric Ring, Green & White Opaque, 16 Piece 58.00
Tea Set, Child's, Jade Transoptic, Stippled Band, 8 Piece 85.00
Tea Set, Child's, Topaz, Transparent, Stippled Band, Covered 135.00
Teapot, Blue 8.00
Tumbler & Saucer, Block Optic 6.00
Vase, Fan, Green, 5 In. 9.00
Vase, Fan, Orange, 5 In. 9.00
Vase, Green, Marble, 5 In. 6.00

ALABASTER, Figurine, Woman, Seated, 19th Century, 15 1/2 In. .... *Illus* 400.00

Alabaster, Figurine, Woman,
Seated, 19th Century, 15 1/2 In.

ALBUM, PHOTOGRAPH, see Photography, Album

Alhambra

Alhambra is a pattern of tableware made in Vienna, Austria, in the twentieth century. The geometric designs are applied in gold, red, and dark green.

ALHAMBRA, Bowl, Design Inside & Out, Signed, 3-Footed 55.00
Nappy, Gold Handle, Signed 45.00
Relish, Elevated Looped Handle, 7 5/8 In. 50.00

ALUMINUM, Ashtray, Siesta Scene, Everlast, 5 1/4 In. 3.50
Ashtray, 6 Incised Flowers, Buenilum, 6 1/2 In. 3.50
Basket, Autumn Bouquet, Handled, Design Aluminum, 13 1/2 In. 10.00
Basket, Bread, Raspberry, Farberware, 12 In. 9.00
Basket, Floral, Crimped Edge, 8 1/2 In. 14.00
Basket, Wild Rose, Handled, Brillianton, 8 In. 5.00
Bowl, Bamboo, Everlast, 10 In. 6.00
Bowl, Bouquets & Bows, Lehman, 13 1/2 In. 9.00
Bowl, Grapes, Hammerkraft, 11 1/2 In. 7.00
Bowl, Ruffled & Crimped, 8 1/2 In. 7.00
Bowl, Ruffled, Leaf Scroll, 14 In. 7.00

Butter, Wooden Knob On Cover 5.00
Candlestick, Petaled, Everlast, 5 1/2 In., Pair 8.00
Candy, Blossoms & Bows, Footed, Covered, Rodney Kent, 6 In. 8.00
Candy, Leaf Cluster, Footed, Covered, Continental, 7 In. 10.00
Case, Cigarette, Pocket, Presto Pak, Army Insignia 6.00
Casserole, Leaf & Floral, Candle Warmer, Everlast, 10 1/4 In. 18.00
Cheese & Cracker, Covered Dish, Tulip, Rodney Kent, 12 In. 10.00
Coaster, Dog .... .75
Coaster, Ducks In Flight .... .50
Coaster, Tulips, Rodney Kent, Set Of 7 .... 7.00
Coffeepot, Black Wood Handle, Club Aluminum Ware 14.00
Creamer, Everlast 4.00
Dish, Arch & Swirl, Canterbury Arts, 9 1/2 In. 4.50
Dish, Candy, Dogwood Bouquet, Footed, Hand Finished, 7 In. 5.00
Dish, Crimped, Flowers, Leaf, Coil Handled, Farber, 7 1/2 In. 3.50
Dish, Daffodils, Handwrought, 20 In. 9.00
Dish, Tulip, Basket Handled, Crimped, Rodney Kent, 7 In. 5.00
Ice Bucket, Insulated, Covered, Hammerkraft 13.00
Ice Bucket, Roses, 2-Handled, Covered, Everlast 12.00
Juicer, Foley, Fits On Top Of Glass 2.50
Lazy Susan, Chrysanthemum, Continental, 18 In. 14.00
Lazy Susan, Daffodils, Glass Insert, Federal Silver, 14 In. 12.00
Lazy Susan, Fruits, Flowers, Cromwell, 14 1/2 In. 12.00
Lazy Susan, Poppy, Wheat, Daffodil, Handwrought, 14 1/2 In. 12.00
Lazy Susan, Scalloped, 8-Petal Flowers, Buenium, 14 1/2 In. 12.00
Lighter, Cigarette, Advertising, Wood Of Texas, Plastic Center 5.00
Percolator, Miro, 3 Quart 15.00
Pitcher, Water, Tulip Design 8.00
Server, Fruits & Flowers, Handle, Cromwell Mark, 8 3/4 In., 4 Piece .. 9.00
Silent Butler, Fruits & Flowers, Cromwell 8.00
Silent Butler, Pinecone, Needles, Everlast 8.00
Silent Butler, Tulips, Rodney Kent 8.00
Sugar & Creamer, Chrysanthemum, Covered, Continental 12.00
Teakettle, Wagner, 2 Quart 14.00
Tray, Acorns, Handled, Continental, 15 In. 10.00
Tray, Bread, Basket Handle, Chrysanthemum, Continental, 13 X 7 In. .. 10.00
Tray, Bread, Tulip, Rodney Kent 8.00
Tray, Chrysanthemum, Applied Leaves On Handles, 13 In. 16.00
Tray, Chrysanthemum, Handled, Continental, 17 In. 12.00
Tray, Crimped, Handled, Cromwell, 10 X 12 In. 9.00
Tray, Engraved Jack-In-The-Pulpits, Florman, 10 X 5 In. 10.00
Tray, Flower Center, Handled, Continental Mark, 5 Part, 12 In. 10.00
Tray, Flower Center, Handled, 14 1/2 In.Diam. 10.00
Tray, Flowers, Porcelain Plate Center, Handled, Farberware, 14 In. ... 10.00
Tray, Flying Ducks, Aluminum Design, 13 X 9 In. 10.00
Tray, Fruits & Flowers, Hand Finished, 14 In. 10.00
Tray, Fruits & Flowers, Keystone, 16 1/2 In. 10.00
Tray, Leaf Handles, Patent July 30, 1946, Continental, 18 X 12 In. 12.00
Tray, Pinecone, Wendell August Forge, 14 In. 20.00
Tray, Pines, Mountains, Handled, 11 1/2 X 9 In. 10.00
Tray, Vegetables, Keyston, 10 X 13 In. 7.00
Tray, 2-Tier, Dogwood, Raspberry, Everlast 8.00

Amber glass is the name of any glassware with the proper yellow-brown shade.
It was a popular color after the Civil War.

AMBER GLASS, Berry Bowl, Master, Leaf & Flower 98.00
Bottle, Clown, Hollow Stopper 85.00
Butter, Block & Lattice, Covered 85.00
Compote, Covered, Amber, 6 In. 695.00
Compote, Daisy & Button With Crossbars, Open 40.00
Cordial Set, Leaf Design Allover, 13 Piece 225.00
Eyecup, Finger Holds, Stem, 8-Panel 210.00

Figurine, Cat On Hamper, Greentown 165.00
Mug, Child's, Bar Handle, Hobnail, Amber, 3 1/2 In. 38.00
Pitcher, Blown Into Mold, Cherry Pattern, 10 In. 135.00
Pitcher, Turned-Down Trefoil Top, Reeded Handle, 8 1/4 In. 65.00
Salt, Hexagonal Cut Sides, Rayed Base 10.00
Sugar, Block & Lattice, Covered 70.00
Table Set, Block & Lattice, 4 Piece 265.00
Tray, Daisy & Button, Handled, Square, 9 1/2 X 11 In. 20.00
Tumbler, Daisy & Button With Crossbars, Rayed Base 22.00
Water Set, Block & Lattice, 5 Piece 175.00
      AMBERETTE, see Pressed Glass, Klondike

*Amberina is a two-toned glassware made from 1883 to about 1900. It was
patented by Joseph Locke of the New England Glass Company. The
glass shades from red to amber.*
   AMBERINA, see also Baccarat; Bluerina; Plated Amberina
AMBERINA, Bottle, Embossed Pattern, Place For Wine Label, Blown, 11 In. 135.00
Bowl, Cranberry To Amber, Fluted, Flowers, Blue, Yellow, & Pink 300.00
Bowl, Dewdrop Pattern, Handled, 9 1/2 In. 75.00
Bowl, Diamond Optic, 4 In. 35.00
Bowl, Inverted Thumbprint, 5 In. 52.50
Bowl, Ruffled, 5 X 2 1/2 In. 140.00
Bowl, Swirl Pattern, Ruffled, 5 X 3 1/2 In. 195.00
Butter Chip 50.00
Butter, Coin Optic Pattern, Celery Stalk Finial, 5 In. 100.00
Carafe, Rigaree 300.00
Cream Plate, Daisy & Button, Scalloped Corners, 5 3/4 In. 110.00
Creamer, Inverted Thumbprint, Squatty, Amber Handle, 5 3/4 In. 375.00
Cruet, Inverted Thumbprint, 3-Way Top, Amber Handle & Stopper 175.00
Cruet, Salt & Pepper Set, Pairpoint, Handled Holder 575.00
Cruet, Vinegar, Swirl Design, Amber Stopper, 5 In. 225.00
Cup, Punch, Amber, Handle, Polished Pontil .... 90.00 To 110.00
Cup, Punch, Diamond-Quilted, Amber Handle, 5 1/2 In. .... 65.00 To 125.00
Cup, Punch, New England, Baby Thumbprint, 2 3/4 In. 125.00
Decanter, Swirl, Bubble Stopper, Florals, Gold Ground, 8 1/2 In. 225.00
Dish, Cheese, Inverted Thumbprint, Amber Knob, 9 X 7 In. 350.00
Dish, Inverted Thumbprint, Covered, 9 In.Diam. 175.00
Figurine, Buddha, Solid, 6 X 4 In. 65.00
Finger Bowl, Diamond-Quilted, Tricornered, Pinched Top, 2 1/8 In. 195.00
Finger Bowl, New England, Ruffled Top 195.00
Jar, Mustard, Pewter Lid & Spoon, Marked, 2 3/4 In. 485.00
Lamp, Hanging, Inverted Thumbprint, Pear Shape 260.00
Mug, Enameled Baby Inverted Thumbprint, Reverse, 3 In. 135.00
Mug, Inverted Thumbprint, Amber Handle, 2 3/4 X 2 1/2 In. 75.00
Pitcher, Baby Thumbprint, Amber Threaded Handle 375.00
Pitcher, Clear Handle, Trifoil Lip, 2 1/2 In. 135.00
Pitcher, Coin Dot, Square, 9 In. 195.00
Pitcher, Coin Optic Pattern, Amber Celery Stalk Handle, 8 In. 200.00
Pitcher, Diamond-Quilted Design, Amber Handle, 8 1/2 In. 350.00
Pitcher, Diamond-Quilted, New England Glass Co., 8 1/2 In. 325.00
Pitcher, Hobnail, 4-Sided Neck, Applied Handle, 7 1/2 In. 99.50
Pitcher, Melon Ribbed, 13 In. 45.00
Pitcher, Paneled Effect, Squared Amber Handle, 7 3/4 In. 195.00
Pitcher, Pontil Mark, 11 In. 145.00
Pitcher, Trefoil Lip & Clear Handle, 2 1/2 In. .... 115.00 To 135.00
Salt & Pepper 150.00
Saltshaker, Honeycomb, Inverted Thumbprint, Pewter Top, 3 1/2 In. 115.00
Spooner, Diamond-Quilted 95.00
Syrup, Silver Plate Underplate, Graduated Color 5000.00
Syrup, Underplate, Plated 5500.00
Tankard, Amber Handle, 4 X 6 3/4 In. 375.00
Tieback, Curtain, Flower Form, Pair 115.00
Toothpick, Daisy & Button, Footed, Flint 210.00

Toothpick, Fuchsia .... 225.00 To 250.00
Tumbler, Baby Inverted Thumbprint, Reverse, 4 In. 130.00
Tumbler, Baby Thumbprint 55.00
Tumbler, Diamond, Deep Fuchsia, Red Shading, 3 1/2 In. 85.00
Tumbler, Mt.Washington 135.00
Tumbler, Reversed, Jeweled, Flowers, Leaves, 4 3/4 In. 75.00
Tumbler, Swirl 120.00
Vase, Amber Coil Trim, Coin Gold Flowers & Leaves, 14 1/2 In. 295.00
Vase, Baby Inverted Thumbprint, Fluted, Ruffled Top, 5 In. 120.00
Vase, Basket Weave Pattern, Ruffled Top, 9 3/4 In. 145.00
Vase, Birds, Butterfly, Limbs, Flowers, 7 In. 295.00
Vase, Inverted Thumbprint, Applied Amber Fluting, Amber Base 225.00
Vase, Jack-In-The-Pulpit, 6 1/2 In. 65.00
Vase, New England, Ribbed Effect, 4 In. 75.00
Vase, Paneled Optic 35.00
Vase, Roman Gold Lilies, Footed, Flared, 12 3/4 In. 450.00
Vase, Ruffled Top, 8 In. 130.00
Vase, Swirl Pattern, Fluted Top, 11 1/4 In. 400.00
Vase, Swirl, Amber Feet & Rigaree Around Neck, Florals, 11 1/2 In. 275.00
Vase, Swirl, Calla Lily Shape, Cranberry To Olive Amber, 13 In. 195.00
Vase, Swirl, Cranberry To Golden Amber, Ruffle Top, Pair, 10 1/8 In. 345.00
Vase, Swirl, Enameled, Signed, 10 In. 300.00
Vase, 17 In. At Middle, Ground Rim, 9 1/2 In. 135.00
Water Set, Inverted Thumbprint, Amber Handle, 5 Piece 325.00
Water Set, Jeweled, Reversed, Clear Handle, Flowers, 7 7/8 In., 5 Pc. 550.00

*American Encaustic Tiling Co. of Zanesville, Ohio, worked from 1879
to 1935. Decorative glazed, embossed, and faience tiles were made.*

AMERICAN ENCAUSTIC TILING CO., Tile, Commemorative, Woman With Wreath, 1899 .. 40.00
Tile, Torches, Garlands, 6 X 11 In., Set Of 4 .... 65.00
Tile, 5-Petal Flower, 6 X 5 1/2 In. 5.00

*Amethyst glass is any of the many glasswares made in the proper dark purple
shade. It was a color popular after the Civil War.*

AMETHYST GLASS, Ashtray, Triangular, 8 In. 12.00
Bowl, Flower, Oblong, 9 1/2 X 4 1/2 In. 6.00
Bowl, Flower, Round, 6 In. 8.00
Bowl, Flower, Square, 5 3/4 In. 7.00
Bowl, Scalloped, 7 1/2 X 1 1/2 In. 38.00
Creamer, Inverted Thumbprint, Clear Handle, Fluted, 4 1/2 In. 85.00
Cruet, Optic, Original Stopper 95.00
Eyecup, Finger Hold, 1 1/2 X 1 3/4 In. 255.00
Finger Bowl, Diamond Pattern, Amber, 5 1/4 In. 60.00
Jar, Bulbous, Swirled Clear Finial, 6 X 11 In. 25.00
Jar, Puff, White Floral Design, Hinged Cover 95.00
Mantel Set, 2 Vases, Bowl, Enameled Leaves, Bowl, 7 1/2 In. 595.00
Pitcher, Bulbous, 7 1/2 In. 25.00
Pitcher, Clear Applied Handle, 11 In. 48.00
Pitcher, Inverted Bubble, Crimp Top, Crystal Handle, 11 In. 150.00
Plate, Flattened Diamond, 10 1/2 In. Square 16.00
Plate, Handled, 10 1/2 In. 10.00
Rose Bowl, Lacy Top, Ground Pontil, 4 1/2 In. 88.00
Vase, Bud, Flowers, Ruffled, Flared Top, 10 In., Pair 95.00
Vase, Fluted Top, Double V Handle, 8 3/4 In. 62.50
Vase, Fluted, 10 In. 10.00
Vase, Ipswich, 6 3/4 In. 60.00
Vase, Ruffled Rim, 6 X 8 In. 18.00
Windowpane, Sculptured Flowers, Addison, 9 7/8 X 5 In. 85.00

AMOS & ANDY, Music, Sheet, Theme Of Radio Program, Check & Double Check 18.00

Puzzle, Lightnin', Brother Crawford, & Kingfish, At O.K. Hotel 75.00
Tablet, Picture On Cover 10.00
Toy, Fresh Air Taxi, Tin, Windup, Original .... 395.00 To 750.00
  AMPHORA, see Teplitz
  ANDIRON AND RELATED FIREPLACE ITEMS, see Fireplace

ANIMATION ART, Cel, Alice In Wonderland, Cheshire Cat, 1951, 15 X 11 In. 220.00
 Cel, Cinderella & Prince Dancing 175.00
 Cel, Doc Holding Lantern, 8 X 8 In. 935.00
 Cel, Don Donald, Donald Serenading Donna, 1937, 8 X 8 In. 495.00
 Cel, Dumbo Taking A Bath, 8 X 7 In. 1320.00
 Cel, Fantasia, Ostrich Ballerina, 11 X 9 In. 192.00
 Cel, Figaro Stalking Fly, 1939, 4 X 5 In. 380.00
 Cel, Grumpy Admiring Himself, 1937, 6 X 8 In. 330.00
 Cel, Jiminy Between 2 Pipes, 1939, 11 X 8 In. 990.00
 Cel, Jiminy Resting In Ashtray, 3 X 3 In. 395.00
 Cel, Jiminy, Pinocchio, 1939, 9 X 7 In. 660.00
 Cel, Little Hiawatha, Hiawatha Hunting Rabbit, 8 X 8 In. 330.00
 Cel, Mother Goose Goes Hollywood, Charlie McCarthy 880.00
 Cel, Pinocchio, Figaro & Celo Smiling, Fishbowl, 9 X 7 In. 412.00
 Cel, Pinocchio, Foulfellow & Giddy, 1939, 9 X 7 In. 412.00
 Cel, Pinocchio, Jiminy In Leaking Bubble, 6 X 7 In. 605.00
 Cel, Pinocchio, Jiminy Underwater, Seahorse, 1939, 8 X 9 In. 660.00
 Cel, Pinocchio, Marionettes, 1939, 7 X 7 In. 192.00
 Cel, Saludos Amigos, Jose Playing Concertina, 7 X 7 In. 440.00
 Cel, Snow White, All 7 Dwarfs, 1937, 7 X 5 In. 1650.00
 Cel, Snow White, Chipmunks, Deer, 8 X 7 In. 825.00
 Cel, Snow White, Doc, Sneezy, Happy, Dopey, 9 X 7 In. 550.00
 Cel, Snow White, Dopey Sitting On Log, 1937, 9 X 7 In. 275.00
 Cel, Snow White, Doves, 1937, 8 X 8 In. 1210.00
 Cel, Snow White, Grumpy Sitting On Barrel, 1937, 5 X 7 In. 385.00
 Cel, Snow White, Queen, Casket, Shows Heart, 7 X 8 In. 2475.00
 Cel, Snow White, Sleepy Yawning, 8 X 7 In. 247.00
 Cel, Society Dog Show, Dachshund, Owner Look Alike, 8 In. 220.00
 Cel, The Beach Picnic, Donald Riding Water Horse, 9 X 9 In. 412.00
 Cel, The Country Cousin, Abner Saying Goodbye, 8 X 8 In. 330.00
 Cel, The Pointer, Mickey Greeting Pluto, 1939, 10 X 8 In. 605.00
 Cel, The Pointer, Mickey, Pluto Embracing, 10 X 8 In. 1320.00
 Cel, The Pointer, Pluto, Bird On His Tail, 1939, 8 X 7 In. 495.00
 Cel, Ugly Duckling, Watching A Frog, 1931, 8 X 6 In. 137.00
  APOTHECARY JAR, see Bottle, Apothecary
  APPLE PEELER, see Kitchen, Peeler, Apple

ARCHITECTURAL, Backbar, Barber, Milk Glass Counter, 3 Beveled Mirrors, 16 Ft. 1500.00
 Backbar, Barber, Single Station, Milk Glass Top, Mirror, 6 Ft. 600.00
 Backbar, Cigarette Store 1785.00
 Backbar, Leaded Windows & Mirrors, Mahogany, 7 Ft. 10 In. 7750.00
 Backbar, Mirror, Columns & Carvings, Golden Oak, 1890, 8 Ft. 6000.00
 Backbar, Pine, 10 Ft. 550.00
 Booth, Telephone, Brownell, Peru, Ind., Double Wall, 1915, Oak 1200.00
 Booth, Telephone, Oak, Raised Panels Inside & Out, C.1920 .... 700.00
 Cabinet, Apothecary, 1860s, Glass Labels & Pulls, 2-Section 600.00
 Cabinet, Medicine, C.1900, Golden Oak 100.00
 Cage, Elevator, Otis, Wrought-Iron, 5 X 5 X 10 Ft. 1200.00
 Column, Base Diam. 30 In., Tapering To 28 In.Top, 22 Ft. 500.00
 Desk, Front, Hotel, Pigeonholes, Marble Top, C.1900, 5 X 4 Ft. 1000.00
 Door, Bifold, Leaded, Oak & Clear, 3 X 7 Ft. 300.00
 Doorbell, Taylor, 1860, Embossed Swivel, Porcelain Knob, Brass 25.00
 Doorknob & Latch Lock, Porcelain, Complete 12.50
 Doorknob, Passage Set, Sandwich Glass, Set 32.00
 Doorknob, Victorian, Engraved Design, Bronze, Set 38.00
 Fan, Ceiling, Emerson, Wooden Blades 100.00
 Fence, 5 Square Posts, Urn Top, Cast Iron, 132 Ft. X 38 In. 1500.00
 Fencing, 3 Ft.Gate & 3 Posts, Cast Iron, 128 Ft. X 27 In. 1300.00

Figure, Court House, 1890s, Zinc, 10 Ft. 3500.00
Gazebo, Wood, Octagonal, Arches, Painted Tin Roof, 7 Ft. 1320.00
Holder, Tumbler, Wall, Wire 5.00
Mantel, Pierced Lotus & Dragon Terminals, Wooden, 5 Ft. 5 In. 247.00
Mirror, Backbar, Carved Wooden Frame 2000.00
Ornament, Oriental, Horned Dragon, Blue & Red Paint, 53 In. 200.00
Post Office Front, Dual Teller Windows, 56 Boxes, 1900s 7000.00
Shelf, Italy, Putti Bust, Shoulder Wings, 17 X 19 In. 175.00
Sink Bathtub, Hip Rails, C.1880 .... 95.00
Store Case, Candy, Lift Top, Glass & Oak 155.00
Toilet Tank, Oak 65.00
Window Vent, Federal, Circular, Scalloped Rim, 32 In. 110.00

 Arequipa Pottery was produced from 1911 to 1918 by the patients of the Arequipa Sanitorium in Marin County Hills, California.

AREQUIPA, Vase, Black, Glaze, Trail Mark, 3 1/2 X 3 In. .... 100.00 To 135.00
    Vase, Blue & Gray, 6 X 5 1/2 In. 195.00
    ARGY-ROUSSEAU, see G. Argy-Rousseau

ARITA, Bowl, Overall Landscape Scene, Petals, 19th Century, 11 1/4 In. 330.00
    Dish, Flowering Peonies Center, Scroll Band, 19th Century, 22 In. 247.00

Art Deco, or Art Moderne, is a style started at the Paris Exposition of 1925, characterized by linear, geometric designs.All types of furniture and decorative arts, jewelry, book bindings, and even games were designed in this style.

ART DECO, Ashtray, Figural, Full-Length Nude, Cast Metal, Brown, 13 In. 80.00
    Ashtray, Fish, Open-Mouthed, 4 1/2 In. 15.00
    Ashtray, Standing, Iron, Nude Emerging From Lily, 22 In. 370.00
    Ashtray, Standing, Posed Nude, Outstretched Arms, 22 1/2 In. 225.00
    Blotter, Desk, Brass & Copper Corners 12.00
    Bookends, Birds, Silver On Bronze, Onyx Base, 10 1/2 In. 100.00
    Bookends, Clowns Sitting, Metal, 5 1/4 X 5 1/4 In. 45.00
    Bookends, Holly & Berries, Iron 15.00
    Bookends, Kneeling Nudes, Gun Metal Gray 30.00
    Bookends, Nude Seated Man, Black, 7 1/2 In. 58.00
    Bookends, Penguin, Steel Base, White, 4 1/4 In. 50.00
    Bookends, Ram's Head, Gold Finish 35.00
    Bookends, Woman's Body 20.00
    Bottle, Perfume, Crystal, Geometrical Body, Stopper, Crystal, 7 In. 50.00
    Bottle, Perfume, Green, Leaf Stopper, 6 3/4 In. 65.00
    Bottle, Perfume, Swirled Design, Metal Top, 4 X 2 1/2 In. 15.00
    Box, Mirrored, Blue 57.50
    Brooch, Oval, Malachite, Checkered Enameling, 2 1/2 In. 50.00
    Bust, Christ & Mary, Metal On Blue Mirrors, Wall Hanging, Pair 25.00
    Candlestick, Gold Gilt, White Metal, Tapered, 4 1/4 In. 20.00
    Chandelier, Chrome Supports, Pink Glass, Pebble Design, 3-Light 60.00
    Compact, Pearl Top, Gold Metal 12.00
    Compote, Yellow Flashed, Clear Floral Design, Black Trim, 12 In. 14.00
    Cordial Set, Cranberry To Clear, Geometric Banding, 8 In. 180.00
    Dresser Plateau, Cobalt Glass, Grecian Lady, Greyhound Logo 45.00
    Figurine, Airplane On Empire State Building, 18 In. 2500.00
    Figurine, Dancing Couple, Claire Volkhart, 1913, 13 1/2 In. 375.00
    Figurine, Egyptian Dancer, Ivory Body, 12 In. 295.00
    Figurine, Nudes, Kneeling, Facing Glass Globe 165.00
    Flower Frog, Frolicking Nude Woman, 12 In. 50.00
    Frame, Picture, Mirrored, Blue 49.00
    Frame, Picture, Standing, Black Marble Base, Brass Arms, 14 X 9 In. 100.00
    Inkwell, Bronzed, Footed, Key Design, Shakespeare Center, 10 In. 115.00
    Inkwell, Brown Veined, Onyx Base, Glass Insert 85.00

Jar, Dresser, Frosted Glass, Blue Metal Top	40.00
Lamp, Bronzed, Snake Charmer Holding Lamp, Marked	150.00
Lamp, Floor, Black Metal Base, Hexagonal Shade	60.00
Lamp, Girl Seated On Pedestal, Leaves, Roses, 14 1/2 In., Pair	350.00
Lamp, Gold Washed, Kiwi Bird, Onyx Plinth, 9 In.	55.00
Lamp, Gray-White Translucent Glass, Pyramid Style, 4 In.	30.00
Lamp, Lady, Elevated Legs, Green Ball Shade, Wired, 19 In.	180.00
Lamp, Nude Dancer, On Wedding Cake, Amber Glass Base, 18 In.	250.00
Lamp, Sculptural, Seated Nude, Amethyst Glass Globe, 8 X 7 In.	275.00
Lamp, Ship, Iridescent Black Base, Chrome Sails	65.00
Lamp, Table, Figural, Nude Dancer, Blue Accent, 9 1/2 In.	175.00
Lamp, Table, Opaque White & Pink, Reed Design	5.00
Lamp, 2-Arm, Calcite Shade	325.00
Letter Opener, Celluloid	12.00
Mirror, Chrome Ship, Blue	35.00
Mirror, Hand, 14 In.	12.00
Mirror, Pocket, Lady's, Blue Beveled Glass, Attached Lipstick	20.00
Money Clip, Raised Aztec God Design	25.00
Nude, Marble Base, Metal, 5 In.	45.00
Opener, Letter, Advertising, Paul's Barber Shop, N.Y., 6 In.	12.00
Pendant, Magnifying Glass, 14K White Gold, 3 Diamonds	290.00
Picture, Silhouette, Black, Orange, Butterflies, 3 In.	22.00
Pitcher, Milk, Gilt & Floral Design, French, 6 1/2 In.	90.00
Plate, Cake, Floral Shape, Yellow & White, Chrome Trim, 12 In.	20.00
Vase, Crystal, Florals, Pastel Colors, Marked Grosz, 8 In.	100.00
Vase, Dancing Figures, Yellow, 8 1/2 In.	33.00
Vase, Opalescent Green, Nude Dancing, 9 In.	39.00

Art glass means any of the many forms of glassware made during the late nineteenth century or early twentieth century. These wares were expensive and production was limited. Art glass is not the typical commercial glass that was made in large quantities, and most of the art glass was produced by hand methods.

ART GLASS, see also separate headings such as Burmese; Nash; Schneider; etc.

ART GLASS, Basket, Amber, Rope Handle, Blue Threading Top	78.00
Basket, Blue, Reeded Handled, Fluted Top, 4 X 3 In.	48.00
Basket, Gold, Wishbone Handle, Yellow Opaque Overshot	150.00
Basket, Multicolor, Thorn Handle	160.00
Bowl, Hanky, Diamond-Quilted, White Opalescent, 6 X 6 In.	135.00
Bowl, Ruffled, Applied Strawberry, Blue To Opalescent, 6 X 5 In.	110.00
Bride's Basket, Pears & Leaves, Pink Inside, Silver Plate Frame	295.00
Candlestick, Blue, Iridescent	160.00
Perfume, Atomizer, Frosted, Pink Glass, Pedestal Foot, 5 In.	35.00
Pitcher, Diamond, Pink To Dark Pink, Clear Handle, 4 In.	50.00
Pitcher, Water, White Design, Pink Cased	165.00
Rose Bowl, Dark Pink Blending To Light, 8-Crimp, 4 1/2 In.	95.00
Shade, Lamp, Gold Iridescent, Ruffled, 5 3/4 In., Pair	70.00
Shaker, Sugar, Blown Twist, Blue, Opalescent	45.00
Shaker, Sugar, Parian Swirl, Green, Opaque, Design	45.00
Shaker, Sugar, White Quilted Phlox, Pink Floral Design	45.00
Vase, Birds, Handled, Textured Ground, Signed Ver-Art, 12 1/2 In.	650.00
Vase, Flower Form, Iridescent Orange, Blue, Green, Ruffled, 13 In.	500.00
Vase, Frosted Figure, Yellow, Rose Ground, French Cameo, 5 1/4 In.	235.00
Vase, Jack-In-The-Pulpit, Gold Swirls, Cranberry Fluting, 9 In.	85.00
Vase, Rose & Green Iridescent, Footed, 10 X 6 In.	200.00
Vase, Threading Throughout, Signed Louis Auriel, 4 1/2 In.	72.50

Art Nouveau, a style characterized by free-flowing organic design, reached its zenith between 1895 and 1905. The style encompassed all decorative and functional arts from architecture to furniture and posters.

ART NOUVEAU, see also Furniture; various Glass categories, etc.

ART NOUVEAU, Bowl, Poppy Design, Shallow, 6 In.	68.00

Buckle, Multicolored Flower & Leaves 85.50
Button, Sterling, Floral Design, Marked, Set Of 5 .... 75.00
Charger, Profile Of Woman, Gold Ground, 16 In. 420.00
Chest, Lift Top, Stile Feet, C.1900, Brass-Mounted, 36 X 20 In. 250.00
Clip, Green, Blue, Yellow, Orange, Spring Hinged, 2 X 3 In. 60.00
Desk, Lap, Wood, Lady's Face In Copper 95.00
Hair Receiver, Floral 45.00
Knife, Butter, Woman & Flower Design, Reed & Barton 20.00
Mirror, Hand, Grapes, Leaves, 6 In. 40.00
Mirror, Hand, Lady's, Brass Floral Frame 125.00
Paper Clip, Desk, Brass Inlaid Wood, Vine Design 95.00
Tray, Card, Girl Feeding Carp, 22K, Pewter, 6 X 12 In. 285.00
Tray, Desk, Seminude, Green Patina 45.00
Vase, Gold, Handled, Signed Silver Craft, 12 In. 28.00
Vase, Gray, Full Figure Nude, Flowing Hair, 9 In. 135.00
     ART POTTERY, see under factory name

AURENE

Aurene glass was made by Frederick Carder of New York about 1904.
It is an iridescent gold glass, usually marked Aurene or Steuben.
    AURENE, see also Steuben
AURENE, Bottle, Cologne, Shape 1414, Signed, 7 1/2 In. 295.00
Bowl, Blue, Signed, 6 In. 495.00
Bowl, Footed, Blue, Signed, 10 In. 695.00
Bowl, Gold Mark, 4 X 10 In. 1295.00
Bowl, Gold, Pink Highlights, Signed, 12 X 3 1/2 In. 275.00
Box, Pagoda Shape Cover, Signed, 6 X 4 1/4 In. 750.00
Box, Powder, Gold, Pagoda Shape Cover, Signed, 6 X 4 1/2 In. 495.00
Cigarette & Match Holder, Iridescent, Signed 175.00
Cigarette Holder, Gold, Signed, 2 1/2 X 2 1/4 In. 135.00
Console Set, Blue, Candleholder, 8 In., 3 Piece 225.00
Dish, Nut, No.139, 5 Feet, Clover Shape, Ruffled Edge 175.00
Juice Set, Ivorene, Cobalt Blue Base & Handle, 9 1/2 In., 7 Piece 390.00
Lamp, Blue, Bronze Dore Base, 16 In. 1350.00
Shade, Gold, Dome Shape, Ribbed, Signed, 6 In. 115.00
Shade, Gold, Purple Iridescent, Ribbed, Signed, 6 In. 95.00
Shade, Gold, Ribbed, 6 In. 120.00
Shade, Gold, 6 In. 85.00
Vase, Applied Handles, Blue, Signed, 12 In. 1250.00
Vase, Blue, Cylinder, Round Foot, Marked, 8 In. 225.00
Vase, Blue, Fluted Handles, Signed, 12 X 6 In. 1250.00
Vase, Blue, Signed, Numbered, 6 1/2 In. 430.00
Vase, Bud, Blue, Cylinder, Round Foot, Marked, 6 In. 225.00
Vase, Bud, Gold, Cylindrical, Blue Ground, Signed, 8 1/4 In. 245.00
Vase, Dimpled Sides, Gold, Marked, 4 In. 225.00
Vase, Double Gourd Shape, Gold Iridescence, Signed, 6 In. 275.00
Vase, Gold, Amphora Shape, Flared Lip, 12 In. 700.00
Vase, Gold, Flare To Tricorner Top, Signed, 4 1/4 In. 175.00
Vase, Gold, Red Highlights, Signed, 8 1/4 X 8 In. 750.00
Vase, Gold, Trumpet Shape, Gold, Blue, Lavender Tones, 11 In. 550.00
Vase, Inverted Bellflower Shape, Marked, 5 1/2 In. 190.00
Vase, Ivorene, Random Threads, Marked, 5 In. 425.00
Vase, Millefiori Florets, Green Leaves & Vines, Gold Ground, 6 In. ... 1500.00
Vase, Optic Rib, Marked, 6 3/4 In. 250.00
Vase, Ribbed & Flared, Scalloped Rim, Marked, 5 In. 325.00
Vase, Ribbed, Marked, 5 1/2 X 5 In. 250.00
Vase, Scalloped Edge, Bulbous, Signed, 2 1/4 X 5 In. 285.00
Vase, Stick, Signed, Blue, 8 1/2 In. 345.00
Vase, Tricorner Stretched Top, Gold, Signed, 4 1/2 In. 175.00
Vase, Trumpet Shape, Rounded Pedestal, Signed, Blue, 9 In. 750.00
Wine, Iridescent Gold, Twisted Stem, Signed 175.00
     AUSTRIA, see Royal Dux; Kauffmann; Porcelain

Auto parts and accessories are collectors' items today.

AUTO, Air Gauge, Ford, For Model A, Watch Face Type, Leather Case	45.00
Ashtray, Ford, 1954	4.50
Gas Pump Globe, Atlantic Imperial Premium, Milk Glass	145.00
Gas Pump Globe, Atlantic Regular, Milk Glass	125.00
Gas Pump Globe, Clark, Plastic Body	75.00
Gas Pump Globe, Frontier Ethyl	150.00
Gas Pump Globe, GLF Quality	150.00
Gas Pump Globe, Hustol	150.00
Gas Pump Globe, Indian Gasoline, Montana, 2-Sided, 6 Ft.Diam.	395.00
Gas Pump Globe, Mobil Flying Red Horse	75.00
Gas Pump Globe, Sinclair, Plastic Body	75.00
Gas Pump Globe, Standard Gold Crown	175.00
Gauge, Air, States For Model A Ford, Suede Case	42.50
Gauge, Tire, Model A	52.50
Gauge, Tire, Schrader, Dated 1923	6.00
Gearshift Knob, Agate	9.50
Headlight, Beveled Glass, Swivel Neck, Battery, C.1905, 5 3/4 In.	35.00
AUTO, HOOD ORNAMENT, see also Lalique	
Hood Ornament, Charging Ram	35.00
Hood Ornament, Lady	28.00
Hood Ornament, Oldsmobile, 1950	45.00
Hood Ornament, Swan, Lighted Wings	15.00
Hood Ornament, Whippet Radiator	25.00
Hood Ornament, Winged Mercury	45.00
Hood Ornament, Wings, Model T Ford	15.00
Hub Cap, Whippet	10.00
Insignia, Studebaker, 10 1/2 In.	15.00
Jack, Ford, Model T	16.50
Jack, 1949 Cadillac, Folding Crank Handle	20.00
Knob, Steering Wheel, Pin-Up Girl Inside	20.00
Lamp, Driving, Dietz	40.00
Lamp, Side, Ford, Model T	45.00
License Plate, Excelsior Springs, Missouri, 1932, Taxi	20.00
License Plate, Florida, 1972	5.00
License Plate, Florida, 1973	5.00
License Plate, Illinois, 1922, Pair	14.00
License Plate, Illinois, 1927, Pair	13.50
License Plate, Illinois, 1931, Pair	12.50
License Plate, Illinois, 1934, Truck, Pair	12.50
License Plate, Illinois, 1935, Pair	10.00
License Plate, Illinois, 1951	5.00
License Plate, Illinois, 1964	5.00
License Plate, Illinois, 1969, State	5.00
License Plate, Michigan, 1914, Porcelain	45.00
License Plate, New Hampshire, 1916	30.00
License Plate, Pennsylvania, 1915, Porcelain, 15 X 6 In.	27.00
License Plate, Quebec, 1960	1.00
License Plate, South Dakota, 1921	11.00
License Plate, Texas, 1974	5.00
License Plate, Vermont, 1915	20.00
License Plate, Vermont, 1959	1.00
License Plate, Wisconsin, 1958, Farm	5.00
License Plate, Wisconsin, 1973	1.00
Nozzle, Gas Pump, Buckeye, 1926, Brass	45.00
Nozzle, Gas Pump, McDonald Dubuque, Brass	40.00
Pump, Tire, Ford, Model T, Brass Barrel	35.00
Rack, Luggage, Running Board	35.00
Radiator, Model A	100.00
Sidelight, Oil, For Model T, Edmond & Jones, Brass Trim, 1914	55.00
Vase, Flower, Pierce Arrow, Pewter	45.00
Vase, Grapevine Design, Pair	65.00
Wrench, Embossed Ford	2.00

Autumn Leaf pattern china was made for the Jewel Tea Company from 1933. Hall China Company of East Liverpool, Ohio, Crooksville China Company of Crooksville, Ohio, Harker Potteries of Chester, West Virginia, and Paden City Pottery, Paden City, West Virginia, made dishes with this design. Autumn Leaf dishes have been made in the 1970s.

AUTUMN LEAF, Bowl, Cereal, Jewel Tea	4.50
Bowl, Hall, 3 1/2 In.	3.75
Bowl, Jewel Tea, Oval, 10 1/2 In.	12.00
Bowl, Jewel Tea, 7 3/4 In.	9.00
Bowl, Mixing, Jewel Tea Co., Set Of 3	30.00 To 35.00
Bowl, Vegetable, Jewel Tea, Handles, Covered, 10 In.	27.00
Bowl, Vegetable, Oval, 10 In.	20.00
Bowl, 7 1/2 In.	10.00
Cake Plate, Jewel Tea	12.00
Casserole, Jewel Tea, Tab Handles, 2-Part	22.50
Clock, Electric, Wall, Hall	30.00
Coffee Grinder, Electric, Jewel Tea	30.00
Coffee Server, Gooseneck	20.00
Coffeepot, Jewel Tea	35.00 To 75.00
Cookie Jar, Covered, Hall	60.00
Creamer, Jewel Tea	10.00
Cup & Saucer	5.00 To 6.00
Dish, Baking, Hall, Individual, Set Of 6	18.00
Dish, Fruit, Coupe	4.50
Dish, Soup, Jewel Tea	5.00
Dripolator, Hall, China, 9 Piece	80.00 To 150.00
Gravy Boat	12.00 To 15.00
Jar, Grease, Covered, Jewel Tea	15.00
Jar, Marmalade, Underplate, Hall	40.00
Mug, Irish Coffee	45.00
Mustard, Jewel Tea, Covered, Underliner	30.00
Pitcher, Jewel Tea, Ice Lip	22.00
Pitcher, Jewel Tea, 2 1/2 Pint, 6 In.	12.00 To 15.00
Pitcher, Milk, Jewel Tea, 5 3/4 In.	15.00
Plate, Jewel Tea, 7 In.	4.00 To 7.00
Plate, Jewel Tea, 8 In.	4.00 To 8.00
Plate, Jewel Tea, 9 In.	5.00
Plate, Jewel Tea, 9 1/2 In.	8.00
Plate, Pie, Jewel Tea, 9 1/2 In.	7.00
Platter, Jewel Tea, 13 3/4 In.	12.00 To 15.00
Platter, Jewel Tea, 14 X 11 In.	11.50
Pot, Bean, Covered	85.00
Range Set, Hall, 4 Piece	28.00
Refrigerator Set, Stacked, 4 Piece	49.50
Salt & Pepper, Range, Jewel Tea	15.00 To 20.00
Salt & Pepper, Scalloped	8.00
Sugar, Jewel Tea, Covered	15.00
Teapot, Hall, Square	45.00 To 50.00
Teapot, Jewel Tea, Aladdin	40.00
Teapot, Jewel Tea, Long Spout	55.00
Tray, Jewel Tea, Glass, Wooden Handles	80.00
Tumbler, Jewel Tea, Frosted, 14 Ounce	15.00

AVON, see Bottle, Avon

Baccarat glass was made in France by La Compagnie des Cristalleries de Baccarat, located 150 miles from Paris. The factory was started in 1765. The firm went bankrupt and began operating again about 1822. Cane and millefiori paperweights were made during the 1860 to 1880 period. The firm is still working near Paris making paperweights and glasswares.

BACCARAT, Bell, Plain Ground, Faceted Ball Handle, Clapper, Marked	95.00

Bobeche, Ribbed Swirl Rose Satin Cased With White, Pair	48.00
Bottle, Blue Flash, Gilt, Fine Cut, 4 1/2 In.	85.00
Bottle, Cologne, Clear To Amberina, Swirl, Stopper, 6 1/2 In.	119.00
Bottle, Cologne, Swirl, Light Blue, 6 In.	48.00
Bottle, Cologne, Swirled Pattern, Stopper, 7 In., Pair	75.00
Bottle, Fine Cut, Gilt Trim, Blue Flash, 4 1/4 In.	85.00
Bottle, Perfume, Clear, Original Label, Turtle Shaped, Signed	50.00
Bottle, Perfume, Dolphin Stopper	115.00
Bottle, Perfume, Figural, White Satin Hand, Marked, 6 In.	165.00
Bottle, Perfume, Rose Teinte, Swirl Pattern, Square, 5 In.	65.00
Bottle, Perfume, Stopper, Label, 3 In.	35.00
Bowl, Blue, Gold Leaves, 3 In.	65.00
Bowl, Rose Teinte, Swirl Pattern, Ormolu Mount, 12 X 7 1/2 In.	225.00
Box, Covered, Marked, Light Blue, 3 1/2 X 3 In.	48.00
Cake Plate, Floral Pattern, Swirled, Footed, 8 X 2 1/2 In.	65.00
Compote, Rose Teinte, Swirl Pattern, 4 X 4 In.	65.00
Decanter, Signed, 13 In.	145.00
Figurine, Cat, Stylized, Marked, 3 1/4 In.	48.00
Figurine, Frog, Full Body, Crystal, 4 1/4 In.	50.00
Figurine, Giraffe, Full Body, 7 1/4 In.	60.00
Figurine, Pelican, Full Body, Crystal, 6 1/2 In.	70.00
Figurine, Squirrel, Full Body, Crystal, 4 1/2 In.	50.00
Goblet, Stem, 4 X 4 In.	18.00
Goblet, Water, Perfection Pattern	30.00
Jar, Scene, Eiffel Tower, Covered, Amberina, Signed	180.00
Lamp, Fairy, Rose Teinte, Pinwheel Pattern, Base, Marked, 4 1/8 In.	195.00
Mayonnaise, Underplate, Ruby, Gold Design, Bowl, 4 3/4 In., 6 1/4 In.	325.00
Paperweight, Anchor Form, 3 3/4 X 4 1/2 In.	35.00
Paperweight, Blue Agate, Opaline Gilt, Circular Design, 2 1/2 In.	45.00
Paperweight, Bumblebee, Fleur De Lis, Gilt, Blue, 2 1/2 In.	70.00
Paperweight, Butterfly Within Garland, On Lace, 3 1/4 In.	3100.00
Paperweight, Cat, 3 1/2 In.	50.00
Paperweight, Clematis & Bud, White, 2 1/2 In.	1300.00
Paperweight, Clichy Bouquet, Flowers, Yellow, Blue, Clear, 2 1/4 In.	2900.00
Paperweight, Concentric, Central Arrow Cane, Red, Green, 2 1/2 In.	385.00
Paperweight, Elephant, 3 X 3 In.	40.00
Paperweight, Flat, Clear, 4 1/2 X 4 1/2 In.	55.00
Paperweight, Floret, 4 Concentric Circles, Pink, Blue, 2 3/4 In.	100.00
Paperweight, Flower, Clear Glass, Salmon Pink, 2 1/4 In.	1200.00
Paperweight, Frog	85.00
Paperweight, Magnum, Cube With Prism Cut Top, Clear, 2 1/2 In.	100.00
Paperweight, Magnum, Cut Flower Form Dome, Clear, 4 In.	55.00
Paperweight, Magnum, Prism Cut, 3 1/2 In.	120.00
Paperweight, Millefiori On Lace, Scattered, 1848, 3 In	1500.00 To 1600.00
Paperweight, Pansy, 5 Green Leaves, 5-Petal Flowers, Star Cut, 2 In.	200.00
Paperweight, Primrose, Millefiori Ring, Blue, White, 2 1/2 In.	1800.00
Paperweight, Primrose, Red & White, Star-Cut Base, 3 In.	1175.00
Paperweight, Sulfide, Abraham Lincoln	200.00
Paperweight, Sulfide, Adlai Stevenson, Ruby Ground, 7 Windows, 2 In.	88.00
Paperweight, Sulfide, Andrew Jackson	50.00
Paperweight, Sulfide, Ben Franklin	400.00
Paperweight, Sulfide, Dwight Eisenhower, Overlay, 1st Edition	500.00
Paperweight, Sulfide, Eleanor Roosevelt, Overlay	150.00
Paperweight, Sulfide, George Washington	200.00
Paperweight, Sulfide, Harry Truman, Overlay	175.00
Paperweight, Sulfide, John F.Kennedy	175.00
Paperweight, Sulfide, Lafayette	200.00
Paperweight, Sulfide, Martin Luther King, Gilded Cameo	125.00
Paperweight, Sulfide, Mount Rushmore, Overlay	300.00
Paperweight, Sulfide, Napoleon Bonaparte, Overlay	175.00
Paperweight, Sulfide, Patrick Henry, Overlay	150.00
Paperweight, Sulfide, Pope Pius XII, Overlay	250.00
Paperweight, Sulfide, Robert E.Lee	200.00
Paperweight, Sulfide, Sam Rayburn, Overlay	300.00

Paperweight, Sulfide, Teddy Roosevelt 75.00
Paperweight, Sulfide, Thomas Jefferson 200.00
Paperweight, Sulfide, Will Rogers, Overlay 175.00
Paperweight, Sulfide, Winston Churchill 600.00
Paperweight, Sulfide, Woodrow Wilson, 1972 .... 60.00
Paperweight, Sulphide, Night, Cobalt Overlay, 7 Windows, 2 3/4 In. 55.00
Paperweight, Trefoil Garland, Arrow & Star Cane, Clear, 3 1/16 In. 675.00
Paperweight, Turtle, Crystal 65.00
Paperweight, Twisted Cane, Signed 250.00
Plate, Pedestal, Clear, Swirl Design, 8 1/2 X 3 In. 85.00
Plate, Scalloped Rim, Expanded Diamonds, Signed, 5 1/4 In. 35.00
Tazza, Signed, Blue, 5 1/4 In.Diam. 35.00
Tray, Rubina, Signed, 7 X 10 In. 100.00
Turtle, Full Lead Crystal, 4 X 1 1/4 In. 60.00
Vase, Cameo, White & Clear, Snake Winding, Marked, 8 In. 75.00
Vase, Teardrop Shape, Slant Cut Opening, 7 In. 45.00
Vase, Teardrop, Signed, 7 In. 50.00
Wine, Dewdrop 35.00
Wine, Perfection Pattern 45.00

BADGE, Buck Jones, Wild West Shows & Roundup Days, Ring Stock 65.00
Cap, Jersey Central Lines, Statue Of Liberty & Lettering, 1 1/2 In. 40.00
Chauffeur, Illinois 21.00
Chauffeur, Michigan, 1929 .... 6.50
Chauffeur, Minnesota, 1920s 6.00
Deputy Sheriff, McLean County, Illinois, Brass Star 60.00
Deputy Sheriff, Passaic County, N.J. 45.00
Deputy Sheriff, Wallet, Michigan 8.00
Deputy Sheriff's Posse, Wyandotte County, Kansas, State Seal 65.00
Hat, Military, Australian Commonwealth, Crown Under Sun 3.50
Hat, Regal Oil Co., Embossed Oil Truck, Porcelain 25.00
Hat, Yellow Cab Co., Pete, 1955 .... 25.00
Inspector's, Board Of Health, Mass., Bold Design, Raised Seal 15.00
Los Angeles County Deputy Sheriff, Bear On Top 55.00
Metropolitan Police, D.C., R.Nixon Inauguration, 1969 .... 140.00
Police, Deputy, Indian Creek, N.Y. 45.00
Police, Omaha 18.00
Police, Reserve, Commander, Albany, 7-Point Star 45.00
Police, San Francisco, Sterling Silver 75.00
Policeman, Glen Carbon, Ill., Enameled Halo Around Seal 17.00
Prosecuting Attorney, Jackson County, County Seal 45.00
San Francisco Police, Sterling Silver 75.00
Steel City Rangers, Gary A.M.A. No.654, Tire & Wings 67.50
Trustee, Peoria, Ill., Gold Plated, Raised Eagle 15.00
Woman's Relief Corps, G.A.R., 1861-65 On Back, Dated 1883 .... 9.00

Metal banks have been made since 1868. There are still banks, mechanical banks, and registering banks (those which show the total money deposited on the face of the bank). Many old banks have been reproduced since the 1950s in iron or plastic.

BANK, Abe Lincoln Stovepipe Hat, Iron, Black Paint, Embossed Pass-Around 95.00
Alphabet Block, Cast Iron, 3 1/4 In. 1475.00
Amherst Stove, Cast Iron 150.00
Amish Boy, Holding Pig, Sitting On Bale Of Hay, 4 5/8 In. 65.00
Andy Gump On Stump, Arcade, Cast Iron, 4 1/2 In. .... 450.00 To 775.00
Apple, Chalk, Polychrome, Circle Design, 3 In. 150.00
Apple, Yellow, Cast Iron 950.00
Armoured Car Savings 35.00
Army-Navy .... *Illus* 300.00
Aunt Jemima, Original Paint, Cast Iron, 5 In. .... 60.00 To 65.00
Auto, Rubber Wheels, Red Paint, Banthrico, Aluminum, 8 In. 40.00
Auto, With People, Cast Iron 475.00
Automat Chocolate, Germany, Tin, 5 3/4 In. 115.00

Baby In Cradle, Bird, Scotty Dog, Original Paint, Metal 65.00
Baby In Cradle, Black, Cast Iron, 3 7/8 In. 925.00
Baby's Book Bank, Key, 1 X 3 X 4 1/4 In. 25.00
Bank Building, Cast Iron, 3 In. 40.00
Bank Building, Cast Iron, 3 3/8 In. 55.00
Bank Building, Cast Iron, 5 1/2 In. 50.00
Bank Building, Columbia, Kenton, Combination Lock, Cast Iron, 5 5/8 In. 200.00
Bank Building, Penny, Cast Iron 30.00
Bank Building, Red Roof, Green, Tin, Square, 4 X 3 X 2 3/4 In. 35.00
Bank Skyscraper, Triangular, Cast Iron, 5 7/8 In. 135.00
Barrel, Brotherhood Of Locomotive Engineers Title & Trust, 1923 .... 40.00
Barrel, Cast Iron, 2 3/4 In. 30.00
Baseball Player .... 150.00 To 165.00
Baseball, Key, Japan, Tin, 3 In. 3.00
Battle Of Gettysburg, 100th Anniversary, Commemorative Bank, Iron, 7 In 40.00
Battleship Kentucky, Cast Iron, 10 1/4 In.Long 450.00
Battleship Maine, Cast Iron, 4 1/2 In.Long 175.00
Battleship Oregon, Cast Iron, 5 In.Long 210.00
Battleship Oregon, Cast Iron, 6 In.Long 325.00
Bear, Snow Crest, Bottle 8.00
Bear, Standing, Stealing Pig, Cast Iron .... 525.00 To 950.00
Bear, Teddy On Side, Cast Iron, 3 7/8 In. 80.00
Bear, With Pot, Hubley, 6 3/4 In. 70.00
Beehive, Bear Robbing Honey, Cast Iron 250.00
Beehive, Figural, Turned 2-Part Wood, 3 In. 19.00
Belt, Coin Slot, Embossed Cowboy, Steerheads, 6-Guns, Metal, 3 X 5 In. 15.00
Benjamin Franklin Thrift 50.00
Big Boy, Figural, Brown Hair, Checkered Overalls 15.00
Bill-E-Grin, Aluminum 65.00
Billiken Shoes Bring Luck, Cast Iron, 4 1/2 In. 65.00
Billiken, Cast Iron, 4 1/4 In. 30.00
Billiken, Original Paint, Cast Iron 58.00
Billy Possum, Cast Iron, 4 7/8 In.Long 1525.00
Bison, Cast Iron 85.00
Bison, Gilt 45.00
Black Boy Head, Double-Faced, Cast Iron 140.00
Black Boy, Nodder, Eating Watermelon, Souvenir, Biloxi 50.00
Black Face With Turban, Pottery .... 25.00 To 45.00
Black Sharecropper, Shoes Off, Cast Iron 60.00
Blackpool Tower, Cast Iron, 7 1/2 In. 85.00
Boat, When My Fortune Ship Comes In, Cast Iron 950.00
Boat, With Child, Dolphin, Cast Iron, 4 1/2 In. 325.00
Boat, With Child, Mermaid, Cast Iron, 4 1/8 In. 275.00
Book, Advertising Insurance Co. 15.00
Book, Save & Insure, Maryland Assurance Corp, Brass Trim, 4 1/2 In. 6.00
Book, Singer Sewing Machine Co., Figural, Leather Bound, Brass Edge 38.00
Boy Scout, Cast Iron 90.00
Brass Bound Book, Springfield, Mass. Institution For Savings, 5 In. 8.00
Brunswick Victrola, Cast Iron 65.00
Buddy Bank, Glass & Tin, Marx, 4 1/4 In. 65.00
Bugs Bunny, Ceramic, 16 In. 90.00
Bugs Bunny, Warner Brothers, White Metal, 5 3/4 In 75.00
Building, Cast Iron, 4 1/2 In. 35.00
Building, Cast Iron, 6 1/2 X 4 1/4 In. 65.00
Building, Hand-Painted Windows, Marbleized Roof, Cast Iron, 5 1/2 In. 75.00
Building, Lookout Turret, Windows, Cast Iron, 4 In. 50.00
Building, Woolworth, Cast Iron, 8 In. .... 65.00 To 95.00
Bus, Well's, Tin 150.00
Bust Of Man, Cast Iron, 5 1/8 In. 55.00
Buster Brown & Tige .... Illus 200.00
Buster Brown & Tige, Cashier Security, Fidelity, Cast Iron, 5 In. 225.00
Buster Brown & Tige, Fidelity Trust Vault, Cast Iron, 6 1/2 In. 335.00
Buster Brown, With Horseshoe, Cast Iron 135.00
Buy War Bonds, World War II, Tin, 4 In. 5.00

Bank, Army-Navy　　　　　　　　　Bank, Buster Brown & Tige

Banks, Camels; Donkeys

(See Pages 14, 15, 18)

Calendar, Speer, Rosebelt, Milwaukee, Wis.	35.00
Calumet, Tin, 4 In.	18.00
Calumet, Tin, 5 1/2 In.	150.00
Camel, Cast Iron, 4 3/4 In.	65.00
Camel, Large ....*Illus*	150.00
Camel, Small ....*Illus*	45.00
Camel, With Pack, Cast Iron, 5 In.	200.00
Campbell Kids, Cast Iron, 3 3/8 In.	120.00 To 225.00
Cannon, Cast Iron, 6 1/2 In.	1225.00
Captain Kidd, Cast Iron	295.00
Cash Register, Arcade, Cast Iron, 3 3/4 In.	70.00
Cash Register, Happy Days, Black & Yellow, 4 In.	10.00 To 20.00
Cash Register, J.Chein, Tin	15.00
Castle, 3 Turrets, 2 Coin Slots, English, Cast Iron, 7 In.	375.00
Cat Head, Brown Ceramic	35.00
Cat With Ball	190.00
Cat With Ball, Cast Iron, 5 5/8 In.	250.00
Cat With Ball, Cast Iron, 5 5/9 In.	145.00
Cat With Bowtie, Cast Iron, 4 3/8 In.	155.00
Cat, Googly-Eyes, Cast Iron	50.00
Cat, Papier-Mache	65.00
Cat, Seated, Fine-Haired, Cast Iron, 4 1/8 In.	100.00
Cat, Sitting, Gilt Paint, Cast Iron, 4 1/8 In.	115.00

Charlie Chaplin, Clear Glass, Polychrome Paint, 3 7/8 In.	65.00
Charlie Chaplin, Next To Barrel, Cast Iron	175.00
Charlie McCarthy, Composition, Mouth Is Money Slot	125.00
Charlie McCarthy, Feed Me, I Save Your Money, Papier Mache, 9 In.	30.00
Charlie McCarthy, Sits On Trunk, 1930s, Pot Metal, Semimechanical	175.00
Chevrolet 27 Years, Chein	28.00
Chevrolet, Oxford Maroon, Banthrico, Cast Aluminum, Rubber Wheels, 7 In.	50.00
Chevy, '54, Banthrico	95.00
Chief Big Moon	850.00
Chinaman, Reclining, Cast Iron	1850.00
Church, Chein, Cast Iron	15.00
Church, Chein, Tin	70.00
Church, Red & Green Paint, Coin Slot, Metal, 12 In.	65.00
Clock, A.C.Williams, Cast Iron, 6 1/8 In.	285.00
Clock, Mechanism & 2 Slots, White Metal, 5 7/8 In.	32.50
Clown, Cast Iron, 6 1/4 In.	75.00
Clown, Chein, Tin	35.00 To 100.00
Clown, Redhead, Riding Pig, Dated 1949, Chalkware, 5 1/2 X 11 In.	32.50
Coffin, Tin	13.00
Commonwealth Three Coin, Dated 1905	55.00
Cottage, Cast Iron, 4 In.	155.00
Cow, Cast Iron, 5 3/8 In.	150.00 To 180.00
Crown, Cast Iron, English, 3 3/4 In.	135.00
Curtis Thrift Bank, Vending, Marx, Boxed, Plastic & Tin, 7 3/4 In.	5.00
Daffy, Warner Brothers, White, Metal, 4 1/4 In.	75.00
Deer, Cast Iron, 9 In.	105.00
Department Of Collection, Trash Can, Semimechanical, 1940s	70.00
Dime Register, Astronaut	45.00
Dime Register, Beehive, Cast Iron, 6 1/2 X 5 1/2 In.	165.00
Dime Register, Capitol	6.00
Dime Register, Captain Marvel	85.00
Dime Register, Chein, Tin	17.50
Dime Register, Circular, Girard Model Works, Tin, 5 1/2 In.Diam.	35.00
Dime Register, Elves Rolling Coins	35.00
Dime Register, Jackie Robinson Daily, Tin, 2 In.	58.00
Dime Register, Keep 'em Sailing	85.00
Dime Register, Magic Pocket	75.00
Dime Register, Magic Round	50.00
Dime Register, Popeye, 1929	10.00 To 35.00
Dime Register, Snow White	45.00
Dime Register, Superman	85.00
Dime Register, Treasury	10.00
Dime Register, Uncle Sam	100.00
Dime Register, Wonderland Of Knowledge	20.00
Dime Savings, Sailor, China	25.00
Dime Tube, Coca Cola, Holds & Counts Dimes	1.50
Dodge, Advertising, Barrel Shape, Tin	48.00
Dog On Tub, Cast Iron	75.00
Dog, Aluminum	35.00
Dog, Basset Hound, Cast Iron, 3 1/4 In.	950.00
Dog, Boston Bull, Hubley, Cast Iron, 4 3/8 In.	105.00
Dog, Boston Terrier, Cast Iron	17.50
Dog, Bulldog, Cast Iron, 3 7/8 In.	75.00
Dog, Bulldog, Ceramic, 7 1/2 In.	65.00
Dog, Bulldog, Seated, Cast Iron	40.00
Dog, Bulldog, Standing, Cast Iron, 5 1/2 In.	80.00
Dog, Cast Iron, 3 3/4 In.	40.00
Dog, Fido, Cast Iron	100.00
Dog, I Hear A Call, Copyright 1900, Cast Iron, 5 1/4 In.	55.00
Dog, Pug, Seated, Cast Iron, 3 1/2 In.	85.00
Dog, Puppy, Hubley, Cast Iron, 4 In.	175.00
Dog, Retriever, Cast Iron, 5 3/4 In.	175.00
Dog, Scotty, Cast Iron, 4 3/4 In.	95.00

Dog, Scotty, Hubley, Cast Iron, 5 1/8 In.	85.00
Dog, Setter, With Pack, Cast Iron	45.00
Dog, Sitting, Hubley, Cast Iron	55.00
Dog, Spitz, Cast Iron	275.00
Dog, St.Bernard, With Pack, Cast Iron	55.00
Dog, With Pack, Cast Iron, 5 1/2 In.	79.00
Donald Duck, Ceramic	12.50
Donald Duck, Figural Composition, 1938, Crown Toy	125.00
Donkey With Blanket, Cast Iron, 5 3/4 In.	445.00
Donkey, Cast Iron, 4 1/2 In.	70.00
Donkey, Saddled & Bridled, Cast Iron	30.00
Donkey, Standing, Original Gilt, Cast Iron, 4 1/2 In.	58.00
Donkey, Turned Head, Saddled, Cast Iron	55.00
Donkey, 4 In. .... Illus	25.00
Donkey, 6 1/2 In. .... Illus	100.00
Dreadnaught, United We Stand, Cast Iron	375.00
Drink Pepsi Cola, Vending, Bottles In Carton, Plastic & Tin, 6 3/4 In.	87.50
Drinker's, Boxed	125.00
Drum, Remember Pearl Harbor, Ohio Art Co., Tin	20.00
Duck On Tub, Cast Iron, Hubley, 5 1/4 In.	90.00
Duck, Cast Iron, 5 In.	100.00
Duck, 2nd National, Tin	65.00
Dutch Girl, Cast Iron, 5 3/8 In.	55.00
Dutch Girl, Cast Iron, 6 1/2 In.	330.00
Dutch Girl, Port Metal, 5 5/8 In.	30.00
Eagle, Cast Iron, 4 In.	425.00
Eagle, Save Your Pennies To Make Dollars, Iron & Tin, 3 1/2 In.	145.00
Elephant On Tub, A.C.Williams, Cast Iron, 5 1/2 In.	105.00
Elephant, Blanket & Seat, Cast Iron, 4 X 3 1/4 In.	65.00
Elephant, Chalkware	15.00
Elephant, Circus, Cast Iron	150.00
Elephant, Gar-Ru, Pot Metal	95.00
Elephant, GOP, Cast Iron, 4 In.	105.00
Elephant, Howdah, Cast Iron, 2 1/2 In.	45.00
Elephant, Howdah, Cast Iron, 3 In.	20.00 To 25.00
Elephant, Howdah, Cast Iron, 6 3/4 In.	45.00
Elephant, Hubley, Cast Iron, 4 3/4 In.	80.00
Elephant, Jumbo Savings Bank, England, Tin, 5 1/4 In.	65.00
Elephant, On Wheels, Cast Iron, 4 In.	185.00
Elephant, On Wheels, With Bell, Hill Brass Co., Cast Iron, 5 1/2 In.	175.00
Elephant, Prosperity McKinley, Teddy, Cast Iron, 2 1/2 In.	475.00
Elephant, Trunk Down, Gilt Paint, Cast Iron, 3 In.	75.00
Elephant, Tusks & Howdah, Cast Iron, 5 X 5 In.	50.00
Elephant, White Metal, 5 1/4 In.	10.00
F.D.R. Bust	35.00
Face With Save & Smile Money Box, On Hat, English, Cast Iron, 4 In.	250.00
Fat Man, Give Billy A Penny, Silver Paint, Cast Iron, 4 3/4 In.	55.00
Ferry Boat On Wheels, Cast Iron, 7 3/4 In.	165.00
Fireman, Cast Iron	185.00
Fireman, Climbing, Marx, Boxed	85.00
Ford, Model T, Cast Iron	100.00
Ford, 2-Door Sedan, Arcade, Replaced Driver, Cast Iron, 6 3/8 In.	115.00
G.E.Refrigerator, Cast Iron, 4 1/4 In.	37.00
Gas Pump, Indicator Needle, Cast Iron, 5 7/8 In.	105.00
Gasoline Pump, Cast Iron	120.00
General Butler, Pat'd. 1878, Stevens, Cast Iron, 6 1/2 In.	550.00
General Pershing, Cast Iron	70.00 To 125.00
General Pershing, Copper Finish, Dated 1918, Metal, 8 In.	55.00
General Sherman, On Rearing Horse, Arcade, Cast Iron, 6 In.	385.00
George Washington, Cast Iron, 6 1/2 In.	68.00
Get Rich Quick, Tin	35.00
Girl & Dog Cart, Marked Sixpenny Piece Bank, Aluminum, 3 1/4 In.	45.00
Globe Of The World, Tin, 4 1/2 In.	3.00

Globe On Bracket, Arcade, Cast Iron, 4 7/8 In. 100.00
Globe, J.Chein & Co., C.1930, Metal, 4 X 4 In. 15.00
Globe, Ohio Art, Tin 10.00
Globe, On Arc Stand, Cast Iron, 5 3/8 In. 70.00
Gloomy Gus, Cast Iron, 4 3/4 In. 65.00
Goats, Two Kids, Cast Iron, 4 1/2 In. 500.00
Golliwog, Cast Iron, 6 1/8 In. 200.00
Goofy, Nodder, Car, Chalk 18.00
Goose, Cast Iron, 5 In. 180.00
Graf Zeppelin, Cast Iron, 8 In. 225.00
Happy Fats, Cast Iron 225.00
Haunted House, Battery, Boxed 25.00
Head, Black Boy, Floppy Hat, Cast Iron, 3 In. 85.00
Hen, Cast Iron, 6 1/4 In. 200.00
Hippopotamus, Cast Iron, Nickel Plated 600.00
Home Saving Bank, Cast Iron, 4 7/8 In. 85.00
Horse, Black Beauty, Cast Iron 40.00
Horse, My Pet, Cast Iron, 4 1/4 In. 105.00
Horse, On Tin Wheels, Cast Iron, 4 3/4 In. 145.00
Horse, On Tub, A.C.Williams, Cast Iron, 5 3/8 In. .... 110.00 To 175.00
Horse, Prancing, Belly Band, Cast Iron, 4 1/2 In. 96.00
Horse, Prancing, Original White & Black Paint 48.00
Horse, Prancing, Rectangular Base, Arcade, Cast Iron, 7 3/4 In. 75.00
Horse, Rearing, Pebbled Base, Cast Iron 50.00
House, Cast Iron, 3 In. 32.00
House, Clear Glass, Tin Bottom, 3 1/8 In. 20.00
House, Double Chimneys, Cast Iron 25.00
Humpty Dumpty, England, Cast Iron 185.00
Ice Cream Freezer, Richmond Cedar Works, Cast Iron, 4 3/8 In. 85.00
Ice Cream Freezer, 5 In. .... Illus 150.00
Indian Chief, Bust, Pot Metal 45.00
Ironstone, Floral Design, Gilt, English, 8 In. 20.00
Jolly Bear Guitarist, Boxed 75.00
Jug, Redware 25.00
Kewpie 45.00
Kitten, Pink Bow Around Neck, Original Paint, Cast Iron 37.50
Lamb, Silver Paint, Cast Iron, 3 1/8 In. 45.00
Let's Build A Dry America, Temperance, Ceramic, Aqua, 4 1/2 In. 35.00
Liberty Bell, Bust Of George Washington, Cast Iron, 3 7/8 In. 25.00
Liberty Bell, Carnival Glass, 4 In. 4.00
Liberty Bell, Cast Iron, 2 3/4 In. 65.00
Liberty Bell, Embossed Glass, 1776, Tin Closure, 4 X 4 1/2 In. 35.00
Liberty Bell, Wooden Base, Centennial Money Bank, Cast Iron, 4 5/8 In. 40.00
Limousine, Battery Operated, Boxed 75.00
Lincoln Bank, Log On Sawbuck, Hatchet, Saw, Steel, 8 1/4 In. 25.00
Lincoln, Embossed, Glass, Tin Top, Abraham Lincoln Picture 6.00
Lindy Bank By G.& T., 1928, Gilded, Cast Aluminum, 6 1/2 In. 65.00
Lion, Cast Iron, 5 1/2 In. .... 40.00 To 55.00
Lion, On Tub, A.C.Williams, Cast Iron, 4 1/4 In. 135.00
Lion, On Tub, A.C.Williams, Cast Iron, 5 1/2 In. 100.00
Lion, On Wheels, Cast Iron 225.00
Lion, Tin Wheels, Cast Iron, 4 3/4 In. 70.00
Little Red Riding Hood & Wolf, Marked Harper 1907, Black, 5 In. 1425.00
Little Red Riding Hood, Hull 195.00
Log Cabin Savings, Towles, Tin 40.00
Log Cabin, Cast Iron, 2 5/8 In. 175.00
Log Cabin, Glass 20.00
Lucky Joe, Black, Glass 14.00
Lucy Atwell Fairy House, Tin 250.00
Mailbox, Air, Original Green Paint, Cast Iron 35.00
Mailbox, Postal Savings, U.S., Bronze Finish, Lock, Cast Iron, 6 3/4 In. 50.00
Mailbox, Save For Defense & Security, Crown Toy Co., Tin, 4 1/2 In. 35.00
Mailbox, U.S. Air Mail & Eagle, Cast Iron, 5 1/2 In. 40.00

Mailbox, U.S. Mail, A.C.Williams, Cast Iron, 5 1/4 In. 75.00
Mailbox, U.S.Mail, Nickel Plated, Cast Iron, 4 In. 45.00
Mammy, Cast Iron, 8 In. 12.00
Mammy, Hubley, Cast Iron, 5 1/4 In. 75.00
Mammy, With Spoon, A.C.Williams, Cast Iron, 5 3/4 In. .... 50.00 To 75.00
Man, Wearing Bowler Hat, Save For A Rainy Day, Wood, 26 In. 1430.00
Man's Head & Arms, Original Paint, Cast Iron, Hall's Excelsior 75.00
Marx Budget 20.00
Mary And Little Lamb, Cast Iron, 4 1/2 In. .... 195.00 To 550.00
Mascot, Boy On Baseball, American & National League Ball, Hubley, 6 In. 1425.00

*Mechanical banks were first made about 1870. Any bank with moving parts is
considered mechanical, although those most collected are the metal banks made
before World War I. Reproductions are being made.*

Mechanical, Artillery, Bronze 500.00
Mechanical, Artilleryman Shooting Into Tree, Cast Iron, Dated 1877 .... 225.00
Mechanical, Atomic, Pot Metal, 1930s 49.00
Mechanical, Automatic Coinsavings, Cast Iron, Bronze Finish, 7 1/4 In. 615.00
Mechanical, Baby In Egg, Voice Box, Cast Iron, 7 1/4 In. 95.00
Mechanical, Bad Accident 1300.00
Mechanical, Bear & Tree Stump 500.00
Mechanical, Billy Goat 3000.00
Mechanical, Black Mammy, Feeding Dish 350.00
Mechanical, Black Man Riding Mule, Book Of Knowledge, 1950s, Cast Iron 80.00
Mechanical, Black Minstrel Face, Original Paint, Germany, Tin, 7 In. 175.00
Mechanical, Boy & Girl Playing Banker, Tin, 5 In. 35.00
Mechanical, Breadwinners 3750.00
Mechanical, Buffalo, Black Paint, Cast Iron, 8 1/2 In. 125.00
Mechanical, Cabin, Cast Iron, 3 5/8 In. .... 285.00 To 325.00
Mechanical, Calumet, Child's Head, Tin, 5 In. 195.00
Mechanical, Captain Kidd Mystery Bank, Lithography, Tin, 4 In. 350.00
Mechanical, Captain Kidd, Cast Iron, 5 3/4 In. 160.00
Mechanical, Chief Big Moon, 1899 ....*Illus* 550.00
Mechanical, Church, Day By Day A Penny A Meal, Chein, Tin, 6 1/2 In. 35.00
Mechanical, Clown, Head, Tongue Accepts Coin 40.00
Mechanical, Clown, Tin, Chein, 5 In. 25.00
Mechanical, Creedmore .... 350.00 To 400.00
Mechanical, Creedmore, J.& E.Stevens, 1877 ....*Illus* 250.00
Mechanical, Crowing Rooster, Cast Iron, 6 1/8 In. 220.00
Mechanical, Dark Town Battery, Cast Iron, 9 7/8 In. 975.00
Mechanical, Dentist, Cast Iron, C.1890, 8 1/2 In. 100.00
Mechanical, Dinah, Cast Iron, 6 1/2 In. 250.00
Mechanical, Dog, Bulldog 450.00
Mechanical, Dog, On Turntable, Cast Iron .... 225.00 To 350.00
Mechanical, Dog, Trick, Cast Iron, 7 1/4 In. 355.00
Mechanical, Donald Duck, 2nd National Duck Bank, Tin, Chein, 6 In. 50.00
Mechanical, Eagle & Eaglets, J.& E.Stevens, 1883 ....*Illus* 300.00
Mechanical, Elephant & Three Clowns 1000.00
Mechanical, Elephant, Chein, Tin, 5 In. 50.00
Mechanical, Elephant, Howdah, Pull Tail .... 160.00 To 225.00
Mechanical, Elephant, Three Stars 600.00
Mechanical, Elephant, Wooden Figure In Howdah, Cast Iron, 5 1/2 In. 275.00
Mechanical, Feed The Kitty, Cast Iron, 7 3/4 In. 50.00
Mechanical, Football, Cast Iron, 10 1/4 In.Long 1300.00
Mechanical, Fortune Teller, Brass Slot, Cast Iron, 6 3/4 In. 65.00
Mechanical, Frog, On Cylindrical Lattice Base, Cast Iron, 4 1/4 In. 200.00
Mechanical, Frog, On Rock 300.00
Mechanical, Frog, On Round Base 450.00
Mechanical, Frogs, Two, Moving Legs, Cast Iron, 9 In. 575.00
Mechanical, Hen & Chick 1600.00
Mechanical, Home Bank, Original Key & Receipt Cards, Tin 260.00
Mechanical, Home Bank, Tin, 6 1/4 In. 105.00
Mechanical, Hoop-La Bank, Cast Iron, 8 3/8 In. .... 275.00 To 650.00

Banks, Three Wise Monkeys; Oriental Camel, Rhinoceros; Ice Cream Freezer

(See Pages 19, 22, 23, 24)

Banks, Mechanical, Chief Big Moon, 1899; Eagle & Eaglets, J.& E. Stevens, 1883; Creedmore,

J.& E.Stevens, 1877

Mechanical, Humpty Dumpty	650.00
Mechanical, Jockey	550.00
Mechanical, Jolly Nigger	200.00
Mechanical, Jolly Nigger, Marked Starke's, Cast Aluminum, 6 1/4 In.	55.00
Mechanical, Kiltie	1100.00
Mechanical, Lighthouse	700.00
Mechanical, Lion Hunter, Cast Iron	1000.00
Mechanical, Little Miss Muffet, Spider In Window, Tin, 4 In.	45.00
Mechanical, Locomotive, Removable Stack Opens When Full, 5 3/4 In.	115.00
Mechanical, Magician	600.00 To 950.00
Mechanical, Memorial Money Bank	700.00
Mechanical, Mickey Mouse, Phone, 1930s	155.00
Mechanical, Monkey	300.00
Mechanical, Monkey, Tin, Chein, 5 1/4 In.	35.00
Mechanical, Monkey, Tips Hat, Chein	16.00 To 45.00
Mechanical, Monkey, With Train, Tin	325.00
Mechanical, Mousetrap, Lithography, Germany, Tin, 6 1/8 In.	20.00
Mechanical, Mule Entering Barn	750.00
Mechanical, National, Gold & Silver Paint, Key, Cast Iron, 6 3/8 In.	455.00
Mechanical, New Bank, Cast Iron, 5 1/2 In.	285.00
Mechanical, North Pole Bank, Flag, Cast Iron, 5 1/4 In.	1600.00
Mechanical, Organ Grinder & Performing Bear	1500.00
Mechanical, Organ, Dated 1881, Cast Iron, 4 In.	435.00
Mechanical, Organ, Monkey	265.00
Mechanical, Owl, Cast Iron, 5 3/4 In.	110.00
Mechanical, Owl, Turns Head, Cast Iron	140.00 To 325.00
Mechanical, Paddy & The Pig	800.00 To 900.00
Mechanical, Parking Meter	62.00
Mechanical, Pay Phone, Cast Iron	225.00
Mechanical, Peg Leg Beggar, Nodding Head, Cast Iron, 5 1/4 In.	700.00
Mechanical, Pelican, Man Thumbing Nose	950.00

Mechanical, Pig Baby In Highchair, Dated 1897, Cast Iron, 5 3/4 In. 475.00
Mechanical, Pig, Drummer, Schuko 1500.00
Mechanical, Pineapple Peter, Hawaii, Dated .... 110.00 To 225.00
Mechanical, Pistol, Sheet Metal 475.00
Mechanical, Plantation, Weedens, Tin 450.00
Mechanical, Pony, Trick 295.00
Mechanical, Professor Pug Frog 2750.00
Mechanical, Punch & Judy .... 475.00 To 995.00
Mechanical, Rabbit, Chein 60.00
Mechanical, Rooster, Gold 300.00
Mechanical, Safe With Watchdog, Old Paint, Cast Iron, 5 7/8 In. 175.00
Mechanical, Safe, Electric 350.00
Mechanical, Sailor 950.00
Mechanical, Santa At Chimney, Cast Iron, 6 In. .... 475.00 To 1000.00
Mechanical, Southern Comfort, Cast White Metal, 8 1/2 In. 25.00
Mechanical, Steer, Moving Horns, Paint, Cast Iron, 6 3/4 In.Long 130.00
Mechanical, Surly Bruin, Cast Iron, 6 3/8 In. 275.00
Mechanical, Sweet Thrift Bank, Tin, 6 In. 165.00
Mechanical, Tammany, 5 3/4 In. .... 150.00 To 175.00
Mechanical, Tank & Cannon, Aluminum 650.00
Mechanical, Teddy & The Bear .... 375.00 To 475.00
Mechanical, Terrier, In Dog House, Tin, 5 In. 55.00
Mechanical, Toad On Stump 345.00
Mechanical, Tricky Pig, Pop-Up Man, Cast Iron, 8 In. 115.00
Mechanical, Uncle Remus Bank, Cast Iron, 4 1/2 In. 55.00
Mechanical, Uncle Sam, Dated 1886 .... 375.00
Mechanical, Uncle Sam, Silver Paint, Red, Blue, Cast Iron, 5 3/8 In. 90.00
Mechanical, Uncle Tom, Cast Iron, 5 1/4 In. 175.00
Mechanical, Uncle Wiggily, Tin, Chein, 5 In. 70.00
Mechanical, Watch Dog Safe 400.00
Mechanical, William Tell .... 125.00 To 475.00
Mechanical, Wireless .... 170.00 To 425.00
Mechanical, World's Fair 900.00
Mickey Mouse, Aluminum, French, 8 1/4 In. 115.00
Middy Bank, Cast Iron, 5 3/8 In. 100.00
Mississippi Sidewheeler Berry Boat, Cast Iron, 7 5/8 In. 185.00
Mr.Peanut, Plastic 5.00
Mulligan The Cop, A.C.Williams, Cast Iron, 5 3/4 In. 300.00
Mulligan The Cop, Cast Iron .... 65.00 To 95.00
Mutt & Jeff, Cast Iron, 5 1/4 In. .... 110.00 To 185.00
Nickel Register, Red Paint, Cast Iron, 4 X 2 7/8 In. 105.00
Nipper, Radio Corp. Of America, Fuzzy Cover, Pot Metal, 5 1/2 In. 65.00
Nursery Rhyme Book, Set Of 4, Tin 80.00
Oil, Havoline, 3 In. 14.00
Old South Church, Cast Iron 525.00
Oriental Camel, 4 In. .... *Illus* 800.00
Our Kitchener Bank, Bust, Lion, Unicorn, Cast Iron, 6 3/4 In. 105.00
Owl, Be Wise, Save Money, Cast Iron, 5 In. 75.00
Owl, Square Base, Vindex, Cast Iron, 4 1/4 In. 100.00
Panda Bear, Cast Iron, Original Paint 35.00
Panda, Aluminum, 4 1/4 In. 155.00
Penny Trust Co, Milk Glass, Tin Top, 2 7/8 In. 25.00
Pepsi Vending Machine 75.00
Pig, Boston Bean, Cast Iron 45.00
Pig, Carnival Glass, 4 In. 3.00
Pig, Cast Iron, 4 In.Long 55.00
Pig, Deckers Iowana, Cast Iron, 4 1/2 In. .... 65.00 To 75.00
Pig, Embossed Bismark Bank, Cast Iron, 7 1/2 In. 85.00
Pig, In Highchair 465.00
Pig, Laughing, Cast Iron, 5 1/4 In. 70.00
Pig, Nickel Plated, 7 1/4 In. 40.00
Pig, Roseville 75.00
Pig, Sitting, Cast Iron 45.00

Pig, Thrifty, Standing, Cast Iron 65.00
Pig, Thrifty, The Wise, Cast Iron, 6 3/4 In. 45.00
Pig, With Bow, Lock, Nickeled Cast Iron, 2 7/8 In. 125.00
Pinocchio, Crown Co., 1940, Composition 75.00
Pirate, Holding Pistols, Sits On Chest, Pot Metal 45.00
Pirate, White, Metal, 6 In. 25.00
Pittsburgh Corning, Glass Block 10.00
Polar Bear, Arcade, Gold, Cast Iron, 5 3/8 In. 55.00
Policeman, Marked Harper 1907, Cast Iron, 5 3/8 In. 1225.00
Porky Pig, Bisque .... 75.00 To 85.00
Porky Pig, Cast Iron, 5 3/4 In. 165.00
Possum, Cast Iron 395.00
Pot, Boston Bean, Cast Iron 45.00
Potato, Cast Iron, 5 1/2 In. 500.00
Presto, Cast Iron 15.00
Professor Pug Frog, Cast Iron, 3 1/4 In. 220.00
Puss 'n Boots, Plaster, 10 In. 22.00
Rabbit, A.C.Williams, Cast Iron, 3 3/4 In. 75.00
Rabbit, Cast Iron, 4 5/8 In. 95.00
Rabbit, Cast Iron, 5 In. 75.00
Rabbit, On Base, Cast Iron, 2 1/4 In. 850.00
Rabbit, 1884 Bank, Cast Iron 450.00
Radio, Cast Iron 75.00
Radio, Glass 20.00
Radio, Majestic, Cast Iron 69.50
RCA Dog 120.00
Red Goose, Tin 160.00
Red Riding Hood, Cast Iron 185.00
Redware, Design 22.50
Refrigerator, Figural, Electrolux 39.00
Refrigerator, G.E.Motor Top, Cast Iron 55.00
Reindeer, Cast Iron, 6 In. 60.00
Rhinoceros .... Illus 225.00
Rival Dog Food, Tin 10.00
Rocking Chair, Cast Iron 600.00
Roller Safe, Cast Iron 70.00
Roly Poly, Clown, Nickel Plated Copper, Weighted 40.00
Rooster, A.C.Williams, Cast Iron, 4 7/8 In. 110.00
Rooster, Cast Iron 185.00
Rooster, Painted Black, Brass 85.00
Rooster, Red Comb, Cast Iron 65.00
Rooster, Weaver, Cast Iron 85.00
Rumpelstiltskin, Do You Know Me, Cast Iron, 6 In. .... 225.00 To 525.00
Safe, Combination Lock, Cupids In Relief, Dated 1911, Cast Iron 35.00
Safe, Globe, Ball & Claw Foot, C.1910, Cast Iron, 5 1/4 In. 85.00
Safe, Heart Design, Twist Pin, Bank Falls Apart, Cast Iron, 3 In. 27.50
Safe, Key Combination Safe No.408, Stevens, Cast Iron, 6 In. 110.00
Safe, Marked Security Safe Deposit, Cast Iron, 4 In. 36.00
Safe, Mickey's Bank, Lithograph, Candy, Tin 130.00
Safe, Security, Patent Feb. 14, 1881, Cast Iron 95.00
Safe, Stork & Baby, J.M. Harper 1907, Cast Iron, 5 5/8 In. 375.00
Safe, The Daisy, Japanned & Gold, Cast Iron, 2 3/16 In. 45.00
Safe, The Daisy, Red & Gold, Cast Iron, 2 3/16 In. 45.00
Sailor, Saluting, Early 20th Century, Cast Iron, 6 In. 100.00
Sailor, Seaman's Bank For Savings, Porcelain .... 18.00 To 22.50
Sailor, Silver, Cast Iron, 5 3/4 In. 140.00
Santa Claus, Banthrico 45.00
Santa Claus, Battery Operated, Tin 165.00
Santa Claus, Chalkware, C.1940, 12 In. 25.00
Santa Claus, In Chair, Cast Iron 55.00
Santa Claus, Plaster 22.00
Santa Claus, Save Your Pennies, Tin, Oval 35.00
Santa Claus, Seated In Chair, Chalkware 18.00

Santa Claus, With Pack, Pot Metal 125.00
Santa Claus, With Tree, Cast Iron, 7 1/4 In. .... 180.00 To 370.00
Santa, Ive's, Cast Iron 700.00
Sea Captain, Figural, Wooden, 9 In. 18.00
Seal, Cast Iron, 4 1/4 In. 200.00
Sharecropper, Cast Iron .... 55.00 To 100.00
Shelf Clock, Cast Iron, 5 5/8 In. 105.00
Shell Service Station, Western Germany, Tin, 5 7/8 In. 50.00
Shell, Cast Iron, 1 1/2 In. 65.00
Shell, 1 Pounder Bank, U.S.A., With Eagle, Brass & Steel, 8 In. 35.00
Shoe House, Bronzed, Pot Metal 8.00
Shoe, Embossed Do It With Shoes For The Kid, Tin, 2 7/8 In. 45.00
Simple Simon, Cast Iron 12.00
Slot Machine 55.00
Smiling Jim, Peaceful Bill, Bronze Plated, Cast Iron, 4 In. 545.00
Snoopy, Glass, 1960 .... 8.00
Soldier, World War I, Cast Iron 395.00
Sport Safe, Cast Iron 65.00
Statue Of Liberty, Cast Iron, 6 In. 50.00
Statue Of Liberty, Cast Iron, 9 1/2 In. 175.00
Stove, Dot, Cast Iron, 4 In. 65.00
Stove, Iron & Tin, 4 1/2 In. 70.00
Stove, Pot Metal 95.00
Streetcar, Main Street, Cast Iron, 6 3/4 In. 170.00
Symmetroscope 80.00
Tally Ho, Horse's Head, Horseshoe, Horn, Iron, 4 1/2 In. .... 90.00 To 125.00
Tank Bank U.S.A. 1918, Cast Iron, 4 3/8 In. 55.00
Tank, Save For Victory, Wooden 22.00
Tank, World War I, Brass 145.00
Tank, 1918, Cast Iron 45.00
Tap-Tap, Lehman 185.00
Teddy Roosevelt, Bust, Cast Iron .... 175.00 To 225.00
Teddy Roosevelt, Rough Rider Costume, Cast Iron, 5 1/8 In. 145.00
Telephone, Little Wonder 110.00
The Capitalist, Cast Iron 500.00
There's Money In Aberdeen Angus, Cast Aluminum, Label, 7 1/2 In. 85.00
Three Little Pigs Bank, Chein, Tin, 3 In. 35.00
Three Wise Monkeys .... *Illus* 190.00
Thrift Book, Mickey Mouse 35.00
Tower Bank, 1891, Cast Iron 550.00
Tower Bank, 1891, Cast Iron, 7 In. 300.00
Tower, Fort, Cast Iron, 4 1/8 In. 85.00
Transvaal Money Box, Paul Krugar, Semimechanical, Cast Iron, 6 In. 390.00
Treasure Chest, Cast Iron 25.00
Trick Box, Wooden, 4 1/4 In. 50.00
Trolley Car, Kenton Co., C.1911, Cast Iron, 5 1/4 In. 185.00
Trolley, Main Street, Cast Iron, 6 3/4 In. 250.00
Truck, Armour's Quality Products, Wooden 30.00
Trunk, With Combination Trap, Nickel Plated Steel, 3 1/2 In.Long 45.00
Turkey, Cast Iron, 3 1/2 In. 75.00
Turkey, Cast Iron, 4 3/8 In. 425.00
Turtle, Coppertone Pot Metal, 5 1/2 In. 265.00
Two-Faced Black Man, Cast Iron, 3 1/4 In. .... 85.00 To 250.00
Two-Faced Woman, Cast Iron 92.00
Uncle Sam, Cast Iron 50.00
Uncle Scrooge, Lying In Bed, Disney Productions, 1961 .... 75.00
Underwood Typewriter, 1940 World's Fair, Tin, Figural 48.00
Universal, 3-Coin, Shonk Co., Chicago, Patent 1905 .... 95.00
Watch Me Grow, Tin .... 45.00 To 85.00
Water Tank, Case, Cast Iron 40.00
Water Wheel, Cast Iron, 4 1/2 In. 750.00
When My Fortune Ship Comes In, Brighton, Cast Iron, 5 3/8 In. 300.00
White City Puzzle Saving Bank, A Pail Of Money, Cast Iron, 3 In. 40.00

Windmill, Red & Yellow, Tin, 3 7/8 In. 35.00
World, Tin 6.00
World's Fair Administration Bldg., 1893, Cast Iron, 5 3/4 In. 350.00
World's Fair, 1964, New York, Tin 15.00
Yellow Cab, Cast Iron 475.00

BANKO, Creamer, Tapestry, 5 In. 65.00
Cup & Saucer, Gray, Geometric, C.1890 .... 45.00
Jar, Covered, Gray Ground, Floral, 20th Century, Signed, 2 In. 55.00
Jug, Gray, Applied Flower, 20th Century, Signed, 2 In. 55.00
Mug, Applied Elephant, Marked 130.00
Pitcher, Tankard, 2 Oriental Women In Detail, 12 In. 425.00
Sugar & Creamer, Tapestry, C.1875, Rope Handled 125.00
Sugar, Gray Ground, Flowers, Leaves, Twist Rope Handled, Marked 45.00
Teapot, Birds, Rose, Snake & Frog On Lid 125.00
Teapot, Chicken, Marked 375.00
Teapot, Faces In Relief 88.00
Teapot, Gray, Floral & Crane Design, Strainer, Rope Handled, C.1860 .... 300.00
Teapot, Pumpkin Shape, Stencil Design, C.1875, Marked 175.00
Teapot, Tapestry, Hexagonal, Marked 150.00
Vase, Gray, Basket Effect, Floral, Pair, 19th Century, Signed, 3 1/2 In. 135.00
Vase, Pagoda, Man In Boat, Birds, Mountains, Bulbous, 5 In. 50.00
Vase, Raised Flowers, Miniature 20.00
Vase, Temple Scene, Brown Glaze, Handled, 5 In. 75.00

BARBER, Bowl, Flanged, Neck Cut-Out, Nickel Over Brass 75.00
Chair, Archer, Rochester, N.Y., Horsehair Padding, Reclines 1500.00
Chair, Carved Horse Legs, Hoofs, Brass Horseshoes, C.1891, Hydraulic 2750.00
Chair, Carved Swans, Red Velvet, C.1878, Walnut 850.00
Chair, Cast Brass Lion's Paws, C.1895, Oak 1500.00
Chair, Child's, Kiddie Car, Hydraulic System 1600.00
Chair, Kern, Victorian Carvings, Burl Overlay 2250.00
Chair, Koch, Carved Horse Leg & Hoof Legs 2950.00
Chair, Koch, Columbia Model, 4-Legged Base, Oak 350.00
Chair, Koken, Hydraulic, Carvings, Brass Legs, Velvet Upholstered 1450.00
Chair, Koken, Hydraulic, 4-Legged, Oak 1850.00
Chair, Koken, Round Bottom & Back, Oak 2250.00
Clipper, Improved Andis Master, Racine, Wis., Patent 1924 .... 35.00
Hat & Coat Rack 325.00
Light, Pole, Glass, Red, Blue Stripes, Signed Marvy, St.Paul, 24 In. 125.00
Pole, Nonrevolving, C.1900 .... 295.00
Pole, Wall-Mount, Acorn Finial, Wooden, 48 In. 395.00
Pole, Wall-Mount, Glass Globe 200.00
Pole, Wooden, 6 Ft. 170.00
Scissors, Lambert, Lakeworth, Florida 15.00

BAROMETER, Aneroid, Wooden Case, Dial 13 In.Diam. 40.00
French, Oak 125.00
Pocket, Short & Mason Co., Leather Case 165.00

BASKET, Acorn-Shaped, Sweetgrass & Splint, 2 X 1 1/2 In. 15.00
Allover Frame Scene, Coil Construction, 13 X 12 In. 38.00
Apple, Splint Handle, Shallow, Carolina, 15 In.Diam. 40.00
Apple, Splint, 1/2 Bushel 35.00
Ash Handle & Ribs, Leather Weavers & Binding, 12 X 9 In. 45.00
Boudoir, Woven Palm, Hinged Cover, Satin Bow, 3 X 6 X 2 In. 12.50
Bread, Rye Straw 55.00
Buttock, Vine Handle, 25 In. 210.00
Buttocks, Splint, High Sides, 8 In. 260.00
Buttocks, Splint, Wooden Handle, 8 X 8 3/4 In. 85.00
Buttocks, Splint, Wooden Handle, 12 X 8 In. 55.00
Buttocks, Splint, Wooden Handle, 14 X 14 In. 85.00
Caddy, Wine, Woven Silver, Handle, Christofle, France, 9 1/4 X 4 1/4 In 65.00

Cat, Wicker 18.00
Cheese, Splint, 24 X 8 In. 385.00
Cheese, 6-Sided, 19 In.Diam. 295.00
Cheese, 28 In.Diam. 247.50
Doll Clothes, Wicker, Braided Handles, Oval, 11 1/2 X 8 X 6 In. 20.00
Eel, Splint Woven, Wooden Buoy Bobber, Hemp Rope, C.1870, 9 X 21 In. ... 140.00
Egg, Child's, Hand-Notched Bentwood Handle, Rim 6 1/2 In., , 14 In.Hig ... 50.00
Egg, Farmer Wife's, Handle, Natural Patina, Rim 10 In. X 12 In. 95.00
Egg, Hand-Carved Handle, Wrapped Rim, C.1870, 7 1/4 X 11 In. 130.00
Egg, Notched Bentwood Handle, Rim 10 In., 14 In.Tall. 65.00
Feather, Bombe-Sided, Cover Slides Up Or Down, 12 In. 65.00
Food Storage, New York State, 19th Century, Hexagonal Openwork ... 145.00
Gathering, Woven Splint, 17 X 27 X 5 1/2 In. 55.00
Hanging, Loom, Weaver, Maine, Cross Handle, Bottom, 15 In., 25 In. High ... 350.00
Herb Drying, Split Oak, 2 Drop Handles, Signed H.Johnson 35.00
Kennel Carry, Victorian, Tin Window, 12 X 20 X 16 1/2 In. 75.00
Melon, Red, 13 X 24 In. 900.00
Melon, Splint, Green, 5 X 6 In. 525.00
Melon, Splint, 2 1/2 X 3 1/4 In. 450.00
Petit Point Design, Narrow Strands, Covered, On Base, Oval, 8 In. ... 55.00
Picnic, Hinged Pine Cover, Bentwood Handles, 10 1/4 X 17 3/4 X 8 In. ... 30.00
Rattan, Chain Link Openwork Sides, 3 3/4 X 3 In. 10.00
Rye Straw, Applied Hickory Base & Handle, 19 X 21 1/2 In. 900.00
Rye Straw, Laced Splint Willow, 15 In. 40.00
Rye, Covered, 3 Ft.Diam. 275.00
Scalloped Rim, Openwork Handles, Wicker, 5 1/4 X 7 1/2 X 2 1/2 In. ... 6.50
Scissor Case, Double Loop Sweetgrass Handles, Tapered, 3 3/4 In. ... 18.50
Sewing, Diamond Shape, Various Weaves, 7 In.Diam. 45.00
Sewing, Straw & Wicker, Bombe-Shaped, Pink Interior, C.1890, 4 In. ... 45.00
Shopping, Victorian, Braided Wicker, Rim, Oval Base, 18 In. 125.00
Splint Feather, Domed Cover Slides Up & Down Handle, 11 X 15 In. ... 135.00
Splint Nose, Bentwood Rim & Handles, 13 3/4 X 15 In. 185.00
Splint, Black, Wall, 3-Pocket, 18 X 10 In. 950.00
Splint, Blue Bands, 2 1/4 X 3 In. 110.00
Splint, Blue, Covered, Cylindrical, 8 In. 275.00
Splint, Blue, Oval, 4 X 4 In. 600.00
Splint, Blue, Yellow Band, 2 1/2 X 3 1/2 In. 140.00
Splint, Brown, Black Dots, Rectangular, 8 1/2 In. 625.00
Splint, Brown, Handled, Rectangular, 5 In. 100.00
Splint, Cone, Fixed Handle, New England, 7 1/2 In. 380.00
Splint, Curlicue Design, Wooden Handle, 12 X 9 In. 35.00
Splint, Diagonal Handled, Rectangular, 5 X 8 In. 120.00
Splint, Dome-Topped Cover, Loop Ring, 7 1/4 X 3 1/2 In. 30.00
Splint, Fish, Rectangular, 7 X 11 In. 50.00
Splint, Fixed Handle, Melon, 8 In. 300.00
Splint, Handled, Polychrome Painted, 7 X 22 In. 200.00
Splint, Melon, Covered, New England, 6 1/2 X 12 1/2 In. 250.00
Splint, Melon, Fixed Handle, Red, 5 X 8 In. 340.00
Splint, Melon, Fixed Handle, 9 X 13 X In. 290.00
Splint, Melon, Fixed Handle, 12 X 15 In. 425.00
Splint, Melon, Green, New England, 4 1/2 In. 110.00
Splint, Melon, Green, 6 X 8 In. 340.00
Splint, Melon, Light Gray, 4 1/4 In. 210.00
Splint, Melon, Red, 6 X 8 In. 650.00
Splint, Melon, 2 1/2 X 4 In. 375.00
Splint, Melon, 5 1/2 X 7 In. 300.00
Splint, Miniature, 3 3/4 X 3 X 1 3/4 In. 25.00
Splint, Notched Handle, Square Base, 11 In. 65.00
Splint, Oval, Handled, New England, 7 In. 500.00
Splint, Pink-Gray, 4 X 3 In. 150.00
Splint, Polychrome, Cylindrical, Covered, 7 In. 375.00
Splint, Polychrome, Cylindrical, Handled, Covered, 10 1/2 In. 375.00
Splint, Polychrome, Cylindrical, Peaked Cover, 10 1/2 In. 500.00

Splint, Polychrome, Cylindrical, 6 1/2 In. 120.00
Splint, Polychrome, Melon, Fixed Handle, 6 1/2 In. 280.00
Splint, Polychrome, Melon, 2 1/2 X 3 In. 750.00
Splint, Polychrome, Melon, 3 X 4 In. 55.00
Splint, Polychrome, Square, 12 X 12 In. 200.00
Splint, Red & Black, Handled, Rectangular, 9 X 11 1/2 In. 90.00
Splint, Red Bands, Covered, Rectangular, 6 1/2 In. 130.00
Splint, Shallow, Cylindrical, 2 1/2 X 7 In. 70.00
Splint, Swing Handle, Cylindrical, 19th Century, 4 1/2 In. 150.00
Splint, Wall, Green, Rectangular, 9 1/2 In. 325.00
Splint, Wall, Polychrome Paint, Rectangular, 10 X 10 In. 500.00
Splint, Wall, Polychrome, 2-Pocket, 28 X 14 In. 3200.00
Splint, Wall, Rectangular, New England, 7 X 10 In. 260.00
Splint, Wall, Rectangular, New England, 11 X 12 In. 460.00
Splint, Wall, Rectangular, 7 In. 80.00
Splint, Wall, Rectangular, 10 X 16 In. 220.00
Splint, Wall, 3-Pocket, White, 31 X 14 In. 950.00
Splint, Wooden Handle, 7 1/2 In. .... 75.00 To 185.00
Splint, Wooden Handle, 8 In. 65.00
Storage, Splint, Cross-Over Top, Square Base, 9 In. Rim, 6 In. High 75.00
Storage, Splint, Red Beet Dye & Natural, New Hampshire, 9 3/4 In. 50.00
Storage, Stovepipe, Squared Bottom, Round Mouth, C.1860, Rim 10 In. 210.00
Sweetgrass, C.1920, Covered, 7 X 3 In. 25.00
Wall, Polychrome, Oval, 6 In. 550.00
Wall, Splint, Black Dots, Diamonds, Rectangular, 9 1/2 In. 850.00
Willow, Cane, Handle, 15 X 17 In. 10.00
Winnowing, Pyramid Pattern, 18th Century, 21 1/4 In. 225.00

BATCHELDER, Tile, Man Spearing Lion, 4 X 4 In. 95.00

BATMAN, Mask, Robin, Flip-Over, 2 In 1, 1966 .... 7.00
Ornament, Bicycle, Full Figure, 1966, Wrapped 12.00
Pin, Enameled, Original Display Card, 1966 .... 6.50
Thermos, 1966 .... 8.00
Toy, Car, Friction, Lithograph, Boxed, 12 In. 125.00

*Battersea enamels are enamels painted on copper and made in the Battersea
district of London from about 1750 to 1756. Many similar enamels are
mistakenly called Battersea.*

BATTERSEA, Box, Green Base, White Interior, Mirror, Oval, 1 1/2 X 1 1/4 In. 235.00
Box, Patch, Dog's Head 225.00
Box, Sky Blue Exterior, White Floral Design, Landscape, 2 1/2 In. 225.00
Box, White Ground, Cobalt Border, White Dots, Oval, 1 3/4 In. 200.00

*Bavaria was a district where many types of pottery and porcelain were made
for centuries. The words "Bavaria, Germany" appeared after 1871.*

BAVARIA, see also Rosenthal
BAVARIA, Bowl, Floral Design, 10 1/4 In. 30.00
Bowl, White, Roses, Scalloped Top, Gold Trim, Marked, 9 In. 36.00
Cracker Jar, Gold, Fruits On Side 35.00
Dish, Candy, Ruby Etched 90.00
Eggcup, Carmen Pattern 15.50
Humidor, Floral, Pipe Finial, China 65.00
Plate, Acorn Design, Round, Open Handled, Schumann, 10 In. 25.00
Plate, Fish, Hand-Painted, Gold Lace Rim, Tirschenreuth, Set Of 6 .... 120.00
Plate, Floral Design Center, Set Of 10, 8 In. 325.00
Plate, Green & Gold, Floral Center, 10 In. 35.00
Plate, Portrait, Cobalt Blue, Gold Rim, 9 In. 125.00
Plate, Portrait, Victorian Woman, Roses, Gold, 6-Sided, 11 1/2 In. 65.00
Plate, Portrait, Woman, Blue, Gold, 1905, ... 30.00
Plate, Rose Design, Round, Scalloped, Louvre, 10 In. 20.00
Platter, Flowered, Gold & Rust, 11 X 9 In. 30.00

Sugar & Creamer, Covered, Green, Rose Design, Hand-Painted, Signed 75.00
Sugar & Creamer, Pastel Roses, Prince Regent Bavaria 35.00
Sugar, Covered, Sheaf Of Wheat, Eschenbach 3.00
    BAYONET, see Sword, Bayonet
    BEACH BABIES, see Sand Babies

BEATLES, Album, Two Virgins, Yoko Ono & John Lennon, 1968, Signed By Lennon 1050.00
  Bandana 15.00
  Book, Coloring 25.00
  Book, Souvenir, A Hard Day's Night 37.25
  Card, Bubble Gum, Set Of 165 .... 200.00
  Cards, Playing, Yellow Submarine, Set 55.00
  Doll, John Lennon, Inflatable 20.00
  Fun Kit 16.50
  Lunch Box, Yellow Submarine 27.50
  Mirror, Pocket, Black & White, 1964 .... 2.50
  Necklace & Bracelet 75.00
  Pillow, 12 X 12 In. 30.00
  Pin, Flasher, Red Background, Says The Beatles, 2 1/2 In. 3.00
  Pinback, Movie Promotional, Help, Red Background, 2 In. 2.00
  Poster, Yellow Submarine, Italian, 1969, 18 1/2 X 26 1/2 In. 300.00
  Ring, Flasher, Gumball, Set Of 4 .... 5.00
  Scarf, Pictures, Signatures, Instruments, Dated 1964, 22 X 22 In. 7.50
  Song Sheet, Scrambled Egg, Signed & Inscribed, 12 X 9 In. 550.00
  Tie Tack, 4 On Guitar, Metal 6.00
  Tray, Photograph Of Each Beatle, Tin, Red 85.00
  Tumbler, Group Picture 25.00
  Wristwatch, Photo Face, Sweep Second Hand, Dated 1964 .... 415.00
    BECK, see Buffalo Pottery

BED WARMER, Center Engraved Bird On Cover, Brass 270.00
  Engraved Bird, Turned Cherry Handle 250.00
  Hinged Copper Pan, Wooden Handle, Salesman's Sample, 9 In. 85.00

Beehive, Austria, or Beehive, Vienna, china includes all the many types of decorated porcelain marked with the famous beehive mark. The mark has been used since the eighteenth century.
    BEEHIVE, see also Royal Vienna
BEEHIVE, Bottle, Cologne, Florals, Gold Top 60.00
  Cracker Jar, Classical Figures, Austria 70.00
  Plate, Cobalt & Blue, Classical Scene, 9 3/4 In. 120.00
  Plate, Portrait, Gold Tracery, Lady Plucking Lyre, 9 3/4 In. 120.00
  Vase, Picture Of Falstaff, Austrian, 8 1/2 In. 60.00

Beer cans have been made since the 1930s. Collectors search for old or new cans.

BEER CAN, Ansell's Mild, Squirrel, British, 5-Pint 18.00
  Budweiser, St.Charles Bicentennial Issue, 1976 .... 5.00
  Buffalo, Gold Can 4.00
  Falstaff, Cone Top 22.00
  Gold Medal, Stegmaier, Cone Top 28.50
  Jet Malt Liquor, Full 15.00
  Koch's, Dunkirk, N.Y., 1 Gallon 6.00
  Kuebler Pilsner, Cone Top 50.00
  National Lager, Flat Top 3.50
  Piel's Real Draft, Woodgrain Test Can 6.00
  Razorback, Set Of 3 .... 5.00
  Ruddles Traditional Draught Bitter, British, 5-Pint 18.00
  Tiger, Brewed For Nigeria, Schmidt 3.50
  Tip Top Ale, Cone Top 28.00
  Whitbread Party King, British, 5-Pint 18.00
  White Bear, Flat Top 1.50

Wildcat Commemorative 1.50
Wisconsin, Premium 1.50

Bells have been made of china, glass, or metal. All types are collected.

BELL, Alarm, Great Lakes Oil Tanker, 11 X 8 In., Brass 8.00
　Boxing Ring, Iron, 12 In. 30.00
　Brass, Wooden Handle, 7 1/2 In. 15.00
　Bronze, Canadian Railroad, Leather Strap, 4 1/2 In. 40.00
　Bronze, Ceremonial, 3 Knob Bed Feet, Pear Shape, 9 1/4 In. 135.00
　Bronze, Decorated With Words, Stand, 32 In. 250.00
　Calliope, 2 Octaves, Cast Iron Stand, Brass 150.00
　Chain Attached To Clapper, Brass, 6 X 5 In. 19.00
　Church, Cast Iron, 38 In.Across 1800.00
　Church, F.Fuller, 1879, Providence, R.I., Bronze, 21 X 18 In .... 900.00 To 950.00
　Door, Gong Type, Dated 1879, Cast Iron 25.00
　Dutch Girl, Brass 25.00
　Farm, Cast Iron, Large 85.00
　Figural, Lady, Dances Tiptoe On Ball, Starburst Base, Brass, 7 3/4 In. 40.00
　Figural, Lady, Full Ruffled Skirt, Bonnet, Brass, 4 1/2 In. 25.00
　For Shafts, Iron Clapper, Brass, 2 7/8 In., Pair 22.50
　Gong, Boxing, Brass, Lever Action, 9 1/4 In.Diam. 68.00
　Hanging, Bird & Floral Design, Iron, 44 X 32 In. 450.00
　Jester Head, Brass, 4 In. 55.00
　Lady, Blue Dress, Green Bow & Fan, Brass, 3 1/4 X 6 In. 75.00
　Lady, Fancy Hairdo, Fan, Hoopskirt, Brass, 5 1/2 In. 68.00
　Napoleon Figural Handle, Brass, 3 1/4 X 6 1/4 In. 75.00
　Navy, 9 In. 125.00
　No.32, Case, Iron 375.00
　Ox, 17th Century, Wooden 75.00
　R.A.F.Benevolent Fund, Stalin, Churchill, & Roosevelt Heads, 5 1/2 In. ... 60.00
　School, Brass, Wooden Handle, 10 In. 80.00
　School, Brass, 4 In. 25.00
　School, Brass, 6 In. 16.00
　School, Brass, 8 1/2 In. 65.00
　School, Hand, Brass 65.00
　School, Handle Marked J.E.W., C.1870, Brass, 8 1/2 X 4 1/2 In. 75.00
　School, Hanger, Cast Iron 495.00
　Schoolmarm's, Turned Walnut Handle, Brass, C.1870, 8 In. 75.00
　Sheep, Cast-Iron Clapper, Sheet Iron, 2 X 2 1/2 X 3 In. 14.50
　Sheep, Small 20.00
　Ship, Clapper, Brass, C.1870, 10 In. 130.00
　Ship, Iron Clapper, Hand-Up Ring, Brass, 5 X 5 1/4 In. 40.00
　Sleigh, Acorn Shape, Brass, Set Of 27 .... 78.50
　Sleigh, Acorn, Loop & Pin, Buckle, C.1870, Strap, 82 In., Set Of 25 .... 200.00
　Sleigh, Original Leather Strap, Brass, Set Of 19 .... 150.00
　Spread-Winged Eagle, Shield, Civil War, Cast Metal, 3 1/2 X 5 1/4 In. ... 125.00
　Store, Coiled Spring, Brass 65.00
　Teacher's, Wooden Handle, 6 In. 12.00
　Town Crier's, Wooden Handle, Brass, 14 In. 225.00
　Tricycle, Embossed Vines, Nickel 12.00
　Trolley 55.00
　Woman With Hands On Hips, French, Signed, Bronze, 6 1/4 In. 45.00

*Belleek china is made in Ireland, other European countries, and the
United States. The glaze is creamy yellow and appears wet. The first
Belleek was made in 1857. All pieces listed are Irish Belleek.
The mark changed through the years. The first mark, black, dates from
1863 to 1890. The second mark, black, dates from 1891 to 1926 and includes
the words "Co.Fermanagh, Ireland." The third mark, black, dates from
1926 to 1946 and has the words "Deanta in Eirinn." The fourth mark,
same as the third mark but green, dates from 1946 to 1955. The fifth mark,
green, dates from 1955 to 1965 and has an R in a circle added in the upper
right. The sixth mark, green, dates after 1965 and the words "Co.
Fermanagh" have been omitted.*

BELLEEK, see also Ceramic Art Co.; Haviland; Lenox; Ott &
Brewer; Willets
BELLEEK, Ashtray, Horseshoe 15.00
  Basket, Double Rodded Edging, Hexagon, 9 1/2 In. 1250.00
  Basket, Henshaw Pattern, 8 In. 1800.00
  Basket, Shamrock, 3 Strand, 5 In.Diam. 390.00
  Basket, 4 Strand, Applied Flowers, Ribbon Mark, Small 175.00
  Basket, 4 Strand, Cloverleaf Shape, Applied Roses, Shamrock, Marked 190.00
  Bowl, Cereal, New Shell, 3rd Black Mark 30.00
  Bowl, Floral Trim, Gold Handles, 6 In. 145.00
  Bowl, Flower, Raised Design, 2nd Black Mark, 3 In. 345.00
  Bowl, Handled, 2nd Black Mark, 2 1/2 X 3 1/2 In. 48.00
  Bowl, Lily Center, 1st Black Mark, 9 In.Diam. 1950.00
  Bowl, Oatmeal, Melon Ribbed, Marked, 2 X 5 In. 40.00
  Bowl, Shamrock Pattern, 3rd Black Mark, 2 X 3 1/2 In. 50.00
  Bowl, Slop, Limpet, 1st Black Mark 45.00
  Box, Heart Shaped, Covered, Green Trim, 2nd Black Mark, 5 In. 220.00
  Box, Trinket, Acorn, Green Mark 64.00
  Box, Trinket, Grate Shape, 3rd Green Mark 85.50
  Box, Trinket, 2nd Black Mark 285.00
  Bread Plate, Limpet, 3rd Black Mark, 5 Colors, 11 1/4 In. 250.00
  Bread Plate, New Shell, 3rd Black Mark, Dark Luster, 10 1/2 In. 145.00
  Brooch, Blue & Yellow Flowers 35.00
  Bust, Clytie, 1st Black Mark, Parian Ware, 11 In. 1775.00
  Butter, Leaf, Open, 3rd Black Mark 35.00
  Butter, Shamrock, 2nd Black Mark, 4 1/4 In. 75.00
  Butter, Shell Pattern, Lidded, 3, Prong Lid Finial, 2nd Black Mark 240.00
  Cabaret Set, Echinus, Pearl, 1st Black Mark 1850.00
  Cabaret Set, Hawthorne Design, 1st Black Mark 2100.00
  Cabaret Set, Tridacna, Pearl, 2nd Black Mark 1200.00
  Cake Plate, Limpet, Handled, Black Mark, 11 1/2 In. 125.00
  Cake Plate, 2-Handled, Tridacna, Green Mark, 10 In. 30.00
  Cake Plate, 4-Strand Weave, 10 1/4 In. 275.00
  Cake Server, Grasses, 1st Black Mark, 11 1/2 In. 250.00
  Candleholder, Celtic, Green Mark 48.00
  Chamberstick, Boy On A Dolphin, Pearl & Biscuit, 1st Black Mark 890.00
  Chocolate Pot, Gold Dragon, Applied Handle, Red Pattern, Marked 165.00
  Coffee Set, Shamrock, Green Mark, 4 Piece 120.00
  Coffeepot, Limpet, 2nd Green Mark 120.00
  Coffeepot, Shamrock Pattern, Harp Handle, 3rd Black Mark 175.00
  Creamer, Girl, Green Mark 25.00
  Creamer, Ivy, Twisted Rope Handle, Marked, 5 In. 250.00
  Creamer, Ribbon, 2nd Black Mark 40.00
  Creamer, Shell, Harp Handle, Green Mark 30.00
  Creamer, Shell, Pink Branch Handle, 1st Black Mark, 4 1/2 In. 195.00
  Creamer, Twig Handle, Pearl Finish, Pink Trim, Black Mark 45.00
  Cup & Saucer, Artichoke, White, 1st Black Mark 145.00
  Cup & Saucer, Chocolate, Shamrock Pattern, Green Mark 41.00
  Cup & Saucer, Demitasse, Floral Design, Gold Trim 25.00
  Cup & Saucer, Demitasse, Shamrock, 2nd Black Mark 70.00
  Cup & Saucer, Demitasse, Shamrock, 3rd Black Mark 68.00
  Cup & Saucer, Demitasse, Tridacna, 2nd Black Mark 70.00
  Cup & Saucer, Echinus, 1st Black Mark, C.1861 .... 120.00
  Cup & Saucer, Grasses, 1st Mark 150.00
  Cup & Saucer, Green Trim, 3rd Black Mark 84.00
  Cup & Saucer, Harp & Shamrock, 2nd Green Mark 42.00
  Cup & Saucer, Harp Handle, 3rd Black Mark 70.00
  Cup & Saucer, Hawthorne, 1st Black Mark 290.00
  Cup & Saucer, Hexagon, Pink Trim, 2nd Black Mark 82.00
  Cup & Saucer, Hexagon, 1st Black Mark 60.00
  Cup & Saucer, Institute Ware, 2nd Black Mark 190.00
  Cup & Saucer, Limpet, Plain, 3rd Black Mark 70.00
  Cup & Saucer, Limpet, 1st Black Mark 60.00

Cup & Saucer, Mask, Black Mark 65.00
Cup & Saucer, Neptune, Green Trim, 2nd Black Mark 84.00
Cup & Saucer, Neptune, Pink Trim, 2nd Black Mark 82.00
Cup & Saucer, Neptune, White, 2nd Black Mark 70.00
Cup & Saucer, Pink & Gold Trim, 2nd Black Mark 125.00
Cup & Saucer, Pink Trim, New Shell, 3rd Black Mark 65.00
Cup & Saucer, Shamrock, Basket Weave, Twig Handle, Marked, Set Of 6 .... 180.00
Cup & Saucer, Shamrock, Green Mark, Set Of 8 .... 240.00
Cup & Saucer, Shamrock, Harp Handle, 3rd Black Mark 84.00
Cup & Saucer, Shamrock, 2nd Black Mark 60.00
Cup & Saucer, Shamrock, 3rd Black Mark .... 48.00 To 54.00
Cup & Saucer, Tridacna, Green Trim, 2nd Black Mark ...... 55.00 To 65.00
Cup & Saucer, Tridacna, Orange Trim, 2nd Black Mark 145.00
Cup & Saucer, Tridacna, Pink Trim, 2nd Black Mark 44.00
Cup & Saucer, Tridacna, Plain, 1st Black Mark On Saucer 55.00
Cup & Saucer, Tridacna, 2nd Black Mark 125.00
Cup & Saucer, White 30.00
Cup, Cone, 2nd Black Mark 55.00
Cup, Harp & Shamrock, 2nd Black Mark 15.00
Cup, Nut, Shell, 3rd Green Mark 23.00
Cup, Tridacna, Green Trim, 2nd Black Mark 30.00
Dish, Heart-Shaped, 2nd Black Mark, 5 X 5 In. 65.00
Dish, Nut, Multicolored Flowers, Ivory Ground, Marked 55.00
Dish, Primrose, 3rd Black Mark 35.00
Dish, Sandwich, Shell-Shaped, 1st Mark 145.00
Dish, Shell, Handled, 3rd Black Mark, 6 In. 30.00
Dish, Shell, Oval, 3rd Black Mark 45.00
Dish, Shell, Purple Coral Trim, Sterling Frame, 1st Black Mark ... 464.00
Ewer, Applied Flowers, Black Mark, 8 In. 135.00
Figurine, Girl With A Basket, 1st Black Mark, 9 In. 950.00
Figurine, Greyhound, 3rd Black Mark 640.00
Figurine, Harp, Tower & Hound 200.00
Figurine, Irish Greyhound, 3rd Black Mark 614.00
Figurine, Leprechaun, Clear, 3rd Black Mark 240.00
Figurine, Lesbia, 1st Mark, 9 In. 600.00
Figurine, Pig, Green Mark, Large 35.00
Figurine, Pig, White, Yellow Ears, Green Mark 70.00
Figurine, Swan, 2nd Black Mark, 4 In. 108.00
Figurine, Tri-Mermaid Globe, 1st Black Mark, 7 3/4 In. 890.00
Flask, Sterling Cover, 1st Black Mark 745.00
Flower Holder, 1st Black Mark, 8 X 8 In. 1450.00
Flowerpot, Applied Flowers, 2nd Black Mark, 3 X 2 5/8 In. 110.00
Flowerpot, Octagonal, 4 1/2 In. 90.00
Footbath, 1st Black Mark, 22 In.Diam. 890.00
Harp, Blue Mark, 5 1/2 In. 295.00
Honeypot, Grasses, 1st Black Mark 600.00
Jam Jar, Shamrock, Covered, Marked 85.00
Jardiniere, Shell, 2nd Black Mark, 9 In. 1750.00
Jug, Pink Trim, 2nd Black Mark, 6 In. 390.00
Kettle, Water, Echinus, 2nd Black Mark, 6 1/2 In. 890.00
Kettle, Water, Grasses, 1st Black Mark, 8 In. 990.00
Lamp Base, Lighthouse Tower, 1st Black Mark 420.00
Lily Center, Pink & Tan, 1st Mark, 9 In. 1950.00
Marmalade Jar, Shamrock, 3rd Black Mark 86.00
Mug, Artichoke, 1st Black Mark 95.00
Mug, Grapes & Leaves, Gold & Green Handle, C.1886 .... 200.00
Mug, Grapes, Foliage, Handled, Artist Signed, Marked, 7 In. 75.00
Mug, Portrait, Bust Of Gentleman, Brown Ground 150.00
Mug, Singing Monk, Rusty Brown To Cream, Signed 85.00
Paperweight, Whippet, 1st Black Mark 1450.00
Pitcher, Autumn Leaves Design 85.00
Pitcher, Cider, Blackberries, Marked, 6 1/2 In. 150.00
Pitcher, Cider, Red & Yellow Apples, Signed 185.00

Pitcher, Ivy, 1st Black Mark, 4 1/2 In.	50.00
Pitcher, Milk, Ivy Pattern, Black Mark, 6 In.	160.00
Pitcher, Milk, Shamrock, Basket Weave, 3rd Black Mark, 4 1/4 In.	115.00
Plaque, Hand-Painted Multicolor Design, 1st Black Mark, 14 In.	1200.00
Plate, Bacchus & Ivy Pattern, 2nd Black Mark, 8 In.	90.00
Plate, Bacchus, Yellow Border, Black Mark, 8 1/2 In.	45.00
Plate, Bread, Limpet, Cob Trim, 6 In.	30.00
Plate, Bread, Neptune, 2nd Black Mark	95.00
Plate, Bread, Shamrock, 2nd Black Mark, 6 1/2 In.	30.00
Plate, Cake, Limpet, Handled, 11 1/2 In.	125.00
Plate, Christmas, 1970	95.00
Plate, Christmas, 1971, Boxed	65.00
Plate, Echinus Pattern, Pink Trim, 1st Black Mark, 9 1/4 In.	118.00
Plate, Green & Gilded, Reticulated, 2nd Black Mark, 9 1/2 In.	425.00
Plate, Harp & Shamrock, 2nd Green Mark, 8 In.	32.00
Plate, Hawthorne, 1st Black Mark, 7 In.	210.00
Plate, Hawthorne, 1st Black Mark, 9 In.	375.00
Plate, Heart-Shaped, Green Mark	25.00
Plate, Leaf, Cob Trim, 6 In.	29.00
Plate, Mask, 3rd Black Mark, 8 In.	53.00
Plate, Neptune, Green Trim, Marked, 5 In.	22.00
Plate, Ruffle Pattern Border, Pink, Gold Edging, Marked, 10 In.	45.00
Plate, Salad, Shamrock, 2nd Black Mark	33.00
Plate, Salad, Tridacna, Green Trim, 2nd Black Mark	32.00
Plate, Sandwich, Shell-Shaped, 1st Black Mark	135.00
Plate, Shamrock, 2nd Black Mark, 8 In.	34.00
Plate, Shamrock, 3rd Black Mark, 8 In.	33.00
Plate, Soup, Tridacna, Gold Trim, 2nd Black Mark, 8 1/2 In.	155.00
Plate, Sydney, Green Trim, 2nd Black Mark, 6 In.	69.00
Plate, Tridacna, Pink Trim, Black Mark, 8 In.	44.00
Plate, Tridacna, Pink Trim, 3rd Black Mark, 7 In.	48.00
Platter, Game Birds Drinking At Stream, 10 1/2 In.	30.00
Pot, Gold Handles & Trim, Black Legs, 2nd Black Mark, 4 In.	150.00
Salt, New Shell, Open, 3rd Black Mark	30.00
Salt, Pink Coral Feet, Marked	18.50
Salt, Star Shape, Green Mark	16.00
Saucer, Light Green Trim, Marked	24.00
Saucer, Tridacna, 3rd Black Mark, Set Of 5	50.00
Snack Set, Tridacna, 3rd Black Mark	125.00
Spill, Spray Of Roses, Buds, & Leaves, 3rd Black Mark, 6 In.	175.00
Stein, Hand-Painted Flowers, Green	75.00
Sugar & Creamer, Basket Weave & Shamrocks, 3rd Black Mark	75.00
Sugar & Creamer, Black Mark	65.00
Sugar & Creamer, Cleary, 1st Green Mark	40.00
Sugar & Creamer, Ivy, 3rd Black Mark, 4 3/4 In.	130.00
Sugar & Creamer, Lily	40.00
Sugar & Creamer, Lotus, 3rd Black Mark	88.00
Sugar & Creamer, Mask, 3rd Black Mark	108.00
Sugar & Creamer, New Shell, 3rd Black Mark	85.00
Sugar & Creamer, Ribbon, 3rd Black Mark	65.00
Sugar & Creamer, Shamrock & Basket, Green Mark	55.00
Sugar & Creamer, Shamrock & Harp, 3rd Black Mark	50.00
Sugar & Creamer, Shamrock, Child's, 4th Green Mark	55.00
Sugar & Creamer, Shamrock, Green Mark	55.00
Sugar & Creamer, Shamrock, 2nd Black Mark	125.00
Sugar & Creamer, Shamrock, 3rd Black Mark	70.00 To 110.00
Sugar, Shamrock, Open, 3rd Black Mark	40.00
Swan, 1st Black Mark, 2 1/2 X 4 3/8 X 3 1/8 In.	165.00
Swan, 3rd Black Mark, 6 In.	120.00
Tazza, Shell, Dolphins, Turquoise, Pearl Base, 1st Black Mark	1650.00
Tea Set, Harp Handles, 3rd Black Mark, 3 Piece	250.00
Tea Set, Neptune, Green, 2nd Black Mark	675.00
Tea Set, Shamrock, Marked	40.00

Tea Set, Tridacna, Pearl, 2nd Black Mark, 8 Piece 1250.00
Teapot, Basket Weave & Cloverleaf, 2nd Green Mark, 6 1/2 In. 55.00
Teapot, Basket Weave & Shamrock, Finial, 4th Black Mark 145.00
Teapot, Blarney Pattern, 2nd Black Mark, Medium Size 450.00
Teapot, Grasses Pattern, 1st Black Mark, 5 1/2 X 4 1/2 In. 450.00
Teapot, Harp & Shamrock, 1st Green Mark 100.00
Teapot, Hawthorne, Yellow Glazing, 1st Black Mark 1050.00
Teapot, Limpet, 1st Green Mark 150.00
Teapot, Neptune, Green Mark 152.00
Teapot, Neptune, Green, 2nd Black Mark 260.00
Teapot, Shamrock, Harp Handled, 3rd Black Mark 240.00
Teapot, Shamrock, 2nd Black Mark 130.00
Teapot, Tridacna, Green Trim, 2nd Black Mark 195.00
Teapot, Tridacna, Pearl, 2nd Black Mark, 8 In. 475.00
Tray, Blarney Pattern, 2nd Black Mark, 15 In. 950.00
Tray, Bread, Basket, 4-Strand Weave, 10 In. 275.00
Tray, Dragon, Brown & Pearl, 1st Black Mark, 15 In.Diam. 1800.00
Tray, For Tea Set, Tridacna, 1st Black Mark 475.00
Tray, Gilded & Pink, 1st Black Mark, 14 In.Diam. 1900.00
Tray, Hawthorne Spider, Amber & Pearl, 1st Black Mark, 14 In.Square 1350.00
Tray, Hexagonal, Green Trim, 2nd Black Mark, 17 In. 1100.00
Tray, Leaf Shape, Green Mark, 5 X 5 In. 34.50
Tray, Pinecone Rim, Pine Tree Center, 2nd Mark, 14 1/4 X 17 1/2 In. 495.00
Tray, Sandwich, Mask, 3rd Black Mark 175.00
Vase, Aberdeen, Applied Flowers, 3rd Black Mark 186.00
Vase, Amphora, Gilding, 1st Black Mark, 7 In. 750.00
Vase, Baluster Flowered, 3rd Black Mark, Pearl, 8 1/2 In. 375.00
Vase, Bird Stump, Pearl, 2nd Black Mark, 12 1/2 In. 1750.00
Vase, Cylinder Shaped, Roses, Pink Ground, Blue Top, 7 In. 85.00
Vase, Dolphin Handled, Yellow, Marked, 6 1/2 In. 35.00
Vase, Fish, Pink Trim, 1st Mark, 7 1/2 In. .... 575.00 To 625.00
Vase, Flying Fish, 1st Black Mark, 2 1/2 X 4 1/2 In. 395.00
Vase, Hoof Tripod, 1st Black Mark, 8 1/2 X 13 In. 695.00
Vase, Jug, Aberdeen, Pearl Luster, 3rd Black Mark, 6 In. 195.00
Vase, Lizard, 1st Mark, 8 1/2 In. 650.00
Vase, Orange Painted Design, 1st Black Mark, 5 In. 1450.00
Vase, Prince Albert, Black Mark, 10 3/4 In. 410.00
Vase, Rathmore, 3rd Black Mark, 7 In. 125.00
Vase, Shell, Coral Bowl, Pink Trim, 2nd Black Mark, 4 1/4 In. 295.00
Vase, Shell, Pearl On Green Coral, 2nd Black Mark, 11 In. 1350.00
Vase, Tree Trunk, Shamrocks, 3rd Black Mark, 6 In. 110.00
Vase, Triple Fish, Multicolor Butterflies, 1st Black Mark 1450.00
Vase, Trunk, 2nd Black Mark, 6 In. 118.00
Vase, White Ground, Yellow & Gold Trim, Applied Grapes, 3 In., Pair 180.00

Bennington ware was the product of two factories working in Bennington, Vermont. Both firms were out of business by 1896. The wares include brown and yellow mottled pottery, Parian, scroddled ware, stoneware, graniteware, yellowware, and Staffordshire-like vases.

BENNINGTON, see also Rockingham
BENNINGTON TYPE, Mold, Food, 10 In.Diam. 95.00

BENNINGTON, Basket, Flower Border, Cream, Oval, 3 X 3 X 3 In. 95.00
Bowl, Flared, 8 X 4 In. 30.00
Bowl, Mottled Brown & Yellow, 5 3/4 In. 110.00
Bowl, 8 In. 95.00
Bust, Parian, Woman With Dove On Shoulder, 5 In. 38.00
Butter Churn, Stylized Leaf Design, 4 Gallon 350.00
Crock, Cobalt Blue Leaf, Signed, 1 Gallon 95.00
Dish, Pudding, 2 1/2 X 9 In.Diam. 65.00
Jug, Batter, E.Norton & Co., Bail Handle, 1 Gallon 175.00

Jug, Signed J.E.Norton, Gray, Gallon 39.00
Mug, Parrot & Lattice 27.00
Pan, Pudding, 8 1/2 In. 50.00
Pitcher, Cow, Covered 375.00
Pitcher, Cupid Playing Lyre, Flower Setting, 8 In. 175.00
Pitcher, Hound Handle, Man's Face, Beard On Spout, Animals 250.00
Pitcher, Milk, 7 3/4 In. 60.00
Plate, Pie, Brown & Yellow, 10 1/4 In. 110.00
Plate, Pie, 10 In. 100.00
Salt Crock, Original Lid 115.00
Teapot, Mandarin Design, Pair 65.00
Teapot, Wire Bail, Wooden Grip, Brown Yellow Glaze 45.00
Vase, Fruit Design, White & Cobalt Blue, C.1850, 5 1/2 In. 18.50
Vase, Parian, 8 In. 150.00
Vase, 9 In. 75.00

Berlin, a German porcelain factory, was started in 1751 by Wilhelm Kaspar Wegely. In 1763 the factory was taken over by Frederick the Great and became the Royal Berlin Porcelain Manufactory. It is still in operation today.

BERLIN, Bowl, Floral Bouquet, 2-Handled, KPM Mark, 12 In. 100.00
Figurine, Shepherd Boy, White, 4 1/2 In. 55.00
Solitaire Set, Floral, Gold Trim, German Script, 5 Piece 350.00
Vase, Bell-Shaped, Scenic Panel, 1820-30, Blue Sceptre Mark, 8 In. 150.00

BESWICK, Figurine, Golden Retreiver 50.00
Pitcher, Scenic, 10 1/2 In. 110.00

BETTY BOOP, Card, Publicity, Fleischer Studio, 1930s, 3 1/4 X 6 1/4 In. 6.50
Doll, Carnival, Feathers, Celluloid, 1940s, 9 In. 12.00
Doll, Dresser 30.00
Doll, Fleischer Studios, Labeled, 1930s, 12 In. 600.00
Doll, Wood & Composition, Sticker, 12 In. 550.00
Figurine, Chalkware, 18 In. 70.00
Hatpin, Art Deco, Glass Head, Pewter Back, Headband, 10 3/4 In. 20.00
Mask, Cardboard, 1931 .... 20.00
Quilt Cover, Doll's Bed, 1930s, 14 X 18 In. 75.00
Valentine, Wooden 100.00
Vase, Wall, Betty Twisting Bimbo's Ear 150.00

BICYCLE, High Wheel, 52 In. 2000.00
License Plate, 1948, Keene, N.H., Tin 3.50
Pattern No.7, Wooden Rims, Light, Tools, & Toe Clips 60.00
Tricycle, Chain Driven, Rubber Tires, Heavy Duty, 1923 .... 175.00
Velocipede, 3 Wheels, Wooden Fenders On Rear Wheels 350.00

Bing & Grondahl is a famous Danish factory making fine porcelains from 1853 to the present. Their Christmas plates are especially well known.

BING & GRONDAHL, Dish, Seagull, Square, High Sided, 8 1/2 X 9 In. 45.00
Figurine, Boy Kissing Girl, 7 1/2 In. 85.00
Figurine, Boy Kneeling, Playing Marbles, No. 1636 .... 85.00
Figurine, Girl & Boy, Reading Book 125.00
Figurine, Girl With Book 65.00
Figurine, King Charles Spaniel 175.00
Figurine, Rooster & Hen, 4 1/2 In. 50.00
Figurine, Seagull, Holding Fish 45.00
Figurine, Swimming Duck, 3 X 4 1/4 In. 50.00
Figurine, Swimming Trout, 2 1/2 X 8 1/2 In. 130.00
Figurine, Trout, 8 1/2 X 2 1/2 In. 130.00

Plate, Christmas, 1904 .... 95.00 To 100.00
Plate, Christmas, 1909 .... 95.00
Plate, Christmas, 1912 .... 75.00
Plate, Christmas, 1913 .... 130.00
Plate, Christmas, 1916 .... 75.00
Plate, Christmas, 1917 .... 90.00
Plate, Christmas, 1920 .... 75.00
Plate, Christmas, 1938 .... 60.00
Plate, Christmas, 1969 .... 20.00
Plate, Mother's Day, 1969 .... 286.00
Vase, Christmas, Blue & White Snow Scene, C.1918, 7 1/4 In. 180.00
Vase, Lily Of The Valley, 7 3/4 In. 75.00
Vase, Seagull, 8 In. 75.00
Vase, Snow Scene, Signed Bahl, 6 1/2 In. 165.00

BINOCULARS, French, Jockey Club, 10-Powder, Nickel Over Brass 18.50

BIRDCAGE, Brass, Wooden Frame, Green & White Paint, 11 1/2 X 16 1/2 X 20 In. 75.00
John Calvin, Carved Finials, C.1850, 25 1/2 In. .... *Illus* 2000.00
Musical, Phalibois, Single Bird, Signed, 10 X 10 X 20 In. 900.00
Peaked Roof, Chimney, Floral Base, Tin & Metal, 7 1/2 X 10 1/2 In. 145.00
Stand, Brass & Iron 110.00
White Wicker, On Pedestal Stand, 70 In. 290.00
2 Stories, 4 Apartments, Bent Twig Design, 24 X 13 X 19 In. 250.00

*Bisque is an unglazed baked porcelain. Finished bisque has a slightly sandy
texture with a dull finish. Some of it may be decorated with various colors.
Bisque gained favor during the late Victorian era when thousands of bisque
figurines were made.*

BISQUE, see also named porcelain factories

BISQUE, Bust, Children, Girl In Blue & Pink, Boy In White, 7 1/4 In., Pair 195.00
Figurine, Baby In Tub, 6 In. .... *Illus* 130.00
Figurine, Black Boy, Floral Setting, German 35.00
Figurine, Monkey, Top Hat, Blue Bowtie, French, 9 1/2 In. 385.00
Slipper, Jewels, Clown Inside, Dog On Toe 45.00
Vase, Fan Shaped, Boy & Girl Figures, Period Costume, Pair 65.00

Birdcage, John Calvin, Carved Finials, C.1850, 25 1/2 In.

Bisque, Figurine, Baby In Tub, 6 In.

*Black amethyst glass appears black until it is held to the light; then a
dark purple can be seen. It has been made in many factories from 1860
to the present.*

BLACK AMETHYST, Ashtray, Square, 3 1/2 In. 25.00
  Atomizer, Perfume, Enamel Flowers 60.00
  Bowl, Console, Thorn & Clover 36.00
  Bowl, Flared, 11 In. 20.00
  Bowl, Horizontal Ribbed, Ruffled, 3-Footed, 10 X 3 In. 25.00
  Bowl, Rolled Edge, Gold Band, 9 In. 22.00
  Bowl, Thorn, 11 1/2 In. 45.00
  Bowl, 6 X 4 In. 27.00
  Candleholder, Round, 3 3/4 X 1 1/2 In., Pair 15.00
  Candleholder, 3 1/2 In., Pair 28.00
  Candleholder, 4 X 6 In., Pair 35.00
  Candleholder, 7 In., Pair 35.00
  Candy, Cloverleaf, Covered, 3-Part, Pierced 12.00
  Cheese & Cracker Set, Pedestal, Sterling Deposit, 10 In. 100.00
  Coaster, 5 In. 2.50
  Compote, Holly 40.00
  Compote, Semidraped Female Stem, 7 1/4 In. .... 30.00 To 32.00
  Console Set, Sterling Deposit 95.00
  Cookie Jar 50.00
  Dish, Lace Edge, 8 1/2 In. 15.00
  Plate, Chop 20.00
  Plate, Grill, 9 In. 5.00
  Rose Bowl, Hobnail 15.00
  Rose Bowl, Poppy 35.00
  Sugar & Creamer 12.50
  Sugar & Creamer, Bearded Man 20.00
  Toothpick, Bees On A Basket 55.00
  Top Hat, Figural, 3 1/2 X 5 In. 20.00
  Tray, Center Handle, 5 1/2 In. 18.50
  Urn, Covered, Footed, 7 1/2 In. 20.00
  Vase, Bulbous, Embossed Flowers 40.00
  Vase, Clipper Ship, Silver Overlay, 7 3/4 In. 20.00
  Vase, Cut To Clear, Flowers, Marked, 12 In. 650.00
  Vase, Diamond Point, Chalice Shape, 11 In. 30.00
  Vase, Dogwood 35.00
  Vase, Fan, Floral Design, Silver Deposit, 9 In. 275.00
  Vase, Fan, Rockwell, Silver Deposit 275.00
  Vase, Fan, 7 1/2 In. 27.00
  Vase, Handled, 8 3/4 In. 20.00
  Vase, L.E.Smith, 6 In. 9.00
  Vase, Leaf & Scroll, Stippled, 5 1/2 X 4 1/2 In. 25.00
  Vase, Painted Flowers, 9 In. 28.00
  Vase, Ribbed Sides, Seagulls In Flight, Silver Overlay, 8 In. 225.00

BLACK, Ashtray, Boy Eating Watermelon 10.00
  Bank, Aunt Jemima, Iron, Boxed 65.00
  Basket, Mammy, Iron, Red Dress, White Basket 55.00
  Bell, Mammy, Bisque, 5 In. .... 6.00 To 8.00
  Bill Hook, Johnson Hat Company, Black Man In Top Hat, Celluloid 7.50
  Box, Cigar, Old Virginia Cheroots, Wood, 1890 .... 35.00
  Box, Recipe, Aunt Jemima, Celluloid 38.00
  Button, Aunt Jemima, Advertising 2.00
  Calling Card Holder, Boy .... *Illus* 1450.00
  Card, Birthday, Comical, Boy Taking Bath, 1920s 1.00
  Condiment Set, Aunt Jemima, Spices, Salt & Pepper, Syrup, 11 Piece 160.00
  Cookie Jar, Aunt Jemima, Celluloid .... 60.00 To 110.00
  Cookie Jar, Chef, Pearl China 75.00
  Cookie Jar, Mammy, Bisque 16.00
  Cookie Jar, Mammy, Celluloid 110.00

(See Page 38)

Black, Calling Card Holder, Boy   Black, Match Holder, Art Deco Waiter

Cruet, Oil & Vinegar, Mammy & Chef	35.00
Doll, Aunt Jemima, Child Diana & Wade, Oilcloth, Boxed	95.00
Doll, Aunt Jemima, Cloth Cutout, Quaker Oats Co., Uncut	45.00 To 65.00
Doll, Bisque, Jointed Arms & Legs	11.00
Doll, Blue Dress, Red Bandana, Cloth, 10 In.	22.00
Doll, Bye-Lo, Baby, Jointed Arms & Legs, Gown, Bisque, 4 In.	11.00
Doll, Gerber Baby, Boxed	35.00
Doll, Girl, Jointed Arms, 3 Ponytails, Bisque, 6 In.	10.00
Doll, Glass Eyes, Lace Outfit, Bisque, 11 In.	32.00
Doll, Happy Baby, Giggles & Coos, 16 In.	18.00
Doll, Mammy, Pappy, Wood, 19th Century, Dressed As Poor Folk, 9 In., Pair	250.00
Doll, Miss Topsy, Bisque	15.00
Doll, Musical Action, Bisque Head & Hands, Music Plays	14.50
Doll, Rag, Little Sister, Detailed Features	25.00
Doll, Rag, 18 In.	90.00
Doll, Uncle Mose, Oilcloth	35.00
Figurine, Bisque, Outhouse With Boy, 2 1/2 In.	8.00
Figurine, Black Drummer, 6 In.	25.00
Figurine, Boy Eating Watermelon, Bisque, 3 In.	3.50 To 5.00
Figurine, Boy On Potty, Boy & Girl In Nighties, Bisque	53.00
Figurine, Boy Smoking Cigar, Holding Hat, Bisque, 9 1/2 In.	235.00
Figurine, Boy Wearing A Jester Suit, Playing Mandolin, 6 In.	235.00

Figurine, Child On Chamber Pot, 2 In. 10.00
Figurine, Child, Pink Turban, Arms Out, 5 In. 4.00
Figurine, Negro Musicians, Bisque, 5 Piece 120.00
Game, Snake Eyes, Wide-Eye Picture On Box, Cards, Chips 22.00
Grocery List, Hanging, Aunt Jemima, I'se Gotta Git, Wooden 28.00
Hat, Aunt Jemima 5.00
Holder, Broom, Figural, Black Man, Iron 155.00
Holder, Card, Bellhop, Full Figure, Floor Standing, 32 In. 145.00
Holder, Pad, Mammy Memo 15.00
Holder, Paper Towel, Aunt Jemima, Wooden 48.00
Holder, Spice, Aunt Jemima 15.00
Holder, String, Mammy .... 35.00 To 45.00
Humidor, Figural, Woman, Gold Earrings, Headdress, 7 In. 65.00
Label, Dixie Boy Fruit, 9 X 9 In. 1.50
Letter Opener, Black Baby & Alligator, Celluloid 25.00
Match Holder, Art Deco Waiter .... Illus 350.00
Pan, Frying, Mammy, Iron, Miniature 10.00
Paper Dolls, Uncle Moses, Aunt Jemima, Uncut 78.00
Picture, Cupid Asleep, Oval Frame, 7 In. 165.00
Pie Bird, Black Chef 25.00
Pie Bird, Mammy .... 24.00 To 25.00
Pincushion, Black Maid, Lace Apron, Rooted Hair, 7 In. 15.00
Plate, Calendar, 1915, Boy Eating Watermelon 35.00
Recipe Box, Mammy 17.00
Salt & Pepper, Aunt Jemima & Uncle Mose .... 7.00 To 15.00
Salt & Pepper, Aunt Jemima, Celluloid, 3 1/2 In. 12.00
Salt & Pepper, Luzianne, Original Green Skirt 22.00
Salt & Pepper, Mammy & Chef, Ceramic 14.00
Salt & Pepper, Mammy & Chef, 4 1/2 In. 14.00
Salt & Pepper, Mammy, Bisque, 3 In. .... 4.00 To 9.00
Salt & Pepper, Mammy, Celluloid, 5 In. .... 3.50 To 5.00
Salt & Pepper, Mammy, 6 In. 18.00
Salt & Pepper, Salty & Peppy, Pearl China, 4 1/2 In. 25.00
Spice Set, Mammy, 6 Piece 75.00
Sprinkler, Lawn, Sambo, Double-Sided, Wooden, 34 In. 175.00
Sugar & Creamer, Aunt Jemima .... 30.00 To 52.00
Sugar & Creamer, Aunt Jemima, Covered, Celluloid 22.50
Sugar & Creamer, Mammy & Mose Handles 25.00
Sugar, Mammy 15.00
Sweeper, Bread Crumb, Mammy, Ceramic 28.00
Syrup, Aunt Jemima, 6 In. 20.00
Tape Measure, Advertising, Aunt Jemima 3.00
Toothpick Holder, Mammy, Bisque, 3 In. .... 2.00 To 3.00
Towel, Kitchen, Black Chef With Lobster 20.00
Toy, Boy Drummer, Black Cotton Hair Over Tin, Grass Skirt, 5 In. 75.00
Toy, Face, Negro, Moving Eyes, Celluloid, 1920s, Kobi 110.00
Whisk Broom, Mammy, 4 1/2 In. 20.00

Blown glass was formed by forcing air through a rod into molten glass.
Early glass and some forms of art glass were hand-blown. Other types of
glass were molded or pressed.

BLOWN GLASS, Bottle, Chestnut, Crimped & Turned-Back Handle, Amber, 7 1/2 In. 50.00
Creamer, Crimped, Turned-Back Handle, 18th Century, 6 1/2 In. 125.00
Funnel, Clear, 9 1/4 In. 8.00
Jar, Apothecary, Knobbed Cover, Pedestal, Blue, 16 In. 60.00
Jar, Sweetmeat, Banded, Cylindrical, Acorn Finial, 9 In. 50.00
Jar, Sweetmeat, Cylindrical, Ringed, Molded Domed Cover, 10 In. 150.00
Pitcher, Aqua, Applied Rolled Foot & Handle, 2 3/4 In. 305.00
Pitcher, Aqua, Threaded Top, Applied Foot & Handle, 3 In. 95.00
Pitcher, Clear, Applied Handle, Pittsburgh, 2 In. 55.00
Pitcher, Clear, Applied Handle, Pittsburgh, 2 3/8 In. 45.00
Pitcher, Clear, Applied Handle, Tooled At Base, 2 1/2 In. 135.00
Pitcher, Pale Green, Applied Threading, 3 1/4 In. 175.00

Pitcher, Wisteria Blue, Variegated, 16 Ribs, Swirled Neck, 4 In. 775.00
Salt, Aqua, Footed, South Jersey, 1 5/8 In. 85.00
Salt, Deep Aquamarine, Hollow Foot, Pittsburgh, 2 3/4 In. 295.00
Vase, Hand Threading At Flared Top, Random Bubbles, Flint, 7 In. 60.00
    BLUE GLASS, see Cobalt Blue
    BLUE ONION, see Onion

*Blue Willow pattern has been made in England since 1780. The pattern
has been copied by factories in many countries, including Germany, Japan, and
the United States. It is still being made. Willow was named for a
pattern that pictures a bridge, birds, willow trees, and a Chinese landscape.*

BLUE WILLOW, Berry Bowl, Allerton, 5 1/2 In. 8.00
Bowl, Allerton, 9 1/2 In. 18.00
Bowl, Burslem, Brown & Stevenson, Square, 10 In. 68.00
Bowl, Oval, 9 In. 35.00
Bowl, Vegetable, Allerton 49.50
Bowl, Vegetable, Venton, Oval, 9 In. 35.00
Bowl, 5 3/4 In. 3.75
Bowl, 9 In. 15.00
Butter Chip, Allerton 15.00
Butter Pat, C.1860 .... 15.00
Butter, Covered 18.00
Cake Plate, Allerton 59.50
Cake Plate, Royal China, 6 1/4 In. 3.00
Cake Plate, 6 In. 2.50
Casserole, Covered 20.00
Charger, 12 3/4 In. 50.00
Creamer .... 5.00 To 9.00
Creamer, Child's 7.50
Creamer, Oak 45.00
Creamer, Sadler 29.50
Cup & Saucer .... 6.50 To 9.00
Cup & Saucer, Allerton 25.00
Cup & Saucer, Demitasse 5.00
Cup & Saucer, Made In Japan 5.00
Cup & Saucer, Scalloped, 1906, Buffalo Pottery 22.00
Cup, Child's, 2 1/8 In. .... 3.50 To 5.00
Cup, Demitasse 4.00
Demitasse Set, Pot, 7 1/4 In., 17 Piece 135.00
Dish, Deep, 9 3/8 In. 45.00
Dish, Soup, Allerton, 8 In. 15.00
Gravy Boat & Underplate, Meakin 15.00
Gravy Boat, Allerton, 8-Sided 35.00
Pitcher, Octagonal Shaped, Marked Mason's, 5 1/2 X 4 1/2 In. 95.00
Pitcher, 7 X 9 In. 50.00
Plate, Allerton, 6 3/4 In. 8.00
Plate, Buffalo, 6 In. 5.00
Plate, Child's, 3 7/8 In. .... 3.50 To 5.00
Plate, Grill, Marked Made In Japan, 10 1/4 In. 10.00
Plate, Grill, Marked Shenango, 10 3/8 In. 12.00
Plate, Grimwades, 7 1/2 In. 13.00
Plate, Homer Laughlin, 10 1/2 In. 5.00
Plate, Luncheon, Stoke On Trent, England, 8 In. 4.00
Plate, Washington Pottery, Staffordshire, 9 1/2 In. 8.00
Plate, 6 In. 1.75
Plate, 9 1/4 In. .... 4.75 To 6.00
Plate, 10 In. 15.00
Platter, Impressed Mark, 15 3/4 X 12 1/2 In. 48.00
Platter, Meat, Child's, Oval, 6 In. 15.00
Platter, Oval, Marked, 10 In. 30.00
Platter, Oval, 12 1/2 X 9 In. 20.00
Platter, Oval, 16 X 12 3/4 In. 58.00
Platter, 14 X 17 In. 70.00

Salt & Pepper	18.50
Saltshaker, Square, Japan, 3 1/4 In.	12.00
Sandwich Server, Royal	6.00
Saucer, Child's	2.00
Soup Dish, Scalloped, Allerton, 9 In.	24.00
Spoon Rest	10.00
Spoon Rest, Double	25.00
Sugar & Creamer, Allerton	39.00
Sugar & Creamer, Child's	18.00 To 18.50
Sugar, Buffalo Pottery	65.00
Sugar, Covered	7.00 To 14.00
Sugar, Meakin	25.00
Tea Set, Child's, 6 Piece	58.00
Teapot, Child's, Covered	20.00
Tray, Oval, 5 1/2 In.	17.00
Tureen, Child's, Covered, 5 1/2 In.	28.00
Tureen, Child's, Covered, 6 X 3 In.	25.00
Tureen, Covered	20.00

Bluerina is a type of art glass which shades from light blue to ruby. It is often called blue amberina.

BLUERINA, Toothpick, Jack-In-The-Pulpit	89.00

The Boch Freres factory was founded in 1841 in La Louviere in eastern Belgium. The wares resemble the work of Villeroy & Boch. The factory is still in business.

BOCH FRERES, Vase, Blue, Yellow, Florals, Gourd Shape, Marked, 12 In.	200.00
Vase, Brown Leaves, Black Twig, White Ground, Marked, 5 In.	120.00
Vase, Brown, Rust, Black, Florals, Orange Ground, Marked, 10 In.	90.00
Vase, Yellow, Black Stripes, Green Floral, Oblong, 12 In.	170.00

Osso China Company was reorganized as Edward Marshall Boehm Inc. in 1953. The company is still working in England and New Jersey.

BOEHM, Bookends, Owls	550.00
Figurine, Bunny, White	150.00
Figurine, Chick, Yellow, 1950s	250.00
Figurine, Chickadee, Fledgling	225.00
Figurine, Cocker Spaniel, Brown & White	450.00
Figurine, Fox, Standing, 4 In.	45.00
Figurine, Goldfinch, Fledgling	140.00
Figurine, Jays, Green	2000.00
Figurine, Little Wren, Marked	550.00
Figurine, Parrot, Red	175.00
Figurine, Rabbits, Pair	300.00
Figurine, Tufted Titmice	900.00
Figurine, Young American Bald Eagle	600.00 To 675.00
Plate, Annual, 1974, Rufous Hummingbird	60.00
Plate, Bird Of Peace, Edward Marshall, Boxed	225.00 To 235.00
Plate, Malvern Bird, Set Of 8	450.00
Plate, Mute Swan	225.00

Bohemian glass is an ornate, overlay, or flashed glass made during the Victorian era. It has been reproduced in Bohemia, which is now a part of Czechoslovakia. Glass made from 1875 to 1900 is preferred by collectors.

BOHEMIAN GLASS, Bell, Clear Handle, Ruby, 6 In.	35.00
Bottle, Teardrop-Shaped Stopper, Pink Center, Flowers, 9 In.	50.00
Bowl, Finger, Vintage Pattern, Cobalt Blue	30.00
Box, Enameled Gold & White Floral Design, 3 1/2 In.	150.00

Chalice, Ruby To Clear, Flying Birds, Marked, 10 In. 110.00
Chalice, Wolf Chasing Deer Scene, Amber, 12 1/2 In., Pair 850.00
Compote, Applied Rosettes, Pedestaled, Red, 4 1/2 In. 45.00
Compote, Geometric Design, Cobalt Blue & White, 6 In. 180.00
Cordial Set, Ruby Cut To Clear, Decanter & 6 Glasses 125.00
Cruet, Ruby To Clear, Clear Applied Notched Handle, 6 In. 85.00
Decanter, Clear, Cut Fluting, Floral Swags, 9 In., Pair 210.00
Decanter, Cobalt Blue To Clear, 51 1/4 In., Pair 350.00
Decanter, Ruby, Deer & Castle, 15 1/2 In. 70.00
Decanter, Stopper, Yellow, Green, Etched, Silver Trim, 10 In. 350.00
Lamp Base, Ewer-Shaped, Gold, Handled, Green, 16 1/2 In., Pair ... 150.00
Teapot, Engraved Deer, Castle, & Scrolls, C.1885 .... 250.00
Urn, Hunting Scene, Covered, Green, 15 In. 145.00
Vase, Bud, Ruby, Floral Design, 7 1/2 In. 45.00
Wine, Vintage Pattern, Stemmed 22.00
    BOOK, see Paper, Book and others
    BOSTON & SANDWICH CO., see Sandwich Glass; Lutz

BOTTLE OPENER, Advertising, Schaeffer Beer 4.00
Alligator, Figural, Polychrome, Cast Iron, 6 1/2 In. 45.00
Baseball Cap, Reingold Beer, Cast Iron 28.00
Beer Drinker 33.00
Bird 15.00
Black Face, Brass 45.00
Black Man's Head, Open Mouth, Wall Mounted 30.00
Black Waiter, Holding 3 Steins, Wooden, 1900s, Original Paint 85.00
Bourbon Street Lady 7.00
Clown, Face, 4-Eyed, Open Mouth, Original Paint, Cast Iron 25.00
Cockatoo On Floor Perch, Iron 18.50
Cowboy 33.00
Crab 12.00
Dachshund, Bronze 25.00
Dolphin, Brass 19.00
Donkey, Original Paint, Cast Iron 48.00
Donkey, Sitting, Iron 18.00
Dragon, Green, Iron 41.00
Drunk, At Sign Post, Mr.Washington, Cast Iron .... 10.00 To 12.00
Drunk, Derby Hat 15.00
Drunk, High Hat 12.00
Drunk, 4-Eyed 19.00
Elephant, Pink, Cast Iron .... 18.00 To 33.00
Elephant, Wooden 28.00
Embossed Scrolls & Ribs, Hollow Handle, Sterling Silver, 6 In. ... 26.00
False Teeth, Wall Mount 12.00
Fish, Hinged 12.00
Four Eyes, Wall Mount, Cast Iron 48.00
Goat, Iron 22.00
Golf Club 5.00
Goose, Canada, Brass 37.00
Hammer, Bronze 15.00
Hampden Mild Ale 1.00
Hessian Soldier 20.00
Horseshoe 15.00
Idol, Sterling Silver 65.00
Indian Boy, Iroquois Beverage 13.00
King Whiskey 8.00
Lady, 4-Eyed 19.00
Lemp St.Louis Beer, Auto Shape 15.00
Lobster 26.00
Lock 26.00
Man, Straw Hat 63.00
Man's Head, Colored, Open Mouth, Wall Mount 30.00
Mermaid, Chero-Cola 35.00

Moustached Man, Double Set Of Eyes, Iron	65.00
Moxie, Metal, Green	10.00
Nude, Brass	37.00
Nude, Canada On Wreath, Chrome	56.00
Nude, Chrome	26.00
Old Snifter, Cast Iron	35.00
Pabst Blue Ribbon, Bottle Shape	12.00
Parrot, Cast Iron	25.00 To 38.00
Parrot, On Perch, Cast Iron	28.00
Parrot, With Can Punch	33.00
Pelican	19.00 To 45.00
Pig's Hind End, Iron	10.00
Seagull On Stump, Multicolored, Iron	35.00
Seahorse, Brass	48.00
Shaeffer Beer	.50
Shovel	15.00
Shrimp	16.00
Standing Man, High Hat, With Corkscrew, Brass	34.00
Stegmaier, Sliding	15.00
Swordfish, Original Paint	65.00
Teeth, Figural, Iron, Wall Mount	45.00
Tennis Racket	10.00
Trout, Cast Iron	20.00 To 22.00
Waiter, Figural, Wood	28.00
Waiter, Holding 3 Beer Steins, Black, Wooden, 1900s	85.00
Whale Tooth, Attached At Point Of Tooth, 5 In.	65.00
Whale, Brass	12.00

Bottle collecting has become a major American hobby. There are several general categories of bottles, such as historic flasks, bitters, household, and figural. For modern bottle prices and more old bottle prices, see the book "The Kovels' Bottle Price List" by Ralph and Terry Kovel.

BOTTLE, Apothecary, Amber, Hollow Blown, Ground Stopper, 11 In.	110.00
Apothecary, Clear, Applied Foot & Ring, Hollow Stopper, 19 In.	110.00
Aqua, Applied Lip, Embossed Aschenbach & Miller, 10 In.	45.00

Avon started in 1886 as the California Perfume Company. It was not until 1929 that the name Avon was used. In 1939 it became Avon Products, Inc. Each year Avon sells figural bottles filled with cosmetic products. Ceramic, plastic, and glass bottles are made in limited editions.

Avon, Betsy Ross, Boxed	20.00
Avon, Hard Hat	4.00
Avon, McConnell, Boxed, 1973	50.00
Avon, Seahorse, Metal Top	10.00
Avon, Spanish Senorita	7.00
Avon, Stagecoach, Boxed	3.00
Baby, Nursing, Acme Graduated	18.00
Baby, Nursing, Comfort	22.00
Barber, Art Glass, Opalescent Swirl, Mushroom Stopper, 11 1/4 In.	150.00
Barber, Bristol, Flowers, Hair Tonic, Gold Lettering	75.00
Barber, Camphor Glass Stopper, Blown, 7 1/2 In.	35.00
Barber, Cut Thumbprint Band & Mirror Block Neck, Vaseline	125.00
Barber, Double Gourd Shape, Green, Stopper, Enameled Flower	75.00
Barber, Enameled Flowers, Stopper, Amethyst	98.50
Barber, Moonstone, Pair	18.00
Barber, Newbros Herpicide, 8 Ounce, 7 3/4 In.	5.50
Barber, Opalescent Stripe, Cranberry	75.00

Beam bottles are made to hold Kentucky Straight Bourbon, made by the James B.Beam Distilling Company. The Beam series of ceramic bottles began in 1953.

Beam, Barney's Slot Machine, Casino	30.00

Beam, Binion's Horseshoe, Casino 10.00
Beam, Cable Car, On Wheels 5.00
Beam, Canteen 14.00
Beam, Coffee Mill 15.00
Beam, Ernie's Flower Cart, On Wheels 30.00
Beam, Figaro 281.00
Beam, Franklin Mint 8.00
Beam, Harolds Club, 1968 .... 32.00
Beam, Hyatt House, Chicago 16.00
Beam, Madame Butterfly 563.00
Beam, San Diego Elephant 21.00
Beam, Showgirl 133.00
Beam, Sports Car Club 11.00
Beam, Travelodge Bear 9.00
Beam, Waterman, Pair 300.00
Beer, Champion, Baltimore Brand, Embossed Boxers, Amber 20.00
Beer, Conrad & Co., Budweiser, C.1870, Aqua 15.00
Beer, Fehr's Kentucky, 4 Horses, Miniature 33.50
Beer, High Life, Milwaukee, Wisconsin, Clear, 4 In. 5.00
Beer, Moehn Brewing Co., Burlington, Iowa, Porcelain Top 6.50
Beer, S.Liebmann's & Sons Brewing Co., N.Y., Aqua, 10 In. 1.00
Bitters, Atwood's Jaundice, Formerly Atwood, 12-Sided .... 1.25 To 6.50
Bitters, Barrel Shape, Wide Lip Flange, Embossed, 9 In. 80.00
Bitters, Bering's Apple Bitters, Amethyst, Square, 9 In. 6.00
Bitters, Dr.Hostetter's Stomach 20.00
Bitters, Dr.Miles Restorative Nervine 10.00
Bitters, Dr.Warren's Herb & Root, Providence, R.I., 5 Star, Aqua 62.50
Bitters, Figural, Bear, Seated, Black Glass, 10 In. 30.00
Bitters, Figural, Fish, Amber Glass, 10 In. 30.00
Bitters, Old Sachem, Amber, C.1860, 9 1/2 In. .... *Illus* 550.00
Bitters, Royal Pepsin Stomach, Amber, 9 In. 95.00
Bitters, Warner's Safe Kidney & Liver Cure, Rochester, N.Y., Amber 250.00
BOTTLE, COCA-COLA, see Coca-Cola, Bottle
Cognac, Authentique Commission Des Liquers De Quebec, No.3, 7 1/4 In 4.50
Cologne, Amber Cut, Stopper, 8 1/2 X 4 1/2 In. 175.00
Cologne, Ball Shape, Cork, 1 3/4 In. 12.00
Cologne, Blue, Atomizer, Notched Panel 30.00
Cologne, Crystal, Hand-Painted, Floral, Bohemian, Stopper, 9 1/2 In. 50.00
Cologne, Flower Stopper, Gold, Enameled Marine Scene, 8 1/2 In. 95.00
Cologne, Pedestal, Black, Green, Dauber, Deco 35.00
Figural, Andy Jackson, Ceramic, Old Hickory Distilling, 11 1/4 In. 15.00
Figural, Auto, Perfume, Blue, Porcelain 125.00
Figural, Baby, Crying, Amethyst, 3-Piece Mold, Dated June 1874 .... 75.00
Figural, Bear, Light Green, C.1870, 10 1/4 In. .... *Illus* 275.00
Figural, Charlie Chaplin, Clear, Sparkline 80.00
Figural, Drakes Plantation, 4 Logs, Amber 45.00
Figural, Fish, Clear, Screw Cap, Ground Lip 25.00
Figural, Jester, Seated, Holding Round Bottle, Open Pontil 120.00
Figural, Jolly Man, Amethyst 40.00
Figural, Jolly Man, Frosted Body, Painted Face 55.00
Figural, Lady Acrobat, Upside Down On Ball, Frosted Glass 55.00
Figural, Lady, Torso, Screw Top, Ground Lip 60.00
Figural, Man In Basket, Milk Glass, Ground Lip 45.00
Figural, Man On Barrel, Embossed Italy, Ground Lip 15.00
Figural, Man On Barrel, Embossed Jim Crown, Rockingham Glaze 50.00
Figural, Man On Barrel, Embossed, Clear, Screw Cap 15.00
Figural, Matador, Old Paint & Clear, 6 1/2 In. 45.00
Figural, Napoleon, Open Pontil 25.00
Figural, Potato, Aqua, Screw Top, Ground Lip 25.00
Figural, Seal, Green, Applied Ring, 9 In. 65.00
Figural, Turk, Seated, Clear, Gloppy Lip 65.00
Flask, Double Eagle, Shield With Stripes, Banner, Green, 1/2 Pint 175.00
Flask, Pretzel, Austria, 1908 .... 65.00

Bottle, Bitters, Old Sachem, Amber, C.1860,
9 1/2 In.

Bottle, Figural, Bear, Light Green, C.1870,
10 1/4 In.

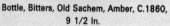

(See Page 43)

Flask, Pumpkin Seed, Free-Blown, Thumbprint, C.1860, 5 1/2 In.	125.00
Flask, Pumpkin, Green Glass, Woven Splint, 1/2 Pint	10.00
Flask, Success To The Railroads, C.1860, Olive Green	250.00
Flask, Washington & Clay, Aqua, Quart	60.00
Flask, West Willington, 1/2 Pint	71.50
Flask, Zanesville, Amber, Chestnut, 10-Diamond, 5 1/2 In.	775.00
Flask, Zanesville, Pinch, Chestnut, Aqua, 2 1/2 In.	105.00
Fruit Jar, Anchor Lightning, Clear, Quart	1.00 To 1.10
Fruit Jar, Atlas E-Z Seal, Aqua, Quart	.50 To 1.00
Fruit Jar, Atlas E-Z Seal, Bail & Cover, Citron Green, 1 Pint	5.00
Fruit Jar, Atlas, Mason, Porcelain Lined Zinc Cover, Aqua, Pint	1.50
Fruit Jar, Ball Perfect Mason, Zinc-Lined Lid, Aqua, Qt.	1.50 To 2.00
Fruit Jar, Gem, Hess Co., Philadelphia	1000.00
Fruit Jar, Kerr, Glass Insert, Aluminum Lid, Clear	12.00
Fruit Jar, Lightning Putnam, Bail & Cover, Aqua, Auart	2.00
Fruit Jar, Masons Maltese Cross, Patent 1858, Covered, 1 Pint	3.50
Fruit Jar, Millville Atmospheric, Aqua, Quart	17.50
Fruit Jar, Millville Atmospheric, 1861, Aqua, Pint	20.00 To 50.00
Fruit Jar, Millville Atmospheric, 1861, Aqua, Quart	55.00
Fruit Jar, Princess, Clear, Quart	5.00
Fruit Jar, Safety Valve, Patent 1894, Cover & Iron Clamp, Aqua	8.50
Fruit Jar, Smalley & Co., Patent 1896, Tin Cover, Amber, Quart	40.00
Fruit Jar, Swayzee's Improved, Green	18.00
Fruit Jar, The Wears Jar, Cover & Clamp, Clear, Pint	2.75
Fruit Jar, Weir, Iron Clamp, Patent 1892, Stoneware, 2 Quart	20.00
Ink, Carter Cathedral, Master, Cobalt Blue, 1/2 Pint	90.00
Ink, Carter, Hexagonal, Gothic Arches, Cobalt Blue, 9 In.	45.00
Ink, Columbian, Blue, C.1850, 4 5/8 In.	*Illus* 330.00

Ink, Pa Carter, Dated 1914 .... 25.00
Ink, Teakettle, Embossed J.& I.E.M., Aqua, 1 3/4 In. 22.50
Ink, Umbrella, Aqua, 8-Sided, Rolled Lip, Open Pontil 15.00
Inkwell, Ma & Pa Carter, Pair 75.00
Insect & Feather Design, Ball Stopper, 6 1/4 In. 12.00
Lincoln, Bank, 9 In. .... Illus 15.00
Medicine, A.A.Cooley, Hartford, Conn., Oval, Olive Green, 4 1/2 In. 100.00
Medicine, Barry's Tricopherous For Skin & Hair, Aqua, 6 1/4 In. 32.50
Medicine, Hagans Magnolia Balm, Milk Glass, 6 In. 15.00
Medicine, Horseshoe, Blue, Quart 5.00
Medicine, Lash's Bitters Natural Laxative Tonic, Label, Amber, 12 In. 15.00
Medicine, Lyon's For The Hair, Katharion, N.Y., Aqua, 6 In. 27.50
Medicine, Mrs.D.A.Allen's World Hair Balsam, N.Y., 7 In. 50.00
Medicine, Querus Cod Liver Oil Jelly, Cylindrical, Aqua, 5 1/2 In. 90.00
Medicine, S.B.Goff's Cough Syrup, Camdem, N.J., Aqua 3.00
Medicine, W.M.Sumerville & Sons, For Horses & Cattle, Aqua 7.00
Milk, AC Oakland, Store Bottle, 1/2 Pint 4.00
Milk, Baby, Baby Face, Brookfield Dairy, Original Cap, 1/2 Pint 20.00
Milk, Borden's Cream, Advertising, Miniature 6.50
Milk, College View Dairy, Northfield, Vermont, Painted Label, 1/2 Pint 1.50
Milk, Dana Farm, Fairhaven, Mass., Painted Label, Quart 20.00
Milk, Excelsior Creamery, Santa Anna, 1/2 Gallon 6.00
Milk, Fairview Dairy, Wellesley Hills, Mass., Farm Scene, Quart 2.00
Milk, Flander's Dairy, Baby Face On Bottle, 1/2 Pint 28.00
Milk, Golden State, 1/2 Pint 5.00
Milk, Hampton Dairy, East Hampton, Embossed, 1/2 Pint 1.50
Milk, Holiday Farms, San Diego, 1/2 Gallon 6.00
Milk, Honey Gardens Dairy, Lebanon, N.H., Painted Label, 1/2 Pint 1.50
Milk, Model Dairy Co., Corry, Pa., 1/2 Pint, Painted Label 1.50
Mineral Water, Spring Water, Whitney Glass Works, WCK Mark, Quart 70.00
Moxie, Embossed, Aqua 12.00
Pabst Beer, Fighter In Ring, Handlebar Mustache, Oversized 275.00
Perfume, Art Deco, Leaf Shape Stopper, Green Crystal, 4 1/2 In. 65.00
Perfume, Bell-Shaped, Cork, Black Glass, France, 1 3/4 In. 12.00
Perfume, Bulbous Base, Chrome Top, 1920s, 4 X 3 In. 15.00
Perfume, Cane Alternating Pattern, Brass Neck, Brass Cap, 2 1/4 In. 35.00
Perfume, Clamshell, Blue, English, C.1870, 2 3/8 In. .... Illus 240.00
Perfume, Enameled Flowers, Gold Foliage, Sapphire Blue, 4 1/4 In. 100.00
Perfume, Green Crystal, Leaf Stopper, 6 3/4 In. 65.00
Perfume, Insect & Feather Design, Ball Stopper, Pressed, 6 1/4 In. 12.00
Perfume, Kaziun, Intaglio Cut, Red Rose Stopper, Signed, 9 1/4 In. 1250.00
Perfume, Purse, Embossed X On Panels, C.1890, 2 5/8 In. 10.00
Perfume, X Pattern, Brass Neck, Glass Stopper, 2 1/4 In. 35.00
Preserve, Blueberry, Amber, 11 1/4 In. .... Illus 200.00
Seltzer, Old Newbury Sparkling Water, C.Leary & Co., Qt .... 5.00 To 8.00
Snuff, Village Scene, People All Around, 3 In. 60.00
Soda, A.W.Rapp, Sapphire .... Illus 625.00
Soda, Blob Top, Aqua, Whittle Marks At Neck, 9 In. 5.50
Soda, Blob Top, Citrate Magnesia, Clear, 7 3/4 In. 3.00
Soda, Hygera Weid, Thompson Mfg.Co., Cherry Phosphate, Aqua, 6 In. 5.00
Soda, John Graf, Amber 20.00
Soda, Mission Beverage, Painted Label 1.10
Soda, Radio Aromatic Ginger Ale, Boston, 16 Ounce, 9 3/4 In. 15.00
Soda, W.M.Dean, Newark, Hutchinson Soda, Teak Green, 7 In. 8.00
Syrup, Ben Franklin, Flask Type, Green 4.00
Water, Congress Water Co., Quart, Green Applied Top, Saratoga, N.Y. ... 25.00
Whiskey, A.M.Binninger & Co., Label, Amber, Quart 62.50
Whiskey, Bourbon Co., Amber, C.1870, 8 3/4 In. .... Illus 300.00
Whiskey, George Noar, Amber, C.1850, 8 3/4 In. .... Illus 360.00
Whiskey, J.F.T.& Co., Amber, C.1850, 7 1/4 In. .... Illus 180.00
Whiskey, Old Classic, Amber, Miniature, Tassel, Stamp Intact 14.00
Whiskey, Old Continental, Amber, C.1870, 9 In. .... Illus 500.00

Bottle, Lincoln, Bank, 9 In.

(See Pages 44, 45)

Bottle, Ink, Columbian, Blue, C.1850,
4 5/8 In.

Bottle, Perfume, Clamshell, Blue, English,
C.1870, 2 3/8 In.

Bottle, Preserve, Blueberry, Amber, 11 1/4 In.

Bottle, Soda, A.W.Rapp, Sapphire

(See Page 45)

Bottle, Whiskey, Bourbon Co., Amber,
C.1870, 8 3/4 In.

Bottle, Whiskey, George Noar, Amber,
C.1850, 8 3/4 In.

Bottle, Whiskey, J.F.T.& Co., Amber, C.1850,
7 1/4 In.

(See Page 45)

Bottle, Whiskey, Old Continental, Amber, C.1870, 9 In.

*Boxes of all kinds are collected. They were made of thin strips of inlaid
wood, metal, tortoiseshell, embroidery, or other material.*

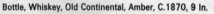

**BOX, see also Ivory, Box; Porcelain, Box; Shaker, Box; Store,
Box; Tin, Box; and various Porcelain categories**

BOX, Baker, Dovetailed, Hinged Cover, Stenciling, 1885	40.00
BOX, BATTERSEA, see Battersea, Box	
Beekeeper's, Glass Bottom, Cover Slide, 4 1/2 X 3 1/2 In.	13.00
Bentwood, Spring-Clip Lid, Burned Design, 4 X 4 In.	45.00
Bible, Leather Covered, Brass Edges, Lined, C.1860, Walnut, 8 1/4 X 13 In.	225.00
Blanket, Pine, Lift Top, Applied Molding, 4-Footed, Red, 12 In.	175.00
Brass Hinges, Lock, C.1860, Crotch Mahogany Over Walnut, 6 X 6 In.	50.00
Bride's, Painted Blue, Polychrome Floral Design, 15 1/2 In.	400.00
Candle, Dovetailed, Original Blue Paint, C.1780	325.00
Candle, Hanging, Walnut, Drawers, C.1800, Slant Lid, 19 In.	750.00
Candle, Octagonal Shape, Leather Hinges, 18th Century, 12 1/4 In.	425.00
Candle, Pinwheel Front, Rectangular, 4 3/4 In.	375.00
Candle, Slide Cover, Thumb Notch, C.1840, New England, Pine, 18 In.	295.00
Candle, Sliding Handled Cover, 8 X 10 In.	210.00
Carved Hearts & Circles, Covered, Oval, 4 X 5 In.	425.00
Cheese, Broadland Cheese Stenciled On Lid, Bentwood, 18 X 8 3/4 In.	85.00
Cheese, Kraft Velveeta, 2-Pound Size	5.00
Cheese, Painted Chrome, Yellow, Basswood, 16 X 9 In.	35.00
Cigar, Bering Habana, Labels & Customs Labels, 7 5/8 X 4 1/2 In.	8.00
Cigar, Musketeers, Hinged, Lock, 3-Compartment, Wooden	10.00
Cigarette, Marble, Art Deco, 5 X 3 1/2 In.	65.00
Collar Stud, Black Faille, Needlepoint Lid, 1 1/2 X 2 In.	15.00
Cribbage, Ivory, Pewter Rim, 3 3/4 X 9 1/2 X 2 1/4 In.	20.00
Document, Brass Handles, Lined, Dated 1879, 12 X 8 X 6 In.	95.00
Document, Original Boston Label, C.1830	110.00
Dome Top, Hinges & Hasps, Japanned, C.1890, Tin, 2 3/4 X 4 X 2 3/4 In.	65.00
Dome Top, Red & Black Sponge Design, Gray Ground, 24 X 12 X 11 In.	195.00
Dome Top, Yellow & Brown Grain Painted, 27 3/4 X 10 3/4 X 9 1/4 In.	95.00
Dough, Maple, New England, Pine Trestle Base	125.00

Fare, Trolley, Brass Front, Lever 75.00
Federal, Pine, C.1800, Rectangular, 7 X 14 In. 50.00
Hanging, Red Paint, Shaped Backboard & Sides, 21 X 7 In. 1500.00
Hat, E Pluribus Unum, White, Red, & Green, Hannah Davis, 20 X 15 X 15 In. 280.00
Hat, Pine, Tricorner, Light Blue-Green, 18 1/2 In. 1400.00
Hat, Swan Handle, Fruit Basket, Hannah Davis, 16 X 12 X 14 In. 395.00
Hearts & Geometric Forms, Spruce Gum, 4 1/4 In. 260.00
Jack Sprat Prunes, Wooden, 10 X 14 In. 15.00
Jewel, Gilt Bronze Ormolu, Marble Top, 2-Drawer, 12 3/4 X 7 X 7 In. 395.00
Jewelry, Openwork Base, Foliage Design, 5 X 8 In. 85.00
Knife, Black Walnut, Coped-Out Handle, Slant Sides, 9 In. 60.00
Knife, Brown, Yellow, & Green Floral Design, 7 X 14 In. 205.00
Knife, Hanging, Pine, Slanted Sides, Red Paint, 13 X 11 In. 725.00
Knife, Mahogany, Dovetailed, Cut-Out Divider, 10 X 14 In. 55.00
Knife, Oak, Slanted Sides, Divider, 7 X 11 In. 60.00
Knife, Pine, Gray, Orange Glaze, 8 X 11 In. 50.00
Knife, Pine, 2-Part, Turned Handle, Brown, 8 1/2 X 14 1/2 In. 50.00
Knife, Scouring, Pine, 5 X 17 In. 120.00
Knife, Turnip-Shaped Grip, Pine & Hardwood, Red Paint, C.1880, 15 1/4 In. 60.00
Knife, White Birch, Hand-Forged Nails, 9 X 12 In. 60.00
Knife, 2-Compartment, Reeded Sides, Painted Green, 13 X 9 X 6 In. 38.00
Leather Covered, Iron Lock, Brass Tacks, 5 X 4 In. 30.00
Letter, Pumpkin Pine, Slant Front, 11 X 11 1/2 In. 65.00
Mahogany, Cartoon Painting, Black Boy, 12 X 5 In. 20.00
Maple, Wire Bail Handle, Covered, 5 1/2 In. 60.00
Metal Banding, Bentwood, Covered, 3 3/4 X 4 In. 22.00
Money, Church, Rectangular Top, 18th Century, 6 X 24 In. 300.00
Norwegian, Birch-Laced Pine, Covered, 13 X 5 X 7 In. 95.00
Orange Slices, Label On Lid, Round, 6 1/2 In. 50.00
Painted Red, Deep, 4 3/4 X 10 X 5 In. 250.00
Pantry, Blue-Green, Single-Lap, Covered, Oval, 6 In. 180.00
Pantry, Covered, Round, Tacked Red, 8 1/2 In. 65.00
Pantry, Green Over Red, Covered, Round, 4 X 7 In. 100.00
Pantry, Light Blue-Green, New England, Single-Lap, 6 1/2 In. 180.00
Pantry, Round, Old Red Paint, 5 3/4 In. 150.00
Pantry, Round, Original Brown Paint, 6 1/2 In. 35.00
Pen, Mahogany, Drawer, Brass Handle, 2 1/2 X 6 1/4 In. 65.00
Pencil, Hinged Lid, 2-Section, 1890, Rectangular, Wooden 5.00
Pill, Round, Sponge Design, Brown On Yellow, 3 1/8 In. 65.00
Pine, Brown & Black Flame Graining, 7 X 13 In. 35.00
Pine, No Nails, Glue & Seams, Covered, 6 5/8 X 3 1/2 In. 195.00
Pine, Red & Black, Yellow Striping, Covered, 6 X 12 In. 40.00
Pine, Spring Lid, Oval, Branded Design, 5 1/2 In. 200.00
Pine, Wall, Lift Top, 2 Compartments, 1 Drawer, Red Paint, 11 In. 150.00
Pine, White, Staple Hinges, 6 X 16 In. 65.00
Pipe, Cherry, Drawer, Circular Hanger, 21 1/2 In. 1600.00
Pipe, Cherry, Ivory Inlaid Heart, 2 Drawers, 16 In. 1600.00
Pipe, Mahogany, Scrolled Pendant, Drawer, Hanger, 24 X 6 In. 1700.00
Pipe, Oak, Hanging, Old Dark Finish, 20 In. 85.00
Pipe, Rectangular Backboard, 18th Century, New England, 20 X 5 In. 1300.00
Pipe, Rectangular, Single Drawer, Green, 18th Century, 21 1/2 In. 1100.00
Rosewood Veneer, Rectangular, Checkerboard Border, 12 X 9 In. 65.00
Rosewood, Grained, 9 X 11 In. 300.00
Salt, Pine, Hanging, Curved Crest, Brown, 8 X 10 In. 75.00
Salt, Pine, Hanging, Stenciled Salt, 4 X 5 In. 25.00
Scouring, Pine, 8 X 15 In. 50.00
Seed, Ferry & Morse, Dovetailed 50.00
Seed, Inside Label, Birds & Flowers, Wooden 65.00
Shoeshine, Hinged Storage Area, C.1880, Pine, 10 1/4 X 21 In. 85.00
Slide Cover, Black Cherry, 8 1/2 X 15 1/2 X 4 3/4 In. 35.00
Stagecoach, Iron Lock, Handles, Leather Covered, C.1840, 20 1/2 In.Long. 175.00
Stamp, Iron, Signed Simpson Iron Works 75.00
Stamp, Wilton, Turtle & Frog, Iron 22.50

BOX, TEA CADDY, see also Tea Caddy
Tea Caddy, Russian Lacquer, Imperial Period, 6 X 6 In.	225.00
Tea Caddy, Victorian, Gilt & Black Lacquer, 8 X 5 In.	60.00
Tea Caddy, Victorian, Rosewood, Brass Inlaid, 12 In.	225.00
Tool, Different Scene On Each Side, Carrying Handle, Pennsylvania	900.00
Turned Wood, Original Red Finish, 2 1/2 In.	235.00
Turned Wood, Wire Bail, Wooden Handle, Old Finish, 3 3/8 In.	205.00
Wallpaper-Covered, Lined With 1806 Newspaper, 5 X 7 In.	90.00
Wooden, Gold Stenciled, Liner, 5 1/2 In.	20.00
Wooden, Yellow Finish, Footed, 6 3/4 In.	110.00
Wooden, Yellow Ground, Original Red Sponged Design, 5 In.	300.00
Wooden, 12-Layered Carved Rings, 3 1/4 X 3 In.	45.00
Writing, Pine & Poplar, Rosewood Bound, 8 X 3 3/4 In.	25.00

BOY SCOUT, Axe & Knife, Combination
BOY SCOUT, Axe & Knife, Combination	38.00
Axe & Sheath, 13 In.	35.00
Book, On The Trail, By Durston, 1921	1.25
Book, Scoutmaster, 1929	15.00
Book, Trailblazers, 1917	9.00
Book, Woodcraft Or How A Patrol Leader Made Good, 1913	8.50
Bookmark, 1930s, Brass	3.50
Bugle, Brass	85.00
Button, Campaign Hat, Blue Ground, 1925, Celluloid	15.00
Camera, Kodak, Metal Bellows, Film 127, Case	60.00
Cap, Red Braid, Patch On Front, Size 7 7/8	3.00
Card, Membership, June 1921	10.00
Catalog, Equiment, Dated 1927	35.00
Drum, Tin, Dated 1907	35.00
First Aid Box, 1942, Tin, Content	12.00
First Aid Kit, Metal Box	10.00
Flashlight	9.00
Game, Sunny Andy Kiddie Kampers, Marble, Tin	195.00
Handbook, Patrol Leaders, 1929	18.00
Handbook, Scout Master, 1936	17.50
Handbook, 1911	22.50
Handbook, 1946	4.50
Handbook, 1946, Rockwell Cover	8.00
Hat & Breeches, C.1933	50.00
Hat, Campaign, Felt	20.00
Hat, Master's, Leather Hat Band & Buckle, Official Emblem, Size 7	27.50
Hatchet	12.00
Holder, Kerchief	4.00
Holder, Match Book, Jamboree, 1950, Copper	27.00
Indian Beadcraft Outfit, Boxed, 1935	45.00
Knife, Ulster, U.S.A.	9.00
Manual, The Bear Club Book, 1943	5.00
Merit Badge, 1943	5.00
Music, Sheet, Scouts On Parade March	5.00
Pin, Flag, 1918	6.00
Pin, Life Member, Enamel Heart	12.00
Signaler, Fleron Official, 1940s, Box	30.00
Songbook, Boys Will Sing, 1938	11.00
Stove, Coleman, Canvas Holder	15.00
Transmitter, Morse Code, Pair	28.00

*Bradley & Hubbard Manufacturing Company made lamps and other metal
work in Meriden, Connecticut, from the mid-nineteenth century.*

BRADLEY & HUBBARD, Bookends, Lion	35.00
Candlestick, Brass, 12 In.	30.00
Chandelier, Pull-Down, Oil, 3 Fonts, Original Shades	400.00
Desk Set, Milk Glass Inkwell, Bronze	75.00

Inkwell, Deco Style, 4-Sided, Brass, 4 1/2 X 2 1/4 In.	40.00
Inkwell, 2 Wells, Hinged Cover, Pewter, 9 X 4 1/2 In.	95.00
Lamp, Banquet, Faceted Jewels In Pierced Shade, Signed	360.00
Lamp, Gone With The Wind, Dated 1896	280.00
Lamp, Hanging, Amberina Shade, Painted Birds, Wired	800.00
Lamp, Library, Pull-Down, Hobnail Shade, C.1890, Signed	1200.00
Lamp, No.4, Metal	90.00
Lamp, Oil, Gone With The Wind, Multipanel Globe	250.00
Lamp, Oil, Table, Bronze Base, Ball Shade	250.00
Lamp, Table, Water Lilies In Relief, Patent 1893, Wired	350.00
Lamp, Table, 275-Piece Leaded Shade, Signed	350.00
Lamp, Turkey Foot, Brass, 36 In.	450.00
Lamp, 6-Panel Chocolate Slag Shade, Ivory Finish, 12 In.	95.00
Letter Opener & Paper Clip, Brass	15.00
Plaque, Wall, Gypsy Girl, 8 In.	65.00
Shade, Lavender, Antique White, 8-Paneled, Metal	175.00

Brass has been used for decorative pieces and useful tablewares since ancient times. It is an alloy of copper, zinc, and other metals.

BRASS, see also Bell; Tool; Trivet; etc.

BRASS, Ashtray, Embossed Logo, Brass	7.00
Ashtray, Figural, Horse, Head & Neck, Mt.Washington, N.H., 4 1/4 In.	5.00
Ashtray, Westinghouse Air Brake, Robot On Top, 10 In.	45.50
Basin, Wash, Flaring Sides, Hammered, Hanging Ring, 11 1/2 In.	70.00
Bed Warmer, English, Pierced, Floral Design, Wood Handle, 43 In.	110.00
Bed Warmer, Pierced, Turned Wood Handle, 18th Century, 45 In., Pair	600.00
Bed Warmer, Tooled Ship On Lid, 10 1/2 In.	70.00
Belt, Linked, 3-Link Forms, Paste Rubies, Incised, 19th Century, 33 In.	75.00
Board, Polishing, Button	14.00
Boiler & Engine, Weeden, Model No. 49, 2 Flywheels, 11 1/2 In.	20.00
Bookends, Knights Of Columbus, 1922	20.00
Bookends, Pagodas	24.00
Bookends, Ship	32.00
Bowl, Cylindrical, Wide Rim, 11 In.	100.00
Bowl, Dragon, Flared, 2 1/2 X 4 In.	9.00
Bowl, Pierced, Claw Feet, Melons & Vines Design, 7 1/2 In.	35.00
Box, Cigarette, Overlaid Silver, Burmese Figures, 3 X 1 3/7 In.	65.00
Box, Diamond-Scored Design On Lid, Switzerland, 7 5/8 X 4 3/8 In.	28.00
Box, Tobacco, Holland, Symbolic Figures, 1 3/8 X 6 1/8 In.	225.00
Box, Trinket, Engraved Flowers, Dragons, Medallions, Lined	145.00
Bracket, Tumbler, Wall Mounting, Victorian, C.1890, 3 3/4 In.	35.00
Bucket, Champagne, Lion Heads	95.00
Bucket, Iron Bail, 8 X 5 In.	79.00
Bucket, Log, 15 In.	330.00
Bucket, Tin Lined, Riveted Iron Mounts, Bail Handle, 3 3/4 In.	38.00
Bucket, Wrought Banding & Bail	100.00
Butter, Flowers, Ivies, Blue & Red Enamel, India, 5 1/2 In.	15.00
Caddy, Spoon, Souvenir, Sidney Harbour Bridge, C.1891	25.00
Cage, Cricket, Indonesian Beehive Shape, Hinged	100.00
Camera, Pocket, Folding, Cased	50.00
Candelabrum, Art Deco, 3-Branch, 5 In.	150.00
Candlestick, Altar, Beehive & Diamond Stems, Drip Pan, 19 In., Pair	200.00
Candlestick, Altar, Triangular Base, 19th Century, 37 In., Pair	225.00
Candlestick, Altar, Turned, 15 In., Pair	110.00
Candlestick, Baluster Shape, C.1800, 9 In., Pair	145.00
Candlestick, Baluster Stem, Drip Pan, Circular Base, 4 In., Pair	275.00
Candlestick, Baluster Stem, Octagonal Dome, 7 In.	150.00
Candlestick, Baluster Stem, Push-Ups, 19th Century, 9 3/4 In., Set Of 4	225.00
Candlestick, Baluster Turned Stem, Octagonal Domed Base, 18th Century	200.00
Candlestick, Baluster Turned Stems, 19th Century, 7 3/4 In., Pair	300.00
Candlestick, Beehive, 1840s, 11 In., Pair	215.00
Candlestick, Belgian, 10 In., Pair	50.00
Candlestick, Candle Socket, Baluster Stem, Domed Base	450.00

Candlestick, Capstan, Molded Socket, Ejector, Flaring Base, 5 In.	375.00
Candlestick, Collapsible, C.1860, 3 1/4 In., Pair	150.00
Candlestick, Continental, Baluster Stem, Drip Pan, Domed, 7 1/2 In.	400.00
Candlestick, Continental, Urn Shaft, Domed Base, 5 1/2 In., Pair	775.00
Candlestick, Dish Base, 7 1/2 In.	70.00
Candlestick, Double Twisted, 10 In.	85.00
Candlestick, Elongated Socket, Ejector, Bell-Form Base, 5 In.	160.00
Candlestick, English, Bell-Bottom, 18th Century, 10 In.	850.00
Candlestick, Engraved, Urn Shape, Animal-Form Handles, 6 In., Pair	650.00
Candlestick, Etched Design, English, 6 3/4 In., Pair	15.00
Candlestick, Federal, Baluster Shaft, Square Base, 6 In., Pair	100.00
Candlestick, Federal, Inverted Trumpet Shafts, Set Of 4	90.00
Candlestick, Footed Base, Teardrop & Saucer Turning, 9 In.	40.00
Candlestick, Gothic Revival, French, Pair	180.00
Candlestick, Knob Stem, Drip Trays, 7 In., Pair	65.00
Candlestick, Mid Drip, Baluster Stem, 18th Century, England, 9 1/4 In.	700.00
Candlestick, Mid Drip, Dome Base, 3-Ring Stem, 17th Century, 7 In.	1900.00
Candlestick, Mid Drip, Multiring, Turned Stem, 18th Century, 6 3/4 In.	1100.00
Candlestick, Mid Drip, Turned Stem, Circular, 18th Century, 9 In., Pair	1450.00
Candlestick, Octagonal Base, Screw-In Stem, 6.1/8 In.	175.00
Candlestick, Pair, Pedestal, Dome Base, 19th Century, 2 3/4 X 1 3/4 In.	60.00
Candlestick, Push-Up, Victorian, Beehive & Diamond Detail, 13 In.	200.00
Candlestick, Push-Up, 17 In.	48.00
Candlestick, Push-Up, 9 3/4 In., Pair	56.00
Candlestick, Queen Anne Base, England, 18th Century, 7 In., Pair	175.00
Candlestick, Queen Anne, Baluster Shape, Marked, England, 18th Century	325.00
Candlestick, Queen Anne, Cupped Bobeches, Knob Stem, 7 5/8 In., Pair	600.00
Candlestick, Queen Anne, Octagonal Base, Baluster Stem, 6 In.	155.00
Candlestick, Queen Anne, Scalloped Base, Elongated, 8 In., Pair	875.00
Candlestick, Queen Anne, Straight Shaft, Scalloped Edge, 9 In.	150.00
Candlestick, Queen Anne, Turned Stem, England, 18th Century, 6 1/2 In.	225.00
Candlestick, Square Base, Paw Feet, Flared Socket, 8 1/2 In.	125.00
Candlestick, Straight Cups, Ring Design, Ejector Holes, 5 In., Pair	600.00
Candlestick, Straight Sided, Square Base, Molded Lip, 6 1/2 In.	275.00
Candlestick, Straight Socket, Square Flat Base, 5 In., Pair	425.00
Candlestick, Telephone, Pair	95.00
Candlestick, Turned Stem, England, 19th Century, 9 1/2 In., Pair	375.00
Candlestick, Turned Stem, 19th Century, England, 9 X 9 1/4 In., Pair	225.00
Candlestick, Urn-Shaped Socket, Mid Drip, Domed Base, 5 In.	475.00
Candlestick, Urn-Shaped Socket, Mid Drip, 5 1/2 In.	550.00
Candlestick, Venetian Glass Shade, C.1860, 2 Ft., Pair	240.00
Candlestick, Victorian Molded Design, Drip Pan, English, 3 1/2 In., Pair	75.00
Candlestick, Victorian, Push-Ups, 10 1/4 In., Pair	120.00
Candlestick, Victorian, Push-Ups, 11 3/4 In., Pair	190.00
Candlestick, 17th Century, Mid Drip, 16 1/2 In., Pair .... *Illus*	1700.00
Centerpiece, Viking Ship Shape, Columned Stand, Footed, 17 In.	40.00
Changer, Coin, Street Car Conductor's, Sam Browne Belt	75.00
Coal Scuttle, Leaf, China, 4 X 3 1/2 In.	8.50
Coaster, Flowers, Ivies, 3 1/2 In.	5.00
Coffeepot, Handled Tray, Tsarist Period, Brass, 9 1/2 In.	95.00
Coffeepot, Hinged Cover, Long Spout, Russian, Signed, 12 X 9 In.	129.00
Coffeepot, Lighthouse Form, 9 1/2 In.	100.00
Coffeepot, Long Spout, Double Eagle, Russian	45.00
Colander, Shallow Pierced Bowl, Hanging Handle, 8 In.	150.00
Compass, Surveyor, English	75.00
Compote, Cow's Head Spout, 3 1/2 In.	10.00
Crumber, Cat Handle, Marked Poorage, Made In England	18.00
Cup, Cyclist's, 1897	20.00
Cup, Dated 1933, Chicago, 3 In.	10.00
Cuspidor, Bulbous Base, 6 1/2 In.	85.00
Cuspidor, Removable Cover, 10 In.	70.00
Cutter & Ashtray, Cigar, Ship's Wheel, 4 3/4 X 9 In.	110.00
Cutter, Cigar, Cigar Shape, Pocket, Brass	15.00

Brass, Candlestick, 17th Century, Mid Drip,
16 1/2 In., Pair

Brass, Jardiniere, Mythological Figural Scenes,
12 X 12 In.

Cutter, Cigar, In Center Of Ashtray, Ship's Wheel, 6 3/4 X 4 3/4 In.	85.00
Dipper, Well-Shaped Handle, 20 In.	65.00
Dish, Candy, Souvenir Of 1915 Panama Pacific Exposition, 5 1/2 In.	14.25
Door Knocker, C-Scroll, Brass Plate, 18th Century, 7 3/4 In.	60.00
Door Knocker, Enameled Sailing Ship, 2 3/4 In.	8.50
Door Knocker, Form Of Lion's Head, English, 2 X 4 1/2 In.	22.00
Door Knocker, Hand Holding Rose, 5 In.	15.00
Duster Gun, Powder End, Wooden Handle, 21 In.	40.00
Ewer, Russian, Signed, 12 X 5 In.	119.00
Fender, Fire, Georgian, C.1820, 36 1/2 In.	70.00
Figurine, Dancer, Nude	55.00
Figurine, Mercury, Marble Base, 21 X 5 1/2 In.	300.00
Frame, Picture, Standing, Mirror Border, 13 X 10 In.	50.00
Furniture, Mirror, Continental Trompe L'oeil, 5 Ft. 3 In., Pair	495.00
Headband, Oxen, Heart, Leather Harness, 9 X 14 In.	40.00
Holder, Toothbrush, Wall Bracket, Gourd Shape, C.1890, 6 In.	45.00
Horn, Fox Hunt, Circular Bend, English, 12 In.Diam.	100.00
Horn, Yachting, Signed Arurelbo	110.00
Jardiniere, Floral Basket Design, Ring Handles, 3-Footed, 9 In.	38.00
Jardiniere, Mythological Figural Scenes, 12 X 12 In. ....*Illus*	225.00
Jardiniere, Sculptured Roses Design, Hammered Texture, 9 X 11 In.	40.00
Kettle, Brass Swing Handle, C.1860, 9 1/2 In.	125.00
Kettle, Rolled Rim, Iron Bail, Round Bottom, 8 In.	275.00
Key, Figural, Opening Day State Fair Of Texas, 1915, Porcelain Top	25.00
Key, Jail	20.00
Knife Sharpener, Wood Base, Nickel Plated, 1908, Philadelphia	25.00
Knocker, Door, Lion, 4 1/2 X 7 1/2 In.	28.00
Knocker, Door, Urn Form, Female Mask Striker, 1830	170.00
Lamp, Binnacle, Double, 13 X 17 In.	75.00
Lamp, Candle, Spring Loaded, Pedestal Base, 12 1/2 In.	50.00
Lamp, Carbide, Just Rite, U.S.A., 4 1/4 In., Pair	15.00
Lamp, Middle Eastern, Spout, Flared Foot, 7 In.	20.00
Lamp, Skater's, Bail, 12 In.	65.00
Lamp, Whale Oil, Gimbal, Conical Hinged Cover, 19th Century, 6 In.	125.00
Lamp, Whale Oil, Maine, Acorn-Shaped Font, Marked Webb, 7 In.	1250.00
Lantern, Eclipse, American La France Fire Dept.	350.00
Lantern, Fire Dept., Pat.1893	50.00
Lantern, Skater's	65.00
Latch, Door, Iron Bar & Keeper, 7 1/2 In.	35.00

Letter Opener, Woman With Long Hair, 6 1/2 In. 35.00
Lock & Key, Scotty Dog 13.00
Lock, Key, Reeses, U.S.A., 2 In. 3.00
Measure, Liquid, Strap Handle, Pouring Lip, 6 1/2 In. 75.00
Microscope, Bausch & Lamb 165.00
Mirror, Hand, Porcelain Back, Bust Portrait Of Blonde Lady 165.00
Mirror, Shaving, Figural, Man 85.00
Money Clip, R.S.Cola 15.00
Mortar & Pestle, 1 1/2 In. 18.00
Nutcracker, Lion Standing Above Shield, English 20.00
Padlock & Key, Champion 6 Lever, Round 40.00
Padlock, Keen Kutter, Figural Emblem, Red Paint 80.00
Padlock, Reese, 2 Keys, Made In U.S.A., 1 1/2 In. 4.00
Padlock, Sprocket 40.00
Pail, Dated 1866 .... 85.00
Pan, Spun, Wide Rim, Rolled, Tapered Sides, 17 1/2 In. 95.00
Paper Clip, Figural, Hand, English 35.00
Paper Clip, Hand With Lacy Cuff, 19th Century 45.00
Pin, Horse Blanket, Embossed 311, 4 3/4 In. 4.50
Planter, Lion Head Ring Handles, 12 In., Pair 75.00
Plaque, Greyhound, Embossed Farnoon Ferry, 22 X 8 1/2 In. 75.00
Plate, Dirk Van Erp, 6 1/4 In. 95.00
Pump, Boat, Embossed Perko, Wooden Grip Handle, 23 In. 22.50
Pump, Tire, Iron Base 40.00
Quadrant, Inlaid Ivory, Oak Case, Sunderland, London, 14 In. 825.00
Rack, Magazine, Art Deco, Cut-Out Fawn 75.00
Rosette, Embossed Concentrics, 1 3/4 In.Diam., Pair 4.50
Samovar, Faceted Inverted Pear Shape, 15 In. 100.00
Samovar, Globular Form, Beaded Border, 15 In. 125.00
Samovar, Lobed Inverted, Pear Shape, 18 In. 125.00
Samovar, Straight Sides, Cylindrical Form, 18 In. 200.00
Sconce, Circular Dish, Drip Plate, Scrolled Support, 8 In., Pair 625.00
Sconce, Wall, Cherub Climbing Leafy Vine, 2-Light, 19 In. 55.00
Sconce, Wall, Cherub Climbing Vine, 2-Arm, 19 In. 55.00
Sconce, Wall, Urn Shape, Scrolled Arm, 8 1/2 In., Pair 200.00
Scoop, Candy, Hang-Up Loop, 9 X 6 In. 40.00
Scoop, Cowl Top, Flat Bottom, 1/2 Pound, 8 In. 30.00
Scoop, Ice Cream .... 16.00 To 25.00
Scoop, Ice Cream, Gilcrist 35.00
Scoop, Tubular Handle, Brass Rivets On Heel, 15 In. 150.00
Shoehorn, English, 9 In. 35.00
Skewer, Figural, Duck Handle, Greek, Brass, 11 In. 4.00
Skimmer, Copper Rivet, Oval Bowl, 7 X 9 In. 240.00
Skimmer, Design, Piercing In Handle & Blade, 20 In. 105.00
Skimmer, Steel Handle, 20 1/2 In. 150.00
Snuffer, Candle, C.1775 .... 35.00
Spatula, Iron Handle, 15 In. 55.00
Spigot, Barrel, 5 In.Wide 18.50
Spittoon, Saloon, 10 X 16 In. 55.00
Spool Rack, 4-Tiered, 8 Spindles, Figure, 17 In. 350.00
Stand, Plant, 4 Spears Hold Vase, C.1880, 13 In. 22.00
Stand, Shoeshine, Footrest, Lady's 25.00
Stand, Smoking, Green Marble, 11 X 28 In. 75.00
Stand, Vase, Spears Curving Out, Acanthus Leaf Design, 13 In. 22.00
Stencil, Alphabet, Circular 60.00
Stencil, Apple Barrel, Extra Selected Kings, 12 X 14 In. 50.00
Stencil, G.S.W., 1 1/8 In.Letters, 3 1/2 X 6 In. 10.00
Tankard, Art Deco, Monkey On Top, Tail Becomes Handle, 15 In. 125.00
Tapper, Soda Fountain, 14 In. 65.00
Tazza, Raised On Bobbin-Form Stem, 19th Century, 16 In. 110.00
Tea Set, Gooseneck Spout, Doubled-Handled Tray, Russian, 4 Piece 125.00
Teakettle, Black Curved Handle, Copper Bottom, Germany, 7 In. 35.00

Teakettle, Cylindrical Body, Floral Design, Swing Handle, 5 In. 450.00
Teakettle, Swinging, Burner Stand, English 135.00
Teapot, Black Wooden Ribbed Handle, Marked S.& Co., 8 In. 35.00
Teapot, Peking Glass Finial, Floral, Miniature, 20th Century, 2 In. 70.00
Teapot, Queen Anne, Pear Shape, Scrolled Spout, 7 In. 260.00
Teapot, Wooden Ribbed Handle, Marked S.& Co., 8 In. 40.00
Telephone, Stick, Marked Western Electric Co., 1904 .... 130.00
Telescope, English, Day Or Night, 3 Draws, Leather Casing 330.00
Telescope, Sun Shade, Admiral David Farragut, U.S.S., Hartford, 32 In. 350.00
Telescope, 3 Sections, Dust Cover, 33 In, ... 65.00
Tongs, Ember, 21 In. 35.00
Tongs, Fireplace, Handled, Knob Finial, Ring Shank, 28 In. 55.00
Tongs, Hanging Ring, Claw Ends, 11 In. 14.00
Tray, Oval, Scalloped, Etched Floral Design, 15 3/4 In. 15.00
Tray, Pin, Wonderful Colorado, Horse's Head In Bottom, Brass 20.00
Trimmer, Wick, Fancy Handles 39.00
Umbrella Stand, Lion Head Side Rings, Ruffled Top & Bas .... 75.00 To 125.00
Urn, Sculptured Scroll Neck, Handles, Ribbed, 13 X 5 1/2 In. 22.00
Vase, Monster Head Handles, Blue, Green, Floral Bands, 11 In. 160.00
Warming Pan, Decorated Top, Turned Wooden Handle, New England, C.1800 .... 170.00
Warming Pan, Iron Handle, Etched Star Design, 44 In. 600.00
Warming Pan, Peafowl, Round, Bird & Scroll Design, 42 In. 200.00
Warming Pan, Pierced, Wooden Handle, 43 In. 275.00
Warming Pan, Turned Wooden Handle, 42 In. 150.00
Whistle, Steam, American Steam Gauge, 1884, 10 1/2 In. 50.00
Whistle, Steam, 1 Tone, Marked Buckeye Brass Works, Dayton, 13 3/4 In. 65.00
Whistle, Steam, 1 Tone, 7 3/4 In. 55.00
Whistle, Steam, 1 Tone, 10 3/4 In. 50.00
Whistle, Steam, 1 Tone, 15 1/2 In. 55.00
Whistle, Steam, 1 Tone, 17 In. 65.00
Whistle, Tuning, Violin, Peerless, 4-Tube 10.00
Whistle, U.S.Army, Chain 15.00
    BREAD PLATE, see various Pressed Glass patterns

*Brides' baskets of glass were usually one-of-a-kind novelties made in
American and European glass factories. They were especially popular about
1880 when the decorated basket was often given as a wedding gift. Cut glass
baskets were popular after 1890. All brides' baskets lost favor about 1905.*

BRIDE'S BASKET, Applied Figural Squirrel, Blue Satin Glass 175.00
  Art Glass, Cranberry Overlay, Silver Plated Holder 85.00
  Bowl, Pale Yellow, Satin Glass 235.00
  Bowl, Pink Overlay 360.00
  Case, Holder, Reds & Cream 175.00
  Cranberry To Pink Bowl, Silver Plated Frame, 9 3/4 In. 295.00
  Custard To Ruby, Silver Plated Frame 200.00
  Custard, Ruby Tips 200.00
  Dark Green, Silver Plated Frame 150.00
  Delaware Pattern, Green & Gold 125.00
  Dish, Pink Overlay, Metal Holder, 7 In. 145.00
  Green, Gold, Silver Plated Frame, Delaware 125.00
  Holder, Pink, Overhead Bail 125.00
  Milk Glass & Blue, Shell Shape Feet, Crimped, 8 In. 20.00
  Orange & White Overlay, Silver Plated Holder, Handle, Signed 175.00
  Pink & Cranberry Ruffled Overlay, Blue Dot Enamel 185.00
  Red Edge, Silver Plated Frame 225.00
  Ruffled Edge, Cased Glass Bowl, Silver Plated Frame 140.00
  Ruffled, Pleated Edge, White To Blue, 12 X 4 In. 125.00
  Scalloped, Silver Plated Frame, Maroon, 9 1/4 X 10 3/4 In. 195.00

BRIDE'S BOWL, Beaded Drape, Red Satin Glass Insert 575.00
  Enameled Scrolls, Silver Plated Holder, 9 X 11 3/4 In. 195.00
  Lattice Edge, Green Shaded To White, 11 1/2 X 4 In. 245.00
  Pink Inside, Hobnail Edge, Silver Plated Holder, Handles 110.00

Pink Overlay, Silver Plated Holder, White Lining, 9 3/4 In.	365.00
Swirl Cranberry, Cased In White	75.00

BRIDE'S BOX, Facing Man & Woman, German Inscription, Green 925.00

> *Bristol glass was made in Bristol, England, after the 1700s. The Bristol glass most often seen today is a Victorian, lightweight opaque glass that is often blue. Some of the glass was decorated with enamels.*

BRISTOL, Biscuit Barrel, Enameled Flowers & Leaves, English, 7 In.	135.00
Bottle, Dresser, Pink, Petticoat Stopper, 10 In.	45.00
Bottle, Perfume, Gold Leaves & Flowers, Gold Stopper, Turquoise	88.00
Bottle, Perfume, Gold Scrolls, Florals, Ball Stopper, 3 7/8 In.	100.00
Box, Jewel, 2 Hand-Painted Dogs On Cover, Round	175.00
Cup, Enameled Remember Me, 4 In.	9.00
Epergne, Enameled Butterflies, Blue	125.00
Jar, Sweetmeat, Enameling, Silver Lid, Bail Handle, Blue	90.00
Lamp, Blue, 12 In.	185.00
Salt, Bucket Shape, Silver Plated Rim & Bail, Gray, 2 In.	58.00
Urn, Aqua, Bird Design, 14 In.	135.00
Vase, Apple Blossom Design	37.50
Vase, Blue, Flower Design, Crimped, 9 In.	15.00
Vase, Blue, Ruffled Rim, Floral Design, 9 X 3 In.	25.00
Vase, Bud, Hummingbird & Flowers, Enamel Paint, 7 1/2 In.	85.00
Vase, Bud, Pale Blue, Gold Band, 6 1/2 In.	8.00
Vase, Enameled Classical Figure, Gold Trim, 9 1/2 In., Pair	195.00
Vase, Frosted White, Gold Floral, Religious Design, 9 1/2 In.	20.00
Vase, Green, Hand-Painted, Ruffled, 11 In.	65.00
Vase, Hand-Painted White & Gold Flower, Deep Blue, 12 In.	65.00
Vase, Hydrangeas, Cream Ground	65.00
Vase, Jewels, Gold Panels & Leaves, Flowers, Turquoise, 7 In.	98.00
Vase, Lilies, Pink Ground, Pair	220.00
Vase, Pink, Flying Sparrow Design, 12 1/2 In., Pair	130.00
Vase, Rose, Foliage, Gold Beading, Brick Neck, 10 1/4 In.	32.00
Vase, Ruffled Overlay, Pink, Hand-Painted, Floral, 5 1/2 In.	45.00
Vase, Ruffled Rim, English, Pair	45.00
Vase, Scenery & Chickens, Brown Trim, Cylinder, 10 In.	45.00
Vase, Victorian Lady, 12 In.	200.00
Vase, White Ground, Hand-Painted Flowers, 9 1/4 In., Pair	115.00
Vase, White, Multicolor Roses, Winter Scene, Ivies, 9 X 5 In.	40.00
Vase, White, Pink Flowers, Brown & Gold Leaves, 7 1/2 In.	22.00
BRITANNIA, see Pewter	

BRONZE, Ashtray, Lady In Canoe, French	30.00
Ashtray, Viennese, Boy With Cigarette & Marble, Marked, 1911	140.00
Austrian, Figurine, Pheasant, Signed, 13 X 6 1/2 In.	450.00
Bookend, Abraham Lincoln Seated, Draped Chair, Plated, 6 X 4 In.	10.00
Bookend, Companions, Dog & Child Reading	55.00
Bookends, Dickens' Bust, Shakespeare's Bust	95.00
Bookends, Egyptian Mummy Design, Signed & Dated 1915	70.00
Bookends, Golfer In Knickers, With Caddy	95.00
Bookends, Indian, Looking Back On Horse	45.00
Bookends, Isadora Duncan, Signed F.F.Ziegler, Dated 1921, 7 In.	500.00
Bookends, Ship, 5 Masts	75.00
Box, Brass Acorn, Hinged Lid, Oak Leaves, 5 1/2 X 4 In.	48.00
Box, 2 Horses, Fighting Gladiators, Covered, 5 X 7 In.	150.00
Brazier, Foo Dog Knop, Tiger, Dragons, Cloud, Swing Handles, 9 In.	475.00
Burner, Incense, Eagle, Japanese, 23 In.	375.00
Burner, Incense, Jade Finial On Rosewood Cover, Dated 1736	1200.00
Bust, Boy, Hat, Double-Tiered Marble Base, Marked, 10 In.	450.00
Bust, C.Kauba, Young Lady Smiling, Signed, Marble Base, 7 1/2 In.	1500.00
Bust, Schiller, Foundry Mark, 6 In.	195.00
Candlestick, Straight Sided, Baluster Shaft, 17th Century, 5 3/4 In.	300.00
Chinese, Son Of Buddha, Gold Overlay, Late Ming Period	580.00

Bronze, Figurine, A.Dressler, Capitoline
Venus, 1867, 21 In.

Bronze, Figurine, E.Villanis, Slave, Removable
Skirt, 15 1/2 In.

Figurine, A.Dressler, Capitoline Venus, 1867, 21 In. ....*Illus* 550.00
Figurine, Athlete, Male, Nude, Red Marble Base, 19th Century, 10 3/4 In 130.00
Figurine, Austria, Boar, 7 In. 600.00
Figurine, Austria, Dog, Doberman, 7 3/4 X 4 3/4 In. 500.00
Figurine, Austria, Frog, Whimsical, Signed, 7 In. 595.00
Figurine, Austria, Mountain Goat, 5 1/4 In. 450.00
Figurine, Bayre, Dog, Hound, Seated, Marked 295.00
Figurine, Bayre, Hunting Dogs, Signed, 6 X 4 In. 375.00
Figurine, Bayre, Lion & Serpent, Signed 995.00
Figurine, Bear, Russian, Gilt, 3 In. 250.00
Figurine, Bouraine, Girl With Deer, Marble Base, 12 3/4 X 23 In. 800.00
Figurine, Bufano, Hand Of Peace, Signed, 15 1/2 In. 7500.00
Figurine, Buffalo, Standing, 8 X 8 In. .... 145.00 To 195.00
Figurine, Bull, Charging Stance, Ivory Horns, 3 X 6 In. 255.00
Figurine, Cat, Walking, Pushing Baby Carriage, 2 Kittens 170.00
Figurine, Child, Eskimo, Marked, 5 In. 190.00
Figurine, Classical, 17 In., Pair 250.00
Figurine, Clown, Kicking Millefiori Ball, Ivory Face, 10 In. 1000.00
Figurine, Crane, Oriental, Standing On Dragon, Marked, 10 In. 475.00
Figurine, D.Chiparus, Exotic Dancer, Onyx Base, Ivory, Signed, 21 In. 7000.00
Figurine, Dog, Borzoi, 10 X 7 In. 125.00
Figurine, Dog, Setter, With Dead Fowl, Marked, 17 X 20 In. 750.00
Figurine, E.Villanis, Slave, Removable Skirt, 15 1/2 In. *Illus*1250.00
Figurine, Elephant, Red Trunk, Ivory Tusks, 7 X 5 In. 175.00

Bronze, Figurine, Elischer, Oriental Woman, C.1825, Base, 9 In.

Bronze, Figurine, L. Alliat, Female, Art Nouveau, 1904, Signed

Figurine, Elischer, Oriental Woman, C.1925, Base, 9 In. .... *Illus* 625.00
Figurine, F.Sicaro, Winged Warrior, Marble Base, 20 1/2 In. 985.00
Figurine, Foo Dog, Seated, Rectangular Plinth, 4 In. 55.00
Figurine, G.M.V.Bareau, Man With Hammer & Anvil, 28 In. 2600.00
Figurine, Hagenauer, Fox, 11 In. 50.00
Figurine, Head Of Women, Marble Base, 8 In. 25.00
Figurine, Hercules, Movable Fig Leaf, 1875, 10 1/4 In. 325.00
Figurine, Horse, Boy Feeding Rabbit 195.00
Figurine, Indian On Horse, C.1900, Marked, 12 X 6 In. 1200.00
Figurine, Infantrymen, Franco-Prussian War, 12 In., Pair 425.00
Figurine, Isidore Jules Bonheur, Horse Prancing, Signed, 15 X 11 In. 1750.00
Figurine, Juan Clara, Girl With Cat, Signed, 10 In. 1400.00
Figurine, Kneeling Nude, Leg Outstretched, Marble Base, 26 X 16 In. 2000.00
Figurine, L.Alliat, Female, Art Nouveau, 1904, Signed .... *Illus* 1600.00
Figurine, Lad, Hat, Signed, 10 X 5 In. 425.00
Figurine, Lion, Tail Extended, Teeth Bared, Marked, 23 In. 200.00
Figurine, Marius Montagne, Young Hermeas, Dated 1867, 27 In. 3900.00
Figurine, Max Kalish, Unemployed, 1930, 16 1/2 In. .... *Illus* 3000.00
Figurine, Mene, Scottish Hunter, Group Of Men, Dead Fox, Dog, 20 In. 2000.00
Figurine, Miroy Freres, Hercules, Tearing Up Tree, Signed, 32 In. 500.00
Figurine, Monkey, Walking On All Fours, Spectacles, Pipe, 2 In. 80.00
Figurine, Nefruari, Gilt, Cold Painted, 1926, Marked, 17 1/2 X 27 In. 2750.00
Figurine, Nude, Slave Bracelet On Upper Arm, 13 1/2 In. 800.00
Figurine, Old Lady With Cat, Signed, 7 In. 85.00
Figurine, P.Mengin, Girl Seated On Rock, Signed, 21 In. .... *Illus* 800.00
Figurine, P.Tereszczuk, Dancing Lady, C.1920, Signed .... *Illus* 1700.00
Figurine, P.Tereszczuk, Female, Ivory Head, 7 1/2 In. .... *Illus* 400.00
Figurine, P.Tereszczuk, Seated Woman, C.1910, 6 1/2 In. .... *Illus* 500.00
Figurine, Parrot, Poised To Attack, Moth, Aloe Plants, Marked, 9 In. 195.00
Figurine, Peacock, Long Plume, Peering Down, Tree, Chinese, 16 In. 160.00
Figurine, Peacock, Male, Standing On Tree, Japanese, 24 In. 8350.00

Figurine, Perillo, Buffalo Hunt 110.00
Figurine, Pheasant, Hen On Clump, 2 Chicks, Marked, 12 In. 325.00
Figurine, Proctor, Tiger, Marked, 1912, 9 X 3 In. 500.00
Figurine, Quail, Red-Brown Patina, On Mound, Marked, 1835-94, 7 1/2 In. 250.00
Figurine, Rocky Mountain Canary, Man & Mule, 1904, 3 1/4 In. 55.00
Figurine, Rudolph Valentino, Role Of Le Gaucho, Wood Base, 10 In. 200.00
Figurine, Tutankhamun, Harpooner, 12 X 10 In. 275.00
Figurine, V.Siefert, Standing Nude, Drinking From Bowl, 11 In. 800.00
Figurine, Vienna, Cat On Basket, C.1890 .... 175.00
Figurine, Vienna, Cat, Pushing Baby Carriage, 2 Kittens Inside 140.00
Figurine, Vienna, Pig, Playing Bass Fiddle, 3/4 In. 155.00
Figurine, Vienna, Pug Dog 97.00
Figurine, Woman, Nude, Teak Plinth, Marked, 20 In. 450.00
Figurine, 2 Leaping Gazelles, Wood Base, 13 X 15 In. 55.00
Four-Leaf Clover, Signed, 6 In. 69.00
Garniture, Dial Inscribed H.Doranlo, French, Clock, 22 In., 3 Piece 775.00
Group, Austria, Pheasants, Joined, 5 1/2 X 4 In. 450.00
Incense Burner, Foo Dog Handle, Monster Feet, 12 In. 175.00
Japanese, Tiger, Signed Chop Mark, 9 1/2 In.Long 750.00
Lamp, Slag Dome, 19th Century, Chinese, 18 In. 725.00
Lamp, Table, 2-Handle, Urn Shape, Bas Relief, 20th Century, 28 1/2 In. 140.00

Bronze, Figurine, Max Kalish, Unemployed,
1930, 16 1/2 In.

Bronze, Figurine, P.Mengin, Girl Seated
On Rock, Signed, 21 In.

(See Page 58)

Bronze, Figurine, P.Tereszczuk, Female, Ivory Head, 7 1/2 In.

Bronze, Figurine, P.Tereszczuk, Seated Woman,
C.1910, 6 1/2 In.

Bronze, Figurine, P.Tereszczuk,
Dancing Lady, C.1920, Signed

Lantern, Coach, Glass Windows, 26 In., Pair	70.00
Medallion, Dante, Round, Raised Bust, 3 In.	35.00
Plaque, Bacchanalian Scene, French, 8 1/4 X 16 3/4 In.	300.00
Plaque, 2-Masted Schooner, 8 X 6 1/2 In.	80.00
Sconce, Wall, Empire, 3 Branches, Flamiform Cap, 9 In., Pair	300.00
Statue, Gazelle, On Base, Gazing Upward, Hollow, 35 In.	1100.00
Table, Garden, Scene Of Orpheus, Tripod Base, 31 X 18 In.	725.00
Urn, Art Nouveau, Pair	350.00
Urn, Dogs & Goddesses, 4 Paw Feet, Scrolled Handled, 18 In., Pair	400.00
Urn, Dragon Handles, Birds, Monster Heads, Bulbous, 17 In.	1050.00
Urn, Temple, Chinese, Carved Wooden Base, Covered, 20 In.	450.00
Vase, Baluster Form, Bas-Relief, Hen & Chicks, C.1900, 12 1/8 In.	120.00
Vase, Baluster Form, Bas-Relief, Violets, 19th Century, 7 1/2 In.	125.00
Vase, Cylinder Shape, Iris Design, 12 1/2 In.	100.00
Vase, Dore Grapes & Vines, Brown Patina, 9 X 5 In.	169.00
Vase, Dragon Handles, Fowl Design, 7 In.	25.00
Vase, Dragons Among Waves, Bulbous, Round Feet, 5 1/2 In.	110.00
Vase, Grapes & Leaves, Gold Dore, 9 1/2 X 5 In.	295.00
Vase, Oriental, Dragon, Bulbous, Flared Base, 15 In.	125.00
Vase, Silver Crest, Ovoid, Applied Sterling Motif, Marked, 9 1/2 In.	60.00
Vase, Silver Overlay, Iris Design, 12 In.	100.00

*Brownies were first drawn in 1883 by Palmer Cox. They are
characterized by large round eyes, down-turned mouths, and skinny legs.*

BROWNIES, Book, Brownies & Other Stories, Palmer Cox Children	27.50
Book, Juvenile Budget, Palmer Cox	28.00
Book, Through The Union, Palmer Cox	39.00
Game, Auto Race, Lithographed Tin, Jeannette Toy Co., 10 1/2 In.	50.00
Game, Brownie Skeet Ball, Miller, Jeannette, Pa.	22.50
Game, Wooden Balls	48.00
Knife, Fork, & Spoon, Palmer Cox, Boxed	75.00
Plate, Palmer Cox	21.50
Spoon	20.00
Stamp Set, Palmer Cox, 11 Piece	75.00
BRUSH MCCOY, see McCoy	

BRUSH, Cookie Jar, Lion, Belmont	25.00
Cookie Jar, Panda	35.00
Cookie Jar, Pig, Formal	55.00

BUCK ROGERS, Atomic Pistol, Daisy	48.00
Battle Cruiser, Yellow & Blue, 1930, 5 In.	25.00
Book, Dangerous Mission, Pop-Up	48.00
Boy, Rocket Ship, Venus Duo Destroyer, Tootsietoy, 1937, Boxed	200.00
Disintegrator	125.00
Gun, Rubber Band	85.00
Gun, Rubber Band, 1940	85.00
Ring, Ring Of Saturn	39.00
Ring, Straight Arrow	26.00
Rocket Pistol, XZ-31, 1934, Boxed	365.00
Rocket Pistol, 25th Century	85.00
Rocket Ship, Flint Cover Missing	225.00
Rocket Ship, Model Kit, 1934	450.00
Strato-Kite, 1946, Unopened	35.00
Watch, Pocket	45.00

*Buffalo pottery was made in Buffalo, New York, after 1902. The company
was established by the Larkin Company, famous manufacturers of soap. The
wares are marked with a picture of a buffalo and the date of manufacture.
Deldare ware is the most famous pottery made at the factory. It is a
khaki-colored transfer-decorated ware.*

BUFFALO POTTERY DELDARE, Bowl, Fruit, Ye Lion Inn, Signed, 8 In. 225.00
Bowl, Fruit, Ye Village Tavern, Signed, 9 In. 425.00
Bowl, The Fallowfield Hunt, The Death, 9 In. 425.00
Bowl, Ye Village Tavern, Signed, 9 1/4 X 3 3/4 In. 400.00
Candlestick, 9 In., Pair 500.00
Charger, An Evening At Ye Lion Inn, 14 In. 325.00
Charger, Fallowfield Hunt, Signed, 14 In. 575.00
Creamer, Breaking Cover 135.00
Creamer, Ye Olden Days, Signed 175.00
Cup & Saucer, The Hunt 200.00
Cup & Saucer, Village Scenes 135.00
Ewer, Ye Lion Inn, 10 X 8 1/2 In. 525.00
Humidor, Ye Lion Inn, Signed, Octagonal, 7 In. 650.00
Mug, At The Three Pigeons, 1909, L.Anna, 4 1/2 In. 250.00
Mug, Dr.Syntax & Counterpart, Dated 1911, 3 1/2 In. 495.00
Mug, Fallowfield Hunt Series, Signed, 4 1/2 In. 250.00
Mug, Lion's Inn 225.00
Mug, Saturday Night At The Buffalo Club, 1911 .... 25.00
Mug, Ye Lion Inn .... 225.00 To 275.00
Pitcher, Annual Rent, Octagonal, 8 In. 475.00
Pitcher, Fallowfield Hunt, Octagonal, 8 In. 265.00
Pitcher, This Amazed Me, Octagonal, 9 In. 510.00
Pitcher, To Demand, 8 In. 475.00
Plaque, Breaking Cover & Ye Lion Inn, Pair 375.00
Plaque, Fallowfield Hunt, 1908, Signed, 12 In. 425.00
Plate, At Ye Lion Inn, 6 1/2 In. 65.00
Plate, Breaking Cover, 7 1/4 In. 95.00
Plate, Card, The Fallowfield Hunt, 1908 .... 210.00
Plate, Chop, Lion's Inn 450.00
Plate, Fallowfield Hunt, Marked, 6 1/4 In. 135.00
Plate, Fallowfield Hunt, Marked, 9 In. .... 95.00 To 275.00
Plate, Fallowfield Hunt, 6 1/4 In. 90.00
Plate, Fallowfield Hunt, 8 1/2 In. 125.00
Plate, Hunt, 7 1/2 In. 100.00
Plate, Olden Times 175.00
Plate, Olden Times, 9 1/2 In. .... 105.00 To 140.00
Plate, The Start, Signed, 9 1/2 In. 175.00
Plate, Town Crier, 8 1/4 In. .... 75.00 To 100.00
Plate, Town Crier, 8 3/4 In. 130.00
Plate, Village Gossips, 10 In. .... 135.00 To 165.00
Plate, Village Scene, 7 3/4 In. 110.00
Plate, Ye Lion Inn, 6 1/2 In. 85.00
Sugar & Creamer, Olden Days 350.00
Sugar & Creamer, Village Life In Olden Days 375.00
Sugar, Scenes Of Village Life In Olden Days 135.00
Sugar, Village Scene, Open 155.00
Teapot, Scenes Of Village Life 75.00
Tile, Tea, Fallowfield Hunt-Breaking Cover, Signed 285.00
Tray, Calling Card, Ye Lion Inn.1909, Signed 220.00
Tray, Dresser, Dancing Minuet, 9 X 12 In. 490.00
Tray, Fallowfield Hunt, Marked, 8 In. 85.00

BUFFALO POTTERY, Bowl, Center Fruit Design, Flowered Rim, White, 9 1/2 In. 14.00
Dish, Vegetable, Blue Willow, 8 X 9 1/2 In. 22.00
Pitcher, Blue Willow, Blue, 4 1/2 In. 75.00
Pitcher, Blue Willow, Dated 1905, 7 In. 225.00
Pitcher, Blue Willow, 1913, 5 In. 75.00
Pitcher, Bluebird, Large 95.00
Pitcher, Chrysanthemum 25.00
Pitcher, Floriana, Dominate Blue, 9 In. 275.00
Pitcher, George Washington .... 375.00 To 395.00
Pitcher, Geranium, Blue 85.00
Pitcher, Gloriana, Blue 350.00
Pitcher, John Paul Jones, 1907, 9 In. .... 325.00 To 450.00

Pitcher, Landing Of Roger Williams 245.00
Pitcher, Marine, Blue On White 535.00
Pitcher, Pilgrim, 9 In. .... 485.00 To 800.00
Pitcher, Robin Hood, Signed, 8 1/4 In. 125.00
Pitcher, Sailor 475.00
Pitcher, The Gunner .... 140.00 To 165.00
Plate, Canton, Green & White 38.00
Plate, Capitol, 10 In. 28.00
Plate, Christmas, 1954 .... 45.00
Plate, Christmas, 1955 .... 45.00
Plate, Game, Deer, 10 In. 28.00
Plate, Game, Moose, 10 In. 28.00
Plate, Independence Hall, 10 In. 28.00
Plate, McKinley Monument, Buffalo, N.Y., 7 1/2 In. 25.00
Plate, Mt. Vernon, 10 In. 28.00
Plate, Niagara Falls 37.50
Plate, Niagara Falls, Blue, 10 In. 20.00
Plate, Trinity Church, New York, Green, 7 In. 75.00
Plate, View Of Thompson Falls, Montana, Green, 7 1/2 In. 50.00
Plate, White House 37.50
Platter, Deer, R.Beck 75.00
Platter, Princess Pattern, 15 In. 30.00
Stamp, Butter, Blue Willow 20.00
Sugar & Creamer, Willow Pattern, 1911 .... 22.00
Tray, Pin, Floral, Gold Rim, 3 1/4 X 6 1/4 In. 24.00

> *Burmese glass was developed by Frederick Shirley at the Mt. Washington*
> *Glass Works in New Bedford, Massachusetts, in 1885. It is a two-toned*
> *glass, shading from peach to yellow. Some have a pattern mold design. A few*
> *Burmese pieces were decorated with pictures or applied glass flowers of*
> *colored Burmese glass.*

BURMESE, see also Gunderson
BURMESE, Basket, Rigaree Bottom, Silver Plated Frame, 6 1/2 In. 325.00
  Basket, Ruffled, Silver Plated Frame, 6 1/2 X 2 1/2 In. 395.00
  Bottle, Teardrop Shape, Pale Rose To Yellow, 6 In. 150.00
  Bottle, 9 In. 195.00
  Bowl, Acid Finish, Oblong, 4 X 5 X 2 In. 195.00
  Bowl, Ruffled, Pink, 9 In.Diam. 85.00
  Fairy Lamp, Signed Clarke Base, 5 In. 275.00
  Lamp, Fairy, Creamy Yellow To Deep Rose, 4 In. 175.00
  Lamp, Fairy, 3 Shades, 2 Vases, Clarke Mirror Base, 6 3/4 In. 1650.00
  Mustard, Scalloped, Yellow To Rose, Brass Top 65.00
  Rose Bowl, Floral Design, Small 385.00
  Toothpick, Enameled Floral 425.00
  Tumbler, Mt.Washington 210.00
  Vase, Applied Rigaree, 5 X 4 In. 1250.00
  Vase, Blue, Forget-Me-Nots, Black Band, 3 1/2 X 3 1/2 In. 275.00
  Vase, Enamel Design Of Daisies & Foliage, Mt.Washington, 7 1/2 In. 345.00
  Vase, Gold & White Daisies, Mt.Washington, 8 In. 345.00
  Vase, Hobnail, 5-Sided Top, Yellow To Pink, 7 1/2 In. 135.00
  Vase, Lily, Acid Finish, Mt.Washington, 15 In. 600.00
  Vase, Lily, Original Label, 14 1/4 In. 550.00
  Vase, Matte Finish, Mt.Washington, 3 In. 475.00
  Vase, Mt.Washington, Gold Enameled, Daisies, 8 In. 625.00
  Vase, Quilt Design, Crimped Edge, Mold Blown, 2 1/2 In. 100.00
  Vase, Ruffled Top, Footed, 4 In. 220.00
  Vase, Trumpet, Crimped Edge, 11 In. 400.00
  Vase, Trumpet, Lily Pad Base, Ribbed, Silver Plated Holder, 9 In. 400.00
  Vase, Trumpet, Turned-Back Rim, Crimped, 11 In. 250.00
  Vase, Turned-In Star-Shaped Neck, 3 1/4 In. 265.00
  Vase, Yellow Edge, Flattened, Mt.Washington, Signed, 7 In. 1050.00
  BURMESE, WEBB, see Webb Burmese

BUSTER BROWN, Bank, With Tige, Iron, Original Paint, 5 1/4 In. 135.00

Book, And The Donkey, Muslin Cloth, Signed Outcault 45.00
Book, Plays Cowboy, 1907 .... 12.00
Bottle, Figural, Hand-Painted Features, Label 45.00
Clicker, Shoe Shape 20.00
Cup & Saucer, Buster And Tige 25.00
Doll, Bisque, Buster Brown Shoe On Back, 3 In. 45.00
Figurine, Tige, Chalkware 25.00
Knife, Several Blades, Large 30.00
Knife, 3-Blade 40.00
Mirror, Pocket 45.00
Mirror, Pocket, Pictures Buster & Tige, Celluloid Back 28.50
Pillow With Tige 85.00
Pinback, Hose Supporters 10.00
Plate, Child's, Buster Having Tea With Girl, 6 1/4 In. 25.00
Roly Poly, Celluloid 45.00
Socks, Boxed .... 45.00 To 75.00
Tin, Cigar, 2 For 5 Cents 45.00
Tin, Mustard, Steinwender Coffee Co., St.Louis 35.00
Whistle, With Tige, Lithograph 15.00
    BUTTER MOLD, see Kitchen, Mold, Butter
    BUTTERMILK GLASS, see Custard Glass

Buttons have been known throughout the centuries, and there are millions of
styles. Only a few types are listed for comparison.

BUTTON, Cameo, Hand-Carved, 18K Gold, Pink 73.00
   Celluloid, 2-Sided, 2 In. 40.00
   Charles Lindbergh, Red, White, & Blue Ribbon, Airplane 30.00
   Copper, Pre-Revolutionary War, Engraved Bow & Concentrics, 1 1/2 In. 10.00
   Duster, Automobile, C.1906 Run-A-Bout Auto, 1 In.Diam. 7.50
   English Royal Coat Of Arms, Brass, Large & Small, Set Of 7 .... 22.00
   Engraved Bow & Concentrics, Pre-Revolutionary War, Copper, 1 1/8 In. 8.50
   Hand-Carved Cameo, Cut Steel Frame, Buckle, C 1800, Set Of 15 .... 145.00
   Mother-Of-Pearl, Original Card, 1930s, Metal Clip, Set Of 4 .... 2.00
   Motorman, Street Railway Uniform, C.1900, 7/8 In., Set Of 6 .... 15.00
   New Hanover City Police, Brass, 5/8 In.Diam. 6.00
   Wild Roses, Meissen 65.00

BUTTONHOOK, Amber & Green Celluloid Handle 3.50
   Art Nouveau Floral, Monogrammed, Sterling Silver 16.00
   Child's, Figural Handle, High-Button Shoes, 3 1/4 In. 18.00
   Claw Holding Marble, Germany, 4 3/8 In. 12.00
   Design, Sterling Silver Handle, Marked, 7 In. 22.50
   Embossed, High-Button, Guilford, Maine, Metal 6.00
   Feather Design On Ivory Handle, 9 3/4 In. 15.00
   Floral Design, Folding 8.00
   Floral, Steel, 3 In. 2.50
   Lady's Leg, Pewter 18.00
   Monogrammed Handle, Sterling Silver, 7 3/4 In. 12.00
   Sterling, Floral Handle, Mark, 6 In. 24.00
   Translucent Amber, Marbleized 3.50

BYBEE, Vase, Pierced, Marked, 5 X 4 In. 35.00

BYRDCLIFFE, Bowl, Multicolored Florals, Pigeon Forge, 7 In. 385.00
    CALCITE, see Steuben

CALENDAR PAPER, Perpetual, Federal Union Insurance Co., Eagle & Flags 115.00
   1866, Hood's Sarsaparilla, Top 10.00
   1888, Hood's Sarsaparilla, Advertising 15.00
   1890, Mass. Mutual Life Insurance, 8 X 6 In. 40.00
   1892, Hood's 10.00
   1893, Home Insurance Co. Of N.Y., Outdoor Scene 38.00
   1893, Singer Sewing Machine Co., 2 Children, Mother 40.00

1894, Hood's	22.00
1894, Horseford	35.00
1894, Palace Steam Laundry, Attached Pad, 8 X 10 3/4 In.	20.00
1895, New York Life Insurance Co.	19.00
1897, Continental Ins. Co.	12.00
1897, Winchester, Framed	395.00
1898, Hood's, 8 1/2 X 10 1/2 In.	39.00
1898, Mezzo, Tinted Flowers	15.00
1898, Winchester Ammunition, Hunter & Elk	575.00
1899, Baker's Extracts	45.00
1899, Winchester Repeating Arms, Hunters & Bear, A.B.Frost	675.00
1900, Opens To 3 Prints, Victorian Girls, Scenic, 9 X 30 In.	30.00
1901, Colgate, Book Form, Beautiful Woman	12.00
1902, Fairy Art, Signed Edward Bisson	15.00
1902, McCormick Harvesting Machine Co., Lady & Equipment	125.00
1902, The Joyful Year, Christmas Theme, 3 Segments	18.50
1902, W.G.Baker, Child & Listing Of All Products	75.00
1903, Dr. Miles, Girl Holding Roses	22.00
1903, Prudential Girl, Framed	25.00
1904, Libby, McNeill, Libby, Girl & Corned Beef	235.00
1905, Tongaline Bitters, Go-Shono Apache Medicine Man	48.00
1906, Pabst Extract, Indian, 36 In.	95.00
1906, Rainier Brewing	12.00
1906, Sleepy Eye Milling Co.	135.00
1906, Triptych-Like Folding Panels, 12 X 21 1/2 In.	30.00
1907, Anthony & Freeport, Kansas, Drugstores	15.00
1907, Child With Robin, Hamphrey	65.00
1908, Christian Herald, Girl In Church Dress	65.00
1908, Die Cut, Water Wheel Mill House, Embossed	27.50
1908, F.Bauernschmidt, American Brewery, Baltimore Streets	200.00
1908, Pabst Extract, Jewel	35.00
1909, Auto Antikamnia Tablet, Girl, Low-Cut Dress	3.50
1909, Blanke's Coffee, 4 Young Women & Flowers	85.00
1910, Anthony & Freeport, Kansas, Drug Stores	15.00
1910, Dr.Simmons Squaw Vine Wine, Maid, Pad, 6 X 11 1/2 In.	32.00
1910, Rev. E.Huber, Illinois, Printed In German	6.75
1911, Antikamnia Tablets, Alice	10.00
1911, Gilt Frame, Motto, Perry Mason Co., 7 1/2 X 11 In.	12.50
1913, Cosmopolitan, Lady & Red Roses, 8 X 32 In.	20.00
1913, Prudential Girl, Framed	25.00
1914, General Store, Black Man With Chickens	28.00
1914, Parker's Garage, Cleveland, O., Woman Watching Repair	45.00
1915, Pabst Extract, Panama Girl, Roll-Up Type	8.00
1915, 6-Part Fan, Red Poinsettias, Scenes	30.00
1916, Sailing Ship, Hand-Painted Title, Salesman's Sample	7.50
1916, Women On Stone Fence, Diamond Shape, 9 In.Square	7.50
1918, Champions Horse Review	135.00
1918, Old Reliable Coffee, Pretty Girl, Pad, 7 X 12 1/2 In.	15.00
1920, Illustrated By Zula Kenyon, 16 X 42 In.	95.00
1920, John Morrell Co.	7.00
1923, Scripture Text	10.00
1925, Anna Woodford	8.00
1925, First National Bank Bandera, Texas, Scene, 7 X 14 In.	12.00
1925, National Meat Market	60.00
1928, Enchantress, Rolf Armstrong	95.00
1928, Rawleigh Cigarettes	5.00
1928, Southern Pacific Lines, 20 X 14 In.	30.00
1931, Goodyear, Brown Town, Minn. Auto Dealership	15.00
1933, Art Deco, Lady, Goodyear & Ford, Pair	25.00
1934, Christian Home	10.00
1936, Currier & Ives, 17 1/4 X 23 1/2 In.	25.00
1937, Mobil Oil	14.00
1938, Burlington Railroad	50.00

1939, Reliance Life Ins.Co. 15.00
1942, Jewel Tea 10.00
1944, Meyer's Fresh Bread, Baker Boy & Girl, Giant Loaves 25.00
1947, Dionne Quintuplets 12.00
1948, Varga 45.00
1949, Esquire 35.00
1949, Parrish, The Village Church, 22 X 16 In. 195.00
1950, Scandinavian Air 8.00
1951, John Morrell Co. 7.00
1951, Parrish, Daybreak, 22 X 16 In. 195.00
1953, Marilyn Monroe, Golden Dreams, Nude 10.00
1953, Marilyn Monroe, Golden Dreams, Nude, Full Color 7.00
1957, Northwest Paper Co., Canadian Mounties 7.00
1959, Hilda, Duane Bryers 10.00
1960, Hummel .... 18.00 To 25.00
1963, Hummel 38.00
1965, Hummel 35.00
1966, Currier & Ives 10.00
1968, Hummel 22.00
1971, Hummel 8.00

Calendar plates were very popular in the United States from 1906 to 1929. Since then plates have been made every year. A calendar, the name of a store, a picture of flowers, a girl, or a scene was featured on the plate.

CALENDAR PLATE, 1907, Cedar Falls, Iowa 30.00
1907, Christmas, Santa Claus Going Down Chinney, 9 In. 45.00
1908, Flowers 30.00
1908, Grundy Center, Iowa 30.00
1908, Maquoketa, Iowa 25.00
1908, Woman In Touring Car, Band B, St.Paul 35.00
1909, E.C.Stiegler & Co., 9 1/2 In. 25.00
1909, E.D.Dorsey, Richmond, W.Va., Roses In Center 30.00
1909, Holly Design, 6 1/2 In. 35.00
1909, Mountain Scene In Wreath Of Flowers 35.00
1909, Seasonal Scene, 8 1/2 In. 22.50
1909, Victorian Lady Center, Orrin D.Clark, Jeweler, 9 In. 60.00
1910, Cupids Ringing In New Year 30.00
1910, Old Swimming Hole, Ohio Advertising, 9 In. 22.50
1910, Sleepy Eye, Minn., Horseshoe & Sailing Boats, 7 1/4 In. 14.00
1911, Ship In Full Sail 23.00
1912, Fruit Center, Months With Cherubs Border, Wisconsin 22.50
1912, Indian Maiden Husking Corn 30.00
1912, Morning Glories, Nebraska Advertising, 8 1/2 In. 27.50
1912, Osgood, Missouri 27.00
1912, Owl On Box, 8 1/2 In. 25.00
1913, Ragged Boy, 7 1/2 In. 25.00
1914, Drug Store Advertising 25.00
1914, Kane 32.00
1918, Flags 30.00
1959, Taylor Smith, White & Gold, 10 In. 8.00

Camark Pottery started in 1924 in Camden, Arkansas. Jack Carnes founded the firm and made many types of glazes and wares. The company was bought by Mary Daniel who still owns the firm. Production in 1983 has been halted but it may soon begin again.

CAMARK, Ashtray, Melon Ribbed, Marked, Maroon, 3 1/4 In. 2.00
Basket, Dogwood Pattern, Sticker, Yellow, 4 1/2 X 3 3/4 In. 6.00
Basket, Double, Leaf Form, Handle, Sticker, Maroon, 4 1/2 X 5 1/2 In. 6.00
Basket, Flared Rim, 2-Handled, Sticker, Cream, 5 X 4 X/2 In. 6.00
Bowl, Apple Green, Tab Handles, Sticker, 4 1/2 In. 3.00
Bowl, Centerpiece, Double-Flared Shell, Turquoise, 12 X 5 1/2 In. 12.00
Bowl, Melon Ribbed, Scalloped, 9 1/2 X 3 In. 7.00

Bowl, Scalloped Rim, Leaf Handles, Sticker, Cream, 12 In.Diam. 12.00
Bowl, Turquoise, Melon Ribbed, Scalloped, 9 1/2 In. 7.00
Candleholder, Yellow Glaze, Deluxe Artware, Paper Label, 5 In., No.269 .... 5.00
Cornucopia, Horizontal Ribbed, Sticker, Cream, 8 X 9 In. 12.00
Creamer, Deco, Sticker, High Gloss Black, 4 1/4 In. 4.00
Ewer, Apple Green, 3 1/4 In. 1.50
Ewer, Melon Rib, Sticker, Turquoise To Plum, 10 In. 25.00
Figurine, Seal, Black 22.50
Holder, Flower, Crane, High Gloss Maroon, 5 X 10 In., Pair 12.00
Holder, Flower, Ducks, Outspread Wings, Sticker, 9 X 5 3/4 In. 12.00
Holder, Flower, Figural, Dancing Nude, Maroon, 9 In. 14.00
Holder, Flower, Maroon, Cranes, Sticker, Pair, 10 X 5 In. 12.00
Holder, Flower, Sticker, White, 3 7/8 X 2 1/2 In. 4.00
Pitcher & Bowl, Relief Fruit, Green, Pitcher 3 1/4 In. 6.00
Pitcher, Bead & Scroll, Bulbous, Sticker, Maroon, 5 1/4 In. 6.00
Pitcher, Cat Climbing Over Top Makes Handle, Label, 8 In. 18.00
Pitcher, Lemon Branch In Relief, Ice Guard, 7 1/2 In. 12.00
Planter, Cream, Fish, Clam, Water Design, Sticker, 10 1/2 In. 12.00
Planter, Double Swan, Sticker, Green, 7 X 7 In. 10.00
Planter, Hand-Painted Flowers, Pink & Green, 3/4 X 5 3/4 In. 12.00
Planter, Relief Fish, Clams, & Water, Cream, Oval, 10 3/4 X 8 3/4 In. 12.00
Pot, Strawberry, Hanging, 8-Cup, Sticker, Yellow, 5 1/2 X 4 3/4 In. 7.00
Vase, Fan, Scalloped Shell, Sticker, Yellow, 10 X 6 In. 12.00
Vase, Gray, Dark Brown, Ring Shoulder Handles, Sticker, 4 1/2 In. 10.00
Vase, Green Vellum Glaze, 6 In. 15.00
Vase, Leaf Form, Flared Split Top, Footed, Sticker, Green, 5 In. 5.00
Vase, Melon Ribbed, Scalloped, 3-Handled, Black, 5 3/4 X 7 In. 5.00
Vase, Ring Shoulder Handles, Sticker, 4 1/4 X 4 1/2 In. 10.00
Vase, Scalloped, Turquoise, 6 1/2 In. 14.00

*Cambridge art pottery was made in Cambridge, Ohio, from about 1895 until
World War I. The factory made brown glazed decorated wares with
a variety of marks including an acorn, the name "Cambridge, " the name
"Oakwood, " or the name "Terrhea."*

CAMBRIDGE POTTERY, Vase, Molded Flowers, Brown, Oakwood, 7 1/4 In. 68.00
Vase, Squat, Brown Nuts On Tree Branch, 3 X 5 1/4 In. 95.00

*Cambridge Glass Company was founded in 1901 in Cambridge, Ohio.
The company closed in 1954, reopened briefly, and closed again in 1958.
The firm made all types of glass. Their early wares included heavy pressed
glass with the mark "Near Cut." Later wares included etched stemware,
crystal, colored, and Crown Tuscan. The firm used a C in a triangle
mark after 1920.*

CAMBRIDGE, Adonis, Bowl, 16 In. 65.00
Apple Blossom, Vase, Green, 12 In. 45.00
Bashful Charlotte, Apple Green, 10 1/2 In. 325.00
Bashful Charlotte, Apple Green, 13 1/2 In. 325.00
Bashful Charlotte, Flower Frog, Pink, 7 In. 85.00
Bashful Charlotte, Flower Frog, 6 1/2 In. 30.00
Bashful Charlotte, Flower Frog, 8 1/2 In. 70.00
Bluejay, Flower Frog 110.00
Bowl, Ebony Frog, Carmen & Ebony 67.50
Bowl, Flying Nude, Seashell, Original Label, 11 In. 155.00
Boy Holding Lamb, Flower Frog, Green, 9 In. 160.00
Calla Lily, Candlestick, 6 1/2 In., Pair 25.00
Caprice, Bonbon, Blue, 2-Handled 27.00
Caprice, Bowl, Console, Blue, 12 X 5 In. 20.00
Caprice, Bowl, Footed, 16 In. 22.00
Caprice, Bowl, Siver Deposit, 4-Footed, 12 In. 40.00
Caprice, Bowl, 4-Footed, 10 1/2 In. 22.00
Caprice, Candleholder, Blue, Pair 125.00
Caprice, Candleholder, 7 In., Pair 25.00

Caprice, Candlestick, Pair 15.00
Caprice, Cruet Set & Tray .... 42.00 To 55.00
Caprice, Cruet, Handled 35.00
Caprice, Cruet, With Tray 42.00
Caprice, Cup & Saucer .... 12.00 To 14.00
Caprice, Cup, Pistachio 30.00
Caprice, Decanter, Blue, Tilt Ball, Stopper, 32 Ounce 65.00
Caprice, Dish, Blue, 3 Part, 7 1/4 In. 48.00
Caprice, Dish, Candy, Covered 30.00
Caprice, Goblet, Blue, 3 Ounce 33.00
Caprice, Goblet, 5 3/4 In. 9.00
Caprice, Luncheon Set, Pink 165.00
Caprice, Plate, Blue, Handled, Footed, 8 In. 27.00
Caprice, Plate, Blue, 14 In. 27.50
Caprice, Plate, 7 1/2 In. 8.00
Caprice, Plate, 8 1/2 In. 6.50
Caprice, Plate, 9 In. 12.00
Caprice, Plate, 9 1/2 In. 32.50
Caprice, Relish 12.00
Caprice, Relish, 3-Section, Blue, 8 1/2 In. 32.00
Caprice, Rose Bowl, Footed, 7 1/2 In. 42.50
Caprice, Salt & Pepper, Sterling Silver Tops 25.00
Caprice, Sherbet, Short 16.95
Caprice, Sugar & Creamer, Tray, Blue 40.00
Caprice, Sugar, Emerald, Signed 4.00
Caprice, Tumbler, Royal Blue, 2 Ounce 25.00
Caprice, Wine, Clear 20.00
Carmen, Cordial, 10 Ounce 20.00
Carnation, Pitcher, Cocktail, Stirrer 165.00
Cascade, Goblet, Wine 10.00
Cascade, Vase, 9 In. 27.50
Cascade, Wine, Yellow, Set Of 6 .... 100.00
Chantilly, Bowl, Flared, 12 1/2 In. 55.00
Chantilly, Cake Plate, 2-Handled, 10 In. 55.00
Chantilly, Cocktail Shaker, Glass Stopper 145.00
Chantilly, Cordial, 1 Ounce 45.00
Chantilly, Decanter, Glass Stopper, Sterling Silver Base 185.00
Chantilly, Dish, Candy, Covered, Sterling Silver Finial 98.00
Chantilly, Goblet, Champagne, 6 In. .... 24.00 To 27.00
Chantilly, Goblet, 7 1/2 In. .... 25.00 To 28.00
Chantilly, Ice Bucket, Sterling Silver Base 125.00
Chantilly, Jug, Ball, Sterling Silver Foot 225.00
Chantilly, Mayonnaise, Underplate 25.00
Chantilly, Mustard, Sterling Silver Base & Lid, 5 In. 35.00
Chantilly, Pitcher, Sterling Base, 24 Ounce 40.00
Chantilly, Salt & Pepper, Sterling Top & Base 27.50
Chantilly, Saltshaker 14.95
Chantilly, Sherbet 26.95
Chantilly, Sugar & Creamer, Sterling Silver Base .... 40.00 To 60.00
Chantilly, Tumbler, Water 26.95
Chintz, Vase, Crown Tuscan, Marked, 12 In., Pair 225.00
Cleo, Bowl, Covered, 7 In. 16.00
Colonial, Butter, Green, Covered, Child's 45.00
Colonial, Creamer, Cobalt Blue, Child's 35.00
Colonial, Creamer, Green, Child's 35.00
Colonial, Cup, Punch, Near Cut 4.50
Colonial, Spooner, Cobalt Blue, Child's 35.00
Colonial, Spooner, Green, Child's 35.00
Colonial, Table Set, Child's, 4 Piece 78.00
Colonial, Table Set, Green, Child's, 4 Piece 125.00
Colonial, Toothpick, Green 30.00
Cornucopia, Vase, Crown Tuscan, 11 In. 68.00
Cornucopia, Vase, Crown Tuscan, 12 In., Pair 125.00

Cornucopia, Vase, Seashell Base, Clear, 8 In.	35.00
Cornucopia, Vase, Shell Base, Crown Tucan, 5 In.	20.00
Cornucopia, Vase, 9 In.	27.50
Cornucopia, Vase, 14 In.	35.00
Daffodil, Sherbet, Crystal	9.50
Decagon, Celery, Blue, Etched, Marked	18.50
Decagon, Cup, Blue	10.00
Decagon, Jug, Ball, Amber, 80 Ounce	48.00
Decagon, Jug, Ball, Amethyst, 80 Ounce	48.00
Decagon, Relish, Green, 3-Section	19.50
Decagon, Sauce, Yellow	12.50
Decagon, Server, Sandwich, Center Handle, Blue	25.00
Decagon, Sugar & Creamer, Amber	15.00
Decagon, Sugar, Blue	11.00
Diane, Goblet, Champagne	21.00
Diane, Goblet, Tall Stem, 10 Ounce	26.00
Diane, Mayonnaise, Sterling Silver Base	32.00
Diane, Plate, 8 In.	8.00 To 16.00
Diane, Salt & Pepper, Footed	45.00
Diane, Sugar & Creamer	40.00
Dianthus, Flower Frog, Pink, 8 1/2 In.	105.00
Doric, Candleholder, Jade, Pair	125.00
Draped Lady, Flower Frog, Clear	55.00
Draped Lady, Flower Frog, Clear, 8 In.	50.00
Draped Lady, Flower Frog, Clear, 9 In.	125.00
Draped Lady, Flower Frog, Crystal Satin, 8 1/2 In.	100.00
Draped Lady, Flower Frog, Crystal, 8 1/2 In.	70.00
Draped Lady, Flower Frog, Green	95.00
Draped Lady, Flower Frog, Green, 8 1/2 In.	100.00
Draped Lady, Flower Frog, Green, 9 In.	95.00
Draped Lady, Flower Frog, Pink, 8 1/2 In.	85.00
Draped Lady, Flower Frog, Pink, 13 In.	225.00
Draped Lady, Flower Frog, Rose, Green	195.00
Eagle, Bookends	125.00 To 150.00
Elaine, Plate, 9 1/2 In.	18.00 To 30.00
Elaine, Sherbet, Set Of 7	125.00
Everglade, Bowl, Blue, 15 In.	185.00
Everglade, Console Set	75.00
Everglade, Plate, 16 In.	46.00
Everglade, Sugar & Creamer, Sterling Silver Bases	49.00
Flower Block, Compote, Farber Ware Holder, 9 In.	75.00
Gadroon, Cake Plate, Crown Tuscan, Footed, 11 In.	38.00
Gadroon, Sugar & Creamer, Individual	40.00
Gloria, Candleholder, Amber, Keyhole, Pair	48.00
Gloria, Mayonnaise, Underplate, Yellow	37.50
Heron, Compote, Farber Ware Holder, 9 In.	75.00
Heron, Flower Frog, 9 In.	49.00
Hunt Scene, Tumbler, Peachblow, 8 Ounce	45.00
Inverted Baby Thumbprint, Lemonade Set, Amber, Signed, 5 Piece	175.00
Inverted Feather, Compote, Marked	40.00
Laurel Wreath, Cocktail, Oyster, No.3700	12.95
Laurel Wreath, Goblet, 6 5/8 In.	18.00
Laurel Wreath, Sherbet, 4 3/4 In.	15.00
Leaf Band, Console Bowl, Blue, 11 1/2 In.	42.00
Log Pattern, Ice Bucket, Green, Marked	35.00
Lynbrook, Cocktail, Oyster	14.95
Lynbrook, Sherbet, Low	14.95
Lynbrook, Tumbler, Footed, 5 Ounce	14.95
Marjorie, Berry Set, 7 Piece	56.00
Martha Washington, Dish, Candy, Pink, Covered	85.00
Martha Washington, Jar, Candy, Covered, Pink	85.00
Mt.Vernon, Brandy	8.00
Mt.Vernon, Finger Bowl	8.00

Mt.Vernon, Sherbet	12.50
Mt.Vernon, Tumbler, Footed, 5 In.	18.00
Mt.Vernon, Tumbler, Water, Flat	8.00
Mt.Vernon, Tumbler, 5 3/4 In.	6.00
Mt.Vernon, Wine	6.00 To 8.00
Nautilus, Vase, Crown Tuscan, Footed, 6 In.	42.50
Nautilus, Wine Set, Crown Tuscan, 7 Piece	220.00
No.622, Sherbet	16.00
Nude Child Holding Lamb, Flower Frog, Vaseline, 9 In.	145.00
Nude Stem, Bowl, Compote, Cobalt Blue, 8 1/2 In.	95.00
Nude Stem, Bowl, Red, Crystal	125.00
Nude Stem, Cocktail, Forest Green, 3 Ounce	62.00
Nude Stem, Cocktail, Gold Cup, Crown Tuscan, 6 In.	90.00
Nude Stem, Compote, Cobalt Blue, Crystal Stem, 9 In.	125.00
Nude Stem, Compote, Crown Tuscan, 8 In.	125.00 To 140.00
Nude Stem, Compote, Farber Ware Holder, 7 3/4 In.	45.00
Nude Stem, Compote, Red Bowl	125.00
Nude Stem, Compote, Shell, Crown Tuscan, 6 In.	95.00
Nude Stem, Compote, Shell, Crown Tuscan, 7 In.Diam.	165.00
Nude Stem, Cordial, Forest Green, 1 Ounce	62.00
Nude Stem, Ivy Bowl, Crown Tuscan, 9 1/2 In.	85.00
Nude Stem, Wine, Amethyst Bowl, 4 Ounce	50.00
Nude Stem, Wine, Black, Clear Bowl	35.00
Nude Stem, Wine, Crown Tuscan	95.00
Octagon, Mayonnaise Set, Gold Overlay, 3 Piece	65.00
Peacock, Pitcher	1000.00
Portia, Bowl, Ruffled Top, Footed, 11 In.	55.00
Portia, Champagne, 5 1/2 In.	22.00
Portia, Cocktail Shaker, Chrome Top & Strainer	125.00
Portia, Plate, 7 1/2 In.	15.00
Portia, Vase, Crown Tuscan, Encrusted Gold, 5 In.	95.00
Pouter Pigeon, Bookend, Frosted, Pair	85.00
Pouter Pigeon, Wine, Farber Ware Holder, Frosted	85.00
Pristine, Dish, Candy, Silver Knob, 3-Part	40.00
Queen Anne, Ice Bucket, Dolphin Footed	47.50
Queen Anne, Plate, Orchid Etched, 10 1/2 In.	42.50
Ram's Head, Bowl, Azurite	350.00
Ram's Head, Bowl, Heliotrope, 12 In.	100.00
Ram's Head, Bowl, 12 In.	120.00
Rose Point, Ashtray, Pair	65.00
Rose Point, Bonbon, 2-Handled	20.00
Rose Point, Bowl, Golden Crested, 2-Handled, 8 In.	35.00
Rose Point, Bowl, Square, Footed, 11 In.	55.00
Rose Point, Box, Cigarette, Covered	45.00
Rose Point, Butter, Covered	135.00 To 150.00
Rose Point, Candleholder, Pair	65.00
Rose Point, Champagne	29.00
Rose Point, Cocktail Shaker, Stopper, 32 Ounce	85.00 To 95.00
Rose Point, Cordial	55.00 To 68.00
Rose Point, Cup & Saucer	35.00
Rose Point, Decanter Set, Amethyst	65.00
Rose Point, Epergne, 4 Piece	65.00
Rose Point, Goblet, Water	20.00
Rose Point, Goblet, 10 Ounce	21.00
Rose Point, Ice Bucket	115.00 To 125.00
Rose Point, Ice Bucket, Handled, Tongs	75.00
Rose Point, Mayonnaise Set, 3 Piece	95.00
Rose Point, Plate, Handled, 13 1/2 In.	75.00
Rose Point, Plate, 7 1/4 In.	17.00
Rose Point, Plate, 8 1/2 In.	12.00
Rose Point, Relish, 2-Part, 7 In.	22.00
Rose Point, Relish, 3-Part	25.00
Rose Point, Relish, 3-Part, Footed, Gold Trim, 12 In.	35.00

Rose Point, Relish, 5-Part .... 50.00 To 75.00
Rose Point, Relish, 5-Section 75.00
Rose Point, Salt & Pepper 30.00
Rose Point, Sherbet .... 18.00 To 29.00
Rose Point, Sherbet, Gold 35.00
Rose Point, Sherbet, Short 17.50
Rose Point, Shrimp Cocktail, Liner 62.50
Rose Point, Sugar & Creamer .... 30.00 To 45.00
Rose Point, Tray, 12 X 5 In. 75.00
Rose Point, Tumbler, Barrel Shape 38.00
Rose Point, Tumbler, Juice, Footed 22.50
Rose Point, Tumbler, Water 28.95
Rose Point, Vase, Bud, 10 In. 42.50
Rose Point, Vase, Keyhole, 12 In. .... 48.00 To 85.00
Rose Point, Vase, Pedestal, Dancing Nudes, 8 X 6 1/2 In. 95.00
Rose Point, Vase, Ring Stem, 12 In. 125.00
Rose Point, Vase, Trumpet Shaped, Crown Tuscan, Gold, 11 In. 125.00
Rose Point, Vase, 12 In. 58.00
Sea Gull, Flower Frog .... 35.00 To 125.00
Seashell, Bowl, Crown Tuscan, Painted Roses, Footed, 10 1/2 In. 95.00
Seashell, Bowl, Crown Tuscan, 3 Shell Feet, 10 In. 43.00
Seashell, Bowl, Footed, Crown Tuscan, 11 In. 75.00
Seashell, Compote, Crown Tuscan 35.00
Seashell, Dish, Crown Tuscan, Footed, 10 1/4 In. 90.00
Seashell, Flower Frog, Blue, 6 In. 35.00
Seashell, Vase, Cornucopia, 9 1/2 In. 45.00
Shell, Compote, Crown Tuscan, 7 X 3 In. 20.00
Swan, Black, Marked, 9 In. 125.00
Swan, Crown Tuscan, 3 In. 35.00
Swan, Green, Signed, 3 1/2 In. 27.50
Swan, Pink, Marked, 7 In. 40.00
Swan, Pink, Signed, 3 1/2 In. 25.00
Swan, Pink, 8 1/2 In. 25.00
Swan, Yellow, Signed, 3 1/2 In. 25.00
Swan, 2 1/4 In. 15.00
Swan, 3 In. 20.00
Tally-Ho, Ice Bucket 20.00
Tally-Ho, Sherbet, Tall 26.00
Turkey, Dish, Red, 2 Piece 125.00
Waverly, Flower Bowl, Crimped, 12 In. 62.50
Wild Rose, Cup, Punch, Red 25.00
Wildflower, Bonbon, Crystal, Footed 12.50
Wildflower, Bowl, Console 35.00
Wildflower, Candleholder, Etched, 2-Light 20.00
Wildflower, Pitcher, Gold Trim 150.00
Wildflower, Sherbet 15.00

Cameo glass was made in much the same manner as a cameo in jewelry.
Parts of the top layer of glass were cut away to reveal a different colored glass
beneath. The most famous cameo glass was made during the nineteenth
century.

CAMEO GLASS, see also under factory names

CAMEO, Bottle, English, Shell Design, Sterling Silver Cap, 2 1/2 In. 750.00
Bottle, Perfume, English, Butterfly On Back, Red & White Layers, 6 In. ... 2750.00
Bottle, Perfume, English, Cut Throughout, 3-Color 2750.00
Bottle, Perfume, English, Lay Down, Leaves, Unger Bros. Top 795.00
Bottle, Perfume, English, Lay Down, Palm Fronds, Butterfly, 9 1/2 In. ... 1750.00
Bottle, Perfume, English, Palm Trees & Leaves, Silver Top, Chain 1750.00
Bottle, Scent, English, Fuchsia, Chartreuse Ground, Marked, 4 1/2 In. ... 1050.00
Bowl, Blown-Out Swirled Body, Chipped Ice Ground, Lorraine, 12 X 6 In. ... 1200.00
Bowl, French, Landscape, Enameled, Pink Opalescent, 5 3/4 X 4 In. 750.00
Flask, Lady's, Floral Design, White To Pink, Signed, 6 X 1 3/4 In. 565.00

French, Biscuit Jar, Silver Plated Top, Rim, & Handle, Sevres, 7 In. 495.00
French, Decanter, Ruby & Amber, Stopper, 12 In. 225.00
Jar, Bonbon, Pink, Florentine, Floral Design, Silver Plate Cover, Rim 225.00
Salt, English, White Flowers, Silver Trim, Blue 750.00
Vase, Blue Ground, Grape Design, Metal Mounting, Signed, 7 3/4 In. 650.00
Vase, English, Bottle, Shell Design, Silver Cap, Olive Green, 2 1/2 In. 650.00
Vase, English, Flowers All Around, Citron Ground, 15 In. .... 1150.00 To 1250.00
Vase, French, Peacock On Fence, Gold Ground, Signed De Veau, 10 In. 1100.00
Vase, French, Swans On Lake, Branches Frame Top, Signed Michel, 8 In. 995.00
Vase, House On Island, Acid Cuttings, Signed De Veau, 4 1/8 In. 395.00
Vase, Orange, Yellow, Brown, Signed Blount, 8 In. 325.00
Vase, White Ground, Floral Design, Urn Shape, English, 3 3/8 In. 1250.00
     CAMPAIGN, see Political

CAMPBELL KIDS, Game, Jigsaw Puzzle 12.00
Knife, Fork, Spoon 30.00
Salt & Pepper 25.00
Spoon, Girl 6.00

*Camphor glass is a cloudy white glass that has been blown or pressed. It
was made by many factories in the Midwest during the mid-nineteenth century.*

CAMPHOR GLASS, Basket, Hand-Painted Design, Yellow 30.00
Candlestick, Brittany Maid & Cavalier, Portieux Glass, Pair 135.00
Decanter, Cancan Girl, Diamond-Quilted Stopper, Gin 22.00
Dish, Candy, Filigree Gilt Base, 3-Footed, Covered 18.00
Jar, Powder, Pink Elephants 35.00
Sugar & Creamer, Rose Colored 59.00
Tumbler, Wild Rose & Bowknot Pattern, Greentown, Ind. 27.50
Vase, White & Blue Enameling, 10 In. 40.00
     CANARY GLASS, see Vaseline Glass

CANDELABRUM, Bronze, Empire Style, 3 Paw Feet, 20 In., Pair 175.00
Iron, Standing, Renaissance, Revolving Cup, 72 In. 150.00
Iron, Standing, 9-Light, 68 In. 650.00
3-Light, Circular Base, Beaded Border, Silver Plate, 15 In., Pair 140.00
5-Light, Foliate Border, Swept Arm, Silver Plate, Pair 230.00

     CANDLEHOLDER, see also Brass and various Porcelain categories
CANDLEHOLDER, Flying Dragon, Wrought Iron, Pair 20.00
Hog Scraper, Iron Ring Wedding Band 220.00
Iron, Adjustable, C-Shaped Legs, 18th Century, 29 In. 375.00
Iron, Tommy, 12 In. 95.00
Iron, Trammel, Cylindrical Drip Pan, 30 In. 850.00
Miner's, Sticking Tommy 25.00
Push-Up, Lip For Chair 60.00
Rushlight, Iron, Scissor Style Clamp, Twisted Shank, 11 In. 275.00

     CANDLESTICK, see also Brass, Candlestick; Pewter, Candlestick;
     Sandwich Glass, Candlestick; and various Porcelain categories
CANDLESTICK, Bell, Queen Anne, Metal, Baluster Shaped Stem, 18th Century, 5 In. 325.00
Candle Cup, Black, Turned Base, 2 1/4 In. 200.00
Carved, Folk Art, Bird On Branch, 19th Century, 8 In. 400.00
Child Figure Holding Stick, Black Amethyst Base, Miniature 45.00
Hog Scraper, Push-Up With Hook, Salmon & Black Paint, 6 1/8 In. 110.00
Iron, Adjustable Stem, Turned Wooden Base, 18th Century, 8 In. 110.00
Iron, Penny Feet, Gooseneck Top, 12 1/4 In., Pair 40.00
Iron, Spring Stem, Tripod Base, 18th Century, American, 6 1/2 In. 150.00
Iron, Twisted Spiral Push-Up, 5 In. 45.00
Oak, Brass Top, 12 3/4 In., Pair 40.00

*Candy containers, especially those made of glass, have been popular since
the late Victorian era.*

CANDY CONTAINER, Airplane .... 55.00 To 265.00

Candy Container, Airplane, 5 In.

Airplane, Spirit Of Goodwill .... 50.00 To 150.00
Airplane, U.S.Army Bomber, Glass .... 15.00 To 20.00
Airplane, USP51, With Candy 35.00
Airplane, 5 In. ....*Illus* 25.00
Alarm Clock 68.00
Amos & Andy 375.00
Auto, Disneyland Main Street Market House 10.00
Auto, Electric Runabout, Tin Closure 30.00
Auto, Electric, Coupe, Dated 1912 .... 44.00 To 50.00
Auto, Rear Trunk 65.00
Auto, Sedan, 12 Vents 80.00
Auto, Station Wagon, No.3 .... 8.00
Auto, Streamlined Touring Car 32.00
Auto, Volkswagen 45.00
Auto, With Tin Wheels 65.00
Bank Building, Tin 25.00
Bank, Barrel, James Candy Co., Papier-Mache, 7 In. 15.00
Barney Google .... 75.00 To 275.00
Baseball Bat, Wooden, 11 In. 6.00
Basket, Sagging 80.00
Bear In Auto 125.00
Bear, On Tub 25.00
Bell, Blue 60.00
Bell, Clear 45.00
Black Cat, Hand-Painted, Papier-Mache, 1915, 7 1/2 In. 35.00
Boat, Battleship On Waves 16.00
Boat, Colorado, 1914 .... 85.00
Boat, Remember The Maine 60.00
Boat, Uncle Sam, Clear, Stanley 17.00
Boot, Aqua Glass, Star On Bottom, 2 3/4 In. 12.50
Boot, Glass, 3 In. 4.00
Boot, Santa's, Decal & Candy 16.00
Boston Kettle 35.00
Bottle, Dolly's Milk 22.00
Bulldog 35.00
Bulldog, Black 45.00
Bulldog, Camphor Glass, 3 In. 12.50
Bureau 175.00
Bus, Victory Lines, Special 70.00
Camera .... 100.00 To 200.00
Cat, Black 35.00
Chamberstick, Plastic Hurricane Shade, Red, 3 In. 25.00
Charlie Chaplin, Borgfeldt 90.00
Charlie Chaplin, Original Paint .... 150.00 To 160.00
Chick & Auto 198.00
Chicken On Nest, Glass 35.00
Chickens 15.00
Church, Cross, Tin 25.00
City Garage, Tin 25.00

Candy Container, Felix The Cat, 5 In.

Candy Container, Dog, U.S.A., Brown, 4 In.

Clock, Mantel	125.00 To 175.00
Clock, Milk Glass	175.00
Clown Dog, Glass, Candy Filled, Screw Top	12.00
Clown, Rockinghorse	145.00 To 200.00
Clown, Spring Head, Papier-Mache	15.00
Colorado	100.00
Cupid	75.00
Dirigible, Los Angeles	65.00 To 90.00
Dog, By Barrel	125.00 To 195.00
Dog, Cobalt	15.00
Dog, Germany	6.00
Dog, U.S.A., Brown, 4 In. *Illus*	30.00
Doll, Flapper, Paper Face	75.00
Dolly Sweeper	375.00
Dolly's Milk	20.00
Don't Park	245.00
Don't Park Here	125.00
Drug Store, Tin	25.00
Drum Mug	30.00
Duck	35.00 To 40.00
Duck, Nodder, Papier-Mache, 7 1/4 In.	10.00 To 20.00
Duck, On Top Of Basket, Tin Slide Closure, Yellow, 2 3/4 In.	45.00
Elephant, 8 In.	5.00
Engine	200.00
Fat Boy On Drum	225.00
Felix The Cat, 5 In. *Illus*	65.00
Felix, German	90.00
Figural, Apple, Wyandotte, Tin	30.00
Fire Engine, Fire Department In Circle	20.00
Fire Engine, Large Boiler	40.00
Fire Truck, Clear, Candy, Cardboard Enclosure	20.00
Floral, Black, Gold Finial, Hand-Painted, 11 In.	28.00
Frog, Figural	27.50
Glass Candlestick Telephone, Pewter, Wood, 1907	52.00
Glass, Battleship, 5 1/2 In.	12.00
Goldfish, Figural, Embossed Scale, 8 3/4 In.	30.00

Goldfish, Fish Scale Embossed, 8 3/4 In.	30.00
Gun, Amber, Candy	24.00
Gun, Glass, Tin Screw Cap, 3 1/4 Ounce, 7 In.	22.00
Gun, Metal Screw Cap, 5 1/2 X 2 1/2 In.	16.00
Gun, Revolver, Diamond In Grip	35.00
Gun, Revolver, Round Butt	22.50
Gun, Revolver, Square Butt	28.00
Gun, Revolver, West Brothers Co.	12.00
Gun, Stought's Whistling Jim	11.00
Gun, Sunker Eye	45.00
Gun, Whistling Jim's	20.00
Happifats	175.00
Happifats, On Drum	195.00
Hat, Fedora, Clambroth	45.00
Hat, Uncle Sam	45.00
Hat, With Tin Brim, Milk Glass	60.00
Hatchet, Red & Silver, Paper Over Cardboard, 7 In.	40.00
Hen	12.50 To 20.00
Hen, Glass	22.00
Hen, Resting With Chick On Side, Papier-Mache, 1915	25.00
Hen, Westmoreland, 2 In.	22.00
Horn, Blue Glass	40.00
Horse & Cart, Embossed Dog	25.00
Horse Spark Plug, 1923	60.00
Horse, 2-Wheeled Cart	12.50
House With Picture Window, Tin	25.00
House, 2-Story, Tin	25.00
Independence Hall	250.00
Iron, Cord	50.00
Jack-O'-Lantern	110.00 To 185.00
Jack-O'-Lantern, Wire Bale, Orange Paint, Slant Eyes	45.00
Jeep	14.00 To 20.00
Jeep, Willy's, Driver, Embossed, 4 1/2 In.	10.50 To 25.00
Jitney Bus	325.00
Kettle, Bean	6.00
Kewpie Doll, Enclosure	65.00
Kewpie, Marked Geo. Borgfeldt	78.00
Kiddie Kar	325.00
Lamp	40.00
Lantern, Barn, Aqua	18.00
Lantern, Barn, Clear	20.00
Lantern, Conductor, Striped Clothes, 3 1/2 In.	20.00
Lantern, Round, Beaded Section, Cover, Bale	24.00
Lantern, Signal, Green	18.00
Lantern, Square, Metal Top, Red Paint	5.00 To 50.00
Lantern, Tin Top & Bottom	4.00
Lantern, Victory	22.00
Learned Fox	95.00
Liberty Bell, Blue	95.00
Liberty Bell, Glass, Wire Bail, Easter Greeting, Candy	28.00
Liberty Bell, Hanger	20.00
Liberty Bell, Metal Bale, Base	50.00
Lighthouse	10.00 To 20.00
Lobster, Papier-Mache, Marked Germany	30.00
Locomotive, Mogul	75.00
Log Cabin	80.00
Log Cabin, Advertising On Door, Wooden	20.00
Log, George Washington's Cherry Tree, Figural, Papier-Mache	24.00
Mailbox, Tin Closure, 11 1/2 In.	40.00
Monkey Lamp	125.00
Moon Mullins	36.00
Mother, Daughter	400.00
Mr.Duck, Papier-Mache	6.00

Mrs.Duck, Papier-Mache	6.00
Mule, Pulling Barrel	65.00
Night Stick, Policeman's, Amber	75.00
Old Locomotive, No.1028	20.00
Old Oaken Bucket, Wire Bail, Embossed Rings & Staves, 3 In.	20.00
Opera Glasses, Milk Glass, Tin Closure	9.00
Opera Glasses, Pewter Holder	35.00
Owl, Original Paint	48.00
Owl, Standing, Original Paint, Dead Eyes	145.00
Owl, Top Closure, 4 1/4 In.	19.00
Pelican, Papier-Mache	22.50
Pencil	65.00
Pencil, Baby Jumbo	75.00
Penny Safe	75.00
Phonograph, Glass Record	200.00
Phonograph, Tin Record	325.00
Piano	350.00
Piano, Gold Paint, Slot For Bank	110.00
Piano, Grand, Concert	56.00
Pickwick Inn, Greenwich, Connecticut, Tin, 1920s, 7 In.	7.00
Pipe, Glass, Amber Mouthpiece	150.00
Pipe, Wicker Bowl	30.00
Pistol, Amber, Screw On Cap	22.00
Pistol, Screw Cover On Barrel	30.00
Porky Pig, White Jacket, Red & White Bowtie, 3 3/4 In.	7.50
Powder Horn	18.00
Princess Theatre, Tin	25.00
Pump	45.00
Pumpkin Head, Witch	350.00
Pumpkin, Orange Design, Straight Eyes, Lid & Bail	55.00
Purse	400.00
Rabbit Mother & Daughter	345.00
Rabbit, Crouching	60.00
Rabbit, Eating Carrot	20.00 To 30.00
Rabbit, Emerging From Egg, Brown, Papier-Mache, 1915	28.00
Rabbit, Nodding Spring Heads, Papier-Mache	10.00
Rabbit, On Dome	250.00
Rabbit, Papier-Mache	6.00 To 30.00
Rabbit, Paws To Body, Gold Paint, 5 1/16 In.	49.50
Rabbit, Pushing Wheelbarrow	150.00
Rabbit, Running On Log	200.00
Rabbit, Standing, 6 In.	4.00
Rabbit, Standing, 6 3/4 In.	17.50
Rabbit, Standing, 8 In.	5.00
Rabbit, With Basket	35.00
Rabbit, 6 In. *Illus*	25.00
Racer 12	40.00
Radio	45.00
Radio, With Speaker	95.00
Railroad Station	200.00
Rapid Fire Cannon	325.00
Reindeer, Leather & Hide, Glass-Eyed, 1895, German Label	75.00
Rooster	175.00
Rooster, On Round Nest	200.00
Sadiron	350.00
Safe	60.00
Santa Claus Boot, Glass, Candy	5.00 To 15.00
Santa Claus Boot, Papier-Mache, Red, 7 3/4 In., Pair	10.00
Santa Claus, Double Cuff, 4 3/8 In.	75.00 To 120.00
Santa Claus, Drum, Celluloid Face	25.00
Santa Claus, Germany, 6 In.	25.00
Santa Claus, In Sleigh, Plaster Face	30.00
Santa Claus, Leaving Chimney	80.00

Candy Container, Rabbit, 6 In.

Santa Claus, Plastic Head	35.00 To 65.00
Santa Claus, Square Chimney	98.00
Santa Claus, Stocking, C.1880, 7 In.	10.00
Schoolhouse, Flag Hanging From Roof, Tin	25.00
Scotty Dog, Clear	12.50 To 20.00
Scotty Dog, Standing, Clear & Frosted, 5 1/4 In.	12.50
Skookum	175.00 To 325.00
Snowman, Papier-Mache	12.50
Spark Plug, Clear	50.00 To 125.00
Spirit Of Goodwill	25.00 To 45.00
Spirit Of Goodwill, Tin Propeller & Closure, Candy	80.00
Spirit Of St.Louis	75.00 To 350.00
Suitcase, Metal Closure	22.00
Suitcase, Milk Glass	30.00 To 48.00
Suitcase, Straps, Wire Handle, Tin Slide On Bottom	35.00
Suitcase, Tin Base & Handle	25.00
Suitcase, Wire Bail	22.00
Sweeper	125.00
Tank, Clear, Candy, Cardboard Enclosure	20.00
Tank, Man In Turret	12.00
Tank, U.S., Victory Glass Toy Div., 4 In.	25.00 To 30.00
Tank, 2 Cannons, Candy, Closure	16.00
Taxi, 6-Vent	60.00 To 65.00
Telephone, Candlestick, Wooden Receiver, Pewter Top, 1907	55.00
Telephone, Clear, Cardboard Enclosure, Victory Glass	25.00
Telephone, French, With Candy	12.00
Telephone, Millstein	15.00
Telephone, Tot	50.00
Top	45.00
Toys & Confectionery, Tin	25.00
Train Engine, Candy, Victory Glass Co.	15.00
Train Engine, Original Candy	15.00
Truck Tire	22.50

Truck, Tin Top	7.50
Turkey	95.00
Village, With Insert	95.00
Washer, Midget	25.00
Watch, Pocket	45.00 To 95.00
Water Wagon, Pulled By Mule	55.00
Wheelbarrow	22.00 To 65.00
Windmill	25.00 To 50.00

CANE, Bamboo, Silver Beads, Embossed Panels, Oriental Figures, 33 In.	36.00
Black Jack, Concealed	60.00
Boot, Silver Studs, Engraved Plate, Niles Tool Works, 35 In.	45.00
Brass Dog's Head Top	85.00
Bulldog Head, China	11.00
Chicago World's Fair	15.00
Eagle Head, Bone	32.50
Foot Carved On It	40.00
Glass, Aqua, Square With Twisted Handle, 76 In.	95.00
Glass, Aqua, Twisted & Straight Ribs, 59 In.	40.00
Glass, Aqua, Twisted, 38 1/2 In.	35.00
Glass, Clear, Gold Interior, 53 In.	45.00
Glass, Clear, Gold Interior, 54 1/2 In.	70.00
Glass, Clear, Hollow Center, Dark Red Liquid, 51 1/2 In.	125.00
Glass, Clear, Red Striped Center, Twisted Handle, 49 1/2 In.	45.00
Glass, Smoke & White Swirl	200.00
Head, Blue & White Striated Glass, Blown, 1 1/4 In.	4.50
Screw-Off Top Holds Flask, Bird's-Eye Maple	160.00
Sword, Staghorn Handle, Silver Mounting, Brass Tip, 35 In.	125.00
Walking Stick, Art Deco, Ivory Nobbed Handle On Ebony	75.00
Walking Stick, Chestnut, 35 3/4 In.	30.00
Walking Stick, Gold Head, From Friends Of St.Patrick's Church, 35 In.	165.00
Wooden, Carved Shaft, Eagle Head Handle, Flying Bird Base, 35 In.	65.00
Wooden, Staghorn Handle, Chased Silver Ferrule, 30 3/4 In.	30.00

Canton china is a blue-and-white ware made near Canton, China, from about 1785 to 1895. It is hand-decorated with Chinese scenes.

CANTON, Basket & Tray, Blue Willow, 9 1/2 In., 9 3/4 In. *Illus*	400.00
Basket, Fruit, Undertray, C.1830, Cobalt Blue, Marked, 9 In.	475.00
Basket, Fruit, Undertray, Signed, Basket, 8 1/2 X 9 3/4 In.	400.00
Bowl, Blue & White, Trees, Vines, Flowers, Oriental People, 3 In.	125.00
Bowl, Mid-19th Century, 9 1/4 In.	180.00
Bowl, Reticulated, Oval, 8 1/2 In.Diam.	295.00
Bowl, 9 1/2 In.	145.00
Carafe, Landscape Design, Elongated Neck, Bulbous, 10 1/2 In.	750.00
Creamer, 3 1/4 In.	65.00 To 75.00
Cup & Saucer, Blue & White, Saucer 6 In.Diam.	50.00
Cup & Saucer, Child's, Blue & White, 4 Sets	75.00
Cup & Saucer, Demitasse, Blue & White, 2 1/4 In.	50.00

Canton, Basket & Tray, Blue Willow, 9 1/2 In., 9 3/4 In.

Cup, Posset, Covered, Twisted Handle 145.00
Dish, Blue & White, Orange Peel Glaze, 8 3/4 In. 55.00
Dish, Bone, Fish Shape, Blue & White, 4 3/4 In. 65.00
Dish, Fish Shape, 5 1/2 In. 35.00
Dish, Hot Water, Octagonal 235.00
Dish, Leaf Shaped, 7 1/2 In. .... 95.00 To 185.00
Dish, Serving, Leaf Shape, 7 3/4 In. 95.00
Dish, Vegetable, Covered, Blue, Oval 375.00
Dish, 9 1/4 In. 145.00
Jar, Ginger, Swiss Pewter Screw Top, China, 19th Century, 8 1/4 In. 100.00
Mug, Cobalt Blue Design, Entwined Strap Handle, 4 In. 225.00
Plate, Dark Blue Scalloped Edge, 8 3/4 In. 75.00
Platter, Blue & White, Lemon Peel Glaze, 11 1/2 In. 115.00
Platter, Oriental Scene, 11 In.Diam. 160.00
Platter, Rectangular, Canton, 14 X 17 In. 170.00
Platter, 12 In.Diam. 200.00
Saltcellar, Rectangular, Cut Corners, Cobalt Blue, 1 1/2 In. 260.00
Sconce, Wall, Round, Ormolu Mounts, Candle Holder On Each, Pair 950.00
Tea Caddy, Blue & White, Great Ape, 7 X 5 In. 125.00
Teapot, Harbor Scene, Individual Size 40.00
Tureen, Boar's Head Handles, Covered 800.00

Capo-di-Monte porcelain was first made in Naples, Italy, from 1743 to 1759. The factory moved near Madrid, Spain, and reopened in 1771 and worked to 1834. Since that time the Doccia factory of Italy acquired the molds and is using the N and crown mark.

CAPO-DI-MONTE, Basket, Flower, Girl, C.1890, 9 1/2 In. 325.00
Bottle, Scent, Blue Crown Mark 95.00
Bowl, Andrea, Covered, 7 1/2 X 6 1/2 X 5 In. 48.00
Box, Angels Playing Instruments, Flowers, 3 X 5 In. 265.00
Box, Applied Roses & Leaves, 2 3/4 In.Diam. 22.00
Box, Brass Trim, Children In Relief, Blue Crown, 1 X 2 X 3 In. 95.00
Box, Children Pulling Chariot, Blue Crown Mark, 2 In. 185.00
Box, Jewelry, Oval, Figural Design, 4 1/2 In. 140.00
Box, Ladies Fixing Hair, Crown Glaze, 2 1/2 X 3 1/2 X 5 In. 135.00
Fernery, Faces At Each End, Oval, 11 In. 185.00
Figurine, Bird, On Tree Stump, C.1886, 6 1/2 In. 130.00
Figurine, Boy & Girl, Flowers, Crown Mark, 1850, 6 1/2 In. 475.00
Figurine, Boy & Girl, Marked, 7 1/2 X 6 In. 135.00
Figurine, Boy & Girl, 6 X 7 In. 125.00
Figurine, Bust Of Cavalier, Marked, 6 In. 125.00
Figurine, Cherub, Porcelain, 6 1/2 In. 225.00
Figurine, Cherubs, Frolicking With Roses, Marked, 6 In. 400.00
Figurine, Grenadier, Full Figure, Standing, 7 In. 169.00
Figurine, Lady, Flowered Dress, By Bench, Blue Cap, 10 In. 125.00
Figurine, Man & Lady, Standing, Arms Separate, 7 1/2 In., Pair 42.00
Figurine, Napoleon's General, Marked, 12 In. 300.00
Figurine, Three Cherubs Frolicking With Garland Of Roses 225.00
Sugar & Creamer, Footed, Crown Mark 90.00
Tazza, Cherubs, Blowing Trumpets, Gold Trim, 14 1/2 X 8 In. 500.00
Urn, Cherub Figures, Blowing Trumpets, Finial, 12 X 20 In. 675.00
Urn, Venus & Neptune, Polychrome, Side Handles, 19 In. 195.00

CAPTAIN MARVEL, Pennant, 1944, Felt 35.00
Puzzle, Original Package, C.1945 .... 7.50
Reflector, Bicycle, Dated 1973, Package 2.50
Watch, 1948, Box With Instructions 110.00

CAPTAIN MIDNIGHT, Badge, Decoder 50.00
Code-O-Gram, Magni-Magic, 1945 .... 50.00
Code-O-Gram, Photomatic, 1942 .... 65.00
Decoder, With Photograph, 1941 .... 35.00
Decoder, 1940s 20.00
Decoder, 1945 .... 18.00

Decoder, 1946 .... 27.50
Decoder, 1948 .... 15.00
Detect-O-Scope 85.00
Pilot Wings, Brass 32.00
Pin, Skelly Flight Patrol 10.00
Tumbler, Plastic 12.50

      CARAMEL SLAG, see Chocolate Glass

      CARD, see also Postcard
CARD, Advertising, American Sewing Machine Co., Boy, Sea, Telescope 3.50
Advertising, American Sewing Machine, Women, We All Want American 4.00
Advertising, Ayer's Cherry Pectoral, Ayer & Co., Girl, Cherries 3.30
Advertising, Babbitt Clothing-Lewiston, Dogs Dressed In Outfits 7.00
Advertising, Belding Bros., Spool Silk, 1876, Black & White, 3 X 5 In. 5.00
Advertising, Chase & Sanborn Coffee, 1889, American Flag 6.00
Advertising, Chase & Sanborn, North American Birds, 1905 .... 7.00
Advertising, Clark's Thread, Alex Of Russia, Palace, 3 X 4 In. 3.75
Advertising, Clark's Thread, 1867, Children Marching, 3 X 4 In. 5.00
Advertising, Consolidated Coffee Co., Embossed, Butterflies 4.00
Advertising, Coricelli Spool Silk, 3 Puppies, Doghouse, 3 X 4 In. 2.50
Advertising, Deep Cool, It's No Work To Wash With Ozone Soap, 1920s 1.00
Advertising, Diamond Yeast, Cherubs, Woman's Shoe, Flowers, 3 X 4 In. 5.00
Advertising, Dixon's Carburet Of Iron Stove Polish, Lady, Tree 5.00
Advertising, Dr.Buckland's Scotch Oats Essence, Woman, 3 Cherubs 3.75
Advertising, Dr.Price's Flavoring Extracts, Water Scene, Cherub 6.00
Advertising, El Palermo Cigar, 1870, Mule, Black & White, 3 X 5 In. 7.50
Advertising, Fairbank Laundry Soap & Gold Dust Washing Powder, Twins 13.00
Advertising, Football, Issued By Coca-Cola & Tampa Police, Set Of 22 .... 10.00
Advertising, Gum, Batman, Set 30.00
Advertising, Gum, Frontier Days, Set 175.00
Advertising, Gum, Kennedy, Set 20.00
Advertising, Gum, Mars Attacks, Set 350.00
Advertising, Gum, Tarzan, Set 30.00
Advertising, Haas Hog Remedy, Hog, School, Teacher, 3 X 5 In. 6.00
Advertising, Hatter & Furrier-Meyer Of Brooklyn, Boy, Girl, Barrow 3.00
Advertising, Hood's Vegetable Pills, Children, Stars, Sky, 1888 .... 11.00
Advertising, Hoyt's German Cologne, Child's Head, Bottle, 2 X 4 In. 5.00
Advertising, Hoyt's German Cologne, Ladies' Calendar For 1889 .... 6.00
Advertising, J & P Coats Thread, Child, Puppy On Ice Pond 3.00
Advertising, J & P Coats Thread, Cow & Frog 2.75
Advertising, J & P Coats Thread, Girl Carrying 2 Dogs, Stream 3.50
Advertising, J & P Coats Thread, Old Crones Sitting Around Gossiping 3.00
Advertising, J & P Coats Thread, 2 Children Carrying Baby, 3 X 4 In. 3.00
Advertising, J & P Coats, 1880, Man & Woman Fishing 1.00
Advertising, Julius J. Wood Starch Co., 1888, Lady, Product 6.00
Advertising, Kings Quick Rising Flours, Children, Tree, Stove, 3 X 4 In. 4.00
Advertising, Kingsford's Oswego Corn Starch, Child Going To Store 2.50
Advertising, Magic Yeast, Lady On Front, Product On Back, 4 X 6 In. 5.00
Advertising, Mason & Hamlin Organ & Piano Co., 4 Models 3.50
Advertising, McLaughlin's Coffee, Die-Cut Animals, Irish Setter 4.00
Advertising, McLaughlin's Coffee, Fox Terrier, Venio 3.00
Advertising, McLaughlin's Coffee, Pointer, Saddleback 4.00
Advertising, McLaughlin's Coffee, Swan, 2 1/2 X 2 1/2 In. 3.00
Advertising, McLaughlin's Coffee, Wavy Coated Retriever, Careth 3.00
Advertising, Merrick Thread, Girl, Long Coat, Bonnet, Spools, 3 X 6 In. 5.00
Advertising, Mrs. Winslow's Soothing Syrup, 1885, 3 X 5 In. 6.00
Advertising, New Home Sewing Machine, Cherubs, Sewing Machine 5.00
Advertising, New Process Starch, Chinese Laundryman, 3 X 4 In. 5.00
Advertising, Paper, Book, Druggist's Circular, Recipes For Medication 24.00
Advertising, Pozzoni's Dove Complexion Powder, Lady, Product, 6 X 9 In. 11.00

Advertising, Queen Of The North Chewing Gum, Soldier, Turkey, Gum 4.00
Advertising, Round Oak Stoves, Dowagiac, Mich., Family, Stove, 1880 .... 7.00
Advertising, Schiller Pianos, Boating Scene, Flowers, 3 X 5 In. 5.00
Advertising, Shoes, Greensfelder, Florsheim, & Co., Child, Geese 5.00
Advertising, Singer Sewing Machine, 1898, American Bird 16.00
Advertising, Smith-Wallace Show Co., Chicago, Winter Scene, 3 X 4 In. 4.00
Advertising, Soapine Soap, Boy In Sailor Suit, 3 X 5 In. 4.00
Advertising, Soapine Soap, Girl On Fan-Shaped Card, 3 X 4 In. 3.50
Advertising, Soapine Soap, Woman, Laundry, Clothes Spell Product 4.00
Advertising, Soapine, Gleeful Child, Tub Of Water, 3 1/2 X 5 In. 4.00
Advertising, Sterling Piano & Organ Co., Organ, Child, Cat 3.00
Advertising, White House Coffee & Tea, Species Of Birds, 1923 .... 6.00
Advertising, Woolson Spice Co., Toledo, 1894, Girl, Flowers, 5 X 7 In. 7.00
Calling, C.1850, Calligraphy, Dove Sitting Amid Florals, White 6.50
Fortune-Telling, 1897-1904, Mile, Set Of 53 .... 14.00
Greeting, Winter Twilight, Parrish, 6 X 7 In. 17.00
Holiday Greeting, Silk Fringed, Chromolithograph, Set Of 9 .... 18.50
Lobby, Movie, George O'Brien, Lawless Valley, 1947, 11 X 14 In. 25.00
Movie, Lobby, Gone With The Wind, 1947, 11 X 14 In. 100.00
Movie, Lobby, Humphrey Bogart, Beat The Devil, 1953, 11 X 14 In. 30.00
Movie, Lobby, Katharine Hepburn, Dragon Seed, 1944, 11 X 14 In. 50.00
Movie, Lobby, Laurel & Hardy, Heroes Of The Regiment, 11 X 14 In. 75.00
Movie, Lobby, Roy Rogers, Twilight In The Sierras, 11 X 14 In. 20.00
New Year, Silk Fringed, Bonneted Girl, Signed Tuck 6.50
New Year, Silk Fringed, Prang, 3 3/4 X 4 1/4 In. 6.50
Playing, Advertising, Hotpoint Electric Kitchen, C.1940 .... 6.00
Playing, Advertising, Strom Machinery Corp., Unbroken, Boxed 1.00
Playing, Brown-Bigelow, 50th Anniversary 4.00
Playing, Century Of Progress, 1934, Boxed 5.00
Playing, Souvenir, 1916 Movie 50.00
Valentine, Accordion Fold, Bouquets, See-Through Center, C.1883 .... 12.50
Valentine, Boy & Girl Cooking At Old Stove, Stand-Up, 8 In. 15.00
Valentine, Calligraphy, Cupids & Bows, C.1845, London, 6 3/8 X 8 1/4 In. 65.00
Valentine, Candy Heart In Wax Paper 3.00
Valentine, Center Urn, See-Through Colors, Boy Blowing Bubbles, Wood 22.50
Valentine, Cherubs, Deer, & Lady, Her Lover, Lacy Envelope, C.1850 .... 22.50
Valentine, Children, Floral, Lacy 10.00
Valentine, Color Puzzle, Girl Peering Out, Wood, 3 1/4 X 4 1/2 In. 35.00
Valentine, Colored Wood Block, Cupid & Lady, C.1850, Strong, 7 In. 55.00
Valentine, Cupid In Boat, Tissue Paper Waves, Dated 1919, Stand-Up 12.00
Valentine, Die Cut Cottage, Boy, Bag Of Valentines For Girl, Fold-Over 6.50
Valentine, Die Cut Girl, Gold Foil Floral, By Wood, 2 3/4 X 3 3/4 In. 22.50
Valentine, Easel Front, Accordion Tabs, Center Rose, 4 1/2 X 6 3/4 In. 7.50
Valentine, Figural Girl, Blue Hat Swivels, Tuck, 6 In. 12.50
Valentine, Floral Lacework, Fabric Leaves, C.1850, Mossman, 5 1/4 In. 22.50
Valentine, Floral Wreath, Embossed Lady & Rabbits, 3 3/4 X 5 3/4 In. 25.00
Valentine, Florals & Snowflakes, Center Child, C.1870, Signed Wood 22.50
Valentine, Flowers, Lovebirds, & Child, Stand-Up 12.00
Valentine, Folding, Lacy Church & Cherubs, Signed Wood, 3 X 3 3/4 In. 22.50
Valentine, Girl Catching Butterflies, Die Cut, Whitney, 5 1/4 In.Square 4.50
Valentine, Girl In Fancy Outfit, Pop-Out, Germany 10.00
Valentine, Hand-Painted Florals, Boy Courting Girl, Signed Taft 22.50
Valentine, Honeycomb Entire Length, Cupid, Hearts, & Arrows, 8 X 11 In. 15.00
Valentine, Lacy Front, See-Through To Woodblock Of Couple, Florals 17.50
Valentine, Lacy Front, 2 Cupids, Die Cut, Handmade, C.1850, 3 3/4 X 5 In. 30.00
Valentine, Lovers & Milling Crowd, Openwork, Gilt, Signed Taft 22.50
Valentine, Medallion Of Couple Teasing Bird, Embossed Bird, Howland 30.00
Valentine, Pinocchio, 1939, Move Hat, Nose Get Longer, 3 X 5 In. 6.95
Valentine, Pope Mfg. Co., Bicycles, Motorcycles, Automobiles, 1903 .... 20.00
Valentine, Romeo & Juliet, Ribbon, Handwritten Poem, 2 3/4 X 3 3/4 In. 35.00
Valentine, Sailor's, Framed, 2 Hearts, Family Shield, Shells, 15 X 18 In. 1325.00
Valentine, Scenic, Die Cut Florals, 3-Layer, Tuck, 3 X 4 3/4 In. 8.50
Valentine, See-Through, Floral Wreath With Affection, Signed Meek 25.00

Valentine, Side Flower Holder, Butterfly Trim, Celluloid, 8 X 9 1/2 In. 12.00
Valentine, Signed S.Garrel, 1908, Embossed 1.50
Valentine, Spinning Wheel, Heart, Girl, To One I Love, 4 X 6 In. 12.50
Valentine, Split Door Shows Victorian Child, Poem, C.1880, 5 3/4 In. 10.00
Valentine, Sunbonnet Stand-Up Figural, Mechanical, Tuck, 7 1/4 In. 22.50
Valentine, Victorian Lady, Pop-Out Shows Doves, Germany, 5 X 8 1/2 In. 12.00
Valentine, Wizard Of Oz, 1939, Scarecrow, Tin Man, Lion, Oz In Love 11.00
Valentine, 2-Layer, Boy In Fauntleroy Suit, Germany, 6 X 5 1/4 In. 7.50
Valentine, 3-D, Lovers In Vintage Auto, 10 X 9 1/2 In. 34.00
    CARDER, see Aurene; Steuben

Carlsbad, Germany, is a mark found on china made by several factories in Germany. Most of the pieces available today were made after 1891.

CARLSBAD, Bowl, Iridescent, Blue, 4 Gold Handles, 6 X 3 In. 125.00
    Cup & Saucer, Demitasse 16.00
    Ewer, Nude Baby Picture, Cobalt Blue, Marked 35.00
    Plate, Art Nouveau Border, Blue, Yellow, & Gold, 8 1/2 In. 15.00
    Plate, Hand-Painted Bird, 8 In. 42.00
    Plate, Hand-Painted, Scalloped Trim, Grapes, 8 In. 25.00
    Vase, Deep Red, Gold Design, Classical Figures, 8 1/2 In. 50.00
    Vase, Floral, Cobalt Blue, Gold Trim, 7 In. 45.00

Carlton ware was made at the Carlton Works of Stoke-on-Trent, England, about 1890. The firm traded as Wiltshaw & Robinson until 1957. It was renamed Carlton Ware Ltd. in 1958.

CARLTON WARE, Biscuit Jar, Floral Design, Silver Plated Top & Handle, Marked 75.00
    Biscuit Jar, Orchids & Foliage, Silver Plated Top & Rim 85.00
    Bowl, Footed, Green, 8 In. 45.00
    Box, Rouge Royale, Flying Duck, Covered, 5 1/4 In. .... 120.00 To 145.00
    Cookie Jar, Enamel Design, Red Roses, Matte Finish, Marked 75.00
    Dish, Lobster 40.00
    Humidor, White Slip Scene, Blue Ground 65.00
    Tray, Single Handle, Cattails & Dragonflies, Enameled 115.00
    Vase, Art Nouveau, Blue Floral, Gold Trim, 6 In. 48.00

Carnival, or taffeta, glass was an inexpensive, pressed, iridescent glass made from about 1907 to about 1925. Over 1,000 different patterns are known. Carnival glass is currently being reproduced. If the letter N for Northwood is included in the description, it appears on the piece of glass.

    CARNIVAL GLASS, see also Northwood
CARNIVAL GLASS, Acanthus, Bowl, Scalloped Edge, Purple, 8 X 3 1/4 In. 75.00
    ACORN BURRS & BARK, see Acorn Burrs
Acorn Burrs, Berry Set, Marigold, 6 Piece 195.00
Acorn Burrs, Cup, Punch, Amethyst 45.00
Acorn Burrs, Cup, Punch, Green 25.00
Acorn Burrs, Cup, Punch, Marigold 13.00
Acorn Burrs, Cup, Punch, Purple 32.00
Acorn Burrs, Cup, Punch, White 35.00
Acorn Burrs, Pitcher, Water, Marigold .... 300.00 To 325.00
Acorn Burrs, Punch Set, Green, 8 Piece 675.00
Acorn Burrs, Spooner, Green 95.00
Acorn Burrs, Spooner, Purple 92.50
Acorn Burrs, Sugar, Marigold, Covered 95.00
Acorn Burrs, Table Set, Marigold, 4 Piece 395.00
Acorn Burrs, Tumbler, Green 35.00
Acorn Burrs, Tumbler, Marigold 39.00
Acorn Burrs, Tumbler, Purple .... 35.00 To 55.00
Acorn Burrs, Tumbler, Signed Northwood, Purple 300.00
Acorn Burrs, Water Set, Marigold, 7 Piece 525.00

Acorn Burrs, Water Set, Purple, 7 Piece 695.00
Acorn, Bowl, Amethyst, 7 In. 55.00
Acorn, Bowl, Cobalt Blue, 8 In. 38.00
Acorn, Bowl, Green, 8 In. 35.00
Acorn, Bowl, Purple, 7 1/2 In. 65.00
Acorn, Bowl, Ruffled Edge, Cobalt Blue, 7 1/2 In. 45.00
Acorn, Bowl, Vaseline Center, Marigold 60.00
    AMARYLLIS, see Tiger Lily
    AMERICAN BEAUTY ROSES, see Wreath of Roses
    APPLE & PEAR, see Two Fruits
Apple Blossom Twigs, Bowl, Peach, 9 In. 195.00
Apple Blossom Twigs, Plate, Ruffled, White, 9 In. 95.00
Apple Blossoms, Bowl, Marigold, 7 In. 36.50
Apple Blossoms, Bowl, Ruffled, Flat Base, Marigold, 7 1/4 In. 30.00
Apple Tree, Pitcher, Water, Marigold 80.00
Apple Tree, Tumbler, Cobalt Blue 55.00
Apple Tree, Tumbler, Fenton, Cobalt Blue 55.00
Apple Tree, Water Set, Marigold, 7 Piece 225.00
    ARGONAUT SHELL, see Nautilus
    AURORA, see Flowers
Australian Swan, Bowl, Ruffled, Signed, Purple, 9 In. 175.00
Autumn Acorns, Bowl, Ribbon Rim, Green, 8 1/2 In .... 50.00 To 72.00
    BANDED MEDALLION & TEARDROP, see Beaded Bull's Eye
Basket, Cobalt Blue, N In Circle 80.00
    BASKETWEAVE & CABLE BAND, see Basketweave & Cable
Basketweave & Cable, Bowl, Marigold, 5 1/2 In. 51.00
Basketweave & Cable, Bowl, Vaseline Base, 5 1/2 In. 35.00
Basketweave & Cable, Plate, Cobalt Blue, 8 In. 10.00
    BATTENBURG LACE NO. 1, see Hearts & Flowers
    BATTENBURG LACE NO. 2, see Captive Rose
    BATTENBURG LACE NO. 3, see Fanciful
Beaded Bull's Eye, Vase, Marigold, 11 In. 23.00
Beaded Cable, Dish, Candy, Footed, Green 40.00
Beaded Cable, Dish, Candy, 3-Footed, Cobalt Blue, 8 In. 45.00
Beaded Cable, Rose Bowl, Aqua .... 225.00 To 295.00
Beaded Cable, Rose Bowl, Blue 75.00
Beaded Cable, Rose Bowl, Green .... 40.00 To 65.00
Beaded Cable, Rose Bowl, Marked, Amethyst 60.00
Beaded Cable, Rose Bowl, Purple .... 65.00 To 67.00
Beaded Cable, Rose Bowl, White .... 100.00 To 150.00
Beaded Cable, Rose Bowl, 3-Footed, Green 75.00
Beaded Cable, Rose Bowl, 3-Footed, Ray Pattern Inside, Red 110.00
Beaded Cable, Rose Bowl, 3-Footed, Ray Pattern, Purple 110.00
Beaded Shell, Berry Set, Purple, 4 Piece 210.00
Beaded Shell, Creamer, Marigold .... 60.00 To 62.00
Beaded Shell, Creamer, Purple .... 40.00 To 90.00
Beaded Shell, Mug, Amethyst 55.00
Beaded Shell, Mug, Marigold 85.00
Beaded Shell, Mug, Purple 85.00
Beaded Shell, Spooner, Marigold 55.00
Beaded Shell, Tumbler, Marigold .... 39.00 To 50.00
    BEADED STAR & SNAIL, see Constellation
Beaded Stars, Compote, Marigold, 5 In. 18.00
Beauty, Bud Vase, Marigold 17.50
Bird With Grapes, Vase, Wall, 8 In. 72.00
Birds & Cherries, Bonbon, Amber 60.00
Birds & Cherries, Bonbon, Amethyst, 2-Handled .... 45.00 To 49.00
Birds & Cherries, Bonbon, Cobalt Blue, 2-Handled, 6 1/2 In. 35.00
Birds & Cherries, Bonbon, Purple 37.00
    BIRDS ON BOUGH, see Birds & Cherries
    BLACKBERRY & CHECKERBOARD, see Blackberry Block
    BLACKBERRY A., see Blackberry
    BLACKBERRY B., see Blackberry Spray

Blackberry Banded, Dish, Candy, Cobalt Blue, 3 1/4 In.	40.00
Blackberry Block, Pitcher, Marigold	275.00
Blackberry Block, Tumbler, Purple	35.00
Blackberry Bramble, Compote, Green	38.00
Blackberry Spray, Basket, Red	250.00
Blackberry Spray, Bowl, Marigold, Fluted, 6 In.	39.00
Blackberry Spray, Hat, Marigold, 6 In.	32.50
Blackberry Wreath, Bowl, Amethyst, 8 1/4 In.	95.00
Blackberry Wreath, Bowl, Amethyst, 10 In.	150.00
Blackberry Wreath, Bowl, Green, 10 In.	50.00
Blackberry Wreath, Bowl, Green, 10 1/2 In.	65.00
Blackberry Wreath, Bowl, Marigold, 7 1/2 In.	34.00
Blackberry Wreath, Bowl, Marigold, 9 In.	65.00
Blackberry Wreath, Bowl, Scalloped, Amethyst, 5 1/2 In.	40.00
Blackberry Wreath, Bowl, Wide Panel, Amethyst, 7 1/2 In.	65.00
Blackberry Wreath, Bowl, 10 1/2 In.	155.00
Blackberry, Compote, Green, Miniature	50.00
Blackberry, Compote, Marigold, 7 In.	25.00
Blackberry, Compote, Purple	45.00
Blackberry, Vase, Hat-Shaped, Red	150.00
Blossoms & Spears, Bowl, Marigold, 4 1/2 In.	10.00
Blueberry, Tumbler, Cobalt Blue	65.00
Bouquet, Pitcher, Marigold	165.00
Bouquet, Tumbler, Cobalt Blue	45.00
Bouquet, Water Set, Marigold, 7 Piece	385.00
Brocaded Acorns, Console Set, Ice Blue, 3 Piece	165.00
Brocaded Daffodills, Sugar & Creamer, Pink	120.00
Brocaded Palms, Bonbon, Gold Trim, Ice Green	40.00
Broken Arches, Punch Set, Marigold, 8 Piece	225.00
Broken Arches, Punch Set, Purple, 8 Piece	675.00
Brooklyn Bridge, Bowl, Marigold, 8 1/2 In.	235.00 To 295.00
Bull's-Eye & Beads, Bowl, Amethyst, 8 X 6 In.	50.00
BUSHEL BASKET, see Basket	
BUSY CHICKENS, see Farmyard	
Butterflies & Bells, Compote, Purple, 4 1/4 X 7 In.	95.00
Butterflies, Bonbon, Marigold	22.00 To 35.00
Butterfly & Berry, Berry Bowl, Green	95.00
Butterfly & Berry, Berry Bowl, Marigold, 10 In.	49.50
Butterfly & Berry, Berry Set, Marigold, 5 Piece	105.00 To 130.00
Butterfly & Berry, Berry Set, Marigold, 7 Piece	210.00
Butterfly & Berry, Berry Set, Purple, 5 Piece	135.00
Butterfly & Berry, Bowl, Amethyst, 8 In.	30.00
Butterfly & Berry, Bowl, Cobalt Blue, 10 In.	85.00 To 100.00
Butterfly & Berry, Butter, Covered, Marigold	80.00
Butterfly & Berry, Creamer, Marigold	45.00
Butterfly & Berry, Creamer, White	55.00
Butterfly & Berry, Pitcher, Water, Marigold	75.00
Butterfly & Berry, Sugar, White	65.00
Butterfly & Berry, Table Set, Marigold, 4 Piece	215.00
Butterfly & Berry, Tumbler, Cobalt Blue	20.00 To 45.00
Butterfly & Berry, Tumbler, Marigold	15.00 To 20.00
Butterfly & Berry, Vase, Cobalt Blue, 10 In.	50.00
Butterfly & Berry, Water Set, Marigold	325.00
Butterfly & Berry, Water Set, Marigold, 7 Piece	225.00 To 325.00
BUTTERFLY & CABLE, see Springtime	
Butterfly & Fern, Tumbler, Cobalt Blue	40.00 To 46.00
Butterfly & Fern, Tumbler, Marigold	25.00
Butterfly & Fern, Water Set, Marigold, 7 Piece	495.00
BUTTERFLY & GRAPE, see Butterfly & Berry	
BUTTERFLY & PLUME, see Butterfly & Fern	
Butterfly & Tulip, Bowl, Marigold, 10 In.	225.00 To 295.00
Butterfly & Tulip, Bowl, Square Footed, Purple	900.00 To 1100.00
Butterfly Bush, Compote, Ruffled, Purple, 4 1/8 X 7 1/2 In.	125.00

Butterfly, Bonbon, Handled, Marigold .... 30.00 To 45.00
Buzz-Saw, Cruet, Marigold 250.00
    CABBAGE ROSE & GRAPE, see Wine & Roses
    CACTUS LEAF RAYS, see Leaf Rays
Cane, Bowl, Marigold, 7 1/2 In. 20.00
Captive Rose, Bonbon, Amethyst 40.00
Captive Rose, Bonbon, Cobalt Blue 23.00
Captive Rose, Bowl, Green, 8 In. 40.00
Captive Rose, Bowl, Green, 9 In. 55.00
Captive Rose, Bowl, Marigold, 9 In. 30.00
Captive Rose, Bowl, Ruffled, Purple, 8 1/2 In. .... 24.00 To 35.00
Captive Rose, Compote, Amethyst 35.00
Captive Rose, Compote, Candy Ribbon Edge, Green 55.00
Captive Rose, Plate, Candy Ribbon Edge, Blue, 9 In. 60.00
Carolina Dogwood, Bowl, Amethyst 12.50
Carolina Dogwood, Plate, Purple, 9 In. 295.00
Caroline, Bowl, Crimped, Peach, 8 In. 100.00
    CATTAILS & FISH, see Fisherman's Mug
    CATTAILS & WATER LILY, see Water Lily & Cattails
Chatelaine, Pitcher, Water, Purple 1300.00
Chatelaine, Tumbler, Purple 350.00
    CHERRIES & HOLLY WREATH, see Cherry Circle
    CHERRIES & MUMS, see Mikado
Cherry & Chain, Bowl, Double Pattern, White, 8 1/2 In. 160.00
Cherry Chain, Plate, Orange Tree Outside, Marigold, 6 1/2 In. 60.00
Cherry Circle, Bonbon, Marigold, 8 1/2 In. 35.00
Cherry Circle, Bowl, 3-Footed, Marigold 35.00
    CHERRY WREATHED, see Wreathed Cherry
Cherry, Bowl, Millersburg, Marigold, 10 In. 120.00
Cherry, Compote, Blue & Gold, 3-Footed, 8 1/4 In. 60.00
Cherry, Tumbler, Green 195.00
    CHRISTMAS CACTUS, see Thistle
Christmas Compote, Compote, Purple 2500.00
    CHRISTMAS PLATE, see Poinsetta
    CHRISTMAS ROSE & POPPY, see Six-Petals
    CHRYSANTHEMUM WREATH, see Ten Mums
Chrysanthemum, Bowl, Cobalt Blue, 8 In. .... 70.00 To 85.00
Chrysanthemum, Bowl, Cobalt Blue, 10 1/2 In. 110.00
Chrysanthemum, Bowl, 3-Footed, Scalloped, Marigold, 10 In. 75.00
Circled Scroll, Tumbler, Marigold .... Illus 325.00
    COCKATOO & GRAPES, see Bird With Grapes
Coin Dot, Bowl, Marigold, 8 1/2 In. 12.00
Coin Dot, Bowl, Marigold, 9 1/2 In. 25.00
Coin Dot, Bowl, Purple, 7 In. .... 20.00 To 40.00
Coin Dot, Plate, Aqua, 9 In. 125.00
Coin Dot, Rose Bowl, Green, Marigold Luster 55.00
Coin Spot, Compote, Peach .... 30.00 To 49.00
    COLONIAL, see Colonial Carnival
Colonial Carnival, Candleholder, Cobalt Blue, 8 1/2 In., Pr. 55.00
Colonial Carnival, Candleholder, Marigold, Pair 85.00
Colonial Carnival, Vase, Marigold, 8 1/2 In. 34.00
Colonial Lady, Vase, Purple 275.00
    COMET, see Ribbon Tie
Concave Diamonds, Tumbler, Ice Blue .... 25.00 To 40.00
Constellation, Compote, White .... 75.00 To 95.00
    CORAL MEDALLION, see Mayan
Corn Bottle, Bottle, Smoky 200.00
Corn Vase, Vase, Ice Green 235.00
Cornucopia, Candleholder, Ice Blue, Pair 165.00
Cosmos & Cane, Spooner, Marigold 65.00
Cosmos Variant, Bowl, Amethyst, 10 In. 85.00
Cosmos, Bowl, Green, 6 In. 40.00
Cosmos, Bowl, Marigold, 9 In. 20.00

Cosmos, Bowl, Marigold, 9 1/2 In. 25.00
Crab Claw, Bowl, Marigold 35.00
Crab Claw, Tumbler, Marigold 45.00
Crackle, Dish, Candy, Covered, Marigold, 7 1/4 In. 20.00
Crackle, Tumbler, Marigold, Set Of 6 .... 80.00
Curved Star, Chalice, Marigold 100.00
Dahlia, Pitcher, Water, Marigold 235.00
Dahlia, Pitcher, Water, Purple 595.00
Dahlia, Sugar, Open, White 40.00
Daisies & Drape, Pitcher, Water, Marigold 135.00
DAISY & LATTICE BAND, see Lattice & Daisy
Daisy & Plume, Compote, Green 50.00
Daisy & Plume, Compote, Ruffled, Marigold, 4 1/2 X 7 1/4 In. 50.00
Daisy & Plume, Compote, Ruffled, Marigold, 6 In. .... 20.00 To 28.00
Daisy & Plume, Rose Bowl, Green .... 60.00 To 65.00
Daisy & Plume, Rose Bowl, Marigold .... 45.00 To 50.00
DAISY BAND & DRAPE, see Daisies & Drape
Dandelion, Mug, Marigold 225.00
Dandelion, Mug, Purple 275.00
Dandelion, Tumbler, Marigold 40.00
Dandelion, Tumbler, Purple 40.00
DIAMOND & CABLE, see Fentonia
Diamond & Daisy Cut, Tumbler, Marigold .... 25.00 To 30.00
Diamond & Daisy Cut, Tumbler, Purple 20.00
Diamond & Daisy, ...
DIAMOND BAND, see Diamond
Diamond Lace, Berry Bowl, Purple, 5 1/2 In. 22.00
Diamond Lace, Bowl, Green, 9 In. 95.00
Diamond Lace, Bowl, Purple, 8 In. 65.00
Diamond Lace, Pitcher, Water, Marigold 175.00
Diamond Lace, Pitcher, Water, Purple .... 155.00 To 200.00
Diamond Lace, Tumbler, Purple .... 40.00 To 50.00
Diamond Lace, Water Set, Purple, 7 Piece .... 365.00 To 425.00
DIAMOND POINT & DAISY, see Cosmos & Cane
Diamond Ring, Bowl, Marigold, 9 In. 25.00
Diamond Ring, Bowl, Ruffled, Smoky, 3 1/4 X 9 1/4 In. 60.00
Diamond, Bell, Marigold 400.00
Diamond, Pitcher, Water, Amethyst 150.00
Diamond, Tumbler, Green, Set Of 5 .... 145.00
Diamond, Tumbler, Purple 65.00
Diving Dolphins, Bowl, Purple 195.00
DOGWOOD & MARSH LILY, see Two Flowers
Dogwood Sprays, Bowl, Dome Base, Peach, 9 1/8 In. 65.00
Dogwood Sprays, Compote, Amethyst 35.00
Dogwood Sprays, Compote, Black Amethyst 85.00
DOLPHINS & FLOWERS, see Diving Dolphins
Double Dolphin, Vase, Fan, Pedestal, Pink 53.00
Double Star, Tumbler, Green .... 45.00 To 55.00
Double-Stem Rose, Bowl, Footed, Marigold, 8 In. .... 28.00 To 30.00
Double-Stem Rose, Bowl, Footed, White 85.00
Dragon & Lotus, Bowl, Amethyst, Footed, 7 1/2 In .... 40.00 To 65.00
Dragon & Lotus, Bowl, Amethyst, 8 1/2 In. 75.00
Dragon & Lotus, Bowl, Amethyst, 9 In. 30.00
Dragon & Lotus, Bowl, Cobalt Blue, 8 In. 50.00
Dragon & Lotus, Bowl, Cobalt Blue, 8 3/4 X 2 1/2 In. 70.00
Dragon & Lotus, Bowl, Cobalt Blue, 10 In. 45.00
Dragon & Lotus, Bowl, Fluted, Marigold, 8 1/2 In .... 45.00 To 50.00
Dragon & Lotus, Bowl, Fluted, Purple, 9 In. 55.00
Dragon & Lotus, Bowl, Red, 8 1/2 In. .... Illus 500.00
DRAPE & TIE, see Rosalind
Drape, Dish, Candy, Ice Blue, Marked N 70.00
Drapery, Basket, Ribbon Candy Edge, Aqua, 8 1/2 In. 23.00
Drapery, Rose Bowl, Purple 85.00

(See Page 85)

Carnival Glass, Circled Scroll, Tumbler, Marigold

Carnival Glass, Dragon & Lotus, Bowl, Red, 8 1/2 In.

Drapery, Rose Bowl, Signed, Aqua	185.00
DUTCHMAN, see Sailing Ship	
Eastern Star, Bowl, Marigold, 8 In.	25.00
Eastern Star, Bowl, Purple, 8 In.	25.00
Eastern Star, Compote, Marigold	15.00 To 27.00
Eastern Star, Plate, Green, 7 In.	90.00
Eastern Star, Plate, Purple, 9 In.	95.00
EGYPTIAN BAND, see Round-Up	
EMALINE, see Zippered Loop Lamp	
Embroidered Mums, Bowl, Ice Green, 8 In.	265.00
Embroidered Mums, Bowl, Marigold, 9 In.	45.00 To 55.00
Embroidered Mums, Bowl, Purple, 9 In.	72.00 To 90.00
FAN & ARCH, see Persian Garden	
Fanciful, Plate, Marigold, 9 1/2 In.	135.00
Fanciful, Plate, Pie Crust Rim, Cobalt Blue, 9 In.	140.00
Fanciful, Plate, Ruffled, White, 8 1/2 In.	165.00
FANTASY, see Question Marks	
Farmyard, Bowl, 6 Ruffles, Purple	1400.00
Fashion, Pitcher, Water, Purple	595.00
Fashion, Punch Bowl, Marigold	85.00
Fashion, Rose Bowl, Marigold, 7 1/2 In.	45.00
Fashion, Tumbler, Marigold	22.00
Feather & Heart, Tumbler, Aqua	85.00
Feather & Heart, Tumbler, Marigold	60.00 To 85.00
FEATHER & HOBSTAR, see Inverted Feather	
FEATHER & SCROLL, see Quill	
FEATHERED SCROLL, see Feathered Serpent	
Feathered Serpent, Bowl, Marigold, 9 In.	48.00
Feathered Serpent, Bowl, Purple, 10 In.	65.00
FENTON'S ARABIC, see Illusion	
FENTON'S BUTTERFLIES, see Butterflies	
Fentonia, Creamer, Marigold	65.00
Fern Panels, Hat, Marigold	20.00
FIELD ROSE, see Rambler Rose	
Field Thistle, Compote, Marigold	195.00

Field Thistle, Pitcher, Water, Marigold 185.00
Field Thistle, Plate, Marigold, 9 In. 298.00
Field Thistle, Spooner, Marigold 55.00
Fieldflower, Pitcher, Marigold 70.00
Fieldflower, Pitcher, Red 75.00
Fieldflower, Pitcher, Water, Amethyst, 9 In. 195.00
Fieldflower, Tumbler, Marigold 35.00
Fieldflower, Water Set, Red, 7 Piece 125.00
Fine Cut & Roses, Bowl, Ice Blue, 3-Footed, 4 In. 135.00
Fine Cut & Roses, Dish, Candy, Cobalt Blue, Footed 95.00
Fine Cut & Roses, Dish, Candy, Green 60.00
Fine Cut & Roses, Dish, Candy, Purple 65.00
Fine Cut & Roses, Dish, Candy, Red 95.00
Fine Cut & Roses, Dish, Candy, White 135.00
Fine Cut & Roses, Rose Bowl, Amethyst .... 68.00 To 75.00
Fine Cut & Roses, Rose Bowl, Marigold .... 50.00 To 70.00
Fine Cut & Roses, Rose Bowl, Marigold, 3-Footed, 4 In. 68.00
Fine Cut & Roses, Rose Bowl, Purple .... 65.00 To 75.00
Fine Cut & Roses, Vase, Cobalt Blue, Ribbed, 16 In. 40.00
Fine Rib, Vase, Cobalt Blue, 17 In., Pair 95.00
Fine Rib, Vase, Green, 7 In. 35.00
Fine Rib, Vase, Green, 10 In. 20.00
Fine Rib, Vase, Pulled-Out Points, Ice Green, 10 In. 65.00
    FINECUT & STAR, see Star & File
    FISH & FLOWERS, see Trout & Fly
Fisherman's Mug, Mug, Amethyst 90.00
Fisherman's Mug, Mug, Marigold .... 165.00 To 195.00
Fisherman's Mug, Mug, Purple .... 85.00 To 110.00
    FISHERMAN'S NET, see Treebark
Fishscale & Beads, Dish, Candy, Marigold, 6 1/2 In. 12.00
Fleur De Lys, Bowl, Footed, Amethyst, 8 1/2 In. .... Illus 250.00
    FLORAL & DIAMOND POINT, see Fine Cut & Roses
Floral & Grape, Pitcher, Green 295.00
Floral & Grape, Pitcher, Marigold .... 70.00 To 125.00
Floral & Grape, Pitcher, Water, Cobalt Blue .... 175.00 To 200.00
Floral & Grape, Pitcher, White 325.00
Floral & Grape, Tumbler, Amethyst, Set Of 4 .... 60.00
Floral & Grape, Tumbler, Cobalt Blue .... 20.00 To 35.00
Floral & Grape, Tumbler, Marigold .... 18.00 To 20.00
Floral & Grape, Tumbler, Marigold, Set Of 12 .... 500.00
Floral & Grape, Tumbler, Purple .... 20.00 To 35.00
Floral & Grape, Water Set, Cobalt Blue, 7 Piece 210.00
Floral & Grape, Water Set, Marigold, 7 Piece 350.00
    FLORAL & GRAPEVINE, see Floral & Grape
Floral & Optic, Bowl, Marigold, 8 1/2 In. 16.00
Floral & Optic, Bowl, Smoky, 3-Footed, 9 In. 65.00
Floral & Optic, Cake Plate, White 28.00
    FLORAL & WHEAT SPRAY, see Floral & Wheat
Floral & Wheat, Bonbon, Marigold, 2-Handled, Pedestal 25.00
Floral & Wheat, Bonbon, Peach 95.00
    FLOWER POT, see Butterfly & Tulip
    FLOWERING ALMONDS, see Peacock Tail
Flowers & Beads, Plate, Marigold, 6-Sided, 7 In. 55.00
Flowers & Beads, Plate, Tricornered, Amethyst, 8 In. 60.00
Flowers, Rose Bowl, Marigold 35.00
Flowers, Rose Bowl, Twig Footed, White 60.00
    FLUFFY BIRD, see Peacock
Flute & Cane, Pitcher, Milk, Cobalt Blue 145.00
Flute & Cane, Pitcher, Milk, Marigold 79.00
Flute & Cane, Tankard, Water, Marigold 189.00
Flute, Berry Bowl, Marigold, 4 1/2 In., Set Of 4 .... 60.00
Flute, Berry Set, Purple, 5 Piece 100.00
Flute, Candleholder, Green, 8 1/2 In., Pair 80.00

Flute, Goblet, Marigold, Set Of 4 .... 40.00
Flute, Sugar & Creamer, Purple 85.00
Flute, Sugar, Amethyst 55.00
Flute, Toothpick, Green .... 70.00 To 75.00
Flute, Toothpick, Marigold 25.00
Flute, Toothpick, Marigold Overlay, Vaseline 295.00
Flute, Vase, Purple, 9 In. 35.00
Folding Fan, Compote, Peach 47.50
Four Flowers, Plate, Peach, 6 In. 60.00
French Knots, Dish, Hat Shaped, Cobalt Blue, 3 1/8 In. 60.00
Fruits & Flowers, Bonbon, Cobalt Blue 60.00
Fruits & Flowers, Bonbon, Purple .... 40.00 To 50.00
Fruits & Flowers, Bonbon, Stemmed, Marigold 50.00
Fruits & Flowers, Bowl, Purple, Footed, 9 In. 60.00
Fruits & Flowers, Compote, Cobalt Blue .... 75.00 To 80.00
Fruits & Flowers, Compote, Green, 2-Handled 50.00
Fruits & Flowers, Plate, Green, 7 In. 100.00
Garden Mums, Water Set, Green, 7 Piece 280.00
Garden Path Variant, Plate, Chop, Green 2000.00
Garden Path, Bowl, Marigold, 9 In. 45.00
Garden Path, Bowl, Purple, 6 In. 165.00
Garden Path, Plate, Chop, Purple, 11 In. 1750.00
Garland, Rose Bowl, Cobalt Blue .... 45.00 To 65.00
Garland, Rose Bowl, Marigold .... 35.00 To 55.00
Georgia Belle, Plate, Marigold, Fluted Edge 75.00
Golden Grapes, Rose Bowl, Marigold .... 25.00 To 45.00
Golden Harvest, Decanter, Stopper, Marigold 95.00
Golden Harvest, Wine, Marigold 25.00
Good Luck, Bowl, Cobalt Blue, 9 In. .... 195.00 To 235.00
Good Luck, Bowl, Marigold, 9 In. .... 70.00 To 85.00
Good Luck, Plate, Purple, 9 In. 160.00
Grape & Cable, Banana Bowl, Amethyst 225.00
Grape & Cable, Banana Bowl, Cobalt Blue .... 185.00 To 225.00
Grape & Cable, Banana Bowl, Marigold .... 95.00 To 150.00
Grape & Cable, Banana Bowl, Purple, 11 1/2 X 7 In. 275.00
Grape & Cable, Bonbon, Marigold 20.00
Grape & Cable, Bonbon, 2-Handled, Amethyst 45.00
Grape & Cable, Bonbon, 2-Handled, Cobalt Blue .... 80.00 To 85.00
Grape & Cable, Bottle, Cologne, Green 105.00
Grape & Cable, Bottle, Cologne, Marigold 150.00
Grape & Cable, Bottle, Cologne, Purple 75.00
Grape & Cable, Bottle, Cologne, Stopper, Amethyst 150.00
Grape & Cable, Bowl, Aqua, 7 1/2 In. 75.00
Grape & Cable, Bowl, Basket Weave Exterior, Purple, 11 In. 150.00
Grape & Cable, Bowl, Console, Cobalt Blue, 11 X 6 1/4 In. 350.00
Grape & Cable, Bowl, Console, Northwood, Purple 350.00
Grape & Cable, Bowl, Footed, Amethyst, 7 1/2 In. 50.00
Grape & Cable, Bowl, Footed, Amethyst, 8 In. .... 42.00 To 65.00
Grape & Cable, Bowl, Footed, Amethyst, 9 In. 50.00
Grape & Cable, Bowl, Footed, Marigold, 8 In. 50.00
Grape & Cable, Bowl, Footed, Marigold, 8 1/4 In. 50.00
Grape & Cable, Bowl, Marigold, 10 In. 80.00
Grape & Cable, Bowl, Punch, Purple 45.00
Grape & Cable, Bowl, Purple, 3-Footed, 10 1/2 X 5 1/4 In. 225.00
Grape & Cable, Bowl, Purple, 5 1/2 In. 38.50
Grape & Cable, Bowl, Purple, 8 1/2 In. 70.00
Grape & Cable, Bowl, Purple, 11 In. 95.00
Grape & Cable, Bowl, Red, 7 In. 375.00
Grape & Cable, Bowl, Red, 7 1/2 In. 450.00
Grape & Cable, Bowl, Red, 8 In. 425.00
Grape & Cable, Bowl, Ruffled, Marigold, 7 In. 45.00
Grape & Cable, Bowl, Serrated, Crimped, Amethyst, 9 In. 87.00
Grape & Cable, Bowl, White, 11 In. .... 195.00 To 265.00

Grape & Cable, Bowl, 3-Footed, Cobalt Blue, 10 In. 155.00
Grape & Cable, Box, Dresser, Purple, Pair 75.00
Grape & Cable, Box, Powder, Marigold 70.00
Grape & Cable, Breakfast Set, Green 140.00
Grape & Cable, Butter, Covered, Marigold .... 150.00 To 185.00
Grape & Cable, Butter, Covered, Purple 95.00
Grape & Cable, Candleholder, Green 100.00
Grape & Cable, Candle Lamp, Northwood, Green .... Illus 450.00
Grape & Cable, Candleholder, Aqua, Pair 225.00
Grape & Cable, Candleholder, Green .... 95.00 To 115.00
Grape & Cable, Candleholder, Marigold 75.00
Grape & Cable, Candleholder, Purple .... 105.00 To 110.00
Grape & Cable, Compote, Covered, Amethyst 495.00
Grape & Cable, Cracker Jar, Covered, Purple 120.00
Grape & Cable, Cracker Jar, Marigold 185.00
Grape & Cable, Creamer, Amethyst 250.00
Grape & Cable, Creamer, Purple, 4 3/4 In. 80.00
Grape & Cable, Cup, Punch, Marigold .... 20.00 To 25.00
Grape & Cable, Cup, Punch, Marked N, Amethyst 22.00
Grape & Cable, Cup, Punch, Purple .... 16.00 To 25.00
Grape & Cable, Decanter, Amethyst 150.00
Grape & Cable, Dish, Hat Shaped, Marigold, 3 1/2 In. 25.00
Grape & Cable, Dish, Sweetmeat, Amethyst 87.50
Grape & Cable, Dish, Sweetmeat, Purple .... 185.00 To 285.00
Grape & Cable, Dresser Set, Northwood, Marigold, 6 Piece 1225.00
Grape & Cable, Hatpin Holder, Amethyst 110.00
Grape & Cable, Hatpin Holder, Marigold .... 100.00 To 145.00
Grape & Cable, Hatpin Holder, Purple .... 75.00 To 175.00
Grape & Cable, Hatpin Holder, White 145.00
Grape & Cable, Humidor, Marigold .... 205.00 To 210.00
Grape & Cable, Jar, Powder, Covered, Marigold 70.00
Grape & Cable, Jar, Powder, Covered, Marked N, Amethyst 70.00
Grape & Cable, Jar, Powder, Green, Covered 70.00
Grape & Cable, Jar, Sweetmeat, Purple 225.00
Grape & Cable, Nappy, Handled, Marigold 50.00
Grape & Cable, Nappy, Marigold .... 50.00 To 55.00
Grape & Cable, Orange Bowl, Purple .... 140.00 To 195.00
Grape & Cable, Pitcher, Purple, 8 1/2 In. 175.00
Grape & Cable, Plate, Footed, Marigold, 9 In. 55.00
Grape & Cable, Plate, Green, 9 In. 95.00
Grape & Cable, Plate, Handled, Purple, 6 1/2 In. 69.50
Grape & Cable, Plate, Marigold, 6 In. 30.00
Grape & Cable, Plate, Purple, 9 In. 95.00
Grape & Cable, Punch Set, Ice Green, 7 Piece 1600.00
Grape & Cable, Punch Set, Marigold, Banquet Size, 10 Piece 1350.00
Grape & Cable, Punch Set, N Mark, Purple, Medium Size 485.00
Grape & Cable, Punch Set, Purple, Banquet Size, 10 Piece 1500.00
Grape & Cable, Spooner, Green 135.00
Grape & Cable, Spooner, Purple 120.00
Grape & Cable, Sugar, Covered, Green 75.00
Grape & Cable, Sugar, Covered, Purple .... 135.00 To 175.00
Grape & Cable, Table Set, Purple, 4 Piece 560.00
Grape & Cable, Tankard, Ice Green 2700.00
Grape & Cable, Tray, Dresser, Marigold .... 125.00 To 150.00
Grape & Cable, Tumbler, Amethyst 25.00
Grape & Cable, Tumbler, Green .... 35.00 To 50.00
Grape & Cable, Tumbler, Marigold .... 40.00 To 75.00
Grape & Cable, Tumbler, Purple .... 25.00 To 32.00
Grape & Cable, Tumbler, Purple, Set Of 6 .... 250.00
Grape & Cable, Vase, Footed, Marigold, 6 1/2 In. 40.00
Grape & Cable, Water Set, Amethyst, 7 Piece 495.00
Grape & Cable, Water Set, Marigold, 7 Piece .... 315.00 To 375.00
Grape & Cable, Water Set, Purple, 7 Piece .... 375.00 To 445.00

Grape & Cable, Whiskey, Amethyst .... 135.00 To 180.00
Grape & Cable, Whiskey, Marigold 140.00
Grape & Gothic Arches, Sugar & Creamer, Cobalt Blue 85.00
Grape & Gothic Arches, Table Set, Marigold, 5 Piece 365.00
Grape & Gothic Arches, Tumbler, Cobalt Blue .... 28.00 To 37.50
Grape & Gothic Arches, Tumbler, Marigold 20.00
Grape & Gothic, Bowl, Cobalt Blue, 6 In. 26.00
Grape Arbor, Bowl, Footed, Marigold, 9 1/2 In. 165.00
Grape Arbor, Pitcher, White 495.00
Grape Arbor, Tumbler, Ice Blue .... 100.00 To 125.00
Grape Arbor, Tumbler, Marigold .... 35.00 To 40.00
Grape Arbor, Tumbler, Purple 49.00
Grape Arbor, Tumbler, White .... 80.00 To 135.00
Grape Arbor, Water Set, Marigold, 7 Piece .... 300.00 To 420.00
   GRAPE DELIGHT, see Vintage
Grape Leaves, Bowl, Daisy & Plume Exterior, Green, 9 In. 60.00
Grape Wreath, Bowl, Bead Center, Green, 9 In. 49.50
Grape Wreath, Bowl, Geometric, Marigold, 10 In. 60.00
Grape Wreath, Bowl, Scalloped, Marigold, 6 1/2 In. 45.00
Grape, Bowl, Console, Turned-Up Points, Northwood, Green 365.00
Grape, Candle Lamp, Metal Holder, N Mark, Marigold 600.00
Grape, Candle Lamp, Northwood, Cobalt Blue 760.00
Grape, Candleholder, Northwood, Marigold, Pair 150.00
Grape, Carafe, Imperial, Purple 130.00
Grape, Cup & Saucer, Imperial, Marigold 50.00
Grape, Cup, Imperial, Marigold 30.00
Grape, Decanter, Imperial, Marigold 75.00
Grape, Decanter, Imperial, Purple 130.00
Grape, Nappy, Fenton, Amethyst 12.00
Grape, Pitcher, Imperial, Marigold 90.00
Grape, Plate, Northwood, Basket-Weave Back, Marigold, 9 In. 55.00
Grape, Plate, Stippled, N Mark, Ice Green, 9 1/2 In. 160.00
   GRAPEVINE DIAMONDS, see Grapevine Lattice
Grapevine Lattice, Plate, Marigold, 7 In. 40.00
Grapevine Lattice, Plate, Scalloped, White, 7 In. 40.00
Grapevine Lattice, Tumbler, Amethyst 45.00
Grapevine Lattice, Tumbler, Marigold, Set Of 6 .... 90.00

Carnival Glass, Grape & Cable, Candle Lamp, Northwood, Green

Carnival Glass, Fleur De Lys, Bowl, Footed, Amethyst,
8 1/2 In.   (See Page 88)

Grapevine Lattice, Tumbler, Purple .... 35.00 To 50.00
Grapevine Lattice, Tumbler, Purple, Set Of 4 .... 200.00
Grapevine Lattice, Water Set, Purple, 6 Piece 295.00
Greek Key, Bowl, Cobalt Blue, 9 In. 20.00
Greek Key, Bowl, Marigold, 9 In. 45.00
Greek Key, Bowl, Octagon Shaped, Dome Footed, Green 45.00
Greek Key, Lampshade, Marigold 35.00
Greek Key, Pitcher, Water, Marigold 475.00
Greek Key, Plate, Green, 9 In. 265.00
Greek Key, Tumbler, Green .... 85.00 To 110.00
Greek Key, Tumbler, Purple .... 90.00 To 110.00
Greek Key, Water Set, Green, 7 Piece 1250.00
Greek Key, Water Set, Marigold, 4 Piece 975.00
Greek Key, Water Set, Purple, 7 Piece 1050.00
Harvest Flower, Tumbler, Marigold 95.00
    HARVEST TIME, see Golden Harvest
Headdress, Compote, Marigold, Rayed Base, 6 X 4 3/4 In. 40.00
Heart & Flowers, Compote, Marigold .... 45.00 To 55.00
Heart & Vine, Bowl, Candy Ribbon Edge, Green, 8 3/4 In. 55.00
Heart & Vine, Bowl, Purple, Ribbon Rim, 8 3/4 In .... 50.00 To 55.00
Heart & Vine, Plate, Cobalt Blue, 9 In. 225.00
    HEART BAND & HERRINGBONE, see Feather & Heart
Hearts & Flowers, Compote, Aqua .... 235.00 To 350.00
Hearts & Flowers, Compote, Ice Blue 190.00
Hearts & Flowers, Compote, Ice Green 265.00
Hearts & Flowers, Compote, Purple 77.00
Hearts & Flowers, Compote, White .... 75.00 To 165.00
Hearts & Flowers, Plate, Green, 9 In. 275.00
Hearts & Flowers, Plate, Marigold, 9 In. 165.00
Hearts & Flowers, Plate, Purple, 9 In. 125.00
Heavy Drape, Plate, Chop, Amber 325.00
Heavy Drape, Plate, Chop, Amethyst 450.00
Heavy Drape, Plate, Chop, Green, 11 In. 190.00
Heavy Drape, Plate, Green, 8 In. 75.00
    HERON & RUSHES, see Stork & Rushes
Heron, Mug, Purple 250.00
    HOBSTAR & TORCH, see Double Star
Holly & Berries, Plate, Cobalt Blue, 9 1/2 In. 75.00
    HOLLY & BERRY, see Holly, Carnival
    HOLLY CHRISTMAS COMPOTE, see Christmas Compote
    HOLLY SPRAY, see Holly Sprig
Holly Sprig, Bowl, Footed, Marigold, 6 1/2 In. 25.00
Holly Sprig, Bowl, Peach, 8 In. 45.00
Holly Sprig, Bowl, Tricornered, Amethyst, 6 1/2 In. 45.00
Holly Whirl, Bowl, Purple, 9 1/2 In. 75.00
Holly Whirl, Bowl, Scalloped, Green, 6 1/2 In. 58.00
Holly Whirl, Bowl, Spider Web Center, Amethyst, 9 In. 68.00
Holly Whirl, Sauce, Peach .... 35.00 To 65.00
Holly, Berry Bowl, Fluted, Cobalt Blue, 9 1/2 In. 45.00
Holly, Bonbon, Cobalt Blue 50.00
Holly, Bowl, Green, 9 1/2 In. .... 60.00 To 65.00
Holly, Carnival, Berry Bowl, Marigold 30.00
Holly, Carnival, Dish, Hat Shaped, Marigold 18.00
Holly, Compote, Candy Ribbon Edge, Marigold, 4 X 5 In. 15.00
Holly, Compote, Footed, Purple, 5 1/4 X 4 1/2 In. 75.00
Holly, Compote, Ruffled, Red 295.00
Holly, Dish, Hat Shaped, Amber .... 85.00 To 125.00
Holly, Dish, Hat Shaped, Red 275.00
Holly, Plate, Cobalt Blue, 10 In. 98.00
Holly, Plate, White, 9 In. 135.00
    HONEYCOMB COLLAR, see Fishscale & Beads
    HORN OF PLENTY, see Cornucopia
    HORSE MEDALLIONS, see Horses' Heads

Horses' Heads, Bowl, Collar Base, Cobalt Blue, 7 In. 110.00
Horses' Heads, Bowl, Collar Base, Green, 7 In. 110.00
Horses' Heads, Bowl, Footed, Marigold, 6 1/2 In. 70.00
Horses' Heads, Bowl, Footed, Marigold, 7 1/2 In. .... 60.00 To 75.00
Horses' Heads, Dish, Nut, Footed, Marigold, 3 1/2 In. 75.00
Horses' Heads, Dish, Nut, Red 875.00
Horses' Heads, Plate, Marigold, 7 1/2 X 1 In. 65.00
Horses' Heads, Rose Bowl, Footed, Cobalt Blue 285.00
Illinois Daisy, Jar, Covered, Marigold 85.00
Illusion, Bonbon, Cobalt Blue 55.00
Illusion, Bonbon, Green 65.00
Imperial Grape, Bowl, Amber, 6 In. 18.00
Imperial Grape, Bowl, Clambroth, 9 In. 25.00
Imperial Grape, Bowl, Footed, Cobalt Blue, 6 In. 65.00
Imperial Grape, Bowl, Green, 5 In. 11.00
Imperial Grape, Bowl, Green, 7 In. 45.00
Imperial Grape, Bowl, Green, 9 1/4 In. 40.00
Imperial Grape, Bowl, Marigold, 10 In. .... 12.00 To 30.00
Imperial Grape, Candleholder, Marigold, 6 1/4 In., Pair 36.00
Imperial Grape, Carafe, Purple 140.00
Imperial Grape, Carafe, White 150.00
Imperial Grape, Compote, Footed, Marigold 22.00
Imperial Grape, Compote, Scalloped & Fluted, Marigold 35.00
Imperial Grape, Cup & Saucer, Green .... 49.00 To 85.00
Imperial Grape, Cup, Punch, Marigold 15.00
Imperial Grape, Cup, Punch, Purple 22.50
Imperial Grape, Decanter, Marigold .... 75.00 To 90.00
Imperial Grape, Decanter, Purple .... 125.00 To 135.00
Imperial Grape, Goblet, Marigold .... 25.00 To 35.00
Imperial Grape, Pitcher, Green, 8 3/8 In. 125.00
Imperial Grape, Pitcher, Marigold 95.00
Imperial Grape, Plate, Purple, 8 In. 275.00
Imperial Grape, Punch Set, Marigold, 7 Piece 135.00
Imperial Grape, Tumbler, Marigold 20.00
Imperial Grape, Tumbler, Purple 39.00
Imperial Grape, Water Set, Green, 7 Piece 275.00
Imperial Grape, Water Set, Marigold, 5 Piece 225.00
Imperial Grape, Wine Set, Marigold, 6 Piece 195.00
Imperial Grape, Wine, Green 25.00
Imperial Grape, Wine, Marigold 20.00
Imperial Grape, Wine, Purple 25.00
    INDIAN ROSE, see Headdress
Inverted Coin Dot, Pitcher, Water, Marigold 145.00
Inverted Coin Dot, Tumbler, Marigold 30.00
Inverted Feather, Cookie Jar, Covered, Green .... 160.00 To 185.00
Inverted Feather, Toothpick, Cobalt Blue 9.50
Iris, Compote, Amethyst 38.00
Iris, Compote, Marigold 50.00
Iris, Goblet, Marigold 55.00
Iris, Herringbone, Butter, Covered, Marigold 27.50
Iris, Herringbone, Creamer, Marigold 7.00
Iris, Tumbler, Amethyst 120.00
    IRISH LACE, see Louisa
Jeweled Heart, Dish, Low, Ruffled, Peach, 6 1/2 In. 35.00
Jeweled Heart, Tumbler, Marigold 65.00
    KIMBERLY, see Concave Diamonds
Kingfisher, Bowl, Purple, 9 1/2 In. .... 135.00 To 150.00
Kingfisher, Toothpick, Purple 25.00
Kittens, Banana Bowl, Marigold 110.00
Kittens, Bowl, Vaseline, 7 In. 185.00
Kittens, Cup, Marigold .... 95.00 To 135.00
Kittens, Plate, Footed, Marigold, 4 1/2 In. 85.00
Kittens, Spooner, Cobalt Blue, 2 1/4 In. .... 200.00 To 250.00

Kittens, Spooner, Marigold, 2 1/2 In. .... 110.00 To 135.00
Kittens, Spooner, Purple 80.00
Kittens, Spooner, White 90.00
Knotted Beads, Vase, Cobalt Blue 17.00
Knotted Beads, Vase, Green 35.00
    LABELLE ELAINE, see Primrose
    LABELLE ROSE, see Rose Show
    LATE IRIS, see Iris, Herringbone
Late Thistle, Tumbler, Cambridge Glass Co., Amethyst 335.00
Lattice & Daisy, Tankard, Marigold, 11 1/2 In. .... 88.00 To 115.00
Lattice & Daisy, Tumbler, Cobalt Blue 50.00
Lattice & Daisy, Tumbler, Marigold .... 10.00 To 22.00
Lattice & Grape, Tankard Pitcher, White 575.00
Lattice & Grape, Tumbler, Cobalt Blue 34.00
Lattice & Grape, Tumbler, Marigold .... 14.00 To 35.00
Lattice & Grape, Tumbler, White 75.00
Lattice & Grape, Water Set, Marigold, 7 Piece 200.00
    LATTICE & GRAPEVINE, see Lattice & Grape
Leaf & Beads, Bowl, Green, Footed, Marked N 60.00
Leaf & Beads, Dish, Candy, Footed, Purple 40.00
Leaf & Beads, Dish, Nut, White 105.00
Leaf & Beads, Rose Bowl, Aqua .... 220.00 To 225.00
Leaf & Beads, Rose Bowl, Footed, Purple .... 65.00 To 95.00
Leaf & Little Flowers, Compote, Green 325.00
Leaf Chain, Bowl, Aqua, 7 1/2 In. 150.00
Leaf Chain, Bowl, Red, 7 In. 450.00
Leaf Chain, Dish, Ruffled, Marigold, 7 In. 38.00
Leaf Chain, Plate, Cobalt Blue 95.00
Leaf Chain, Plate, Green, 9 In. .... 75.00 To 110.00
    LEAF MEDALLION, see Leaf Chain
    LEAF PINWHEEL & STAR FLOWER, see Whirling Leaves
Leaf Rays, Nappy, Handled, Heart Shaped, Marigold 20.00
Leaf Rays, Nappy, Ruffled, Handled, Amethyst 32.00
Leaf Tiers, Pitcher, Footed, Marigold 295.00
Leaf Tiers, Tumbler, Footed, Marigold 50.00
Lion, Bowl, Marigold, 6 In. .... 95.00 To 105.00
Lion, Bowl, Marigold, 7 In. 125.00
Lion, Bowl, Marigold, 7 1/2 In. 95.00
Lion, Plate, Cobalt Blue, 7 In. 120.00
Lion, Plate, Marigold, 7 1/2 In. 350.00
Little Barrell, Bottle, Perfume, Green 80.00
Little Fishes, Bowl, Footed, Marigold, 9 In. 99.00
Little Flowers, Berry Bowl, Cobalt Blue, 8 In. 65.00
Little Flowers, Bowl, Amethyst, 10 In. 95.00
Little Flowers, Bowl, Red, 9 In. 1250.00
Little Flowers, Dish, Nut, Cobalt Blue 75.00
Little Flowers, Plate, Marigold, 6 1/2 In. 90.00
Little Flowers, Rose Bowl, Marigold 35.00
Little Stars, Bowl, Marigold, 9 In. 95.00
Little Stars, Bowl, Purple, 8 In. 80.00
Loganberry, Compote, Fluted, Covered, Marigold 40.00
Loganberry, Vase, Green, 3 1/2 In. 140.00
    LOOP & COLUMN, see Pulled Loop
    LOOPED PETALS, see Scales
Lotus & Grape, Bonbon, Green 45.00
Lotus & Grape, Bonbon, 2-Handled, Marigold, 4 X 4 X 2 1/2 In. 35.00
Louisa, Bowl, 3-Footed, Purple, 8 1/2 In. 30.00
Louisa, Dish, Shell, Footed, Purple, 6 3/8 In. 30.00
Louisa, Rose Bowl, Amber 60.00
Louisa, Rose Bowl, Amethyst .... 45.00 To 50.00
Louisa, Rose Bowl, Purple .... 40.00 To 70.00
Lustre Flute, Sugar & Creamer, Green 25.00
Lustre Rose, Bowl, 3-Footed, Marigold, 7 1/4 In. 12.00

Lustre Rose, Spooner, Marigold 30.00
Lustre Rose, Sugar & Creamer, Marigold 60.00
Lustre Rose, Tumbler, Green 18.00
Lustre Rose, Tumbler, Marigold .... 20.00 To 40.00
Lustre Rose, Water Set, Cobalt Blue, 7 Piece 165.00
Lustre Rose, Water Set, Marigold, 7 Piece .... 160.00 To 189.00
    MAGNOLIA & POINSETTIA, see Water Lily
    MAINE COAST, see Seacoast
Many Fruits, Bowl, Punch, Purple 450.00
Many Fruits, Punch Set, Marigold 350.00
Many Stars, Bowl, Amethyst, Millersburg, 9 1/2 In. 175.00
Maple Leaf, Berry Set, Marigold, 7 Piece 150.00
Maple Leaf, Bowl, Berry, Master, Pedestal, Purple 95.00
Maple Leaf, Pitcher, Amethyst 175.00
Maple Leaf, Pitcher, Purple 200.00
Maple Leaf, Sherbet, Amethyst 21.00
Maple Leaf, Tumbler, Amethyst 35.00
Maple Leaf, Tumbler, Cobalt Blue 35.00
Maple Leaf, Tumbler, Marigold .... 20.00 To 35.00
Maple Leaf, Tumbler, Purple .... 30.00 To 42.50
Maple Leaf, Water Set, Purple, 7 Piece .... 375.00 To 395.00
    MARYLAND, see Rustic
Mayan, Bowl, Purple, 8 1/2 In. 60.00
    MELINDA, see Wishbone
Memphis, Bowl, Punch, Purple 400.00
Memphis, Cup, Punch, Green .... 28.00 To 65.00
Memphis, Cup, Punch, White 60.00
Memphis, Pitcher, Green 90.00
Memphis, Punch Set, White, 8 Piece 850.00
Mikado, Compote, Marigold .... 135.00 To 150.00
Mikado, Compote, White 550.00
Milady, Pitcher, Tankard, Cobalt Blue 675.00
Milady, Tumbler, Cobalt Blue 75.00
Morning Glory, Tumbler, Green 750.00
    MULTI FRUIT & FLOWERS, see Many Fruits
    MUMS & GREEK KEY, see Embroidered Mums
Nautilus, Compote, Dome Footed, Purple, 4 X 4 X 6 1/2 In. 200.00
    NESTING SWAN, see Swan, Carnival
No Dragon, Strawberry, Plate, Marigold, 9 1/4 In. .... *Illus* 1900.00
Northern Star, Dish, Collar Base, Rayed, Marigold, 6 1/4 In. 40.00
Northern Star, Tray, Card, Marigold, 6 1/4 In. 30.00
    OAK LEAF & ACORN, see Acorn
    OAK LEAF BROCADE, see Brocaded Acorns

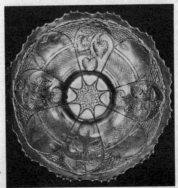

Carnival Glass, No Dragon, Strawberry, Plate,
Marigold, 9 1/4 In.

Octagon, Pitcher, Milk, Marigold 85.00
Octagon, Pitcher, Water, Marigold, 8 In. 70.00
Octagon, Sherbert, Marigold 50.00
Octagon, Tumbler, Marigold 25.00
Octagon, Vase, Marigold, 8 In. .... 30.00 To 55.00
Octagon, Wine, Marigold 12.00
    OLD FASHION FLAG, see Iris
    OLE CORN, see Corn Bottle
Open Rose, Bowl, Fluted, White, 10 In. 65.00
Open Rose, Bowl, White, 9 1/4 In. 34.00
Open Rose, Plate, Green, 9 In. 50.00
Optic & Buttons, Cake Plate, Marigold 15.00
Orange Peel, Cup, Punch, Amethyst 15.00
    ORANGE TREE & CABLE, see Orange Tree Orchard
    ORANGE TREE & SCROLL, see Orange Tree Variant
Orange Tree Orchard, Pitcher, Water, White 400.00
Orange Tree Variant, Tumbler, Cobalt Blue 60.00
Orange Tree, Bowl, Candy Ribbon Edge, Cobalt Blue, 9 In. 30.00
Orange Tree, Bowl, Fluted Edge, Marigold, 2 1/2 X 8 1/2 In. 40.00
Orange Tree, Bowl, Punch, Whimsey, Marigold 385.00
Orange Tree, Bowl, Ruffled Edge, Cobalt Blue, 9 X 2 1/4 In. 65.00
Orange Tree, Bowl, Ruffled, Amber, 8 1/2 In. 75.00
Orange Tree, Bowl, White, 8 In. 77.50
Orange Tree, Bowl, 3-Footed, Amethyst 13.50
Orange Tree, Compote, Marigold 28.00
Orange Tree, Creamer, Footed, White 95.00
Orange Tree, Creamer, Purple .... 45.00 To 65.00
Orange Tree, Cup, Marigold 8.00
Orange Tree, Cup, Punch, Cobalt Blue 18.00
Orange Tree, Cup, Punch, White 35.00
Orange Tree, Goblet, Cobalt Blue 45.00
Orange Tree, Hatpin Holder, Cobalt Blue .... 110.00 To 145.00
Orange Tree, Hatpin Holder, Green 275.00
Orange Tree, Jar, Powder, Covered, Cobalt Blue 80.00
Orange Tree, Jar, Powder, Covered, Marigold 70.00
Orange Tree, Loving Cup, Marigold .... 90.00 To 165.00
Orange Tree, Loving Cup, Peacock Tail Interior, White 240.00
Orange Tree, Mug, Amethyst 25.00
Orange Tree, Mug, Cobalt Blue .... 12.00 To 50.00
Orange Tree, Mug, Marigold .... 15.00 To 45.00
Orange Tree, Mug, Red 350.00
Orange Tree, Orange Bowl, Footed, Marigold 75.00
Orange Tree, Plate, Cobalt Blue, 9 In. 95.00
Orange Tree, Plate, Green, 9 In. 275.00
Orange Tree, Plate, White, 9 1/2 In. 73.00
Orange Tree, Punch Bowl & Base, Marigold 80.00
Orange Tree, Punch Set, Cobalt Blue, 10 Pieces 360.00
Orange Tree, Punch Set, White, 7 Piece 700.00
Orange Tree, Rose Bowl, Marigold 45.00
Orange Tree, Rose Bowl, Twig Feet, Red 450.00
Orange Tree, Spooner, Footed, White 125.00
Orange Tree, Sugar & Creamer, Amethyst 135.00
Orange Tree, Sugar, Purple 65.00
Orange Tree, Tumbler, Cobalt Blue .... 45.00 To 65.00
Orange Tree, Water Set, Footed, White, 7 Piece 465.00
Orange Tree, Wine, Cobalt Blue 40.00
Orange Tree, Wine, Marigold .... 17.50 To 25.00
Oriental Poppy, Pitcher, Water, Purple 550.00
Oriental Poppy, Tumbler, Green 50.00
Oriental Poppy, Tumbler, Ice Blue .... 145.00 To 165.00
Oriental Poppy, Tumbler, Marigold .... 35.00 To 42.00
Oriental Poppy, Tumbler, Purple 40.00
Oriental Poppy, Water Set, Amethyst, 7 Piece 675.00

PANELED BACHELOR BUTTONS, see Milady

Pansy, Bowl, Overlapping Arches On Back, Purple	45.00
Pansy, Nappy, Handled, Marigold	20.00
Pansy, Plate, Ruffled, Amethyst, 9 In.	95.00
Pansy, Sugar & Creamer, Marigold	40.00
Panther, Berry Set, Marigold, 7 Piece	350.00
Panther, Bowl, Berry, Cobalt Blue, 9 In.	275.00
Panther, Bowl, Berry, Footed, Green, 9 In.	275.00 To 450.00
Panther, Bowl, Berry, Marigold, 5 In.	20.00 To 35.00

PARROT TULIP SWIRL, see Acanthus

Pastel Swan, Dish, Swan Shaped, Green	30.00
Peach & Pear, Bowl, Fruit, Marigold, 12 In.	65.00
Peach, Tumbler, Cobalt Blue, N Mark	55.00
Peach, Tumbler, Green, N Mark	25.00 To 30.00
Peach, Water Set, Green, 6 Piece	210.00
Peach, Water Set, White, 7 Piece	950.00
Peacock & Dahlia, Bowl, Marigold, 6 In.	75.00
Peacock & Grape, Bowl, Amethyst, 8 1/2 In.	48.00
Peacock & Grape, Bowl, Cobalt Blue, 8 In.	50.00 To 60.00
Peacock & Grape, Bowl, Cobalt Blue, 9 X 2 1/4 In.	75.00
Peacock & Grape, Bowl, Green, 9 In.	65.00 To 125.00
Peacock & Grape, Bowl, Marigold, 8 1/2 In.	35.00
Peacock & Grape, Bowl, Ruffled Edge, Green, 3 1/4 X 8 In.	65.00
Peacock & Grape, Bowl, Ruffled, Marigold, 9 In.	38.00
Peacock & Grape, Bowl, Vaseline, 8 In.	495.00
Peacock & Grape, Plate Footed, Amethyst, 9 In.	210.00
Peacock & Grape, Plate, Footed, Green, 9 1/2 In.	250.00
Peacock & Urn, Berry Set, White, 6 Piece	250.00
Peacock & Urn, Bowl, Amethyst, 7 1/2 In.	350.00
Peacock & Urn, Bowl, Amethyst, 8 1/2 In.	225.00
Peacock & Urn, Bowl, Berry Exterior, Cobalt Blue, 8 In.	90.00
Peacock & Urn, Bowl, Berry, Marigold	37.50
Peacock & Urn, Bowl, Cobalt Blue, 9 In.	85.00 To 95.00
Peacock & Urn, Bowl, Green, 9 In.	225.00 To 250.00
Peacock & Urn, Bowl, Marigold, 10 In.	150.00
Peacock & Urn, Bowl, Marigold, 8 In.	1050.00
Peacock & Urn, Bowl, Purple, 10 In.	175.00
Peacock & Urn, Bowl, Ruffled Edge, Marigold, 9 In.	82.00
Peacock & Urn, Bowl, White, 10 In.	210.00
Peacock & Urn, Compote, Cobalt Blue	65.00
Peacock & Urn, Compote, Marigold	45.00
Peacock & Urn, Plate, Beaded Berry Exterior, White	85.00
Peacock & Urn, Plate, Chop, Purple	800.00
Peacock & Urn, Plate, Cobalt Blue, 9 In.	210.00
Peacock & Urn, Plate, Green, 9 In.	210.00
Peacock & Urn, Plate, Marigold, 9 1/2 In.	165.00
Peacock At Fountain, Berry Set, Cobalt Blue, 7 Piece	265.00
Peacock At Fountain, Bowl, Punch, Marigold	250.00
Peacock At Fountain, Bowl, Punch, Purple	425.00
Peacock At Fountain, Butter, Covered, Marigold	160.00
Peacock At Fountain, Creamer, Marigold	70.00
Peacock At Fountain, Hatpin Holder, Purple	175.00
Peacock At Fountain, Orange Bowl, Marigold	135.00 To 145.00
Peacock At Fountain, Orange Bowl, N Mark, Cobalt Blue	225.00
Peacock At Fountain, Pitcher, Amethyst	350.00
Peacock At Fountain, Pitcher, Cobalt Blue, 8 3/8 In.	400.00
Peacock At Fountain, Pitcher, Water, Marigold	175.00 To 195.00
Peacock At Fountain, Pitcher, Water, Purple, 9 3/4 In.	265.00
Peacock At Fountain, Spooner, Amethyst	10.00
Peacock At Fountain, Sugar, Marigold	95.00
Peacock At Fountain, Sugar, Purple	90.00
Peacock At Fountain, Table Set, Marigold, 4 Piece	275.00
Peacock At Fountain, Table Set, Purple, 4 Piece	560.00

Peacock At Fountain, Tumbler, Amethyst .... 48.00 To 50.00
Peacock At Fountain, Tumbler, Cobalt Blue .... 30.00 To 50.00
Peacock At Fountain, Tumbler, Marigold 24.00
Peacock At Fountain, Tumbler, Purple 35.00
Peacock At Fountain, Water Set, Blue, 7 Piece .... 350.00 To 365.00
Peacock At Fountain, Water Set, Marigold 365.00
Peacock At Fountain, Water Set, Signed, Purple, 7 Piece 535.00
    PEACOCK ON FENCE, see Peacock
Peacock Tail, Bonbon, Marigold 29.00
Peacock Tail, Bowl, Cobalt Blue, 9 In. 65.00
Peacock Tail, Bowl, Marigold, 10 In. 20.00
Peacock Tail, Compote, Amethyst 65.00
Peacock Tail, Compote, Cobalt Blue .... 30.00 To 48.00
Peacock Tail, Nappy, Amethyst 25.00
Peacock, Bowl, Marigold, 8 In. 32.00
Peacock, Bowl, Marigold, 9 In. 75.00
Peacock, Plate, Amethyst, 9 In. 165.00
Peacock, Plate, Ice Green, 9 In. 250.00
Peacock, Plate, Marigold, 9 1/2 In. 145.00
Peacock, Plate, Northwood, Ice Green, 9 1/2 In. .... 235.00 To 245.00
Peacock, Plate, Purple, 9 1/2 In. 190.00
Peacock, Plate, White, 8 1/2 In. 295.00
Peacock, Plate, White, 9 1/2 In. 240.00
Peacock, Tumbler, Amethyst 65.00
Peacock, Tumbler, Cobalt Blue 35.00
Peacock, Tumbler, Purple 65.00
Peacock, Vase, Purple, 8 In. 25.00
Peacock, Water Set, Fluted, Amethyst, 7 Piece 1500.00
Persian Garden, Bowl, Ice Cream, White, 6 In. .... 45.00 To 65.00
Persian Garden, Bowl, Punch, Purple 40.00
Persian Garden, Bowl, Ruffled, White, 5 In. 60.00
Persian Garden, Bowl, White, 11 In. .... 110.00 To 235.00
Persian Garden, Bowl, 6-Petal, White, 8 In. 45.00
Persian Garden, Plate, Chop, Purple 2000.00
Persian Garden, Plate, Marigold, 6 1/2 In. .... 30.00 To 50.00
Persian Garden, Plate, Marigold, 7 In. 60.00
Persian Garden, Plate, Peach, 6 1/2 In. 55.00
Persian Garden, Plate, Purple, 6 In. 135.00
Persian Garden, Plate, White, 6 1/2 In. 85.00
Petals, Bowl, White, 8 1/2 In., Set Of 6 .... 50.00
    PINE CONE WREATH, see Pine Cone
Pineapple, Bonbon, Peach, 5 In. 60.00
Pineapple, Pitcher, Marigold, 4 1/2 In. 42.00
Pineapple, Plate, Purple, 8 In. 95.00
Pinecone, Plate, Green, 6 In. .... 45.00 To 75.00
Pinecone, Plate, Marigold, 6 1/2 In. .... 35.00 To 55.00
Pinecone, Plate, Scalloped Rim, Amethyst, 6 In. 65.00
Poinsetta, Bowl, 3-Footed, Marigold, 8 1/2 In. 85.00
Poinsetta, Pitcher, Milk, Green 70.00
Poinsetta, Pitcher, Milk, Marigold .... 55.00 To 80.00
Poinsetta, Pitcher, Milk, Purple 145.00
Poinsetta, Pitcher, Milk, Smoky 125.00
    POLKA DOT, see Inverted Coin Dot
Polo Ashtray, Ashtray, Aqua 20.00
Polo Ashtray, Ashtray, Marigold 17.50
Pond Lily, Bonbon, Cobalt Blue 35.00
Pond Lily, Bonbon, 2-Handled, White .... 70.00 To 75.00
    PONY ROSETTE, see Pony
Pony, Bowl, Marigold, 8 1/2 In. .... 55.00 To 60.00
Pony, Bowl, Marigold, 9 In. 58.00
Pony, Plate, Marigold, 9 In. 65.00
    POPPY SCROLL, see Poppy
Poppy, Bowl, Marigold, 7 In. 20.00

Poppy, Dish, Pickle, Marigold .... 39.00 To 45.00
Primrose, Bowl, Green, 10 In. 85.00
Primrose, Bowl, Marigold, 10 In. 85.00
Primrose, Bowl, Purple, 10 In. .... 85.00 To 110.00
    PRINCESS LACE, see Octagon
Pulled Loop, Vase, Marigold, 11 1/2 In. 12.00
Pulled Loop, Vase, Marigold, 12 In. 18.00
Pulled Loop, Vase, Peach, 10 In. 34.00
Puzzle, Bonbon, Footed, Purple 35.00
Puzzle, Bonbon, Footed, White 55.00
Question Mark, Bonbon, Handled, White 45.00
Question Mark, Bonbon, 2-Handled, Marigold, 5 1/8 In. 25.00
Question Mark, Compote, White, 6 X 3 In. 45.00
Question Mark, Compote, 2-Handled, Marigold, 7 In. 35.00
Quill, Tumbler, Marigold 75.00
Rambler Rose, Pitcher, Water, Aqua 325.00
Rambler Rose, Tumbler, Amethyst 45.00
Rambler Rose, Tumbler, Cobalt Blue 35.00
Rambler Rose, Tumbler, Marigold .... 18.00 To 22.00
Rambler Rose, Water Set, Marigold, 7 Piece 125.00
Ranger, Pitcher, Milk, Marigold 30.00
Ranger, Water Set, Marigold, 7 Piece 1600.00
Raspberry, Pitcher, Milk, Marigold .... 98.00 To 115.00
Raspberry, Pitcher, Water, Ice Green 2500.00
Raspberry, Saucer, Purple 68.50
Raspberry, Tumbler, Amethyst .... 32.00 To 35.00
Raspberry, Tumbler, Green .... 10.00 To 55.00
Raspberry, Tumbler, Purple .... 35.00 To 50.00
Raspberry, Water Set, Marigold, 7 Piece 225.00
Rays & Ribbon, Bowl, Green, 10 In. 72.50
Rays & Ribbon, Bowl, Purple, 10 In. 55.00
Ribbon Tie, Bowl, Cobalt Blue, 8 In. 40.00
Ribbon Tie, Bowl, Marigold, 9 In. 47.50
Ribbon Tie, Bowl, Ruffled Edge, Green, 9 In. 75.00
Ripple, Bowl, Green, 9 In. 35.00
Ripple, Vase, Amethyst, 8 1/2 In. 40.00
    ROBIN RED BREAST, see Robin
Robin, Mug, Marigold .... 49.00 To 55.00
Robin, Pitcher, Water, Marigold 295.00
Robin, Tumbler, Marigold 58.50
Robin, Water Set, White, 7 Piece 75.00
Rococo, Bowl, Marigold, 5 In. 27.00
Rosalind, Bowl, Amethyst, 10 1/2 In. 80.00
Rosalind, Bowl, Ruffled, Purple, 10 In. 110.00
    ROSE & RUFFLES, see Open Rose
Rose Garden, Pitcher, Marigold 900.00
Rose Panels, Compote, Marigold, 6 3/4 X 9 In. 75.00
Rose Show, Plate, Cobalt Blue, 9 In. 190.00
Rose Show, Plate, Purple, 9 3/4 In. 265.00
Rose Spray, Compote, Marigold 30.00
Rose Spray, Compote, White 75.00
    ROSES & LOOPS, see Double-Stem Rose
Round-Up, Plate, Marigold, 9 In. 110.00
Rustic, Vase, Marigold, Scalloped & Fluted, 12 In. 15.00
Rustic, Vase, Purple, 11 In. 18.00
S-Repeat, Creamer, Purple 64.00
S-Repeat, Cup, Punch, Amethyst 35.00
    SAILBOAT & WINDMILL, see Sailboats
Sailboats, Bowl, Ruffled, Rainbow, Marigold, 6 In. 60.00
Sailboats, Plate, Cobalt Blue, 6 In. 250.00
Sailboats, Wine, Marigold .... 25.00 To 28.00
Sailing Ship, Plate, Marigold, 7 In. 40.00
Scale Band, Pitcher, Marigold 55.00

Scale Band, Water Set, Marigold, 6 Piece 235.00
Scales, Bowl, Marigold, 6 1/2 In. 20.00
     SCROLL EMBOSSED, see Eastern Star
     SEA LANES, see Little Fishes
Seacoast, Tray, Pin, Green 150.00
     SHASTA DAISY, see Garden Mums
Shell & Jewel, Sugar & Creamer, Covered, Green 40.00
     SHELL & SAND, see Shell, Carnival
     SHELL & WILD ROSE, see Wild Rose
Shell, Carnival Bowl, Green, 7 In. 40.00
Ship & Stars, Plate, Marigold, 8 In. 20.00
Singing Birds, Bowl, Berry, Marigold 34.00
Singing Birds, Butter, Covered, Amethyst .... 160.00 To 175.00
Singing Birds, Creamer, Marigold 65.00
Singing Birds, Creamer, Purple .... 40.00 To 80.00
Singing Birds, Mug, Amethyst .... 52.00 To 65.00
Singing Birds, Mug, Cobalt Blue .... 55.00 To 75.00
Singing Birds, Mug, Ice Blue 550.00
Singing Birds, Mug, Lavender 135.00
Singing Birds, Mug, Marigold .... 40.00 To 60.00
Singing Birds, Mug, Purple .... 45.00 To 65.00
Singing Birds, Pitcher, Marigold 225.00
Singing Birds, Pitcher, Water, Northwood, Green 250.00
Singing Birds, Spooner, Marigold 65.00
Singing Birds, Sugar, Covered, Marigold .... 60.00 To 75.00
Singing Birds, Sugar, Covered, Purple 80.00
Singing Birds, Tumbler, Ice Green 55.00
Singing Birds, Tumbler, Marked N, Green 35.00
Singing Birds, Tumbler, Purple .... 30.00 To 47.00
Singing Birds, Water Set, Green, 7 Piece .... 495.00 To 625.00
Single Flower, Bowl, Candy Ribbon Edge, Peach 40.00
Six Petals, Bowl, Peach, 8 1/2 In. 65.00
Six Petals, Bowl, Red, 8 1/2 In. 45.00
Six Petals, Bowl, White, 8 1/2 In. .... 42.00 To 50.00
Ski-Star, Bowl, Compass Pattern Outside, Peach, 10 1/2 In. 300.00
Ski-Star, Bowl, Dome-Footed, Peach, 9 In. 68.00
Ski-Star, Bowl, Purple, 11 In. 85.00
Ski-Star, Bowl, Ruffled, Peach, 5 1/2 In. 42.00
Ski-Star, Bowl, Ruffled, Peach, 10 1/2 In. 95.00
Soda Gold, Spittoon, 6-Sided Base, Marigold, 4 X 7 In. 25.00
Soda Gold, Water Set, Flat Bottom, Marigold, 7 Piece 285.00
     SPIDER WEB, see Soda Gold
Split Diamond, Butter, Marigold 75.00
     SPRING FLOWERS, see Bouquet
Springtime, Bowl, Berry, Purple, 4 1/2 In. 60.00
Springtime, Butter, Amethyst, Marked N 40.00
Springtime, Butter, Marigold 165.00
Springtime, Pitcher, Purple 450.00
Springtime, Pitcher, Water, Marigold .... 275.00 To 325.00
Springtime, Water Set, Marigold, 7 Piece 700.00
Stag & Holly, Bowl, Cobalt Blue, 7 1/2 In. 160.00
Stag & Holly, Bowl, Cobalt Blue, 10 In. 225.00
Stag & Holly, Bowl, Footed, Amber, 11 In. 425.00
Stag & Holly, Bowl, Footed, Green, 9 In. 95.00
Stag & Holly, Bowl, Footed, Marigold, 11 In. .... 120.00 To 125.00
Stag & Holly, Bowl, Footed, Marigold, 7 1/2 In. 50.00
Stag & Holly, Bowl, Footed, Purple, 10 In. 85.00
Stag & Holly, Bowl, Footed, Vaseline, 11 In. 235.00
Stag & Holly, Bowl, Green, 10 In. 225.00
Stag & Holly, Bowl, Marigold, 10 In. .... 85.00 To 110.00
Stag & Holly, Bowl, Marigold, 13 In. 95.00
Stag & Holly, Bowl, Scalloped Edge, 3-Footed, Cobalt Blue 175.00
Stag & Holly, Bowl, 3-Footed, Green, 8 In. 100.00

Stag & Holly, Plate, Chop, Footed, Marigold, 12 In. 195.00
Stag & Holly, Rose Bowl, Footed, Cobalt Blue 685.00
Stag & Holly, Rose Bowl, Marigold 185.00
Star & File, Creamer, Marigold 20.00
Star & File, Wine, Marigold 38.00
Star Of David & Bows, Bowl, Amethyst, 9 In. 40.00
Star Of David & Bows, Bowl, Dome Base, Marked, Amethyst, 7 In. 75.00
Star Of David & Bows, Bowl, Marigold, 7 1/2 In. 30.00
Star Of David & Bows, Bowl, Smoky, 8 In. 28.00
Star Of David & Bows, Pitcher, Milk, Clambroth 45.00
Star Of David & Bows, Pitcher, Milk, Marigold .... 20.00 To 45.00
Star Of David & Bows, Pitcher, Milk, Smoky .... 45.00 To 50.00
Star Of David & Bows, Tankard, Marigold 25.00
Star Of David & Bows, Tumbler, Marigold 16.00
    STAR OF DAVID MEDALLION, see Star of David & Bows
Starflower, Pitcher, Cobalt Blue 1100.00
    STIPPLED CLEMATIS, see Little Stars
    STIPPLED DIAMOND & FLOWER, see Little Flowers
Stippled Flower, Bowl, Peach, 7 In. .... 28.00 To 55.00
    STIPPLED LEAF & BEADS, see Leaf & Beads
    STIPPLED LEAF, see Leaf Tiers
    STIPPLED ORANGE, see Orange Peel
    STIPPLED POSY & PODS, see Four Flowers
Stippled Rays, Bonbon, Flat Base, Scalloped Edge, Marigold 25.00
Stippled Rays, Bowl, Amethyst, 6 In. 20.00
Stippled Rays, Bowl, Amethyst, 8 1/2 In. .... 33.00 To 35.00
Stippled Rays, Bowl, Dome Foot, Green, 10 In. 60.00
Stippled Rays, Bowl, Fluted, Purple, 6 In. 35.00
Stippled Rays, Bowl, Fruit, Purple, 10 1/2 In. 28.00
Stippled Rays, Bowl, Green, 6 1/4 In. 25.00
Stippled Rays, Bowl, Green, 10 In. 35.00
Stippled Rays, Bowl, Marked N, Amethyst, 9 1/4 In. 70.00
Stippled Rays, Bowl, Northwood, Purple, 9 In. 47.00
Stippled Rays, Bowl, Red, 5 In. 195.00
Stippled Rays, Bowl, Ruffled, Crimped, Amethyst, 8 In. 38.00
Stippled Rays, Bowl, Ruffled, Fluted, Square, Green, 10 1/2 In. 60.00
Stippled Rays, Bowl, Ruffled, Marigold, 8 1/2 In. 35.00
Stippled Rays, Sherbet, Marigold 32.50
Stippled Rays, Sugar & Creamer, Footed, Marigold 38.00
Stippled Rays, Sugar & Creamer, Marigold 27.50
    STIPPLED RIBBONS & RAYS, see Rays & Ribbons
Stork & Rushes, Cup, Marigold 32.50
Stork & Rushes, Cup, Punch, Marigold 16.00
Stork & Rushes, Dish, Candy, Hat Shaped, Marigold 25.00
Stork & Rushes, Mug, Marigold .... 18.00 To 35.00
Stork & Rushes, Tumbler, Cobalt Blue .... 25.00 To 49.00
Stork & Rushes, Tumbler, Marigold .... 20.00 To 30.00
Stork & Rushes, Tumbler, Purple 35.00
Stork & Rushes, Vase, Marigold, 7 In. 24.00
Stork & Rushes, Water Set, Cobalt Blue, 7 Piece 450.00
Stork, Vase, Marigold, 7 1/2 In. .... 30.00 To 45.00
    STRAWBERRY, see Wild Strawberry
    SUNFLOWER, see Dandelion
    SUNFLOWER & WHEAT, see Fieldflower
Sunflower Diamond, Vase, Marigold, 12 In. 65.00
    SUNFLOWER-WHEAT-CLOVER, see Harvest Flower
Sunflower, Bowl, Spatula Footed, Amethyst, 8 1/4 In. 87.00
Sunflower, Bowl, 3-Footed, Marigold, 7 In. 45.00
Swan, Carnival, Bowl, Amethyst, 10 In. 425.00
Swan, Carnival, Bowl, Green, 8 In. 275.00
Swan, Carnival, Bowl, Marigold, 10 In. 170.00
Swan, Dish, Covered, Marigold 125.00

Swirled Hobnail, Rose Bowl, Purple .... 225.00 To 295.00
TADPOLE, see Tornado
Tankard Pitcher Set, Marigold, 6 Piece 195.00
Target, Vase, Marigold, 10 In. 13.00
Target, Vase, Peach 40.00
Ten Mums, Bowl, Cobalt Blue, 10 In. 95.00
Ten Mums, Bowl, Scalloped, Cobalt Blue, 10 1/2 In. 125.00
Ten Mums, Pitcher, Water, White 1150.00
Ten Mums, Water Set, Cobalt Blue, 7 Piece 1250.00
Thistle & Lotus, Bowl, Marigold, 7 In. 45.00
Thistle & Thorn, Creamer, Marigold 22.00
Thistle & Thorn, Dish, Nut, Marigold .... 25.00 To 35.00
Thistle, Bowl, Cobalt Blue, 2 1/2 X 8 In. 55.00
Thistle, Bowl, Green, 8 In. 55.00
Thistle, Bowl, Marigold, 6 1/2 In. 47.00
Thistle, Bowl, Marigold, 9 In. 22.00
Thistle, Bowl, Ruffled, Amethyst, 8 3/4 In. 50.00
Thistle, Compote, Pie Crust Edge, Green 65.00
Three Fruits, Bowl, Basket Weave Outside, Marigold, 8 1/2 In. 45.00
Three Fruits, Bowl, Booted, Stippled, Aqua, 9 In. 340.00
Three Fruits, Bowl, Grape Border, Marigold, 8 1/2 In. 35.00
Three Fruits, Bowl, Green, 9 1/2 In. 45.00
Three Fruits, Bowl, Scalloped, Purple, 8 3/4 In. 84.00
Three Fruits, Bowl, White, 9 In. 125.00
Three Fruits, Plate, Green, 9 1/4 In. 110.00
Three Fruits, Plate, Marigold, 9 1/2 In. 75.00
Three Fruits, Plate, Purple, 9 1/4 In. 89.00
Three Fruits, Plate, Stippled, Marigold, 8 3/4 In. 80.00
Three Fruits, Plate, 12-Sided, Amethyst, 1 1/2 X 9 1/4 In. 125.00
Three Fruits, Plate, 12-Sided, Marigold .... 55.00 To 100.00
Thumbprint & Oval, Vase, Marigold 98.00
Tiger Lily, Pitcher, Water, Amethyst 29.50
Tiger Lily, Pitcher, Water, Marigold 100.00
Tiger Lily, Tumbler, Green 28.00
Tiger Lily, Tumbler, Marigold .... 18.00 To 39.00
Tornado, Vase, Marigold, 6 1/2 In. 180.00
Tornado, Vase, Purple 39.00
Tree Trunk, Vase, Aqua, 10 In. 35.00
Tree Trunk, Vase, Cobalt Blue, 13 In. 40.00
Tree Trunk, Vase, Funeral, Green, 13 In., Pair 175.00
Tree Trunk, Vase, Marigold, 11 In. 10.00
Tree Trunk, Vase, Purple, 13 1/2 X 6 In. 75.00
Tree-Of-Life, Pitcher, Water, Marigold 35.00
Treebark, Epergne, Peach .... 185.00 To 200.00
Treebark, Pitcher, Marigold .... 25.00 To 60.00
Treebark, Tumbler, Marigold .... 10.00 To 20.00
Treebark, Vase, Cobalt Blue, 6 1/2 In. 25.00
Trout & Fly, Bowl, Amethyst, 9 1/8 In. 300.00
Trout & Fly, Bowl, Marigold, 9 In. .... 225.00 To 250.00
TWO BAND, see Scale Band
Two Flowers, Bowl, Footed, Marigold, 10 In. 70.00
Two Flowers, Bowl, Ruffled Rim, Footed, Marigold, 10 In. 40.00
Two Flowers, Plate, Marigold, 9 In. 495.00
Two Flowers, Rose Bowl, Spatula Footed, Marigold 40.00
Two Fruits, Bonbon, Divided, Handled, Cobalt Blue 70.00
Victorian, Bowl, Peach, 11 In. 2350.00
Victorian, Bowl, Purple, 11 In. 250.00
Vineyard, Pitcher, Water, Marigold 65.00
Vineyard, Tumbler, Marigold .... 16.00 To 28.00
Vineyard, Water Set, Marigold, 7 Piece .... 275.00 To 325.00
Vintage Banded, Mug, Marigold 30.00
Vintage, Bowl, Cobalt Blue, 9 In. .... 45.00 To 75.00
Vintage, Bowl, Fluted, Purple, 9 In. 55.00

Vintage, Bowl, Grape Cluster, Center Leaf, Green, 8 1/2 In. 65.00
Vintage, Bowl, Green, 9 In. 30.00
Vintage, Bowl, Red, 10 In. 450.00
Vintage, Bowl, Ruffled, Marigold, 8 3/4 In. 30.00
Vintage, Bowl, Ruffled, Purple, 6 In. 35.00
Vintage, Candleholder, Marigold 20.00
Vintage, Compote, Ruffled, Pedestal, Amethyst, 7 In. 60.00
Vintage, Dish, Nut, Footed, Marigold 38.00
Vintage, Dish, Nut, 3-Footed, Cobalt Blue 49.00
Vintage, Dish, Nut, 6-Footed, Amethyst .... 70.00 To 72.00
Vintage, Dish, Nut, 6-Footed, Purple 65.00
Vintage, Epergne, Lily, Amethyst 90.00
Vintage, Epergne, Marigold 100.00
Vintage, Ferner, 3-Footed, Cobalt Blue 45.00
Vintage, Jar, Powder, Covered, Marigold 40.00
Vintage, Plate, Amethyst, 7 In. 110.00
Vintage, Plate, Cobalt Blue, 7 1/2 In. 55.00
Vintage, Plate, Marigold, 7 1/2 In. .... 55.00 To 125.00
Vintage, Rose Bowl, Cobalt Blue .... 40.00 To 85.00
Vintage, Rose Bowl, Footed, White 80.00
Vintage, Rose Bowl, Purple .... 60.00 To 85.00
Vintage, Rose Bowl, White .... 55.00 To 60.00
Vintage, Wine, Purple, Set Of 6 .... 140.00
     WAFFLE BAND, see Lustre Flute
Waffle Block, Punch Set, Marigold, 8 Piece 100.00
Water Lily, Dish, Crimped, Footed, Marigold, 6 1/2 In. 18.00
Water Lily, Sauce, Footed, Red 375.00
Waterlily & Cattails, Banana Boat, Marigold, 11 In. 110.00
Waterlily & Cattails, Bowl, Banana, Marigold 225.00
Waterlily & Cattails, Sauce, Marigold, 5 1/2 In. 25.00
Waterlily & Cattails, Toothpick, Marigold 80.00
Waterlily & Cattails, Tumbler, Marigold .... 12.00 To 26.00
Waterlily & Cattails, Water Set, Marigold, 7 Piece 485.00
Whirling Leaves, Bowl, Amethyst, 9 In. 85.00
Whirling Leaves, Bowl, Green, 9 1/2 In. 65.00
Whirling Leaves, Bowl, Green, 11 In. 80.00
Whirling Leaves, Bowl, Marigold, 11 In. 60.00
Whirling Leaves, Bowl, Tricornered, Marigold, 10 In. 85.00
Wide Panel, Goblet, Marigold 25.00
Wide Panel, Rose Bowl, Marigold 12.00
Wild Blackberry, Bowl, Marigold, 8 In. 65.00
     WILD GRAPES, see Grape Leaves
Wild Rose, Bowl, Footed, Green, 11 In. 85.00
Wild Rose, Bowl, Open Heart Edge, Marigold, 7 X 3 3/4 In. 58.00
Wild Rose, Bowl, Openwork Edge, Green, 5 1/2 In. 50.00
Wild Rose, Dish, Heart Shaped, Footed, Green 40.00
Wild Rose, Lamp, 3 Lady Medallion, Amethyst 1500.00
Wild Strawberry, Berry Set, N Mark, Marigold, 6 Piece 149.00
Wild Strawberry, Bowl, Fluted, Purple, 6 In. 75.00
Wild Strawberry, Bowl, Purple, 9 In. 78.00
Wild Strawberry, Compote, Amethyst, 4 X 6 1/2 In. 265.00
Wild Strawberry, Plate, Amethyst, 8 1/2 In. 120.00
Wild Strawberry, Plate, Basket Weave Outside, Amethyst, 9 In. 125.00
Wild Strawberry, Plate, Green, 9 In. .... 65.00 To 95.00
Wild Strawberry, Plate, Handled, Green, 7 1/2 In. 100.00
Wild Strawberry, Plate, Handled, Marigold, 7 1/2 In. 85.00
Wild Strawberry, Plate, Marigold, 9 In. 60.00
Wild Strawberry, Plate, Marked N, Marigold, 8 1/2 In. 55.00
Windflower, Bowl, Marigold, 8 In. 55.00
Windflower, Bowl, Purple, 8 3/4 In. 45.00
Windflower, Nappy, Handled, Marigold .... 25.00 To 35.00
Windflower, Plate, Cobalt Blue, 9 In. .... 95.00 To 110.00
Windflower, Plate, Marigold, 8 In. 65.00

Windflower, Plate, Marigold, 9 In. .... 35.00 To 75.00
Windflower, Sauce, Marigold 50.00
Windflower, Sauce, Purple 80.00
    WINDMILL MEDALLION, see Windmill
Windmill, Pitcher, Water, Marigold 75.00
Windmill, Tumbler, Marigold 15.00
Wine & Roses, Goblet, Marigold 35.00
Wishbone & Spades, Bowl, 3-Footed, Marigold, 8 In. 65.00
Wishbone & Spades, Plate, Chop, Purple .... 695.00 To 800.00
Wishbone, Bowl, Footed, Amethyst, 8 1/2 In. 68.00
Wishbone, Bowl, Footed, Cobalt Blue, 8 In. 60.00
Wishbone, Bowl, Footed, White, 8 1/2 In. 475.00
Wishbone, Bowl, Green, 8 In. 85.00
Wishbone, Bowl, Pie Crust Edge, Marigold, 9 1/2 In. 50.00
Wishbone, Plate, Footed, Marigold, 9 In. 195.00
Wishbone, Plate, Footed, Purple, 9 In. 125.00
Wishbone, Tumbler, Marked N, Amethyst 130.00
Wishbone, Tumbler, Purple 135.00
    WISTERIA & LATTICE, see Wisteria
Wisteria, Tumbler, Ice Blue 400.00
Wreath Of Roses, Bonbon, Amethyst 28.00
Wreath Of Roses, Bonbon, 2-Handled, Green 40.00
Wreath Of Roses, Compote, Marigold .... 25.00 To 38.00
Wreath Of Roses, Compote, 2-Handled, Cobalt Blue, 8 In. 45.00
Wreath Of Roses, Cup, Punch, Green 15.00
Wreath Of Roses, Punch Set, Cobalt Blue, 10 Piece 350.00
Wreath Of Roses, Punch Set, Vintage Interior, Purple, 8 Pc. 380.00
Wreath Of Roses, Rose Bowl, Marigold .... 35.00 To 40.00
Wreathed Cherry, Banana Boat, White .... 90.00 To 125.00
Wreathed Cherry, Bowl, Banana, Purple, 12 1/4 In .... 90.00 To 150.00
Wreathed Cherry, Creamer, Purple 65.00
Wreathed Cherry, Pitcher, Gold Trim, White 375.00
Wreathed Cherry, Tumbler, Purple 45.00
Zig-Zag, Pitcher, Enamel Design, Green 265.00
Zig-Zag, Pitcher, Enamel Design, Ice Green 360.00
Zippered Loop Lamp, Lamp, Marigold .... 325.00 To 365.00

CAROUSEL, Bear, Wood, Carved 4000.00
Children's, Limonair Band Organ, 34-Key, 8 Music Books 6500.00
Clown, Hand-Carved Wooden Face 225.00
Crest, Gilded Wood Carving, 7 Ft.Long 185.00
Horse, Happy Jumper, Herschell, Spillman, Brass Pole, Cream Colored 2600.00
Horse, Mangel, Metal Kiddie 250.00
Horse, Spillman 2250.00
Horse, Stander 4200.00
Pony & Cart, Mangel 50.00
Seat, Ferris Wheel, Yellow 1200.00
Seat, Swan, Attached Pair 1200.00

CARRIAGE, Baby, Heywood 300.00
Baby, High Wheel, Velvet Upholstered, Parasol, 1890s, Reed 550.00
Baby, Wicker, Extra Large 675.00
Baby, With Umbrella, Wicker 850.00
Brougham, 2-Passenger 2800.00
Buggy, Doctor's 600.00
Buggy, Double, Iron & Wooden Handles, Wooden Wheels 650.00
Buggy, Jump Seat 1400.00
Child's Pull, Brass Label, Smith & Hunt, Guilford, Vt., 1874 .... 450.00
Cutter, 1-Horse, Red Leather Upholstered 1500.00
Hearse, Horse-Drawn 4700.00
Hotdog Stand, Sidewalks Of N.Y., Wooden Wheels, Umbrella 1800.00
School Bus, Horse-Drawn 3500.00
Sleigh, Clamshell, Ryegate, Vermont 220.00

Stroller, Child's, Wicker 195.00
Stroller, Wicker 150.00
Surrey, Touring 1150.00
Surrey, 1873 .... 5000.00
U.S.Mail, Horse-Drawn 700.00
Wagon, Businessman's, Spring 1200.00
Wagon, Delivery, With Umbrella 800.00
Wagon, Grain, C.1885 .... 575.00

*Cased glass is made with one thin layer of glass over another layer or layers
of colored glass. Many types of art glass were cased. Cased glass is
usually a well-made piece by a reputable factory.*

CASED GLASS, Vase, Pink, Gold Dust, Air Traps, 9 X 5 In. 119.00

CASH REGISTER, Amount Of Sale Plate On Front, Wooden 800.00
  Michigan, Model 79, Candy Store, Brass Plated 450.00
  National, Barbershop, 5 Cents To 1 Dollar, 15 Cent Haircut 550.00
  National, Floor Model, 5-Drawer, Brass & Oak 1800.00
  National, Model 3, Mahogany, Brass Trim, C.1891 .... 2000.00
  National, Model 5, Pinwheel Design, Candy Store Size, Brass 900.00
  National, Model 44, Brass 450.00
  National, Model 130b, 1 Dollar 550.00
  National, Model 211, Barbershop, Adding, Cast-Iron Keys 650.00
  National, Model 311, Candy Store, Brass 900.00
  National, Model 313, Ice Cream Parlor 750.00
  National, Model 327, Original Marquee, Nickel Plated 975.00
  National, Model 336, Print-Out Device, 1 Cent To 3 Dollars 250.00
  National, Model 337 .... 850.00
  National, Model 349, Double Drawer 795.00
  National, Model 411, Crank Style, Small 450.00
  National, Model 522-2c 2500.00
  National, Model 542-5, Floor Model, Brass Feet, Oak 1000.00
  National, Snub Nose, Brass 425.00
  National, White Marble Slab, Brass, Oak Trim, C.1900 .... 900.00
  Ohmer, Clock 85.00
  Premier Jr. 125.00
  St.Louis, Candy Store Size, Brass 450.00
  Sun, Display Case Ends, Tally, Combination Lock, 1880 .... 595.00
  3 Oak Drawers, Marble Top, Brass, Early 1900 .... 3250.00

*Castor sets have been known as early as 1705. Most of those found today
date from Victorian times. A castor set usually consists of a silver plated
frame that holds three to seven condiment bottles. The pickle castor is a
single glass jar about six inches high, held in a silver frame. A cover and
tongs were kept with the jar. They were popular from 1890 to 1900.*

CASTOR SET, see also various Porcelain and Glass categories
CASTOR SET, 4-Bottle, Beaded Trim, Silver Plated Frame, 9 1/2 In. 50.00
  4-Bottle, Clear, Shield, Stopper, Pewter Stand 95.00
  4-Bottle, Cut & Etched, Wilcox Silver Plated Frame 110.00
  4-Bottle, Drape Pattern, Miniature 70.00
  4-Bottle, Electroplated Square Frame, 8 In. 88.00
  4-Bottle, Opalescent, Stripe, Sterling Silver Spoon 135.00
  4-Bottle, Revolving, Etched Floret, Pewter Frame, 10 In. 125.00
  4-Bottle, Swirl Design, Gothic Arch Bottles, Pewter Top 95.00
  4-Bottle, Thumbprint, Ruby 275.00
  5-Bottle, Center Handle, Cut-Out Figural Flowers, Wm. Rogers 140.00
  5-Bottle, Gothic Bottles, I.Trask, Pewter 195.00
  5-Bottle, Pewter Holder 60.00
  5-Bottle, Revolving, Mercury Glass, Dated 1861 .... 135.00
  5-Bottle, Rotating Stand, Silver Plated Frame 90.00
  5-Bottle, Victorian, Silver Plated, Lily-Of-The-Valley Design 115.00
  6-Bottle, Cut & Etched, Silver Plated Holder 150.00
  6-Bottle, Decorated Holder, Ornate Bail, Middletown 185.00

6-Bottle, Engraved, Silver Plated Holder, Meriden, 15 1/4 In. 85.00
6-Bottle, Etched Bottles, Garden Scene Skirt, Meriden Holder 165.00
6-Bottle, Etched, Original Stoppers, Silver Plated Stand 95.00
6-Bottle, Silver Plated Holder, Loop Bail 350.00

CASTOR, PICKLE, see also various Glass categories

CASTOR, Pickle, Bell Shape Bottle, Enameled Floral, Rubena 110.00
Pickle, Cane Pattern Insert, Cranberry Glass, Meriden Frame & Tongs 150.00
Pickle, Clear Insert, Tongs, Footed, Rogers 70.00
Pickle, Cranberry Inverted Thumbprint Jar, Silver Plated Loop Frame 260.00
Pickle, Daisy & Button Insert, Rockford Silver Holder 225.00
Pickle, Diamond Insert, Tongs, Silver Plated Frame, 11 In. 85.00
Pickle, Diamond-Quilted Pattern, Tongs, Silver Plated 225.00
Pickle, Double 75.00
Pickle, Double Inserts, Fork, Silver Plated Holder 125.00
Pickle, Double, Footed, Silver Plated Frame, Handle 45.00
Pickle, Embossed Birds & Flowers, Paneled Insert, Silver Plated Lid 75.00
Pickle, Enameled Jar, Silver Plated Holder & Tongs, Southington 185.00
Pickle, Enameled, Blue 295.00
Pickle, Glass Insert, Silver Plated Holder 65.00
Pickle, Inverted Thumbprint, Allover Enameling, Rubena, Frame 395.00
Pickle, Inverted Thumbprint, Figure 8 Form, Cranberry, 5 In. 60.00
Pickle, Mother-Of-Pearl Jar, Green & Gold 300.00
Pickle, Reverse Swirl, Frame & Tongs, Opalescent Blue 145.00
Pickle, Rose In Snow Pattern 95.00
Pickle, Royal Ivy Jar, Bowknot Frame, Clear 150.00
Pickle, Royal Oak, Cranberry, Frosted, Marked Northwood 250.00
Pickle, Rubena Jar, Enameled 325.00
Pickle, Rubena To Clear, Royal Oak, Silver Plated Frame 225.00
Pickle, Ruby Glass Insert, Footed Frame, Tongs, Silver Plated 275.00
Pickle, Thumbprint, Cranberry Glass, Silver Plated Holder 135.00
Pickle, Thumbprint, Ruby Glass, Etched 450.00
Pickle, Victorian, Silver Plated Handle & Fork 66.00
Pickle, Windows Pattern, Cranberry Opalescent 225.00
CATALOG, see Paper, Catalog
CAUGHLEY, see Salopian

The firm Cauldon Limited worked in Staffordshire, Great Britain,
and went through many name changes. John Ridgway made porcelain at
Cauldon Place, Hanley, until 1855. The firm of John Ridgway,
Bates and Co. of Cauldon Place worked from 1856 to 1859. It became
Bates, Brown-Westhead, Moore and Co. from 1859 to 1862. Brown-
Westhead, Moore and Co. worked from 1862 to 1904. About 1890 this firm
started using the word "Cauldon" or "Cauldon ware" as part of the mark.
Cauldon Ltd. worked from 1905 to 1920, Cauldon Potteries from 1920
to 1962.

CAULDON, see also Indian Tree
CAULDON, Plate, Gold Border, 9 In., Set Of 12 .... 125.00
Spooner, Blue & White 35.00

Celadon is a Chinese porcelain having a velvet-textured green-gray glaze.
Japanese, Korean, and other factories also made a celadon-colored glaze.

CELADON, Bowl, Oval, Skirted, 9 X 7 In. 110.00
Figurine, Boy, Holding Peach, 4 1/2 In. 50.00
Jardiniere, Everted Rim, Corner Feet, Green Glaze, 15 1/2 In. 110.00
Lamp, Ginger Jar, 1920s 175.00
Planter, Blue & White Scroll, Rectangular, Scroll Feet, 7 In. 110.00
Planter, Blue Lozenges, Scrolls, Scroll Feet, 7 X 10 X 7 In. 70.00
Planter, Blue, Rice Pattern 30.00
Planter, Enameled Lozenges, Scrolled, Footed, 7 X 10 In .... 85.00 To 110.00
Teapot, White Flowers, Dark Green Leaves, Squatty, 4 3/4 In. 135.00
Umbrella Stand, Scroll Band Top, Blue Carp, 25 In. 950.00
Vase, Animal Handles, Cobalt Blue, 9 In. 150.00
Vase, Ovoid, Pale Green Crackled Glaze, C.1900, 12 In. 200.00

Vase, 2 Deer Head Handles, 10 In. 325.00

CELLULOID, Box, Dresser, Art Deco 65.00
  Box, Dresser, Kittens, Pilgrims, 5 In. 32.50
  Box, Ring, Velvet Lined, Ivory, 1 1/4 X 1 1/2 In. 16.00
  Calendar, 1904, Compliments Of The Daily News 8.00
  Doll, Nude, Red Hair, K In Star, Arms Move, 6 In. 15.00
  Dresser Set, Art Deco, Black & Amber Outlining, Pearlized Green 79.00
  Dresser Set, Child's, Green 22.00
  Dresser Set, Green, Black, Gold, Footed Box, Oval Mirror 20.00
  Dresser Set, Including Clock, Ivory, 31 Piece 269.00
  Dresser Set, Mirror, Comb, & Brush 18.00
  Dresser Set, 2 Frames, Perfume, Working Clock, 10 Piece 125.00
  Figurine, Dog, 3 In. 6.00
  Hair Receiver, Amber 8.00
  Hair Receiver, Gold Trim, Amber 5.00
  Hair Receiver, White, Round, 4 In. 10.00
  Hairpin, Arrow Center, Amber, Set Of 4 .... 6.00
  Manicure Set, Oilcloth Case 8.00
  Mirror & Brush, Hand-Painted Bouquet 12.00
  Mirror, Hand, Beveled Glass 6.50
  Mirror, Hand, Green Pearlized, 13 In. 15.00
  Mirror, Hand, Ivory, Beveled Glass 10.00
  Mirror, Shaving, Beveled Glass, Easel Back 15.00
  Nail Set, Amber & Ivory 25.00
  Napkin Ring, Ivory, Round 2.00
  Powder Box & Hair Receiver, Covered, 4 3/4 In.Diam. 6.50
  Powder Jar, Amber, 4 1/2 In. 8.00
  Santa In Sleigh, 2 Reindeer, Boxed 200.00
  Shaving Set, Folding, Soap Insert, Badger Brush, Beveled Mirror 40.00
  Shoehorn, Ivory Handled 3.00
  Shoehorn, Snakeskin Design, Green, 1930s, 16 In. 6.00
  Sweeper Set, Crumb, Fuller 15.00
  Toilet Set, Leather Case, 7 Piece 35.00
  Traveling Set, Complete With Traveling Clock 18.00
  Vanity Set, Tortoiseshell, Boxed 18.00

The Ceramic Art Company of Trenton, New Jersey, was established in 1889 by J. Coxon and W. Lenox, and was an early producer of American Belleek porcelain.

CERAMIC ART CO., Candlestick, Hand-Painted, Art Nouveau, Marked, 6 1/2 In. 125.00
  Condiment Set, Orange Trees, Fruits, Palette Mark 40.00
  Condiment Set, Palette Mark, Gold Rim 40.00
  Dish, Nut, Oval, Pedestal, Handled, Floral, Palette Mark 55.00
  Pitcher, Tankard, Flowers, Palette Mark, 1902 .... 215.00
  Salt, Gold Scalloped Rim, Apple Blossoms, Palette Mark 12.00
  Salt, Rose, Palette Mark, Set Of 6 .... 50.00
  Tankard, Red, Green, & Purple Grapes, White Ground, 14 In. 250.00
  Tray, Dresser, Floral Design, Gold, Palette Mark, 8 X 11 In. 69.50
  Vase, Ball Shape, Green, Florals, Palette Mark, 9 In. 295.00
  Vase, Cream, Gold Side Handles, American, 12 In. 75.00
  Vase, Flowers & Gold Gilt, Handled 450.00

Chalkware is really plaster of Paris decorated with watercolors. The pieces were molded from known Staffordshire and other porcelain models and painted and sold as inexpensive decorations.

CHALKWARE, Ashtray, Pink 4.00
  Bookends, Little Miss Muffet, 7 In. 28.00
  Bookends, Ship 18.00
      CHALKWARE, FIGURINE, see also Kewpie
  Figurine, Boy, Chinese, With Lute, Black Pants, 5 1/2 In. 5.00
  Figurine, Cat, Black Brows & Tail, Brown Coat, Yellow Eyes, 5 In. 355.00

Figurine, Child With Toy, 8 1/2 In. 90.00
Figurine, Dog, Bulldog 20.00
Figurine, Dog, Mastiff 23.00
Figurine, Dog, Spaniel, Black & White, 4 1/2 In. 5.00
Figurine, Dog, Spaniel, Black & White, 5 In. 5.00
Figurine, Dog, Spaniel, Red, Black, & Brown, 7 1/4 In., Pair 220.00
Figurine, Dog, Spaniel, 19th Century, Hollow, 8 1/2 In. 225.00
Figurine, Dog, 1 Standing, 1 Sitting, Polychrome, 7 In., Pair 250.00
Figurine, Dopey, 3 1/2 In. 12.00
Figurine, Girl, Navy Uniform, Remember Pearl Harbor, 1944 .... 11.00
Figurine, Girl, Standing Holding Skirt Out, Lace, 16 In. 70.00
Figurine, Grumpy, 3 1/2 In. 12.00
Figurine, Little Girl, Nude, 10 1/2 In. 10.00
Figurine, Mae West 30.00
Figurine, Owl, Brown, 9 In. .... 18.00 To 180.00
Figurine, Parrot, 13 1/2 In. 18.00
Figurine, Pup, Hound, 5 1/2 In. 3.00
Figurine, Rooster, Carnival, 12 In. 12.00
Figurine, Sailor Boy, 1934, 8 In. 8.00
Figurine, Sailor Girl, 9 In. 6.00
Figurine, Sailor Girl, 10 In. 18.00
Figurine, Scotty 10.00
Figurine, Snow White, Carnival, 14 In. 17.00
Figurine, Snow White, 5 In. 15.00
Figurine, Squirrel, Yellow-Green, Red Tail, 7 In. 660.00
Figurine, Stag, Recumbent, Brown, 17 In. 400.00
Figurine, Woodpecker, On Tree Trunk 28.00
Holder, String, Boy In High Hat 15.00
Holder, String, Girl Wearing Dutch Hat 15.00
Light, Ma & Pa Sitting Beside Fireplace 30.00
Mantel Ornament, Fruits & Leaves, Red, Green, Yellow, Black, 14 In. 1430.00
Vase, Fruit, 10 1/2 In. 12.00
Vase, Squirrel & Fruit, 9 In. 12.00

CHARLIE CHAPLIN, Box, Pencil, Tin .... 30.00 To 50.00
Figurine, 1915, 9 In. 2500.00
Knife, Pocket 65.00
Mirror, Pocket 85.00
Paper Doll, Cutout, Complete 30.00
Plate, Warwick China 65.00
Toy, Windup, Cast-Iron Feet 525.00
Toy, Windup, Tin 85.00
Toy, Windup, Walks, Composition & Metal, 1920s, 11 In. 650.00
Whistle, Tin, Painted 15.50

CHARLIE MCCARTHY, Bank, Mouth Moves, Metal, 1938 .... 95.00
Costume, Detective 12.00
Doll 265.00
Doll, Dummy, Juro, 1963 .... 50.00
Doll, Walker 150.00
Figurine, Chalkware, 12 In. .... 38.00 To 40.00
Game, Radio 15.00
Money, Play, Pack Of 20 .... 5.00
Puppet, Hand, Ideal 24.00
Radio 145.00
Spoon 19.00
Spoon, Figural 9.50
Teaspoon, Silver Plated .... 7.00 To 7.50
Toy, Crazy Car .... 225.00 To 325.00
Toy, Drives Benzine Buggy, Windup, Marx, 1930s 275.00
Toy, In Car, Windup 280.00
Toy, Walker .... 125.00 To 175.00

Chelsea grape pattern was made before 1840. A small bunch of grapes in a raised design, colored with purple or blue luster, is on the border of the white plate. Most of the pieces are unmarked. The pattern is sometimes called Aynsley or Grandmother. Chelsea sprig is similar but has a sprig of flowers instead of the bunch of grapes.

CHELSEA GRAPE, Cake Plate, White & Lavender, 10 In.	33.00
Cup & Saucer	22.00
Cup, 12-Sided, Pink Luster	24.00
Saucer	8.00
Teapot, 10 In.	85.00

CHELSEA KERAMIC ART WORKS, see Dedham

Chelsea porcelain was made in the Chelsea area of London from about 1745 to 1784. Recent copies of this work have been made from the original molds.

CHELSEA, Figurine, Boy Going To Market, Gold Anchor Mark, 7 In.	195.00
Figurine, Cats, Black & White, Red & Gold Pillows, Marked, 3 In.	130.00
Figurine, Court Jester, Gold Anchor, C.1780, 9 In.	375.00

Chinese export porcelain is all the many kinds of porcelain made in China for export to America and Europe in the eighteenth and nineteenth centuries.

CHINESE EXPORT, see also Canton; Celadon; Nanking

CHINESE EXPORT, Basket, Hilly Landscape, Buddha, Cricket, Fruits, 10 In.	412.00
Bottle, Famille Rose, Figure & Boy Attendants, 9 3/4 In.	220.00
Bowl, Barber's, Red, Black, Robin Flying, C.1750, 14 1/4 In.	990.00
Bowl, Black, Yellow, Redman-O'-War, Sea, Clouds, C.1785, 10 In.	770.00
Bowl, Famille Rose, Center Scene Medallion, 10 1/8 In.	330.00
Bowl, Fox Hunting, Strolling Figures, C.1790, 11 In.	990.00
Bowl, Lotus, Pink To Yellow, Blue Ribbon, C.1760, 5 In.	770.00
Bowl, Lotus, Pink, Red Edge, Hibiscus Spray, C.1760, 6 In.	330.00
Bowl, Mandarin Design, Oriental Figures, River, 9 In.	770.00
Bowl, Punch, Porcelain, 18th Century, 11 X 4 3/4 In.	375.00
Bowl, Punch, Sprig Design, Diaperwork Border, C.1790, 11 In.	275.00
Bowl, Stylized Floret, Flower Clusters, 9 3/8 In.	425.00
Bowl, Tobacco Leaf Pattern, Rose, Yellow, Blue, 10 In.	1320.00
Bowl, Waste, Lotus, Pink Petals, Red Scrolls, C.1760, 5 In.	632.00
Box, Artichoke, Overlapping Leaves, Floral Spray, 3 In.	220.00
Box, Condiment, 4-Section, Scene On Cover	75.00
Box, Snuff, Swans, Dogs, Pig, Arms Of Lewin Of Hartford, 2 In.	2200.00
Candlestick, Fruits & Flowers, Red, Puce, Brown, 4 In.	660.00
Charger, Blue, White Ground, Florals & Birds, 12 In.	90.00
Charger, Famille Rose, 19th Century	650.00
Charger, Quail Pattern, C.1725, Red, Blue, Yellow, 14 In., Pair	1540.00
Cistern, Basin, Wall, Famille Verte, C.1700, 17 In.	4950.00
Coffeepot, Polychrome, Diaperwork, Pistol Grip Handle, 7 In.	525.00
Condiment Set, Famille Rose, Landscapes & Maidens, 9 Piece	192.00
Console Set, Japonica, C.1765, 3 Piece	1200.00
Cooler, Wine, Bouquets, Sprigs, Shell Handle, 5 In., Pair	1450.00
Cooler, Wine, Red, Yellow, Green, Blue, Floral, C.1780, 6 In., Pai	2750.00
Dish, Armorial, Arms Of Sir Archibald Campbell, 13 In.	1200.00
Dish, Blue, Kidney Shaped, Fitzhugh, 10 In., Pair	385.00
Dish, Condiment, Shell Shaped, Arms Of Duncan, C.1798, 3 In.	1200.00
Dish, Famille Rose, Aqua, Red, Pink, Spearhead Band, 8 In.	605.00
Dish, Famille Rose, Birds, Lotus, Scroll Rim, 15 1/4 In.	625.00
Dish, Hot Water, Armorial, Arms, Van Wenckum, C.1785, 10 In.	825.00
Dish, Hot Water, Brown, Carnation Sprig, 11 In., Pair	467.00
Dish, Serving, Blue & White, Butterflies, C.1770, 14 In.	275.00
Dish, Serving, Domed Cover, Berry Handle, Fitzhugh, 10 In.	275.00
Dish, Vegetable, Lozenge Shaped, Red, Butterflies, 11 In.	330.00
Figurine, Pigeons, White, Black Eyes, 6 1/2 In., Pair	935.00
Figurine, Quail, White, Blue Eyes, Rockwork Base, 6 In., Pair	522.00

Figurine, Stag, Recumbent, Monkey With Peach, C.1830, 8 In. 1200.00
Flask, Moon, Dragons Encircled By Floral Scrolls, 11 3/4 In. 660.00
Garden Seat, Barrel, Florals, Gourds, 18 In., Pair 1650.00
Garden Seat, Elephant Form, Polychrome, 18 In., Pair 1540.00
Garden Seat, Flambe, Pierced Flower Panels, 18 1/4 In. 330.00
Garden Seat, Shou Medallions, Bats & Fruit, 18 In., Pair 180.00
Inkstand, Painted Flowers, C.1800, 10 In. 225.00
Jar, Famille Rose, Bombe Sides, Warrior Scene, Yellow, 17 In. 1320.00
Jar, Famille Rose, Phoenix & Floral Panels, Cover, 16 In. 275.00
Jar, Ginger, Famille Rose, Birds, Peonies, Rocks, 4 In. 440.00
Jar, Ginger, Famille Rose, Pink Diaper Ground, Figures, 9 In. 385.00
Jar, Ginger, Polychrome Design, 2 Scenes 195.00
Jar, Prunus Extending Over Sides, Green, Covered, 12 In., Pair 220.00
Jardiniere, Blue & White, Peony Sprays, C.1770, 7 In. 880.00
Jug, Helmet Shape, Sprig, Blue Design Lip Border 185.00
Mug, Bamboo & Pheasants, Wang Hing, No.90, 6 X 4 In. 1650.00
Mug, Cylindrical, Loop Handle, Floral, C.1800, 4 1/2 In. 250.00
Mug, Porcelain, Entwined Strap Handle, C.1800, 4 1/2 In. 200.00
Mug, 3 Figures, Animal, River, Blossoms, Dolphin Handle, 5 In. 410.00
Planter, Underplate, Scenic Design, 10 In., Pair 350.00
Plate, Aesop's Fables, Fox Attacking Rooster, C.1810, 9 In. 525.00
Plate, Amorous, Man, Woman, River, C.1740, 9 In., Pair 825.00
Plate, Armorial, Arms Of Frederick, C.1724, 8 In., Pair 1650.00
Plate, Blue, Deer, Bonsai Tree, Peonies, C.1740, 9 In. 60.00
Plate, Blue, Red & Gold Florals, Cream Ground, 9 In. 55.00
Plate, Brown, Lion Rampant, Crest, Apricot, 9 In., Pair 525.00
Plate, Carmine, Violet, & Green, 9 In., Pair 95.00
Plate, Comedy, Harlequin Holding Letter, C.1725, 8 In. 385.00
Plate, Famille Rose, Green, Blue, Red, Yellow, Set Of 6 .... 1045.00
Plate, Judgment Of Paris, C.1755, Paris, Venus, Apple, 9 In. 770.00
Plate, Les Oies De Frere Philippe, C.1740, 8 In. 330.00
Plate, Soup, Armorial, Arms Of Mercer, C.1755, 9 In., Pair 1100.00
Platter, Armorial, Arms Of Elder, C.1775, 16 1/2 In. 2100.00
Platter, Armorial, Arms Of Wright, Blue, Black, Rose, 11 In. 155.00
Platter, C.1840, Floral Spray, Red, Blue, Yellow, 14 In. 325.00
Platter, Rose, Purple, Red, Green, Floral Sprays, 10 In. 275.00
Pot, Brush, Famille Verte, Calligraphy Mark, 4 3/4 In., Pair 125.00
Saltcellar, Tobacco Leaf Pattern, Red, Blue, Aqua, 4 In., Pair 1210.00
Sugar, Twined Leaf Handles, Gilt Berry Finial, Rose Cluster 365.00
Tea Set, Cabbage & Butterfly, Famille Rose Trim, 11 Piece 285.00
Tea Set, 50 Piece 1400.00
Teabowl & Saucer, Child's, Brown, Eagle Emblem, Star Border 330.00
Teabowl & Saucer, Famille Verte, Fluted, C.1720, Leaf Mark 220.00
Teabowl & Saucer, Lotus, Pink Peonies, Rose Petals, 5 In. 465.00
Teabowl & Saucer, Man Fishing, River, 2 In. 495.00
Teabowl & Saucer, Shields, Purple, Red, Black Crest, 3 In. 140.00
Teapot, C.1800, Flower Border, Entwined Handle, 5 In. 50.00
Teapot, Famille Rose, Birds, Flowers, Figural Knob & Spout 475.00
Teapot, Famille Rose, Green, Red, Purple, C.1740, 4 1/4 In. 715.00
Teapot, Famille Rose, Wicker Carrying Case 77.50
Teapot, Fitzhugh, Orange & Brown, Fruits, Flowers, 6 In. 1100.00
Teapot, Fruit Strap Handle, 1860s 130.00
Teapot, Lotus, Overlapping Petals, C.1760, 4 In. 385.00
Teapot, Red Flowers, Yellow Buds, C.1745, Covered, 4 1/2 In. 605.00
Tray, Spoon, C.1825, Orange & Gilt Birds & Butterflies, 7 In. 260.00
Tureen, Floral Festoons, Hare's Head Handles, Lid, 13 1/2 In. 935.00
Tureen, Pomegranate-Shaped, Parrots, Rose To Yellow, 5 In. 770.00
Tureen, Soup, Cricket, Fruit, Flowers, Red, Yellow, Back, 12 In. 1650.00
Tureen, Soup, Famille Rose, Pheasants, Songbirds, 15 In. 880.00
Vase, Famille Rose, Birds, Trees, Qianlong, 22 3/4 In., Pair 2550.00
Vase, Famille Rose, Dragon & Phoenix Medallions, 23 1/2 In. 935.00
Vase, Famille Rose, Warriors & Dragons, 18 In., Pair 340.00
Vase, Flowering Trees & Birds, 22 In. 275.00

Vase, Mandarin Design, River, Diaper Ground, C.1785, 9 In., Pair 2860.00
Vase, Scene Of Scholar & Students, Red Seal Mark, 11 1/4 In. 90.00

Chocolate glass, sometimes mistakenly called caramel slag, was made by the Indiana Tumbler and Goblet Company of Greentown, Indiana, from 1900 to 1903.

CHOCOLATE GLASS, Basket, Art Nouveau, Handled, 12 In. 29.00
  Berry Bowl, Geneva, Master, 8 1/2 X 5 1/4 In. 125.00
  Berry Set, Leaf Bracket, 7 Piece 310.00
  Bowl, Berry, Geneva, Oval, 8 1/4 In. 105.00
  Bowl, Cactus, 6 In. 85.00
  Bowl, Chrysanthemum Leaf, 4 In. 120.00
  Bowl, Fruit, Geneva, 9 1/2 X 6 In. 150.00
  Butter, Cactus, Covered 195.00
  Butter, Daisy Pattern, Covered 210.00
  Butter, Leaf Bracket, Covered 185.00
  Celery, Leaf Bracket, 5 1/2 X 11 In. 95.00
  Compote, Jelly, Cactus 55.00
  Compote, Jelly, Geneva 65.00
  Compote, Melrose, Scalloped, 6 In. 265.00
  Cruet, Cactus, Original Top 165.00
  Cruet, Leaf Bracket, Original Stopper 165.00
  Cruet, Wild Rose With Bowknot, Stopper 275.00
  Cup, Punch, Shuttle 50.00
  Dish, Sauce, Fish Lid, Dolphin 150.00
  Figurine, Dolphin, Sawtooth Edge Around Mouth 180.00
  Frappe, Dewey 65.00
  Holder, Hat Pin, Orange Tree, Pair 575.00
  Lamp, Wild Rose With Festoon, 8 1/2 In. 575.00
  Mug, Cactus, 3 1/2 In. 115.00
  Mug, Herringbone Buttress .... 35.00 To 55.00
  Mug, Herringbone Buttress, Set Of 5 .... 255.00
  Mug, Serenade 130.00
  Nappy, Masonic .... 60.00 To 110.00
  Pitcher, Water, Heron 450.00
  Pitcher, Water, Paneled 250.00
  Sauce, Dewey 45.00
  Sauce, Leaf Bracket 35.00
  Slipper, With Kittens, Hobnail 8.50
  Stein, Castle Scene, Spout, Greentown .... 110.00 To 165.00
  Stein, Herringbone Buttress, Greentown 45.00
  Stein, Indoor Drinking Scene, Greentown 125.00
  Sugar & Creamer, Covered 50.00
  Sugar, Leaf Bracket 45.00
  Sugar, Wild Rose & Bowknot 65.00
  Syrup, Cord Drapery, Original Lid 145.00
  Table Set, Dewey, Individual Size, 4 Piece 335.00
  Table Set, Leaf Bracket, 4 Piece 225.00
  Tankard, Creamer, Shuttle 35.00
  Tankard, Strigal, 6 1/4 In. 75.00
  Toothpick, Cactus 65.00
  Tumbler, Cactus .... 40.00 To 45.00
  Tumbler, Leaf Bracket .... 40.00 To 60.00
  Tumbler, Lemonade, Cactus 65.00
  Tumbler, Shuttle 85.00
  Tumbler, Shuttle, Greentown 85.00
  Tumbler, Uneeda Biscuit, Greentown .... 90.00 To 115.00
  CHRISTMAS PLATE, see Collector Plate

CHRISTMAS TREE, Light Bulb, Betty Boop 65.00
  Light Bulb, Character, Three Men In A Tub 5.00
  Light Bulb, Clown, Masked, Figural 15.00
  Light Bulb, Comic Strip Characters, Boxed, 6 Figures 200.00

Light Bulb, Cotton Clad Wires, Button Slide Clasps, C.1920 .... 6.00
Light Bulb, Dirigible, Figural 11.00
Light Bulb, Embossed Tree Shape, Set Of 6 .... 10.00
Light Bulb, Horse In Horseshoe 15.00
Light Bulb, House, Figural 8.00
Light Bulb, House, Figural, 6-Sided, Milk Glass 20.00
Light Bulb, Lion With Tennis Racket 15.00
Light Bulb, Little Boy Blue 10.00
Light Bulb, Madza, Figural, String Of 8 .... 40.00
Light Bulb, Mickey Mouse, Noma, Boxed 175.00
Light Bulb, Moon Mullins, Figural 28.00
Light Bulb, Mother Goose 10.00
Light Bulb, Parrot, Figural, Milk Glass, 4 In. 10.00
Light Bulb, Pinocchio, Figural 15.00
Light Bulb, Pocket Watch, Figural 15.00
Light Bulb, Queen Of Hearts 15.00
Light Bulb, Santa Claus 20.00
Light Bulb, Santa Claus Christmas Tree, Glass 5.00
Light Bulb, Santa Claus, Milk Glass, Red Robe, 4 In. 20.00
Light Bulb, Santa Claus, Plastic, C.1940, 3 In. 6.50
Light Bulb, Santa Claus, 2-Faced 45.00
Light Bulb, Santa Claus, 9 In. 75.00
Light Bulb, Santa With Pack, Figural 10.00
Light Bulb, Smitty, Figural, Original Paint 35.00
Light Bulb, Snowman 20.00
Ornament, Air Balloon, Blown, Crinkle Wire, Spun Glass, 7 In. 30.00
Ornament, Airedale 15.00
Ornament, Angel, Figural, Cream, Plastic, 4 In. 5.00
Ornament, Angel, Golden Hair, Chromolitho, C.1880 .... 15.00
Ornament, Angel, Pressed Cotton 3.00
Ornament, Angel, Wax, 4 In. 40.00
Ornament, Baby, Blown, 3 1/2 In. 85.00
Ornament, Baby, Wrapped In Crinkle Wire, 5 In. 15.00
Ornament, Ball With Horns, Silver, Concave Dimples, 2 In. 15.00
Ornament, Ball, Fluted, Snowman, Yellow Tree, Celluloid, 3 In. 20.00
Ornament, Ball, Mercury Glass, Gold, Large, Hanger 15.00
Ornament, Balloon, Figure, C.1900, 6 1/2 In. .... *Illus* 145.00
Ornament, Bell, Cobalt Blue 22.00
Ornament, Bell, Embossed Santa, Milk Glass, 2 1/2 In. 10.00
Ornament, Bird, Angel Hair Tail, Red Wings, Glass, 5 In. 30.00
Ornament, Bird, Figural, Angel Hair Tail, Black Beak, 4 In. 18.50
Ornament, Bird, Pink Cotton 3.00
Ornament, Bird, Pink, Purple Beak, Glass, 7 In. 25.00
Ornament, Birds, Clip-On, Pair 10.00
Ornament, Blue Bells, Blown Glass, 1 1/2 X 2 In. 7.50
Ornament, Boy On Sled, Celluloid, Tin, 3 In. 25.00
Ornament, Boy, Glass, German, C.1920, 4 In. .... *Illus* 27.50
Ornament, Candle Holder, Flower, Fish, Clip, Tin, Set Of 5 .... 22.50
Ornament, Candle Holder, Victorian, Tin Cups, Set Of 6 .... 60.00
Ornament, Carrot 60.00
Ornament, Cello, Figural, Pink, Black Design, Glass, 5 In. 30.00
Ornament, Cello, Rose, Victorian, Glass, 6 In. 22.50
Ornament, Charlie Chaplin, C.1920, 2 3/4 In. .... *Illus* 220.00
Ornament, Clown, Red Suit, Yellow Collar, Milk Glass, 2 In. 22.50
Ornament, Deer, Blown, C.1900, Glass 15.00
Ornament, Dirigible, Propellers, Crinkle Wire, C.1880, 6 In. 20.00
Ornament, Dog, Glass, 3 1/2 In. 20.00
Ornament, Father Christmas, Top Hat, Beard, Stand, 18 In. 85.00
Ornament, Fiddle, Gold, Red Strings, Blown Glass, 3 In. 20.00
Ornament, Fox 15.00
Ornament, Fox Terrier 15.00
Ornament, Grapes, Purple, Green Leaves, Glass, 2 1/4 In. 12.50
Ornament, Happy Santa, Lighted Eyes, Battery, 9 In. 55.00
Ornament, Heart, Silver, Hobnail Design, Blown Glass, 2 In. 15.00

Christmas Tree, Ornament, Balloon, Figure, C.1900, 6 1/2 In.

Christmas Tree, Ornament, Charlie Chaplin, C.1920, 2 3/4 In.

Christmas Tree, Ornaments, Boy, Glass, German, C.1920, 4 In.; Little Miss Muffet, C.1920, 3 3/4 In. *(See Page 114)*

Ornament, Horn, Figural, Silver & Green, Glass, 4 In. 22.50
Ornament, Horn, White, Hot Pink Keys, Blown Glass, 6 In. 30.00
Ornament, House, Figural, Bay Windows, Silver, Gold, C.1900 .... 25.00
Ornament, Lamb, Wooly, Germany, Small 15.00
Ornament, Lantern, Green & Red, Convex Diamonds, 2 In. 5.00
Ornament, Lantern, Japanese, Milk Glass, Hand-Painted 10.00
Ornament, Lion, Holding Tennis Racket, Glass 10.00
Ornament, Little Miss Muffet, C.1920, 3 3/4 In. .... *Illus* 27.50
Ornament, Mandolin, Figural, Green, White Strings, Glass 30.00
Ornament, Melon Shaped, Victorian, White, Glass, 3 In. 12.50
Ornament, Mushroom, Green, Paper Flower, Glass, 2 In. 12.50
Ornament, Mushroom, Victorian, Red, Glass, 3 In. 16.50
Ornament, Orange, Pink, Dimpled Skin, Glass, 1 In. 10.00
Ornament, Owl, C.1930, Glass, 3 1/2 In. .... *Illus* 13.75
Ornament, Owl, C.1945, Green Glass, 3 1/2 In. .... *Illus* 5.50
Ornament, Parrot, Yellow, Red Beak, Glass, 4 In. 18.50
Ornament, Peach, Crinkle Wire, C.1890, 4 In. 29.00
Ornament, Pear 70.00
Ornament, Pekingese 15.00
Ornament, Pineapple 85.00
Ornament, Pinecone, Glass, 2 1/4 In. 6.00
Ornament, Santa Claus, Papier-Mache, Dressed In Felt, 4 In. 25.00
Ornament, Santa Claus, Pressed Cotton & Chenille, 4 In. 5.00
Ornament, Santa Claus, Red Suit, Papier-Mache Face, 5 In. 22.50
Ornament, Santa Claus, 2-Faced, Full Figured, Glass, 3 In. 18.50
Ornament, Santa, Clapper, Double-Faced, Papier-Mache 20.00
Ornament, Santa, Embossed Paper, Blue, 13 In. 18.00
Ornament, Santa, Going Down Chimney, Papier-Mache, 10 In. 25.00
Ornament, Santa, On Bike, Tin & Rubber, 5 In. 20.00
Ornament, Santa, On Skis, Metal, 3 In. 15.00
Ornament, Santa, Paper Sack, 6 In. 70.00
Ornament, Santa, Papier-Mache, Cloth Suit, 5 1/2 In. 20.00
Ornament, Santa, Red Suit, Pipe Cleaner, 6 3/4 In. 16.50
Ornament, Santa, Stand-Up, Embossed Paper, 11 In. 40.00
Ornament, Santa, Standing, Red Suit, Milk Glass, 3 In. 15.00
Ornament, Santa, With Chimney, C.1895, Paper, 7 In. 5.00
Ornament, Santa, With Pack, C.1900, Germany, 14 In. 85.00

Christmas Tree, Ornaments, Owls, C.1930, Glass, 3 1/2 In.; C.1945, Green
Glass, 3 1/2 In.

Christmas Tree, Ornament, St.Nicholas, German, C.1890, 15 In.

Ornament, Santa, With Reindeer, Tin & Celluloid	18.00
Ornament, Scotty	15.00
Ornament, Snow White & Seven Dwarfs, Papier-Mache, Glitter	182.00
Ornament, St.Bernard	15.00
Ornament, St.Nicholas, German, C.1890, 15 In. ....*Illus*	330.00
Ornament, Star, Foil-Covered Cardboard, Blue Glass Beading	3.00
Ornament, Star, Treetop, Figural, Glass	750.00
Ornament, Sugar Bowl, Silver, Green, Leaves, Handled, 4 In.	28.00
Ornament, Swan, Green, Long-Necked, Glass, 4 3/4 In.	25.00
Ornament, Trumpet, Gold, Green, Blown Glass, 3 1/2 In.	22.50
Ornament, Tuba, White, Red, Green, Blown Glass, 4 In.	22.50
Ornament, Umbrella, Hot Pink, C.1890, 9 In.	30.00
Stand, North Bros., Philadelphia, Pa., Iron	25.00
CHRISTMAS, Santa Claus, Cotton Stuffing, 24 In.	95.00
Santa Claus, Mechanical, Rubber Face, Tin Body, 10 In.	30.00
Santa Claus, On Skis, Tin, Mechanical, 5 In.	25.00
Santa Claus, Straw Stuffing, Wooden Base, 19 In.	35.00

Art Deco chrome items became popular in the 1930s. Collectors are most interested in pieces made by the Chase Brass and Copper Company of Waterbury, Connecticut.

CHROME, Ashtray, Black Amethyst Glass, Tooled, Slide Top, 3 3/8 X 2 7/8 In.	8.00

Ashtray, Open-Mouthed Fish Center, Hamilton Product, 4 1/2 In.Diam. 15.00
Basket, Openwork, Glass Insert, 3 Sections, 5 X 4 1/2 In. 12.00
Buckle, Belt, Man's, Art Deco, 1 3/4 In. 5.00
Candlestick, Prismatic Glass Balls, 17 In. 28.00
Candlestick, S-Curve, Wood Base, 9 1/2 In. 10.00
Cigarette Lighter, Musical, Starlite, Mosaic Front, 2 1/2 In. 25.00
Cigarette Lighter, Novelty, Johnson's Wax Tower, Art Moderne, 6 In. 35.00
Cigarette Lighter, Scotty Dog, Brown, 3 X 2 1/2 In. 15.00
Cigarette, Jar & Lighter, Table, Brass Lined, Green Trim 32.00
Cigarette, Lighter, U.S. Air Force Insignia 5.00
Cocktail Set, Covered Shaker, 6 Footed Cordials, Tray 30.00
Cocktail Set, Shaker, Cups, & Tray, Boxed 40.00
Cocktail Set, Tray, 6 Cocktails, Chase 40.00
Cocktail Set, Tray, 6 Stemmed Cordials 25.00
Cocktail Shaker, Art Deco, Chase Co. 23.00
Cocktail Shaker, Curved Red Handle, Covered, 12 In. 18.00
Cocktail Shaker, Grape Leaf Cluster Etch Band, Handled, 11 In. 10.00
Cocktail Shaker, Hammered, 6 Flared Goblets 45.00
Coffee Set, Norman Bel Geddes, 9 Piece 650.00
Compote, Female Nude, Cambridge Glass Insert, Farber Ware, 7 3/4 In. 40.00
Crumber Set, Manning Bowman, 2 Piece 12.00
Dispenser, Cordial, Keg On Pedestal, 6 Mugs 15.00
Dispenser, Liqueur, Deco Sphere, 6 Shot Glasses 25.00
Lazy Susan, Center Handle, 2-Tier, 16 Original Tumblers 36.00
Lazy Susan, Center Handle, 18 Original Tumblers 35.00
Loveseat, Tubular, Brown Vinyl Cushion 20.00
Pencil, Mechanical, Rib Lead Design, 5 1/2 In. 12.00
Silent Butler, Amber Glass Insert, Farber Ware, Signed 18.00
Stand, Smoking, Art Deco 25.00
Stand, Smoking, Black Metal Foot & Top, 5 Posts, 14 X 25 In. 50.00
Stand, Smoking, Lighter, Jar, Glass Tray 225.00
Tea Strainer, Queen Elizabeth II Coronation 15.00
Tray, Geometric, Red, White, & Black, Hand-Painted 49.00
Tray, Mint, Basket Handle, Farber Ware, 7 X 5 3/4 In. 6.00
Tray, Serving, 5 Section Glass Liner, Ivorine Handle 35.00
Tray, 9 X 4 1/2 In. 3.50
Vase, Bud, Art Deco, Cylinder, 9 In., Pair 20.00
Vase, Farber Ware Holder, Orange, 9 In. 18.00

CIGAR STORE FIGURE, Indian Chief, Full Headdress, 6 Ft. 5000.00
Indian, Dated 1910 ....4000.00
Indian, Original Paint, 250 Pounds, 7 1/2 Ft. 3500.00
Scouting Chief, Late 1800s, Wooden 3700.00

*Cinnabar is a vermilion or red lacquer. Some pieces are made with hundreds
of thicknesses of the lacquer that is later carved.*

CINNABAR, Box, 3 In.Square 50.00
Jar, Hand-Carved, Village All Around, Covered, 6 In., Pair 85.00

*Civil War mementos are important collectors' items. Most of the pieces
are military items used from 1861 to 1865.*

CIVIL WAR, Bayonet, Leather Sheath, Brass Trimmed, 29 1/2 In. 45.00
Bayonet, Springfield, Leather Scabbard 35.00
Box, Cartridge, Round 25.00
Breastplate, Brass Clipped Corners, War Eagle Center, 4 X 2 In. 65.00
Buckle, Belt, Officer's, Sword, U.S. Eagle 65.00
Buckle, Snake 75.00
Buttons, Brass, U.S. Cavalry, Set Of 3 .... 1.50
Cannonball, From Fort Sumner, 25 Pounds, Pair 50.00
Canteen, Confederate, All Wood, Round 65.00

Canteen, GAR, Dark Gray, Cork, Loopets, Tin, C.1875 .... 45.00
Canteen, With Design 110.00
Cap, Billed, G.A.R., Gold Band, Insignia, C.1880 .... 45.00
Cap, Peaked, Band Of Gold, Square Peak, 1880 .... 65.00
Case, Cartridge, Black Leather, 40 Ammo Rounds, 6 X 7 X 2 In. 125.00
Cup, Collapsible, Tin Case 65.00
Discharge, 1863, John Farnum, Private Regiment Of N.J. 25.00
Drum, U.S. Infantry Crest, Rosewood Sticks, 13 In. 385.00
Flag, Confederate Battle, 13 Stars, Wool, 22 X 17 In. 1000.00
Flag, Signal, Navel, C.S.S. Sumner, 48 X 50 In. 300.00
Fuse, Wooden, For Mortar Shell 25.00
Hat Wreath, Brass, With Hooks 15.00
Headdress, Navy, Black Velour, Velvet Edging, Gold Band, 1860 .... 95.00
Humidor, Cigar, Presented To Grant, Chinese Black & Gold, 10 In. 950.00
Knife, Bowie Type, Handmade, 6 In. 45.00
Lamp, Nurse's, Tole Painting, Tin 210.00
Mirror, Brass, Pocket, 3 X 4 In. 35.00
Mug, Drinking, Handle Embossed U.S., Tin, 4 In. 25.00
Plaque, Soldier Standing, Rifle, Fixed Bayonet, Iron, 8 In. 45.00
Plate, Cartridge Box, Round 25.00
Print, McClellan At Antietam, 1862, 9 3/4 X 12 3/4 In. 8.50
Quilt, Soldier's, Crazy Patch, Feather Stitching 125.00
Rosette, Horse, Hooks, Round, Copper 20.00
Southern Cross, Awarded Poindexter, Photograph With Flag 150.00
Sword & Scabbard, Cavalry, Dated 175.00
Sword, American, Eagle Leather Holder, 1864 .... 175.00
Sword, Rooster Hilt, Stamped US & NC 285.00
Telescope, Extension, General's, Tin 150.00
Uniform, Naval Officer's, Black Wool, Silk Lined, Gold Eagle, 1860 .... 265.00
    CKAW, see Dedham

*Clambroth glass, popular in the Victorian era, is a grayish color and is
semiopaque like clambroth.*

CLAMBROTH, Bottle, Barber, Cork & Porcelain Stopper, Set Of 3 .... 38.00
Bottle, Barber, Octagonal Neck, Stopper 18.00
Bottle, Scent, Blue, Petal Stopper, Pair 1700.00
Candlestick, Dolphin, Petal Socket 550.00
Candlestick, Petal & Loop 215.00
Celery, Star Medallion 38.00
Eggcup, Cable, Flint 550.00
Jar, Antiseptic, Covered, 7 In. 12.00
Jar, Cream, Nickel Plated Lid, Covered, 4 In. 20.00
Sugar Shaker, 10 Panels 15.00
Taster, Whiskey, Barred Oval, 2 1/8 In. 125.00
Taster, Whiskey, Lacy, 1 3/4 In. 145.00
Toothpick, Button Arches, Souvenir 30.00
Tumbler, Sterilizer 20.00
Vase, Corset Shape, Black Band, Ribbed, 9 In. 35.00

*Clarice Cliff was a designer who began working at several English
factories in the 1920s. She died in 1972.*

CLARICE CLIFF, Bowl, Brown Leaves, 10 In. 60.00
Bowl, Hand-Painted Flowers In Straw Basket, Oval 25.00
Chamberstick, Tonquin, 8 1/2 In. 30.00
Holder, Brush, Red, English Scene, 10 In. 35.00
Honey Pot, Art Deco, Covered, Marked, 4 1/4 In. 125.00
Honey Pot, Gay Day, Bizarre, 3 3/4 In. 195.00
Jar, Jam, Art Deco, Celtic Harvest, Nickel Plated Lid, Marked 95.00
Jar, Jam, Marked Bizarre, 3 In. 195.00
Jar, Sweetmeat, Raised Florals, Marked, 4 In. 125.00
Mask, Wall, Woman 250.00
Plate, Harvest Pattern, 10 In. 10.00
Plate, Large Basket Of Flowers, 10 In. 22.00

Plate, Ophelia Pattern, 10 In.	7.50
Plate, Queen Elizabeth I, 11 In.	30.00
Platter, Harvest Pattern, 12 In.	12.00
Platter, Tonquin Pattern, Royal Staffordshire	20.00
Sifter, Sugar, My Garden, 5 1/2 In.	195.00
Sugar Shaker, Art Deco, Floral, Marked Bizarre, Marked, 5 In.	125.00
Vase, Bizarre, Circular Stripes, Marked, 4 3/4 X 6 1/2 In.	195.00
Vase, Raised Florals, Marked, Cream & Blue Ground, 8 1/2 In.	175.00
Vase, Raised Parakeets, Protruding Parakeets, 12 1/2 In.	195.00

Clewell ware was made in limited quantities by Charles Walter Clewell of Canton, Ohio, from 1902 to 1955. Pottery was covered with a thin coating of bronze, then treated to make the bronze turn different colors. Pieces covered with copper, brass, or silver were also made. Mr. Clewell's secret formula for blue patina bronze was burned when he died in 1965.

CLEWELL, Vase, Footed, Incised Base, Coppery Green Glaze, 8 1/2 X 2 1/4 In.	175.00

Clews pottery was made by George Clews & Co. of Brownhill Pottery, Tunstall, England, from 1806 to 1861.

CLEWS, see also Flow Blue

CLEWS, Plate, Christmas Eve, C.1820, Wilkie, Blue & White, 9 In.	365.00
Plate, Dr.Syntax Drawing After Nature, Dark Blue	135.00
Plate, Landing Of Lafayette, Signed, Blue & White, 9 In.	425.00
Plate, Landing Of Lafayette, 9 In.	310.00
Platter, C.1810, Marked	285.00
Platter, Tavern Scene Center, Octagonal, Blue & White, 13 X 18 In.	285.00

The Clifton Pottery was founded by William Long in Clifton, New Jersey, in 1905. He worked there until 1908, making a line called Crystal Patina. The Clifton pottery made art pottery. Another firm, the Chesapeake Pottery, sold majolica marked "Clifton ware."

CLIFTON, Bowl, Gray-Green, Crystal Patina, 6 X 2 In.	35.00
Candlestick, Indian Ware, Squat, 4 1/4 In.	45.00
Humidor, Geometric Indian Relief At Rim & Lid, 5 1/2 In.	125.00
Teapot, Crystal, Covered	72.00
Teapot, Green, Crystal Patina, Covered, 5 3/4 /n.	80.00
Teapot, Indian Ware, Mottled Yellow Luster, Gold Trim	36.00
Vase, Crystalline, 1906, Yellow & Green, Artist Signed, 7 In.	145.00
Vase, Indian Ware, 6 In.	60.00

CLOCK, Advertising, AC Spark Plugs, 16 X 16 In.	75.00
Advertising, Alarm, Mr.Peanut, Yellow Face	57.00
Advertising, Baird, Molliscorium, Label	750.00
Advertising, Benrus Watch Co., Porcelain Sockets, Metal	450.00
Advertising, Calumet Baking Powder, Regulator	400.00
Advertising, Canada Dry Sport Cola, 13 X 18 In.	20.00
Advertising, Carstairs White Seal Whiskey	70.00
Advertising, Charlie Tuna	30.00
Advertising, Dari-Delite, Electric Neon Clock Co., Cleveland, Ohio	250.00
Advertising, Dr.Pepper, Lighted, 1975, 12 X 18 In.	29.00
Advertising, Electric Postal Telegraph, Hammond, 15 In. Dial	45.00
Advertising, Ever-Ready, Shaving, Man's Face, Tin	700.00
Advertising, Fenn's That Good Ice Cream, Wood & Plastic	95.00
Advertising, Gem Razor Blade	800.00
Advertising, Goodrich Tire	28.00
Advertising, Gulf Gas, Convex Glass Front, 1940-50, 15 In.Diam.	275.00
Advertising, Gulf Oil Co., Electric	175.00
Advertising, Harvard Beer, Reverse Painting, Factory	750.00
Advertising, Humphreys Jewelers, Sessions, Schoolhouse, Oak	400.00
Advertising, International Tailoring	365.00

Advertising, Ithaca, Wall, 5 Cent & 10 Cent Cigars 1200.00
Advertising, Joe Louis, World's Champion, Boxing Gloves Each Side 200.00
Advertising, Joe's Market, Buffalo, N.Y., Stoneware 65.00
Advertising, Keebler, Bobbing Bird, Shape Of House, Windup 20.00
Advertising, Keeney, Magic 350.00
Advertising, Lewis Red Jacket Bitters, Center Indian, C.1888 .... 475.00
Advertising, Lucky Strike, Schoolhouse 875.00
Advertising, Lucky Strike, Wall, Key Wind, Time & Strike, Walnut, C.1900 .... 1050.00
Advertising, Lux, Beer Drinkers 25.00
Advertising, Lux, Happy Days, Mechanical 155.00
Advertising, Mince Meat 350.00
Advertising, Mobil Gas, Inserts 200.00
Advertising, New York City Silk Importers, Enameled, Brass 65.00
Advertising, Old Chartres Whiskey .... 85.00 To 150.00
Advertising, Old Dutch Cleanser, Regulator 550.00
Advertising, Old Mr. Boston 325.00
Advertising, Orange Crush 25.00
Advertising, Pabst Blue Ribbon Beer .... 45.00 To 185.00
Advertising, Pan American Exposition, Frying Pan Shape 245.00
Advertising, Parry's Buggies, Time & Strike, Oak 1100.00
Advertising, R.C.A. Victor, Tin Lithograph, C.1910 .... 1000.00
Advertising, Reed's Tonic, Golden Oak Case, C.1865 .... 1000.00
Advertising, Royal Crown Cola, Diamond Shape .... 56.00 To 65.00
Advertising, Seagram Whiskey, 14 X 14 In. .... 35.00 To 75.00
Advertising, Sidney, Rotating Advertising Panels, Mahogany, C.1886 .... 4800.00
Advertising, Sky Chief, Glass Panel, 12 X 4 In. 10.00
Advertising, Spartan Radio, 18 1/2 In. 135.00
Advertising, Star Brand Shoes, Gilbert, Bronze 60.00
Advertising, Starkist Foods, Sorry Charlie, Lux 35.00
Advertising, Texaco Diesel Chief, Inserts 75.00
Advertising, Time To Polish, Red Devil, Electric, 15 X 15 In. 125.00
Advertising, Trade, Cast Iron, Face 12 In. 250.00
Advertising, Waterbury, Regulator, 2 Star Radiator Solder, Oak 450.00
Advertising, Whistle Soda, Pixie Pointing To Pop, Electric, C.1930 .... 175.00
Advertising, 7-Up, Glass & Metal 35.00
Alarm, Animated, Early Bird 75.00
Ampichron, Piano Attachment, Tuning Diagram, Wooden Box 1400.00
Animated, Early Bird Catches The Worm 285.00
Ansonia, Baghdad, Regulator 1500.00
Ansonia, Ball Swinger 495.00
Ansonia, Banjo 250.00
Ansonia, Blue & White Flowers, Dresden China 325.00
Ansonia, Calendar, Long Drop, Time & Strike 475.00
Ansonia, Gingerbread, Shelf 180.00
Ansonia, Hand-Painted, Royal Bonn Case, Gilt Trim, 13 In. .... *Illus* 500.00
Ansonia, Mantel, Brass, Large 300.00
Ansonia, Mantel, Open Escapement, Porcelain Dial, Iron 150.00
Ansonia, Mantel, Time & Strike, Open Escapement, Iron Case 175.00
Ansonia, Marbleized Design, Iron, 22 X 11 In. .... *Illus* 90.00
Ansonia, Marchioness Model, Open Escapement, Rhinestones On Dial 675.00
Ansonia, Model A, School, Time & Strike, Walnut 325.00
Ansonia, Open Escapement, Onyx With Gilt Design 250.00
Ansonia, Porcelain, Royal Bonn Case, C.1890, 11 3/4 In. 290.00
Ansonia, School, All Original, C.1800 .... 385.00
Ansonia, School, Calendar, Time & Strike, Walnut 350.00
Ansonia, School, Long Drop 500.00
Ansonia, School, Time & Strike, Short Drop, Walnut 275.00
Ansonia, Shelf, Time & Strike, 8-Day, Oak 140.00
Ansonia, Shelf, 8-Day, Royal Bonn China 380.00
Ansonia, Swinging Doll & Tree, Dated April 29, 1889 .... 425.00
Ansonia, Time & Strike, 12 In.Dial 250.00
Ansonia, Triumph, Cupids On Sides, Walnut 295.00
Ansonia, Unique Model, Iron Case, Time & Strike 75.00
Ansonia, Wall, 30-Hour, Brass Works, Veneered Case, C.1840, 25 1/2 In. 265.00

(See Page 119)

Clock, Ansonia, Hand-Painted, Royal Bonn Case, Gilt Trim, 13 In.

Clock, Ansonia, Marbleized Design, Iron, 22 X 11 In.

Ansonia, Walnut, Brass Trim, Cathedral Style, 6 X 7 In.	45.00
Ansonia, Welcome Model, Porcelain Dial, 8-Day, Time & Strike	295.00
Atkins & Downs, Stenciling, 30-Hour, Wooden Works	260.00
Atkins, Shelf, Reverse Glass, 8-Day, Time & Strike, Rosewood	285.00
Automaton, Wall, Ship's Rock, Clock In Tower, C.1830	575.00
Baby Ben, Dresser, Celluloid Holder	20.00
Banjo, Alarm, Federal, Mahogany, 8-Day, C.1820, 35 1/2 In.	350.00
Banjo, Federal, Mahogany & Eglomise, Acorn Finial, C.1810, 39 In.	990.00
Banjo, Federal, Mahogany & Eglomise, American Eagle, C.1815, 42 In.	2450.00
Birge & Fuller, Twin Steeple, 8-Day, C.1844, 25 In. *Illus*	2100.00
Birge & Mallory, Triple Decker, 8-Day, Brass Movement	250.00
Black Shoeshine Boy, Animated	185.00
Boardman & Wells, Stenciled Columns, 30-Hour, Wooden Works	260.00
Boston Clock Co., Mantel, Colored Inlaid Marble, Tandem Wind Movement	150.00
Boston Clock Co., Mantel, Rip Van Winkle	495.00
Boston Clock Co., Tandem Wind, Marble Case, Damascened Movement	225.00
Bracket, Ebonized, Painted Dial, 18th Century, 16 1/4 In.	1450.00
Calculagraph, Key Wind, Telephone Co.	79.00
Carillon, 13-Bell, 8 Tunes, Angelus Chimes, C.1840, 3 1/2 Ft.	3250.00
Carriage, Brass, C.1900, 4 1/2 In.	385.00
Carriage, Brass, C.1900, 5 1/2 In.	465.00
Carriage, Hour Repeater, Brass, Late 19th Century, 5 1/4 In.	475.00
Cartel, French, Bronze Dore, 19th Century, 2 In.Long	260.00
Case, Federal, Mahogany, Arch Cornice, Inlaid Door, C.1800, 81 In.	900.00
Case, Inlaid, New England, Face Portrait Of Justice, C.1800, 83 In.	1100.00
Case, Mahogany, Quebec, C.1820	3000.00
Case, Pine, Brass Face, Moon Dial, Arch Bonnet, 86 In.	1500.00
Charles Stratton, 30-Hour, Wooden Works, Mahogany Case, Dated 1840	260.00
Chelsea Co., Boston, Ball Footed, Pedestal Base, Round, 5 In.	90.00
Chelsea, Banjo, Reverse Painted Glasses, Signed	1275.00
Chippendale, Tall Case, Walnut, Arched Door, C.1800, 8 Ft.	2420.00
Connecticut Clock Mfg., School, 8-Day, Mahogany	190.00
Continental Model, Blinking Eye, Cast Iron, 17 In.	800.00
Cuckoo, Walnut, 8 Men, Weight Driven, 33 X 22 In.	3880.00
D. Pratt & Sons, Shelf, 30-Hour Ogee, Fancy Dial	140.00
D.P.Davis, Banjo, Weight, All Original	2000.00
Daniel Pratt Jr., 30-Hour, Wooden Works, Mahogany Columns, Dated 1842	230.00
Daniel Pratt, Double Decker, 30-Hour, Wooden Works, Mahogany Case	325.00
Daniel Pratt, Reverse Ogee, Reverse Painted Border, 30-Hour, 27 In.	240.00
David Wood, Grandfather, 18th Century	9000.00
Edward Barnes, Flat Ogee, 30-Hour, Wooden Works	150.00
Eli Terry, Regulator, Alarm, 1-Day	100.00
Elisha Hotchkiss, Shelf, 30-Hour, Wooden Works, Stenciled Columns	230.00

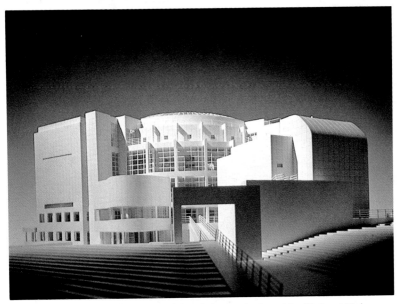

Model of the new High Museum of Art, Atlanta, designed by Richard Meier.
Exterior view from Peachtree Street, *Ezra Stroller © ESTO*

Clock, Mantel Set, Marble, Bronze, Gilt, Silver, Semiprecious Stones,
American, C. 1875, 3 Piece

Cabinet, Ebonized Cherry,
Herter Brothers,
C. 1880, 60 In.

Lantern, Copper & Stained
Glass, Pair, Marked Karl Kipp,
C. 1915, 11½ In.

Fireplace Andirons, Brass, Iron & Gilt, Washington in Uniform, American, C. 1850, 19¾ In.

Pedestal, Egyptian Revival, Ebonized Cherry, Gilt, C. 1875, 42 In.

KTK Lotusware Vase, East Liverpool, Ohio, C. 1895, 8¼ In.

Chesapeake Pottery, Pilgrim Vase, Transfer-Printed Floral Design, 18½ In.

Ott & Brewer Pitcher, Egg-Shaped, Ducks & Flowers, Marked, C. 1880, 13¼ In.

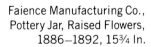

Faience Manufacturing Co., Pottery Jar, Raised Flowers, 1886–1892, 15¾ In.

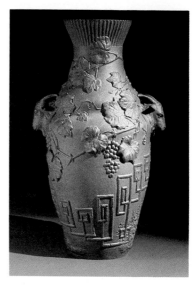

Tiffany Box, Copper & Enamel,
Jellyfish Pattern, Multicolored,
Marked, C. 1900, 4¼ In.

Ott & Brewer Pottery Vase, Bacchic
Design, Marked Broome,
1876, 17¾ In.
(Top right)

Rookwood Vase, Maria
Longworth Nichols,
Signed, 17¼ In.

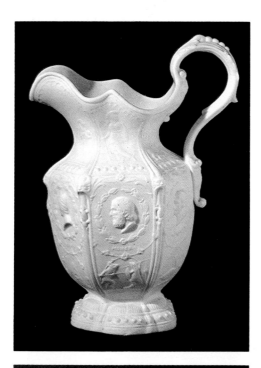

Union Porcelain Works
Pitcher, Six Medallions,
Greenpoint, New York,
C. 1876, 9 In.

Union Porcelain Works,
Pitcher, Rococo Revival,
Marked WB & BR's,
C. 1853, 7⅝ In.

Royal Flemish Vase, Flowers, Leaves, & Scrolls, Marked, 13⅜ In.

Art Glass Vase, Hobbs & Brockunier, C. 1886, 7⅞ In., Base: 3¼ In.

Universal City Plate, Taxile Doat, St. Louis, 1914, 9¼ In.

Empire, Mahogany, Eagle Crest, 30-Hour Movement, C.1830, 36 In.	325.00
English, Regency Style Case, Fusee Movement, C.1830	200.00
Ephraim Downs, 30-Hour, Wooden Works, Footed	420.00
F.Kroeber, Regulator, No.33	3000.00
Felix The Cat, Animated Eyes & Tail, 15 In.	20.00
Florence Droeber, Mantel, Time & Strike, 8-Day	275.00
French, Calendar, Mother-Of-Pearl Design, Silk String Suspension	900.00
French, Carriage, Time, Alarm	200.00
French, Champleve, Crystal Regulator, 8-Day, Time & Strike, 13 1/4 In.	1990.00
French, Colored Marble Inlay, Visible Escapement	145.00
French, Crystal Regulator, Barometer Below Clock, Engraved Mask	100.00
French, Crystal Regulator, Bow Front	395.00 To 450.00
French, Crystal Regulator, Mercury Pendulum, Porcelain Dial	325.00
French, Crystal Regulator, Time & Strike, 8-Day, Brass Case, 10 In.	450.00
French, Lion On Top, Nude Woman Each Side, Key Wind, Alabaster	125.00
French, Mantel, Late 19th Century, Gilt Metal, 21 1/2 In.	250.00
French, Mantel, Ornamented With Putti & Lovebirds, Bronze, 15 In.	600.00
French, Mantel, Visible Escapement, Inlaid Marble	135.00
French, Mercury Pendulum, Porcelain Dial, Brass & Glass	325.00
French, Pinwheel, Jeweler's, Regulator	4500.00
French, Regulator, Bow Front	395.00
French, Regulator, Crystal, Black Star & Frost, Mercury Pendulum	275.00
French, Regulator, Crystal, Bow Front, Porcelain Dial, Mercury Pendulum	365.00
French, Regulator, Mercury Pendulum, Gold Hands	350.00
French, Regulator, Mercury Pendulum, Porcelain Dial	325.00
French, Repeater Verge Strike, Hour & 1/2 Hour	1100.00
French, Wag-On-Wall, Brass Pendulum, 8-Day, Strike, 1800	500.00
French, Wall, Mother-Of-Pearl Inlaid, 19th Century	350.00
French, Wall, Westminster, Fruitwood	325.00
George Hoff, Lancaster, Pa., Walnut	1000.00
George III, Grandfather, Painted Face, C.1800, Signed, Oak, 85 In.	350.00
German, Bracket, Westminster Chime	100.00
German, Shelf, 2 Brass Pillars, 30-Hour Stem Wind, 5 X 9 In.	110.00
Gilbert, Alarm, Chimes At Hour & 1/2 Hour, Wooden	190.00
Gilbert, Art Nouveau Woman, Garlands, Gold Finish Bronze, 10 In.	225.00
Gilbert, Banjo, Figure-8 Style, Barometer & Thermometer	195.00
Gilbert, Calendar, Time & Strike, Maranville, Rosewood	675.00
Gilbert, Cottage, Time & Strike, 8-Day	125.00

Clock, Birge & Fuller, Twin Steeple,
8-Day, C.1844, 25 In.

Gilbert, Eastlake, Mantel, Etched Birds & Grapes 245.00
Gilbert, Gingerbread, Egyptian Model, Oak 160.00
Gilbert, Gingerbread, 8-Day, Pressed Oak Case 150.00
Gilbert, Mantel, Mission Oak 95.00
Gilbert, Mantel, Pendulum Driven 45.00
Gilbert, Mantel, Time & Strike, Camelback, Mahogany 60.00
Gilbert, No.10, Regulator 1500.00
Gilbert, Ogee, Mahogany 185.00
Gilbert, Parlor, Carved Crest, Sides, & Base, 8-Day, Walnut 240.00
Gilbert, Regulator, Calendar Movement, Time Only, Oak 275.00
Gilbert, Regulator, Wall, Miniature 150.00
Gilbert, School, C.1900 .... 275.00
Gilbert, Shelf, Ogee, 30-Hour, Reverse Painted Glass, Paper, 28 3/4 In. 285.00
Gilbert, Shelf, Pillared, Regulator Pendulum, Walnut 250.00
Gilbert, Wall, Cylinder Pendulum 125.00
Gilbert, 8-Day, Chrome Case, Art Deco, 6 1/2 In. 28.00
Grandfather, Federal, Brass Finials & Dial, American, C.1810, 80 In. 800.00
Grandfather, Finials & Pediment Hood, Brass Dial, England, 81 1/2 In. 450.00
Grandfather, Walnut, Ogee Feet, Columns, Arched Door, 91 In. 2600.00
Gustav Becker, Balloon 225.00
Gustav Becker, Bracket, Westminister, Silvered Dial, Mahognay, 16 In. 750.00
Gustav Becker, Regulator, 2-Weight, Carved Case 400.00
Hammond, Black & White Onyx, Mantel, Rectangular Case, 7 In. 70.00
Hammond, Electric Silver Dial, Calendar Windows, Manual Day & Date 60.00
Heller Movement, 8-Tune, Swiss Chalet, Strikes, 20 In. 3900.00
Hersheide, Grandfather, Tubular Bell Chime, Mahogany 3000.00
Hiram Hunt, Stenciled Column & Splat, 30-Hour, Wooden Works 220.00
Horace Tifft, Banjo 880.00
Horse, Gold & Silver Finish, Marbleized Base 25.00
Hotchkiss & Benedict, Weight Driven, Brass Works, Black & Gold Dial 675.00
Howard, Banjo , Rosewood 4600.00
Howard, Damascene, Pendulum Bob, Dial 12 In. 1275.00
Howard, Figure-8, No.2, Rosewood Case 4600.00
Howard, Figure-8, No.65 .... 950.00
Howard, No.27, White Marble 1900.00
Howard, No.70, Walnut Case 1375.00
Howard, Pendulum, Cut Glass Regulator 300.00
Howard, Regulator, Second Hand, Mercury Pendulum, Mahogany, 53 X 19 In. 1650.00
Imperial, Regulator, Store, Battery Operated, Mahogany 175.00
Ingraham, Banjo, 8-Day, Spring Driven, 2-Note Chime, 31 In. 200.00
Ingraham, Calendar, Wall, Meridian Time 300.00
Ingraham, Cornell, Shelf, 8-Day, Half & Hour Strike, 10 In. 85.00
Ingraham, Grecian, Bird's-Eye Maple, C.1870, 14 1/2 In. .... *Illus* 200.00
Ingraham, Grecian, 8-Day, Original Label, Rosewood Case 250.00
Ingraham, Kitchen, 8-Day, Oak 135.00
Ingraham, Long Drop, Time & Calendar, Oak 325.00
Ingraham, Mantel, Rounded Sides, 6 Free Standing Pillars, Black 90.00
Ingraham, Mantel, Side Lion Heads, Wood Case, 17 X 11 In. .... *Illus* 60.00
Ingraham, Regulator, Alliance, Time & Strike, Oak 450.00
Ingraham, Regulator, Store, Time & Calendar, Oak 325.00
Ingraham, School, Time Only, Oak 275.00
Ingraham, Shelf, Gingerbread, 8-Day, Walnut 150.00
Ingraham, Steeple, Brass Springs, 8-Day, Gothic Style, Signed 230.00
Ingraham, Steeple, Fuzee, 30-Hour, Gothic 310.00
Ingraham, Wall, Ionic Mosaic, Time & Strike, Walnut & Chestnut Case 325.00
Ingraham, Wall, Meridian, Time & Strike, Rosewood 350.00
Ingraham, Wall, Reverse Painted Glass, 8-Day, Time & Strike 275.00
Ingraham, 8-Day, Oak, Kitchen, Shelf, Chimes, Gilt, Tin Face 165.00
Ingram, Wall, Bartholdi, Walnut, 44 In. 650.00
Ithaca, Calendar, D Dial, Rosewood Case 1500.00
Ithaca, Calendar, Double Dial, Farmer's Model No.10 .... 750.00
Ithaca, Calendar, Farmer's Pattern, Walnut, C.1865, 26 In. .... *Illus* 600.00
Ithaca, Calendar, Original Roller Papers, Walnut Case 675.00

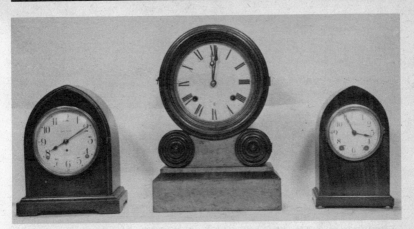

Clocks, Seth Thomas, Gothic, Beehive Top, Walnut, 10 1/4 In.; Ingraham, Grecian, Bird's-Eye Maple, C.1870, 14 1/2 In.; Seth Thomas, Shelf, Gothic, Convex Glass, 9 1/2 In.
(See Pages 125, 126)

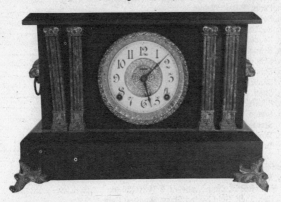

Clock, Ingraham, Mantel, Side Lion Heads, Wood Case, 17 X 11 In.

Ithaca, Model O, Bank, Wall	4200.00
J.C.Brown, Steeple, 30-Hour, Signed Movement & Dial	160.00
Jaeger Le Coultre, Cube Shape, Frosted Glass, Weights, 9 X 7 In.	300.00
Janghaus, Mantel, Time, Strike, & Calendar, Westminster Chime, Mahogany	175.00
Jasper, Maiden, Water Lilies, Blue, White, Number Impressed, 5 In.	72.00
Jerome & Co., Hanging, Victorian Gingerbread, 8-Day	240.00
Jerome, Cottage, Upside Down Movement, Glass Design, Labels	240.00
Jerome, Steeple, 8-Day, C.1850, Mahogany	275.00
Jeromes & Darrow, Triple Decker, Wooden Works	360.00
John Polsey, Banjo, Weight Driven, Signed	1250.00
Jonas Fitch, Pepperill, Mass., 1770, Tall Case	2500.00
Jonathan Frost Jr., 30-Hour, Wooden Works, Mahogany Columns	240.00
Jonathan Frost, Steeple, Strike & Alarm, Reverse Painting	225.00
Junghans, Carriage, Musical, 2 Tunes, Triple Dial	108.00
Junghans, Mantel, Time, Strike, & Calendar, Westminster Chimes, Mahogany	350.00
Kearney, Pillar & Scroll	990.00
Kitchen, Walnut, Overlay Trim, New Hampshire	125.00

L.F.& W.W.Carter, Double Dial Calendar, Burl Case 750.00
Lincoln, Regulator, Time & Strike 1050.00
Lux, Cuckoo, Animated Bird, 30-Hour 35.00
Mantel, Beveled Glass, Trapezoid Face, Amber, Chrome Trim, 8 X 14 In. 200.00
Mantel, Black, Gargoyle Handled 65.00
Mantel, Gingerbread, Walnut 135.00
Mantel, Marble & Bronze, Architectural Form, Black, 16 In. 175.00
Marble & Onyx, Bronze Lady, Flowing Robe, Ivory Face, Art Deco 1800.00
Maritime Clock Co., Ship's Bell, 8-Day, Brass Case, 6 In.Diam. 365.00
Miller, Calendar, Regulator, Wall, Double Dial, Rosewood, 53 In. 3500.00
New England, Banjo, Painted Scene Of The Constitution Escape 1000.00
New Haven Clock Co., Banjo, Mahogany Case, 22 In. 80.00
New Haven Whitney, Banjo, 29 In. .... 135.00 To 235.00
New Haven, Banjo, Brass Rope Trim, 30-Day, 40 In. 575.00
New Haven, Banjo, Miniature, 12-Day 125.00
New Haven, Banjo, Pendulum Movement, 8-Day, 29 In. 195.00
New Haven, Banjo, Time & Strike 350.00
New Haven, Banjo, Time Only, Mahogany 225.00
New Haven, Banjo, Walnut, 26 In. 155.00
New Haven, Banjo, 30-Day 400.00
New Haven, Banjo, 8-Day, 25 In. 150.00
New Haven, Elfrida, Regulator 1200.00
New Haven, Gingerbread, Time & Strike, Barometer & Thermometer, Oak 190.00
New Haven, Lily Of The Valley & Cupids, Green Jasperware, 5 1/2 In. 75.00
New Haven, Parlor, 8-Day, Walnut 180.00
New Haven, Regulator, Beveled Glass, 8-Day, Time & Strike, 26 In. 250.00
New Haven, Regulator, Octagonal, Long Drop 300.00
New Haven, Regulator, Wall, Jeweler's, Glass Sides, Walnut 2950.00
New Haven, School, Miniature, 5 In. Dial 125.00
New Haven, School, Strike, Octagonal Drop, Oak 250.00
New Haven, School, 8-Day, Time & Strike, Octagonal 250.00
New Haven, Shelf, Camelback, Time & Strike, Mahogany 65.00
New Haven, Shelf, 30-Hour, Ogee, Reverse Painted Tablet 140.00
New Haven, Silvered Dial, Florals, White Ground, China Case, 8 1/2 In. 130.00
New Haven, Statue, Poetry 350.00
New Haven, Statue, Saxon 450.00
New Haven, Time & Calendar, Rosewood 340.00
New Haven, Time & Strike, Inlaid, Walnut 325.00
New Haven, Traveling, Alarm, Box & Papers 50.00
Novelty, Sessions, Airplane Shape, Electric, Art Deco, 9 1/2 X 21 In. 110.00
Ogee, 8-Day, Mahogany 235.00
Orrin Hart, Shelf, Bristol, Conn., Labeled, C.1830, 35 In. 120.00
Plymouth, 8-Day, Shelf, Gold Leafed Glass, Ebonized Case 295.00
R. & A., Regulator 275.00
Regulator, French, Brass & Crystal, Gold Hands, Pendulum 350.00
Regulator, Keyhole, Waltham 1200.00
Remco Co., Cuckoo, Pinky Lee, Boxed 30.00
Revival, Rococo, Continental, 16 In. 150.00
Sambo, Blinking Eye, Cast Iron, C.1860, 15 1/2 In. 500.00
Saturn, Regulator 850.00
Sawing Style, Banjo, Mahogany .... 650.00 To 875.00
School, Black Forest, Germany, 8-Day, 12 In. 295.00
Sessions, Airplane Shape, Chrome, Rubber Wheels, 1930s, 3 X 21 In. 130.00
Sessions, Alarm, Electric, Ivory Celluloid Case, 7 1/4 X 4 1/4 In. 14.00
Sessions, Banjo, Cape Cod 95.00
Sessions, Banjo, Time & Strike, Lighthouse & Ship, 35 In. 275.00
Sessions, Banjo, 5-Day, Large 300.00
Sessions, Banjo, 8-Day, Mt.Vernon Case 225.00
Sessions, Gingerbread, 8-Day, Serpent Design, Oak 150.00
Sessions, Mantel, Black, Time & Strike 75.00
Sessions, Mantel, Celluloid Dial, Time & Strike 75.00
Sessions, Mantel, Hour Chime, Half Hour Strike, Wooden, Black 125.00
Sessions, Mantel, 8-Day 100.00
Sessions, No.5, Regulator 1100.00

(See Page 122)

Clock, Ithaca, Calendar, Farmer's
Pattern, Walnut, C. 1865, 26 In.

Sessions, No.6, Regulator	1200.00
Sessions, Regulator, Store, Time & Calendar	400.00
Sessions, Shelf, Pillars, Walnut	45.00
Seth Thomas Yale, Golden Oak, 8-Day, Kitchen	175.00
Seth Thomas, Adamatine, Mantel, 8-Day, Marbleized Case, Gilt Feet	140.00
Seth Thomas, Banjo, 8-Day, Time & Strike, 29 In.	195.00
Seth Thomas, Boston City Series	275.00
Seth Thomas, Calendar, Double Dial, Rosewood Veneer Case, 2 In.	890.00
Seth Thomas, Carriage, Brass Folding Handle, Roman Numerals, Brass	145.00
Seth Thomas, Column Weight, 3-Hour	175.00
Seth Thomas, Cottage, 3-Sided Top, Rosewood, Miniature	110.00
Seth Thomas, Eclipse, Hanging, Gingerbread	425.00
Seth Thomas, Free Standing Columns, White Adamatine	125.00
Seth Thomas, Gallery, Oak, Dial 12 In.	195.00 To 250.00
Seth Thomas, Gallery, 8-Day, Pendulum Movement, 16 X 16 In.	150.00
Seth Thomas, Gothic, Beehive Top, Walnut, 10 1/4 In. *Illus*	95.00
Seth Thomas, Gothic, 8-Day, Cathedral Gong, Mahogany, 11 In.	125.00
Seth Thomas, Iron Weight Pulleys, Wooden Works, 1840, 35 In.	1800.00
Seth Thomas, Kitchen, Time, Strike, & Alarm, Oak & Metal	175.00 To 200.00
Seth Thomas, Long Drop, Double Wind, 30-Day, Walnut, 32 In.	420.00
Seth Thomas, Mantel, Lyre Movement, Rosewood	275.00
Seth Thomas, Mantel, Time & Strike, Adamatine Finish	65.00
Seth Thomas, No.2 Regulator, Oak	795.00 To 850.00
Seth Thomas, No.6, Regulator	1500.00
Seth Thomas, No.30, Regulator	1150.00
Seth Thomas, Ogee, Mahogany & Bird's-Eye Maple Case	250.00
Seth Thomas, Outside Bell, Replaced Dial	385.00
Seth Thomas, Parlor Calendar, No.3, Original Dials, Paper	900.00
Seth Thomas, Pillar & Scroll, Brass Finials, Reverse Painting, 24 In.	375.00
Seth Thomas, Pillar & Scroll, Mahogany, C.1890, Three-Quarter Size	340.00
Seth Thomas, Regulator, Golden Oak Case	2500.00
Seth Thomas, Regulator, Reverse Painted Glass, Rosewood, 16 X 32 In.	475.00
Seth Thomas, Regulator, 2-Weight, Mahogany	785.00
Seth Thomas, Regulator, 3-Weight	975.00
Seth Thomas, Regulator, 54 In. Drop	1995.00

Seth Thomas, School, Reo Model, 8-Day, Time & Strike, Brass Trim 395.00
Seth Thomas, School, Time Only, Oak 275.00
Seth Thomas, School, Time Only, Rosewood Case 275.00
Seth Thomas, Shelf, Flat Ogee, 30-Hour Movement, Rosewood, 15 1/2 In. 170.00
Seth Thomas, Shelf, Gothic, Convex Glass, 9 1/2 In. .... *Illus* 45.00
Seth Thomas, Shelf, Ogee, 30-Hour, Split Door, C.1870, Maple, 15 3/4 In. 195.00
Seth Thomas, Shelf, Rosewood, Lyre Movement 160.00
Seth Thomas, Shelf, Time & Strike, Lyre Movement, Original Label 140.00
Seth Thomas, Shelf, 30-Hour, Brass Works, Reverse Painting, 15 3/4 In. 195.00
Seth Thomas, Shelf, 8-Day, Time & Strike, Reverse Glass ....:............... 125.00 To 150.00
Seth Thomas, Shelf, 8-Day, Walnut Case 130.00
Seth Thomas, Short Case, Carved Splat, Columns, & Feet 750.00
Seth Thomas, Short Drop, 30-Hour Wooden Works, Stenciled Columns 300.00
Seth Thomas, Sonora, Wall, Slag Glass Paneled Door, Mahogany 975.00
Seth Thomas, Sonora, 8-Bell, Inlaid Gothic Case 750.00
Seth Thomas, Steeple, 8-Day, Time & Strike 145.00
Seth Thomas, Stenciled, 30-Hour, Wooden Works, Label 240.00
Seth Thomas, 30-Hour, Columns, Mahogany 125.00
Shelf, Eastlake, 1875-1900, Black, Gilt Trim, 20 In. .... *Illus* 80.00
Shelf, Eastlake, 1875-1900, Brass Movement, Walnut, 21 In. .... *Illus* 80.00
Shelf, Mahogany, Ogee, Tin Face, Weights, Mirror Glass, 15 X 26 In. 125.00
Silas Hoadley, Grandfather, Door Marked, Repaired 1869 .... 5250.00
Silas Hoadley, Stenciled Columns, Ivory Bushed Movement, 30 In. 360.00
Smith & Blakesley, Triangular Columns, 30-Hour, Wooden Works 220.00
Standard Calendar Clock Co., Ogee With Calendar, Gold Leaf 280.00
Standard Electric Time Co., Master, Dark Oak, 19 X 48 In. 450.00
Strauss Brothers, Cast Iron 2250.00
Stromberg, Master, Electric, 5 Ft.Long 525.00
Stromberg, Time Punch, Electric .... 50.00 To 65.00
Swiss, Chalet, 3-Dimensional People, Amimals, Birds At Windows, Iron 750.00
Swiss, Cuckoo, Musical, 6-Tune Brass Plate, 20 X 34 In. 1900.00
Table, Bakelite, Oval, Art Deco, 3 3/4 X 4 In. 30.00
Tall Case, Federal, Inlaid Mahogany, Rocking Ship, C.1800, 8 Ft. 9350.00
Tall Case, Federal, Mahogany, Brass Dial, Arched Door, C.1785, 7 Ft. 4225.00
Tall Case, Federal, Pine, Scalloped Skirt, Bracket Feet, 7 Ft. 1760.00
Tall, New Haven Clock Co., Arts & Crafts, C.1915, 84 In. .... *Illus* 225.00
Tall, Timothy Chandler, Concord, New Hampshire, 82 In. .... *Illus* 3000.00
Teddy Bear, Animated, Key Wind, German 25.00
Terhune & Edwards, Iron Front, 30-Hour 130.00
Terry & Andrews, Shelf, 30-Hour, Ogee, Weight, Stenciled Tablet 140.00
Terry, Stenciled Columns & Glass Splat, 30-Hour, Wooden Works, 27 In. 375.00
Thomas Willard, Grandfather, Walnut, C.1790 .... 990.00
Thos.Snow, Grandfather, Recoil Anchor Escapement, C.1811, 8 Ft. 1 In. 1870.00
    CLOCK, TIFFANY, see Tiffany, Clock
Topsy, Blinking Eye, C.1860, 1-Day, Cast Iron, 16 1/2 In. 500.00
Travel, Art Deco, Oval Bakelite Frame, 3 3/4 X 4 In. 30.00
Treasure Island, Banjo 495.00
Umbria, Regulator, 30-Day, Time & Strike 950.00
Vienna, Regulator, 2-Weight, Tiger Oak, Walnut Burl Accents 450.00
W.S.Johnson, Empire, 8-Day, Brass Spring, Miniature 220.00
W.S.Johnson, Ogee, Internal Alarm, Beveled Door, 30-Hour, Wooden Works 150.00
W.S.Johnson, Shelf, 8-Day, Lyre Movement, Signed 260.00
W.S.Johnson, Shelf, 30-Hour, Ogee, Tablet of Flowers 140.00
Wag-On-Wall, Wooden Face, Floral Design, White Ground, 17 In. 300.00
Wall, Brass, Repousse, Victorian 125.00
Wall, Eastlake, Satinwood Inlay, Mahogany, 16 X 36 In. .... *Illus* 160.00
Wall, French, Brass Enamel Face, Polychrome 300.00
Wall, Lattice Trim, Mission Oak, 30 In. 120.00
Wall, Profile Of Columbus, World's Fair, 1893, 14 1/2 In. .... *Illus* 85.00
Wall, Stencil Design, Marquetry, Mahogany Veneer, 30 In. .... *Illus* 180.00
Waterbury, Banjo, Reverse Painted Glasses, Porcelain Dial, 42 In. 500.00
Waterbury, Calendar, Large 400.00
Waterbury, Carriage, Brass Case, Beveled Glass Front, Alarm 120.00
Waterbury, Carriage, Brass, 3 In. 125.00

Clock, Shelf, Eastlake, 1875-1900,
Black, Gilt Trim, 20 In.

Clock, Shelf, Eastlake, 1875-1900,
Brass Movement, Walnut, 21 In.

Clock, Tall, New Haven Clock Co., Arts
& Crafts, C.1915, 84 In.

Clock, Tall, Timothy Chandler, Concord,
New Hampshire, 82 In.

(See Page 126)

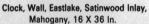

Clock, Wall, Eastlake, Satinwood Inlay,
Mahogany, 16 X 36 In.

Clock, Wall, Profile Of Columbus,
World's Fair, 1893, 14 1/2 In.

Waterbury, Carriage, Half Hour Strike, Repeater With Alarm	425.00
Waterbury, Gingerbread, 8-Day, Oak Case	150.00
Waterbury, Kitchen, Walnut	100.00
Waterbury, Mantel, Open Escapement, Porcelain Dial, Mahogany	180.00
Waterbury, Marine, Octagon Oak Case, 7 In.Dial	100.00
Waterbury, No.3, Regulator	1350.00
Waterbury, No.11, Regulator	2250.00
Waterbury, School, Oak	240.00 To 350.00
Waterbury, Short Drop, Time Only, Rosewood Veneer, Dial 12 In.	350.00
Waterbury, Statue, Man Holding Rabbit, Louis XV Model, 18 In.	265.00
Waterbury, Time, Strike, & Alarm, 30-Hour, Walnut	120.00
Waterbury, Timer, Turn On Coal Furnace	100.00
Welch Verdi, A Frame Movement, 15-Day, Rosewood	495.00
Welch, Calendar, Octagonal, Rosewood	375.00
Welch, Calendar, Perpetual, Double Dial	850.00
Welch, Calendar, Time Only, Golden Oak	450.00
Welch, Gothic, Shelf, Glass Pendulum, Time & Alarm, Rosewood, 12 In.	150.00
Welch, Hanging, Blue Painted China, Bird & Flowers	235.00
Welch, Kitchen, 30-Hour, Walnut	150.00
Welch, Mantel, Porcelain Dial, Visible Escapement, Marble	145.00
Welch, Oak Gingerbread, Reverse Painting, Battleship, C.1900	185.00
Welch, Regulator, Store, Oak	235.00
Welch, Regulator, Time & Strike, 30-Hour, Rosewood	170.00
Welch, School, Mahogany	170.00
Welch, School, Oak, 1884-1903, 17 1/2 X 28 In. *Illus*	140.00
Welch, School, Time Only, Octagonal Case, 26 X 18 In.	285.00
Welch, Shelf, 30-Hour, Ogee, Painted Tablet, Signed Movement	130.00
Weldon, Ogee, Wooden Works, C.1840, Original Mirror, 25 1/2 In.	395.00
Western Clock Mfg. Co., Mantel, Art Nouveau	95.00
Western Horse, Gear, United Brass Plated, White Metal, 11 X 7 In.	25.00

Clock, Wall, Stencil Design, Marquetry,
Mahogany Veneer, 30 In.
(See Page 126)

Clock, Welch, School, Oak, 1884-
1903, 17 1/2 X 28 In.

Westminster, Chime, Bracket, German	100.00
Whitney, Banjo, Reverse Painted Glass, 33 In.	190.00
Willard Type, Banjo, C.1815	1750.00
William And Mary, Case, Molded Cornice, Marked, 18th Century, 84 In.	1600.00
Williams, Orton-Preston & Co., 30-Hour, Wooden Works	240.00
Wizard, Token Dispensing, Trade Stimulator	1100.00
Wood, Alarm, Animated, 1959	155.00

Cloisonne enamel was developed during the tenth century. A glass enamel was applied between small ribbonlike pieces of metal on a metal base. Most Cloisonne is Chinese or Japanese.

CLOISONNE, Bottle, Snuff, Blue Ground, Flowers & Butterflies	125.00
Bowl, Silver Gilt, Inverted Rim, Marked, 3 1/2 In.	800.00
Bowl, Turquoise Ground, Flowers & Fruits, 9 In.	350.00
Bowl, White, Blue, Red, Yellow, Flowers, Pair	135.00
Box, Archaic Pattern, Quail Form, 5 1/4 X 3 In., Pair	650.00
Box, Blue Flower Design, Covered, 3 X 3 In.	85.00
Box, Cigarette, Button Feet, Polychrome Chrysanthemum, Cover	45.00
Box, Cigarette, Matching Matchbox	65.00
Box, Cigarette, 19th Century, Opaque, 3 In.	70.00
Box, Green Ground, White Flowers & Stem, Oval, 3 1/2 In.	58.00
Box, Green, 6 1/2 X 5 X 2 In.	75.00
Box, On Satsuma, Enameled Beading, Lift-Off Cover, 3 1/4 In.Diam.	195.00
Box, Orange Flower Design, Covered, Marked China, 3 1/2 X 3 In.	85.00
Box, Red, Blue & Pink Flowers, 4 Parts, 5 X 7 In.	125.00
Box, Snuff, Floral Scroll, Covered, 3 In.	225.00
Box, 20th Century, Opaque, 1 5/8 X 5 1/2 In.	125.00
Buckle, Enamel On Copper, 2-Part, 2 1/4 X 1 1/4 In.	70.00
Candlestick, Pale Blue, Floral & Scroll, 8 In., Pair	85.00
Candlestick, Turquoise Ground, Lotus Blossoms, Pair, 8 In.	275.00
Censer, Bird, Movable Breast & Head Cover, 9 1/2 In., Pair	660.00
Charger, Blue Ground, Birds, Flowers, 12 In.	380.00
Charger, Flowers & Leaves, Birds In Flight, Blue Ground, 11 In.	450.00
Charger, Long-Legged Birds, Gray-Green Ground, 11 3/4 In.	475.00
Clasp, Belt, Silver, Bronze, Turquoise Tones, Pair	500.00
Cup, Sake, Blue, Flowers, Set Of 5	60.00

Dish, Mutton Jade Insert, Flowers, Black Ground, Chinese, 4 1/2 In. 75.00
Figurine, Cockerel, Leg On Trunk, Turquoise Ground, 17 1/2 In., Pr. 1600.00
Figurine, Horse, Prancing, Blue, Enamel Scrollwork, 5 X 6 In., Pair 825.00
Figurine, Horse, Walking, Blue Ground, Scrolls, 5 X 6 In. 735.00
Figurine, Horses, Walking, Pastel Colors, 5 X 6 In., Pair 685.00
Ginger Jar, Flowers, Chinese, Black Ground, 11 1/2 In. 275.00
Gourd, Scenic Panels, 8 In., Pair 472.00
Humidor, Blossoms, 19th Century, Sponge Holder, Black Ground, 6 In. 195.00
Jar, Butterflies, Goldstone, Green, Black, Covered, 4 In. 295.00
Jar, Flowers & Butterflies, Goldstone Flecks, C.1890, 4 In. 225.00
Jar, Polychrome Leaves & Flowers, Brass Flower Finial, 4 3/4 In. 120.00
Jar, Twisted Wire, Covered, 3 X 3 In. 160.00
Jar, 7 Medallions, White Outlined, Brass Feet, Covered, 2 1/2 In. 140.00
Jardiniere, C.1840, 3 1/2 X 2 In., Pair 325.00
Lamp, Oil, Frosted Ball Shade, Herons & Florals, 24 In. 1495.00
Match Holder, Leaf 125.00
Matchbox Holder, Rust 8.00
Napkin Ring, 2 Dragons, Flaming Pearl, Brass 35.00
Planter, Barrel Shape, 3 Butterfly Feet, C.1880, 8 1/4 In. 835.00
Planter, Moriage Trim, Marked 175.00
Planter, Overall Floral Design, Scalloped Rim, 6 In. 160.00
Planter, Polychrome Enamels, Blue Ground, 10 1/4 In., Pair 275.00
Plate, Silver Wire Design, Butterflies, 9 1/2 In. 275.00
Salt, 3 Feet 16.00
Smoking Set, Floral, 3 Piece 60.00
Snuff Bottle, Flowers & Butterflies, Blue Ground 125.00
Teapot, Bronze Mongoose On Cover, Handle, Spout, 4 1/2 In. 500.00
Teapot, Twist Wires, Shield-Shaped Sections, 3 3/4 In. 245.00
Teapot, Two K-Claw Dragons, Gold Clouds, 6 1/4 In. 180.00
Toothpick, Red, Blue Flowers, Green Ivy, Yellow Ground 1 1/2 In. 40.00
Toothpick, Turquoise Ground, Floral Design, Marked China, 1 3/4 In 22.00
Tray, Forest Green, Berries, Brass Filagree, Round, 6 In. 60.00
Tray, Polychrome Floral & Butterfly, Blue Enamel Back, 12 In. 130.00
Urn, Chinese, Covered, Mountain, Camels, Butterfly, 3 X 3 In. 75.00
Urn, Green Ground, White, Yellow, Flowers, 6 1/2 In. 115.00
Urn, 3-Toed Dragon On Cover, Some Goldstone, 2 1/2 In.Diam. 145.00
Vase, Akasuke, Pink & White Roses, Bird, Palm, 3 1/2 In. 315.00
Vase, Bamboo Design, Black & White, 4 X 4 In. 75.00
Vase, Birds & Flowers, 12 In. 295.00
Vase, Black Ground, Dragons, Waves, Lappets, 10 1/4 In. 150.00
Vase, Black Ground, Flowers, 6 3/4 In. 160.00
Vase, Black, White Bamboo Design, Bulbous, 4 In. 75.00
Vase, Blue & Green, Florals 495.00
Vase, Blue & Purple Irises, Ice Blue Ground, 6 In. 450.00
Vase, Blue Flowered, 7 In. 325.00
Vase, Blue Ground, Brass Scroll, Red, Orange, Blue, 4 In. 35.00
Vase, Blue Irises On Yellow Ground, 3 3/4 In. 250.00
Vase, Crystal, Fish Design, Green, Plique-A-Jour, 5 1/4 In. 590.00
Vase, Dark Blue Ground, Dragons, Round, 10 1/2 In., Pair 1250.00
Vase, Dark Blue, 8 In., Pair 135.00
Vase, Dragon, Blue Ground, Square Sides, 10 1/2 In., Pair 1250.00
Vase, Dragon, Tan Ground, 10 In. 275.00
Vase, Fish Scale Pidgeon Blood, Blooming Tiger Lily, 7 In. 135.00
Vase, Floral Design, Crackle Glaze, C.1890, 3 1/2 In. .... *Illus*   90.00
Vase, Floral Design, Melon-Shaped, Black Ground, 5 In., Pair 785.00
Vase, Flowers & Butterflies, Goldstone & Blue, 1890, 5 In. 195.00
Vase, Flowers & Geometrics, Multicolored, 12 In. 225.00
Vase, Flowers & Stems, Light Green Ground, 5 1/4 In. 70.00
Vase, Flowers, Black Ground, 6 In., Pair 240.00
Vase, Flowers, Leaves, Blue Ground, C.1890, 3 3/4 In. .... *Illus*   100.00
Vase, Foil Flowers, Lavender & Orange, Black Ground, 3 In. 75.00
Vase, Goldstone & Blue Panels, Flowers, Butterflies, 5 In. 195.00
Vase, Green & White Fish Scale Ground, Flowers, Leaves, 7 In. 190.00

Cloisonne, Vase, Floral Design, Crackle Glaze,
C.1890, 3 1/2 In.

Cloisonne, Vase, Flowers, Leaves, Blue Ground,
C.1890, 3 3/4 In.

Vase, Lavender Flowers On Black, 5 In., **Pair** 75.00
Vase, Melon-Shaped, Chrysanthemum, Peony, & Wisteria, 5 In. 785.00
Vase, Mid-19th Century, Japanese, 15 1/2 In., Pair 550.00
Vase, Multicolored Flowers & Birds, 10 In. 275.00
Vase, Multicolored Mons, Dark Blue Ground, 4 In., Pair 395.00
Vase, Multicolored Mons, Turquoise Ground, 4 In., Pair 450.00
Vase, Panel With Flowers, Foil, & Goldstone, Dark Ground, 8 In. 185.00
Vase, Pearlized White, Mum Design, Fish Scale, 5 In. 365.00
Vase, Pigeon Blood Ground, Floral Design, Trees, Tiger Lily, 7 In. 145.00
Vase, Pigeon Blood, Cone Shape, Birds, 9 1/2 In., Pair 180.00
Vase, Pigeon Blood, 3 1/2 In. 80.00
Vase, Pink & White Flowers, Green Ground, 6 In. 225.00
Vase, Pink, White, Red Flowers, Black Ground, Pair 55.00
Vase, Roses & Leaves, Pigeon Blood Ground, 8 1/2 In. 155.00
Vase, Serpent Handles, Japanese, 15 In. 350.00
Vase, Spring Scroll Cloisons On Blue, Flowers, 3 1/4 In. 85.00
Vase, Swans On Lake, Fish Scale, 5 In. 45.00
Vase, White Herons, Green Foil Ground, C.1890, 3 3/4 In. 100.00
Vase, Yellow, Red, & Blue Florals, Cloud Cloisons, 4 In. 50.00
    CLOTHING, see Textile

Cluthra glass is a two-layered glass with small air pockets that form white
spots. The Steuben Glass Works of Corning, New York, made it after
1903. Kimball Glass Company of Vineland, New Jersey, made Cluthra
from about 1925.
    CLUTHRA, see also Steuben
CLUTHRA, Vase, Baluster Top, Jade & White, Signed Kimble, 12 In. 300.00
    Vase, Cylindrical Gourd Form, Signed, 7 3/4 In. 140.00

Coalport ware has been made by the Coalport Porcelain Works of
England from 1795 to the present time.
    COALPORT, see also Indian Tree
COALPORT, Box, Trinket, White With Roses, C.1891, 1 1/2 X 4 In. 50.00
    Candlestick, King's Ware, Black Crown Mark, 4 In., Pair 30.00
    Cup & Saucer, Cobalt Blue, Gold Design, Birds, Flowers 20.00
    Cup & Saucer, Demitasse, Blue 60.00
    Cup & Saucer, Gold Interior, 4 Gold Feet, C.1890, Miniature 58.00

Cup & Saucer, Indian Tree 20.00
Cup & Saucer, 10 Panels, Hand-Painted Birds, Demitasse 400.00
Dessert Set, Castle Scenes, Green, Gold Edges, C.1820, 14 Piece 1895.00
Egg, Porcelain, Hard Paste, 2 1/2 X 3 X 4 1/2 In. 50.00
Plate, Hand-Painted, Floral Center, Marked Thomas Dixon, 10 In., Pr. 350.00
Plate, Hand-Painted, Kenilworth Castle, Signed P.Simpson, 9 1/2 In. 168.00
Plate, Hand-Painted, Windsor Castle, Signed Simpson, 9 1/2 In. 168.00
Urn, Oriental Coloring, 1810-1820, 6 X 9 In. 595.00
Vase, Gold Ground, Turquoise Dots, Lion Head Handled, 6 In. 445.00

Cobalt blue glass was made using oxide of cobalt. The characteristic bright dark blue identifies it for the collector. Most cobalt glass found today was made after the Civil War.

COBALT BLUE, see also Shirley Temple

COBALT BLUE, Bottle, Perfume, Floral, Gold Trim, Stopper, 2 1/2 X 6 In. 85.00
Bottle, Perfume, Paneled Overlay, 6 1/2 In. 75.00
Box, Hinged, Enamel Design, Glass & Brass, 4 In.Diam. 75.00
Box, Jewel, Silver Ormolu, Enameled Design, 4 1/2 X 4 1/2 In. 379.00
Box, Puff, Hand-Painted Boy & Girl, Marked, 4 1/2 In.Diam. 48.00
Box, White Dot Enamel, Green Flowers, Hinged, 3 1/2 X 2 1/2 In. 80.00
Butter, Gold Design Of Angels, Rayed Bottom, Covered 125.00
Carafe, Pink Scrolls, Flowers, Clear Cut Stopper, 2 X 4 In. 125.00
Decanter, Crystal Stopper, Polished Base 75.00
Ewer, Allover Gilt & Enamel, Blue, 6 In. 48.00
Ewer, White Enamel Floral Design, 11 1/2 In. 85.00
Eyecup, Fishbowl Style, Wooden Stem 55.00
Pitcher, Advertising, Seagram's V.O.Canadian 5.00
Pitcher, Gold Band, White Dots, Cobalt Blue Handle, 2 In. 65.00
Pitcher, Water, Clear Reeded Handle 48.00
Pitcher, Water, Opalescent, Swirl, Northwood 225.00
Salt & Pepper, Fine Rib Pattern 10.00
Spittoon 65.00
Vase, Floral Medallion, Gold Trim, Signed, 11 In. 85.00
Vase, French, 3 Eagles, Wings Form Feet, Silver Footed, 7 1/4 In. 195.00

Coca-Cola advertising items have become a special field for collectors.

COCA-COLA, Ashtray, Coke Logo, Glass, 1951 .... 10.00
Bank, Tin 65.00
Bank, Vending Machine, Boxed 75.00
Banner, Cloth, Red, White Squares, 18 X 43 In. 5.00
Barrel, Syrup, Label, 1920s 75.00
Blotter, Bottle On Both Ends, 1920s 20.00
Blotter, Coke Time, From Canada 11.00
Book, Flower Arranging, Book 2, 1941 .... 9.00
Booklet, Lindbergh, 1929 .... 20.00
Bottle Opener, Hanging 10.00
Bottle Opener, Star X, Cast Iron, Wall Mount, Boxed 3.00
Bottle Opener, 1935 .... 10.00
Bottle Protector, Prevents Drips, 1932, A Great Drink With Lunch 1.25
Bottle Protector, Prevents Drips, 1932, Thirst Asks Nothing More 1.25
Bottle, Amber 40.00
Bottle, Amber, Kentucky 23.00
Bottle, Circleville Pumpkin Show, Coke Logo, Filled 3.50
Bottle, Display, 1923, 20 In. 145.00
Bottle, Miniature, 3 In. 1.00
Bottle, Seltzer, Etched, Blue, C.1930 .... 28.00
Bottle, Soda Water, Clear, Coca-Cola Marking 6.00
Bottle, Spanish, Case Of 12, 3 In. 12.00
Bottle, 1951 .... 4.00
Bowl, Pretzel, Aluminum, 1935 .... 60.00
Box, Recipe, Complete With Recipes, Coke Logo 6.00
Calendar, 1921 .... 300.00
Calendar, 1926, Year & Month Sheets, 10 X 19 In. .... 250.00 To 350.00

Calendar, 1933 .... 275.00
Calendar, 1953, Girls In Uniform, 12 X 22 In. 48.00
Calendar, 1955, 15 X 17 In. 30.00
Cap, Flexible, Plastic, Used To Twist Off Caps 4.00
Cards, Nature Study, Boxed .... 6.00 To 35.00
Changer, Coin, Coke Red Key, 1940s 95.00
Check, 1940s 7.00
Clock, C.1950 .... 55.00
Clock, 1910, Regulator .... 950.00 To 985.00
Coaster, Instructs How To Drink From Bottle, 1940's 2.50
Coin-Operated Machine, Bottle Dispenser, 10 Cent Slot, 1930s 150.00
Cooler, Glascock, Please Pay The Clerk, 1929 .... 425.00
Cooler, 1938 .... 325.00
Dispenser, Fountain, 1938 .... 325.00
Dispenser, Fountain, 1950s 75.00
Dispenser, Fountain, 1960 .... 100.00
Dispenser, Syrup, Wheeling Pottery Co. 1850.00
Door Push, Brass, 1901 .... 65.00
Fairy Lamp, Red, Art Glass 59.00
Fan, Made Of Raffia Palm, Marked 20.00
Game, Cribbage Board, Advertising 45.00
Glass, C.1905, Set Of 6 .... 725.00
Glass, Shot, Coke Adds Life To Parties 4.00
Holder, Pin, Sprite Boy, 2 1/4 In. 1.50
Ice Pick & Bottle Opener, Combination, Written In Script, With Ad 45.00
Jug, Syrup, Paper Label, And Cap 7.50
Key Chain, Miniature Coke Can, Boxed 2.00
Key Chain, T-Shirt Shaped Fob, Have A Coke And A Smile 1.50
Lighter, Cigarette, Bottle Shape, 1938 .... 10.00
Lighter, Cigarette, Bottle Shape, 2 1/2 In. 20.00
Marker, Street, Drink Coca-Cola, Safety First, Brass, 1900 .... 60.00
Megaphone 20.00
Menu Blackboard, Specials Today, Logo, Tin, Dated 1931, 18 X 24 In. 160.00
Mirror, Boxed, 18 X 12 In. 12.00
Mirror, 1914, Pocket 195.00
Mirror, 1916, Pocket 200.00
Neckerchief, Kit Carson 23.50
Ornament, Christmas, Santa, Set Of 4 .... 12.00
Pad, Bridge, Royal Bottling Works, Ontario 5.00
Paperweight, 12-Sided 15.00
Pencil, Red With Black Logo 1.00
Poster, Girl, 14 1/2 X 20 1/2 In. 3.00
Radio 180.00
Record, 45 RPM, Commercial Songs, Set Of 4 .... 20.00
Ruler, Wood, Golden Rule, 12 In. 1.75
Screwdriver, Advertising, 4 In. 1.50
Shade, Leaded 3500.00
Sharpener, Pencil, Bottle Shape, Cast Iron, 1930s .... 22.00 To 30.00
Sign, Christmas, Coke Bottle, Tin, 1923, 19 X 27 In. 115.00
Sign, Drugstore, Double-Faced Porcelain, Dated, 5 X 42 In. 250.00
Sign, Embossed, Tin, 1940, 19 1/2 X 27 1/2 In. 75.00
Sign, Fountain Service, Dated 1935, Pediment Top, 5 Ft. X 45 In. 300.00
Sign, Fountain Service, Porcelain, 27 X 14 In. 150.00
Sign, Porcelain, Double Sided 150.00
Sign, Tin, Policeman & School Stop Sign, 5 Ft. 200.00
Sign, 1939, 56 X 32 In. 145.00
Spoon, Demitasse, Gold, Drink Coca-Cola 5, 4 In. 10.00
Stand, Playtown, Wooden Stand, Cash Register, Food, Plates 50.00
Thermometer, Bottle Shaped, Tin, 16 In. 10.00
Thermometer, Bottle Shaped, Tin, 1950s, 17 In. 30.00
Thermometer, Bottle Shaped, 30 In. 50.00
Thermometer, Green Border, Wooden 275.00
Thermometer, Plastic, 16 In. 10.00
Thermometer, Sign Of Good Taste, 8 X 27 In. 45.00

Thermometer, 1939 .... 30.00
Thimble, Glass, Ruby Red 5.00
Thimble, Yellow, Red Logo, Plastic 2.00
Toy, Bus, Double Decker, Coke Logo On Side 6.00
Toy, Truck, Buddy-L, Coke Logo, Boxed 15.00
Toy, Truck, Coke Logo On Side 4.00
Toy, Truck, Yellow, Sprite Boy, 1949 .... 75.00
Trade Card, Different Birds, 1933, Set Of 11 .... 9.00
Tray, Tip, 1912, Girl With Rose In Hat 125.00
Tray, Tip, 1914, Betty .... 65.00 To 120.00
Tray, 1909, Coca-Cola Girl, Oval, Large 500.00
Tray, 1909, Coca-Cola Girl, Red Border, Modern Reproduction 6.00
Tray, 1917, Elaine .... 75.00 To 135.00
Tray, 1921, Summer Girl 150.00
Tray, 1923, Flapper Girl 100.00
Tray, 1924, Smiling Girl 250.00
Tray, 1925, Girl At Party .... 95.00 To 125.00
Tray, 1926, Sports Couple .... 150.00 To 275.00
Tray, 1927, Curb Service 135.00
Tray, 1929, Girl In Swimsuit Holding Glass .... 120.00 To 139.00
Tray, 1930, Bathing Beauty 135.00
Tray, 1931, Boy With Dog, Norman Rockwell .... 167.50 To 350.00
Tray, 1932, Girl In Yellow Bathing Suit 285.00
Tray, 1934, O'Sullivan & Weismuller .... 90.00 To 262.50
Tray, 1935, Madge Evans 100.00
Tray, 1936, Hostess .... 60.00 To 115.00
Tray, 1937, Running Girl .... 45.00 To 85.00
Tray, 1938, Girl In Yellow Dress & Hat .... 35.00 To 55.00
Tray, 1939, Springboard Girl .... 48.00 To 80.00
Tray, 1940, Sailor Girl Fishing 48.00
Tray, 1941, Girl Ice Skater .... 50.00 To 55.00
Tray, 1942, Two Girls At Car .... 48.00 To 75.00
Tray, 1943, Girl With Wind In Her Hair 35.00
Tray, 1950, Girl With Menu 18.00
Tray, 1958, Picnic Basket 12.00
Tray, 1961, Be Really Refreshed 10.00
Wallet, Pigskin 22.00
Waste Can, Original Condition 135.00

Coffee grinders of home size were first made about 1894. They lost favor by the 1930s.

COFFEE GRINDER, Ahner, Lap, Wooden, Vienna, Black Boy Holding Sign Brazil 65.00
Arcade, Hanging, Crystal 75.00
Arcade, Lap, Iron Top, Wooden .... 55.00 To 70.00
Arcade, No.3, Original Glass On Bottom 100.00
Arcade, Wall, Original Paint .... 42.00 To 48.00
Brasil, Black Boy On Side, Made In Austria 20.00
Dovetailed Drawer, Mahogany, Inlay, Iron Crank, 12 In. 200.00
Electric, Store 275.00
Embossed Imperial, Small Eagle, Cast Iron Top, Wooden 50.00
Enterprise, Double Wheel, Eagle, Stencils, Dated 1873, 17 In. 425.00
Enterprise, No.7, Original Stenciling 425.00
Enterprise, Patent July 12, 1898, Wheels 11 In. 275.00
Golden Rule, Covered 150.00
Hand, Dovetailed, Maple, Iron Hopper, 7 1/2 X 9 In. 95.00
J.Wright, Inc., Wrightsville, Pa., Drawer, Wheels, 6 3/4 In. 150.00
Lap, Square Wood Box, Drawer, Iron Cup & Shank, 7 In. 57.00
Original Paint, C, 1920 .... 85.00
Regal, Wall 40.00
S.H. Co., St.Louis, Clamps On Table 120.00
Universal 109, Tabletop, Tin, Drawer, C.1905, 5 X 5 In. 60.00
Wall, Glass, Cover, Marked Arcade 57.50
Wall, Iron & Tin Hopper, Wooden Grip, 6 X 8 In. 45.00

COIN SPOT, Compote, Canary Opalescent 45.00
  Lamp, Chevron Base, Vaseline Opalescent 125.00
  Lamp, Globular, Cranberry, 4 In. .... 90.00 To 270.00
  Pitcher, Bell Shape, Opalescent Blue 130.00
  Pitcher, Green Opalescent, 10 In. 98.00
  Pitcher, Reeded Handle, Opalescent, Periwinkle Blue 125.00
  Pitcher, Water, Bulbous, Rope Handle, Clear Opalescent 95.00
  Pitcher, Water, C.1880, Large 125.00
  Pitcher, Water, Hobbs, Opalescent Blue 145.00
  Pitcher, Water, Victorian, 1880, Green Opalescent 95.00
  Pitcher, Water, White On Clear 115.00
  Sugar Shaker, Rubena, Opalescent 225.00
  Syrup, Blue Opalescent 100.00
  Syrup, Bulbous Base 86.50
  Syrup, Original Lid, Blue 100.00
  Syrup, Swirl, White Opalescent 75.00
  Syrup, 9 Panels, Green Opalescent 85.00
  Tumbler 24.00
  Vase, Cylindrical Shape, Purple To Clear, 12 X 4 In. 85.00
  Water Set, Fluted Top, Burlington Mark, Cranberry, 7 Piece 325.00
  Water Set, Opalescent Green, 7 Piece 250.00

COIN-OPERATED MACHINE, Advance, Shocker 125.00
  Arcade, Ball Grip, Globe, 5 Cent 1995.00
  Arcade, Football, Poland 875.00
  Arcade, Peppy The Clown 750.00
  Booze Barometer, Sobriety Tester, 5 Cent 165.00
  Caille, 4 Reel Sphinx, 25 Cent 2900.00
  Candy, Windmill, Cast Iron Stand, Oak Case 600.00
  Card, Exhibit Supply, Model D, Claw Legs, Oak 450.00
  Cigarette, Hol-E-Smoke, Countertop, 1 Cent 225.00
  Cigarette, Lucky Strike Cigarettes, Drop Coin Here 750.00
  Cigarette, Mercury, Deluxe, 1 Cent 260.00
  Claw, Merchantman Digger, Floor Model 1450.00
  Coin Changer, Hopkins & Robinson, Walnut Table 295.00
  Electricity Is Life, Cast Iron Shocker 950.00
  Fortune Teller Mills, Success, 5 Cent .... 700.00 To 1000.00
  Fortune Teller, Grandma, Handle On Side 4500.00
  Fortune Teller, Granny, Wax Head, Hands .... 3500.00 To 4195.00
  Fortune Teller, Janco, 10 Cent, Walnut, 1920s 2395.00
  Fortune, Donkey Delivers Card From Mine On Track 2500.00
  Game, Bally, Submarine Light Gun, C.1963, 5 Cent 235.00
  Grip & Shock, Caille, Floor Model, Eureka 2300.00
  Grip Test, Globe Mfg. Co., Stained Glass Top 1100.00
  Gum Ball & Gypsy Fortune-Teller, 14 X 14 X 5 In. 500.00
  Gum Ball, Advance, 1 Cent .... 75.00 To 85.00
  Gum Ball, Basketball, 1 Cent 89.00
  Gum Ball, Bluebird, Penny Drop, Decals, Steel Cabinet 325.00
  Gum Ball, Bluebird, With Marque 175.00
  Gum Ball, Bluebird, 3 For 1, 1 Cent 150.00
  Gum Ball, Columbus, Model A 165.00
  Gum Ball, Comet, 5 Cent 750.00
  Gum Ball, Ford, Cup & Marque 65.00
  Gum Ball, National, 5 Cent 90.00
  Gum Ball, Watling, Front Slot, 1 Cent 1450.00
  Gum Ball, Watling, Twin, Front Vendor, 1 Cent 2400.00
  Gum Ball, Yankee, Trade Stimulator, 1 Cent 145.00
  Gum, Mills, 1 Cent 100.00
  Gum, Official Sweepstakes, Arcade 900.00
  Gum, Pulver, Yellow Kid, 1 Cent .... 375.00 To 475.00
  Gum, Short's, Original Mirror & Paint, 20 1/2 In. 395.00
  Gum, Zeno, Wall Bracket, Labels Inside, 1 Cent, Wood 495.00
  Horse Race, Evans, 4 Horses, 7 Coin Slots 1850.00

Knautty Peek, Sailor's Paradise, 1 Cent, 46 In.High 345.00
Lighter, Eldred, Jump Spark 250.00
Lighter, Fluid Dispenser 495.00
Love Tester, Measure Sex Appeal, 25 Cent 1150.00
Match, Diamond Matches, 1 Cent 400.00
Match, Kelley Mfg., 4 Cent 465.00
Merchandiser, Northwestern, 1931, 1 Cent 90.00
Mills, Lion Front, 5 Cent 1300.00
Mills, Golf Ball, 25 Cent 2195.00
Mills, Operator's Bell, 1910, 5 Cent 4995.00
Mills, Puritan, Complete, Locks, Keys 650.00
Movie, Mills, Panogram 16mm, Wooden Cabinet, 1930s 750.00
Movie, 8mm, C.1948, 52 Cent, 6 Ft. 475.00
Mutoscope, Clamshell, Base & Signboard, Cast Iron 1200.00
Mutoscope, Peep Show, Cast Iron 1500.00
Mutoscope, Treasure Island Digger, Table Model 1150.00
Nickelodeon, Western Electric, Selectra Model B 3000.00
Peanut, Advance, Football Globe 175.00
Peanut, Atlas Bantam 45.00
Peanut, Climax, No.10, 1 Cent 675.00
Peanut, Columbus P-Nut 125.00
Peanut, Columbus, Model A 165.00
Peanut, Columbus, Model B, 1 Cent 90.00
Peanut, Columbus, Penny Peanut, Glass Dome, Cast Iron 275.00
Peanut, Electric, 1920, 1 Cent 285.00
Peanut, Lincoln, Claw Feet, Original Decal, Cast Iron 650.00
Peanut, Lincoln, Light-Up Stained Glass Top, Iron 1495.00
Peanut, Mabey, Dixie Cup Side Vendor, 5 Cent 225.00
Peanut, Northwestern, 1 Cent 90.00
Peanut, Selmon, Original Decal, Cast Iron, 1 Cent 275.00
Peanut, Superior, Decal 275.00
Perfume Vendor, Container For 25 Cents 50.00
Personality Tester, Shake Hands With Uncle Sam 1495.00
Pinball, Bally, Traffic, 1934 .... 275.00
Pinball, Gottleib, Sky Jump, C.1974, 25 X 55 X 70 In. 750.00
Pinball, Gottlieb, Hurdy Gurdy 400.00
Pinball, Grotchen, Pok-O-Reel 150.00
Pinball, Jennings, Sportsman, 5 Cent 650.00
Pinball, Kenney, Red Hot, Paris Buildings, 1936 .... 800.00
Pittsburgh Penny Drop, Silver Ball, 1930s 50.00
Punching Bag, Mills 500.00
Scale, Jockey, Toledo, Lollipop Design, Beveled Glass 695.00
Scale, National, 1891 .... 1495.00
Shocker, Mills, Firefly, 1 Cent 175.00
Shooting Dice, Jolly, Negro, C.1920, 5 Cent 300.00
Skill Crane, 1 Play 10 Cents, 2 Play, 25 Cents 550.00
Skill, A.J.D.Lattimer, Game-O-Skill, 5 Cent 595.00
Slot, A.B.T., Big Game Hunt 275.00
Slot, Baby Grand, Full Payout With Jackpot, 5 Cent 1395.00
Slot, Baby Jacks .... 850.00 To 880.00
Slot, Baker's Racers 5500.00
Slot, Bally, Double Bell .... 300.00 To 3000.00
Slot, Bally, Double, 5 To 25 Cent 2800.00
Slot, Berger, 5-Way, Electric, Floor Model 5500.00
Slot, Black Cherry, 10 Cent 1650.00
Slot, Bronze Chief, 25 Cent 1450.00
Slot, Buckley, Pointmaker, Electric 495.00
Slot, Buckley, Track Odds 1500.00
Slot, Caille, Aristocrat Roulette, 25 Cent 4500.00
Slot, Caille, Our Baby, 5 Cent .... 4500.00 To 5000.00
Slot, Caille, Poker, Cast Iron 2795.00
Slot, Caille, Puck, Upright, 5 Cent 7995.00
Slot, Caille, Roulette, 25 Cent 4500.00
Slot, Caille, Royal Jumbo, Counter, Cast Iron, 5 Cent 2795.00

Slot, Caille, Sphinx, 5 Cent	1600.00
Slot, Caille, Superior, Counter, 5 Cent, 1928	2200.00
Slot, Challenger, 5 & 25 Cent	1100.00
Slot, Chas. Fey, Logo Front, 5 Cent	1800.00
Slot, Clawson, Penny Drop, C.1885	495.00
Slot, Columbia, 25 Cent	495.00
Slot, Diamond, 10 Cent	1495.00
Slot, Diamond, 25 Cent	1995.00
Slot, Gable, Fox, Musical Movement, 1908, 5 Cent	9000.00
Slot, Garden City Gem	135.00
Slot, Groetchen, Champion	200.00
Slot, Groetchen, Klix	150.00
Slot, Groetchen, Mercury	150.00
Slot, Groetchen, Sparks	250.00
Slot, Hightops, 777	950.00
Slot, Jackson, Never Lose	350.00
Slot, Jennings, Club Chief, Floor Model, 25 Cent	1950.00
Slot, Jennings, Club Special, Floor Model, 5 Cent	975.00
Slot, Jennings, Dutch Boy, 5 Cent	875.00 To 1450.00
Slot, Jennings, Dutch Boy, 25 Cent	1500.00
Slot, Jennings, Golfball Payout, 25 Cent	1400.00
Slot, Jennings, Little Duke	1350.00 To 1895.00
Slot, Jennings, National, Twin Jackpot, 5 Cent	1400.00
Slot, Jennings, Op-Bell, Mints Of Quality, 5 Cent	1500.00
Slot, Jennings, Operator's Bell, Wooden Front, 10 Cent	1450.00
Slot, Jennings, Operator's Bell, 1923, 25 Cent	2250.00
Slot, Jennings, Puritan Maid, 1 Cent	495.00
Slot, Jennings, Silver Club Chief, 1 Cent	1195.00
Slot, Jennings, Silver Club, 1938, 5 Cent	925.00
Slot, Jennings, Today Vendor, Coin Return, 5 Cent	2195.00
Slot, Jennings, Tri-Plex, Plays 5, 10, & 25 Cents	3750.00
Slot, Jennings, Victoria Peacock, 5 Cent	1400.00
Slot, Jennings, Victory Chief, Doughboy Front, 10 Cent	1000.00
Slot, Jennings, 4-Reeler, Light-Up Front, 25 Cent	1395.00
Slot, Mills, Bell Box	1200.00
Slot, Mills, Blue Bell High Top	1050.00
Slot, Mills, Bursting Cherry, 5 Cent	1300.00
Slot, Mills, Bursting Cherry, 25 Cent	1300.00
Slot, Mills, Castle, Skyscraper Coin Head, 5 Cent	2395.00
Slot, Mills, Check Boy, 5 Cent	3800.00 To 5000.00
Slot, Mills, Chicago, Upright, 5 Cent	8995.00
Slot, Mills, Dewey, 5 Cent	6000.00 To 8500.00
Slot, Mills, Diamond Front, 5 Cent	925.00
Slot, Mills, F.O.K., Front Vendor With Eagles	1500.00
Slot, Mills, Firebird, Q.T.Bell, 5 Cent	900.00
Slot, Mills, Gold Award, Castle Front	1200.00
Slot, Mills, Gold Diamond Front, 10 Cent	1050.00
Slot, Mills, Golden Falls, 10 Cent	950.00
Slot, Mills, Golden Falls, 25 Cent	950.00
Slot, Mills, Golfball, Pays Up To 20 Balls, 25 Cent	2395.00
Slot, Mills, Gooseneck With Side Vendor, 1922, 5 Cent	1450.00
Slot, Mills, Hi-Top, 10 Cent	975.00
Slot, Mills, Hi-Top, 25 Cent	1175.00
Slot, Mills, Hi-Top, 50 Cent	1600.00
Slot, Mills, Horsehead Bonus, 10 Cent	1600.00 To 1800.00
Slot, Mills, Lion Front, 5 Cent	1300.00
Slot, Mills, Melon Bell, 1937, 5 Cent	2200.00
Slot, Mills, On-The-Square, 5 Cent	7500.00
Slot, Mills, Operator's Bell, 1921, 5 Cent	1595.00
Slot, Mills, Operator's Bell, 50 Cent	1995.00
Slot, Mills, Puritan Bell, 25 Cent	600.00
Slot, Mills, Puritan, Cash Register Shape, 5 Cent	650.00
Slot, Mills, Q.T.Bell, Triangle Front, 5 Cent	850.00
Slot, Mills, Q.T.Bell, 5 Cent	1000.00

Slot, Mills, Silver Dollar Hi-Top 1850.00
Slot, Mills, Single Torch, 5 Cent 1450.00
Slot, Mills, Vest Pocket, 5 Cent 395.00
Slot, Mills, War Eagle, 5 Cent .... 1450.00 To 1600.00
Slot, Pace, Bantam, 1 Cent 1050.00
Slot, Pace, Bantam, 10 Cent 950.00
Slot, Pace, 1928, 25 Cent 1350.00
Slot, Pace, 5 Cent .... 1000.00 To 1400.00
Slot, Pulver, Cop & Robber 495.00
Slot, Puritan Girl 900.00
Slot, Rock-Ola, Hold & Draw 375.00
Slot, Rock-Ola, Reserve, Pure Mint Co., 5 Cent 1900.00
Slot, Rock-Ola, Super Triple, Skill Stops, 5 Cent 1395.00
Slot, Roll-A-Top, C.1933, 10 Cent 2300.00
Slot, Roman Head, 50 Cent 1650.00
Slot, Schall, Alaskan, Counter Wheel, 1896 .... 4800.00
Slot, Silent Sphinx 1250.00
Slot, Silver King, 25 Cent, Delayed Payoff 1495.00
Slot, Silver Moon Chief, 5 Cent 1395.00
Slot, Sittman & Pitt, Little Card Machine, Cast Iron 2500.00
Slot, Standard Chief, 10 Cent 1250.00
Slot, Superior, 4 Reel, 5 Cent 1250.00
Slot, Watling, Baby Gold Award, 5 Cent 1895.00
Slot, Watling, Bird Of Paradise, Roll-A-Top, 25 Cent 3000.00
Slot, Watling, Brownie, With Jackpot, 5 Cent 2300.00
Slot, Watling, Checkerboard, Roll-A-Top, 10 Cent 2750.00
Slot, Watling, Gumball Front, 1 Cent 1850.00
Slot, Watling, Roll-A-Top, Matching Stand, 5 Cent 3950.00
Slot, Watling, Treasury, 10 Cent 3000.00
Slot, Watling, Twin Jackpot, Fortune Strips, 1 Cent 1850.00
Slot, Watling, Twin Jackpot, 5 Cent 1200.00
Slot, Watling, 4 Column 3500.00
Stamp, Schermack, 1 Cent & 3 Cent 100.00
Stamp, U.S., 5 & 10 Cent Stamps 45.00
Stamp, 3 Three Cent Stamps For 10 Cents, Glass Sides 135.00
Stimulator, Fey Midget 400.00
Stimulator, Mills, Electricity Is Life 3500.00
Strength Tester, Barbell, Floor Model, Oak, C.1920 .... 650.00
Strength Tester, Barbell, Floor Model, 1 Cent 500.00
Strength Tester, Gottlieb, Counter Top, 1 Cent 185.00
Strength Tester, Mills 450.00
Trade Stimulator, Daisy, Cigar 325.00
Trade Stimulator, Mercury Deluxe, Full Of Tokens 265.00
Trade Stimulator, Whirlwind 325.00
Trade Stimulator, 2-Wheel Bicycle 2000.00

*Collector plates are modern plates produced in limited editions. Some will
be found listed under the company. Pictures and more price information can
be found in "Kovels' Price Guide for Collector Plates, Figurines,
Paperweights and Other Limited Editions."*

COLLECTOR PLATE, Angel With Black Eye, 1975 .... 79.50
   COLLECTOR PLATE, BING & GRONDAHL, see Bing & Grondahl
Goebel, Mother's Day, Cats, 1976 .... 45.00
Haviland, Chase Of Unicorn, 1973 .... 105.00
Haviland, Christmas, 1972 .... 115.00
Lalique, Dreamrose, Annual, 1966 .... 185.00
Lenox, Wild Life, 1973 .... 85.00
Lenox, Wood Thrush, 1970 .... 245.00
Limoges, Flight Into Egypt, 1975 .... 69.00
Pickard, Christmas, 1976 .... 135.00
Rockwell, Butter Girl, 1973 .... 115.00
Rockwell, Cobbler, 1978 .... 135.00
Rockwell, Toy Maker, 1977 .... 200.00

Rosenthal, Christmas, 1971, Madonna & Child 1195.00
Royal Bayreuth, Young Americans, 1974 .... 109.00
      COLLECTOR PLATE, ROYAL COPENHAGEN, see Royal Copenhagen
Wedgwood, Innocence, 1977 .... 85.00
Wedgwood, Paul Revere's Ride, 1973 .... 112.50
Wedgwood, Windsor Castle, 1969 .... 199.00

      COMIC ART, CELLULOID, see also Celluloid; Disneyana
COMIC ART, Dream Of Rarebit Fiend, 1904, Sunday, Winsor McCay, Framed 650.00
Sketch, Pencil, Betty Boop, 1937 .... 120.00
Skippy, Merry Christmas Card, Signed, 1931 .... 7.50

Commemoration items have been made to honor members of royalty and those of great national fame. World's fairs and important historical events are also remembered with commemorative pieces.
      COMMEMORATIVE, see also Coronation; World's Fair

COMMEMORATIVE, Bell, Prince Charles, Lady Diana, 5 1/4 In. 28.00
Cover, Pillow, Tapesty, King George VI, Maroon Ground 45.00
Cup & Saucer, Great World War, 1919 .... 22.00
Cup & Saucer, King George V, Shelley, 2 3/4 In. 60.00
Cup & Saucer, Prince Charles, Lady Diana, Crown Staffordshire 55.00
Dessert Set, Queen Victoria Diamond Jubilee, 3 Piece 45.00
Jar, Queen Elizabeth, Prince Philip, Royal Seal, Wedgwood 250.00
Medallion, Sir Winston Churchill, Sterling Silver, 2 In. 100.00
Medallion, Wright Bros. On Front, Airplane On Back, 2 In. 15.00
Mug, Edward VIII 28.00
Mug, Great World War, 1919 .... 22.00
Mug, The Royal Marriage 29 July 1981, 5 In. 35.00
Pitcher, Admiral Dewey, Pattern Glass, 9 In. 75.00
Pitcher, Columbus, 1492-1892, Etched Picture, Clear 125.00
Plaque, Brass, Queen Elizabeth II, Silhouette, 9 In. 29.00
Plate, Col.Lindbergh, 1927, 8 1/2 In. 35.00
Scarf, Silk, Admiral Dewey 25.00
Spoon, Souvenir, The Royal Wedding, Portraits In Bowl, 4 In. 7.00

Coors ware was made by a pottery in Golden, Colorado, owned by the Coors Beverage Company. It was produced from the turn of the century until the pottery was destroyed by fire in the 1930s. The name "Coors" is marked on the back.

COORS, Bean Pot, Pink Flowers, Yellow, Covered, 6 In. 20.00
Cup, Custard, Rosebud 3.00
Mortar & Pestle .... 15.00 To 25.00
Pitcher, Rosebud, Label, Turquoise, Covered 23.50
Teapot, Rosebud, Covered 35.00

W.T.Copeland & Sons, Ltd., ran the Spode Works in Staffordshire, England, from 1847 to 1976. Copeland & Garrett was the firm name from 1833 to 1847.
      COPELAND SPODE, see also Flow Blue; Spode
COPELAND SPODE, Bottle, Picture Of Mayflower, Brown Mark 65.00
Coffeepot, White Classical Figures, Brown Ground, 7 1/2 In. 70.00
Figurine, Mallard, Wingspan 10 In. 250.00
Pitcher, Cameo, Blue & White, 1890, 9 In. 65.00
Pitcher, Hunters, Horses, & Dogs, Squatty, 5 1/4 In. 75.00
Pitcher, Reynold, 5 In. 35.00
Plate, Iris, Signed, 9 In. 10.00
Plate, Jefferson Barracks, St.Louis, 1840, 10 1/2 In. 15.00
Plate, Mountain & Lake Scene, Cobalt Border, 8 In. 135.00
Plate, Plover, Blue & White, 10 1/4 In. 40.00
Plate, Wild Ducks, Blue & White, 10 1/4 In. 40.00
Teapot, Fitzhugh, Blue & White 98.00

Water Set, Hunters, Horses, & Dogs, 5 Piece 135.00

COPELAND, see also Copeland Spode; Spode

COPELAND, Compote, Indian Tree, Orange, Brown, Marked, 4 X 8 In. 42.00
Cup & Saucer, Maid Milking, Brown, Haystacks, Marked 32.00
Dish, Soup, Gold & Turquoise Rim, 1851-85 .... 8160.00
Figurine, Diana On Lion, Parian, C.1840, 9 X 9 3/4 In. 450.00
Figurine, Ophelia, Parian, Signed Art Union, 11 In. 400.00
Mug, Friendship, Hunting Scenes, 3-Handled, White Bisque, 7 1/2 In. 135.00
Pitcher, Lily Of The Valley, Parian, 6 In. 125.00

COPPER LUSTER, see Luster, Copper

COPPER, Ashtray, Art Deco, Soaring Eagle, Mountains, & Lake, 3 1/4 In. 12.50
Bed Warmer, Iron Ferrule, Pierced Top, Flowers, 10 1/2 In. 175.00
Bells, Sleigh, Acorn Shape, String Of 25 .... 200.00
Binnacle, Whale Oil Lamp Attached At Side, 10 In. 150.00
Bowl, Fruit Mold Design, Handmade, 14 X 12 In. 98.00
Box, Storage, Square, Slant Sides, Tin Lid, 13 X 12 In. 78.00
Bucket, Bail Handle, Lapped Seam, 12 X 6 In. 60.00
Bucket, Berry, Tin Lining, 5 1/2 In. 40.00
Chamberstick, Figural, Porpoise Handles, 4 1/2 In. .... 25.00 To 30.00
Coffeepot, Gooseneck Spout, Wooden Handle, Marked Rome, 9 In. 30.00
Coffeepot, Nickel Plated, Gooseneck Spout, Wooden Handle, 10 Cup 50.00
Dispenser, Hot Water, Barber's, Tin Lined, 2 Gallon, 9 X 14 In. 95.00
Dispenser, Syrup, Ice Cream Parlor, Embossed Boston, C.1870, 7 In. 85.00
Filler, Inkwell, Schoolhouse, C.1860, Toucan Shaped, Pint 65.00
Funnel, Brewery, Lap Seams, Hand-Up Hook, C.1850, 10 In. 60.00
Funnel, Spun, Rolled Rim, Wire-Looped Hang Up, 5 3/4 In. 35.00
Holder, Rushlight, Spring Clamp, Footed, 4 Arched Legs, 8 In. 325.00
Inkstand, Embossed Reindeer, 4 In. 59.00
Kettle, Jam, 22 1/4 In. 140.00
Ladle, Hammered, Iron Rattail Handle, 16 In. 140.00
Ladle, Wooden Handle, 16 In. 35.00
Lamp, Dovetailed Construction, Hinged Lid, 7 1/2 In. 20.00
COPPER, MOLD, see Kitchen, Mold
Mug, Drinking, 2-Handled, Early 1800s, 10 In. 85.00
Mug, Lapped Seams, Handle, C.1860, 3 1/4 In. 60.00
Pan, Curved Handle, Wooden Side Handle, 10 1/2 In. 50.00
Pan, Rolled Rim, Tapering Sides, Footed, 6 3/4 In. 90.00
Pistol Flask, 5 In. 30.00
Pitcher, Middle Eastern, Spout Flap, Hinged Lid, 14 In. 385.00
Pitcher, Milk, 9 1/2 In. 75.00
Plaque, Abraham Lincoln, 1809-1909, Signed Keating, 5 X 3 1/2 In. 59.00
Pot, Handled, Dovetailed, 8 1/2 In. 120.00
Samovar & Stand, Alcohol Burner, Tinned Interior, 12 In, ... 50.00
Sconce, Wall, Scalloped Shape, Single Arm, 19th Century, 12 In., Pair 150.00
Shaker, Salt, Cone Shaped, Brass Top, 8 1/2 In. 45.00
Snuffer, Candle, C.1860, 18 In. 75.00
Steamer, Hot Dog, Queen Anne Legs, Double Top, 11 X 17 X 11 In. 300.00
Stein, Pewter Handle & Base, Etching, 12 In. 50.00
Still, Tin Vat, Copper Coil, Handled, C.1880, 10 Gallon, 11 X 21 In. 150.00
Teakettle, Bail Handle, Wood Grip, C.1900, 1/2 Gallon 40.00
Teakettle, Bail Handle, Wooden Pull, C.1900, 1/2 Gallon 40.00
Teakettle, Brass Handle, Acorn Finial, 11 In. 85.00
Torch, Jeweler's, Brass Wick Cap, Embossed L.K., 8 In. 50.00
Vase, Hand-Hammered, 5 In. 5.00
Vase, Opaque Enamel, Shield Shape, Birds, Dragons, 3 7/8 In. 50.00
Vase, Revere, Rome, N.Y., 8 In. 25.00
Vat, Brass Spigot, Concentric Lines, 10 X 14 In. 65.00
Water Can, Gooseneck Spout, 6 1/2 In. 20.00

Coralene glass was made by firing many small colored beads on the outside of glassware. It was made in many patterns in the United States and Europe in the 1880s. Reproductions are made today.

CORALENE, JAPANESE, see Japanese Coralene

CORALENE, Bride's Bowl, Mother-Of-Pearl, Silver Plated Holder, 9 1/2 In.	750.00
Plaque, Water Crocus, Gold Beaded Trim, Pastel Ground, 9 In.	160.00
Vase, Art Nouveau Design, Cobalt Blue Rim, Green Ground, 8 1/2 In.	325.00
Vase, Cobalt Blue & Gold, 9 In.	375.00
Vase, Gold Dots, Pink & Green, 1909, 6 X 4 1/2 In.	135.00
Vase, Green, Pink To Lavender, Gold Trim, 13 1/2 In.	475.00
Vase, Lemon Yellow Overlay, Yellow Beading, White Lining, 9 3/4 In.	465.00
Vase, Lilies & Leaves, Gold Trim, Openwork Handles, 8 1/4 In.	200.00
Vase, Snowflake, Blue Satin, Mother-Of-Pearl, 4 3/4 In.	450.00
Vase, Star Pattern, Stars At Diamond Intersections, 5 1/8 In.	650.00
Vase, Wheat Pattern, Gold Diamond-Quilted, White Lining, 3 1/4 In.	425.00

The Cordey China Company was founded in 1942 by Boleslaw Cybis in Trenton, New Jersey. The firm produced gift shop items. Production stopped in 1950 and Cybis Porcelains was founded.

CORDEY, Ashtray, Rococo, Gold On Cream, Signed, 6 In.	23.00
Box, Blue, 3 In.	32.00
Box, No.6053	45.00
Box, Red, Covered, Bluebird Mark, 7 1/2 In.	95.00
Bust, Lady, Applied Curls, Lace & Gold Trim, 15 In.	475.00
Bust, Lady, Full Arms & Hands, Lace & Gold Trim, 20 X 15 In.	475.00
Bust, Lady, No. 5001	99.00
Bust, Lady, No. 5027	99.00
Bust, Napoleon, No.5038, Striped Vest, Purple Cockade Hat, 7 1/2 In.	75.00
Bust, Young Lady, Blue On White Dress, Gold Crown, 6 1/2 In.	55.00
Candleholder, Oriental Woman, Blown-Out Design, 6 1/2 In.	25.00
Console Set, Roses & Petals, Bowl 9 1/2 X 12 1/2 In.	110.00
Figurine, Bird, Wings Spread On Top Of Flower, 9 In.	100.00
Figurine, Flying Bird, Tree Stump Base, Signed, 9 In.	120.00
Figurine, Frenchman, Lace On Costume, No.5020, 6 3/8 In.	85.00
Figurine, Girl, Gathering Fruit In Skirt, No.304, 10 In.	150.00
Figurine, Lady, Ball Gown, Lace Trim, Roses, No.4217, Signed, 13 In.	125.00
Figurine, Lady, Green Dress, Red Hat, Long Hair, No.302, 16 1/2 In.	220.00
Figurine, Lady, Red, Pink Attire, Signed, 16 In.	125.00
Figurine, Lady, Roses In Hair, Hoop Skirt, 10 In.	65.00
Figurine, Male, Decorated, 16 In.	125.00
Figurine, Man & Woman, Burgundy & Pink Outfits, Marked, 16 In., Pr.	195.00
Figurine, Man & Woman, Colonial Costume, Lace, Gold Trim, 14 In., Pair	375.00
Figurine, Man, On Tree Stump, Festooned With Roses, Marked, 11 In.	190.00
Lamp, Vanity, Colonial Man & Woman, Original Sticker, Pair	135.00
Plaque, Wall, Cherubs & Flowers, Pair	175.00
Shelf, Wall, Yellow Rose, Gold Trim, Pair	150.00
Vase, Black, 8 In.	25.00
Vase, Oriental Lady, No.090, Signed, 9 In.	40.00

CORKSCREW, Antler Tip, Sterling Silver Fittings, Handmade, 2 1/2 X 3 In.	25.00
Boy, Nude, Naughty	50.00
Keen Kutter, Wooden Handle	10.00
Man In Formal Wear, Original Paint, Wooden	40.00
Pig, Figural, Silvery Metal	18.00
Sailing Vessel, Brass	24.00
Stag Handle, Elk Horns, Brass	40.00
Stag Horn	18.00
Tomahawk, Embossed, Cast Iron	20.00

Coronation cups have been made since the 1800s. Pottery or glass with a picture of the monarch and date have been souvenirs for many coronations.

CORONATION, see also Commemorative
CORONATION, Ashtray, George VI, 1937 .... 20.00
  Beaker, Elizabeth II 10.00
  Dish, Fruit, George VI, 1937, Glass, 9 3/4 In. 30.00
  Mug, Coffee, Queen Elizabeth, 1963, Staffordshire, 4 In. 10.00
  Mug, Edward VIII, 1937, 3 1/2 In. 35.00
  Mug, Elizabeth II 12.50
  Mug, George VI, 1937 .... 20.00 To 25.00
  Mug, 1911 .... 28.00
  Picture, Queen Elizabeth, Tin, Red, 2 1/2 X 3 1/2 In. 6.00
  Plate, Edward VIII, Spode 35.00
  Plate, Edward VIII, 1937, Portrait, 7 In. 20.00
  Plate, Edward VIII, 1937, 10 In. 25.00
  Plate, Queen Elizabeth II, 1953, Minton, Square 25.00
  Plate, 1937, Wedgwood, Blue On Cream, 9 1/2 In. 90.00
  Tumbler, George V, 1935 Silver Jubilee, Myott 30.00

Cosmos pattern glass is a pressed milk glass pattern with colored flowers.

COSMOS, Bottle, Cologne, Stopper, Pink Band 225.00
  Butter, Covered .... 185.00 To 195.00
  Castor, Pickle, Silver Plated Frame, Pink Band 425.00
  Lamp Base, Kerosene, Milk Glass 45.00
  Lamp Base, Yellow, Pink, & Green 100.00
  Lamp, Crystal, 8 In. 50.00
  Lamp, Gold, Miniature, Pair 35.00
  Lamp, Pink .... 325.00 To 395.00
  Pickle Castor .... *Illus* 230.00
  Pitcher, Water 275.00
  Pitcher, Water, Bulbous, Beige Band 225.00
  Pitcher, Water, Drilled For Lamp 65.00
  Salt & Pepper 125.00
  Salt & Pepper, Blue Glass 85.00
  Salt & Pepper, Milk Glass 80.00
  Salt, Original Tin Top 50.00
  Sugar & Creamer, Milk Glass 245.00
  Syrup 295.00
  Table Set, Pink Band, 3 Piece 315.00
  Tumbler 220.00
  Vase, Pink, White Flowers, Signed, 7 1/2 In. 95.00

COUNTRY STORE, see Store

Cosmos, Pickle Castor

COVERLET, Blue & Gold, Navy Blue Ground, Flowers, 86 X 100 In. 330.00
  Bride's, White, Pinapple, Blossoms, Dated 1798, 88 X 84 In. 880.00
  Circles & Stand-Up Center, Crocheted, Double Bed 60.00

Double Weave, Delhi, New York, 1847, Blue & White	400.00
Floral Medallion, Animals, Birds, Beige Ground, 86 X 75 In.	600.00
Geometric, Wool, Coral, Brown & Beige, 68 X 74 In.	85.00
Green & Yellow Overshot, Trundle Bed Size	275.00
Jacquard Weave, Blue & White, 80 X 76 In.	85.00
Jacquard, Blue & White, Tulips, Blossoms, 1824, 92 X 76 In.	330.00
Jacquard, Blue, Green, Red, White, Pots Of Flowers, 83 In.	185.00
Jacquard, Floral Design, White, Blue, Red, 1876, 75 X 89 In.	115.00
Jacquard, Floral, Blue, White Floral, 1866, 74 X 92 In.	200.00
Jacquard, J.Hamelton, Northemberland Co., 1841, 86 X 78 In.	475.00
Jacquard, Red, White, Green, Blue, Rose Center, 70 X 96 In.	250.00
Jacquard, Woven By William Nye, Lebanon, Pa., 1850	650.00
Jacquard, Woven & Red & White, 19th Century, 86 X 76 In.	300.00
Linsey-Woolsey, Floral, Leaf Pattern, Green, 18th Century	600.00
Linsey-Woolsey, Geometric Pattern, Green, 18th Century	225.00
Linsey-Woolsey, Green, Floral & Leaf Design	600.00
Linsey-Woolsey, Green, Geometric Pattern	250.00
Linsey-Woolsey, Homespun, Brown & White, 66 X 96 In.	195.00
Old Rose Pattern, Crocheted, 82 X 92 In.	145.00
Overshot, Tricolor, Blue, White Border, Red, 72 X 76 In.	180.00
Single Weave, Red, White, 2 Piece, 78 X 100 In.	90.00
Snail's Trail Design, White Overshot, Black Wool	225.00
Snowballs & Double Pine Tree Border, Double Weave	245.00
Summer & Winter Pattern, Signed, Dated 1833, Double Size	875.00
Wool & Cotton, Green, Red, Blue, 90 X 80 In.	55.00
Wool, Mauve & Black On Cream, Small	85.00
Woven, 1857	700.00

 Cowan pottery was made in Cleveland, Ohio, from 1913 to 1931. Most pieces of the art pottery were marked with the name of the firm in various ways.

COWAN, Ashtray, Spade Shaped, Scrolled, Beige, 2 1/2 In.	2.00
Bowl, Blue Luster, 12 In.	45.00
Bowl, Console, Delphinium, Marked, 10 3/4 X 8 X 2 1/2 In.	22.00
Bowl, Flared Top, Blue Luster, 7 X 3 In.	35.00
Bowl, Flower Frog, Rainbow Blue, 9 1/2 X 8 1/2 X 3 1/8 In.	22.00
Bowl, Marigold Luster, Marked, 7 1/2 X 2 1/2 In.	16.00
Bowl, Pedestal, Green, 9 In.	39.00
Bowl, Rainbow Blue, Marked, 9 1/2 X 2 1/2 In.	22.00
Bowl, Rainbow Blue, 1924, Stamp Mark, 8 In.	18.00
Bowl, Seahorse Base, Marked, Ivory Outside, Green Inside, 6 X 3 1/4 In.	22.00
Bowl, Sweet Pea, Blue Luster, 3 3/8 In.	18.00
Bowl, Sweet Pea, Delphinium Blue, Marked, 5 1/2 X 3 1/4 In.	15.00
Candleholder, Art Deco, Orange, 5 X 2 In., Pair	55.00
Candleholder, Cream White, Impressed, 2 In., Pair	15.00
Candleholder, Cream White, Impressed, 4 In., Pair	17.00
Candleholder, Impressed, Cream White, 2 In., Pair	15.00
Candleholder, Impressed, Cream White, 4 In., Pair	17.00
Candleholder, Light Green, 4 1/2 X 1 1/2 In., Pair	15.00
Candleholder, Seahorse, Marked, Ivory, 4 1/4 In.	8.00
Candleholder, Seahorse, Pink, Pair	30.00
Candleholder, Triple, White, Pair	32.00
Candlestick, Dolphin, White, Pair	30.00
Compote, Boat Shaped, Ivory Out, Lavender In, Marked	27.50 To 30.00
Compote, Seahorse	35.00
Dish, Soap, Pedestal, 3 X 6 In.	25.00
Figurine, Dancing Girl, Art Nouveau, Signed, White	65.00
Holder, Card, Impressed, Cream White, 3 In.	13.00
Lamp, Ink Mark, Orange Luster, 9 In.	115.00
Vase, Ali Baba Style, Marked, Blue, 4 3/4 X 5 1/4 In.	28.00
Vase, Ali Baba Style, Marked, Rainbow Blue, 3 1/2 X 4 In.	18.00
Vase, Apple Blossom, Cylindrical, Marked, 5 3/4 In.	30.00
Vase, Bird, Lime Green, 6 1/2 In.	30.00

Vase, Black Stamp, Blue Luster, 5 X 2 1/4 In. 15.00
Vase, Blue Gloss, 8 In. 55.00
Vase, Blue Luster, Black Stamp, 5 X 2 1/4 In. 15.00
Vase, Blue Luster, Ink Mark, 4 In. 12.00
Vase, Blue Luster, Marked, 6 7/8 In. 20.00
Vase, Blue Luster, 6 In. 10.00
Vase, Blue Luster, 9 1/2 X 8 In. 110.00
Vase, Cream & Blue, Marked, 11 1/2 In. 28.00
Vase, Fan Shaped, Seahorse Base, Cream, 6 In. 35.00
Vase, Orange Luster, Ink Mark, 5 In. 20.00
Vase, 1924 Logan Medal Vase, Marked, Blue Luster, 7 1/2 X 8 1/4 In. 50.00

CRACKER JACK, Bear 20.00
Book, Encyclopedia Of The Planets 2.00
Bookmark, Picture Of Dog, Metal 22.00
Boxcar, Tootsietoy 10.00
Cart, Marked, Tin & Wood 30.00
Charm, 25 Charms & Chain 75.00
Fortune-Telling Wheel, Paper 8.00
Handkerchief With Donkey 35.00
Horse & Wagon 65.00
Moon Mullins, Tin Standup 20.00
Pin, Black Lady 35.00
Police Badge 3.00
Sled, Tin 30.00
Spinner 10.00
Trolley, Toonerville, 1 1/2 In. 275.00
Watch, Pocket, Tin 15.00
Wheelbarrow, Tin 60.00
Whistle .... 7.00 To 12.00

> Crackle glass was originally made by the Venetians, but most of the ware
> found today dates from the 1800s. The glass was heated, cooled, and refired
> so that many small lines appeared inside the glass. It was made in many
> factories in the United States and Europe.

CRACKLE GLASS, see also Fry

CRACKLE GLASS, Bowl, Console, Light Blue 13.00
Decanter, Pinched, Pink, 10 1/2 In. 120.00
Lemonade Set, Green Handle & Finial, C.1920, 7 Piece 135.00
Pitcher, Bulbous, Clear Applied Handle, Cranberry, 5 5/8 In. 95.00
Shade, Torpedo, Vaseline, 3 In. 30.00
Vase, Enameled Marine Plants, 6 In. 75.00

> Cranberry glass is an almost transparent yellow-red glass. It resembles
> the color of cranberry juice.

CRANBERRY GLASS, see also Northwood; Rubena Verde; etc.

CRANBERRY GLASS, Atomizer, Gold & White Enameling 135.00
Bell, Cut Handle, 11 1/2 In. 325.00
Bell, Engraved Butterfly & Flower, Clear Handle 45.00
Bell, Wedding, Clear Handle, Ribbon Design, 11 1/2 In. 300.00
Berry Set, Delaware, Gold Trim, 7 Piece 215.00
Bottle, Cologne, Gilt Greek Key Design, 4 1/2 In. 75.00
Bottle, Cologne, Gold Floral Design, Stopper, 7 X 3 1/4 In. 135.00
Bottle, Perfume, Flowers, Gold Leaves, Bulbous, 5 1/2 In. 125.00
Bottle, Perfume, Roses, Forget-Me-Nots, Gold Trim, 5 5/8 In. 110.00
Bottle, Perfume, Stopper, Thistle Design, 4 3/4 X 2 In. 115.00
Bottle, Perfume, 3-Section, Faceted Stopper, 4 3/4 In. 135.00
Bowl, Crystal Applied Garlands, Scroll Feet, Pontil, 5 In. 350.00
Bowl, Diamond Optic, Crimped, 10 In. 65.00
Bowl, Finger, 4 X 1 3/4 In. 25.00
Bowl, Flashed To Clear, Celery Stalk Feet, 9 X 5 In. 40.00
Bowl, Silver Plated Holder, Swan Handles, 15 1/4 In. 195.00
Bowl, 3-Corner Top, Berry Pontil, Footed, 3 3/4 X 4 In. 175.00
Bowl, 6-Sided, Pressed Pattern, 8 In. 15.00

Box, Clear Finial, Gold Bands, Covered, 2 3/4 X 4 1/2 In.	95.00
Box, Enameled Flowers	120.00
Box, Patch, Enameled Figure Of Girl, 2 In.	225.00
Box, Patch, Floral, Gold Trim, Hinged Cover, 2 X 1 In.	125.00
Bride's Bowl, Ruffled Snow Crest Edge, 10 In.	17.50
Butter, Hollow Knob Finial, Covered, 5 3/4 In.	95.00
Butter, Inverted Thumbprint, Dated 1893, Covered, 5 1/2 In.	150.00
Candleholder, Entwined Vaseline Dolphin, 10 1/2 In.	225.00
Compote, Gold Design, Clear Stem, 12 In.	200.00
Creamer, Applied Handle & Feet, 4 In.	35.00
Creamer, Clear Rigaree Center, Fluted Top, Footed, 4 3/8 In.	68.00
Cup & Saucer, Gold Bands, Enameled Violets, Gold Handle	110.00
Cup & Saucer, Gold Trim, Bands, & Garlands, Enameled Edge	80.00
Cup, Punch, Chicago, 1905, 2 In.	20.00
Decanter Set, Original Stopper, 7 Piece	18.00
Dish, Jam, Apple Shaped, Silver Plated Holder, 5 X 5 1/4 In.	125.00
Dish, Jam, Double, Silver Plated Frame, 11 In. .... 145.00 To	155.00
Dish, Jam, Intaglio Engraved, Silver Plated Holder, 4 In.	110.00
Dish, Soap	65.00
Epergne, Brass Mountings, Ruffled Base & Center, 20 3/4 In.	395.00
Epergne, Clear Rigaree, Threaded Base, 21 In.	150.00
Epergne, 4 Flowers, 12 In.	235.00
Ewer, Allover Enameled Flowers, Gold Trim, 4 3/4 In.	165.00
Flask, Bellow Shaped, C.1890	125.00
Goblet, 5 1/2 In.	47.50
Hat, Silver Plated Brim, 4 1/4 X 2 5/8 In.	110.00
Inkwell, Double, Silver Plated Holder	265.00
Jar, Alma, 1919, Covered	24.00
Jar, Coin Spot, Covered, 10 In.	225.00
Jar, Enameled & Gold Design, Covered, 4 1/2 X 5 In.	145.00
Jar, Powder, Enameled Design	75.00
Knife Rest	145.00
Lamp, Hanging, Hall, Hobnail, Brass, 14 In.	885.00
Mantel Set, Enamel Outlined Leaves, Dots, 8 3/4 In., 3 Piece	650.00
Pitcher, Clear Handle, 11 1/2 In.	190.00
Pitcher, Frosted, Gold Leaf Design, Handled, 3 7/8 In.	85.00
Pitcher, Inverted Thumbprint, Clear Handle, 9 In.	165.00
Pitcher, Inverted Thumbprint, Square Mouth, 5 7/8 In.	110.00
Pitcher, Ribbed, Applied Clear Handle, 9 In.	135.00
Pitcher, Ribbed, Vaseline Handle, 4 1/2 X 3 1/4 In.	75.00
Pitcher, Roll-Over Ruffled Rim, Clear Handle, 9 In.	140.00
Pitcher, Scrolls, Applied Jewels, Gold Trim, 5 1/4 In.	85.00
Pitcher, Swirl Pattern, Clear Handle, 7 In.	98.00
Pitcher, Tankard Shaped, Reed Handle, Round Mouth, 9 1/4 In.	165.00
Pitcher, Water, Clear Reeded Handle, 9 3/8 In.	165.00
Pitcher, Water, Enameled Lilies Of The Valley, 11 3/8 In.	225.00
Pitcher, Water, Inverted Thumbprint	265.00
Pitcher, Water, Leaf Umbrella, Spatter	245.00
Pitcher, Water, Opalescent, Swirl, Northwood	225.00
Plate, Dinner, Grape & Leaf Border, 8 3/4 In.	55.00
Rose Bowl, Floral Design, 3 X 3 1/2 In.	118.00
Rose Bowl, Gold Decoration, 2 1/2 In.	30.00
Rose Bowl, 8-Crimp Top, Enameled Forget-Me-Nots, 3 In.	118.00
Salt & Pepper, Thistle Pattern, 3 1/2 In.	35.00
Saltshaker, Bulbous, Inverted Thumbprint, Original Top	43.00
Saltshaker, Emu Bird Shape, Crystal Applique, Silver Plated	125.00
Saltshaker, Leaf Mold	60.00
Saltshaker, Leaf Umbrella	30.00
Saltshaker, Opaque Threading, Clear Shell Feet, 2 3/4 In.	59.00
Saltshaker, Vaseline Trim, Silver Plated Holder, 3 1/8 In.	100.00
Spooner, Leaf Mold, Spatter	65.00
Sugar & Creamer, Florals, Gold Leaves, Pedestal, 2 1/4 In.	165.00
Sugar Shaker, Cut Panels, Silver Plated Top, 5 1/4 In.	55.00
Sugar Shaker, Paneled, Silver Plated Top	75.00

Sugar Shaker, Ribbed Opal, Lattice	95.00
Syrup, Baby Thumbprint, Burlington Mark	125.00
Toothpick, Frazier, Enamel Trim	45.00
Toothpick, Inverted Thumbprint	50.00
Toothpick, Lattice Ribbed Opal	85.00
Toothpick, Venetian, Polished Rim	70.00
Tumbler, White & Yellow Dot Flowers, Leaves, 3 3/4 In.	30.00
Urn, Gold Leaves, Flowers, Covered, Finial, 18 1/2 In.	295.00
Vase, Applied Spiral Trim, Heart Shape Top, 9 In.	95.00
Vase, Applique Pinecone & Crystal Handle, 7 1/8 In.	85.00
Vase, Blossoms, 2 X 4 1/2 In.	195.00
Vase, Crystal Applied Leaves, 8 3/4 X 4 1/4 In.	118.00
Vase, Crystal Flowers, Tricorn Top, Footed, 5 X 4 In.	195.00
Vase, Cylinder Shaped, Gold Decoration, 9 1/2 In.	65.00
Vase, Enamel Outlined Gold Flowers, 6 5/8 In., Pair	188.00
Vase, Enameled Oak Leaves & Acorns, Snail Feet, 3 1/8 In.	295.00
Vase, Enameled Scene, Gold Flowers, Blue Dots, 9 In.	195.00
Vase, Enameled, Flowers, Cylinder Shape, 15 In.	165.00
Vase, Enameled, Lacy Design, 8 3/8 In., Pair	145.00
Vase, Floral Design, Pedestal, 8 1/2 X 4 1/4 In.	165.00
Vase, Gold & Enamel Flowers, Bulbous, 7 X 6 1/2 In.	175.00
Vase, Gold Flowers, Outlined In Enamel, 6 5/8 In., Pair	188.00
Vase, Gold Leaves, Enameled Flowers, Blue Center, 11 In.	165.00
Vase, Gold Scroll Foliage, White Enamel Dots, 3 In.	50.00
Vase, Gold Scrolls & Leaves, Enameled Flowers, 11 1/2 In.	295.00
Vase, Jack-In-The-Pulpit, Clear Rigaree At Center, 10 In.	125.00
Vase, Lattice Pattern, Dogwood Enameling, 6 In.	155.00
Vase, Lilies Of The Valley, White Enamel, 6 3/4 In., Pair	135.00
Vase, Optic Ribbed, Crimped Top, 6 1/4 X 4 In.	55.00
Vase, Ruffled Trumpet Top, Crystal Base, Pair, 12 In.	125.00
Vase, Sanded Gold Leaves, Enamel Outlining, 4 X 7 In.	165.00
Vase, Sanded Gold Leaves, Florals, 5 X 11 In.	145.00
Vase, Straight Top, Fenton, 5 1/2 In.	25.00
Vase, Swirl, Ruffled Edge, 7 In.	75.00
Water Set, Daisy & Fern, 8 Piece	325.00
Water Set, Inverted Thumbprint, 5 Piece	600.00
Water Set, White Spatter, Burlington Mark, 6 Piece	185.00
Wine Set, Clear Handle & Base, Handled, 6 Piece	95.00
Wine, Arcadia Pattern, Teardrop Stem, Cranberry, 7 In.	385.00
Wine, Hollow Stem, 5 In.	65.00
Wine, Swirled Bowl, Clear Foot & Stem	28.00

*Creamware, or queensware, was developed by Josiah Wedgwood about 1765.
It is a cream-colored earthenware that has been copied by many factories.*

CREAMWARE, see also Wedgwood
CREAMWARE, Basket & Undertray, 19th Century, Basket 11 1/2 In., Pair 130.00
    CROESUS, see Pressed Glass, Croesus

*Crown Derby is the nickname given to the works of the Royal Crown
Derby factory, which began working in England in 1859. An earlier and
more famous English Derby factory existed from 1750 to 1848. The two
factories were not related. Most of the porcelain found today with the
Derby mark is the work of the later Derby factory.*

    CROWN DERBY, see also Royal Crown Derby

CROWN DERBY, Cup, Derby Posies	8.00
Figurine, Lady On Ram, Wearing Glasses	300.00
Figurine, Sealyham Dog	35.00
Plate, Floral Center, Green, Gold, Blue, 8 3/4 In., Pair	120.00
Plate, Mikado, Blue, 10 1/4 In.	30.00
Rose Jar, Gold Design, Pink Ground, 1875 Period, 6 In.	250.00
Shrimp Dish, Imari Colors, 10 In.	250.00
Vase, Gold Floral Design, Dots At Top Rim, Marked, Yellow, 10 In.	250.00

Crown Milano glass was made by Frederick Shirley about 1890. It had a plain biscuit color with a satin finish. It was decorated with flowers, and often had large gold scrolls.

CROWN MILANO, Biscuit Jar, Burmese Color Ground, Floral, Handle, Label, 7 In. 695.00
Biscuit Jar, Encrusted Gold Florals, Signed, 8 In. 900.00
Biscuit Jar, Floral & Leaf Pattern, Rose To Custard, 8 In. 275.00
Biscuit Jar, Gold Encrusted Design, Burmese, Crown Mark 495.00
Biscuit Jar, Green, Brown Lily, Butterfly, Silver Lid, Marked 700.00
Biscuit Jar, Jeweled & Beaded, Marked 650.00
Biscuit Jar, Mottled Blue Pansies, Melon Ribbed 650.00
Biscuit Jar, Mums, Signed MW, Covered 485.00
Bowl, Blue Puffed-Out Flower Panels, Marked, 5 X 2 In. 175.00
Cracker Jar, Applied Red Jewels 400.00
Cracker Jar, Blown-Out Pebbles, Starfish, & Jewels 1250.00
Cracker Jar, Boy In 18th Century Garb, Raised In Gold, Signed 850.00
Dish, Sweetmeat, Burmese, Gold Floral, Mt.Washington Lid, Signed 875.00
Dish, Sweetmeat, Gilt, Signed 525.00
Dish, Sweetmeat, Melon Ribbed, Silver Plated Handle, 4 In. 195.00
Dish, Sweetmeat, Metal Lid, Initialed M.W. 450.00
Dish, Sweetmeat, Queen's Design, Marked, 4 In. 450.00
Ewer, Coral & Burgundy, Signed, 11 X 8 1/2 In. 1950.00
Ewer, Enameled Thistles & Foliage, Gold Outline, 10 In. 1850.00
Humidor, Leaves & Acorns, Sponge Holder Inside Lid, Yellow 575.00
Muffineer, Bouquet Of Flowers, Melon Shape, Ribbed, 4 In. 550.00
Rose Bowl, Encrusted Raised Gold, Mums, White Ground, 5 1/2 In. 550.00
Shaker, Melon Shape, Ribbed, Floral Design, Marked, 4 1/4 In. 550.00
Sugar & Creamer, Florals, Gold Drape & Tassel, Signed 300.00
Sugar Shaker, Melon Shape, Floral Design, Marked, 4 In. 490.00
Syrup, Floral, Raised Dots, Silver Plated Lid, Handle, 5 3/4 In. 985.00
Tray, Thistles Outlined In Raised Gold, Marked, 9 1/2 X 7 In. 1150.00
Vase, Children Scene, White Satin Ground, Purple Mark, 13 In. 1250.00
Vase, Ducks, Frank Guba, Marked, 10 In. 1450.00
Vase, Flowers, Leaves, Ivory, Gold Trim, 10 1/2 In. 495.00
Vase, Gold Ivy, Signed, 7 In. 475.00
Vase, Mums & Buds, Raised Gold, Gray & White, 5 1/2 X 5 1/2 In. 750.00
　　CROWN TUSCAN, see Cambridge

Cruets of glass or porcelain were made to hold vinegar or oil. They were especially popular during Victorian times.

　　CRUET, see also various Glass sections
CRUET, Cranberry Glass, Clear Handle & 3-Petal Clear Stopper 95.00
Cranberry Glass, Enameled Lilies Of The Valley, Clear Stopper, 8 In. 145.00
Cranberry Glass, Inside Ribbing 65.00
Cranberry Glass, Thumbprint Pattern 75.00
Cut Glass, Sheffield Holder, Set Of 4 .... 95.00
Set, Original Bottles, Silver Plated Holder, 16 1/2 In. 175.00

CT GERMANY, Cuspidor, Hand-Painted, Falcon Crest, C.1880 .... 45.00

Cup plates are small glass or china plates that held the cup while a gentleman of the mid-nineteenth century drank his coffee or tea from the saucer. The most famous cup plates were made of glass at the Boston and Sandwich factory located in Massachusetts.

CUP PLATE, Anchor, 24 Large Beads With Reels, Clear, 3 1/16 In. 65.00
Bunker Hill, Chain Pattern, 76 Scallops, 3 5/8 In. 14.00
Bunker Hill, Drape Pattern, 53 Scallops, 3 9/16 In. 15.00
Bunker Hill, Sandwich Glass, Flint 16.50
Bunker Hill, Scalloped, Clear 25.00
Cadmus, Sandwich Glass 45.00
Clipper Ship, Sandwich Glass 22.00

Eagle, Clear 45.00
Eagle, Lacy, Plain Rim, Clear, 3 7/16 In. 22.00
Eagle, 78 Scallops, Clear, 3 1/2 In. 29.00
Ft.Feire, Log Cabin 65.00
Heart, Sandwich Glass 50.00
Henry Clay 50.00
Log Cabin, 61 Scallops, 3 1/16 In. 31.00
Log Cabin, 66 Scallops, 3 1/4 In. 27.00
No Name Clay, 25 Scallops, 3 5/8 In. 10.00
Purple, Sandwich Glass 35.00
Ship, 23 Bold Scallops, 3 5/8 In. 12.00
Sunburst, No Center Dot, 50 Scallops, Clear, 3 In. 18.00
Sunburst, 61 Scallops, 3 1/16 In. 18.00
Victoria, Clear 65.00
13 Hearts In Shoulder, 54 Scallops, Clear, 3 1/4 In. 18.00

*Currier & Ives made the famous American lithographs marked with their
name from 1857 to 1907.*

CURRIER & IVES, Abraham Lincoln, 16th President 80.00
American Express Train, River Steamer 8500.00
American Homestead, Four Seasons .... 465.00 To 500.00
American Homestead, Spring 68.00
American Patriot's Dream, The Night Before The Battle 175.00
American Scenery .... 125.00 To 168.00
American Speckled Brook Trout 765.00
Among The Pines 285.00
Apples & Plums 65.00
Art Gallery, Centennial Exhibition 1876 .... 135.00
Autumn On Lake George 145.00
Base Hit 375.00
Battle At Antietam, Md. 170.00
Battle At Cedar Mountain 165.00
Battle Of Baton Rouge, La. 195.00
Battle Of Cedar Creek, Va. 135.00
Battle Of Malvern Hill 58.00
Battle Of Mill Spring, Ky. 140.00
Battle Of Spotsylvania, Va. 175.00
Battle Of The Wilderness, Va. 140.00
Best Likeness 135.00
Black-Eyed Beauty 45.00
Blackfish Nibble 225.00
Bluefishing 30.00
Bombardment & Capture Of Fredericksburg, Va. 67.00
Boss Of The Road 55.00
Bound To Shine 55.00
Bouquet Of Roses .... 54.00 To 75.00
Brave Wife 85.00
Burning Of The Steamship Austria 235.00
Butt Of The Jokers 250.00
Card, A Bare Chance 48.00
Card, Horse-Drawn Wagons, Advertising, 1880, Set Of 5 .... 350.00
Card, Hunting Theme, No Advertising 80.00
Catterskill Fall .... 145.00 To 165.00
Celebrated Trotting Mare Lula 185.00
Central Park, The Bridge .... 295.00 To 375.00
Central Park, Winter Skating Pond 650.00
Chappaqua Farm, Residence Of Horace Greeley 165.00
Childhood's Happy Days .... 285.00 To 288.00
Children In The Woods 60.00
City Hall, N.Y. 185.00
Clara 45.00
Col. Elmer E. Ellsworth .... 48.00 To 85.00
Col. Michael Corcoran, At The Battle Of Bull Run, Va. 145.00
Coming From The Trot 4000.00

Copped At A Cock Fight 225.00
Cottage By The Cliff 148.00
Cottage Life, Summer 175.00
Darktown Fire Brigade, Under Full Steam 195.00
Darktown Trotter Ready For The Word 225.00
Darktown Yacht Club, Hard Up For A Breeze 195.00
Day Before Marriage, The Bride's Jewels 75.00
Deathbed Of The Martyr President, Abraham Lincoln 60.00
Deer In The Woods .... 225.00 To 235.00
Deer Shooting 165.00
Draw Poker, Getting 'em Lively 225.00
Drive Through The Highlands 300.00
Dwight L.Moody, The American Evangelist 28.00
Ella 25.00
Fall Of Richmond, Va., Night Of April 2nd, 1865 .... 170.00 To 175.00
Falls Of Niagara, From Clifton House 145.00
Fashionable Turn-Outs In Central Park 4400.00
Fast Team, Out On The Loose 215.00
Fast Trotters On Harlem Lane, New York 5200.00
First Pants 145.00
First Ride 75.00
First Trot Of The Season .... 1650.00 To 1950.00
First Under The Wire 325.00
Fort Pickens, Pensacola Harbor, Fla. 190.00
Fort Sumter, Charleston Harbor, S.C. 245.00
Foul Tip 200.00
Fox Hunting, The Death 850.00
Fox Hunting, The Meet 800.00
Frontier Settlement 695.00
Fruit Vase, Ornate White Vase 95.00
Fruits Of The Tropics 90.00
Fruits, Autumn Varieties 95.00
General Francis Marion Of S.C. 250.00
General Grant & Family .... 50.00 To 85.00
General James A. Garfield .... 48.00 To 60.00
General U.S. Grant, Nation's Choice For President 45.00
Glengariff Inn, Ireland 75.00
God Bless Father And Mother 60.00
Going To The Trot 4200.00
Grand Horse St. Julien, The King Of Trotters .... 195.00 To 300.00
Grand National Republican, Banner, 1876, Hayes & Wheeler 135.00
Grand United Order Of Odd Fellows, Chart 85.00
Grandpa's Cane 30.00
Great Fire At Boston, 1872 .... 195.00
Great International Boat Race, 1869 .... 895.00
Grottoes Of The Sea, People Around Fire 60.00
Group Of Flowers 80.00
Happy Family 145.00
Harvest 198.00
He Is Saved 40.00
High Bridge At Harlem, N.Y. 495.00
Home In The Country 495.00
Home In The Wilderness .... 475.00 To 495.00
Home Of Washington, Mt.Vernon, Va. 195.00
Home On The Mississippi 395.00
Homeward Bound 575.00
Hot Race To The Wire 450.00
Household Treasures 48.00
Hudson Highlands 225.00
Hues Of Autumn 165.00
Hundred-Leaf Rose 20.00
Hunter's Shanty 395.00
Idlewild, On The Hudson 195.00
Impending Crisis Or Caught In The Act 165.00

In The Mountains 175.00
In The Woods 110.00
Indian Lake, Sunset 495.00
Infant Brood 295.00
Ingleside Winter .... 450.00 To 465.00
Jane 55.00
Lake George, Black Mountain 90.00
Lake George, N.Y. 185.00
Lake Memphremagog, Owl's Head 165.00
Landscape, Fruit & Flowers 1750.00
Lapped On The Last Quarter 400.00
Life Of A Sportsman, Camping In The Woods 365.00
Light Of The Swelling 50.00
Lismore Castle, County Waterford 9.00
Little Harry, Cat On Chair 32.00
Little Lizzie 42.00
Look At Papa 35.00
Love Is The Lightest 48.00
Lovers' Reconciliation 60.00
Lt.Gen. Winfield Scott, General In Chief Of The U.S. Army 58.00
Major Gen. Benj. F. Butler 65.00
Mammoth Iron Steamship, Great Eastern 80.00
Mansion Of The Olden Time 165.00
Mayflower Saluted By The Fleet 525.00
Midnight Race On The Mississippi 425.00
Mill In The Highlands 275.00
Miniature Ship, Red, White, & Blue 195.00
Moonlight, The Castle 75.00
Moonlight, The Ruins 68.00
Moosehead Lake 165.00
Morning Of Life 75.00
Morning Star 50.00
Moss Roses & Buds .... 85.00 To 135.00
Most Holy Catholic Faith 25.00
Mother's Blessing 135.00
Mother's Dream 38.00
Mountain Spring, West Point 695.00
Mountaineer's Home 325.00
Mrs. Lucretia R. Garfield .... 45.00 To 48.00
Mud S., De Great Record Buster 400.00
My Little Playfellow 20.00
My Little White Kittens 65.00
My Little White Kitties Playing Dominoes 85.00
My Pony And Dog 100.00
My Three White Kitties, Learning Their ABC's 44.00
Narrows, New York Bay, From Staten Island 325.00
Natural Bridge 85.00
New Suspension Bridge, Niagara Falls 235.00
New York Bay From Bay Ridge, Long Island 350.00
New York Ferry Boat, Fulton 600.00
New-Fashioned Girl 65.00
Niagara Falls, From Goat Island, Moonlight .... 165.00 To 195.00
Niagara Falls, From The Canada Side 125.00
Night By The Campfire .... 295.00 To 325.00
Night Express, The Start 2495.00
No You Don't 85.00
No, No, Fido 44.00
Noontide, A Shady Spot 145.00
Not Caught 195.00
O Dat Watermillon 200.00
Off The Port 575.00
Old Blandford Church, Petersburg, Va. 145.00
Old Farm House .... 625.00 To 645.00
Old Ruins 75.00

Old Windmill	30.00
On The Owago	135.00
On The St. Lawrence, Indian Encampment	225.00 To 285.00
Outlet Of Niagara River	110.00
Pacing Wonder, Little Brown Jug Of Chicago	600.00
Pacing Wonder, Sleepy Tom	475.00
Pair Of Nutcrackers	95.00
Papa's Darlings	58.00
Partridge Shooting	285.00
Peerless Goldsmith Maid	725.00
Pic-Nic Party	796.00
Pilot Boat In A Storm	425.00
Placid Lake	195.00
President Lincoln At Home, Reading Scriptures To Wife	75.00
Pride Of The West	28.00
Prize Trotter	500.00
Queen Of The Turf, Lady Thorn	210.00
Railroad Suspension Bridge, Near Niagara Falls	495.00
River Side	125.00 To 135.00
Roadside Mill	165.00
Rocky Mountain, Buffalo Herd In Foreground	365.00
Rural Lake	245.00
Saratoga Springs	215.00
Scenery Of The Wissahickon	185.00
Search The Scriptures	35.00
Shooting On The Beach	945.00
Shooting On The Prairie	745.00
Sibyl's Temple	38.00
Siege & Capture Of Vicksburg, Miss., July 4th, 1863	135.00
Silver Cascade	145.00
Silver Creek, California	345.00
Sinking Of The Steamship Ville De Havre	195.00
Skating Scene, Moonlight	795.00
Sleepy Hollow Bridge	245.00
Sleepy Hollow, Church	595.00
Source Of The Hudson, Indiana Pass	235.00
Spirit Of The Union	125.00
Sports Whot Lost Their Tin	450.00
Squirrel Shooting	395.00
St. Peter Receiving The Keys	25.00
Stag At Bay	160.00
Stoppin Place On The Road	8500.00
Stratford On Avon	48.00
Striped Bass	145.00
Summer In The Country	135.00
Summer Morning, Children, River	185.00
Summer Morning, Two Couples Boating, Mill In Distance	160.00
Summer Noon	220.00
Sunny South	145.00
Sunnyside, The Residence Of The Late Washington Irving	950.00
Surrender Of Genl. Joe Johnston Near Greensboro, N.C.	140.00
Sweet Springtime	24.00
Taking Breath	45.00
Taking It Easy	38.00
Tantallon Castle	185.00
Terrific Combat Between The Monitor & Merrimac	488.00
There's A Mousie	75.00
Through To The Pacific	695.00
To The Rescue	40.00
Tomb Of Kosciusko, West Point	145.00
Trenton High Falls	145.00
Trotters On The Snow	495.00
Trotting Stallion, Namebrind Gift	425.00
Trout Pool	625.00

Trout, Just Caught 350.00
Two Little Fraid Cats .... 54.00 To 58.00
U.S. Post Office, New York 285.00
Under Cliff, On The Hudson 165.00
Valley Falls, Virginia 175.00
View From Fort Putnam, West Point, Hudson River 245.00
View On Hudson River 125.00
View On The Roundout .... 195.00 To 295.00
Vigilant, Defender Of America's Cup 160.00
Washington's Reception By The Ladies 165.00
Watkins Glen 240.00
We Parted On The Hillside Amid The Winter's Snow 105.00
Which Of Us Will You Marry? 65.00
Winning Hands Down With A Good Second 345.00
Winter Morning, Feeding The Chickens 2650.00
Wreck Of The Atlantic .... 125.00 To 145.00
Yacht Meteor Of New York 295.00
Yankee Doodle On His Muscle 345.00
Yosemite Falls, California 195.00
Young Cadets 48.00

CURRIER, Battery, New York, By Moonlight 475.00
Battle Of Buena Vista 1847 .... 130.00
Battle Of Cerro Gordo 125.00
Burning Of The Clipper Ship Golden Light 950.00
Burning Of The Henry Clay Near Yonkers 185.00
Capitol At Washington 175.00
Check, Keep Your Distance, 1853 .... 3500.00
City Hall, N.Y., View From The Park In Front 225.00
Clipper Ship Great Republic, Broadside View 295.00
Constitution & Guerriere 130.00
Death Of Major Ringgold 75.00
Death Of Major Ringgold, Battlefield, Horse, Officer 75.00
Declaration .... 30.00 To 55.00
Declaration Of Independence 145.00
Dreadful Wreck Of The Mexico On Hempstead Beach, Jan. 2nd, 1837 .... 1495.00
Esther, 3/4 Length Figure 55.00
Father & Child 56.00
Father's Pride, Mother & Son, Victorian Sofa 65.00
Flower Vase 95.00
General Taylor At The Battle Of Resaca De La Palma 40.00
General Z. Taylor, Hero Of The Rio Grande 95.00
George M Dallas, The People's Candidate For Vice President 75.00
Grand National Democratic Banner, Polk & Dallas 165.00
Grand National Whig Banner 160.00
Harvest Field 295.00
James K. Polk, Eleventh President .... 80.00 To 85.00
Morning Prayer 35.00
Naval Bombardment Of Vera Cruz 165.00
New England Homestead, Framed, 16 1/2 X 20 1/2 In. 35.00
New York Clipper Ship Challenge 395.00
Presidents Of The United States, Washington To Polk .... 37.00 To 125.00
Royal Mail Steamship Persia 875.00
Sacred Heart Of Jesus .... 16.00 To 20.00
Santa Anna's Messengers Requesting Gen. Taylor To Surrender 110.00
Sons Of Temperance, Love, Purity, & Fidelity 32.00
Spaniel 225.00
Steamship Wedding Day 65.00
Storming Of The Bishop's Palace 80.00
Susanna 55.00
The Steamship President, Largest In The World 265.00
Theodore Frelinghuysen, Hurrah, Hurrah, The Country's Risin 48.00
Tomb Of General W.H.Harrison 175.00
Vase Of Flowers 195.00

View Of The Distributing Reservoir On Murray's Hill 365.00
View Of The Park, Fountain & City Hall 185.00
Washington Family 145.00
Washington In The Field 185.00
Water Rail Shooting 375.00
Wild Duck Shooting, Long Island Hunting Series 5500.00
Wm.Penn's Treaty With The Indians .... 38.00 To 125.00

Custard glass is an opaque glass sometimes known as buttermilk glass.
It was first made in America after 1886 at the La Belle Glass Works,
Bridgeport, Ohio.

CUSTARD GLASS, see also Maize
CUSTARD GLASS, Alba, Sugar Shaker, Green 75.00
Argonaut Shell, Banana Boat 150.00
Argonaut Shell, Compote, Jelly 95.00
Argonaut Shell, Creamer, Northwood 125.00
Argonaut Shell, Pitcher, Signed, Northwood 325.00
Argonaut Shell, Saltshaker 150.00
Argonaut Shell, Spooner .... 60.00 To 110.00
Argonaut Shell, Sugar, Covered 65.00
Argonaut Shell, Tumbler, Gold 65.00
Argonaut Shell, Tumbler, Set Of 6 .... 60.00
Argonaut Shell, Water Set 500.00
Argonaut Shell, Water Set, 7 Piece 500.00
Beaded Cable, Rose Bowl, Northwood, Pinched, Nutmeg Stain 75.00
Beaded Circle, Salt & Pepper 255.00
Bees On Basket, Toothpick 58.00
Bees On Basket, Toothpick, Green 38.00
Cane Insert, Tumbler, Gold Trim 50.00
Cherry Sprig, Butter 230.00
Cherry Sprig, Salt & Pepper, Gold 145.00
Cherry Sprig, Sugar 55.00
Chrysanthemum Sprig, Berry Bowl, Signed, 7 1/2 In. 425.00
Chrysanthemum Sprig, Berry Bowl, 7 1/2 In. 200.00
Chrysanthemum Sprig, Butter 275.00
Chrysanthemum Sprig, Celery .... 700.00 To 800.00
Chrysanthemum Sprig, Compote, Jelly .... 65.00 To 90.00
Chrysanthemum Sprig, Compote, Jelly, Blue 40.00
Chrysanthemum Sprig, Creamer 100.00
Chrysanthemum Sprig, Creamer, Blue .... 275.00 To 300.00
Chrysanthemum Sprig, Cruet .... 200.00 To 225.00
Chrysanthemum Sprig, Pitcher, Water 315.00
Chrysanthemum Sprig, Salt & Pepper, Northwood 135.00
Chrysanthemum Sprig, Sauce, Blue 75.00
Chrysanthemum Sprig, Sauce, Gold Rim, 3 1/2 X 5 In. 50.00
Chrysanthemum Sprig, Sauce, Northwood, Signed 195.00
Chrysanthemum Sprig, Spooner 100.00
Chrysanthemum Sprig, Sugar & Creamer 145.00
Chrysanthemum Sprig, Sugar & Creamer, Signed, Gold Trim 850.00
Chrysanthemum Sprig, Table Set, Blue, 4 Piece 1450.00
Chrysanthemum Sprig, Table Set, 4 Piece 650.00
Chrysanthemum Sprig, Tray, Pin 20.00
Chrysanthemum Sprig, Tumbler 55.00
Chrysanthemum Sprig, Tumbler, Blue 295.00
Chrysanthemum Sprig, Tumbler, Gold Trim 55.00
Chrysanthemum Sprig, Tumbler, Northwood, Set Of 4 .... 125.00
Chrysanthemum Sprig, Water Set, Blue, 5 Piece 1100.00
Chrysanthemum Sprig, Water Set, Hand-Painted, 7 Piece 500.00
Cupid, Box, Ring, Hinged, 2 1/2 In. .... 225.00 To 295.00
Delaware, Creamer, Blue 40.00
Delaware, Jar, Powder, Jeweled Lid, Green With Gold 175.00
Delaware, Toothpick, Color Stain Flowers, Clear With Gold 75.00
Delaware, Toothpick, Green With Gold 80.00
Delaware, Toothpick, Rose Stain With Gold 110.00

Delaware, Tray, Pin, Green Enamel, 6 In. .... 50.00 To 65.00
Diamond With Peg, Dish, Sauce, Ludlow, Vt., Signed Crystol 35.00
Diamond With Peg, Glass, Shot 75.00
Diamond With Peg, Mug 45.00
Diamond With Peg, Mug, Milwaukee, Wisconsin 45.00
Diamond With Peg, Saltshaker 35.00
Diamond With Peg, Spooner, Rose, Conneaut, Pa. 50.00
Diamond With Peg, Toothpick 50.00
Diamond With Peg, Tumbler, Rose Design 58.00
Diamond With Peg, Vase, 6 In. 50.00
Diamond With Peg, Water Set, Roses, 6 Tumblers 325.00
Diamond With Peg, Wine, Roses, Gold 60.00
Diamond With Peg, Wine, Stratton, Me., 6-Sided 32.00
Double Loop, Sugar, Northwood 60.00
Dragon & Lotus, Bowl, Fenton 85.00
Everglades, Spooner 125.00
Fan, Butter, Covered, Gold Trim 40.00
Fan, Water Set, 7 Piece 500.00
Fandango, Basket, Floral & Butterfly, Handle, 13 In. 175.00
Fandango, Tray, Ice Cream 80.00
Fentonia, Butter, Covered, Nutmeg Trim 215.00
Fine Cut & Roses, Rose Bowl, Nutmeg Stain, 3 Feet 135.00
Geneva, Berry Set, Oval, Red & Green, 7 Piece 325.00
Geneva, Creamer 80.00
Geneva, Sauce, Gold & Green, Round 48.00
Geneva, Sauce, Oval 50.00
Georgia Gem, Berry Bowl, 7 1/2 In. 75.00
Georgia Gem, Berry Set, Clear & Green, 7 Piece 180.00
Georgia Gem, Butter, Covered 95.00
Georgia Gem, Butter, Sugar & Creamer, Covered 220.00
Georgia Gem, Creamer .... 45.00 To 50.00
Georgia Gem, Creamer, Floral Design 75.00
Georgia Gem, Saltshaker, Souvenir, Maine, Green 20.00
Georgia Gem, Shade, Dome Shape, 18 X 7 In. 150.00
Georgia Gem, Sugar, Covered 70.00
Georgia Gem, Toothpick 80.00
Georgia Gem, Toothpick, Gold Trim 55.00
Georgia Gem, Toothpick, Green .... 32.00 To 65.00
Georgia Gem, Tumbler, Enameled Flower 55.00
Georgia Gem, Tumbler, Souvenir, Gettysburg, Green 45.00
Grape & Cable, Bottle, Cologne 500.00
Grape & Cable, Bowl, Centerpiece, Brown 250.00
Grape & Cable, Bowl, Orange, Northwood, Signed, Nutmeg 425.00
Grape & Cable, Cup, Punch, Brown 40.00
Grape & Cable, Dish, Candy, Nutmeg 45.00
Grape & Cable, Sauce, Footed, Nutmeg Stain 45.00
Grape & Cable, Sauce, Nutmeg Stain, Footed 45.00
Grape & Cable, Sugar, Clear 105.00
Grape & Gothic Arches, Bowl, Berry, Green, 7 1/2 In. 40.00
Grape & Gothic Arches, Goblet 55.00
Grape & Gothic Arches, Goblet, Nutmeg Stain 70.00
Grape & Gothic Arches, Spooner, Nutmeg Stain 75.00
Grape & Gothic Arches, Table Set, Green, 4 Piece 200.00
Grape & Gothic Arches, Tumbler 45.00
Grape & Gothic Arches, Vase, Northwood, Marked 85.00
Grape & Gothic Arches, Water Set, Green, 10 Piece 225.00
Grape Arbor, Vase, Hat Shape, N Mark, Nutmeg Stain, 5 1/4 In. 30.00
Grape Arbor, Vase, Hat Shaped, Nutmeg Stain, Marked, 5 In. 27.00
Harvard, Creamer, Green, Souvenir Of Zion City 20.00
Harvard, Toothpick .... 28.00 To 45.00
Harvard, Toothpick, Blue 25.00
Heart & Thumbprint, Sugar 35.00
Horseshoe & Clover, Toothpick, Green 26.00
Intaglio, Berry Set, Green Trim, 7 Piece .... 175.00 To 225.00

Intaglio, Bowl, Berry, Green Trim, 7 1/2 In. 65.00
Intaglio, Bowl, Fruit, Gold Trim, Large 115.00
Intaglio, Compote, Footed, Green & Gold Design, 9 X 6 In. 195.00
Intaglio, Compote, Jelly 85.00
Intaglio, Cruet, Green, Gold Design, Original Stopper 375.00
Intaglio, Saltshaker, Northwood, Blue 75.00
Intaglio, Saltshaker, Pair 100.00
Intaglio, Sauce, Blue Trim 20.00
Intaglio, Spooner 110.00
Intaglio, Sugar, Blue & Gold 30.00
Intaglio, Table Set, Gold Trim, Green .... 450.00 To 585.00
Intaglio, Tumbler, Gold & Green Decoration 65.00
Intaglio, Tumbler, Gold Trim, Green, Set Of 6 .... 180.00
Intaglio, Tumbler, Green 55.00
Intaglio, Tumbler, Green & Gold 55.00
Inverted Fan & Feather, Butter, Covered 200.00
Inverted Fan & Feather, Pitcher, Gold Trim, Green 165.00
Inverted Fan & Feather, Saltshaker, Blue 175.00
Inverted Fan & Feather, Spooner 135.00
Inverted Fan & Feather, Toothpick 450.00
Inverted Fern & Feather, Bowl, Gold Trim, 9 3/4 In.Diam. 195.00
Iris, Cruet .... 450.00 To 475.00
  IVORINA VERDE, see Winged Scroll
Jack-In-The-Pulpit, Vase, Green, Ruffled Low 30.00
Jackson, Berry Bowl, Blue, 7 1/2 In. 75.00
Jackson, Berry Bowl, 7 1/2 In. 75.00
Jackson, Creamer 75.00
Jackson, Cruet 135.00
Jackson, Pitcher 195.00
Jackson, Pitcher, Water 195.00
Jackson, Sugar 40.00
Jackson, Tumbler .... 42.00 To 45.00
Jefferson Optic, Berry Set, Green & Clear, 7 Piece 200.00
Jefferson Optic, Saltshaker, Pingree, N.D. 35.00
Jefferson Optic, Sugar, Covered 90.00
  LITTLE GEM, see also Georgia Gem
Little Gem, Creamer 45.00
Lotus & Grape, Bonbon, Handled, Pink 45.00
Louis XV, Banana Boat 150.00
Louis XV, Banana Boat, Blue 165.00
Louis XV, Bowl, Fruit 140.00
Louis XV, Butter 200.00
Louis XV, Butter & Spooner 200.00
Louis XV, Butter, Covered, Gold Trim 150.00
Louis XV, Creamer .... 55.00 To 85.00
Louis XV, Creamer & Spooner 150.00
Louis XV, Cruet 175.00
Louis XV, Salt & Pepper, Original Top 185.00
Louis XV, Saltshaker, Green 20.00
Louis XV, Sauce .... 28.00 To 45.00
Louis XV, Sauce, Blue 45.00
Louis XV, Spooner .... 55.00 To 95.00
Louis XV, Spooner, Ruffle 75.00
Louis XV, Sugar, Covered 130.00
Louis XV, Tumbler .... 40.00 To 55.00
  MAIZE, see Maize
Maple Leaf, Banana Boat 200.00
Maple Leaf, Berry Bowl, 7 1/2 In. .... 350.00 To 450.00
Maple Leaf, Butter, Covered 110.00
Maple Leaf, Butter, Covered, Blue 400.00
Maple Leaf, Creamer, Gold Trim 105.00
Maple Leaf, Dish, Jelly 375.00
Maple Leaf, Salt & Pepper 500.00
Maple Leaf, Spooner, Gold & Green 95.00

Maple Leaf, Spooner, Gold Trim .... 85.00 To 95.00
Nestor, Pitcher, Water, Blue 118.00
Peacock At Fountain, Ice Cream, Master, Nutmeg Stain 175.00
Peacock At Urn, Dish, Ice Cream, Master, Nutmeg Design 195.00
Pier & Wave, Bowl, 5 1/2 In. 25.00
Plain Band, Toothpick, Souvenir 35.00
Prayer Rug, Bonbon, 2-Handled 35.00
Prayer Rug, Bowl, 7 1/2 In. 25.00
Prayer Rug, Nappy, Green 15.00
Prayer Rug, Plate, Green, 7 1/2 In. 8.00
Ribbed Thumbprint, Pitcher, Souvenir, Toronto, Handled 30.00
Ribbed Thumbprint, Toothpick, Souvenir, Rosebuds 48.00
Ring Band, Berry Bowl, Green, 7 1/2 In. 50.00
Ring Band, Bowl, Cambridge, Green, 10 1/2 X 3/4 In. 10.00
Ring Band, Bowl, Condiment, Ladle, McKee, Green 40.00
Ring Band, Butter, Gold Bands 160.00
Ring Band, Toothpick, Gold .... 50.00 To 65.00
Ring Band, Tumbler, Gold & Green Band, Signed, Heisey 65.00
Smocking, Bell 40.00
Smocking, Mug, Embossed Rose, Goofus Gold 30.00
Thumbprint Band, Tumbler, Revere Beach, 1908, Heisey Mark 38.00
Thumbprint, Tumbler, Rose Design, Ribbed 25.00
Tiny Thumbprint, Toothpick, Souvenir 50.00
Tiny Thumbprint, Vase, Picture, Souvenir, 5 1/2 In. 18.00
Trailing Vine, Butter, Blue 70.00
Vermont, Relish, Pink Enamel, 8 1/2 In. 37.50
Vermont, Toothpick, Green With Gold .... 50.00 To 85.00
Vermont, Vase, Enamel Trim 65.00
Victoria, Spooner 85.00
Wild Bouquet, Toothpick, Decorated, Custard With Gold 550.00
Wild Bouquet, Toothpick, Northwood 475.00
Winged Scroll, Berry Bowl, 8 1/2 In. 95.00
Winged Scroll, Butter, Covered .... 100.00 To 225.00
Winged Scroll, Creamer .... 60.00 To 90.00
Winged Scroll, Jar, Dresser 80.00
Winged Scroll, Jug, Gold Design, 1/2 Gallon 245.00
Winged Scroll, Ring Tree, Low 100.00
Winged Scroll, Spooner 90.00
Winged Scroll, Sugar & Creamer 100.00
Winged Scroll, Table Set, Gold Trim, Heisey, 4 Piece 385.00
Winged Scroll, Toothpick .... 85.00 To 100.00
Winged Scroll, Tray, Dresser, Rose Design 75.00
Winged Scroll, Tray, Green, 5 1/2 X 8 1/2 In. 40.00
Winged Scroll, Tray, Pin 15.00
Winged Scroll, Tray, 8 1/2 In. 75.00

*Cut glass has been made since ancient times, but the large majority of the
pieces now for sale date from the brilliant period of glass design, 1880 to
1905. These pieces had elaborate geometric designs with a deep miter cut.*

CUT GLASS, see also listings under factory name

CUT GLASS, Ashtray, Sphere, Hobstars, Pineapples, Crosshatching 20.00
Ashtray, Sunburst Pattern Underside, Square, 5 X 2 1/2 In. 50.00
Banana Bowl, Expanding Star Pattern 225.00
Basket, Cosmos Spray, 12 In. 165.00
Basket, Fans, Fern-Filled Vesicas, Double Handle, 6 In. 225.00
Basket, Queen's Lace Pattern, 9 1/2 X 7 X 9 1/2 In. 255.00
Bell, Dinner, Hobstars, 6 In. 275.00
Bell, Hobstars, Diamond & Cone, Prism Cut Top, 4 In. 225.00
Berry Bowl, Princess, 8 In. 275.00
Biscuit Barrel, Silver Plated Mounts, 5 1/2 In. 175.00
Biscuit Jar, Hobstars & Blaze, Rayed Base, 9 1/2 In. 625.00
Boat, Harvard Pattern, 4 In. Long 75.00
Bottle, Barrel Shape, Diamond Cut, Cranberry To Clear, 7 In. 175.00
Bottle, Bureau, Stopper, Cut Cane Design, Square Panel, Canary, 6 In. 155.00

Bottle, Dresser, Diamond & Hobstars, Faceted Neck, 7 In. 195.00
Bottle, Orgy Scene, 16-Ray Base, Floral Deisgn, 9 In. 150.00
Bottle, Perfume, English, Lay Down, Blue, 4 1/4 In. 125.00
Bottle, Perfume, Flute & Strawberry, Sterling Hinged Top, 3 3/4 In 95.00
Bottle, Perfume, Yellow, Hobstar Bottom, 5 In. 200.00
Bottle, Perfume, 8-Sided, Diamond Shape, Stopper, 6 3/4 In. 45.00
Bottle, Scent, Panel Cut Stopper, English, 2 X 3 1/4 In. 35.00
Bottle, Whiskey, Draped & Swagged Pattern, 12 1/2 In. 575.00
Bottle, X Pattern, Brass Neck, Hinged, Glass Stopper, 2 1/4 In. 35.00
Bowl, Bands Of Zipper Beveling, Hobstar Medallion, 8 1/4 In. 95.00
Bowl, Canoe In Iowa Pattern, 9 In. 150.00
Bowl, Creswick Pattern, Hobstars, Diamonds, 8 X 3 In. 75.00
Bowl, Creswick Pattern, Scalloped, 8 1/2 In. 75.00
Bowl, Diamond, Fan, Russian, Hobstar Bottom, 2 X 2 3/4 In. 60.00
Bowl, Dorflinger's Parisian Pattern, 14 X 7 In. 850.00
Bowl, Fan & Hobstars, Star Bottom, 8 1/2 In. 125.00
Bowl, Finger, Button, Scalloped Rim, Russian, 2 3/4 X 5 1/4 In. 150.00
Bowl, Finger, Renaissance, Dorflinger, 24-Star Base, Set Of 4 .... 120.00
Bowl, Fruit, Cane Pattern, Floral Design, Cylindrical Form, 8 In. 65.00
Bowl, Fruit, Hobstar, Fan, Notched Panel Design, 10 In. 125.00
Bowl, Harvard Pattern, Signed J.Hoare, 8 X 4 In. 295.00
Bowl, Harvard Pattern, Turned-In Sides, Oval, 11 X 7 X 4 1/2 In. 395.00
Bowl, Harvard Vesicas, Star Radiant, 2-Handled, 7 In.Diam. 475.00
Bowl, Heart & Hobstar, 4 X 8 In. 285.00
Bowl, Hobstar Chain, Engraved Stem, Base, Signed, 6 X 8 In. 800.00
Bowl, Hobstar, Fans, Chair Bottom Pattern, Footed, 7 3/4 In. 35.00
Bowl, Hobstars, Hobnails, Zippers, Crosshatching, Signed, 8 In. 185.00
Bowl, Hobstars, Teardrop Stem, 9 X 9 In. 550.00
Bowl, Intricate Cutting, Signed Hoare, 10 X 2 1/2 In. 495.00
Bowl, Pinwheel Design, Feathered Fan, Notched Rim, 9 In. 45.00
Bowl, Punch, Keystone Pattern, 10 Cups, 12 In. 1350.00
Bowl, Ripley Pattern, Floral & Leaves, 8 X 3 3/4 In. 65.00
Bowl, Rose, Strawberry Diamond, Fan, Hobstar Base, 4 In. 165.00
Bowl, Salad, Russian & Pillars, Hobstar Bottom, 9 In. 695.00
Bowl, Singing Birds Pattern, Signed Fry, 8 1/2 In. 285.00
Bowl, Sunburst & Button, 7 In. 80.00
Bowl, Wassail, Silver Stand, 6 Hobstars, Silver Top, 17 X 10 In. 1900.00
Box, Dresser, Cherub, Roses & Leaves, Sterling Lid, 4 In. 135.00
Box, Flashed Ruby Cut, Cane Pattern, Rectangular, 5 X 7 In. 300.00
Box, Heart Shape, Hobstars, Hobnail, Fan, Covered, 6 In. 135.00
Box, Intaglio Cut, Sterling Silver Lid, Monogrammed 55.00
Box, Jewel, Harvard Pattern, Rayed Base, Hinged Lid, 7 X 4 1/4 In. 875.00
Box, Patch, Sterling Top 55.00
Box, Powder, Hobstar On Base & Lid, 3 X 5 In. 225.00
Box, Puff, Gravic Cut, Green To Clear, Thumbprint & Leaves, 5 In. 135.00
Butter Chip, Crosshatch & Fan, Sawtooth Edge, 3 1/4 In. 17.50
Butter Pat, Crosshatch & Fan 18.00
Butter, Flower, Leaves, & Strawberry Diamond, Covered 375.00
Butter, Hobstars, Crosshatching, Dorflinger, Signed, Domed Top 285.00
Butter, Wild Roses & Hobstars, Covered 200.00
Cakestand, Hobstars & Fan, Crosshatched Vesicas, 7 X 9 In. 1100.00
Candlestick, Flowers & Leaves, Hollow Stem & Base, 8 1/2 In. 65.00
Candlestick, Hobstars & Strawberry Diamond, Green Cut To Clear 625.00
Candy, Hobstars, Pinwheels, Crosshatching, 7 In. 15.00
Candy, Scalloped Rim, 2-Handled, 8 In. 95.00
Candy, Strawberry, Diamond & Fan, Footed, 5 In. 45.00
Canoe, Harvard Pattern, 11 1/2 In.Long 400.00
Carafe, Bright Cut, 8 1/2 In. 110.00
Carafe, Diamond & Fan, Paneled & Notched Neck, 8 In. 85.00
Carafe, Fan & Strawberry, 8 1/2 In. 70.00
Carafe, Harvard Pattern, Cut Neck 350.00
Carafe, Hobstars, Crosshatched, Diamonds 110.00
Carafe, Hobstars, Step Cut 8-Prism Neck, 9 In. 150.00
Carafe, Water, Pineapple & Hobstar, 8 1/2 In. 395.00

Castor Set, Set Of 6, Sheffield Silver Frame 225.00
Celery, Boat Shape, Hobstar Pattern, Scalloped, 12 In. 45.00
Celery, Empress Pattern, Scalloped & Serrated, 11 1/2 In. 65.00
Celery, Hobnail Diamonds, Hobstars, Russian, 11 X 4 1/2 In. 45.00
Celery, Russian Pattern, Folded-In Sides, 11 In.Long 325.00
Celery, Wedgemere Pattern, 12 3/4 X 5 1/2 In.Wide 295.00
Chalice, Strawberry Fan, Diamonds, Crosshatching, 6 In. 135.00
Chamberstick, 24-Point Hobstar On Base, 3 X 7 In. 600.00
Champagne, Encore, Teardrop Stems, Hobstar Base, Pair 195.00
Cheese, Underplate, Covered, Cane & Fan, 9 In. 450.00
Clock, Boudoir, Harvard Pattern 325.00
Coffeepot, Chain, Meridan Glass Company 800.00
Cologne, Brass Cap, Inside Stopper, 2 1/4 In. 35.00
Cologne, Stopper, French Ivory Holder, 4 1/2 In. 35.00
Compote, Allover Prism Cut, Scalloped Rim, Rayed Base, 7 1/2 In. 110.00
Compote, Bull's-Eyes, Cut Base, Expanding Stem, 9 1/4 In. 230.00
Compote, Butterflies, Stemmed, 9 In. 95.00
Compote, Comet Pattern, 5 1/2 X 8 In. 625.00
Compote, Cut Flowers & Foliage, Rayed Base, 4 1/2 X 6 1/4 In. 35.00
Compote, Hobstar, Cane, Star, & Crosshatching, Stemmed, 8 X 6 In. 325.00
Compote, Hobstars, Hobstar Base, 9 X 6 In. 175.00
Compote, Hobstars, Pinwheels, & Hobnail, Signed Maple City, 5 In. 250.00
Compote, Leicester, Signed Clark, 5 1/2 X 5 3/4 In. 250.00
Compote, Teardrop In Stem, Scalloped, Hobstar, 8 5/8 In. 215.00
Compote, Vesicas, Cane, & Crosshatching, Pillar Stem, 8 In. 325.00
Compote, 6-Sided Stop Cut, 7 1/2 In. 195.00
Condiment Set, Ornate Silver Plated Stand, Set Of 6 .... 295.00
Cooler, Champagne, Large, 12 Pound, 9 1/2 X 9 In. 3050.00
Cordial, Double Teardrop In Stem, 4 1/2 In. 310.00
Cruet, Cane Diamonds, Zipper, & Fan, Rayed Base, Stopper, Pair 695.00
Cruet, Strawberry & Fan, St.Louis Cut Handle, 3-Lip, 6 1/2 In. 125.00
Cruet, Strawberry, Diamonds & Fans, Stopper, Handle, 9 In. 37.50
Cruet, Trumpet Shape, Strawberry Diamond & Fan, Stopper, 8 In. 38.00
Cruet, Zipper 35.00
Decanter, Amethyst Cut To Clear, 17 In. 295.00
Decanter, Basket Pattern, Honeycomb Neck, Stopper, 13 In. 895.00
Decanter, Captain's, Comet Pattern, Small 450.00
Decanter, Cranberry Cut To Clear, 15 In. 295.00
Decanter, Delft Pattern, Signed Hoare, 12 1/2 In. 395.00
Decanter, Double Cut, Knobs On Neck, Light Green, 12 In. 1200.00
Decanter, Fans, Hobstars, & Diamonds, Fluted Neck, 10 1/2 In. 250.00
Decanter, Geometrics & Scalloped Hobstar Foot, Stopper, 16 In. 850.00
Decanter, Gothic Design, Handle, Stopper, 14 In. 275.00
Decanter, Hobstars, Handle, 12 In. 450.00
Decanter, Moorish Revival Design, Burgundy, White, Crystal, 11 In. 645.00
Decanter, Nailhead Diamond Pattern, 12 In. 535.00
Decanter, Regency, Stopper, C.1820, 8 In., Pair 80.00
Decanter, Stopper, Bulls-Eye, Honeycomb Cut, 13 In. 125.00
Decanter, Vintage, Chain Of Hobstars, Tuthill, 12 In. 425.00
Decanter, Wine, Teardrop Stopper, 13 In. Tall 950.00
Decanter, 3-Ring Neck, Downward Cutting, 11 In., Pair 80.00
Dessert Set, C.1935, Germany, 7 Piece 550.00
Dish, Butter, Heart Shape, Russian Pattern, 7 1/2 In. 145.00
Dish, Cheese, Russian Pattern, Dome Cover 350.00
Dish, Expanding Star, Sawtooth Edge, 8 In. 30.00
Dish, Heart Shape, Star In Oval Diamond Field, 8 In. 95.00
Dish, Hobstar Rosettes, Oval, 7 X 4 In. 70.00
Dish, Hobstars & Cane, Shamrock Shape, 7 1/2 X 7 In. 175.00
Dish, Pickle, Cut Allover, 7 X 4 In. 35.00
Dish, Russian Pattern, Mt.Washington Cranberry Buttons, 6 1/2 In. 275.00
Dish, Shell Pattern, 6 In.Diam. 825.00
Doorknob, Allover Cut In 8-Point Hobstars, Brass Fittings, Pair 225.00
Eggcup, Bellflower, With Shield, Flint 495.00
Eggnog Bowl, 2 Piece, 9 X 9 In. 425.00

Epergne, Thumb-Molded Bowl, Scalloped, Flaring Base, 16 In. 200.00
Ewer, Thumbprint, Diamond Block, Star Bottom, 12 In. 125.00
Fernery, Allover Cut, Footed, 5 X 7 In.Diam. 55.00
Fernery, Hobstars & Nailhead Diamonds, 7 1/4 X 4 In. 75.00
Goblet, Hobstars, 24-Point Star Base, Etched Stem 35.00
Goblet, Lobmeyr, Lady In Lavender Gown, 6 In. Tall 100.00
Goblet, Teardrop Stem, 16-Point Hobstar Feet, 5 3/4 In., Set Of 6 .... 600.00
Hair Receiver, Harvard & Notched Prisms, Sterling Top 150.00
Hair Receiver, Star, Diamond, & Fan, Sterling Lid, 4 1/2 In. 110.00
Hat Stand, Cut Knob On Top & Base, Metal Holder, 21 In. 125.00
Holder, String, Zipper & Prism, Silver Top 160.00
Holder, String, Zipper & Prism, Sterling Silver Top 160.00
Honey Pot, Vertical Prism, Rayed Base, 4 1/2 In. 165.00
Humidor, Cigar, Pinwheels, Vertical Notch, Hobnail, 9 In. 725.00
Humidor, Satin Intaglio & Thumbprint, Rayed Bottom, 8 In. 425.00
Humidor, Tobacco, Brilliant, Satin Intaglio, C.1910, 8 In. 425.00
Ice Bucket, Harvard, 5 1/4 X 7 In. 225.00
Ice Bucket, Sunburst Pattern, 6 1/2 X 4 1/2 In. 400.00
Inkwell, Faceted Cut Hinged Lid, Enameled Flowers, Blue, 2 1/4 In. 135.00
Inkwell, Hobstars, Strawberry, & Diamond, Sterling Silver Top 275.00
Inkwell, Miter Star Leaf Fan, Sterling Silver Lid, 13 1/2 X 5 In. 200.00
Inkwell, Multifaceted Lid, Sapphire Blue 95.00
Inkwell, Silver Plate Hinged Cover, Square, 3 1/2 In. 75.00
Inkwell, Square, Hinged Faceted Cover, 3 In. 150.00
Inkwell, Sterling Ornate Hinged Top, 4 1/2 In. 60.00
Inkwell, Vaseline Cube, Separate Lid, 3 In. 75.00
Jar, Cigar, Hobstars & Blaze, Rayed Base, Hollow Cover, 9 1/2 In. 725.00
Jar, Pill, Feathered Buzz, Rayed Base, 4 1/2 In. 125.00
Jar, Powder, Sterling Silver Cover, Girl & Boy In Swing 95.00
Jar, Tobacco, Pineapple & Hobstar, Gorham Silver Lid 495.00
Juice, American Pattern, Hobstar Base, Set Of 6 .... 375.00
Knife Rest, Cube Cut, Solid 21.00
Knife Rest, Large, Allover Cut 40.00
Knife Rest, Pinwheel & Ladder, 4 1/2 In. 38.00
Knife Rest, Stars On End On Knob, 4 In. 15.00
Lamp, Brilliant Cut, Hobstars, 2-Light, 10 In. 1800.00
Lamp, Dorflinger, Mushroom Shape, Cut Prisms, Sticker, 2 1/4 Ft. 3500.00
Lamp, Fluid, Silver Plated, 30 In. 200.00
Lamp, Intaglio Daisies, Deep Cut Leaves, Prisms, 13 In. 495.00
Lamp, Prisms, Harvard & Floral Pattern, 23 In. 650.00
Lamp, Swirl, Oil, Zipper Cut Base, Crosshatching, 36 In. 1500.00
Loving Cup, 3-Handled, Sterling Top, 6 In. 450.00
Mayonnaise Set, Chain Of Hobstars, Scalloped Rims, Star Center 250.00
Muffineer, Vesicas, Fans, & Crosshatching, Green, 6 In. 200.00
Mustard, Hobnail Pattern 55.00
Napkin Ring, Harvard Pattern 75.00
Napkin Ring, Hobstars, Diamonds, Fan, 3 In. 90.00
Nappy, Deep Cutting Allover, 6 In. 45.00
Nappy, Feathered Hobstar 65.00
Nappy, Hobstar, Handles, Sawtooth Edge, 5 In. 15.00
Nappy, Hobstars Within Allover, Scalloped, 6 In. 50.00
Paperweight, Obelisk, Intaglio Enameled Urn Of Flowers, 6 In. 85.00
Paperweight, Pineapple & Fan, Recessed Center 75.00
Perfume, Green, Dauber 38.00
Pitcher, Champagne, Daisies, Hobstar Base, 7 1/2 X 13 In. 325.00
Pitcher, Champagne, Fan, St.Louis Cut Handle, 12 In. 325.00
Pitcher, Champagne, Sterling Collar, 9 3/4 In. 195.00
Pitcher, Harvard Pattern, Notched Handle, 10 In. 195.00
Pitcher, Heart Pattern, Double Notch Handle, 10 In. .... 450.00 To 475.00
Pitcher, Hobnail & Fan, Double Notch Handle, 7 1/2 In. 80.00
Pitcher, Hobstar, Crosscut, Diamond, Fan, Signed, 9 In. 265.00
Pitcher, Hobstar, Fan, & Thatch, Rayed Base, 10 In. 220.00
Pitcher, Hobstars, Slashes, & Strawberry, Notched Handle, 10 In. 150.00
Pitcher, Lemonade, Floral & Cane Design, Notched Spout, 10 In. 110.00

Cut Glass, Punch Bowl, Sunbursts, Hobstars,
& Cane Bands, C.1900

Pitcher, Martini, Brilliant Cut, 9 In.	295.00
Pitcher, New England Middlesex Pattern, Strap Handle	265.00
Pitcher, Triple-Notched Handle, 32-Point Hobstar Base, 14 In.	475.00
Pitcher, Water, Florence Star, Set On Low Standard	650.00
Pitcher, Water, Monarch Pattern, Ball Shape, Signed Hoare	225.00
Plate, Berkshire Pattern, 9 In.	250.00
Plate, Ice Cream, Sinclair, 5 1/2 In., Set Of 12	600.00
Plate, Leaf Shape, Large & Small Hobstars & Fans, 7 X 9 In.	115.00
Plate, Primrose Comet, Tuthill, 10 In.	1000.00
Platter, Ice Cream, Harvard Pattern, 8 X 13 1/2 In.	395.00
Punch Bowl, Sunbursts, Hobstars, & Cane Bands, C.1900	*Illus* 1400.00
Punch Set, Hobstars & Fan, 10 Cups, Bowl 14 In.Diam.	875.00
Relish, Hunt's Royal Pattern, 7 1/2 In.	85.00
Rose Bowl, Hobstars, Diamond, & Fan, Hobstar Bottom	495.00
Rose Bowl, Russian Pattern, Plain Buttons, 3 In.	125.00
Salt, Crosscut, Strawberry Diamonds, Fans, 24-Point Star	16.00
Shaker, Cocktail, Cut Design, Waffle, Sterling Cover, 10 In.	195.00
Sugar & Creamer, On Pedestal, Knobbed Stem With Teardrop, 6 In.	2500.00
Sugar & Creamer, Thumbprint Handle, Pinwheels, Sawtooth Bottom	85.00
Sugar Shaker, Hobstar Base, Sterling Silver Collar, 4 7/8 In.	135.00
Sugar Shaker, Wilcox Sterling Silver Collar & Lid, 1890	95.00
Syrup, Grapes, Leaves, & Vines, Sterling Silver Overlay, 10 In.	100.00
Syrup, Hobstars, Fan, & Zipper, Sterling Silver Band, 10 In.	125.00
Syrup, Pinwheel, Strawberry Diamond Design, Sheffield Top	165.00
Tazza, Hobstars & Cane, 24-Point Base, 8 1/2 X 8 In.	595.00
Toothpick, Button Arches, Red Flashed	25.00
Toothpick, Zipper Pattern	30.00
Tray, Banana, Fan & Hobnail, Scalloped Tooth Rim, 12 X 5 1/2 In.	265.00
Tray, Calling Card, Pineapple Pattern, Sterling Silver Rim, 6 In.	145.00
Tray, Cornwall, Marked Sinclair, 10 In.	425.00
Tray, Hobstars & Diamond Points, Round, 12 In.	275.00
Tray, Ice Cream, Sawtooth Scallops, Hobstars, & Fan, 14 X 7 1/2 In	175.00
Tray, Pansy, Tuthill, Russian Border, 11 X 6 1/2 In.	2200.00
Tumbler, Hobstars, Fan	25.00
Tumbler, Pinwheel, Single Miter Cane, Signed Clark, Set Of 6	250.00
Tumbler, Strawberry Diamond With Fan, 4 In.	25.00
Tumbler, Strawberry Diamond, Pinwheels, 4 In.	25.00
Vase, Corset Shape, Hobstars, Clear Thumbprints, Maple City, 8 In.	185.00
Vase, Corset Shape, Hobstars, Engraved Butterflies, 5 1/2 X 11 In.	175.00
Vase, Corset Shape, Miter Cut, Crosshatched Waist, 12 In.	85.00

Vase, Cosmos, 10 In.	65.00
Vase, Fan Shape, Acid Cut, Clear To Green, Marked, 7 3/4 In.	169.00
Vase, Flared, Navarre, Signed, 11 1/2 X 7 3/4 In.	475.00
Vase, Fruit Pattern, Etched, Crystal, 10 In.	127.00
Vase, Genoa Pattern, Signed Clark, 6 1/2 In.	650.00
Vase, Harvard, Trumpet Shape, Hobstars & Fans, 12 X 4 3/4 In.	115.00
Vase, Hobstar & Chain, Scalloped Rim, Urn Shape, 12 In.	160.00
Vase, Hobstars & X-Cut Vesicas, 32-Star Base, Corset Shape, 12 In.	275.00
Vase, Hobstars Alternate With Quadruple X Cut, 12 In.	325.00
Vase, Hourglass Shape, Pinwheel Design, Scalloped, 9 In.	45.00
Vase, Lotus, Solid Green, Egginton, 16 In.	2000.00
Vase, Melon Shaped, Step Cut Neck, Vertical Vesicas, 13 3/4 In.	575.00
Vase, Notched Prisms, 12 In.	75.00
Vase, Portrait, Gravic Cut Rose On Back, Dated 1906, 8 1/2 In.	295.00
Vase, Queen's Pattern, Trumpet Shape, Marked, 14 In.	650.00
Vase, Rose Pattern, Crystal, Etched Rose, 14 In.	138.00
Vase, Russian Variation, Buzz, Flared Top, Rayed Bottom, 14 In.	350.00
Vase, Star & Feather, Marked, 16 In.	975.00
Vase, Sunburst Pattern, Faceted Knob, Petal Foot, 10 1/4 In.	625.00
Vase, Trumpet, Clear Green, Frosted Roses, Leaves, 10 1/2 In.	65.00
Vase, Trumpet, Hobstars, Fan, Crosshatching, 10 In.	110.00
Vase, Trumpet, Pinwheels, 12 In.	75.00
Vase, Trumpet, Strawberry Diamond Fan, 12 In.	125.00
Vase, Trumpet, Vintage Cutting, Dorflinger Blank, 12 1/2 In.	110.00
Vase, 2-Handled, Hobstars, Vesicas, Step Cut Neck, 10 1/2 In.	675.00
Wine, Diamond Fan, Blue, Ball Stem, 24-Point Star Base, Set Of 6	1200.00
Wine, Hobstars, Strawberry, Diamond, Fans, Signed, 4 In., Set Of 4	200.00
Wine, Morning Glory Pattern, Intaglio Cut	65.00
Wine, Red To Clear, Tulip Shape, Double Teardrop Stem, 8 1/2 In.	369.00
Wine, Russian, Cranberry To Clear, Hobstar Button	275.00
CZECHOSLOVAKIA, Bank, Teapot, Pottery, 3 1/2 In.	30.00
Box, Dresser, Hinged, Woman, Puppy, & Flutist, Signed, 4 In.	95.00
Canister Set, Blue Hummingbirds, Pearlized, 9 Piece	165.00
Clock, Mantel, Glazed Pottery, Blue, Green, Yellow, 10 In.	60.00
Coffeepot, Art Deco, Ceramic	35.00
Figurine, Couple Dancing Tango, Orange, Green, Cream, 13 In.	190.00
Figurine, Pair, Boy In Blue, Girl With Bonnet, Sitting, 6 In.	30.00
Jug, Baroque, Green, Enamel Design, 9 1/4 In.	100.00
Lamp, Hand-Painted Porcelain, Green Crystal, 11 In.	320.00
Salt, Hand-Painted Flowers, Porcelain, Marked	10.00
Toothpick, Playing Card Design	35.00
Vase, Green Glass, Blue Serpent Wrap	65.00

D'Argental is a mark used by the St. Louis, France, glassworks. The firm made multilayered, acid-cut cameo glass in the late nineteenth and twentieth centuries. D'Argental is the French name for the city of Munzthal, home of the glassworks. Later they made enameled etched glass. Compagnie des Cristalleries de St. Louis is still working.

D'ARGENTAL, Atomizer, Perfume, Bleeding Heart Pattern, Coin Spot	48.00
Vase, Bay & Mountains, Gold Ground, Signed, 9 3/4 In.	995.00
Vase, Bird & What Scene, Frosted Gold Ground, Signed, 4 X 17 In.	995.00
Vase, Boat Scene, Purple To White Ground, Signed, 5 3/4 In.	650.00
Vase, Castle Scene, Frosted Gold Ground, Signed, 12 1/8 In.	995.00
Vase, Deer Drinking In Forst, Yellow To Pink, Signed, 8 3/4 In.	995.00
Vase, Gondola Venice Scene, 3 Acid Cuttings, Signed, 5 3/4 In.	695.00
Vase, Landscape Along Bay, Frosted Blue Ground, Signed, 9 1/2 In.	995.00
Vase, Landscape Scene, Chateau, Gold Ground, Chateau, 12 1/4 In.	995.00
Vase, Landscape Scene, 3 Acid Cuttings, Signed, 4 X 11 5/8 In.	1100.00
Vase, Maroon To Rose Landscape, Gold Frosted, Signed, 3 1/2 In.	550.00
Vase, Pine Trees & Mountain Lake, Gold Ground, Signed, 9 3/4 In.	995.00
Vase, Scenic, Gold & Magenta Ground, Signed, 8 X 3 1/2 In.	695.00

Vase, Scenic, House In Forest, White Ground, Signed, 6 7/8 In. 650.00
Vase, Trees On Bay, Low Mountains, Frosted Blue, Signed, 9 1/2 In. 995.00
Vase, Trees, Moon, & Clouds, Brown Shades, Signed, 11 3/4 In. 1150.00

D'AURYS

D'Aurys is a mark found on French cameo glasswares of the nineteenth century.

D'AURYS, Vase, Tree Landscape, Green, Red, 8 In. 450.00
DAGUERREOTYPE, see Photography, Daguerreotype
DANISH CHRISTMAS PLATE, see Bing & Grondahl; Royal Copenhagen

Jean Daum started a glassworks in Nancy, France, in 1875. The company, now called Christalleries de Nancy, is still working. The "Daum Nancy" mark has been used in many variations.

DAUM NANCY, Bottle, Cologne, Winter Scene, Mottled Stopper, Signed, 5 1/4 In. 1100.00
Bottle, Florals, Sterling Silver Top & Cup, Signed, 5 7/8 In. 450.00
Bowl, Mottled Streaks, Pinched, Chartreuse, Signed, 5 X 2 1/2 In. 150.00
Bowl, Winter Scene, Black Trees, Gold Ground, Signed, 6 In. 698.00
Bowl, Winter Scene, Mottled Gold Ground, Signed, 4 1/2 In. 975.00
Bowl, Winter Scene, Signed, 5 3/4 X 2 1/2 In. 825.00
Bowl, Yellow, Leaves & Blueberries, 3 X 5 1/2 In. 485.00
Bowl, 4-Leaf Clover Shaped, Red Bleeding Hearts, Marked, 6 In. 325.00
Box, Berries & Leaves, Lemon Mottled Ground, 6 1/2 X 4 1/2 In. 1250.00
Box, Berries, Leaves, Lemon Mottled Ground, Lid, Signed, 4 1/2 In. 1250.00
Box, Berries, Lemon Mottled Ground, Signed, 3 1/2 X 4 1/2 In. 750.00
Box, Red Flowers, Leaves, Gold Design, Signed, 3 X 3 In. 495.00
Lamp, Table, Peaches & Leaves, Tangerine, Orange, & Green, 14 In. 4250.00
Rose Bowl, Winter Scene, Gold Frosted Ground, Signed, 5 X 6 In. 1250.00
Rose Bowl, Winter Scene, Mottled Gold Ground, Signed, 5 1/2 In. 1100.00
Salt, Tub Shape, Lavender, Pink Flowers 395.00
Salt, Tub Shape, Sailboats 425.00
Toothpick, Oval, Fuchsia, Signed 400.00
Tumbler, Allover Floral, Cameo Cased, Yellow Roses, Marked, 5 In. 500.00
Tumbler, Barrel Shaped, Cameo, Floral, Signed, 2 1/4 In. 250.00
Tumbler, Floral Cameo Design, Marked, 5 In. 500.00
Tumbler, Mistletoe, Frosted, 5 In. 55.00
Tumbler, Scenic, Trees & Forest Glade, Signed 540.00
Vase, Autumn Scenic, Enameled, Blue Ground, Signed, 9 1/8 In. 1500.00
Vase, Blown-Out Bubble Glass, Majorelle Frame, 11 In. 250.00
Vase, Boats & Sunset, Flattened Oval, Gold, Signed, 4 3/4 In. 695.00
Vase, Boats, Mottled Gold Ground, Enameled, Oval, Signed, 4 In. 695.00
Vase, Carved, Enameled Thistle Design, 5 In. 325.00
Vase, Cornflowers, Mottled Pink Ground, Signed, 7 In. 1250.00
Vase, Dark Green To Orange, Trees, Lake, Marked, 8 1/2 In. 950.00
Vase, Deep Green To Clear, Gold Floral Design, Marked, 4 In. 295.00
Vase, Enameled Flowers & Leaves, Iridescent, Signed, 10 1/2 In. 325.00
Vase, Enameled Violets & Leaves, Mottled White & Orange, 3 In. 695.00
Vase, Flowers & Leaves, Apricot, Gold Trim, 7 In. 1200.00
Vase, Green Ground, Purple Leaves, Marked, 6 In. 265.00
Vase, Green Leaves & Peaches, Coral Ground, Signed, 19 In. 1695.00
Vase, Green Summer Scene, Flattened Oval, Signed, 4 3/4 In. 795.00
Vase, Green To Orange, Trees Reflected In Lake, 8 In. 950.00
Vase, Lavender, Pink, Brown, Marked, 22 In. 195.00
Vase, Mottled Lavender, Pink, & Brown, Signed, 22 In. 195.00
Vase, Orange, White, & Gold, Majorelle Frame, Signed, 13 In. 395.00
Vase, Poppy Design, Silver Mounting, Signed, 5 X 3 1/4 In. 1000.00
Vase, Raine Scene, Diamond Shape, Green & Pink, Signed, 7 3/8 In. 1000.00
Vase, Scenic, Fox & Raven, Textured Glass, Green, Signed, 8 In. 995.00
Vase, Scenic, Pedestal, Gold Frosted Ground, Signed, 13 3/4 In. 995.00

Vase, Stick, Bulbous Base, Violets, Frosted Ground, Signed, 5 In. 595.00
Vase, Summer Scene, Blue Sky, Blue Ground, Signed, 11 7/8 In. 1250.00
Vase, Summer Scene, Blue Sky, Frosted, Marked, 5 In. 975.00
Vase, Summer Scene, Chartreuse Ground, Signed, 6 1/2 In. 795.00
Vase, Summer Scene, Enameled, Flattened Oval, Signed, 8 1/2 In. 850.00
Vase, Summer Scene, Forest, Chartreuse Ground, Marked, 4 In. 850.00
Vase, Summer Scene, Green Mottled Ground, Signed, 6 1/2 In. 795.00
Vase, Swans Scene, Mottled Blue Ground, Signed, 4 1/2 In. 2200.00
Vase, Trees & River, Mottled Gold Ground, Signed, 13 3/4 In. 995.00
Vase, Trees, River & Mountains, Gold Ground, Signed, 9 1/4 In. 1595.00
Vase, Urn Shaped, Deep Red, Black Spattering, 8 In. 150.00
Vase, Violets & Green Leaves, Frosted Ground, Signed, 5 In. 595.00
Vase, Winter Scene, Flattened Cylinder, Gold, Signed, 6 1/2 In. 875.00
Vase, Winter Scene, Flattened Cylinder, Signed, 6 1/2 In. 850.00
Vase, Winter Scene, Gold Frosted, Enameled, Signed, 9 5/8 In. 1895.00
Vase, Winter Scene, Gold Ground, Barren Forest, Marked, 5 In. 895.00
Vase, Winter Scene, Gold Mottled Ground, Signed, 14 1/8 In. 1650.00
Vase, Winter Scene, Mottled Gold Ground, Signed, 13 7/8 In. 1100.00
Vase, Winter Scene, Snow, Trees, Orange Sky, Marked, 6 In. 925.00

*Davenport pottery and porcelain were made at the Davenport factory in
Longport, Staffordshire, England, from 1793 to 1887. Earthenwares,
creamwares, porcelains, ironstone wares, and other products were made.
Most of the pieces are marked with a form of the word "Davenport."*

DAVENPORT, Cup & Saucer, Floral Design, Pink Luster, Marked 250.00
Gravy Boat, Underplate, Blue, White, Impressed Anchor, C.1844 .... 95.00
Mustard, Turquoise & Gold, Silver Plated Cover, Marked, 3 1/4 In. 58.00
Tureen, Sauce, Fruit Finial, Paw Feet, 1805-20, 4 1/2 X 7 In., Pair 200.00
Tureen, Underplate, Blue, White, Gothic, C.1844, 5 3/4 In. 75.00
Vase, Butterflies, Thistles, Lion Heads At Sides, Marked, 6 1/2 In. 275.00

DAVY CROCKETT, Badge, Indian Scout 5.00
Bowl, Bear In Bottom, Milk Glass 15.00
Bowl, Bear In Center, Milk Glass 12.00
Button, Crossed Muskets, Coonskin Hat & Dead Bear, C.1950 .... 12.50
Doll 30.00
Hat 5.00
Mug .... 5.00 To 20.00

*De Vez is a name found on special pieces of French cameo glass made by
the Cristallerie de Pantin about 1890. Monsieur de Varreux was the art
director of the glassworks and he signed pieces "de Vez."*

DE VEZ, Bowl, Gondola Venice Scene, Frosted Gold Ground, Signed, 12 7/8 In. 1995.00
Bowl, Mountain & Lake Scene, Diamond Shape, Gold, Signed, 3 1/2 In. 695.00
Trees With Fruit, Mountains, House, Green To Pink, Signed, 6 In. 795.00
Vase, Amethyst On Alabaster, Signed, 5 X 5 1/2 In. 765.00
Vase, Bird Scene, Frosted Gold Ground, Signed, 5 1/2 X 7 7/8 In. 875.00
Vase, Boat Scene, Branches Frame Top, Green, Signed, 10 In. 895.00
Vase, Boat Scene, Vines Frame Top, Signed, 4 1/4 In. 495.00
Vase, Boat Scene, Yellow To Frosted Pink Ground, Signed, 9 7/8 In. 695.00
Vase, Boats, Mountains, Blue Frosted Ground, Signed, 9 1/4 In. 795.00
Vase, Cut Mountains, Water, & Tree Landscape, Pink, Signed, 6 1/8 In. 575.00
Vase, Fishermen & Boats Scenic, Signed, 4 X 7 1/2 In. 1895.00
Vase, Fishing Scene, Branch Framed, Gold Ground, Signed, 4 1/4 In. 695.00
Vase, Gondola, Venice Ground, Signed, 6 1/8 In. 795.00
Vase, Green To Rose Sailboats, Signed, 10 In. 995.00
Vase, House On Island, Branches Frame Scene, Signed, 5 1/4 In. 525.00
Vase, Intaglio Cut Girl & Nubian Maid, Pink, Signed, 20 In., Pair 9000.00
Vase, Man In Rowboat, Leaves & Berries Border, Signed, 10 1/2 In. 1350.00
Vase, Mosque & Palm Trees, Gold Frosted Ground, Signed, 11 3/4 In. 1100.00
Vase, Mountains, Trees, &birds In Sky, Yellow, Signed, 6 3/4 In. 695.00
Vase, Orange Trees With Fruit, Mountains, Blue, Signed, 6 In. 795.00

Vase, Roman Temple Scene, Pearly Translucent Ground, Signed, 9 In. 1050.00
Vase, Sailboat Scene, Pink Translucent Ground, Signed, 17 3/4 In. 2100.00
Vase, Sailboats In Mountain Cove, Blue To Yellow, Signed, 9 7/8 In. 695.00
Vase, Scenic Lake & Village, Roses On Rim, Signed, 16 1/2 In. 2250.00
Vase, Swans Scene, Gold Ground, Flowers & Vines, Signed, 9 5/8 In. 850.00
Vase, Trees, Water, & Mountains, Gold Ground, Signed, 3 X 6 1/2 In. 695.00
Vase, Venice Scene Through Pillars, Gold Ground, Signed, 11 3/4 In. 1350.00
Vase, Waterfall Scene, Rocks, Yellow Ground, Signed, 17 1/8 In. 2250.00

*Decoys are carved or turned wooden copies of birds. The decoy was
placed in the water to lure flying birds to the pond for hunters.*

DECOY, Back Bay Canvasback, Mason, Pair 400.00
Black Duck, Ben Schmidt, 1950 .... 695.00
Black Duck, Charles Hart 4000.00
Black Duck, Frank Schmidt 125.00
Black Duck, Glass Eyes, 14 In. 30.00
Black Duck, Mason 135.00
Black Duck, Mason Premier, Original Paint 325.00
Black Duck, Snake Head, Glass Eyes, Old Paint, 15 In. 70.00
Bluebill Drake, Alert Head, 13 In. 30.00
Bluebill Hen, Ward Bros., 1936 .... 2350.00
Bluebill, Ken Anger, 1940, Pair 1395.00
Bluebill, Mason Challenge, Pair 4500.00
Bluebill, Turned Head, Glass Eyes 110.00
Bluebill, Ward Bros., 1972, Pair 3100.00
Bluewing Teal, Texas 125.00
Butterball Drake, Glass Eyes, Original Paint, 11 1/4 In. 55.00
Canada Goose, Balsa & Pine, 18 1/2 In. 45.00
Canada Goose, East Coast, C.1900, Tack Eyes, Original Paint 550.00
Canada Goose, George Boyd, Canvas 4250.00
Canada Goose, Glass Eyes, Original Paint, 13 In. 80.00
Canada Goose, Glass Eyes, 16 1/2 In. 145.00
Canada Goose, Madison Mitchell, Original Paint 275.00
Canada Goose, T.J.Hooker, Hollow, Glass Eyes, Painted 200.00
Canvasback Drake, Gus Moak, Balsa Body 150.00
Canvasback Drake, Saginaw Bay, 16 In. 30.00
Canvasback Drake, Wisconsin, Oversize 65.00
Canvasback Duck, Madison Mitchell, 1950, Pair 300.00
Canvasback Duck, Stevens, N.Y., Original Paint 295.00
Canvasback Hen, Mason, Original Paint 140.00
Coot, Branded L.J.R., Glass Eyes, 11 In. 100.00
Curlew, Elmer Crowell 8000.00
Decoy, Yellowlegs, Preening, Elmer Crowell 3500.00
Duck, Black, Glass Eyes, 14 In. 30.00
Duck, Black, Snake Head, Glass Eyes, Old Paint, 15 In. 70.00
Duck, C.W.Stevens, Woodsport 310.00
Duck, Carved, Hollow, Pair 395.00
Duck, Dappled Head, Orange Bill, Green & White Feathers 120.00
Duck, Glass Eyes, Painted Black Body, White Feathering, 14 1/2 X 5 In. 65.00
Duck, Pascagoula, Miss. 50.00
Duck, Pudgy, Glass Eyes, White Wings, C.1880, 7 1/2 In. 65.00
Duck, Stick-Up, Tin 30.00
Duck, Turned Head, Glass Eyes, Painted Wings & Tail, 11 In.Long 65.00
Duck, Wooden Head, Cork Body 25.00
Goldeneye Duck, Barrows, Wooden 375.00
Goldeneye, Mason Challenge, Pair 2500.00
Goose, Black Head, Neck Feathers, Hand-Scorped, C.1890, Pine, 17 1/4 In. 125.00
Goose, Brant, Pine, Black Head, White Neck, C.1890, 17 In. 125.00
Goose, Brant, 2 Piece, Black Head, Gray Body, C.1890, 17 In. 125.00
Goose, Chunky Body, Black & White, Cedar, 11 In. 130.00
Goose, Extended Head & Neck, White Tail, C.1890, 26 1/2 In.Long 165.00
Goose, Fat Bodied, Primitive Carved, 20-Piece Head, Cedar, 22 X 10 In. 135.00
Goose, Gray & White Paint, Teal Underside, Wooden, 22 1/2 In.Long 125.00

Goose, Gray & White, 22 1/2 In.	125.00
Goose, Head In Retracted Neck, Black & White, Cedar, 20 1/2 In.Long	125.00
Goose, New Hampshire, Canvas Covered	400.00
Goose, Pratt, Original Paint, Wooden	150.00
Goose, Retracted Neck, Fat Body, Black & White, Cedar, 20 In.	125.00
Goose, Stick-Up, Flat, Black & White, C.1890, 23 In.	135.00
Goose, Stick-Up, Wooden Ground Stake, C.1890, Tin, 23 X 30 In.	175.00
Green-Winged Teal Drake, Glass Eyes, 1890, Original Paint, 11 In.	110.00
Lesser Yellowlegs, Elmer Crowell	3600.00
Loon, Original Black & White Paint	125.00
Mallard Drake, C.1910, 15 1/2 In.	60.00
Mallard Drake, Evans, Original Paint	150.00
Mallard Drake, Hollow, Illinois Riber, C.1890, Glass Eyes	175.00
Mallard Drake, Hollow, Turned Head, Glass Eyes, 16 In.	40.00
Mallard Drake, Mason	150.00
Mallard Hen, Armstrong, Canvas	55.00
Mallard Hen, Glass Eyes, 16 1/2 In.	40.00
Mallard Hen, Hollow, Illinois River, C.1910, 17 In.	75.00
Mallard, Cork	15.00
Mallard, Green Head, White Body, Glass Eyes, 15 In.	40.00
Mallard, Victor	40.00
Mallard, Victor Veri-Lite	30.00
Merganser Drake, Mason Premier	2500.00
Merganser, Cedar, Hollow, C.1899, 16 1/4 In.	250.00
Merganser, Mason Challenge, Pair	5000.00
Merganser, Willie Ross, Pair	5000.00
Owl, Papier-Mache	30.50
Pigeon, Hollow, Glass Eyes, New Jersey, 14 In.	175.00 To 200.00
Pigeon, Papier-Mache	15.00
Pintail Drake, Shang Sheeler	4500.00
Pintail Duck, Feathered Body, Wooden, Painted Black, 15 In.Long	25.00
Pintail Hen, Ward Bros., 1932	9700.00
Plover, Geroge Boyd	3000.00
Red-Breasted Merganser, Elmer Crowell	3750.00
Redhead Drake, Charles Medera	295.00
Redhead Drake, Herters, Balsa & Pine, Glass Eyes, 15 3/4 In.	30.00
Redhead Drake, William Cramner, 1950	295.00
Redhead, Mason Challenge, Pair	3500.00
Redhead, Robert Sellers, 1945, Pair	575.00
Ruddy Duck, Glass Eyes, Mustard Beak & Feathers, 12 1/2 X 6 3/4 In.	65.00
Shorebird, Folding, Tin, 12 In.	45.00
Shorebird, Yellow Legs, Feeding Position, 12 1/2 In.	250.00
Shorebird, 9 In.Long	100.00
Snow Goose, White, Black, Gray, Orange Bill, 9 In.	275.00
Swan, Herter	650.00
Swan, Maryland, C.1900	950.00
Whistler Drake, Frank Dewis, Humpback	85.00
Widgeon Drake, Shand Wheeler	6750.00
Yellowlegs, Carved & Painted, 32 1/2 In.	175.00

Chelsea Keramic Art Works was established in 1872 in Chelsea, Massachusetts, by members of the Robertson family. The factory closed in 1889, and was reorganized as the Cheisea Pottery U.S. in 1891. It became the Dedham Pottery of Dedham, Massachusetts, in 1895. The factory closed in 1943. It was famous for its crackleware dishes, which picture blue outlines of animals, flowers, and other natural motifs.

DEDHAM, Bowl, Rabbits, 5 3/4 In.	90.00
Plate, Elephants, 7 1/4 In.	200.00
Plate, Horsechestnut, 7 1/2 In.	95.00 To 125.00
Plate, Mushroom, 8 1/2 In.	125.00
Plate, Polar Bears, 8 1/2 In.	165.00
Plate, Poppy, 8 1/2 In.	125.00 To 195.00
Plate, Rabbit, Marked, 8 1/2 In.	60.00

Plate, Snowtree, 10 In. 200.00
Plate, Water Lilies, 7 1/2 In. 125.00

> *Degue is a signature found acid etched on pieces of French glass made in*
> *the early 1900s. Cameo, moldblown, and smooth glass with contrasting*
> *colored rims are the types most often found.*

DEGUE, Bowl, Rose, Green Crackle Glass, Marked, 4 1/2 In. 75.00
Vase, Boat & House Scene, Royal Blue To Rose, Signed, 3 X 5 1/2 In. 525.00
Vase, Scenic, Peach & Orange Ground, Signed, 5 1/2 In. 525.00

FDEjAℑTE
NAℑCℑ
> *Delatte glass is a French cameo glass made by Andre Delatte. It was*
> *first made in Nancy, France, in 1921. Lighting fixtures and opaque*
> *glassware in imitation of Bohemian opaline were made.*

DELATTE, Vase, Bird On Branch Scenic, Handled, Signed, Green Ground, 6 1/2 In. 850.00
Vase, Magenta Florals & Leaves, Mottled Ground, Signed, 4 1/4 In. 425.00
Vase, Magenta Florals, Mottled Ground, Signed, 4 1/4 In. 398.00
Vase, Maroon Cut To Rose Landscape, Pedestal, Signed, 9 1/2 In. 995.00
Vase, Maroon Cut To Rose Landscape, White Ground, Signed, 9 1/2 In. 995.00
Vase, Mauve Trees & River, Salmon Ground, Signed, 7 1/2 In. 675.00
    DELAWARE, see Custard Glass; Pressed Glass
    DELDARE, see Buffalo Pottery Deldare

> *Delft is a tin-glazed pottery that has been made since the seventeenth*
> *century. It is decorated with blue on white or with colored decorations.*
> *Most of the pieces sold today were made after 1891, and the name "Holland"*
> *appears with the Delft factory marks.*

DELFT, Ashtray, Bowl, Self-Closing Lid, Holland, 4 X 4 In. 12.00
Ashtray, K.L.M.Airlines 24.00
Ashtray, Plunger Action Chrome Top, 4 X 4 In. 15.00
Bowl, Blue Stylized Floral Design, Holland, 4 X 8 In. 175.00
Bowl, Blue, Chinoiserie Design, Footed Base, 13 In. 1400.00
Bowl, Windmills, Farm Scene, German, 10 X 3 In. 90.00
Brick, Flower, Blue & White, Leafy Scroll Design, 2 1/2 X 5 In. 100.00
Brick, Flower, C.1800, Blue, Landscape Scene, 2 1/2 X 4 3/4 In. 275.00
Charger, Blue, Oriental Bridge, Flowers, Trees, 13 In. 310.00
Charger, Floral Design, Floral Border, Polychrome, Holland 400.00
Charger, Lambeth, C.1750, Red, Yellow, Green, Parrot On Branch, 13 In. 325.00
Charger, Manganese & Yellow, Noah's Ark, Tulip Border, 13 In. 675.00
Coffee Grinder, Wall 125.00
Creamer, Cow, 4 In. 12.00
Creamer, Lighthouse, Blue 18.00
Creamer, Sailboat, Blue 18.00
Cup, Posset, Bulbous Form, Double Handle, Holland, 18th Century, 5 In. 475.00
Decanter, Liqueur, Windmill Scene, Stopper, 7 1/2 In. 10.00
Dish, C.1740, Blue Axe Mark, 14 In. 725.00
Figurine, Cow & Nursing Calf, Oval Stand, Blue, 5 1/2 X 4 In. 65.00
Holder, Hatpin, Wall Hanging, Holds 6, Blue & White, 3 X 4 In. 75.00
Holder, Pipe, Blue & White, Seated Woman Form, Wearing Bonnet, 5 In. 110.00
Jar, Apothecary, Urn Shaped, Blue Peacock, Holland, Marked, C.1800, 9 In. 3500.00
Jar, Ginger, Ovoid, Foo Dog Finial, 12 In. 225.00
Jug, Milk, Stylized Floral Design, Yellow-Green, Ocher, Blue 175.00
Jug, Puzzle, Floral Design, Putti, Pedestal, Holland, 9 In. 350.00
Muffineer, Blue & White, Domed Top, 8-Sided, 6 3/4 In. 30.00
Mug, Blue & White, Windmill Scene, Floral, 4 3/4 In. 15.00
Mug, Windmill Scene, Floral, Blue & White, 4 3/4 In. 15.00
Mug, Windmill, Scene, Holland 4.00
Pitcher, Crossed Sword Mark, 3 3/4 In. 35.00
Planter, Blue & White, Allover Floral, 12 In., Pair 600.00
Plaque, Blue, Signed, Bach Holland, 15 1/2 In. 175.00
Plaque, Men Sitting Around Barrel, Smoking, Oak Frame, 11 1/2 X 8 In. 125.00

Plaque, Picture Of Rembrandt, Wood Frame, 10 X 8 In. 115.00
Plaque, Portrait, Woman, Flow Blue, Artist Name, 16 1/2 In. 425.00
Plaque, Wall, Blue Windmill, Harbor Scene, 9 In 50.00
Plaque, Windmills, Cottage, Figures In Boat, Blue & White, 14 In. 75.00
Plate, Blue & White, Leaf & Berry Design, Set Of 10, 9 In. 300.00
Plate, Blue & White, Rocky Island, Pagodas, C.1760, 10 In. 100.00
Plate, Blue & White, 5 1/4 In. 125.00
Plate, Chinoiserie Center, Diapering & Vine Border, English 155.00
Plate, Floral Border, Oriental Landscape, Blue, Gray, C.1760, 9 In. 85.00
Plate, Lady In Landscape, Mountains, Ireland, 8 7/8 In. 500.00
Plate, Ships & Windmills, Blue & White, Royal Sphinx, 10 In. 18.00
Plate, Windmill Scene, 10 In. 60.00
Plate, Winter Dutch Canal Scene, Pierced, 15 In. 75.00
Platter, Architectural Landscape, Floral Rim, 16 In. 250.00
Punch Bowl, Painted Floral Design, Paste, Early 19th Century, Signed 500.00
Salt & Pepper, Dutch Man & Lady, Marked 25.00
Tea Caddy, Twin, Ship & Windmill Scene, Floral Tray, 8 1/2 X 4 1/4 In. 40.00
Tile, Blue & White, Women, Animals, Framed, 11 X 10 In. 300.00
Toby, Lady, Polychrome, Marked 615.00
Tray, Pin, Pierced Border, Marked, 4 In. 20.00
Tray, Tea, Blue & White, Ship & Windmill, Floral, 8 X 4 In. 40.00
Tulipiere, Blue & White Tin Glaze, C.1765, 31 In. 1450.00
Urn, Blue Floral, Covered, C.1900, 10 1/2 In. 125.00
Veilleuse, Blue & White, Fruit, Foliate, Marked, C.1770, 9 In. 385.00
Wall Pocket, Birds, Yellow, Blue, & Green, Signed 55.00

DENTAL, Cabinet, Glass Topped, Oak 895.00
Cabinet, Mirror Back, O-Section Top, Marble Base, 63 In. 1200.00
Cabinet, Roll Top, Oak 1500.00
Chair, Cabinet, & Tools, 1923 .... 3000.00
Chair, Columbia, C.1905 .... 1500.00
Sterilizer, American Sundries Co., Papers & Box, Stoneware 48.00
Sterilizer, 8 1/2 In.Diam., 5 In.High 35.00
Toothpick, Rectractable, 14K Gold, 2 1/4 In. 113.00
    DENTIST, see Medical

> *Depression glass was an inexpensive glass manufactured in large quantities*
> *during the 1920s and early 1930s. It was made in many colors and patterns by*
> *dozens of factories in the United States. The name "Depression glass"*
> *is a modern one. For more descriptions, history, pictures, and prices of*
> *Depression glass, see the book "The Kovels' Illustrated Price*
> *Guide to Depression Glass and American Dinnerware."*

DEPRESSION GLASS, Adam, Ashtray, Pink 17.00
Adam, Bowl, Green, 4 1/2 In. 10.00
Adam, Bowl, Pink, Covered, 9 In. .... 25.00 To 39.00
Adam, Bowl, Pink, Oval, 9 1/2 In. 15.00
Adam, Bowl, Pink, 4 1/2 In. 9.00
Adam, Butter, Pink, Covered .... 65.00 To 75.00
Adam, Cake Plate, Green 14.00
Adam, Cake Plate, Pink .... 11.00 To 18.00
Adam, Candleholder, Green, Pair 57.50
Adam, Candleholder, Pink, Pair .... 32.00 To 52.00
Adam, Coaster, Green, 3 1/2 In. 12.00
Adam, Creamer, Green 10.00
Adam, Creamer, Pink 10.00
Adam, Cup, Pink 12.00
Adam, Dish, Candy, Pink, Covered .... 45.00 To 50.00
Adam, Pitcher, Pink, 8 In. 25.00
Adam, Plate, Green, 6 In. 3.75
Adam, Plate, Grill, Green .... 8.00 To 10.00
Adam, Plate, Pink, Square, 7 3/4 In. 9.00
Adam, Plate, Pink, Square, 9 In. 14.00
Adam, Plate, Pink, 6 In. 4.25

Adam, Plate, Pink, 7 3/4 In. 7.00
Adam, Relish, Pink, 2-Part 12.00
Adam, Salt & Pepper, Green 67.50
Adam, Salt & Pepper, Pink .... 35.00 To 40.00
Adam, Saltshaker, Pink 19.00
Adam, Sherbet, Green 15.00
Adam, Sherbet, Pink .... 12.00 To 36.00
Adam, Sugar & Creamer, Pink, Covered .... 22.00 To 25.00
Adam, Sugar, Pink 9.50
Adam, Sugar, Pink, Covered .... 21.00 To 23.00
Adam, Tumbler, Pink, 4 1/2 In. 16.00
Adam, Tumbler, Pink, 5 1/2 In. 25.00
Adam, Vase, Pink 150.00

AMERICAN BEAUTY, see English Hobnail

American Pioneer, Cup, Crystal 5.00
American Pioneer, Ice Bucket, Crystal 30.00
American Sweetheart, Bowl, Cereal, Monax, 6 In. 8.00
American Sweetheart, Bowl, Console, Cobalt Blue, 18 In. 850.00
American Sweetheart, Bowl, Console, Red, 18 In. 650.00
American Sweetheart, Bowl, Oval, Pink 20.00
American Sweetheart, Creamer, Monax 7.00
American Sweetheart, Creamer, Monax, Footed, Gold Rim 12.50
American Sweetheart, Cup & Saucer, Monax 10.00
American Sweetheart, Cup & Saucer, Pink .... 10.00 To 13.50
American Sweetheart, Cup, Monax 12.00
American Sweetheart, Dish, Soup, Pink 20.00
American Sweetheart, Pitcher, Pink, 80 Ounce 325.00
American Sweetheart, Plate, Blue, 15 1/2 In. 350.00
American Sweetheart, Plate, Pink, 6 In. .... 2.00 To 2.50
American Sweetheart, Plate, Pink, 8 In. 5.50
American Sweetheart, Plate, Red, 7 In. 65.00
American Sweetheart, Plate, Server, Monax, 15 1/2 In. 135.00
American Sweetheart, Plate, Server, Pink, 12 In. 10.00
American Sweetheart, Plate, Server, Red, 12 In. 125.00
American Sweetheart, Platter, Monax, 13 In. 30.00
American Sweetheart, Platter, Pink, 13 In. 15.00
American Sweetheart, Salt & Pepper, Pink 225.00
American Sweetheart, Saltshaker, Pink 125.00
American Sweetheart, Sherbet, Pink 8.00
American Sweetheart, Soup, Cream, Monax 45.00
American Sweetheart, Soup, Cream, Pink 20.00
American Sweetheart, Sugar & Creamer, Monax 10.00
American Sweetheart, Sugar & Creamer, Pink 15.00
American Sweetheart, Sugar & Creamer, Red 145.00
American Sweetheart, Sugar, Monax 6.50
Anniversary, Bowl, Crystal, 5 In. 3.00
Anniversary, Bowl, Pink, 9 In. 7.50
Anniversary, Butter, Pink, Covered 35.00
Anniversary, Creamer, Pink 5.00
Anniversary, Cup, Crystal 1.25

APPLE BLOSSOM, see Dogwood

Aunt Polly, Butter, Blue, Covered 150.00
Aunt Polly, Dish, Candy, Green 13.00
Aunt Polly, Tumbler, Blue, 8 Ounce 14.00

AURORA, see Petalware

Avocado, Sugar & Creamer, Green 55.00
Avocado, Sugar, Green 16.50

BALLERINA, see Cameo
BANDED CHERRY, see Cherry Blossom
BANDED FINE RIB, see Coronation
BANDED PETALWARE, see Petalware
BANDED RAINBOW, see Ring
BANDED RINGS, see Ring
BASKET, see No. 615

Adam

American Sweetheart

American Sweetheart

Beaded Block, Plate, Blue, Square, 7 3/4 In.	6.00
Beaded Block, Plate, Green, Square, 7 3/4 In.	4.00
Beaded Block, Plate, Pink, Square, 7 3/4 In.	4.00
Beaded Block, Sugar & Creamer, Pink	18.00
BELMONT, see Rose Cameo	
BLOCK, see Block Optic	
Block Optic, Bottle, Water, Green	5.00 To 8.00
Block Optic, Bowl, Green, 5 1/4 In.	5.00
Block Optic, Butter, Green, Covered, 1 Pound	27.50
Block Optic, Cup & Saucer, Pink	6.50
Block Optic, Cup, Green	4.00 To 6.00
Block Optic, Dish, Candy, Green, Covered	24.00
Block Optic, Plate, Green, 6 In.	2.00 To 4.00
Block Optic, Plate, Pink, 8 In.	2.50
Block Optic, Plate, Yellow, 6 In.	2.00
Block Optic, Plate, Yellow, 8 In.	3.50
Block Optic, Salt & Pepper, Green	20.00
Block Optic, Saucer, Green, 6 1/4 In.	3.00
Block Optic, Saucer, Yellow, 6 1/4 In.	5.00
Block Optic, Sherbet, Green, Cone Shaped	4.00
Block Optic, Sherbet, Pink	3.50 To 4.00
Block Optic, Sugar & Creamer, Green	14.00 To 15.00
Block Optic, Sugar & Creamer, Pink	12.00 To 20.00
Block Optic, Sugar & Creamer, Yellow	16.00
Block Optic, Sugar, Green	7.50
Block Optic, Tumbler, Green, 5 1/2 In.	8.00
Boopie, Goblet, Water, Green	4.50
Boopie, Sherbet, Green, Footed	4.50
BOUQUET & LATTICE, see Normandie	
Bowknot, Cup, Green	7.00
Bowknot, Plate, Green, 7 In.	6.00
Bowknot, Tumbler, Crystal, Footed	9.00

BRIDAL BOUQUET, see No. 615

Bubble, Bowl, Crystal, 4 In.	2.00
Bubble, Cup & Saucer, Blue	3.50
Bubble, Cup, Blue	2.50
Bubble, Plate, Blue, 6 In.	1.50 To 3.00
Bubble, Plate, Blue, 9 1/2 In.	4.00
Bubble, Plate, Crystal, 6 3/4 In.	2.50
Bubble, Plate, Grill, Blue	8.50
Bubble, Saucer, Blue	1.00 To 1.50
Bubble, Sugar & Creamer, Blue	26.00
Bubble, Sugar, Green	4.50

BULLSEYE, see Bubble
BUTTONS & BOWS, see Holiday
CABBAGE ROSE, see Sharon

Cameo, Bowl, Green, Footed, 12 In.	20.00
Cameo, Bowl, Green, 8 1/4 In.	16.00
Cameo, Bowl, Yellow, 5 1/2 In.	20.00
Cameo, Butter, Green, Covered	135.00
Cameo, Cake Plate, Green	10.00 To 13.50
Cameo, Candleholder, Green, Pair	65.00 To 75.00
Cameo, Cookie Jar, Green	25.00
Cameo, Creamer, Yellow	10.00 To 12.50
Cameo, Cup & Saucer, Green	10.00 To 12.50
Cameo, Cup & Saucer, Yellow	9.00
Cameo, Decanter, Green	40.00
Cameo, Dish, Candy, Green	75.00
Cameo, Dish, Candy, Yellow	55.00
Cameo, Dish, Soup, Green	22.50 To 28.00
Cameo, Goblet, Water, Green	30.00
Cameo, Mayonnaise Set, Green	17.00
Cameo, Pitcher, Green, 6 In.	38.00
Cameo, Plate, Green, 5 1/2 In.	4.00
Cameo, Plate, Green, 6 In.	2.50 To 3.50
Cameo, Plate, Green, 10 In.	10.00 To 12.00
Cameo, Plate, Grill, Green	5.00 To 10.00
Cameo, Plate, Grill, Yellow	4.00 To 10.00
Cameo, Plate, Yellow, 6 In.	1.25 To 2.00
Cameo, Plate, Yellow, 10 In.	6.00
Cameo, Platter, Green, Closed Handle	13.00
Cameo, Relish, Green	15.00
Cameo, Salt & Pepper, Green	55.00
Cameo, Saucer, Green	4.00
Cameo, Sherbet, Green	8.00 To 9.50
Cameo, Sugar & Creamer, Green, 3 1/4 In.	24.50 To 25.00
Cameo, Sugar & Creamer, Green, 4 1/4 In.	28.50
Cameo, Sugar & Creamer, Yellow	21.00
Cameo, Sugar, Green	10.00
Cameo, Tumbler, Green, Footed, 4 3/4 In.	16.00
Cameo, Tumbler, Green, 3 Ounce	35.00
Cameo, Tumbler, Green, 11 Ounce	20.00
Cameo, Tumbler, Green, 3 3/4 In.	16.00
Cameo, Tumbler, Green, 5 In.	16.00
Cameo, Tumbler, Yellow, Footed, 4 3/4 In.	10.00
Cameo, Tumbler, Yellow, Footed, 9 Ounce	20.00
Cameo, Vase, Green, 8 In.	17.50 To 20.00
Cameo, Wine Set, Green, Decanter, 5 Wine Goblets	275.00
Candlewick, Ashtray, Crystal, Heart Shaped, 6 1/2 In.	10.00
Candlewick, Bowl, Crystal, Handled, 7 In.	14.00
Candlewick, Bowl, Crystal, Handled, 10 In.	21.00
Candlewick, Butter, Crystal, Covered, Round, 5 1/2 In.	19.00
Candlewick, Marmalade, Crystal, Covered, Metal Ladle	10.00
Candlewick, Plate, Crystal, 8 In.	15.00
Candlewick, Relish, Crystal, Oval	11.00 To 16.00
Candlewick, Sugar & Creamer, Tray, Crystal	22.00

Bubble

Cameo

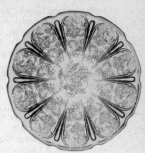

Cherry Blossom

Cape Cod, Sherbet, Crystal	1.50
Cape Cod, Tumbler, Ruby, 5 In.	18.00
Caprice, Cup, Blue	18.00
Caprice, Ice Bucket & Tongs, Crystal	35.00
Caprice, Tumbler, Blue	25.00
CHAIN DAISY, see Adam	
CHERRY, see Cherry Blossom	
Cherry Blossom, Berry Bowl, Delphite	10.00
Cherry Blossom, Berry Bowl, Green	9.00 To 10.00
Cherry Blossom, Berry Bowl, Pink	8.00 To 9.00
Cherry Blossom, Bowl, Console, Pink, Footed	40.00
Cherry Blossom, Bowl, Green, Footed, 8 1/2 In.	15.00
Cherry Blossom, Bowl, Green, 10 1/2 In.	38.00
Cherry Blossom, Bowl, Pink, Footed, 10 1/2 In.	20.00 To 30.00
Cherry Blossom, Bowl, Pink, 8 1/2 In.	16.00
Cherry Blossom, Bowl, Vegetable, Pink, 9 In.	20.00 To 22.00
Cherry Blossom, Butter, Pink, Covered	60.00 To 80.00
Cherry Blossom, Cake Plate, Green	15.00 To 17.00
Cherry Blossom, Cake Plate, Pink	16.00 To 22.00
Cherry Blossom, Coaster, Green	9.00
Cherry Blossom, Creamer, Delphite, Child's	30.00
Cherry Blossom, Creamer, Green	8.00 To 12.00
Cherry Blossom, Creamer, Pink	9.00 To 12.00
Cherry Blossom, Cup & Saucer, Delphite, Child's	30.00
Cherry Blossom, Cup & Saucer, Green	17.00
Cherry Blossom, Cup & Saucer, Pink	14.50 To 24.00
Cherry Blossom, Pitcher, Green, Straight Sided	30.00
Cherry Blossom, Pitcher, Pink, 8 In.	30.00 To 38.00
Cherry Blossom, Plate, Grill, Green	14.00 To 15.50
Cherry Blossom, Plate, Grill, Pink	15.00 To 15.50
Cherry Blossom, Plate, Pink, 6 In.	5.00
Cherry Blossom, Plate, Pink, 7 In.	9.00 To 13.00
Cherry Blossom, Plate, Pink, 9 In.	10.50 To 11.00
Cherry Blossom, Plate, Sandwich, Pink	18.00
Cherry Blossom, Plate, Sherbet, Pink	4.50
Cherry Blossom, Platter, Pink, Divided, 13 In.	32.00 To 38.00
Cherry Blossom, Platter, Pink, Oval, 11 In.	18.00 To 20.00
Cherry Blossom, Sherbet, Footed, Green	10.50
Cherry Blossom, Sherbet, Pink	10.00 To 11.00
Cherry Blossom, Sugar & Creamer, Green, Covered	22.00
Cherry Blossom, Sugar & Creamer, Pink, Covere	28.50 To 40.00
Cherry Blossom, Sugar, Delphite	16.00
Cherry Blossom, Sugar, Green	10.00
Cherry Blossom, Sugar, Pink, Covered	20.00 To 30.00
Cherry Blossom, Tea Set, Delphite, Child's, 14 Piece	275.00
Cherry Blossom, Tray, Pink, Handled, 10 1/2 In.	15.00
Cherry Blossom, Tumbler, Pink, Footed, 4 1/2 In.	22.00

Cherry Blossom, Tumbler, Pink, 3 1/2 In. .... 8.50 To 12.00
Cherry Blossom, Tumbler, Pink, 4 1/4 In. 14.00
Cherry Blossom, Water Set, Green 125.00
Cherry Blossom, Water Set, Pink, 7 Piece 150.00
   CHERRY-BERRY, see also Strawberry
Cherry-Berry, Sugar, Pink 10.00
Circle, Bowl, Green, Flared, 5 1/4 In. 2.75
Circle, Cup, Green 3.00
Circle, Goblet, Green, Water 5.00
Circle, Sherbet, Green 4.00
   CIRCULAR RIBS, see Circle
Cloverleaf, Creamer, Black 9.50
Cloverleaf, Cup & Saucer, Black 14.00
Cloverleaf, Cup & Saucer, Green .... 6.00 To 7.00
Cloverleaf, Cup, Pink 4.50
Cloverleaf, Plate, Grill, Green 15.00
Cloverleaf, Plate, Pink, Octagon, 7 In. 4.00
Cloverleaf, Salt & Pepper, Green .... 22.50 To 25.00
Cloverleaf, Sherbet, Footed, Green .... 5.00 To 6.50
Cloverleaf, Sherbet, Pink 4.50
Cloverleaf, Sugar & Creamer, Black 22.00
Cloverleaf, Sugar, Black 9.50
Cloverleaf, Sugar, Green 4.00
Colonial Block, Goblet, Green, 5 3/4 In. 6.00
Colonial, Bowl, Crystal, 9 In. 10.00
Colonial, Bowl, Vegetable, Crystal, Oval 8.50
Colonial, Butter, Green, Covered .... 22.00 To 35.00
Colonial, Candleholder, Opaque White 12.50
Colonial, Creamer, Green, 5 In. 14.00
Colonial, Cup, Pink 6.00
Colonial, Goblet, Green, 4 In. 18.00
Colonial, Pitcher, Water, Pink, 54 Ounce 28.50
Colonial, Plate, Green, 10 1/4 In. 30.00
Colonial, Plate, Grill, Green 18.00
Colonial, Sherbet, Pink, Footed 7.50
Colonial, Tumbler, Pink, 4 In. 7.50
Colonial, Whiskey, Pink .... 6.00 To 7.50
Columbia, Butter, Crystal, Metal Cover 12.00
Columbia, Cup & Saucer, Crystal 4.50
Columbia, Plate, Crystal, 6 In. .... 1.00 To 1.50
Comet, Plate, Green, 6 In. 2.00
Coronation, Berry Set, Ruby, 7 Piece 27.50
Coronation, Cup, Pink .... 2.25 To 5.00
Coronation, Plate, Sherbet, Pink 1.50
Coronation, Sherbet, Pink, Footed 3.50
Cosmos, Water Set, Iridescent, 7 Piece 55.00
Cremax, Plate, Floral Decal, 6 1/4 In. 4.50
Cremax, Saucer, Cream 3.50
Cube, Dish, Candy, Covered, Pink 20.00
   CUBIST, see also Cube
Cubist, Bowl, Pink, 4 1/2 In. 3.50
Cubist, Bowl, Pink, 6 1/2 In. 6.00
Cubist, Salt & Pepper, Green 22.50
Cubist, Saltshaker, Pink 12.50
Cubist, Saucer, Pink 1.50
Cubist, Sugar & Creamer, Pink 3.50
Cubist, Sugar, Crystal .... .75
Cubist, Sugar, Pink 6.00
   DAISY, see No. 620
   DAISY PETALS, see Petalware
   DIAMOND, see Windsor
   DIAMOND PATTERN, see Miss America
   DIAMOND POINT, see Petalware

Diamond Quilted, Bowl, Pink, 6 3/4 In.	5.00
Diana, Plate, Green, 8 In.	3.00
Diana, Saucer, Pink	1.25
Dogwood, Bowl, Pink, 8 1/2 In.	27.50 To 30.00
Dogwood, Cake Plate, Green, 13 In.	50.00
Dogwood, Cake Plate, Pink, 12 In.	40.00
Dogwood, Creamer, Pink	12.00 To 15.00
Dogwood, Cup & Saucer, Green	18.00
Dogwood, Cup & Saucer, Pink	8.50 To 12.00
Dogwood, Cup, Green	8.00
Dogwood, Plate, Green, 8 In.	4.00
Dogwood, Plate, Grill, Pink	12.50
Dogwood, Plate, Pink, 6 In.	3.50
Dogwood, Plate, Pink, 8 In.	3.50 To 8.00
Dogwood, Plate, Server, Monax, 12 In.	18.00
Dogwood, Saucer, Pink	4.00
Dogwood, Sherbet, Pink	15.50 To 17.00
Dogwood, Sugar & Creamer, Green	60.00
Dogwood, Sugar & Creamer, Pink	21.00
Dogwood, Sugar, Pink	7.50 To 15.00
Dogwood, Tumbler, Pink, 3 1/2 In.	4.50
Dogwood, Tumbler, Pink, 4 In.	4.50
Doric & Pansy, Bowl, Ultramarine, 10 In.	30.00
Doric & Pansy, Plate, Pink, 6 In.	6.00
Doric & Pansy, Sugar, Pink, Child's	19.50
Doric & Pansy, Tray, Green, 10 In.	17.00
Doric, Delphite, Sherbet	20.00
Doric, Dish, Candy, Green, Covered	28.00
Doric, Dish, Candy, Pink, Center Handle	7.50
Doric, Dish, Candy, Pink, Covered	22.00 To 30.00
Doric, Pitcher, Green, 6 In.	20.00
Doric, Plate, Pink, Handled, 10 In.	8.00
DOUBLE SWIRL, see Swirl	
DRAPE & TASSEL, see Princess	
English Hobnail, Bowl, Pink, 4 1/2 In.	14.00
English Hobnail, Bowl, Pink, 4 3/4 In.	12.50
English Hobnail, Candleholder, Pink, 3 1/2 In., Pair	25.00
English Hobnail, Compote, Green, Footed, 8 In.	25.00
English Hobnail, Goblet, Crystal, Square Base, 6 In.	10.00
English Hobnail, Goblet, Pink, 6 1/4 In.	20.00
English Hobnail, Lamp, Amber, 9 1/2 In.	75.00
English Hobnail, Pepper Shaker, Crystal	15.00
English Hobnail, Plate, Crystal, 8 In.	6.00
English Hobnail, Plate, Green, 8 In.	10.00
English Hobnail, Plate, Pink, 8 In.	7.50 To 10.00
English Hobnail, Saltshaker, Pink	25.00
English Hobnail, Tumbler, Crystal, 5 In.	9.00
English Hobnail, Tumbler, Pink, 5 In.	17.50
Fairfax, Plate, Pink, 6 In.	2.75
Fairfax, Plate, Pink, 7 In.	3.75
Fairfax, Saucer, Green	4.00
FAN & FEATHER, see Adam	
FINE RIB, see Homespun	
FLAT DIAMOND, see Diamond Quilted	
Floragold, Bowl, Iridescent, Ruffled, 8 1/2 In.	4.00
Floragold, Bowl, Iridescent, 9 1/2 In.	16.00
Floragold, Candleholder, Iridescent, Pair	27.50
Floragold, Creamer, Iridescent	6.00
Floragold, Dish, Candy, Iridescent, 4-Legged	4.00
Floragold, Tumbler, Iridescent, 5 In.	9.00
Floral, Bowl, Green, 7 1/2 In.	7.50
Floral, Bowl, Pink, 4 In.	8.00
Floral, Butter, Pink, Covered	52.50 To 65.00

Floral, Candleholder, Green, Pair 28.50
Floral, Candleholder, Pink, Pair 22.50
Floral, Coaster, Green 7.50
Floral, Creamer, Pink 7.00
Floral, Cup, Green 7.00
Floral, Dish, Candy, Green, Covered .... 22.00 To 27.50
Floral, Dish, Candy, Pink, Covered .... 22.50 To 25.00
Floral, Plate, Green, 6 In. 3.50
Floral, Plate, Green, 8 In. 6.50
Floral, Relish, Green 9.00
Floral, Relish, Pink 8.00
Floral, Salt & Pepper, Green 32.50
Floral, Salt & Pepper, Pink .... 26.00 To 32.00
Floral, Sherbet, Green 8.50
Floral, Sherbet, Pink 7.50
Floral, Sugar & Creamer, Pink, Covered 22.00
Floral, Sugar, Green 7.00
Floral, Tray, Green, 6 In. 15.00
Floral, Tray, Pink, 6 In. 8.00
Florentine No.1, Bowl, Green, 8 1/2 In. 13.50
Florentine No.1, Cup, Green 3.75
Florentine No.1, Plate, Green, 8 1/2 In. 4.50
Florentine No.1, Salt & Pepper, Pink .... 40.00 To 50.00
Florentine No.1, Sherbet, Green 5.50
Florentine No.1, Sherbet, Pink 7.50
Florentine No.1, Sugar & Creamer, Green, Covered 20.00
Florentine No.1, Tumbler, Green, Footed, 5 In. 12.00
Florentine No.2, Ashtray, Green, 5 In. 15.00
Florentine No.2, Butter, Amber, Covered 85.00
Florentine No.2, Coaster, Pink 11.00
Florentine No.2, Cup & Saucer, Amber 10.00
Florentine No.2, Cup, Amber 7.00
Florentine No.2, Plate, Amber, 6 In. 3.00
Florentine No.2, Plate, Amber, 8 1/4 In. 6.50
Florentine No.2, Platter, Amber, 11 In. 10.00
Florentine No.2, Salt & Pepper, Green 30.00
Florentine No.2, Soup, Cream, Green 7.50
Florentine No.2, Soup, Cream, Pink .... 6.00 To 8.50
Florentine No.2, Tumbler, Amber, 12 Ounce 22.50
Florentine No.2, Tumbler, Water, Green 10.00
     FLOWER BASKET, see No. 615
Flower Garden With Butterflies, Bowl, Console, Blue 95.00
Flower Garden With Butterflies, Cup & Sauce .... 125.00 To 145.00
Flower Garden With Butterflies, Plate, Green, 8 In. 20.00
Flower Garden With Butterflies, Sherbet, Blue 55.00
Flower Garden With Butterflies, Vase, Pink, 10 In. 125.00
Forest Green, Cup 2.00
Forest Green, Sugar 2.00
     FROSTED BLOCK, see Beaded Block
Fruits, Cup & Saucer, Green 5.50
Fruits, Plate, Green, 8 In. 3.00
Fruits, Saucer, Green 2.00
Fruits, Tumbler, Green, 4 In. 6.50
Georgian, Bowl, Green, 4 1/2 In. 4.00
Georgian, Bowl, Green, 5 3/4 In. 8.00
Georgian, Bowl, Green, 6 1/2 In. .... 37.50 To 45.00
Georgian, Bowl, Green, 7 1/2 In. 28.00
Georgian, Butter, Green, Covered .... 55.00 To 60.00
Georgian, Cup & Saucer, Green 7.50
Georgian, Cup, Green 6.00
Georgian, Plate, Green, 6 In. .... 1.50 To 3.00
Georgian, Plate, Green, 8 In. 4.50
Georgian, Plate, Green, 8 1/2 In. 5.50
Georgian, Plate, Green, 9 1/4 In. 13.50

Cubist

Dogwood

Floral

Floral

Florentine No. 1

Florentine No. 2

Georgian, Saucer, Green 2.50
Georgian, Sherbet, Green .... 6.00 To 6.50
Georgian, Sugar & Creamer, Green, Covered .... 25.00 To 39.00
Georgian, Sugar, Green .... 5.00 To 8.00
Georgian, Tumbler, Green, 4 In. 27.00
    GLADIOLI, see Royal Lace
    HAIRPIN, see Newport
    HANGING BASKET, see No. 615
Heritage, Bowl, Crystal, 9 In. 4.00
Heritage, Bowl, Crystal, 10 1/2 In. 10.00
Heritage, Plate, Crystal, 11 In. 4.00
    HINGE, see Patrician
Hobnail, Lamp Base, Crystal 20.00
Holiday, Bowl, Pink, 10 In. 12.00
Holiday, Butter, Pink, Covered 30.00
Holiday, Candleholder, Pink 22.50
Holiday, Dish, Soup, Pink 20.00
Holiday, Pitcher, Pink, 6 3/4 In. 37.50
Holiday, Platter, Pink 12.00
Homespun, Butter, Pink, Covered 35.00
Homespun, Cup & Saucer, Pink 7.00
Homespun, Plate, Pink, Child's 8.50
Homespun, Sherbet, Pink 4.00
Homespun, Tumbler, Pink, Footed, 4 In. .... 6.00 To 8.00
    HORIZONTAL RIBBED, see Manhattan
    HORIZONTAL ROUNDED BIG RIB, see Manhattan
    HORIZONTAL SHARP BIG RIB, see Manhattan
    HORSESHOE, see No. 612
    IRIS & HERRINGBONE, see Iris
Iris, Bowl, Iridescent, Beaded, 8 In. 9.50
Iris, Bowl, Iridescent, Ruffled, 5 1/4 In. 20.00
Iris, Butter, Iridescent, Covered 30.00
Iris, Creamer, Crystal 4.00
Iris, Cup & Saucer, Iridescent 10.00
Iris, Cup, Crystal, Demitasse 28.00
Iris, Cup, Iridescent 8.00
Iris, Plate, Crystal, 5 1/2 In. 5.00
Iris, Sandwich Server, Crystal 10.00
Iris, Saucer, Crystal, Ruffled 4.50
Iris, Sherbet, Iridescent 6.50
Iris, Sugar & Creamer, Iridescent, Covered 16.00
Iris, Tumbler, Crystal, Footed, 6 In. 10.00
Iris, Tumbler, Iridescent, Footed, 6 In. .... 9.50 To 10.00
Iris, Vase, Iridescent, 8 In. 12.00
Jack Frost, Lemonade Set, Crystal, 7 Piece 36.00
Jadite, Bowl, Green, 6 In. 4.00
Jubilee, Plate, Yellow, 8 3/4 In. 7.50
June Tumbler, Crystal, 11 Ounce 20.00
June, Bowl, Console, Crystal, Rolled Edge, 12 In. 35.00
June, Candleholder, Crystal, Pair 35.00
    KNIFE & FORK, see Colonial
Lace Edge, Bowl, Pink, Ribbed, 9 1/2 In. 12.00
Lace Edge, Bowl, Pink, 6 1/2 In. 7.50
Lace Edge, Bowl, Pink, 7 3/4 In. 11.50
Lace Edge, Bowl, Pink, 9 In. .... 5.50 To 10.00
Lace Edge, Butter, Pink, Covered 45.00
Lace Edge, Candleholder, Pink, Pair 135.00
Lace Edge, Compote, Pink, Footed .... 12.00 To 18.00
Lace Edge, Creamer, Pink 10.00
Lace Edge, Cup & Saucer, Pink 22.00
Lace Edge, Dish, Candy, Pink, Covered 20.00
Lace Edge, Flower Bowl & Frog, Pink 15.00
Lace Edge, Plate, Pink, 10 1/2 In. 15.00
Lace Edge, Relish, Pink .... 12.50 To 13.50

Holiday   Iris, Beaded Edge   Iris, Ruffled Edge

Lace Edge, Tumbler, Pink, 4 1/2 In. .... 7.50 To 8.00
    LACY DAISY, see No. 618
Laurel, Bowl, Jade, 9 In. 8.50
    LILY MEDALLION, see American Sweetheart
    LINCOLN DRAPE, see Princess
    LOOP, see Lace Edge
    LORAIN, see No. 615
Lotus, Saltshaker, Green, Footed 12.00
    LOUISA, see Floragold
    LOVEBIRDS, see Georgian
    LYDIA RAY, see New Century
Madrid, Bowl, Amber, 5 In. .... 3.50 To 4.00
Madrid, Bowl, Amber, 7 In. 6.50
Madrid, Bowl, Amber, 10 In. 16.00
Madrid, Bowl, Console, Pink, 11 In. 7.00
Madrid, Butter, Amber, Covered .... 40.00 To 75.00
Madrid, Cookie Jar, Amber 8.00
Madrid, Cookie Jar, Pink 32.00
Madrid, Creamer, Amber 10.00
Madrid, Cup & Saucer, Amber 6.00
Madrid, Cup & Saucer, Blue 12.50
Madrid, Cup & Saucer, Pink 7.50
Madrid, Dish, Soup, Crystal, 7 In. 4.00
Madrid, Gravy Boat, Amber 400.00
Madrid, Pitcher, Amber, Square, 8 In. 25.00
Madrid, Pitcher, Green, Square, 8 In. 95.00
Madrid, Plate, Amber, 6 In. 3.50
Madrid, Plate, Amber, 7 1/2 In. 6.50
Madrid, Plate, Amber, 9 In. 6.00
Madrid, Plate, Amber, 10 1/2 In. .... 20.00 To 28.00
Madrid, Plate, Blue, 9 In. 12.00
Madrid, Plate, Green, 9 In. 7.00
Madrid, Plate, Grill, Green 6.00
Madrid, Platter, Green 15.00
Madrid, Salt & Pepper, Crystal, Footed, Pair 38.00
Madrid, Salt & Pepper, Green 47.50
Madrid, Saucer, Amber .... 2.00 To 2.25
Madrid, Sherbet, Amber .... 3.00 To 8.00
Madrid, Sherbet, Green 6.50
Madrid, Soup, Cream, Amber 12.00
Madrid, Sugar & Creamer, Amber, Covered .... 35.00 To 48.00
Madrid, Sugar & Creamer, Green 15.00
Madrid, Sugar, Amber .... 2.75 To 4.00
Madrid, Tumbler, Amber, 5 1/2 In. 13.00
    MAGNOLIA, see Dogwood
Manhattan, Bowl, Crystal, 4 1/2 In. 4.25
Manhattan, Bowl, Crystal, 7 1/2 In. 6.00

Manhattan, Bowl, Pink, Footed, 5 1/2 In. 5.00
Manhattan, Cup & Saucer, Crystal 10.50
Manhattan, Plate, Crystal, 6 In. .... 1.75 To 2.00
Manhattan, Plate, Crystal, 10 1/4 In. 5.50
Manhattan, Salt & Pepper, Crystal 13.00
Manhattan, Sherbet, Crystal .... 4.00 To 4.50
Manhattan, Sugar & Creamer, Pink 18.00
Manhattan, Tumbler, Pink, 5 1/4 In. 7.50
    MANY WINDOWS, see Roulette
Mayfair Federal, Creamer, Amber 9.00
Mayfair Open Rose, Bowl, Blue 45.00
Mayfair Open Rose, Bowl, Fruit, Blue 85.00
Mayfair Open Rose, Bowl, Green, 11 3/4 In. 15.00
Mayfair Open Rose, Bowl, Pink, Flared 20.00
Mayfair Open Rose, Bowl, Pink, Handled, 10 In. .... 16.00 To 20.00
Mayfair Open Rose, Bowl, Pink, 5 In. 10.00
Mayfair Open Rose, Bowl, Pink, 5 1/2 In. .... 10.00 To 11.00
Mayfair Open Rose, Bowl, Pink, 7 In. 12.00
Mayfair Open Rose, Bowl, Pink, 10 In. 12.00
Mayfair Open Rose, Bowl, Vegetable, Pink, Oval .... 14.00 To 15.00
Mayfair Open Rose, Butter, Blue, Covered 250.00
Mayfair Open Rose, Cake Plate, Pink 15.00
Mayfair Open Rose, Celery, Pink 15.00
Mayfair Open Rose, Cookie Jar, Pink, Lid 25.00
Mayfair Open Rose, Creamer, Blue 37.50
Mayfair Open Rose, Creamer, Pink .... 9.50 To 11.50
Mayfair Open Rose, Cup & Saucer, Pink 15.00
Mayfair Open Rose, Cup, Pink .... 9.00 To 10.00
Mayfair Open Rose, Dish, Candy, Pink, Covered .... 25.00 To 33.00
Mayfair Open Rose, Goblet, Pink, 5 3/4 In. .... 29.50 To 35.00
Mayfair Open Rose, Pitcher, Crystal, 6 In. 15.00
Mayfair Open Rose, Pitcher, Pink, 6 In. .... 20.00 To 29.00
Mayfair Open Rose, Pitcher, Pink, 8 1/2 In. 45.00
Mayfair Open Rose, Plate, Grill, Blue, 9 1/2 In. 32.50
Mayfair Open Rose, Plate, Grill, Pink, 9 1/2 In. 17.00
Mayfair Open Rose, Plate, Pink, 6 In. .... 6.00 To 7.50
Mayfair Open Rose, Plate, Sherbet, Pink 7.00
Mayfair Open Rose, Platter, Blue, Oval 55.00
Mayfair Open Rose, Platter, Pink 16.00
Mayfair Open Rose, Relish, Pink, 4-Part .... 15.00 To 20.00
Mayfair Open Rose, Salt & Pepper, Pink .... 35.00 To 40.00
Mayfair Open Rose, Sandwich Server, Pink 20.00
Mayfair Open Rose, Sherbet, Pink .... 10.00 To 12.00
Mayfair Open Rose, Soup, Cream, Pink 28.00
Mayfair Open Rose, Sugar & Creamer, Pink 22.00
Mayfair Open Rose, Tray, Green, Handled, 12 In. 18.00
Mayfair Open Rose, Tray, Serving, Pink, Center Handle 25.00
Mayfair Open Rose, Tumbler, Pink, Flat, 4 1/4 In. 18.50
Mayfair Open Rose, Tumbler, Pink, Flat, 9 Ounce 17.50
Mayfair Open Rose, Tumbler, Pink, Footed, 10 Ounce 22.50
Mayfair Open Rose, Tumbler, Pink, Footed, 5 1/2 In. 22.50
Mayfair Open Rose, Tumbler, Pink, Footed, 6 1/2 In. 27.50
Mayfair Open Rose, Vase, Blue .... 80.00 To 85.00
Mayfair Open Rose, Vase, Pink 95.00
Mayfair Open Rose, Wine, Pink, 4 1/4 In. 45.00
    MEADOW FLOWER, see No. 618
    MEANDERING VINE, see Madrid
Miss America, Bowl, Crystal, 6 1/4 In. 5.00
Miss America, Bowl, Fruit, Pink 40.00
Miss America, Bowl, Green, 6 1/4 In. 8.50
Miss America, Cake Plate, Crystal 12.00
Miss America, Cake Plate, Pink 25.00
Miss America, Celery, Pink 12.50
Miss America, Compote, Crystal 12.00

Madrid

Mayfair Open Rose

Miss America

Moderntone

Miss America, Compote, Pink	13.00 To 15.00
Miss America, Cup & Saucer, Crystal	7.50 To 10.00
Miss America, Cup, Green	6.50
Miss America, Goblet, Crystal, 5 1/2 In.	15.00
Miss America, Goblet, Pink, 5 1/2 In.	27.50
Miss America, Plate, Grill, Crystal	6.00
Miss America, Plate, Grill, Pink	12.00
Miss America, Plate, Pink, 8 1/2 In.	8.00 To 10.50
Miss America, Plate, Pink, 10 In.	14.00
Miss America, Platter, Crystal	9.50
Miss America, Relish, Crystal, 4-Part, 9 In.	7.00 To 11.50
Miss America, Relish, 5-Part, 11 3/4 In.	12.50 To 25.00
Miss America, Salt & Pepper, Crystal	35.00
Miss America, Salt & Pepper, Pink	20.00
Miss America, Saucer, Pink	2.55 To 3.50
Miss America, Sherbet, Pink	8.00
Miss America, Sugar & Creamer, Crystal	12.00
Miss America, Tumbler, Crystal, 4 1/2 In.	8.00
MODERNE ART, see Tea Room	
Moderntone, Ashtray, Cobalt Blue, 5 1/2 In.	10.00 To 12.00
Moderntone, Bowl, Cobalt Blue, 5 In.	7.50
Moderntone, Butter, Cobalt Blue, Covered	50.00
Moderntone, Creamer, Cobalt Blue	10.00
Moderntone, Cup & Saucer, Cobalt Blue	7.50
Moderntone, Plate, Cobalt Blue, 6 In.	2.50
Moderntone, Plate, Cobalt Blue, 7 In.	4.00 To 4.50
Moderntone, Plate, Cobalt Blue, 9 In.	6.00
Moderntone, Plate, Cobalt Blue, 10 3/4 In.	10.00
Moderntone, Salt & Pepper, Cobalt Blue	16.00 To 22.50
Moderntone, Sherbet, Amethyst	3.50
Moderntone, Sherbet, Cobalt Blue	6.00
Moderntone, Sugar & Creamer, Cobalt Blue	10.00
Moondrops, Ashtray, Red	25.00

Moondrops, Berry Bowl, Red, 4 In. 8.00
Moondrops, Bowl, Vegetable, Red 20.00
Moondrops, Cake Plate, Red, 11 In. 40.00
Moondrops, Cup & Saucer, Red .... 10.00 To 18.00
Moondrops, Goblet, Red, 4 In. 12.00
Moondrops, Platter, Red, 12 In. 18.00
Moondrops, Soup, Cream, Amethyst 10.00
Moondrops, Sugar & Creamer, Green 10.00
Moondrops, Sugar & Creamer, Red 25.00
Moonstone, Bottle, Cologne, Crystal, Stopper 15.00
Moonstone, Bowl, Crystal, 9 1/2 In. 10.00
Moonstone, Bowl, Green, Crimped, 8 In. 7.00
Moonstone, Box, Powder, Crystal 13.50
Moonstone, Candleholder, Green 5.50
Moonstone, Creamer, Crystal 6.50
Moonstone, Dish, Candy, Crystal, Covered 12.50
Moonstone, Plate, Crystal, 6 In. 2.75
Moonstone, Sherbet, Crystal .... 5.50 To 6.00
Moonstone, Sugar & Creamer, Crystal .... 10.00 To 18.00
Moonstone, Vase, Crystal, 3 1/2 In. 10.00
New Century, Butter, Green, Covered 43.00
New Century, Tumbler, Crystal, 5 In. 7.00
Newport, Cup & Saucer, Amethyst 6.00
Newport, Platter, Amethyst 9.00
Newport, Sherbet, Amethyst 13.00
Newport, Soup, Cream, Amethyst 7.00
No.610, Bowl, Green, 8 1/2 In. 28.00
No.610, Bowl, Pink, Oval, 9 1/2 In. .... 35.00 To 40.00
No.610, Bowl, Yellow, 4 3/4 In. 20.00
No.610, Creamer, Green 18.00
No.610, Creamer, Pink .... 7.50 To 17.00
No.610, Creamer, Yellow 19.00
No.610, Relish, Pink, 4-Part 30.00
No.610, Saltshaker, Crystal 30.00
No.610, Sugar & Creamer, Pink 35.00
No.612, Bowl, Yellow, 7 1/2 In. 15.00
No.612, Creamer, Green .... 10.00 To 12.00
No.612, Cup, Green 7.00
No.612, Plate, Green, 9 1/2 In. 7.00
No.612, Relish, Yellow 9.00
No.612, Saucer, Green 2.00
No.612, Sugar, Green 15.00
No.615, Bowl, Yellow, 6 In. .... 20.00 To 40.00
No.615, Creamer, Yellow 15.00
No.615, Cup, Yellow 13.00
No.615, Plate, Green, 10 In. 29.50
No.615, Plate, Yellow, 7 3/4 In. .... 9.50 To 10.00
No.615, Platter, Yellow, 11 1/2 In. .... 25.00 To 30.00
No.615, Sherbet, Green .... 6.50 To 14.00
No.615, Sherbet, Yellow .... 24.00 To 28.00
No.615, Sugar & Creamer, Green .... 20.00 To 24.50
No.616, Cup, Crystal 6.00
No.616, Sandwich Server, Crystal, 12 In. 9.00
No.618, Bowl, Crystal, 7 1/2 In. 5.50
No.618, Cup & Saucer, Crystal 8.50
No.618, Sherbet, Crystal 12.00
No.618, Tray, Amber, Rectangular 10.00
No.620, Bowl, Crystal, 4 1/2 In. 1.75
No.620, Bowl, Green, 7 1/2 In. 4.00
No.620, Ice Bucket, Green, Metal Handle 22.00
No.620, Plate, Amber, 8 3/8 In. .... 3.00 To 5.50
No.620, Plate, Amber, 9 3/4 In. 5.00
No.620, Plate, Crystal, 8 3/8 In. 2.00
No.620, Plate, Grill, Crystal, 10 3/8 In. .... 3.00 To 4.00

No.620, Relish, Amber, O Part, Footed .... 10.00 To 16.00
No.620, Soup, Cream, Amber .... 4.00 To 5.50
No.620, Soup, Cream, Crystal 2.50
No.620, Tumbler, Crystal, Footed, 4 1/2 In. 4.50
Normandie, Bowl, Pink, 5 In. 4.50
Normandie, Cup & Saucer, Pink 6.50
Normandie, Cup, Iridescent .... 4.00 To 5.50
Normandie, Cup, Pink .... 4.00 To 5.00
Normandie, Sherbet, Iridescent 4.00
Normandie, Sherbet, Pink 4.00
Old Cafe, Bowl, Pink, 4 1/4 In. 2.00
Old Cafe, Cup, Red 5.50
Old Cafe, Plate, Pink, 10 In. 13.00
Old Cafe, Saucer, Crystal 2.00
Old English, Bowl, Console, Green, 11 In. 20.00
Old English, Eggcup, Crystal 3.00
    OLD FLORENTINE, see Florentine No. 1
    OPEN LACE, see Lace Edge
    OPEN ROSE, see Mayfair Open Rose
    OPEN SCALLOP, see Lace Edge
    OPTIC DESIGN, see Raindrops
    ORIENTAL POPPY, see Florentine No. 2
Oyster & Pearl, Bowl, Crystal, 10 In. 11.00
Oyster & Pearl, Candleholder, Red 27.50
Oyster & Pearl, Plate, Pink, 13 1/2 In. 8.00
    PANELED ASTER, see Madrid
    PANELED CHERRY BLOSSOM, see Cherry Blossom
    PARROT, see Sylvan
Patrician, Bowl, Amber, Oval, 10 In. 14.00
Patrician, Butter, Amber, Covered 45.00
Patrician, Cup, Green 4.50
Patrician, Plate, Grill, Amber 7.00
Patrician, Salt & Pepper, Pink 60.00
Patrician, Saucer, Green 2.50
Patrician, Sherbet, Amber .... 5.00 To 5.50
Patrician, Soup, Cream, Amber 9.50
Patrician, Tumbler, Amber, Footed, 5 1/4 In. .... 20.00 To 24.00
Patrician, Tumbler, Amber, 4 In. 15.00
    PETAL, see Petalware
    PETAL SWIRL, see Swirl
Petalware, Bowl, Pink, 9 In. 8.00
Petalware, Cup & Saucer, Monax 6.00
Petalware, Plate, Monax, 9 1/2 In. 5.50
Petalware, Sugar, Monax 3.50
    PINEAPPLE & FLORAL, see No. 618
    PINWHEEL, see Sierra
    POINSETTA, see Floral
Popeye & Olive, Banana Boat, Red, Footed 35.00
Popeye & Olive, Sherbet, Red 15.00
    POPPY NO. 1, see Florentine No. 1
    POPPY NO. 2, see Florentine No. 2
    PRIMUS, see Madrid
Princess Feather, Plate, Crystal, 8 In. 5.00
Princess Feather, Sugar & Creamer, Crystal 15.00
Princess, Bowl, Green, 9 In. 17.00
Princess, Bowl, Pink, 5 In. 11.00
Princess, Cake Plate, Pink 10.00
Princess, Cookie Jar, Green, Covered .... 25.00 To 35.00
Princess, Creamer, Green .... 7.50 To 10.00
Princess, Cup & Saucer, Amber 5.00
Princess, Cup & Saucer, Green .... 8.00 To 10.50
Princess, Cup & Saucer, Pink .... 8.50 To 11.00
Princess, Cup, Green 6.00
Princess, Cup, Pink .... 4.00 To 6.50

Princess, Dish, Candy, Green, Covered .... 20.00 To 22.50
Princess, Dish, Candy, Pink, Covered 28.00
Princess, Pitcher, Green, 8 In. 29.00
Princess, Plate, Green, 6 In. 4.00
Princess, Plate, Green, 8 In. .... 7.00 To 8.00
Princess, Plate, Green, 9 In. .... 14.50 To 15.00
Princess, Plate, Grill, Topaz, 10 1/4 In. 6.00
Princess, Platter, Green .... 12.00 To 18.00
Princess, Salt & Pepper, Green .... 30.00 To 32.50
Princess, Saltshaker, Green 12.00
Princess, Sherbet, Green .... 12.50 To 24.00
Princess, Sherbet, Pink .... 8.00 To 9.50
Princess, Tumbler, Amber, 5 1/4 In. 12.00
Princess, Tumbler, Green, Footed, 5 1/4 In. 22.50
Princess, Tumbler, Green, 4 In. 18.50
Princess, Tumbler, Green, 5 In. 16.00
Princess, Tumbler, Pink, Footed, 5 1/4 In. 14.50
Princess, Tumbler, Pink, 3 In. 12.50
Princess, Vase, Green, 8 In. 15.00
Princess, Vase, Pink, 8 In. 15.50
    PROVINCIAL, see Bubble
    PYRAMID, see No. 610
Queen Mary, Cup, Pink .... 4.00 To 5.50
Queen Mary, Plate, Crystal, 12 In. 6.50
Raindrops, Cup, Green 4.00
    RASPBERRY BAND, see Laurel
    REX, see No. 610
    RIBBED, see Manhattan
Ribbon, Plate, Green, 6 1/4 In. 7.00
Ribbon, Salt & Pepper, Green 12.00
Ring, Decanter & Stopper, Crystal 12.00
Ring, Pitcher, Crystal, 8 In. 8.00
Ring, Salt & Pepper, Crystal 9.00
Rock Crystal, Bowl, Console, Crystal 30.00
Rock Crystal, Candleholder, Crystal, 2-Part, Pair 35.00
Rock Crystal, Pitcher, Crystal, 9 In. 160.00
Rock Crystal, Plate, Crystal, 11 In. 10.00
Rock Crystal, Sugar & Creamer, Red 40.00
Rose Cameo, Saucer, Green 3.50
Rose Cameo, Tumbler, Green, 5 1/4 In. 8.00
    ROSE LACE, see Royal Lace
Roulette, Cup & Saucer, Green 4.00
Roulette, Cup, Green 3.00
Roulette, Plate, Green, 8 In. 3.00
Royal Lace, Berry Bowl, Pink, 10 In. .... 15.00 To 16.00
Royal Lace, Bowl, Console, Green, Fluted 35.00
Royal Lace, Butter, Green, Covered 225.00
Royal Lace, Butter, Pink, Covered 95.00
Royal Lace, Cookie Jar, Crystal, Covered 26.00
Royal Lace, Cookie Jar, Pink, Covered 30.00
Royal Lace, Creamer, Green 12.00
Royal Lace, Cup & Saucer, Pink 11.00
Royal Lace, Cup, Cobalt Blue 20.00
Royal Lace, Plate, Cobalt Blue, 8 1/2 In. 25.00
Royal Lace, Plate, Cobalt Blue, 10 In. 9.00
Royal Lace, Plate, Crystal, 10 1/2 In. 10.00
Royal Lace, Plate, Grill, Cobalt Blue .... 16.00 To 20.00
Royal Lace, Platter, Cobalt Blue, 13 In. 39.00
Royal Lace, Salt & Pepper, Green 85.00
Royal Lace, Salt & Pepper, Pink .... 34.00 To 55.00
Royal Lace, Soup, Cream, Cobalt Blue .... 12.00 To 28.00
Royal Lace, Soup, Cream, Pink 10.00
Royal Lace, Sugar & Creamer, Cobalt Blue 125.00
Royal Lace, Sugar & Creamer, Pink, Covered 55.00

No. 612

No. 612

Normandie

Patrician

Princess

Royal Lace

Royal Lace

Royal Lace

Royal Lace, Sugar, Covered, Pink 18.00
Royal Lace, Tumbler, Pink, 4 1/2 In. 8.00
Royal Ruby, Bowl, Salad, 11 1/2 In. 20.00
Royal Ruby, Bowl, 4 1/4 In. 3.50
Royal Ruby, Bowl, 8 1/2 In. 8.50
Royal Ruby, Cup & Saucer 3.50
Royal Ruby, Cup, Punch 2.00
Royal Ruby, Ice Bucket & Tongs 30.00
Royal Ruby, Sugar & Creamer, Covered 18.00
Royal Ruby, Tumbler, 3 1/2 In. 4.00
Royal Ruby, Tumbler, 5 1/4 In. 4.00
    RUSSIAN, see Holiday
S Pattern, Bowl, Crystal, 6 In. 5.00
S Pattern, Plate, Crystal, 8 In. 4.00
    SAIL BOAT, see White Ship
    SAILING SHIP, see White Ship
    SAWTOOTH, see English Hobnail
    SAXON, see Coronation
    SHAMROCK, see Cloverleaf
Sharon, Bowl, Amber, 5 In. .... 4.00 To 5.50
Sharon, Bowl, Amber, 8 1/2 In. .... 3.50 To 10.00
Sharon, Bowl, Amber, 10 1/2 In. 15.00
Sharon, Bowl, Pink, 10 1/2 In. 13.00
Sharon, Butter, Green, Covered 60.00
Sharon, Butter, Pink, Covered .... 33.00 To 37.50
Sharon, Cake Plate, Pink .... 14.00 To 18.00
Sharon, Cookie Jar, Green, Covered 25.00
Sharon, Creamer, Amber 8.00
Sharon, Creamer, Pink .... 9.00 To 15.00
Sharon, Cup & Saucer, Amber .... 9.00 To 10.00
Sharon, Cup & Saucer, Pink .... 11.00 To 12.50
Sharon, Dish, Candy, Amber, Covered 30.00
Sharon, Dish, Candy, Pink, Covered 33.00
Sharon, Plate, Amber, 6 In. 3.00
Sharon, Plate, Amber, 9 1/2 In. 8.00
Sharon, Plate, Green, 6 In. 3.50
Sharon, Plate, Pink, 7 In. 15.00
Sharon, Plate, Pink, 9 1/2 In. 10.00
Sharon, Platter, Pink 15.00
Sharon, Salt & Pepper, Amber 30.00
Sharon, Salt & Pepper, Green 40.00
Sharon, Salt & Pepper, Pink .... 32.00 To 38.00
Sharon, Saucer, Green 2.50
Sharon, Sherbet, Pink .... 8.00 To 12.00
Sharon, Soup, Cream, Amber 15.00
Sharon, Soup, Cream, Pink .... 21.00 To 27.00
Sharon, Sugar, Green, Covered 27.00
Sharon, Sugar, Pink, Covered .... 24.00 To 30.00
Sharon, Tumbler, Pink, 4 1/8 In. .... 18.00 To 19.00
Sharon, Tumbler, Pink, 5 1/4 In. 27.50
Sharon, Tumbler, Pink, 6 1/2 In. 28.00
    SHELL, see Petalware
Sierra, Plate, Dinner, Pink 6.00
    SMOCKING, see Windsor
    SNOWFLAKE, see Doric
Spiral Flutes, Butter Tub, Green, Handled 12.00
    SPIRAL OPTIC, see Spiral
Spiral, Dish, Candy, Green, Covered 8.50
Spiral, Ice Tub, Green, Covered 9.00
Spiral, Plate, Green, 8 In. 1.50
    SPOKE, see Patrician
Starlight, Creamer, Crystal 4.50
    STRAWBERRY, see also Cherry-Berry

Strawberry, Creamer, Pink 10.00
Strawberry, Sugar, Green 10.00
Sunflower, Cake Plate, Green .... 5.00 To 8.00
Sunflower, Cake Plate, Pink 7.00
Sunflower, Cup & Saucer, Pink 9.00
Sunflower, Sugar & Creamer, Pink 12.50
Swirl, Bowl, Ultramarine, Handled, Footed, 10 In. 25.00
Swirl, Bowl, Ultramarine, 5 1/2 In. 7.00
Swirl, Bowl, Ultramarine, 7 In. 15.00
Swirl, Butter, Pink, Covered 95.00
Swirl, Candleholder, Ultramarine, Pair 22.50
Swirl, Creamer, Ultramarine 8.00
Swirl, Cup & Saucer, Ultramarine 8.00
Swirl, Ice Bucket, Amber, Metal Handle .... 16.50 To 32.50
Swirl, Plate, Ultramarine, 6 1/2 In. 2.50
Swirl, Plate, Ultramarine, 9 1/4 In. 8.00
Swirl, Salt & Pepper, Ultramarine 24.00
Swirl, Sherbet, Pink 4.50
Swirl, Sugar & Creamer, Ultramarine 14.00
Swirl, Vase, Ultramarine, 8 1/2 In. 15.00
    SWIRLED BIG RIB, see Spiral
    SWIRLED SHARP RIB, see Diana
Sylvan, Creamer, Green .... 16.50 To 20.00
Sylvan, Cup & Saucer, Green 30.00
Sylvan, Cup, Green 22.50
Sylvan, Plate, Green, Square, 7 In. 22.50
Sylvan, Platter, Green 20.00
Sylvan, Sugar & Creamer, Green, Covered 75.00
    TASSELL, see Princess
Tea Room, Bowl, Amber, Oval, 9 In. 35.00
Tea Room, Relish, Green, 2-Part 10.00
Tea Room, Sugar & Creamer, Green, 4 In. 24.00
Tea Room, Sugar & Creamer, Pink 24.00
Tea Room, Vase, 6 In. 20.00
Thistle, Plate, Green, 8 In. 9.50
    THREE PARROT, see Sylvan
Trojan, Cake Plate, Handled, Topaz 17.50
Trojan, Plate, Topaz, 9 In. .... 10.00 To 12.00

Sharon   Swirl

Sylvan

Windsor

Trojan, Sugar & Creamer, Topaz	29.00
Twisted Optic, Candleholder, Pink, Pair	9.00 To 12.00
Twisted Optic, Plate, Pink, 8 In.	3.00
Twisted Optic, Sherbet, Amber	1.50
Twisted Optic, Sherbet, Pink	4.00

    VERNON, see No. 616
    VERTICLE RIB, see Queen Mary
    VIVID BANDS, see Petalware
    WAFFLE, see Waterford

Waterford, Ashtray, Crystal, Post Cereal	25.00
Waterford, Butter, Crystal, Covered	24.00
Waterford, Cake Plate, Pink, Handled	8.00 To 8.50
Waterford, Cup & Saucer, Crystal	3.50
Waterford, Goblet, Crystal, 5 1/4 In.	7.00
Waterford, Plate, Crystal, 14 In.	3.50
Waterford, Plate, Pink, Handled, 10 1/4 In.	12.00
Waterford, Plate, Pink, 9 1/2 In.	8.50 To 9.00
Waterford, Salt & Pepper, Crystal	12.00
Waterford, Sherbet, Crystal, Footed	5.00

    WEDDING BAND, see Moderntone

White Ship, Cocktail Shaker	35.00
White Ship, Ice Bucket, Holder & Tongs	24.00

    WILDFLOWER, see No. 618
    WILDROSE, see Dogwood
    WINDSOR DIAMOND, see Windsor

Windsor, Ashtray, Pink	12.00 To 28.00
Windsor, Berry Bowl, Green	5.00
Windsor, Bowl, Pink, 5 3/8 In.	8.00
Windsor, Bowl, Pink, 8 1/2 In.	7.00
Windsor, Coaster, Green	11.00
Windsor, Cup & Saucer, Green	8.50
Windsor, Plate, Pink, 13 1/2 In.	12.50
Windsor, Salt & Pepper, Pink	18.00 To 20.00
Windsor, Saltshaker, Green	15.00
Windsor, Sandwich Server, Pink, Handled, 10 1/4 In.	6.50
Windsor, Sugar & Creamer, Crystal, Covered	10.00
Windsor, Sugar & Creamer, Green, Covered	22.00
Windsor, Tray, Pink, 13 3/4 In.	16.50

    WINGED MEDALLION, see Madrid

 Derby porcelain was made in Derby, England, from 1756 to the present. The factory changed names and marks several times. Chelsea Derby (1770-1784), Crown Derby (1784-1811), and the modern Royal Crown Derby are some of the most famous periods of the factory.

DERBY, see also Chelsea; Crown Derby; Royal Crown Derby

DERBY, Figurine, 3-Figure, 1779 Mark	1200.00

Plate, King's, Gold, Pair, C.1825, 10 In. 375.00
Platter, Meat, Mid-19th Century, Orange & White 50.00

DEVEZ, Vase, Black Flowers & Leaves, Pink Ground, Pedestal, 6 In. 250.00
Vase, Glass, Cameo, Ovoid, Landscape, Amethyst, Signed, 12 1/4 In. 600.00

DEVILBISS, Atomizer & Perfume Bottle, Orchid, Black, Art Deco Design, Set 75.00
Atomizer, Etched Amber Glass, 7 In. 60.00
Bottle, Perfume, Gold Trim, Cranberry 85.00
Bottle, Perfume, White Satin Glass, Gold Trim, Signed 60.00
Bottle, Perfume, 18K Gold Overlay, Boxed 150.00
Lamp, Nude Girl With Butterfly Wings Shade, Bronze Base 175.00

DICK TRACY, Badge, Crime Stopper .... 11.00 To 25.00
Badge, Detective Club .... 8.00 To 22.50
Book, Comic, Popped Wheat Giveaway, 1940 .... 8.00
Book, Detective, 1946 .... 10.00
Book, Encounters Facey 6.00
Camera, Seymour Co., Chicago 20.00
Car, Patrol 60.00
Car, Windup, Siren & Light, Marx, 1950s 55.00
Card, Membership, Junior Crime Stopper 5.00
Compass, Rodeo Boots, Celluloid 8.00
Crime Stopper Set, Badge, Handcuffs, Nightstick .... 18.00 To 30.00
Decoder, Slide Rule, Boxed 28.00
Dress-Up Kit, 1940, Boxed 30.00
Game, Crime Stopper, Boxed 45.00
Game, Detective, Chester Gould, 1937 .... 18.50
Game, Super Detective Mystery Card Game, 1941, Lithographed Box 20.00
Handcuff, For Junior, Original Cartoon Store Display, 1946 .... 20.00
Lamp, Table, Chalkware Base, Shape Of Tracy, 1930s 250.00
Magnifying Glass, Folding Case 12.00
Pistol, Clicker 25.00
Puzzle, Ball Bearing 20.00
Tommy Gun .... 20.00 To 25.00
Toy, Squad Car, Windup, Boxed 75.00
Wings, Air Detective, Gold 10.00
Wrist Radio, Boxed 17.00
     DICKENS WARE, see Royal Doulton; Weller

DIONNE QUINTUPLETS, Dish, Feeding, Picture Of Girls, Metal 15.00
Paper Dolls, Clothes, 1936 .... 15.00
Postcard, 1939 .... 20.00
Spoon, Set, Silver Plated 80.00

    Walt Disney and his company introduced many comic characters to the world.
    Collectors search for examples of the work of the Disney Studios and the
    many commercial products modeled after his characters. These collectibles
    are called Disneyana.

DISNEYANA, Ashtray, Figural, Three Little Pigs, 1930s .... 65.00 To 75.00
Autograph Album, Zips Around 3 Sides, Mickey Mouse, 1960s 4.50
Bank, Book, Mickey Mouse, 1936, Zell Productions, Red 85.00
Bank, Bugs Bunny, Ceramic, 16 In. 100.00
Bank, Bugs Bunny, Metal 15.00
Bank, Cinderella, Ceramic 20.00
Bank, Donald Duck, Figural, Crown Toy, 1938 .... 125.00
Bank, Donald Duck, Registering 90.00
Bank, Dumbo .... 15.00 To 16.00
Bank, Goofy, Nodder, Chalkware 30.00
Bank, Mickey Mouse, Glass .... 30.00 To 45.00
Bank, Pinocchio, Disney Enterprises 65.00
Bank, 3 Pigs, We Save Our Coins, So Who's Afraid Of The Wolf 30.00
Bedspread, Mickey Mouse & Donald Duck, Pacific 12.00

Belt Buckle, Clock Faced, Blue, Nickel Over Brass, 26 In. 75.00
Belt Buckle, Mickey Mouse, 1940s 20.00
Blackboard, Mickey Mouse, Standing, Shelf Folds, 3 1/2 Ft. 225.00
Blocks, Mickey Mouse, Set Of 9, 1930s 35.00
Book, Adventures Of Mickey Mouse, Book I, 1931 .... 125.00
Book, Big Little Book, Donald Duck, Set Of 3 .... 55.00
Book, Big Little Book, Mickey Mouse & The Sacred Jewel 25.00
Book, Big Little Book, Mickey Mouse To Draw & Color, 320 Pictures 40.00
Book, Big Little Book, Mickey The Detective 25.00
Book, Clarabelle Cow, 1938 .... 18.00
Book, Coloring, Pinocchio 15.00
Book, Coloring, Silly Symphony 30.00
Book, Donald's Lucky Day, Whitman, 1939 .... 30.00
Book, Jiminy Cricket, 1940 .... 3.95
Book, Mickey Mouse Map Of The United States, 1939 .... 55.00
Book, Mickey Mouse, Hardcover, 1931 .... 50.00
Book, Mickey Mouse, Pop-Up 175.00
Book, Mickey Presents Walt Disney's The Golden Touch, 1937 .... 28.00
Book, Minnie Mouse, Blue Ribbon, Pop-Up, C.1933 .... 335.00
Book, Paint, Mickey Mouse, 1946 .... 25.00
Book, Paint, Snow White, 1938 .... 10.00
Book, Paper Doll, Mickey & Minnie Steppin' Out, 1977, Uncut 3.50
Book, The Tortoise & The Hare, Whitman, 1935 .... 20.00
Bottle, Perfume, Mickey Mouse 31.00
Bowl, Disney, Rose Design, Vernon Kilns 50.00
Box, Crayon, Mickey Mouse, Chein, 5 X 3 1/2 X 3 In. 5.00
Box, Paint, Mickey Mouse, 1930s 60.00
Bracelet, Mickey & Minnie, 1932 .... 25.00
Bracelet, Mickey Mouse, Die-Cut Figures, 1930s 70.00
Bracelet, Pinocchio, Various Characters 33.00
Button, Mickey Mouse, Buy Cote's Master Loaf 2.00
Camera, Figural, Bugs Bunny, Boxed .... 45.00 To 50.00
Camera, Mick-A-Matic Mickey Mouse, Boxed .... 135.00 To 140.00
Card, Membership, Mickey Mouse Club, 1930s 200.00
Cards, Playing, Dopey, Boxed 6.50
DISNEYANA, CEL, see Animation Art
Chest, Toy, Mickey Mouse, 1932, Odora Co. 295.00
Clock, Alarm, Bugs Bunny 225.00
Clock, Alarm, Mickey Mouse, Celluloid Case, Ingersoll 225.00
Clock, Alarm, Woody Woodpecker, Animated 375.00
Clock, Animated, Bambi, Bayard 185.00
Clock, Animated, Bugs Bunny, Eating Carrot, Ingraham 125.00
Clock, Animated, Mickey, Donald, Pluto, Bayard 65.00
Clock, Animated, Pluto 150.00
Clock, Mickey Mouse, Ingersoll, 1940s 250.00
Clock, Pluto, Bones Hands 15.00
Clock, Wall, Donald Duck, Germany 20.00
Coloring Set, Snow White, Whitman, 1938, 40 Pages, Boxed 35.00
Cookie Cutter, Mickey Mouse, Boxed 10.00
Cookie Jar, Alice In Wonderland 40.00
Cookie Jar, Dumbo Turnabout 52.00
Cookie Jar, Goldilocks 50.00
Cookie Jar, Mickey & Minnie, Turnabout .... 35.00 To 60.00
Cookie Jar, Winnie The Pooh, Walt Disney 22.00
Creamer, Donald 20.00
Creamer, Dumbo 18.00
Cuff Links, Mickey Mouse 5.00
Cup, Mickey Mouse, Signed Walt Disney, C.1930 .... 15.00
Dish, Mickey & Minnie, Helpmates, Tin 8.00
Display, Mickey Mouse & Pluto, 26 In. 125.00
Doctor's Kit, Donald Duck, Original Box 24.00
Doll Dishes, Mickey Mouse, Tin, Boxed, 6 Piece 55.00
Doll, Cinderella, Olive Green, 14 In. 60.00
Doll, Dopey, Composition, Original Clothes, Dated 1938 .... 195.00

Doll, Ferdinand The Bull, Jointed, Ideal	35.00
Doll, Mickey & Minnie Mouse, Vinyl, Jointed, Signed Disney, 9 In.	15.00
Doll, Mickey Mouse, Black Rubber	45.00
Doll, Mickey Mouse, Cloth, Checked Jacket, Striped Pants, 15 In.	15.00
Doll, Mickey Mouse, Cloth, Straw Stuffed, C.1930s, 14 In.	265.00
Doll, Mickey Mouse, Cloth, 1930s, 11 In.	280.00
Doll, Mickey Mouse, Cloth, 1930s, 14 In.	175.00
Doll, Mickey Mouse, Handmade, C.1930, 13 In.	85.00
Doll, Mickey Mouse, Straw Stuffed, C.1930, 13 In.	325.00
Doll, Mickey Mouse, Stuffed, 11 In.	200.00
Doll, Mickey Mouse, Sun Rubber	75.00
Doll, Mouseketeers, Girl & Boy	40.00
Doll, Pinocchio, Composition, 10 In.	75.00
Doll, Pluto, Blows Horn	150.00
Doll, Snow White, Boxed, 1977	80.00
Doll, Snow White, Composition, Original Dress, Knickerbocker	65.00
Doll, 3 Little Pigs, Original Clothes By Madame Alexander	2050.00
Dollhouse, Carry-All, Marx	65.00 To 95.00
Drinking Straw, Mickey Mouse, Sunshine, Boxed	10.00
Easel, Mouseketeer	100.00
Figurine, Doc, Bisque, 3 In.	18.00
Figurine, Donald Duck, Carnival, 1930s, 14 In.	38.00
Figurine, Donald Duck, Chalkware, 7 In.	12.00
Figurine, Donald Duck, Long Beak, Bisque, 3 In.	28.00
Figurine, Donald Duck, On A Scooter, Bisque	65.00
Figurine, Dopey, Bisque, 5 In.	30.00
Figurine, Ferdinand & Bullfighter, 1938	135.00
Figurine, Happy, Wooden, 3 In.	35.00
Figurine, Mickey & Minnie Mouse, Bisque, 2 3/4 In., Pair	95.00
Figurine, Mickey & Minnie Mouse, Celluloid, 5 In., Pair	350.00
Figurine, Mickey Mouse Riding Pluto, Bisque, 2 1/4 In.	68.00
Figurine, Mickey Mouse, Ceramic, Playing Saxophone, 1930s	20.00
Figurine, Mickey Mouse, Christmas, Bisque, 1979	200.00
Figurine, Mickey Mouse, Hands On Hips, Bisque, 2 1/2 In.	25.00
Figurine, Mickey Mouse, Movable Limbs, 13 1/2 In.	55.00
Figurine, Mickey Mouse, Porcelain, 1930s, 3 3/4 In.	65.00
Figurine, Mickey Mouse, Rubber, Movable Arms, Legs, Head	60.00
Figurine, Mickey Mouse, With Drum, Bisque, 3 1/2 In.	28.00
Figurine, Mickey Mouse, With Tennis Racket, Bisque	15.00
Figurine, Minnie Mouse, With Accordion, Bisque, 3 1/4 In.	12.00
Figurine, Minnie Mouse, Wooden, 6 In.	225.00
Figurine, Pinocchio, Bisque, 3 In.	38.00
Figurine, Pinocchio, Pressed Wood, 5 In.	15.00
Figurine, Pluto, Ceramic, 5 In.	18.00
Figurine, Sneezy, With Violin, Bisque, 4 1/2 In.	85.00
Figurine, Snow White & 7 Dwarfs, Bisque, 6 1/2 In.	200.00
Figurine, Snow White & 7 Dwarfs, Complete Set, Britains	500.00
Figurine, Snow White, Bisque, 4 In.	20.00
Film, Movie Jecktor, Silly Symphony, Boxed	15.00
Fork, Mickey Mouse, Silver Plated, I.Wilkins, 6 1/4 In.	13.50
Game Board, 3 Little Pigs, 1933	25.00
Game, Bagatelle, Mickey Mouse	160.00
Game, Card, Mickey Mouse Old Mail, 1937, Box	45.00
Game, Circus	185.00
Game, Ferdinand The Bull, 1938	36.00
Game, Library Card, Mickey Mouse, 1946	25.00
Game, Mickey Mouse Circus	185.00
Game, Mickey Mouse Coming Home, Board & Box	85.00
Game, Mickey Mouse Scatter Ball, Boxed, 1934, Marx	125.00
Game, Mickey, Minnie, Donald, Goofy, Loony	18.00
Game, Rocket, Tomorrowland	22.00
Glass, Grumpy	12.00
Globe, World	85.00
Hairbrush, Donald Duck	30.00

Hand Car, Donald Duck & Pluto, Clockwork, 1936-37 ....*Illus* 650.00
Handkerchiefs, Mickey Mouse, Boxed 45.00
Holder, Placecard, Doc, Sirocco, Wooden Platform, 1 1/2 In. 25.00
Horn, Party, Mickey & Minnie, Marx 45.00
House, Mickey Mouse, Cardboard, Original Envelope, 2 1/2 Ft. 275.00
Kaleidoscope, Mickey Mouse 25.00
Kaleidoscope, Mickey Mouse, Minnie, Pluto, Donald, 9 In. 85.00
Knife, Pen, Mickey Mouse, Chicago World's Fair 1933 .... 35.00
Lamp Base, Donald Duck, Ceramic 55.00
Lamp, Donald Duck, Wooden 60.00
Lamp, Mickey Mouse Sitting On Chair, By Soreng Manegold, 1936 .... 75.00
Lamp, Wall, Donald Duck, Yellow Umbrella, Metal, 12 In. 55.00
Light, Mickey Mouse, Disney Enterprises, Boxed 150.00
Light, Mickey Mouse, Noma, Boxed 110.00
Lunch Box, School, Walt Disney 12.00
Lunch Pail, Pinocchio, Round, 1940 .... 25.00
Lunch Pail, School Bus 5.00
Mask, Gepetto, Premium Of Gillette 1939 .... 12.00
Mask, Pinocchio & Jiminy, Pair 20.00
Minnie Mouse, High-Heeled Papier Mache Shoes, 12 In. 150.00
Minnie Mouse, Strumming Lute, Bisque, 3 In. 45.00
Mirror, Mickey Mouse, Pocket 2.50
Mug & Bowl, 3 Little Pigs 75.00
Mug, Bugs Bunny, Figural 20.00
Pail, Sand, Donald Duck, Ohio Art Co., 1939 .... 69.00
Pail, Sand, Mickey & Minnie, 1930s, Ohio Art 45.00
Paint Set, Donald Duck .... 9.00 To 12.00
Pen, Fountain, Mickey Mouse, Inkograph Co. 30.00
Pencil, Mechanical, Mickey Mouse, Figural Top, Decal .... 40.00 To 55.00
Picture, Reverse Painting, 3 Pigs Dancing, Building, Wolf 36.00
Pin, Mickey Mouse, Buy Cote's Master Loaf 2.00
Pitcher, Dumbo, Ceramic, 1 Quart 25.00
Planter, Alice In Wonderland, Double 20.00
Planter, Mickey Mouse, Luster Ware, Playing Saxophone, 4 In. 50.00
Planter, Porky Pig, Ceramic 25.00
Planter, Thumper 16.00
Poster, Buy A Bond, Framed 40.00
Poster, Mickey's Good Deed, 1930s, 28 X 41 In. 3575.00
Poster, Mickey's Nightmare, 1930s, 28 X 41 In. 4125.00
Poster, Silly Symphony, Bugs In Love, 1930s, 28 X 41 In. 1045.00
Poster, Silly Symphony, The Bears & The Bees, 28 X 41 In. 550.00
Poster, The Klondike Kid, 1930s, 28 X 41 In. 7700.00
Poster, Touchdown Mickey, 1930s, 28 X 41 In. 3025.00
Poster, Trader Mickey, 1930s, 28 X 41 In. 4950.00
Poster, War, Donald & Horace As Riveters, 12 X 19 In. 90.00
Poster, Wayward Canary, 1930s, 28 X 41 In. 4400.00
Potty Chair, Mickey Mouse 20.00
Projector, Keystone, Mickey Mouse, 1935, Box & Catalogue 135.00
Projector, Movie, Mickey, Boxed 80.00
Puppet, Hand, Dopey, Yellow Felt Hat, Felt Body, Composition Head 20.00
Puppet, Mickey & Minnie, Strings, Hand Holders, 13 In., Pair 250.00

Disneyana, Hand Car, Donald Duck & Pluto,
Clockwork, 1936-37

Puppet, Mickey Mouse, Display, 26 In. 125.00
Puppet, Pluto, Display, 26 In. 125.00
Puzzle, Mickey, Minnie, Goofy, & Donald Duck 6.50
Puzzle, Snow White, Whitman, 1938, Boxed 40.00
Rattle, Mickey Mouse, Celluloid 150.00
Record, Mickey Mouse Club, We're The Mouseketeers 6.00
Ring, Mickey Mouse, Sterling Silver 50.00
Roller Skates, Mouseketeer 30.00
Rug, Mickey Mouse, Donald Duck, Pluto, Rowboat, 3 X 4 Ft. 250.00
Rug, Mickey Mouse, 1930s .... 150.00 To 225.00
Salt & Pepper, Donald Duck 18.00
Salt & Pepper, Mickey & Minnie Mouse, On Bench 25.00
Salt & Pepper, Thumper, White, Leeds China 6.00
Scooter Jockey, Mickey Mouse 140.00
Seed Packet, Donald Duck Peas, Donald Farming Peas, 1977 .... 2.00
Seed Packet, Mickey Mouse & Minnie Mouse, Daisy, 1977 .... 2.00
Seed Packet, Mickey Mouse Radish, Mickey Pulling Wagon, 1977 .... 2.00
Seed Packet, Pinocchio Sunflower Seeds, Litho, Hanger, 1977 .... 2.00
Seed Packet, 7 Dwarfs Marigolds, Litho, Cardboard Hanger 2.00
Sheet Music, Mickey Mouse's Birthday Party, Loose Cover 7.00
Sketch, Fantasia, Dancing Mushrooms, 12 X 10 In., Set Of 5 .... 357.00
Slate, Magic, Wall Hung, Donald Duck, Wooden Pencil 15.00
Sled, Mickey Mouse, Decal, 32 In. 200.00
Slippers, Mickey Mouse, 1940s 15.00
Soap, Funny Bunnies, 1930s, Boxed 40.00
Sparkler, Mickey Mouse 275.00
Spinner, Porky Pig, Umbrella 165.00
Spoon & Fork, Mickey & Minnie, Stainless Steel, 1970's 5.00
Spoon, Demitasse, Donald Duck, Figural, Silver Plate 6.00
Spoon, Demitasse, Mickey Mouse, Figural, Silver Plate 6.00
Spoon, Mickey Mouse, Silver Plate 20.00
Spoon, Mickey, Figural, Pewter, Shovel Shaped 6.50
Stand, Christmas Tree 50.00
Stationery, Mickey Mouse, 1930s 35.00
Store Display, Donald Duck On Trapeze, Windup, Linemar 325.00
Tablet, School, Mickey Mouse, Disney Gang Driving Old Car, 60-Page 1.50
Tea Set, Child's, Peter Pan, 23 Piece 285.00
Tea Set, Child's, Snow White & 7 Dwarfs, Marked 135.00
Tea Set, Mickey Mouse & Minnie Mouse 40.00
Tea Set, Mickey Mouse, Luster Ware, 1930s, 18 Piece 375.00
Tea Set, Peter Pan, China, Marx, 23 Piece 295.00
Tea Set, Snow White, 1930s 275.00
Toothbrush Holder, Donald Duck 165.00
Toothbrush Holder, Donald Duck, Bisque, Siamese 250.00
Toothbrush Holder, Donald Duck, Mickey & Minnie 235.00
Toothbrush Holder, Mickey Mouse & Minnie Mouse .... 65.00 To 125.00
Toothbrush Holder, Mickey Mouse Wiping Pluto's Nose, Bisque 80.00
Toothbrush Holder, Mickey Mouse, Bisque 60.00
Toothbrush Holder, Minnie Mouse, Bisque, 1930s 275.00
Toothbrush Holder, Minnie Mouse, Movable Arm 225.00
Toothbrush Holder, Three Little Pigs .... 60.00 To 75.00
Top, Mickey Mouse, Characters All Around, 12 In. 125.00
Top, Mickey Mouse, Tin, 6 Panels Of Mickey, 5 In. 20.00
Toy, Disneyland Ferris Wheel .... 150.00 To 190.00
Toy, Donald Duck Duet 425.00
Toy, Donald Duck Rubber Car 35.00
Toy, Donald Duck, Drummer .... 175.00 To 250.00
Toy, Donald Duck, Hops, Linemar 125.00
Toy, Donald Duck, Sun Rubber, 7 1/2 In. 18.00
Toy, Donald The Skier, Windup 250.00
Toy, Drum Set, Mickey Mouse, 1950 .... 50.00
Toy, Ferris Wheel, Windup, Tin, Chein .... 210.00 To 350.00
Toy, Fire Truck, Battery Operated, Lithographed Tin, 18 In. 400.00
Toy, Fire Truck, Mickey Mouse, Sun Rubber 26.00

Toy, Fire Truck, Rubber	22.00
Toy, Hand Car, Mickey Mouse, Lionel	450.00 To 475.00
Toy, Hopping Donald Duck, Linemar	125.00
Toy, Little Big Wheel, Mickey Mouse, Motor Noise, Boxed	50.00
Toy, Locomotive, Mickey Mouse, Battery Operated, Boxed	100.00
Toy, Mail Plane, Mickey Mouse	32.00
Toy, Mickey Mouse & Donald Duck In Fire Truck	35.00
Toy, Mickey Mouse In Tractor	38.00
Toy, Mickey Mouse Playing Xylophone, Celluloid, Tin	325.00 To 435.00
Toy, Mickey Mouse, Acrobat	100.00
Toy, Mickey Mouse, Dance-A-Tune, Boxed	15.00
Toy, Mickey Mouse, Drummer, Battery Operated, Linemar	250.00
Toy, Mickey Mouse, Magician, 1976	45.00
Toy, Mickey Mouse, On Rocking Horse, Japan	1200.00
Toy, Mickey Mouse, Pie-Eyed, Sieberling Hard Rubber	58.00
Toy, Mickey On Trapeze, Pie-Eyed	35.00
Toy, Mickey The Magician, Tin, Cloth, & Plastic, Battery, 5 1/4 In.	500.00
Toy, Minnie Mouse In Rocker, Windup, Mar Line, Tin, 6 3/4 In.	75.00
Toy, Minnie Mouse, In Rocking Chair, Linemar	200.00
Toy, Mouse In Tractor, Sun Rubber	35.00
Toy, Movie-Vuer, Mickey Playing Piano, Pie-Eyed, Film Boxed	40.00
Toy, Newsreel, With Sound, Mickey Mouse Club, Mattel, Boxed	175.00
Toy, Nurse Kit, Minnie Mouse	15.00
Toy, Pinocchio, Rubber, Squeeze, Seiberling	70.00
Toy, Pinocchio, Walker	175.00
Toy, Pluto In Top Hat	190.00
Toy, Pluto, On A Stick, Fisher Price	35.00
Toy, Pluto, Pop-Up Kritter	25.00
Toy, Pluto, Stuffed, Character Novelty, 12 In.	60.00
Toy, Pluto, Wooden, String Operated, 1936	40.00
Toy, Popeye With Punching Bag, J.Chein, Windup, Tin, 6 3/4 In.	155.00
Toy, Print Shop, Mickey Mouse, 1930s, Boxed	275.00
Toy, Projector, Mickey Mouse Club	28.00
Toy, Pull, Donald Duck With Xylophone, 1938	150.00
Toy, Pull, Donald Duck, Fisher	75.00
Toy, Pull, Mickey Mouse, Fisher Price	100.00
Toy, Racer, Mickey Mouse, Windup, Boxed	225.00
Toy, Railroad, Mickey Mouse, Melody, Boxed	325.00
Toy, Roller Coaster, Disneyland, Mechanical, Chein	325.00
Toy, Roller Coaster, Mickey Mouse, Chein	85.00
Toy, Squeeze, Dumbo, Dell	15.00
Toy, Stamp Pad, Mickey Mouse	25.00
Toy, Straight Shooter, Donald Duck	95.00
Toy, Suitcase, Mickey Mouse	14.00
Toy, Talkiejector, Mickey Mouse, 1 Film	245.00
Toy, Television Playhouse	135.00
Toy, Train Set, Mickey Mouse, Wooden, 5 Piece	65.00
Toy, Train, Disneyland Express	95.00
Toy, Unicorn, Fantasia, Ride-Em, Rubber	300.00
Toy, Walking Popeye With Parrot Cage, Marx, Windup, Tin, 8 In.	65.00
Toy, Xylophone, Mickey Mouse, Fisher Price, 1939	38.00
Tray, Mickey Mouse Club	95.00
Tumbler, Coachman, Red-Orange, Verse On Back, 5 In.	10.00
Tumbler, Donald Duck, 1930s	12.50
Tumbler, Grumpy, Blue, Verse On Back, 5 In.	10.00
Tumbler, Pluto	3.00
Tumbler, Snow White, Black, Verse On Back, 5 In.	15.00
Tumbler, Ugly Duckling, Yellow & Blue, Verse On Back, 5 In.	10.00
Umbrella, Donald Duck, Pink, 4 Pictures Of Donald, Marked	155.00
Umbrella, Figural, Mickey Mouse	18.50
Wall Pocket, Donald Duck Cowboy	20.00 To 25.00
Wallpaper Trim, Mickey, Minnie, 3 Nephews, Pluto, Goin' To Picnic	15.00
Watch Fob, Mickey Mouse, Leather Strap	25.00 To 45.00
Watch, Pocket, Mickey Mouse, 1933	150.00 To 200.00

Watering Can, Rooster, Mickey, 5 In. 75.00
Wristwatch, Bugs Bunny, Carrot Hands 45.00
Wristwatch, Cinderella, Slipper, Boxed 250.00
Wristwatch, Mickey Mouse Club, Swiss 75.00
Wristwatch, Mickey Mouse, Ingersoll, New Strap 150.00
Wristwatch, Mickey Mouse, Ingersoll, 1950s 22.00
Wristwatch, Mickey Mouse, Red Band 65.00
Wristwatch, Mickey Mouse, Turning Head, 1946 .... 200.00
Wristwatch, Mickey Mouse, U.S.Time 15.00
Wristwatch, Mickey Mouse, 1933 .... 250.00 To 350.00
Wristwatch, Mickey Mouse, 1947 .... 75.00
    DOCTOR, see Medical

*Doll entries are listed by marks printed or incised on the doll, if
possible. If there are no marks, the doll is listed by the name of the
subject or country.*

DOLL, A.B.G., Baby, Philadelphia Shepherd, 21 In. 1000.00
A.B.G., Toddler, Character Face, Fully Jointed, 16 In. 475.00
A.B.G.1352, Baby, 19 In. 335.00
A.B.G.1361, Baby, Breather, 27 1/2 In. 792.00
A.B.G.1361, Character Baby, Sleep Eyes, Teeth, 21 1/2 In. .... 550.00 To 565.00
A.B.G.1367, Baby, Pierced Nostrils, 21 In. 350.00
A.M., Bisque, Open Mouth, Jointed, Wooden Body, Marked 130.00
A.M., Dream Baby, Sleep Eyes, Cloth Body, 8 1/2 In. 225.00
A.M., Open Mouth, Blue Eyes, Compositon Jointed Body, Dressed 18 In. 135.00
A.M.246, My Dearie, 23 In. 325.00
A.M.323, Googly Blue Eyes To Side, Composition Body, Dressed, 10 In. 650.00
A.M.323, Googly, 7 In., Pair 1000.00
A.M.326, Prized Baby, Toddler Boy, Sleep Eyes, Navy Suit, 13 In. 495.00
A.M.341, Baby, Flange Neck, Set Eyes, Bisque, Original Gown 225.00
A.M.341, Dream Baby, Cloth Body, 14 In. 250.00
A.M.341, Dream Baby, Puppet On A Pillow 225.00
A.M.345, My Dream Baby, Kiddie Joy, 21 In. 600.00
A.M.351, Pillow Baby, Closed Mouth, Bed 350.00
A.M.352, Baby Love, Boy, Composition Body, 18 In. 575.00
A.M.370, Bisque, Kid Body, Sleep Eyes, 4 Teeth, Open Mouth, 20 In. 250.00
A.M.390, Ball-Jointed Body, Dressed, 17 In. 325.00
A.M.390, Bisque Head, Stick Body, Sleep Eyes, Beige Coat, 15 In. 240.00
A.M.390, Bisque, Brown Eyes, Ball-Jointed, 26 1/2 In. 295.00
A.M.390, Boy, Blonde Hair, Brown Eyes, Pink Velvet Suit, 24 In. 350.00
A.M.390, Brother & Sister, Bisque, 36 In., Pair 1200.00
A.M.390, Gibson Girl, 22 In. 295.00
A.M.390, Mohair Wig, Sleep Eyes, Hand-Crocheted Outfit, 10 In. 235.00
A.M.390, Original Blonde Hair, Brown Eyes, Pink Dress, 24 In. 350.00
A.M.971, Character, Baby, 18 In. 475.00
A.M.996, Breather, Flirty Eyes, 21 In. 525.00
Advertising, Rag, Tastykake 15.00
    DOLL, ALEXANDER, see Doll, Madame Alexander
Amberg, Child, Swivel Waist, Marked, 1929, 15 In. 150.00
American Character, Toddler Butterball, 19 In. 55.00
American Character, Tressy 15.00
    DOLL, ARMAND MARSEILLE, see Doll, A.M.
Arranbee, Nancy, Roller Skates, 2 Dresses & Coats, Bathing Suit, Case 175.00
Baby Brother & Sister, Yarn Hair, Pair 100.00
Baby Skeezix, Oilcloth 45.00
Baby, Composition, On Tummy, Holds Rattle, Japan, Glass Eyes, 9 In. 50.00
Barney Google, Original Tux Jacket, Cloth, 12 In. 50.00
Barry Goldwater, Boxed 10.00
Bebe, Closed Mouth, 19 In. 1950.00
Bebe, Composition Body, 12 In. 950.00
Belton, Bisque Head, Paperweight Eyes, Jointed Body, Dressed, 13 1/2 In. 1150.00
Belton, Bisque Head, Paperweight Eyes, Silk Dress, 15 1/2 In. 1195.00
Belton, Bisque, Brown Paperweight Eyes, Dressed, 24 In. 2395.00

Belton, Fashion, Closed Mouth, Swivel Neck, 14 In. 900.00
    DOLL, BERGMANN, see also Doll, S & H; Doll, Simon & Halbig
Bergmann, Ball-Jointed Body, Human Hair Wig, Red Velvet Dress, 23 In. 425.00
Bergmann, Boy, Brown Eyes, Dressed, 38 In. 1500.00
Bergmann, Brown Set Eyes, Chunky Body, Blue Silk Dress, 28 In. 695.00
Bergmann, Brown Sleep Eyes, 30 In. 700.00
Bergmann, Girl, Sleep Eyes, Pink Silk Dress, 28 In. 595.00
Bergmann, Sleep Eyes With Lashes, Ball-Jointed Body, 18 In. 395.00
Bergmann, Walter Shausen, Dark Hair, Blue Eyes, Pink Lace Outfit, 26 In. 450.00
Bess Truman, Papier-Mache, Inaugural Gown, Hand-Painted, 9 In. 85.00
Betsy McCall, Ideal 45.00
Bisque, Baby, Angel Winged, Movable Arms, High Boots, C.1880, 3 In. 130.00
Bisque, Brown Hair, Pink Bow, Molded Face, Chubby Body 45.00
Bisque, China Hands & Feet, Cloth Body, Blonde Hair, Striped Dress, 14 I 375.00
Bisque, Fat Apple Cheeks, Blue Eyes, Cloth Body, C.1880, 9 In. 110.00
Bisque, Kid Body, Black Molded Hair, Turned Head, 11 In. 150.00
Bisque, Movable Arms, Painted Hair & Face, C.1925 .... 20.00
Bisque, Puritan, Real Hair, Felt Hat, Boy & Girl, 4 3/4 In., Pair 75.00
Bisque, Wide-Eyed, Fat Tummy, Movable Arms, Germany, 4 1/2 In. 65.00
Black Baby, Composition, Dressed, 12 In. 50.00
Bru, Nurser, Dressed 5800.00
Bruno Schmidt 209, Character Baby, Flirty, 27 In. 1045.00
Buddy Lee, Western Clothes 125.00
Bye-Lo, Baby, Blue Eyes, Head, 15 In. 800.00
Bye-Lo, Bisque Head, Grace Storey Putnam, Signed, 17 In. 450.00
Bye-Lo, Bisque, Brown Sleep Eyes, 22 In. 950.00
Bye-Lo, Bisque, Movable Head, Arms, & Legs, Sleep Eyes, Blue Shoes, 7 In. 450.00
Bye-Lo, Celluloid Hands, Composition, 13 In. .... 200.00 To 285.00
Bye-Lo, Celluloid Hands, Molded Head, Silk Dress & Slip, 9 1/2 In. 350.00
Bye-Lo, Painted Hair & Face, Cradle, Marked, 4 1/2 In. 350.00
Bye-Lo, Stamped Body, Head, 14 1/2 In. 800.00
Bye-Lo, Twins, Blue-Eyed & Brown-Eyed, 14 In., Pair .... 750.00 To 1150.00
Candy Kids, Boy & Girl, Pair 200.00
Casimir Bru, Mannequin, C.1880, 46 In. 5750.00
Celluloid, Boy, Crepe Paper Base, Wire Stand, 1920s, 9 In. 15.00
Celluloid, Costumed Boy, Germany, Turtlemark, 3 In. 12.00
Celluloid, Flapper, Risque Skirt, 4 In. 6.50
Character, Mechanical, Soldier Boy, Bisque, Brown Suit, Germany, 9 In. 375.00
Charlie Chaplin, Boxed 195.00
Charlie McCarthy, Walker 175.00
Chase, Baby, Jointed, Dressed, Marked, Early 1890s, 27 In. 525.00
Chase, Baby, 12 In. 175.00
Chatty Cathy, Original Tagged Dress 35.00
China Head, Black Hair, Center Part, Soft Hands & Feet, 12 In. 75.00
China Head, Yellow Hat, Pink Ribbon, Rose, Germany, 3 1/4 In. 28.00
Cloth, George Washington, Painted Composition Head, 21 In. 35.00
Clown, Wax Head, Painted Features, 15 In. 65.00
Columbia, Turned Shoulder Head, Red Mohair Wig, Dressed, 23 In. 375.00
Composition, Cloth Body, Blonde Hair, Painted Features, 1920s, 15 In. 39.00
Cornhusk, Country Lady, 7 In., Pair 25.00
Cuno & Otto Dressel, Bisque, Set Brown Eyes, Human Hair Wig, Bib, 24 In. 275.00
D * R 101, Bisque, Braided Buns Above Ears, Dressed, 17 In. 2000.00
Dave Clark, Rock & Roll Dolls, Remco, 4 In., Set Of 5 .... 48.00
Dolley Madison, China Head, 30 In. 400.00
Dolley Madison, Leather Boots, Old Dress, Pink Luster, 24 In. 550.00
E.Denamur, Bisque Head, Ball-Jointed Body, Crocheted Dress, Hat, 21 In. 1150.00
Effanbee, Alice, Storybook, 11 In. 20.00
Effanbee, Anne Shirley, Bride, Original Outfit, 21 In. 125.00
Effanbee, Anne Shirley, Ice Skates, Composition 145.00
Effanbee, Baby, Sleep Eyes, 1924, 21 In. 55.00
Effanbee, Bobsey Twins, Freddie & Flossie, School Outfits, Plaid, Pair 38.50
Effanbee, Campfire Girl, 1957, All Original, 8 In. 35.00
Effanbee, Cinderella, Storybook, 11 In. 20.00
Effanbee, Dutch Girl, Original Clothes, Heart Bracelet, 1940s, 9 In. 125.00

Effanbee, Dy-Dee, Applied Ears, 11 1/2 In. 30.00
Effanbee, Gigi, Through The Years, Set Of 6 .... 200.00
Effanbee, Girl, With Watering Can, 1981 .... 125.00
Effanbee, Hans Brinker, Storybook, 11 In. 20.00
Effanbee, Jack & Jill, Storybook, 11 In., Pair 40.00
Effanbee, John Wayne, Cowboy, 1981 .... 50.00
Effanbee, Kissy, 15 In. 35.00
Effanbee, Lambkins, Bracelet, Original Clothes 185.00
Effanbee, Lawrence Welk's Champagne Lady, Vinyl & Plastic, 18 In. 65.00
Effanbee, Miss Revlon, Platinum Hair 55.00
Effanbee, Patricia, Blonde Yarn Hair, Marked, Boxed 425.00
Effanbee, Patricia, Braids, Composition, 14 In. 160.00
Effanbee, Patsy Ann, Composition, Original Wig, 19 In. 125.00
Effanbee, Patsy Ann, Roller Skates, Tagged Dress, 19 In. 165.00
Effanbee, Patsy Baby, Twin Boy & Girl, All Original, Pair 250.00
Effanbee, Patsy Joan, 14 In. 125.00
Effanbee, Patsy, All Original, 14 In. .... 75.00 To 150.00
Effanbee, Patsy, Jr., Composition, 11 In. 125.00
Effanbee, Patsy, Jr., Sleep Eyes, Nude, 12 In. 65.00
Effanbee, Renoir's Girl With Watering Can 95.00
Effanbee, Rosemary, 26 In. 165.00
Effanbee, Skippy, Composition, All Original 395.00
Effanbee, Suzette, Painted Face, Braids, Dress, 11 1/2 In. .... 65.00 To 85.00
Effanbee, Sweetie Pie, All Original, 20 In. 125.00
Effanbee, Tinkerbell, 1978 .... 35.00
Effanbee, Wicked Witch, Boxed 55.00
Ellis, Composition Head, Jointed Wooden Body, Metal Hands & Feet 650.00
Emmett Kelly, Ventriloquist 45.00
Faith Wick, Mrs. Wiggs Of The Cabbage Patch, Porcelain, Original 300.00
Faith Wick, Party Time Boy & Girl, Pair 80.00
Fanny Brice, Tagged 215.00
Fashion, Swivel Head, Kid Body, Closed Mouth, Original Clothes, 14 In. 1400.00
Flat Top, Cloth Body, Black Hairdo, Porcelain Arms, C.1858, 13 In. 165.00
Foxy Grandpa, Papier-Mache, 1901 .... 68.00
Fran Schmitt, Toddler, Straight Leg, Velvet & Crepe Outfit, 15 1/2 In. 525.00
French, Bisque Arms, Original Wig, Clothes, Extra Outfit, 14 In. 1450.00
French, Bisque Head & Shoulders, Leather Body, 11 1/2 In. 875.00
French, Bisque Head, Kid Body, Dressed, 12 In. 850.00
French, Bisque Head, Paperweight Eyes, Ball Jointed, Silk Dress, 16 In. 2100.00
French, Bisque Swivel Head, Leather Body, Tafetta Dress, 14 1/2 In. 1195.00
French, Bisque, Kid Body, Marked, Original Clothes, 18 In. 95.00
French, Bisque, Punchinello, Original Silk Costume 1800.00
French, Bisque, Swivel Head, Rose Silk Dress, Parasol, 12 In. 1150.00
French, Boudoir, Blonde, Composition & Cloth, Dressed, 27 In. 65.00
French, Cherie, Limoges, Marked, 16 In. 700.00
French, Chunky Body, Sleep Eyes, Dressed, 26 In. 750.00
French, La Donte, Blonde Hair, Pale Blue Moire Gown, 18 In. 750.00
French, Open Mouth, Ball-Jointed, Marked, 24 In. 950.00
Frozen Charlotte, Bisque, Penny Doll, 1 1/8 In. 20.00
Frozen Charlotte, Boxed, 2 In. 35.00
Frozen Charlotte, Painted Head, Molded Hair, Pink Luster Head, 15 In. 275.00
Frozen Charlotte, Pink Luster Face & Body, Molded Hat, 2 1/2 In. 150.00
Frozen Charlotte, Pink Luster Face, Gold Slippers, 4 1/2 In. 150.00
Frozen Charlotte, Pink Luster, 3 1/2 In. 100.00
    DOLL, FULPER, see also Doll, Horsman
Fulper, Baby, Blue Sleep Eyes, 20 In. 695.00
Fulper, Boy, Open Mouth, Kid Body, Wooden Arms, Marked, 9 1/2 In. 450.00
Fulper, Girl, Pink Linen Dress, Hat To Match, 22 In. 600.00
G.Borgfelt, Swivel Head, Open-Close Eyes, Ball-Jointed Body, 24 In. 350.00
G.I.Joe, Original Clothes 20.00
Gebruder Heubach No.7118, Character, Glass Eyes, 13 1/2 In. 495.00
Gebruder Heubach, Girl, Bisque, Sleep Eyes, Open Mouth, Red Dress, 21 In. 735.00
Gebruder Krauss No.8192, Character Girl, Ball-Jointed Body, 21 In. 735.00
Gebruder Krauss, Bisque, Fashion, Open Mouth, Original Body & Wig 375.00

Gebruder Krauss, Pouty Girl, Dressed, 7 In. 350.00
Georgene Averill, Bonnie Babe, 14 In. 850.00
Gerber, Baby, Black 20.00
German, Bisque Head, Jointed Composition Body, 1912, Dressed, 24 In. 425.00
German, Boy, Celluloid, Original Costume, Turtle Mark, 3 In. 20.00
German, Boy, Leather Hands & Feet, Kid Body, Signed 200.00
German, Dollhouse Family, Cloth Bodies, Bisque Heads, 4 Piece 600.00
German, Fashion, Lady, Bisque, C.1870, 23 In. .... *Illus* 1250.00
German, Fashion, Lady, Turned Head, Brown Sleep Eyes, 15 1/2 In. 695.00
German, Happifats, Boy, C In Circle Mark, Bisque, 4 1/4 In. 150.00
German, Happifats, Pink Dress, 3 1/2 In., Pair 450.00
German, Mechanical, Soldier Boy, Head Moves Side To Side, C.1900, 9 In. 375.00
German, No.2, Paperweight Eyes, Heavy Brows, Jointed Body, 16 In. 370.00
German, No.196, Bisque, Fur Eyebrows, 30 In. 795.00
German, Tilted Head, Marked, 6 In. 650.00
German, Wanda, Walker, All Original, Instructions, Boxed, 18 In. 165.00
Ginny, Party Dress & Hat, Pink, Brunette, 1954-1956 .... 110.00
Girl Scout, Brownie Uniform, Fluffy Wig, Vinyl, 8 In. 40.00
Gladdy, Painted Clay Head, 20 In. 950.00
Goebel, Bisque Socket Head, Sleep Eyes, Composition Body, 17 In. 175.00
Googly, Bisque Head, Glass Sleep Eyes, Baby Body, Incised 163, 13 In. 2000.00
Handwerck & Halbig, Bisque, Ball-Jointed, Sleep Eyes, 22 In. 295.00
Handwerck & Halbig, Girl, White Clothing, Original Wig, 33 In. 1400.00
Handwerck, Ball-Jointed, Pierced Ears, Human Hair, Signed, 24 In. 425.00
Handwerck, Bisque Head, Kid Body, Brown Eyes, Open Mouth, 11 In. 295.00
Handwerck, Bisque Head, Open Mouth, Teeth, Open-Close Eyes, 19 In. 595.00
Handwerck, Bisque, Kid Body, 17 In. 275.00
Handwerck, Boy, Brown Eyes, George Washington Velvet Suit, 23 In. 400.00
Handwerck, Brown Set Eyes, Brown Wig, Pink Dress, 33 1/2 In. 1100.00
Handwerck, Catherine The Great Dress, 32 In. 1650.00
Handwerck, Girl, Bisque Head, Open-Close Eyes, Blonde Wig, 19 In. 595.00
Handwerck, Girl, Long Blonde Mohair Wig, 31 In. 895.00
Handwerck, Open Mouth, Blue Glass Eyes, Blonde Human Hair, 13 1/2 In. 295.00
Handwerck, Pierced Ears, Blue Eyes, 28 In. 775.00
Handwerck, Pierced Ears, Old Dress, 33 In. 1000.00
Handwerck, Queen Louise, Red Velvet Outfit, 26 In. 775.00
Hasbro, Flying Nun, Original Costume, 1967 .... 25.00
Hasbro, That Kid, 1967, 14 In. 75.00
HEbee, Bisque, Blue Booties With Ribbons, 7 In. 650.00
Heubach Koppelsdorf 342, Baby, Bent Limb, Flirty Eyes, 26 In. 525.00
Heubach Koppelsdorf 399, Character Baby, Black, 12 In. 450.00
Heubach Koppelsdorf 6969, Pouty Boy, Composition & Bisque, 18 In. 2100.00
Heubach Koppelsdorf 7602, Baby, Closed Mouth, Intaglio Eyes, Dressed 695.00
Heubach Koppelsdorf, Baby, Bent Limb, Sleep Eyes, Molded Tongue, 20 In. 465.00
Heubach Koppelsdorf, Baby, Bisque, Gray Eyes, Open Mouth, 11 In. 535.00
Heubach Koppelsdorf, Baby, Blue Sleep Eyes, Blonde Wig, 10 In. 275.00
Heubach Koppelsdorf, Baby, Closed Mouth, 7 1/2 In. 290.00
Heubach Koppelsdorf, Baby, Pants & Jacket, Tam, Jointed, 8 1/2 In. 475.00
Heubach Koppelsdorf, Bisque Head, Jointed Oilcloth Body, Outfit, 12 In. 165.00
Heubach Koppelsdorf, Scot's Outfit, All Original, 10 In. 125.00
Heubach Koppelsdorf, Set Blue Eyes, 1900-1908, 26 In. 350.00
Heubach Koppelsdorf, Toddler, 20 In. 335.00
Heubach, Baby, Bisque Head, Jointed Body, Dressed, 11 1/2 In. 475.00
Heubach, Bisque Head, Arms, Cloth Body, Blue Eyes, Signed, 21 In. 225.00
Heubach, Blue Eyes, Wheat Hair, White Lawn Dress, Pink Bonnet, 24 In. 350.00
Heubach, Pouty Boy, Flopped Hair, Intaglio Eyes, 11 In. 375.00
Heubach, Toddler, 17 In. 295.00
Holz-Masse, Girl, Undressed 145.00
Horsman, Betsy McCall, Original Outfit, 29 In. 50.00
Horsman, Billiken, 1909, 12 In. 175.00
Horsman, Boy, Stuffed, Vinyl 22.00
Horsman, Campbell Kid, Original Clothes, 1910, 11 In. 100.00
Horsman, Girl, Crier, Red Wig, Brown Eyes, Open Mouth, Blue Dress, 20 In. 85.00

Horsman, Hansel & Gretel, 1957, 15 In., Pair 175.00
Horsman, Living Bye Bye Baby, Boxed 50.00
Horsman, Marked EIH, Inc., Co., 19 In. 50.00
Horsman, Mary Poppins, Tagged Clothes, 26 In. 75.00
Horsman, Poor Pitiful Pearl, Dress, Socks, 1963, 17 In. .... 30.00 To 38.50
Ideal, Betsy Baby, Layette, 1964, Boxed 35.00
Ideal, Bizzy Lizzy, Original 20.00
Ideal, Bonnie Braids, Marked 45.00
Ideal, Boy, Flirty Eyes, Molded Brown Hair, Crawler Outfit, 20 In. 35.00
Ideal, Deanna Durbin, Composition, Original Tagged Dress, 20 In. 385.00
Ideal, Jiminy Cricket, Flexible, Wooden, 8 In. 55.00
Ideal, Mary Hartline, Bisque, Storybook, 7 In. 15.00
Ideal, Patsy Baby, Painted Eyes, Dress 95.00
Ideal, Patty Playpal, Blonde Hair 60.00
Ideal, Sara Ann, Original Dress 65.00
Ideal, Shirley Temple, 1973, Vinyl, 16 In. 120.00
Ideal, Snoozie, Sleep Eyes, 20 In. 40.00
Ideal, Toni, Original Dress, 15 In. 55.00
    DOLL, INDIAN, see Indian, Doll
    DOLL, J.D.K., see also Doll, Kestner
J.D.K., Baby, Painted Blue Eyes, Molded Hair, 14 In. 750.00
J.D.K., Hilda, 5-Piece Bent Limb Baby Body, 16 1/2 In. 2700.00
J.D.K., Toddler, Sleep Eyes, Open-Close Mouth, Jointed, Dressed, 14 In. 895.00
J.D.K., Twitter Tongue, 33 In. 1499.00
J.D.K.143, Character, Bent Limb, Jointed Body, Bisque Head, 8 In. 325.00
J.D.K.152, Baby, The Talker, Brown Eyes, 16 In. 640.00
J.D.K.211, Baby, Sleep Eyes, Open-Close Mouth, 22 In. 700.00
J.D.K.211, Character Baby, Fur Wig, White Romper, 14 In. 495.00
J.D.K.221, Googly, Composition Body, Blonde Wig, 12 In. 1095.00
J.D.K.221, Toddler, Googly Sleep Eyes, 13 In. 3350.00
J.D.K.226, Baby, Bisque Head, Sleep Eyes, 2 Upper Teeth, Marked, 14 In. 400.00
J.D.K.243, Oriental Baby, 13 In. 1300.00
J.D.K.260, Toddler, Stamped Body & Wig, Leather Shoes, 22 In. 795.00
Jane Withers, 20 In. 550.00
Japan, Betty Boop, 7 In. 12.00
Japan, Bisque, Movable Arms, Bow In Hair, Painted Features, Dress, 5 In. 28.00
Joe Palooka, Jointed, Wooden, 5 1/2 In. 42.50
Julia, Diahann Carroll, Mattel, 1968, Box 37.50
Juliet, Brown Velvet Gown, 12 In. 35.00
Jumeau, Baby, Black, Closed Mouth, Plaid Silk Dress, Has Toy, 18 In. 3500.00
Jumeau, Baby, Closed Mouth, Blue Eyes, French Curls, 15 In. 2200.00
Jumeau, Bisque Head, Glass Sleep Eyes, Ball-Jointed, Silk Dress, 25 In. 995.00
Jumeau, Bisque Head, Glass Sleep Eyes, Silk Dress, Marked, 22 In. 995.00
Jumeau, Bisque Head, Open Mouth, Ball-Jointed, Dressed 24 1/2 In. 995.00
Jumeau, Bisque Head, Open Mouth, Teeth, Pigtails, Marked 1907, 29 In. 1800.00
Jumeau, Bisque Head, Paperweight Eyes, Jointed Body, Marked .... 1450.00 To 3600.00
Jumeau, Bisque Head, Paperweight Eyes, Pierced Ears, 15 In. 3300.00
Jumeau, Bisque Head, Sleep Eyes, Ball-Jointed, Underclothes, 27 In. 1150.00
Jumeau, Bisque Head, Sleep Eyes, Underclothes, 22 In. 995.00
Jumeau, Bisque, Open Mouth, Paperweight Eyes, 23 In. 1795.00
Jumeau, Bisque, Paperweight Blue Eyes, Ball-Jointed, Dressed, 21 In. 1495.00
Jumeau, Blue Paperweight Eyes, Ecru Silk Dress, Body Sticker, 18 In 1400.00
Jumeau, Blue Set Eyes, Bisque, Pink Dress, Apron, 16 In. 475.00
Jumeau, Boy, 2 Rows Of Teeth, Paperweight Eyes, Straight Wrist, 17 In. 975.00
Jumeau, Chunky Body, Sleep Eyes, Human Hair Wig, C.1907, 25 In. 1850.00
Jumeau, Closed Mouth, Bisque Head, Paperweight Eyes, 26 In. 3000.00
Jumeau, Closed Mouth, Blue Eyes, 27 In. 4950.00
Jumeau, Closed Mouth, Brown Eyes, Pierced Ears, 16 In. 2500.00
Jumeau, Closed Mouth, Brown Eyes, 17 In. 3450.00
Jumeau, Compostion Jointed Body, Bisque Head, Marked, 32 In. 3300.00
Jumeau, Girl, Original Wig & Dress, Marked, 15 In. 1885.00
Jumeau, Head Turns, Throws Kiss, Pink Silk Dress, Pull String, 23 In. 1800.00
Jumeau, Laughing, Bisque Head, Sleep Eyes, 2 Upper Teeth, 27 In. 2400.00
Jumeau, Laughing, Composition, 14 In. .... *Illus* 1300.00

Jumeau, Long Curls, Paperweight Eyes, Slit Mouth, Marked No.9, 23 In. 1650.00
Jumeau, Open Mouth, Blue Eyes, 24 In. 2350.00
Jumeau, Open Mouth, Blue Glass Eyes, Bisque, Pink Dress, Bonnet, 15 In. 545.00
Jumeau, Open Mouth, Carousel, Silk Dress, 32 In. 3500.00
Jumeau, Open Mouth, Paperweight Eyes, Old Silk Clothes, 14 In. 995.00
Jumeau, Open Mouth, Pierced Ears, Ball-Jointed Body, 1907, 29 In. 1975.00
Jumeau, Paperweight Eyes, Human Hair Wig To Hips, Yellow Dress, 31 In. 1100.00
Jumeau, Walker, Composition Body, Legs Move Head Side To Side, 23 In. 1600.00
Jumeau, Yellow Cotton Dress, Blue Bathing Shoes, New Wig, Marked, 26 In. 1400.00
Juno, Tin Head, Leather Body, 13 In. 75.00
K * R 109, Pouty, Brown Eyes, Pink Satin Lace Dress, Shoes, 14 In. 4950.00
K * R 115, Toddler, Blue Sleep Eyes, Painted Hair, 14 In. 795.00
K * R 117, Character Girl, Brown Hair, Blue Eyes, 26 In. 1200.00
K * R 117, Child Like Expression, Original Dress, 30 In. 2000.00
K * R 117N, Mein Liebling .... *Illus* 7250.00
K * R 122, Character Baby, 23 In. 995.00
K * R 122, Chubby Body, 2o 1/2 In. 850.00
K * R 126, Baby, Flirty Eyes, 26 In. 765.00
K * R 126, Bisque Head, Spring Tongue, Jointed Body, Dressed, 17 In. 375.00
K * R 126, Brown Sleep Eyes, Christening Dress, 29 In. 2000.00
K * R 126, Chubby Baby, Flirty Eyes, 25 1/2 In. 1450.00
K * R, Baby, All Original, 22 In. 550.00
K * R, Blue Sleep Eyes, 5-Piece Body, Painted-On Shoes, 10 In. 195.00
K * R, Character, Girl, Flirty Sleep Eyes, Celluloid, Marked, 19 In. 300.00
K * R, Princess Elizabeth, All Original, 20 In. 2600.00
K * R, Sleep Eyes, Ball-Jointed, Voice Box, Yellow Dress, 31 In. 850.00
Kallus, Baby Bouquet, Original Clothes, 16 In. 1995.00
Kathe Kruse, Anillie, 19 In. 325.00
Kathe Kruse, Astrid, 10 In. 140.00
Kathe Kruse, Bear, Brown, 21 In. 125.00
Kathe Kruse, Boy, Celluloid, 18 In. .... *Illus* 550.00
Kathe Kruse, Boy, Cloth, Original Wrist Tag, 19 In. 695.00
Kathe Kruse, Boy, Molded Muslin, Original Clothes, 19 In. 650.00
Kathe Kruse, Cissette, Blue Flowered Dress 100.00
Kathe Kruse, Du Mein, Baby 335.00
Kathe Kruse, Girl, Red Braids, Freckles, 1974, Boxed, 9 In. 185.00
Kathe Kruse, Gisela, 19 In. 325.00
Kathe Kruse, Julie, 20 3/4 In. 450.00
Kathe Kruse, Martina, 19 In. 325.00
Kathe Kruse, Molded Muslin, Painted Head, Jointed Body, Marked, 21 In. 450.00
Kathe Kruse, Otto, 19 In. 325.00
Kathe Kruse, Pauline, 19 In. 325.00
Kathe Kruse, Regina, 20 3/4 In. 375.00
Kathy Kruse, Boy & Girl, Turtlemark, Stands, 1959, 9 In., Pair 665.00
Kathy Kruse, Yorgel, 19 In. 325.00
Ken, Football Player, Mattel 55.00
    DOLL, KESTNER, see also Doll, J.D.K.
Kestner 136, Girl, Brown Sleep Eyes, Checked Outfit, Straw Hat, 24 In. 595.00
Kestner 146, Open Mouth, Ball-Jointed, Blue Sleep Eyes, 24 In. 450.00
Kestner 146, Sleep Eyes, Bisque, Ball-Jointed, White Dress, 28 In. 695.00
Kestner 147, Kid Body, Dress & Pantaloons, Bisque, 21 In. 350.00
Kestner 147, Paperweight Eyes, Ivory Dress & Hat, 20 In. 385.00
Kestner 151, Baby, Open-Close Mouth, Brown Eyes, 12 In. 395.00
Kestner 151, Character Baby, Solid Dome, 12 1/2 In. 485.00
Kestner 164, Blue Eyes, Ball-Jointed Body, Long Blonde Curls, 30 In. 575.00
Kestner 164, Brown Hair & Eyes, Red Velvet Dress & Hat, 25 In. 575.00
Kestner 166, Kid Body, Human Hair Wig, Sleep Eyes, 20 In. 475.00
Kestner 168, Carved Teeth, Sleep Eyes, Jointed, Boxed, 19 In. 350.00
Kestner 171, Bisque, Ball-Jointed, Original Wig, Antique Dress, 28 In. 495.00
Kestner 171, Daisy, Bisque Head, Stamped Jointed Body, French Curls 995.00
Kestner 171, Daisy, Sleep Eyes, Human Hair Wig, Ball-Jointed, 28 In. 395.00
Kestner 171, Girl, 31 In. 600.00
Kestner 211, Baby, Life Size 500.00

Dolls, Germany, Fashion, Lady, Bisque, C.1870, 23 In.;
Kathe Kruse, Boy, Celluloid, 18 In.

(See Pages 196, 197)

Doll, Jumeau, Laughing, Composition, 14 In.

Doll, K * R 117N, Mein Liebling

Kestner 214, Character, Brown Eyes, Blonde Human Hair Wig, 25 In. 600.00
Kestner 247, Baby, Hilda Look-Alike, Bent Limb, Sleep Eyes, 19 In. 1000.00
Kestner 257, Character Baby, 20 In. 595.00
Kestner 260, Character Girl, Blue Satin Dress & Hat, 22 In. 600.00
Kestner, Baby, All Bisque, Open-Close Mouth, Original Pate & Wig, 7 In. 675.00
Kestner, Bisque, Closed Mouth, C.1885, 21 In. .... *Illus* 2300.00
Kestner, Celluloid Head, Glass Sleep Eyes, Blonde, Turtle Mark, 5 In. 15.00
Kestner, Closed Mouth, Kid Body, Sleep Eyes, Blue Lace Dress, 20 In. 1400.00
Kestner, Closed Mouth, 21 In. 675.00
Kestner, Gibson Girl, Ecru Silk & Lace Dress, 10 In. 1100.00
Kestner, Kid Body, Brown Stationary Eyes, Marked, 14 In. 695.00
Kestner, Open Mouth, Jointed Kid Body, Bisque, Long White Dress, 20 In. 495.00
Kestner, Open-Close Mouth, Leather Body, 13 In. 375.00
Kestner, Sleep Eyes, Open Mouth, Jointed, Blue Silk Dress, 7 In. 295.00
    DOLL, KEWPIE, see Kewpie, Doll
Kiddie Toy, Bisque Head, Sleep Eyes, Cloth Body, Dressed, Marked, 19 In. 550.00
Kley & Hahn, Character Baby, 5-Piece Bent Limb Body, 20 In. 750.00
Kley & Hahn, Character Boy, Toddler Body, Wobbly Tongue, 18 In. 795.00
Kley & Hahn, Walker, 33 In. 1000.00
Lenci, Boy, All Original, Mountain Climber, Knapsack, 14 In. 495.00
Lenci, Corinne, 20 In. 245.00
Lenci, Deborah, Numbered, 18 In. 255.00
Lenci, Girl, Side Glance Eyes, 1930s, 27 1/2 In. 195.00
Lenci, Mouse, Felt, Tagged, 15 In. 75.00

(See Page 199)

Doll, Kestner, Bisque, Closed Mouth, C.1885, 21 In.

Lenci, Stefania, Signed & Numbered, 18 In.	255.00
Lenci, Susannah, 20 In.	245.00
Lenci, Swivel Head, Jointed Shoulders, All Felt, Dressed, 20 1/2 In.	250.00
Lissy Meg, Blue Dress, 12 In.	185.00
Little Genius, Hard Plastic, Organdy Dress & Bonnet, 12 In.	55.00
Little Lulu, Felt, 1940s, 11 In.	35.00
Madame Alexander, Agatha Portrait, 1967, 8 In.	650.00
Madame Alexander, Agatha, Dressed In Lavender, Boxed	285.00
Madame Alexander, Agatha, Turquoise	350.00
Madame Alexander, Agatha, Wrist Tag, 1979, Boxed	225.00 To 395.00
Madame Alexander, Alexanderkins, 1953	25.00
Madame Alexander, Alice In Wonderland, Costume Tagged, 14 In.	295.00
Madame Alexander, Amish Girl, 8 In.	500.00
Madame Alexander, Amy, Boxed, 8 In.	45.00
Madame Alexander, Antony & Cleopatra, Pair	105.00
Madame Alexander, Babs Skater, Original Clothes, 14 In.	200.00
Madame Alexander, Baby Brother, 14 In.	65.00
Madame Alexander, Baby Genius, Cloth Body, All Original, 19 In.	150.00
Madame Alexander, Baby McGuffey, 11 In.	115.00
Madame Alexander, Baby Sister, 14 In.	65.00
Madame Alexander, Beth, Straight Leg, Non-Walker, 1973-75, 8 In.	125.00
Madame Alexander, Beth, Walker, Plastic, Green Taffeta Dress, 14 In.	185.00
Madame Alexander, Betsy McCall, 1961, 8 In.	125.00
Madame Alexander, Betsy Ross, 8 In.	45.00
Madame Alexander, Black Cynthia, 18 In.	575.00
Madame Alexander, Boy & Girl, Austrian, 8 In., Pair	85.00
Madame Alexander, Boy, Argentinian, 8 In.	575.00
Madame Alexander, Boy, Indian, 8 In.	500.00
Madame Alexander, Boy, Peruvian, 8 In.	525.00
Madame Alexander, Bride, 14 In.	70.00
Madame Alexander, Buster Brown	135.00
Madame Alexander, Caroline, Original Pink Dress, Tagged	225.00 To 300.00
Madame Alexander, Cheri, All Original, 18 In.	250.00
Madame Alexander, Cissette, Ball Gown	250.00
Madame Alexander, Cissy, Theater Dress & Coat	200.00
Madame Alexander, Cornelia, 1976	495.00
Madame Alexander, Cowboy, 8 In.	450.00
Madame Alexander, Deanna Durbin, 18 In.	125.00

Madame Alexander, Degas Girl, 21 In.	58.00
Madame Alexander, Dionne Quintuplets, Strollers, Set Of 5	975.00
Madame Alexander, Dolley Madison	175.00
Madame Alexander, Dryper Baby, 1950s, 10 In.	30.00
Madame Alexander, Elise, Ballerina, Blue, 17 In.	250.00
Madame Alexander, Elise, Ballerina, Pink Outfit, 15 1/2 In .... 140.00 To	185.00
Madame Alexander, Elise, Ballerina, Silver, 17 In.	75.00
Madame Alexander, Elise, Ballerina, 1957, Boxed, 15 1/2 In.	225.00
Madame Alexander, Elise, Bride, 21 In. .... 110.00 To	135.00
Madame Alexander, Elise, Bridesmaid, Boxed .... 130.00 To	190.00
Madame Alexander, Elise, Original Dress & Hat, 1960, 14 In.	95.00
Madame Alexander, Enchanted Doll, Certificate, Boxed, 8 In .... 275.00 To	350.00
Madame Alexander, Fisher Quints, Original Wrappers, 8 In., Set Of 5	370.00
Madame Alexander, Floradora, 13 In.	225.00
Madame Alexander, Gainsborough, 1978, Boxed	325.00
Madame Alexander, Girl, Hawaiian, Bent Knee .... 350.00 To	475.00
Madame Alexander, Girl, Hungarian, Bent Knee, Crown Of Jewels, 8 In.	110.00
Madame Alexander, Girl, Indian, 8 In.	500.00
Madame Alexander, Girl, Irish, Boxed, 8 In.	100.00
Madame Alexander, Girl, Korean, Maggie Face, 8 In.	375.00
Madame Alexander, Girl, Mexican, Boxed, 8 In.	100.00
Madame Alexander, Girl, Netherlands, 8 In.	37.00
Madame Alexander, Girl, Swedish, Bent Knee, 8 In.	75.00
Madame Alexander, Girl, Yugoslavian, Boxed, 8 In.	100.00
Madame Alexander, Godey, 1977, Boxed, 21 In. .... 475.00 To	595.00
Madame Alexander, Goya, 21 In.	295.00
Madame Alexander, Grandma Jane, Blue Check Dress, Glasses, 13 In.	125.00
Madame Alexander, Heidi	60.00
Madame Alexander, Huggums, Blue Pinafore, Large	85.00
Madame Alexander, Jacqueline Kennedy, Riding Outfit, Boxed, 21 In.	850.00
Madame Alexander, Japanese Bride, 12 In.	50.00
Madame Alexander, Jo, Boxed, 8 In.	45.00
Madame Alexander, Jo, Boxed, 12 In.	60.00
Madame Alexander, Josephine, Pinky	75.00
Madame Alexander, Laurie, Bent Knees, Original Clothes, 1966, 8 In.	200.00
Madame Alexander, Laurie, 1973, Marked Alex, 8 In.	125.00
Madame Alexander, Liesel, Sound Of Music, 14 In.	140.00
Madame Alexander, Lissy, Bride, 1957, Boxed	325.00
Madame Alexander, Lissy, Bridesmaid, Blue Gown	225.00
Madame Alexander, Little Butch, Vinyl, Blonde Hair, Yellow & White Suit	65.00
Madame Alexander, Little Lord Fauntleroy	100.00
Madame Alexander, Little Women & Laurie, 12 In., Set Of 5 .... 325.00 To	385.00
Madame Alexander, Lucinda, 1979, 14 In.	70.00
Madame Alexander, Mabel, 15 In.	240.00
Madame Alexander, Margaret O'Brien, All Original, 14 1/2 In.	400.00
Madame Alexander, Margaret O'Brien, Dressed, 1946, 21 In.	650.00
Madame Alexander, Marionette, Bashful	125.00
Madame Alexander, Marmie, Molded, 1963, 12 In.	75.00
Madame Alexander, Marta, Sound Of Music, 8 In.	150.00
Madame Alexander, Martha Randolph	175.00
Madame Alexander, Mary Mine, 12 In.	85.00
Madame Alexander, Mary Mine, 18 In.	100.00
Madame Alexander, Mary Todd Lincoln	150.00
Madame Alexander, Mary, Mary, 1965-1972, 8 In.	125.00
Madame Alexander, McGuffey Ana, Little Betty Face, 1935-39, 10 In.	175.00
Madame Alexander, McGuffey, All Original, 14 In.	250.00
Madame Alexander, Melanie, Dressed In White, Boxed	285.00
Madame Alexander, Melanie, Pink	300.00
Madame Alexander, Mimi, Scotch Costume, Jointed Wrist & Waist, 30 In.	325.00
Madame Alexander, Miss Muffet, 8 In.	45.00
Madame Alexander, Napoleon	60.00
Madame Alexander, Napoleon, Josephine, 12 In., Set Of 2 .... 135.00 To	150.00
Madame Alexander, Orphan Annie	225.00
Madame Alexander, Peter Pan, Amberg Body, Dressed, Sculptured Hair	350.00

Madame Alexander, Pinky, Blue Boy, Pair 125.00
Madame Alexander, Pinky, 8 In. 60.00
Madame Alexander, President's Wives, Louisa Adams, 1st Set 195.00
Madame Alexander, President's Wives, Martha Randolph, 1st Set 195.00
Madame Alexander, President's Wives, Martha Washington, 1st Series 300.00
Madame Alexander, President's Wives, Polk, Boxed 135.00
Madame Alexander, President's Wives, 1st Set, Boxed .... 1375.00 To 1500.00
Madame Alexander, President's Wives, 2nd Set, Boxed .... 650.00 To 775.00
Madame Alexander, Prince Philip, Hard Plastic, Tagged, 1953, 18 In. 350.00
Madame Alexander, Princess Elizabeth, All Original, 14 In. 225.00
Madame Alexander, Princess Elizabeth, Composition, Blue Dress, 23 In. 350.00
Madame Alexander, Priscilla, Bent Knee, Basket 265.00
Madame Alexander, Priscilla, 8 In. 350.00
Madame Alexander, Puddin, 21 In. .... 50.00 To 85.00
Madame Alexander, Pussy Cat, Silk Coat & Hat, Tagged, 1972, 14 In. 125.00
Madame Alexander, Pussy Cat, 20 In. 65.00
Madame Alexander, Rabbit, Original Clothes 225.00
Madame Alexander, Red Boy, 8 In. 60.00
Madame Alexander, Renoir Girl, 1968 .... 225.00
Madame Alexander, Romeo 60.00
Madame Alexander, Romeo & Juliet, Pair 125.00
Madame Alexander, Scarlett, Floral Dress, Straw Hat, 8 In. 275.00
Madame Alexander, Scarlett, Green Velvet Outfit, 21 In. 300.00
Madame Alexander, Scarlett, White Organdy Dress, Green Sash, 8 In. 75.00
Madame Alexander, Skater, 8 In. 300.00
Madame Alexander, Sleeping Beauty 70.00
Madame Alexander, Sonja Henie, Bride, Composition, White Dress, 20 In. 295.00
Madame Alexander, Sonja Henie, Original Dress & Skates, 14 In. 200.00
Madame Alexander, Sweet Sue Sophisticate, 14 In. 75.00
Madame Alexander, Sweet Tears, Dress, Pacifier, 1965, 9 In. .... 95.00 To 165.00
Madame Alexander, Victoria, Christening Dress 85.00
Madame Alexander, Victoria, 20 In. .... 65.00 To 70.00
Madame Alexander, Winnie Walker, Large 175.00
Madame Alexander, Yvonne, Quintuplet, Paper Booklet, Pin, 11 In. 275.00
Mama, Brown Celluloid Over Tin Eyes, Blonde Wig, 1920-30's, 22 In. 95.00
Mary Ann, 21 In. 200.00
Mary Lee, 21 In. 200.00
Mattel, Barbie, Bubble Cut, Bride, 1962 .... 35.00
Mattel, Barbie, No.3, Bubble Haircut .... 85.00 To 150.00
Mattel, Barbie, No.75, Blonde Ponytail 55.00
Mattel, Dick Van Dyke, Rag, Voice String 30.00
Mattel, Dr.Doolittle, 1976, 16 In. 75.00
Mattel, Skipper, Bendable Legs, 1965 .... 35.00
Mattel, Skooter, 1965 .... 20.00
Mego, Batman, Magnetic, 12 1/2 In. 18.00
Mexico, Composition Head, Cloth Body, Blouse & Skirt, C.1920, 12 In. 28.00
Milk Bottle, Black Mammy, Original Clothes, 1910 .... 35.00
Milliner's Model, Papier-Mache Shoulders, Head, Kid Body, Dressed 550.00
Miss Revlon, 2 Dresses 48.00
Mona Lisa, Smiling, French Fashion, 20 In. 2200.00
Morimura Bros., Baby, Bent Limb, 14 In. 175.00
Morimura Bros., Bisque Socket Head, Sleep Eyes, Jointed, Dressed, 15 In. 275.00
Mr.Bluster, Squeak Toy, Rubber, Original Box, 6 In. 25.00
Music, Madame Hendren, Cylinder, 2 Records 325.00
Mutt & Jeff, Ball-Jointed 250.00
Nippon, Bisque, Movable Hands, 3 In. 40.00
Nippon, Boy, Bisque, 4 1/4 In. 30.00
Nippon, China Head, Kidskin, Cloth Body, Incised Mark, 15 In. 100.00
Nippon, Molded Blonde Hair, Movable Arms, Dress, 5 1/4 In. 45.00
Norah Wellings, Black Child, Glass Eyes, Hoop Earrings, 13 1/2 In. 165.00
Norah Wellings, Polynesian Girl, Glass Eyes, Label, 18 In. 150.00
Oriental, Ceremonial, Headdress, Papier-Mache Head, 28 In. 250.00
        DOLL, PAPER, see Paper Doll

Papier-Mache, Black Child, Jointed, Hair, C.1885, 6 1/2 In. 200.00
Papier-Mache, Boy, Glass Eyes, 15 In. 950.00
Papier-Mache, Child, Turned Head, Paperweight Eyes, Mohair Wig, 19 In. 275.00
Papier-Mache, Cloth Body, Blonde Hair, German, 18 In. 95.00
Papier-Mache, German, Brown Wig, Painted Eyes, 5-Piece Body, 9 In. 95.00
Papier-Mache, Girl, Molded Blonde Hair, 11 1/2 In. 65.00
Parian, Bisque Head, Molded Hair, Painted Eyes, Cloth Body, 20 1/2 In. 450.00
Parian, Girl, Molded Blonde Hair, Exposed Ears, 13 In. 175.00
Parsons Jackson, Baby Boy, Signed, Fully Dressed, 14 In. 395.00
Pat-O-Pat, Claps Hands, Cloth 100.00
Paul Revere, Bisque Head, Marked PRP No.2, Blue Eyes, Pink Dress 155.00
Penny Farthing, Jointed, Painted Face, Hands, & Feet, Carved Pine, 10 In. 35.00

DOLL, PINCUSHION, see Pincushion Doll

Quaker Oats Crackle, Photo Giveaway 65.00
Queen Louise, Brown Eyes, Red Hair, White Dress & Hat, 23 1/2 In. 300.00
R & A, Girl, Bisque Swivel Head, Leather Body, 14 In. 275.00
Rag, Cat, Printed On Fabric 45.00
Rag, Cream-O-Wheat, Black Man, Printed On Fabric, 17 In. .... 55.00 To 95.00
Rag, Elmer Fudd 20.00
Rag, Gauze Face, 9 In. 150.00
Rag, Harold Lloyd, Printed On Fabric 95.00
Rag, Soldier, Painted By S.Finburgh, 1915, 18 In. 65.00
Revalo, Toddler Boy, 14 1/2 In. 400.00
Revere Pottery, Bisque Head, Glass Eyes, C.1920, 12 In. .... *Illus* 110.00
Revlon, Raving Beauty, Paper Flyer, Boxed, 17 In. 145.00
Roly Poly, Oriental, 3 In. 15.00
Ruth, China, Turned Head, Old Dress, 30 In. 450.00

DOLL, S & H, see also Doll, Bergmann; Doll, Simon & Halbig

S & H 126, Toddler, Flirty Eyes, Dressed, 24 In. 625.00
S & H 139, Girl, Black, 10 1/2 In. 495.00
S & H 170/4, Clown, Bisque, Jointed Composition Body .... *Illus* 1200.00
S & H 949, Brown Hair & Eyes, Orange Chemise Dress, 12 In. 375.00
S & H 1009, Bisque, Set Eyes, Ball-Jointed, 25 1/2 In. 450.00
S & H 1009, Original Hair, Brown Eyes, Red Lace Dress & Hat, 18 In. 600.00
S & H 1009, Swivel Neck, Fashion Body, Bisque Lower Arms, 24 In. 695.00
S & H 1078, Bisque Head, Pierced Ears, Jointed Body, Dressed, 11 1/2 In. 325.00
S & H 1079, Blue Eyes, Blonde Wig, Dress & Hat, 31 In. .... 750.00 To 800.00
S & H 1079, Brown Sleep Eyes, Blonde, Pink Taffeta Dress, 26 In. 650.00
S & H 1079, French Body, Sleep Eyes, Dressed, 26 In. 285.00
S & H 1079, Stamped On Jumeau Body, Sleep Eyes, Satin Dress, 26 In. 700.00
S & H 1159, Gibson Girl, Blue Eyes, Dark Lashes, 18 In. 1150.00
S & H 1249, Santa Claus, Marked, 32 In. 2250.00
S & H 1249, Santa Claus, Sleep Eyes, Blonde Mohair Wig, 17 In. 450.00
S & H 1469, Lady, Sleep Eyes, Ball-Jointed, Navy Top, White Skirt, 14 In. 375.00
S & H, Baby, Taffy Curls, Brown Eyes, Green Taffeta Dress & Hat, 25 In. 475.00
S & H, Bisque Head, Blue Eyes, Open Mouth, Jointed, Blue Dress, 23 In. 495.00
S & H, Blue Eyes, Human Hair, Gold Brocade Gown, Mink Trim, 23 In. 375.00
S & H, Girl, Black, Toddler, Original Clothes & Wig, 9 In. 350.00
S & H, Girl, Fur Eyebrows, 33 In. 1250.00
S & H, Hanna, Baby, Sleep Eyes, Braids, White Dress & Bonnet, 24 In. 775.00
S & H, Oriental, Bisque Head, Glass Eyes, Open Mouth, Jointed, 13 In. 1900.00
S.F.B.J., Baby, Laughing, Open-Close Mouth, Bisque, White Dress, 23 In. 2175.00
S.F.B.J., Bisque Head, Glass Sleep Eyes, Underclothes, 22 In. 995.00
S.F.B.J., Brown Eyes, Pierced Ears, 20 In. 1000.00
S.F.B.J., Jumeau Face, Set Eyes, Ball-Jointed, Dressed, 29 1/2 In. 1095.00
S.F.B.J.60, Black Girl, 15 In. 600.00
S.F.B.J.60, Sleep Eyes, Dark Satin Dress & Bonnet, 22 In. 725.00
S.F.B.J.224, Character Boy, Paperweight Eyes, Toddler Body, 14 1/2 In. 1500.00
S.F.B.J.235, Blue Eyes, 21 In. 1850.00
S.F.B.J.236, Laughing Jumeau, Character Baby, 23 In. 2175.00
S.F.B.J.236, Toddler Boy, Laughing, 14 In. 1395.00
S.F.B.J.251, Toddler Boy, Sleep Eyes, 18 In. 1700.00
S.F.B.J.251, Toddler, Human Hair Wig, Black Velvet Suit, 27 In. 3450.00

S.F.B.J.252, Pouty Baby, Skin Wig, 8 In. 2700.00
S.F.B.J.256, Bisque, Boy, Composition Body, 18 1/2 In. .... *Illus* 2700.00
S.F.B.J.301, Bisque Head, Ball-Jointed Body, Velvet Dress, Muff, 22 In. 995.00
S.F.B.J.301, Bisque, Sleep Eyes, Silk Dress, Lace Trim, 31 In. 1295.00
S.F.B.J.301, Jumeau Body, Bisque, French Girl, 18 In. 625.00
S.F.B.J.301, Open Mouth, Glass Eyes, Bisque Head, Ball-Jointed, 22 In. 1050.00
Schmidt 1272, Toddler, Straight Legs, Bisque Teeth, Breather, 16 In. 595.00
Schoenhut, Baby, Wooden, Dated 1911 .... 225.00
Schoenhut, Baby, 11 In. 350.00
Schoenhut, Boy, Original, Wig, Marked, 1911, 17 In. 250.00
Schoenhut, Girl, All Original, Stand, 16 In. 450.00
Schoenhut, Girl, 19 In. 375.00
Schoenhut, Maggie & Jiggs .... 440.00 To 800.00
Schoenhut, Pouty Boy, Brown Corduroy Suit, 16 In. 575.00
Schoenhut, Pouty Face, Sailor Dress, 22 In. 395.00
Schoenhut, Santa Claus, Roly Poly, 7 1/2 In. 195.00
Schoenhut, Teddy Roosevelt 925.00
Schoenhut, Walker, Pouty Baby Face, Original Wig & Underwear, 17 In. 450.00
Schoenhut, Wooden, Open Eyes, Blonde, Blue & White Check Dress, 21 In. 850.00
    DOLL, SHIRLEY TEMPLE, see Shirley Temple
    DOLL, SIMON & HALBIG; see also Doll, Bergmann; Doll, S & H
Simon & Halbig 1039, Walks & Flirts, Bisque, Dressed, 24 In. 895.00
Simon & Halbig 1159, Swivel Head, Dressed, Gibson Hair Style, 17 In. 895.00
Simon & Halbig 1294, Baby, Flirty Eyes, 16 In. 650.00
Simon & Halbig, Blue Sleep Eyes, Open Mouth, Jointed, Silk Dress, 32 In. 1900.00
Snuffy Smith, Cloth 12.00
Southern Girl, Composition Body, Brown Hair, 11 In. 170.00
Steiff, Santa Claus, Original Paper Label, 12 In. 350.00
Steiner, Baby, Bisque, Sleep Eyes, Old Clothes & Wig, 18 In. 250.00
Steiner, Bisque Head & Arms, Clockworks, Dressed, Arms Move, 14 In. 2450.00
Steiner, Bisque Head, Paperweight Eyes, Jointed, Marked, 14 1/2 In. 2300.00
Steiner, Bisque, Paperweight Eyes, Underclothes & Shoes, 11 1/2 In. 1995.00
Steiner, Girl, Bisque Head, Composition Jointed Body, Marked, 16 In. 2695.00
Steiner, Wire Eyed, Closed Mouth, Signed, 28 In. 6800.00
Steiner, Wire Eyed, Open Mouth, A Series, Marked, 27 In. 2495.00
Strobel & Wilkin, Googly, All Original .... *Illus* 2600.00
Strobel & Wilkin, Googly, Glass Eyes, Fat Toddler Body, 7 In. 495.00
Sun Rubber, Baby, 13 In. 35.00
Sun Rubber, Cindy Lee, Baby, Bent Limb, Jointed, 11 In. 12.00
Superman, 24 In. 80.00
Sweetie Pie, Flirty Eye, Fur Wig, 18 In. 75.00
Terra-Cotta, Fisherman's Wife, Original Dress, 11 1/2 In. 125.00
Tete Jumeau, Open Mouth, Pale Bisque, 32 In. .... *Illus* 2100.00
Tete Jumeau, Paperweight Eyes, Pale Bisque, 24 In. 3000.00
Tiny Tears, Plastic Face, Rubber Body, 1950, 13 In. 35.00
Tiny Tears, 1956, 11 In. 22.50
Tommy Tucker, Flirty Eye, Fur Wig, 14 In. 50.00
Topsy Turvy, One White, One Black, Pair 850.00
Topsy Turvy, Straw Body, Black & White, W.D.Co., 11 1/2 In. 165.00
Troll, Eccky, Dated 1964, 12 In. 85.00
Tutti & Todd, Sundae Treat 75.00
Unis 301, Jumeau Mold, Open Mouth, Brown Eyes, 31 In. 1999.00
Unis, Malata, 9 In. 300.00
Unis, Wood & Composition Body, Silk Dress, Marked, 29 In. 900.00
Vogue, Baby Dear, 1965, 25 In. .... 45.00 To 65.00
Vogue, Baby Hilary 20.00
Vogue, Ginny, Black 15.00
Vogue, Ginny, Walker, 6 Outfits & Trunk 85.00
Vogue, Hug-A-Bye, 16 In. 40.00
Vogue, Littlest Angel, 1977, 15 In. 35.00
Vogue, Miss Jill, 15 In. 25.00
Vogue, Picture Girl 18.00

Doll, S & H 170/4, Clown, Bisque,
Jooined Composition Body

(See Page 203)

Doll, Revere Pottery, Bisque Head, Glass Eyes,
C.1920, 12 In.

(See Page 203)

Doll, S.F.B.J., Bisque, Boy, Composition Body,
18 1/2 In.

(See Page 203)

Doll, Strobel & Wilkin, Googly, All Original

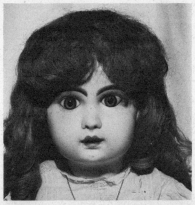

Doll, Tete Jumeau, Open Mouth, Pale Bisque, 32 In.

Vogue, Twins, Boy & Girl, 24 In., Pair 60.00
Vogue, Wee Imp 55.00
Vollendam, Philadelphia Baby, 21 In. 950.00
Walker, Child, Bisque Head, Composition, Jointed, Sleep Eyes, 34 In. 1050.00
Wax Shoulders, Head, Glass Eyes, Kid Body, Dressed, 24 In. 350.00
    DONALD DUCK, see Disneyana

*Iron doorstops have been made in all types of designs. The vast majority of
the doorstops sold today are cast iron and were made from about 1890 to
1930. Most of them are shaped like people, animals, flowers, or ships.*

DOORSTOP, Airedale, Tan With Brown 50.00
Aunt Jemima .... 65.00 To 97.00
Basket Of Red Poppies, Signed, Hubley, 8 In. 28.00
Basket Of Tulips & Jonquils 50.00
Blacksmith, Brass Plated 40.00
Boston Bull, Full Figure, 5 In. 75.00
Boston Bull, Full Figure, 8 1/2 In. 80.00
Boston Terrier, Sitting, One Ear Up, Red Paint, 8 In. 60.00
Bull Terrier, Brass Studded Collar, 10 X 9 1/2 In. 125.00
Bulldog, Sitting, Some Original Paint 90.00
Bulldog, Standing, 10 In. 65.00
Butler, Black Man 90.00
Cape Cod House, Fence 45.00
Cat, Black, Red Bow 85.00
Cat, Black, 9 In. 70.00
Cat, Blue & White, 8 In. 45.00
Cat, Full Figure Sitting, Black, Green Eyes, 7 1/4 In. 65.00
Cat, Reclining, Black, 9 1/2 In. 35.00
Cat, Siamese, Full Figure, Original Paint, Brown To Tan 90.00
Cat, Sitting, Hubley 65.00
Cat, Tail Up, White, 9 X 11 In. 95.00
Clipper Ship, 3 Masts, 4 Sails, Beige & Brown, 11 In. 27.50
Coach, Bronze, Signed, 2 Prongs For Balance, 8 In. 140.00
Cockatoo, Red, Yellow, Green, Signed Noyes & Co., 7 In. 58.00
Cockatoo, Signed Albany Forge, 12 In. 65.00
Cockatoo, White, Dated 1882, 12 In. 75.00
Colonial Lady, Black Dress, Holding Yellow Hat, 11 1/2 In. 45.00
Colonial Lady, Cobalt Blue & Pastels 68.00
Conestoga Wagon, 10 3/4 X 8 1/2 In. 80.00
Cottage & Trees, Original Paint, 5 1/2 X 8 In. 85.00
Cowboy 48.00
Daisy Basket, Flat Back, 9 1/2 In. 60.00
Dog, Art Deco, Flat Back, Signed, 6 1/2 In. 20.00
Dog, Scotty, Leaning On Fence, Flat Back, 4 1/2 X 4 1/2 In. 35.00
Drum Major, Full Figure 125.00
Duck 90.00
Dwarf, Holding Lantern & Keys, 9 1/2 In. 135.00
Elephant, White, Flat Back, 7 In. 40.00
Fawn 65.00
Fireside Cat, Hubley 50.00
Fisherman, Old Salt, Full Figure, 11 In. 150.00
Flower Basket, Daisies & Petunias 35.00
Flower Basket, Delphiniums, Roses 35.00
Flower Basket, Hospitality, 8 In. 25.00
Flower Basket, Marigolds, Hubley No.315, 7 3/4 In. 65.00
Flower Basket, Pansy Bowl, Hubley No.256, 7 In. 75.00
Flower Basket, Poppies In Yellow-Orange Pot 25.00
Flower Basket, Zinnias, Hubley No.267, 7 1/4 In. 55.00
Flower Pot, Poppies 30.00
Flower Pot, Tulips, Original Paint .... 50.00 To 70.00
Fox Terrier, Facing Front 85.00
Fox Terrier, Hubley 65.00
Fox Terrier, Wirehaired, Full Figure, 8 In. 75.00

Fox Terrier, Wirehaired, Tan & Black, 8 X 9 In. 70.00
Frog On Base, Alice In Wonderland, 6 1/2 In. 145.00
Frog, Green Paint .... 20.00 To 45.00
Frog, 3 1/2 In. 55.00
Galleon 28.00
General Robert E. Lee, 7 1/4 In. 75.00
German Shepherd, 9 1/2 In. 42.00
Golfer In Knickers, Putting, Flatback 175.00
Heron, Blue Paint, Orange Bill & Leg, 7 In. 60.00
High-Button Shoe, Lady's 30.00
Horse, Black, Parade Saddle 19.00
Horse, Full Body 30.00
Horse, Hubley, Black .... 45.00 To 50.00
House, White Picket Fence 35.00
Indian Chief Head, Flat Back, Original Paint, 6 In. 48.00
Jockey Cap, Red Paint 35.00
Jockey, Black, Ring In Hand, 11 1/2 In. 50.00
Jockey, Black, 13 In. 80.00
Kittens 95.00
Knight On Horseback, Marked, 7 In. 55.00
Lady Holding Hat & Scarf, 11 In. 55.00
Lady Wearing Hat & Scarf, Full Figure, 6 1/2 In. 65.00
Lighthouse On Rocks, Flat Back, 10 In. 65.00
Mail Coach & Horses 75.00
Mammy, Bank, Full Figure, 5 1/2 In. 85.00
Mammy, Black, 13 In. 80.00
Mammy, Full Figure, Blue Skirt, Hubley, 2 1/2 In. 50.00
Mammy, Full Figure, Green Skirt, Signed Hubley, 12 In. 245.00
Mammy, Full Figure, Red Skirt, Hubley, 8 1/b In. 135.00
Mammy, Full Figure, 6 3/4 In. 125.00
Mammy, Full Figure, 9 In. 115.00
Mayflower Ship, 11 1/2 In. 35.00
Nasturtiums 37.00
Organ Grinder & Monkey, 1940s, 9 3/4 In. 135.00
Pan With Flute On Mushroom, Flat Back, 7 1/4 In. 115.00
Parrot, 6 1/4 In. 75.00
Peacock, Flat Back, 1920s, 7 In. 125.00
Pelican 22.50
Penguin In Top Hat, Full Figure, Hubley No.463, 10 In. 150.00
Pheasant, Original Paint, 8 X 7 In. 110.00
Policeman With Baton, Cartoon Figure, Signed, 8 In. 130.00
Poppies, Flat Back, 7 In. 55.00
Punch & Baby, Flat Back, 7 In. 85.00
Rabbit Seated, Full Figure, 12 X 10 In. 85.00
Rabbit, White, Seated, 13 X 12 In. 175.00
Raging Bull 35.00
Ram 90.00
Red Riding Hood & Wolf 75.00
Rooster, 7 In. 50.00
Santa Maria Ship 35.00
Scotty, 8 In. 45.00
Setter 85.00
Shepherd Dog, Flat Back, Black Paint, 6 In. 25.00
Skier, Full Figure, Female With Skis, 12 1/2 In. 195.00
Stagecoach, Flat Back, 8 In. 60.00
Storybook, Drum Major, Full Figure, 12 1/2 In. 165.00
Storybook, Dwarf, Full Figure, 13 1/2 In. 300.00
Storybook, Lady In Canoe, Flat Back, 4 1/4 X 9 3/4 In. 155.00
Sunbonnet Girl, 6 In. 40.00
Terrier, White, Tan, & Brown, 5 In. 50.00
Terrier, 7 1/2 In. 35.00
Terrier, 8 1/2 In. 55.00
Tiger Lilies, Art Deco 42.00
Totem Pole, Skinny, Flat Back, Original Paint, 7 1/2 In. 110.00

Turtle	57.50
Vase, Daisies	35.00
Vase, Nasturtiums	40.00
Vase, Tulips	35.00
Welsh Corgi, Original Brown Paint, White Chest & Paws, 10 In.	95.00
Windmill, Flat Back, 7 In.	65.00
Wolfhound, Black & White Marking, 1 1/2 X 7 1/2 In.	135.00

DORFLINGER, Decanter & 2 Cordials, Middlesex, Emerald To Clear 1500.00

Doulton pottery and porcelain were made by Doulton and Co. of Burslem, England, after 1882. The name "Royal Doulton" appeared on their wares after 1902.

DOULTON, see also Royal Doulton

DOULTON, Ashtray, Advertising, Lambeth, Stoneware, Cobalt Blue, Mark, 4 1/2 In.	65.00
Biscuit Jar, Burslem, Band Of Birds & Animals, Silver Plated Rim	195.00
Biscuit Jar, Burslem, Birds & Animals On Turquoise Band, 7 3/4 In.	195.00
Biscuit Jar, Burslem, Melon-Section Shaped, Silver Plated Top	118.00
Biscuit Jar, Burslem, Satin Tapestry Finish, Silver Plated Handle	125.00
Biscuit Jar, Pink Flowers, Green Leaves, Silver Plated Top, Handle	118.00
Bowl, Burslem, Willow Pattern, Blue & Gold, 1891 Mark, 10 In.	140.00
Bowl, Flow Blue, Wateau, 2 1/4 X 3 3/4 In.	40.00
Candleholder, Allover Flowers, Bands, Marked, 10 1/4 In., Pair	125.00
Cookie Jar, Burslem, Embossed Design, Snakeskin Ground, 1891 Mark	145.00
Cracker Jar, Burslem, Blown Body, Brass Fittings, Signed	179.00
Creamer, Faience Ware, Blue Bands & Handle, Center Flower, 4 1/8 In.	95.00
Foot Warmer, Beige Ground, Lambeth	95.00
Jardiniere, Lambeth, Cobalt Blue Rim, Marbleized Floral, 7 In.	225.00
Jardiniere, Lambeth, Relief Floral, Dated 1882, Green, 7 3/4 In.	175.00
Jug, Hunting, Lambeth, Egyptian, Brown Glaze, Beige Center Band, 7 In.	125.00
Jug, Lambeth, Beading, Rosettes, & Curlicues, Green & Blue, 7 In.	225.00
Jug, Lambeth, Raised Enameled Flowers, Tan Ground, 3 Handles, 6 In.	185.00
Jug, Lambeth, Scroll Design, Dated 1874, Signed, Green, 7 1/2 In.	150.00
Jug, Lambeth, Swirling, Olive Ground, Dated 1874, Signed, 7 1/2 In.	150.00
Lamp, Oil, Lambeth, Edith Oupton, 1881	450.00
Pitcher, Lambeth, Hunting Scenes, 6 1/2 In.	48.00
Pitcher, Lambeth, Incised Design, Dated 1876, 8 In.	165.00
Pitcher, Lambeth, Verse Around Top & Base, Marked, 7 1/2 In.	110.00
Pitcher, Lambeth, 4 Portrait Medallions, Marked, 8 In.	155.00
Pitcher, White, Floral, Green Chicken Skin Ground, 9 In.	50.00
Plaque, Christ Rideth Into Jerusalem, Terra-Cotta, 9 X 9 In.	650.00
Plate, Spanish Armada, 10 1/2 In.	40.00
Plate, Sunflower, C.1879, 10 In.	25.00
Plate, Watteau, Flow Blue, 7 1/2 In.	22.00
Pot, Demitasse, Lambeth, Raised Dutch Figures, 2-Tone Brown	30.00
Teapot, Aqua & White Flowers, Tapestry Ground, Marked, 5 1/4 In.	195.00
Teapot, Blue Bands, Spout, & Handle, Green Leaves Band, Marked	195.00
Tray, Burslem, Floral, Gold Border, Marked, 10 X 13 In.	85.00
Vase, Barkis, Marked, Square, 4 X 7 In.	165.00
Vase, Blue Cornflowers, Gold Leaves & Trim, Signed, 5 3/4 In., Pair	265.00
Vase, Burslem, Hand-Painted, Lace-Impressed Bottom, Floral	100.00
Vase, Carrara, Stylized Flowers, Blue, Red, & Green, 7 3/4 In.	550.00
Vase, Farm Scene, Brown, Orange, Gold, Marked, 12 In.	650.00
Vase, Girl With Basket Of Flowers, Gold Trim, Marked, 8 1/4 In.	275.00
Vase, Lady Playing Horsy With Girl, Gold Trim, Marked, 9 In.	395.00
Vase, Lady With Hat, Girl In Front, Gold Trim, Marked, 12 3/8 In.	475.00
Vase, Lambeth, Apple Blossoms & Foliage, Signed, Dated 1877, 9 In.	235.00
Vase, Lambeth, Donkeys Grazing, Blue, Brown, Hannah Barlow, 10 3/4 In.	350.00
Vase, 6 Incised Goats, Signed Hannah Barlow, Stoneware, 9 In.	495.00

DR. SYNTAX, see Adams; Staffordshire

Moriage is a type of decoration on Japanese pottery. Raised white designs are applied to the ware. Dragonware is a form of moriage pottery. White dragons are the major raised decorations. The background color is gray and white, orange and lavender, or orange and brown. It is a twentieth-century ware.

DRAGONWARE, Ashtray, Individual, Gray & White, 3 X 2 In.	12.50
Ashtray, Round, Gray & White, 6 In.	30.00
Box, Square, Gray & White, Covered, 5 X 4 In.	40.00
Cup & Saucer, Child's, Gray & White	14.00
Sake Set, Decanter, Gray & White, 6 X 2 1/2 In., 7 Piece	75.00
Teapot, Figural, Elephant, 6 3/4 In.	48.00

Dresden china is any china made in the town of Dresden, Germany. The most famous factory in Dresden is the Meissen factory.

DRESDEN, see also Meissen

DRESDEN, Ashtray, Gold Trim, Marked, 5 1/2 In.	50.00
Bottle, Perfume, Blue, Green, Gilt, Floral, 1 1/2 X 3 1/4 In.	60.00
Bowl, Floral Design, Marked, 9 In.	55.00
Bowl, Raised Floral Bouquets, 3 Standing Angels, 13 X 6 In.	450.00
Candleholder, Column Shaped, White Ground, Floral, 7 In., Pair	120.00
Candleholder, Flowers & Fruits, Gold Trim, Signed, 8 1/4 In., Pair	225.00
Compote, Garlands & Ribbons, Footed, Marked, 7 X 3 1/2 In.	125.00
Compote, Multifloral, Reticulated, 8 1/2 X 5 1/2 In.	165.00
Cup & Saucer, Cloverleaf Shaped, Pink, White, Figures, Flowers	65.00
Cup & Saucer, Portrait, Yellow	165.00
Cup & Saucer, Wreath, Dated 1845	10.00
Figurine, Ballerina, Applied Flowers	55.00
Figurine, Beggar Woman, Signed, 6 1/2 In.	150.00
Figurine, Couple Dancing, Lacy Dress, Marked	35.00
Figurine, Frolicking Children, Polychrome, 9 In.	250.00
Figurine, Monkey Band, C.1890, Set Of 8	1100.00
Figurine, Parrot, On Tree Stump, Signed, 6 1/2 In., Pair	280.00 To 335.00
Figurine, Parrot, Seated On Tree Stump, Signed, 6 1/2 In.	150.00
Figurine, Rooster & Hen, Marked	38.00
Figurine, Woman Dressed In 18th-Century Costume, Yellow, 6 In.	90.00
Figurine, Woman, Wearing Pink, Green, Blue Dress, Bouquet, 7 In.	145.00
Figurine, Young Girl, Wearing Bonnet, Basket Of Flowers, 4 In.	135.00
Fruit Stand, Figural, Lovers, Scroll Feet, 14 In.	275.00
Hatpin Holder, Saucer Shaped, Pears & Flowers	45.00
Jar, Pomade, Egg Shaped, Lattice Top, Rose Medallion On Side, 7 In.	120.00
Lamp, Figures, Painted Flowers, 19th Century, Electric *Illus*	375.00
Mug, Blue, White, Floral, Marked Donath, 1872, 3 1/2 X 3 1/4 In.	85.00
Plate, Multicolored Floral, Perforated Edges, 1875, 6 1/2 In.	55.00
Plate, People & Flowers, 7 1/2 In.	55.00
Ramekin, Underplate, Florals, Gold, Covered, Signed, 3 1/4 X 1 1/2 In.	85.00
Tray, Serving, Hunt Scene, Floral Cluster, Cartouche Shaped, 20 In.	200.00

Duncan & Miller is a term used by collectors when referring to glass made by the George A. Duncan and Sons Company or the Duncan and Miller Glass Company. These companies worked from 1893 to 1955 when the use of the name "Duncan" was discontinued and the firm became part of the United States Glass Company.

DUNCAN & MILLER, Adoration, Iced Tea	15.00 To 19.00
Adoration, Sherbet	14.00 To 19.00
Astaire, Goblet, Crystal, 5 1/2 In.	6.50
Button Panel, Water Set, Gold Trim, 7 Piece	125.00
Candlewick, Mayonnaise	20.00
Candlewick, Plate, 8 In.	4.00
Canterbury, Basket, 6 In.	30.00
Canterbury, Bowl, Crimped, Chartreuse, 10 In.	24.00
Canterbury, Bowl, Scalloped Edge, Blue, 7 1/2 In.	35.00
Canterbury, Compote, Crystal	8.00
Canterbury, Plate, Crystal, 7 3/4 In.	4.50
Canterbury, Rose Bowl	35.00

Dresden, Lamp, Figures, Painted Flowers,
19th Century, Electric

(See Page 209)

Canterbury, Tumbler, 5 Ounce	6.00
Canterbury, Vase, Blue Opalescent, 6 In.	20.00
Caribbean, Bowl, Console, Handled, Oval, Footed, 11 In.	35.00
Caribbean, Bowl, 4 In.	8.00
Caribbean, Bowl, Serving, 9 In.	30.00
Caribbean, Bowl, Serving, 12 In.	35.00
Caribbean, Cup & Saucer	24.00
Caribbean, Dish, Candy, Covered	75.00
Caribbean, Goblet, 3 3/4 In.	20.00
Caribbean, Goblet, 4 In.	20.00
Caribbean, Iced Tea, 5 In.	20.00
Caribbean, Jelly Set, Center Handle, 5 Piece	105.00
Caribbean, Plate, Bread & Butter	6.00
Caribbean, Plate, Dinner, Sapphire Blue	40.00
Caribbean, Plate, Handled, 6 In.	7.00
Caribbean, Plate, Sandwich, 2-Handled	25.00
Caribbean, Plate, Torte, 13 In.	25.00
Caribbean, Plate, 2-Handled, 8 In.	12.00
Caribbean, Plate, 8 In.	12.00
Caribbean, Punch Set	350.00
Caribbean, Sauce	9.00
Caribbean, Sherbet, Footed	20.00
Caribbean, Smoking Set, Amber, 5 Piece	40.00
Caribbean, Sugar & Creamer, 3 In.	30.00
Caribbean, Tumbler, Old-Fashioned	35.00
Caribbean, Vase, Mushroom, 7 In.	25.00
Caribbean, Vase, Trumpet, Footed, 7 In.	25.00
Chanticleer, Goblet, 8 1/2 Ounce	18.00
Clover, Bowl, Berry, C.1888, Emerald Green	55.00
Cornucopia, Vase, 3 Feathers, Pink Opalescent	120.00

Dove, 11 1/2 In.	250.00
Dover, Sherbet, Ruby	15.50
Duck, Ashtray, Crystal	38.00
Duck, 4 In.	40.00
First Love, Console Set, 2-Branch Candleholder, Fluted Bowl	80.00
First Love, Goblet, 5 In.	14.00 To 16.00
First Love, Pitcher	115.00
First Love, Relish, Teardrops, 6 X 12 In.	24.00
First Love, Salt & Pepper	27.50
Fish, Ashtray, Blue	35.00
Fluted, Bowl, Blue Opalescent, 11 In.	55.00
Fruit & Flower, Epergne, 12 In.	40.00
Georgian, Cup, Ruby	7.00
Georgian, Water Set, Pink, 7 Piece	36.00
Graded Diamond & Sunburst, Rose Bowl, 5 1/2 In.	28.00
Hobnail, Basket, Pink Opalescent, 10 1/2 In.	75.00
Hobnail, Bottle, Cologne, Pink, 6 1/2 In., Pair	50.00
Hobnail, Bowl, Salad, 12 In.	65.00
Hobnail, Goblet, 9 Oz.	9.00
Hobnail, Ivy Ball, Red	30.00
King Arthur, Pitcher, Water	35.00
Laguna, Relish, Pink, 9 In.	40.00
Language Of Flowers, Iced Tea	16.95
Language Of Flowers, Tumbler	16.95
Mardi Gras, Bottle, Water	40.00
Mardi Gras, Creamer	16.00
Mardi Gras, Decanter	60.00
Mardi Gras, Jar, Mustard, Pewter Top	20.00
No.30, Syrup	38.00
Sandwich, Candleholder, 4 In., Pair	12.00
Sandwich, Goblet, Chartreuse, 5 3/8 In.	15.00
Sanibel, Dish, Blue Opalescent, 10 1/2 In.	45.00
Sanibel, Relish, Blue, 9 In.	40.00
Sanibel, Tray, Hors D'oeuvre, 13 In.	45.00 To 55.00
Sawtooth, Compote, Footed	20.00
Shell, Blue, 14 In.	75.00
Shell, Console Set, Blue Opalescent, 14 In., 3 Piece	75.00
Shell, Plate, Pink Opalescent, 14 In.	43.00
Swan Ruby, 7 In.	28.00
Swan, Chartreuse, 11 1/2 In.	65.00
Swan, Crystal Neck, Black, 13 In.	55.00
Swan, Crystal Neck, Green, 13 In.	45.00 To 55.00
Swan, Crystal Neck, Ruby, 13 In.	45.00 To 50.00
Swan, Crystal, 5 In.	20.00
Swan, Crystal, 8 In.	15.00
Swan, Crystal, 12 In.	25.00
Swan, Green, Open Back, 10 1/2 In.	40.00 To 50.00
Swan, Peach Opalescent, 12 1/2 In.	95.00
Swan, Red, 10 In.	40.00
Swan, Spread Wing, Blue Opalescent, 12 In.	175.00
Swan, Spread Wing, Pink Opalescent, 12 1/2 In.	225.00
Swan, Sylvan, Blue Opalescent, 7 In.	30.00
Swan, Sylvan, Vaseline Opalescent, 6 1/2 In.	40.00
Swirl, Cornucopia, Crystal, 14 In.	25.00
Tavern, Basket, 11 In.	38.50
Tavern, Basket, 13 In.	48.50
Teardrop, Celery, 11 In.	10.00
Teardrop, Cruet Set, Crystal, 5 Piece	35.00
Tepee, Toothpick	38.00 To 45.00
Trumpet, Candelabrum, Prisms	35.00

*Durand glass was made by Victor Durand from 1879 to 1935 at several
factories. Most of the iridescent Durand glass was made by Victor*

Durand, Jr., from 1912 to 1924 at the Durand Art Glass Works in Vineland, New Jersey.

DURAND, Bottle, Perfume, King Tut, 8 In.	350.00
Bowl, Finger, Underplate, Amethyst	80.00
Champagne, Rib Design, Amber Stem, Blue Twist, 6 In.	115.00
Compote, Iridescent, Stretched Rim, Signed, 7 1/2 X 6 1/2 In.	295.00
Cup & Saucer, Ruby Peacock	395.00
Lamp, Brass, Paw Feet, Leaf Mounts, Gold, Pink, & White, 17 In., Pair	900.00
Lamp, Night, Blue Opalescent Shade, Silver Plated Base, 6 In.	225.00
Lamp, Shade, Peacock Feather, Green Border, Gold Webbing, 8 X 5 In.	120.00
Lamp, Shade, Torchere, Vine & Leaf, Iridescent Gold, Green, Pair	650.00
Plate, Bridgeton Rose, D.Link Engraver, 8 In.	300.00
Tazza, Gold Iridescent, Blue Highlights, Signed, 7 3/4 X 6 1/2 In.	395.00
Vase, Blue & White, Signed, 6 1/2 In.	1100.00
Vase, Blue Iridescent, Art Deco Shape, Marked, 7 In.	375.00
Vase, Blue Iridescent, Classic Shape, Signed, 6 In.	650.00
Vase, Blue Iridescent, Flared Top, Signed, 7 In.	300.00
Vase, Blue Iridescent, Floral, Signed, 10 In.	850.00
Vase, Blue Iridescent, Silver Design, Signed, 7 In.	425.00
Vase, Crackle Glass, Blue & White, Gold Aurene Interior, 9 1/2 In.	500.00
Vase, Crackle Glass, Blue & White, 9 In.	400.00
Vase, Dark Blue, White Leaves & Vines, Signed, 10 In.	850.00
Vase, Gold Ground, Green Pulls, White, Ruffled Top, Signed, 6 3/4 In.	385.00
Vase, Gold Iridescent, Classic Shape, Everted Lip, Marked, 8 In.	500.00
Vase, King Tut, Gold, Green, 12 1/2 In.	950.00 To 1100.00
Vase, King Tut, Orange, Blue, Marked, 10 In.	325.00
Vase, King Tut, Orange, Bulbous, Marked, 10 In.	325.00
Vase, King Tut, Pink & Lavender, Green, 12 1/2 In., Pair	1500.00
Vase, Opalescent Feathers, Gold, Flared Base & Shoulder, 7 In.	325.00
Vase, Orange Iridescent, Flared Top, Signed, 2 3/8 X 6 In.	235.00
Vase, Orange Iridescent, Marked, 6 3/4 In.	285.00
Vase, Orange Iridescent, Polished Pontil, Marked, 6 In.	235.00
Vase, Peacock Feather, Green, 7 In.	350.00
Vase, Ruffled Top, 4-Color, Signed, 7 In.	825.00
Wine, Peacock Feather, Ruby & White, Yellow Footed Stem, 5 1/2 In.	395.00
Wine, Ruby Peacock, Pale Spanish Yellow Stem & Base, 5 In.	450.00
Wine, Ruby Ribbed, Yellow Stem, Footed, 7 In.	250.00

ELFINWARE, Basket, Yellow, Applied Flowers, 4 In.	32.00
Cup, Nut, Swan, 2 In.	18.00
Shoe, Man's, 4 X 2 In.	75.00

ELVIS PRESLEY, Key Chain, Guitar Shape	3.50
Music Box, Statue On Top, Love Me Tender	45.00
Poster, Movie, Girls, Girls, Girls, 14 X 36 In.	25.00
Record, Army Interview, 1958, Set Of 3	35.00
Scarf, Signed Sincerely, Elvis, Silk, 42 In.	6.00
Sheet Music, Don't Be Cruel	15.00
Sneaker, Pictures & Signature	50.00
Spoon, Palladium Concert, England, Gold	25.00
Tape Measure, Heart Shaped	2.00
ENAMEL WARE, see Graniteware	

ENAMEL, Russian, Scoop, Sugar, Multicolored Blues, Reds, & Whites, 1891, 5 In.	625.00
END OF DAY GLASS, see Spatter Glass	

ES Germany porcelain was made at the factory of Erdmann Schlegelmilch from 1861 to 1925 in Suhl, Germany. The porcelain was sold decorated or undecorated.

ES GERMANY, Bonbon, Red Roses	19.00
Bowl, Cloverleaf Shape, Hand-Painted Roses, 9 1/2 In.	70.00

Chocolate Pot, Rose Design, 9 1/4 In. 95.00
Dish, Pin, Wing Shape, Gold Design, Madame Recamier, 7 In. 87.00
Plate, Portrait, Gold Rococo Rim, 6 Blown-Out Flowers, 9 1/2 In. 139.00
Relish, Portrait, Gold Border, Marked, 8 1/2 In. 30.00
Rose Jar, Portrait, Iridescent, 7 1/2 In. 69.00
Sugar & Creamer, Covered, Floral Top, Green Mark, Peacocks 75.00
Tray, Blackcap Chickadee, Hand-Painted, Marked, 13 In. 125.00
Vase, Iris, Multicolored, Handled, Gold Rim, 12 In. 82.00
Vase, Portrait, 2-Handled, 11 In. 250.00

ES PRUSSIA, Dish, Lobster, Floral Design, Lobster Handle, 12 In. 85.00
Dish, Pin, Wing Shaped, Portrait Madame Recamier, Gold Design 87.00
Hair Receiver, Yellow Roses 32.50
Hatpin Holder, Floral Design, 7 In. 65.00
Plate, Roses, 6 In., Set Of 3 .... 40.00
Vase, Roses, Tan To Brown Ground, 10 In. 85.00

ETLING, Compote, Opalescent, Molded Floral, Gold Stand, Signed, 6 X 8 In. 149.00
ETRUSCAN MAJOLICA, see Majolica

FAIENCE, Box, Watteauesque Scene, Blue Ground, Covered, 8 In. 100.00
Figurine, Mendicant, Standing, Basket On Back, 6 In. 950.00
Vase, Baluster, Pair Of Lovers, Covered, 12 In., Pr. 100.00

*Fairings are small souvenir china boxes that were sold at country fairs
during the nineteenth century.*

FAIRING, Box, Baby On Dresser Looking In Mirror .... *Illus* 85.00
Box, Fireplace With Watch On Top, Covered 59.00
Box, Trinket, Red Riding Hood & Wolf On Lid, 2 1/2 X 3 In. 65.00
Figurine, A Party Of Four, 5 1/4 In. 85.00
Figurine, Little Red Riding Hood, 4 1/2 In. .... *Illus* 70.00
Mirror, Dresser, Lion Head Design 22.00

Fairing, Figurine, Little Red Riding Hood, 4 1/2 In.

Fairing, Box, Baby On Dresser Looking
In Mirror

FAMILLE ROSE, see Chinese Export

FAN, Advertising, Cherry Blossom Tea 15.00
  Advertising, Moxie, Girl 15.00
  Advertising, Opal Coffee, Paper 17.00
  Advertising, Radio Corp. Of America, Speaker & Tube Pictured, Cardboard 12.50
  Advertising, 666 Salve, Singing Baby & Birds, Cardboard & Stick 6.00
  Art Deco, Pastel Butterfly, Seminude, Cardboard 14.00
  Ceiling, Guth, Stained Glass Panels 175.00
  Ceiling, Westinghouse, Brass Blades & Housing 30.00
  Ceiling, 3-Speed, Diehl, Heavy Duty, Four 5 In.Blades, C.1920s, 22 In. 75.00
  Chinese, Cardboard, Painted 85.00
  Circus, Hand-Tinted, Van Amburgh & Co., 1864 .... 65.00
  Embroidered, Bone, Silk 30.00
  Folding, Black Silk, 9 In. 25.00
  French, Hand-Painted Butterflies, Black Lace & Silk 110.00
  French, Lady's, Hand-Painted Butterflies, Black Lace & Silk 110.00
  General Putnam, Cardboard 4.00
  Gold Oriental Figures, Lacquered & Silk 110.00
  Hand-Painted, Celluloid, Silk 75.00
  Hand-Painted, Signed, Silk & Ivory 65.00
  Mandarin, One Thousand Faces, Gold Lacquered Box 1500.00
  Mourning, Large 35.00
  Organdy, Black, Silver Sequins, Carved Wood Sticks, 8 1/2 In. 35.00
  Ostrich Feathers, Pink Rosebuds, Gray Sticks, Brown & White 75.00
  Ostrich Feathers, Variegated Deep To Pale Yellow 65.00
  Parlor, Lumina Tree 395.00
  Tangerine Ostrich Feather & Tortoiseshell 90.00
  Tortoiseshell & Tassel, Black Plumes 75.00
  Tortoiseshell, Ostrich Feathers 65.00
  Victorian, Velvet Handle, Red Design 30.00
  White Ostrich Feathers, Celluloid 20.00

FEDERZEICHNUNG, Vase, Brown, Marked, 6 X 9 In. 1600.00
  Vase, Brown, 6 3/4 In. 1500.00
  Vase, Satin Glass, 10 1/2 In. 1850.00

*Fenton Art Glass Company, founded in Martins Ferry, Ohio, by
Frank L.Fenton, is now located in Williamstown, West Virginia. It
is noted for early carnival glass produced between 1907 and 1920.
Many other types of glass were also made.*

FENTON, Acorn, Bowl, 7 1/2 In. 30.00
  Baby Coin Spot, Salt & Pepper, Cranberry, Pair 40.00
  Baby Thumbprint, Cruet, Vaseline 37.00
  Beaded Melon, Bottle, Green, Stopper, 5 1/2 In. 35.00
  Big Cookies, Basket, Wicker Handle, Jade 75.00
  Big Cookies, Cookie Jar, Peking Blue 125.00
  Bird, Ashtray, Crystal 10.00
  Blackberry, Banded, Nappy, Marigold 20.00
  Blue Dot, Ivy Ball, Milk Glass Base, 8 1/2 In. 30.00
  Butterfly & Berry, Bowl, Amethyst, Claw-Footed, 9 In. 20.00
  Butterfly & Berry, Bowl, Red, Footed, 9 In. 20.00
  Chessie, Box, Candy, Rosaline .... 95.00 To 225.00
  Coin Dot, Basket, Cranberry, 5 In. 65.00
  Coin Dot, Lamp, Cranberry Opalescent, 22 In. 200.00
  Coin Dot, Sugar & Creamer, Cranberry Opalescent 50.00
  Coin Dot, Vase, White, 7 X 2 In. 30.00
  Cornucopia, White Opalescent, 3 1/2 In. 8.00
  Crest, Bowl, Aqua, 7 In. 18.00
  Crest, Bowl, Peach, Ruffled, 7 In. 22.50
  Crest, Bowl, Peach, 10 In. 45.00
  Crest, Cake Plate, Footed, Silver 15.00
  Crest, Cake Plate, Gold, 12 In. 18.00

Crest, Candlestick, Tall, Silver, Pair	15.00
Crest, Compote, Crimped, Gold	22.00
Crest, Compote, Gold, 7 In.	18.00
Crest, Plate, Dinner, Ivory	40.00
Crest, Plate, Salad, Ivory	30.00
Crest, Rose Bowl, Ivory	32.00
Crest, Vase, Crystal, 6 In.	10.00
Crest, Vase, Emerald, 8 In.	24.00
Crest, Vase, Fan, Rose, 4 In.	20.00
Crest, Vase, Peach, Double Crimp, Crystal Edge, C.1940	32.50
Crest, Vase, Spiral Optic, Blue, Snow, 8 In.	25.00
Daisy & Button, Vase, Emerald Opalescent, 8 In.	20.00
Daisy & Button, Vase, Milk Glass, Footed, 8 In.	18.00
Daisy & Fern, Syrup, Cranberry, Metal Top	55.00
Daisy & Scroll, Plate, Blue, 8 1/2 In.	28.00
Dancing Ladies, Vase, Flare Top, Ruby, 9 In.	125.00
Dancing Ladies, Vase, Periwinkle Blue, 9 In.	95.00
Diamond Lace, Epergne, C.1949	95.00
Diamond Lace, Epergne, Carnival, 3-Horn	75.00
Diamond Lace, Epergne, Opalescent	50.00
Diamond-Quilted, Basket, Cranberry, 8 In.	55.00
Dish, Dolphin, Lilac	35.00
Dolphin, Compote, Shell, Milk Glass	12.00
Dolphin, Vase, Fan, Handled, Jade	35.00
Dolphin, Vase, Fan, Velda Rose, Handled	25.00
Dot Optic, Vase, Blue, 9 In.	38.00
Federation Of Women's Clubs, Bicentennial, Plate, Set Of 4	85.00
Fenton, Coin Spot, Vase, Cranberry, 7 In.	35.00
Fern & Daisy, Cruet, Cranberry, Round	50.00
Fern & Daisy, Pickle Castor, Cranberry, Silver Holder	150.00
Fern & Daisy, Sugar Shaker, Cranberry	45.00
Fine Rib, Banana Bowl, 10 In.	60.00
Fine Rib, Vase, Marigold, Scalloped, Fluted, 10 In.	10.00
Fish, Paperweight	20.00
Garland, Rose Bowl, Footed	50.00
Grape & Cable, Bowl, 7 1/2 In.	30.00
Green Turtle, Flower Bowl, No.509	60.00
Handkerchief, Vase, Orange	12.50
Handkerchief, Vase, Plum Opalescent, 7 1/2 In.	55.00
Hanging Heart, Rose Bowl, Blue	24.00
Hanging Heart, Vase, Custard, 5 In.	25.00
Hat, Blue Opalescent	18.50
Hobnail, Atomizer, White Opalescent	15.00
Hobnail, Basket, Piecrust Crimped, 10 In.	24.50
Hobnail, Basket, Turquoise, 7 In.	35.00
Hobnail, Bonbon, Blue Opalescent, 6 In.	12.50
Hobnail, Bowl, Blue Opalescent, Ruffled Rim, 9 3/4 In.	18.00
Hobnail, Bowl, Blue, Ruffled Edge, 11 In.	50.00
Hobnail, Bowl, Cranberry, Ruffled Edge, 9 In.	80.00
Hobnail, Bowl, Crimped, Opaque Turquoise, 9 In.	55.00
Hobnail, Bowl, Green, Wavy Edge, 8 1/2 In.	60.00
Hobnail, Bowl, Plum, Ruffled Edge, 8 1/4 In.	75.00
Hobnail, Candleholder, Amber Opalescent, 4 In., Pair	20.00
Hobnail, Candleholder, Cranberry, Handled, Opalescent	45.00
Hobnail, Creamer, Blue	15.00
Hobnail, Cruet, Blue Opalescent, 3 In.	30.00
Hobnail, Epergne, Blue Opalescent, 4 Piece	60.00
Hobnail, Epergne, Yellow Opalescent	30.00
Hobnail, Juice Set, 7 Piece	65.00
Hobnail, Kettle, Pink Milk Glass	12.50
Hobnail, Mayonnaise Set, White	15.00
Hobnail, Mustard, Covered, Blue	15.00
Hobnail, Pitcher, Cranberry, 4 1/2 In.	45.00
Hobnail, Pitcher, Juice, Blue Opalescent	95.00

Hobnail, Pitcher, Water, 80 Ounce, Cranberry Opalescent, 4 Tumblers 375.00
Hobnail, Rose Bowl, White, 6 1/2 In. 42.00
Hobnail, Salt & Pepper, Cranberry Opalescent 15.00
Hobnail, Salt & Pepper, Yellow Opalescent 18.00
Hobnail, Shoe, Blue 18.00
Hobnail, Sugar & Creamer, Blue 22.00
Hobnail, Sugar & Creamer, Blue Opalescent 15.00
Hobnail, Sugar & Creamer, Yellow Opalescent 20.00
Hobnail, Sugar, Covered, Blue 15.00
Hobnail, Tumbler, Blue, 5 Ounce 9.00
Hobnail, Vase, Blue Opalescent, Footed, 5 1/2 In. 22.00
Hobnail, Vase, Bud, Plum Opalescent 35.00
Hobnail, Vase, Cranberry, 6 X 5 In. 40.00
Hobnail, Vase, Fan Shape, Blue, 8 X 8 In. 30.00
Hobnail, Vase, Green, Ruffled Edge, 6 In. 22.00
Hobnail, Vase, Ruffled, Blue Opalescent, 4 1/2 In. 18.00
Lamb's Tongue, Candy, Covered, Green 35.00
Late Coin Spot, Pitcher, Lemonade, Green Opalescent, 4 Tumblers 185.00
Leaf & Chain, Plate, Cobalt Blue, 8 In. 75.00
Lily Of The Valley, Compote, Blue Opalescent 22.50
Lily Pad, Bowl, Rosaline, 8 In. 42.50
Lincoln Inn, Iced Tea, Red, Set Of 8 .... 185.00
Lincoln Inn, Sherbet, Jade 8.00
Lincoln Inn, Tumbler, Red, 4 Ounce 15.00
Lotus & Grape, Bonbon, Green 45.00
Mandarin, Candlestick, Red, Pair 40.00
Mandarin, Vase, Burmese 150.00
Mongolian, Jar, Green 110.00
Mongolian, Vase, Peacocks, Green, 7 1/2 In. 95.00
No.950, Candlestick, Aqua, Pair 40.00
Novelty Shoe, Ashtray, Royal Blue 18.00
Nude Lady, Flower Frog, Pink 90.00
Nude Lady, Flower Frog, Red, Pair 85.00
Old Glory, Tray, Crystal, 10 X 8 In. 45.00
Peacock, Vase, Periwinkle Blue, 7 1/2 In. 95.00
Petticoat, Cake Plate, Label, Footed, 12 In. 30.00
Pineapple, Bowl, Crystal Satin, Triangle, 7 In. 15.00
Pinecone, Bowl, White Opalescent, 7 In. 50.00
Rib Optic, Bowl, Turquoise Opaque, Cupped, 9 1/2 In. 22.00
Rib Optic, Tumbler, Blue Opalescent 18.00
Rustic, Vase, Mother-Of-Pearl, 10 In. 12.00
Sailboat, Dish, Candy, Marigold, 6 In. 18.00
Shoe, Blue Opalescent 15.00
Spiral, Rose Bowl, Cranberry 95.00
Stalking Lion, Bowl, Custard Glass 85.00
Swan, Figurine, Green 14.00
Swan, Rosaline, Open 25.00
Teardrop, Salt & Pepper, Milk Glass 25.00
Thistle, Banana Boat, 4-Footed, Green 200.00
Thistle, Bowl, Amber, 9 In. 125.00
Threaded Diamond Optic, Basket, 7 In. 18.00
Thumbprint, Basket, Crimped, Black, 8 In. 33.00
Thumbprint, Sugar Shaker, Cranberry 45.00
Thumbprint, Syrup, Metal Top, Cranberry 55.00
Valencia, Candy, Covered, Blue 14.50
Vintage, Compote, Amethyst 45.00
Water Lily & Cattail, Bowl, White 35.00
Water Lily & Cattail, Plate, Scalloped Edge, Crystal, 11 In. 20.00
Water Lily, Jardiniere, White Satin 15.00
White House, Plate, Fruit & Floral Edge, Blue, 10 In. 150.00
Wild Rose, Biscuit Jar, Cranberry, Silver Lid 85.00
Wild Rose, Bottle, Barber, Decorated & Signed 55.00
Wild Rose, Fairy Lamp, Artist Signed, 3 Piece 65.00

Fiesta dinnerware was introduced in 1936 by the Homer Laughlin China Co., redesigned in 1969, and withdrawn in 1973. The simple design was characterized by a band of concentric circles, beginning at the rim. Cups had full-circle handles until 1969, when partial-circle handles were made. Harlequin and Riviera were related wares. For more information and prices on American dinnerware, see the book "The Kovels' Illustrated Price Guide to Depression Glass and American Dinnerware."

FIESTA, Ashtray, Dark Blue	25.00
Ashtray, Gray	25.00
Ashtray, Green	25.00 To 35.00
Ashtray, Old Ivory	25.00
Ashtray, Red	30.00
Ashtray, Rose	25.00
Ashtray, Turquoise	35.00
Ashtray, Yellow	25.00 To 35.00
Bowl, Covered, Kitchen Kraft, Red, 7 1/2 In.	25.00
Bowl, Fruit, Blue, 11 1/2 In.	45.00 To 55.00
Bowl, Gray, 7 1/4 In.	10.00
Bowl, Green, 4 3/4 In.	5.50
Bowl, Nested Set	375.00
Bowl, Old Ivory, 4 3/4 In.	5.50
Bowl, Old Ivory, 6 In.	8.00
Bowl, Red, 6 In.	16.00
Bowl, Red, 8 1/2 In.	18.00
Bowl, Red, 9 1/2 In.	25.00
Bowl, Salad, Yellow, 8 In.	50.00
Bowl, Turquoise, 4 3/4 In.	5.50
Bowl, Turquoise, 5 1/2 In.	6.50
Bowl, Turquoise, 8 1/2 In.	10.00
Bowl, Turquoise, 9 In.	30.00
Bowl, Yellow, 4 3/4 In.	5.50
Bowl, Yellow, 5 1/2 In.	6.50
Bowl, Yellow, 7 1/4 In.	10.00
Bowl, Yellow, 8 1/2 In.	13.00
Cake Plate, Kitchen Kraft, Green	20.00
Candleholder, Bulb, Marked, Dark Blue, Pair	35.00
Candleholder, Bulb, Old Ivory, Pair	14.00
Candleholder, Bulb, Turquoise, Pair	40.00
Candleholder, Tripod, Dark Blue	45.00
Carafe, Covered, Dark Blue	75.00
Carafe, Turquoise	80.00
Carafe, Yellow	48.00
Casserole, Covered, Old Ivory	60.00
Casserole, Covered, Rose	60.00
Casserole, Covered, Yellow	30.00 To 55.00
Casserole, Dark Blue	50.00
Casserole, Green	50.00
Casserole, Kitchen Kraft, Yellow	45.00
Casserole, Old Ivory	75.00
Coffeepot, After Dinner, Yellow	59.50
Coffeepot, Covered, Chartreuse	32.00
Coffeepot, Covered, Yellow	32.00 To 45.00
Coffeepot, Dark Blue	30.00
Coffeepot, Gray	35.00
Coffeepot, Green	25.00
Coffeepot, Light Green	42.00
Coffeepot, Red	65.00 To 120.00
Coffeepot, Rose	39.50 To 65.00
Compote, Fruit, Turquoise, 12 In.	75.00
Compote, Fruit, Yellow, 12 In.	75.00
Compote, Sweetmeat, Turquoise	28.50
Creamer, Red	15.00

Creamer, Yellow	8.00
Cup & Saucer, After Dinner, Dark Blue	16.00
Cup & Saucer, After Dinner, Dark Green	85.00
Cup & Saucer, After Dinner, Red	35.00
Cup & Saucer, After Dinner, Yellow	22.00 To 25.00
Cup & Saucer, Chartreuse	17.50
Cup & Saucer, Dark Blue	12.00 To 17.50
Cup & Saucer, Dark Green	14.00
Cup & Saucer, Green	12.00 To 20.00
Cup & Saucer, Red	14.00 To 20.00
Cup & Saucer, Turquoise	12.00 To 17.50
Cup & Saucer, Yellow	12.00 To 17.50
Egg Cooker, Chartreuse	25.00
Egg Cooker, Red, Crystal Bowl Insert	35.00
Egg Cooker, Red, Hankscraft	45.00
Gravy Boat, Green	21.00
Gravy Boat, Old Ivory	18.00
Gravy Boat, Red	18.00 To 42.50
Gravy Boat, Turquoise	29.50
Gravy Boat, Yellow	13.00 To 29.50
Jar, Juice, Green	10.00
Jar, Refrigerator, Covered, Yellow	35.00
Jug, Ivory, 2 Pint	17.00
Jug, Kitchen Kraft, Old Ivory	20.00
Jug, Turquoise, Half Gallon	20.00
Jug, Yellow, Half Quart	20.00
Mug, Chartreuse	30.00 To 35.00
Mug, Dark Blue	30.00
Mug, Green	35.00
Mug, Tom & Jerry, Green	18.00
Mug, Tom & Jerry, Yellow	18.00
Mug, Turquoise	25.00 To 30.00
Mug, Yellow	25.00 To 29.50
Mustard, Red	75.00
Mustard, Turquoise	55.00
Pitcher, Dark Blue	26.00
Pitcher, Disc, Old Ivory	22.00
Pitcher, Disc, Red	45.00
Pitcher, Ice Lip, Dark Blue	38.00
Pitcher, Ice Lip, Red	35.00 To 59.50
Pitcher, Ice Lip, Yellow	45.00
Pitcher, Juice, Yellow	12.00 To 18.00
Pitcher, Rose, Large	20.00
Pitcher, Tilt, Red	30.00
Pitcher, Yellow, 2 Pint	39.50
Plate, Chartreuse, 10 In.	11.00
Plate, Chop, Chartreuse, 14 In.	20.00
Plate, Chop, Red, 15 In.	25.00
Plate, Chop, Yellow	10.00
Plate, Cobalt, 10 In.	6.50
Plate, Dark Blue, 9 1/4 In.	3.50
Plate, Dark Green, 6 In.	3.00
Plate, Dark Green, 10 In.	11.00
Plate, Green, 9 1/4 In.	3.50
Plate, Grill, Cobalt	12.00
Plate, Grill, Red	20.00
Plate, Old Ivory, 9 In.	5.00
Plate, Old Ivory, 10 In.	8.00
Plate, Red, 6 In.	4.00 To 7.50
Plate, Red, 7 In.	2.00 To 8.50
Plate, Red, 9 In.	2.50 To 12.00
Plate, Red, 10 In.	15.00
Plate, Turquoise, 6 In.	3.00

Plate, Turquoise, 7 In. 7.50
Plate, Turquoise, 9 In. 6.00
Plate, Turquoise, 10 In. 5.50
Plate, Yellow, 9 In. .... 2.50 To 6.00
Plate, Yellow, 9 1/4 In. 3.50
Platter, Medium Green 20.00
Platter, Red 18.00
Refrigerator Stacking Set, Red Lid 85.00
Relish, Blue 65.00
Relish, Dark Blue, Sectioned 45.00
Relish, Dark Blue, 10 3/8 In. 60.00
Relish, Green 65.00
Relish, Red 75.00
Relish, Red, 4 Inserts, Blue, Turquoise, Green, & Yellow 75.00
Relish, Turquoise 55.00
Salt & Pepper, Light Green 6.00
Salt & Pepper, Medium Green 10.00
Salt & Pepper, Red 10.00
Salt & Pepper, Turquoise 8.00
Salt & Pepper, Yellow 8.00
Soup Plate, Green 99.50
Soup, Cream, Green .... 12.00 To 13.00
Soup, Cream, Old Ivory 12.00
Soup, Cream, Turquoise 12.00
Soup, Cream, Yellow 12.00
Soup, Dish, Chartreuse 15.00
Soup, Dish, Green .... 12.00 To 15.00
Soup, Dish, Turquoise 10.00
Soup, Dish, Yellow 12.00
Soup, Onion, Cobalt, Covered 125.00
Soup, Onion, Old Ivory, Covered 145.00
Sugar, Covered, Red .... 20.00 To 25.00
Syrup, Covered, Turquoise 85.00
Syrup, Ivory Handle, Yellow 95.00
Syrup, Lid, Green .... 50.00 To 115.00
Syrup, Red 100.00
Syrup, Round, Red 195.00
Syrup, Turquoise .... 99.50 To 125.00
Teapot, Dark Green 50.00
Teapot, Green 25.00
Teapot, Green, Small 40.00
Teapot, Red 50.00
Teapot, Red, Large .... 45.00 To 65.00
Teapot, Turquoise .... 24.00 To 50.00
Teapot, Yellow 45.00
Tray, Figure 8 Shape, Turquoise 125.00
Tumbler, Antique Gold 25.00
Tumbler, Dark Blue 20.00
Tumbler, Juice, Green 13.00
Tumbler, Juice, Red 22.50
Tumbler, Juice, Turquoise 13.00
Tumbler, Juice, Yellow 13.00
Tumbler, Light Green 20.00
Tumbler, Old Ivory .... 15.00 To 20.00
Tumbler, Red .... 19.00 To 25.00
Tumbler, Turquoise, 10 Ounce 30.00
Tumbler, Water, Dark Blue 20.00
Tumbler, Water, Turquoise 20.00
Utility Tray, Turquoise 15.00
Utility Tray, Yellow 15.00
Vase, Bud, Dark Blue 35.00
Vase, Bud, Red 30.00
Vase, Bud, Turquoise 25.00

Vase, Bud, Yellow 18.00
Vase, Green, 8 In. 65.00

*Findlay, or onyx, glass was made using three layers of glass. It was
manufactured by the Dalzell Gilmore Leighton Company about 1889 in
Findlay, Ohio. The silver, ruby, or black pattern was molded into the glass.
The glass came in several colors, but was usually white or ruby.*

FINDLAY ONYX, Bowl, 2 3/4 X 8 In.Diam. 720.00
  Celery, Cream & Platinum 350.00
  Spooner 465.00
  Sugar Shaker, Original Top 425.00

FIREFIGHTING, Badge, Calhoon Fire Dept., Banner Type, Nickel Plated Brass 45.00
  Bucket, Marked M.Laighton 1806, Leather, Pair 750.00
  Bucket, Marked P.Brown, Leather, Light Brown, 13 In. 210.00
  Bucket, Marked Wm.P.Benedict 1945, Relief, Leather, Pair 700.00
  Bucket, No.1, J.Stackpole 1809,Leather, C.1890, 13 In. 325.00
  Extinguisher, Auto, Atomized Fire Powder, Tin, 15 In. 15.00
  Extinguisher, Copper & Brass, 2 1/2 Gallon 25.00
  Extinguisher, Harden, Hand Grenade, Blue, Contents 110.00
  Extinguisher, Pioneer, 22 In. 8.00
  Helmet, Brass Eagle, Liberty No.5, Reading, Pa., White 150.00
  Helmet, Defiance Hook & Ladder Co., Brass 300.00
  Helmet, Dunbarton Fire Dept., Leather 75.00
  Helmet, English, Brass 200.00
  Helmet, New South Wales, Brass 275.00
  Lamp, Pole, 6-Sided, Dated 1878 .... 1800.00
  Lamp, Side, Steam Fire Engine, Marked Newton 3, 19 In., Pair 1300.00
  Lantern, Dietz King, Slide-Over Cage, Nickel On Brass 235.00
  Lantern, Presentation, 1865, Nickel 300.00
  Nozzle, Akron, Brass 65.00
  Pitcher, Presented To S.E.Whitcomb, H.& L.Co., Silver Plated 250.00
  Rattle 70.00
  Searchlight For Fire Truck 30.50

FIREPLACE, Andirons & Screen, Hand-Forged Brass, Screen, 64 X 45 X 9 In. 1000.00
  Andirons, Ball Top, Brass, 14 1/2 In., Pair 75.00
  Andirons, Ball Top, Snake Feet, 18th Century, Brass, 17 In. 295.00
  Andirons, Brass Ball Finials, Spit Holder, 26 In. 225.00
  Andirons, Brass Eagle Finial, Iron Knob, 18th Century, 22 In. 500.00
  Andirons, Brass Knob, Arched Feet, 18 In., Pair 500.00
  Andirons, C.1775, Brass, 19 1/4 In. 500.00
  Andirons, Cylindrical Loop, Shoe Foot, Tapering Shaft, 13 In., Pair 225.00
  Andirons, Federal Bell, Metal, Baluster Turned Stem, C.1795, 16 In. 350.00
  Andirons, Federal, Bell, Metal, Lemon Top Finial, C.1800, Pair 400.00
  Andirons, Federal, Brass & Iron, Conical Top, Ball, C.1800, 19 In. 495.00
  Andirons, Gooseneck, Arched Feet, Iron, 12 1/2 In., Pair 350.00
  Andirons, Gooseneck, Faceted Heads, 15 In., Pair 150.00
  Andirons, Gooseneck, 18th Century, Wrought Iron 225.00
  Andirons, Hessian Soldier, Iron, 12 In., Pair 250.00
  Andirons, Hessian Soldiers, 17 In., Pair 425.00
  Andirons, Indian Shape, Early 19th Century, Cast Iron, 16 In. 295.00
  Andirons, Iron & Brass, Arched Legs, Penny Feet, Pair 475.00
  Andirons, Lily Pad, Brass 190.00
  Andirons, Penny Feet, Brass Finials, C.1750, Wrought Iron 500.00
  Andirons, Ram's Horn Finials, Straight Bar, Penny Feet, 14 In., Pair 125.00
  Andirons, Ring Finials, Arched Legs, Penny Feet, 14 In., Pair 100.00
  Andirons, Ring Top, Bedroom Size, 10 X 11 In. 39.00
  Andirons, Scrolled Finials, Arched Legs, Penny Feet, 10 In., Pair 120.00
  Andirons, Urn & Finial Top, Penny Feet, C.1790, Brass 445.00
  Andirons, Urn Finial, Signed R.Wittingham, Brass, 16 In. 400.00
  Andirons, Urn Shape, Arched Penny Feet, 17 In., Pair 210.00

Bellows, Painted Ship Facade, Brass & Leather Findings, 18 In. 875.00
Broom, Hearth, Birch, 27 1/2 In. 160.00
Broom, Hearth, C.1810, Birch Splint, 41 In. 150.00
Chestnut Roaster, Iron, Slide Lid, 35 In.Handle 125.00
Corn Popper, Sliding Wire Lid, 27 In. 10.00
Crane, C.1860, 24 In. 175.00
Crane, Ram's Head Curl End, 18th Century, Forged Iron, 21 In. 95.00
Crane, 18th Century, Hand-Forged Iron, 24 In. 95.00
Fender, Brass Poker & Tongs, C.1800, 48 In. 325.00
Fender, George III, 19th Century, England, Brass, 47 In., Pair 550.00
Fender, Pierced, Bowfront, C.1860, Steel, Pair 120.00
Fender, Regency, Serpentine Front, Pierced, C.1810, Steel 165.00
Fender, Victorian, Pierced, 19th Century, Paw Feet, Brass 125.00
Fire Surround, Silver Metal, Victorian, 19th Century 40.00
Fireback, Coat Of Arms Of George II, Dated 1746, 36 X 34 In. 880.00
Fireback, English, C.1700, Black Painted, 26 X 23 In. 192.00
Footman, Brass, Iron, Pierced Brass Plate, C.1800, 11 1/2 X 16 In. 250.00
Frypan, Chamfered Handle, Extruded Loop End, Wrought Iron, 44 In. 225.00
Grate, George III, Brass & Iron, Figures, Fruit Tree, 32 In. 192.00
Grate, Iron, 18 X 12 In. 20.00
Hod, Coal, Liner, Covered, Wooden 85.00
Oven, Biscuit, Sheet Iron 45.00
Peel, Bread, Hand-Forged Iron, Cannonball End, C.1860, 37 1/2 In. 45.00
Potholder, Swivel, Hand-Forged 14.00
Roasting Meat Rack, Brass 85.00
Saucepan, Straight Handle, Footed, Cast Iron, Pot 5 1/4 X 4 In. 40.00
Screen, George IV, 3-Panel Chinese Silk, Mahogany, 46 In. 192.00
Screen, Louis XV, Floral & Acanthus Design, Walnut, 37 1/2 In. 200.00
Screen, Mahogany, Framed, Carved Feet, Floral & Birds, 26 In. 105.00
Screen, Pedestal, Needlepoint Face, Tripod Base, 4 Ft. 75.00
Screen, Victorian, Biblical Scene, Painted Tole, 27 X 47 In. 325.00
Shovel & Tongs, Lemon Finials, Iron Arms, Brass Shovel, 30 In. 195.00
Shovel, Ash, Ram's Horn Handle, Cast Iron 60.00
Sifter, Ash, Wooden 45.00
Toaster, Hearth, Rotating, 18th Century, Hand-Wrought Iron 325.00
Toaster, Iron, Flip Style, 24 In. Handle 89.00
Toaster, Rack Of Arched Bars, 18th Century, Wrought Iron, 20 In. 300.00
Toaster, Swivel, Wrought Iron 125.00
Tongs, For Removing Hot Coals, C.1850, Hand-Forged Iron, 18 1/4 In 30.00
Tongs, Hearth, Cannonball Finial, Iron, 19 3/4 In. 30.00
Tongs, Iron, 17 1/2 In. 13.00
Tool Set, George III, 5 Piece, Brass, 26 1/2 In. 350.00
Tools, Ram's Horn Handle, Knob Handle, 18th Century 120.00
Trammel Chain & Pot Hook, Hand-Forged, C.1830, Adjustable, 80 In. 100.00
Waffle Iron, Hand-Forged Long Handle 135.00

Fischer porcelain was made in Herend, Hungary. The factory was founded in 1839, and has continued working into the twentieth century. The wares are sometimes referred to as Herend porcelain.

FISCHER, Ewer, Beads & Roundels Allover, Covered, Signed, Blue, 9 1/2 In. 200.00
Ewer, Blue, Beige Ground, Gold Trim, Marked, 9 In. 200.00
Jar, Multicolored Floral, Outlined In Gold, Covered, Marked, 9 In. 255.00
Tray, Shell Shape, Reticulated, Gold Trim, 13 1/2 X 8 1/2 In. 215.00
Vase, Gold & Blue, Gourd Shape, 10 1/2 In. 135.00

FISHING, Box, Tackle, Heddon 22.50
Bucket, Minnow, Wire & Mesh 18.00
Catalog, Bristol, 1920s 38.00
Creel, Birchbark 75.00
Creel, Bombe-Sided, Hinged Cover, C.1890, 11 3/4 X 7 1/2 In. 40.00
Fly Reel, Bone Handle, Nickel Silver Over Brass, 2 1/4 In.Diam. 26.00
Fly Rod, Winchester, No.6040 .... 150.00
Hooks, Pflueger, Wooden Box 3.50

Lure, Airex, Ablette 5.00
Lure, Airex, Godart 5.00
Lure, Beul Spinner, Feathered Treble Hook 3.00
Lure, Heddon, Hi-Tail 6.00
Lure, McDonald, Lif-Lik Merry Minnow 6.00
Lure, P. & K., Bucktail Spinner 5.00
Lure, Paw Paw Bait Co., Indian-Pictured Box 10.00
Lure, Pedigo, Airedale Plug 10.00
Lure, Pflueger, Colorado Spinner, Small 1.50
Lure, Russelure 3.00
Lure, Shakespeare, Glo-Lite Pup 6.00
Lure, Tony Accetta, River Devil 6.00
Lure, True Temper, Speed Shad 6.00
Lure, Weber, Little Sam 6.00
Lure, Weber, SN2 .... 6.00
Reel, Atlas Portage, No.60 .... 15.00
Reel, Brothers Sentrie 10.00
Reel, Deep Sea, Single Action, Brass 55.00
Reel, Heddon, Lone Eagle, No.206 .... 12.50
Reel, Meisselbach, 1907 .... 25.00
Reel, Pflueger Trump, 1943 .... 15.00
Reel, Pflueger, Nobby 10.00
Reel, Pflueger, Trusty 10.00
Reel, Rev-ONoc 15.00
Reel, Shakespeare, Kazoo, Brass 25.00
Reel, South Bend Cast-O Reno, No.5 .... 11.00
Reel, Winchester, Brass, Small 50.00
Rod, Fly, South Bend, C.1910, Original Case 45.00
Rod, Fly, Wooden Case 15.00
Rod, Premax, Case, 3 Piece 25.00
Rod, Richardson, Metal 15.00
Tray, Minnow, Shakespeare, Glass 30.00
     FLAG, see Textile, Flag

FLASH GORDON, Book, Big Little Book, Perils Of Mongo 12.50
Book, In The Water World Of Mongo, Whitman, 1937 .... 19.00
Compass 10.00
Display, Pioneer Belts, Cardboard, 14 X 15 In. 75.00
Space Compass, On Card 5.50

Flow blue, or flo blue, was made in England about 1830 to 1900. The plates were printed with designs using a cobalt blue coloring. The color flowed from the design to the white plate so the finished plate had a smeared blue design. The plates were usually made of ironstone china.

FLOW BLUE, Berry Bowl, Waldorf 24.00
Bone Dish, Dundee, Ridgway 27.00
Bone Dish, Lakewood, Wedgwood 39.00
Bowl, Ayr, Round, 8 1/2 In. 50.00
Bowl, Carlton, Enclosed Scroll Handles, Florals, 9 1/2 In. 57.50
Bowl, Cereal, Conway, New Wharf 31.50
Bowl, Cereal, Corey Hill, E.Walley 36.00
Bowl, Cereal, Poppy 30.00
Bowl, Cereal, Touraine 28.00
Bowl, Cobalt Blue, Blue Rose To Center, 6 In. 18.00
Bowl, Colonial, Oval, 10 1/2 In. 55.00
Bowl, Conway, 10 In. 45.00
Bowl, Delamere, Alcock, 9 In. 50.00
Bowl, Fairy Villas, 6 1/4 In. 55.00
Bowl, Melbourne, Grindley, Oval, 9 X 6 1/2 In. 47.00
Bowl, Nelson, England, 10 1/2 In. 35.00
Bowl, Pansy, England, 10 In. 45.00
Bowl, Rose, Grindley, 1880, 4 1/2 In. 18.00

Bowl, Rose, Grindley, 6 In.	18.00
Bowl, Rose, 8 In.	7.00
Bowl, Roslyn, Oval, 6 X 8 In.	45.00
Bowl, Serving, Oriental Scene, Flowers, Curved Handles, 9 In.	35.00
Bowl, Soup, Kyber, Adams, 9 In.	45.00
Bowl, Soup, Mikado	35.00
Bowl, Soup, Nonpareil	35.00
Bowl, Soup, Peking, 1845	30.00
Bowl, Soup, Virginia	30.00
Bowl, Soup, Wild Rose, Impressed, Blue Mark	24.00
Bowl, Touraine, Stanley, 8 In.	38.00
Bowl, Touraine, Stanley, 9 1/2 In.	50.00
Bowl, Ubertas, Prussia, 9 In.	30.00
Bowl, Valencia, Marked S. Hancock, 2 1/4 X 9 1/4 In.	65.00
Bowl, Vegetable, Candia, Handled, C.1910, 11 1/2 In.	110.00
Bowl, Vegetable, Dahlia, 10 In.	48.00
Bowl, Vegetable, Gala, Covered, Semi Porcelain, 7 1/2 X 12 In.	90.00
Bowl, Vegetable, Lonsdale, 9 3/4 In.	45.00
Bowl, Vegetable, Lorne, Covered, 12 In.	40.00
Bowl, Vegetable, Melbourne, Open, Oval, 9 In.	55.00
Bowl, Vegetable, Nankin, M & V, 10 In.	140.00
Bowl, Vegetable, Nonpareil, 9 1/2 In.	85.00
Bowl, Vegetable, Oregon, Open, Oval, Johnson Bros., 9 In.	48.00
Bowl, Vegetable, Seville, 10 X 7 1/2 In.	75.00
Bowl, Vegetable, Touraine, Covered, Stanley, 9 1/4 In.	200.00
Bowl, Vegetable, Yedo, Ironstone, Covered	250.00
Bowl, Waldorf, 7 1/2 In.	52.00
Bowl, Waldorf, 9 In.	38.00
Butter Chip, Argyle	29.00
Butter Chip, Grace	18.00
Butter Chip, Hamilton, Maddock	12.00
Butter Chip, Linda	12.00
Butter Chip, Lotus, Set Of 11	185.00
Butter Chip, Melbourne	20.00
Butter Chip, Melbourne, Grindley	20.00
Butter Chip, Morning Glory	16.50
Butter Chip, Princeton	15.00
Butter Chip, Sydney, New Wharf Pottery	17.00
Butter Chip, Waverly, Maddock	15.00
Butter, Denton, Covered, Grindley	100.00
Butter, Melbourne, Covered, Insert	150.00
Canister, Covered, Floral Design, Blue Delft, 7 1/4 In.	35.00
Chamber Pot, Saskia, Ridgway	125.00
Chamber Pot, Savory, Wood & Sons	110.00
Cheese Dish, Blossom, Wedgwood	150.00
Chop Plate, Hong Kong, 9 In.	24.00
Condiment Set, Blue Flowers, Gold Trim, 5 1/4 In., 3 Piece	85.00
Creamer, Crumlin, Myott	65.00
Creamer, Indian, Pratt	159.50
Creamer, La Belle	35.00
Creamer, Lobelia	75.00
Creamer, Madras	90.00
Creamer, Melbourne	100.00
Creamer, Nonpareil	50.00
Creamer, Touraine	200.00
Creamer, Touraine, Stanley	200.00
Cup & Saucer, Bouquet	35.00
Cup & Saucer, Brunswick	45.00
Cup & Saucer, Colonial	22.00
Cup & Saucer, Conway, New Wharf	35.00
Cup & Saucer, Dahlia	56.50
Cup & Saucer, Dahlia, Handleless	75.00
Cup & Saucer, Ebor, Ridgway	107.50
Cup & Saucer, Haddon	49.00

Cup & Saucer, Haddon, Grindley	47.00
Cup & Saucer, Hofburg	30.00
Cup & Saucer, Italia, W. & E.Corn	65.00
Cup & Saucer, La Belle	35.00 To 55.00
Cup & Saucer, Lancaster, Corn	45.00
Cup & Saucer, Lotus, Grindley	36.00
Cup & Saucer, Manilla, Podmore Walker, Handleless	140.00
Cup & Saucer, Melbourne	20.00
Cup & Saucer, Morning Glory, Handleless	110.00
Cup & Saucer, Mush	49.00
Cup & Saucer, Nonpareil	65.00
Cup & Saucer, Oregon, Handleless	85.00
Cup & Saucer, Oriental, J. & G.Walker, Handleless	120.00
Cup & Saucer, Ormonde	27.00
Cup & Saucer, Osborne	54.00
Cup & Saucer, Seaweed, Burshstroke	75.00
Cup & Saucer, Shanghai, Handleless	85.00
Cup & Saucer, Somerset, Grindley	36.00
Cup & Saucer, Sydney, New Wharf Pottery	52.00
Cup & Saucer, Togo	45.00
Cup & Saucer, Touraine, Alcock	45.00 To 55.00
Cup & Saucer, Waldorf, New Wharf Pottery	45.00
Cup & Saucer, Waldorf, Wood & Son	40.00
Cup & Saucer, Watteau, New Wharf Pottery	27.00
Cup & Saucer, Windsor	44.00
Cup Plate, Kyber, Adams	32.00
Cup Plate, Tonquin, Heath	48.00
Eggcup, Madras, New Wharf Pottery	50.00
Gravy Boat & Underplate, Melbourne	100.00
Gravy Boat, Argyle, Grindley	55.00
Gravy Boat, Chiswick	35.00
Gravy Boat, Dorothy, Tray, Johnson Bros.	86.00
Gravy Boat, Duchess, Tray, Grindley	85.00
Gravy Boat, Excelsior, Fell	125.00
Gravy Boat, Nonpareil	60.00
Gravy Boat, Olympia	51.00
Gravy Boat, Scinde	165.00
Gravy Boat, Tivoli	100.00
Gravy Boat, Touraine	125.00
Gravy Tureen, Springtime, Tray, Cauldon	150.00
Jardiniere, Blue Floral Pattern, C.1890, 8 1/2 X 10 In.	150.00
Jug, Bird & Flowers, Gold Trim, 7 3/4 X 4 1/2 In.	70.00
Jug, Milk, Wagon Wheel, Child's	139.50
Mug, Kin Shan	145.00
Pitcher & Bowl, Genevese	650.00
Pitcher, Blue Danube, 7 In.	115.00
Pitcher, Harvest, Hancock & Sons, 6 1/2 In.	55.00
Pitcher, Hofburg, 6 In.	80.00
Pitcher, Kona, 8 In.	85.00
Pitcher, Marie, 8 In.	125.00
Pitcher, Milk, Roseville, Hughes & Son	117.50
Pitcher, Milk, Wagon Wheel	138.00
Pitcher, Oyama, 6 X 5 In.	175.00
Pitcher, Tulips, Ford, 7 In.	110.00
Plaque, Mythological Woman, Ormolu Frame, 13 In.Diam., Pair	395.00
Plate, Acantha, 8 In.	14.00 To 15.00
Plate, Acantha, 9 In.	18.00
Plate, Acantha, 10 In.	15.00
Plate, Alaska, 7 3/4 In.	28.00
Plate, Amoy, 7 In.	45.00
Plate, Arcadia, 10 In.	35.00
Plate, Argyle, 10 In.	35.00
Plate, Arms Of The State Of New York, Mayer, 9 7/8 In.	495.00
Plate, Belmont, Wedgwood, 14 In.	85.00

Plate, Bentick, 10 In. 41.00
Plate, Carlton, 10 1/2 In. 85.00
Plate, Challinor, Pelew, 9 1/2 In. 25.00
Plate, Chapoo, 7 1/2 In. 60.00
Plate, Chapoo, 8 1/2 In. 75.00
Plate, Chapoo, 9 1/2 In. 80.00
Plate, Chinese Plant, Wood, 9 In. 57.00
Plate, Chinese, Dimmock, 9 1/4 In. 55.00
Plate, Chiswick, Ridgway, 10 In. 25.00
Plate, Clytie, Turkey Center, 10 In. 40.00
Plate, Clytie, 8 In. 39.50
Plate, Conway, New Wharf Pottery, 10 In. 45.00
Plate, Conway, 10 In. 50.00
Plate, Corean, Mulberry, 7 3/4 In. 44.00
Plate, Country Scenes, 7 In. 22.00
Plate, Dahlia, 9 7/8 In. 42.50
Plate, Dresden, Furnival, 6 1/4 In. 16.00
Plate, Dresden, Hancock, 9 X 12 In. 32.00
Plate, Excelsior, 9 In. 37.00
Plate, Fairy Villas, Adams, 10 In. 50.00
Plate, Fairy Villas, 7 3/4 In. .... 20.00 To 45.00
Plate, Fairy Villas, 9 In. 45.00
Plate, Fern, 8 1/2 In. 50.00
Plate, Ford City, C.1880, 10 In. 75.00
Plate, Formosa, Walker, 6 1/2 In., Set Of 5 .... 275.00
Plate, Hampton Sprays, 5 3/4 In. 20.00
Plate, Indian Jar, 10 1/2 In. 85.00
Plate, Indian, 7 In. 40.00
Plate, Indian, 9 In. 60.00
Plate, Kyber, 7 1/4 In. 32.00
Plate, Kyber, 9 In. 45.00
Plate, La Belle, Wheeling, 9 In. 45.00
Plate, La Belle, 9 1/2 In. 68.00
Plate, Lahore, Phillips, 7 1/2 In. 40.00
Plate, Lancaster, New Wharf Pottery, 8 In. 32.50
Plate, Lancaster, 8 In. 32.00
Plate, Leicester, 10 In. 32.00
Plate, Lois, 8 In. 35.00
Plate, Lonsdale, 10 In. 47.50
Plate, Loraine, 9 1/4 In. 35.00
Plate, Madras, Davenport, C.1844, 9 In. 32.50
Plate, Mandarin, Maddock, 7 1/2 In. 42.00
Plate, Mandarin, Pountney Bristol, 10 1/2 In. 22.50
Plate, Marie, Grindley, 9 In. 25.00
Plate, Marie, 10 In. 37.50
Plate, Melbourne, 6 1/2 In. 30.00
Plate, Melbourne, 8 In. 8.00
Plate, Melbourne, 8 3/4 In. 15.00
Plate, Moorish Castle, Wedgwood, 9 In. 50.00
Plate, Nankin, M & V, 8 In. 45.00
Plate, Ning Po, 8 1/2 In. 65.00
Plate, Nonpareil, Burgess & Leigh, 6 3/4 In. 28.00
Plate, Nonpareil, Burgess & Leigh, 7 1/8 In. 36.00
Plate, Nonpareil, Burgess & Leigh, 10 In. 60.00
Plate, Nonpareil, 6 In. 25.00
Plate, Nonpareil, 6 3/4 In. 20.00
Plate, Nonpareil, 7 1/2 In. 45.00
Plate, Nonpareil, 8 3/4 In. 36.00
Plate, Nonpareil, 9 In. 40.00
Plate, Nonpareil, 10 In. 40.00
Plate, Normandy, 10 In. .... 48.00 To 50.00
Plate, Pekin, Dimmock, 10 1/4 In. 65.00
Plate, Rhone, 7 In. 28.50
Plate, Rose, Grindley, 1880, 5 1/2 In. 18.00

Plate, Scinde, Alcock, 9 1/2 In. 55.00
Plate, Scinde, 6 In. 45.00
Plate, Scinde, 7 1/4 In. .... 45.00 To 55.00
Plate, Scinde, 8 In. 18.00
Plate, Scinde, 9 In. 60.00
Plate, Scinde, 9 3/4 In. 30.00
Plate, Scinde, 10 In. 55.00
Plate, Seville, 9 1/2 In. 55.00
Plate, Shanghai, 7 1/2 In. 50.00
Plate, Shanghai, 8 1/2 In. 55.00
Plate, Shell, Challinor, 9 1/2 In. 75.00
Plate, Shusan, 7 In. 40.00
Plate, Splendid, 8 In. 40.00
Plate, Temple, Podmore Walker, 8 3/4 In. 92.50
Plate, Tokyo, K.& Co., 14 In. 88.00
Plate, Tonquin, Adams, 10 1/4 In. 70.00
Plate, Tonquin, 7 1/2 In. 60.00
Plate, Tonquin, 10 1/2 In. 90.00
Plate, Touraine, Alcock, 7 1/2 In. .... 30.00 To 40.00
Plate, Touraine, Alcock, 9 In. .... 38.00 To 42.00
Plate, Touraine, Alcock, 10 In. 45.00
Plate, Touraine, Stanley, 9 In. 28.00
Plate, Touraine, Stanley, 10 In. 70.00
Plate, Touraine, 6 1/2 In. .... 22.00 To 25.00
Plate, Touraine, 8 3/4 In. .... 28.00 To 40.00
Plate, Vista, 10 In. 57.00
Plate, Waldorf, New Wharf Pottery, 8 3/4 In. 35.00
Plate, Waldorf, New Wharf Pottery, 9 1/4 In. 37.00
Plate, Waldorf, New Wharf Pottery, 9 1/2 In. 35.00
Plate, Waldorf, Wood & Sons, 10 In. 37.00
Plate, Waldorf, 7 1/2 In. 40.00
Plate, Waldorf, 10 In. .... 30.00 To 50.00
Plate, Wampa, Ivanhoe, Wedgwood, 10 In. 75.00
Plate, Wentworth Pattern, 9 3/4 In. 18.00
Plate, Whampoa, 10 1/2 In. 55.00
Plate, Wilmington Water Tower, 8 In. 30.00
Plate, Yedo, Ironstone, 9 1/4 In. 35.00
Plate, Yedo, 15 1/2 In. 175.00
Platter, Arcadia, 16 In. .... 89.00 To 95.00
Platter, Astoria, 12 X 9 In. 75.00
Platter, Beauties Of England & Wales, 15 X 19 1/2 In. 110.00
Platter, Carlton, F.Winkle & Co., 13 1/2 X 16 1/2 In. 100.00
Platter, Chapoo, 16 In. 295.00
Platter, Chen-Si, 15 3/4 In. 80.00
Platter, Chinese Jar, 8-Sided, 20 X 16 In. 165.00
Platter, Constance, W.A.A.& Co., 13 1/2 X 10 3/4 In. 70.00
Platter, Eclipse, Johnson Brothers, 14 1/2 In. 50.00
Platter, Eclipse, 14 In. 90.00
Platter, Flowers, 16 1/2 X 11 In. 65.00
Platter, Formosa, Mayer, 12 1/2 X 9 1/2 In. 275.00
Platter, Formosa, 18 X 14 In. 250.00
Platter, Fulton, 12 1/2 X 9 1/4 In. 78.00
Platter, Gironde, 20 X 13 In. 150.00
Platter, Glenmore, 16 1/4 X 18 1/2 In. 80.00
Platter, Loretta, Alcock, 13 X 17 In. 90.00
Platter, Lorne, Oval, 18 In. 50.00
Platter, Melbourne, 14 In. 90.00
Platter, Nonpareil, Burgess & Leigh, 12 X 10 In. 90.00
Platter, Nonpareil, 15 X 12 1/2 In. 125.00
Platter, Pelew, 10 3/4 In. 120.00
Platter, Pelew, 18 1/2 X 12 In. 350.00
Platter, Persian, 14 X 10 In. 110.00
Platter, Turkey Design, 18 X 13 1/2 In. 155.00

Platter, Waldorf, New Wharf Pottery, 10 3/4 X 8 3/4 In.	40.00
Platter, Watteau, 10 1/2 In.	100.00
Platter, Whampoa, 15 1/2 In.	160.00
Platter, Yedo, 17 1/2 In.	235.00
Relish, Chusan, Shell Shape, Amoy	65.00
Relish, Waverly, Grindley	65.00
Ring Tree, Upright Hand, Romantic, Staffordshire, England	75.00
Sauce, Amoy	40.00
Sauce, Argyle, Johnson	21.50
Sauce, Fairy Villas, Adams	14.00
Sauce, Madras	20.00 To 25.00
Sauce, Marie, Grindley	16.00
Sauce, Nonpareil, 5 1/2 In.	20.00
Sauce, Tonquin, Adams	45.00
Sauce, Tonquin, Heath, 5 In.	42.00
Sauce, Touraine	12.50 To 20.00
Saucer, Alaska	12.00
Saucer, Conway, New Wharf Pottery, Set Of 4	98.50
Saucer, Florida, Johnson Bros., Set Of 3	18.00
Saucer, Lorne	5.00
Saucer, Nonpareil, 6 In.	15.00
Saucer, Seville	8.00
Saucer, Touraine, Stanley	16.00
Soup, Andorra, Johnson Bros.	26.00
Soup, Cashmere, 9 1/4 In.	75.00
Soup, Chein-Ki, 10 1/2 In.	90.00 To 95.00
Soup, Chen-Si, 10 1/2 In.	80.00
Soup, Hong Kong, Meigh, 10 1/4 In.	85.00
Soup, Kyber, Adams, 9 In.	65.00
Soup, La Belle	32.00
Soup, Lorne	25.00
Soup, Lorne, 8 3/4 In.	18.00
Soup, Marie, Grindley, 8 3/4 In.	30.00
Soup, Moselle, Flanged, 8 3/8 In.	28.00
Soup, Nonpareil, 8 3/4 In.	65.00
Soup, Roseville, Flange, Hughes & Son	37.50
Soup, Touraine, Alcock	45.00
Soup, Touraine, 9 In.	35.00
Soup, Waldorf, 9 In.	40.00
Sugar & Creamer, Tonquin, Heath, Covered	350.00
Sugar, Amoy	145.00
Sugar, Chinese	50.00
Sugar, Marguerite	75.00
Sugar, Melbourne, Covered	100.00
Sugar, Milan	75.00
Sugar, Savoy, Johnson	25.50
Sugar, Scinde, Covered	50.00
Syrup, La Belle, Brass Lid	95.00
Tea Set, California	400.00
Teapot, Amoy	375.00
Teapot, Chapoo	395.00
Teapot, Oriental	25.00
Teapot, Scinde, Alcock	300.00 To 325.00
Tile, Tea, Souvenir, Beatrice, Nebraska	24.00
Toilet Set, Scroddle, Ewer, Covered Toothbrush, Covered Soap	625.00
Tureen, Vegetable, Lorraine, Covered	85.00
Tureen, Vegetable, Mikado, Covered, Wilkinson	126.00
Tureen, Vegetable, Norwich, Covered, Grindley	95.00
Wash Set, Flower Pattern, Empress, Pitcher & Bowl	250.00
Waste Bowl, Ashburton, Grindley	49.50
Waste Bowl, Dahlia, Dark Flow	119.50
Waste Bowl, Oxford, 6 In.	55.00
Waste Bowl, Touraine, Stanley	40.00

FLYING PHOENIX, see Phoenix Bird

Folk art is listed in many sections of the book under the actual name of the object. See categories such as Box; Cigar Store Indian; Weather Vane; Wooden; etc.

FOLK ART, Basket, Rigid Overhead Handle, Sawtooth Rim, Tinsmith-Made	175.00
Block, 3 Hand-Carved Balls Inside, Wooden, 6 1/2 In.	6.00
Box, Handkerchief, Pyrography, Woman's Head	15.00
Figurine, Horse, Saddle, Hardwood, 7 In.	35.00
Figurine, Leghorn Chicken, Applied Wings, Wire Legs, 9 In.	50.00
Figurine, Movable Arms, Hand-Scorped, Big Nose, Gray Hair, 8 In.	40.00
Figurine, Old Man & Lady, Hand-Carved, 5 In., Pair	45.00
Figurine, Squirrel, Sitting On Cut Log, C.1910, Pine, 3 X 3 3/4 In.	40.00
Lemon Slice, Papier-Mache, Sanded Finish, Yellow, 1900s, 48 In.	15.00
Oxen, Carved, Pair	85.00
Paperweight, Carved Coal, Depicts Coal Mine, 5 X 4 1/2 In.	20.00
Shooting Gallery Figures, Bear, Lion, Elephant, Iron, 12 In.	75.00
Silhouette, Pressed Sea Moss, Designs & Wreaths, 5 In.Diam., Pair	10.00
Stand, Tree, Picket Fence Around Animals & Man, 17 X 17 In.	250.00
Toy, Cat & Birdcage, Mechanical, Wooden	300.00
Toy, Dog, Platform, Hand-Scorped, C.1930, 9 3/4 X 2 3/4 X 7 In.	100.00
Toy, Ram, Hand-Carved & Scorped, C.1930, Wheels, 5 1/2 X 10 1/2 In.	185.00
Troika, 3-Horse Hitch, Carriage, Driver & Passenger, Original Paint	400.00
Ugly Man, Hand-Scorped, Movable Arms, High Glaze Paint, 7 In.	40.00
Werewolf, Wolf's Head On Man's Body, Right Arm Moves, 7 1/2 In.	40.00
Whirligig, Black Mammy Washing Clothes	175.00
Whirligig, Cowboy On Bucking White Mule	465.00
Whirligig, Man Sawing Wood	100.00 To 140.00
Whirligig, Man With Paddle Hands, Maine	1800.00
Whirligig, Pecking Bird	100.00
Whirligig, 2 Black Men Dancing On Platform At End Of Stick	385.00
Whirligig, 2 Boys On See Saw	225.00
Wreath, Hair, Flowers, Butterflies, Shadowbox Frame, 1850s	195.00

Foo dogs are mythical Chinese figures, part dog and part lion. They were made of pottery, porcelain, carved stone, and wood.

FOO DOG, Figurine, Mounted As Lamps, 10 In., Pair	50.00
Ginger Jar, Rust On White, Porcelain	225.00
Planter, Underplate, Royal Court Scene, Blue Ground, Porcelain	280.00
Teapot, Tail Handle, Dog Leaning Upright, C.1900, 6 1/2 In.	110.00

FOOT WARMER, A Warm Friend, Logan Pottery	75.00
Brass Fittings, Copper	36.50
Charcoal Drawer, Rug-Covered	35.00
Cherrywood, Tin Lid, Brass Porthole Vents, 9 1/2 X 4 3/4 In.	300.00
Cherrywood, Tin, Diamonds & Circles	130.00
Clark Heater No.2, Charcoal Tray	20.00 To 24.00
Copper, Handmade, Signed Overlay, Footed, Square	55.00
Dorchester Pottery, Signed, Dated 1912	100.00
Pierced Tin, Wooden Frame	120.00
Punched, Maple Frame, Coals Cup, Tin	125.00
Slab Of Soapstone, Wire Bail, 6 X 9 In.	22.50
Stoneware, Applied Floral Decoration, Tan Glaze, 13 3/4 In.	45.00
Stoneware, Loop For Use As Horse Tether, Round	10.00
Stoneware, Wire Bail, Rectangular	22.50
Walnut	165.00
Wooden, Scalloped Detail, Applied Diamonds, Red & Black, 12 In.	45.00

Fostoria glass was made in Fostoria, Ohio, from 1887 to 1891. The factory was moved to Moundsville, West Virginia, and most of the glass seen in shops today is a twentieth-century product.

FOSTORIA, see also Milk Glass

FOSTORIA, Airedale, Vase, 10 In.	18.00

American Lady, Cocktail 9.00
American Lady, Cordial, 1 Ounce 10.00
American Lady, Goblet, Water 10.00
American Lady, Goblet, Wine 8.00
American Lady, Goblet, 10 Ounce 18.00
American Lady, Whiskey, 2 Ounce 9.00
American, Bonbon, 3-Footed, Red, 7 In. 55.00
American, Bonbon, 3-Footed, 7 In. 12.00
American, Bowl, Oval, 11 3/4 In. 30.00
American, Bowl, Serving, Handled, 9 In. 20.00
American, Bowl, 3-Footed, 10 1/2 In. 22.00
American, Butter, Domed 65.00
American, Cake Plate, Square 47.00
American, Celery 12.00
American, Compote, Covered, 9 In. 22.00
American, Creamer 8.00
American, Cruet, 7 Ounce 18.00
American, Cup & Saucer, Footed .... 9.50 To 10.00
American, Cup, Footed 6.00
American, Dish, Candy, Red, Hexagonal Foot, Covered 75.00
American, Dish, Candy, 3-Footed, 7 In. 3.50
American, Dish, Serving, 4-Part, 9 X 6 In. 28.00
American, Goblet, Cocktail, Flared, Footed, 3 Ounce 5.00
American, Goblet, 9 Ounce .... 7.00 To 8.00
American, Goblet, 10 Ounce 12.50
American, Ice Cream Set 85.00
American, Jug, 40 Ounce 30.00
American, Liquor Set 50.00
American, Mayonnaise & Underplate 16.00
American, Mustard Jar, Covered 33.00
American, Nappy, Handled, 3-Cornered, 5 In. 7.50
American, Nappy, Square, 4 1/2 In. 5.00
American, Oyster Cocktail, 4 1/2 Ounce 5.00
American, Pitcher, Barrel-Shaped, Ice Lip, 1 Gallon 110.00
American, Pitcher, Ice Lip, 3 Pint 45.00
American, Plate, Torte, 12 In. 20.00
American, Plate, 6 In. 5.00
American, Plate, 9 1/2 In. 18.00
American, Punch Set, Tray, 11 Cups, Bowl, 1 1/2 Gallon 135.00
American, Relish, 3-Part, 11 In. 22.00
American, Salt & Pepper 10.00
American, Sherbet, Flared Top 5.00
American, Sherbet, Low, 5 Ounce 4.00
American, Sugar & Creamer 8.00
American, Sugar & Creamer, Covered 18.00
American, Sugar & Creamer, Individual 15.00
American, Sundae, 5 Ounce 4.00
American, Sundae, 6 Ounce 5.00
American, Tea Set, 4 Piece 14.00
American, Toothpick 15.00
American, Toothpick, Hat-Shaped 15.00
American, Tumbler, Flared, 5 1/4 In. 13.00
American, Tumbler, Iced Tea, 12 Ounce 12.00
American, Tumbler, 5 Ounce 5.00
American, Vase, Bud, Flared, 6 In. 8.00
American, Vase, Bud, Red 45.00
American, Vase, Square, 6 1/2 In. 15.00
American, Wedding Bowl, Covered 75.00
Arcadia, Sugar 12.00
Atlanta, Lamp 165.00
Baroque, Bowl, Flared, 7 In. 15.00
Baroque, Bowl, Handled, 10 1/2 In. 25.00
Baroque, Bowl, Handled, 16 In. 32.00
Baroque, Cake Plate, Handled 15.00

Baroque, Candleholder, Double, 8 1/2 In., Pair 40.00
Baroque, Candleholder, 5 1/2 In., Pair 12.00
Baroque, Celery, Oval, 10 1/2 In. 14.00
Baroque, Creamer, Chintz Etched 10.00
Baroque, Dish, Candy, Blue, Footed 12.00
Baroque, Goblet, 5 1/2 In. 7.50
Baroque, Goblet, 6 In. 8.50
Baroque, Ice Bucket 45.00
Baroque, Relish, Divided, 12 In. 20.00
Baroque, Sherbet 6.50
Baroque, Sugar, Azure, Individual 6.00
Baroque, Vase, Ice Blue, 6 1/2 In. 35.00
Beverly, Sherbet, Twisted Stem, Green Bowl, Set Of 6 .... 54.00
Buttercup, Bowl, Console 38.50
Buttercup, Candleholder, Triple, Pair 65.00
Buttercup, Tumbler, Iced Tea, 12 Ounce 25.00
Cellini, Goblet, 7 Ounce 8.00
Century, Cup & Saucer, Crystal 15.00
Century, Goblet, 10 Ounce 8.00
Century, Sherbet, 4 1/2 In. 6.00
Chanticleer, Figurine 195.00
Chapel Bells, Goblet, Wine 18.00
Chapel Bells, Sherbet 18.00
Chapel Bells, Tumbler, Water 18.00
Chintz, Candleholder, 2-Light 12.00
Chintz, Creamer 6.50
Chintz, Cruet 32.00
Chintz, Goblet, Champagne, 5 1/2 In. 17.00
Chintz, Goblet, Wine, 4 1/4 In. 12.00
Chintz, Ice Bucket 40.00
Chintz, Nappy, Etched, Handled 16.00
Chintz, Plate, 7 1/2 In. 11.00
Chintz, Relish, 3 Part 23.00
Chintz, Sugar & Creamer, Individual 22.50
Chintz, Tray, Handled, 11 In. 39.00
Colony, Goblet, Water 8.00
Colony, Oyster Cocktail 7.00
Colony, Sherbet .... 6.00 To 6.50
Colony, Tumbler, 9 Ounce 8.00
Colony, Vase, Cupped, 7 In. 12.00
Corsage, Oyster Cocktail 14.00
Corsage, Tumbler, Iced Tea 19.00
Corsage, Tumbler, Water 19.00
Cube, Sugar & Creamer 2.00
Double Snail, Pitcher, 5 1/4 In. 50.00
Edgewood, Butter, Covered 45.00
Elephant, Jar, Dresser 15.00
Fairfax, Bowl, Handled, Pink, 5 1/2 In. 5.00
Fairfax, Creamer, Topaz 8.00
Fairfax, Cup & Saucer, Amber, 2-Footed 6.00
Fairfax, Cup & Saucer, Azure Blue 6.00
Fairfax, Cup & Saucer, Pink, Footed .... 6.00 To 8.00
Fairfax, Cup, Topaz 8.00
Fairfax, Plate, Amber, 8 In. 15.00
Fairfax, Plate, Chop 3.50
Fairfax, Plate, Pink, 7 In. 2.75
Fairfax, Plate, Topaz, 6 In. 2.50
Fairfax, Plate, Topaz, 7 In. 3.50
Fairfax, Plate, Topaz, 9 In. 6.00
Fairfax, Platter, Green, 10 1/2 In. 10.00
Fairfax, Relish, Topaz, 8 1/2 In. 8.00
Fairfax, Saucer, Topaz 3.00
Fairfax, Sherbet, Topaz, Footed 14.00
Fairfax, Sugar & Creamer, Green 10.00

Fairfax, Sugar & Creamer, Individual	15.00
Fairfax, Sugar, Green, Footed	8.00
Fairfax, Sugar, Topaz	8.00
Fairfax, Tumbler, Topaz, 5 Ounce	20.00
Fairfax, Tumbler, Topaz, 9 Ounce	14.00
Fern, Console Set, Etched, Sticker, 3 Piece	60.00
Fern, Goblet, Cocktail, Oyster	10.00
First Love, Sugar, Individual	10.00
Fountain, Plate, Luncheon, Green	4.00
Grape, Creamer, Acid Etched	1.50
Handkerchief, Bowl, Blue Opalescent	45.00
Hartford, Bottle, Perfume, 4 1/2 In.	35.00
Heather, Goblet, Wine, Blue	21.00
Heather, Sherbet, Blue	21.00
Heather, Tumbler, Water, Blue	21.00
Heirloom, Candelabra, 3-Candle, Prisms, Rock Crystal, Pair	125.00
Heirloom, Candleholder, Pink Opalescent, 9 1/2 In., Pair	35.00
Heirloom, Candleholder, White, 9 1/2 In., Pair	15.00
Heirloom, Candleholder, 9 1/2 In., Pair	35.00
Heirloom, Celery, Pink Opalescent	35.00
Heirloom, Flower Frog, Pink Opalescent, 10 In.	25.00
Heirloom, Vase, Blue, 10 In.	14.00
Heirloom, Vase, Opalescent Blue, 10 In.	20.00
Heraldry, Goblet, 6 1/2 In.	7.00
Heraldry, Sherbet	6.00
Holly, Goblet, Wine, 6 In.	25.00
Holly, Goblet, 8 In.	24.00
Holly, Plate, 8 1/2 In.	15.00
Holly, Sherbet, 5 1/4 In.	20.00
June, Bowl, Blue, Footed, 12 In.	65.00
June, Bowl, Console, Yellow, 12 In.	30.00
June, Bowl, Handled, Blue, 9 In.	35.00
June, Candleholder, Pinwheel Handles, 5 In., Pair	25.00
June, Cordial, Topaz	55.00
June, Cup & Saucer	20.00
June, Goblet, Champagne, Blue	20.00 To 39.00
June, Goblet, Champagne, Topaz	22.00
June, Mayonnaise Set	24.00
June, Oyster Cocktail, Blue	25.00
June, Plate, Topaz, 6 In.	5.00 To 6.50
June, Plate, Topaz, 7 1/2 In.	10.00
June, Plate, Topaz, 10 In.	27.00
June, Relish, Divided	24.00
June, Sherbet, Blue	30.00 To 39.00
June, Sugar & Creamer	20.00
June, Sugar, Topaz	20.00
June, Tumbler, Iced Tea, Blue	30.00
Lafayette, Bowl, 12 In.	14.00
Lafayette, Celery, Oval, 11 1/2 In.	13.00
Lafayette, Plate, 6 In.	4.00
Laurel, Goblet, 9 Ounce	10.00
Louis XVI, Table Set, Green, 4 Piece	385.00
Lyre, Bowl, Oval, 10 1/2 In.	12.50
Mayfair, Plate, Blue, 7 In.	5.00
Mayfair, Plate, Ebony, 7 In.	5.00
Mayfair, Plate, Green, 9 In.	4.00
Mayfair, Plate, Pink, 5 3/4 In.	2.00
Mayflower, Goblet, Champagne	12.00
Meadow Rose, Goblet, Champagne	14.00
Meadow Rose, Sherbet, Footed	12.00 To 14.00
Midnight Rose, Cake Plate, Handled, Etched	17.50
Mt.Vernon, Tumbler, Water	18.00
Navarre, Candleholder, Double, Pair	35.00
Navarre, Compote, 6 In.	18.00

Navarre, Cordial .... 10.00 To 40.00
Navarre, Dish, Pickle, 9 In. 9.00
Navarre, Goblet, Champagne 14.00
Navarre, Goblet, Water .... 12.50 To 24.00
Navarre, Goblet, 10 Ounce .... 12.00 To 15.00
Navarre, Plate, Handled, 10 In. 18.00
Navarre, Relish, 4-Part, 12 In. 22.00
Navarre, Sherbet 14.00
Navarre, Sherbet, Low 18.00
Navarre, Shrimp Icer & Liner 45.00
Navarre, Sugar & Creamer 16.00
Navarre, Vase, Footed, 9 1/2 In. 35.00
Oriental, Goblet, Wine, 5 1/4 In. 18.00
Oriental, Sherbet, 4 1/4 In. 10.00
Pioneer, Cake Set, Amber, Server, 10 1/2 In., 5 Piece 15.00
Pioneer, Relish, Green, 3-Part 12.00
Pioneer, Saucer, Green 1.25
Priscilla, Butter, Emerald & Gold, Covered 125.00
Priscilla, Custard, Handled, Footed 7.00
Priscilla, Soup, Cream, Underplate, Amber 8.00
Priscilla, Table Set, Gold Trim, Green, 4 Piece 275.00
Rambler, Bowl, Handled, 10 In. 25.00
Rearing Horse, Bookend .... 25.00 To 30.00
Romance, Creamer, 3 In. 10.00
Romance, Sherbet 18.00
Romance, Sugar & Creamer 37.00
Romance, Sugar, 3 In. 10.00
Romance, Tumbler, Water 18.00
Rosalie, Goblet, 7 In. 15.00
Rosby, Punch Set, Bowl, Stand, & 29 Cups, 1910 .... 315.00
Rosby, Water Set, Pitcher, 2 Quart, 7 Piece 135.00
Round Robin, Creamer 1.50
Royal, Bowl, Amber, Oval, 9 In. 30.00
Royal, Soup, Cream, Amber 9.00
Royal, Sugar, Flat, Amber 7.00
Seal, Frosted 65.00
Seneca, Goblet, Water 6.50
Seneca, Oyster Cocktail 5.00
Seneca, Sherbet 5.50
Seville, Plate, Amber, 8 1/2 In. 6.00
Shirley, Sugar & Creamer 10.00
Sonata, Compote, Green, 8 In. 10.00
Springtime, Plate, Torte, 13 In. 32.00
Swirl, Console Set, Ultramarine, 3 Piece 40.00
Swirl, Goblet, Cocktail, Ice Blue 24.00
Trojan, Goblet, Water, Amber 25.00
Trojan, Plate, Yellow, 8 1/4 In. 75.00
Trojan, Vase, Yellow, 8 In. 62.00
Vernon, Dish, Candy, 3-Part, Covered, Green 85.00
Versailles, Bowl, Console, Footed, 12 In. 25.00
Versailles, Bowl, Console, Green, Footed 30.00
Versailles, Compote, Topaz, 6 In. 25.00
Versailles, Cup & Saucer, Pink 20.00
Versailles, Dish, Candy, Pink, Covered 50.00
Versailles, Dish, Candy, Pink, 3-Part 40.00
Versailles, Goblet, Water, Blue 25.00
Versailles, Goblet, Wine, Green, Clear Stem 24.00
Versailles, Ice Bucket, Pink, Handled 45.00
Versailles, Pail, Whipped Cream, Blue 60.00
Versailles, Plate, Lemon, Green, 2-Handled 12.00
Versailles, Plate, Pink, 6 1/4 In. 4.00
Versailles, Plate, Pink, 7 3/4 In. 6.50
Versailles, Plate, Pink, 9 1/4 In. 12.00
Versailles, Plate, Topaz, 9 In. .... 10.00 To 12.00

Versailles, Plate, Topaz, 10 1/2 In. 25.00
Versailles, Salt & Pepper, Pink 65.00
Versailles, Saucer, Green 5.00
Versailles, Sherbet, Topaz 16.00
Versailles, Tumbler, Green, 6 In. 18.00
Vesper, Candleholder, Green, 9 In., Pair 135.00
Vesper, Vanity Set, Powder Jar & Attached Perfume 135.00
Victoria, Dish, Lobster 35.00
Vintage, Compote, C.1904, Covered, 8 1/2 In. 45.00
Willowmere, Goblet, Water 16.00
Yeoman, Creamer 22.50
    FOVAL, see Fry Foval
    FRAME, see Furniture, Frame

Francisware is an amber hobnail glassware made by Hobbs Brockunier and Company, Wheeling, West Virginia, in the 1880s.

FRANCISWARE, Bowl, Frosted Hobnail, Square, 7 1/2 In. 65.00
  Pitcher, Water, Child's 125.00
  Pitcher, 7 1/4 In. 125.00
  Sauce, 6 In.Square 20.00
  Toothpick, Frosted .... 45.00 To 55.00

Frankart, Inc., New York, New York, mass-produced nude "dancing-lady" lamps, ashtrays, and other decorative Art Deco items in the 1920s and 1930s. They were made of white lead composition and spray-painted. "Frankart Inc." and the patent number and year were stamped on the base.

FRANKART, Ashtray, Cowgirl On Rearing Horse, Bronzed, 7 X 6 In. 35.00
  Ashtray, Horse, Standing 65.00
  Ashtray, Nude, No.T301 .... 105.00
  Bookends, Cast Metal, Stylized Head Of Woman, 6 1/2 In. 80.00
  Bookends, Dutch Boy & Girl, Bronzed .... 45.00 To 58.00
  Bookends, Springer Spaniels, Bronzed Finish, Signed 45.00
  Candlestick, Nudes, Original Paint, 12 In., Pair 270.00
  Figurine, Nude, 12 In. 140.00
  Lamp Base, Nude, Octagonal, 7 In. 110.00

Frankoma Pottery was originally known as The Frank Potteries when John F. Frank opened shop in 1933. The factory is now working in Sapulpa, Oklahoma.

FRANKOMA, Bowl, Brown, 6 In. 10.00
  Bowl, 1-Handled, Impressed Mark, Bronze, 3 3/4 X 2 1/2 In. 5.00
  Candleholder, Black Glazed, 5 In. 6.00
  Candleholder, Blue-Green Impressed Over Seal, 1 1/2 In., Pair 22.00
  Console Set, Green, 3 Piece 35.00
  Cookie Jar, Brown & Green 20.00
  Cornucopia, Footed, Mottled Pink, 7 In. 9.00
  Dish, Clamshell Shape, 5-Footed, Green, 7 In.Diam. 6.00
  Dish, Rectangular, Green & Bronze, 9 1/2 X 5 3/4 In. 8.00
  Flask, Aztec Design, Thong Through Ceramic Loops, 6 1/2 X 6 In. 15.00
  Jug, Blue Green, 5 1/2 In. 6.00
  Jug, Tan, 7 In. 8.00
  Mug, Donkey, Yellow 11.00
  Mug, Elephant, Brown Satin 7.00
  Mug, Elephant, Red, With Black 8.00
  Mug, 1968 G.O.P. Elephant 55.00
  Pitcher, Black Glaze, 2 In. 5.00
  Pitcher, Brown & Cream, Set Of 6 Tumblers, 9 In. 55.00
  Pitcher, Milk, Aztec Relief, Handle, 4 3/4 In. 2.00
  Pitcher, No.553, Blue, 2 In. 8.00
  Pitcher, Rounded, Black, 2 In. 5.00
  Planter, Ball Shape, Blue & Brown 7.50
  Planter, Duck 27.50

Planter, Mottled Green & Brown .... 5.00 To 8.00
Plate, Christmas, 1965, White, First Edition 225.00
Plate, Christmas, 1967 .... 45.00
Plate, Christmas, 1968 .... 18.00
Plate, Christmas, 1970 .... 18.00
Plate, Easter, 1972 .... 9.00
Plate, Jesus The Carpenter, Brown To Tan, 6 In. Diam. 7.00
Plate, Oklahoma, 1907, Gold Sticker, Bronze, 8 1/2 In. 12.00
Plate, Prairie Chicken 35.00
Sign, Dealer, Red 22.50
Sugar & Creamer, Green With Brown, 2 In. 4.00
Sugar & Creamer, Plain Design 8.00
Sugar, Aztec Relief, Handle, Bronze 6.00
Teapot, Green, Bronze, Covered, 6 In. 15.00
Vase, Bud, Cream & Tan, 6 In. 8.00
Vase, Bulbous, Green, 6 In. 25.00
Vase, Cylindrical, Green, 10 X 4 In. 10.00
Vase, Footed, High Gloss Green, 2 1/2 X 8 In. 7.00
Vase, Free Form, Label, Rose, 7 1/2 X 6 In. 6.00
Vase, Shell Shape, Scalloped Rim, 6 In. 8.00
Wall Pocket, Acorn 13.00
Wall Pocket, Shoe, Brown & Tan, 6 In. 7.00
　　　　　FRUIT JAR, see Bottle, Fruit Jar

Fry glass was made by the H.C.Fry Glass Company of Rochester,
Pennsylvania. It includes cut glass, but the famous Fry glass today is
the foval, or pearl, art glass. This is an opal ware decorated with colored
trim. It was made from 1922 to 1933.

FRY FOVAL, Basket, Delft Blue Handle, Blue Opalescent, 8 1/4 In. 300.00
Bowl, Fruit, Delft Blue Pedestal, 13 In. 275.00
Candlestick, Barley Sugar Twist Stem, Blue Glass, 10 In., Pair 220.00
Cup & Saucer, Cobalt Handle, Ground Pontil 79.00
Cup & Saucer, Green Jade Handle 65.00
Shade, Trumpet Flair, 4 In., Pair 100.00
Sugar & Creamer, Corset Shape, Pearly Opalescent, 3 In. 135.00
Tumbler, Lemonade, Pedestal, Jade Green 45.00

　　　　　FRY, see also Cut Glass

FRY, Bowl, Hobstar & Fan Pattern, Signed, 8 In. 110.00
Champagne, Allover Cut 25.00
Fernery, 3-Footed, Signed, 8 In. 185.00
Plate, Divided, Heat Resistant, Opalescent, 10 1/2 In., Set Of 3 .... 45.00

Fulper is the mark used by the American Pottery Company of
Flemington, New Jersey. The art pottery was made from 1910 to 1929.
The firm had been making bottles, jugs, and housewares from 1805. Doll
heads were made about 1928. The firm became Stangl Pottery in 1929.

FULPER, Ashtray, Green & Brown Flambe Glaze, 2 1/2 X 9 In. 75.00
Basket, Rope Handle, Blue Drip Glaze, 9 1/2 In. 48.00
Bowl, Bulbous, 3 Shoulder Handles, Crystalline Mottled, 6 1/2 In. 140.00
Bowl, Coil, Brown, Dark Blue & Red Glaze, 10 In. 300.00
Bowl, Console, Sky Blue Flambe, Marked, 40 X 16 X 3 1/2 In. 65.00
Bowl, Crystalline Green Over Pea Green, Oval, 12 X 7 In. 85.00
Bowl, Flambe Interior, 10 In. 80.00
Bowl, Flower Frog, Shell Shape, 1912, 11 1/2 In. 85.00
Bowl, Flower, Green, Gold Crystalline Geometric Design, 10 In. 95.00
Bowl, Footed, Flemington Stamp, Green & Black, 8 X 2 1/4 In. 95.00
Bowl, Green Over Blue & Cream, Marked, 8 1/2 X 2 In. 40.00
Bowl, Mottled Green Glaze, 11 X 2 3/4 In. 115.00

Bowl, Peg Legs, Flemington Stamp, Blue Gray, 8 X 2 1/4 In. 85.00
Bowl, Purple Over Rose, Stamp, 8 3/4 X 4 3/8 In. 90.00
Bowl, Scarab Frog, 8 In. 48.00
Bowl, 3-Footed, Marked, Metallic Green Streaking, 10 1/2 X 3 3/8 In. 65.00
Candleholder, C.1910, Mahogany Flambe To Blue, 5 X 5 In., Pair 125.00
Candleholder, Flowers & Moths, Satin Finish, Marked 35.00
Candleholder, Gun Metal Glaze, 5 In. 5.00
Candleholder, Side Handles, Marked, Green Into Rose, 5 X 3 In. 35.00
Candlestick, Blue, Crystalline, 8 In. 115.00
Candlestick, Brown Matte, 2 1/4 X 5 In. 50.00
Candlestick, Twist Shape, Speckled Copper Oxide Green, 8 In., Pair 80.00
Centerpiece, Green, Yellow, Blue, Oval, 11 1/2 X 9 1/2 In. 285.00
Chamberstick, Flambe, Cobalt Blue, High Glaze 47.50
Chamberstick, Lavender 60.00
Chamberstick, Purple 35.00
Compote, Crystalline, 12 X 4 In. 120.00
Creamer, Ink Stamp, Gun Metal Over Gray, 3 3/8 X 1 1/2 In. 25.00
Crock, Leaf Design, Cobalt Blue 125.00
Dish, Crystalline, Oval, Green, 2 X 7 In. 38.00
Dish, Flared & Scalloped Rim, Footed, Copper Oxide Green, 7 1/2 In. 38.00
    FULPER, DOLL, see Doll, Fulper
Ewer, Wisteria Blue Flambe & Matte Glaze, Marked, 4 1/2 In. 35.00
Flower Frog, Fish, Flambe 55.00
Flower Frog, High Gloss, Green Over Beige, 7 X 3 1/4 In. 30.00
Flower Frog, Metallic Green Over Tan, 4 1/4 In.Diam. 34.00
Flower Frog, Orange Flambe 75.00
Flower Frog, Scarab, Marked, Gun Metal Gray, 2 X 1 1/2 In. 15.00
Flower Frog, Swan, Cream Running Over Blue, 6 1/2 X 4 1/2 In.Diam. 55.00
Flower Frog, Swan, 6 In. 40.00
Flower Frog, Women In Canoe, Marked, 8 In. 125.00
Jar, Powder, Cleopatra Finial, Blue Base .... 175.00 To 225.00
Jar, Powder, Figural, Deco Lady, Purple, Signed 145.00
Jug, Charcoal, Blue-Green, Rust Specks, 2 Handles, 6 In. 125.00
Lamp, Blue, Crystalline 120.00
Lamp, Figural, Perfume 185.00
Lamp, Fluted, Footed, Green Into Rose, 25 1/2 In. 130.00
Lamp, Perfume, Ballerina, Pink .... 160.00 To 190.00
Lamp, Perfume, Ballerina, Yellow 195.00
Lamp, Perfume, Bird 395.00
Lamp, Perfume, Parrot, 11 In. 395.00
Lamp, Perfume, Signed Martin Stangl 200.00
Mug, Green Glaze, Old Mark 65.00
Mustard, Coiled, Gun Metal, 3 Handles 280.00
Pitcher, Brown & Black, High Glaze, 5 1/4 In. 150.00
Pitcher, Coil, Green, Gold & Charcoal Glaze, 6 In. 300.00
Pitcher, Coils Of Clay, Brown & Black, 5 1/4 In. 150.00
Rose Bowl, Green Crystalline Over Amber Flambe, Marked, 7 In.Diam. 110.00
Sconce, Candle, Handled, 7 X 4 In. 75.00
Tile, Kidney Beans & Circle Inside Raised Edge, Maroon, 7 In. 40.00
Urn, Greek, Rust, Blue, Ivory Glaze, 9 1/2 In. 510.00
Urn, 3-Handled, Gray, Blue Flambe, 7 In. 105.00
Vase, Beehive, Shoulder Handles, Black Luster, 6 1/2 X 5 1/4 In. 110.00
Vase, Black Over Brown, 5 In. 60.00
Vase, Blue Crystalline, 3-Handled, Marked, 8 1/2 In. 125.00
Vase, Blue, Volcanic Glaze, 6 1/2 In. 70.00
Vase, Brown & Black, 7 In. 175.00
Vase, Brown Drip Over Blue Luster, Bulbous, 4 In. 50.00
Vase, Brown Jewels On Italian Green, Mirror Luster, 7 In. 75.00
Vase, Brown To Green Glaze, 4 In. 60.00
Vase, Bulbous, Shoulder Handles, Green Over Rose, 7 1/2 In. 90.00
Vase, Cat's Eye, Cream, Rust, Charcoal Glaze, Copper Dust, 6 In. 175.00
Vase, Chinese Blue & Olive, C.1930, 9 In. 275.00
Vase, Crystalline, Blue & Gold, 5 X 6 In. 60.00
Vase, Crystalline, Green, 10 In. .... 150.00 To 210.00

Vase, Cylinder-Shaped, Black, Blue, 8 In. 50.00
Vase, Famille Rose, 8 1/2 In. 65.00
Vase, Fan, Charcoal Black, Blue-Green & Mustard, Flambe Glaze, 7 In. 200.00
Vase, Fan, Raised Bands, Drip Glaze, Marked, 6 X 3 1/2 In. 35.00
Vase, Green & Blue Over Mauve, Bulbous, 3-Handled, 7 In. 70.00
Vase, Green Drip Glaze Over Mauve, 7 In. 85.00
Vase, Handled, Pink To Brown, 4 In. 65.00
Vase, High Gloss Green Over Matte Rose, Marked, 4 1/2 X 3 In. 45.00
Vase, Horizontal Ribs, Marked, Black Flambe & Crystal, 3 1/2 In. 30.00
Vase, Ivory To Mahogany Flambe, Marked, C.1912, 7 X 4 1/2 In. 100.00
Vase, Leopard Skin, Crystalline, 13 In. 285.00
Vase, Nude, Flowers Encircled By Frogs, 5 1/2 In. 135.00
Vase, Ovoid, Turquoise Drip, Green, 6 X 3 1/2 In. 30.00
Vase, Raspberry & Gray, 7 3/4 In. 85.00
Vase, Round, Mottled Blue Glaze, 3 1/2 In. 25.00
Vase, Sculptured Fronds, Marked, Footed, Mottled Blue, 8 In. 45.00
Vase, Silver Threading, Green Glaze, 6 1/2 In. 65.00
Vase, Stick, Purple, 8 1/2 In. 40.00
Vase, Turquoise & Mustard, Flambe Glaze, 5 1/2 X 3 1/2 In. 55.00
Vase, Vertical Mark, Blue Streaking Into Purple, 6 3/4 X 4 1/2 In. 85.00
Vase, White Drip Over Brown, 8 1/4 In. 100.00
Vase, 3-Handled, Mottled Brown & Black, 7 In. 150.00
Wall Pocket, Acorn-Shaped, Blue With Gold, 7 In. 85.00
Wall Pocket, Bird, Yellow Feathers, Gray Ground, Marked, 9 In. 125.00
Wall Pocket, Figural, Parrot, Glaze, Original Green Sticker, 10 In. 80.00

FURNITURE, Armchair, Arrow Back, Child's, Green, Yellow Striping, Gilded 75.00
Armchair, Ash, 3 Vertical & Horizontal Spindles, 43 In. 2000.00
Armchair, Carved & Inlaid Walnut, C.1890 .... 220.00
Armchair, Carved Walnut, Leaf & Nut Crest, C.1860 .... 600.00
Armchair, Child's, Georgian Style, C.1900, Rush Seat ....*Illus* 375.00
Armchair, Chippendale, Carved, Wooden Seat, C.1780, Oak 275.00
Armchair, Chippendale, Interlaced Splat, Mahogany 250.00
Armchair, Chippendale, Mahogany, Carved Back, Dolphin Feet 650.00
Armchair, Chippendale, Mahogany, Claw & Ball Feet 605.00
Armchair, Chrome Frame, Padded Seat, White Cotton Duck 175.00
Armchair, George III, Japanned, Caned Backrest 70.00
Armchair, George III, Ladder Back, Yew, Rush Seat 175.00
Armchair, George III, Mahogany, Arched Crest, 38 1/2 In. 400.00
Armchair, George III, Oak, Wheat Sheaf Forms Splat 192.00
Armchair, Hand-Carved, Needlepoint Seat & Back, C.1800 .... 2000.00
Armchair, Hepplewhite, Shieldback, Mahogany, Leaf Legs 600.00
Armchair, Jacobean, Walnut, Open, Striped Fabric 350.00
Armchair, Ladder Back, Ash, Post Legs, C.1680, 45 In. 1100.00
Armchair, Ladder Back, Ball Feet, Delaware Valley, 4 Slat 1700.00
Armchair, Ladder Back, Cherry, Hickory, Maple 75.00
Armchair, Ladder Back, Maple & Ash, 18th Century, 46 In. 1100.00
Armchair, Ladder Back, Mushroom, Sausage Turned Legs, 44 In. 400.00
Armchair, Ladder Back, New England, Splint Seat, Red Paint, 42 In. 200.00
Armchair, Ladder Back, 4 Slats, Black Paint, C.1700, 47 In. 1600.00
Armchair, Lady's, Victorian, Carved Walnut, Finger-Carved 195.00
Armchair, Louis XV, Gilt Wood, Needlepoint Panel, Black 357.00
Armchair, Louis XVI, Shieldback, Acanthus Carved Legs, Pair 375.00
Armchair, Lyre Back, Cane Seat, French, Gilt 70.00
Armchair, Massachusetts, Maple & Ash, C.1680, 43 In. ....*Illus* 1800.00
Armchair, Oak & Ash, Post Back, Rush Seat, C.1680, 43 In. 7000.00
Armchair, Open Baluster Splat, Mahogany, C.1760 .... 375.00
Armchair, Provincial, Rush Seat, Oak, Georgian, Pair 625.00
Armchair, Queen Anne, Maple, Spanish Feet, C.1740, 40 In. 2000.00
Armchair, Queen Anne, Molded, Spooned Crest, Maple, 1740, 40 1/2 In. 2000.00
Armchair, Queen Anne, Needlepoint Covered, Pad Feet, Mahogany 325.00
Armchair, Queen Anne, Spanish Feet, Maple, 1740-60 .... 950.00
Armchair, Queen Anne, Spanish Feet, Rush Seat, C.1750 ....*Illus* 1700.00
Armchair, Queen Anne, Spanish Feet, Yoke-Shaped Crest, C.1750 .... 1700.00

Furniture, Armchair, Child's, Georgian Style, C.1900, Rush Seat

Furniture, Armchair, Massachusetts, Maple & Ash, C.1680, 43 In.

Armchair, Queen Anne, Walnut, Brown Needlepoint Seat, Trifid Feet 440.00
Armchair, Sculptured Chinese Teakwood, Dragon Head Arms 1150.00
Armchair, Sheraton, Arched Crest, Polychrome Floral, 36 In., Pair 500.00
Armchair, Slat Back, Plain Stiles, 17th Century, 42 In. 1600.00
Armchair, Slat Back, Rush Seat, New England, C.1700, 42 In. 500.00
Armchair, Spanish, Walnut, Leather Seat 125.00
Armchair, Spindle Back, Saddle Seat, Elm, Georgian 550.00
Armchair, Vase-Shaped Splat, Slip Seat, Mahogany, George III 550.00
Armchair, Victorian Gothic, Arched Crest, Rosewood 200.00
Armchair, Victorian, Stick-Form Splat, Out-Scrolled Arms, Oak 220.00
Armchair, William & Mary, Banister Back, C.1720, 48 1/2 In. 350.00
Armchair, William & Mary, Banister Back, Maple, Ash, C.1740, 50 In. 2100.00
Armchair, William & Mary, C.1700, 48 1/4 In. .... *Illus* 950.00
Armchair, William & Mary, C.1740, Maple & Ash, 50 In. .... *Illus* 2100.00
Armchair, William & Mary, Carved Volute, C.1700, 51 In. 1100.00
Armchair, Windsor, Ash & Maple, Bamboo Legs, Brown, 37 In. 250.00
Armchair, Windsor, Baluster & Spindle Backrest, 3-Legged 120.00
Armchair, Windsor, Bamboo, Old Black Paint, Gold Striping, 18 In. 125.00
Armchair, Windsor, Bow Back, Ring & Reel Legs, Red Paint, 37 In. 150.00
Armchair, Windsor, Bow Back, Saddle Seat, Red Paint, 41 In. 200.00
Armchair, Windsor, Bow Back, Saddle Seat, Ting & Reel Legs, 37 In. 400.00
Armchair, Windsor, Bow Back, 7 Spindles, 34 In. 550.00
Armchair, Windsor, Comb Back, English, 19th Century, Pine 300.00
Armchair, Windsor, Comb Back, 7 Spindles, C.1790 .... 1320.00
Armchair, Windsor, Continuous Arms, 18th Century 600.00
Armchair, Windsor, Lady's, Fan Crest, Ash & Pine, 18th Century 2500.00
Armchair, Windsor, New England, Hickory & Fruitwood .... *Illus* 1200.00
Armchair, Windsor, Philadelphia Style, Saddle Seat, Pair 1200.00
Armchair, Windsor, Pine, Step-Down, C.1810 .... 475.00

Furniture, Armchair, Queen Anne, Spanish Feet, Rush Seat, C.1750

Furniture, Armchair, William & Mary, C.1700, 48 1/4 In.

Furniture, Armchair, William & Mary, C.1740, Maple & Ash, 50 In.

(See Pages 236, 237)

Furniture, Armchair, Windsor, New England, Hickory & Fruitwood

Armchair, Windsor, Vase-Shaped Leg Turnings, Maple 550.00
Armchair, Windsor, Wheel Back, Elm & Yew, George III 1100.00
Armchair, Windsor, Writing, Bow Back, Black Paint, C.1800, 38 In. 800.00
Armchair, Windsor, 19th Century, Elm, George III 715.00

Armchair, Windsor, 9 Turned Spindles, Shaped Seat, C.1780 .... 357.00
Armchair, Wing, Federal, Inlaid Mahogany, Loose Cushion, C.1800 .... 1100.00
Armchair, Wing, Federal, Mahogany, Arched Crest, Scrolled, C.1790 .... 990.00
Armchair, 3 Shaped Slats, Turned Ash, C.1690, 42 1/4 In. 1100.00
Armoire, Art Nouveau, Carved Walnut, C.1880, 98 In. 1000.00
Armoire, Cameo Glass, Mahogany, Rosewood, 37 1/2 In. .... *Illus* 2100.00
Armoire, Coromandel, Chinese, Early 19th Century 2050.00
Armoire, French Provincial, Oak, 2 Doors, 4 Shelves, 78 In. 1500.00
Armoire, Provincial, Fruitwood, 1 Door, 75 X 35 In. 1200.00
Bed, American Rococo, Rosewood, C.1840, 7 Ft.6 In. X 60 In. 1500.00
Bed, Arched Headboard, American, Pine, 41 1/2 X 76 1/2 In. 50.00
Bed, Baby, 1930s, All Metal 125.00
Bed, Cannonball, Tiger Maple, Double 1250.00
Bed, Canopy, Brass Crown On Top, Iron & Brass, 73 In. X 8 1/2 Ft. 2400.00
Bed, Canopy, Chinese, Scroll & Leaf, Forms 3 Drawers, 86 In. 1400.00
Bed, Canopy, Federal, Maple & Pine, C.1800, 83 1/2 In. 950.00
Bed, Canopy, Federal, Red Paint, C.1800, Square Posts, 79 X 73 In. 2000.00
Bed, Cutout Beaded Headboard, C.1800, 76 X 50 In. 525.00
Bed, Double, Eastlake, Rosette Design, C.1880 .... 135.00
Bed, Empire, Four-Poster, Carved, Mahogany, 56 1/2 X 82 In. 1050.00
Bed, Federal, Arched Headboard, Square Posts, 56 X 47 In. 225.00
Bed, Federal, Mahogany, Square Four-Poster, C.1810, 4 X 6 Ft. 1870.00
Bed, Federal, Painted, Chamfered Post, C.1800, 48 In. High 300.00
Bed, Federal, Press, Painted Blue, 18th Century, 50 1/2 In. 1500.00
Bed, Federal, Red Paint, Turned Posts, 20 X 74 In. 375.00
Bed, Four-Poster, Carved Mahogany, C.1840, 54 X 76 1/2 In. 1000.00
Bed, Four-Poster, Federal, Cherry, Reeded, C.1850, 56 In. 1430.00
Bed, Four-Poster, Maple, Turned Posts, Blue Paint, 56 X 68 In. 120.00
Bed, Four-Poster, Pine & Maple, Old Red Paint, 77 X 53 In. 350.00
Bed, Four-Poster, Rope, C.1830, 3/4 Size 1550.00
Bed, Four-Poster, Turned Posts, Shaped Headboard, Mahogany, 80 In. 725.00
Bed, Hired Man's, Birch & Pine, Block & Turned Posts, Red Paint 150.00
Bed, Murphy, Beveled Mirror, Oak, C.1900 .... 1000.00
Bed, Murphy, Victorian, Oak, Scroll Ornament, Oval Mirror 375.00
Bed, Pencil Post, Pine Headboard, Birch Frame, C.1820, 15 In. 300.00
Bed, Pencil Posts At Head, 19th Century, Old Red Stain, Small 1200.00
Bed, Rope, C.1840, Grain Painted 275.00
Bed, Rope, Cherry, Turned Posts, Acorn & Ball Finials, 50 In. 300.00
Bed, Rope, Poplar, Turned Posts, Scalloped Footboard 375.00
Bed, Rope, Scrolled Headboard, Brass Bolts, 55 X 79 In. 350.00
Bed, Rope, Sheraton, Maple, Bobbin Spindles, Urn Design, 52 In. 325.00
Bed, Rope, Tester, Cherry, C.1850 .... 1650.00
Bed, Rope, Texas Primitive, Mattress, C.1825, Double 750.00
Bed, Sleigh-Type, Twin 145.00
Bed, Tall Post, Federal, Mahogany, C.1830, 88 X 56 In. 1100.00
Bed, Tester, Arched Canopy, C.1810, Original Red Finish 2100.00
Bed, Tester, Maryland, C.1820, Poplar With Old Red Stain 2200.00
Bed, Tester, Pencil Post, Arched Crest, American, Pine, 59 X 84 In. 800.00
Bed, Tester, Pencil Post, Cherry, C.1770 .... 1400.00
Bed, Trundle, Maple & Pine, Molded Crest, Paneled Headboard, 20 In. 250.00
Bedroom Set, Art Deco, Bachelor Chest, Drop-Front Secretary, 3 Pc. 1975.00
Bedroom Set, Eastlake Style, Marble Tops, Walnut, 1860s, 3 Piece 3500.00
Bedroom Set, Eastlake, Folding Telescope Bed, Desk, Beveled Mirror 2800.00
Bedroom Set, French Style, C.1910, 10 Piece .... *Illus* 3500.00
Bedroom Set, Louis XIV, Rosewood Veneer, 8 Piece 1500.00
Bedroom Set, Satinwood, C.1910, 5 Piece 1550.00
Bedroom Set, Spoon-Carved Cherry, 3 Piece 650.00
Bedstep, William XIV, Mahogany, 3 Red Leather Treads, 17 In. 495.00
Bench, Bucket, Old Green Paint 495.00
Bench, Bucket, Old Red Over Green 695.00
Bench, Bucket, Walnut 235.00
Bench, Cobbler's, Pine, 7 Drawers, Shoe Vise, 1858, Blue, 44 In. 525.00
Bench, George I Style, Molded Apron, Pad Feet, C.1900, 18 In. 100.00
Bench, Mammy, Plant Seat, Baby Guard, Blue, 49 In. 215.00

Furniture, Armoire, Cameo Glass, Mahogany, Rosewood, 37 1/2 In.

(See Page 239)

Furniture, Bedroom Set, French Style, C.1910, 10 Piece

Bench, Mortised, Traces Of Brown Paint, 84 In.	5.00
Bench, Pennsylvania, 58 X 17 1/2 In.	155.00
Bench, Piano, Geometric Form, Iron Base, Muslin Cover, 24 In.	35.00
Bench, Piano, Marble Claw Feet, Circular, Roses & Flowers	78.00
Bench, Pine, Square Nail, Blue Paint, 16 X 22 In.	40.00
Bench, Poplar, Shelf, Ends Mortised, Split, 13 1/2 X 17 In.	165.00
Bench, Water, Poplar, Top Shelf, Red Paint, 43 In.	425.00
Bibliotheque, Louis XV, Inlaid Marquetry, Tulipwood	425.00
Bidet, Mid-19th Century, Mahogany	135.00
Book Press, Provincial, Frieze Drawer, Oak, 26 X 53 In.	200.00
Bookcase, & Cabinet, Mission Oak, Stickley Bros., 56 In.	610.00
Bookcase, Dwarf, Breakfront, George III, Mahogany	500.00
Bookcase, Eastlake, Drop Front, C.1875, Walnut & Burlwood	1075.00
Bookcase, Empire, Inlaid Mahogany, Mullioned Doors, 8 Feet	660.00
Bookcase, Library, Chippendale, Acanthus Leaf Design, 3 Shelves	1000.00
Bookcase, Oak & Glass, 4 Shelves, C.1900, 58 In.	300.00
Bookcase, Original Glass & Brasses, C.1890, Oak, 4 1/2 X 6 1/2 Ft.	595.00
Bookcase, Pine, 7 Shelves, Wood Screws, Brown, 76 X 44 In.	275.00
Bookcase, Queen Anne, Lift-Up Slide-In Glass Doors, C.1890, Walnut	1250.00
Bookcase, Rope Twist Sides, Drawer In Base, Oak	595.00
Bookcase, Victorian, 2 Doors, 2 Shelves, Bottom Drawer, 6 Ft.	695.00
Bookcase, Victorian, 3 Glazed Doors, Mahogany & Oak, 54 X 87 In.	800.00
Bookshelves, Victorian, Glass Front, Oak	170.00
Box, Bentwood, Round, Wire Bail, Red, 11 1/2 X 6 1/4 In.	85.00
Box, Blanket, Child's, Original Red, 30 X 11 X 13 In.	195.00
Box, Blanket, Miniature, Dovetail Construction, C.1700, 8 X 17 In.	1800.00
Box, Collection, Dark Varnish Finish, 4 1/2 X 13 1/2 In.	22.50
Box, Decorated, Pine, Scandinavian, 19th Century, 3 X 4 1/4 In.	240.00
Box, Domed Top, Dovetailed, Poplar, C.1800, 5 1/4 X 7 1/4 In.	1700.00
Box, Knife, Hepplewhite, Silver Escutcheon, Matched, Pair	4200.00
Box, Miniature, Decorated, Dome Top, Poplar, C.1800, 4 X 8 1/2 In.	200.00

Box, Pipe, Curved, Cherry, New England, C.1700, 7 1/4 X 20 1/2 In. 1350.00
Box, Storage, Pine, Oval, Spring Lid, Blue, 6 3/4 X 12 1/2 In. 125.00
Box, Writing, Slant Top, George III, Fitted, Mahogany, 30 In. 290.00
Breakfront, Adams, 3 Central Drawers, Painted Satinwood, 34 In. 275.00
Breakfront, Carved Cherrywood, C.1890, 6 X 7 Ft. 520.00
Breakfront, Dwarf Bookcase, George III, Mahogany 500.00
Breakfront, Regency, Rosewood, Gilt Metal Mounted, 2-Part 1750.00
Buffet, Beveled Mirror, Tiger Oak, 1900 .... 285.00
Buffet, Cloister Style, C.1910, Mission Oak 975.00
Buffet, Edwardian, Mahogany, Green Marble, 3 Drawers, 42 In. 1200.00
Buffet, Provincial, Paneled Doors, Scroll Feet, Oak, 45 X 41 In. 450.00
Bureau Bookcase, George III, Sloping Lid, Mahogany, Small 925.00
Bureau Bookcase, Queen Anne, Sloping Lid, Inlaid Walnut, 85 In. 2200.00
Bureau, Chippendale, 4 Graduated Drawers, Bracket Base, Cherry 2200.00
Bureau, Dutch, Slant Top, 3 Drawers, Paw Feet, 42 In. 1100.00
Bureau, George III, Mahogany, Slant Front, Shell Inlaid, 40 In. 1210.00
Bureau, George III, Slant-Front, Fitted Inside, Mahogany, 41 In. 1100.00
Bureau, Louis XV, Kingwood & Tulipwood, 28 X 43 In. 2400.00
Bureau, Regency, 5 Drawers, Mahogany, Ball Feet, 43 In. 250.00
Cabinet, Bow Front, Biedermeier, Walnut, Ebony Columns, 36 In. 950.00
Cabinet, Bow Front, Biedermeier, Walnut, 5 Doors, 37 In. 675.00
Cabinet, Continental, Leaded Upper Glass Doors, 19th Century, Oak 325.00
Cabinet, Continental, Upper Glass Doors, Oak, 44 1/4 X 93 In. 300.00
Cabinet, Corner, Hanging, Georgian, Mahogany, Door, 36 1/2 In. 110.00
Cabinet, Corner, Inlaid Mahogany, C.1790, 4 Ft. 2 In. 660.00
Cabinet, Corner, Paneled Door, Plinth Base, Pine, 23 X 93 In. 225.00
Cabinet, Corner, Round Front, Walnut 300.00
Cabinet, Demilune, Italian, Carved Wood, Bun Feet, 34 In. 2000.00
Cabinet, Dwarf, Victorian, Mahogany, Paneled Doors, 51 In. 200.00
Cabinet, File, Step Back, 25 Drawers On Base, Oak 370.00
Cabinet, Filing, 7 Drawers, Oak 75.00
Cabinet, George III, Gentleman's, Mahogany, 37 In. 330.00
Cabinet, Gilt Bronze, 19th Century, French 7250.00
Cabinet, Hanging, Molded Cornice & Bottom, 18th Century, Oak 250.00
Cabinet, Hoosier Type, Oak 325.00
Cabinet, Hoosier, Meal & Flour Bins, Pine, C.1895 .... 895.00
Cabinet, Hoosier, Zinc Top, 3 Slag Panels At Top, Oak 525.00
Cabinet, Inlaid Oak, 2 Doors, Bleached Oak, 44 In. 350.00
Cabinet, Jelly, 1 Drawer, 2 Doors, Lock & Key, Grain Painted 495.00
Cabinet, Kitchen, Pine, 2 Piece, 5 Drawers, 71 3/4 In. 445.00
Cabinet, Louis XV, Walnut, Marble Top, 33 In. 750.00
Cabinet, Louis XVI, Vitrine, Mahogany & Gilt Bronze 5250.00
Cabinet, Medicine, Towel Bar, Pine 55.00
Cabinet, Music, Vernis Martin, Gilt Mounts, C.1900, Painted, Bombe 250.00
Cabinet, Nut & Bolt, Revolving, 96 Drawers, Pine 1100.00
Cabinet, Piano Roll, Beveled Glass Doors, Large 275.00
Cabinet, Regency, Rosewood, Metal Mounted, 11 In. 650.00
Cabinet, Sliding Doors, 7 Drawers, Korean, Wood, 28 3/4 In. 550.00
Cabinet, Storage, Regina, Holds 15 1/2 In.Discs, Oak, 20 X 34 In. 600.00
Cabinet, Storage, Regina, 20 In. Discs, Mahogany 600.00
Cabinet, Vitrine, Inlaid Mahogany, Hinged Top, 29 1/2 In. 3650.00
Cabinet, Vitrine, Louis XVI, 1 Drawer, 1 Shelf, 53 1/2 In. 425.00
Cabinet, Wall, Hanging, Pine, Door, Wrought Hinges, 18 In. 175.00
Cabinet, What Not, Victorian, Ebonized & Burl Walnut, 49 In. 175.00
Cabinet, William & Mary, Japanned, 2 Sections, Arched, 2 Doors 1100.00
Cabinet, William IV, Rosewood, 54 X 48 In. 700.00
Candlestand, Birch & Poplar, Walnut Post, 27 1/2 In. 150.00
Candlestand, Chippendale, Maple & Cherry, Mid-18th Century 375.00
Candlestand, Chippendale, Maple, Brown Finish, C.1770, 26 In. 3500.00
Candlestand, Chippendale, Round Top, Cherry, C.1770, 25 In. 450.00
Candlestand, Chippendale, Square Top, Tripod Base, Cherry, C.1770 .... 575.00
Candlestand, Chippendale, Tilt Top, Machogany, C.1755, 27 In. 7000.00
Candlestand, Chippendale, Turned Post, Cherry, C.1780, 27 In. High 900.00
Candlestand, Country, Walnut, Spider Legs, Spade Feet, 25 In. 105.00

Candlestand, Dish Top, Chippendale, C.1780, 26 In. 275.00
Candlestand, Federal, Birch, Spider Legs, C.1790, 28 In. 300.00
Candlestand, Federal, Birch, Tilt Top, Diamond Dot, C.1800, 27 In. 1000.00
Candlestand, Federal, Cherry, Turned Post, C.1810, 16 1/2 In. 700.00
Candlestand, Federal, Mahogany, Urn-Shaped Post, C.1800, 27 In. 250.00
Candlestand, Federal, Tilt Top, Maple & Cherry, 25 In. 1430.00
Candlestand, Federal, Tilt Top, Tiger Maple, Tripod Base, C.1800 .... 450.00
Candlestand, George III, Dish Top, Pad Feet, 27 1/2 In. 175.00
Candlestand, Greco-Roman Revival, Cherry, C.1830, 28 In. 400.00
Candlestand, Hepplewhite, Tilt Top, Maple & Birch 200.00
Candlestand, Maple, Figured, Snake Foot, Tilt Top 575.00
Candlestand, Pine & Hardwood, T Base, Octagonal Top, Red, 26 In. 1800.00
Candlestand, Pine & Maple, Cross Base, Old Red Paint, 24 1/2 In. 5000.00
Candlestand, Queen Anne, Inlaid Walnut, 1760-70, 27 In. 1100.00
Candlestand, Queen Anne, Mahogany, 3 Footed, C.1760, 27 In. 900.00
Candlestand, Regency, Tripod Base, C.1810, Mahogany 240.00
Candlestand, Snake Feet, Oval, C.1800, Oak, 24 In. 225.00
Candlestand, Weighted Conical Base, Crimped Pan, 19 In. 325.00
Case, Display, Twin Steeples 1000.00
Cassone, Italian, Carved Walnut, 22 X 62 In. 600.00
Chair Table, Round Top, C.1830, Pine 885.00
Chair Table, William & Mary, Square Top, Rounded Corners, 36 In. 3000.00
Chair, Arrow Back, Stenciled Design, Yellow Paint, Set Of 6 .... 1870.00
Chair, Arrow-Shaped Front Stretcher, Stenciled, Set Of 6 .... 2950.00
Chair, Belter Type, Rosewood 950.00
Chair, Bentwood, Open Back, Curved Arms, 3 1/4 X 4 1/4 In. 28.00
Chair, Boudoir, Victorian, Upholstered, 19th Century, Pair 125.00
Chair, Bow Back, C.1800, Saddle Seat, Bamboo Legs, 36 In. 325.00
Chair, Child's, Adirondack 85.00
Chair, Child's, Fanback, Wicker 105.00
Chair, Child's, Folding, Slatted 30.00
Chair, Child's, French, Needlepoint Covering, 27 In. .... *Illus* 325.00
Chair, Child's, Turned Legs & Spindles, Brown, 20 In. 45.00
Chair, Child's, Walnut, Diamond Design, C.1800, 23 1/4 In. 150.00
Chair, Child's, Windsor, Yellow Paint, Rose Design Crest, 26 In. 145.00
Chair, Chinese, Teakwood, C.1870, 37 In. .... *Illus* 600.00
Chair, Chippendale, Carved Ears, Rush Seat, Pair 750.00
Chair, Chippendale, Carved Mahogany, Claw Feet, C.1760 .... 3580.00
Chair, Chippendale, Side, Shaped Crest Rail, 18th Century, 38 In. 800.00
Chair, Chippendale, Spanish Feet, Maple, C.1750 .... 1200.00
Chair, Chippendale, Walnut, C.1770, Crest, Claw Feet 660.00
Chair, Continental, Walnut, 45 In., Pair .... *Illus* 750.00
Chair, Corner, Groge III, Oak, Spoonbill Form Top, Drop-In Seat 220.00
Chair, Corner, Maple & Ash, Splint Seat, 33 1/2 In. 2600.00
Chair, Corner, Queen Anne, Mahogany, C.1760, Horseshoe Back, 35 In. 500.00
Chair, Corner, Wicker, Curlicue Top 225.00
Chair, Corner, Wicker, Heywood, Wakefield 425.00
Chair, Country, Slat, Crest, Cane Seat, Pair 70.00
Chair, Cut From Round Log, Curved Back, Plywood Seat, 24 X 35 In. 125.00
Chair, Desk, Walnut, Caned, Victorian 450.00
Chair, Dining, Arts & Crafts, L. & J.G.Stickley, Oak, Set Of 8 .... 600.00
Chair, Dining, George III, Plank Seat, Oak, Set Of 4 .... 325.00
Chair, Dining, Ladder Back, Chippendale, Set Of 12 .... 2900.00
Chair, Dining, Louis XVI, High Sides, Set Of 6 .... 600.00
Chair, Dining, Plank Seat, Oak, Set Of 6 .... 450.00
Chair, Dining, Regency, Applied Eagles On Back Rail, Set Of 6 .... 2100.00
Chair, Dining, Victorian, Walnut, Set Of 6 .... 750.00
Chair, Eames, Charles, Oak, Black Iron Legs, 1940s 85.00
Chair, Eastlake, Metal Castor Wheels, 1890s, Walnut 125.00
Chair, Empire, American, Mahogany, C.1900, Set Of 3 .... 425.00
Chair, Empire, Italian, Walnut, Urn-Form Splat, 35 In. 100.00
Chair, Federal, Mahogany, C.1790, Plum Carved Splat, Pair 1650.00
Chair, Federal, Pineapple Design, Rush Seat, C.1830, 32 In. 85.00
Chair, George I, Mahogany, Slip Seat, Pad Feet 100.00

Clockwise: Furniture, Chairs, Child's, French, Needlepoint Covering, 27 In.; Chinese, Teakwood, C.1870, 37 In.; Hall, Carved Oak, Angels, C.1880; Hall, Oak, Rams' Heads, C.1880; Continental, Walnut, 45 In., Pair

Chair, George III, Blind Fret Carved, Mahogany, Set Of 4	900.00
Chair, George III, Mahogany, Square Back & Seat, C.1780	200.00
Chair, George III, Needlepoint Slip Seat, Mahogany	165.00
Chair, George III, Slip Seat, Square Legs, Mahogany	140.00
Chair, George III, Square Back & Seat, Mahogany, C.1780	200.00
Chair, Greco-Roman, Japanned, C.1840, Set Of 8	425.00
Chair, Hall, Carved Oak, Angels, C.1880	*Illus* 300.00
Chair, Hall, Oak, Rams' Heads, C.1880	*Illus* 300.00

Chair, High Back, Child's, C.1915, Original Red Paint, Pair 98.00
Chair, High, Oak, Carved Back, Cane Seat, Folds Into Rocker 650.00
Chair, High, Plank Seat, Curved Arms, Spindle Back, 36 In. 35.00
Chair, Ice Cream, Child's, Copper 100.00
Chair, Japanese, Carved Hardwood, Flowers, Mt.Fuji 250.00
Chair, Kem Weber, Chrome, Blue Upholstery 600.00
Chair, Kindergarten, Oak, Bentwood, Pair 48.00
Chair, Ladder Back, Ash & Hickory, 3 Slats, Splint Seat 140.00
Chair, Ladder Back, Country, Reeded Seat, C.1820 .... 85.00
Chair, Ladder Back, Flared Posts, Woven Seat 40.00
Chair, Ladder Back, Maple & Ash, Rush Seat, 42 In. 325.00
Chair, Ladder Back, Maple, C.1730, 42 In. 100.00
Chair, Ladder Back, Original Red Paint, Pair 750.00
Chair, Ladder Back, Pine-Pegged, Original Rush Seat, C.1800 .... 135.00
Chair, Ladder Back, Slat Back, 18th Century, 42 1/2 In. 225.00
Chair, Ladder Back, Turned Legs, Black Painted, 45 In. 800.00
Chair, Ladder Back, 3 Slats, 1851, Tiger Maple, Set Of 8 .... 1450.00
Chair, Laminated Walnut, Pair 1500.00
Chair, Lyre & Dolphin, Fruitwood, C.1810, Anthemion Crest 550.00
Chair, Meetinghouse, Masonic Emblem, Set Of 4 .... 500.00
Chair, Moravian, Carved Flowers & Hearts, Walnut, Dated 1830 .... 1250.00
Chair, Morris, Oak 125.00
Chair, Morris, Oak, Gray Upholstered Back & Seat 450.00
Chair, Morris, Signed Stickley, 1912-18 .... 1000.00
Chair, Oak & Ash, Carver Type, Rush Seat, 40 1/2 In. 4400.00
Chair, Oak, Leaf Carved Crest, Jacobean Style, 50 1/2 In. 80.00
Chair, Parlor, Arm, Blue Velour, C.1920, Dark Wood 30.00
Chair, Photographer's, Victorian, Wicker, White 285.00
Chair, Pierced, Carved, Indian, 19th Century .... Illus 550.00
Chair, Plank Seat, Original Paint, Set Of 6 .... 1000.00
Chair, Plank Seat, Pine, Cluster Of Flowers, C.1825, Set Of 6 .... 1000.00
Chair, Plank, Pink, Gilt Scroll, C.1830, Set Of 6 .... 1750.00
Chair, Pool Hall, High 125.00
Chair, Potty, Child's, Wing Style, Curving Arms, 21 In. 50.00
Chair, Pressback, Eastlake, Grape & Leaf Design, Walnut 225.00
Chair, Pressback, Oak, Set Of 6 .... 95.00 To 150.00
Chair, Pressback, Plank Seat, Oak 50.00
Chair, Queen Anne, Crest Rail, Black Paint, C.1730, Pair 1300.00
Chair, Queen Anne, Cupid's Bow Crest Rail, Spoon Back 750.00
Chair, Queen Anne, Grained, Square Seat, C.1730, 39 In. 4400.00
Chair, Queen Anne, Maple, Crest On Splat, C.1750, 40 In. 300.00
Chair, Queen Anne, Maple, Rush Seat, Vase-Shape Splat, C.1740 .... 800.00
Chair, Queen Anne, Maple, Spoon Crest, Spanish Feet, 40 In. 1000.00
Chair, Queen Anne, Maple, Turned & Painted, Black, C.1730 .... 1320.00
Chair, Queen Anne, New England, C.1730, Black, 41 In. .... Illus 650.00
Chair, Queen Anne, Spanish Feet, New England, C.1730, 41 In. 650.00
Chair, Queen Anne, Spanish Feet, Vase-Shaped Splat, 42 In. 750.00
Chair, Regency, Mahogany, Scroll Back, Saber Legs, C.1820 .... 50.00
Chair, Regency, Scroll Back, Slip Seat, Saber Legs, Mahogany 50.00
Chair, Sedan, Italian, Scene Of Virgin, Leather Sides, 62 In. 2500.00
Chair, Shaker, Tape Seat, Labeled, 34 In. 175.00
Chair, Slat Back, Ash, 4 Arched Slats, Green, 40 In. 900.00
Chair, Slat Back, Birch & Ash, Sausage-Turned Stiles, 41 In. 375.00
Chair, Slat Back, Button Feet, C.1700, 43 1/2 In. 600.00
Chair, Slat Back, Maple & Ash, Turned Stiles, 33 In. 400.00
Chair, Slat Back, Maple & Oak, 17th Century, 32 In. 150.00
Chair, Slat Back, Pilgrim, Rush Seat, 33 1/2 In. 600.00
Chair, Slat Back, Rush Seat, Button Feet, C.1700, 42 In. 750.00
Chair, Slat Back, Rush Seat, Turned Feet, Black, 44 In. 375.00
Chair, Slat Back, Sausage Turnings, Yellow Over Red, C.1750, Pair 385.00
Chair, Slat Back, Sausage-Turned Stiles, Rush Seat, 42 In. 475.00
Chair, Slipper, Victorian, Carved Mahogany 125.00
Chair, Spindle, Plank Bottom, Rabbit Ear, Set Of 6 .... 450.00
Chair, Split Banister, Painted 325.00

Furniture, Chair, Pierced, Carved,
Indian, 19th Century

Furniture, Chair, Queen Anne, New
England, C.1730, Black, 41 In.

Chair, Spoon Back, Carved Crest, Spanish Feet 495.00
Chair, Stickley, Rush Seat, Arched Apron, Signed, Set Of 7 .... 2500.00
Chair, Thonet, Bentwood, Blonde Wood, Vinyl Seats, Set Of 4 .... 70.00
Chair, Thumb Back, Putty Grain Painted, Eagle Stencil, Set Of 6 .... 1825.00
Chair, Victorian, Balloon Back, Carved Crest, Upholstered, Set Of 4 .... 900.00
Chair, Victorian, Walnut, Carved, Needlepoint Set 165.00
Chair, Victorian, Walnut, Flower Heads, Pierced Heart, C.1860 .... 110.00
Chair, Wallace Nutting, Brace Back 400.00
Chair, Wicker, Circular Back, Curlicues .... *Illus* 450.00
Chair, Wicker, Corner 450.00
Chair, Wicker, High Center Splat .... *Illus* 475.00
Chair, Wicker, Round Seat, Rolled Top .... *Illus* 180.00
Chair, Wicker, Spindles, Knobs, Scrolls .... *Illus* 375.00
Chair, William & Mary, Arched Crest, Maple, C.1700, 44 In. 2100.00
Chair, William & Mary, Banister Back, C.1720, 42 In. 500.00
Chair, William & Mary, Banister Back, C.1720, 44 In. 1200.00
Chair, William & Mary, Banister Back, C.1740, 44 In. 175.00
Chair, William & Mary, Banister Back, Carved Crest 800.00
Chair, William & Mary, Banister Back, Dutch Carved, C.1720, 44 In. 3300.00
Chair, William & Mary, Banister Back, New England, C.1700 .... 250.00
Chair, William & Mary, Banister Back, 42 In., Pair 1100.00
Chair, William & Mary, Black, C.1700, 47 1/2 In. .... *Illus* 6500.00
Chair, William & Mary, Block & Vase Turned Legs, Black, 42 In. 650.00
Chair, William & Mary, Boston, Black, C.1720, 42 In. .... *Illus* 1500.00
Chair, William & Mary, Cane Back & Seat, Spanish Feet, 43 In. 650.00
Chair, William & Mary, Carved Crest, C.1700, 47 1/2 In. 6500.00
Chair, William & Mary, Crest, Curved Stiles, Turned Feet 1250.00
Chair, William & Mary, Crest, Upholstered, Turned Feet, 42 In. 1100.00
Chair, William & Mary, Curved Stiles, Turned Feet, 43 In. 900.00
Chair, William & Mary, Grain Painted, Upholstered, 41 In. 1300.00
Chair, William & Mary, Maple & Ash, Banister Back, 47 In. 300.00
Chair, William & Mary, Maple, Boston, C.1700, 42 In. 2250.00
Chair, William & Mary, Maple, Spanish Feet, C.1700, 44 In. 1200.00
Chair, William & Mary, Maple, Turned Stiles, Black, 45 In. 1300.00
Chair, William & Mary, Molded Crest, Block Legs, 43 In. 900.00

Furniture, Chairs, Wicker, Round Seat, Rolled Top; Circular Back, Curlicues; Spindles, Knobs, Scrolls

Furniture, Chair, William & Mary, Black,   Furniture, Chair, William & Mary, Boston,
C.1700, 47 1/2 In.   Black, C.1720, 42 In.

(See Page 245)

Chair, William & Mary, Molded Crest, 18th Century, 45 In.	175.00
Chair, William & Mary, New England, C.1700, 45 In. .... *Illus*	2750.00
Chair, William & Mary, New England, C.1720, 44 In. .... *Illus*	3300.00
Chair, William & Mary, Oak, Leaf Carved Top	192.00
Chair, William & Mary, Vase Finials, Black Paint, Pa., 46 In.	2200.00
Chair, William & Mary, Vase-Turned Legs, 42 1/2 In.	750.00
Chair, William & Mary, Walnut, Fleur-De-Lis Front, 37 In.	175.00

Chair, Windsor, Bow Back, Bamboo Legs, Saddle Seat, C.1800, Pair 200.00
Chair, Windsor, Bow Back, Woodbury, Conn., Inscribed 395.00
Chair, Windsor, Bow Back, 7 Spindles, C.1790, Pair 990.00
Chair, Windsor, Bow Back, 7 Turned Spindles, Pair 880.00
Chair, Windsor, Continuous Arm, Knuckle Arms, Green Paint, 36 In. 800.00
Chair, Windsor, Fanback, Saddle Seat, Reel Legs, 37 In. 200.00
Chair, Windsor, Fanback, Saddle Seat, Vase & Reel Legs 875.00
Chair, Windsor, Fanback, Saddle Seat, 35 1/2 In., Set Of 6 .... 1600.00
Chair, Windsor, Fanback, Signed Custer, 18th Century 1850.00
Chair, Windsor, Foliage Design, Black, Set Of 3 .... 330.00
Chair, Windsor, George III, Yew, Pair 450.00
Chair, Windsor, Philadelphia, Comb Back, Serpentine Arms 9500.00
Chair, Windsor, Writing Arm, Drawer, Bamboo-Turned, 17 3/4 In. 800.00
Chair, Windsor, 2 Step-Down, Brown, C.1800, 35 In. 400.00
Chair, Windsor, 7 Spindles, C.1810, Set Of 6 .... 5775.00
Chair, Windsor, 7-Spindle Back, Red Paint 475.00
Chair, Windsor, 9 Spindles, Pipe-Stem Turnings, Upholstered Seat 1095.00
Chair, Wing, Chippendale, Ball & Claw, Red Silk Cover 1200.00
Chair, Wing, Chippendale, Mahogany, Claw & Ball Feet, 41 In. 175.00
Chair, Wing, Federal, Cherry, Carved Crest, C.1810, 45 1/2 In. 800.00
Chair, Wright, Frank Lloyd, Mahogany, Geometric Design, Set Of 6 .... 2500.00
Chaise Longue, Louis XVI, Gold Damask Cover, Painted 300.00
Chaise, Louis XVI, Gilt Wood, Gadrooned Crest, 36 In., Pair 175.00
Chaise, Wicker, Blue Cushions 350.00
Chenet, Louis XV, Cherub, 19th Century, Bronze Dore, Pair 500.00
Chest Of Drawers, Bowfront, Federal, Cherry, C.1810, 37 X 42 In. 1300.00
Chest Of Drawers, Rosewood, Gold Acanthus Leaf Stenciling 1850.00
Chest-On-Chest, C.1830, Mahogany 2500.00
Chest-On-Chest, Chippendale, Bracket Feet, C.1830, English 2400.00
Chest-On-Chest, Federal, Cherry, 7 Drawer, Bracket Feet, 6 Ft. 3190.00
Chest-On-Chest, Korean, Elm, Brass Mounts, 62 In. 325.00
Chest-On-Chest, William & Mary, Original Japanning 5500.00
Chest-On-Frame, Queen Anne, Cabriole Legs, C.1760, 39 In. High 3100.00
Chest-On-Stand, Baroque, Walnut Cupboard Door, 67 In. 1000.00
Chest-Over-Chest, American Chippendale, Fluted Columns, C.1773 .... 2600.00
Chest, Adams, Lingerie Slides, Painted Satinwood, 34 X 54 In. 325.00
Chest, Adams, Painted Satinwood, Lingerie Slides, 54 In. 325.00
Chest, African Mahogany, Birch, Poplar, Pine, C.1810, 6 Drawer 1850.00
Chest, American Sheraton, 4 Drawer, Mahogany, 41 In. .... *Illus* 1000.00
Chest, Apothecary, Pine, 10 Cockbeaded Drawers, 20 In. 775.00
Chest, Apothecary, 15 Drawer, Pine 550.00
Chest, Apothecary, 36 Labeled Drawers, 3 1/2 X 2 1/2 Ft. 875.00
Chest, Banded Inlay Around Drawers, Original Brasses, C.1802 .... 4200.00
Chest, Blanket, Bootjack Ends, Snipe Hinges, 18th Century, Red 365.00
Chest, Blanket, Bootjack Ends, 18th Century, 2 Drawer, Red Paint 1050.00
Chest, Blanket, Bun Foot, 2 Drawer, 1720-40 .... 5500.00
Chest, Blanket, Carved & Painted Poplar, C.1781, 26 In. 2090.00
Chest, Blanket, Chippendale, Pine, C.1780, 3 False Drawers, 59 In. 900.00
Chest, Blanket, Inlaid Walnut, 2 Drawer, C.1800, 30 In. 1760.00
Chest, Blanket, Lock & Butt Hinges, Grain Painted 425.00
Chest, Blanket, Lock & Strap Hinges, 6-Board, Pine 340.00
Chest, Blanket, Pennsylvania, Ogee Feet 1210.00
Chest, Blanket, Pilgrim, Oak, 1 Long Drawer, 1670-90, 27 X 44 In. 1320.00
Chest, Blanket, Pine, Bracket Feet, Iron Strap Hinges, 15 In. 225.00
Chest, Blanket, Pine, C.1720, 32 X 29 In. 475.00
Chest, Blanket, Pine, Cutout Bracket, Turned Feet, 21 In. 220.00
Chest, Blanket, Pine, Cutout Feet, Till Lid, Green, 30 In. 250.00
Chest, Blanket, Pine, Dovetailed, Red & Black Graining, 15 In. 325.00
Chest, Blanket, Pine, Dovetailed, Red Paint, Handles, 18 X 17 In. 95.00
Chest, Blanket, Pine, Dovetailed, Red Paint, 13 X 23 In. 175.00
Chest, Blanket, Pine, Green Paint, C.1810, 25 X 49 In. 500.00
Chest, Blanket, Pine, Lift Top, Bootjack Feet, 46 In. 660.00
Chest, Blanket, Pine, Lift Top, Red & Black, 25 In. 225.00
Chest, Blanket, Pine, Red, Yellow Stars, 14 X 29 In. 385.00

Furniture, Chair, William & Mary,
New England, C.1700, 45 In.

Furniture, Chair, William & Mary,
New England, C.1720, 44 In.

(See Pages 246, 247)

Furniture, Chest, American Sheraton, 4 Drawer,
Mahogany, 41 In.

Furniture, Chest, Child's, American
Empire, Mahogany, 12 X 6 In.

Chest, Blanket, Pine, Scalloped Feet, Iron Strap Hinges, Red	155.00
Chest, Blanket, Pine, Yellow Tulip, House, Trees, 5 X 10 In.	2420.00
Chest, Blanket, Pine, 1 Drawer, Red Paint, 36 X 44 In.	500.00
Chest, Blanket, Poplar, Dovetailed, 2 Drawer, Blue, Red, 50 X 30 In.	175.00
Chest, Blanket, Secret Drawer, Old Green Over Old Red Paint	225.00
Chest, Blanket, Shaker, Hancock	2050.00
Chest, Blanket, Smoke Decorated, Lift Top, 19th Century, 30 1/2 In.	1300.00
Chest, Blanket, Strap Hinges, Till, Old Red Paint	575.00
Chest, Blanket, Till, Butt Hinges, Flame, Grain Painted	395.00
Chest, Blanket, White Oak, Iron Tack Design, 24 In.	200.00
Chest, Blanket, William & Mary, C.1700, 37 1/2 X 35 1/2 In.	1900.00
Chest, Blanket, William & Mary, Pine, Lift Top, Bracket Legs, 36 In.	1750.00
Chest, Blanket, 3 Drawer, Lift-Top, Ogee Curved Skirt, C.1765, Pine	1150.00
Chest, Blanket, 6-Board, Strap Hinges, Mahoganized Paint, Small	600.00
Chest, Bowfront, Cockbeaded Drawers, Cherry	990.00

Chest, Bowfront, Federal, Birch & Mahogany, C.1810, 37 In. 1050.00
Chest, Bowfront, Federal, Mahogany, 4 Drawer, C.1800, 34 In. 750.00
Chest, Bowfront, Federal, Maple, French Foot, C.1800, 34 In. 450.00
Chest, Bowfront, George III, 2 Short & 3 Long Drawers, Mahogany 300.00
Chest, Bowfront, Oak Lined, Mahogany, C.1825, 41 X 39 X 21 In. 780.00
Chest, Butternut, 4 Drawer, Scalloped Base, 40 X 39 1/2 In. 200.00
Chest, Campaign, C.1776, Wooden, Small 85.00
Chest, Camphorwood, Lift Top, Brass-Bound, 19 X 41 In. 475.00
Chest, Charles II, Paneled Drawers, English, Oak, 37 1/2 X 43 In. 1100.00
Chest, Cherry & Tiger Maple, C.1820, 41 1/2 X 21 1/2 X 50 1/2 In. 1400.00
Chest, Child's, American Empire, Mahogany, 12 X 6 In. ....*Illus* 575.00
Chest, Child's, English, 19th Century, 17 1/2 In. ....*Illus* 475.00
Chest, Child's, 3 Drawer, C.1850, 3 Ft. 120.00
Chest, Chippendale, Birch, 4 Drawer, Red Paint, C.1800, 32 In. 900.00
Chest, Chippendale, Cherry & Mahogany, Claw & Ball Feet, 32 In. 600.00
Chest, Chippendale, Mahogany, C.1780, 34 In. ....*Illus* 1900.00
Chest, Chippendale, Mahogany, C.1790, 44 X 37 X 21 In. 1100.00
Chest, Chippendale, Mahogany, 4 Drawer, C.1790, 36 In. 1400.00
Chest, Chippendale, Mahogany, 5 Drawer, Cock Beading, C.1760, 36 In. 475.00
Chest, Chippendale, Maple, 6 Drawer, C.1780, 56 In. 2100.00
Chest, Chippendale, Miniature, Rectangular, 10 X 17 In. 400.00
Chest, Chippendale, Miniature, Walnut, 19th Century, 6 1/2 In. 275.00
Chest, Chippendale, Serpentine Front, Mahogany, C.1780, 37 X 42 In. 1200.00
Chest, Chippendale, Tiger Maple, 4 Drawer, C.1800, 30 In. 500.00
Chest, Chippendale, Walnut, 4 Cock-Beaded Drawer, C.1790, 33 In. 1540.00
Chest, Chippendale, 5 Drawer, Fluted Quarter Columns, Walnut 6250.00
Chest, Chippendale, 6 Drawer, Carved Walnut 1760.00
Chest, Commonwealth, Fruitwood & Oak, Bun Feet, 36 In. 1430.00
Chest, Domed Top, Spanish Marquetry, 19 In. 1000.00
Chest, Dower, Painted, Basswood, Floral Motif, C.1780, 21 X 51 In. 1300.00
Chest, Dower, Pennsylvania, Floral Design, Green, Black Grained 8500.00
Chest, Dower, Pennsylvania, Grab Lock & Key, Red Paint 1450.00
Chest, Dower, Tulip Hinges, Penna., 1788, 52 X 24 1/2 X 19 1/2 In. 2500.00
Chest, Empire, Bowfront, Mahogany On Pine, Rope Column, 37 In. 450.00
Chest, Empire, Cherry, Bowfront, 4 Drawers, Turned Feet 450.00
Chest, Empire, Cherry, 4 Drawer, Roped Quarter Columns 425.00
Chest, Empire, Mahogany, Crossbanded Doors, C.1815, 4 Ft. 1750.00
Chest, Empire, Mahogany, Plinth Base, C.1820, 31 1/2 In. 475.00
Chest, England, Handles, Iron-Mounted Oak, 19th Century, 21 1/2 In. 275.00
Chest, English, Baroque Oak, 2 Short, 1 Long Drawers, 45 In. 660.00
Chest, Federal, Cherry & Mahogany Veneer, 3 Drawers, C.1810, 36 In. 925.00
Chest, Federal, Inlaid Mahogany, Bowfront, C.1790, 37 In. 1540.00

Furniture, Chest, Chippendale, Mahogany,
C.1780, 34 In.

Furniture, Chest, Child's, English, 19th
Century, 17 1/2 In.

Chest, Federal, Mahogany & Maple, 4 Drawer, C.1800, 36 In. 1700.00
Chest, Federal, Mahogany, Cock Beading, 4 Drawer, C.1800, 40 In. 300.00
Chest, Federal, Mahogany, Cock-Beaded Drawers, C.1815, 48 In. 990.00
Chest, Federal, Mahogany, Rectangular Top, Bracket Feet, 40 In. 440.00
Chest, Federal, Mahogany, Swell Front, C.1810, 37 In. 500.00
Chest, Federal, Mahogany, 4 Drawer, French Feet, C.1800, 40 In. 350.00
Chest, Federal, Mahogany, 5 Drawer, Rosewood Inlay, 42 X 23 In. 300.00
Chest, Federal, Maple, 6 Drawer, Bracket Feet, 4 Ft. 5775.00
Chest, Federal, Walnut, 4 Drawer, French Feet, C.1800, 33 In. 1900.00
Chest, Federal, Walnut, 4 Drawer, French Feet, 38 In. 425.00
Chest, Federal, Walnut, 5 Drawer, Cornice, Bracket Feet, 5 Ft. 3575.00
Chest, Flat Top, Black Over Mustard Yellow Paint, 27 1/2 X 13 In. 225.00
Chest, Fluted Legs, Cookie Corner Top 400.00
Chest, George III, Bracket Feet, Mahogany, 27 X 34 In., Pair 600.00
Chest, George III, Inlaid Mahogany, 3 Drawer, C.1800, 59 In. 200.00
Chest, George III, Mahogany, Bracket Feet, C.1790, 34 In. 660.00
Chest, George III, Mahogany, Bracket Feet, C.1800, 34 In. 880.00
Chest, George III, Mahogany, 3 Drawer, C.1810, 40 X 40 In. 750.00
Chest, George III, Mahogany, 3/4 Gallery, 7 Drawer, 50 In. 350.00
Chest, George III, 5 Drawer, England, Mahogany, C.1790, 36 In. 1320.00
Chest, George III, 7 Graduated Drawers, Mahogany, 26 X 50 In. 350.00
Chest, Greco-Roman Revival, Mahogany & Bird's-Eye Maple, 45 In. 150.00
Chest, Handkerchief Drawers, American, Walnut, 44 In.Wide 225.00
Chest, Hepplewhite, Bird's-Eye & Tiger Maple, New England 2200.00
Chest, Hepplewhite, Bowfront, Inlay, Original Brasses 4200.00
Chest, Hepplewhite, Cherry With Maple Inlay, New Hampshire 2700.00
Chest, Hepplewhite, Cherry, French Footed, C.1815 .... 1250.00
Chest, Hepplewhite, Swell Front, Inlaid, Replaced Brasses 2700.00
Chest, Hepplewhite, 6 Drawer, Original Brass, Pennsylvania, Walnut 1200.00
Chest, Iron Carrying Handles, Iron Shop Sign, Elm, 33 X 16 In. 300.00
Chest, Joined Oak & Pine, Red Stain, Stile Feet, 26 X 40 In. 2100.00
Chest, Korean, Elm, Brass Mount, Low, 25 In. 325.00
Chest, Korean, Sliding Drawer Beside Door, Base Drawers, 45 In. 440.00
Chest, Mahogany, Bowfront, C.1800, 40 X 26 In. 300.00
Chest, Mahogany, Bowfront, Federal Style, 20th Century 750.00
Chest, Military, Brassbound, Chestnut Lined, 38 X 19 In. 1200.00
Chest, Mule, Empire, Pine, Turned Feet, 2 Drawer, 40 In. 400.00
Chest, New England, Serpentine Front, Mahogany, C.1780, 39 X 34 In. 5500.00
Chest, New England, 4 Drawer, Cherry, C.1800, 44 1/2 X 44 1/2 In. 425.00
Chest, New York Hepplewhite, Fluted Columns 1250.00
Chest, Pillar Front, Tiger Maple 700.00
Chest, Pine, 2 Drawer, Button Pulls, Blue-Gray Paint, C.1815, 9 In. 1200.00
Chest, Pine, 3 Drawer, Cutout Base, 30 X 29 In. 250.00
Chest, Pine, 4 Drawer, Perimeter Molding, 38 X 43 In. 175.00
Chest, Seaman's, Painting Of Sailing Ship On Lid, Strap Hinges 425.00
Chest, Seaman's, Secret Drawer, Dovetailed, Pine 200.00
Chest, Serpentine Front, Bird's-Eye Maple, 4 Drawer, 32 In. 90.00
Chest, Sheraton, Bow Front, Mahogany, Applied Beading, 41 In. 450.00
Chest, Sheraton, Cherry, Reeded Post, 4 Drawer, 41 In. 800.00
Chest, Sheraton, 5 Graduated Drawers, Tiger Maple, 3/4 Size 800.00
Chest, Shoe, Sliding Door Opening, 3 Drawer, 26 1/2 X 11 1/2 In. 275.00
Chest, Spanish, Walnut, Lattice Design, 44 X 76 In. 2400.00
Chest, Spice, Hepplewhite, Kentucky, Cherry, Walnut Door, 27 In. 2500.00
Chest, Spice, 8 Drawer, Alligator Finish 210.00
Chest, Spool, 2 Drawer, Walnut 165.00
Chest, Studded & Hinged, Brass Dome Top, 21 In. 250.00
Chest, Sugar, Amish, Dovetailed Case, 19th Century, Grained 475.00
Chest, Traveling, Handles, 4 Drawer, 2 Part, C.1810, 33 X 42 In. 875.00
Chest, Victorian, Domed Top, C.1870, 29 X 20 X 21 In. 80.00
Chest, Victorian, Figured Drawer Front, 5 Drawer 495.00
Chest, Victorian, Marble Top, 3 Drawer, C.1860, 54 In. 325.00
Chest, Victorian, Mirror, 5 Drawer, C.1850, Spiegel Co., 38 X 66 In. 450.00
Chest, Victorian, Walnut, Splashboard, 3 Drawer, 36 In. 330.00
Chest, Walnut, 4 Drawer, Brass Pulls, C.1840, 13 In. 150.00

Chest, Wardrobe, Handles, 2-Door, 6 1/4 X 3 7/8 In. 28.00
Chest, William & Mary, Pine, Paneled Drawers, Turned Feet, 34 In. 1100.00
Chest, William & Mary, 3 Drawer, Bun Feet, Molded Edge, 35 In. 3000.00
Chest, 2 Drawer, Diagonal Striping, Pennsylvania, Red Over Black 2400.00
Chest, 2 Drawers Over 5, Pine Lined, C.1790, Oak, 40 X 54 In. 975.00
Chest, 3 Drawer, Cutout Sides, Blue, 11 3/4 X 8 1/2 X 16 In. 150.00
Chest, 3 Drawer, One-Board Top, Original Red Grain Finish 650.00
Chest, 3 Graduated Drawers, Cherry, C.1825 .... 425.00
Chest, 4 Drawer, Fitted Top Drawer, C.1780, 33 1/4 In.Wide 3000.00
Chest, 4 Drawer, Maine, Red & Black, Grain Painted, 17 X 7 1/2 In. 165.00
Chest, 5 Drawer, Mahogany, C.1800, 38 1/2 X 42 In. 200.00
Chiffonier, Marble Top, French, Parquetry Inlaid, 53 1/2 In. 1800.00
China Cabinet, Curved Glass Front, Mirror Back, Oak, 57 X 71 In. 1300.00
China Cabinet, Glass Doors, Drawers, Lebanon, Penn., C.1810, Cherry 2900.00
China Cabinet, 4 Door, Beveled Mirror, Oak, 4 3/4 X 6 1/4 Ft. 1100.00
Clothes Press, Victorian, Mahogany, 3 Drawer, C.1860, 75 In. 450.00
Clothes Press, Victorian, Slides, 3 Drawer, Mahogany, 49 X 75 In. 450.00
Coatrack, C.1890, Bentwood 165.00
Commode, Bi-Level, Mirror, Oak 300.00
Commode, Eastlake, Walnut, Marble Top, Original Hardware 450.00
Commode, Greco-Roman Revival, Mahogany Veneer, C.1830, 35 In.High 800.00
Commode, Italian Directoire, Walnut, 2 Drawer, 35 In. 500.00
Commode, Italian, Directoire, Inlaid Fruitwood, 34 In. 475.00
Commode, Louis XV, Provincial, Fruitwood, Hoof Feet, 32 In. 2500.00
Commode, Louis XVI Style, Parquetry, Gilt Bronze Mounts 6750.00
Commode, Marble Top, C.1865, Walnut 220.00
Commode, Swedish Marquetry, Marble Top, D-Shaped, Pair 5750.00
Commode, Victorian, English, Carved, Mahogany 180.00
Commode, Victorian, Marble Top, Walnut, C.1765 .... 240.00
Console, Louis XVI, Gilt Wood, Green Marble Top, 38 In. 500.00
Cradle, American, Pine, 19th Century, 36 In. 985.00
Cradle, Hooded, Mahogany, Double Rockers, 40 In. 200.00
Cradle, Mortise & Tenon Posts, Walnut 375.00
Cradle, New York, Curly Maple 575.00
Cradle, Pine, Curved Hood, Red-Black Paint, 30 X 41 In. 100.00
Cradle, Pine, Scalloped Head & Foot, Blue Paint, 36 In. 225.00
Cradle, Poplar, Cutout Rockers, Dark Finish, 41 In. 135.00
Cradle, Redwood, C.1850, 37 1/2 X 14 In.Wide 185.00
Cradle, Spool-Turned 275.00
Cradle, Tiger Maple & Cherry, Pewter Screws 650.00
Cradle, Wicker .... *Illus* 1700.00
Credenza, Italian, Walnut, 4 Doors, Plinth Base, 46 In. 1500.00
Crib, Brass & Iron 125.00
Crib, One Hinged Drop Side, Cherry 350.00
Crib, Swinging, Cast Iron, White 150.00
Cupboard, Apothecary, Pine, 12 Drawers, 3 Shelves, 77 In. 1100.00
Cupboard, Ash, Board Door, High Feet, 26 1/2 X 16 X 42 1/4 In. 250.00
Cupboard, Beaded Edges, Original Red Paint, C.1820 .... 2200.00
Cupboard, Birchwood & Pine, Ring-Turned Colonettes, C.1825, 7 Ft. 2650.00
Cupboard, Butternut, Paneled Doors, Dovetailed, Red, 72 3/4 In. 325.00
Cupboard, Chimney, Adz-Hewn, Green Paint Over Yellow, Walnut & Oak 485.00
Cupboard, Chimney, Butterfly Hinges, Rose-Head Nails, 1730-50, Pine 2100.00
Cupboard, Chimney, Gray Painted 725.00
Cupboard, Chimney, New York, Spotted Blue Paint 1250.00
Cupboard, Chimney, Pine, Red Finish, Connecticut, C.1730 .... 2100.00
Cupboard, Corner, Amish, Walnut, 12 Panes, 2 Drawers 3000.00
Cupboard, Corner, Barrel Back, 3 Shelves, Pine, 88 In., 2 Piece 1500.00
Cupboard, Corner, Barrel Front, Pine, 2 Doors, Iron Hinges, 73 In. 3300.00
Cupboard, Corner, Cherry, 1 Piece, Bracket Feet, 8 Panes, 85 In. 2000.00
Cupboard, Corner, Cherry, 2 Piece, Cutout Feet, 89 In. 1550.00
Cupboard, Corner, Chippendale, Cherry, C.1780, 89 In. High 2500.00
Cupboard, Corner, Chippendale, Cherry, Mullioned Doors, 7 Ft. 3850.00
Cupboard, Corner, Chippendale, Pine, C.1780, Flat Cornice, 81 In. 650.00
Cupboard, Corner, Federal, Cherry & Maple, Arched Doors, 7 Ft. 1650.00

(See Page 251)

Furniture, Cradle, Wicker

Cupboard, Corner, Federal, Cherry, Cornice, Bracket Feet, 7 Ft. 2580.00
Cupboard, Corner, Federal, Pine, Mullioned Doors, 7 X 4 Ft. 1320.00
Cupboard, Corner, Georgian, Pine, Shell Form, 6 Ft. 7 In. 176.00
Cupboard, Corner, Georgian, Shaped Shelves, Inlaid Oak, 5 Ft. 8 In. 715.00
Cupboard, Corner, Glass Doors, Walnut, 49 X 74 In. 950.00
Cupboard, Corner, Hanging, Glazed Door, Pine, 30 X 38 In. 120.00
Cupboard, Corner, Kentucky, Walnut, 37 1/2 In. X 6 Ft. 9 In. 2250.00
Cupboard, Corner, Molded & Carved, Pennsylvania, C.1780 .... 3950.00
Cupboard, Corner, Pennsylvania, Blue Paint, C.1835 .... 2200.00
Cupboard, Corner, Pennsylvania, 19th Century, Red Finish 8700.00
Cupboard, Corner, Pine & Ash, 2 Piece 550.00
Cupboard, Corner, Pine, Hanging, Cornice, Molding, Brass Knob 360.00
Cupboard, Corner, Pine, Hanging, Reeded Molding, 42 In. 210.00
Cupboard, Corner, Pine, 77 X 55 In. 1350.00
Cupboard, Corner, Two 8-Pane Doors On Top, Cherry 1995.00
Cupboard, Corner, Two 8-Pane Doors, 2 Drawer, Green & Red Paint 1700.00
Cupboard, Corner, Walnut, Glass Doors, 48 X 74 In. 950.00
Cupboard, Corner, Walnut, Hanging, Paneled Door, Brass Knob, 53 In. 250.00
Cupboard, Country, Pine, Flat Top, 1 Door, Cutout Bootjack, 66 In. 800.00
Cupboard, Dutch Door, Pine, 42 X 72 In. 465.00
Cupboard, English, Mahogany, Inlay, 2 Drawers, 10 In. 95.00
Cupboard, Federal, Grain Painted, 18th Century, 84 In. High 1800.00
Cupboard, George I, Provincial, Oak, 38 X 41 In. 770.00
Cupboard, Georgian, Oak, Rectangular Top, 4 Ft. 1 In. 550.00
Cupboard, Hanging, Cherry & Tiger Maple, 3 X 3 Ft. 410.00
Cupboard, Hanging, Drawer, Glass-Paned Door, Red, 12 X 11 X 21 In. 235.00
Cupboard, Hanging, George III, Ebony Swags, Oak, 4 Ft. 1 In. 302.00
Cupboard, Hanging, Molded Cornice, 18th Century, 27 X 23 In. 2400.00
Cupboard, Hanging, Pine, Double Slat Door, Red Paint, 31 In. 4200.00
Cupboard, Hanging, Walnut, Base & Cornice Molding, 29 In. 185.00
Cupboard, Jam, 2 Drawer, 2 Doors, Original Red Paint 375.00
Cupboard, Jelly, Burkey, Hamburg, Pa., Grain-Painted Chestnut 435.00
Cupboard, Jelly, Butternut, Double Paneled Doors, 55 X 43 In. 400.00
Cupboard, Jelly, Maple, Cutout Feet, Doors, Red, 45 X 45 In. 375.00
Cupboard, Jelly, Pennsylvania, Smoked Paint 750.00

Cupboard, Jelly, Sponge-Painted Panels, Butternut 400.00
Cupboard, Jelly, Walnut, Tin Sides, Top Drawer, C.1820, 42 In. 595.00
Cupboard, Jelly, 2 Drawer, 2 Doors, Original Red Paint 375.00
Cupboard, New York, 1800-10, Pumpkin Pine 950.00
Cupboard, North Carolina, Original Red Paint, C.1850 .... 1450.00
Cupboard, Paneled Walnut, C.1840, 78 In. 9500.00
Cupboard, Pennsylvania Dutch, Old Red Paint, 2 Piece 1595.00
Cupboard, Perimeter Molding, Batten Door, 3 Shelves, 76 In. 450.00
Cupboard, Pine & Poplar, 2 Panel Doors, 7 Drawer, 72 In. 1550.00
Cupboard, Pine & Poplar, 2 Panel Doors, 7 Drawers, 72 In. 1550.00
Cupboard, Pine, Flat Cornice, 2 Doors, Blue, 66 X 34 In. 6500.00
Cupboard, Pine, Frame Molding, Cornice, Red & Yellow, 35 In. 200.00
Cupboard, Pine, Board Door, Top Cutout, Blue, 38 3/4 X 75 In 2450.00
Cupboard, Pine, Towel Rack, Cornice, Double Doors, 69 X 37 In. 2200.00
Cupboard, Poplar, Dovetailed, Paneled Door, 30 1/4 X 18 1/4 In. 195.00
Cupboard, Queen Anne, Corner, Country 3300.00
Cupboard, Raised-Panel Doors, Rattail Hinged, Butternut 3800.00
Cupboard, Scalloped Doors, Pine 695.00
Cupboard, Standing, Pine, 2 Doors, Natural Color, 76 In. 650.00
Cupboard, Step Back, Canadian, C.1850 .... 715.00
Cupboard, Step Back, Pine, 41 X 74 In. 658.00
Cupboard, Wall, Empire, 2 Piece, Walnut & Maple, 2 Drawer, 93 In. 900.00
Cupboard, Wall, Federal, Walnut, 2 Part, C.1825, 7 Ft. 2 1/2 In. 2875.00
Cupboard, Wall, Hanging, Maple & Pine, Painted Red, 34 X 22 In. 600.00
Cupboard, Wall, Maple & Walnut, 89 X 46 In. 475.00
Cupboard, Wall, Pine, 1 Piece, 1 Door, 3 Open Shelves, Brown Paint 200.00
Cupboard, Wall, Pine, 1 Piece, Board & Batten Doors, 75 In. 165.00
Cupboard, Wall, Poplar, Red & Black Graining, Doors, 73 In. 525.00
Cupboard, Wall, Poplar, 2 Piece, 2 Bins, 3 Drawers, 75 In. 1600.00
Cupboard, Wall, Poplar, 3 Drawer, Top 6 Glass, 54 X 86 1/2 In. 1300.00
Cupboard, Wall, 2 Piece, Batten Doors, Red, 45 X 79 In. 800.00
Cupboard, Welsh, Black Walnut, C.1850 .... 1275.00
Cupboard, Welsh, Open Shelves Above Drawers, Pine, 77 In. 425.00
Cupboard, York, Pennsylvania, Blue 495.00
Cupboard, 2 Doors Above Large Drawer, Pine 1500.00
Cupboard, 2 Glass Doors & 2 Drawers Beneath, Ash 295.00
Cupboard, 4-Pane, Step Back, Mustard Grained 2800.00
Cupboard, 8-Pane, Pennsylvania, Pine, C.1830 .... 2700.00
Daybed, Empire, Maple 148.50
Daybed, Victorian, Curved Crest, Velvet Upholstery, 80 In. 165.00
Desk, Birch, Fan Pendant, Original Pulls, 39 X 31 In. 4800.00
Desk, Butler's, Empire, Inlaid Mahogany, C.1825, 45 1/2 In. 250.00
Desk, C Curve, Chair, Walnut & Mahogany, C.1910, 60 In. 1395.00
Desk, Campaign, Victorian, Brass-Mounted Mahogany, 36 X 40 In. 1100.00
Desk, Child's, Eastlake, Walnut, Slant Top, C.1860, 38 In. 225.00
Desk, Child's, Roll Top, Maple 95.00
Desk, Child's, Slant Top Raises, Birch Chair 75.00
Desk, Child's, String Inlay, Beaded Top, Maine, Cherry, 19 X 28 In. 225.00
Desk, Chippendale, Block Front, Mahogany, 4 Drawer, 41 In. 625.00
Desk, Chippendale, Curly Maple, C.1780, 42 In. ....*Illus* 5250.00
Desk, Chippendale, Slant Front Top, Original Brasses 4500.00
Desk, Chippendale, Slant Front, Cherry, 4 Drawer, C.1780 .... 1800.00
Desk, Chippendale, Slant Front, Cherry, 4 Drawer, Ogee Feet, 43 In. 1100.00
Desk, Drop Front, Eastlake 695.00
Desk, Drop Front, Oak, Crafters, C.1910, 46 In. ....*Illus* 200.00
Desk, Drop Front, 3 Drawers, Oak 375.00
Desk, Empire, Drop Leaf, Serpentine Front, Claw Feet, Oak 1500.00
Desk, Empire, Slant Front, Mahogany, 1 Drawer, 23 X 42 In. 225.00
Desk, Fall Front, Leather-Covered Surface, C.1850 .... 625.00
Desk, Federal, Boston, Mass., C.1830, Mahogany 1350.00
Desk, George III, 3 Drawers, Square Legs, 30 In. 350.00
Desk, Gustav Stickley, Oak 1000.00
Desk, Japanese, Caned Hardwood, C.1900, 55 X 45 In. 1500.00
Desk, Kneehole, George III, Bracket Feet, Mahogany, 39 X 33 In. 1980.00

Desk, Lap, Art Nouveau Silver Design 175.00
Desk, Lap, Brass Corners & Plaque, Fitted, Walnut, 9 X 13 1/2 In. 120.00
Desk, Lap, Brass Key & Accents, Walnut, 11 1/2 X 8 In. 65.00
Desk, Lap, Dovetailed, C.1850, Pine 100.00
Desk, Lap, Gilded Cupids & Cherubs On Cover, Black Lacquer 32.00
Desk, Lap, Mother-Of-Pearl Inlay, Velvet Liner, 16 X 9 1/2 X 5 In. 295.00
Desk, Lap, Mother-Of-Pearl Insert, 2 Wells, Walnut, 13 1/2 X 5 In. 162.00
Desk, Lap, Star-Patterned Cover, Grained 22.00
Desk, Lap, Victorian, Brassbound, Mahogany, Rectangular, C.1860 .... 120.00
Desk, Lap, Victorian, Brassbound, Rosewood 250.00
Desk, Lap, Victorian, Brassbound, Walnut, 15 1/2 X 6 1/2 In. 100.00
Desk, Lap, Victorian, Rosewood, Brassbound, Rectangular 250.00
Desk, Lap, Victorian, Square-Legged Stand, Walnut, 17 1/2 X 8 In. 300.00
Desk, Lap, 2 Inkwells, Pewter Tops, Walnut, C.1861, 12 X 8 1/2 In. 65.00
Desk, Lift-Top, Pennsylvania, C.1830, Small 1500.00
Desk, On Frame, Queen Anne, New England, C.1750, 43 In. ....*Illus* 7500.00
Desk, Partner's, Oak-Paneled, Leather, Top, C.1880, 60 X 30 In. 1250.00
Desk, Partner's, Victorian, Mahogany, C.1900, 56 X 34 1/2 X 30 In. 2300.00
Desk, Partner's, Victorian, Mahogany, 67 X 39 1/2 X 31 1/2 In. 1800.00
Desk, Pine, 3 Drawer, Fold-Down Lid, 49 In. 400.00
Desk, Queen Anne, Slant Front, 4 Cabriole Legs, Birch, C.1750 .... 7500.00
Desk, Queen Anne, Step-Down Interior, C.1775, Cherry 3750.00
Desk, Roll Top, Carved Pulls, 33-Drawer Interior, Oak 3875.00
Desk, Roll Top, Cherry, 29 X 42 X 43 In. 1150.00
Desk, Roll Top, S Curve, Mahogany, Bronze Pulls, 66 X 40 In. 4800.00
Desk, Roll Top, 43 Drawer, Brass Hardware, Columns, Fluted, 66 In. 6500.00
Desk, S Roll Top, Andrews & Co., Chicago, Mahogany, 40 X 66 In. 4800.00
Desk, S Roll Top, Carved, Mahogany, 66 X 40 In. 4800.00
Desk, S Roll Top, Leather Top, Carved, Walnut, 47 X 47 In. 3000.00
Desk, S Roll Top, Oak, 48 In. 1275.00
Desk, S Roll Top, 10 Drawer, 22 Slots, Chair, Oak, 54 X 50 In. 2600.00
Desk, School, Double, C.1910 .... 110.00
Desk, Schoolmaster's, Cherry 395.00
Desk, Schoolmaster's, New Hampshire, Blue Over Green Paint, 4 Ft. 650.00
Desk, Schoolmaster's, Original Paint, Pine 225.00
Desk, Schoolmaster's, Pine, Slant Lift Lid, Dated 1843, 40 In. 200.00
Desk, Schoolmaster's, 1800, Walnut 850.00
Desk, Secretary, Oxbow, Mahogany, Chippendale, C.1770, 80 X 23 In. 4000.00
Desk, Secretary, Walnut, C.1840 .... 1575.00
Desk, Slant Front Top, Greco-Roman Revival, C.1830, 43 1/2 In. 700.00
Desk, Slant Front, Bracket Feet, New England, Maple 1500.00
Desk, Slant Front, Chippendale, Cherry, Ogee Feet, C.1760, 44 In. 6100.00
Desk, Slant Front, Chippendale, Maple & Pine, Miniature, C.1780 .... 2200.00
Desk, Slant Front, Chippendale, Maple, C.1780, Document Drawer 2100.00
Desk, Slant Front, Chippendale, Old Brasses, Maple, 37 In.Wide 3700.00
Desk, Slant Front, Chippendale, Reverse Serpentine, Mahogany 4000.00
Desk, Slant Front, Chippendale, Walnut, Bracket Feet, 42 In. 1000.00
Desk, Slant Front, Federal, Cherry, C.1780, 45 X 40 In. 2200.00
Desk, Slant Front, Federal, Pine, 4 Drawer, Bracket Feet, 39 In. 900.00
Desk, Slant Front, Figured Cherry, 1780-1815 .... 3500.00
Desk, Slant Front, George II, Mahogany, 9 Drawer, 40 In. 900.00
Desk, Slant Front, Georgian, Mahogany, 8 Drawer, 35 In. 800.00
Desk, Slant Front, Maple, William & Mary, C.1700, 38 In. 7000.00
Desk, Slant Front, New England, Cherry 4200.00
Desk, Slant Front, Pine, Bow Drawer, 45 In. 700.00
Desk, Slant Front, Queen Anne, Pine, Red Stain, C.1750, 40 In. 1350.00
Desk, Slant Front, Tiger Maple 6200.00
Desk, Slant Front, Walnut, Ogee Feet, 4 Drawer, 32 In. 1050.00
Desk, Slant Front, 1780-1815, Cherry 3500.00
Desk, Slant Top, Victorian, Mahogany, Leather, 7 X 26 In. 275.00
Desk, Tambour Cylinder, C.1860, 6 Drawer, Mahogany, 32 X 38 In. 225.00
Desk, Traveling, Victorian, Gold-Tooled Leather Surface, C.1860 .... 192.00
Desk, Trustee's, Shaker 2500.00
Desk, Victorian, Adjustable Top, C.1870, Walnut, 42 1/2 X 33 In. 650.00

Furniture, Desk, Chippendale, Curly
Maple, C.1780, 42 In.
(See Page 253)

Furniture, Desk, Drop Front, Oak, Crafters,
C.1910, 46 In.
(See Page 253)

Furniture, Desk, On Frame, Queen Anne,
New England, C.1750, 43 In.

Desk, Wells Fargo, Secret Drawer, 9 Drawer, 9 Doors, Walnut	3000.00
Desk, Wooton, S Curve Roll Top, Rotary Pedestal, Oak, 60 In.	4000.00
Dining Set, Chippendale Style, Carved Mahogany, 11 Piece	2900.00
Dining Set, Chippendale, C.1900, 8 Chairs	4800.00
Dining Set, Claw Foot, 3 Leaves, 4 Chairs, Oak, 45 In.Diam.	500.00
Dough Tray, Stretcher Base, C.1840, Original Finish	850.00
Dresser, Eastlake, Burled Walnut, Marble Top, Lamp Shelves	450.00
Dresser, Federal, Maple, 4 Drawer, 36 X 42 In.	90.00
Dresser, Kitchen, 2 Doors, 3 Drawer, Open Shelves, Pine	750.00
Dresser, Lower Doors, Upper 2 Drawer, English, Stained Pine, 7 Ft.	1100.00
Dresser, Marble Insert, Glove Drawers, 3 Drawer, 1870s	210.00
Dresser, Marble Top, Candlestands, Walnut, 43 X 80 In. *Illus*	500.00
Dresser, Marble Top, Eastlake, 3 Drawer, Tilt Mirror, 40 In.	160.00
Dresser, Marble Top, Stenciled Design, Secret Skirt Drawer, C.1870	850.00
Dresser, Pine, 2 Drawer, Doors, 6 Ft. 7 In.	1430.00
Dresser, Plate Rack, Lower Drawer, England, Pine, 6 Ft. 11 In.	550.00
Dresser, Plate Rack, 2 Frieze Drawers, England, Pine, 5 Ft. 7 In.	660.00
Dresser, Victorian, Marble Top, Beveled Mirror, English	225.00
Dresser, Victorian, Marble Top, Serpentine Front, Mahogany, 74 In.	425.00
Dry Sink, American, Cherry, C.1800	525.00

Dry Sink, High Back, Dovetailed Drawers, Chamfered Doors 690.00
Dry Sink, Pine, Cupboard Doors & Drawers, 6 Ft. 1 In. 175.00
Dry Sink, Pine, Primitive, 18 1/2 X 50 X 28 1/2 In. 90.00
Dry Sink, Pine, 30 In.Wide 485.00
Dry Sink, Reversed Design Of Gallery On Apron, C.1860, Blue Paint 1150.00
Dry Sink, 2 Drawer, 2 Doors, Dovetailed, Pine & Poplar 525.00
Easel, Victorian, Oak, Spool-Turned Trim 65.00
Etagere, Black & Gilt Lacquered Designs, Oriental, 77 1/2 In. 1100.00
Etagere, Carving, Beveled Mirrors, 8 Shelves, 6 Ft.Tall 600.00
Etagere, Inlaid Landscape, L.Majorelle, Nancy, 68 In. ....Illus 5300.00
Etagere, William IV, Mahogany, C.1835, Spiraltwist Legs 325.00
Etagere, 3 Shelves, Spiral Twist Supports, C.1835, Mahogany 325.00
Fire Screen, Louis XV, Carved Walnut, Floral Design, 37 In. 200.00
Footstool, Floral Design, Ocher Ground 460.00
Footstool, French Provincial, Carved, 8-Legged, Walnut, 28 In.Long 350.00
Footstool, French Provincial, 6-Legged, Walnut, 27 In.Long 215.00
Footstool, Iron Base, Needlepoint Seat, 15 X 8 In. 45.00
Footstool, Wicker 95.00
Frame, Crisscross Leaf Corners, Gilt Liner, 11 X 9 In. 14.00
Frame, Gilt Liner, Walnut, 14 1/2 X 12 1/2 In. 36.00
Frame, Marbleized Green, Gold Lines, C.1880, 8 3/4 X 10 3/4 In., Pr 48.00
Frame, Shadowbox, Gold Liner, Walnut, 18 3/4 X 19 3/4 In. 90.00
Frame, Walnut, 48 1/2 X 38 1/2 In. 150.00
Hall Seat, Lion Heads On Arms, Carved Jack Frost On Back, Oak 1375.00
Hall Tree, Iron, Victorian, Floral Design 175.00
Hat Rack & Mirror, 3 Hooks, Cupid & Flowers, 18 X 18 In. 85.00
Hat Rack, Bentwood 65.00
Hat Rack, Expandable, Oak 25.00
High Chair, Arrow Back 95.00
High Chair, Caned Seat, Thonet, Bentwood 350.00
High Chair, Ladder Back, Maple, 18th Century, 38 1/2 In. 2500.00
High Chair, Painted, 2-Slat Back, 18th Century, 32 1/2 In. 800.00
High Chair, Rush Seat, 18th Century, 39 In. ....Illus 750.00
High Chair, Splint Seat, Shaped Arms, 18th Century, 40 In. 350.00
High Chair, Windsor, Bamboo, 36 In. 160.00
Highboy, American Centennial, Ball & Claw Feet, Mahogany 1400.00
Highboy, C.1760, English Oak, 36 X 18 X 62 1/2 In. 2750.00
Highboy, Chippendale, Secret Drawer, American, Mahogany, 83 In. 950.00
Highboy, Map Drawer In Molding, C.1700, Yew 3500.00
Highboy, Queen Anee, Cherry, Flat Top, 1760, Pad Feet, 6 Ft. 7975.00
Highboy, Queen Anne, Cherry, 4 Drawer, Mirror, 31 In. 385.00
Highboy, Queen Anne, Walnut, Trifid Feet, C.1780, 6 Ft. 2640.00
Highboy, Queen Anne, 2 Section, Flat Molded Cornice, C.1760, 67 In. 5500.00
Highboy, William & Mary, Maple & Pine, C.1710, 60 In. 7500.00
Highboy, William & Mary, Poplar & Maple, C.1700, 57 In. 925.00
Highboy, William & Mary, Tiger Maple, Secret Drawer, C.1740, 71 In. 4700.00
Huntboard, North Carolina, 1810, Red Paint, Yellow Pine 2500.00
Hutch Table, Lift-Up Seat, Mitered Breadboard Ends, Seats 6 .... 1400.00
Hutch, Pine, 2 Shelves, Bootjack Ends, Green, 70 In. 1700.00
Hutch, Pine, 3 Shelves, Spoon Rack, Red Paint, 60 In. 1500.00
Hutch, Step Back, Pine, 5 Shelves, 70 X 53 In. 525.00
Hutch, Welsh, Pine, C.1800, 50 X 19 X 83 In. 850.00
Linen Press, Atlantic Origin, Softwood & Hardwood, 48 X 76 In. 3200.00
Linen Press, Pine, C.1820, 6 Ft. 39 In. X 23 In. 2150.00
Living Room Set, Black Lacquered, Japanese, 5 Piece 9750.00
Love Seat, Edwardian, Loop Arms, Tufted Back, 46 In. 125.00
Love Seat, Mahogany, Leaf Carved Frame, Victorian 375.00
Love Seat, Wicker 625.00
Lowboy, Chippendale, Mahogany, 3 Drawer, Square Legs, 29 In. 750.00
Lowboy, Queen Anne, Burl Walnut Veneered, Maple 2600.00
Lowboy, William & Mary, Maple, 3 Drawer, Brass Pulls, Bell Legs 1100.00
Lowboy, 3 Frieze Drawers, Walnut, 35 X 1 1/2 X 29 In. 300.00
Mirror, American, Arched Crest, Rectangular Opening, Grain Painted 550.00
Mirror, Baroque, 19th Century, Dutch, Gilt Metal, 43 X 52 1/2 In. 525.00

Furniture, Dresser, Marble Top, Candlestands,
Walnut, 43 X 80 In.   *(See Page 255)*

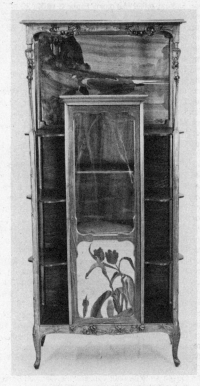

Furniture, Etagere, Inlaid Landscape,
L. Majorelle, Nancy, 68 In.

Furniture, High Chair, Rush Seat,
18th Century, 39 In.

Mirror, Beveled Plate, 19th Century, Gilt Wood 38 In.	150.00
Mirror, Bilbao, Figure Medallion, C.1790, Marble & Gilt Wood	750.00
Mirror, Chippendale, Mahogany, Scrolled Frame, 25 In.	250.00
Mirror, Chippendale, Mahogany, Swan's Neck Pediment, 4 Ft.	1650.00
Mirror, Chippendale, Wall, Veneered, Mahogany, 18th Century, 26 In.	125.00
Mirror, Convex, Regency, Gold Painted, 44 In.	220.00
Mirror, Courting, Angular Crest, Reverse-Painted Glass, 17 In.	1450.00
Mirror, Courting, Reverse-Painted Stylized Flowers, Bark Frame	625.00
Mirror, Courting, Stylized Flowers, Gilt Liner, 17 X 12 In.	450.00

Mirror, Eagle, Abalone Inlay, C.1880, Cast Iron, 13 X 10 In. 45.00
Mirror, Empire, Gilt, C.1840, Sailboat Panel, 22 X 12 In. 70.00
Mirror, Empire, Reverse Painting Of Ships, 13 X 26 In. 25.00
Mirror, Federal, Gilt, C.1820, Polychrome Panels, 21 In. 195.00
Mirror, Federal, Inlaid Mahogany Eagle, C.1800, 30 In. 3300.00
Mirror, Federal, Maple & Gilt, Phoenix Crest, 40 In. 240.00
Mirror, Federal, Pine Eglomise, Horse & Rider Panel, 22 In. 330.00
Mirror, George II, Gilt Eagle, Mahogany, 24 In. 547.00
Mirror, George II, Mahogany, C.1745, 14 1/2 X 24 1/2 In. 220.00
Mirror, Gilt Wood, 2 Part, Pine Frame, Leaf Design, 47 In. 150.00
Mirror, Hall, Victorian, Walnut, Black Paint 40.00
Mirror, Italian, Gilt & Gesso, Urn Surmount, 33 In. 200.00
Mirror, Italian, Wreathed With Flowers, Marble Top, Wrought Iron 725.00
Mirror, Louis XV, Carved Gilt Wood, Scrolled Crest, 38 In. 650.00
Mirror, Louis XVI, Pierced Crest, Laurel Design, 42 In. 100.00
Mirror, Mahogany Veneer, Gilt, 44 X 22 In. 850.00
Mirror, Neoclassical Style, Italy, Scrolled Ends, 48 In. 200.00
Mirror, Overmantel, Federal, Gilt Wood, 33 X 22 In. 250.00
Mirror, Pier, Victorian, Dated 1866, 34 X 11 Ft. 4 In., Pair 1600.00
Mirror, Pier, With Console, Rococo, Carved & Gilt, 38 1/2 X 85 In. 1300.00
Mirror, Pine, Rectangular, Cut Corners, 10 3/4 X 6 1/2 In. 200.00
Mirror, Plateau, Beveled Glass, Silver Plated Frame & Feet, 12 In. 85.00
Mirror, Plateau, Beveled Glass, Silver Plated Rim & Feet, 14 In. 60.00
Mirror, Plateau, Chains & Leaves, Grapes, Gilt, 14 1/4 In. 120.00
Mirror, Plateau, Double Beveled, Signed Eureka 85.00
Mirror, Plateau, Engraved Base, Double Beveled Glass, 17 1/2 In. 165.00
Mirror, Plateau, Floral, Double Beveled, 12 1/4 In. 85.00
Mirror, Plateau, Gilt Edge, Oval, 10 1/2 X 16 1/2 In. 50.00
Mirror, Plateau, Scroll Feet, Double Beveled Edge, 4 X 9 3/4 In. 45.00
Mirror, Plateau, Scrollwork Sides, Animal Claw Feet, 11 1/2 In. 75.00
Mirror, Queen Anne, Carved Crest, Gilded Shell, C.1730, 15 X 10 In. 650.00
Mirror, Queen Anne, Cutout Crest, Mahogany, 14 X 28 In. 145.00
Mirror, Queen Anne, High Crest, Pine Frame, Red, 19 In. 2300.00
Mirror, Queen Anne, Mahogany, C.1760, Bird's Head, 24 In. 1650.00
Mirror, Queen Anne, Pine Frame, Black, Shaped Crest, 16 In. 1300.00
Mirror, Queen Anne, Pine, Painted, Etched Glass Overlay, 1750s 600.00
Mirror, Queen Anne, Scrolled Crest, 28 In. 400.00
Mirror, Queen Anne, Scrolled, Mahogany On Pine, 14 X 24 In. 375.00
Mirror, Queen Anne, Walnut Molding, 2-Part Glass, 33 X 15 In. 2000.00
Mirror, Queen Anne, Walnut Veneer, Pine, Scrolled Crest, 26 In. 500.00
Mirror, Regency Style, Arched Plate, Gilt Wood, 47 In. 425.00
Mirror, Scroll, Poplar, 18 X 33 In. 70.00
Mirror, Shaving, Empire, Grain Painted Over Veneer 145.00
Mirror, Shaving, Federal, C.1820, Baluster Posts, 19 In. 110.00
Mirror, Shaving, Victorian, Walnut 385.00
Mirror, Sheraton, Reverse Painting Of Fisherman 225.00
Mirror, Venetian, Deco, Pink, 15 In.Diam. 75.00
Mirror, William & Mary, Mahogany, C.1730, 46 X 18 In. 1350.00
Mirror, William & Mary, Painted, Pine, C.1700, 21 X 12 1/2 In. 550.00
Mirror, William & Mary, Walnut, Arched Crest, C.1720, 36 In. 900.00
Mirror, William & Mary, Walnut, Cutout Crest, 26 In. 400.00
Parlor Set, Belter Type, Laminated Rosewood, 3 Piece 4750.00
Parlor Set, Belter Type, Laminated Rosewood, 6 Piece 9500.00
Parlor Set, Carved Lions' Heads, Oak, 5 Piece 2495.00
Parlor Set, French, Carved, Cabriole Legs, Caned & Upholstered 500.00
Parlor Set, Massive, Carved Walnut, C.1876, 4 Matched Pieces 4500.00
Pedestal, Edwardian, Mahogany Inlaid, 42 1/2 In. 375.00
Pedestal, Gold Design, Red Lacquered, Chinese 225.00
Pew, Church, Walnut 125.00
Piano, Child's, Cherry, Marked Schoenhut 65.00
Pie Safe, Hand-Punched Tin, Grain Painted 335.00
Pie Safe, Pierced Tin Sides, Oak 185.00
Pie Safe, Pine & Poplar, Shenandoah Valley, 8 Eagle Tins 1150.00
Pie Safe, Pine, Scalloped Base, 1 Drawer, 75 In. 325.00

Pie Safe, Tin Panels, Star Design, Old Red Paint, 34 In. 610.00
Pie Safe, Urn Design, Punched Tin Panels, Virginia, Walnut 1700.00
Pie Safe, 12 Tin Panels, Drawer, Red, 41 X 55 In. 450.00
Pine, 1 Board Door, Shelves, Red, 25 X 74 In. 230.00
Plant Stand, Heart Design, C.1870 .... 385.00
Plant Stand, Mother-Of-Pearl Inlay, Carved, Teakwood 225.00
Pool Table, August Jungblut, 3 Slates, Oak, Accessories 5000.00
Post Office, General Store, Letter Window, Brass Boxes, Locks, Oak 200.00
Potty Chair, Sponge-Painted 200.00
Rack, Spoon, Drawer & Till, Hand-Carved, Cherry, 13 X 24 In. 2500.00
Rocker & Sofa, Limbert, Mission 750.00
Rocker, Armchair, Shaker, No.7, Spindle Back, Tape Seat 225.00
Rocker, Boston, Stenciling On Crest, Turned Legs 35.00
Rocker, Child's, Comb Back, Red Paint, 19 In. 65.00
Rocker, Child's, Country Origin, Plank Seat, 19th Century, Yew 120.00
Rocker, Child's, Crabed Arms, Pressed Back, Oak, 15 X 26 In. 225.00
Rocker, Child's, Hoop Back, Pine & Poplar, C.1880 .... 125.00
Rocker, Child's, Shaker, Mt.Lebanon, New York 425.00
Rocker, Child's, Upholstered, Oak 25.00
Rocker, Child's, Wicker, 1920s 125.00
Rocker, Ladder Back, 3 Slats, Turned Finial 45.00
Rocker, Maple, Shaker, No.3, Labeled Shaker, Tape Seat, 34 In. 280.00
Rocker, Oak, High Spindle Back, Board Seat, Original Finish 65.00
Rocker, Oak, Incised Scroll Back 95.00
Rocker, Pilgrim Style, Maple, Slat Back, C.1860 .... 500.00
Rocker, Platform, Eastlake, American Walnut 120.00
Rocker, Platform, Wicker 495.00
Rocker, Shaker, Splint Seat, Red Paint, 41 In. 1100.00
Rocker, Shaker, Tape Seat, Mt.Lebanon, N.Y., 48 In. ....*Illus* 7250.00
Rocker, Shaker, Watervliet, Old Red 400.00
Rocker, Shaker, 3 Shaped Slats, Tape Seat, 34 In. 110.00
Rocker, Sheraton, Rabbit Ear Back, 3 Slats 120.00
Rocker, Slat Back, Original Splint Seat, 19th Century, Red 170.00
Rocker, Spindle Back, Rush Seat, C.1830 .... 90.00
Rocker, Twisted Spindles, Pearl Inlays, Mahogany 280.00
Rocker, Wicker, Rolled Arms, Cane Seat 195.00
Rocker, Wicker, Wooden Seat, Victorian 60.00
Rocker, Windsor, Bow Back, Knuckle Arm, Saddle Seat, 35 In. 225.00
Rocker, Windsor, Elm, Early 19th Century 550.00
Rocker, Windsor, Stick, Old Black Paint 185.00
Rocker, Wing, Round Legs, Shaped Crest, 44 In. 325.00
Rocker, Wing, Upholstered, Red Stain, 45 In. 1000.00
Salon Set, Edwardian, Inlaid Satinwood, 43 In. 650.00
Screen, Fan & Shell Design, Floral Border, Mahogany, C.1850, Pair 875.00
Screen, Pole, Victorian, Carved, 19th Century, Mahogany 175.00
Screen, 4-Panel, Chinese, 19th Century, 21 1/2 X 78 In. 2500.00
Screen, 4-Panel, Woven Wicker 750.00
Seat, Wagon, Maple & Basswood, Rear Leg, C.1825, 29 In. 300.00
Seat, Window, Hepplewhite Style, 8 Legs, 68 1/2 In. ....*Illus* 600.00
Secretaire, Regency, Drop Front, Fluted Columns, Mahogany, 41 In. 450.00
Secretary Bookcase, Burled Drawers, 45 X 101 In. ....*Illus* 1300.00
Secretary Bookcase, Chippendale, Maple & Cherry, C.1790, 6 Ft. 5500.00
Secretary Bookcase, Curved Glass, Oak 450.00
Secretary China Cabinet, Hand-Carved, Oak 575.00
Secretary Desk, Curved Glass, Mirror Above Desk, Oak 400.00
Secretary Desk, Victorian, 4 Cupboards, Burl Walnut, C.1865, 68 In. 3800.00
Secretary, Cylinder Front, Biedermeier, Mahogany, C.1830 .... 1500.00
Secretary, Eastlake, Victorian, Brick & White Cornice Tiles 700.00
Secretary, Fall Front, Mahogany, Brass Mounted, Empire, C.1825 .... 2310.00
Secretary, Fall Front, Mahogany, Continental, 4 Ft. 4 In. 880.00
Secretary, Federal, Birch, Paneled Doors, C.1810, 67 In. 700.00
Secretary, Federal, Mahogany & Bird's-Eye Maple, C.1795, 51 In. 500.00
Secretary, Federal, Mahogany & Veneer, C.1810, 57 X 38 In. 375.00
Secretary, Fretted Doors, Barley Twist Stand, Oak, 36 X 86 In. 850.00

Furniture, Seat, Window, Hepplewhite Style, 8 Legs, 68 1/2 In.

Furniture, Rocker, Shaker, Tape Seat, Mt.Lebanon, N.Y., 48 In.

Furniture, Secretary, Hepplewhite, Writing
Surface, 2 Part

Furniture, Secretary Bookcase, Burled Drawers, 45 X 101 In.

(See Page 259)

Secretary, Hepplewhite, Writing Surface, 2 Part	*Illus*	2000.00
Secretary, Roll Top, Cylinder, Walnut, 68 1/2 In. X 11 Ft. 11 In.		9000.00
Secretary, Sheraton, Bookcase Top, Mahogany, 66 In.	*Illus*	1100.00
Secretary, Sheraton, Flame Mahogany Drawer Fronts, C.1810		1595.00
Secretary, Twist Stand, Leaded Glass, C.1910, Oak, 35 X 79 In.		695.00
Server, D-Shaped, Mahogany, 1 Drawer, C.1800, 28 In.		500.00
Server, Hepplewhite, 2 Drawer, Pine		299.00
Server, Mahogany & Cane, C.1900, 43 In.	*Illus*	250.00
Settee & Chair, Wicker	*Illus*	850.00
Settee & 2 Armchairs, Wicker	*Illus*	3000.00
Settee, Adam Style, Satinwood		1900.00
Settee, Camel Back, Chippendale, Claw Feet, 54 In.		400.00

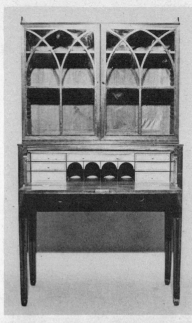

Furniture, Server, Mahogany & Cane, C.1900, 43 In.

Furniture, Secretary, Sheraton, Bookcase Top, Mahogany, 66 In.

Furniture, Settee & Chair, Wicker

Settee, Camel Back, Chippendale, Mahogany, Claw Feet, 6 Ft. 425.00
Settee, Federal, C.1800, Landscape Cover, Caned Seat, 5 Ft. 1540.00
Settee, Greco-Roman Revival, Cane Seat, Saber Legs, C.1830, 35 In. 200.00
Settee, Plank Seat, Foliate Design, Ocher Ground, 5 Ft. 1100.00
Settee, Plank Seat, Pine, C.1840, Clusters Of Fruits, 5 Ft. 2100.00
Settee, Plank Seat, Pine, Turned Legs, 5 Ft. 10 In. 625.00
Settee, Wicker .... *Illus* 1000.00

Settle, Cupboard Door Below, Round Back, Oak, 27 In. 400.00
Settle, Painted, Pine, Curved Back, 18th Century, 64 In. High 650.00
Settle, Pine, Curved, Shoe Feet, 76 X 62 In. 850.00
Settle, Pine, Double Lift Seats, Red, 49 X 57 In. 1000.00
Settle, Shaped Arms & Shoe Feet, Curved, Pine 2300.00
Settle, William & Mary, Carved, Lift Seat, C.1900, Oak 335.00
Sewing Stand, Wicker 135.00
Sewing Stand, 1-Drawer, Tray, 1920, Spool Holders 50.00
Shaving Stand, Eastlake, Marble Top, 2-Drawer, 68 In. .... *Illus* 275.00
Shelf, Hanging, Crescent-Shaped Shelves, Mahogany, C.1900, 36 In. 165.00
Shelf, Wall, Hanging, Pine, Cupboard Doors, Flat Top, 39 In. 600.00
Shelf, Wall, Hanging, Pine, 4 Shelves, 23 X 18 In. 375.00
Shelf, Wall, Hanging, 2 Tier, Scalloped Sides, 19 In. 70.00
Shelf, Wall, Mahogany, 3 Tier, 23 X 25 In. 275.00
Shelf, Wall, Oak, 3 Shelves, 2 Drawer, Shaped Sides, 38 In. 525.00
Shelf, Wall, Pine, 3 Shelves, Scalloped Ends, 20 In. 300.00
Shelf, Wall, Pine, 3 Shelves, Shaped Sides, Green, 30 X 20 In. 250.00
Shelf, Wall, 3 Tier, Shaped Sides, Grain Painted, 38 In. 900.00
Shelf, 3 Tier, Hanging, Molded Pediment, Oak, 26 X 38 In. 100.00
Shelf, 3 Tier, Wicker 325.00
Shelves, Pine, Bootjack Ends, Scalloped Top, 10 X 40 In. 85.00
Sideboard, Bowfront, Beveled & Etched Mirrors, Mahogany, C.1867 .... 2800.00
Sideboard, Bowfront, Federal, Inlaid Mahogany, C.1810, 5 Ft. 1320.00
Sideboard, Federal, Inlaid Mahogany, C.1790, 6 Ft. 7 In. 1980.00
Sideboard, Federal, Mahogany, C.1790, Double Door, 37 X 67 In. 2600.00
Sideboard, Federal, Mahogany, C.1790, 2 Drawer, Bowed Doors, 40 In. 2310.00
Sideboard, French, Beveled Mirror, Marble Top, Walnut, 61 X 22 In. 200.00
Sideboard, George II, Mahogany, C.1800, Bowfront, 30 X 40 In. 350.00
Sideboard, George III, Satinwood, Mahogany, C.1790, 36 In. 1045.00
Sideboard, German, Beveled Leaded Doors, 98 X 64 In. 975.00
Sideboard, Hepplewhite, Bowfront, Mahogany, 55 In. 650.00
Sideboard, Hepplewhite, 2 Tier, 6 Drawer, Mahogany, 72 X 43 In. 8000.00
Sideboard, Original Brasses, Quarter-Sawed Oak, 65 X 25 X 70 In. 4000.00
Sideboard, Stickley Bros., Original Hardware, Quarter-Sawed Oak 500.00
Sideboard, Variegated Marble Top, Austrian, Walnut, 94 X 40 In. 2900.00
Sideboard, Wicker, 3 Drawer, Open Sides .... *Illus* 950.00
Sideboard, 2 Small Drawers, Large Drawer, 2 Doors In Base, Oak 550.00
Sink, Tray, Pine & Poplar, Paneled Doors, Zinc-Lined Well, 34 In. 300.00
Smoking Stand, Copper Lined, Carved Oak 550.00
Sofa, Classical Revival, Mahogany, C.1820, 82 In.Long .... *Illus* 5000.00
Sofa, Country, Pine Legs, Blue-Gray Hopsacking, 78 In. 550.00
Sofa, Ebonized & Piece Carved, Cameo Back, Center Medallion 1800.00
Sofa, Empire, Brocade, Carved Mahogany, C.1890 .... 1500.00
Sofa, Federal, Mahogany, Scroll Arms, Reeded Posts, 78 In. 700.00
Sofa, Finger-Carved Cameo Back, Walnut 280.00
Sofa, Greco-Roman Revival, Mahogany, Carved Eagle, C.1830, 33 In. 375.00
Sofa, Late Empire, C.1840, Mahogany 450.00
Sofa, Mission, Oak, Stickley, Settle Bench Type, 6 Ft. 550.00
Sofa, Neoclassical, Carved Mahogany, C.1830, 98 In. 400.00
Sofa, Sheraton, Pineapple Carving, Salem, Mass. 3500.00
Sofa, Wicker, C.1920 .... 360.00
Spice Chest, 18 Drawer, Original Lettering, 44 1/2 X 16 X 38 In. 375.00
Stand, Book, Country, C.1800, Curved Crest, Slant Top, 8 1/2 In. 470.00
Stand, Butternut Base, Spider Legs, Cherry Top, 23 In. 250.00
Stand, Butternut, Cherry Legs, 2 Drawer, Red, 17 X 28 In. 90.00
Stand, Corner Basin, Federal, Maple, C.1780, Scrolled Legs, 40 In. 330.00
Stand, Corner Basin, George III, Drawer, Platform Shelf, C.1790 .... 247.00
Stand, Corner Basin, George III, Hinged Top, Mahogany, 4 1/3 Ft. 550.00
Stand, Drop Leaf, Cherry 450.00
Stand, Fern, Neoclassical, Inset Marble Top, Fruitwood, 45 1/4 In. 275.00
Stand, Flower, Handle, Wicker 175.00
Stand, Hepplewhite, Cherry, Square Legs, Drawer, 29 In. 125.00
Stand, Hepplewhite, Mahogany, 1 Drawer, Massachusetts 650.00
Stand, Light, Ratchet Shelf, Late 19th Century 45.00

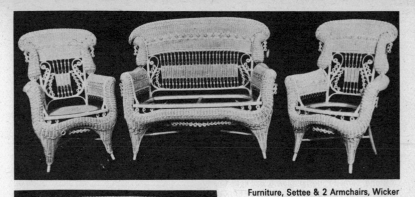

Furniture, Settee & 2 Armchairs, Wicker

Furniture, Settee, Wicker

Furniture, Sideboard, Wicker, 3 Drawer, Open Sides

Furniture, Shaving Stand,
Eastlake, Marble Top,
2-Drawer, 68 In.

(See Pages 260, 261)

Furniture, Sofa, Classical Revival, Mahogany, C.1820, 82 In.Long

Stand, Marble Top, Teak, C.1900, 20 In. 100.00
Stand, Oriental Carved, Marble Top, Rosette Shape, 18 In. 325.00
Stand, Pine, Square Legs, Drawer, Board Top, Red, 29 In. 55.00
Stand, Reading, George IV, Mahogany, C.1820, 30 In. 935.00
Stand, Sheraton, Turned Legs 250.00
Stand, Sheraton, 1 Drawer, Pine 90.00
Stand, Sheraton, 2 Drawer, Maple 545.00
Stand, Spider Leg, Cherry & Birch 475.00
Stand, Teak, Marble Top, C.1900, Paw Feet, 31 1/2 In. 225.00
Stand, Teak, Marble Top, Fish & Floral Design, 30 In. 250.00
Stand, Tilt Top, Chippendale, Mahogany, Snake Feet, C.1780, 28 In. 875.00
Stand, Tilt Top, Inlaid, Cherry 775.00
Stand, Turned Legs, Tiger Maple 350.00
Stand, Turned Pedestal, Claw & Ball Feet, Cherry 2000.00
Stand, Turned Pedestal, Snake Feet, 18th Century, Cherry 450.00
Stool, Chippendale, Mahogany, Acanthus Carved Legs, Pair 440.00
Stool, Cricket, Plank Top, Button Feet, Pine, 6 X 12 X 7 In. 130.00
Stool, Ice Cream Parlor, Iron Pedestal, Iron Back, Set Of 4 .... 275.00
Stool, Organ, Oak 110.00
Stool, Piano, High Back, Ball & Claw Feet, Fluted Legs 125.00
Stool, Pierced Square Top, 19th Century, England, Elm, 19 In. 100.00
Stool, Pine & Poplar, Square Legs, Brown, 8 1/2 In. 40.00
Stool, Pine, Stenciled, Yellow Bird & Fruit, 12 In. 140.00
Stool, Rush Seat, 3 Footed, Triangular, 18 In. 150.00
Stool, Sheraton, Mahogany, Cloth Covering, 18 In. 175.00
Stool, Switchboard Operator's, Wicker Seat, Revolving 250.00
Stool, Turned Legs, 24 In. 35.00
Stool, William & Mary, Maple & Pine, Square Top, 18 In. 550.00
Stool, William & Mary, Rectangular Tip, Birch, C.1700, 15 1/2 In. 400.00
Swing, Wicker 350.00
Table, Ambulante, Louis XVI, C.1900, Marble Top, 38 In. 100.00
Table, Banquet, Federal, Veneer, Cherry, Mahogany, C.1820, 29 1/2 In 1700.00
Table, Banquet, Federal, 3-Part, Mahogany, 14 Legs, 29 X 109 In. 1900.00
Table, Banquet, George III, C.1800, Mahogany, Square Legs, 28 In. 350.00
Table, Banquet, Greco-Roman Revival, Mahogany, 29 X 54 In. 2300.00
Table, Barley Twist Legs, Oak, Closed 43 In.Square 450.00
Table, Bedside, George II, Mahogany, C.1800, 30 In. 750.00
Table, Bedside, Provincial, Fruitwood, 1 Drawer, 29 In. 275.00
Table, Billards, Cover Of 3 Leaves For Dining, Inlaid Edge 1200.00
Table, Breakfast, C.1800, Mahogany, 4 Ft. 1 In. X 26 1/2 In. 715.00
Table, Breakfast, Cherry, Drop Leaf, Turned Legs, 30 In. 715.00
Table, Breakfast, Federal, Mahogany, C.1810, D-Shaped Leaves 330.00
Table, Breakfast, George III, Mahogany, Saber Leg 425.00
Table, Breakfast, Tilt Top, William IV, Burl Walnut, 31 In. 450.00
Table, Breakfast, Victorian, Walnut, Oval, Foliate Scrolls, 18 In. 1400.00
Table, Butler's Tray, Chippendale 6500.00
Table, Card, D-Shaped, George I, Mahogany, Leather Top, 28 In. 2200.00
Table, Card, Demilune, Regency, Burl Walnut, 28 In. 350.00
Table, Card, Duncan Phyfe, Full Eagle On Globe Below 3600.00
Table, Card, Empire, Curly Maple, Pedestal Base, 28 In. 525.00
Table, Card, Empire, Inlaid Mahogany, C.1815, Animal Carved Legs 2450.00
Table, Card, Federal, Inlaid Mahogany & Maple, C.1790, 29 In. 1980.00
Table, Card, Federal, Inlaid Mahogany, C.1790, 28 In. 1950.00
Table, Card, Federal, Inlaid Mahogany, C.1790, 29 In. 1540.00
Table, Card, Federal, Inlaid Mahogany, C.1790, 29 X 35 In. 1650.00
Table, Card, Federal, Inlaid Mahogany, Reeded Legs, 29 In. 550.00
Table, Card, Federal, Mahogany, C.1810, Inlaid Edge, 30 In. 800.00
Table, Card, Fluted Legs, Country, Birch 550.00
Table, Card, Fold Top, Cherry, & Birch, Federal, 29 X 36 In. 2400.00
Table, Card, George III, Mahogany, C.1780, Hinged Top, 29 In. 385.00
Table, Card, Greco-Roman Revival, Mahogany, C.1815, 30 In. 2000.00
Table, Card, Greco-Roman Revival, Mahogany, C.1820, 29 1/2 In. 350.00
Table, Carved Teak, Indian, C.1900, Temples, Berries, 30 In. 200.00
Table, Center, Louis Philippe, 19th Century, Rosewood 225.00

Furniture, Table, Center, Victorian, Marble Top, C.1870

Table, Center, Victorian, Ball & Claw Feet, C.1910, Walnut 345.00
Table, Center, Victorian, Carved Walnut, Marble Panel .... 440.00 To 467.00
Table, Center, Victorian, Marble Top, C.1870 ....*Illus* 880.00
Table, Charles II, Oak, Cylindrical Legs, 35 In. 600.00
Table, Chinese Teak, Mother-Of-Pearl Inlay, 35 In. 1700.00
Table, Chinese, Shelf Below, Hoof Feet, 31 X 11 In. 250.00
Table, Chrome Legs, U-Shaped, Black Lacquer, 30 In. 50.00
Table, Chrome Rails, Bi-Level, Black Lacquer, 23 X 25 In. 90.00
Table, Coffee, French, Smoked Mirror Glass Top, 19 In. 200.00
Table, Console, Demilune, Louis XVI, Palmettes, Scrolls, 30 In. 70.00
Table, Console, Federal, Pine, C.1800, Green Paint, 33 In. 300.00
Table, Console, Federal, Tiger Maple, C.1810, 28 In. 800.00
Table, Console, Victorian, Marble Top, 19th Century, Rosewood 1300.00
Table, Country, Hardwood, Pembroke, 16 1/4 X 41 3/4 In. 700.00
Table, Country, Hepplewhite, Pine, Dark Finish, 39 1/2 In. 50.00
Table, Country, Oak, Tripod Base, Pine Top, 42 1/2 X 26 1/2 In. 525.00
Table, Country, Pine, 1 Drawer, 30 In. 95.00
Table, Demilune, Pine, 3 Square Legs, 26 In. 600.00
Table, Dice, Turned Legs 1800.00
Table, Dining, Federal, Cherry, 3-Part, Drop Leaves, 28 In. 2400.00
Table, Dining, Federal, Drop Leaf, Cherry, C.1795, 28 1/2 In. 425.00
Table, Dining, Federal, Mahogany, D-Shaped Ends, 28 X 44 In. 500.00
Table, Dining, Federal, Mahogany, Drop Leaves, C.1810, 28 In. 350.00
Table, Dining, Federal, Mahogany, Drop Leaves, Reeded Legs, 29 In. 2860.00
Table, Dining, Federal, Mahogany, 4 Drawer, Red Paint, C.1810, 32 In. 220.00
Table, Dining, Federal, Mahogany, 6 Legs, C.1790, 29 X 46 In. 250.00
Table, Dining, Frank Lloyd Wright, Mahogany, Copper Design, 29 In. 2500.00
Table, Dining, George III, Horseshoe, Mahogany, 65 In.Diam. 1500.00
Table, Dining, Greco-Roman Revival, Mahogany, C.1830 ....*Illus* 1750.00
Table, Dining, Victorian, Leaves, Carved, Oak .... 700.00 To 1200.00
Table, Dining, Victorian, Oak Extension, Drop Leaves, 25 X 42 In. 225.00
Table, Dining, Victorian, Turned Legs, Mahogany, 50 X 28 In. 75.00
Table, Directoire, Fruitwood, Brass Gallery, Marble Top, 28 In. 700.00
Table, Dish Top, Cherry, Chippendale, C.1760, 34 1/2 In. 250.00
Table, Dressing, Gentleman's, George I, Mahogany, 23 X 15 In. 330.00
Table, Dressing, George III, 3 Drawer, Oak, 32 X 28 In. 715.00
Table, Dressing, Massachusetts, Walnut, Maple, 29 In. ....*Illus* 2500.00
Table, Dressing, New England, C.1810, Stenciling & Paint 685.00
Table, Dressing, Victorian, Beveled Mirror, English, Mahogany 525.00
Table, Drop Leaf, Butterfly Leaves, C.1810, Cherry 495.00

Table, Drop Leaf, Child's, Walnut, Trestle Legs, C.1880, 8 X 16 In. 135.00
Table, Drop Leaf, Chippendale, Maple, Swing Legs, 28 In. 100.00
Table, Drop Leaf, Empire, Inlaid & Turned Mahogany, 28 In. 250.00
Table, Drop Leaf, English, Baroque, Oak, Bobbin Legs, 27 In. 660.00
Table, Drop Leaf, English, Baroque, Oak, 32 X 26 1/2 In. 1650.00
Table, Drop Leaf, Federal, Birch, C.1800, 27 X 45 In. 350.00
Table, Drop Leaf, Federal, Cherry, C.1820, 30 In. 250.00
Table, Drop Leaf, Federal, Maple & Mahogany, C.1810, 28 In. 660.00
Table, Drop Leaf, Federal, Tiger Maple, Turned Legs, 29 In. 425.00
Table, Drop Leaf, George I, Provincial, Oval Top, 26 1/2 In. 825.00
Table, Drop Leaf, George I, Snake Feet, Walnut, 35 1/2 X 26 In. 225.00
Table, Drop Leaf, Queen Anne, Cabriole Legs, C.1775, Tiger Maple 2200.00
Table, Drop Leaf, Queen Anne, Mahogany, Cutout Ends, 42 In. 300.00
Table, Drop Leaf, Queen Anne, Rounded Leaves, Oak & Walnut, 28 In. 100.00
Table, Drop Leaf, Queen Enne, Mahogany, Pad Feet, 28 In. 300.00
Table, Drop Leaf, Tiger Maple, 4 1/2 X 3 Ft. 1150.00
Table, Drop Leaf, William & Mary, Gateleg Base, Oak, 44 X 27 In. 250.00
Table, Drop Leaf, 1 Drawer, C.1840, Solid Cherry 200.00
Table, Drum, George III, Mahogany, Leather Top, C.1800, 29 In. 1200.00
Table, Drum, Greco-Roman Revival, Circular Top, C.1830, 31 X 46 In. 2100.00
Table, Eastlake, Rose Marble Top, Walnut 325.00
Table, Eastlake, Walnut, C.1880, 16 X 22 In. 90.00
Table, Farm, Lift-Off Top, Cherry Legs, Walnut, 37 X 66 In. 1975.00
Table, Farm, Pine, 65 X 39 In. 565.00
Table, Farm, Plank Top, Pine, C.1870, 6 1/2 Ft. X 32 In. 600.00
Table, Federal, Inlaid Mahogany, 6 Legs, 32 X 28 In. 150.00
Table, Game, George IV, Parquetry Top, Frieze Drawer, 28 In. 330.00
Table, Game, Lift Top, Regency, Rosewood, 1 Drawer, 28 X 26 In. 1300.00
Table, Game, Louis XV, Black Lacquer, Dore Bronze, 27 In. 400.00
Table, Game, Louis XV, Mahogany, Leather Top, 29 In. 2100.00
Table, Game, Regency, C.1830, Mahogany, 30 X 36 X 18 In. 2000.00
Table, Game, Sheraton, Mahogany, Serpentine Front, C.1800 .... 1300.00
Table, Gateleg, Oak, C.1720, 58 X 58 In. 3500.00
Table, Gateleg, William & Mary, Mahogany & Maple, 1 Drawer, 26 In. 400.00
Table, Gateleg, William & Mary, Maple & Pine, 26 X 43 In. 300.00
Table, Gateleg, William & Mary, Maple, C.1700, 38 X 48 In. 3750.00
Table, Gateleg, William & Mary, Maple, 8 Legs, 1 Drawer, 26 In. 2300.00
Table, Gateleg, William & Mary, Oak, Sausage Legs, C.1730, 41 In. 120.00
Table, Gateleg, 1 Drawer, Oval Top, Maple, C.1725 .... 9000.00
Table, George I, Mahogany, Marble Top, 27 In. 165.00
Table, George III, Frieze Drawer, Oak, 32 X 27 In. 440.00
Table, George III, Inlaid Mahogany, Round, 21 In. 70.00
Table, George III, Mahogany, Inlaid Diamond Design, 27 In. 250.00
Table, George III, Oak, Square Top, Drawer, 26 In. 275.00
Table, George III, Tilt Top, Bleached Mahogany, 23 X 29 In. 220.00
Table, George III, Trestle-Form Feet, C.1900, 30 X 32 In. 165.00
Table, Georgian Provincial, 1 Drawer, Oak, 27 X 28 In. 275.00
Table, Gustav Stickley, No.629, 1907, Round, 30 In. .... *Illus* 650.00
Table, Harvest, Drop Leaf, Red Wash, C.1800, 8 Ft. 5500.00
Table, Harvest, Pine, 5 Turned Legs, 2-Board Top, 12 Ft. 695.00
Table, Hepplewhite, Pine & Poplar, Old Red Finish, 38 In. 210.00
Table, Hepplewhite, Tiger Maple 1700.00
Table, Hepplewhite, 2 Drawer, Opening From Opposite Sides, Poplar 235.00
Table, Hutch, American, Pine, Planked Box Seat, 30 In. 495.00
Table, Hutch, Pine & Maple, Oval, Square Legs, 46 In. 600.00
Table, Hutch, Pine, Lift Lid In Seat, 36 X 46 X 29 In. 525.00
Table, Hutch, Pine, Shoe Feet, Red Paint, 26 In. 3000.00
Table, Hutch, Poplar, Lid In Seat, Dark Patina, 27 X 48 3/4 In. 350.00
Table, Hutch, 1 Drawer, Pine, 19th Century, 29 X 56 3/4 In. 2100.00
Table, Ice Cream Parlor, Round, Oak, Iron Legs, 25 In. 70.00
Table, Indo-Portuguese, Ivory & Wood Inlaid, Birds, 23 In. 275.00
Table, Inset Polychrome Carved Panels, Oriental, Lacquered, 18 In. 225.00
Table, Italian, Inlaid Mahogany, 2 Drawers, 29 In. 400.00
Table, Italian, Walnut, 4 Drawers, 33 X 102 In. 1500.00

Furniture, Table, Dining, Greco-Roman Revival, Mahogany, C.1830

Furniture, Table, Dressing, Massachusetts, Walnut,
Maple, 29 In.   *(See Page 265)*

Furniture, Table, Gustav Stickley, No.629, 1907,
Round, 30 In.

(See Page 265)

Table, Library, L.& J.G.Stickley Decal & Label, Oak, 48 X 29 In.	600.00
Table, Library, Regency, Mahogany, False Drawer, C.1820, 27 In.	300.00
Table, Limbert, Cutout Heart, C.1910, 29 In. .... *Illus*	600.00
Table, Low, Chinese, Hardwood, Ribbon Scrollwork, 20 In., Pair	400.00
Table, Low, Side, Kittinger Co., Ebonized Bamboo Legs, Pair	300.00
Table, Maple, 3 Drawers, Splayed Base, Breadboard Top, 36 1/2 In.	1250.00
Table, Marble Top, Victorian, Walnut, C.1875, 29 In.	330.00
Table, Mission Oak, Round, 54 In.	300.00
Table, Nesting, 1940s, Carved Teak, Set Of 4 .... *Illus*	375.00
Table, Parlor, Polychrome Iron, 8 Legs, Marble Top, 22 In.	175.00
Table, Parlor, Victorian, Gray Marble Top, 31 In.	200.00
Table, Pedestal, Dark Pine, 4 Scroll Carved Feet, 20 In.	35.00
Table, Pembroke, Federal, Cherry, C.1790, Square Legs, 27 X 31 In.	250.00
Table, Pembroke, Geroge III, Mahogany, C.1800, Drawer, 27 In.	620.00
Table, Pembroke, Maple, 1800-20, 29 In.	700.00
Table, Pembroke, Oak, C.1810, 36 X 19 In.	250.00
Table, Pembroke, Sheraton, With Leaves Up 49 In.Across	600.00
Table, Pier, Empire, Mahogany, Marble Top, 1825, Mirror Plate, 38 In.	2530.00
Table, Pier, Marble Top, Empire, Mahogany, C.1830, 32 In.	225.00
Table, Pine Top, 1 Drawer, Cherry	496.00
Table, Queen Anne, Drop Leaf, Shaped Skirt, Oval Top	2200.00
Table, Queen Anne, Maple, 1 Drawer, Pad Feet, C.1750, 28 In.	1300.00

Table, Queen Anne, Oak, 54 In.Diam. 300.00
Table, Queen Anne, Pad Feet, Mahogany, Closed 36 In.Square 375.00
Table, Queen Anne, Porringer Top, Maple, C.1750, 26 In. High 3250.00
Table, Refectory, Baroque, English, Oak, 7 Ft. 3 In. X 29 1/2 In. 3300.00
Table, Refectory, C.1890, Oak, 32 X 72 In. 360.00
Table, Refectory, Carved Base, Oak, C.1870, 37 X 48 In. 500.00
Table, Refectory, English, Pine, 8 Ft. 7 In. X 30 In. 770.00
Table, Refectory, French Provincial, Oak Parquetry, 71 X 29 In. 425.00
Table, Roulette, Claw Feet 2700.00
Table, Roulette, 1890, Mason, Claw Feet 4200.00
Table, Sawbuck, Pine & Oak, Rectangular Top, Red Paint, 27 In. 300.00
Table, Sawbuck, Pine, Rectangular Top, Old Red Paint, 24 In. 300.00
Table, Sawbuck, Pine, X-Crossed Brace Legs, 29 In. 175.00
Table, Sawbuck, Rectangular Top, Pine, 19th Century, 28 In. High 550.00
Table, Sawbuck, Walnut, Rectangular, Top, 30 In. 250.00
Table, Serving, Federal, Maple, Drop Leaves, 2 Drawers, 28 In. 475.00
Table, Serving, Queen Anne, C.1775, Cherry, 26 1/2 X 26 In. 3200.00
Table, Sewing, Empire, Mahogany, 28 1/2 X 21 1/2 In. .... Illus 1300.00
Table, Sewing, Federal, Bird's-Eye Maple, 28 1/4 In. .... Illus 4000.00
Table, Sewing, Federal, Cherry & Bird's-Eye Maple, C.1820, 29 In. 200.00
Table, Sewing, Federal, Mahogany, 2 Drawer, 30 X 22 In. .... Illus 3500.00
Table, Sewing, Federal, Mahogany, 29 1/4 X 21 1/4 In. .... Illus 2300.00
Table, Sewing, Federal, 1 Drawer, Maple, C.1810, 28 X 19 In. 400.00
Table, Sewing, George IV, Silk-Lined Basket, Mahogany, C.1830 .... 495.00
Table, Sewing, Lady's, Hand-Painted Design, 18th Century 2900.00
Table, Sewing, Mahogany, Federal, 30 X 15 1/2 In. .... Illus 3500.00
Table, Sewing, Mahogany, 2 Drawer, Drop Leaf, Rope Leg, Ball Feet 750.00
Table, Sewing, Pine & Butternut, Removable Breadboard, 28 In. 160.00
Table, Sewing, Poplar Base, Pine Top, Drop Leaf, Red Paint, 27 In. 675.00
Table, Sewing, Queen Anne, Walnut & Butternut, Duck Feet, 2 Drawer 400.00
Table, Sewing, Stretcher Base, One-Board Top 295.00
Table, Sewing, Tiger Maple, Plank Top, 1820-40, 29 In. 275.00
Table, Tavern, Box Stretcher, 17th Century 1750.00
Table, Tavern, Cherry, Country, Box Stretcher 500.00
Table, Tavern, Federal, Cherry & Pine, C.1800, 1 Drawer, 27 In. 425.00
Table, Tavern, Federal, Pine, C.1800, Square Legs, 25 In. 400.00
Table, Tavern, Pegged Tapered Legs, Tiger Maple & Pine 950.00
Table, Tavern, Pine & Maple, Trestle Base, Shoe Feet, C.1700, 25 In. 2400.00
Table, Tavern, Pine, Sausage Turned Legs, 1720-60, 29 In. 550.00

Furniture, Table, Nesting, 1940s,
Carved Teak, Set Of 4

(See Page 267)

Furniture, Table, Limbert, Cutout
Heart, C.1910, 29 In.

Furniture, Table, Sewing, Empire, Mahogany,
28 1/2 X 21 1/2 In.

Furniture, Table, Sewing, Federal, Bird's-Eye
Maple, 28 1/4 In.

Furniture, Table, Sewing, Federal, Mahogany,
29 1/4 X 21 1/4 In.

Furniture, Table, Sewing, Federal,
Mahogany, 2 Drawer, 30 X 22 In.

Furniture, Table, Sewing, Mahogany, Federal,
30 X 15 1/2 In.

(See Page 270)
Furniture, Table, Tavern, William &
Mary, C.1720, Red, 24 1/2 In.

Table, Tavern, Pine, Shelf, Brown Paint, 28 X 28 In. 270.00
Table, Tavern, Pine, Shelf, Red Paint, 19 X 30 In. 255.00
Table, Tavern, Provincial, Iron Bail, C.1750, 27 In. 275.00
Table, Tavern, Queen Anne, Maple, Button Feet, C.1750, 31 In. 1500.00
Table, Tavern, Queen Anne, Oval Top, Splay Legs, C.1750, 26 In. 6000.00
Table, Tavern, William & Mary, Birch, C.1700, 48 X 26 In. 125.00
Table, Tavern, William & Mary, C.1720, Red, 24 1/2 In. .... *Illus* 4500.00
Table, Tavern, William & Mary, Cherry & Pine, C.1700, 26 In. 3800.00
Table, Tavern, William & Mary, Maple, Block Legs, 25 In. 5000.00
Table, Tavern, William & Mary, Maple, Molded Skirt, 22 In. 1600.00
Table, Tavern, William & Mary, Maple, Pine, Splay Leg, 1740, 24 In. 225.00
Table, Tavern, William & Mary, Oak & Pine, C.1730, 25 In. 325.00
Table, Tavern, William & Mary, Oak, Rounded Corners, 13 In. 225.00
Table, Tavern, William & Mary, Pine & Maple, Black Paint, 22 In. 1500.00
Table, Tavern, William & Mary, Pine & Maple, C.1700, 24 In. 3600.00
Table, Tavern, William & Mary, Pine & Maple, 1 Drawer, Red, C.1700 .... 7000.00
Table, Tavern, William & Mary, Pine, Maple, C.1720, 24 1/2 X 22 In. 4500.00
Table, Tavern, Windsor, Maple & Pine, Breadboard Top, 23 In. 300.00
Table, Tavern, 1 Drawer, Red Paint, 1800s .... 125.00 To 175.00
Table, Tavern, 1 Drawer, Turned Legs, Red Paint, 2 1/2 Ft.Square 345.00
Table, Tavern, 1 Drawer, Turned Oak & Pine, 22 1/2 In. High 825.00
Table, Tea, Chippendale, Cherry, C.1770, Dish Top, Pad Feet, 28 In. 525.00
Table, Tea, George I, Mahogany, Drop Leaf, Duck Feet, 28 In. 400.00
Table, Tea, George III, Hinged Rectangular Top, Mahogany, 29 In. 400.00
Table, Tea, Mother-Of-Pearl Top, Open-Worked Apron, Chinese, 24 In. 75.00
Table, Tea, Queen Anne, Maple, Pad Feet, 25 In. 250.00
Table, Tea, Tilt Top, Chippendale, Mahogany, C.1760, 25 In. 300.00
Table, Tea, Tilt Top, George III, 27 In. 275.00
Table, Tea, Tilt Top, Queen Anne, Cherry & Maple, 28 In. 715.00
Table, Tilt Top, Chippendale, Mahogany, Snake Feet, C.1780, 28 In. 600.00
Table, Tilt Top, Federal, Cherry, & Mahogany, C.1770, 27 In. 300.00
Table, Tilt Top, Federal, Mahogany, Saber Legs, C.1810, 21 In. 200.00
Table, Tilt Top, George III, Inlaid Oak, Scrolled Feet, 28 In. 385.00
Table, Tilt Top, George III, Irish, Mahogany, 29 X 28 In. 650.00
Table, Tilt Top, George III, Mahogany, Snake Feet, C.1770, 24 In. 440.00
Table, Tilt Top, Georgian, England, Mahogany, 28 In. 220.00
Table, Tilt Top, Inlaid Stones, Ivory, & Scene, Chinese, Teak Base 425.00
Table, Tilt Top, Maple, Pine Top, Cutout Shoe Feet, 28 In. 200.00
Table, Tilt Top, Trifid, Queen Anne, Walnut, Pad Feet, 29 In. 800.00
Table, Tilt Top, Victorian, Burl Walnut Top, 39 X 53 In. 995.00
Table, Tilt Top, 2-Board Top, Maple 385.00
Table, Tray Top, 1 Drawer, New England, Cherry 475.00
Table, Tripod, Federal, Maple & Mahogany, 26 X 14 In. 66.00
Table, Tripod, Federal, Pine, S-Shaped Legs 80.00
Table, Tripod, Federal, Red Painted Pine, 3 Legs, C.1810 .... 250.00
Table, Tripod, George III, Dish Top, Elm, 20 X 27 In. 220.00
Table, Tripod, George III, Tilt Top, Mahogany, 17 X 26 In. 325.00
Table, Tripod, George III, 3 Scrolled Legs, Snake Feet, 28 In. 165.00
Table, Tripod, Scalloped Apron, Ohio 485.00
Table, Tuckaway, William & Mary, Oval Top, 24 In. 3000.00
Table, Victorian, Carved Mahogany, Gray Marble Top, 17 In. 275.00
Table, Victorian, Marble Top, Oval, Carved, Rosewood 950.00
Table, Victorian, Marble Top, Oval, Walnut, C.1870 .... 225.00 To 375.00
Table, Victorian, Rosewood, 28 X 48 In. 500.00
Table, Walnut, Turned Legs, 2 Drawer, 29 In. 115.00
Table, Wicker, Round Top .... *Illus* 975.00
Table, Wicker, Square Top .... *Illus* 450.00
Table, Wicker, 20 X 30 X 36 In. 75.00
Table, William & Mary, Maple & Cherry, C.1720, 26 X 34 1/2 In. 4250.00
Table, William & Mary, Pine & Beechwood, 42 X 53 In. 300.00
Table, Wine Tasting, George III, Mahogany, 28 X 80 In. 1800.00
Table, Writing, Art Nouveau, Louis Majorelle, 30 In. .... *Illus* 1500.00
Table, Writing, Dutch, Inlaid Walnut, Frieze Drawer, 32 In. 400.00
Table, Writing, Kidney Shaped, Louis XVI, Marble Top, 24 In. 150.00

Furniture, Table, Wicker, Square Top ; Chair, Wicker, High Center Splat ; Table, Wicker, Round Top

Furniture, Table, Writing, Art Nouveau, Louis Majorelle, 30 In.

Table, Writing, Lady's, Wolfgang Hoffmann Design, 29 In.	220.00
Table, Writing, Victorian, Leather Surface, Pine & Mahogany, 28 In.	300.00
Table, 2 Leaves, Extends To 120 In., Mahogany, 60 In.Diam.	595.00
Table, 2 Tier, Gilt-Metal Mounted, Oval, Mahogany	80.00
Table, 7 Leaves, Pedestal, 48 In., Oak	375.00
Taboret, Marble Top, Chinese, Teak	250.00
Taboret, Teak, Chinese, Carved, 19 X 16 In., Pair	475.00
Tea Cart, Walnut	125.00
Towel Rack, Oak, 20 In.Across, 2 Piece	30.00
Umbrella Stand, Walnut, Victorian, Brass Rail, 30 In.	35.00
Wardrobe, Double Door, Carved Top, C.1915, Golden Oak	325.00
Wardrobe, Shelves, Hooks, Yellow & Brown, 84 In.	300.00
Wardrobe, Victorian, Triple, Mid-19th Century, English, Mahogany	1300.00
Washstand, Carved, Oak	95.00
Washstand, Federal, Cherry, Cup Holes, 1 Drawer, C.1800	225.00
Washstand, Marble Top, C.1865, Back Splash, Walnut, 40 1/4 In.	225.00
Washstand, Marble Top, Victorian	250.00

Washstand, Pine, English, Mahogany, Marbleized Bowl, 32 In. 200.00
Washstand, Pine, Grape Design, Bowl Hole, Yellow, C.1810, 37 In. 150.00
Washstand, Pine, Red, 27 X 24 In. 50.00
Washstand, Sheraton, Mahogany, Marble Top, 32 X 26 In. 200.00
Washstand, Solid Top, Drawer Base, Painted Green 50.00
Washstand, Victorian, Marble Top, 1 Drawer, 2 Doors, Rosewood 550.00
Washstand, 2 Doors & 2 Drawers, Oak 125.00
Wigstand, George I, 2 Drawer, Mahogany, 32 In. .... 150.00 To 375.00
Wigstand, Man's, Carved Oak, 15 In. 2600.00
Workbench, Dental, Drawer Area, Tools, Oak, 36 X 45 In. 650.00

G-ARGY-
ROUSSEAU

Gabriel Argy-Rousseau, born in 1885, was a French glass artist
who produced a variety of objects in Art Deco style. His mark,
"G. Argy-Rousseau," was usually impressed.

G.ARGY-ROUSSEAU, Tray, Scarabs, Pate-De-Verre, 5 In. 1200.00
Vase, Art Deco Geometrics, Green, Gray, 8 In. 1500.00

Galle

Galle glass was made by the Galle factory, founded in 1874 by Emile
Galle of France. The firm made cameo glass, furniture, and other
Art Nouveau items, including some pottery. After Galle's
death in 1904, the firm continued in production until 1931.

GALLE POTTERY, Vase, Florals, Leaves, Handles, Brown Ground, Signed, 11 In. 1250.00
Vase, Melon Form, Dark Green Shading, Signed, 4 1/2 In. 325.00

GALLE, Atomizer, Perfume, Purple Flowers, Pastel Ground 600.00
Atomizer, Red Fire, Yellow Ground 795.00
Bottle, Perfume, Signed, 4 1/2 In. 475.00
Bowl, Cut Leaves & Flowers In Green & Brown, Footed, 8 1/2 X 4 In. 1100.00
Bowl, Leaves & Flowers, Pink, Green, & White Ground, 8 1/2 X 4 In. 975.00
Bowl, Man In Boat On River, Clover Top, Signed, Brown & Gold, 3 3/8 In. 850.00
Bowl, Scenic Design, Gilt Trim, Blue, Signed, 9 1/2 X 5 1/4 In. 225.00
Box, Cut Flowers Inside & Outside, Lavender, Green, & Frost, 4 1/2 In. 795.00
Coupe, Stag Hunt Scene, Brown Enamel, C.1878 .... 900.00
Decanter, Green, Seaweed & Castle, Double Lip, Marked, 9 In. 500.00
Decanter, Milky To Rose, Magnolia Blossom, Marked, 11 In. 500.00
Lamp, Grapevine Design, Orange & White 8 In. Base, Marble & Brass 400.00
Night-Light, Red Bleeding Hearts, Gold Ground, Electrified 1250.00
Pitcher, Bleeding Hearts & Leaves, Frosted Handle, Signed, 3 In. 850.00
Pitcher, Boat Scene, Light & Dark Blue, Gold Trim, Marked, 6 In. 375.00
Plate, Sea-Life Scene, Signed, 9 1/2 In. 2950.00
Shade, Red Floral, 7 In. 550.00
Tray, Enameled Peacock Design, Triangle, Signed 400.00
Tray, Leaf Shape, Pond Scene, Frog, 16 In. 1950.00
Tumbler, Woman, Enameled, Signed, 4 1/2 In. .... 340.00 To 450.00
Vase, Apricot, Light & Dark Green Leaves, Signed, 5 1/2 In., Pair 1050.00
Vase, Avocado Ferns On White, Signed, 4 In. 175.00
Vase, Banjo Shape, Green Ferns, Frosted, Signed, 6 1/2 In. 495.00
Vase, Berries & Leaves, Red & Orange, Signed, 8 In. 800.00
Vase, Blown-Out Hyacinth, Yellow & White Ground, 11 In. .... 3750.00 To 5500.00
Vase, Blue Petals To Lavender Leaves, Signed, Frosted Ground, 7 In. 725.00
Vase, Boat Shape, Blue & Gold, Beach Scene, 9 In. 95.00
Vase, Bottle Shape, Leaf & Flower, Signed, 10 1/2 In. 1295.00
Vase, Bud, Satin Glass, Bowl, Jack-In-The-Pulpit, Jeweled, 7 In. 179.00
Vase, Burgundy To Brown Blossoms, Leaves, Signed, Frosted Brown, 10 In. 1475.00
Vase, Enameled Fish, 11 In., Pair 275.00
Vase, Enameled Over Cameo, Trefoil Neck, Green & Brown, 10 In. 1750.00
Vase, Floral Design, Green, Yellow, & Orange, Signed, 6 1/2 In. 600.00
Vase, Floral, Chartreuse To Purple To Blue, Signed, 13 1/8 In. 1100.00
Vase, Floral, Gold Ground, Signed, 7 3/4 In. 1150.00
Vase, Flowers, Leaves, Gold Ground, 4 X 3 In. 475.00
Vase, Frosted Ground, Orange Flowers, Marked, 5 1/2 In. 565.00
Vase, Frosted Pink To Apricot, Leaves, Green, Yellow, Marked, 12 In. 1265.00

Vase, Frosted To Frosted Gold Ground, Roses, Marked, 7 In. 895.00
Vase, Fruit Design, 3 Acid Cuttings, Signed, Amber, 6 7/8 In. 1995.00
Vase, Ginkgo Leaves, Mahogany, Frosted Pink & Green, Marked, 6 In. 775.00
Vase, Goldenrod & Leaves, White Ground, 12 3/4 In. 1795.00
Vase, Green Ground, 2-Tone Cameo Flowers, Signed, 6 1/4 In. 895.00
Vase, Lake Scene, Brown, Tan, White, 6 In. 875.00
Vase, Lake Scene, Cut-In Brown, Green Ground, Signed, 4 1/2 In. 795.00
Vase, Lavender Leaves & Flowers, White Ground, Signed, 8 In. 585.00
Vase, Leaf Design, Orange, Marked, 3 In. 385.00
Vase, Lily Pads & Buds At Base, Background Trees, Signed, 5 7/8 In. 650.00
Vase, Magenta Ground, Purple To Frosted, Flowers, Marked, 21 In. 2950.00
Vase, Orange Floral, Frosted, Marked, 3 In. 285.00
Vase, Orange Flowers, Flattened Shape, Frosted, Signed, 5 1/2 In. 575.00
Vase, Orange Irises Cut To Frosted Ground, Signed, 2 3/4 In. 325.00
Vase, Pink To Clear, Flowers, Leaves, Yellow & Orange, Marked, 5 In. 775.00
Vase, Polished Berries, Leaves, 6 1/2 In. 450.00
Vase, Pond With Water Lilies, Foliage, Signed, Chartreuse, 13 1/2 In. 1100.00
Vase, River & Tree Landscape, Signed, Brown To Pink Ground, 9 7/8 In. 995.00
Vase, River Running Between Riverbanks, Brown, Signed, 6 3/4 In. 800.00
Vase, Rosy Red, Cherry Clusters, Yellow Ground, Signed, 18 In. 2800.00
Vase, Salmon Pink, Violet, Terra Verde, Marked, 13 In. 700.00
Vase, Stick, Pansy-Type Flowers Over White, Silver Leaves, 3 1/2 In. 345.00
Vase, Trees Framing Scene In Panels, Signed, Brown To Green, 9 7/8 In. 1100.00
Vase, Violet To Frosted, Flowers, Peach Ground, Marked, 13 In. 1000.00
Vase, Water Lilies On Water, Lavender, Violet, & Blue, Signed, 7 3/4 In. 1500.00
Vase, White, Violet Cameo Flowers, Leaves, Marked, 8 In. 595.00
Wine, Clear, Amber Tint, Leaf & Flowers, Marked, Footed, 2 3/4 In. 25.00

Game plates are any type of plate decorated with pictures of birds, animals, or fish. The game plates usually came in sets consisting of twelve dishes and a serving platter. These game plates were most popular during the 1880s.

GAME PLATE, Birds, Scalloped Gold Border, Limoges, 12 In. 175.00
Fish, Hand-Painted, Green Rim, Set 350.00

GAME, Ali Baba & The Forty Thieves, J.H.Singer, 1880, Complete 85.00
Alley Oop, 1937, Royal Toy Co., Illustrated Container 20.00
Ally Sloper, Milton Bradley, 1904 .... 30.00
As The World Turns 8.00
Authors, Lithograph Box, Instructions, Parker Bros. 12.50
Auto Race, Metal, 4 Cars 12.00
Automobile, Touring, Original Version .... 6.00 To 14.00
Ball & Gear, 8 Balls, Glass Top, Pocket, 3 X 4 In. 30.00
Barber Pole, Lithograph Label, Parker Bros., 6 In.Square 45.00
Barney Google, Original Box, Book Of Directions 75.00
Baseball, Official, 296 Cards, 1969, Milton Bradley 120.00
Baseball, Spinner, Original Box, C.1912 .... 22.00
Billy Whiskers, Board 25.00
Bing Crosby, Board, 1947 .... 22.00
Birds On The Fence, Shooting, Popgun 85.00
Board, Checker, Folding, Wooden, 1910 .... 12.00
Board, Checker, Red & Dark Mustard 155.00
Board, Checker, Separate Storage Section, Oak, 13 X 19 In. 160.00
Board, Cribbage, Hand-Carved Roses, Pins Included, Ivory, 7 In. 45.00
Board, Cribbage, Priests Indigestion Powder, Advertising 65.00
Board, Parcheesi, C.1879 .... 550.00
Board, White Squares On Yellow Graining, Folding, Wooden 110.00
Brownie Auto Race, Marble Game, Color Lithograph, Tin, 10 In. 50.00
Cavalcade Derby, Boxed, 1940s 30.00
Charlie McCarthy's Radio Party, Spinner, C.1938 .... 35.00 To 45.00
Chinese Star Checkers, Wooden Board, Milton Bradley, 1938, 17 X 19 In. 20.00
County Fair, Merry-Go-Round, Side Show, Freaks, 1936 .... 44.00
Criss-Cross, Pinball, Tin 12.00

Croquet Set, Wooden Stand, C.1920 .... 30.00
Dice Cage, 3 Dice, 10 In. 95.00
Dick Tracy Detective, Board, Comic Strip Characters, Boxed 18.50
Dominoes, Ebony & Ivory, Set 25.00
Donkey Party, Muslin, Donkey Image, Tails, Whitman, 1930s 5.00
Donkey Party, Saalfield, Original Envelope, Cloth Donkey, 1926 .... 15.00
Drawing Set, James Bond, Electro 65.00
Dutch Boy & Girl Tenpins, Parker Bros., 1921, Boxed 35.00
Eliot Ness 15.00
Ferdinand The Bull, Boxed, 1938 .... 20.00
Fibber McGee & Molly, 1940 .... 9.00 To 15.00
Fish Pond, 1890s, Original Box 75.00
Fish, Lithographed Box & Cover, Slotted Gameboard, Milton Bradley 12.50
Football, Lindstrom 22.00
Fortune-Teller, Lithographed Box, Figural Witch, 1905, Milton Bradley 40.00
Garden Of Eden, 1925 .... 12.50
Gee Whiz, Horse Race, Complete With Box, 29 In. .... 50.00 To 78.00
General Grant's Wooden Board, C.1870, Small Swirls, Set Of 32 .... 225.00
Go Bang, 1905, Lithograph Cover Of Child & Firecrackers, Milton Bradley 12.50
Have Gun, Will Travel 15.00
Hee-Haw, Instructions, Boxed, Milton Bradley 17.50
Hockey, Mechanical, Eagle, Tin, Mechanical Players 24.00
Horse Race, Milton Bradley 10.00
Horse Race, 8 Lead Horses & Riders, Jeu De Course, Spring Operated 275.00
Howdy Doody, 3-Ring Circus, Clarabell's Nose Lights Up, Electric 33.00
I Don't Know, Milton Bradley, C.1890, Boxed 20.00
Jack And The Bean Stalk, Spinner, Parker Bros., 1895, Boxed 25.00
Kennedy's, Original Box 40.00
Lead Horse, Course, Spring Operated, C.1880s 210.00
Life Of The Party 10.00
Lindy Flying 25.00
Lindy, 1927 .... 12.00
Mah-Jong, Ivory, Wood Box, Sliding Lid, 100 Pieces 110.00
Marble Coaster, Trucker's, Original Unopened Box 25.00
Peggity, Parker Bros. 15.00
Pit, 1903, Parker Bros., Complete 7.50
Poker Chips, Clay, 6-Sided, Section For Cards, 10 X 5 In. 135.00
Presidents, Original Box, Dated 1894 .... 18.00
Prince Valiant, Crossbow Pistol, 1948, Boxed 45.00
Puzzle, Amos & Andy, 1932 .... 55.00
Puzzle, Bonnie Braids 7.00
Puzzle, Folger's Coffee, Unopened Can 15.00
Puzzle, Hi-Speed Gas, Dated 1931, Fishing Scene 10.00
Puzzle, Hood's Sarsaparilla, Rainy Day, Horses, & Carriage .... 25.00 To 50.00
Puzzle, Hoppy, The Marvel Bunny 9.50
Puzzle, Locomotive, Original Box, 1900 .... 65.00
Puzzle, Norman Rockwell 3.00
Race Horse, Murad Cigarette, Board, 25 X 24 In. 75.00
Race Track, 8 Lead Horses, 2 Tracks, Wooden Box, France, 11 1/2 In. 115.00
Radio Quiz, Milton Bradley 12.00
Ranger, 1936 .... 15.00
Rin Tin Tin, Spinner, Cards, & Plastic Pieces, Transogram 8.00
Shakespeare, Fireside Fame Co., Boxed 4.50
Shakespeare, 1901, Instructions, Complete, Boxed 12.50
Shooting Gallery, Schoenhut 75.00
Skor-It Poosh-M-Up, Marble 14.00
Snake Eye 15.00
Snuffy Smith 8.50
Space Patrol, Planets For Score, Spinning Disc, Metal Plunger 4.00
Spot Shot, Tin, Marble 30.00
Straight Arrow, National Biscuit Co., Boxed 35.00
Table Tennis, Milton Bradley, Boxed 20.00
Target, Lone Ranger 75.00
Target, Wood Cannon, Figures, Wooden 65.00

This Is Your Life	15.00
Tiddlywinks, Cup, Winks, 1915, Germany	5.00
Toonerville Trolley, Board	18.00
Toy Town Telegraph Office, C.1920, Parker Bros., Lithographed Box	30.00
Uncle Sam's Postman, Milton Bradley, 1895, Lithograph Of Uncle Sam, Box	45.00
Uncle Wiggly, Wobbie Wobble Duck Pond	42.00
Walton Family	6.00
Wheel, Carnival, 30 In.Diam.	165.00
Whippet Dog Race, Board, Wooden Dogs, Rabbits, & Children, Pressman	28.00
Who's On First, Abbott & Costello	15.00

The Gardner porcelain works was founded in Verbilki, outside Moscow, by the English-born Francis Gardner in 1766. Gardner made porcelain tablewares, figurines, and faience.

GARDNER, Teapot, Rose, Floral, Handle, Russian, Mark, 5 1/4 In.	125.00

Gaudy Dutch pottery was made in England for America from about 1810 to 1820. It is a white earthenware with Imari-style decorations of red, blue, green, yellow, and black. Only sixteen patterns of Gaudy Dutch were made: Butterfly, Carnation, Dahlia, Double Rose, Dove, Grape, Leaf, Oyster, Primrose, Single Rose, Strawflower, Sunflower, Urn, War Bonnet, Zinnia, and No Name. Other similar wares are called Soft Paste, Gaudy Ironstone, or Gaudy Welsh.

GAUDY DUTCH, Bowl, Waste, Dove, C.1820, 5 In.	330.00
Cup & Saucer, Carnation, Handleless	450.00
Jug, Milk, Sunflower, C.1820, 4 In.	605.00
Plate, Grape, C.1825, Marked, 9 In., Pair	330.00
Tea Service, Grape, C.1825, 6 In.	1320.00
Teabowl & Saucer, Grape, C.1825, Pair	440.00

Gaudy Welsh is an Imari-decorated earthenware with red, blue, green, and gold decorations. It was made after 1820.

GAUDY WELSH, Cup & Saucer, Carnation Pattern	55.00
Cup & Saucer, Grape & Lily Pattern, Cup, 2 1/4 In.	55.00
Cup & Saucer, Wagon Wheel Pattern	50.00
Cup, Saucer, & Underplate, Oyster Pattern	48.00
Pitcher, Oyster Pattern, Squatty, 3 1/2 X 3 1/4 In.	50.00
Pitcher, Wagon Wheel Pattern, 8 In.	115.00
Plate, Grape Pattern, Square, 8 1/2 In.	65.00
Sugar & Creamer, Grape & Lily Pattern, Covered, C.1840	165.00
Tea Set, Lavender, 9 Piece	300.00

In the late nineteenth century Geisha Girl porcelain was made in Japan for export. It was an inexpensive porcelain often sold in dime stores or used as free premiums. Pieces are sometimes marked with the name of a store. Japanese ladies in kimonos are pictured on the dishes. Borders of red, blue, green, gold, brown, or several of these colors were used. Modern reproductions are being made.

GEISHA GIRL, Bowl, Fruit, Blue Trim, 9 In.	30.00
Bowl, Rose, 3 Scrolled Feet, Crimped Edge	28.00
Box, Powder, Covered	16.00
Chocolate Pot	75.00
Chocolate Pot, Nippon, 9 1/2 In.	65.00 To 95.00
Chocolate Set, Nippon, Cobalt Trim, 6 Cups & Saucers	200.00
Creamer	4.50
Cup & Saucer	7.00
Hair Receiver, Red Trim	15.00
Jar, Powder, Red, Gold Overlay	18.00
Match Holder, Hanging, 3 1/2 X 2 1/2 In.	25.00
Match Holder, Wall, Double	30.00
Tea Set, Nippon, 11 Piece	75.00
Teapot, Covered	16.00
Toothpick Holder	12.50

Gene Autry was born in 1907. He began his career as the singing cowboy in 1928. His first movie appearance was in 1934, his last in 1958.

GENE AUTRY, Badge, Club, Official	15.00
Badge, Flying A Brand	5.00
Book, Coloring, Oversized, 1950	20.00
Book, Gene In Law Of The Range, Whitman, 1939	12.00
Book, Punch-Out, Uncut, 1941, Merrill	15.00
Book, Songs, Words & Music, Dated 1938, 95 Pages	10.00
Button, Sunbeam Bread	8.00
Display, Double Mint Gum, 1941	45.00
Gun, Cap, Kenton	40.00
Gun, Cast Iron, Boxed	95.00
Holster, Cuffs & Spurs, Boxed	30.00
Holster, Flying A Ranch, Metal	30.00
Lunch Box, With Thermos	35.00
Rain Boots	30.00 To 65.00
Wristwatch, Boxed	135.00

Black and blue decorated Gibson Girl plates were made in the early 1900s. Twenty-four different 10 1/2-inch plates were made by the Royal Doulton Pottery at Lambeth, England. These pictured scenes from the book "A Widow and Her Friends" by Charles Dana Gibson. Another set of twelve 9-inch plates featuring pictures of the heads of Gibson Girls had all-blue decoration.

GIBSON GIRL, Bowl, Portrait, Marked, 8 1/2 In.	75.00
Calendar, 1905	65.00
Miss Diggs Is Alarmed	85.00
Pillow, Signed	35.00
Pitcher, Water	235.00
Plate, Day After Arriving, Journey's End	65.00 To 80.00
Plate, Message From The Outside World	65.00
Plate, Miss Babbles, Authoress, Calls & Reads Aloud	65.00 To 75.00
Plate, She Becomes A Trained Nurse	75.00
Plate, She Contemplates The Cloister	65.00 To 75.00
Plate, She Decides To Die In Spite Of Dr.Bottles	65.00 To 75.00
Plate, She Goes To Fancy Dress Ball	65.00
Plate, She Is Disturbed By A Vision	67.50
Plate, She Is Subject Of Hostile Criticism	75.00
Plate, She Longs For Seclusion	80.00
Plate, She Looks For Relief Among The Old Ones	50.00 To 75.00
Plate, They Take A Morning Run	90.00
Plate, Winning New Friends	85.00

GILLINDER   *Gillinder pressed glass was first made by William T. Gillinder of Philadelphia in 1863. Many glass items were made for the Centennial.*

GILLINDER, Vase, Held By Hand, Fluted, Philadelphia Centennial, 8 1/2 In.	40.00

GIRL SCOUT, Knife, Brownie	5.00
Pail, Lunch, Tin, Litho On Sides & Top, 4 X 6 X 3 In.	45.00
Patch, Winged Propeller, Yellow & Green	1.00
Penknife, 4 Blades, Green Plastic Handle, Scout Seal	12.50
Statue, 1953, Copperplated	38.00

GLASSES, Lorgnette, Marcasite, Chain	275.00
Lorgnette, Openwork, Ring At End, Vermeil Sterling Silver Mark	135.00
Lorgnette, Tortoiseshell, 6 Loose Rings, Chain, 10 3/4 In.	85.00
Pince-Nez, Folding, Chain	20.00

W. Goebel Porzellanfabrik of Oeslau, Germany, now Rodental, West Germany, has made many types of figurines and dishes. The firm is still working.

GOEBEL, see also Hummel

GOEBEL, Ashtray, Disney's Thumper, Full Bee With V	75.00
Bust, Madonna, White, Crown Mark, 10 1/2 In.	85.00
Condiment Set, Monk, Mustard, Salt, & Pepper, Holder	58.00
Creamer, Cow, Bell Around Neck	25.00
Decanter, Friar Tuck With 4 Children	100.00
Figurine, Snow White & The Seven Dwarfs, 3 To 4 In.	175.00
Figurine, Snow White, 6 1/2 In.	95.00
Figurine, Spaniel, V Mark, 3 In.	15.00
Match Holder, Friar Tuck, Striker, Full Bee	38.00
Pitcher, Friar Tuck & Cardinals, 2 1/2 In.	48.00
Table Set, Friar Tuck On Tray, Full Bee, 4 Piece	45.00

Goldscheider
Wien

Porcelain has been made by three branches of the Goldscheider family.
The family left Vienna in World War II and started factories in
England and in Trenton, New Jersey.

GOLDSCHEIDER, Ashtray, Terra-Cotta, Art Deco Bust	110.00
Figurine, Blanche, 6 1/2 In.	55.00
Figurine, Collie, 6 In.	25.00
Figurine, Dancer, Raised Skirt, 12 In.	125.00
Figurine, Dog Head, 5 X 10 In.	30.00
Figurine, Girl, Floral Dress, Scotty Dog, Marked, 9 In.	95.00
Figurine, Horse, Chinese Ming, 11 1/2 X 11 1/2 In.	250.00
Figurine, Lady With Fan, Roses In Hair, Signed, 11 In.	45.00
Figurine, Lady, Holding Basket Of Fruit, 8 In.	65.00
Figurine, Man With Violin, 9 In.	60.00
Figurine, New Bonnet, 9 In.	35.00
Figurine, Precious Moments, Praise The Lord, 9 In.	45.00
Figurine, Rooster, 11 In.	65.00
Figurine, Scotty, 5 In.	25.00
Figurine, Singer Sewing Machine, Music Box, 100th Anniversary	375.00
Figurine, Spaniel, 5 In.	25.00
Figurine, U.S.A.Southern Belle, 11 In.	55.00
Figurine, Woman, Art Deco, With Fawn, 10 In.	200.00

GONDER, Planter, Swan, Mottled, Yellow, 5 In.	16.00
Vase, Chinese Blue, Crackle, Marked, 21 In.	95.00
Vase, Figural Leaves & Flowers, Blue Luster, 11 X 8 3/4 In.	22.00
Vase, Swans Around Base, Scalloped, 2-Tone Brown, 8 In.	20.00

Goofus glass was made from about 1900 to 1920 by many American factories.
It was originally painted gold, red, green, bronze, pink, purple, and other
bright colors.

GOOFUS GLASS, Bowl, Red Roses, Green Leaves, Gold Trim	33.00
Bowl, Red, Gold, Iris, 7 1/2 In.	10.00
Compote, Gold To Pink, Red Roses	24.00
Creamer, Peach & Clear, Gold & Purple Fruits, Marked Northwood	47.50
Plate, Apples, 8 1/2 In.	12.00
Plate, Grapes, 7 1/2 In.	8.00
Vase, Roses, Pair, 7 In.	40.00

W.H.COSS

Goss china has been made since 1858. English potter William Henry
Goss first made it at the Falcon Pottery in Stoke-on-Trent. In 1934
the factory name was changed to Goss China Company when it was taken
over by Cauldon Potteries. Production ceased in 1940. Goss china resembles
Irish Belleek in both body and glaze. The company also made popular
souvenir china.

GOSS, Cup & Saucer, Arms Of Jack Newbury	35.00
Cup & Saucer, Crest	35.00
Cup & Saucer, Pinch Purse, Llandudno Crest	35.00
Pitcher, Salisbury Leather Gill, 1658, 3 In.	30.00

Pitcher, Slant-Sided, Red Shield, 3 In. 27.00
Shoe, First Size Worn By Queen Victoria, Blue Trim Crest, 4 1/4 In. 47.50

327
SCHOONHOVEN
HOLLAND
COREL
E
Pottery has been made in Gouda, Holland, since the seventeenth century. Two firms, The Zenith pottery, established in the eighteenth century, and the Zuid-Hollandsche pottery, made the brightly colored Art Nouveau wares marked "Gouda" from 1880 to about 1940.

GOUDA, Candlestick, Handled, House Mark, 7 In. 125.00
Charger, Art Deco Flowers, Green Rim, 12 In. 130.00
Compote, Daisies, Footed, 10 In.Diam. 98.00
Dish, Candy, Covered, Art Deco, Marked, 6 In. 125.00
Dish, Green Leaf, House Mark, 8 X 8 In. 34.00
Ewer, Handled, Stylized Flowers, 4 3/4 In. 75.00
Figurine, Girl, Squatting, Signed, Black, 8 In. 85.00
Humidor, Black Base, Orange, Blue, & Green, Marked, 7 3/4 In. 175.00
Humidor, Brown-Black Ground, Design, Marked, 7 1/4 X 5 1/2 In. 155.00
Inkwell, Attached Tray, High Glaze, 6 In.Diam. 140.00
Jar, Tobacco, Covered, 6 In. 145.00
Jardiniere, Art Nouveau, Rust, Royal Blue, & Mustard, 5 1/2 X 4 1/2 In. 75.00
Jardiniere, Leaf Design, Blue, Black, Rust, Yellow, Marked, 4 In. 100.00
Match Holder With Striker On Base, 2 In. 75.00
Pitcher, Art Nouveau, Yellow, Tan, & Black, Regina, 6 In. 85.00
Plaque, Anniversary, Dated June 1878, 11 In. 145.00
Rose Bowl, Ivora Pattern, Black, Marked 60.00
Sugar, Art Deco Design, 2 X 4 In. 28.00
Vase, Art Nouveau, Handled, Iris Design, House Mark, 8 In. 155.00
Vase, Baluster, Art Deco Florals, 5 1/2 In. 28.00
Vase, Bulb Shape, Floral, Gray Ground, Marked, 3 In. 20.00
Vase, Cobalt Blue, Green, & Rust Flowers, Blue Mark, 11 1/2 In. 125.00
Vase, Danier Pattern, Paper Label, 6 1/2 In. 85.00
Vase, Dark Blue, Orange, & Green, 8 1/2 In. 95.00
Vase, Handled, Cobalt On Black, Floral Design, Marked, 5 1/4 In. 58.00
Vase, Kaffa Pattern, 8 1/2 In. 85.00
Vase, Orange & Brown, 7 In. 45.00
Vase, Stick, Long Neck, Marked, 7 In. 45.00
Vase, Stylized Pine Boughs, Black & Gold, Ovoid, C.1900 .... 115.00

Graniteware is an enameled tinware that has been used in the kitchen from the late nineteenth century to the present. Earlier graniteware was green or turquoise blue, with white spatters. The later ware was gray with white spatters. Reproductions are being made in all colors.

GRANITEWARE, Basin, Child's, White, Kidney Shape, Black Rim, 4 X 6 In. 5.00
Basin, Green, 8 1/2 In. 14.00
Basin, Wash, Blue & White, Marbleized, 17 In. 28.00
Basin, Wash, Child's, Blue & White, Black Rim, Hang-Up Hole 12.50
Basin, Wash, Child's, Gray On Gray, 11 In. 12.50
Basin, Wash, Child's, Gray, 11 In. 8.50
Basin, Wash, Gray, Brass Gromet, Flanged Rim, 12 In. 10.00
Basin, Yellow & Green, Oval, 17 In. 12.00
Bathtub, Baby's, Gray Blue, White Dots, Oval, 13 X 18 In. 25.00
Bathtub, Child's, Yellow, Green Trim, Painted Animals, 27 In. 75.00
Boiler, Coffee, Blue & White Speckles, Navy Filter, 8 In. 28.50
Boiler, Coffee, Country Inn, Gray, Wireball Handle, Domed Cover 22.50
Boiler, Coffee, Gray On Gray, Blue Rim, Dome Cover, Grip Handle 40.00
Boiler, Coffee, Gray, Wide Spout, Bail Handle, 1 Gallon 45.00
Boiler, Coffee, White, Black Handle, Hinged Cover, Half Gallon 18.00
Bowl, Blue & White, White Interior, Black Rim, 5 In. 14.50
Bowl, Blue Swirl, 10 1/2 X 7 1/2 In. 14.00
Bowl, Child's, White, Blue Rim, Marked Germany, 4 In. 22.50
Bowl, Feeding, Child's, Baby Blue, Bunny Rabbit, 8 In. 30.00
Bowl, Gray, Child's, Gray On Gray, 5 1/4 In. 8.50
Bowl, Green On Green, Straight Sides, 9 1/2 In. 7.50

Bowl, Mixing, Black Speckled, 7 X 3 In. 12.50
Bowl, Mixing, Gray, 6 1/2 In. 6.00
Bowl, Mixing, Gray, 9 In. 9.00
Bowl, Mixing, Marbleized Yellow & White, 9 1/2 X 5 In. 22.00
Bowl, Mixing, Sky Blue, Black Rim, 11 In. 10.00
Bowl, Mixing, White, Blue Rim, 10 In. 6.00
Bowl, Soup, Child's, White, Blue Rim, Marked Kickums, 7 In. 7.50
Bucket, Dinner, Gray, Oval 79.00
Bucket, Ice, Green, Swing Handle, Paw Feet, Covered, 18 In. 145.00
Bucket, Tin Lid, Gray, 6 In. 29.00
Cake Plate, Gray, Dark Gray Speckled, 9 In. 6.50
Can, Cream, Gray Covered Bail, Wooden Handle 17.50
Can, Milk, Gray On Gray, Side Handle, 1 Gallon 22.50
Can, Milk, Gray, Dome Top, Handled, Half Gallon 35.00
Can, Milk, Gray, Grip Handle, 1 Quart 30.00
Can, Milk, White, Strap Handle, Domed, L & G Mfg., Half Gallon 25.00
Can, Oil, Gray, 2 Quart 10.00
Candlestick, Floral, White, Lavender Blossoms, Ring Handle, 2 In. 35.00
Canister, White, Blue Lettering, Barley, 6 1/2 In. 45.00
Canner, Gray, 6 Quart 38.00
Chamber Pot, Child's, Sky Blue 35.00
Chamber Pot, Gray, 9 1/2 In. 24.50
Chamber Pot, Navy 4.00
Coffeepot, Black Trim Around Rim 15.00
Coffeepot, Black, White Dots, Dome Cover, 10 Cup 45.00
Coffeepot, Blue & White Swirled, 11 In. 25.00
Coffeepot, Blue & White, 4 1/2 X 7 In. .... 11.50 To 28.00
Coffeepot, Blue Marbleized, Bail 35.00
Coffeepot, Blue, Bulbous, Gooseneck Spout, 7 In. 50.00
Coffeepot, Brown & White, Gilt-Washed, Pewter Handle, 11 In. 165.00
Coffeepot, Camp, Gray 45.00
Coffeepot, Child's-Egg Blue & White, 4 In. 30.00
Coffeepot, Gooseneck Spout, Blue, 8 In. 22.00
Coffeepot, Gooseneck Spout, Teal & White Swirl 24.00
Coffeepot, Gooseneck, Chocolate Brown, Covered, Black Rim 40.00
Coffeepot, Gooseneck, Gray, Pewter Spout & Cover, 9 In. 135.00
Coffeepot, Gooseneck, Tin Top, Gray Mottled, 1 Quart 37.00
Coffeepot, Gray, Bail, Wooden Grip, 1 1/2 Gallon 18.00
Coffeepot, Gray, Bail, 13 In. .... 31.00 To 40.00
Coffeepot, Gray, Leopard-Spotted, Pewter Rim, 8 In. 150.00
Coffeepot, Gray, Pint .... 18.00 To 26.00
Coffeepot, Gray, Semidomed, Wooden Pull, 5 In. 25.00
Coffeepot, Gray, Tin Lid, Bail, & Side Handle, 11 1/2 In. 28.00
Coffeepot, Gray, 1 Gallon 25.00
Coffeepot, Pink, Blue Morning Glories, Pewter Trim, 1880 .... 195.00
Coffeepot, Robin's-Egg Blue, White Interior, 8 In. 22.50
Coffeepot, Statue Of Liberty, Pewter Trim, 9 1/2 In. 225.00
Coffeepot, Swirl, Teal & White, 11 1/2 In. 37.50
Coffeepot, White Interior, Brown Outside, 9 1/2 In. 24.00
Colander, Aqua 13.50
Colander, Footed, Black & White, 10 In. 10.00
Colander, Footed, Gray, 11 In. 10.00
Colander, Gray On Gray, Pedestal Base, Handleless, 4 In. 12.50
Colander, Gray, Footed Base, Dovetailed Bottom, 4 In. 18.50
Colander, Gray, Footed, 2 Handled, 10 In. 22.00
Colander, Mottled Green 11.00
Colander, Pearl Gray, Half-Inch Draining Holes, 9 In. 12.50
Cooker, Lid & Handles, Gray, 12 1/2 X 7 In. 25.00
Creamer, Bail, Gray, Pint 30.00
Cup & Saucer, Robin's-Egg Blue & White, 1 1/2 In. 22.50
Cup & Saucer, White, Blue Band, Signed Germany, 2 In. 35.00
Cup, Coffee, Mottled Gray, Quart Size, 5 1/2 In. 12.50
Cup, Custard, Chocolate Brown, White Interior, Germany, 3 In. 12.50
Cup, Handled, Farmer's, Gray, 5 In. 12.50

Cup, Peacock Blue, White Band, 5 Gold Lines, 2 1/2 In. 25.00
Cup, Swirled, Blue & White 12.00
Cup, Swirled, Red & White 19.50
Cup, White & Black 4.00
Cuspidor, Cobalt Blue, Gold Concentric Bands, 8 X 5 In. 65.00
Dish, Apple Pie, Black & White, 11 In. 12.50
Dish, Child's, Blue, Dutch Boy, Goose, Windmill, 8 In. 30.00
Dish, Deep, Green, Boy Picking Apples, Tree, Barefoot, 7 In. 35.00
Dish, Feeding, Pea Green, Nursery Rhyme, 7 In. 60.00
Dish, Soap, Shell & Scroll Pattern, Gray 25.00
Dish, Soap, Wall Mounted, Gray On Gray 22.50
Dish, Soap, White, Removable Strainer, Hang-Up Slot, 5 X 3 In. 16.50
Dishpan, Turquoise & White Swirl 35.00
Dispenser, Coffee, Gray 165.00
Double Boiler, Gray, Tin Cover 10.00
Double Boiler, Green & White, Marbleized 19.00
Double Boiler, White, Black, & Blue Trim 12.00
Egg Poacher, Gray, 5 Holes 115.00
Egg Poacher, 7-Egg, White & Black, White Interior, Cover, 8 In. 75.00
Funnel, Brown & White, Marbleized, Round, Handled, 5 X 5 In. 25.00
Funnel, Fruit Jar, Gray On Gray, Handled .... 12.50 To 22.50
Funnel, Gray, 6 5/8 In. 7.00
Funnel, Gray, 8 1/2 In.Diam. 18.00
Funnel, Handle, Gray, 4 1/2 X 5 In. 18.00
Holder, Soap, Blue & White Swirl, Wall, Back Splash 25.00
Kettle, Canning, Covered, 2-Handled, 13 X 10 In. 18.00
Kettle, Covered, Mottled Blue, 2 1/4 Gallon 35.00
Kettle, Jelly, Gray, Bail Handle, Wooden Grip, Marked M.K.G. 25.00
Kettle, Tea, White, Red Enameled Wood Handle, 1 Gallon 12.50
Kettle, Wood & Wire Handle, Gray, 8 1/2 In. 10.00
Ladle, Brown & White, 14 1/2 In. .... 8.00 To 10.00
Ladle, Cocoa, Curved Handles, 8 1/2 In. 12.00
Ladle, Dark Blue Spatter 12.50
Ladle, Gray On Gray, 5 X 8 In. 22.50
Ladle, Gray, Hooked Handle, 12 3/4 In. 22.50
Ladle, Light Blue, White Interior Bowl, End Hook, 15 In. 6.50
Ladle, Milk Skimmer, Gray, Concave Bowl, Draining Holes, 10 In. 20.00
Ladle, White & Blue, 12 In. 12.00
Ladle, Windsor, Gray, Pearl Gray Handle, 14 In. 18.50
Lamp Shade, Forest Green, White Interior, Black Rim, 5 In. 30.00
Lunch Pail, Miner's, Gray 65.00
Lunch Pail, Round, Covered, Gray 22.00
Measure, Gray, Pint 24.00
Measure, Gray, Quart 18.00
Measure, Liquid, White, Blue Numerals, Pouring Lip, 6 In. 14.50
Mold, Food, Fluted, 16 Scallops, Gray 30.00
Mold, Pudding, Gray, Fluted, Shallow 20.00
Muffin Tin, Blue 35.00
Muffin Tin, Gray, 6 Holes 12.00
Muffin Tin, Gray, 8 Holes 26.00
Muffin Tin, Gray, 9 Holes 18.00
Muffin Tin, Gray, 12 Holes, 14 X 10 In. 25.00
Mug & Plate, Child's, Robin's-Egg Blue, Children, Begging Dog 80.00
Mug, Child's, Creamy Yellow, Boy, Dog Begging, German Mark 40.00
Mug, Child's, Green, Nursery Rhyme, Mary, Lamb, Marked Sweden 30.00
Mug, Child's, Pink, Nursery Rhyme, Mary And Lamb, 2 3/4 In. 40.00
Mug, Coffee, Cobalt Blue & White, 4 In. 10.00
Mug, Coffee, Gray, Handled, 3 X 2 In. 12.50
Pail, Berry, Child's, Blue & White 15.00
Pail, Berry, Gray, Bail Handle, 2 Quart, 6 In. 35.00
Pail, Berry, Tin Lid & Bail, 4 X 4 1/2 In. 34.00
Pail, Blueberry, Child's, Sky Blue, White Interior, Wire Handle 18.50
Pail, Child's, Gray, Wooden Handle, 3 In. 65.00
Pail, Cream, Gray, Cover, Bail Handle, 8 In. 55.00

Pail, Milk, Blue, Swing Handle, Gray Domed Cover	35.00
Pail, Milk, Dark Gray, Striped On Gray, Covered, Half Gallon	25.00
Pan, Baking, Dark Gray, Light Gray Spots, 7 X 12 In.	15.00
Pan, Baking, Side Wire Pull, Gray, 8 X 10 1/2 X 2 In.	14.00
Pan, Blue Gray, Flanged Rim, 4 1/2 In.	8.50
Pan, Blue Gray, White Speckled, Black Rim, 6 In.	6.50
Pan, Bread, Gray, 11 1/2 X 6 In.	20.00
Pan, Butter-Melting, Blue, Pouring Lip, White Interior, 5 In.	10.00
Pan, Cake, Angel Food, Gray	20.00
Pan, Draining, Navy Blue & White Speckled, Set Of 3	40.00
Pan, Draining, White, Red Border, 10 In.	8.50
Pan, Frying, Cobalt Blue, Pouring Lip, White Interior, 5 Quart	40.00
Pan, Frying, Gray Mottled, Agate Handle, Large	34.50
Pan, Frying, Gray On Gray, 10 In.	18.50
Pan, Frying, 1 Egg, Black & White Speckled, Black Exterior, 5 In.	12.50
Pan, Green & White Speckled, Black Rim, 14 In.	15.00
Pan, Green & White, Marbleized, Bail, 10 In.	32.00
Pan, Jelly, Turquoise & White	18.00
Pan, Loaf, Gray, Folded Corners, Slant Side, 5 X 9 In.	6.00
Pan, Milk, Gray, 13 1/2 In.	10.00
Pan, Pudding, Blue & White, Black Rim, 12 In.	15.00
Pan, Pudding, Blue & White, White Interior, Black Rim, 10 In.	15.00
Pan, Pudding, Brown, White Swirls, 7 1/4 In.	16.50
Pan, Pudding, Chocolate Brown & White, 10 In.	30.00
Pan, Pudding, Dark Brown, Snow White Speckles, 13 In.	24.50
Pan, Pudding, Gray On Gray, Flange Rim, 10 In.	6.00
Pan, Pudding, Gray On Gray, Flanged Rim, 8 1/2 In.	10.00
Pan, Pudding, Gray On Gray, Signed LTG Mfg., 6 1/2 In.	12.50
Pan, Pudding, Gray On Gray, 11 In.	8.50
Pan, Pudding, Lavender Blue, White Cotton Ball Speckles, 10 In.	12.50
Pan, Pudding, Powder Blue & White, Black Rim, 12 In.	24.50
Pan, Red, White, & Black, Columbian Stamping Co., 18 In.	30.00
Pan, Sky Blue, White Interior, U Handles, 15 In.	15.00
Pan, Tube, Cobalt, 14 Flutes, White Inside	24.00
Perculator, Beige, Green Trim, 3-Part, 9 Cups	18.50
Pie Plate, Black & White, White Dots, 9 In.	10.00
Pie Plate, Blue & White, White Interior, Black Rim, 8 In.	14.50
Pie Plate, Blue & White, White Interior, 9 3/4 In.	7.50
Pie Plate, Blue & White, 10 In.	13.00
Pie Plate, Gray On Gray, 8 3/4 In.	5.00
Pie Plate, Green & White, White Interior, 8 3/4 In.	15.00
Pie Plate, Individual, Gray, 6 X 1 In.	5.00
Pie Plate, Sky Blue, White Interior, 8 3/4 In.	5.00
Pie Plate, Swirled, Blue & White, 9 In.	12.00
Pitcher, Cream, Doll's, White, Blue Band, Gold Trim, 2 In.	45.00
Pitcher, Measuring, Tray, 1 Quart	26.00
Pitcher, Water, Blue & White, Marked Geder, 10 In.	45.00
Pitcher, Water, White, Gray Speckles, Black Rim, 8 In.	22.50
Plate, Child's, Light Green, Dutch Children Center	10.00
Plate, Child's, Nursery Rhyme, Mary & Lamb Design, 8 In.	22.50
Plate, Cobalt Blue Tulips, Stars, Triangles, Set Of 6, 9 In.	90.00
Plate, Gray, 8 In.	6.00
Plate, Soup, Green Edge, 8 1/2 In.	4.00
Platter, 8-Sided, White	17.50
Pot, Bail Handle, Gray, 7 1/2 In.	15.00
Pot, Gray On Gray, U Handles, Covered, 10 In.	14.50
Pot, Handled, Chocolate Brown, White Speckles, 7 3/4 In.	12.50
Potty, Child's, Beige & Green	8.00
Potty, Gray, Original Label	10.00
Rack, Utensil, Blue & White	68.00
Roaster, Covered, Handles, Gray, 13 X 17 1/2 In.	28.00
Roaster, Lavender Blue, White Cotton Ball Speckles, 9 In.	15.00
Saucepan, Blue, White Interior, 2 Quart	22.50
Saucepan, Chocolate Brown & White, Eagle Mark, 5 In.	20.00

Saucepan, Gray & Brown, Pouring Spout, 9 In.	7.50
Saucepan, Navy & White, Flanged Rim, 10 In.	15.00
Scoop, Druggist's, Gray	48.00
Shaving Mug, White Flowers	5.00
Skillet, Gray, 8 1/2 In.	20.00
Skimmer, Gray	24.00
Skimmer, White, Blue Handle & Rim, 12 In.	12.50
Skimmer, Yellow Spatter, Brown Handle	25.00
Spatula, Gray	38.00
Spittoon, Gray, Iron	22.00
Spittoon, Russet, Black Rim, Cover, 2 Piece, 10 In.	40.00
Spoon, Basting, Cobalt Blue, 13 In.	6.50
Spoon, Blue Swirl, 13 1/2 In.	12.00
Spoon, Long-Handled, Gray, 16 In.	10.00
Spoon, Mixing, Long-Handled, Gray Mottled	11.00
Strainer, Gray On Gray, 10 In.	10.00
Strainer, Gray, Tab-Footed, Round, 7 3/4 In.	14.00
Strainer, Rim Hook, Blue & White Speckled	22.00
Strainer, Rim Hook, Gray	13.00
Sugar, Handles, Covered, White & Blue	12.00
Tea Set, Child's, Soldier, White, Red Trim, Sweden, 4 Piece	20.00
Tea Set, Light Blue Spatter On White, Miniature, 11 Piece	150.00
Teakettle, Avocado Green, Black Rim, White Interior, 5 In.	22.50
Teakettle, Gray	20.00
Teakettle, Mottled Green	26.00
Teakettle, Wrought Iron Range Co., Swivel Cover, 4 Quart	35.00
Teapot, Blue, Gooseneck Spout, 3 1/8 In.	50.00
Teapot, Bulbous, Tin Top, Light Green	23.00
Teapot, End-Of-Day, Rainbow, Black Spout & Handle, 4 Cup	150.00
Teapot, Grass Green, Gooseneck Spout, Black Rim, 4 Cup	30.00
Teapot, Green & White Speckle, Brass Collar, Germany, 8 Cup	175.00
Teapot, Green, Gooseneck, Dome, Handled, 4 In.	30.00
Teapot, Morning Glory, Dome Top, Ribbed Spout, Pewter Trim	250.00
Teapot, Orange, Gooseneck, Black Handle, 3 Cup	35.00
Teapot, Orange, Gooseneck, Dome Cover, 2 Cup	22.50
Teapot, Pea Green, Gooseneck, Domed, White Interior, 4 Cup	22.50
Teapot, Red, Gooseneck, Black Rim, 5 In.	35.00
Teapot, Ultramarine Blue, Gooseneck, Black Rim, 4 1/2 In.	40.00
Teapot, White & Red, Gooseneck, Red Handle, 7 1/2 In.	22.50
Teapot, White, Blue Trim, 2 Cup	8.00
Tray, Cobalt Blue, White Speckle, Flanged Rim, 12 In.	20.00
Tray, Robin's-Egg Blue & White, 25 X 19 In.	40.00
Tray, Swirled, Blue & White, 17 3/4 In.	45.00
Washboard, Cobalt Blue Mottling	50.00

Greentown glass was made by the Indiana Tumbler and Goblet Company of Greentown, Indiana, from 1894 to 1903. In 1899, the factory name was changed to National Glass Company. A variety of pressed, milk, and chocolate glass was made.

GREENTOWN, see also Chocolate Glass; Custard Glass; Holly Amber; Milk Glass; Pressed Glass

GREENTOWN, Berry Bowl, Leaf Bracket, Footed	39.50
Bowl, Holly, 10 X 4 In.	155.00
Bowl, Mitted Hand	45.00
Butter, Crystal, Covered, Footed	75.00
Butter, Dewey, Amber	60.00
Butter, Dewey, Covered, Vaseline	90.00
Butter, Teardrop & Tassel, Green, Covered	110.00
Compote, Cactus	130.00
Compote, Clear, Cord Drapery, 6 1/2 X 8 1/2 In.	48.00
Compote, Open, Peacock Feather	26.00
Compote, Viking, Covered, Large	72.00
Cordial, Austrian, Vaseline	135.00
Creamer, Child's, Austrian, Blue	75.00

Rifle, Winchester, Model 1873, Octagon Barrel, Walnut Stock, 24 In.	150.00
Rifle, Winchester, 1866, Saddle Ring Carbine	850.00
Rifle, Winchester, 22 Caliber, Pump Action, Model 1890	235.00
Rifle, Winchester, 30-30, Cowl Front Sign, Marlin Lever Action	120.00
Shotgun, Double Barrel, Engraved, C.1875, German	345.00
Shotgun, Double Barrel, Wells Fargo	500.00
Shotgun, Muzzle-Loading, 4-Gauge Muzzle, Market	600.00
Shotgun, Percussion, Single Round Barrel, Walnut Stock, 43 In.	130.00
Shotgun, W.& C.Scott, Hammerless, Double, Engraved	250.00

Gunderson glass was made at the Gunderson Pairpoint Works of New Bedford, Massachusetts, from 1952 to 1957. Gunderson Peachblow is especially famous.

GUNDERSON, Cornucopia, Marina Blue, Clear Bubble Ball Base, 11 In.	110.00
Decanter, Peachblow, Small	75.00
Salt & Pepper, Peachblow, C.1880	125.00
Vase, Fruits, Gold Leaves, 9 1/2 In.	175.00

GUTTA-PERCHA, see also Photography, Daguerreotype Case

GUTTA-PERCHA, Mirror, Raised Flower Border, Handle	35.00
Pin, Mourning, Oval Under Glass, C.1873, Gold Frame	110.00

The Haeger Brick and Tile Company of Dundee, Illinois, was founded in 1871 by David Haeger. His son Edmund H. Haeger decided to produce an art pottery in 1914. The name of the firm was changed to The Haeger Potteries, Inc. The firm is still in operation.

HAEGER, Bowl, Centerpiece, Pink, Blue, Green, Ivies, Flowers, 23 1/4 In.	20.00
Console Set, Pink Over Plum, Grape & Leaf Design	60.00
Console Set, Waves, Swans In 2 Poses, 7 1/2 In.Tall, 3 Piece	18.00
Cornucopia, Basket Weave, Green, 14 In.	20.00
Cornucopia, Footed Shell, Label, 8 X 5 In.	8.00
Dish, Leaf, Green, Blue, Philodendron Design, 13 In.	18.00
Planter, Figural, Girl Leans Over Pool, Ivory, 11 1/2 X 10 In.	32.00
Planter, Figural, Gold, Basin In Lap, Braids, 11 1/4 X 9 3/4 In.	25.00
Planter, Free-Form Oval, Cream	6.00
Planter, Madonna & Child, White, 11 1/2 In.	9.00
Vase, Abstract Design, Brown, Beige, & White, 10 In.	10.00
Vase, Bud, Eggshell, Silver Sticker, 7 1/4 In.	8.00
Vase, Gray Brown, Leaf-Form Beaded Spirals, 9 1/2 In.	5.00
Vase, Modernistic Deer, Green Sticker, Cream, 7 In.	10.00
Vase, Swordfish, Pink, Blue-Green, 13 X 9 In.	25.00
Vase, White & Green, 11 In.	10.00
Windowbox, Mottled Green, Impressed Mark, 16 X 6 X 4 1/2 In.	10.00

HALL'S
SUPERIOR
QUALITY
KITCHENWARE

Hall China Company started in East Liverpool, Ohio, in 1903. The firm made all types of wares, including Autumn Leaf pattern dishes. It is still working.

HALL'S
MADE IN
U.S.A.
CHINA

HALL, see also Autumn Leaf

HALL, Bowl, Red Poppy, 7 1/2 In.	10.00
Bowl, Red Poppy, 8 1/2 In.	12.00
Bowl, Tavern, 7 1/2 In.	15.00
Casserole, Orange Blossom	10.00
Casserole, Red Poppy, Covered, 8 1/2 In.	15.00
Casserole, Rose Parade, 2 Handled	22.00
Coffeepot, Floral Decal, Drip-O-Lator, Porcelain, 8 Cup	15.00
Coffeepot, Red Poppy, Drip-O-Lator Inset, 8 Cup	22.00
Cookie Jar, Banded, Chinese Red	30.00
Cookie Jar, Pink, Gold Trim	60.00
Creamer, Autumn Leaf	5.50
Creamer, Red Poppy	9.00

Creamer, White Inside, Red Outside, 6 In. 5.00
Cup, Custard, Orange Blossom 3.50
Dish, Refrigerator, Made For Westinghouse, Covered, Blue 4.00
Dish, Refrigerator, Orange, Covered, Westinghouse 6.00
Dispenser, Water, Jadite, Chrome Spigot 32.00
Gravy Boat, Red Poppy 14.00
Jar, Grease, Red Poppy, Covered 9.50
Jug, Ball, Chinese Red 12.00
Jug, Ball, Powder Blue 10.00
Jug, Banded, Chinese Red 15.00
Jug, Poppy 12.50
Jug, Red Carafe, Covered, Round 20.00
Jug, Sani-Grid, Chinese Red 10.00
Pepper, Crocus 5.00
Pie Plate, Rose Heather 8.00
Pitcher, Cream, Tilt, 7 In. 8.00
Pitcher, Red Poppy 8.00
Pitcher, Westinghouse, Covered, Blue, 8 3/4 In. 17.50
Salt & Pepper, Poppy 12.50
Salt & Pepper, Red Poppy, Handled, Pair 15.00
Spittoon, Brown 25.00
Spittoon, Green 15.00
Sugar, Red Poppy, Covered 11.00
Teapot, Disraeli, Pink 10.00
Teapot, Donut, Red Poppy 38.00
Teapot, Hollywood, Maroon, Gold Trim 18.00
Teapot, Individual, Celeste Blue 10.00
Teapot, Melody, Green 27.00
Teapot, Parade, Canary 12.00
Teapot, Red Sani-Grid, 6 Cup 17.00
Teapot, Star, Turquoise 12.00
Teapot, Surfside, Emerald Green 25.00
Teapot, Westinghouse, Blue 28.00
Tile, Tea, Green, 6 In. 3.50
Toothbrush Holder, Excelsior Pattern, 2 Piece 28.50
Warmer, Casserole, Autumn Leaf, Oval 16.00

HALLOWEEN, Candy Container, Black Cat, Papier-Mache 32.00
Candy Container, Old Witch, Papier-Mache, 8 1/4 In. 46.00
Display, Stand-Up, Salem Witch, Die Cut, Germany, 16 In. 49.00
Doll, Witch, Tagged Coca-Cola, Stuffed, 28 In. 55.00
Figure, Cat, Black, 2 Smaller Cats Inside, Wooden, 4 In. 20.00
Figure, Man Holding Pumpkin, Chenille, 5 In. 35.00
Jack-O'-Lantern, Papier-Mache, Paper Eyes, Teeth, 5 X 6 In. 38.00
Jack-O'-Lantern, Papier-Mache, 7 X 10 In. 15.00
Mask, Bashful, Happy, Sneezy, & Dopey, By Fishback 100.00
Mask, J.F.Kennedy, Plastic 50.00
Mask, Mickey Mouse & Minnie Mouse, Pair 50.00
Postcard, Tuck, Clapsaddle, Set Of 10 .... 48.00
Pumpkin, Papier-Mache, Germany, 2 1/4 In. 35.00
Pumpkin, Papier-Mache, Split Design Hooks Together, 6 In. 35.00
Sparkler, On Card, Metal 75.00

Hampshire pottery was made in Keene, New Hampshire, between 1871 and 1923. Hampshire developed a line of colored glazed wares as early as 1883, including a Royal Worcester-type pink, olive green, blue, and mahogany.

HAMPSHIRE, Candlestick, Green, 5 1/4 In. 60.00
Lamp Base, Oil, Handles, 5 3/4 In. 85.00
Lamp, Cadmon Robertson, Brass Parts, 9 In. 98.00
Mug, Transfer Portrait Of Indian, Marked 115.00
Pitcher, Yankee Doodle, 11 In. 145.00

Stein, Green Matte, 7 In.	45.00
Vase, Cylinder, Green, 5 In.	28.00
Vase, Indian Type Design, Dark Green, 4 In.	30.00
Vase, Mottled Blue & Green Glaze, 7 1/2 In.	70.00

Philip Handel worked in Meriden, Connecticut, about 1885 and in New York City from about 1900 to the 1930s. His firm made art glass and other types of lamps.

HANDEL, Candleholder, Windmill Scene, Marked, C.1920, 8 1/2 In.	550.00
Hair Receiver, Hand-Painted Florals	125.00
Humidor, Cigar, Indian Portrait, Full Headdress	325.00
Humidor, Horse & Dog, Pewter Lid With Pipe For Handle, Signed	250.00
Humidor, Shriner's Design, Man On Camel, Emblem, Signed, 6 In.	575.00
Humidor, 3 Horses Drinking, Signed	72.00
Lamp, Arab & Camel, Artist Initialed	6750.00
Lamp, Art Deco, Bronze Lady, Parchment Shade, C.1890, Label	1500.00
Lamp, Bronze, Hearts & Vines Shade, Gold Iridescent, 10 X 56 In.	1500.00
Lamp, Floor, Organ, Green Leaded Shade, Bronze	2000.00
Lamp, Green & Yellow Shade, 12 In.	1400.00
Lamp, Green Slag, Emerald Green Jewels, Marked	1250.00
Lamp, Hall, Hanging, Cranberry Etched Globe, Signed	1250.00
Lamp, Mica Shade, Signed, 20 In.	880.00
Lamp, Obverse & Reverse Painted Scenic Shade, Signed, 21 In.	800.00
Lamp, Raspberry Branches, Ocher Ground, Shade, 21 X 16 In.	2190.00
Lamp, Reverse-Painted Shade, Daffodil, Signed, 22 In.	*Illus* 2700.00
Lamp, Sunset Landscape Scene, Signed, 16 In.	3200.00
Lamp, Table, Art Deco, Parchment Shade, Lady Bronze Statue, C.1893	1500.00
Lamp, Table, Hand-Painted Florals, Brass Base, Signed, 19 1/2 In.	850.00
Lamp, Table, Ivy Leaf & Berry Border Shade, Signed, 14 In.	1200.00
Lamp, Table, Signed, Forest Scene On 16 In.Shade	900.00
Lamp, Yellow Centered Blossoms, Bronzed Base, C.1910, Signed, 24 In.	2300.00
Night-Light, Reverse Painted Parrots, Flowers, Signed, 7 1/2 In.	800.00
Shade, Dragonfly, Signed Shade & Base, 11 X 18 In.	1600.00
Shade, Leaded, Geometric Starred, Tag, 19 In.	900.00
Shade, Leaded, Squash, Leaves, & Gourds, 3-Light Base, 17 3/4 In.	1100.00

Handel, Lamp, Reverse-Painted Shade, Daffodil,
Signed, 22 In.

Harlequin dinnerware was produced by the Homer Laughlin Company from 1938 to 1964, and sold without trademark by the F.W. Woolworth Co. It has a concentric ring design like Fiesta, but the rings are separated from the rim by a plain margin and cup handles are angular in shape.

HARLEQUIN, Ashtray, Basket Weave, Yellow	15.00
Dish, Nut, Red	5.00
Eggcup, Double, Blue	12.50
Eggcup, Double, Rose	12.50
Eggcup, Green	7.00
Eggcup, Mauve	12.00
Figurine, Donkey, Blue	58.00
Figurine, Donkey, Maroon	40.00
Figurine, Maverick Cat	15.00
Sauceboat, Turquoise	5.00
Sugar & Creamer, Yellow	6.00

HATPIN HOLDER, see also Porcelain and various Porcelain categories

HATPIN HOLDER, Arms Of Wales In Red & Yellow, Cymru Am Byth, Porcelain	35.00
Flowers & Gold Leaves, English Pottery, Lavender, 5 3/4 In.	35.00
Pansies, Fluted Foot, Germany, 3 5/8 X 5 In.	35.00
Pink Roses, Green Foliage, German, 3 1/4 X 5 In.	30.00

HATPIN, Beehive Shape, Victorian, Faceted Black Glass Head, 11 In.	16.50
Blue Glass Head, Relief Of Spider, 10 1/2 In.	18.50
Diamond-Shaped Brass Head, Concentrics, 7 3/4 In.	8.50
Faceted Amber Glass, 1/ 1/2 In.	18.50
Filligree Brass, Blue Enameled Flower, 6 In.	20.00
Mercedes Symbol On Purple Carnival Glass, 10 1/2 In.	16.50
Reticulated Gold-Filled Ball, 7 3/4 In.	6.50
Rhinestones, Oval, Large	12.00
Ruby Glass Ball With Hobs In Gilt, 5 5/8 In.	4.50
Turquoise, Gold Pin, Oval, Large	10.00
3 Gilted Florals With Brilliants, Enameled	15.00
6-Pointed Star, Ruby Center Stone, Halo Of Brilliants	20.00

HAVILAND & CO.

Haviland china has been made in Limoges, France, since 1842. The factory was started by the Haviland Brothers of New York City. Other factories worked in the town of Limoges making a similar chinaware.

HAVILAND, Bone Dish, Green Flowers On White	15.00
Bowl, Pink Floral Design Inside & Out, Gold, 9 1/2 In.	50.00
Bowl, Vegetable, Chrysanthemum	40.00
Box, Candy, Spray Of Gilt Berries, Covered, Round	28.50
Butter Chip, Floral	7.00
Butter Chip, Floral, Set Of 10	35.00
Butter Chip, Garlands Of Pink Roses, Set Of 8	40.00
Butter, Baltimore Rose, Covered, Pink	150.00
Butter, Frontenac Pattern, Covered	49.50
Butter, Garlands Of Pink Roses, Insert, Green & Gold	47.50
Cake Plate, Baltimore Rose	60.00
Cake Plate, Malmaison	45.00
Casserole, Sprays Of Blue Flowers, Gold Handles, Covered	35.00
Chamberstick, Porcelain, Gold Ring Handle, Painted Floral	65.00
Charger, Bluebirds, 1 On Flight, 2 On Limb, Gold Trim, 14 In.	375.00
Charger, Peaches On Branches, Bluebirds, Gold Rim, 14 In.	375.00
Chocolate Pot, Clover, Monogram In Gold	110.00
Chocolate Pot, Floral, Gold Trim, 10 1/2 In.	125.00
Chocolate Pot, Floral, 10 In.	110.00
Chocolate Pot, Flowers, Scalloped Base & Top, Gold Trim	89.50
Chocolate Pot, Hand-Painted Ribbons, Gold Base, Signed, 10 1/2 In.	180.00
Chocolate Pot, Princess	150.00
Chocolate Pot, Ribbon Handle & Design,	179.00
Chocolate Set, Covered, Decorated, Limoges, 11 In., 5 Piece	90.00
Coffeepot, Flower Design, France, 8 In.	85.00

Coffeepot, Gold Decoration	65.00
Coffeepot, Trailing Vines, Berry Finial, Star On Spout, Footed	89.00
Compote, Art Nouveau Design, Gold & Blue, 9 X 4 1/2 In.	70.00
Cracker Jar, Orchid, Pink, Violet, & Green Ground	140.00
Cup & Saucer, Belfort	8.00
Cup & Saucer, Chrysanthemum	12.00
Cup & Saucer, Encrusted Gold Scroll Border	30.00
Cup & Saucer, Floral & Gold	70.00
Cup & Saucer, Marie	15.00
Cup & Saucer, Meadow Visitors Pattern, Green Mark	27.00
Cup & Saucer, Pink & Yellow Roses, Gold Flared Edges	12.00
Cup & Saucer, Princess	35.00
Dessert Set, Wild Roses & Forget-Me-Nots, Tray, 12 1/2 In., 7 Piece	95.00
Dish, Cheese, Cornflower Pattern, Gold Trim, Marked, 10 X 7 In.	160.00
Dish, Leaf Shaped, Baltimore Rose, Handle, Gold Trim, 8 X 9 In.	39.50
Dish, Pickle, Sponged Gold, Scalloped Rim, Florals, 10 X 3 1/2 In.	10.00
Gravy Boat, Princess	55.00
Gravy Boat, Underplate, White & Pink Flowers	25.00
Hair Receiver, Gilt Design, Lavender & Brown	28.00
Plate, Chrysanthemum, 8 1/2 In.	10.00 To 12.00
Plate, Dropped Rose, Scalloped Edge, Pink, 8 1/2 In.	35.00
Plate, Fish, Underwater Scene, Scalloped Rim, Signed, 1899, 9 In.	65.00
Plate, Fruit, Set Of 6, 8 1/2 In.	75.00
Plate, Oyster, Blue Flower, Gold Scalloped Rim, 5 Shell	28.00
Plate, Oyster, Brown, Rust, Flowers & Berries, 4 Shell	28.00
Plate, Oyster, 5-Section, Shells & Seaweed, Salmon Ground, 8 1/2 In.	55.00
Plate, Pansies, Purple & Yellow, Smoke-Tone Ground, 8 1/2 In.	40.00
Plate, Pink & Yellow Roses, 10 1/2 In.	12.00
Plate, Portrait, Baby, Gold Applique, Green Border, Initialed, C.1881	110.00
Plate, Wild Roses, Scalloped Gold Rim, Oval, 13 1/2 In.	35.00
Plate, Yellow Roses, Signed Stoner, 8 1/2 In.	35.00
Platter, Forget-Me-Nots, Gold Handles, 14 X 9 1/2 In.	35.00
Platter, Marie, 12 In.	25.00
Platter, Rose Border, Well, 16 1/2 X 12 1/2 In.	45.00
Platter, Turkey, Garland Of Roses, 18 In.	95.00
Ramekin, With Underplate, Porcelain, Violets, Mark, Limoges France	72.00
Salt Dip, Pink, Baltimore Rose	48.00
Salt, Norma	35.00
Sauceboat, With Attached Underplate, Covered, Roses	68.00
Sugar & Creamer, Belfort	18.00
Sugar & Creamer, Frontenac Pattern, Covered	29.50
Tea Set, Gold Trim, 3 Piece	150.00
Teapot, Pink Clover, Green Leaf Design, Gold Trim, Ranson	65.00
Tray, Dresser, Pink & Violet Flowers, Oval, 11 1/4 X 8 3/4 In.	34.00
Tray, Floral Drapes, Princess, Sedan Chair, Palace, Marked, 9 In.	235.00
Tray, Hand-Painted Roses, Gold Rim, Signed, 8 In.	20.00
Tray, Sprays Of Blue Flowers, Gold Handles, 12 1/2 In.	35.00

 T.G.Hawkes & Company of Corning, New York, was founded in 1880. The firm cut glass made at other firms until 1962. Many pieces are marked with the trademark, a trefoil ring enclosing a fleur-de-lis and two hawks.

HAWKES, see also Cut Glass

HAWKES, Bottle, Cologne, Venetian Pattern, Sterling Silver Top, Small	345.00
Bottle, Whiskey, Thistle Pattern, Sterling Silver Shot Top, Signed	135.00
Bowl, Allover Hobstars, 8 In.	225.00
Bowl, Cheese, Round, Covered, Marked, 9 3/4 In.	300.00
Bowl, Floral Swags & Vines, Signed, 8 In.	130.00
Bowl, Gravic Iris, Signed, 8 In.	450.00
Bowl, Shallow, Serrated Rim, Marked, 2 1/2 In.	175.00
Bowl, Strawberry, Diamond Points, Hobstars, 8 1/4 X 4 1/4 In.	145.00
Bowl, 5-Petal Flowers & Leaves, Signed, 5 X 16 In.	165.00
Box, Cigarette, Covered, Pedestal, Engraved Flowers, Trefoil Mark	47.00

Box, Cigarette, Flower Engraved, Covered, Mark 50.00
Butter Chip, Crossed Ellipticals Of Strawberries, Signed, Set Of 6 .... 165.00
Carafe, Queen's Pattern, St.Louis, Cut Neck, Signed, 7 1/4 In. 1000.00
Champagne, Hollow Stem, Rock Crystal, Signed, Set Of 12 .... 595.00
Cocktail Shaker, Blank, Cut In Crosscut, Marked 350.00
Cocktail Shaker, Etched Rooster, Sterling Silver Top 175.00
Cocktail Shaker, Paneled Design, Silver Plated Cover, Marked, 12 In. 75.00
Cologne Bottle, Venetian, 6 In. 395.00
Compote, Engraved Floral & Leaf Underside, Signed, 5 1/4 X 7 In. 250.00
Compote, Floral Cut, Signed, 4 In. 60.00
Cordial, Gladys Pattern, Signed, Set Of 4 .... 195.00
Cruet, Engraved Oil, Vinegar, Floral, Dated .... 38.00 To 65.00
Cruet, Trumpet Shape, Sterling Stopper, Floral Design, Signed, 7 In. 75.00
Decanter, Icicle & Diamond Point, Marked, 12 In. 425.00
Dish, Candy, Trefoil Shape, Silver Overlay Garland, Handled 75.00
Dish, Grazia Pattern, Flared Rim, Double Signed, 10 1/4 In. 50.00
Finger Bowl, Rock Crystal, Set Of 12 .... 350.00
Goblet, Gravic Pattern, Signed, Set Of 5 .... 250.00
Goblet, Three Fruits Pattern, Signed, 6 3/4 In. 100.00
Ice Bucket, Etched Leaves, Vines, Marked, Green 150.00
Inkwell, Powder Box Shape, Signed, Yellow, 3 X 1 3/4 In. 275.00
Jar, Cigar, Hobstars, Fans, & Crosscut Diamonds, Signed, 8 1/2 In. 375.00
Jar, Jam, Crystal, Floral Engraving, Sterling Silver Knob 45.00
Match Holder, Striker, Signed 95.00
Mixer, Martini, Engraved Leaf & Berries Design, Marked, 16 In. 110.00
Pitcher, Emerald Green, 1 Tumbler, 10 1/2 In. 175.00
Pitcher, Free-Blown, Gold Banding, Applied Handle, Signed, 7 In. 175.00
Plate, Cut & Rye Pattern, Signed, 8 1/2 In. 46.00
Plate, Delft Diamond, Set Of 8, Signed, 8 In. 250.00
Plate, Grecian Pattern, 6 7/8 In. 375.00
Rose Bowl, Wheel-Engraved Festoon, Gold Band, Apple Green, Signed 75.00
Sugar & Creamer, Strawberry Pattern, 16 Point Star Base, Signed 350.00
Syrup, Flutes & Hobstars, Sterling Silver Top, Signed, 5 In. 275.00
Tazza, Cut Floral, Green Stem & Foot, 7 In. 105.00
Tray, Classic Pattern, Signed, Oval, 10 1/4 X 7 In. 350.00
Tumbler, Brunswick, Signed 70.00
Tumbler, Middlesex, Signed 36.00
Vase, Cut Design, Crystal, 12 1/2 In. 275.00
Vase, Fan, Acid Cut, Clear To Green, Marked, 7 1/4 In. 175.00
Vase, Green, Enameled Crystal, White Design, 13 In. 200.00
Vase, Green, Fan, Engraved Grape Leaves, 7 In. 95.00
Vase, Marine Scene, Sailboats, Marked, 12 In. 295.00
Vase, Navarre, Hobstar Base, 12 1/2 In. 595.00
Vase, Star Pattern, Signed, 8 In. 48.00
Wine, Blooming Flowers, Chevrons, Garland, Marked, 8 1/2 In. 120.00

*Heintz Art Metal shop made jewelry, copper, silver, and brass in
Buffalo, New York, from 1915 to about 1935. It became Heintz
Brothers Manufacturers about 1935.*

HEINTZ ART, Bookend, Copper, Sterling Silver Overlay, Pair 45.00
Frame, 5 X 7 In. 60.00

*Heisey glass was made from 1896 to 1957 in Newark, Ohio, by A. H.
Heisey and Co., Inc. The Imperial Glass Company of Bellaire,
Ohio, bought some of the molds and the rights to the trademark. Some
Heisey patterns have been made by Imperial since 1960. After 1968 they
stopped using the "H" trademark.*

HEISEY, see also Custard Glass

HEISEY, Albemarle, Cocktail 17.50
Albemarle, Goblet 17.50
Albemarle, Goblet, Chateau Cutting, 8 Ounce 28.00
Albemarle, Goblet, 8 Ounce 20.00

Alexandrite, Vase, 6 In. 250.00
Arcadia, Compote, 5 1/2 In. 52.50
Banded Flute, Compote, Footed, Marked, 10 1/2 In. 110.00
Banded Flute, Sherbet, 3 Bands, 4 1/2 In. 10.00
Beaded Panel & Sunburst, Bowl, Punch 125.00
Beaded Panel & Sunburst, Cracker Jar, Covered 165.00
Beaded Panel & Sunburst, Syrup 45.00
Beaded Swag, Goblet, Roses, Souvenir, Rock City, Illinois 65.00
Beaded Swag, Goblet, Souvenir, Custard 75.00
Beaded Swag, Pitcher, Milk, White Opalescent 175.00
Beaded Swag, Pitcher, Milk, White Opalescent Design 175.00
Beaded Swag, Spooner, Enameled Flower 75.00
Beaded Swag, Sugar, Covered, Floral Design 90.00
Beaded Swag, Tumbler, White Opalescent 30.00
Beau Knot, Ashtray, Moongleam, 4 In. 22.50
Candleholder, Krystol, Handled, Dated 1907, Marked, Miniature, Pair 32.00
Caprice, Candleholder, Pair 32.00
Carcassonne, Cordial, Sahara, 1 Ounce 38.00
Carcassonne, Goblet, Old Colony Etch 12.50
Cleopatra, Goblet, Fairacre 25.00
Coarse Rib, Plate, Flamingo, 7 In. 8.00
Coarse Rib, Relish, Metal Basket, Amber, 13 In. 45.00
Colonial, Compote, Floral Garland, Footed, Marked, 10 1/2 In. 79.00
Colonial, Compote, Footed, 8 In. .... 36.00 To 49.00
Colonial, Compote, Footed, 9 1/2 X 8 In. 45.00
Colonial, Cordial, Marked 15.00
Colonial, Cruet, Original Stopper, Marked 45.00
Colonial, Cup & Saucer 10.00
Colonial, Goblet, Marked 20.00
Colonial, Goblet, Original Wooden Shipping Box, Marked, Set Of 9 .... 150.00
Colonial, Jug, Marked, 3 Pint 46.00
Colonial, Jug, 3 Pint 46.00
Colonial, Pitcher, Bulbous, Sterling Silver Overlay, 5 In. 60.00
Colonial, Pitcher, Water, Marked 125.00
Colonial, Pitcher, Water, 1 Quart 40.00
Colonial, Pitcher, Water, 3 Quart 65.00
Colonial, Plate, Star Bottom, Marked, 5 1/2 In. .... 4.00 To 7.00
Colonial, Punch Set, Bowl, Pedestal, 7 Cups, Marked 225.00
Colonial, Relish, Marked, 10 X 7 In. 19.00
Colonial, Sherbet, Marked .... 8.00 To 50.00
Colonial, Sugar & Creamer, Tray 35.00
Colonial, Tray, Crystal, 10 In. 20.00
Colonial, Tray, Rayed Center, Marked, 10 1/2 In. 26.00
Colonial, Vase, Flower Shape, Cobalt Blue, 9 In. 300.00
Colonial, Vase, Handled, Footed, Cobalt Blue, 8 In. 325.00
Colonial, Vase, Sweet Pea, Flared, 5 1/2 X 6 In. 18.00
Colonial, Vase, Trumpet, Frosted, 10 In. 25.00
Colonial, Wine Set, Silver Overlay, Decanter & 6 Glasses, Marked 85.00
Colonial, Wine, Clear, 2 1/2 Oz. 8.50
Columbia, Candleholder, Crimped, Marked, Pair 42.00
Comet, Wine, Square Base, 3 1/4 In. 8.50
Continental, Celery, 12 X 4 1/2 In. 35.00
Continental, Relish, 9 X 3 3/4 In. 30.00
Cornucopia, Vase, Cobalt Blue, 8 In. 160.00
Country Club, Whiskey, 1 1/2 Ounce 20.00
Crystal, Candelabra, 3-Arm, Scrolling, Baluster, 22 In., Pair 250.00
Crystal, Sugar Loaf Holder, Double, Marked 40.00
Crystolite, Bowl, Marked, 12 In. 35.00
Crystolite, Bowl, Signed, 8 1/2 In. 16.00
Crystolite, Box, Cigarette, 3 In. 17.50
Crystolite, Candleholder, Hurricane 18.00
Crystolite, Candleholder, 3-Light, Pair .... 55.00 To 70.00
Crystolite, Candlestick, 4 In. 35.00
Crystolite, Compote, 5 In. 18.00

Crystolite, Creamer 15.00
Crystolite, Cruet 28.00
Crystolite, Dish, Candy, Covered, Marked, 7 In.Diam. 40.00
Crystolite, Dish, Shell Shape, Covered, Footed .... 22.00 To 25.00
Crystolite, Ice Bucket 35.00
Crystolite, Plate, 7 1/2 In. 7.00
Crystolite, Plate, 8 1/4 In. 15.00
Crystolite, Punch Cup 7.00
Crystolite, Relish, 3-Part, Oval, 13 In. .... 20.00 To 28.00
Crystolite, Sherbet, Blown, 6 Ounce .... 8.00 To 10.00
Crystolite, Soda, Blown, 12 Ounce 15.00
Crystolite, Sugar & Creamer 35.00
Diamond Point, Bonbon 30.00
Dish, Lemon, Floral Cutting, Dolphin Finial Cover, Farberware Holder 50.00
Dolly Madison, Sugar & Creamer, Rose Cutting 42.00
Dolphin, Bowl, Pink, Footed 18.00
Dolphin, Candlestick, Flamingo, 1-Light, Petticoat, Pair 225.00
Double Rib & Panel, Mustard, Covered, Marked 50.00
Duquesne, Tumbler, Soda, Chintz Etched, 5 Ounce 12.00
Empress, Bowl, Dolphin Foot, 11 In., No.1401 .... 20.00
Empress, Bowl, Sahara, 10 In. 50.00
Empress, Candlestick, Sahara, Dolphin-Footed, Pair 295.00
Empress, Compote, Oval, 8 In. 75.00
Empress, Cup & Saucer .... 15.00 To 35.00
Empress, Cup & Saucer, Sahara 38.00
Empress, Dish, Lemon, Classic Etched, Covered 75.00
Empress, Goblet 39.75
Empress, Nut Cup, Dolphin-Footed, Sahara 24.00
Empress, Pitcher, Water 145.00
Empress, Plate, Round, Moongleam, 8 In. 15.00
Empress, Plate, Square, Marked, 6 In. 8.00
Empress, Plate, Square, 8 1/2 In. 18.75
Empress, Sugar, Pink, Dolphin-Footed, 3-Handled 10.00
Empress, Vase, Flamingo, Footed, 9 In. 90.00
Fancy Loop, Compote, 7 In. 75.00
Fancy Loop, Plate, Dinner, 8 3/4 In. 25.00
Fancy Loop, Saltshaker .... 11.00 To 16.00
Fancy Loop, Toothpick, Clear 60.00
Fancy Loop, Toothpick, Gold Trim, Green .... 65.00 To 75.00
Fandango, Bowl, 8 In. 50.00
Fandango, Cruet 48.00
Fandango, Toothpick .... 75.00 To 85.00
Fern, Bowl, Oval, Footed, Marked, 11 In. 31.50
Fern, Plate, Belvedere Etching, 8 In. 15.00
Figurine, Bull 1200.00
Figurine, Clydesdale .... 285.00 To 450.00
Figurine, Donkey 175.00
Figurine, Elephant, Set Of 3 .... 625.00
Figurine, Gazelle 1200.00
Figurine, Geese, Set Of 3 .... 350.00
Figurine, Giraffe, Looking Back .... 95.00 To 125.00
Figurine, Giraffe, Looking Forward, 11 In. 145.00
Figurine, Goose, Wings Half Up .... 58.00 To 86.50
Figurine, Goose, Wings Up .... 65.00 To 100.00
Figurine, Hen 375.00
Figurine, Plug Horse, Oscar 75.00
Figurine, Pony, Kicking, Blue 20.00
Figurine, Pony, Rearing, Imperial, Blue 20.00
Figurine, Pouter Pigeon 450.00
Figurine, Ringneck Pheasant .... 100.00 To 175.00
Figurine, Ringneck Pheasant, Pair 225.00
Figurine, Rooster 450.00
Figurine, Rooster, Fighting 125.00
Figurine, Scotty .... 65.50 To 85.00

Figurine, Sparky 85.00
Figurine, Sparrow 60.00
Figurine, Tropical Fish 1200.00
Figurine, Wood Duck 500.00
Fish, Bookend, Pair .... 85.00 To 195.00
Flat Panel, Cruet 38.00
Floral, Console Set, Moongleam, 12 In., 3 Piece 250.00
Floral, Dish, Lemon, Dolphin Finial Cover, Farberware Holder 50.00
Fox Chase, Cocktail, 1 Quart, 3 Piece 125.00
Fox Chase, Mug, Beer 150.00
Fox Chase, Tumbler 45.00
Frontenac, Tankard, Etched, 3 Pint 180.00
Goose, Cocktail, Stemmed 120.00
Graceful, Cocktail, Oyster, Harvester Cut 17.50
Grandeur, Goblet, Sabrina Etching 20.00
Grandeur, Plate, Sabrina Etching, 6 In. 6.00
Grape, Candlestick, Pair .... 115.00 To 200.00
Grape, Mustard, Sterling Silver Cover 60.00
Greek Key, Banana Bowl 25.00
Greek Key, Bowl, Marked, 8 1/2 In. 45.00
Greek Key, Bowl, 3 1/2 X 8 1/2 In. 24.00
Greek Key, Butter, Covered 165.00
Greek Key, Cruet 45.00
Greek Key, Dish, Banana Split 24.00
Greek Key, Dish, Dresser, Blue Jade, Metal Rim, 4 1/2 In. 60.00
Greek Key, Goblet 85.00
Greek Key, Jar, Fruit, Covered, 2 Quart 225.00
Greek Key, Pitcher, Silver Overlay, Marked, 8 3/4 In. 125.00
Greek Key, Pitcher, Water, Clear 110.00
Greek Key, Plate, 5 In. 12.00
Greek Key, Plate, 9 1/4 In. 45.00
Greek Key, Punch Bowl, Stand 650.00
Greek Key, Punch Cup 9.00
Greek Key, Punch Cup, Marked 35.00
Greek Key, Relish, Oval, 12 In. 48.00
Greek Key, Relish, Oval, 9 In. 38.00
Greek Key, Sherbet, 4 1/2 Ounce .... 9.00 To 17.00
Greek Key, Spooner 85.00
Greek Key, Tray, French Bread, 12 In. 150.00
Greek Key, Tumbler, Iced Tea, Flat Bottom 75.00
Hohinoor, Vase, Ball, Taper, Label, 6 In. 30.00
Horsehead, Bookend, Frosted, Pair 210.00
Horsehead, Box, Cigarette 50.00
Horsehead, Dish, Cigarette 55.00
Horseshoe, Cake Stand, 7 In. 40.00
Ipswich, Candleholder, Prisms & Inserts, Pair 125.00
Ipswich, Champagne, Sahara, 4 Ounce 23.00
Ipswich, Cocktail, Crystal, 4 Ounce 10.00
Ipswich, Cruet, Stopper 45.00
Ipswich, Goblet, Footed, Marked 15.00
Ipswich, Plate, Square, 8 In. 17.50
Ipswich, Tumbler, Footed, Sahara, 5 Ounce 18.00
Ipswich, Vase, Candle, Prisms & Inserts 125.00
Ipswich, Vase, Prisms, Footed, Pair 350.00
Jamestown, Goblet, Barcelona Cut 22.50
Kalonyal, Candlestick 25.00
Kalonyal, Compote, Pedestal, 10 In. 85.00
King Arthur, Champagne, Moongleam Stem 15.00
King Arthur, Goblet, Moongleam Stem 22.50
Kingfisher, Flower Block, Moongleam 220.00
Lariat, Box, Cigarette 16.00
Lariat, Candlebrum, 2-Light, Pair 40.00
Lariat, Cocktail, Moonglo Cut, 4 In. .... 22.50 To 27.00
Lariat, Cocktail, Stemmed, 4 Ounce 22.00

Lariat, Compote, 4 1/2 In. 10.00
Lariat, Dish, Candy, Covered, 7 In. 45.00
Lariat, Goblet, Moonglo Cut Stem, 5 3/4 In. 30.00
Lariat, Jelly Set 25.00
Lariat, Punch Set, Bowl & 10 Cups 175.00
Lariat, Punch Set, Bowl, 15 Piece 395.00
Lariat, Relish, 2-Part, 7 In. 15.00
Lariat, Sugar 8.00
Lariat, Sugar & Creamer, Tray .... 15.00 To 20.00
Lariat, Tray, For Sugar & Creamer 12.50
Lariat, Tumbler, Juice, Moonglo Cut Stem, 5 1/2 In. 25.00
Lariat, Vase, Cut Floral & Leaves Design, 7 In., Pair 60.00
Lariat, Vase, Fan, Clear, Sterling Etch, Bird Decoration 45.00
Locket On Chain, Wine, Ruby, Gold Trim 375.00
Minuet, Candlestick, 2-Light, Single 65.00
Minuet, Cocktail, Oyster, 3 1/2 In. 30.00
Minuet, Goblet, 8 In. .... 38.50 To 42.50
Minuet, Sherbet, 6 1/4 In. 30.00
Minuet, Sugar, Dolphin Footed, 3-Handled 30.00
Minuet, Tumbler, Footed, 5 1/4 In. 30.00
Minuet, Tumbler, Iced Tea, Footed, 6 7/8 In. 38.50
Minuet, Wine, 6 In. 31.00
Monticello, Goblet, Water, 6 1/4 In. 22.00
Monticello, Wine, 4 1/4 In. 35.00
Moonglo, Cocktail Shaker 50.00
Narrow Flute, Candlestick, 7 In. 38.00
Narrow Flute, Celery, Clear, 9 In. 20.00
Narrow Flute, Mustard, Marked, Covered 27.50
Narrow Flute, Nut Cup, Oval, Set Of 6 .... 45.00
Narrow Flute, Plate, 5 In. 4.00
Narrow Flute, Salt, Individual 9.50
New Era, Candlestick, Prisms, 9 In., Pair 125.00
No.2, Candelabrum, 9 In. 110.00
No.2, Candlestick, 9 In. 80.00
No.21, Candlestick, 9 In. 30.00
No.112, Candlestick, Pair, Moongleam 37.50
No.125, Candlestick 250.00
No.458, Basket 98.00
No.459, Basket, 7 In. 100.00
Oceanic, Candlestick, 5 In., Pair 22.00
Oceanic, Celery, Marked, Pink, 1i 1/2 X 4 In. ... 25.00 To 27.50
Oceanic, Celery, Pink, 12 X 4 In. 25.00
Oceanic, Compote 62.50
Oceanic, Ice Bucket 67.50
Oceanic, Relish, Marked, Pink, 6 1/2 X 3 1/2 In. ... 16.50 To 20.00
Oceanic, Salt & Pepper 12.00
Octagon, Bonbon, Moongleam, 6 In. 10.00
Octagon, Dish, Nut, Flamingo 10.00
Octagon, Salt, Master, Flamingo 6.00
Old Dominion, Goblet, Flamingo 25.00
Old Dominion, Wine, Sahara 28.00
Old Sandwich, Candlestick 28.00
Old Sandwich, Cocktail, Oyster 12.50
Old Williamsburg, Bowl, Berry, Marked, 4 1/2 In. 4.50
Old Williamsburg, Sherbet 17.00
Old Williamsburg, Tumbler, Iced Tea 20.00
Old Williamsburg, Tumbler, Water 20.00
Omega, Tumbler, Waltz Cut, 5 Ounce 17.50
Orchid Etch, Bowl, Crystal, 12 In. 32.50
Orchid Etch, Bowl, 12 1/2 In. 60.00
Orchid Etch, Candlestick, Double, 6 In. 75.00
Orchid Etch, Candlestick, 4 In. 45.00
Orchid Etch, Celery, Clear, Frosted, Marked 35.00
Orchid Etch, Celery, 12 In. 35.00

Orchid Etch, Champagne	20.00
Orchid Etch, Cocktail, Oyster	31.00
Orchid Etch, Compote, Footed, 6 In.	25.00
Orchid Etch, Compote, 6 In.	30.00
Orchid Etch, Creamer, 3 In.	25.00
Orchid Etch, Goblet, Crystal, 10 Ounce, 6 In.	25.00
Orchid Etch, Goblet, Footed, 5 1/2 In.	25.00
Orchid Etch, Goblet, Water	20.00
Orchid Etch, Goblet, 10 Ounce	24.00 To 28.00
Orchid Etch, Goblet, 13 Ounce	24.00
Orchid Etch, Mayonnaise Set, 3 Piece	45.00
Orchid Etch, Plate, Torte, Crystal, 14 In.	45.00
Orchid Etch, Plate, 7 In.	15.00
Orchid Etch, Plate, 7 1/2 In.	27.00
Orchid Etch, Plate, 7 3/4 In.	28.00
Orchid Etch, Relish, 3-Part, 11 1/2 In.	48.00
Orchid Etch, Relish, 8-Compartment, 11 In.	35.00
Orchid Etch, Sherbet, 4 In.	16.00
Orchid Etch, Soda, Footed, 12 Ounce	20.00 To 28.00
Orchid Etch, Sugar & Creamer	55.00 To 65.00
Orchid Etch, Tumbler, Iced Tea	29.00
Oxford, Goblet	17.50
Oxford, Sherbet	12.50
Palmetto, Goblet	25.00
Paperweight, Rabbit	95.00
Peacock, Goblet, Bobwhite, 10 Ounce	25.00
Peerless, Dish, Ice Cream, Ruffled Top	25.00
Peerless, Goblet, Water, 7 In.	15.00 To 27.00
Peerless, Toothpick	29.00 To 32.00
Peerless, Wine	8.00
Pied Piper, Cordial, 1 Ounce	32.00
Pied Piper, Goblet, 10 Ounce	22.00
Pied Piper, Plate, Double, Etched Claret Stem, C.1925	32.50
Pied Piper, Tumbler, 12 Ounce	15.00
Pillows, Bowl, Signed, 8 In.	42.00
Pineapple & Fan, Creamer, Green	35.00
Pineapple & Fan, Cruet, Green, Gold Trim	135.00
Pineapple & Fan, Dish, Honey, Underplate, Marked	20.00
Pineapple & Fan, Mug, Emerald Green, Gold Trim	50.00
Pineapple & Fan, Spooner, Gold Trim, Clear	45.00
Pineapple & Fan, Spooner, Green	62.00
Pineapple & Fan, Sugar, Green	35.00 To 45.00
Pineapple & Fan, Sugar, Hotel, Gold Trim	75.00
Pineapple & Fan, Toothpick	68.00
Pineapple & Fan, Vase, Marked, 6 In.	32.50
Pineapple & Fan, Vase, 12 In.	50.00
Pinwheel & Fan, Bowl, Signed, 8 1/4 In.	55.00
Plain Band, Table Set, Child's	325.00
Plantation Ivy, Goblet, 6 In.	25.00
Plantation Ivy, Mayonnaise Set, 2 Piece	65.00
Plantation Ivy, Plate, 8 1/2 In.	16.00
Plantation Ivy, Sherbet, 4 1/4 In.	20.00
Plantation Ivy, Tumbler, Iced Tea, Footed	26.00
Plantation, Butter, Covered, 1/4 Pound	55.00
Plantation, Cake Stand, 14 X 4 3/4 In.	145.00
Plantation, Candleblock, Marked	25.00
Plantation, Candleholder, 2-Light, Ivy Etch	55.00
Plantation, Candleholder, 3-Light, Pair	155.00
Plantation, Candlestick	65.00
Plantation, Compote, 11 1/2 X 7 In.	125.00
Plantation, Cruet	35.00 To 75.00
Plantation, Mayonnaise, Double	25.00
Plantation, Pitcher, Water	125.00
Plantation, Relish, 3 Part, Oval	47.50

Plantation, Wine 35.00
Plantation, Wine, 3 Oz. 27.50
Pleat & Panel, Bowl, Cut Flowers Pink, 8 In. 15.00
Pleat & Panel, Sugar & Creamer 24.00
Pointed Oval In Diamond Point, Sugar 25.00
Prince Of Wales, Bowl, Berry, Oval, 11 In. 35.00
Prince Of Wales, Punch Cup 24.00
Prince Of Wales, Sugar & Creamer, Covered, Ruby Flashed 145.00
Prince Of Wales, Toothpick, Clear & Gold 55.50
Prince Of Wales, Toothpick, Marked 65.00
Priscilla, Compote, Jelly, Handled, Footed, 5 In. 32.50
Priscilla, Custard, 5 Ounce 6.00
Priscilla, Vase, Hawthorne, 8 In. 125.00
Prison Stripe, Tumbler 50.00
Provincial, Oil & Vinegar 32.50
Provincial, Pitcher, Water, Ice Lip, Signed 80.00
Punty & Diamond Point, Compote 58.00
Punty Band, Relish, Marked 65.00
Punty Band, Salt & Pepper 56.50
Punty Band, Salt & Pepper, Floral Decoration 80.00
Punty Band, Shaker, Souvenir, Ruby Flashed 30.00
Punty Band, Toothpick 55.00
Punty Band, Toothpick, Ruby Flashed, Souvenir 35.00
Punty Band, Wine, Ruby, Revere Beach, 1906, Marked 32.00
Puritan, Bowl, Clear, Footed, 8 X 8 1/2 In. 30.00
Puritan, Compote, Jelly, Footed, 5 In. 16.00
Puritan, Dish, Ice Cream, 5 1/2 In. 6.00
Puritan, Goblet, Clear, 6 Ounce 13.00
Puritan, Sherbet, 4 1/2 In. 5.00
Queen Ann, Bowl, Lion Head, Dolphin Footed 300.00
Queen Ann, Bowl, Punch, 2 Piece 395.00
Queen Ann, Cake Plate, Handled, Marked, 12 In. 27.50
Queen Ann, Candlebra, Single, Pair 75.00
Queen Ann, Console Set, 3-Light Candleholder, Rose Of Peace Etch 60.00
Queen Ann, Goblet, Everglade Cutting, 10 Ounce 28.00
Queen Ann, Mustard, Flamingo, 3 Piece 55.00
Queen Ann, Plate, Orchid Etch, 10 1/2 In. 32.00
Queen Ann, Plate, Sahara, 8 In., Square 14.00
Queen Ann, Punch Set, Bowl & 12 Cups, Marked 550.00
Rib & Panel, Champagne 9.00
Rib & Panel, Cruet, Oil 25.00
Rib & Panel, Sugar & Creamer, Marked 28.00
Rib & Panel, Vase, Footed, 9 1/2 In. 35.00
Ribbed Octagon, Bowl, Flamingo, Oval, 9 In. 27.00
Ridgeleigh, Bowl, Punch, Set Of 14 Cups, 10 1/2 X 6 In. 175.00
Ridgeleigh, Box, Cigarette, Covered 17.00
Ridgeleigh, Cake Set, Marked, 16 In. 65.00
Ridgeleigh, Candleholder, Marked, 11 In., Pair 175.00
Ridgeleigh, Candlestick 28.00
Ridgeleigh, Compote, Jelly, 2-Section, Marked 49.50
Ridgeleigh, Creamer, Individual 14.00
Ridgeleigh, Creamer, Sugar, & Tray, Marked 35.00
Ridgeleigh, Cruet, Original Stopper 24.50
Ridgeleigh, Nappy, Marked, 4 1/2 In. 12.50
Ridgeleigh, Plate, Silver Overlay, Marked, 13 1/4 In. 30.00
Ridgeleigh, Plate, 8 1/2 In. 75.00
Ridgeleigh, Punch Cup, Marked, Set Of 6 .... 55.00
Ridgeleigh, Sherbet, 4 In. 15.00
Ridgeleigh, Sherbet, 5 In. 17.00
Ridgeleigh, Smoke Set, Cigarette Holder, 4 Ashtrays 45.00
Ridgeleigh, Sugar, Individual 10.00
Ring Band, Butter, Custard, Covered 110.00
Ring Band, Pitcher, Water, Souvenir Of State Fair, 1906 .... 245.00
Ring Band, Toothpick, Custard .... 55.00 To 58.00

Ring Band, Tumbler, Lidgerwood 55.00
Ring Band, Tumbler, Popham Beach, Maine, Gold Floral 145.00
Rococo, Salt & Pepper, Crystal 75.00
Rooster Head, Cocktail Shaker 75.00
Rooster, Cocktail Shaker .... 65.00 To 75.00
Rooster, Cocktail Shaker, 11 In. 39.00
Rooster, Decanter, 8 Glasses 136.00
Rooster, Vase 100.00
Rosalie, Bowl, Console, Dolphin Footed 35.00
Rosalie, Goblet 27.50
Rose Etch, Bowl, Footed, 5 1/2 In. 28.00
Rose Etch, Bowl, Fruit, Crimped, 12 In. 85.00
Rose Etch, Candelabrum, Triple, Marked 195.00
Rose Etch, Candleholder, 2-Light, Pair 85.00
Rose Etch, Candleholder, 3-Light .... 45.00 To 90.00
Rose Etch, Celery, Invert Panel, 4 X 11 1/2 In. 30.00
Rose Etch, Champagne 30.00
Rose Etch, Claret, 4 Ounce 75.00
Rose Etch, Cocktail, Oyster, 3 Ounce 23.00
Rose Etch, Compote, Jelly, Footed, 2-Handled, 6 In. 28.00
Rose Etch, Creamer 19.00
Rose Etch, Creamer, Star Bottom, Marked 40.00
Rose Etch, Dish, Candy, Covered, 5 1/2 In.Diam. 35.00
Rose Etch, Goblet, Water 32.00
Rose Etch, Goblet, 9 Ounce .... 28.00 To 45.00
Rose Etch, Mayonnaise Set, 3 Piece 65.00
Rose Etch, Plate, 8 1/2 In. .... 18.50 To 27.00
Rose Etch, Plate, 14 In. 85.00
Rose Etch, Relish, 3-Part 38.00
Rose Etch, Relish, 5-Compartment, Silver Plated Trim, 13 In. 50.00
Rose Etch, Sherbet .... 15.00 To 30.00
Rose Etch, Sugar & Creamer 50.00
Rose Etch, Sugar, Cut & Etched, Marked, Large 40.00
Rose Etch, Syrup 29.00
Rose Etch, Tumbler, Iced Tea 45.00
Rose Etch, Tumbler, Juice, Footed, 5 Ounce .... 23.00 To 40.00
Rose Etch, Tumbler, Water, 9 Ounce .... 30.00 To 40.00
Rose Etch, Wine, 3 Ounce 85.00
Sahara, Sugar & Creamer, Empress 75.00
Sandwich Star, Ashtray 5.25
Sea Horse, Cocktail, Crystal 150.00
Skier, Glass, Juice, Etched, Footed 65.00
Spanish, Candlestick, 7 In., Pair 85.00
Spanish, Candlestick, 9 In., Pair 125.00
Spanish, Goblet, Cobalt Blue, 10 Ounce 85.00
Stanhope, Cup & Saucer 9.00
Stanhope, Sugar & Creamer 23.00
Suez, Goblet 15.00
Sunburst, Punch Bowl & Base 140.00
Sunburst, Syrup, 13 Ounce 98.00
Swan Song, Nut Set, Master & 8 Individual 175.00
Swan, Candlestick, Moongleam, 6 1/2 In., Pair 350.00
Tally Ho, Cocktail Shaker, Etched 75.00
Tally Ho, Cocktail Shaker, Hand-Painted Scene, 3 Pint 55.00
Tally Ho, Cocktail, Etching 45.00
Tally Ho, Tumbler, 5 In. .... 45.00 To 48.00
Thumbprint & Panel, Candleholder, Sahara, Double 60.00
Titania, Goblet, Spanish Stem, 7 1/2 In. 47.00
Titania, Plate, 8 1/2 In. 24.00
Touraine, Cup 10.00
Twist, Compote, Pink, 5 In. 27.50
Twist, Cruet, Flamingo 70.00
Twist, Nappy, Marked, 4 In., Set Of 6 .... 45.00
Twist, Pitcher, Pint 110.00

Twist, Plate, Marked, 4 1/2 In.	35.00
Twist, Plate, Moongleam, Marked, 7 In.	5.00
Twist, Sherbet, Footed, Flamingo, Marked	12.50
Twist, Wine, Moongleam, 4 Ounce	30.00
Victoria, Goblet, Footed, 5 In.	15.00
Victoria, Tumbler, Marked, 12 Ounce	12.00
Victorian, Bar Glass, Sahara, 2 Ounce	50.00
Wampum, Bowl, Console, 12 In.	35.00
Wampum, Plate, Sandwich, 12 In.	15.00
Warwick, Cornucopia, Clear, Pair	60.00
Waverly, Bowl, Floral, Orchid Etch, 12 In.	40.00
Waverly, Bowl, Oval, 8 X 2 In.	48.00
Waverly, Box, Powder, Man Behind Woman On Sleigh	18.00
Waverly, Butter, Covered	75.00
Waverly, Butter, Sea Horse Finial	35.00
Waverly, Compote	75.00
Waverly, Creamer	10.00
Waverly, Goblet, 6 In.	18.00
Waverly, Mayonnaise, Footed	30.00
Waverly, Plate, Torte, Orchid Etch, 14 In.	40.00
Waverly, Relish, Oval, 3 Part	40.00
Waverly, Relish, 3-Section, Orchid Etch, 11 In.	30.00
Waverly, Sugar & Creamer, Crystal	20.00
Waverly, Tumbler, Iced Tea, 6 7/8 In.	18.00
Wedding Band, Juice	21.00
Wedding Band, Sherbet	21.00
Whirlpool, Champagne, 5 Ounce	15.00
Whirlpool, Compote, Jelly, Footed	18.00
Whirlpool, Compote, 6 In.	16.00
Whirlpool, Cruet, Pair	40.00
Whirlpool, Goblet, 10 Ounce	20.00
Whirlpool, Plate, Torte, Clear, 10 In.	35.00
Whirlpool, Tumbler, Footed, 9 Ounce	18.00
Whirlpool, Tumbler, Iced Tea, 12 Ounce	20.00
Whirlpool, Tumbler, Juice, Footed, 5 Ounce	15.00
Winged Scroll, Spooner, 2-Handled	60.00
Winged Scroll, Table Set, Custard, Gold Trim, Covered	385.00
Winged Scroll, Toothpick, Custard	95.00
Yeoman, Bowl, Green, Panel, Ribbed, Scalloped, Footed, 11 In.	35.00
Yeoman, Sugar & Creamer, Marked	47.50
Yeoman, Sugar, Covered, Marked	27.00

HEREND, see Fischer

Gebruder Heubach, a German firm working from 1820 to 1925, is best known for bisque dolls and doll heads, their principal products. They also manufactured bisque figurines, including piano babies, beginning in the 1880s, and glazed figurines in the 1900s.

HEUBACH, Dish, Jasper, Green & White, Indian, Marked, 4 1/4 In.	65.00
Doll, Bisque, Cloth Body, Paperweight Eyes, 4 Teeth, Marked, 21 In.	360.00
Ewer, Scenic Design, Green, Pair	110.00
Figurine, Baby, In High Chair, Pulling Off Sock, Bisque, 5 In.	78.00
Figurine, Boy & Rabbit, Girl With Bird, Nightshirt, 12 1/2 In., Pair	475.00
Figurine, Boy Holding Shovel & Leaning On Sea Wall, Marked	65.00
Figurine, Boy, Chinese, Holding Bowl, White Tunic, Marked, 7 In.	80.00
Figurine, Child, Japanese, Holding Parasol, Marked	65.00
Figurine, Colonial Gentleman, Standing, Blue & White, Marked, 8 In.	50.00
Figurine, Dog, Shaggy, Sitting On Haunches, White, Marked, 5 1/2 In.	185.00
Figurine, Dog, Sitting, Hound, Gray & White, 3 1/2 In.	90.00
Figurine, Dog, White, Black, Standing, 5 X 5 In.	175.00
Figurine, Dutch Boy & Girl, Seated, Blonde Hair, Marked, 7 In., Pair	235.00
Figurine, Dutch Girl & Boy, Standing In Front Of Egg, Marked, 9 In.	140.00
Figurine, Dutch Girl, Red Dress, 6 In.	118.00
Figurine, Dutch Girl, Seated, Blue, 6 In.	120.00

Figurine, Girl, With Basket, Black Hair, Marked, 9 In. 245.00
Figurine, Indians, Bow & Arrow, Hatchet, Green Jasperware, 4 In. 75.00
Figurine, Lute Player, Mint Green, 9 1/2 In. 175.00
Figurine, Man With Monkey, 15 In. 450.00
Figurine, Peasant Girl With Basket, White Clothes, Marked, 9 In. 225.00
Figurine, Pirate Boy, Signed, 8 1/2 In. 95.00
Figurine, Rabbit, Pink Eyes, Marked, 3 X 5 In. 100.00
Figurine, Rabbit, Sitting On Haunches, Marked, 3 1/2 X 5 1/2 In. 125.00
Figurine, Setter, Standing, Long Hair, Gray & White, Marked, 10 In. 155.00
Figurine, Setter, White, Gray, Base, Marked, 5 X 10 In. 175.00
Figurine, Spaniel, Gray & White, Marked, 2 X 5 1/2 In. 140.00
Tobacco Jar, Figural, Boy, Bisque, Signed 145.00
Tray, Sea Gull, Full Figure, Gray White 75.00
Vase, Attached Dutch Girl, Marked, 6 1/2 In. 85.00

H⬡**I**⬡**G**

*Higbee glass was made by the J.B.Higbee Company of Bridgeville,
Pennsylvania, about 1900.*

HIGBEE, see also Pressed Glass
HIGBEE, Basket, Reeded Handle, Arrowhead, Oval 55.00
Butter, Paneled Thistle, Footed, Square, Marked, 5 3/4 In.Square 25.00
Sherbet, Pineapple & Fan, Embossed Bee, Sawtooth Edge 10.00
Spooner, Hawaiian Lei, 2-Handled, Marked 15.00
Table Set, Hawaiian Lei Pattern, Child's, Marked, 4 Piece 100.00
    HISTORIC BLUE, see Adams; Clews; Ridgway; Staffordshire

*Hobnail glass is a pattern of glass with bumps in an allover pattern.
Dozens of hobnail patterns and variants have been made. Reproductions
of many types of hobnail glass can be found.*
    HOBNAIL, see also Fenton; Francisware
HOBNAIL, Cruet 40.00
Cruet, Aqua Opalescent 37.00
Cruet, Cranberry Opalescent 42.00
Pitcher, Water, Four-Corned Top, Opalescent, Hobbs 265.00
Pitcher, Water, White Opalescent, Square Mouth 159.00
Syrup, Hobbs Brockunier, 1884, Amber 250.00

⊕

*Hochst, or Hoechst, porcelain was made in Germany from 1746 to 1796.
It was marked with a six-spoke wheel.*

HOCHST, Jug, Baluster, Rhineland Scene, Marked, 7 In. 300.00

*Holly amber, or golden agate, glass was made by the Indiana Tumbler and
Goblet Company from January 1, 1903, to June 13, 1903. It is a pressed
glass pattern featuring holly leaves in the amber-shaded glass.*

HOLLY AMBER, Cruet, Original Stopper 395.00
Relish, 4 5/8 X 4 3/8 X 1 7/8 In. 375.00

*Hopalong Cassidy was named William Lawrence Boyd when he was born
in Cambridge, Ohio, in 1895. His first movie appearance was in 1919,
but the first Hopalong Cassidy film was not until 1934. Sixty-six films
were made. In 1948 William Boyd purchased the television rights to the
movies, then later made 52 new programs. In the 1950s Hopalong Cassidy
was seen in comics, records, toys, and other products. Boyd died in 1972.*

HOPALONG CASSIDY, Badge, Sheriff, Star-Shaped, Brass 7.00
Badge, Star, Metal 9.00
Banner, Theater, 1936, Large 150.00
Belt, Switch A Buckle, Original Package 25.00
Billfold 20.00
Binoculars .... 15.00 To 25.00

Book, Coloring, Sticker, Stencil 12.00
Camera, Box 30.00
Can, Popcorn, Advertising 22.00
Cereal Bowl, White, Pictures Hoppy .... 20.00 To 35.00
Chinese Checkers 75.00
Chow Set, Original Box 65.00
Container, Milk, Cartons From California, 1970s 2.50
Dental Kit, Covered With Pictures, Complete 100.00
Drum 30.00
Field Glasses, Boxed 28.00
Game, Board, Combat 8.00
Game, Dominoes, Boxed 20.00
Game, Lasso, Boxed 35.00
Girl's Outfit, Shirt, Skirt, Kerchief, Plastic Gun, Holster 40.00
Hair Oil 18.00
Hat Rack 45.00
Holder, Tie, Metal Bolo 9.00
Horseshoe, Good Luck, 1950, Hoppy Signature & Bar 20 Ranch 3.00
Lamp, Bullet 120.00
Leather Cuffs, Boxed 25.00
Lunch Box, Thermos 15.00
Mirror, Picture, Advertising, 6 X 4 In. 12.50
Money Clip, Brass, Embossed 8.00
Mug .... 6.00 To 10.00
Napkins, Packaged 12.50
Night-Light, Holster 110.00
Pencil Box 20.00
Pin, Pistol 13.00
Plaque, Wall, Good Luck Horseshoe, Plastic 25.00
Plate 25.00
Pocketknife .... 20.00 To 40.00
Poster, Advertising Bond Bread, 21 X 27 In. 55.00
Puzzle, Set Of 4 .... 45.00
Radio 90.00
Revolver, Holster, Wyandotte, 9 In. 66.00
Ring, Good Luck, Bar 20, 1949, Post Cereal 25.00
Roller Skates, Rollfast, Attached Spurs, Boxed 125.00
Salt & Pepper 7.00
Slide, Steer Head 13.00
Stationery 4.00
Television, 4 Film Strips, 1950, Automatic Toy 160.00
Thermos, Dated 1950 .... 7.00 To 11.00
Toy, Shooting Gallery, Windup 65.00
Toy, Twirling Lariat On Rocking Horse, Windup, Tin 75.00
Trading Cards, Wild West, From Post Cereal, 26 Cards 75.00
Tumbler, Juice 12.00
Tumbler, Milk Glass, Black Picture 7.00
Watch .... 15.00 To 17.00
Watch, On Saddle, Original Box 75.00
Wrist Band, Leather, Studded 15.00
Wristwatch, Original Band & Buckle .... 45.00 To 85.00

HOWDY DOODY, Book, Coloring 6.00
Clock, Talking Alarm 20.00
Doll, Jointed, Wood, Original Label, 12 In. 90.00
Doll, With N.B.C. Mike, Wood Jointed 18.00
Flasher Color Rings, Set Of 7 .... 9.00
Key Chain, Puzzle, NBC Mike 5.00
Neckerchief 28.00
Night-Light 15.00
Ring, Light-Up 8.00
Shoe Polish, Box .... 6.00 To 12.00
Timekeeper, Picture, Howdy & Clock, Packaged, 10 X 18 In. 7.50

Toy, Magic Piano, Original Box 125.00
Toy, On Trapeze, Windup, Tin 25.00

Hull pottery is made in Crooksville, Ohio. The factory started in 1903
as the Acme Pottery Company. Art pottery was first made in 1917.

HULL, Ashtray, Serenade, Large 23.00
Bank, Little Red Riding Hood .... 195.00 To 225.00
Basket, Bow Knot, 12 In. 100.00
Basket, Continental, Orange 20.00
Basket, Dogwood, 7 1/2 In. 30.00
Basket, Ebb Tide, Turquoise, 16 In. 30.00
Basket, Flower, Brown & Yellow, 10 1/2 In. .... 45.00 To 85.00
Basket, Magnolia, Brown & Cream, 10 1/2 In. .... 65.00 To 85.00
Basket, Pink & Green, 12 1/2 X 8 In. 15.00
Basket, Pink Flower, USA & Numbered, Green, 8 1/2 In. 40.00
Basket, Rose & Green, 1 1/2 In. 8.00
Basket, Serenade, Blue, 6 1/2 In. 24.00
Basket, Speckled Pink & Gray, 8 3/4 In. .... 20.00 To 25.00
Basket, Tokay, 8 In. 18.00
Basket, Wild Flower, 8 In. 26.00
Basket, Woodland, Turquoise & Gray, 10 1/2 In. 38.50
Basket, Woodland, 8 3/4 In. 27.50
Bowl, Bow Knot, 13 1/2 In. 26.00
Bowl, Console, Blossom Flite, Ring Handles, Footed, 1955, Pink 25.00
Bowl, Console, Blossom Flite, 16 1/2 In. 18.75
Bowl, Console, Bow Knot, Blue & Green, 13 1/2 In. 32.00
Bowl, Console, Dogwood, 11 1/2 In. 35.00
Bowl, Console, Woodland, Pink, 14 In. 10.00
Bowl, Console, Yellow & Green Flowers 28.00
Bowl, Imperial, Green Basket Weave, 9 In. 5.00
Bowl, Magnolia, Gold Trim, High Gloss, 6 1/2 In. 15.00
Bowl, Rose, Iris, 4 In. 15.00
Bowl, Sugar, Magnolia, Covered, Gloss, 3 3/4 In. 11.00
Bowl, Tom & Jerry, Gold Lettering, 12 Mugs 255.00
Bowl, Utility, Early, Crazing Inside 12.00
Box, Window, Woodland, 10 1/2 In. 22.00
Bulb Bowl, Triple, Green & Tan 10.00
Butter, Little Red Riding Hood, Covered .... 110.00 To 115.00
Candleholder, Blossom Flite, Handled, Pair 14.00
Candleholder, Bow Knot, Blue, Pair 48.00
Candleholder, Narcissus, 6 In., Pair 24.00
Candleholder, Open Rose, 6 1/2 In., Pair 25.00
Candlestick, Ebb Tide, Shrimp, Green 25.00
Candlestick, Magnolia, Matte Pink, Pair 22.00
Candlestick, Woodland, High-Gloss Chartreuse & Rose, Pair 15.00
Canister, Flour, Little Red Riding Hood .... 195.00 To 250.00
Canister, Sugar, Little Red Riding Hood 195.00
Casserole, Hen, Brown, Covered, Oval, 8 In. 45.00
Casserole, Utility, Covered, Early 12.00
Compote, Butterfly, Square, White, 4 3/4 X 5 1/4 In. 13.00
Console Set, Bow Knot, 3 Piece 68.00
Console Set, Magnolia, No.268, Bowl, 12 1/2 In., 3 Piece .... 45.00 To 58.00
Console Set, Open Rose, Bowl, 12 In.Diam., 3 Piece 42.00
Console Set, Woodland, Pink, Bowl, 14 In., 3 Piece 31.00
Cookie Jar, Basket, Closed 65.00
Cookie Jar, Bouquet 50.00
Cookie Jar, Cinderella 125.00
Cookie Jar, Goldilocks 85.00
Cookie Jar, Little Red Riding Hood .... 35.00 To 75.00
Cookie Jar, Mickey & Minnie Mouse, Turn About 95.00
Cornucopia, Blossom Flite, Marked C In Circle 16.00
Cornucopia, Bow Knot, 7 1/2 In. 20.00
Cornucopia, Double, Bow Knot 60.00

Cornucopia, Double, Magnolia, Matte Pink To Blue, 8 X 12 1/2 In. 33.00
Cornucopia, Handled, White, 6 1/2 In. 12.00
Cornucopia, Magnolia, 8 1/2 In. .... 15.00 To 18.00
Cornucopia, Pink & Green 18.00
Cornucopia, Signed, Fuchsia Lining, Green 14.00
Cornucopia, Sunglow, 8 1/2 In. 12.50
Cornucopia, USA 64 .... 12.00
Cornucopia, Water Lily, 6 1/2 In. .... 18.00 To 28.00
Cornucopia, Wild Flower, Pink To Blue, 7 1/2 In. 16.00
Cornucopia, Wild Flower, Yellow To Pink, 7 1/2 In. 16.00
Cornucopia, Wild Flower, 10 X 8 1/2 In. .... 18.00 To 22.00
Cornucopia, Woodland, Matte Finish, 11 In. .... 18.00 To 20.00
Cornucopia, Woodland, Yellow & Green, Decorator's Mark 22.00
Cornucopia, Woodland, 5 1/2 In. 8.00
Cornucopia, 8 1/2 In. 18.00
Cracker Jar, Little Red Riding Hood 150.00
Creamer, Bow Knot, 4 In. 19.00
Creamer, Dark Green Handle, Lime Green 5.00
Creamer, House 'n Garden, Brown 3.50
Creamer, Little Red Riding Hood 35.00
Creamer, Pig, With Beret 12.00
Creamer, Serenade, Pink 7.00
Cruet, House 'n Garden, 6 1/2 In. 3.00
Dish, Butterfly, Heart Shape 12.00
Dish, Candy, Pink 22.50
Ewer, Blossom Flite, No.T-3 .... 26.00
Ewer, Blue To Cream, Rose Matte, Floral, Marked, 5 1/2 In. 18.00
Ewer, Bowknot, 13 1/2 In. 65.00
Ewer, Bowknot, No.B-1, 5 1/2 In. 26.00
Ewer, Iris, 13 1/2 In. 145.00
Ewer, Magnolia, Beige, Yellow, 7 In. 29.00
Ewer, Magnolia, 1946-47, 4 3/4 In. .... 17.00 To 27.50
Ewer, Parchment & Pine, 14 In. 75.00
Ewer, Rosella, 7 In. .... 18.00 To 25.00
Ewer, Rosella, 9 X 6 1/2 In. 15.00
Ewer, Tulip, 12 In. 39.00
Ewer, Water Lily, Brown To Beige, 5 1/2 In. 14.00
Ewer, Water Lily, Gold Trim, 5 1/2 In. 28.00
Ewer, Water Lily, 13 1/2 In. 55.00
Ewer, Wild Flower, Blue To Pink, 5 1/2 In. .... 20.00 To 23.50
Ewer, Wild Flower, Brown, Yellow, 8 1/2 In. .... 30.00 To 39.00
Ewer, Wild Flower, Pink & Blue, 13 1/2 In. 135.00
Ewer, Woodland, Matte & Two-Tone, 5 1/2 In. 60.00
Ewer, Woodland, 6 1/2 In. 25.00
Jar, Grease, Sunglow, 5 In. .... 10.00 To 12.00
Jardiniere, Fluted, Shades Of Green, 9 X 9 In. 15.00
Jardiniere, Iris, Blue To Pink, 5 1/2 In. 23.00
Jardiniere, Tulip, Large 100.00
Jardiniere, Water Lily, 5 In. .... 15.00 To 19.00
Jardiniere, Water Lily, 8 1/2 In. 100.00
Jug, Milk, Heather Rose 10.00
Mug, Alpine, H In Circle Mark, 6 In. 22.00
Mug, Happy Days Are Here Again 10.00
Mug, House 'n Garden, Brown, Ovenproof, 3 1/2 In. 3.00
Mug, Stoneware, Village Scene .... 19.00 To 37.00
Mustard, Little Red Riding Hood .... 75.00 To 105.00
Mustard, Spoon, Little Red Riding Hood 115.00
Pitcher, Bow Knot, 5 1/2 In. 22.50
Pitcher, Bow Knot, 6 1/2 In. 25.00
Pitcher, Butterfly, Footed, C In Circle, 8 1/2 In. 16.00
Pitcher, Floral, Pink & Blue Matte, 7 1/2 In. 25.00
Pitcher, House 'n Garden, Brown, 9 1/2 In. 12.00
Pitcher, Magnolia, Matte Yellow & Rose, 7 In. 25.00
Pitcher, Magnolia, 4 3/4 In. 12.00

Pitcher, Milk, House 'n Garden, Brown, 6 3/4 In. 8.00
Pitcher, Open Rose, Large 45.00
Pitcher, Sunglow, Pink, 24 Ounce 10.00
Planter, Art Nouveau, Figural, Woman Holding Dress To Side 35.00
Planter, Bucket, Tan, Bail Handled, 7 1/4 In. 6.00
Planter, Butterfly, Cream, Gold Rim, Scalloped, 13 In. 12.00
Planter, Chalice, Dark Green, Spiral Bowl, Bead Stem, 4 3/4 In. 4.00
Planter, Dog With Yarn, 5 1/2 X 8 In. 7.50
Planter, Duck With Bandanna, 5 X 7 In. 65.00
Planter, Flared, High-Gloss Mottled Green, 10 X 7 X 2 3/4 In. 14.00
Planter, Free-Form Heart, Gray-Green Over Pink, 11 1/2 X 2 1/2 In. 15.00
Planter, Fruits, Ivory, 8 3/4 In. 8.00
Planter, Hanging, Teacup With Bow 30.00
Planter, Madonna With Child .... 5.00 To 16.00
Planter, Marked, Cream, 11 1/4 X 5 1/2 X 3 In. 10.00
Planter, Peanut Shape, High-Gloss Green, 8 X 4 X 2 1/4 In. 14.00
Planter, Scrolled Medallions, Yellow & Green, 9 1/2 X 4 1/4 X 4 In. 10.00
Planter, Siamese Cat & Kitten 16.00
Planter, St.Francis, Ivory, 11 1/4 In. 10.00
Planter, Swan, Light Green 12.00
Planter, Telephone, 9 In. 95.00
Planter, Wall, Little Red Riding Hood 175.00
Planter, Windows Pattern, Blue Outside, Yellow Inside, 12 X 6 1/2 In. 12.00
Plate, Hand-Painted Florals, Signed & Dated, 7 1/2 In. 14.00
Salt & Pepper, Sunglow, 2 3/4 In. 14.00
Saltshaker, Little Red Riding Hood .... Illus 17.50
Saucer, House 'n Garden, Brown, 6 In. .... 1.00 To 2.50
Sugar & Creamer, House 'n Garden, Green, Covered 10.00
Sugar & Creamer, Little Red Riding Hood 85.00
Sugar & Creamer, Magnolia, Matte 22.00
Sugar, Magnolia, Covered, High-Gloss, Gold Trim, 3 3/4 In. 9.00
Sugar, Serenade, Open, Pink 5.00
Swans, Green, 7 In., Pair 30.00
Tea Set, Daisy, Green, 3 Piece 35.00
Tea Set, Magnolia, Gold Outlined, Gloss, 3 Piece 46.00
Tea Set, Parchment & Pine, Green, 3 Piece 48.00
Tea Set, Water Lily, 3 Piece 75.00
Teapot, Blossom Flite, Pink, 14 In. 26.00
Teapot, Colonial Man's Head, Hat, 5 In. 28.00
Teapot, Elephant, Black Man Lid, Reed Handled, 7 In. 29.00
Teapot, Little Red Riding Hood .... 75.00 To 110.00
Teapot, Magnolia, Matte, 6 1/2 In. 28.00
Urn, Serenade, Yellow, 5 In. 12.00
Vase, Blue Glaze, Flower On Pink Ground, Gold Handles, 8 In. 5.00
Vase, Bow Knot, Blue & Pink, 8 1/2 In. 30.00

Hull, Saltshaker, Little Red Riding Hood

Vase, Bow Knot, Footed, Blue To Green, 8 1/2 In. 26.00
Vase, Bow Knot, Turquoise, Square, Fan Rim, Side Handled, 8 1/2 In. 25.00
Vase, Bulbous Shaped, Bark Handled, Matte Pastel, 5 1/2 In. 26.00
Vase, Butterfly, 3-Footed, Triangular, 10 In. 20.00
Vase, Calla Lily, 6 In. 25.00
Vase, Calla Lily, 7 1/2 In. 48.00
Vase, Calla Lily, 8 In. 26.00
Vase, Camellia, Handled, Squatty, Blue To Pink, 8 1/2 In. 25.00
Vase, Camellia, Matte, Oval, 6 1/2 In. 18.00
Vase, Coil, Green, 5 1/2 In. 15.00
Vase, Coil, Green, 7 In. 25.00
Vase, Continental, Green, Open Gourd, 14 In. 20.00
Vase, Cornucopia, Wild Flower, 8 1/2 In. 20.00
Vase, Deer & Trees, Fan Shape, White, Pink Panel 33.00
Vase, Flamingo, Yellow, Green, Magenta, 9 X 6 In. 25.00
Vase, Granada, Label, Pink & Blue, 9 In. 15.00
Vase, Iris, Peach, 8 1/2 In. 26.00
Vase, Iris, 7 In. 17.00
Vase, Magnolia, Dusty Rose, 15 In. 70.00
Vase, Magnolia, High-Gloss, 11 In. 30.00
Vase, Magnolia, Matte Pink & Blue, 10 1/2 In. .... 25.00 To 26.00
Vase, Magnolia, Matte Yellow & Rose, 12 1/4 In. 46.00
Vase, Magnolia, Matte, No.3, 8 1/2 In. 20.00
Vase, Magnolia, Matte, Yellow Flowers, 1946-47, 4 3/4 In. 27.50
Vase, Magnolia, No.1, Matte Pink, 8 1/2 In. 18.00
Vase, Magnolia, Side-Handled, Footed, High-Gloss, 6 1/2 In. 14.00
Vase, Magnolia, 4 3/4 In. .... 10.00 To 17.00
Vase, Magnolia, 5 1/2 In. .... 12.00 To 24.50
Vase, Magnolia, 8 1/2 In. .... 18.00 To 22.00
Vase, Mardi Gras, No.47, Granada, 9 In. 14.00
Vase, Mardi Gras, No.49, Granada, 9 In. 20.00
Vase, Mardi Gras, 6 In. 8.00
Vase, No.73 .... 14.00
Vase, Open Rose, Fan-Shaped, 8 1/2 In. 38.00
Vase, Open Rose, No.120, 6 1/4 In. .... 16.00 To 36.00
Vase, Open Rose, White, 4 3/4 In. .... 11.00 To 15.00
Vase, Orchid, Blue, 4 1/4 In. 22.00
Vase, Orchid, 6 In. .... 18.00 To 35.00
Vase, Orchid, 8 In. 19.00
Vase, Pillow, Leaf Relief, Mottled Pink Over Green, 5 X 3 3/4 X 6 In. 10.00
Vase, Poppy, 6 1/2 In. 45.00
Vase, Rosella, Base Handles, 8 1/2 In. .... 15.00 To 25.00
Vase, Rosella, R-7, 6 1/2 In. 14.00
Vase, Rosella, 6 1/2 In. 15.00
Vase, Rosella, 8 1/2 In. 25.00
Vase, Serenade, Yellow, 6 1/2 In. 55.00
Vase, Stoneware, Marked 40 H 25.00
Vase, Sunglow, 5 1/2 In. 12.00
Vase, Suspended, Dogwood, 6 1/4 In. 40.00
Vase, Thistle, Pink, 6 1/2 In. .... 30.00 To 41.00
Vase, Tulip, 6 In. 17.00
Vase, Unicorn, 11 1/2 In. 35.00
Vase, Urn, Green Coil, 5 1/2 In. 15.00
Vase, Wall, Green Speckle, 7 1/2 In. 12.00
Vase, Water Lily, Base Handles, Footed, Matte Pink & Green, 8 1/2 In. 30.00
Vase, Water Lily, Brown To Yellow, 9 1/2 In. 26.00
Vase, Water Lily, L-1, 5 1/2 In. 14.00
Vase, Water Lily, 6 1/2 In. .... 15.00 To 18.00
Vase, Water Lily, 10 In. 26.00
Vase, Wild Flower, Blue, Pink, 9 1/2 In. 36.00
Vase, Wild Flower, Brown, Pink, 10 1/2 In. .... 22.00 To 38.00
Vase, Wild Flower, Decorator Mark, 7 1/2 In. 18.00
Vase, Wild Flower, No.78, 8 1/2 In. 22.00
Vase, Wild Flower, W-1, 5 1/2 In. 12.00

Vase, Wild Flower, W-4, 6 1/2 In. 16.00
Vase, Wild Flower, W-5, 6 1/4 In. 14.00
Vase, Woodland, High-Gloss Chartreuse & Rose, 7 1/2 In. 18.00
Vase, Woodland, Speckled Pink To Green, 11 In. 28.00
Vase, Woodland, Speckled Pink, 8 In. 20.00
Vase, Woodland, Two-Tone, 6 1/2 In. 17.50
Vase, Woodland, W-8, 7 1/2 In. 14.00
Vase, Woodland, 7 1/4 In. 20.00
Vase, 3-Part, Black, 10 In. 20.00
Wall Pocket, Bow-Knot, 8 In. 55.00
Wall Pocket, Half Cup & Saucer 30.00
Wall Pocket, Little Red Riding Hood 150.00
Wall Pocket, Red Riding Hood .... 150.00 To 175.00
Wall Pocket, Sunglow, Butterflies, Pink 15.00
Watering Can, Rose Design, Blue & Peach 20.00

*Hummel figurines, based on the drawings of Berta Hummel, are made by the
W. Goebel Porzellanfabrik of Oeslau, Germany, now Rodenthal, West
Germany. They were first made in 1934. The mark has changed through the
years. The following are approximate dates for each of the marks: "Crown"
mark, 1935 to 1949; "U.S. Zone, Germany," 1946 to 1948; "West
Germany," after 1949; "full bee," 1950 to 1959; "stylized bee," 1960 to 1972;
"three line mark," 1968 to 1979; "vee over gee," 1972 to 1975; "new mark,"
1979 to present.*

HUMMEL, Bookends, No.60/A & B, Farm Boy & Goose Girl, Stylized Bee 240.00
Candleholder, No.37, Herald Angels, Stylized Bee 95.00
Figurine, No.2/II, Little Fiddler, Vee Over Gee 500.00
Figurine, No.3/II, Bookworm, Vee Over Gee, 8 In. 500.00
Figurine, No.6/0, Sensitive Hunter, Full Bee 125.00
Figurine, No.7/0, Merry Wanderer, Stylized Bee 83.00
Figurine, No.9, Begging His Share, Full Bee 285.00
Figurine, No.10/I, Flower Madonna, Blue, Full Bee, 9 1/2 In. 225.00
Figurine, No.10/III, Flower Madonna, White Closed Halo, Full Bee 200.00
Figurine, No.12/I, Chimney Sweep, Stylized Bee .... 80.00 To 105.00
Figurine, No.15/0, Hear Ye, Hear Ye, Full Bee 170.00
Figurine, No.15/0, Hear Ye, Hear Ye, Stylized Bee 78.00
Figurine, No.16/2/0, Little Hiker, Stylized Bee 60.00
Figurine, No.21/0, Heavenly Angel, Full Bee, 4 3/4 In. 125.00
Figurine, No.47/0, Goose Girl, Full Bee, 4 In. 55.00
Figurine, No.47/3/0, Goose Girl, Full Bee, 4 3/4 In. 140.00
Figurine, No.49/3/0, To Market, Stylized Bee 85.00
Figurine, No.56/B, Out Of Danger, Full Bee 145.00
Figurine, No.57/0, Chick Girl, Full Bee .... 100.00 To 120.00
Figurine, No.57/0, Chick Girl, New Mark 48.00
Figurine, No.57/0, Chick Girl, Stylized Bee, 3 1/2 In. 79.00
Figurine, No.63, Singing Lesson, Full Bee 110.00
Figurine, No.63, Singing Lesson, Stylized Bee, 3 In. .... 90.00 To 100.00
Figurine, No.65, Farewell, Stylized Bee, 4 3/4 In. 145.00
Figurine, No.67, Doll Mother, Stylized Bee, 4 3/4 In. 85.00
Figurine, No.69, Happy Pastime, Full Bee .... 80.00 To 120.00
Figurine, No.71, Stormy Weather, Full Bee .... 300.00 To 370.00
Figurine, No.74, Little Gardener, Stylized Bee .... 60.00 To 90.00
Figurine, No.74, Little Gardener, Vee Over Gee 49.00
Figurine, No.82/0, School Boy, Full Bee 130.00
Figurine, No.83, Angel Serenade, Crown Mark, 5 1/2 In. 325.00
Figurine, No.84/0, Worship, Full Bee 100.00
Figurine, No.86, Happiness, Stylized Bee 52.00
Figurine, No.87, For Father, Stylized Bee 125.00
Figurine, No.89/I, Little Cellist, Crown 295.00
Figurine, No.94/I, Surprise, Stylized Bee, 5 1/2 In. 125.00
Figurine, No.96, Little Shopper, Full Bee 110.00
Figurine, No.98/0, Sister, Stylized Bee, 5 1/4 In. 100.00

Figurine, No.99, Eventide, Stylized Bee 110.00
Figurine, No.110/0, Let's Sing, Stylized Bee 48.00
Figurine, No.110/0, Let's Sing, Three Line Mark, 3 In. 60.00
Figurine, No.112/3/0, Just Resting, Full Bee 70.00
Figurine, No.118, The Postman, Full Bee 170.00
Figurine, No.123, Max & Moritz, Vee Over Gee 65.00
Figurine, No.128, Baker, Stylized Bee 65.00
Figurine, No.130, Duet, Full Bee 150.00
Figurine, No.130, Duet, Stylized Bee 145.00
Figurine, No.131, Street Singer, Full Bee .... 120.00 To 132.00
Figurine, No.131, Street Singer, Stylized Bee, 5 1/4 In. 60.00
Figurine, No.132, Star Gazer, Full Bee .... 145.00 To 150.00
Figurine, No.135, Soloist, Full Bee 80.00
Figurine, No.142/I, Apple Tree Boy, Full Bee, 6 In. .... 135.00 To 140.00
Figurine, No.142/3/0, Apple Tree Boy, Stylized Bee 90.00
Figurine, No.150/2/0, Happy Days, Stylized Bee .... 70.00 To 120.00
Figurine, No.152/B/II, Umbrella Girl, Full Bee, 8 In. 650.00
Figurine, No.152/B/0, Umbrella Girl, Stylized Bee 400.00
Figurine, No.154/0, Waiter, Stylized Bee 80.00
Figurine, No.154/0, Waiter, Vee Over Gee 84.00
Figurine, No.170/III, School Boys, New Mark 900.00
Figurine, No.171, Little Sweeper, Stylized Bee 52.00
Figurine, No.175, Mother's Darling, Crown Mark 270.00
Figurine, No.175, Mother's Darling, Full Bee 135.00
Figurine, No.175, Mother's Darling, Vee Over Gee 78.00
Figurine, No.177/III, School Girls, Vee Over Gee .... 1000.00 To 1250.00
Figurine, No.178, Photographer, Three Line Mark, 5 In. 115.00
Figurine, No.179, Coquettes, Full Bee 165.00
Figurine, No.186, Sweet Music, Full Bee 117.00
Figurine, No.195/2/0, Barnyard Hero, Stylized Bee .... 82.00 To 85.00
Figurine, No.195/2/0, Barnyard Hero, Three Line Mark 80.00
Figurine, No.196/I, Telling Her Secret, Full Bee 300.00
Figurine, No.196/I, Telling Her Secret, Stylized Bee 180.00
Figurine, No.196/I, Telling Her Secret, Three Line Mark, 6 1/2 In. 225.00
Figurine, No.196/0, Telling Her Secret, Three Line Mark, 5 In. 125.00
Figurine, No.198/I, Home From Market, Stylized Bee 105.00
Figurine, No.198/I, Home From Market, Three Line 95.00
Figurine, No.198/2/0, Home From Market, Full Bee .... 70.00 To 100.00
Figurine, No.199/I, Feeding Time, Vee Over Gee 80.00
Figurine, No.201/2/0, Retreat To Safety, Stylized Bee, 6 In. 120.00
Figurine, No.201, Retreat To Safety, Full Bee 125.00
Figurine, No.217, Boy With Toothache, Full Bee, 5 1/2 In. 125.00
Figurine, No.238/B, Angel With Accordion, Full Bee 80.00
Figurine, No.256, Knitting Lesson, Vee Over Gee 190.00
Figurine, No.261, Angel Duet, Vee Over Gee 70.00
Figurine, No.285, Accordion Boy, Stylized Bee 100.00
Figurine, No.308, Little Tailor, Stylized Bee 160.00
Figurine, No.314, Confidentially, Vee Over Gee 95.00
Figurine, No.319, Doll Bath, Three Line Mark 100.00
Figurine, No.322, Little Pharmacist, Three Line Mark 122.00
Figurine, No.345, A Fair Measure, Vee Over Gee 99.00
Figurine, No.347, Adventure Bound, Vee Over Gee 1200.00
Figurine, No.353/I, Spring Dance, Vee Over Gee 225.00
Figurine, No.363, Big Housecleaning, Vee Over Gee 105.00
Figurine, No.369, Follow The Leader, New Mark 330.00
Figurine, No.369, Follow The Leader, Vee Over Gee 389.00
Figurine, No.381, Flower Vendor, Vee Over Gee 85.00
Figurine, No.385, Chicken Licken, Vee Over Gee 95.00
Figurine, No.387, Valentine Gift, Vee Over Gee, 5 In. 225.00
Lamp, No.44/A, Culprits, Full Bee 275.00
Lamp, No.44/B, Out Of Danger, Full Bee .... 275.00 To 325.00
Plaque, No.137, Child-In-Bed, Full Bee 75.00
Plate, Christmas, 1971 .... 145.00

LORENZ
HUTSCHEN REUTER

GERMANY

Hutschenreuther Porcelain Company of Selb, Germany, was established in 1814 and is still working.

HUTSCHENREUTHER, Cake Plate, Green & Floral, Gold Engraved	67.00
Coffee & Tea Set, Fruits, 36 Piece	265.00
Coffee Server, Margarite	35.00
Dessert Set, Hand-Painted Narcissus, Artist Signed, 3 Piece	30.00
Figurine, Bear, Germany, 6 In.	70.00
Figurine, Bird, Finch, Red, Green, Tan, 3 1/2 X 3 In.	45.00
Figurine, Canary, On Stump, Worm In Beak, 5 In.	140.00 To 210.00
Figurine, Cherub, Standing On Gold Ball, Signed, 6 In.	95.00
Figurine, Dachshund, Standing, Tan & Brown, 8 1/2 In.	145.00
Figurine, Elephant	35.00
Figurine, Fawn, Feeding, White Tail, Artist, Signed, 5 In.	125.00
Figurine, Nude Woman, 13 In.	65.00
Figurine, Parakeet, On Tree Stump, Blue, 7 In.	110.00
Figurine, Parakeet, On Tree Stump, Yellow, 7 In.	110.00
Figurine, Pekingese, Standing, Cream, 3 1/2 X 4 1/2 In.	60.00
Figurine, Poodle, Sitting, Signed, White, 6 1/2 In.	80.00
Figurine, Spaniel, Springer	125.00
Figurine, Stallion, Rearing, Nude Maiden, Marked, 12 In.	275.00
Flower Arranger, White, Children, 8 Piece, Signed, 5 1/2 In.	225.00
Plate, Hand-Painted Floral Center, Gold Rim, 10 1/2 In.	22.50
ICEBOX, see Kitchen, Icebox	
ICON, Apocalypse, Vision Of St. John, Greek, 8 In.	150.00
Brass With Vermeil, C.1900	170.00
Cathedral Type, Opened, 5 1/2 X 8 1/2 In.	62.50
Christ, Saints, Old Man, Child, Russian, 12 X 8 In.	100.00
Russian, Triptych Of Deesis, 18th Century, Brass, 7 X 2 7/8 In.	325.00
Russian, Virgin, 19th Century, 14 1/8 X 11 7/8 In.	375.00
Saint, Porcelain, Encased In Glass & Brass	150.00

Imari patterns are named for the Japanese ware decorated with orange and blue stylized flowers. The design on the Japanese ware became so characteristic that the name Imari has come to mean any pattern of this type. It was copied by the European factories of the eighteenth and early nineteenth centuries.

IMARI, Bottle, Saki, Scalloped Foot, Scenic, Signed, Blue & White, 5 1/2 In.	28.00
Bowl, Bird & Floral Design, 9 3/4 In.	80.00
Bowl, Blue, Orange, Gilt Peony, Silver Rims, Marked, 3 In.	100.00
Bowl, Floral Design, Birds, Swags, Footed, 8 1/2 In.	100.00
Bowl, Florals, Pomegranates, C.1820, Blue & Red, 4 X 9 In.Diam.	275.00
Bowl, Melon Shaped, Panel With Scenes, Scalloped Edge, 9 1/4 X 4 In.	145.00
Bowl, Scalloped Edge, 10 In.	165.00
Bowl, Scalloped, Blue, Red, Gold, Scene, 19 Century, 5 1/2 In.	110.00
Bowl, Square Center-Design Panels, Diaper Ground, Blue, 15 In.	250.00
Bowl, 8 1/2 In.	70.00
Charger, Allover Pattern, 14 1/2 In.Diam.	380.00
Charger, Bird & Flower Design, Multicolor, 14 1/2 In.	310.00
Charger, Bird & Garden Scenes, Scalloped Border, 10 In.	75.00
Charger, Blue & White, C.1830, 15 In.	325.00
Charger, Blue & White, Chrysanthemum, Scrolls, Marked, 12 In.	150.00
Charger, Blue & White, Floral, Bluebirds, 12 In.	165.00
Charger, Blue & White, 18 In.	295.00
Charger, C.1865, Blue & White, 14 In.	450.00
Charger, Circular Flower Medallion, Shaped Panels, 17 7/8 In.	300.00
Charger, Eagle, Scenic Ground, C.1850, Blue & White, 18 1/2 In.	495.00
Charger, Flower Panels, Green, C.1880, 14 In.	165.00
Charger, Gold Trim, Blue & White, 16 In.	200.00

Charger, Molded Carp Rising From Waves, Prunus Blossoms, 24 1/2 In. 440.00
Charger, Multicolored Blossoms, 14 In. 325.00
Charger, Panels Of Birds & Garden Scenes, Scalloped, 10 In. 70.00
Charger, Scalloped, Basket Of Flowers Center, 12 In. 165.00
Charger, Six Panels, 14 In. 295.00
Cup & Saucer, Demitasse, Maddock Majestic 10.00
Dish, Fish Shape, Blue & White, Scale Details, C.1860, 10 In. 190.00
Jar, Ginger, Original Wooden Lid 150.00
Jar, Temple, Blues, Oranges, C.1840, 21 In. 1100.00
Jardiniere, Floral, Rust & Cobalt, 19th Century, 6 1/2 X 6 1/8 In. 200.00
Plate, Blue & Red Alternating Panels, 8 In. 50.00
Plate, Blue & Red Panels, 8 1/4 In. 50.00
Plate, Blue, White, Scene, C.1900, 8 1/2 In. 195.00
Plate, Butterflies, Blue Medallion Center, Set Of 4 .... 200.00
Plate, Carp Against Mt.Fuji, Meiji Period, 14 In. 950.00
Plate, Cellular Brocade Design, Center Medallion, 7 In. 50.00
Plate, Cellular Brocade Pattern, Kylin Medallion, 8 In. 50.00
Plate, Diamond-Shaped, Folding Fan In Crest, Birds, Floral, 11 In., Pr. 650.00
Plate, Medallion Of Riverscape, Floral Medallion Rim, 14 7/8 In., Pair 880.00
Plate, Peacocks Center, Gold Flecks, 12 In. 150.00
Plate, Scalloped, O Naga Doni Bird, Blue, 19th Century, 9 1/2 In., Pair 110.00
Plate, 3-Paneled, 10 In. 80.00
Platter, Diamond-Shaped, Floral Border, Rust, Blue, Yellow, 9 In. 100.00
Platter, Flower Design, Oval, Multicolor, 13 1/2 X 10 1/2 In. 260.00
Platter, Scalloped Edge, Oval, 12 X 15 In. 275.00
Urn, Temple, 18 In. 1250.00
Vase, Flared Lip, Ovoid Ribbed Body, Rust Color, 18th Century 90.00
Vase, Scenes, C.1850, 12 In. 600.00

*Imperial Glass Corporation was founded in Bellaire, Ohio, in 1901.
It became a division of Lenox, Inc., in 1977 and was sold to Arthur
R. Lorch in 1981. It was sold again in 1982.*

IMPERIAL, Bookend, Eagle 75.00
Bowl, Hat Shaped, Orange, 11 In. 35.00
Candlewick, Cake Plate 69.00
Candlewick, Candleholder 12.50
Candlewick, Plate, 8 In. 35.00
Candlewick, Relish, Round, 2-Part 12.50
Candlewick, Saltshaker 9.50
Candlewick, Sugar 9.50
Candlewick, Sugar & Creamer 20.00
Candlewick, Sugar & Creamer, Tray, 22K Gold Trimmed 30.00
Cape Cod, Candlestick, 5 1/2 In., Pair 15.00
Cape Cod, Sherbet 5.00
Cape Cod, Wine 5.00
Colonial, Goblet, Marked, 8 Ounce 8.00
Coreopsis, Sugar, Ruby & Clear 60.00
Daisy & Button With V Ornament, Spooner 42.50
Dragon, Candleholder, Figural, Frosted, Pair 325.00
Dragon, Candleholder, Frosted, Signed Virginia B.Evans, 1960s, Pair 325.00
Figurine, Swan, 4 1/2 In. 15.00
Freehand, Vase, Amber Over Gray, 12 In. 125.00
Freehand, Vase, Yellow, White Pull-Ups, Orange Interior, 11 In. 185.00
Jewel, Vase, Amber, Marked, 5 In. 75.00
Jewel, Vase, Amethyst, Signed, 6 In. 75.00
Stretch, Vase, Old German Cross Mark, Signed 60.00
Tradition, Wine, Blue 7.00

*Indian Tree is a china pattern that was popular during the last half of
the nineteenth century. It was copied from earlier patterns of English
china that were very similar. The pattern includes the crooked branch of a*

*tree and a partial landscape with exotic flowers and leaves. It is colored
green, blue, pink, and orange.*

INDIAN TREE, Cake Stand	21.00
Cup & Saucer, Burslem	20.00
Cup & Saucer, Demitasse, Fluted	22.00
Cup & Saucer, Johnson Bros.	20.00
Dish, Soap, 3 Piece	35.00
Gravy Boat, Brownfield & Son, C.1856	62.00
Pitcher, Gold Trim, Bulbous, 8 1/4 In.	25.00
Plate, Burslem, 10 1/2 In.	20.00
Plate, Johnson Bros., 10 1/2 In.	20.00
Plate, 10 In.	7.00
Platter, Vegetable, Oval, 10 In.	35.00

*Indian art from North America has attracted the collector for many years.
Each tribe has its own distinctive designs and techniques. Baskets, jewelry,
and leatherwork are of greatest collector interest.*

INDIAN, Armband, Fully Beaded, Germantown, Pair	225.00
Ashtray, Santa Clara, Effigy Of A Bird, 7 In.	38.00
Bag, Bird & Flower Design, Beaded, Buckskin, Fringed	195.00
Bag, Cornhusk, Nez Perce, Geometric Design, 18 X 13 In.	325.00
Bag, Fetish, For Umbilical Cord, Beaded	125.00
Basket, Black Triangle Border, Cylindrical, 3 In.	50.00
Basket, Brown Animals, 4 Red Bands, Covered, Round, 4 X 2 1/2 In.	200.00
Basket, C.1900, 18 X 10 In.	55.00
Basket, Canadian, Splint & Sweetgrass, Covered, 9 X 3 In.	15.00
Basket, Coil, Red, 11 In.	60.00
Basket, Coiled Straw, Arrowhead Pattern, 3 Colors, 11 X 4 1/4 In.	45.00
Basket, Coiled Straw, Red, Green, & Lavender Dyes, 11 3/4 X 2 1/4 In.	35.00
Basket, Horsehair, 3/4 In.	14.00
Basket, Hupa, Geometric Design, 7 1/4 In.	220.00
Basket, Maine, Hat-Shaped, Top Comes Off, C.1940, Brim 6 3/4 In.	25.00
Basket, Moose, Bear, & Bird Design, Birchbark, 11 In.	40.00
Basket, Northeast, Curlicue Waist, Top 9 1/2 X 4 1/2 In.	35.00
Basket, Northeast, Natural & Red Splinting, C.1890	85.00
Basket, Northeast, Storage, Loop Side Handled, Plaited, 13 1/2 In.	25.00
Basket, Northeast, Sweetgrass & Green Dyed Splint, Handle, 9 1/2 In.	65.00
Basket, Northwest, Loops & Curlicues, Bentwood Handle, 12 In.	60.00
Basket, Papago, Horsehair, 3/4 In.Diam.	13.50
Basket, Passamaquoddy, Sewing, Splint & Sweet Grass, 9 X 4 3/4 In.	45.00
Basket, Passamaquoddy, Shopping, Blue & Beige Splint, C.1940, 9 In.	60.00
Basket, Penobscot, Curlicue, Wrapped Rim, 7 3/4 In.Rim	25.00
Basket, Penobscot, Storage, Red Dye, Bentwood Handle, Top 10 1/2 In.	30.00
Basket, Sewing, Wide & Narrow Splint, Curlicue Trim, 5 In.	35.00
Basket, Sewing, Wide & Narrow Splints, Green, 12 In.Top Diam.	27.50
Basket, Splint, Curly Design At Rim & Sides, Square, 8 1/2 In.	30.00
Basket, Storage, Round Top, Square Bottom, C.1870, Opening 9 3/4 In.	22.50
Basket, Vermont, Natural, Green, & Orange, Marked 1914, 5 X 3 In.	35.00
Basket, Woodland, Splint, Blue & Orange, 11 1/2 In.	95.00
Basket, Work, Curlicue, Sweet Grass Cover, 2-Tier	45.00
Basket, Yei Figures, Flared, C.1900, 8 X 4 In.	150.00
Basket, Yurok, Step Design, C.1910, 10 X 7 In.	345.00
Belt, Ceremonial, Beaded Red, Green, Blue, & Yellow, 1/4 X 30 In.	150.00
Belt, Sioux, Horsehair	125.00
Belt, Woven Horsehair, Germantown	100.00
Belt, 12 Plain & 4 Stamped Conchos, Plains, C.1925, German Silver	650.00
Blanket, Chief, 3rd Phase, C.1880, Saxony Red, Black, & Tan, 72 X 57 In.	4500.00
Blanket, Figural, Soldiers & Ducks, Double-Faced, 60 X 102 In.	450.00
Bowl, Dragon Design All Around, Signed Susana, 7 X 4 1/2 In.	175.00
Bracelet, Turquoise, Thunderbird Arrowheads	35.00
Burial Pot, Mississippi Culture, Ribbed, 5 X 5 In.	200.00
Button, Zuni, Pottery	15.00
Cradle Board, Ponca, Cloth & Leather, Beads & Shells, 30 X 14 In.	240.00

Cradle Board, Walapai, Reed With Cloth, C.1920 .... 200.00
Doll Cradle, Splint, Painted, Pine Rockers, C.1830, 6 X 8 X 16 In. 275.00
Doll, Baby, Real Hair, 8 In. 25.00
Doll, Cat, Cherokee, Calico, 5 X 11 In. 95.00
Doll, Doeskin, Beaded Dress & Moccasins, Braided Hair, 12 1/2 In. 100.00
Doll, Navajo, Corn Grinding, 5 X 4 In. 12.00
Doll, Squaw, Papoose, Black Hat, Turquoise Skirt, Beads, Mini, 2 In. 10.00
Figurines, Chief & Squaw Kissing, Magnetized, 5 In. 15.00
Frame, Beaded, Germantown 20.00
Frame, Splint & Sweet Grass, Braided Loops, C.1940, 3 1/2 X 3 3/4 In. 22.50
Jar, Fire & Snake Design, Signed Maria & Santana, 5 1/2 In. 2000.00
Jar, Wedding, Acoma, 1930s, 7 In. 40.00
Jug, Wedding, Seneca-Cayuga, 2-Neck, Pottery 75.00
Mace, Livingston County, Ky., Sandstone, 5 X 21 In. 725.00
Moccasins, Arapaho, Child's, Beaded 25.00
Moccasins, Fully Beaded, Germantown 150.00
Moccasins, Sioux, Beaded, High Tops 250.00
Moccasins, Sioux, Chief's, Beaded 125.00
Napkin Ring, Northeast, Birch, Sweet Grass Edge, 2 In., Set Of 6 .... 10.00
Necklace, Navajo, Squash Blossom, 17 Stones, Sterling, Marked 600.00
Pendant, Etched Both Sides, Tennessee, Slate, 7 X 8 3/4 In. 250.00
Pillbox, Silver, Coral Stone On Cover, 1 X 1 1/2 In. 25.00
Pincushion, Beadwork, Inscribed & Dated 1856 .... 45.00
Pipe, Council, Kankakee, Illinois, Gray Granite, 4 X 3 X 11 In. 1250.00
Pot, Cochiti, 1920s, 9 In. 120.00
Pot, Theresa Wild Flower, Miniature, 1 1/4 In. 75.00
Pottery, Jemez Pueblo, 1 X 1 1/2 X 3 In. 6.50
Pouch, Beaded, Leather, C.1920, 6 In. 45.00
Rope, Woven Horsehair, 25 In. 140.00
Rug, Navajo, Butterfly Design, 1930, Red, Gray, & Natural, 32 X 57 In. 135.00
Rug, Navajo, Double-Faced Twill, Geometric Pattern, 30 X 50 In. 195.00
Rug, Navajo, Red, Black, Gray, & White, 50 X 60 In. 750.00
Rug, Navajo, Storm Pattern, Red, White, Black, C.1940, 5 X 3 Ft. 125.00
Rug, Navajo, Two Gray Hills, 1930s, 37 X 56 In. 365.00
Rug, Navajo, 3 Ft. 8 In. X 7 Ft. 2 In. 210.00
Rug, New Mexico, Chief's Pattern, Hand Woven, 5 1/2 Ft.Long 600.00
Rug, New Mexico, Whirling Thunder Design, C.1915, 5 Ft. 5 In.Long 600.00
Rug, Rio Grande, 4 Ft. X 2 Ft. 6 In. 125.00
Sheath, Knife, Sioux, Beadwork 75.00
Tom-Tom, Iroquois, Original Sheepskin Head 140.00
Trade Silver, 4 Different Pieces 325.00
Vase, Signed Lula Yound, Black On Red, 8 In. 65.00
Vase, Wedding, Bear Paw Design, 8 In. 90.00
Vest, Plains, Rawhide, C.1900 .... 155.00
Vest, Sioux, Beaded, Leather 650.00
Whistle, Bone 10.00

INKSTAND, Arch Of Triumph, Art Deco, French 35.00
Victorian, 19th Century, Brass 55.00

INKWELL, see also Brass, Inkwell; Pewter, Inkwell; and various
Porcelain categories
INKWELL, Bear Head, Wearing Blue Cap, Red Collar, Metal, 4 In. 45.00
Blown, Paperweight Base, Mushroom Stopper, 4 In. 75.00
Blown, 3-Mold, Hinged Lid, Blue Opaque 55.00
Bow, Polychrome, Boy Feeding Baby Chicks, C.1785 .... 250.00
Brass & Glass, Pen Holder At Back, Hinged Glass Well 35.00
Brass, Double Dome Lids, Glass Insert, 8 X 3 1/2 In. 110.00
Bronze, Horses & Nymphs, Italian, C.1800 .... 525.00
Bronze, Nude Woman Lid, Red Marble, French, 4 1/2 X 5 1/4 In. 195.00
Cat Head, Hinged, Glass Eyes, Wooden, 4 1/2 In. 39.50
Clear, Pressed, Reservoir, Mixing Ball, W.E.Lewis Mfg., 1892, 4 1/4 In. 20.00
Cone Shaped, Pottery, Paneled, Sides, Mark Josiah Jonson, 2 1/4 In. 80.00
Cut Glass, Amber Cube, Hinged Lid, 2 1/4 In. 110.00

Cut Glass, Melon Shaped, Hinged Sterling Top, 5 In. 185.00
Figural, Skirted Lady Holding Key, Head Lifts, Bronze, 7 In. 225.00
Hard Rubber Pen Dip Device, 1894 .... 25.00
Lady Seated On Barge, French, Porcelain, 12 In. 135.00
Phrenology, F.Bridges 350.00
Sengbusch Self-Closing, Patent 1904 .... 25.00
Serpents, Woman's Heads, Art Nouveau 300.00
Stag Head, Brass Antlers Beside Well 65.00
    INKWELL, TIFFANY, see Tiffany, Inkwell
Traveling, Screw Top Lignum Vitae Cylinder, Blown Glass Liner 22.00
Turtle, Signed J.& I.E.M., Clear 40.00
White Enameled Flowers, Sapphire Blue 110.00

*Insulators of glass or pottery have been made for use on telegraph or
telephone poles since 1844.*

INSULATOR, Armstrong, Clear 1.00
Bell Telephone Co., Dated 1893, Aqua 3.00
Bell Telephone Co., Dated 1893, Green 3.00
Brookfield Telephone, Aqua, 3 In. .... .50
Electric Connector, Blue Porcelain 1.00
Hemingray, No.21, Green 1.50
Hemingray, No.42, Green 1.50
Hemingray, Plain, Green 1.00
Lapp, 1928, Telephone, 4 In. 2.00
Whitall Tatum, No.1, Green 2.50
Whitall Tatum, No.2, Purple 10.00
Whitall Tatum, No.9, Clear 1.50
    IRISH BELLEEK, see Belleek

    IRON, see also Kitchen; Tool; Store
IRON, Agitator, Breaking Up Sugar In Barrel, Wooden Handle, 14 1/2 In. 50.00
Anvil, Oil Field, Large 275.00
Ashtray, Bowlers, C.1890 .... 32.00
Bolt, Slide, Rectangular Backplate, Ellipse At End, 11 3/4 In. 120.00
Bookend, Clipper Ship, 5 1/4 X 5 1/2 In., Pair 10.00
Bookend, Empty Saddles, Signed Verona, Pair 20.00
Bookend, Horse, Rearing, With Wings, 4 X 4 In., Pair 28.00
Bookend, Indian Warrior On Horse, Maxfield Parrish, 3 3/4 X 4 In., Pair 20.00
Bookend, Liberty Bell, Pair 18.00
Bookend, Lincoln Profile, 4 3/4 In., Pair 14.00
Bookend, Mayflower, Pair 15.00
Bookend, Ship, Marked Victory A.Galleon, 18th Century, Pair 15.00
Bookrest, Adjustable Rests, Zigzag Design, 19th Century, 25 In.Long 110.00
Bookstand, Revolving, Victorian 475.00
Boot Scraper, Double Scroll & Curled Top, 18th Century, 8 1/2 In. 60.00
Boot Scraper, Fastening Holes, 6 1/2 X 1 1/4 In. 10.00
Boot Scraper, Witch 60.00
Bootjack, Lacy Words, Try It 65.00
Bootjack, Musselman's Plug Tobacco 125.00
Bootjack, Naughty Nellie, Original Paint 75.00
Bowl, Footed, Red & Black Paint, 6 X 4 In. 20.00
Bracket, Window Shelf, Screwless & Removable, 1899, Pair 8.50
Bust, Gladiator, 9 In. 39.00
Candlesnuffer, Scissor Shaped, Footed, C.1800 .... 50.00
Card Holder, Figural, Black Servant, Dressed In Tuxedo 350.00
Card Holder, Figural, Moor 1450.00
Coal Carrier, Handle, 8 X 14 In. 15.00
Compote, Fruit, Lacy Pedestal, Hexagonal, C.1860, 6 X 7 In. 65.00
Crescent, Outhouse 25.50
Crown, Meat, Ring Supporting 4 Hooks, 18th Century, 14 In. 225.00
Crucifix, Applied Design, 37 In. 150.00
Curling, Marcel Wave, Handle, Iron 12.00
Dish, Leaf, Bronzed Finish, 5 Grape & Leaf Vine, 10 In. 49.00
Door Handle, Long Points, Oval Plates, 17 In. 210.00

Door Knocker, Amish Couple, Animated Eyes 20.00
Door Knocker, Flower Basket .... 20.00 To 30.00
Door Knocker, Flowers 18.00
Door Knocker, Hand & Ball, Black, 6 1/4 In. 25.00
Door Knocker, Inside, Parrot, Original Paint 25.00
Door Knocker, Lady's Hand Clutching Ball, 4 In. 57.00
Door Knocker, Parrot, Original Paint 35.00
Door Knocker, Woodpecker 35.00
Figurine, Eagle, Case 2500.00
Figurine, Michelin Man, 1920's, 14 In. 2000.00
Figurine, Stable Boy, Bareheaded, Hitching Post, 36 In. 550.00
Figurine, Stable Boy, Black, Ragged Trousers, Polychrome, 49 In. 1045.00
Flatiron, Dover No.62 .... 25.00
Fluting Iron, Flat Base, Wooden Handle, Heat Slug 35.00
Fluting Iron, Hinged, 1 Piece 50.00
Fly Box, Stamped Simpson Iron Co. 79.00
Fork, Butchering, Hand-Forged, Handle 15.00
Fork, Curved Hanging Hook, 20 1/2 In. 25.00
Fork, Eye Hanger, Tooled Initials, 23 1/2 In. 35.00
Fork, Meat, Ribbed Handle, Hanging Hook, 32 1/2 In. 350.00
Fork, Turned Walnut Handle, 16 1/2 In. 45.00
Fork, Twisted Handle, Rattail End, 18th Century, 16 1/2 In. 100.00
Fork, 2-Tined, Punched Handle, 29 In. 225.00
Frog, Garland Stove, Strike Match On Mouth 75.00
Furnace, The Williamson Heating Co., Salesman's Sample 850.00
Gate Sculpture, Father Neptune, Red Paint, C.1860, 11 X 16 In. 295.00
Girandoles, Mirrored, Etched, Scroll Base, 15 In. 600.00
Griddle, Flat Disc, Curving Support, Hanging Ring, 20 In. 180.00
Griddle, Hanging, Curved Arm, Flat Plate, 16 3/4 In. 200.00
Griddle, Hanging, Swivel Hook, 13 In. 49.00
Griddle, With Rim, Hanging, 18th Century, 16 In. 175.00
Handcuff, American Handcuff Co., Pair 20.00
Hinge, Double "C" Curve, Snake Head Tip, 18th Century, Pair 118.00
Hitching Post, Broom, 1960, 56 In. 225.00
Hitching Post, Horse Head With Ring, C.1860 .... 140.00
Holder, Pipe, Naughty Woman 35.00
Hook, Beam, Hand-Forged, 5 In. 10.00
Hook, Spikes, Wall Insertion, Designed Crests, 6 In., Pair 55.00
Horse's Head, Carousel, Inscribed Bonnie Bright Eyes 300.00
Horseshoe, Says Good Luck, Biggs & Koch K.C. Hides 35.00
Jockey Boy, With Stand, 36 In. 295.00
Kettle, Camp, 2 Ears, Bail Handle, Tripod Base, 11 In. 55.00
Kettle, Gooseneck, Bail Handle, 4 In. 300.00
Kettle, Gypsy, 11 1/4 X 10 In. 20.00
Kettle, Open, Bail Handle, 5 1/4 In. 100.00
Kettle, Raised Bands, Double Ears, Bail Handle, 6 In. 110.00
Kettle, Tilting, Cylindrical Body, Gooseneck Spout, 8 In. 200.00
Kettle, Tilting, Gooseneck Spout, Cylindrical Body, Covered, 9 In. 775.00
Kettle, Twisted Bail Handle, 6 1/4 In. 275.00
Ladle, Deep Bowl, Long Handled, 44 In. 600.00
Ladle, Deep Bowl, Rattail Handle, 15 In. 140.00
Ladle, Hooked Handle, 2 Quart 50.00
Ladle, Marked Lasayre & Son, Newark, 17 In. 15.00
Ladle, Primitive, 14 3/4 In. 25.00
Ladle, Straining Bowl, Well-Shaped Handle, 18 In. 25.00
Ladle, Wooden Handle, 15 1/2 In. 20.00
Lamp, Kerosene, Brass Font, Signed Venus 45.00
Latch, Spear Ends, 18th Century, 18 1/2 In. 310.00
Leg Irons, American Munitions Co., Pair 50.00
Mailbox, Griswold 72.50
    IRON, MATCH HOLDER, see Match Holder
Matchbox, Self-Closing, Dated 1864, 2 X 3 1/4 In. 28.50
Measure, Cooper's, 7 1/2 In. 17.50

Mortar & Pestle, Bell	90.00
Mortar & Pestle, Flared Rim, 6 3/4 X 6 3/4 In.	35.00
Nippers, Sugar, 9 In.	45.00
Nut Grinder, Tin, Climax	35.00
Padlock, Embossed Navy, Nickel Plated	20.00
Padlock, Prison, Large	15.50
Pail, Jailer's, Late 1800s, Covered	50.00
Pan, Fry, Cylindrical, 3 Legs, Rattail Handle, 9 In.	325.00
Paper Clip, Indian Head	75.00
Planter, Embossed Flowers, Vines, & Scrolls, French, 19 X 8 1/2 In.	125.00
Porringer, Reticulated Handle, Marked W.Bullock & Co., Half Pint	130.00
Rack, Utensil, Handing, Scrollwork, 5 Hooks, 16 In.	105.00
Sadiron, Child's Size, Snap-On Cover, 1900	25.00
Sadiron, Child's, Asbestos, Dated May 23, 1900, 2 Piece	37.50
Sadiron, Child's, Removable Wooden Handle	45.00
Sadiron, Colebrook, Wooden Handle, Maltese Cross Trivet, Pair	40.00
Sadiron, Enterprise, Wooden Handle, E Trivet	40.00
Sadiron, Williams, Wooden Handle, 4 Irons	30.00
Sconce, Scroll Back, Double Candle Arm, Pair, 17 In.	110.00
Seat, Tractor, Champion	40.00
Seat, Tractor, Hoosier Implement	45.00
Shelf, Kettle, Cabriole Legs, Reticulated Top, 11 1/4 In.	65.00
Spittoon, Porcelain Cover	30.00
Spittoon, White Enamel Trim	25.00
Stand, Kettle, Trifid Base, Penny Feet, 13 In.	150.00
Toaster, Flattened Handle, Loop, Curved Holder, 4 Footed	120.00
Toaster, Ram's Horn Handle, 18th Century, 17 In.	300.00
Tongs, Pipe, America, 18th Century, 17 1/2 In.	850.00
Tongs, Pipe, Curved Handle, Fleur-De-Lis Springs, 14 In.	550.00
Tongs, Pipe, Curvilinear Handgrip, 18th Century, 19 In.	475.00
Tongs, Pipe, England, 18th Century, 15 1/4 In., Pair	300.00
Trammel, Chain, Adjustable, 18th Century, 32 In.	30.00
Trammel, Chain, 38 In.	50.00
Trammel, Chain, 56 In.	80.00
Trammel, Saw Tooth, Adjustable Crane, Fleur-De-Lis Top	140.00
Trammel, Wrought, With Wood, American, 18th Century, 38 1/2 In.	100.00
Trammel, 18th Century, 34 In.	75.00
Urn, Garden, Mid-19th Century, Large	200.00
Utensil, Copper Blade Has Holes, 23 1/2 In.	55.00
Wheel, Measuring, 8 In.	40.00
Windmill Weight, Bull	350.00
Windmill Weight, Horse	165.00 To 300.00
Windmill Weight, Horse, Mounted In Wooden Block, 16 X 17 In.	350.00
Windmill Weight, Horse, Numbered 58G	245.00
Windmill Weight, Rooster, 19 1/2 In.	395.00

Ironstone china was first made in 1813. It gained its greatest popularity during the mid-nineteenth century. The heavy, durable, off-white pottery was made in white or was decorated with any of hundreds of patterns. Much flow blue pottery was made of ironstone. Some of the decorations were raised.

IRONSTONE, see also Chelsea Grape; Gaudy Ironstone; Moss Rose; Staffordshire; Wedgwood

IRONSTONE, Bone Dish, Blue & White, Jersey Pattern	20.00
Bone Dish, Eggplant Shape, Marked J.Edwards	30.00
Bowl & Plate, White, Oval	15.00
Butter Chip	8.00
Coffee Urn, Stand, Red Cliff	50.00
Coffeepot, Spring Pattern, Furnival & Sons	45.00
Coffeepot, Wood & Sons, White With Cobalt Blue	55.00
Cup & Saucer, Centennial 1876	90.00
Dish, Soap, Embossed, 2 3/4 X 2 7/8 In.	12.00
Ewer, Hope & Carter	130.00
Ewer, Scalloped Decagon, J.Wedgwood	130.00

Jug, Hot Water, Pewter Lid, Blue Floral, 12 In. 155.00
Ladle, Stalk Handle, 10 In. 45.00
Ladle, White, 11 In. 24.00
Pitcher & Bowl, Wheeling Pottery, White 75.00
Pitcher, Alfred Meakin, 12 1/2 In. 75.00
Pitcher, Mellor & Co., 8 In. 20.00
Pitcher, Milk, Chinese Shaped, Booth, 8 1/4 In. 55.00
Pitcher, Milk, Shell Embossed, Mellor Taylor 64.00
Pitcher, Water, J.G.Meakin, 10 In. 35.00
Pitcher, Water, Sheaf Of Wheat, Baker Bros. 65.00
Pitcher, Windmill & Bush, Blue & White 100.00
Pitcher, 8-Paneled, Vista Pattern, Blue Transfer, Mason, 7 In. 60.00
Planter, Wheat & Clover, 18 In. 45.00
Plate, Baltimore Dairy Lunch, Cow's Head Center, 7 In. 14.00
Plate, Blue, Orange, Pink, 7 3/4 In., Pair 16.50
Plate, Corn & Oats, Wedgwood, 7 In. 12.00
Plate, Gothic Type, Adams, 9 1/2 In. 17.00
Plate, Imari Colors, Mason, 10 1/4 In. 125.00
Platter, Blue, Orange, Pink, Floral Design, 17 In. 275.00
Platter, Grape Design, Adams, 18 In. 27.00
Platter, Sprig Pattern, Grindley & Co., 10 X 14 In. 30.00
Platter, Vienna, 16 In. 16.00
Platter, White Leaf Design, Marked, 15 In. 12.00
Platter, White, Gold Trim, Flowers In Center 65.00
Relish, Lily Of The Valley 38.00
Shaving Mug, Lily Of The Valley 41.00
Sugar & Creamer, Ming Tree 17.50
Sugar, Covered, Alfred Meakin 35.00
Syrup, Decorated, Victorian, 1879 .... 125.00
Syrup, White 37.50
        IRONSTONE, TEA LEAF, see Tea Leaf Ironstone
Tea Set, Child's, Handleless Cups, 14 Piece 95.00
Tea Set, Child's, 1851, Bud Knob, 6 Cups & Saucers 95.00
Tea Set, Miniature, 15 Pieces 25.00
Tile, Grape Design 8.00
Tureen, Blue & White, Covered, C, 1825, 14 In. 385.00
Tureen, Covered, 10 In. 50.00
Tureen, Sydenham Tulip Pattern, T.& R.Boote, England, Large 450.00
Tureen, Vegetable, Covered, White, Pedestal, Handled, Mark 75.00
Tureen, Vegetable, Handles, Covered, Marked, 6 1/2 X 10 1/2 In. 40.00
Vase, Brush, Hawthorn 57.00

        IVORY, see also Napkin Ring; Netsuke
IVORY, **Ball,** Mystery, One Ball Inside Another, Elephants Hold Ball On Trunk 75.00
Ball, Mystery, 6 Layer, 1 Inside Another, 3 Elephants Hold Ball 80.00
Beads, Graduating Sizes, Ivory Clasp, American, 24 In. .... 37.50 To 100.00
Bottle, Snuff, Sages & Attendants In Garden, Stopper 110.00
Box, Bust Of Young Woman In Profile, 2 1/2 In. 135.00
Box, Sugar, Oval, Medallion & Fernery, Hinged, 3 X 4 In. 125.00
Bracelet, Group Of Skulls 90.00
Brushpot, Ovoid Form, Fixed Ring Handles, 5 3/4 In. 475.00
Bust, Lady Wearing Bonnet, Victorian, 4 1/4 In. 450.00
Candlestick, Figure, C.1920, 7 1/2 In., Pair 225.00
Case, Card, Carved Scene, 3 Horses, Trees, & Barn, C.1880, French 300.00
Case, Card, Figures, Trees, Pagodas, 19th Century 175.00
Cricket Cage, Gourd Shape, Pierced Cover 195.00
Doctor's Lady, Lying, Movable Ivory Bracelet, 4 In. $ 70.00 To 85.00
Doctor's Lady, Reclining On Wooden Couch, 4 In.Long 75.00
Doctor's Lady, Reclining, 6 In. 150.00
Elephant Tusk, 2 X 23 In. 175.00
Figurine, Bird, Cardinal, 3 3/4 In. 90.00
Figurine, Boy, Sitting On Tree Stump Holding Frog 150.00
Figurine, Chinnan & Dragon, Fierce Expression, Dragon Over His Head 110.00

Ivory, Figurine, Lord On Throne, Chinese, 19th Century, 10 In.

Ivory, Tankard, Continental, Mid-19th Century, Covered *(See Page 316)*

Figurine, Clam Seller, Holding Fan & Clams, 10 1/4 In.	250.00
Figurine, Cupid, Kneeling, 2 1/2 In.	150.00
Figurine, Dancer, Polychrome, 14 In.	950.00
Figurine, Devil Man, 5 1/2 In.	390.00
Figurine, Dragon Stick Man, Boy, & Stork, 8 In.	360.00
Figurine, Eagle With Snake, 7 In.	325.00
Figurine, Elephant, Beak Base, Small	26.00
Figurine, Elephant, Mounted On Rosewood, 17 In.	225.00
Figurine, Elephant, 1 1/4 In.	12.00
Figurine, Fisherman & Fisherwoman, Holding Bamboo Rods, 6 In., Pair	235.00
Figurine, Fisherman, Holding Basket, Bamboo Rod In Hand, 11 3/8 In.	660.00
Figurine, Foo Dog, Sitting, Head To Rear, 1 3/4 X 3/4 X 1 1/2 In.	75.00
Figurine, Geisha, 2 1/2 In.	135.00
Figurine, Hotei, Seated, Holding Fan In Left Hand, Corpulent Stomach	110.00
Figurine, Hotei, Smiling Expression, Holding Sack Over Back	85.00
Figurine, King & Queen, 11 In.	430.00
Figurine, Kwan Yin, 10 1/2 In.	375.00
Figurine, Longevity, Boy Riding Deer, 12 In.	450.00
Figurine, Lord On Throne, Chinese, 19th Century, 10 In. *Illus*	300.00
Figurine, Man Holding Matchlock Gun, 19th Century, Signed, 10 In.	575.00
Figurine, Man Sitting Over Lying Tiger, Polychrome, 2 1/4 In.	95.00
Figurine, Nine Elephants, Mounted On Rosewood, 17 In.Long	225.00
Figurine, Old Man With Boy, 10 In.	300.00
Figurine, Old Man With Flower Basket, 14 In.	320.00 To 376.00
Figurine, Old Man With Lotus Flower, 11 In.	220.00
Figurine, Old Man, Boy Holding Goose, 10 1/2 In.	285.00
Figurine, Sage, Chinese, Metal Base, 7 1/2 In.	70.00
Figurine, Seated Wise Man, Holds Fan & Scroll, 5 In.	160.00
Figurine, Sennin, Holding Hat Over Shoulder Formed From Frond	80.00

Figurine, Sennin, Holding Peach & Basket Of Flowers, Leaf Robe 415.00
Figurine, Sennin, Seated On Rock, Gourds Over Shoulders 330.00
Figurine, Warrior Fighting Dragon, Pearl In Hand, 2 1/4 In. 110.00
Figurine, Wise Man With Staff, Lady With Flowers, 12 In., Pair 485.00
Holder, Cigarette, Shape Of Eagle's Claw 20.00
Letter Opener & Pen Set, Holder Gold Metal, Egyptian, 9 1/8 In. 75.00
Mask, Fierce Expression, Stylized, Black Pigments 85.00
Pagoda, With People In Garden, Teak Stand, 13 1/2 In.Wide 1050.00
Plaque, Head, African, C.1920, 6 In. 175.00
Portrait, Karl II Of Brunswick, Curly Wig, Rondel, 1 7/8 In. 90.00
Portrait, Mustachioed Gentleman, 12K Gold Frame, 3 1/4 In. 100.00
Portrait, Princess Sophia, Duchess De Bourbon, C.1830, 1 3/4 In. 250.00
Salt & Pepper, Carved, Pair 65.00
Shoehorn, Signed Tiffany & Co., Union Square 125.00
Skull, Human, Spring-Attached Movable Jaw, 2 In. 185.00
Spoon, Opium, Shovel End, 3 3/4 In. 12.50
Stretcher, Glove 10.00
Tankard, Continental, Mid-19th Century, Covered .... *Illus* 4250.00
Thimble, Needle, Spool, & Scissors 15.00
Triptych, Gothic Style, Crucifixion, 18th Century, 7 In. 170.00
Tusk, Rosewood Stand, Carved, 38 In. 1875.00
Tusk, Warriors, Women, Children, Climbing Mountain, 18 In. 875.00
Vase, 2 Women, Child, Deer, Woods, Greek Key Rim, C.1900, 5 In. 300.00

JACK ARMSTRONG, Airplane, P-40 Model, In Envelope 29.00
Book, Mystery Eye, 1936 .... 8.00
Flashlight, Bullet 15.00
Flashlight, Red Torpedo 10.00
Flashlight, Whirling Disc Gun, Book 38.00
Hike-O-Meter, Blue 14.00
Mile-O-Meter, Wheaties 15.00
Telescope, Explorer 22.50

Jack-In-The-Pulpit vases were named for their odd trumpetlike shape that resembles the wild plant called jack-in-the-pulpit. The design originated in the late Victorian years.

JACK-IN-THE-PULPIT, Epergne, Clear, 17 In. 195.00
Vase, Enameled Flowers, Green, 16 In. 65.00
Vase, Gilt-Dusted Pink Ruffle, Clear, 10 1/2 In. 42.00
Vase, Gold Enameled Flowers, Electric Blue, 6 In. 30.00
Vase, Pink Ruffle, Pale Green, 8 In. 47.00
Vase, Purple Ruffle, White Bristol, 7 In. 47.00

Jackfield ware was originally a black glazed pottery made in Jackfield, England, from 1750 to 1775. A yellow glazed ware has also been called Jackfield ware. Most of the pieces referred to as Jackfield are black pieces made during the Victorian era.

JACKFIELD, Bowl, Tea, Saucer, Black Glazed, Flowers, C.1750, 4 1/2 In. 400.00
Dish, Condiment, Heart Shape, Black Glaze, C.1790, 4 1/2 In. 400.00
Dish, Cover Hen, Black, Gold, 7 1/2 In. 75.00
Figurine, Dog, Spaniel, Pair, Black 425.00
Jug, Milk, Glossy Black, Paw Feet, Silver Shape, 4 3/4 In. 400.00
Jug, Milk, Pear Shape, Mask & Paw Feet, Bird Design, 6 In. 550.00
Teapot, Deep Black, Domed Cover, Knob Finial, Ovoid, 5 In. 200.00
Teapot, Globular Form, Brown, Birds, Insects, Flowers, 4 In. 650.00
Teapot, Globular Form, Mask & Claw Feet, Applied Vines, 5 In. 500.00

JADE, Bowl, Spotted Apple Green, Teak Stand 125.00
Box, Cigarette, Carved, Hinged Lid, 4 X 3 In. 95.00
Burner, Incense, Elephant Heads, Rings, 6 In. 150.00
Figurine, Chrysanthemum, Wood Stand 190.00

Japanese Coralene is a ceramic decorated with small raised beads and dots. It was first made in the nineteenth century. Later wares made to imitate coralene had dots of enamel.

JAPANESE CORALENE, Vase, Flowers, Leaves, Blue, Orange, 10 In.	140.00
Vase, Seaweed Design, 8 In.	100.00

Jasperware is a fine-grained pottery developed by Josiah Wedgwood in 1755. The jasper was made in many colors including the most famous, a light blue. It is still being made.

JASPERWARE, see also various art potteries; Wedgwood

JASPERWARE, Figurine, 2 Boys Fighting	85.00
Plaque, Couples, Scrolls, 5 1/2 In.	35.00

JEWELRY, Bar Pin, Art Deco, Cloisonne Look, Blue & Peach, Brass Frame, C.1920	18.00
Bar Pin, Art Nouveau, Rose On Scroll, 1940s, Sterling, 2 1/4 In.	22.00
Bar Pin, Ball Pendant, Embedded Rhinestones, 1940s, 2 1/4 In.	7.00
Bar Pin, Filigree, Aquamarine & 2 Oriental Pearls, Platinum, French	275.00
Bar Pin, Horse's Head & Horseshoe, 14K Gold, 1 5/8 In.	52.00
Bar Pin, Latticed, Large Citrine, Catch	48.00
Bar Pin, Square-Cut Amethyst, 14K Gold	50.00
Bar Pin, Studded With 5 Diamonds, Filigree White Gold, 2 3/4 In.	600.00
Bar Pin, Victorian, Faceted Siberian Amethyst Center, English	115.00
Beads, Black Jet & Crystal	20.00
Bracelet, Amber Bakelite, 1/2 In.Wide	10.00
Bracelet, Art Deco, Block, Alternating Diamonds & Sapphires, 18K	1175.00
Bracelet, Art Deco, Carved Carnelians, Yellow Gold, Flexible	600.00
Bracelet, Art Deco, Oval & Ribbed Link, 14K Gold	90.00
Bracelet, Black Enamel, Egyptian Scenes, 1950s	20.00
Bracelet, Charm, Medallions & Gothic Crosses, Imitation Stones	6.00
Bracelet, Diamond & Pearl, Graduated Sections, Late 19th Century	2800.00
Bracelet, Elastic Mesh, Covered With Brass Buttons, 1930s	30.00
Bracelet, Gold Filled, S Link Design, 7 In.	20.00
Bracelet, Ivory Carved In Deco Lines, Bakelite, 1/2 In.Wide	12.00
Bracelet, Olive Green Carved In Deco Lines, Bakelite, 3/8 In.Wide	10.00
Bracelet, Shaded Agate Bakelite, Carved Deco Lines, 3/8 In.Wide	10.00
Bracelet, Single Strand Rhinestones, Cotton Ribbon, 13 In.	17.00
Bracelet, Sterling Silver Twisted Into Letter B, C.1920	20.00
Bracelet, Sterling Silver, Twisted Into Letter A, C.1920	20.00
Bracelet, Sterling, Marcasite, Floral	85.00
Bracelet, Victorian, Gold & Onyx, C.1880, Pair	775.00
Bracelet, 3 Carved Citrine Cameos, Flexible	750.00
Bracelet, 3 Center Diamonds, Flexible Bezels, Platinum Mounting	1500.00
Brooch & Earrings, Flower Form, Baguette & Round Diamonds	4400.00
Brooch, Abstract Sheath Design, 7 Emeralds, Gold	*Illus* 250.00
Brooch, Amber Faceted Stone, Brass Filigree Edge, 1920s, 1 3/4 In.	24.00
Brooch, Art Deco, Blue China Center, Hawk On Side, C.1925, 2 3/4 In.	100.00
Brooch, Cameo, Sardonyx, 19th Century	*Illus* 325.00
Brooch, Carved Flowers On Filigree Ground, Celluloid, 2 3/4 In.	26.00
Brooch, Carved Flowers, Gray & Blue, Celluloid, 2 X 2 1/4 In.	20.00
Brooch, Colored Plastic Stones, Brass Flower, 1 X 3 In.	9.00
Brooch, Crescent Moon, 23 Garnets, 3 Enameled Flowers, 18K Gold	202.00
Brooch, Crown Shape, 5 Large Diamonds, 71 Small Diamonds, C.1900	3025.00
Brooch, Mosaic Cherub, C.1860	*Illus* 250.00
Brooch, Parrot, Set With Diamonds & Rubies, 14K Gold	*Illus* 800.00
Brooch, Scarab Bezel Center, Scrolled & Engraved, 1 In.	225.00
Brooch, Topaz In Gold Rim, 1930s, 1 1/4 In.	35.00
Brooch, 3 Pearl-Centered Flowers, 7 Rubies In Each, 18K Gold	325.00
Brooch, 6 Diamonds Set As Bouquet, Platinum	1700.00
Brooch, 7 Leaves, Gold, 1920s, 1 X 2 In.	7.50
Buckle & Tie Clip, Monogram, Sterling Silver, Swank, Case	35.00
Buckle, Art Deco, Fake Cut Steel Beads, Gray Metal, 3 1/2 In.	10.00

(See Page 759)

Jewelry: *top row, from left to right:* Brooch, Parrot, Set With Diamonds and Rubies, 14K Gold; Brooch, Abstract Sheath Design, 7 Emeralds, Gold. *Bottom row, from left to right:* Necklace, Pearl, Jade & Onyx, Single Strand, 20 1/2 In.; Watch, Merano, Lady's, 30 Diamonds & Rubies Trim, 14K Gold; Watch, Omega, Lady's, Geometric Face, 14K Gold On Sterling; Pendant, Oriental Cat Design, Blue Enamel On Silver; Necklace, Green Beads, Interspersed Coins, Mid-Eastern

(See Page 317)

Jewelry, Brooches, Cameo, Sardonyx, 19th Century;
Mosaic Cherub, C.1860

Buckle, Shoe, Twisted Leaf, Brass Color, 1 X 2 1/2 In.	6.00
Cape Pin, Comet Shape, Embedded Rhinestones, Apex Art Nouveau Co.	30.00
Case, Cigarette, Ribbed Design, Tiffany & Co., 14K Yellow Gold	600.00
Chain, Diamond, 12 Collet Set, 18K Gold Curb Link, 14 1/2 In.	855.00
Chain, Rope, 14K Gold, 26 In.	145.00
Charm, Bull, Emerald Eyes, Ring In Nose Holds Bell, 1950s, 2 1/2 In.	10.00
Charm, Donkey, Big Ears, Onyx, 1 1/4 X 3/4 In.	9.00
Choker, Diamond & Seed Pearl, Center Yellow Sapphire, Platinum	3400.00
Choker, Faceted Black Glass Beads, Seed Bead Separators	20.00
Choker, Iridescent Blue Rhinestones, 5 Flowers, 14 In.	12.00
Clip, Art Deco Flower, Metal Encased, Celluloid, Pin Back, 2 1/4 In.	12.00
Clip, Dress, Deco, Pave Rhinestones & Cobalt Baguettes, 2 1/8 In.	10.00
Clip, Dress, Triangular Shape, Art Deco, Bakelite	8.00
Cross, Raised Center, Garnets & White Sapphires, 14K Gold, 2 In.	82.00
Cross, Small Diamond, Hollow, 14K Gold	20.00
Cuff Links, Art Deco, Black Enamel & Silver Metal Squares, C.1930	15.00
Earrings, Art Deco, Mirror-Back Stone, Silver Metal	12.50
Earrings, Art Nouveau Flower, Leaves, Gold Filled On Silver, 3 In.	25.00

Earrings, Cameo, Victorian, Carnelian Ground, 14K Gold, Oval 310.00
Earrings, Faceted Black Glass, Button Shape, 1930s, Screw Back 6.00
Earrings, Filigree Over Disc, Silver Button Type, 1930s 10.00
Earrings, Frosted Spatter Glass Dangles, Clip & Screw Back 4.00
Earrings, Hoop, Wires, 14K Gold 80.00
Earrings, Millefiori-Type Flowers, White China, 1950s, Clip 4.00
Earrings, Pear & Baguette Rhinestones, Screw Back, 1 1/4 In. 7.00
Earrings, Plastic Flowers, Green Leaves, 1950s, Screw Back 4.00
Earrings, Red Plastic Triangles In Silver Square, 1950s 6.00
Earrings, Square-Cut Garnets, White Sapphire, Flower Top, 18K Gold 185.00
Earrings, 3 Intertwined Circles, Gold Design, Spain, 1950s, Clip Back 5.00
Earrings, 3 Sapphires At End Of Gold Bars, Screw Back, 3/4 In. 15.00
Earrings, 10 MM. Pearl, Marvella, Clip & Screw Back 2.00
Hatpin, Victorian, Brass, Blue Enameled, Flower, 6 In. 20.00
Hatpin, Victorian, Ruby Glass Ball, 5 1/2 In. 5.00
      JEWELRY, INDIAN, see Indian
Jewelry, Pin, Rhinestone-Studded Crescent, 1950s, 2 In. 7.50
Locket, Center Diamond In Sunburst, Monogram On Back, 14K Gold 175.00
Locket, Double, Photograph Of Lincoln & Jefferson, C.1860 .... 150.00
Locket, Engraved Bail & Beveled Glass, English, C.1860 .... 140.00
Locket, Pocket Watch Shape, Daguerreotype Portrait, 1850s 95.00
Locket, Rose Diamond In Starburst Center, Monogrammed, 14K Gold 150.00
Necklace, Art Deco Blue China Beads, Scarabs, Engraved, Gold, 36 In. 30.00
Necklace, Baltic Amber, 24 In. 85.00
Necklace, Black China Beads, Dimpled, 1950s, 56 In. 20.00
Necklace, Cut Amber, European, 29 In. 150.00
Necklace, Embossed Brass Links, Flowers, 1940s, 16 In. 30.00
Necklace, Emerald Center, 6 Seed Pearls, 14K Gold, 17 In. 395.00
Necklace, Faceted Black Glass Beads, Marked Germany, 15 In. 17.00
Necklace, Faceted Crystal Beads, Black Disc Separators, 1920s 45.00
Necklace, Fake Pearls, Knot Between Each Bead, 1950s 15.00
Necklace, Flapper, Colored Glass Beads, Shimmies As Spacers, 42 In. 25.00
Necklace, Gold & Diamond, French Etruscan Revival Gold 6900.00
Necklace, Green Beads, Interspersed Coins, Mid-Eastern .... *Illus* 40.00
Necklace, Opal & Diamond, Stylized Leaves, 18K Gold, Fitted Box 7150.00
Necklace, Pearl, Jade, & Onyx, Single Strand, 20 1/2 In. .... *Illus* 35.00
Necklace, Pendant Drop, 3-Strand, Dangling, 21 In. 25.00
Necklace, Scrolling Mounts, Rose-Cut Diamonds, 19th Century, Gold 400.00
Necklace, Single Strand, 115 Natural Pearls, Platinum Clasp 4125.00
Necklace, Victorian, 2-Strand, Tassle, Engraved Leaves, 9K Gold 290.00
Necklace, 1-Inch Solid Links, Applied Beads, Copper, 1950s, 18 In. 23.00
Necklace, 3-Strand Diamond-Cut Bar Link, 18K Gold, 26 In. 475.00
Necklace, 18K Gold, Carved Emerald Beads, Chinese 3000.00
Pendant, Cameo, White Gold Filigree Frame, 14K Gold 290.00
Pendant, Carved Tourmaline, C.1750, Chinese 2000.00
Pendant, Chinese Goddess, Clouds, Ivory, Carved Front & Back, 2 In. 95.00
Pendant, Christ Head, 14K Gold, 7/8 In. 31.00
Pendant, Concave, 24K Gold, Tiffany & Co. 160.00
Pendant, Cultured Pearl, Small Diamond & Pearl Drop, 14K Gold 35.00
Pendant, Devil's Head, Ruby Eyes, 14K Gold 39.00
Pendant, Free-Form Flower, Turquoise Glass Center, Chain, 11 In. 20.00
Pendant, Frog, Diamond Eyes, 14K Gold 75.00
Pendant, Heart, Florentine, 15K Gold 40.00
Pendant, Moonstone, Hanging Freshwater Pearl, C.1860, Chain 250.00
Pendant, Oriental Cat Design, Blue Enamel On Silver .... *Illus* 25.00
Pendant, Peridot & Seed Pearl, Barrel Clasp, Chain, English, C.1860 .... 325.00
Pendant, Seed & Cultured Pearl Drop, 14K Gold 85.00
Pendant, Square-Cut Sapphire Center, Diamond At Top, 14K Gold 410.00
Pendant, Star Burst Shape, 12 Diamonds, Clustered Pearls, 14K Gold 160.00
Pendant, Woven Hair, Cross Form, 2 X 2 1/4 In. 20.00
Pendant, 4-Section, Center Diamond, Black & White Enamel, Topaz 289.00
Pendant, 4-Section, Garnets, 14K Gold, 5 1/4 In. 140.00
Pendant, 4-Section, Teardrop With Diamonds, 14K Gold 113.00
Pendant, 5-Section, Tourmalines, 2 Diamonds, 14K Gold, 2 1/8 In. 200.00

Pin, Art Deco, Diamond Shape, Rhinestone Initials HDL 20.00
Pin, Art Deco, Enamel On Gold, Embossed Band, 1 X 2 3/4 In. 35.00
Pin, Art Deco, Faceted Mirror-Back Blue Stone, Silver Metal 20.00
Pin, Art Nouveau Lines, Filigree Sterling, Monogram 25.00
Pin, Art Nouveau, Bird Of Paradise, Enameled, Reds, Blues, 5 1/4 In. 65.00
Pin, Art Nouveau, Cutout Flower, Leaves, Danecraft, 2 3/8 In. 40.00
Pin, Art Nouveau, Flower & Leaves, 1950s, 1 1/2 X 3 1/2 In. 6.00
Pin, Art Nouveau, Flying Bird In Wishbone, Sterling, 3/8 X 7/8 In. 28.00
Pin, Bar, Center Cabochon Lapis, Encircled By 18 Diamonds, Gold 275.00
Pin, Bird In Flight, Marked GJ, 1920s, Sterling Silver 20.00
Pin, Black Glass Baguettes, Round Rhinestones, 3/4 X 2 In. 10.00
Pin, Bulldog, Gold, Ruby Eyes, 3/4 In. 400.00
Pin, Butterfly, Imitation Marcasites, 1940s, 1 X 3/4 In. 10.00
Pin, Camel, Filigree, Leda & Swan, 4 Sapphires, 1 7/8 In. 600.00
Pin, Cameo, Octagonal Shape, 10K Gold, 1 1/2 In. 135.00
Pin, Carved Mother-Of-Pearl, Man On Water Buffalo, 1 X 1 1/4 In. 12.50
Pin, Cockatiel, Long Tail, Marked Guatemala, 1940s, 1/2 X 2 1/2 In. 10.00
Pin, Copper Flower, Green Glass Stone Center, 1950s, 2 1/8 In. 10.00
Pin, Diana, Unger Bros., Sterling Silver, 1 1/2 In. 85.00
Pin, Dragon, Gold, Pearl, Ruby, & Diamond, 1 1/4 In. 750.00
Pin, Embossed Brass Bow & Streamers, Blue Glass Stone, C.1930 .... 20.00
Pin, Embossed Brass Filigree, Center Topaz, 1920s, 1/2 X 1 In. 22.50
Pin, Filigree Fan, Rhinestones In Center, 1930s, 1 3/4 In. 17.50
Pin, Five Petal Flower, Rose Stone, Sterling Craft By Coro, 1930s 30.00
Pin, Gold Bowl, Ruby Suspended On Gold Chain, 1950s, 1 In. 10.00
Pin, Gold Wreath Design, Seed Pearls, 10K Yellow Gold 30.00
Pin, Gold, Birds, Victorian, Pearl & Diamond, 1 3/4 In. 900.00
Pin, Grand Piano, White Enamel, 1930s, 1/2 X 1 In. 18.00
Pin, Hammered Copper, 2 Brass Circles, C.1925, 1 X 2 1/2 In. 10.00
Pin, Metal Sword, Pave Rhinestone Plume, 1920s, 3 1/4 In. 20.00
Pin, Mexican Figure, Native Costume, Sterling, 1925, 1 1/2 In. 25.00
Pin, Mother-Of-Pearl, 4 Carved Pineapples Overlapped, 2 In. 10.00
Pin, Mother, Gold Wire On Mother-Of-Pearl Leaf 15.00
Pin, Red Lamb, Painted Eyes, Celluloid, 1930s, 1 1/2 X 3/4 In. 8.00
Pin, Rhinestone Flowers, Triangular Shape 14.00
Pin, Silver Cameo On Coral Plastic, Brass Frame, C.1920, 1 1/4 In. 25.00
Pin, Tigereye, Scalloped Openwork, 1 1/2 In. 15.00
Pin, Victorian, Seed Pearls, Floral, 10K Yellow Gold, 3/4 In. 41.00
Pin, 2 Oak Leaves Form Circle, Sterling Silver, 1 1/2 X 1 1/4 In. 10.00
Pin, 3 Interlocked Rings, Ball In Center, 1930s, 1 3/4 X 2 1/4 In. 26.00
Ring, Art Deco, Center Pearl, Ringed By Rose Diamonds, 18K Gold 145.00
Ring, Art Deco, Cluster Of 7 Burmese Rubies, 14K Gold 395.00
Ring, Blue Enamel, Surrounded By 22 Rose-Cut Diamonds, 18K Gold 395.00
Ring, Calibrated Sapphires, Rose Diamonds, C.1920, 8-Sided 285.00
Ring, Cameo, Yellow Gold Setting, Coral Stone 120.00
Ring, Center Diamond, Caliber Emeralds, C.1930, Platinum Mount 1500.00
Ring, Cluster, Victorian, 14K Gold, Sapphires & Seed Pearls 115.00
Ring, Cluster, 18K Gold, 7 Rose Diamonds, C.1880 .... 130.00
Ring, Collet Set Ruby, Large Diamond, 6 Small Diamonds, Platinum 1100.00
Ring, Crescent Moon & Clover, Bohemian Garnets, 14K Gold 175.00
Ring, Dark Garnet, Old European, 18K, Yellow Gold 117.00
Ring, Diamond Solitaire, 6 Shoulder Diamonds, C.1930, Platinum 1500.00
Ring, Dome-Shaped Marcasite 65.00
Ring, Engagement, 14K Yellow Gold, Round Cut Diamond, .25 Carat 125.00
Ring, Heart Shape, Diamond Inset, 10K Yellow Gold 45.00
Ring, Heart, Cluster 5 Diamonds & Rubies, 14K 90.00
Ring, Human Hair Woven, Victorian, Grape Cluster Look 12.50
Ring, Link Design, 14K Antique Gold, 7/16 In. Wide Band 71.00
Ring, Man's, World War I Insignia, Sterling Silver 35.00
Ring, Man's, 18K Gold, Star Sapphire & Diamond 400.00
Ring, Mizpah, Victorian, Dated 1884, 9K Gold 80.00
Ring, Oval Aquamarine Diamond Each Side, Filigree, 14K Gold 240.00
Ring, Pearl, 14K Gold, 1 Pearl, 4 X 4 3/4 Mm. 50.00

Ring, Persian Turquoise, Art Nouveau Mounting, 14K Gold 140.00
Ring, Sapphire & Diamond, C.1915, Platinum Mount 1500.00
Ring, Wedding, Rope & Ribbon, Pearl Center, 14K, Yellow Gold 97.00
Ring, 2 Diamonds, European Cut, 22 Small Diamonds, Platinum 2700.00
Ring, 5 Pearls, 4 Mm., 14K Gold 100.00
Safety Pin, Bar Of 8 Rose-Cut Diamonds, Ruby Center, C.1900 .... 185.00
Stickpin, Brass-Framed Orange & Gold Stone 10.00
Stickpin, Cameo, Woman's Face, 15K Gold, Coral 210.00
Stickpin, Cameo, 14K Gold 45.00
Stickpin, Framed Brown Aventurine Stone, Brass Frame, 3 In. 12.50
Stickpin, Freshwater Pearls, Rose Diamond Drop, 14K Yellow Gold 45.00
Stickpin, Gold Calla Lily, With Pearl Center 35.00
Stickpin, Gold-Filled Knot, 3 In. 6.50
Stickpin, Oval, Gold-Colored, Engraved Crossbar, 3 In. 5.00
Stickpin, Wishbone With Pearl, 10K 28.00
Stickpin, Zodiac, Silver Plated, Half Moon, Arrow, 3 In. 6.50
Stickpin, 2-Petal Flower, Cultured Pearl, 14K Gold, 9/16 In.Diam. 26.00
Tie Bar, Applied Horse Head, Georg Jensen 30.00
Tie Clip, Black & White Stripes In Glass, Imitation Marcasites 12.00
Tie Tack, Lady's Hand Holding White Sapphire, 14K Gold, 7/8 In. 25.00
JEWELRY, WATCH, see Watch
Watch Chain, Man's, Crossbar, Double Twist Textured 32.00
Watch Chain, Rose Gold, C.1890, 16 In. 650.00
Watch Chain, 15K Gold, 5 Diamonds, 18 In. 195.00

*John Rogers statues were made from 1859 to 1892. The originals were
bronze, but the thousands of copies made by the Rogers factory were of
painted plaster. Eighty different figures were made.*

JOHN ROGERS, Group, Bath, C.1870, 27 In. 2100.00
Group, Council Of War, C.1868, 24 In. .... 500.00 To 1000.00
Group, Courtship In Sleepy Hollow, C.1868, 16 1/2 In. 850.00
Group, One More Shot, C.1865, 23 1/2 In. 450.00
Group, Parting Promise, C.1878, 22 In. 425.00
Group, School Days, C.1877, 21 1/2 In. 700.00

*Jugtown pottery refers to pottery made in North Carolina as far back as
the 1750s. In 1915 Juliana and Jacques Busbee set up a training and
sales organization for what they named Jugtown Pottery. In 1921 they
built a shop at Jugtown, North Carolina, and hired Ben Owen as a
potter in 1923. The Busbees moved the Village Store where the pottery
was sold and promoted to 37 East 60th Street in New York City.
Juliana Busbee sold the New York store in 1926 and moved into a log
cabin near the Jugtown Pottery. The pottery closed in 1958. It reopened
and is still working.*

JUGTOWN, Candlestick, High-Glaze Orange 45.00
Jug, Cattails, Flower In Cobalt Blue, 1 Gallon 135.00
Jug, Mustard, Handled 48.00
Teapot, Green, 5 1/2 In. 65.00
Vase, Chinese Glaze, Squatty, Blue & Wine, 4 In. 95.00
Vase, Flambe, Chinese Styling, Blue & Wine, Glazed, 3 3/4 In. 125.00

*Kate Greenaway, who was a famous illustrator of children's books, drew
pictures of children in high-waisted Empire dresses. She lived from 1846
to 1901. Her designs appear on china, glass, and other pieces.*

KATE GREENAWAY, Book, Alphabet 55.00
Book, Child's, Illustrated 15.00
Bride's Basket, Girl With Dog, Silver Plated 90.00
Cover, Ironing Board, Embroidered 25.00
Mug, Silver Plated, Rogers Bros. 22.00
Plate, Children Playing With Fruit, Birds, 9 In. 95.00
Plate, Silver, Glass Cruet In Holder 75.00

Salt & Pepper, Silver Plated Top 32.00
Saltshaker, Bonnet, Hands In Pockets, Gold Trim, 4 1/2 In. 60.00
Tea Set, Child's 150.00
Toothpick, 3 Girls With Muffs, Sitting On Rim, Bisque 55.00

> *Kauffmann refers to the type of work done by Angelica Kauffmann, a*
> *painter and decorative artist for Adam Brothers in England between 1766*
> *and 1781. She designed small-scale pictorial subjects in the neoclassic*
> *manner. Most porcelains signed "Kauffmann" were made in the 1800s.*

KAUFFMANN, Bowl, Beehive, Signed, 2 X 10 In. 135.00
  Box, Classical Scene, 2 3/4 In. 55.00
  Celery, Portrait, Burgundy Scalloped Rim, Beehive Mark, 14 In. 75.00
  Plate, Imperial Russian, Gold Trim, 10 In., Pair 150.00
  Toothpick, Garden Scene, Hand-Painted, 3 Maidens, Signed 150.00
    KAYSERZINN, see Pewter

KELVA   *Kelva glassware was made by the C.F.Monroe Company of Meriden,*
Connecticut, about 1904. It is a pale pastel painted glass decorated with
flowers, designs, or scenes.

KELVA, Box, Apple Blossoms, Pink, 2 1/4 X 2 1/2 In. 195.00
  Box, Blown-Out Rose, Hexagonal, Pink & Red 350.00
  Box, Blue, Pink Flowers, Lined, Marked, 4 1/2 In. 350.00
  Box, Dark Green, Pink & White Flowers, Lined, Signed, 8 In. 775.00
  Box, Jewel, Enameled Flowers, Silver Trim, Lined, Signed, 8 In. 725.00
  Dish, Blue Ground, Pink & White Roses, Open, 6 1/2 In. 115.00
  Dish, Pin, Blue 150.00
  Dish, Pin, Green, Pink Flowers, Ormolu Trim & Handles 165.00
  Jar, Tobacco, Cranberry, Floral, White Beads, Silver, Signed, 5 X 4 In. 395.00
  Salt & Pepper, Dark Green Speckled Ground, Floral, Signed 125.00
  Salt & Pepper, Mottled Green, Pink Flowers, Signed 225.00
  Vase, Green, Pink, Silver Plated, Ormolu Feet, Marked, 14 In. 475.00

> *Kemple glass was made by John Kemple of East Palestine, Ohio, and*
> *Kenova, West Virginia, from 1945 to 1970. The glass was made from old*
> *molds. Many designs and colors were made. Kemple pieces are usually*
> *marked with a K on the bottom.*

KEMPLE, Toothpick, Indian Head, White, 3 1/2 In. 15.00

> *Kenton Hills Pottery was founded in 1937 in Erlanger, Kentucky.*
> *In 1945 all molds were destroyed and the factory was closed.*

KENTON HILLS, Lamp, Bear-Shaped, Lotus Design, Signed, 12 1/2 X 6 In. 385.00
  Lamp, Vase, Lotus, Peach & Beige, Hentschel, 12 1/2 X 6 In. 250.00

> *Kew Blas is the name used by the Union Glass Company of Somerville,*
> *Massachusetts. The name refers to an iridescent golden glass made from the*
> *1890s to 1924.*

KEW BLAS, Pitcher, Gold & Green Feathering, 4 1/8 In. ....*Illus* 650.00

Kew Blas, Pitcher, Gold & Green Feathering, 4 1/8 In.

Vase, Allover Pulled Feather On Gold, Signed, 7 1/2 In. 425.00
Vase, Opal Ground Top, Gold Feather Design, Signed, 5 In. 375.00

Kewpies were first pictured in the "Ladies' Home Journal" by Rose O'Neill. The pixielike figures were a success, and Kewpie dolls started appearing in 1911. Kewpie pictures and other items soon followed.

KEWPIE, Bell, Figural, Brass .... 29.00 To 39.00
  Box, Confection, Black, 2 Kewpies, 1 Pushing Other On Swing, 6 In. 45.00
  Box, Soap, Kewpie In Washbasin, Marked Rose O'Neill, 1917 .... 17.50 To 20.00
  Charm, Ivory Like, Rose O'Neill 100.00
  Clock, Blue & White, Dome, Marked 275.00
  Clock, Blue, Jasperware, Marked, 6 In. 600.00
  Cookbook, Jell-O 25.00
  Creamer, Green & White, Jasperware, 7 Kewpies, Marked .... 175.00 To 189.00
  Doll, Bisque, Label, 10 1/2 In. 375.00
  Doll, Bisque, Movable Arms, Heart Sticker 185.00
  Doll, Black, Celluloid, Paper Label, 3 In. .... 50.00 To 60.00
  Doll, Blue Wings, Stamped Rose O'Neill, Red Label, 6 In. 155.00
  Doll, Cameo, Jointed, Boxed 65.00
  Doll, Celluloid, Occupied Japan, 3 In. .... 6.50 To 15.00
  Doll, Celluloid, Rose O'Neill, Sticker, 4 In. 40.00
  Doll, Civil War Soldier, With Vase & Flowers, Bisque, 6 In. 450.00
  Doll, Cloth Body, Composition Head, 17 In. 150.00
  Doll, Cuddle, 20 In. 55.00
  Doll, Cutie, 3 1/2 In. 12.00
  Doll, Farmer, Bisque 65.00
  Doll, Jointed Arms & Legs, Bisque, Paper Label, 5 In. 575.00
  Doll, Jointed Arms, Bisque, 2 1/4 In. 7.50
  Doll, Jointed Arms, Black, Vinyl, 4 1/2 In. 2.00
  Doll, Painted, Chalk Hands, Signed Rose O'Neill Kewpie, Germany 12.00
  Doll, Pin-Jointed, Original Sunsuit 150.00
  Doll, Rubber, Head Turns, Black 15.00
  Doll, Scootles, Bisque, Fat Roly Poly Dimpled Legs, 5 In. 12.00
  Doll, Scootles, Composition, Baby Body, 5 Piece, Rose O'Neill, 13 In. 85.00
  Doll, Thinker, Oily Bisque, Rose O'Neill, 4 In. 350.00
  Doll, Thinker, Rose O'Neill, Signed, 4 In. 235.00
  Doll, Traveler, Bisque, Signed, 3 1/2 In. 235.00
  Doll, Wedding Cake, Bisque, Bride & Groom, 3 In. 145.00
  Doll, Wedding Cake, Bride & Groom, Celluloid, C.1920, 2 1/2 In. 40.00
  Doodle Doggie, Bisque, 2 1/2 In. 6.00
  Figurine, Kewpie With Flower, Bisque, Seated, 1 3/4 In. 240.00
  Flannel, C.1914, Signed .... 12.00 To 30.00
  Hair Receiver, Jasperware, Action Kewpies, Signed Rose O'Neill 250.00
  Hatpin Holder, Blue Jasperware, 3 White Kewpies, Signed Rose O'Neill ... 325.00
  Hugger, Rose O'Neill, Sticker, Japan, 3 1/2 In. 195.00
  Mug, 3 3/8 In. 135.00
  Napkin, Paper, Canned Foods, Flesh Tones, White Ground, 13 In. 15.00
  Plate, Royal Rudolstadt, Signed Rose O'Neill, 9 Action, 7 3/4 In. 100.00
  Plate, 8 Action Kewpies, Marked Rose O'Neill, 9 1/2 In. 175.00
  Postcard, Canceled 1918, Gibson 25.00
  Print, Chemist With Vials, Microscope, Signed Rose O'Neill 45.00
  Salt & Pepper, Silver Plated Holder, Signed, 3 In. 90.00
  Soap, Marked, Boxed, 4 3/4 In. 200.00
  Sweeping, Signed, 3 1/2 In. 175.00
  Thimble, Marked 35.00
  Tin, Candy 19.00
  Tin, Talcum 65.00
  Whistle, Figural, Brass 18.50
      KIMBALL, see Cluthra
      KING'S ROSE, see Soft Paste

      KITCHEN, see also Iron; Store; Tool; Wooden
KITCHEN, Baker, Potato, Tin, C.1909 .... 23.00

Basket, Egg, Wire	15.00
Basket, Massillon Wire Basket Co., Ohio, Red Bottom, 11 1/2 In.	48.00
Bean Slicer & Pea Huller, Vaughan's, Table Clamp, Wooden Handle	35.00
Beater, Carpet, Wireware, Maple Handle	18.50
Beater, Rug, Wireware, Batwing Shape, Wooden Handle, C.1927	22.50
Beater, Rug, Wooden Handle	12.00
Blender, Dough, Red Wooden Handle, Diamond Mark	3.00
Blender, Pastry, Ardalt, Green Handle	6.00
Board, Cutting, Arched Top, Hanging Hole, 19th Century, 29 X 8 In.	38.00
Board, Cutting, Attached Handle, Oak, Wall Hung	12.50
Board, Cutting, Bird's-Eye Maple, 7 3/4 X 14 In.	30.00
Board, Cutting, Pig Shape, Wooden, 11 1/2 In.	4.00
Board, Cutting, Pig Shape, 15 1/2 X 7 1/2 In.	15.00 To 22.00
Board, Cutting, Pig Shape, 6 X 11 In.	40.00
Board, Cutting, Pine, Wall Hung, 18 X 20 In.	15.00
Board, Cutting, Slate, Circular Form, Arrow-Shaped Handle, 17 In.	500.00
Board, Ironing, Sleeve, Wooden, Pine, 21 X 6 In.	10.00
Board, Scrub, Hand-Carved Corrugation, 19th Century, 1 Piece	230.00
Board, Springerle, Man, Goat, Child, Mother, Horse, Applewood, 8 In.	135.00
Board, Wash, Pine, 11 X 24 In.	65.00
Book, Recipe, Advertising, Mazola Salad Bowl Picture, 1939	8.00
Bottle, Hot Water, Rubber, Red Riding Hood, Dunlop	160.00
Bowl, Butter, Hand-Hewn, Oblong, 10 X 23 In.	55.00
Bowl, Cast Iron, 9 In.	48.00
Bowl, Wireware, Victorian, Folding, Germany, Footed, 7 X 4 In.	40.00
Box, Biscuit, Embossed H & P, Tin, 8 X 9 X 5 In.	13.00
Box, Cake, Japanning, Pinholed To Base, Tinware, C.1890, 13 X 10 In.	30.00
Box, Cheese, Draft, 1 Pound	10.00
Box, Cheese, Mel-O'bit	5.00
Box, Dough, Poplar, Blue, Red Trim On Lid, 12 X 10 In.	115.00
Box, Egg Carrying, Wire Bail, Wooden, Apple Green, 12 In.Square	75.00
Box, Knife, Open Lift Handle	30.00
Box, Pantry, Copper Nails, Wooden Pegs, Covered, Bentwood, 6 1/2 In.	30.00
Box, Pantry, Light Blue, Red Evergreens, Christmas Tree Design	140.00
Box, Pantry, Paper Lining, Wooden Pegs, Painted Gray, 8 X 3 1/2 In.	100.00
Box, Recipe, Oak, Tin Hinged, 3 X 5 In.	6.50
Box, Spice, Blue-Green Paint, Covered, Oval, 4 5/9 In.	250.00
Box, Spice, Bright Green, Copper Tacks, Covered, 4 5/8 In.	150.00
Box, Spice, Dark Blue, Single-Lap, Oval, Covered, 5 1/2 In.	240.00
Box, Spice, Gray-Blue, Round, Covered, 5 3/8 In., Pair	300.00
Box, Spice, Gray, Black Smoke Grained Design, 4 5/8 In.	180.00
Box, Spice, Green, Black Bands, Oval, Covered, 3 5/8 In.	300.00
Box, Spice, White, Copper Tacks, Oval, Covered, 6 1/4 In.	160.00
Box, Spice, 2 Shaped Fingers, Red, Initials B.C., 4 3/4 In.	150.00
Box, Spice, 8 Inner Canisters, Round Wooden Box	150.00
Bread Board, Carved Border & Word Bread, Maple, 9 1/2 In.Diam.	53.00
Bread Board, Carved, Round, Wooden	35.00
Bread Board, Cutout Handle, Round, 19 X 22 In.	85.00
Bread Board, Floral & Leaf Design, Word Bread Carved In, 11 In.	25.00
Bread Board, Give Us This Day Our Daily Bread, 11 In.	65.00
Bread Board, Hand-Carved Maple, Octagonal, Concentric Lines, C.1870	65.00
Bread Board, Handle, Hanging Hole, Pine, 30 X 8 In.	65.00
Bread Board, Hardwood, Girl In Fancy Dress On Side, 4 X 12 In.	275.00
Bread Board, Square Nails, Raised Sides	18.00
Bread Board, Wooden, Carved Word Bread	35.00
Broiler, Rotating, Fireplace, Iron, 3-Footed, 11 In.	150.00
Brush, Birch, Hearth, 20 1/2 In.	130.00
Brush, Bottle, Wooden Handle, 12 In.	2.00
Bucket, Berry, Copper, Tin Lining, 5 1/2 In.	40.00
Bucket, Sugar, Over & Under Bentwood Ring, 8 X 7 3/4 In.	35.00
Bucket, Sugar, Staved, Finger Bands, Red, 11 In.	75.00
KITCHEN, BUTTER MOLD, see Kitchen, Mold, Butter	
Butter Paddle, Palette, Rectangular, Walnut, 9 X 16 In.	75.00
Cabinet, Spice, 4-Drawer, Meyer Brothers	375.00

Cake Breaker, Green Celluloid Handle 6.00
Can Opener, Iron, 1892 .... 13.00
Can Opener, Peerless, Iron, 1890 .... 10.00
Can Opener, Ram's Head, Maple Handle, Iron, C.1880, 6 In. 50.00
Candy Thermometer, White, Wood Handle 12.00
Canister, Urn Finial, Barrel Shaped, Covered, 9 In. 400.00
Carpet Sweeper, Banner Logo 20.00
Carpet Sweeper, British, Wooden 45.00
Carrier, Butter, Wire Bail, Wooden Cover, Round, Blue 140.00
Carrier, Butter, Wooden Pinned Flat Bail, Covered 120.00
Carrier, Egg, Gardner, 1889, 2 Dozen 50.00
Cherry Pitter, Clamp-On, Enterprise 32.00
Cherry Pitter, Clamps, Iron, Rollman, Model No.3 .... 15.00
Cherry Pitter, Double, Table Mounted, Tin-Coated Iron, 3 3/4 Pounds 35.00
Cherry Pitter, Enterprise 16, Double 35.00
Cherry Pitter, Goodell, 1895, Iron 35.00
Cherry Pitter, Mechanical, Patent 1917 .... 34.00
Cherry Pitter, Mt.Joy 35.00
Cherry Pitter, New Britain 45.00
Cherry Pitter, Rollman Mfg. Co., Mechanical 34.00
Cherry Pitter, Rollman Mfg.Co., Clamp-On, Cast Iron 36.00
Chopper, Food, Advertising, C.F.Wiggen, Fine, Food Ware 20.00
Chopper, Food, Anchor Shaped, Iron, C.1860, 7 3/4 In. 45.00
Chopper, Food, Bentwood Handle, Hand-Forged Curved Blades 65.00
Chopper, Food, Blonde Oak Grip, Iron Blade, C.1840, 9 In. 65.00
Chopper, Food, Chunky Wooden Handle, Iron Blade, C.1860 .... 40.00
Chopper, Food, Country Kitchen, Wall Hung, Gray Tin Blade, C.1880 .... 12.50
Chopper, Food, Crescent Shape, Double, Iron Divider, C.1880 .... 8.50
Chopper, Food, Crescent-Bladed Rocker, 2-Handled, 10 In. 40.00
Chopper, Food, Curved Oak Handle, Iron Blade, C.1840, 8 In. 60.00
Chopper, Food, Dated 1898, Iron & Tin 13.00
Chopper, Food, Half Round, T-Shaped Wooden Handle, 6 In. 30.00
Chopper, Food, Hand, Closed Style, Wooden Handle, 8 In. 22.00
Chopper, Food, Hand, Marked Universal, T-Stem, Steel Blade 16.50
Chopper, Food, Hand, Wooden Handle, C.1830, 6 In. 45.00
Chopper, Food, Iron Handle & Grips 6.50
Chopper, Food, Iron Shank, Turned Handle, Signed Bingham, C.1880 .... 16.50
Chopper, Food, Maple Handle, Bulbous, Iron Blade, 9 In. 40.00
Chopper, Food, Maple Handle, Iron Blade, C.1860, 6 In .... 35.00 To 45.00
Chopper, Food, Moon Shape, Cathedral Arched, 3-Stemmed Shank, 4 In. .. 35.00
Chopper, Food, Oak Handle, Crescent Shape, Iron Blade, C.1840 .... 40.00
Chopper, Food, Signed Blade, Moon Shape, Wooden Handle 15.00
Chopper, Food, Wishbone Handle, Iron, Tin Blade, C.1880 .... 14.50
Chopper, Food, Wooden T-Handle, Iron, C.1880 .... 40.00
Chopper, Meat, Pail & Gears, Cast Iron 75.00
Churn, Butter, Barrel Shape, Wooden, Large 275.00
Churn, Butter, Barrel, Iron Bands, 12 X 48 In. 295.00
Churn, Butter, Glass, Square 35.00
Churn, Butter, Red Paint, 11 3/4 In. 650.00
Churn, Butter, Rolling Box, Iron Locking Bar, Crank, Pine, 3 Gallon 250.00
Churn, Butter, Stand, Oak Barrel, 3 Gallon 135.00
Churn, Butter, Table Model, Vermont 110.00
Churn, Butter, Tabletop Drum, 9 X 15 In. 65.00
Churn, Butter, Tin Dasher, Handles, Funnel Top, Slant Sides, 18 In. 250.00
Churn, Butter, Wood Staved Barrel, Old Blue Paint, C.1870, 10 Gallon 325.00
Churn, Butter, 2-Woman, Marked Ride-Out Lord, 1880, 21 X 13 In. 350.00
Churn, Cream, Footed Tin Cylinder, Wooden Crank Handle, 6 X 8 In. 85.00
Churn, Dazey, Glass, 1 Quart 45.00
Churn, Dazey, In Frame, Tin & Wooden, Dated 1912 .... 50.00
Churn, Dazey, 1922, 1 Gallon 45.00
Churn, Glass, Metal Paddles, Wooden Handle, 4 Quart 35.00
Churn, Stave Constructed, Iron Bands, 31 In. 150.00
Churn, Tabletop, Tin, Iron Works 38.00
Churn, Wapakoneta, Ohio, Bentwood, 4 Gallon, 1882 .... 240.00

Cleaver, Meat, Black Wooden Handle, Nickle On Brass, 1900 .... 10.00
Cleaver, Tenderizer Top, Wooden Handle 27.50
Clothes Sprinkler, Cat, Black & White, Blue Marble Eyes 12.50
Clothes Sprinkler, Dutch Girl 8.00
Clothes Sprinkler, Elephant 12.00
Clothes Sprinkler, Merry Maid Granny 8.00
      KITCHEN, COFFEE GRINDER, see Coffee Grinder
Coffee Mill, Electric, Aluminum, Hobart 150.00
Coffee Mill, Elna, Tin 45.00
Coffee Roaster, Handle, Iron, 2-Part, 1849-59, 9 In. 80.00
Coffee Server, Stopper, Wood Handle, Gladding-McBean, Turquoise 25.00
Colander, Gray, Tin, Side Handles, 9 3/4 In. 12.50
Cookware, Chuck Wagon, Ladle, Strainer, Oak Grip, Iron, 30 In. 25.00
Cookware, Chuck Wagon, Looped For Hearth, Iron, 14 In. 30.00
Corer & Slicer, Apple, Dandy, 1913 .... 9.00
Corer, Apple, Bone .... 6.00 To 8.00
Corer, Grapefruit, Builtrite 6.00
Corkscrew, Handled, Wood, Grape-Welch, Westview, New York 15.00
Corkscrew, Iron Harp Bottle Rest, Walnut Handle, Brass Grommet 22.50
Cover, Fly Screen, 6 In. 35.00
Creamer, Restaurant, Toddle House, Food You Enjoy, 2 Ounce 55.00
Crimper, Pie, Brass, Wooden Handle 18.00
Crimper, Pie, French, 1930s 5.00
Crimper, Pie, With Wheel, Steel Wire 6.00
Crimper, Pie, Wooden, Bone Shell, 5 In. 22.00
Cruet, Pair, Mepoco Ware, Pearlized, Cobalt Decor, 10 In. 48.00
Curd Breaker, Slant Side Hopper, Crank Handle, Wooden Roller, Teeth 150.00
Cutter, Biscuit-Doughnut, Red Applied Metal Handle 5.00
Cutter, Biscuit, Bisquick, Celluloid, Pair 10.00
Cutter, Biscuit, Concentric Lines To Handle, Tinware, 4 In. 55.00
Cutter, Biscuit, Handled, Tin, 2 In. 2.00
Cutter, Biscuit, Knob Handle, Maple, 3 3/4 In.Diam. 130.00
Cutter, Biscuit, Red Knob, 2 3/4 In. 3.50
Cutter, Bread, 20th Century, French, 26 X 17 1/2 X 9 In. 55.00
Cutter, Cabbage, Barrel Top, Oak Frame, Pine Center, C.1880 .... 165.00
Cutter, Cabbage, The Indianapolis Kraut Cutter, Dated 1905, 2 Piece 45.00
Cutter, Cabbage, 3 Blades, Maple, 26 In. 45.00
Cutter, Cabbage, 30 Degree Angled Blade, Wooden, Dorsay Mfg., 16 In. 22.50
Cutter, Cookie, Aluminum, Red Wooden Handle, Star Shaped 4.00
Cutter, Cookie, A1, Green Wooden Handle 5.00
Cutter, Cookie, Bird In Flight, Tin, C.1890, 1 X 3 In. .... 8.50 To 12.00
Cutter, Cookie, Bird, Perched, Tin 12.00
Cutter, Cookie, Bird, Standing, Tin, C.1930, 2 X 3 In. 10.00
Cutter, Cookie, Birds, Set Of 3 .... 26.00
Cutter, Cookie, Boy, Tin, 3 X 2 In. 6.50
Cutter, Cookie, Card Suits, Tin, Set Of 4 .... 22.00
Cutter, Cookie, Cat, Seated, Tin .... 15.00 To 22.00
Cutter, Cookie, Chick, Standing, Looking Skyward, Gray, Tin, C.1860 .... 14.00
Cutter, Cookie, Chick, Standing, 1930s, 2 1/2 X 2 1/2 In. 10.00
Cutter, Cookie, Chick, Tin .... 15.00 To 18.00
Cutter, Cookie, Circle, Tin, 4 In. 10.00
Cutter, Cookie, Club, Dark Gray, Tin, 3 X 3 In. 14.50
Cutter, Cookie, Club, Tin, 3 Graduated Sizes 14.00
Cutter, Cookie, Cow, Tin 18.00
Cutter, Cookie, Cresecent Moon, Tin, 1 3/4 X 2 1/2 In. 2.50
Cutter, Cookie, Diamond, Gray, Tin, Arch Handled, C.1880, 2 X 3 In. 12.50
Cutter, Cookie, Diamond, Tin 3.00
Cutter, Cookie, Dog, Running, Gray, Tin, 2 X 4 In. 22.50
Cutter, Cookie, Dog, Standing, Tin, C.1930s, 2 X 3 In. 10.00
Cutter, Cookie, Dog, Tin .... 15.00 To 25.00
Cutter, Cookie, Duck, Davis Baking Powder, Tin 8.00
Cutter, Cookie, Duck, Tin, 4 In. .... 10.00 To 16.00
Cutter, Cookie, Dutchman, Handled, Tin, 4 3/4 In. 24.50
Cutter, Cookie, Eagle, Tin .... 15.00 To 30.00

Cutter, Cookie, Easter Cross, Tin, 2 3/4 In. 5.00
Cutter, Cookie, Figural, Gingerbread Man, Tin, 3 X 5 In. 18.50
Cutter, Cookie, Fish, Tin, 1 1/4 X 2 5/8 In. 5.00
Cutter, Cookie, Flower, Scalloped, Wall Hung, 1 In. Center 10.00
Cutter, Cookie, Fluted, Aluminum, 3 1/4 In. 5.00
Cutter, Cookie, Gingerbread Boy, Wooden Knob, 2 In. 10.00
Cutter, Cookie, Heart, Big Strap Handle, 1 In. 34.00
Cutter, Cookie, Heart, Tin, 1 3/4 X 1 3/4 In. 6.00
Cutter, Cookie, Heart, Tin, 4 In. 15.00
Cutter, Cookie, Hen, Standing, Tin, Large, Medium, & Miniature, Set Of 3 .... 20.00
Cutter, Cookie, Horse, Tin .... 10.00 To 23.00
Cutter, Cookie, Lion, Aluminum 3.00
Cutter, Cookie, Lion, Flat, Handle, Tin, 4 X 3 In. 10.00
Cutter, Cookie, Man, Standing, 7 In. 40.00
Cutter, Cookie, Minnie Mouse, Tin 15.00
Cutter, Cookie, Mummy, Tin, C.1860 .... 22.50
Cutter, Cookie, Mushroom, Tin, 1 X 2 In. 7.50
Cutter, Cookie, Peasant Man With Hat, Tin 24.50
Cutter, Cookie, Penguin, Tin 21.00
Cutter, Cookie, Pilgrim, Tin 20.00
Cutter, Cookie, Rabbit, Aluminum 3.00
Cutter, Cookie, Rabbit, Handled, Tin 11.50
Cutter, Cookie, Rabbit, Leaping, Tin, 4 In. 13.00
Cutter, Cookie, Rectangular, Fluted, Applied Handle, Aluminum 4.00
Cutter, Cookie, Round, Red Wooden Handle, Aluminum 4.00
Cutter, Cookie, Santa Claus, Walking, Sack On Back, Tin, 2 X 3 In. 5.00
Cutter, Cookie, Santa's Boot, Tin, C.1900, 2 3/4 X 3 In. 8.50
Cutter, Cookie, Scalloped, Flower, Petal Rim, Tin 8.50
Cutter, Cookie, Scotty Dog, Red Wooden Handle, Aluminum 6.00
Cutter, Cookie, Spade, Dark Gray, Tin, Arched Handle, C.1880 .... 12.50
Cutter, Cookie, Squirrel, Sitting On Haunches, Gray, Tin, 2 X 2 In. 22.50
Cutter, Cookie, Star, Aluminum 3.00
Cutter, Cookie, Star, Copper, Cylindrical Sleeve, 2 In. 20.00
Cutter, Cookie, Star, Tin .... 4.00 To 8.50
Cutter, Cookie, Tea Biscuit, Aluminum, Green, Wooden Handle 4.00
Cutter, Cookie, Walking Parson Reading The Good Book, Tin 25.00
Cutter, Cookie, Woman, Long Dress, Tin 35.00
Cutter, Cookie, 10-Petal Flower, Handle, Tin, 3 3/4 In.Diam. 10.50
Cutter, Dough, Wood Handle, Iron Wheel, Hand Forged 29.00
Cutter, Doughnut, Elongated Knob Handle 85.00
Cutter, Doughnut, Maple, Treen, 2 Holes To Each Side, C.1870, 4 In. 70.00
Cutter, Doughnut, Rumford 6.50
Cutter, Doughnut, Strap Handle 7.00
Cutter, Doughnut, Tin 15.00
Cutter, Doughnut, Wooden Handle, Aluminum, 2 3/4 In. 3.00
Cutter, Heart, Diamond, 6-Sided, Tin 50.00
Cutter, Kraut, Wooden, Small 10.00
Cutter, Slaw, Cherry, Molded Edge, Hanging Crest, 7 X 19 In. 25.00
Cutter, Slaw, Iron Blade, 6 1/4 X 18 In. 18.00
Cutter, Slaw, Kraut Kutter, 1905 .... 45.00
Cutter, Slaw, Maple & Ash, Carved Heart, 8 1/2 X 25 In. 25.00
Cutter, Slaw, Poplar, Steel Blade, Heart Cutout, 7 X 18 In. 115.00
Cutter, Slaw, Walnut, Hanging Crest, 21 1/4 In. 25.00
Cutter, Slaw, Wing Screw Tightener, Wall Hung, Wooden, 6 X 17 In. 18.50
Cutter, Vegetable, Green, Wooden Handle 4.00
Cutter, Vegetable, Maple Board, Square, 12 In. 20.00
Dipper, Chocolate, Gray, Wire & Twisted Wireware, 8 1/2 In. 6.00
Dipper, Cup-Shaped, Hooklike Handle, 3 3/4 In. 160.00
Dipper, Gray, Pump Handle Strap, Slant Sided, 1 Quart, 15 In. 17.50
Dipper, Hand-Scorped, Bilateral Pours, Burl, 6 X 3 1/2 In. 125.00
Dipper, Water, Gourd, Straight Handle, Holds 2 Cups 12.50
Dipper, Water, Tin, Shaker Style, Tubular Handle, Gray, 8 In. 22.50
Drainer, Cheese, Round, Wooden, Pierced Holes, 9 X 3 In. 75.00
Dutch Oven, Flanged Top, Covered, 2 Spouts, 19th Century 150.00

Dutch Oven, Griswold, No.8	45.00
Dutch Oven, Iron, 18th Century, 9 1/4 In.	375.00
Dutch Oven, Lid Holds Coal, Marked, 3-Legged, C.1870, 12 In.	150.00
Egg Boiler, 5 Open Rings, Loop Handle, Pewter	60.00
Egg Box, Wooden, Holds 5 Dozen, 1884	85.00
Egg Holder, Twisted Wire	25.00
Egg Holder, Wire, Holds 4 Eggs	17.00
Egg Poacher, Fry Pan Shaped, 5 Cups, Dark Gray, Tin, 10 X 3 In.	40.00
Egg Separator, Embossed Jewel Stoves & Ranges, Gray, Tin	12.50
Egg Separator, Watkins, Advertising, Tin	6.50
Eggbeater, Cast Iron, 1910	18.00
Eggbeater, Dover, Cast Iron, 12 In.	12.00
Eggbeater, Dover, 1891, Small Blades	15.00 To 25.00
Eggbeater, Fits Onto 3-Cup Pitcher	5.00
Eggbeater, Holt's Dover, Hand Style, Late 1800s, Cast Iron	20.00
Eggbeater, Log Handle, Coil Crank, C.1908, 12 1/2 In.	15.00
Eggbeater, Red & White, Painted Wooden Handle, Hi Speed, Ekco, A & J	4.00
Eggbeater, T-Shaped, Red & White, Wooden Handle, 1936-37, Patented	5.00
Eggbeater, Tin	6.00
Eggbeater, Turbine, Tin, Wood, 13 In.	12.00 To 15.00
Eggbeater, Wall Mount, 1885	62.00
Eggbeater, 4-Geared, Iron, Tin Blades, Wood Handle, Boston	16.50
Extractor, Meat Juice, 1898	20.00
Flour Grinder, Arcade, Original Paint & Decal	85.00
Fork & Spoon, Bird's-Eye Maple, Butterfly Design, C.1900, 10 In.	20.00
Fork, Flesh, Hearth, Iron, C.1870, 18 In.	22.50
Fork, Flesh, 2-Tined, Iron, Wooden Handle, 12 In.	12.50
Fork, Flesh, 3-Tined, Wireware, Wall Hung, 15 In.	5.00
Fork, Pickle, Green Celluloid Handle	3.00
Fork, Pickle, Twisted Wire, Long Handle	6.00
Fork, Toasting, Twisted Handle, Tin	10.00
Funnel, Bottle, Dark Gray, Tin, 4 1/2 In.	3.00
Funnel, Cider, Wood, 1 Piece, 8 1/2 X 20 In.	85.00
Funnel, Dark Gray, Tin, Narrow Spout, 5 In.	12.50
Funnel, Fruit Jar, Porcelain	9.00
Funnel, Glass	6.00
Funnel, Jar, Canning, Dark Gray, Tin, 3 3/4 In.	5.00
Funnel, Maple Syrup, Wooden, 1 Piece	95.00
Funnel, Tin Lined, Copper	45.00
Funnel, Tin, 1 3/4 X 1 7/8 In.	20.00
Grater, Food, Clamp-On, 1870	47.50
Grater, Gray, Wall Hung, Tin, 5 1/4 In.	5.00
Grater, Knuckle Duster, Hand, Gray, Tin, Arched Handle, 3 X 4 In.	7.50
Grater, Lemon, English, 7 3/8 In.	12.00
Grater, Nutmeg, Dark Gray, Hinged, Tin, 2 X 5 In.	12.50
Grater, Nutmeg, Edgar, Pat.1896	38.00
Grater, Nutmeg, Glass Jar, Crank Built Into Red Lid	5.00
Grater, Nutmeg, Gray, Tin, Wall Hung, 5 1/8 In.	12.50
Grater, Nutmeg, Hanging, Tin	6.50
Grater, Nutmeg, Hinged Iron Rasp, Knob Handle, Round	85.00
Grater, Nutmeg, Little Rhody	34.00
Grater, Nutmeg, Silas Pierce, Tin, Small	15.00
Grater, Nutmeg, Spring Action	55.00
Grater, Nutmeg, The Boyer, Tin	49.00
Grater, Nutmeg, Tin & Wood, Mechanical, 1868	115.00
Grater, Nutmeg, Wooden, Dated 1888, 4 1/2 X 2 In.	75.00
Grater, Scoop Type, Wood Handle	4.00
Grater, Slaw, Steel	7.50
Grater, Soap, Fels Naptha, Tin	4.00
Grater, Spice, Revolving, Lorraine	18.00
Grater, Tin, Flat, Combo, Ekco, C.1935	6.00
Grater, Tin, Flat, Curved Ends, Large Hole	4.00
Grater, Veg-E-Grater, Knapp-Monarch, 5 X 12 In.	15.00
Grater, Vegetable, Cream City, Tin	9.00

Griddle, Heart Design, Pennsylvania Dutch, Cast Iron 57.50
Grinder, Food, Clamps, Dated 1899 .... 12.00
Grinder, Food, Universal, Table Clamp, C.1897 .... 10.00
Grinder, Meat, Keen Kutter, Dated 1906 .... 9.00
Grinder, Meat, Keen Kutter, Steel 8.00
Grinder, Meat, Larkin 8.50
Grinder, Meat, 1 Blade, E.C. Simmons, Keen Kutter, 1906, 5 Pounds 25.00
Grinder, Poppyseed, Kosmos, Cast Iron, Green 48.50
Grinder, Sausage, All Wood 145.50
Grinder, Sausage, Keen Kutter 40.00
Grinder, Sausage, Miles, Patent 1964 .... 20.00
Holder, Broom, Holding, Wire 33.50
Holder, Broomstick, 3 Slots, Iron 35.00
Holder, Matchbox, Red & White, Tin, Wall Hanging 6.00
Holder, Pie, Twisted Wire, Holds 4 .... 25.00
Ice Breaker, Steel, 1950 .... 3.00
Ice Cream, Freezer, No.3 Black Tin, Gold & White, King & Co. 55.00
Ice Pick, Arcade, Signed 10.00
Ice Pick, Iron, 4-Sided Handle, Marked Run Right To Reads 35.00
Ice Tongs, Marked Sturde, Iron, 18 In. 20.00
Icebox, Northey Duplex, 4 Door, Oak, 4 X 2 1/2 X 6 Ft. 350.00
Icebox, Parlor, Carved Lions' Heads On Corners, Golden Oak 1100.00
Icebox, Walk-In, Brass Hardware, Oak, 6 X 5 X 8 Ft. 7 In. 700.00
Iron, Flat, Rounded Heel, 5-Pointed Star Embossed, 4 1/2 Pounds 35.00
Iron, Sleeve, Grand Union Tea Co. 30.00
Iron, Tailor's, Iron, Twisted Handle, 13 Pounds 30.00
Iron, Wafer, Geometric Floral Design, 3 3/4 X 23 In. 40.00
Iron, Waffle, Fleur-De-Lis Pattern, Cast Iron 65.00
Iron, Waffle, Heart Shape 45.00
Iron, Waffle, Sunburst Design, Cradle, Cast Iron 25.00
Iron, Waffle, Wagner's, Bail, 1925, 2 Piece 15.00
Jar, Beater, E.C.Reed, North English, Iowa, Blue Stripe 65.00
Jar, Stoneware, Marked Hall 25.00
Kettle, Apple Butter, Tongue & Grooved Copper 225.00
Kettle, Bail Handle, Flanged Lips, Marked, Wagner, 8 In. 40.00
Kettle, Butter, Copper, 30 Gallon 165.00
Kettle, Candy, Rolled Edge, Brass Around Middle, Iron Handles, Copper 225.00
Kettle, Copper, 22 In.Diam. 165.00
Kettle, Doughnut Shape, Bail Handle, Black, Iron, 10 In. 30.00
Kettle, Dutch Oven, Cast Iron, Bail Handle, Trivet, Griswold 35.00
Kettle, Graniteware, Brown & White Mottled, 12 In. 25.00
Kettle, Jelly, American Brass Kettle Mfg., 12.1/2 In.Diam. 65.00
Knife Sharpener, Red Wooden Handle, 9 In. 3.00
Knife, Bread, B.T.Babbit, Wooden Handle 7.50
Knife, Chopping, Wishbone Wooden Handle, Iron, Tin Chopper 18.50
Knife, Curd, Pistol Grip Handle, 1 Piece Hand-Carved Pine, 25 In. 75.00
Knife, Pallet, Red & White Wooden Handle 4.00
Ladle, Cast Iron, 14 In. 10.00
Ladle, Colonial, Pouring Lip, Rattail Loop, Iron, 27 In. 45.00
Ladle, Cream, Tin, C.1926 .... 7.00
Ladle, Deep Bowl, Long Handle, Wooden, 16 1/2 In. 125.00
Ladle, Deep Bowl, Long Handle, Wooden, 18th Century, 17 1/4 In. 70.00
Ladle, Double-Spouted Bowl, Rattail Handle, Iron, C.1870, 14 In. 15.00
Ladle, Enameled, White 5.00
Ladle, Pickle, Glass, Wood Handle 12.00
Ladle, Pouring, Iron, C.1890, Wall Hung, 13 In. 6.00
Ladle, Soup, Sheet Iron Bowl, Iron Shank, Black, Wooden Handle, 12 In. 15.00
Ladle, Soup, Wooden Handle, Marked A & J 3.00
Ladle, 1924, Tin 6.00
Lemon Squeezer, Metal, White 5.00
Lid, Grease, Dragonfly 125.00
Lifter, Pie, Pat'd July 15, 1924, Steel 20.00
Lifter, Pie, Wood & Wire 15.00
Lifter, Pot, Hook Ends, Swivel Hanger, Hand-Forged 20.00

Mallet, Concentric Lines, Wooden, 4 In. 6.50
Masher, Potato, Bell Shaped, Wooden, 12 In. 6.50
Masher, Potato, Country Wood, 6 In. 8.00
Masher, Potato, Green & White Handle, Wooden 5.00
Masher, Potato, Lignum Vitae, Bell Shaped, Maple, 11 1/2 In. 60.00
Masher, Potato, Maple, Knob Handle, 13 In. 6.50
Masher, Potato, Mushroom Topped, Maple 12.50
Masher, Potato, Pestle-Turned Handle, Walnut 10.00
Masher, Potato, Red & White Wooden Handle, Wavy Blade 5.00
Masher, Potato, Sunbonnet Jointed Doll Handle, Wooden, 13 1/2 In. 12.00
Masher, Potato, Wooden .... 8.00 To 12.50
Masher, Potato, Wooden Handle, Wire, 10 3/4 In. 4.50
       KITCHEN, MATCH SAFE, see Match Safe
Measure, Bentwood, Dry, Double Rimmed, 12 In. 35.00
Measure, Bentwood, Hand-Forged, 9 1/2 X 5 1/2 In. 25.00
Measure, Bentwood, Tin Banded, 15 X 7 In. 30.00
Measure, Dry, Bentwood Rim Ring, Hunter Green, 12 1/4 X 6 3/4 In. 75.00
Measure, Dry, Bentwood, Round, Stamped E.B.Frye, 5 1/2 X 3 3/4 In. 30.00
Measure, Dry, Chamfered Lapping, E.B.Frye, Wilton, N.H., 7 X 4 1/2 In. 25.00
Measure, Dry, N.S.Wilkings, Oak Bentwood, C.1890, 11 1/4 X 6 1/4 In. 45.00
Measure, Gray, Wrap-Around Pour Lip, Strap Handle, C.1880, Half Gallon 10.00
Measure, Liquid, Dark Gray, Pouring Lip, Strap Handle, Tin, 1 Gal. 22.50
Measure, Liquid, Hand-Spun, Corset Waist, Brass, C.1860, 6 1/2 In. 45.00
Measure, Liquid, Pouring Lip, Copper, Strap Handle, Copper Rivets 80.00
Measure, Mug Shape, Tinsmith Made, 5 3/4 X 4 1/4 In. 38.00
Measure, Old Nails, Oak Bentwood, 15 1/2 X 7 3/4 In. 35.00
Measure, Old Nails, Signed, Oak Bentwood, 9 1/4 X 5 1/4 In. 30.00
Measure, Quart, Tin 12.00
Measure, Thick Rim, Dry, 1865, 8 X 14 1/2 In. 20.00
Measure, Tin Bands, Thick Rim, Dry, 7 X 11 1/4 In. 16.00
Measure, Tin Straps, Double Rim, Oak Bentwood, C.1880, 15 X 7 3/4 In. 45.00
Meat Fret, Double-Ended Point, Black Enameled Handle, 10 In. 7.50
Meat Press, Iron, 2 Tenderizers, Serrated, 10 In. 15.00
Mill, Food, Foley, Tin & Steel 6.00
       KITCHEN, MOLD, see also Pewter, Mold; Tin, Mold
Mold, Aspic, Bell, Scalloped Edge, Marked, 11 In. .... *Illus* 70.00
Mold, Aspic, Marked 5, Copper, 5 1/4 X 7 In. .... *Illus* 60.00
Mold, Aspic, Ring, Gray, Tin, Oval, 6 X 9 In. 22.50
Mold, Aspic, Turtle, Copper, 6 3/8 X 3 1/4 In. .... *Illus* 62.50
Mold, Bread, Diamond, Gray, Tin, 9 In. 15.00
Mold, Butter Box, 5 Pound 85.00
Mold, Butter Box, 8 Miniature Squares 120.00
Mold, Butter, Acorn & Leaf Design, Wooden, 1 1/2 In. 38.00
Mold, Butter, Beaver, Round, 2 3/4 X 3 1/8 In. 24.00
Mold, Butter, Carved Pinwheel, Plunger Box, 3 In.Diam. 100.00
Mold, Butter, Child's, Pine 22.50
Mold, Butter, Cow, Glass, Wooden Handle 34.00
Mold, Butter, Cow, Maple, 3 Piece 110.00
Mold, Butter, Cow, Wooden Handle, Glass, 4 1/2 In. 60.00
Mold, Butter, Double Sheaf Of Wheat, Box & Press, 3 Piece 45.00
Mold, Butter, Dovetailed Corner, Oblong, 5 1/2 X 3 X 3 1/2 In. 12.00
Mold, Butter, Eagle, Double Sided, Wood, 6 In. 210.00
Mold, Butter, Eagle, Wood, 4 In. 80.00
Mold, Butter, Fern 45.00
Mold, Butter, Flowers & Leaves, Wooden, 1 Pound 80.00
Mold, Butter, Flowers, Brass Clasp, Square 28.00
Mold, Butter, Grapes, Sheaf Of Wheat, Ear Of Corn Design, 5 3/4 In. 125.00
Mold, Butter, Hand-Carved Wheat Pattern, Locking Device, 1 Pound 150.00
Mold, Butter, Homemade, 5 3/4 X 3 1/2 X 3 7/8 In. 10.00
Mold, Butter, Maple, Thistles & Acorn, Brass Corner Hook 60.00
Mold, Butter, Oblong, Brass Handle, Brass Screws, 7 X 4 X 4 In. 12.00
Mold, Butter, Pine Twig Design, Large 65.00
Mold, Butter, Pineapple, Double Flairs, Round, Large 35.00
Mold, Butter, Pineapple, Pine 50.00

Kitchen, Mold, Aspic, Bell, Scalloped
Edge, Marked, 11 In.

Kitchen, Mold, Aspic, Marked 5, Copper,
5 1/4 X 7 In.

Kitchen, Mold, Aspic, Turtle, Copper,
6 3/8 X 3 1/4 In.

Mold, Butter, Pinwheel & Tulip, Wood, 4 1/2 In.	150.00
Mold, Butter, Plunger-Style, 3 Piece, Thistle Pattern	55.00
Mold, Butter, Plunger, Sheaf Of Wheat	45.00
Mold, Butter, Pomegranate Pattern, Wooden Case & Plunger	34.00
Mold, Butter, Rose, Round	100.00
Mold, Butter, Sheaf Of Wheat, Plunger, Miniature	45.00
Mold, Butter, Sheaves Of Wheat, Hand-Carved, Maple, 3 1/2 X 5 3/8 In.	85.00
Mold, Butter, Skinny Cow, Plunger	160.00
Mold, Butter, Star, Double	32.00
Mold, Butter, Stylized Flower, Wooden, Half Pound	40.00
Mold, Butter, Sunflower, Scored Diamond Center, 3 1/2 In.	50.00
Mold, Butter, Swan Looking Skyward, Carved, Maple, 3 3/4 In.Diam.	165.00
Mold, Butter, Swan, Round, 3 1/2 In. X 3 In. High	23.00
Mold, Butter, Thistles & Acorn Sprays, Maple, 4-Part, 1 Pound	60.00
Mold, Butter, Veined Leaves, Berries, Hand-Carved, 3 1/4 X 5 1/2 In.	50.00
Mold, Butter, Wooden Box, Initials F.B., 4 Quarters, 6 X 6 In.	75.00
Mold, Butter, 2 Acorns, Leaf, 4 In.Diam.	68.00
Mold, Butter, 3 Elm Leaves, Triple Concentric Lined Rim, Maple, 2 Pc.	65.00
Mold, Butter, 3 Leaves & Concentric Circles, Wooden, 2 1/2 In.	60.00
Mold, Butter, 8-Point Star, Round, 3 1/4 X 4 In.	14.00
Mold, Cake, Ladyfinger, Tin	12.00
Mold, Cake, Lamb, Cast Iron	30.00 To 65.00
Mold, Cake, Lamb, Iron	37.00
Mold, Cake, Mixed Fruits Top, Tin, Gray, 3 Piece, C.1870, 5 X 6 1/2 In.	130.00
Mold, Cake, Rabbit, Aluminum, 10 In.	25.00
KITCHEN, MOLD, CANDLE, see also Tin, Mold, Candle	
Mold, Candle, Pine, Tin, New England, 19th Century, 11 In. *Illus*	650.00
Mold, Candle, 2-Stand, Handled	42.00
Mold, Candy, Hen	7.00
Mold, Cheese, Pennsylvania, Tin, Side Handle, 3 Footed, 4 X 5 In.	50.00
Mold, Chocolate, Angel, 4 In.	3.25

Mold, Chocolate, Arrow, With 4 Hearts, 4 In. 3.25
Mold, Chocolate, Auto, 2-Door Coupe, 5 In. 4.50
Mold, Chocolate, Banana Shape 18.50
Mold, Chocolate, Baseball Catcher, With Mitt, 3 In. 4.50
Mold, Chocolate, Basket, 4 X 3 In. 20.00
Mold, Chocolate, Basket, 6 X 3 1/2 In. 25.00
Mold, Chocolate, Bugs Bunny, Sitting, High Button Shoe, 9 In. 20.00
Mold, Chocolate, Bugs Bunny, 9 1/2 In. 20.00
Mold, Chocolate, Button Face, Round, Tin, 7 X 13 In. 22.00
Mold, Chocolate, Chicken, Nesting, Tin, 5 X 6 In. 35.00
Mold, Chocolate, Christmas Bell, 4 In. 3.50
Mold, Chocolate, Christmas Ornament, Tin, 3 In. 30.00
Mold, Chocolate, Christmas Tree, 4 In. 3.50
Mold, Chocolate, Christmas Tree, 6 1/2 In. 30.00
Mold, Chocolate, Christmas Wreath, 4 In. 3.50
Mold, Chocolate, Clown, Side View, 4 In. 3.25
Mold, Chocolate, Cowboy With Lasso, Hinged, 5 1/2 X 5 1/2 In. 45.00
Mold, Chocolate, Cupid, 4 In. 3.25
Mold, Chocolate, Easter Bunny, Sitting On Egg, Tin, C.1880, 4 In. 35.00
Mold, Chocolate, Easter Bunny, Sitting, Paws On Basket, 7 In. 35.00
Mold, Chocolate, Easter Bunny, Sitting, 3-D, C.1880, 4 In. 40.00
Mold, Chocolate, Easter Egg, Good Luck Four-Leaf Clover, 3 X 4 In. 35.00
Mold, Chocolate, Easter Egg, Hen On Nest, Chicken, Rabbits, 1 1/2 In. 66.00
Mold, Chocolate, Egg, Gray, Tin, 2 X 4 In. 20.00
Mold, Chocolate, Egg, Stainless, 8 X 3 1/2 In. 4.00
Mold, Chocolate, Egg, Tin, Set Of 4 .... 10.00
Mold, Chocolate, Eggs, Crackled, 10 X 5 In. 20.00
Mold, Chocolate, Eggs, Fluted, 12 X 6 In. 20.00
Mold, Chocolate, Elephant, Dumbo, 5 In. 4.50
Mold, Chocolate, Figural, Bunny, Sitting, 4 X 3 In. 20.00
Mold, Chocolate, Figural, Hen Sitting On Nest, Marked Germany 20.00
Mold, Chocolate, Four Rabbits 55.00
Mold, Chocolate, Girl, Old-Fashioned, 2 In. 2.00
Mold, Chocolate, Halloween, Jack-O'Lantern, Owl, Witch, 1 1/2 In. 66.00
Mold, Chocolate, Hen Setting On Nest, Iron, 4-Mold, 3 X 10 X 2 In. 45.00
Mold, Chocolate, Hens, 6 Setting In Basket, 13 X 8 In. 20.00
Mold, Chocolate, Hippopotamus, 1 1/2 In. 2.00
Mold, Chocolate, Horse, Trotting, 5 In. 4.50
Mold, Chocolate, Indian On Horse, Marked Reich, 6 X 5 In. 52.00
Mold, Chocolate, Indian, With Headdress, Bow & Arrow, 5 In. 4.50
Mold, Chocolate, Jack-O'Lantern, 5 In. 6.00
Mold, Chocolate, Jester, 2 In. 2.00
Mold, Chocolate, Kewpie Doll, Marked Reich, 5 X 3 3/4 In. 50.00
Mold, Chocolate, Kewpie Doll, 4 In. 3.25
Mold, Chocolate, Lambs, 4 Standing, Pewter, 2 Piece 45.00
Mold, Chocolate, Lambs, 4 Stylized, 13 X 7 1/2 In. 20.00
Mold, Chocolate, Laying Hen, Full Figured, 5 X 4 In. 45.00
Mold, Chocolate, Leaf, Oak, 4 In. 3.25
Mold, Chocolate, Marzipan, Tin Plated, 3 X 3 In. 22.50
Mold, Chocolate, Mickey Mouse, Hinged, 6 1/2 X 3 1/2 In. 35.00
Mold, Chocolate, Mother Hen With Bonnet, 5 X 4 1/2 In. 32.00
Mold, Chocolate, Polar Bear, Hinged, 4 1/4 X 2 1/2 In. 30.00
Mold, Chocolate, Poodle, Smiling, Hinged, 3 1/2 X 3 1/2 In. 30.00
Mold, Chocolate, Pumpkin, 4 In. 3.25
Mold, Chocolate, Puss In Boots, 4 In. 3.25
Mold, Chocolate, Rabbit Emerging From Egg, 5 In. 4.50
Mold, Chocolate, Rabbit Holding Basket With 2 Eggs, 13 X 7 In. 20.00
Mold, Chocolate, Rabbit, Display, Holding Basket, 21 In. 250.00
Mold, Chocolate, Rabbit, Orchestra Conductor, Hinged, 5 X 3 In. 28.00
Mold, Chocolate, Rabbit, Sitting In Leaf, 13 X 8 In. 20.00
Mold, Chocolate, Rabbit, Sitting, 15 X 8 In. 30.00
Mold, Chocolate, Rabbit, Standing, Basket In Paws, 13 X 7 In. 20.00
Mold, Chocolate, Rabbit, Standing, Basket On His Back, , 15 X 8 In. 30.00
Mold, Chocolate, Rabbit, Standing, Grass, Basket On Back, 17 X 7 In. 35.00

Mold, Chocolate, Rabbit, Standing, 10 X 5 In. 48.00
Mold, Chocolate, Rabbit, 5 Side By Side, Standing, C.1880, 3 X 6 In. 35.00
Mold, Chocolate, Rabbits, 2 .... 55.00
Mold, Chocolate, Rabbits, 8, 11 X 11 In. 20.00
Mold, Chocolate, Reindeer, Stylized, 13 X 6 In. 20.00
Mold, Chocolate, Rooster 24.00
Mold, Chocolate, Rumpelstiltskin, 2 In. 2.00
Mold, Chocolate, Runabout Roadster, C.1930, 3 X 5 In. 10.00
Mold, Chocolate, Santa Atop Chimmey, 5 1/2 In. 48.00
Mold, Chocolate, Santa Head, 3 X 3 In. 6.25
Mold, Chocolate, Santa Heads, 3 Rows Of 15 .... 70.00
Mold, Chocolate, Santa, Figural, 2 Piece, Copper, 7 In. 175.00
Mold, Chocolate, Santa, Jolly, 8 In. 35.00
Mold, Chocolate, Santa, Reindeer, Sleigh & Tree, 6 In. 10.00
Mold, Chocolate, Santa, With Pack & Tree, 6 In. 30.00
Mold, Chocolate, Shell, Scalloped, 8 X 8 In. 40.00
Mold, Chocolate, Squirrels, 9 X 7 In. 20.00
Mold, Chocolate, St.Nicholas, 4 In. 24.00
Mold, Chocolate, St.Nicholas, 6 In. 30.00
Mold, Chocolate, Sunflower, 4 In. 3.25
Mold, Chocolate, Teddy Bear, 4 In. 3.25
Mold, Chocolate, Turkey, 4 X 5 In. 20.00
Mold, Chocolate, Valentine, Hearts, Arrow, Cupid Standing, 1 1/2 In. 66.00
Mold, Chocolate, Valentine, To My Valentine, 5 X 6 In. 20.00
Mold, Chocolate, Witch Riding Broom, 5 In. 4.50
Mold, Cookie, Bird Design, On Branch, 5 Stars, Iron, 3 X 5 In. 110.00
Mold, Cookie, Grecian Warrior Bust, Iron, 6 In. 75.00
Mold, Fish, Ironstone, 15 In. 85.00
Mold, Fish, Kreamer, Tin 18.00
Mold, Fish, Tin, With Loop, 10 3/8 In. 15.00
Mold, Food, Basket Of Fruit, Copper, Tin Lined, 9 X 6 X 2 In. 50.00
Mold, Food, Cluster Of Fruit, Tin, Oval, 6 X 8 In. 30.00
Mold, Food, Copper, Cone Center, Swirled Design, 8 In. 45.00
Mold, Food, Cornucopia, Impressed, Oval, Copper, 3 X 4 X 1 1/2 In. 40.00
Mold, Food, Earthworm Crest, Tin, 8 1/2 X 3 1/2 In. 25.00
Mold, Food, Figural, Fish, Embossed, Tin, 2 X 5 X 1/2 In. 10.00
Mold, Food, Fruit, Copper 90.00
Mold, Food, Oval, Mold Impression, Soft Paste, C.1820, 5 X 6 In. 45.00
Mold, Food, Pear, Copper & Tin 70.00
Mold, Food, Rose, Copper 85.00
Mold, Food, Swirled Design, Cone Center, Copper, 8 In. 45.00
Mold, Food, Three Fruits, Copper 85.00
Mold, Food, Turk's Head, Tin, 4 1/2 X 2 1/2 In. 6.00
Mold, Footed, Ear Of Corn, Gray, Tin, 4 1/2 X 7 In. 125.00
KITCHEN, MOLD, ICE CREAM, see also Pewter, Mold, Ice Cream
Mold, Ice Cream, Horn Shape, Tin, Large 30.00
Mold, Ice Cream, Krazy Kat, Metal, 2 Piece 26.00
Mold, Ice Cream, Santa Claus, Griswold, Cast Iron 125.00
Mold, Ice Cream, U.S. Flag 80.00
Mold, Jell-O, Different Patterns, Aluminum, 2 1/2 X 2 In., Set Of 12 .... 12.00
Mold, Maple Sugar, Bear, 6 1/2 X 5 1/4 X 1 1/8 In. 8.00
Mold, Maple Sugar, Beaver, 11 X 5 1/2 X 1 1/4 In. 11.00
Mold, Maple Sugar, Crouching Rabbit, 7 1/2 In. 8.00
Mold, Maple Sugar, Hand-Hewn, Makes 3-Pound Blocks, 19 X 4 In. 85.00
Mold, Maple Sugar, House 100.00
Mold, Maple Sugar, Jay Bird Topknot, 6 3/4 X 5 1/2 X 1 1/8 In. 8.00
Mold, Maple Sugar, Round, 2 1/2 X 1 1/2 In. 20.00
Mold, Maple Sugar, Turkey, Tail Feathers Fluffed, 6 X 5 X 1 1/8 In. 8.00
Mold, Maple Sugar, Wooden Pegged 45.00
Mold, Maple Sugar, 6 Section 6.00
Mold, Marzipan, Veined Leaf Form, Copper, C.1800, 3 X 1 1/2 In. 55.00
Mold, Muffin, Cast Iron 18.00
Mold, Peacock, Copper, Tin Lining, 4 1/4 In. 85.00
Mold, Pudding, Apple, Brown Rim, Fluted Sides, 3 X 4 In. 20.00

Kitchen, Mold, Candle, Pine, Tin, New England,
19th Century, 11 In.

Kitchen, Mold, Pudding, Gothic Arches On
Sides, Copper, 16 Ounce

Kitchen, Mold, Pudding, 6-Column,
Copper, 6 1/4 X 4 5/8 In.

Mold, Pudding, Columned, Fluted Skirt, Copper, Marked Britain, 6 In.	100.00
Mold, Pudding, Flower Shaped, Fluted, Tin, 3 1/2 X 1 1/2 In.	4.50
Mold, Pudding, Gothic Arches On Sides, Copper, 16 Ounce .... *Illus*	45.00
Mold, Pudding, Grape, Octagonal	40.00
Mold, Pudding, Lion Resting On Paws, Fluted Skirt, Copper, 5 X 7 In.	140.00
Mold, Pudding, Melon, Tin, Marked Kreamer, 6 1/2 X 5 In.	15.00
Mold, Pudding, Ring, Dovetailed Copper, 18th Century, 8 1/4 X 4 In.	140.00
Mold, Pudding, Teddy Bear, Standing, C.1850, 4 1/2 X 8 1/2 In.	125.00
Mold, Pudding, 6-Column, Copper, 6 1/4 X 4 5/8 In. .... *Illus*	57.50
Mold, Springerle, Boy On Horse, Blowing Trumpet, 5 X 3 In.	192.00
Mold, Springerle, Lion, Roaring, Parrot In Flower Tree, 4 X 4 In.	150.00
Mold, Springerle, 2 Sided, Ram, Squirrel Eating Nut, 6 X 5 In.	330.00
Mold, Springerle, 12 Squares, Baker, Barrel Maker, Shoemaker, 7 In.	195.00
Mold, Springerle, 15 Squares, Animals, Fruits, Human Figures, 10 In.	385.00
Mortar & Double-Headed Pestle, Maple, Spice, 6 1/2 In.	45.00
Mortar & Pestle, Carved Lignum Vitae, 19th Century, 2 Piece	125.00
Mortar & Pestle, Curly Maple, 8 1/4 In.	180.00
Mortar & Pestle, Lignum Vitae, Mortar 8 1/2 In.	150.00

Mortar & Pestle, Turned, 3 1/4 In.	140.00
Mortar & Pestle, Walnut, 7 1/4 In.	125.00
Opener & Lifter, Canning Jar, Iron & Wireware	6.50
Opener, Clam & Oyster, Brass, Iron Blade, 7 In.	35.00
Opener, Jar & Bottle, Screw Type, Green, Wooden Handle, Edlund, C.1930	5.00
Opener, Jar & Can, Champion, Ratchet Clamp, Cast Iron, 1873	85.00
Opener, Sealer, Jar	6.00
Oven Peel, Carved, England, 3 1/2 In.	80.00
Paddle, Butter, Corrugated, Wooden	8.50
Paddle, Butter, Flat Corrugated Surface, 8 3/4 X 2 In.	3.00
Paddle, Butter, Hand-Carved Handle, Shaped End	85.00
Paddle, Butter, Maple, C.1880, 3 3/4 X 10 1/4 In., Pair	30.00
Paddle, Butter, Maple, Curved Handle, 8 1/4 In.	60.00
Paddle, Butter, Maple, Scooped Top	12.50
Paddle, Butter, Maple, Wall Hung, Wide Blade, 11 In.	6.50
Paddle, Butter, Oak, Wide Blade, 12 X 4 1/2 In.	14.50
Paddle, Stirring, Carved Maple, 13 1/2 In.	10.00
Paddle, Syrup, Maple, 34 3/4 In.	20.00
Pail, Cream, Gray, Target Embossed Cover, Bail Handle, 3 Gallon	22.50
Pail, Handle & Lid, Ring Design, Tin, 4 1/4 X 6 In.	15.00
Pail, Jelly, Spun Brass, Size 13	75.00
Pail, Milk, Strap Handle, Wire Bail, Cover, 4 Quart	16.50
Pail, Milk, Swing Handle, Cover, Tin, 6 Quart	16.50
Pan, Baking, Biscuit, Gray, Tin, 6 Molds, 6 3/4 X 10 In.	4.50
Pan, Baking, Bread, Clamps, Ribbed, Round, 2 Piece	30.00
Pan, Bread Rising, Tin, Large	15.00
Pan, Bread, Double, Windows In One End, Tin	65.00
Pan, Bread, 6-Unit, Tin, 13 X 19 In.	20.00
Pan, Breadstick, 11 Molds, Finger Holes, Wagner Ware, 7 X 15 In.	22.50
Pan, Bundt, Cast Iron	55.00
Pan, Cake, Advertising, G.Urban Milling Co., Buffalo, N.Y.	24.00
Pan, Cake, Cone Center, Fluted Sides, Tin, 8 X 2 3/4 In.	5.00
Pan, Cake, Swan's Down Angel Food, Patent December 1923, Tin	8.00
Pan, Corn Stick, Griswold, Nickel Coated	12.00
Pan, Corn Stick, 5 Section, Cast Iron, 6 1/2 X 6 3/4 In.	12.00
Pan, Crispy Corn Stick, Griswold, No.273, Cast Iron	25.00
Pan, Deep Frying, Griswold, No.8, Cast Iron, 11 X 16 In.Long	15.00
Pan, Flan, Fluted, German, Tin, 11 3/4 In.	12.00
Pan, Frying, Gray, Pour Lip, Marked Acme, 1876, 4 X 6 In.	5.00
Pan, Frying, Majestic Cookware, Hanging Ring, Wooden Handle	5.00
Pan, Frying, Wearever	10.00
Pan, Loaf, Tin, Ekcoloy-Silver Beauty, 1 Pound, Hanging Loop	4.00
Pan, Muffin, Griswold, 11 Holes, Finger Openings Each End, Cast Iron	15.00
Pan, Muffin, Iron, 1859	25.00
Pan, Muffin, Shell Design, Iron	45.00
Pan, Plum Pudding, Tin, 2 Piece	25.00
Pan, Sauce, Hearth, Iron, 3-Footed, 4 In.	50.00
Pan, Tart, Dark Gray, Tinware, 4 3/8 In.	3.00
Pan, Tube, Tinover Copper, Fluted, 8 In.	20.00
Parer & Corer, Apple, Tin, 1884	12.00
Pastry Blender, Androck, Red Wooden Handle	5.00
Pastry Jigger, Hand-Forged Iron Shaft, Brass Wheel, Wooden Handle	44.00
Pastry Jigger, 18th Century, Faceted Ball End, Iron, 5 3/4 In.	50.00
Pastry Whip, Brass	40.00
Pea Sheller & Bean Slicer, Table Clamp	12.00 To 35.00
Peeler, Apple, Barlow	30.00
Peeler, Apple, Clamp-On, Marked Goodell	18.00
Peeler, Apple, Crank With Spikes, Table Clamp, Wooden, 9 1/2 In.	95.00
Peeler, Apple, Dated 1878	25.00
Peeler, Apple, Goodell, White Mountain Apple, No.3, Iron	37.50 To 45.00
Peeler, Apple, Hudson, Cast Iron, Patent 1882	45.00
Peeler, Apple, Iron, Reading Hardwood Co., 11 In.	35.00
Peeler, Apple, Keen Kutter, Dated 1898	65.00
Peeler, Apple, Little Star, Cast Iron	23.00 To 35.00

Peeler, Apple, Maple, C.1850, 13 In. 50.00
Peeler, Apple, Monroe, Iron, 1856 .... 50.00
Peeler, Apple, Reading, Cast Iron, 1868 .... 40.00
Peeler, Apple, Reading, Pa., Mechanical 35.00
Peeler, Apple, Scott, Iron, 1868 .... 60.00
Peeler, Apple, Wooden 225.00
Peeler, Apple, 3 Gears, Sinclair Scott Co. 45.00
Peeler, Peach, Mechanical, Sayre, N.J., Cast Iron 65.00
Peeler, Peach, Sinclair, Scott, Mechanical, Cast Iron, 1883 .... 60.00
Peeler, Potato, Advertising Morton Salt 15.00
Peeler, Potato, Hamlinite, 1920 .... 17.00
Peeler, Potato, Painted, Tan & Red, Wooden Handle 1.50
Picker, Cranberry, Wooden Toothed, 3 X 6 X 10 In. 150.00
Pie Bird, Blue & White 12.00
Pie Bird, Cream & Pink, Green Trim 12.00
Pie Bird, Rooster 12.00
Pie Plate, Deep Dish, Marked Crisco, Tin, 10 In. 8.50
Pie Server, Stainless Steel, Red Celluloid Handle, Marked Sta-Brite 4.00
Pin, Wild Flower, Crockery, Elkport, Iowa 165.00
Pitcher, Wooden, 1 Piece, Slant Sides, 1 3/4 In. 8.00
Pot, Candy, Copper 125.00
Pot, Riveted Ring Handles, Brass Plate Over Copper, 4 X 5 1/2 In. 32.50
Press, Cookie, Tin & Wood, Dark Gray, T-Shaped Cylinder, 10 In. 50.00
Press, Lard, Pine, Leather End Hinge, 32 3/4 In. .... 18.50 To 25.00
Press, Lard, Pine, Leather Hinged, Iron, 24 In. 12.50
Press, Lard, Pine, Whittled Handle, 5 X 18 In. 20.00
Press, Meat Juice, Frary, Clark Columbia, Late 1800s 25.00
Print, Butter, Small Eagle, Turned Handle, 3 In. 50.00
Pump, Molasses, Crank, Brass, Talley's Enterprise 35.00
Rack, Drying, Pine, Shoe Feet, White, 41 X 42 In. 45.00
Rack, Folding, Oak, 5 Horizontal Bars, 30 X 31 In. 80.00
Rack, Pie, Wall, Cast Iron 70.00
Rack, Pie, Wire 25.00
Reamer, Porcelain, White, Pink Rose Transfer 10.00
Roaster, Apple, 2-Tier, Handled, Tin 350.00
Roaster, Coffee, Shape Of Skillet, Hand Crank, Italy, 10 In. 35.00
Roaster, Fowl, Sheet Iron 170.00
Roaster, Fowl, 2 Rows Of Hooks, Drip Pan, Handled, Tin 195.00
Roller, Butter, Birch, Geometric Pattern 150.00
Roller, Cookie, Maple, Corrugated Grooves, C .1880, 18 In. 45.00
Roller, Towel, Green Enamel, Iron 10.00
Rolling Pin, Advertising, Crockery, West Point, Nebraska 150.00
Rolling Pin, Advertising, Froemming & Haack, Fern, Iowa 140.00
Rolling Pin, Advertising, P.F.Hannahen, Walton, Iowa 140.00
Rolling Pin, Advertising, Stoneware 195.00
Rolling Pin, Bakery Shop, 2-Man, Maple, 1-Piece, 42 In. 60.00
Rolling Pin, Bird's-Eye Maple .... 10.00 To 40.00
Rolling Pin, Blown Clear Glass 30.00
Rolling Pin, Blue Stripe, Crockery, Hansen's Store 165.00
Rolling Pin, Bonanza, Crockery 155.00
Rolling Pin, Brown Stripe, Grand Junction General Store 140.00
Rolling Pin, Carved Ducks, Owls, Wood 45.00
Rolling Pin, Child's, Wooden Handles, 1 1/4 X 9 In. 3.50
Rolling Pin, China, Ivy Leaf 24.00
Rolling Pin, Clambroth, Wooden Handles 85.00
Rolling Pin, Clarion, Iowa, Blue Stripe, Glass 140.00
Rolling Pin, Cobalt Blue Glass, 12 3/4 In. 60.00
Rolling Pin, Concentric Lines To Handle, 1 Piece, Maple, 18 In. 13.00
Rolling Pin, Crockery, Advertising, Novoo, Illinois 135.00
Rolling Pin, Curly Maple, 1 Piece, 18 1/2 In. .... 20.00 To 25.00
Rolling Pin, Floral, China, Harker 35.00
Rolling Pin, Glass, Cork Stopper, 1900-20 .... 25.00
Rolling Pin, Glass, Gray Tin Screw Cap, 16 In. 22.50
Rolling Pin, Glass, Green, 15 In. 75.00

Rolling Pin, Glass, Green, 19 In. 50.00
Rolling Pin, Glass, Open At One End 50.00
Rolling Pin, Harkerware, Blue Cameo 40.00
Rolling Pin, Harkerware, Petit Point 38.00
Rolling Pin, J.F.Reilly Groceries, Hardware, & Implements, Crockery 175.00
Rolling Pin, John H.Merrit Quality Groceries, Crockery 160.00
Rolling Pin, Killians, Wahoo, Nebraska, Crockery, Handle 145.00
Rolling Pin, King, Cinticalu Co., Cincinnati, Ohio 65.00
Rolling Pin, Maple & Applewood, Carved With Animals, 8 1/2 In. 250.00
Rolling Pin, Maple, Enameled Handles, C.1930, 18 In. 8.50
Rolling Pin, Maple, Grip Handles, C.1880, 1 Piece, 21 In. 22.50
Rolling Pin, Maple, Rattail Hang-Up Loop, 1 Piece, 26 In. 35.00
Rolling Pin, Maple, Separately Turning Handles, 19 1/2 In. 12.50
Rolling Pin, Maple, 1 Piece, C.1860, 17 In. 22.50
Rolling Pin, Maple, 17 In. 12.00
Rolling Pin, Marked Cambridge, Dated, Milk Glass 125.00
Rolling Pin, Milk Glass 55.00
Rolling Pin, Milk Glass, Wooden Handles, Pink 37.00
Rolling Pin, Munsing, Green 15.00
Rolling Pin, Murphyboro, Illinois, Stoneware 145.00
Rolling Pin, Nailsea Glass, Pink & White 160.00
Rolling Pin, Newman Grove, Nebraska, Blue Stripe, Stoneware 145.00
Rolling Pin, Noodle, Small, Wooden 28.00
Rolling Pin, Opaline Glass, Plain 60.00
Rolling Pin, Opaline Glass, Ships & Sayings 80.00
Rolling Pin, Petit Point 85.00
Rolling Pin, Poppy Design 65.00
Rolling Pin, Robt.F.McAfee, Dealer In Groceries, Crockery 165.00
Rolling Pin, Roll-Rite, Clear, Tin Cap, 14 In. 12.50
Rolling Pin, Roosters, Foxes, Lambs, Maple & Applewood, 15 In. 140.00
Rolling Pin, Save Your Dough 110.00
Rolling Pin, Screw-Type Cap, Jadite 69.50
Rolling Pin, Spatterware, Red & Blue 145.00
Rolling Pin, Tiger Maple, Concentric Lines, 17 In. 12.50
Rolling Pin, Tiger Maple, Stripes, 1 Piece, 18 1/2 In. 30.00
Rolling Pin, Tiger Maple, 3 Piece, Turned Handles, 16 In. 30.00
Rolling Pin, Wild Flower Design, Crockery 165.00
Rolling Pin, Wood, Grooved 45.00
Rolling Pin, Wooden Axle, 19 In. 8.00
Rolling Pin, Wooden, Green Handle 10.00
Rolling Pin, Wooden, Grooved, Side Handles, 16 In. 110.00
Rolling Pin, Yellowware 95.00
Rolling Pin, 1 Handled, 11 In. 10.00
Sadiron, Cast Iron, Marked, 3 1/2 X 3 3/4 In. 45.00
Sadiron, Child's, Asbestos, Dated May 23, 1900, 2 Piece 37.50
Sadiron, Child's, Asbestos, Removable Top 20.00
Saltbox, Hinged Lid, Wooden, Hanging, Marked Guernsey Cooking Ware 50.00
Saltbox, Lidded, Wooden, Porcelain, Wall 47.50
Scale, Egg 15.00
Scaler, Fish, Wooden Handle 5.00
Scoop, Apple Butter, Open Handle, 1 Piece, Pine 150.00
Scoop, Burl, Cup Shape, Cone Handle, 18th Century, 6 In. 250.00
Scoop, Burl, Oval, Shallow, Stubby Handle, 6 1/2 In. 250.00
Scoop, Butter, Carved Maple, 1 Piece, 8 1/2 X 4 3/4 In. 35.00
Scoop, Butter, Maple, Concave Bowl, 4 1/2 X 5 1/2 In. 35.00
Scoop, Candy, Brass, Half Pound, Copper Loop 40.00
Scoop, Candy, Fruit And Greenery Design, Brass, 11 In. 35.00
Scoop, Carved Floral Design On Handle, 8 In. 140.00
Scoop, Cowl Top, Flat Bottom, Hold Half Pound, Brass, 8 In. 30.00
Scoop, Cylindrical, 18th Century, 4 1/4 In. 175.00
Scoop, Flour Barrel, Gray, Barrel Shaped, Tin, 12 In. 12.50
Scoop, Flour, Wooden, 1 Piece Of Wood 20.00
Scoop, Golden Sun Coffee 35.00
Scoop, Hand-Hewn, 18th Century, Tiger Maple, 10 In. 140.00

Scoop, Ice Cream, Aluminum, 9 In. 6.50
Scoop, Ice Cream, Gilchrist, No.31, 11 1/4 In. 35.00
Scoop, Ice Cream, Hamilton Mfg.Co., Wooden Handle, Brass, 11 In. 18.50
Scoop, Ice Cream, Tin 23.00
Scoop, Loop Handle, Flat Base, Tin, 1 Pound, 5 X 6 X 2 In. 18.50
Scoop, Tubular Handle, Brass, 15 3/4 In. 150.00
Scoop, Tubular Tin Handle, Holds 10 Pounds, C.1870, 9 X 5 In. 25.00
Seeder, Raisin, Enterprise, Mechanical, Cast Iron, 1897 .... 35.00
Seeder, Raisin, Gem, Iron, 1895 .... 25.00 To 40.00
Seeder, Raisin, Mechanical, Auburn, Maine 35.00
Sharpener, Knife, Hang Up, Pine Slab, Double Row, 1 X 7 In. 6.50
Sharpener, Knife, Wire Handle, Twisted Ends, Round Hone 10.00
Sharpener, Knife, Wooden Handle, Green, Marked A & J 7.50
Shaver, Ice, Wrightville Howe Co., Pa. 45.00
Sieve, Horsehair, 19th Century 110.00
Sifter, Baker's, J.H.Day Co., Wooden, Brushes & Screen 125.00
Sifter, Flour, Arched Hinged Handle, Wooden, Signed & Dated 1873 .... 175.00
Sifter, Flour, Bromwell's 3 Cup Measuring Sifter, Crank Handle 18.00
Sifter, Flour, Bromwell's, Tin, Green Wood Knob, 3 Cup Size 5.00
Sifter, Flour, Hand Held, Green Wooden Handle 4.00
Sifter, Flour, Hoosier 32.50
Sifter, Flour, Myers Bros. Coal, Tin 30.00
Sifter, Flour, Squeeze Handle, Foley, Tin 10.00
Sifter, Flour, Wall Mount, Crocus Pattern 22.50
Sifter, Flour, Wooden, 1861 .... 95.00
Sifter, Grain, Copper Screening, Wooden 15.00
Sifter, Pink & Black, Erickson Mfg., Tin, 2-Cup 7.50
Skewer, Figural, Duck Handle, Greece, 11 In. 4.00
Skillet, Griswold, Square 42.50
Skillet, Iron, 9 3/4 X 29 In. 35.00
Skillet, Long Handle, 3 Legs, Cast Iron 45.00
Skillet, No.4, Cast Iron, 6 In. 12.00
Skillet, Purple & White Swirl, Iron 40.00
Skillet, 2 Pour Lips, Grooved, American, Cast Iron, 11 In. 12.00
Skimmer, Brass Ferrule, Iron Handle, C.1880, 27 In. 50.00
Skimmer, Cream, Shell Shape, Brass-Rimmed Filter Hole In Center 160.00
Skimmer, Hand-Punched, Wrought-Iron Handle, Brass, 22 In. 75.00
Skimmer, Iron, Brass Edge, 22 In. 45.00
Skimmer, Iron, Handled, 27 In. 130.00
Skimmer, Iron, 18 1/2 In. 30.00
Skimmer, Sorghum, Wooden Handle, Tin Scoop 35.00
Slicer, Vegetable, Fluted Tin Blade, Wooden Handle 9.50
Slicer, Vegetable, Wooden, Hanging, Dated 1898, 20 In. 35.00
Slide Rule, Rumford Baking Powder, For Cooking 3.00
Soap Saver, Wire, Twisted Wire Handle .... 12.50 To 15.00
Spatula & Flesh Fork, Turned Wooden Handles, C.1890, 12 In. 10.00
Spatula, Embossed Rumford Baking Powder, 11 In. 10.00
Spatula, Hearth, Iron, Twisted Handle, 17 In. 600.00
Spatula, Iron, Twisted Handle, Rattail End, 20 In. 190.00
Spatula, Iron, Twisted Handle, 19 In. 25.00
Spatula, Wooden Handle, Iron Shank, C.1860, 2 X 4 In. 15.00
Spice Box, 4 Canisters, Round Stenciled Box, Tin 28.00
Spice Box, 6 Covered Boxes Inside, Labeled, Tin 50.00
Spice Box, 7 Small Tins Inside, Tin 45.00
Spice Box, 8 Canisters, Wooden 150.00
Spice Box, 8 Round Covered Boxes, Tin Band, Maple, Dated 1858 .... 175.00
Spice Box, 8-Drawer, Pine 110.00
Spice Rack, Hanging, 7 Labeled Wooden Canisters, 1870 .... 260.00
Spice, Chest, Hanging, 8-Drawer, Scalloped Top, Old Red Paint 120.00
Spit Turner, Clockwork, C.1800, 13 1/2 In. 125.00
Spoon & Fork, Florals, Wooden, Handcarved, 10 In. 20.00
Spoon Rest, Pan Shaped, Ceramic, Marked, Morton 4.00
Spoon, Basting, Androck, Red Wooden Handle 3.00
Spoon, Basting, Gray, Wall Hung, Iron Handle, Tin Bowl, C.1790 .... 5.00

Spoon, Basting, Wall Hung, Aluminum, Germany, Mueller & Co., 14 In. 30.00
Spoon, Basting, 1 Piece, Gray, Iron, C.1890, 13 In. 5.00
Spoon, Burlwood, Tapered Handle, 18th Century, 3 1/2 In. 300.00
Spoon, Chevron Design, Iron, 21 In. 50.00
Spoon, Hasty Pudding, Hand-Hewn Pine, 18 In. 45.00
Spoon, Hearth, Iron Whitesmith-Finished Handle, 18 In. 125.00
Spoon, Iron, Long Handled, 18th Century, Rattail End, 17 In. 100.00
Spoon, Iron, Pointed End, Round Bowl, 8 In. 110.00
Spoon, Iron, Primitive, 13 1/2 In. 35.00
Spoon, Iron, Spear Form, Hanging Holes, 25 In. 50.00
Spoon, Iron, Twisted Handle, 17 1/2 In. 35.00
Spoon, Maple, Hand-Carved, Hang-Up Hook, C.1860, 13 In. 60.00
Spoon, Marrow, 19th Century, Cherry, 10 In. 85.00
Spoon, Nickled Iron, 11 1/2 In. 8.00
Spoon, Tea Caddy, Squeeze Action, Nickel Plated 10.00
Squeezer, Lemon, Hinged Fulcrum Action, Iron, 9 In. 18.50
Squeezer, Lemon, Hinged, Wooden .... 28.00 To 45.00
Squeezer, Lemon, Iron, Ironstone Insert 30.00
Squeezer, Lemon, Maple, C.1870, 12 In. 50.00
Squeezer, Lemon, Pierced Aluminum Insert, Hinged, 11 In. 34.00
Squeezer, Lemon, Wood, Legged 125.00
Squeezer, Lemon, Wooden, 2-Part 40.00
Squeezer, Lemon, Wooden, 11 In. 25.00
Stamp, Butter, Acorn & Leaf Design, Wooden, 4 3/4 In. 40.00
Stamp, Butter, Acorn On Branch, Hand-Carved, 2 5/8 In. 30.00
Stamp, Butter, Bird, Looking Backwards, Raised Wings, Round, 4 In. 260.00
Stamp, Butter, Cherry Pattern, Pine 35.00
Stamp, Butter, Chicken, Round, Wooden, 3 7/8 In. 255.00
Stamp, Butter, Cow & Eagle, 18th Century, Hand-Carved 250.00
Stamp, Butter, Cow, Hand-Carved 175.00
Stamp, Butter, Cow, 18th Century, Hand-Carved 350.00
Stamp, Butter, Eagle With Leaf Border, Round, Wooden, 3 3/4 In. 135.00
Stamp, Butter, Eagle With Star, Round, Wooden, 4 1/2 In. 300.00
Stamp, Butter, Eagle, Baby, With Arrow In Talon, Wooden, 4 In. 295.00
Stamp, Butter, Eagle, Knob Handle, Maple, 3 1/2 In. 250.00
Stamp, Butter, Eagle, Red Paint, Turned Handle, 3 3/8 In. 200.00
Stamp, Butter, Eagle, Round, Wooden, 4 3/4 In. .... 85.00 To 195.00
Stamp, Butter, Fan, Figural 195.00
Stamp, Butter, Flower 25.00
Stamp, Butter, Flower With Ferns, Hand-Carved 65.00
Stamp, Butter, Flower, Side Handle, 3 1/2 In. 13.00
Stamp, Butter, Leaf, Wooden, 4 5/8 In. 50.00
Stamp, Butter, Lollipop, Wooden, Tulip, 9 In. 325.00
Stamp, Butter, Pineapple & Tulips, Turned Handle, 3 3/4 In. 65.00
Stamp, Butter, Pinwheel, Heart, 2-Sided, Wooden, Handled, 3 1/2 In. 200.00
Stamp, Butter, Pomegranate, Flower, Leaves, Almond Shaped, 6 In. 325.00
Stamp, Butter, Pot Of Flowers, 3 3/4 In. 45.00
Stamp, Butter, Primitive Eagle, Red Paint, Turned Handle, 4 In. 300.00
Stamp, Butter, Roller, Leaf Design, Wooden, 5 1/2 In. 185.00
Stamp, Butter, Stars, Hearts, Leaf, Pinwheel, Wooden, 3 X 5 In. 145.00
Stamp, Butter, Stylized Crosshatched Tulip & Flower, Wooden, 3 In. 45.00
Stamp, Butter, Stylized Tulip & Heart, Oblong, Wooden, 4 1/2 In. 345.00
Stamp, Butter, Stylized Tulip, Round, Wooden, 4 1/8 In. 195.00
Stamp, Butter, Swan, Round, 4 In. 30.00
Stamp, Butter, Swastika Pattern, Round, Hand-Carved, 3 1/2 In. 175.00
Stamp, Butter, Swimming Swan, Mid-19th Century 100.00
Stamp, Butter, Tulip & Heart, Double, Wooden, 4 1/4 In. 55.00
Stamp, Butter, Tulip & Heart, Wooden, 3 3/4 In. 150.00
Stamp, Butter, Tulip & Leaves, Round, Wooden, 4 3/8 In. 45.00
Stamp, Butter, Tulip & Leaves, Turned Handle, 2 3/4 In. 50.00
Stamp, Butter, Tulip & Other Flowers, 1 Piece, 4 3/4 In. 145.00
Stamp, Butter, Tulip & Star, 1 Piece, Wooden Handle, 4 In. 175.00
Stamp, Butter, Tulip, Finger Grips, 4 1/4 In. 50.00
Stamp, Butter, Tulip, Flowers, Turned Handle, Wooden, 5 In. 135.00

Stamp, Butter, Tulip, Turned Handle, 3 1/2 In. 125.00
Stamp, Butter, Wild Flower & Fern, 3 3/4 In. 45.00
Steamer, Clam, 2 Screen Shelves, Sliding Door, Copper, 18 1/2 In. 150.00
Stirrer, Apple Butter, Wooden .... 20.00 To 25.00
Stove Plate, Hudson River Valley, Cast Iron, 25 1/2 X 24 In. 975.00
Strainer, Cheese, Round, Footed, Tin 33.00
Strainer, Cream, Brass Wire, Pedestal Base, Hang-Up Hook, 4 X 2 In. 16.50
Strainer, Gray, Tin, Concentric Lines, C.1860, 11 In. 25.00
Strainer, Heart-Shaped, Footed, Tin 85.00
Strainer, Milk, Tin 6.00
Strainer, Tea, Birdcage, Brass Wire Handle, Cup Hook 10.00
Strainer, Tea, Salada Tea, Brass Screen, Green Handle, 8 In. 6.50
Strainer, Wooden Handle 5.00
Strainer, Yellow Wooden Handle 3.00
String Holder, Wire, 2 Spindle 79.00
Sugar Shaker, Hand-Pierced, Handled, Tinsmith Made, 3 X 4 In. 40.00
Sugar Shaker, Tin 12.00
Sweeper, Bissel, Floor, Oak 25.00
Tea Warmer, Lithophane, Brass Holder, Original Burner, 4 1/2 X 5 In. 235.00
Teakettle, Cast Iron 35.00
Teakettle, Child's, Iron 65.00
Teakettle, Handmade, Name On Handle, Copper 85.00
Teakettle, Spherical, Ribbed Domed Cover, Bail Handle, Iron, 8 In. 300.00
Teakettle, Whistling, Enamel Handle, Germany, Brass, 7 X 7 In. 35.00
Tenderizer, Maple, 1 Piece, C.1810, 8 1/2 In. 35.00
Tin, Biscuit, Queen Elizabeth On Horse, Huntley & Palmer 20.00
Toaster, Bread, Rotating, 4 Arched Feet, Ring Handle, 18th Century 125.00
Toaster, Stove Top, Flat Wire, 14 X 10 In. 6.00
Toaster, Wire Frame, Maltese Cross Pattern, Wooden Handle, 18 In. 29.00
Tongs, Ice, Cast Iron, Country Store 10.00
Tongs, Tin, Marked Vaughan-Chicago 2.00
Trimmer & Crimper, Pie Crust, Brass 35.00
Trimmer, Pice Crust, Brass, Wooden Handle 15.00
Turner, Cake, Large Blade, Wooden Handle, A & J 3.00
Vacuum Cleaner, Winchester 65.00
Waffle Iron, Child's 65.00
Waffle Iron, 2-Section, Wooden Handle, 21 In. 30.00
Wash Stick, Hand-Carved, Diamond Center, 27 In. 15.00
Wash Stick, Maple, Wall Hung, 32 In. 22.50
Washboard, Blue Stenciled Tree Stump Top, Glass Insert, 8 X 18 In. 16.00
Washboard, Corrugated Glass, Wooden Frame, 12 1/2 X 24 In. 14.00
Washboard, Metal & Wooden 10.00
Washboard, National, Wood Frame, Brass, Embossed Tin Soap Saver 14.00
Washboard, Pine, 11 X 24 In. 65.00
Washboard, Stenciled Capitol Building, Wood, Metal Insert 10.00
Washboard, 1940s War Effort, Wooden, 12 X 18 In. 14.00
Washing Machine, Dated 1883 .... 145.00
Whisk, Baker's, Wireware, 18 In. 16.50
Whisk, Screw-Type, Single Handle 15.00
Whisk, Wire, Green Wooden Handle 4.00
Wringer, Ash, Turned Handle, Hinged End, Wm.D.Slaw, J.M.D., 21 1/2 In. ... 17.50

KNIFE, Advertising, Anheuser-Busch, Peep Sight 175.00
Barlow, Pocket 20.00
Bowie & Sheath, Herter's Improved, 10 In. 15.00
Bowie & Sheath, Horn Grip, 11 In. 15.00
Bowie, Bone Handle, Marked L.F. & C., Blade 6 In. 75.00
Bowie, Collins, V-44, Survival, Green Grip 75.00
Bowie, Jos.Allen, 8 1/2 In. 40.00
Bowie, Mexican, Engraved Blade, 13 In. 15.00
Bowie, Sheffield, Challenge, 10 In. 48.00
Bowie, Sheffield, Milbro, 10 1/4 In. 40.00
Bowie, Sheffield, Wade, & Butcher, 10 1/4 In. 45.00
Bowie, Wade & Butcher, 9 In. 45.00

Bullet, No.R4353, Pocket	750.00
Camillus American Wildlife, No.11, Pocket	50.00
Case, XX, Moose, No.6275SP, Pocket	75.00
Character, Babe Ruth, Mottled Black & Gray, 1 Blade, 2 1/4 In.	45.00
Cigar Cutter, Super Knife Patented, Hook For Key Chain, Metal	10.00
Crooked, Carved Handle, All Original	65.00
Crown Cutlery, N.Y., Black Wooden Handle, 2 Blades, Pocket	5.00
Double Blade, Florals & Beading, Sterling Silver, 2 3/8 In.	23.00
Embossed, Nude Girl Riding Tiger, 2-Blade, Sheffield, U.S.A., 2 3/8 In.	65.00
Fairmont Cutlery, 2 Blades, Marbleized Handle, Pocket, 2 1/2 In.	12.00
Farrier's, Bone Handle	15.00
Filipino, Carved Horse Head Grip, Scabbard, 22 2n.	25.00
Folding Race, Brass Handle, New York Knife Co., Walden	49.00
Folding, Bell From Maggie, 1873, Sterling Silver, Chain, 7 1/2 In.	35.00
Folding, John 8 Scotch Whiskey, On Keychain	5.00
Hay, Double Handle, Large	12.00
Hunting, Leather Sheath, 9 In.	25.00
Hunting, Mundail, Germany, Bone Handle, 10 1/2 In.	30.00
Hunting, U.S.Army, 1880	95.00
Ivory Handle, 2 Blades, 2 In.Long	6.00
Jack, Advertising, E.H.Best & Co., 2 Blades, Cut Design, 3 1/2 In.	12.50
John West & Co., Chicago, 1920, Pocket	20.00
Ka-Bar, Hunter, 8 In.	10.00
Lady's, Sterling Silver, Pocket	32.00
Leaf Blade, Congo, 1o 1/2 In.	50.00
Machete, Case, No.XX, Folding, World War II, Guard	75.00
Nu-Grape, Opener Combination, Pocket	35.00
Purina Checkerboard, 3-Blade, Pocket, 3 3/8 In.	17.50 To 25.00
Remington, Humback, 5 Blade	450.00
Remington, Hunter, 8 1/2 In.	25.00 To 30.00
Remington, No.R2045, Pocket	60.00
Remington, No.R2203, Pocket	85.00 To 95.00
Remington, No.R6391, Pocket	110.00 To 150.00
Stiletto, Tapered Neck, C.1910, Stainless Steel, Closed 3 In.	7.50
Texas Ranger, 1973, Wooden Case	100.00
Winchester, No.2079, Pocket	75.00
Winchester, No.2907	80.00
2 Blade, Beading & Floral Design, Sterling Silver, Pocket, 2 7/8 In.	28.00
2 Blade, Embossed Scroll, Sterling Silver, Pocket, 2 3/8 In.	22.00

KNOWLES, TAYLOR & KNOWLES, see KTK; Lotus Ware

KOCH, Bowl, Apple, 10 In.	49.00
Bowl, Grapes, Marked, 12 In.	60.00
Bowl, Peaches On Cream Ground, 12 In.	60.00
Creamer, Apples, Water Ground	37.00
Plate, Apples & Grapes, Signed, 8 1/2 In., Pair	75.00
Plate, Apples, Green & Brown Ground, Signed, 7 1/2 In.	38.00
Plate, Apples, Leaves & Blossom, Signed, 8 1/2 In.	55.00
Plate, Cake, Grapes, Handled, 11 In., Marked	60.00
Plate, Colored Fruit, White Ground, Signed, 7 1/2 In.	22.00
Plate, Grapes, 6 In., Marked	30.00

Korean ware is a heavy-glazed pottery usually featuring three-dimensional figures of people and animals as decorations. Dull orange and gray-blue are favored colors. Korean ware is still being made.

KOREAN WARE, Bowl, Lion, Mountains, Orange Background, 6 In. Diameter	75.00
Vase, Raised Boy Figures Climbing Mountain, 9 3/4 In.	225.00

𝒦.𝒫.𝓜

Most dealers and collectors use the term "KPM" to refer to Berlin porcelain, but the same initials were used alone and in combination with other symbols by several German porcelain makers. They include the Konigliche Porzellan Manufaktur of Berlin, initials used in mark 1823-1847; Meissen, 1723-1724 only; Krister Porzellan Manufaktur in

Waldenburg, after 1831; Kranichfelder Porzellan Manufaktur in Kranichfeld, after 1903; and the Kister Porzellan Manufaktur in Scheibe, after 1838.

KPM, Box, Powder, Gold & Floral Painting, Round, 3 In. 55.00
Bust, Lady, Renaissance, Marked Wagner, 5 1/4 In. 2750.00
Cup & Saucer, Cake Plate, Pink Floral Design, Gold Trim, Porcelain 20.00
Dish, Divided, White, Gold Trim 40.00
Dish, Shell, Divided, Handle 42.00
Figurine, Dachshund, Begging Position, Blue Scepter Mark 200.00
Figurine, Monk, Reading Bible, Scepter Mark, 1872, 7 1/2 X 6 1/4 In. 1870.00
Figurine, Ruth Standing With Wheat, Signed A.Schref, 9 X 5 3/4 In. 1540.00
Gravy Boat, Underplate, White 18.00
Plaque, Lion & Maiden, C.1920, 13 X 10 1/4 In. 3900.00
Plate, Eagle Lace, C.1880, Cream & Gold 80.00
Platter, Lady & Man, Gold Lattice, Marked, 12 1/2 X 17 3/4 In. 495.00
Salt, Gold Design In Center, Gold Rim, Oval, Set Of 4 .... 39.50
Sugar & Creamer, Diamond-Shape, Forget-Me-Nots On Ivory, Gold Handles 92.00
Sugar & Creamer, Flowered Middle Band, Diamond Shape, Gold Handles 97.00

K.T.&k.
CHINA
KTK are the initials of the Knowles, Taylor and Knowles Company of East Liverpool, Ohio, founded by Isaac W.Knowles in 1853. They made Lotus Ware. The firm merged with American Ceramic Corporation in 1928. The company closed in 1934.

KTK LOTUS WARE, see Lotus Ware
KTK, Pitcher, Gold Design, 6 1/2 In. 385.00
Pitcher, Pancake, Geometric On White, Cover, 6 1/2 In. 55.00

KU KLUX KLAN, Banner, Grand Dragon's Band, No.41, Ohio, Brass Eagle, Case 200.00
Card, 1920s 7.50
Match Holder, Book Shaped, Celluloid Over Tin, 1 3/4 In. 88.00
Match Holder, Figure On Horse, Celluloid Over Tin, 7 1/8 In. 85.00
Medalette, Silver, Dated 1866, Crown Over Crest 35.00
Medalette, Silver, Spread Winged Eagle, Burning Cross 25.00
Membership Card, Issued July 1928, Signed C.W.Hewitt 150.00
Newsletter, Office Of Grand Dragon, 1929 .... 10.00
Seal, Notary, Spokane 115.00
Tag, Key, Silver, Embossed Klansman On Horse 25.00

Kutani ware is a Japanese porcelain made after the mid-seventeenth century. Most of the pieces found today are nineteenth century.

KUTANI, Ashtray, Elephant, 6 3/4 X 4 1/2 In. 38.00
Bowl, Fruit, Oriental Garden Scene, 10 1/2 In.Diam. 55.00
Charger, Hand-Painted Battle Scene, 18 In.Diam. 695.00
Cup & Saucer, Birds Of Paradise, Demitasse 240.00
Cup & Saucer, Brocade, Raised Gold & Enamel Beading 18.00
Cup & Saucer, Scenic & Floral, Medallions 48.00
Dish, Fish-Shaped, Crabs, Birds, & Scrolls, Late 18th Century 295.00
Dish, Heart-Shaped, One Thousand Faces Pattern 85.00
Dish, Shell-Shaped, Tailed Bird On Branch, Iron Red & Gilding, 8 In. 220.00
Figurine, Elephant, Ashtray On Back, Matchbox On Side, 6 In. 42.00
Figurine, Lady Seated Playing Mandolin, 6 In. 32.00
Jar, Ginger, 6 In. 95.00
Pitcher, Bird Form, Bird's Head Spout With Mouth Open 130.00
Pitcher, Birds & Flowers, C.1840, 6 In. 150.00
Plate, Oriental Garden Scene, Script Mark, 10 In. 12.00
Plate, Thatched Roof Huts, Leaping Fish, Gold Border, Signed, 10 In. 35.00
Syrup, Allover Brocade, Raised Gold & Enamel Beading 30.00
Tea Set, Lake & Mountain Scene, Gold Rim, Lithophane Cups, 12 Piece 150.00

LACQUER, Box, Dresser, Mt.Fuji, Pagoda, & Bridge, Lock, 7 X 7 3/4 X 3 In. 10.00
Box, Pen, Figural & Calligraphic Reserves, C.1900, Persian, 9 In. 160.00
Chest, Painted Medallions On Top Of Dignitaries, Stand, 36 X 18 In. 990.00
Chest, Polychrome Figures On Terraces, 4 Ft. 11 In. X 3 Ft. 385.00
Inro, Carved Side Panel, Figure Of Boy, Reverse Dragon, Glass Ojime 250.00
Inro, Rising Scaly Dragon, Netsuke Form Of Seated Figure 215.00

R. LALIQUE   LALIQUE 🖋

Lalique glass was made by Rene Lalique in Paris, France, between
the 1890s and his death in 1945. The glass was molded, pressed, and
engraved in Art Nouveau and Art Deco styles. Pieces were marked
with the signature "R. Lalique." Lalique glass is still being made.
Pieces made after 1945 bear the mark "Lalique."

LALIQUE, Ashtray, Antheor, Nude Mermaid, Frosted, Signed	325.00
Ashtray, Pheasant	80.00
Ashtray, 8 Girls' Faces Form Rim, 4 1/4 In.Diam.	90.00
Atomizer, Seminude Women, Green Wash, Le Parisien	350.00
Atomizer, Seminude Women, 4 1/2 In.	125.00
Atomizer, 6 Nude Women	230.00
Bookend, Hirondelles, Frosted Bird, Pair	375.00
Bottle, Cologne, Floral Design, Jaytho, Signed, 4 3/4 In.	169.00
Bowl & Plate, Coquilles, Signed, Plate, 6 1/2 In.	345.00 To 550.00
Bowl, Beaded Circles, Art Deco, 8 In.	185.00
Bowl, Chicoree, Opalescent, Signed, 8 In.	170.00
Bowl, Coquille, Opalescent, 6 1/2 X 5 1/4 In.	225.00
Bowl, Coquille, Shell Feet, Opalescent, 9 In.	275.00
Bowl, Fish Border, Allover Bubbles, Signed, 13 3/4 In.	450.00
Bowl, Greyhounds, Marked, 9 X 3 In.	375.00
Bowl, Impressed Flower Circles Overall, Marked, 10 In.	335.00
Bowl, Jaffa Pattern, Underplate, Amber, Bowl, 5 1/2 In.	850.00
Bowl, Leaves Around Border, Signed, 12 In.Diam.	300.00
Bowl, Lily Pads, Frosted To Clear, 11 1/2 In.	400.00
Bowl, Mistletoe, Marked, Numbered, 9 1/2 In.	495.00
Box, Powder, 3 Dancing Nudes On Lid, Signed D'Orsay, 3 3/4 In.	225.00
Chandelier, 12 Lights, C.1925	3500.00
Clock, Floral Design	1400.00
Clock, Lily Of The Valley, Frosted & Clear, 5 X 5 In.	750.00
Figurine, Angel Fish, Green-Blue, Impressed, 2 1/4 X 2 In.	95.00
Figurine, Bear, Polar, 3 In.	65.00
Figurine, Cat, Reclining	457.00
Figurine, Cockatoo, Iridescent, Signed, 11 1/2 In.	950.00 To 1050.00
Figurine, Doe	85.00
Figurine, Fish, Blue, Marked, 2 X 2 In.	110.00
Figurine, Frog, Large	125.00 To 190.00
Figurine, Hedgehog, 2 1/2 X 5 In.	170.00
Figurine, Madonna & Child, Black Base, Signed, 14 In.	495.00
Figurine, Salamander, Green, 7 In.	179.00
Figurine, Turtle, Amber, 5 In.	210.00
Figurine, Wild Boar	85.00
Knife Rest, Marked France	60.00
Panel, Virgin & Child, Intaglio Cut Figures, Signed, 13 1/2 In.Tall	950.00
Paperweight, Chrysis, Frosted Nude, 5 1/2 In.	225.00 To 425.00
Paperweight, Deer	99.00
Paperweight, Deer With Diana	115.00
Paperweight, Ram, Frosted	45.00
Paperweight, Salamander, Green	99.00
Pendant, Red To Tops Of Yellow, Signed, Amberina	875.00
Perfume, Allover Thorny Brambles, Signed, 3 3/4 X 4 1/4 In.	225.00
Perfume, Applied Rose, Clear Frieze, Signed, 5 1/2 In.	175.00
Perfume, Cactus Pattern, Frosted, Blue Centers	250.00
Perfume, Dahlia, Black Enameled Design, 7 In.	159.00
Perfume, Deux Fleurs	75.00
Perfume, Doves, 4 In.	65.00
Perfume, Lily-Of-The-Valley Stopper	85.00
Perfume, Moon & Star, Stopper, 3 3/4 In.	395.00
Perfume, Stopper, Frosted, Green Beaded Swags, Art Deco, 5 1/2 In.	175.00
Perfume, Thorn, Epines, Brown Wash, 3 3/4 In.	365.00
Perfume, Thorn, Epines, Mauve Ground, Signed, 5 In.	475.00

Perfume, 2 Doves On Ground Glass Topper, Signed 140.00
Perfume, 4 Panels Frosted Ladies, 4 Frosted Panels, Signed 165.00
Plate, Annual, 1969, Original Box, 8 1/2 In. 95.00
Plate, Annual, 1970, Peacock, Original Box, 8 1/2 In. 95.00
Plate, Black, 7 In. 75.00
Plate, Convolvulus, Amber 250.00
Plate, Coquille, Shells Form Feet, Opalescent, 12 In. 250.00
Plate, Crescent Shape, Molded Design, Signed, 6 X 8 In. 135.00
Plate, Dancing Nude, 10 In. 210.00
Seal, Birds In Center, Pierced Branches, Marked, 2 In. 50.00
Sherry, Clear, 6 Frosted Recessed Females, Marked, 4 In. 60.00
Stand, Teakwood, Monnaie Du Pape, 10 1/2 In. 1350.00
Toothpick, Petal Design, Black Flower Base, Signed, 2 In. 85.00
Tray, Pin, Molded Center Lovebirds, Signed 55.00
Tumbler, Liquor, Art Nouveau Fish Design, Signed 55.00
Vase Mold, Polished Berries, Frosted, Spherical, Signed 629.00
Vase, Amethyst, Berry & Vine Design, Marked, 6 3/4 In. 350.00
Vase, Caramel Yellow, Eagles, Nudes, Classic Shape, Marked, 10 In. 1200.00
Vase, Dahlias, Frosted, 10 In. 900.00
Vase, Escargot, Snail, Frosted White, Signed, 12 In. 850.00
Vase, Formose Pattern, Red, Signed, 7 In. 2200.00
Vase, Horse Design, Marked, 7 In. 235.00
Vase, Ormeaux, Elm Tree, Opalescent, Round, 6 3/4 In. 485.00
Vase, Robins & Cherries, Signed, 6 X 6 In. 425.00
Vase, Tournesol Pattern, Gray Ground, Silver Rim, Marked, 4 In. 335.00
Vase, 20 Frosted Raised Birds, Marked 285.00
Wine, Children Around, Different Positions, Marked, 1 3/4 In., Pr. 75.00
Wine, Male & Female Dancing Nude Stem, Signed, 5 3/4 In. 65.00
Wine, Silhouette, 2 Dancing Nude Women, 6 In. 75.00

LAMP, see also Bradley & Hubbard, Lamp; Burmese, Lamp; Handel,
Lamp; Pairpoint, Lamp; Tiffany, Lamp

LAMP, Aladdin, Alacite, Acorn, Table 40.00
Aladdin, Alacite, Electric, Red Ground, Leaf Motif, Marked, 15 In. 35.00
Aladdin, Alacite, Gold Band Around Base, Green, Tree Design, Pair, 15 In. 70.00
Aladdin, Alacite, Lady With Leopard 200.00
Aladdin, B-1, Pulldown, Nickel 125.00
Aladdin, B-20, Gold Luster Finish 170.00
Aladdin, B-26, Alacite, Decalmania 165.00
Aladdin, B-51, Washington Drape, Green 69.00
Aladdin, B-62, Lincoln Drape, Ruby Crystal Shade, 10 1/4 In. 375.00
Aladdin, B-75, Alacite, Lincoln Drape, Tall .... 100.00 To 110.00
Aladdin, B-77, Ruby Crystal, Lincoln Drape, Tall 350.00
Aladdin, B-80, Beehive .... *Illus* 50.00
Aladdin, B-82, Beehive, Amber Crystal, No.601 Shade 200.00
Aladdin, B-82, No.601 Shade 200.00
Aladdin, B-83, Beehive, Ruby Red 200.00
Aladdin, B-83, Ruby Crystal 190.00
Aladdin, B-87, Rose Moonstone, Vertique 100.00
Aladdin, B-88, Yellow Moonstone, Vertique .... 225.00 To 240.00
Aladdin, B-92, Green Moonstone, Vertique 95.00
Aladdin, B-99, Venetian, Original Shade, Clear 120.00
Aladdin, B-112, Table, Rose Moonstone, Cathedral 100.00
Aladdin, B-114, Corinthian, White Moonstone 70.00
Aladdin, B-115, Green Moonstone 100.00
Aladdin, B-130, Ivory, Oriental 65.00
Aladdin, B-136, Chromium 140.00
Aladdin, B-137, Bronze 160.00
Aladdin, Blown-Out Flowers & Base Glass, Painted Ground, Electric 65.00
Aladdin, G-16, Figure, Alacite .... 200.00 To 275.00
Aladdin, G-24, Cupid Alacite 80.00
Aladdin, Hanging, Log Cabin Shade 200.00
Aladdin, Hanging, Model B, Parchment Shade 75.00

Aladdin, Lincoln Drape, Cobalt Blue, 1976, Boxed 50.00
Aladdin, M-9, Table, Burner 60.00
Aladdin, No.2, Brass, Table 125.00
Aladdin, No.3, Table, Dimpled, 3 Small Dents 170.00
Aladdin, No.5, Hanging 150.00
Aladdin, No.6, Table, Chippendale Shade 125.00
Aladdin, No.9, Nickel Over Brass, Shade 160.00
Aladdin, No.109, Amber Crystal, Burner .... 65.00 To 75.00
Aladdin, No.202, Cased Green Shade 1000.00
Aladdin, Student, Gooseneck 27.50
Aladdin, Table, Milk Glass Shade, Chrome Over Brass 85.00
Alcohol, Meteor 60.00
Angle, Hanging, 4-Burner 450.00
Angle, Pull-Down Canopy, Nickel Finish, 24 In. 425.00
Animated, Revolving, Laurel & Hardy, 1971, Boxed 37.50
Art Deco, Fry Glass Shade, Brass 50.00
Art Deco, Girl Seated On Pedestal, Roses At Top, 14 1/2 In. 195.00
Art Deco, Gray White Translucent Glass, 3-Step Base, 3 In. 30.00
Art Deco, Millefiori Ball Shade, Ballerina Balancing Shade, 25 In. 650.00
Art Nouveau, Frosted Candle, Flame Shape, Metal Stand, 9 1/2 In., Pair 150.00
Banquet, Allover Violets On Globe, Brass Base, 15 3/4 In. 295.00
Banquet, Baby Thumbprint, Ruffled Rim, Blue 130.00
Banquet, Blown-Out Lion Heads, 4 Blown-Out Medallions, 24 In. 595.00
Banquet, Consolidated Bulging Loops, White 125.00
Banquet, Duplex, Doric Column Base, Cranberry Font, Frosted Shade 675.00
Banquet, Florette, Green Satin Glass, Miniature 195.00
Banquet, Gold Overlay On Crystal Ball Shade, Marble Base, 32 In. 300.00
Banquet, Nouveau, Red Slag Shade, Jewels, Brass Base, Electrified, 39 In. 3250.00
Banquet, Pink Flowers On Base & Globe, Cherubs, Miniature 325.00
Banquet, Rippled Rim Shade, Cranberry 120.00
Banquet, Wrought Iron, Ball Shade, 22 In. 150.00
Berry, Conforming Stand, Oval Lamp, 19th Century, Tin, 6 1/2 In. 100.00
Betty, Crimped Edge Pan, Saucer Base, Tin, 8 In. 215.00
Betty, Double, Hand-Punched Tin, 6 In. 165.00
Betty, Iron, Square, Corner Spouts, 3 In. 45.00
Betty, Iron, Swan Finial, American, 18th Century, 6 In. 130.00
Betty, Iron, Twisted Hanger, Scroll Design, 1/ 3/4 In. 75.00
Betty, Saucer Base, Black, Tin, 8 3/4 In. 110.00
Betty, Tin, On Stand, 9 1/2 In. 325.00
Betty, Wrought & Cast Iron, Swivel Hook, Brass Shield, 3, 1/2 In. 195.00
Boudoir, Colonial Figures, Wired, Germany, 8 1/2 In. 18.00
Boudoir, Fabric Inserts, Metal Shade, Painted, 13 1/2 In., Pair 145.00
Boudoir, Fenton, 12 In. 85.00
Boudoir, Latticework Ground, Signed Base .... *Illus* 500.00
Boudoir, Stratford Shade, Fully Signed .... *Illus* 800.00
Boudoir, Swag-Trimmed Shade, Crystal Beading & Fringe, 18 In., Pair 175.00
Bracket, Floral Dots & Lines On Font, 1876, 12 1/2 In. 40.00
Bracket, Oil, Faceted Band At Top, Blown Chimney, 14 In. 20.00
Bracket, Tin Reflector, Oil, Marked, Black, 13 1/2 In. 60.00
Bracket, Victorian, Candle, Frosted To Clear Shade, Brass, 14 X 14 In. 125.00
Bracket, Wall, Cranberry Shade, Oil, Reflector 195.00
     LAMP, BRADLEY & HUBBARD, see Bradley & Hubbard, Lamp
Buggy, Clear Bull's-Eye Globe, Whitney Carriage Co., 6 3/4 In. 22.50
Buggy, Dietz Union, Dated 1907 .... 37.00
Buggy, Dietz, Buckeye, Bail Handle, Square Tube, 1892 .... 45.00
Buggy, Dietz, Night Driver's Friend, Style A, Pair 125.00
Buggy, Hinged Reflector Port, Wire Bail, Tin, 9 1/2 In. 45.00
Buggy, Rayo, No.80, Brass Burner, Dated April 10, 1906 .... 55.00
Buggy, Reed, No.2 Special, Red Japanned Finish 55.00
Candle, Tin & Glass, Cylindrical Carrying Ring, 10 In. 300.00
Candle, Tin & Glass, Square Sides, Reticulated Top, 8 In. 525.00
Candle, Wrought Iron, Rectangular Pan, 2 Sockets, 13 3/4 In. 190.00
Carriage, Brass Eagle Finial, 19th Century, Brass, 30 In., Pair 250.00
Cast Metal, Hexagonal One-Story Pagoda Form, 20th Century, 12 1/2 In. 130.00

Lamp, Aladdin, B-80, Beehive

Lamps, Boudoir, Stratford Shade, Fully Signed; Latticework Ground, Signed Base

Chandelier, Art Nouveau, Leaded Glass, 19th Century, 20 In.	375.00
Chandelier, Candle, 9 Light, Tin, Electrified	150.00
Chandelier, Globe, Honeycomb Optic, Melon Ribs, Wire Frame, 16 X 10 In.	240.00
Chandelier, Iron, Circular Form, Scalloped Edge, 19th Century, 19 In.	350.00
Chandelier, Wooden, Central Turned Post, With Tin, Fluted Drips, 22 In.	750.00
Chandelier, Wooden, 3 Iron Scroll Arms, Red Paint, 23 In.	325.00
Coach, Copper Trim, Beveled Glass, 13 3/4 In.	25.00
Coal Oil, Round Bottom, Bracket	16.00
Cornelius & Co., Cut Glass Prisms, Bronze Rococo Base, 1849, 16 3/4 In.	425.00
LAMP, COSMOS, see Cosmos, Lamp	
Crusie, Double, Twisted Hanger, Iron, 6 In.	45.00
Crusie, Iron, Double, European, Twisted Hanger, 5 1/2 In.	35.00 To 50.00
Crusie, Iron, Double, Hanging Chain, 4 1/2 In.	110.00
Crusie, Iron, Double, Ram's Horn Scrolled Handle, 11 In.	180.00
Cut Glass Shade, Worm Gear Wick Raiser, Brass Font, Signed, 24 In.	795.00
Cut Glass, Floral & Leaf Pattern, Mushroom Top, 1 Light, 19 In.	1600.00
Cut Glass, Mushroom Top, 2 Side Lights, 21 In.	2250.00
Cut Glass, Prism, Frosted & Cut Dome Shade, 20 1/2 In.	750.00
Desk, Art Nouveau, Figural, Bronze, Signed Raoul Larche	5100.00
Desk, Marble Insert, C.1915, Paper Shade, Brass	85.00
Desk, Parker Pen, Wood Base, C.1950	45.00
Electric, Art Deco Girl, Palm Tree, Vienna Bronze	595.00
Electric, Clown Base, Animals Around Shade, Camphor Glass	75.00
Electric, Hobstars, Flowers, & Leaves, Matching Dome Shade, 20 In.	695.00
Electric, Holding Lamp, Multicolored Globe Shade, Pot Metal	65.00
Electric, Japanese Lady Holding Branch With 6 Lights, C.1920, Metal	900.00
Electric, Jester Musicians, Flanking Spherical Glass Globe	95.00
Electric, Lady On Metal Ball, End-Of-Day Globe, Art Nouveau, 24 In.	160.00
Electric, Oriental Lady Standing By Tree, 1930s, 14 In.	125.00
Electric, Red Goose Shoes, Plaster Of Paris, 20 In.	125.00
Electric, Rogers Bros., Silver Plated, Grape Pattern, Leaded Shade	1200.00
Electric, Sea Gulls, Wings Framing Amber Shade, Art Deco, Metal, 9 In.	55.00
Emeralite, No.9, Shade, Desk	185.00
Emeralite, Original Glass Shade, Brass, Desk	175.00
Fairy, Acid Finish, Webb Burmese, Clarke Base, 4 X 3 In.	175.00
Fairy, Autumn Leaf, Hand-Painted, Fenton, Burmese Glass	69.00
Fairy, Blue Satin, White Thread Base, Daisy & Button, 5 In.	185.00
Fairy, Blue, Frosted, Opalescent Swirl, Enameled Foral, 3 X 3 1/2 In.	550.00
Fairy, Blue, Frosted, Verre Moire, Clarke, 4 7/8 X 6 1/8 In.	425.00

Fairy, Burmese, Polished Pontil, 6 In.	285.00
Fairy, Candy-Striped Overlay, 5 1/4 In., 3 Part	395.00
Fairy, Clarke, Cricklite, Cut, Standard, Gilt Fittings, 15 3/4 In.	415.00
Fairy, Clear Base, Satin Glass Top, Design, Marked Germany, 4 In.	165.00
Fairy, Cranberry, Diamond Point Shade, Marked, 3 In.	35.00
Fairy, Craquelle, Ruby Red, Signed Clarke, 8 In.	345.00
Fairy, Diamond-Quilted, Marked Clarke Base, Rose, 3 5/8 In.	145.00
Fairy, Double Baby Face, Base Marked Clarke, Emerald Green, 4 1/4 In.	195.00
Fairy, Frowning Nun, Bisque, 3 In.	195.00
Fairy, German Dog, Bisque, Glass Eyes, Blue Bow, 3 1/2 In.	170.00
Fairy, Little Miss Muffet, White Porcelain, Gold Design, Lithophane	295.00
Fairy, Mother-Of-Pearl, Floral Design, Clarke Mark, 3 3/4 X 4 In.	295.00
Fairy, Owl, Glass Eyes, White Porcelain, RS Germany	250.00
Fairy, Sandwich Overshot, 9 Protruding Ribs, O Shade, Clarke Base	85.00
Fairy, Satin Glass, Blue	375.00
Finger, Bulbous Knobs, Concave Sadiron Shape Bowl	28.00
Finger, C.1900, Brass & Copper, 7 In.	25.00
Finger, Coal Oil, Pair	55.00
Finger, Coolidge Drape, Pedestal, Cobalt Blue	250.00
Finger, Double Wedding Band	50.00
Finger, Empress, Pedestal, Green	70.00
Finger, Heart Pattern, Custard Glass, Green	210.00
Finger, Little Buttercup, Camphene Burner, Ruby Shade	80.00
Finger, Loop Handle, Brass Collar, Marked B.& A.Hornet, 7 3/4 In.	65.00
Finger, Loop Handle, Half Pint Reservoir, Brass, 3 3/4 In.Diam.	18.50
Finger, Peacock Feather Pattern, Blue	275.00
Finger, Peanut, Cut Glass, Emerald Green	65.00
Floor, Champleve	2500.00
Floor, Iron, Painted White, 5 1/3 In.	40.00
Fluid, Pressed Glass & Marble, 8 In.Pair	40.00
Fluid, Pressed Glass, 9 1/4 In., Pair	40.00
Gas, Wall, Gas Shade, Iron Bracket, C.1850	350.00
Gone With The Wind, Blown-Out Floral, Red Satin Glass, Electrified	250.00
Gone With The Wind, Bluebird, Pale Gold Ground	295.00
Gone With The Wind, Cactus Design, Hand-Painted Shade	95.00
Gone With The Wind, Cord & Drapery Pattern, Red Satin Glass, 22 In.	650.00
Gone With The Wind, Flower Panels, Blue Ground, Electric, 21 1/2 In.	650.00
Gone With The Wind, Hand-Painted Iris On White, Green Tint	450.00
Gone With The Wind, Hand-Painted Shade, Cast Iron Footed, 19 In.	165.00
Gone With The Wind, Oil, Yellow Ball Shade	225.00
Gone With The Wind, Patented 1892, Florals, Pink & White	275.00
Gone With The Wind, Raised Water Lily, Pink & Green, Electrified	395.00
Gone With The Wind, Red & White Peonies, Blue & Red Ground	250.00
Gone With The Wind, Red Roses On White, Russet Tint	395.00
Gone With The Wind, Red Satin, Regal Iris, 27 In.	750.00
Gone With The Wind, Red Satin, Roses & Ruffles Pattern	645.00
Gone With The Wind, Thistle Pattern	400.00
Gone With The Wind, Victoria Pattern, Red Satin Glass, Large	875.00
Gorham, Lion's Head, Copper With Brass Handle, Marked, 4 3/4 In.	30.00
Grease, Saucer Base, Glazed Pottery, Mid-Eastern, 7 In.	100.00
Hall, Candle, Hanging, Clear Glass Shade, 19th Century, 13 In.	300.00
Hall, Hanging, Ruby Ball, Chains	265.00
Hall, Regal Iris, Red Satin	450.00
Hall, Regency Style, Blown Glass, C.1900, 30 In.	165.00
Hand, Amethyst Shade, Brass, Small	95.00
Hand, Birch Leaf, Footed	60.00
Hand, Black Tin, C.1900, Large	32.00
Hand, Bull's-Eye, Footed, Safety Handle, Green	160.00
Hand, Diamond Sunburst	65.00
Hand, Dorothy	60.00
Hand, Erin Fan, Footed	55.00
Hand, Erin Fan, Footed, Green	140.00 To 175.00
Hand, Feather Duster	60.00
Hand, Peacock Feather	55.00

Hand, Peacock Feather, Blue, Flat 85.00
Hand, Ripley, Footed 95.00
Hand, Snowflake Pattern, Clear Ring Handle, Flat Base, White Opalescent 235.00
Hand, Zippered Loop, Footed 70.00
    LAMP, HANDEL, see Handel, Lamp
Hanging, Amberina Swirl & Hobnail Shade 2350.00
Hanging, Argand, Double, France, Deep Red, Blown Glass Drip Catcher 300.00
Hanging, Brass Plated Iron, C.1870 .... 450.00
Hanging, Bull's-Eye Ball, Satin Glass, Red 350.00
Hanging, Daisy & Button, Brass Ceiling Plate, Tri-Pulley, 30 In. 375.00
Hanging, Hobnail, Cranberry Glass, 14 In. 850.00
Hanging, Mother-Of-Pearl Satin Glass, Pink Diamond-Quilted, 16 1/2 In. 895.00
Hanging, Original Green Overlay Shade, Nickel Plated, 39 In. 285.00
Hanging, Pink-Cased Shade & Font, Brass 275.00
Hanging, Ribbed Reflector Glass, Tin 32.50
Hanging, Vestal, Octagonal, Cranberry 325.00
Hanging, 4 Quezal Feathered Shades, Brass 1250.00
Heat, English, Brass Base, Blue Opalescent Swirl Shade 225.00
Hurricane, Candle, Wire Frame, Givens, Corpus Christi, Tex., 1894, Tin 65.00
Hurricane, Cranberry, Milk Glass Base, Fenton, 11 In., Pair 139.00
Jefferson, Domed Shade With Scenic Design, Bronze Base, Signed 800.00
Jefferson, Swedish Verde Finish, Signed 200.00
Jefferson, Winter Scene, Reverse On Glass, 16 In. 500.00
Jeweler's, Brass, Glass Ball, Aqua, Tin Base 30.00
Kerosene, Beaded Drape, Red Satin Glass, Signed & Dated, 19 In. 275.00
Kerosene, Bracket, Blown Chimney, Brass Burner, 14 1/2 In. 22.50
Kerosene, Brass Bracket, Etched Shade, Plume & Atwood, Unique, Pat., 1877 .... 175.00
Kerosene, Brass Font, Marked Venus, Iron 45.00
Kerosene, Buckle, Electric Blue, Burner, Chimney, Miniature 150.00
Kerosene, Bull's-Eye & Fleur-De-Lis, Marble Base 110.00
Kerosene, Bull's-Eye, Safety Handle 140.00
Kerosene, Bull's-Eye, Miniature 100.00
Kerosene, Champleve, Round Urn, Bronze 165.00
Kerosene, Circular Wick Holder, Brass, 11 1/2 In. 75.00
Kerosene, Cobalt Blue Twinkle Base & Burner, Miniature 50.00
Kerosene, Columbia Pattern 25.00
Kerosene, Coolidge Drape, Burner 79.00
Kerosene, Cut Out Letters, Confections, 6-Sided, Copper 900.00
Kerosene, Greek Key, Finger 45.00
Kerosene, Greek Key, Miniature 100.00
Kerosene, Little Buttercup 70.00
Kerosene, Milk Glass, Floral Design, Miniature 28.00
Kerosene, Moon & Star 175.00
Kerosene, Ogee Reeded Stem, Clear Glass Font, 9 1/2 In., Pair 35.00
Kerosene, Opalescent Pattern, White, Full Size 85.00
Kerosene, Parrot, Porcelain, Gray, Yellow Shade, Chimney, 12 X 5 3/4 In. 425.00
Kerosene, Patterned Font, Brass & Iron Base 50.00
Kerosene, Pedestal, Snowflake Design On Base, 8 1/2 In. 25.00
Kerosene, Porcelain Owl With Glass Eyes, Yellow Shade, 13 In. 395.00
Kerosene, Rayo Tin 95.00
Kerosene, Roman Key, No.2 .... 37.50
Kerosene, Roses On Base & Globe, Red Satin Glass, 13 In., Pair 550.00
Kerosene, Shell Pattern, Milk Glass, Pastels, Large 85.00
Kerosene, Signed Trinkle Lamp, With Star, Amethyst Glass 140.00
Kerosene, Spanish Lace, Applied Handle, Ribbed Pattern, Hand 295.00
Kerosene, Tiny Miller, Wall, Nickel Over Brass 70.00
Kerosene, 4-Arm, Original Chimneys, Embossed 1295.00
Lard, Oval Font, Wide Burner, 19th Century, Tin, 6 3/4 X 5 3/4 In. 100.00
Lard, Tin Patent, I. Smith, Marked, Wing Nut Holding Top, 5 3/4 In. 60.00
Library, Hand-Painted Shade, Oil Burner, Prism, Pull-Down 300.00
Marriage, 2 Clear Glass Fonts, Milk Glass Base .... *Illus* 255.00
Miner's, Carbide, Justrite, Tank Straps On Belt 30.00
Miner's, Folding, Stonebridge 45.00
Miner's, Honda, Safety, Brass & Aluminum 100.00

Miner's, Spout & Hook, Signed T.F.Leonard, Tin 33.00
Miner's, Sunshine, Signed Imperial 35.00
Miner's, Taylor & Boogie, Cast Iron 65.00
Miner's, Teapot, Tin, Marked Frostburg 65.00
Miner's, Wolf Safety, Brass, 12 In. 125.00
Moran & Hastings, Art Nouveau, Leaded, 29 In. 3500.00
Night-Light, Gun & Holster 90.00
Night-Light, Ribbed Style No.1, Glow, Clear Base, Red Shade 85.00
Nutmeg, Brass Handle & Retainer Band, Cobalt Blue, 6 1/2 In. 125.00
Nutmeg, Cobalt 60.00
Oil, Beaded Drape, Red Satin Glass 800.00
Oil, Beaded Heart, Clear, 7 In. 110.00
Oil, Beaded Heart, Clear, 9 1/2 In. 85.00
Oil, Beaded Peacock, 12 X 15 1/4 In. 475.00
Oil, Bellflower, Flint 125.00
Oil, Bicycle, Nickel Over Brass 45.00
Oil, Blown Clear Chimney, Brass Collar, Hink's No.2 Duplex, 14 In. 100.00
Oil, Brass, Marked Standard Oil Co. 150.00
Oil, Brass, Marked Standard Oil Of Kentucky 125.00
Oil, Bull's-Eye & Diamond Point 60.00
Oil, Bull's-Eye, Green 160.00
Oil, Bull's-Eye, Green, Flat 125.00
Oil, Bull's-Eye, Green, Footed .... 135.00 To 150.00
Oil, Bull's-Eye, Miniature 75.00
Oil, Canadian, Bull's-Eye, Green, 8 In. 145.00
Oil, Canadian, Heart Shape, Green, 9 In. 145.00
Oil, Cathedral, Amber Base, 16 In. 185.00
Oil, Cathedral, Blue Base, 16 In. 185.00
Oil, Christmas Tree Pattern, Milk Glass, Miniature 165.00
Oil, Coin Spot, Fan Base, 8 1/2 In. 195.00
Oil, Coolidge Drape .... 60.00 To 80.00
Oil, Coolidge Drape, Cobalt Blue 135.00
Oil, Drop-Wick, Blown Glass, Lacy Base, 6 1/4 In. 190.00
Oil, Duncan, Ribbed Band 70.00
Oil, Feather Duster With Sawtooth, Iron Base, 21 1/2 In. 75.00
Oil, Feather Duster, Blue Stand 165.00
Oil, Figural, Woman Holding Urn, C.1865 .... 145.00
Oil, Grapes & Leaves, Milk Glass, Blue, Miniature 38.00
Oil, Greek Key, Depression Glass, Pink, Miniature .... 45.00 To 55.00
Oil, Greek Key, Miniature 95.00
Oil, Hand-Painted Florals, Kosmos Brenner, 8-Panel Cast-Iron Base 65.00
Oil, Iron, Baker's, Saucer Base, 18th Century, 3 1/2 In. 500.00
Oil, King's Crown, Beaded Drape Font, 10 1/2 In. 125.00
Oil, Little Buttercup, Clear 65.00
Oil, Loop, Amethyst 750.00
Oil, Loop, Cobalt Blue, Pair 950.00
Oil, Milk Glass, Miniature, Chimney 20.00
Oil, Moon & Star, Blue, Amber 190.00
Oil, Nellie Bly, Miniature 120.00
Oil, Panel & Drape, 6 1/2 In. 50.00
Oil, Paneled Bull's-Eye, Glass Pedestal & Base 79.00
Oil, Parlor, Soapstone Base, Tin Well, Blown Chimney, 6 1/4 In. 65.00
Oil, Pearl Glass, Camphor, Marked, 4 1/2 In. 60.00
Oil, Pewter Cupid Holding Lamp, Ruby Inverted Thumbprint Shade 450.00
Oil, Pink Dolphin, Pair 300.00
Oil, Pleat & Panel 55.00
Oil, Prince Edward, Squatty, Green, 10 In. 150.00
Oil, Prism Pattern On Base 44.00
Oil, Rayo, Victorian, Ribbed Milk Glass Half Shade, 21 In. 135.00
Oil, Roman Key Design Around Base, 1911 .... 45.00
Oil, Satin Milk Glass, Pink Design, Miniature 195.00
Oil, Sawtooth, Blown Chimney, Cast Iron Base, 21 1/2 In. 75.00
Oil, Snowflake, Blue Opalescent, 7 1/2 In. 210.00
Oil, Star & Punty, Electrified, 10 In. 115.00

Oil, Swirl Glass, Miniature	45.00
Oil, Thousand Eye, Amber	165.00
Oil, Thumbprint, Handle, Clear, 7 1/2 In.	60.00
Oil, Tin, Clear Blown Font, Conical Base, 10 1/2 In.	295.00
Oil, Torpedo, Clear, Pair	160.00
Oil, Torpedo, Clear, 8 In.	90.00
Oil, Washington Drape, Glass Shade, Miniature	75.00
Oil, Wedding Pattern, 8 In.	155.00
Oil, Zippered Loop	70.00

LAMP, PAIRPOINT, see also Pairpoint, Lamp

Pairpoint, Octagonal Glass Insert, Reverse Painting	750.00
Patinated Copper, Mica Shade, Dirk Van Erp, C.1910, 11 In.	*Illus* 1850.00
Peg Bracket, 12 Panels, Brass Base & Collar, E.N.& Co., 13 1/2 In.	50.00
Peg, Blown Glass, Wooden Stand, 5 In.	125.00
Peg, Peachblow Swirl Rib, White-Cased Shade, Brass Holder, 22 1/2 In.	165.00
Perfume, Clear Fount, Swirl Pattern, Ball Shade	20.00
Perfume, Hand-Painted Gold & Enamel Florals, 14 In.	70.00
Petticoat, Filler Tub, Peg For Converting To Candle, C.1800, 4 In.	60.00
Petticoat, Handle, C.1830, Tin, 4 In.	50.00
Phoebe, Iron, Double, Hanging Hook	55.00
Piano, Art Nouveau, Bronze, 16 In.	165.00
Piano, Brass	400.00
Piano, Camphor Glass Base, Clear Flower & Leaf Globe, 9 In., Pair	55.00
Piano, Elephant, Trunk Forms Legs, Rose Floral Shade	1800.00
Pittsburgh, Reverse Painted Scenic Waves, C.1920, 21 1/2 In.	800.00
Rushlight, Iron, Standing, Scroll Top, 18th Century, American, 26 In.	125.00
Rushlight, Iron, Twisted Stem, 18th Century, 8 3/4 In.	100.00
Rushlight, Tripod Base, Brass Wafer At Base, Scrolled, Iron, 13 In.	275.00
Sandwich Glass Overlay, Figured Brass Stem, Bail Font, 9 In.	375.00
Sandwich Glass, Camphene, 9 1/2 In., Pair	210.00
Sandwich Glass, Cranberry, Milk Glass Base, Whale Oil, 11 1/2 In.	450.00
Sandwich Glass, Tulip Design, Brass Fittings, 11 In.	150.00
Sandwich Glass, Whale Oil, Cut Pink To White To Clear, C.1860	375.00

LAMP, SATIN GLASS, see Satin Glass, Lamp

Shade, Fairy, Seaweed, Satin Glass, Blue, 4 1/4 X 3 1/2 In.	133.00
Shade, Hanging, Painted White, For Aladdin Lamp	75.00
Skater's, Nickel Over Brass, Patent 1917, 10 In.	75.00
Skater's, Perko Wonder, Junior, Tin & Ruby Wash	45.00
Sparking, Camphene Burners, Cone Shape, Tin & Pewter, Pair	275.00
Sparking, Handled, 4 In., Pair	350.00
Splint Holder, Tripod, Wrought, Scrolled Feet, 18th Century, 13 3/4 In.	150.00
Store, Hanging, The Rochester, Milk Glass Shade, 14 In.	225.00
Store, Kerosene, Cutout Ice Cream, Candy, Soda, Copper	900.00
Student, Blue Satin Shade	975.00
Student, Butterscotch Shade, 24 In.	*Illus* 350.00
Student, Empress Model, Dated 1870, German Student Lamp Co., N.Y.	495.00
Student, Frosted Reverse-Painted Shade	245.00
Student, Manhattan, Original Shade, C.1876, 7 In.	425.00
Student, Swivel Neck, Brass Base, Patent 1911, Signed Bryant, 18 In.	150.00
Table, Cameo, Boat, Lake, & Trees, Orange Ground, 20 In.	*Illus* 1400.00

LAMP, TIFFANY, see Tiffany, Lamp

Vapo-Cresolene, Burner, Chimney, Iron Base	30.00 To 44.00
Wedding, Ripley, Blue & White Clambroth, Patterned Base	1350.00
Whale Oil, Blown Hobnail, Turnip Shaped, 10 In., Pair	125.00
Whale Oil, Brass, Top Ring Handle, 3 Wicks, 20 In.	185.00
Whale Oil, Etched, Blown, Pressed Glass, C.1840, 7 3/8 In.	125.00
Whale Oil, Glass & Tin, Cranberry, Pierced Base, 15 In.	325.00
Whale Oil, Pear-Shaped Fonts, Cylindrical Supports, Tin, 7 In.	310.00
Whale Oil, Peg, Lemon-Shaped Font, Tin, 4 In.	140.00
Whale Oil, Peg, Petticoat, Brown Japanning, Tin, 4 1/2 In.	75.00
Whale Oil, Petal Font, Clear Glass, Domed Top, C.1840, 11 1/2 In.	110.00
Whale Oil, Pewter, Double Bull's-Eye, C.1780, 11 In.	695.00
Whale Oil, Pierced Tin Spread, Steeple Top, 2 Wick, 17 1/2 In.	195.00

Lamp, Marriage, 2 Clear Glass Fonts,
Milk Glass Base
(See Page 348)

Lamp, Patinated Copper, Mica Shade,
Dirk Van Erp, C.1910, 11 In.

Lamp, Table, Cameo, Boat, Lake, & Trees,
Orange Ground, 20 In.

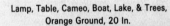

Lamp, Student, Butterscotch Shade, 24 In.

Whale Oil, Ribbed Font, Pewter Top, Double Wick, 6 1/2 In. 95.00
Whale Oil, Ribbed Wafer, Urn-Shaped Font, C.1840, 8 1/4 In. 80.00
Whale Oil, Square Pedestal, Intaglio Grapes On Font 150.00
Whale Oil, Urn-Type, Double Burner, Cobalt Blue, C.1840 .... 450.00
Whale Oil, 3 Spout, Brass, Miniature 295.00
Whale Oil, 10-Paneled Globe, 2 Wick Burner, Tin, 10 In. 365.00

LANTERN, Adams & Westlake, Queen, Brass 100.00
Adlake, Railroad, Battery, Aluminum, Black Handle 10.00
Angle Lamp Co., Round Font, Fleur-De-Lis Design 265.00
Barn, Ham & Co., No.00, Brass 110.00
Best Light Co., Canton, Ohio, Dated 1900, Frosted Glass 195.00
Buhl, No.275, Hurricane, Brass Bottom, Embossed Globe 45.00
C.T.Ham, Railroad, Bell Bottom, No.39, Brass 375.00
Clear Glass Globe, Wrist Ring, Oil Burner, 19th Century, 13 In. 185.00
Coleman, No.242A, Solid Brass, Nickel Font, Green Top 25.00
Coleman, Table, Gasoline, Brass Font, Brown Wood Handle 145.00
Dennis & Wheeler, Dated Nov. 19, 1874 .... 45.00
Dietz, Comet, Red Paint, Marked Globe 15.00
Dietz, Crystal, Glass Font, Square Tube Model, Dated 1888 .... 100.00
Dietz, Hy-Lo, Red Globe, Dated 1910 .... 26.00
Dietz, King Fire Dept. 89.00
Dietz, Little Giant, 70-Hour Font, Tin Finish, Dated 1946 .... 18.00
Dietz, Little Wizard, Red Globe, Blue, 11 1/2 In. 25.00
Dietz, Mill, Red Paint, Square Tube, Dated Sept. 1940 .... 75.00
Dietz, Monarch, Red Glove, Black Paint, Dated 5-7-1930 .... 25.00
Dietz, No.2, D-Lite, Brass Burner, Tin Finish, Dated 5-8-1945 .... 25.00
Dietz, No.39, Standard, Dated 1910 .... 30.00
Dietz, No.39, Steel Clad, Red Globe, Bright Tin Finish 42.50
Dietz, No.100, Seattle Engineering Dept, Red Globe, Key Burner 18.00
Dietz, U.S. Brass Tubular, Dated 1879, 11 In. 100.00
Dietz, Vesta, Clear Globe, Dated May 4, 1909, 11 In. 35.00
Dominion Tubular Lamp, Square Lift, No. 0, Blue Japanned Finish 55.00
Embury, Elgin, Clear, No.10, E Marked On Globe, Brown Paint 23.00
Embury, No.2, Airpilot, Green Paint, Globe Marked E, Kerosene 25.00
Embury, No.61, Brass Font, Red Globe, Tin Finish 65.00
Frank M.Ford, Kerosene, 1871 .... 100.00
Henry Clay, Tin 2500.00
Hubbard Spencer Bartlett Co., Brass Font, Red Japanned Finish 65.00
Hughes Bros., Scranton, Pa., C.1850, 11 In. 120.00
Love-Lite, Perfume Lamp, Original Shade 30.00
Marswell, No.2, Cold Blast, Scrolled Chain Design, Brass Cap 40.00
Naugatuck, Brass, Flame Spreader, Dated 1890, Clear Shade 145.00
Neil City Lantern Co., Ruffled Frame, Red Paint 40.00
Paull's Leader, Original Green Paint, No.2 Font 25.00
Pierced Tin, Reverse, Candle 135.00
Police, Bull's-Eye Lens 85.00
Police, Sliding Hatch, Magnifying Bull's-Eye Lens, Tin 30.00
Prisco, No.2, Pritchard Strong Co., Buggy Lantern, Tin Finish 55.00
    LANTERN, RAILROAD, see Railroad, Lantern
Rayo Hot Blast, Marked 15.00
Sg & L Co., O.K. Tubular, Globe Tips Back, Square Tube Model 55.00
Ship, Anchor, Brass, Electric, Griffiths & Sons, No.7817, 12 X 11 In. .. 110.00
Ship, Anchor, Copper, Brass Trim, Signed, Sea Horse, 15 X 10 In. 120.00
Ship, Anchor, Copper, Electric, Signed, Sea Horse, No.4711, 13 X 11 In. 110.00
Ship, Anchor, Not Under Command Insert, Clear, Red Lens, 14 X 10 In. ... 145.00
Ship, Masthead, Steel, Brass Trim & Oil Burner, Signed, 21 X 13 In. 85.00
Ship, Not Under Command Lens, Oil, Brass Trim & Burner, 20 X 10 In. 105.00
Ship, Passageway Lights, Cabin, Brass, Oil Fonts, 14 X 6 In., Pair 125.00
Ship, Port, Starboard, Clear Lens, Red, Green, 15 X 8 In. 50.00
Ship, Port, Tin, Painted Red, Brass, Window, Bail, Label 85.00
Ship, Red & Green Lenses, Stell Body, Brass Trim, 18 X 13 In., Pair 150.00
Ship, Running Light, Brass, Trim, Green, Red Lens, 12 X 10 In., Pair 140.00

Ship, Running Light, Copper Body, Electric, Side Bracket, 15 X 13 In. 125.00
Ship, Signal, Bull's-Eye Lens, Brass Trim & Burner, 15 X 18 In. 58.00
Ship, Signal, Galvanized Body, Brass Trim & Burner, Oil, 17 X 9 In. 58.00
Ship, Starboard Running Light, Copper, Brass Oil Burner, 20 X 14 In. 145.00
Street, Dietz, No.3, Complete 195.00
Wolfe Safety Lamp Co., M.U., Reflecting Mirror, 11 In. 120.00

*Le Verre Francais cameo glass was made in France between 1920 and
1933 by the C. Schneider factory. It is mottled and usually
decorated with floral designs, and bears the incised signature
"Le Verre Francais."*

LE VERRE FRANCAIS, Night-Light, Stylized Florals, 15 1/2 X 6 In. 700.00
  Plate, Red Center, Signed Charder, 13 3/4 In. 1175.00
  Urn, Art Deco, Textured Yellow, Signed, 10 1/2 In. 550.00
  Vase, Bell-Shape Flowers, Leaves, 7 In. 300.00
  Vase, Cameo, Orange Flowers, Frosted Ground, Signed, 3 In. 195.00
  Vase, Cameo, Orange Ground, Brown Design, Signed, 5 In. 395.00
  Vase, Tortoiseshell Geese, Yellow Ground, Signed, 19 In. 1250.00

LEATHER, Boot, Child's, General Grant Embossed On Front, 19th Century 125.00
  Box, Hat, Clasp Dated '07, Initials MAS 85.00
  Cuffs, Cowboy's, Studs, Pair 40.00
  Holster, Texas Ranger, Pocket, Badge 750.00
  Money Bag, Compliments Of Miner's State Bank, Frontenac, Kansas 17.50
  Pouch, Tobacco, Lion Head With Ring In Nose 30.00
  Pouch, Tobacco, Silver Dragon Clasp, Oriental 475.00
  Saddle, Advertising, E.W.Fluke, Ice, Coal, & Feed, Folded 12 X 16 In. 200.00
  Saddle, Oriental, Japan, Black, Brass Strips, Iron Rings, 21 In. 700.00
  Strop, Razor, 2 Piece 14.00
  Whip, Braided & Linked, Wooden Handle, 53 In. 20.00

LEEDS POTTERY,

*Leeds pottery was made at Leeds, Yorkshire, England, from 1774 to 1878.
Most Leeds ware was not marked. Early Leeds pieces had distinctive
twisted handles with a greenish glaze on part of the creamy ware. Later
ware often had blue borders on the creamy pottery.*

LEEDS, Candlestick, Soft Paste, Baluster Form, Pierced, 18th Century, 10 In. 140.00
  Dish, Vegetable, Creamware, Blue Design 35.00
  Jug, Armorial, Silver, Eagle & Sailboats, 1810-1815, 8 In. .... *Illus* 200.00
  Pitcher, Jug Shaped, Tan, Floral, 6 Sided, Signed, 7 1/4 In. 475.00
  Plate, Impressed Feather, Tassel, & Shell Edge, C.1820, 10 In. 75.00
  Teapot, Beehive, 10 1/2 In. 80.00

*The Geo. Zoltan Lefton Company has imported porcelains to be sold in
America since 1940. The pieces are often marked with the Lefton name.*

LEFTON, Figurine, Pixie, Seated 12.00
  Figurine, Pixie, Seated On Toadstool, 4 In. 5.00
  Pitcher, Cream, Figural, Washington Bust 25.00

*Legras was founded in 1864 by Auguste Legras at St. Denis, France.
It is best known for Art Nouveau and cameo glass wares. Legras merged
with Pantin in 1920 and became the Verreries et Cristalleries de St.
Denis and de Pantin Reunies.*

LEGRAS, Bowl, Allover Enameled Cherries & Foliage, Basket Shape, Signed 275.00
  Bowl, Basket Shape, Enameled, Signed, 8 In. 275.00
  Bowl, Winter Snow Scene, 3 X 3 1/4 In. 125.00

Cracker Jar, Cameo, Burgundy, Florals	795.00
Rose Bowl, Art Deco Raised Design, Flecked Interior, 6 In.	450.00
Vase, Allover Cranberry Leaves, Etched Ground, Signed, 11 1/2 In.	650.00
Vase, Applied Pink Apple Blossoms & Foliage, 19 In.	950.00
Vase, Ball Shape, Cameo, Lavender, Berries, Leaves, 6 In.	350.00
Vase, Enameled Multicolored Florals, Yellow, Signed, 10 1/2 In.	250.00
Vase, Frosted Etched Ground, Cranberry Leaves, Cameo, 11 In.	650.00
Vase, Lake & Mountain Scene, Signed, Brown & Orange, 8 1/2 In.	585.00
Vase, Maroon Flowers, Frosted Ground, Signed, 8 1/4 In.	550.00
Vase, Orange To Maroon, Signed, 6 In.	395.00
Vase, Polished Orange Chrysanthemum Leaves, Cut To Custard, 5 In.	325.00
Vase, Purple Ivy, Peach Ground, Cameo, Marked, 11 1/2 In.	550.00
Vase, Seaweed Pattern, Russet, Cream, Brown, Cameo, 14 In.	875.00
Vase, Stylized Flower Carving, Yellow & Brown, Cameo, Pair	995.00

Lenox china was made in Trenton, New Jersey, after 1906. The firm also makes a porcelain similar to Belleek.

LENOX, see also Ceramic Art Co.

LENOX, Ashtray, World's Fair, 1939, Blue & White	50.00
Atomizer, Penguin	65.00
Bottle, Scotch, Cobalt, Silver Overlay, Matching Stopper	265.00
Bouillon Cup & Underplate, Ming	18.00
Bowl, Green & Gold Trim, White Handle, Covrered, 3 X 7 In.	100.00
Bowl, Melon Ribbed, Crimped Top, Green, Marked, 12 In.	40.00
Bowl, Nautilus Shell, Gold Trim, Green Mark, 6 In.	35.00
Bowl, Ruffled Rim, Coral, 6 1/4 X 4 In.	85.00
Bowl, Shell Shaped, Green Wreath Mark, 9 In., Pair	45.00
Bowl, Shell Shaped, Scalloped, Gold Trim, Marked, 6 1/4 In.	55.00
Bowl, Summer Bouquet, Gold Band, Marked, 7 In.	38.00
Bowl, Swan, Gilt Design, Green Mark, 9 1/2 In.	350.00
Box, Cigarette, Pink, Marked, Raised Gold Trim	35.00
Box, Cigarette, Wheat Pattern, Gold Mark	30.00
Box, Cigarette, World's Fair, 1939	50.00
Box, Green, Gold, White Feather Finial, 7 X 3 In.	100.00
Box, Handle, Green, Gold Trim, 2 X 7 In.	100.00
Box, Powder, Wheat Pattern On Lid, 8 X 3 3/4 In.	75.00
Box, Powder, Woman's Head Finial, Art Deco, 4 1/2 X 4 In.	125.00
Breakfast Set, Green Mark, 8 Piece	110.00
Candlestick, Roses, Gold Trim, Signed & Dated, 10 In.	95.00
Candlestick, Silver Overlay, 7 In., Pair	35.00
Coffeepot, Cobalt, Sterling Overlay, 9 In.	195.00
Coffeepot, White, Sterling Silver Overlay, Palette Mark, 6 3/4 In.	175.00
Creamer, Footed, Square Base, Marked, 5 3/4 In.	75.00
Creamer, Hawthorne, Black Wreath Mark	65.00
Creamer, King Tut	225.00
Cup & Saucer, Bouillon, Gold Rim, Sterling Silver Holder	32.50
Cup & Saucer, Bouillon, Set Of 12, Cobalt, Etched Gold Band	540.00
Cup & Saucer, Cobalt, Hexagon Shape, Marked	60.00
Cup & Saucer, Golden Wreath	25.00
Cup & Saucer, Green & Ivory	25.00
Cup & Saucer, Green, Ivory, Demitasse	22.00
Cup & Saucer, Hexagonal Shape, Cobalt Blue, Marked	60.00
Cup & Saucer, Ming, Black Mark	28.00 To 37.50
Cup & Saucer, Pie Crust Edge, Maroon Band, Marked, Demitasse	15.00
Cup & Saucer, Sheraton	25.00
Cup & Saucer, Square Base Cup	55.00
Cup & Saucer, Sterling Silver Holder, Demitasse, 6 Sets	150.00
Cup & Saucer, Sterling Silver Holder, Gold Trim, Demitasse, 6 Sets	125.00
Cup & Saucer, Wheat Pattern, Cobalt Blue, Marked	25.00
Cup & Saucer, White, Ribbed, Black Wreath Mark, Demitasse	16.00
Dessert Set, Green Mark, 7 Piece	97.00

Dip, Celery, Fluted, Deep Scoop, 2 Ball Feet, Green, Wreath Mark 35.00
Dish, Bird Shape, Open Body On Square Pedestal, Green 60.00
Dish, Gravy, Leaf Pattern, Platinum Edging, Marked, 8 In. 20.00
Dish, Green Mark, 6 1/4 X 3 1/2 In. 30.00
Dish, Nut, Multicolored Flowers, Pedestal, Palette Mark, Ivory 68.00
Dish, Shell, Green Wreath Mark, 2 X 6 In. 38.00
Dish, Shell, White Handle At End, Green Mark, Pink, 9 X 5 In. 49.50
Dish, Soup, Blue Tree Pattern, 1920s 25.00
Dish, Soup, Ming 20.00
Figurine, Bird, Celadon Green, Marked, 6 1/2 In. 75.00
Figurine, Bird, Green, Tail Up, 3 3/4 In. 45.00
Figurine, Bird, Green, Tail Up, 6 1/2 In. 65.00
Figurine, Bird, White, Tail Down, 3 1/2 In. 14.00
Figurine, Bird, Wings Up, Blue 18.00
Figurine, Colonial Lady, Bisque .... 140.00 To 200.00
Figurine, Crinoline Lady, Green Wreath Mark 475.00
Figurine, Dog, Schnauzer, Seated, Green, Wreath Mark 95.00
Figurine, Girl, Sitting On Box, Pink Apron, Pink Bowls, 3 In. 225.00
Figurine, Lady, Nude, White Bisque, Marked, 12 In. 375.00
Figurine, Leda & The Swan .... 175.00 To 200.00
Figurine, Llama, Green Wreath Mark 275.00
Figurine, Penguin, White 85.00
Figurine, Robin, Tail Down, Green, 5 In. 30.00
Figurine, Robin, Tail Up, 5 1/2 In. 20.00
Figurine, Swan, Closed Back, Green Wreath Mark, 5 X 4 In. 30.00
Figurine, Swan, Coral Pink, 4 1/2 In. 20.00
Figurine, Swan, Green Mark, 8 1/2 In. 45.00
Figurine, Swan, Open Wings Up, White, Green Mark, 4 1/2 In. 32.00
Figurine, Swan, Pink, Marked, 3 In., Pair 25.00
Holder, Cigarette, Oval, Fluted, Marked, 3 In. 10.00
Honey Pot, Beehive Shape, Applied Bees, Green Wreath Mark 55.00
Inkwell, Fluted, Pink 75.00
Inkwell, Ruffled, White Edge 60.00
Lamp, Salmon-Pink, White, Handles, Footed, Brass Base, 24 In. 85.00
Mug, Art Nouveau Woman With Butterfly Wings, Palette Mark, 5 In. 100.00
Mug, B.P.O.E., Elk, Handle, Pink 95.00
Pitcher, Cottage, Gold Mark 55.00
Pitcher, Cream, Bulbous, Swirl Base, C Scroll Handle, Marked, 4 In. 30.00
Pitcher, Fluted, Cream With Gold 12.00
Pitcher, Pink, White Handle 225.00
Pitcher, William Penn, White Handle, Pink Ground 195.00
Plate, Annual, 1973, Raccoons 60.00
Plate, Cinderella Pattern, Marked, 10 1/2 In. 20.00
Plate, Cretan, 6 In. 4.00
Plate, Cretan, 8 1/2 In. 7.00
Plate, Fish, C.1906, Marked 95.00
Plate, Loyal Sons Of St.Patrick, Shamrock Border, 9 In. 75.00
Plate, Meadowlark, 1973 .... 50.00
Plate, Olympia, Platinum, 10 1/2 In. 15.00
Plate, Orchard Pattern, 8 1/2 In. 10.00
Plate, Rufous Hummingbird 50.00
Plate, 1970, Woodthrush, First Edition, Original Box 195.00
Platter, Roslyn, 12 In. 40.00
Ramekin, Pierced Sterling Silver Holder, Marked, Set Of 8 .... 275.00
Salt & Pepper Mill, Hourglass Shape, Lourent Pattern, 6 In. 35.00
Salt & Pepper, Du-All, White 18.00
Salt & Pepper, Pheasant 40.00
Salt & Pepper, R.C.A.Victor Dog, Nipper .... 16.50 To 25.00
Salt Spoon, Scoop Shaped, Set 100.00
Saucer, Cretan 4.00
Shot Glass, Brown & Sterling Overlay, 2 1/4 In. 65.00
Slipper, Victorian, Green Mark, 6 In. 110.00
Smoke Set, Rose, 5 Piece 42.00
Sugar & Creamer, Commemorative, Washington's 200th Birthday, Marked 125.00

Sugar & Creamer, Cretan 15.00
Sugar & Creamer, Hawthorne, Covered, Black Wreath Mark 75.00
Sugar & Creamer, Wheat Pattern, Cobalt Blue 35.00
Tea Set, Art Nouveau, Sterling Silver Overlay, 14 Piece 700.00
Tea Set, Hawthorne Pattern, Black Mark, 4 Piece 200.00
Tea Tile, Rose Pattern .... 45.00 To 50.00
Teapot, Hawthorne, Black Wreath Mark 100.00
Teapot, Ming Pattern, Art Deco Shape 85.00
Teapot, Silver Plate Cover & Handle, White Glaze, Dirigible Mark 65.00
Toby Jug, George Washington 325.00
Toby Jug, William Penn, Mask Handle, Green Wreath .... 110.00 To 175.00
Toby Jug, William Penn, Polychrome, 6 1/2 In. 275.00
Urn, Gold Handles, Rims, & Sides Of Base, Marked, White, 5 1/2 In. 98.00
Vase, Acanthus, Ivies, Ivory Luster, Marked, 8 1/2 In. 32.00
Vase, Allover Seascape, Cylindrical, Palette Mark, 15 1/2 In. 285.00
Vase, Berries, Gold Trim, Palette Mark, 9 In. 80.00
Vase, Bulge Pink Body, Ring Handles, Flared Top, White, 5 3/4 In. 60.00
Vase, Chalice Shape, Embossed Design, Green Wreath Mark, 7 In. 65.00
Vase, Claw Feet, Pedestal, Bulbous Base, Green Wreath Mark, 5 In. 34.00
Vase, Dog, Marked, 8 In. 295.00
Vase, Floral Center, Purple Borders, Marked, 8 In. 95.00
Vase, Grecian, Winged Female, Busts As Handle, 12 In., Pair 110.00
Vase, Half-Round, Handle, Green Wreath Mark, 7 In. 18.00
Vase, Ivory, Pink Base, Square, Marked, 9 In. 69.00
Vase, Lady With Fan Figure, Pocket In Rear For Flowers, Marked, 9 In. 195.00
Vase, Morning Glories In Relief, Gold Rim, Gold Mark, 7 In. 35.00
Vase, Oriental Dancing Girls, Gold Petals, Green Mark, 10 1/4 In. 259.00
Vase, Rose Pattern, Figural Swan Handles, 11 In. 80.00
Vase, Swan Handles, Green Mark, 10 1/2 In. 75.00
Vase, Trumpet, Ribbed, Square Base, Green Mark, 8 1/2 In. 45.00
Water Set, Gold Leaf Design, Gold Handle & Trim, Palette Mark, 7 Piece 235.00

LETTER OPENER, Adams Pattern, Sterling Silver Handle, Whiting, 9 1/4 In. 25.00
  Anaconda Copper 15.00
  Atlantic Sponge & Chamois Corp., N.Y., 9 1/4 In. 10.00
  Bankers Trust, Jacksonville, Fla., E.L.Kennedy, President 10.00
  Bone, Vertical Etched Stripes, 10 In. 8.00
  Chicken Claw, Brass 24.00
  Concord, Shield, Raised Florals, N.H.Seal, Sterling Silver 17.50
  Craftsman Studios, 1930s, Copper 16.00
  IBM Will Cut Your Expenses, Bronze 38.00
  Indian, Full Bodied, Copper 28.00
  Lacy Plastic Handle, Elephant End 12.00
  Lady's, Mother-Of-Pearl 6.00
  Mardi Gras, 1910, Brass 80.00
  McCormick Harvesting Machines, Aluminum 5.00
  Meadow Rose Pattern, Sterling Silver Handle, Wallace, 8 In. 25.00
  Mother-Of-Pearl Blade, Art Nouveau Handle, 7 1/2 In. 10.00
  Mother-Of-Pearl Blade, Silver Sterling Handle, Art Deco 17.00
  O'Brien Registered Patent Attorney, Brass, 8 In. 8.00
  Padlock On Top, Yale & Towne, Door Closer At Bottom 65.00
  Paul's Barber Shop, N.Y.C., Art Deco, Metal, 6 3/4 In. 12.00
  Richbrau Beer, Dated 1915, With Knife 27.00
  Rooster Head, Art Deco, Sterling Silver 28.00
  Rose Pattern, Sterling Silver Handle, Wallace, 8 In. 20.00
  Spear-Shaped, Monogram, Sterling Silver, Kirk, 5 3/4 In. 20.00
  Uneeda Biscuit Co. 22.50
  Waverly Pattern, Sterling Silver, Wallace, 7 1/4 In. 22.50
  Woman With Long Hair, Art Nouveau, Brass, 6 1/2 In. 30.00
  Yale Lock 65.00
  100th Skowhegan Fair, 1838-1938, Brass, 8 In. 8.00

Libbey   The Libbey Glass Company has made glass of many types from 1892 to the present.

LIBBEY, Berry Bowl, Master, Blue Trim	175.00
Bowl, Glenda Pattern, Signed, 9 In.	325.00
Bowl, Lovebirds, Marked, 9 In.	650.00
Bowl, Notched Prisms, 12-Point Hobstars, 7 3/4 X 4 In.	185.00
Bowl, Swirled, Crystal, Signed, 9 In.	50.00
Bowl, Wisteria, Love Birds, 8-Sided, 3 In. ....*Illus*	650.00
Bowl, 3 Curled Feet, Signed, 8 1/2 X 4 1/2 In.	195.00
Candlestick, Intaglio Cut Floral On Stem, Signed, 10 In.	75.00
Carafe, Irregular Hobstars, Fans, & Miters, Signed, Large	125.00
Carafe, 32-Rayed Bottom, Signed, 8 In.	100.00
Case, Rabbit, Silhouette Pattern, Crystal, 10 In.	150.00
Champagne, Continental, Stem, Engraved Foot, Signed, 7 In.	38.00
Champagne, Diamond & Feather, Hollow Stem, Signed	90.00
Champagne, Silhouette, Opalescent, Squirrel Stems, Signed, Set Of 4	250.00
Compote, Art Deco Cut, Signed, 9 X 5 In.	60.00
Compote, Geometrics, Knobbed & Flared Stem, Signed, 10 1/2 In.	565.00
Cup & Saucer, World's Fair, 1893, Leaf Shape, Camphor Glass, Marked	98.00
Decanter, Corinthian, Side Handle	325.00
Decanter, Hobstar & Fan Design, Notched Neck, Marked, 13 In.	250.00
Dish, Crossed Bars, Signed, 8 In.	175.00
Dish, Ice Cream, Hobstars, Strawberries, Signed, 8 In.	160.00
Goblet, Black Panther Silhouette Stem, Clear Top & Foot, 7 In.	125.00
Goblet, Harvard Pattern, Double Teardrop, 7 1/2 In.	150.00
Goblet, Intaglio Pattern, Notched Stem, Signed, Set Of 10	400.00
Goblet, Water, Garland Pattern	35.00
Nappy, Heart Pattern, Signed, 7 In.	125.00
Paperweight, Woman's Face With Flowing Hair, 1890	175.00
Pitcher, Poppy, Marked, 8 In.	1100.00
Plate, Sultana Pattern, Signed, 11 3/4 In.	575.00
Relish, Allover Brilliant Cut, Signed, Oval	85.00
Rose Bowl, Hobstars, Strawberries, & Fans, 5 X 6 In.	350.00
Sugar & Creamer, Lovebirds, Marked	375.00
Toothpick, Little Lobe	110.00
Tray, Flower Design, Beaded Crossbars, Signed, 12 In.Diam.	695.00
Tray, Ice Cream, Princess Pattern, 18 In.	495.00
Tumbler, Knickerbocker, Signed	29.00
Vase, Bud, Amberina, Pontiled, 6 3/4 In.	350.00
Vase, Hobstar & Inverted Thumbprint Design, Marked, 10 In.	60.00
Vase, Sweet Pea, 6 1/4 X 9 1/2 In.	525.00
Wine, Intaglio Cut Floralon Bowl, Signed	35.00
Wine, Stem, Engraved Foot, Signed, 5 In.	35.00
Wine, Stem, Engraved Foot, Signed, 6 3/4 In.	40.00

Libbey, Bowl, Wisteria, Love Birds, 8-Sided, 3 In.

LIGHTER, Cigarette, Airplane, Chrome, Art Deco	55.00
Cigarette, Bedford, Chrome, Square, Flannel Cover	2.75
Cigarette, Dunhill, Round, Gold Bottom, Boxed	7.00
Cigarette, Figural, Camera, Movable Legs	10.00
LIGHTING DEVICES, see Candleholder; Candlestick; Lamp; etc.	

Lightning rod balls are collected for their variety of shape and color. These glass balls were at the center of the rod that was attached to the roof of a house or barn to prevent lightning damage.

LIGHTNING ROD, Ball, Milk Glass, Blue	15.00
Ball, Transparent Amber, Swirl	67.50

Limoges porcelain has been made in Limoges, France, since the mid-nineteenth century. Fine porcelains were made by many factories, including Haviland, Ahrenfeldt, Guerin, Pouyat, Elite, and others.

LIMOGES, see also Haviland

LIMOGES, Ashtray, Matchbox Holder, Gold Trim, Marked	10.00
Basket, Sugar, White Roses, White Ground, Gold Trim	35.00
Berry Set, Gold Scalloped Rim, Pink & Yellow Roses, Marked, 7 Piece	95.00
Bowl, Blue, Yellow, Parrots & Fruits, 10 In.	65.00
Bowl, Cloverleaf Shape, 3-Sectioned, Gold Handle, Marked, 11 In.Diam.	50.00
Bowl, La Seynie, Raised Gold Rim, 6 X 1 1/4 In.	5.00
Bowl, Punch, Hand-Painted, Signed Grandmama Lily Mae Staples	525.00
Bowl, Scalloped, Gold Scroll Handle, Hazelnuts, 7 1/2 X 6 In.	35.00
Bowl, Twisted Rope Edge, Iris, Marked, 10 3/8 In.	48.00
Bowl, Vegetable, Covered, 7 X 9 1/2 In.	12.00
Box, Powder, Covered, Multicolored Roses, 5 In.	55.00
Box, Powder, Pansy Design, Tan Ground	50.00
Box, Powder, Portrait, Footed	65.00
Box, Sardine, Swimming Fish On Cover, Marked, Green	28.00
Box, Turtle Shape, Covered, 3 X 5 In.	30.00
Butter, Frontenac Pattern, Pink Roses, Gold Trim, 3 Piece	49.50
Butter, Old Abbey, Domed	25.00
Cachepot, Hand-Painted Yellow & Purple Hollyhocks, C.1891	115.00
Cake Set, Violets, Lily Of The Valley, Gold Trim, 7 Piece	195.00
Candleholder, Blue Scallop Edge, Open Handle, Boy, Girl, Gilt Trim	49.00
Chamberstick, Yellow, Floral, Gold Handle, Rim	95.00
Charger, Hand-Painted Castle Scene, Scalloped Edge, 13 In., Pair	330.00
Charger, Hand-Painted Full Figure Lady, Signed DuBois, 13 In.	375.00
Chocolate Pot, Floral With Gold	70.00
Chocolate Pot, Roses, Pastels, 12 In.	225.00
Chocolate Set, Art Deco, 8-Sided Pot, Signed, 5 Piece	155.00
Chocolate Set, Greek Key The Athena, Hold Handle, Marked, 11 Piece	160.00
Chocolate Set, Roses & Bumblebee On Flowers, Signed, 13 Piece	590.00
Chocolate Set, Tray, Beige, Initialed K.S.F., Star Mark	160.00
Chocolate Set, Tray, 14 1/2 X 11 1/4 In., 6 Piece	165.00
Cider Set, Grapes & Leaves, Signed, Tray, Pitcher, 4 Mugs	195.00
Cider Set, Hand-Painted, 7 Piece	375.00
Coffee Set, White, Green Border, Pink Flowers, Gold Trim	225.00
Coffeepot, Floral, Beaded Handle, Triangular Shape, Marked	125.00
Coffeepot, Gold Spout, Handle, & Finial, White, 8 3/4 In.	48.00
Creamer, Child's, Crystal	18.00
Cup & Saucer, Avignon Pattern	13.00
Cup & Saucer, Bouillon, Elite Pattern	15.00
Cup & Saucer, Cream Soup, Elite Pattern, Violet Design	28.50
Cup & Saucer, White, Gold Border Design, Gold Handles	12.00
Cup, Tea, Orchid Design	3.50
Dish, Celery, Pinecones, Hand-Painted, 13 X 6 In.	45.00
Dish, Nut, Hand-Painted, Rosebud Florals, 2 1/2 X 3 In., Set Of 6	45.00
Dish, Olive, Antique Gold Trim, Gold Fruit, Marked, 9 In.	18.00
Dish, Pancake, Pink Roses, Covered, Gold Ribbon Knob	90.00

Dish, Pancake, 2 Piece, Lavender Floral, 9 1/2 In.	65.00
Dish, Pink & Blue Floral Design, 3 X 6 In.	20.00
Dish, Set Of 6, Pink, Blue, Floral, 3 1/4 X 2 1/4 In.	90.00
Dish, Vegetable, Green, Pink & White Roses, White Ground, 8 In.	45.00
Dresser Set, Daisies & Gold Trim, Candlesticks, Covered Boxes, 5 Pc.	150.00
Dresser Set, Gold & Cobalt Blue Trim, Flowers, 6 Piece	175.00
Dresser Set, Lavender Daisies, Gold Trim, Tray, 12 1/2 X 8 In., 6 Pc.	185.00
Dresser Set, 6 Piece, Scalloped Tray, Gold & Cobalt Trim	195.00
Ewer, Baroque Design, Gold Interior, Clover Blossoms, 13 In.	150.00
Feeder, Invalid, Blue & Gold Flowers	42.00
Fish Set, Hand-Painted, With Gold, Set Of 6 Plates	120.00
Fish Set, Yellow, Seashell Design, Signed, Platter 24 In., 7 Piece	525.00
Fruit Set, Fruits & Flowers, Butterflies, Double Mark, Haviland Co.	150.00
Game Plate, Bird On Limb, Gold Border, Signed, 9 7/8 In.	95.00
Game Plate, Gold Edge, Scalloped, Glazed, 9 1/2 In.	45.00
Game Set, C.1906, Plate 9 1/2 In., 10 Piece	1200.00
Gravy Boat, Roses, White Ground	35.00
Hair Receiver & Powder Box, Bluebirds & Robins, Gold Trim, Footed	179.00
Hair Receiver, Wild Roses, Gilt Cobweb	42.00
Holder, Place Card, Dove, White	18.00
Jardiniere, Tray, Roses, Handled, Pansies, 10 In.	95.00
Jug, Hand-Painted Grapes	68.00
Lamp, Banquet, Cupid Design	375.00
Lemonade Set, Green, Gold, Art Deco Shaped Pitcher, 7 Piece	185.00
Letter Cache, Gold Handles, Ball Feet, Pink & Lavender	395.00
Match Holder, Brownie Design	35.00
Mug, Flowers, Purple Grapes, Covered, C.1880	250.00
Nappy, Roses & Leafings, Artist Signed, Handled	25.00
Oyster Plate, Cream Ground, Roses, 9 In.	100.00
Oyster Plate, Gold Design, Cream	34.00
Oyster Set, Well Platter, 5 Plates, Signed	125.00
Pin, Portrait, Porcelain, Oval, Blue, Signed	40.00
Pitcher, Cider, Berries Design	65.00
Pitcher, Cider, Cream, Pink Flowers, Marked	45.00
Pitcher, Cider, Flowers, Dated June 3, 1884	42.00
Pitcher, Cider, Fruit Design, Marked, 8 1/2 X 6 In.	125.00
Pitcher, Cider, Hand-Painted Apples & Foliage, Dated 1907, 5 1/2 In.	95.00
Pitcher, Clover Blossoms, Baroque Design, 1903, Signed, 12 3/4 In.	150.00
Pitcher, Dragon, Grape Design, Green, Marked, 15 In.	395.00
Pitcher, Grape Clusters, Gold Rim, Signed, 12 3/4 In.	169.00
Pitcher, Grape Design, Figural Dragon Handle, Signed, 15 In.	375.00
Plaque, Duck, Pheasant, Signed, Pair	225.00
Plaque, Fighting Stags, 13 In.	495.00
Plaque, Hand-Painted Fish, Artist Signed, Marked, 13 In.	155.00
Plaque, Hand-Painted Lady, Frame, Signed, 1907	2000.00
Plaque, Hand-Painted Wild Duck, Gold Rim, Signed, 9 1/2 In.	100.00
Plaque, Indian Girl, Gold Rococo Border, Signed DuBois, 13 In.	275.00
Plaque, Indian Girl, Scalloped Edge, Artist Signed, 13 In.Diam.	325.00
Plaque, Pheasant In Flight, Gold Rococo Border, Signed	125.00
Plaque, Portrait, White Rock Lady, Marked, 15 1/2 In.	350.00
Plaque, Wall, Indian Girl, Gold Rococo, Marked, 13 In.	215.00
Plate, Art Nouveau, Butterfly, Hand-Painted, Signed, Pair	110.00
Plate, Bird Center, Gold Edge, Each Different, 8 1/4 In., Set Of 12	1200.00
Plate, Bud, 2 Geese, Orange, Blue & Yellow Ground, Marked, 10 In.	95.00
Plate, Cavalier, Musical Instrument, 10 In.	75.00
Plate, Cherubs Drinking Wine, Eating Grapes, 8 In.	65.00
Plate, Chop, Old Abbey, White Ground, Gold Trim, Lacy Border, 12 In.	42.00
Plate, Coronet, Artist Signed, 10 In.	150.00
Plate, Daisies Trailing Design, Gold Band, 10 1/2 In.	85.00
Plate, Fish, Gold Rococo Edge, Artist Signed, 9 In.	45.00
Plate, Flambe, Fish, Gold Edge, Signed Pubu, 10 1/2 In.	55.00
Plate, Flowers, Gold Trim, Marked & Dated, 9 In.	40.00
Plate, Fruit Design, Gold Rococo Edge, 11 1/4 In., Pair	295.00
Plate, Fruit, Coronet, Gold Border, Marked, 15 In.	225.00

Plate, Fruit, Coronet, Gold Rococo Border, Marked, 13 In. 150.00
Plate, Gold & Cobalt Blue Edge, White, 10 1/2 In., Set Of 10 .... 125.00
Plate, Hand-Painted Flowers, Signed J.K.McGarry, 1903 .... 35.00
Plate, Hand-Painted, Birds, Sky, Building, 11 1/4 In. 90.00
Plate, Hand-Painted, Dog Stalking Pheasant, Signed, 13 1/4 In. 195.00
Plate, Indian Chief Portrait, Coronet 95.00
Plate, Leaf, Whiteware, Curved Handle, 2-Part, Signed, 11 In. 50.00
Plate, Leaves, Acorns, Gold Trim, Marked, 8 1/2 In. 55.00
Plate, Mallard In Clover, Signed, Gold Rim, 9 In. 48.00
Plate, Morman Temple, Hand-Painted, 7 In. 48.00
Plate, Oyster, Blue, Roses, Set Of 6 .... 240.00
Plate, Oyster, Cream Ground, Roses, 9 In. 10.00
Plate, Oyster, Elite Mark, Roses, Gold Trim 45.00
Plate, Oyster, Hand-Painted, Marine Figures, C.1835, 9 In., Set Of 6 .... 360.00
Plate, Pink Morning Glories, Blue Ground, 7 1/4 In. 10.00
Plate, Portrait Of Composer, Gold Design Rim, Marked, 9 5/8 In. 195.00
Plate, Portrait Of Lady, Bench Scene, 10 In. 75.00
Plate, Portrait Of Musketeer, Hand-Painted, Gold Edge, 10 1/2 In. 105.00
Plate, Portrait, Cavalier & Maiden, Signed, 10 In., Pair 200.00
Plate, Raised Gold Scroll, Floral, 8 1/2 In. 32.00
Plate, Sweet Pea, Coronet, Signed, 9 1/2 In. 22.50
Plate, Wild Flying Turkeys, Artist Signed, Brown & Orchid, 9 In., Pr. 22.00
Plate, 3 Orange Poppies, Ivory, 8 1/2 In. 22.00
Platter, Asparagus, Fluted Rim, Gold Trim, Marked, 17 In. 70.00
Platter, Baltimore Rose, Gold Trim, Oval, 11 1/2 In. 39.50
Platter, Fish, Oval, Blue & Gold, Lilac Flowers, 9 X 22 In. 195.00
Platter, Game Bird, Quail, Gold Scalloped Border, 14 In. 175.00
Platter, Quail, Gold Scalloped Border, 14 1/2 In., Pair 185.00
Platter, Red Circle, White, Gold Rim, Marked, 11 In. 10.00
Punch Bowl, 8 Cup, Footed, Hand-Painted, Floral, 14 3/4 In. 695.00
Ramekin & Underplate, Garland Of Roses, Gold Edge 79.50
Ring Tree, Rose Flowers, Marked, 3 X 3 In. 18.00
Salt & Pepper, Pink Floral Design, Gilded Top, 3 1/2 In. 30.00
Shoe, High, Gold Flower Design, Porcelain 45.00
Soup, Red Roses, Blue & Gold Scrolls 4.50
Stein, Blackberries, Leaves, & Blossoms, 5 3/4 In. 45.00
Sugar & Creamer, Black, Floral & Gold Leaf, Signed 65.00
Sugar & Creamer, Child's, Allover Design, Crystal 35.00
Sugar & Creamer, Lilac Clusters, Gold Rims, Marked 79.00
Sugar & Creamer, Oval Shape, Pink Floral, Marked 92.00
Sugar & Creamer, Roses, Gold Trim, Marked 50.00
Tankard, Art Nouveau, Sterling Silver Overlay, Green 70.00
Tankard, Berries, 11 In. 195.00
Tankard, Blackberries, Dogwood Flowers, Lilac, Marked, 15 In. 275.00
Tankard, Dark Green, Dragon Shape, Purple Grapes, Marked, 15 In. 350.00
Tankard, Dragon Handle, Green & Brown Ground, Dated, 15 In. 350.00
Tankard, Grape Design, 12 In. 275.00
Tankard, Maroon, Green, Yellow Berries, 11 In. 110.00
Tankard, Purple Berries, Handled, 11 In. 195.00
Tea Set, Blueberry Pattern, Artist Signed 92.00
Tea Set, Gold & Silver Design, 1902, 3 Piece 95.00
Tea Set, Nasturtiums On Green Body, 3 Piece 37.50
Tea Set, Roses, Gold Trim, Silver Luster, Marked 75.00
Tea Set, Vignaud Pattern, Hand-Painted Roses, Signed, 3 Piece 75.00
Teapot, Sugar, French Rose, Gold Work, Pedestal, 6 1/4 In. 79.00
Tray, Apple Blossoms, Scalloped, Gold & Green, 12 X 8 1/2 In. 39.50
Tray, Cupids, Gold Border, Marked AK, 11 X 7 In. 95.00
Tray, Dresser, Apple Blossom Design, Artist Signed, 12 X 9 In. 40.00
Tray, Dresser, Boat Shape, Gold Trim, Pink Roses, Handles, 15 In.Long 70.00
Tray, Dresser, Green, Pink, Floral, Gold Rim, 12 X 9 In. 38.00
Tray, Dresser, Hand-Painted Forget-Me-Nots 40.00
Tray, Dresser, Purple Violets, Gold Rim, 11 1/4 X 8 In. 40.00
Tray, George & Martha Washington, Mt.Vernon, Marked, 11 X 7 1/2 In. 45.00
Tray, Hand-Painted Center Scene, Scalloped Corners, 14 1/2 X 9 In. 235.00

Tray, Horse Scene, Enameled, 5 1/2 X 3 1/2 In. 24.00
Tray, Magenta Flowers, Blue Ground, Gold Bark Handles, 11 In.Diam. 79.00
Tray, Pen, Floral; 8 3/4 In.Long 25.00
Tray, Perfume, Tea Roses, Artist Signed, Porcelain, 12 In. 45.00
Tureen, Roses, Floral Garland, Gold 62.00
Vase, Alders & Flowers, Floral Panels, Marked, 5 1/4 In. 335.00
Vase, Beige Ground, Floral, Green Twisted Handle, 12 In. 300.00
Vase, Bud, Amethyst Over White, 8 In. 28.00
Vase, Fuchsia Flowers, Birds, 15 1/2 In. 155.00
Vase, Hand-Painted, Floral Design, Gold Handles, Marked, 7 In. 130.00
Vase, Hand-Painted, Poppy Design, Ovoid, Bavarian, 8 1/2 In. 55.00
Vase, Hummingbird, Wisteria Design, 15 In. 185.00
Vase, Lizard Handles, Hand-Painted, White Roses, Signed, 9 In. 145.00
Vase, Ruby, Wrought-Iron Holder, 12 In. 24.00
Vase, Yellow Mottled, 14K Gold Leaf Handle & Base Ring, 4 1/2 In. 12.50

LINDBERGH, Airplane, Paper 35.00
   Pillowcase 45.00
   Pin, Enamel 30.00
   Pin, Lapel, Spirit Of St.Louis 60.00
   Plaque, Bronze, 12 In. 65.00

Lithophanes are porcelain pictures made by casting clay in layers of various thicknesses. When a piece is held to the light, a picture of light and shadow is seen through it. Most lithophanes date from the 1825-1875 period. A few are still being made.

LITHOPHANE, Candle Shield, Boy Lolling On Grass, Goat & Castle, 9 In. 250.00
   Cup & Saucer, Demitasse, Thousand Eye Pattern, Set Of 4 .... 35.00
   Cup & Saucer, Dragon 20.00
   Cup, Hand-Painted, Young Lady Leaning Out Of Window, 2 3/8 In. 85.00
   Cup, Nut, Admiral's Cap Shape, Admiral Schley 135.00
   Cup, Salvation Army, Portrait Of General Booth, 2 7/8 In. 110.00
   Lamp, Fairy, Little Miss Muffet, Candle In Cup Mold, 2 Piece 295.00
   Lamp, 5 Panel, Genre Of Children, Signed KPM, Pair 1895.00
   Lamp, 5 Panel, Pictures Of Children, Signed PPM, Brass Base 995.00
   Lamp, 6-Sided, Children, Women, & Angels, Pewter Base, 26 In. 1050.00
   Panel, Boy Holding Yarn For Grandmother, 6 1/2 X 5 5/8 In. 130.00
   Panel, Boy Leaning Over Wall Talking To Maid, 4 5/8 X 3 7/8 In. 77.50
   Panel, Doe & Buck, Great Antlers, In Stream, 5 X 4 1/4 In. 145.00
   Panel, Draped Lady Smelling Flower, 4 5/8 X 3 7/8 In. 77.50
   Panel, Girl Smells Flower, Leaded Glass, KPM, 7 1/4 X 5 7/8 In. 365.00
   Panel, Man With Lute, Ship, Beehive Mark, 8 1/8 X 6 1/4 In. 250.00
   Panel, Mother & Child, 4 Cherubs In Clouds, 7 5/8 X 6 1/8 In. 175.00
   Panel, Mother Holding Child, KPM, Framed, 5 7/8 X 4 1/2 In. 160.00
   Potty, Naked Little Boy, Gold Lettered, C.1880, 2 X 1 1/2 In. 85.00
   Shade, Mother Bear With Downed Buck, Cubs At Stream, 10 1/2 In. 150.00
   Shade, 4 Scenes Divided By Medallions, Clambroth, 22 In. 2250.00
   Stein, Bicycle, Wheel Each Side, Man & Woman On Bicycles 595.00
   Stein, Figural, Monk, Girl, Decollete Shoulders, Flower In Hair 365.00
   Stein, Scene Of Dancing Couple, Gold Handle, Hand-Painted 195.00
   Stein, Tyrolean Seated At Table, Lady Standing, Pewter Lid 275.00
   Stein, Wife Holding Child, Looking At Father, 5 3/4 In. 120.00
   Stein, 1/2 Liter, Faust In Red 185.00

LITHYALIN, Bottle, Perfume, C.1830, Brown To Terra-Cotta, 5 In. 125.00

LITTLE ORPHAN ANNIE, Book, Annie & The Lucky Knife, Harold Gray 12.00
   Jigsaw Puzzle, Original Box 20.00
   Mug, Glasbake, 1975 .... 10.00
   Shake-Up, Ovaltine 25.00
   Stove, Child's 35.00

Liverpool, England, was the site of several pottery and porcelain factories from 1716 to 1785. Some earthenware was made with transfer decorations. Sadler and Green made print-decorated wares from 1756. Many of the pieces

*were made for the American market and featured patriotic emblems such as
eagles, flags, and other special-interest motifs.*

LIVERPOOL, Bowl, Ships, Coat Of Arms, 10 In. 850.00
   Jug, Apotheosis Of Washington, 10 3/4 In. .... *Illus* 900.00
   Jug, Masonic 500.00
   Pitcher, Black, Landscape, 9 In. 200.00

LOCKE ART, Biscuit Jar, Peach Leaves, Shading To Cream, Shrubhill Works 75.00
   Goblet, Ivy Design, Twisted Stem, 6 1/2 In. 50.00
   Sherbet, Pansy Cutting, Footed, Signed 95.00
   Tray, Kalana Lily, 10 In.Diam. 115.00
   Tumbler, Poppy Design, Signed, 4 1/2 In. 65.00

Liverpool, Jug, Apotheosis Of
Washington, 10 3/4 In.

*Johann Loetz-Witwe bought a glassworks in Austria in 1840. He died in
1848 and his widow ran the company, then in 1879 his grandson took over.
Loetz glass was varied. Most collectors recognize the iridescent gold
glass similar to Tiffany, but many other types were made. The firm closed
in World War II.*

LOETZ, Basket, Blue-Green Mottling, Fruit Design 120.00
   Biscuit Barrel, Green 200.00
   Biscuit Barrel, Pewter Bail & Top, Green Iridescent, Signed, 7 1/2 In. 300.00
   Biscuit Barrel, Verre-De-Soie Base, Amethyst Threading 195.00
   Bowl, Attached To Turtle, Crackled Luster, Blue Base, Fluted, 9 1/4 In. 275.00
   Bowl, Centerpiece, Ruffled, Overall Points, Metal Stand, C.1900, 8 In. 160.00
   Bowl, Gold Ribbed Flared Top, Iridescent, 2 1/2 X 6 1/4 In. 100.00
   Bowl, Iridescent, Tripod, Handled, Leaf Decor, Marked, 10 X 3 1/2 In. 125.00
   Bowl, Paneled, Onionskin Edge, Blue-Green Iridescent, 2 X 9 In. 250.00
   Bowl, Purple Highlights, 2 1/2 X 6 1/4 In. .... 135.00 To 160.00
   Inkwell, Amber Iridescent, Green-Blue Threaded Glass, Hinged 125.00
   Inkwell, Cranberry Iridescent, Hinged Brass Lid, Brass Tray 125.00
   Inkwell, Drape Pattern, Iridescent, Salmon Ground, Signed 75.00
   Inkwell, Hinged Lid, Iridescent 195.00
   Inkwell, Lion's Head, Brass Lid, Iridescent, Signed 225.00
   Jar, Sweetmeat, Spiderweb, Iridescent Green, Bail Handle 475.00
   Rose Bowl, Melon-Shaped, Threaded, Amethyst 155.00
   Shade, Blue, Silver, Iridescent, Random Pull-Up, Pair 250.00
   Toothpick, Green Iridescent 150.00
   Vase, Amethyst & Green, Ribbed, Ruffled Top, Signed, 10 In. 190.00
   Vase, Art Nouveau, Silver Overlay, C.1900, 4 3/4 In. 435.00
   Vase, Blue & Green Iridescent, Brass Collar, 7 In. 95.00

Vase, Blue & Green, Sterling Silver Art Deco Overlay, 4 In. 395.00
Vase, Blue Threading, Iridescent Gold, 8 1/2 In. 115.00
Vase, Blue-Green Iridescent Oil Spot, Pierced Brass Collar, 7 1/2 In. 95.00
Vase, Chartreuse & Brown, Pedestal Foot, Chalice-Shaped, Marked 575.00
Vase, Corset-Shaped, Iridescent, 10 In. 125.00
Vase, Cranberry, Marked, 4 1/2 In. 175.00
Vase, Double Gourd, Blue-Green Interior, 5 1/2 In. 175.00
Vase, Floriform, Aquamarine, Iridescent & Marbleized 195.00
Vase, Gold Dust, Apple Green, Flower-Form Opening, 14 X 7 In. 350.00
Vase, Gold Flecks, Pinched-In Top, Iridescent Green, 8 In. 175.00
Vase, Gold Iridescent, Polished Pontil, 9 In. 95.00
Vase, Gold Iridescent, Random Dots, Raised, 6 In. 225.00
Vase, Gold Oil Spots, Pinched Top, 6 1/2 In. 350.00
Vase, Gold Raindrop Body, Blue Threading, Ruffled Rim, 8 In. 225.00
Vase, Gold, Green & Red, Tapered Cylinder, 6 1/4 In. 95.00
Vase, Gold, Silver Overlay, Dimpled, Ruffled, 4 1/2 In. 375.00
Vase, Gourd Shape, Purple, Green, Serpent Entwined, 9 1/2 In. 125.00
Vase, Gourd Shape, Scalloped Rim, Green, 8 1/2 In. 45.00
Vase, Green Iridescent, Austria, Signed, 5 3/8 In., Pair 325.00
Vase, Green, Cylinder, Snakeskin Design, 7 In. 70.00
Vase, Green, Iridescent, 6 1/2 In., Pair 95.00
Vase, Green, Purple Spots, Marked, 6 In. 750.00
Vase, Green, Raised Veins, Allover Pattern, 5 1/2 In. 75.00
Vase, Green, Threading, Signed, 7 1/2 In. 475.00
Vase, Green, Threading, 8 3/4 In. 225.00
Vase, Iridescent Blue & Green, Trees With Oranges & Leaves, 14 In. 350.00
Vase, Iridescent Reds, Blues, 10 1/4 In. X 6 1/2 In. 425.00
Vase, Orange & Gold Iridescent, Twisted, 8 In. 75.00
Vase, Pulled Colors, Green, 6 In. 93.00
Vase, Pulled Loops, Overall Silver, Tortoiseshell, 5 1/2 In. 120.00
Vase, Red Iridescent, Signed Sterling Overlay, 1895, 4 1/4 In. 325.00
Vase, Red, Opal Feathers, Yellow Raindrops, 1900, 12 In. 400.00
Vase, Silver Overlay, Ovoid, Amber, Floral, Vine, 8 In. 460.00
Vase, Trumpet, Pulled Feathers, Ruffled Top, 12 1/2 In. 350.00
Vase, Wavy Gold Design, Ruffled Top, 12 1/2 In. 650.00

> *The Lone Ranger is a fictional character introduced on the radio in*
> *1932. Over three thousand shows were produced before the series ended*
> *in 1954. In 1938 the first Lone Ranger movie was made. Television shows*
> *were started in 1949. The Lone Ranger appears on many products and*
> *was even the name of a restaurant chain for several years.*

LONE RANGER, Badge, Deputy .... 10.00 To 15.00
Badge, Deputy, Secret Compartment, 1949 .... 25.00
Badge, Original Display Card, 1950s, Set Of 12 .... 35.00
Badge, Safety Club 10.00
Book, Hi Ho Silver 22.00
Box, Pencil 15.00
Brush, Clothes 12.00
Flashlight, Boxed 18.00
Guitar 135.00
Gun, Tin 12.00
Harmonica, Magnus, Original Box 37.50
Knife, Pocket 45.00
Paperweight, Snow .... 15.00 To 35.00
Pin, Safety Scout, Silver Cup 22.00
Puzzle, Story, Parker 65.00
Ring, Atom Bomb, 1947 .... 18.00 To 35.00
Ring, Flashlight 22.00
Ring, Movie Film 20.00
Scarf, Scene On Horseback, Used As Mask, 3 Ft. X 4 3/4 In. 29.00
Statue, Carnival Chalkware .... 22.50 To 28.00
Statue, With Silver, 1938 .... 45.00

Longwy Workshop of Longwy, France, first made ceramic wares in 1798. The workshop is still in business. Most of the ceramic pieces found today are glazed with many colors to resemble cloisonne or other enameled metal.

LONGWY, Bowl, Pink Florals, Blue Ground, Medallion Center, Marked, 11 In. 120.00
  Soup, Cream, Cobalt Blue Ground, Marked, 3 3/4 In. 80.00
  Sugar Shaker, Blue Ground, Floral, Metal Top, 5 In. .... 85.00 To 90.00
  Sugar Shaker, Red Ground, Geometric, Metal Top, 5 In. .... 85.00 To 90.00
  Tile, Enameled Design, Wooden Frame, 8 X 8 In. 65.00
  Tile, Floral, Pair 195.00
  Vase, Cylinder, Turquoise Mosaic Ground, Flowers, Marked, 9 In., Pr. 100.00

Lonhuda Pottery Company of Steubenville, Ohio, was organized in 1892 by William Long, W.H. Hunter, and Alfred Day. Brown underglaze slip-decorated pottery was made. The firm closed in 1896.

LONHUDA, Vase, Top Loop Handle, Leaf & Bud Design, 5 3/4 In. 135.00

Lotus Ware was made by the Knowles, Taylor & Knowles Company of East Liverpool, Ohio, from 1890 to 1900.

LOTUS WARE, Creamer, Bamboo Style Handle, Fishnet Design, Signed, 3 In. 190.00
  Dish, Shell Shape, Roses, Pastels, 8 X 8 1/2 In. 275.00
  Sugar, Hand-Painted Flowers, White Ground 175.00
  Syrup, Hand-Painted Flowers, Brass Top & Spout, Signed 325.00
  Vase, Applied Flowers, Leaves, Green & White, 6 1/2 In., Pair 1500.00

J.&J.G.LOW *Low art tiles were made by the J. and J.G. Low Art Tile Works of Chelsea, Massachusetts, from 1877 to 1902. A variety of art and other tiles were made.*

LOW, Tile, Blue Design, 6 X 6 In. 30.00
  Tile, Lady, Flowing Hair, Brown, 6 X 6 In. 35.00

The Lowestoft factory in Suffolk, England, worked from 1757 to 1802. They made many commemorative gift pieces and small, dated, inscribed pieces of soft paste porcelain.
  LOWESTOFT, see also Chinese Export
LOWESTOFT, Bowl, Willow Design, Polychrome Enamel, Blue, 5 1/2 In. 175.00
  LOY-NEL-ART, see McCoy

LUDWIGSBURG, Bowl, Central Bouquet, Sprigs, Polychrome, C.1760, Marked, 10 In. 375.00

Luneville, a French faience factory, was established in 1731 by Jacques Chambrette. It is best known for its fine biscuit figures and groups and for large faience dogs and lions. The early pieces were unmarked. The firm was acquired by Keller and Guerin and is still working.

LUNEVILLE, Bowl, Finger, Red Poppies, Flow Blue Ground 65.00
  Bowl, Purple Irises, Tricorn-Shaped, Cream, 7 X 6 In. 115.00
  Compote, Rooster Center, Clover & Butterflies, 9 3/4 X 5 1/2 In. 63.00
  Vase, Silver & Gold Design, Collar, Underwater Foliage, 8 1/2 In. 1950.00

Lusterware was meant to resemble copper, silver, or gold. It has been used since the sixteenth century. Most of the luster found today was made during the nineteenth century.

LUSTER, Canary, Mug, Child's, Red Transfer Man & Children On Horses, 2 In. 125.00

Luster, Silver, Jugs, Sir Francis Burdett Portrait, 4 3/4 In.; Boxers, 1810-1815, 4 3/4 In.
(See Page 366)

Copper, Bowl, Blue Band, Gold Design, 6 1/4 X 3 1/4 In.	52.00
Copper, Chocolate Set, Blue Band, 5 Piece	195.00
Copper, Creamer, Flowers, Pink Neck, Bulbous, 3 In.	22.00
Copper, Creamer, Gold Design, 3 In.	30.00
Copper, Goblet, Floral Enamel	45.00
Copper, Mug, Blue Floral Band	80.00
Copper, Mug, Pink Luster Band, Blue Outer Band, Handle, 3 In.	40.00
Copper, Pitcher, Allerton, 5 In.	50.00
Copper, Pitcher, Coaching Scene, Stoke-On-Trent, 2 1/4 In.	12.00
Copper, Pitcher, Dancers, Blue Trim, 6 In.	125.00
Copper, Pitcher, Dancing Youth, Maiden, Blue Trim, 7 In.	65.00
Copper, Pitcher, Diamond-Quilted, 6 1/2 In.	75.00
Copper, Pitcher, Embossed Hunt Scene, Blue Band	95.00
Copper, Pitcher, Milk, Oriental	65.00
Copper, Salt, Open, Flint, Blue Enamel	25.00
Copper, Saltshaker, Copper Sand Base, Beaded Trim, Footed, 5 In.	15.00
Copper, Sugar & Creamer, Blue Band, Raised Polychome Children	75.00
LUSTER, COPPER, TEA LEAF, see Tea Leaf Ironstone	
Copper, Tea Set, Griffin Handle, C.1840, Cobalt Blue, 4 Piece	175.00
LUSTER, FAIRYLAND, see Wedgwood	
Gold, Pitcher, Pink, White Flowers, Green Leaves, 6 1/2 In.	78.00
Gold, Washbowl & Pitcher, Paneled, Pre-1830, Bowl 13 1/2 In.	225.00
Pink, Creamer, Fruits & Floral Band, Gravy Boat Shape, 3 X 6 In.	25.00
Pink, Cup & Saucer, Drape With Flowers, Handleless	40.00
Pink, Cup & Saucer, Faith, Hope, & Charity, Red & Green	50.00
Pink, Cup & Saucer, Floral	45.00
Pink, Cup & Saucer, Floral & Geometric Design	30.00
Pink, Cup & Saucer, Fruit Floral Pattern	25.00
Pink, Cup & Saucer, Gold Trim, Blown Out, Gold Grapes	45.00
Pink, Cup & Saucer, Hanging Drape, Red & Green Floral	30.00
Pink, Cup & Saucer, House, C.1820	40.00
Pink, Cup & Saucer, With Kind Regards, Gold Trim	15.00
Pink, Dessert Set, Impressed Numbers, 25 Piece	695.00
Pink, Mug, Monkeys & Clowns	35.00
Pink, Pincushion, Lady With Legs	65.00
Pink, Pitcher, Ship Northumberland, Bridge Over Wear, Motto, 8 1/4 In.	140.00
Pink, Pitcher, Underplate, Swirled	27.50
Pink, Plate, Brown, Green Floral, Silver Luster Leaves & Border	15.00
Pink, Plate, House, 6 1/2 In.	35.00
Pink, Plate, Red Flowers, Green Leaves, 7 In.	15.00
Pink, Plate, Shepherd Boy, C.1820, 7 1/4 In.	48.00
Pink, Plate, 2-Tone Pink Design, Green Dots, Scalloped, 9 In.	35.00

Leeds, Jug, Armorial, Silver, Eagle & Sailboats, 1810-1815, 8 In. *(See Page 353)*; Luster, Silver, Jug, Puzzle, Pinwheel Design; Luster, Silver, Vase, Painted Scenes, Marked, 9 7/8 In.

Pink, Shaving Mug, Applied Flower	27.50
Pink, Tea Service, C.1820, 12 Piece	200.00
Pink, Tumbler, Souvenir, D.Webster Birthplace, Hand-Painted, Germany	12.50
Silver, Creamer	55.00
Silver, Cup & Saucer	25.00
Silver, Jug, Bird Perched On Boughs, C.1815, 4 In.	192.00
Silver, Jug, Boxers, 1810-1815, 4 3/4 In. ....*Illus*	750.00
Silver, Jug, Grapevines, Aqua, Red, C.1815, 5 In.	375.00
Silver, Jug, Grapevines, Yellow, C.1810, Marked, 5 In.	175.00
Silver, Jug, Puzzle, Pinwheel Design ....*Illus*	175.00
Silver, Jug, Sir Francis Burdett Portrait, 4 3/4 In. ....*Illus*	300.00
Silver, Loving Cup, 2-Handled, C.1850, 4 1/2 In.	55.00
Silver, Tea Set, Scroll Handles, Gadrooned Lower Body, England, 3 Pc.	550.00
Silver, Vase, Painted Scenes, Marked, 9 7/8 In. ....*Illus*	350.00

LUSTER, SUNDERLAND, see Sunderland

Lustre Art Glass Company was founded in Long Island, New York, in 1920 by Conrad Vahlsing and Paul Frank. The company made lampshades and globes that are almost indistinguishable from those made by Quezal.

LUSTRE ART, Shade, Gold Zipper Over Opal On Gold, Signed	150.00
Shade, Gold Zipper Over Pulled Design, Ruffled, Signed	175.00
Shade, Lily, Gold Iridescent, Signed	175.00
Shade, Opalescent Feather, Green Edge On Gold, Signed, Pair	225.00

Lustres are mantel decorations, or pedestal vases, with many hanging glass prisms. The name really refers to the prisms, and it is proper to refer to a single glass prism as a lustre. Either spelling, luster or lustre, is correct.

LUSTRES, Mantel, Ruby Overlay, Hand-Painted Roses, Pair	225.00

Lutz glass was made in the 1870s by Nicholas Lutz at the Boston and Sandwich Company. He made a delicate and intricate threaded glass of several colors. Other similar wares are referred to as Lutz.

LUTZ, Dish, Nut, Applied Raised Enamel Flowers	35.00

Petrus Regout established the De Sphinx pottery in Maastricht, Holland, in 1836. The firm was noted for its transfer-printed earthenware. Many factories in Maastricht are still making ceramics.

MAASTRICHT, Bowl, Batter	20.00
Bowl, Stick Spatter, Green	55.00
Bowl, Stick Spatter, Red	55.00
Plate, Abbey, 8 In.	20.00
Plate, Native Selling Fruit From Horseback, Blue, 8 1/4 In.	38.00

Maize glass, sold by the W.L.Libbey & Son Company of Toledo, Ohio, was made by Joseph Locke in 1889. It is pressed glass formed like an ear of corn. Most pieces were made for household use.

MAIZE, Celery, Gold Enameled Leaves, 4 1/8 X 6 1/2 In.	145.00
Celery, Green Enameled Leaves, Opaque Ground, 4 1/4 X 6 1/2 In.	125.00
Salt & Pepper, Glass, Green Leaves	175.00
Salt & Pepper, Glass, Yellow Leaves	150.00
Sugar Shaker, Blue Leaves	135.00
Tumbler, Gold Leaves	60.00
Vase, Iridescent Staining, 6 In.	60.00
Vase, 6 1/2 In.	92.00

Majolica is any pottery glazed with a tin enamel. Most of the majolica found today is decorated with leaves, shells, branches, and other natural shapes and in natural colors. It was a popular nineteenth-century product.

MAJOLICA, see also Wedgwood

MAJOLICA, Basin, Spanish, 18th Century, 18 1/2 X 5 In.	395.00
Basket, Green, 3 Birds, Flowers, Handled, 10 In.	650.00
Biscuit Jar, Sphinx Finial, Silver Plated Top, C.1875, 7 5/8 In.	275.00
Bowl, Twisted Handles, Footed, 10 3/4 In.	95.00
Box, Sardine, Molded Overlapping Fish On Lid, 8 X 7 1/4 In.	85.00
Box, Sardine, Natural Color Fish, Blue & White, 9 X 7 X 4 1/2 In.	135.00
Box, Sardine, Underplate, Lavender	200.00
Box, Sardine, Underplate, 3 Fish Cover, 8 X 7 1/2 In.	70.00
Butter, Birds & Apple Blossoms, Covered, Marked, 8 1/2 X 5 In.	75.00
Cake Plate, Grape Leaf Pattern	90.00
Cake Plate, Yellow & Brown Basket Weave Stem, 4 1/2 X 9 In.	50.00
Candleholder, Mottled Green, Conical Snuffer Stand, 6 1/2 In.	45.00
Charger, Classical Design, Figures, Seaside, 18 In.	250.00
Cigarette Dispenser, Blue, Woman & Man Figures, Metal Holder	45.00
Compote, Pedestal Lily Pad, Geor.Jones	225.00
Compote, Veined Leaf Center, Splotched Color Edge, 9 1/2 In.	50.00
Creamer, Blackberry	25.00
Creamer, Dogwood, Branch Handle, Pewter Lid, Glazed Interior	75.00
Creamer, Ear Of Corn, 4 1/2 In.	29.00
Creamer, English Cottage	175.00
Creamer, Lavender, Butterfly Spout, Marked, 4 1/2 In.	45.00
Creamer, Rustic, Pink Interior, Small	22.00
Cup & Saucer, Floral, Green, Yellow, Blue Bands	60.00
Cup, Red Leaves, Avalon	23.00
Dish, Sardine, Fish On Lid, 8 X 7 In.	85.00
Doughbox, Acorns & Oak Leaves, Shenandoah Valley	3500.00
Ewer, Oriental Inspired Floral Vines, Yellow On Brown, 14 In.	20.00
Ewer, Wood Pedestal Base, Mid-19th Century, 54 In., Pair	2150.00
Figurine, Frog Musicians, Pair	*Illus* 300.00
Humidor, Bacchus, 7 3/4 In.	150.00
Humidor, Boy's Head With Cap & Cigarette	78.00
Humidor, German Bowler, 6 1/2 In.	130.00
Humidor, Head Of Child, Green Glaze, Ribbon Finial, 5 1/2 In.	65.00
Humidor, Smiling Monk In Brown Cowl, 7 In.	95.00
Jardiniere, Nude Woman, 4-Footed, 7 1/4 In.	110.00
Jug, Molasses, Sunflower, Blue, Etruscan	170.00
Jug, Multicolored, Handled, 3 1/2 In.	125.00
Jug, Tan, Blue, & Brown, Old Saying, C.1865, 7 1/2 In.	190.00
Liquor Set, Heart-Shaped Decanter, Barnyard Scenes, Marked, 7 Piece	125.00
Match Holder, Castle Form, 4 X 7 In.	85.00

Mug, Lily, Etruscan 75.00
Nappy, Leaf Shaped, Twig Handle, Green, 7 1/2 In. 18.00
Pitcher, Albino, Etruscan, 4 1/2 In. 85.00
Pitcher, Brown Ground, Green, Yellow, Leaves, 7 1/2 In. 80.00
Pitcher, Burgundy Lined, Grape Design, 3 Nude Children, 8 In. 90.00
Pitcher, Cockatoo, Bamboo Handle, Marked, 9 In. 135.00
Pitcher, Embossed Fish Design On Side, 4 1/2 In. 50.00
Pitcher, Fish, Tail Forms Handle, Mouth Spout, Green, 10 1/2 In. 75.00
Pitcher, Fish, Tail Forms Handle, Mouth Spout, Pink, 13 1/2 In. 75.00
Pitcher, Fish, Tail Forms Handle, Pink, 9 3/4 In. .... 60.00 To 75.00
Pitcher, Flowers & Leaves, Turquoise Interior, Cream, 4 X 5 3/4 In. 45.00
Pitcher, Fox & Goose 75.00
Pitcher, Grapes & Leaves, Bark Handle, Lavender Interior, 5 In. 38.00
Pitcher, Green, Birds, 4 In. 35.00
Pitcher, Monkey, Carrying Leaves On Back, Branch Handle, 5 3/4 In. 110.00
Pitcher, Monkey, Graduated Set Of 4 .... Illus 935.00
Pitcher, Pug Dog, Brown, Black, Dark Red Collar, 8 In. 45.00
Pitcher, Rooster, Pours Through Bill, 10 3/4 In. 65.00
Pitcher, Syrup, Mustard Ground, Hinged Pewter Lid, 4 In. 65.00
Pitcher, Turquoise Tree Bark Ground, Leaf On Sides 35.00
Pitcher, Water, Seaweed, C.1880 .... 250.00
Pitcher, Yellow, Deer, 8 In. 85.00
Plate, Asparagus Spears Center, Footed, 8 In. 35.00
Plate, Basket Weave, Flowers & Raspberries, 10 1/2 In. 50.00
Plate, Blackberry, Clifton, 10 In. 32.00
Plate, Bread, Floral, Handled, Marked 60.00
Plate, Cauliflower, Etruscan, 7 In. 60.00
Plate, Cauliflower, Etruscan, 9 In. 85.00
Plate, Deer & Hound, Aqua Center, Brown Border, 8 In. 22.00
Plate, Floral, 9 In. 40.00
Plate, Leaf Pattern, Green, Brown, & Yellow, 8 In. 24.00
Plate, Leaf, Green, Brown, & Red, 12 In. 25.00
Plate, Leaf, Green, Brown, & Yellow, 8 In. 24.00
Plate, Leaf, Green, Orange, Salamander, Beetle, 10 X 9 In. 85.00
Plate, Raised Leaf, Etruscan, 7 3/4 In. 35.00
Plate, Scalloped, Grape, Set Of 8, Marked, 7 3/4 In. 150.00
Plate, Seaweed, Pink Shell, 8 In. 40.00
Plate, Water Lily, 8 1/2 In. 25.00
Platter, Basket Weave, Flowers, Open Handle, 10 X 14 In. 70.00
Platter, Begonia Leaf, Green, Pink, & Brown, 9 X 11 1/4 In. 38.00
Platter, Floral & Leaves On Rim, Water Lily Pads, 11 7/8 In. 75.00
Platter, Leaf, Green, Yellow, & Pink, 9 X 12 In. 67.00
Platter, Olive Green, Blackberries, Leaves, Marked, 13 X 9 In. 60.00
Platter, Oyster, Beige Ground, Sea Design, Shell Feet, 15 3/4 In. 175.00
Punch Bowl, Red Ribbon With Bow & Flowers, 14 X 7 In. 200.00
Relish, Vases & Flowers, Lavender Edge, Oval, 6 X 10 In. 60.00
Shelf, Hanging, Leaves & Branches 350.00
Sugar & Creamer, Cauliflower 53.50
Sugar Shaker, Cone, Green 60.00
Sugar, Cauliflower, Covered, Etruscan 75.00
Sugar, Pineapple, Covered 75.00
Tea Set, Cauliflower, Etruscan, 3 Piece 235.00
Tea Set, Pineapple, Leaf Finials, 4 Piece 125.00
Teapot, Cauliflower, Etruscan 250.00
Teapot, English Cottage 95.00
Tray, Blue Ground, Raised Grapes, Green Leaves, 9 X 5 In. 45.00
Tray, Ferns & Cattails, Yellow, Green, & Cobalt Blue, 15 In. 65.00
Tray, Lavender, Rose, & Green, 11 1/4 X 3 In. 30.00
Tray, Leaf Shaped, Open Stem Handle, Green Center, 9 1/2 X 12 In. 75.00
Tray, Mustard Ground, Floral, Round, 5 Servers, Marked, 6 1/2 In. 95.00
Umbrella Stand, C.1900 .... 240.00
Vase, Applied Flower Buds, Leaves, 8 In. 60.00
Vase, Flying Birds, Pink Lining, Dark Blue 65.00
Vase, Man & Women On Each Side, Ram's Head Handles, 13 In. 90.00

Majolica, Figurine, Frog Musicians, Pair   Majolica, Pitcher, Monkey, Graduated Set Of 4

(See Pages 367, 370)

Marble Carving, Two Boys On Sofa,
Signed Vanucci, 16 X 11 In.

Vase, Monkey, Marked, 10 In.	240.00
Vase, Portrait Panels, Blue Ground, Leaf Scroll, 14 In., Pair	400.00
Wall Pocket, Scenery, Heart Shaped, Signed	32.00
MALACHITE, Figurine, Cat, Green, 3 1/2 In.	28.00
Vase, 6 Full Figure Nudes, 12-Sided Footing, 5 In.	125.00
MAP, American Railroads, Rand McNally, 1955, Wall, 38 X 51 In.	39.00
Asia Minor, A.S.S.Union Press, 1830, 5 1/4 X 6 1/2 In.	3.50
Boston, Railway, Rand McNally, 1910, 17 1/2 X 26 1/4 In.	12.50
Chart, Schoolhouse, Reading	400.00
Florida, Johns River, 1884, 26 X 36 In.	20.00
Iowa, Shipper Guide, Pocket, 1915	8.00
Maine, Geological, Somerset County & Moosehead Lake, 1903-56, Set Of 16	50.00
New Hampshire, Geological, Mineral Distribution, 1870, 13 1/4 X 22 In.	4.00
New Hampshire, Gold Fields, 7 Colors, 7 3/4 X 7 3/4 In.	8.50
New Hampshire, Granite Deposits, 1870, 13 1/2 X 22 In.	8.50
Northwest Europe, Linen Backed, Dated 1914, War Office	75.00
Ohio, Hand-Colored, Engraved, John Kilbourn, 1821, 20 X 21 In.	295.00
Yosemite, 1874, With Guide Book	25.00

MARBLE CARVING, Aphrodite, C.1900, Signed Philippe Fiaschi, White, 21 1/2 In. 775.00
Bust, Madonna, Gray Veining 100.00
Maiden, Flowing Dress, Italian, Marked Caradossi, 30 In. 900.00
Mercury, Victorian, White, Playing Pipes, 40 In. 800.00
Two Boys On Sofa, Signed Vanucci, 16 X 11 In. .... *Illus* 1100.00

> *Marbles of glass were made during the nineteenth century. Venetian swirl,*
> *clear glass, sulfides, and marbles with frosted white animal figures embedded*
> *in the glass were popular. Handmade clay marbles were made in many places,*
> *but most of them came from the pottery factories of Ohio and Pennsylvania.*
> *Occasionally, real stone marbles of onyx, carnelian, or jasper can be found.*

MARBLE, Akro Agate, Original Cardboard Box, Tri Color, Set Of 100 .... 60.00
Bennington Type, Blue 1.00
Bennington Type, Brown 1.00
Clay, Mottled, Bag Of 54 .... 7.50
Clay, 1 In. 1.00
Onionskin, Mica, Boxed, Set Of 9 .... 375.00
Porcelain, 1 In. 4.00
Ribbon Core, 7/8 In., Set Of 6 .... 20.00
Ribbon Swirls To Divided Core, Alternating Ribbons 30.00
Sulfide, Annie .... 35.00 To 37.50
Sulfide, Anteater, 1 1/4 In. 85.00
Sulfide, Bat, 1 7/8 In. 85.00
Sulfide, Bear, Begging, 1 1/2 In. 85.00
Sulfide, Bear, Cub, 1 3/8 In. 75.00
Sulfide, Bear, 1 5/8 In. 65.00
Sulfide, Betty 45.00
Sulfide, Bimbo .... 35.00 To 37.50
Sulfide, Bobcat, 1 15/16 In. 90.00
Sulfide, Bull, Standing, 1 5/8 In. 75.00
Sulfide, Bullfrog, White 65.00
Sulfide, Cat, Lying Down, 1 5/8 In. 80.00
Sulfide, Cat, Sitting, 1 3/4 In. 50.00
Sulfide, Cow, Grazing, 1 3/8 In. 65.00
Sulfide, Cow, Standing, 2 1/4 In. 75.00
Sulfide, Dog, Barking, 1 1/2 In. 65.00
Sulfide, Dog, Collie, 1 3/8 In. 60.00
Sulfide, Dog, Pointer, 1 1/2 In. 60.00
Sulfide, Dog, Sitting, 1 11/16 In. 75.00
Sulfide, Dog, St. Bernard, 1 1/2 In. 85.00
Sulfide, Donkey, 2 1/8 In. 112.00
Sulfide, Eagle, 1 3/8 In. 105.00
Sulfide, Elephant, 1 3/8 In. 65.00
Sulfide, Emma .... 35.00 To 48.00
Sulfide, Frog, 1 3/16 In. .... 70.00 To 85.00
Sulfide, Goat, 1 1/2 In. 50.00
Sulfide, Horse, Prancing, 1 3/4 In. 95.00
Sulfide, Horse, Rearing, 1 5/8 In. 85.00
Sulfide, Koko 40.00
Sulfide, Lamb, 1 1/4 In. 50.00
Sulfide, Lion, Crouching, 1 7/8 In. 65.00
Sulfide, Lion, Silver, 2 In. 90.00
Sulfide, Lion, Standing, 1 1/2 In. 60.00
Sulfide, Man-Ape, 1 11/16 In. 90.00
Sulfide, Monkey, With Hat, Begging, 1 3/8 In. 95.00
Sulfide, Moon Mullins 85.00
Sulfide, Owl, Standing 135.00
Sulfide, Parrot, 1 7/16 In. 75.00
Sulfide, Pig, 5 3/4 In. 65.00
Sulfide, Rabbit, Sitting Down, 1 1/2 In. 40.00
Sulfide, Rabbit, 1 1/2 In. 40.00
Sulfide, Razorback Pit, 1 1/4 In. 60.00
Sulfide, Rooster, 1 3/8 In. 50.00

Sulfide, Sandy	35.00
Sulfide, Sheep, Grazing, 1 5/8 In.	50.00
Sulfide, Sheep, Standing, 1 3/8 In.	55.00
Sulfide, Skeezix .... 35.00 To	40.00
Sulfide, Smitty	48.00
Sulfide, Squirrel, Hunched Over, Eating, 1 1/2 In.	80.00
Sulfide, Squirrel, On All Fours, 1 1/8 In.	65.00
Sulfide, Squirrel, With Acorn, 1 3/8 In.	55.00

The Marblehead Pottery was founded in 1905 by Dr. J. Hall as a rehabilitative program for the patients of a Marblehead, Massachusetts, sanitarium. Two years later it was separated from the sanitarium, and it continued operations until 1936. Many of the pieces were decorated with marine motifs.

MARBLEHEAD, Pitcher, Schooner & Galleon Medallions, Waves At Rim, 6-Color	600.00
Tile, Sailing Ship, Blue & White	135.00
Vase, Blue-Gray, 3 1/2 In.	45.00
Vase, Bulbous, Blue Matte, 3 1/2 In.	65.00
Vase, Bulbous, Blue, 4 1/2 In.	58.00
Vase, Flower, Leaf Band, Marked, X.1909, Matte Green, 4 1/2 In.	395.00
Vase, Incised Harpoon Design, Brown Flambe Glaze, 5 X 6 In.	400.00
Vase, Stylized Waves Encircling Top, Marked, Black Glaze, 6 In.	400.00
MARINE, see Nautical	

Martinware is a salt-glazed stoneware made by the Martin Brothers of Middlesex, England, between 1873 and 1915. Many figural jugs and vases were made.

MARTIN BROTHERS, Pitcher, Lotus, 8 In.		135.00
Pitcher, Shellfish & Octopus, Signed, 10 In.	*Illus*	800.00
Pot, Ribbed, Blue & Green Swags, Signed, 4 In.	*Illus*	125.00
Vase, Bird Design, Cream, Signed, 11 3/4 In.	*Illus*	350.00
Vase, Blue, 4 1/2 In.		30.00
Vase, Flowers, Footed, Signed, 10 In.	*Illus*	75.00
Vase, Molded Fish, Signed, 9 3/8 In.	*Illus*	700.00
Vase, Swag, Blue, 1909, Signed, 7 In.	*Illus*	175.00

Martin Brothers, Pot, Ribbed, Blue & Green Swags, Signed, 4 In.; Pitcher, Shellfish & Octopus, Signed, 10 in.; Vase, Molded Fish, Signed 9 3/4 In.

Martin Brothers, Vases, Swag, Blue, 1909, Signed, 7 In.; Bird Design, Cream, Signed, 11 3/4 In.; Flowers, Footed, Signed, 10 In.

(See Page 371)

> *Mary Gregory glass is identified by a characteristic white figure painted on dark glass. It was made from 1870 to 1910. The name refers to any glass decorated with a white silhouette figure and not just the Sandwich glass originally painted by Miss Mary Gregory.*

MARY GREGORY, Berry Bowl, 2 Girls, 1 Boy, Tinted Faces, 9 1/2 In.	95.00
Bottle, Barber, Woman, Scenery, Amethyst	180.00
Bottle, Perfume, Boy Chasing Butterfly, Tinted, Blue, 5 3/4 In.	158.00
Bottle, Perfume, Boy, Sapphire, Ball Stopper, 5 3/4 In.	158.00
Bottle, Perfume, Cut Panels, Sapphire Blue, 5 1/2 In.	158.00
Bottle, Perfume, Girl, Cranberry, 4 5/8 In.	165.00
Bowl, Girls, Gold Notched Rim, Pontil, 3 X 12 In.	350.00
Bowl, Punch, Covered, Green, 12 In. *Illus*	105.00
Box, Boy Picking Flowers, Lime Green, Hinged, 3 1/4 X 3 1/2 In.	165.00
Box, Boy With Hat, Flowers, Sapphire Blue, 3 X 6 1/4 In.	195.00
Box, Boy, Covered, Amethyst, 4 In.	105.00
Box, Double Figure On Lid, Amber, Ormolu Feet, 5 1/2 In.	395.00
Box, Double Figure, Green, Lift-Off Lid, 3 X 2 In.	145.00
Box, Girl, Cranberry, 3 1/4 X 2 In.	180.00
Box, Green, Footed, Hinged	95.00
Box, Patch, Boy, Cobalt Blue, Hinged, 2 X 1 In.	175.00
Box, Patch, Girl, Sapphire Blue, Hinged, 2 X 1 1/4 In.	175.00
Box, Pill, Hearts, Boy, & Flowers, Amethyst	450.00
Box, Sapphire Blue, Ruffled Top, 8 1/2 In.	225.00
Carafe, Water, Boy With Hoop, Cranberry, 7 7/8 In.	175.00
Cruet, Boy Picking Rose, Lime Green, Flattened Shape, 7 In.	145.00
Cruet, Young Boy, Amber, 3-Petal Top, 9 1/4 In.	195.00
Ewer, Girl, Cranberry, Clear Applied Handle, 5 1/2 In.	145.00
Ewer, Girl, Cranberry, Clear Handle, 3 1/8 X 10 1/4 In.	195.00
Mug, Boy, Sapphire Blue, 3 3/8 In.	88.00
Mug, Girl, Amethyst, Stained Handle, 3 1/2 In.	60.00
Mug, Girl, Cranberry, Clear Handle, 3 In.	88.00
Pitcher, Girl With Basket, Sapphire Blue, 2 1/4 I	165.00 To 175.00
Pitcher, Girl With Bird, Cranberry, Applied Handle, 7 1/4 In.	225.00

Mary Gregory, Bowl, Punch, Covered, Green, 12 In.

Pitcher, Girl, Green, Inverted Thumbprint, Handle, 3 3/4 In. 1250.00
Pitcher, Young Seated Girl, Cranberry, Clear Handle, 3 3/4 In. 175.00
Tray, Card, Young Girl, Black Amethyst, Turned-Up Rim, 7 X 9 In. 165.00
Tumbler, Boy Blowing Horn, Sapphire Blue, 4 1/2 In. 65.00
Tumbler, Boy, Amber 75.00
Tumbler, Butterfly Catcher, Blue 85.00
Tumbler, Facing Girl, Boy, Sapphire Blue, 3 In., Pair .... 95.00 To 110.00
Tumbler, Girl With Balloon, Cranberry, 3 In. 65.00
Urn, Girl, Flowers, Cobalt Blue, Covered, 14 1/4 In. 325.00
Vase, Boy & Girl, Cobalt Blue, 10 In., Pair 245.00
Vase, Boy & Girl, Honey Amber, 7 In., Pair 145.00
Vase, Boy Feeding Bird, Chartreuse Green, White Dot Band, 9 In. 195.00
Vase, Boy Holding Hat, Cranberry, 4 1/4 In. 110.00
Vase, Boy Standing On Branch, Cranberry, 9 1/2 In. 195.00
Vase, Boy With Bubble Blower, Cranberry, 5 3/4 In. 110.00
Vase, Boy With Cane, Letter In Hand, Cranberry, 7 3/4 In. 150.00
Vase, Boy With Hoop & Stick, Pink Overlay, 9 1/2 In. 175.00
Vase, Boy With Riding Crop, Cranberry, 5 In. 95.00
Vase, Boy, Cobalt Blue, Ruffled, 9 1/8 In. 165.00
Vase, Boy, Cranberry, 3 In. 110.00
Vase, Boy, Olive Green, 7 1/2 In. 65.00
Vase, Bud, Boy, Cranberry, 8 3/4 In. 118.00
Vase, Bud, Young Boy, Sapphire Blue, Pedestal Foot, 7 In. 110.00
Vase, Child Holding Flower, Blue, Fluted, 6 1/2 In. 45.00
Vase, Child In Riding Outfit, Lime Green, 6 In. 85.00
Vase, Cylinder, Girl, Cobalt Blue, 10 In. 75.00
Vase, Facing Girl & Boy, Cranberry, 8 3/4 In., Pr. .... 365.00 To 495.00
Vase, Facing Girl & Boy, Sapphire Blue, 6 1/2 In., Pair 195.00
Vase, Girl Feeding Birds, Nest In Tree, Cranberry, 12 In. 295.00
Vase, Girl Holding Flowers, Amber, 7 In. 95.00
Vase, Girl With Basket, Lime Green, 4 In. 89.00
Vase, Girl, Amber, Ruffled, 8 1/4 In. 85.00
Vase, Seated Boy Holding Sprig, Emerald Green, 9 In. 105.00
Vase, Young Girl With Basket, Cobalt Blue, 5 In. 75.00

Modern Freemasonry started in seventeenth-century England. The
fraternal order was introduced in the American colonies in the 1730s.
Symbols including the trowel, square, level, and plumb rule, pillars,
columns, arches, the letter "G," beehive, five pointed star, compass, and
eye have special meaning and are often pictured on Masonic material.
Masonic Shrine glassware was made from 1893 to 1917.

MASONIC, Backdrop, Painted, Cloth 275.00

Bookend, Black Metallic Luster, Emblem Molded On Body, Pair 15.00
Bookend, Relief Emblems, Bronzed Cast Iron, Pair 18.50
Chalice, Syria Temple, San Francisco, June 10, 1902 .... 50.00
Champagne, Louisville, Ky., 1909 .... 55.00
Champagne, New Orleans, 1910 .... 30.00
Champagne, Rochester, N.Y., 1911 .... 55.00
Champagne, Syria Shrine, Rochester & Pittsburgh, 1911 .... 125.00
Cuff Links, Emblem, Gold Filled, Pair 3.50
Cup & Saucer, Eastern Star, Symbol, Gold Stars & Rim 10.00
Cup, Saucer, Sugar, & Creamer, Star Emblem 35.00
Goblet, Shriner, Syria, 1908 .... 37.50
Knife, Scottish Rites, 100th Anniversary, Pocket 20.00
Mug, Atlantic City, July 13 & 14, 1904, 5 In. 50.00
Mug, Niagara Falls, 1905, 3-Handled 125.00
Mug, Osman Temple, February 14, 1916 .... 45.00
Mug, Shriner, Saratoga, 1903, Indian 125.00
Orange Cup, Embossed Syria, Pittsburgh 20.00
Pin, Moslem Temple, 1907, Enameled 15.00
Plate, Syria Shrine, Los Angeles, 1906 .... 35.00 To 52.00
Platter, Emblem, Olive Branch Lodge No.84, Westville, Blue Lines 32.00
Tray, Tip, Grain Belt Shriners 35.00
Tumbler, Cincinnati, 1893, Small 35.00
Watch Fob, Cedar Rapids, Dated 1906 .... 30.00
Watch Fob, Grand Lodge Of Iowa, 1906 .... 35.00
Watch Fob, Lalla Rookh Grotto, 1916 .... 15.00
Wine, Cranberry, St.Paul, 1908 .... 60.00
Wine, Shrine Commemorative Of 1900 .... 28.00
Wine, St.Paul, Minn., 1908 .... 60.00
Wine, 1st Grand Session, G.F., N.D., 1909 .... 20.00

J.MASSIER fils

> *Massier pottery is iridescent French art pottery made by Clement
> Massier in Golfe-Juane, France, in the late nineteenth and early
> twentieth centuries. It is characterized by a metallic luster glaze.*

MASSIER, Jardiniere, Tree Scene, Copper Luster, 14 1/2 In. ....*Illus* 450.00
    Vase, Iridescent Gold, Leaves, 8 In. 250.00

    MATCH HOLDER, see also Iron, Match Holder; Staffordshire, Match
    Holder; Store, Match Holder
MATCH HOLDER, Alligator, Iron, Striker 50.00
Bald Man, Open Mouth For Ashes, Star & Crown Mark, 3 3/8 In. 70.00
Bisque, Striker, Shuttered Windows, Wall, Germany, 3 1/4 In. 32.00
Black Boys & Watermelon, Pot Metal, 3 In. 50.00
Bliss & Galbreath Home Furnishers 22.00
Bliss Native Herbs, Wall, Tin 45.00
Boy Seated On Stone Wall, Bisque, 2 X 3 1/2 In. 42.00
Boys With Watermelon & Bale Of Cotton, Iron 65.00
Bronze, Monkey, Signed 450.00
Bulldog, Hand-Carved 35.00
Cat & Pigeon, Fingered Oval, Decoupage, Brass, 1841, 14 1/2 In. 90.00
Ceresota Boy, Tin 95.00
Dated 1896, Double, Iron 55.00
DeLaval, Wall, Tin 55.00
Devil & Grapes, Vines & Grapes, Double Pocket, Iron, 6 In. 85.00
Dockash Stoves, Wall 32.00
Elephant, Blue Glass, Signed Baby Mine, 3 1/2 X 4 In. 57.00
Embossed Lady's Slippers, Twin, Wall, Tin & Brass 28.00
Geisha Girl, Wall, Double 27.50
Hanging Dead Game Animals, Double, Wall, Iron, 9 In. 95.00
Hinged Lid, Spring Dispenser, Wall, Iron, 3 X 5 In. 38.00
Hunting Scene, Wall, Iron 50.00
Ideal Family Flour, Wall, Tin 22.00
Judson Whiskey, Child Serving Father 44.50

Massier, Jardiniere, Tree Scene, Copper
Luster, 14 1/2 In.

Milwaukee Binders & Mowers, Tin, Red, White, & Blue 30.00
Nude Baby, Bronze, Tabletop, 4 3/4 X 5 1/2 In. 250.00
Old Judson, Wall, Tin 48.00
Open Branch, Flower Back, Wall, Iron 30.00
Pall Mall, Famous Cigarettes, Brass, 3 In. 32.00
Pedestaled, Dark Maple, 4 1/4 In. 15.00
Penny, Cloisonne 18.00
Safe Home Matches, Wall, Tin 75.00
Scalloped Top, 19th Century, Pine, Blue Paint, Wall, 7 X 11 In. 65.00
Sharples, Multilithograph, Woman 100.00
Slippers, Brass 12.00
Three Pigs, Brass 45.00
W.W.Nichols Clothing, Wall, Tin 28.00
Wilson Bros. Grinding Mills, Easton, Pa., Embossed 48.50

MATCH SAFE, see also Silver-Sterling, Match Safe
MATCH SAFE, A.Barrett & Sons, English, Gold 375.00
Acorns & Oak Leaves, Sterling Silver, 4 1/2 In. 20.00
Altoona Brewery, Pa., Stamp Case, 1892, Silver Plated · 35.00
Anheuser-Busch, St.Louis, Embossed A .... 40.00 To 65.00
Arm & Hammer Soda, Gutta-Percha 35.00
Art Nouveau, Chrome Bound, Nude Standing Woman, Flowing Hair 48.00
Blue Hardstone Snap, Plaid Pattern, Sterling Silver, 2 In. 50.00
Boy With Cap, Carrying Urn, Marked, Bronze, 9 In. 500.00
Bulldog, Hinged Derby Hat, Striker Head, Silver Plated 45.00
Diamond Match, Iron 100.00
Dog Head, Sterling Silver, 2 1/4 In. 60.00
Eggplant, Figural, Silver Plated 80.00
Eisendrath Glove & Mitten Co., Tin 28.00
F.E.Hathaway & Son, Oldest Shoe Store, Boston, 1905, Metal 40.00
Fallen Suspenders, Hinged Cover, Metal, 1886, 3 3/4 In. 32.00
Flower & Leaf, Sterling Silver, 2 3/4 In. 110.00
Franklin Life Insurance 15.00
Geometric & Flowers, Sterling Silver, Hinged 48.00
Gillette Blades, Steel 8.00
Gillette Blades, Striker, Chrome 7.00
Hub, Oneonta, N.Y. 25.00
Neptune, Sterling Silver, 2 1/2 In. 60.00
Odd Fellows Fraternal, Embossed, Nickel Over Brass 35.00
Pabst Blue Ribbon Beer 35.00
Phoenix Brewery, St.Louis, Eagle 45.00
Plume & Leaf, Sterling Silver, 1 1/4 In. 50.00
Repousse Sailing Ship, Sterling Silver, 2 1/2 In. 60.00
Repousse Vase, Sterling Silver, 2 3/4 In. 45.00
Scout, Tubular 5.00
Scrolls & Flowers, Sterling Silver 37.50
Serpentine Pattern, Sterling Silver, 2 3/4 In. 60.00
Spaniel Head, Sterling Silver, 2 1/4 In. 60.00
Unger Bros., Embossed Floral & Scroll, Cupid 175.00
Union Made Blue Label Cigars, Celluloid Wrap, 1905, Labeled 14.00
United Hatters, Celluloid, Nickel Over Brass 28.00
Val Blatz 37.00

MATSUNOKE, Bowl, Cranberry, No.15353, 2 5/8 X 6 In. 135.00
Vase, Frosted Glass, Berry Pontil, Footed, Signed, 4 1/2 In. 1250.00
Vase, 8 In. 450.00
Vase, 43 Florets, Berry Pontil, Signed, 4 1/4 In. 1250.00

*McCoy pottery is made in Roseville, Ohio. The J.W. McCoy
Pottery was founded in 1899. It became the Brush McCoy Pottery
Company in 1911. The name changed to the Brush Pottery in 1925. The
Nelson McCoy Sanitary and Stoneware Company was founded in
Roseville, Ohio, in 1910. This firm made art pottery after 1926. In 1933
it became the Nelson McCoy Pottery. Pieces marked "McCoy" were
made by the Nelson McCoy Company.*

MCCOY, Ashtray, Green & Brown Bird On Side, 10 In. 4.00
Ashtray, Swan, Green With Bowtie 4.00
Bank, Eagle, Emigrant Industrial 8.00
Bank, Seaman's Saving, White Sailor 8.00
Bank, Williamsburg Savings 8.00
Basket, Green, Yellow, Tan, Handled 16.00
Basket, Hanging, Basket Weave, Turquoise, 9 X 4 In. 12.00
Basket, Leaves, Red Berries, Green 25.00
Basket, Serenade, Yellow, 6 X 7 In. 20.00
Bean Pot, Covered, Brown Glaze 28.00
Bowl, Console, Maroon & Chartreuse, 10 In. 8.00
Bowl, Console, Maroon Froth Over Mottled Gray, 10 X 6 In. 10.00
Bowl, Dark Blue, 7 1/2 In. 4.00
Bowl, Paneled, Brown, 7 1/2 X 7 In. 15.00
Bowl, Pink & Gray, Flecked, 10 In. 7.00
Bowl, Red Roses, Gold Trim, Scalloped Rim, 4 3/4 In. 8.00
Bowl, Zuniart, 2 1/2 X 2 1/2 In. 38.00
Box, Window, Scalloped Rim, Tan, Marked, 10 X 4 3/4 X 3 In. 6.00
Carafe, Pink Lid, Black 28.00
Coffeepot, El Rancho Bar-B-Que .... 18.00 To 30.00
Console Set, Parchment & Pine 40.00
Cookie Jar, Animal Crackers, 1959-60 .... 40.00
Cookie Jar, Apple, 1950-64 .... 12.00 To 23.00
Cookie Jar, Baby Pig 28.00
Cookie Jar, Bananas, 1950-52 .... 40.00
Cookie Jar, Basket Of Fruit 35.00
Cookie Jar, Bear Hiding Cookie 20.00
Cookie Jar, Bear, 1942-45 .... 25.00 To 35.00
Cookie Jar, Bushel Basket, Fruit Top 35.00
Cookie Jar, Cabin .... 25.00 To 35.00
Cookie Jar, Caboose, 1961 .... 45.00
Cookie Jar, Car, Antique 40.00
Cookie Jar, Cat In Pink Basket 28.00
Cookie Jar, Cat Seated With Ribbon 35.00
Cookie Jar, Chef's Head, 1962-64 .... 50.00
Cookie Jar, Chiffonier 40.00
Cookie Jar, Chinese Lantern 18.00
Cookie Jar, Chipmunk, 1959-62 .... 20.00 To 50.00
Cookie Jar, Christmas Tree, 1959 .... 150.00
Cookie Jar, Circus Horse, Black, 1962 .... 40.00 To 55.00
Cookie Jar, Clown Bust, 1943-49 .... 20.00
Cookie Jar, Clown In Barrel, 1953-56 .... 40.00
Cookie Jar, Coffee Grinder, 1961-64 .... 10.00 To 25.00
Cookie Jar, Cookie Bank 38.00
Cookie Jar, Cookie Cabin, 1957-60 .... 20.00 To 40.00
Cookie Jar, Cookstove, Black, 1962-64 .... 15.00
Cookie Jar, Cookstove, White, 1962-64 .... 12.00 To 45.00
Cookie Jar, Covered Wagon, 1959-62 .... 22.00 To 60.00
Cookie Jar, Dog, Mac, 1967 .... 30.00 To 40.00
Cookie Jar, Duck On Basket, 1956 .... 30.00 To 40.00
Cookie Jar, Dutch Boy, 1945 .... 20.00

Cookie Jar, Dutchman 28.00
Cookie Jar, Engine, 1963-64 .... 35.00
Cookie Jar, Fireplace 35.00
Cookie Jar, Friendship Seven .... 30.00 To 40.00
Cookie Jar, Frontier Family .... 18.00 To 22.00
Cookie Jar, Globe, 1959 .... 25.00 To 65.00
Cookie Jar, Grandfather Clock, 1962-64 .... 30.00 To 35.00
Cookie Jar, Granny, 1972-73 .... 29.00
Cookie Jar, Have A Happy Day, Yellow, 1971-75 .... 25.00 To 45.00
Cookie Jar, Hen On Nest, 1959 .... 30.00 To 40.00
Cookie Jar, Hobbyhorse, 1950-51 .... 40.00
Cookie Jar, Honey Bear, 1953-55 .... 11.00 To 35.00
Cookie Jar, Indian Head, 1954-56 .... 75.00 To 100.00
Cookie Jar, Kitten In Basket, 1956-69 .... 15.00 To 35.00
Cookie Jar, Kookie Kettle 12.00
Cookie Jar, Lamb In Basket, 1956-57 .... 25.00 To 35.00
Cookie Jar, Little Clown .... 25.00 To 30.00
Cookie Jar, Lollipops, 1958-60 .... 10.00 To 35.00
Cookie Jar, Lovebirds, Kissing Penguins, 1945 .... 35.00
Cookie Jar, Mammy, 1939 .... 65.00
Cookie Jar, Milk Can, Brown 15.00
Cookie Jar, Milk Can, White 15.00
Cookie Jar, Monk, 1970 .... 6.00
Cookie Jar, Mr.& Mrs.Owl, 1953-55 .... 10.00
Cookie Jar, Old Shoe 22.00
Cookie Jar, Owl, Woodsy, 1972-74 .... 20.00 To 35.00
Cookie Jar, Panda Bear 26.00
Cookie Jar, Panda, Upside-Down 28.00
Cookie Jar, Pears, 1957 .... 18.50 To 38.00
Cookie Jar, Pig In Cookie Sack 28.00
Cookie Jar, Pineapple, 1955-57 .... 14.00 To 32.00
Cookie Jar, Pinecones On Basket .... 25.00 To 30.00
Cookie Jar, Puppy, 1961-62 .... 16.00 To 40.00
Cookie Jar, Puss 'n Boots .... 28.00 To 45.00
Cookie Jar, Raggedy Ann 20.00
Cookie Jar, Rooster, 1955-57 .... 25.00 To 30.00
Cookie Jar, Snow Bear, 1965 .... 35.00
Cookie Jar, Soldier Boy 28.00
Cookie Jar, Squirrel On Log 30.00
Cookie Jar, Strawberry, 1955-57 .... 24.00
Cookie Jar, Teapot, Brown, 1971 .... 15.00
Cookie Jar, Teapot, Copper Luster, 1971 .... 18.00
Cookie Jar, Tepee, 1957-59 .... 60.00 To 120.00
Cookie Jar, Touring Car .... 25.00 To 35.00
Cookie Jar, Turkey, 1959-60 .... 65.00 To 75.00
Cookie Jar, Turtle, Brown 20.00
Cookie Jar, W.C.Fields, 1972-74 .... 45.00 To 60.00
Cookie Jar, Wishing Well, Wish I Had A Cookie, Brown, 1961-70 ...... 20.00
Cookie Jar, Yellow Cylinder 25.00
Cooler, Water 35.00
Creamer, Ceramic, 6 In. 10.00
Dish, Candy, Pink & White, Scalloped, Square, Covered, 6 3/4 In. 10.00
Dish, Candy, Serenade, Turquoise, Covered 24.00
Dish, Dog, To Man's Best Friend His Dog, 7 1/2 In. 18.00
Dish, Green & White, Footed, 6 X 3 In. 4.00
Dish, Hunting Dog, Green 15.00
Dish, Leaf, Brown, Tokay Shape, 13 1/2 In. 9.00
Ewer, Pale Green, Grapes, Brown & Ivory Ground, 9 In. 27.00
Fernery, Brown & Green, 8 3/4 X 4 1/2 X 3 1/4 In. 6.00
Figurine, Swan, Blue & Gold, 8 X 6 In. 25.00
Flower Holder, White Bird, Marked NM, 10 In.Long 7.00
Flowerpot, Attached Saucer, Pink, 4 In. 3.00
Flowerpot, Green, Basket Weave, 3 1/4 In. 3.00
Flowerpot, Green, Cream Matte, Icicles, 3 3/4 In. 3.00

Flowerpot, Green, Greek Key, 4 In. 4.50
Flowerpot, Green, Long Leaves & Dots, 3 1/2 X 3 1/2 In. 5.00
Flowerpot, Pink Roses, Quilted Bottom, 5 In. 4.00
Flowerpot, Turquoise, Basket Weave, 4 1/4 In. 4.50
Flowerpot, Turquoise, 4 In. 5.00
Flowerpot, White, 4 In. 5.00
Flowerpot, Yellow, Basket Weave 3.00
Gravy Boat, Green 3.00
Jardiniere, Leaf Pattern, Bow Handle, Blue, 7 X 7 3/4 In. 22.50
Jardiniere, Pinecone, Green, Tan, Cream, 7 1/4 In. 9.00
Jardiniere, Pink, Floral & Leaf, Ribbed 4.00
Jardiniere, Relief Roses, Rose 12.00
Jardiniere, Sylvan, 4 1/2 In. 22.00
Jardiniere, White Vertical Flutes, 5 X 3 In. 3.00
Jug, Olympia, Ear Of Corn 165.00
Lamp, Boots .... 25.00 To 35.00
Mug, Davy Crockett 20.00
Mug, Green, Banded Barrel, 4 1/2 In. 5.00
Pitcher & Bowl, White & Blue, Pitcher, 6 In. 10.00
Pitcher, Fish, Handled, Green 30.00
Pitcher, Grapes & Leaves, Green, White, & Brown 45.00
Pitcher, Iced Tea, El Rancho 45.00
Pitcher, Kissing Dutch, Green 25.00
Pitcher, Parrot, Handled 18.50
Pitcher, Serenade, Blue 22.00
Pitcher, Yellow, Raised Grapes, 8 1/2 In. 23.00
Planter, Bird & Strawberry, Green & Brown 18.00
Planter, Butterfly 15.00
Planter, Dark Green, Fluted, 6 X 3 In. 4.00
Planter, Grapes, 10 1/2 In. 12.00
Planter, Green, 3 In. 3.00
Planter, Lamb, Blue Bow At Neck 10.00
Planter, Mailbox 18.00
Planter, Pelican, Blue, Marked NM, 6 In. 7.00
Planter, Pink, Black Base 3.00
Planter, Rooster 12.00
Planter, Shell, Handled, Footed, Cream, 6 X 7 1/2 In. 12.00
Planter, Shoe, Blue, Marked NM, 2 In. 4.00
Planter, Shoe, Purple, Marked NM, 2 In. 4.00
Planter, Turtle .... 6.50 To 15.00
Planter, Yellow, Basket Weave 8.00
Plate, Ovenproof, Embossed Mark, Brown, 6 1/2 In. 2.00
Punch Bowl, Green, Ladle, 12 Cups, 13 In. 95.00
Shoe, Baby, Pink 7.00
Sprinkler, Turtle 30.00
Sugar & Creamer, Parchment & Pine 15.00
Tankard, Indian Peace Sign 45.00
Tankard, Shaded Green, Banded Barrel, 8 In. 21.00
Tea Set, Acorn, 3 Piece 22.00
Tea Set, Daisy, 3 Piece .... 40.00 To 45.00
Tea Set, English Ivy, 3 Piece 25.00
Tea Set, Ivy, 3 Piece .... 30.00 To 43.50
Tea Set, Pinecone, 3 Piece .... 34.00 To 50.00
Tea Set, Willow, Green, 3 Piece 35.00
Teapot, Grandma 25.00
Teapot, Grecian 30.00
Teapot, Pinecone 20.00
Teapot, White Blossoms & Gold Flowers, Gold Trim, Marked, Covered 18.00
Tureen, Soup, El Rancho 30.00
Umbrella Stand, Dark Green To Chocolate Brown, No.61 .... 130.00
Urn, Brown Onyx, 6 1/2 In. 25.00
Vase, Arrowhead Leaf Relief, Yellow, 7 1/2 In. 12.00
Vase, Art Deco, Gold Design, 6 In. 24.00
Vase, Blue Onyx, 7 1/2 In. 17.00

Vase, Bud, Florastone, Blue, 9 5/8 In. 60.00
Vase, Butterfly, Blue, 9 In. 9.00
Vase, Butterfly, White, 7 In. 13.00
Vase, Butterfly, Yellow, Footed, 9 In. 16.00
Vase, Fan, Red Flowers, Chartreuse Ground, 8 1/4 In. 12.00
Vase, Grape, 9 1/2 In. 12.00
Vase, Green Leaves, Tan Matte, 6 In. 12.00
Vase, Onyx, Green & Blue Handled, 8 1/2 In. 25.00
Vase, Paneled, Brown, 7 1/2 X 7 In. 15.00
Vase, Springwood, Square Top, Turquoise, 7 3/8 In. 9.00
Vaso, Thistle, Blue, Side Handles, 6 1/2 In. 20.00
Vase, Urn, Green, Footed, 6 In. 7.00
Vase, Vesta, 8 In. 40.00
Vase, Wild Flower, Yellow, Tan, Footed, Side Handle, 6 1/2 In. 14.00
Wall Pocket, Blossom Time 15.00
Wall Pocket, Rustic Glaze 85.00
Wall Pocket, Sunflower, Bird On Top, Yellow & Green 10.00
Wall Pocket, Yellow Bird On Top, Flower 14.00
Wall Pocket, Yellow, Floral Design, Pair 20.00

PRESCUT
The McKee name has been associated with various glass enterprises in the United States since 1836, including J. & F. McKee (1850), Bryce, McKee & Co. (1850 to 1854), McKee and Brothers (1865), and National Glass Co. (1899). In 1903 the McKee Glass Company was formed in Jeanette, Pennsylvania. It became McKee Division of the Thatcher Glass Co. in 1951, and was bought out by the Jeanette Corporation in 1961. Pressed glass, kitchenware, and tableware were produced.

MCKEE, see also Custard Glass
MCKEE, Banana Bowl, Autumn, Green 30.00
Bowl, Daisy & Button, 1886, Blue 65.00
Bowl, Laurel, French Ivory, 11 In. 20.00
Candlestick, Rock Crystal, Double, Pair 20.00
Creamer, Comet .... 22.50 To 35.00
Goblet, Rock Crystal, Footed, Pink, 5 1/2 In. 22.00
Jar, Candy, Skokie, Covered, Green 32.50
Punch Bowl, Red Letters & Scroll, 12 Mugs 55.00
Sailboat, Ship's Wheel & Anchor, Red, 3 1/4 X 3 1/2 In. 10.00
Sherbet, Rock Crystal, Pink, 4 3/4 In. 18.00
Spooner, Champion, Ruby 45.00
Sugar, Open, Toltec, Milk Glass 8.00
Tankard, Rock Crystal, Clear, 11 1/2 In. 135.00
Toothpick, Colonial, Emerald Green 40.00
Toothpick, Yutec 20.00
Tumbler, Bottoms Up, Coaster 75.00
Tumbler, Gladiator, Green 30.00
Vase, Jadite, Nudes, Triangular, 8 In. 15.00
MECHANICAL BANK, see Bank, Mechanical

MEDICAL, Bag, Doctor's, Leather 25.00
Bag, Needles, Medicines, Log Book In Italian, Small 52.00
Bag, Nurse's, Leather, Red Interior, 10 1/2 X 8 X 5 1/2 In. 45.00
Bag, 20 Instruments, Alligator 145.00
Bleeder, Wiehand & Snowden, Philadelphia, Brass, 2 In. 95.00
Burner, Alcohol, Folding, Tin, 3 X 2 In. 25.00
Cabinet, Sterilization, Metal & Glass 500.00
Device, Used To Burn Wound To Stop Bleeding, Civil War 25.00
Dispenser, Dosage, Gilbertson & Sons, London, C.1870, Treen, 3 In., Set 100.00
Ear Horn, With Hose, Bakelite, 42 In. 50.00
Ear Horn, 38 In. Hose 65.00
Eyecup, Fishbowl Style, Green 90.00
Eyecup, Glasco, Long Neck 20.00
Eyecup, John Bull's, Dated 1917, Green 28.00
Eyecup, Short Stem, Ceramic, 2 X 7 7/8 In. 220.00

Eyecup, Tulip Shape	35.00
Eyecup, Wyeth, Cobalt Blue	8.00
Eyecup, 8-Panel, Green	100.00
Feeder, Invalid, China, White	12.00
Feeder, Invalid, Copenhagen, Blue & White, 3 1/4 X 3 In.	45.00
Feeder, Invalid, Florals, Red & Gold Trim, Porcelain, 2 1/2 In.	40.00
Feeder, Invalid, Onion Pattern, Germany	18.00
Feeder, Invalid, Painted Red Cross, Gold Trim, Marked Germany, China	20.00
Feeder, Invalid, Pink Luster Design, Flowers, Gold Trim, 2 1/4 In.	35.00
Feeder, Invalid, Violets, Porcelain, 3 1/2 X 2 1/4 In.	30.00
Fleam, Surgeon's, Blood Letting	95.00
Glass Eye, Ophthalmologist's	50.00
Injection Bottle, Kilmer's Herbal Extract Uterine, Box, Contents	65.00
Instrument, Bloodletting, Spring-Loaded, Leather Case	95.00
Knife, Surgeon's, Ebony Handle, Marked Robinson	30.00
Machine, Horizontal Suppository, Armstrong Cork Co.	150.00
Machine, Magneto-Electric, 1890s	125.00
Microscope, Dated 1900, Spencer Optical Co., Brass	85.00
Microscope, Henry Crouch, Brass, 13 1/2 In.	325.00
Mold, Suppository, 12 Cavity, Aluminum, Boxed	25.00
Mortar & Pestle, Mushroom Knob, Treen, Mortar, 9 In.	80.00
Mortar & Pestle, Pour Spout, C.1880, L.& C.Yarnall, Stoneware, Small	35.00
Nose Cup, Patent 1901	50.00
Ophthalmoloscope, 1900s, Brass	28.00
Pill Roller, Wood & Brass, 2 Piece	150.00
Saw, Surgeon's, Pre-1920	34.00
Scalpel, Rosewood Handle	30.00
Spoon, Medicine, Sterling Silver	55.00
Spoon, Top Opening, Side Spout, Sheffield Hallmark, 1917	20.00
Surgical Kit, Rosewood Case, Ivory Handle, Civil War, Dated 1863	275.00
Syringe, Veterinarian's, Pewter, Turned Wooden Handle, Plunger	20.00
Table, Mortician's, Portable	75.00

Meerschaum pipes and other pieces carved of meerschaum, a soft mineral, date from the nineteenth century to the present time.

MEERSCHAUM, Holder, Cigar, Amber Stem, Case, 3 In.	25.00
Holder, Cigar, Barking Terrier, Hand-Carved, C.1880, 4 1/2 In.	75.00
Holder, Cigar, Horses, Case	75.00
Pipe, Bacchus Head Bowl, Yellow Amber Stem, 17 In.	295.00
Pipe, Boston Bull Chained To Doghouse, 4 In.	135.00
Pipe, Carved Horse In Crook Of Shank, C.1875, Case	55.00
Pipe, Carved Nude, Cupid, 5 X 2 In.	95.00
Pipe, Carved Stallions, Amber Stem, Fitted Case	110.00
Pipe, Dragon Claw Holding Egg, Amber Stem	225.00
Pipe, Figures Of Venus & Cupid, 2 Doves, 5 3/4 In.	120.00
Pipe, Head Of Coolie, C.1870, Case	225.00
Pipe, Ivory Bowl, Gold Trim, Amber Stem, Boxed	175.00
Pipe, Lion's Head Bowl, Carved Amber Stem	195.00
Pipe, Negro Head, Silver Scalloped Band, Leather Case, 4 In.	255.00
Pipe, Nude Lady, Arms Folded Over Head, Case, Large	175.00
Pipe, Two Hounds, Case, 10 X 3 1/2 In.	350.00

Meissen is a town in Germany where porcelain has been made since 1710. Any china made in that town can be called Meissen, although the famous Meissen factory made the finest porcelains of the area.

MEISSEN, see also Dresden; Onion

MEISSEN, Bowl, Cobalt Ground, Raised Gold, Marked, 12 In.	379.00
Bowl, Florals Inside & Outside, Gold Trim, Crossed Swords, 9 3/4 In.	75.00
Bowl, Raised Gold Leaves, Crossed Swords, 12 X 8 In.	48.00
Bowl, Scalloped Rim, Floral Design, Gilded, Marked, 3 X 4 1/2 In.	185.00
Bowl, White Ground, Red, Pink, Yellow, Blue, Floral, 3 X 4 In.	185.00
Button, Wild Rose Design, Hand-Painted	65.00
Candlestick, Chamber, Dancing Figure, 18th-Century Dress, 9 In.	375.00

Candlestick, Cobalt, White, Gold, 12 In.	95.00
Charger, Raised Branches & Leaves, White, Crossed Swords, 10 In.	195.00
Charger, White Ground, Raised Leaf Design, Gold, Marked, 11 In.	295.00
Cup & Saucer, Coffee, Floral, Gold Edge, Marked	79.50
Cup & Saucer, Floral Reserve, Raised Gilt Floral Sprigs	75.00
Cup & Saucer, Floral, Insets, Scalloped, Gold Edge, Marked	90.00
Cup & Saucer, Gold & Cobalt Blue	99.50
Cup & Saucer, White & Cobalt Blue, Gold Trim, Marked	99.50
Cup & Saucer, White Ground, George Washington, Demitasse, Marked	70.00
Dish, Gold Design & Finial, Covered, Crossed Swords, 4 1/2 In.	125.00
Dish, Sweetmeat, Reclining Gallants Holding Bowl, Marked, 11 In., Pr.	950.00
Figurine, Boy, Turkish Costume, Holding Walking Stick, 5 In.	250.00
Figurine, Cupid, Foot Caught In Trap, Marked, 7 1/2 In.	675.00
Figurine, Dog, Border Collie, Marked, 3 X 6 In.	250.00
Figurine, Dog, English Bull, Marked, 3 X 6 In.	225.00
Figurine, Dog, Sitting, Black & White, Spaniel Type, Red Collar	344.00
Figurine, Europa, Seated, Bull, Attendants, Flowers, Marked, 8 In.	300.00
Figurine, Gentleman & Lady, Under Tree, 5 1/4 In.	475.00
Figurine, Girl With Goat, Marked	795.00
Figurine, Group Of Cherubs Sculpting & Painting, 8 In.	2500.00
Figurine, Man In Fur Coat, 9 In.	390.00
Figurine, Man, Woman, 2 Putti, Garland, Courting Scene, 8 In.	400.00
Figurine, Pug Dog, Marked, 3 X 6 In.	250.00
Figurine, Summer & Winter, 9 1/2 In., Pair	350.00
Figurine, Woodsman & Maiden, Beneath Tree, Marked, 8 In.	700.00
Figurine, 2 Figures, 18th-Century Dress, Fruit Tree, Marked, 9 In.	450.00
Gravy Boat, Crossed Swords	140.00
Nappy, Fluted, Gold Leaf Over Wild Roses, 6 In., Pair	45.00
Pitcher, Gold, Floral Design, Ribbed, Scalloped, 8 In.	150.00
Plate, Center Birds, Insects On Border, Crossed Swords, 7 1/2 In.	75.00
Plate, Chinese Down At Harbor, Marked	295.00
Plate, Gold Design On Rim, White, Crossed Swords	49.50
Plate, Relief Scrolls, Gold Trim, Crossed Swords	275.00
Platter, Cobalt Blue & Gilt Border, C.1900, Marked, 19 In.	175.00
Salt, Double, Figural, Cherubic, Seated On Shell, Marked, 6 Pairs	550.00
Salt, Molded Base, Polychrome Spray, C.1760, Pair, 1 1/2 X 4 1/4 In.	625.00
Shoe, Cherubs, Ruffles	170.00
Teapot, Ball Shape, Allover Floral Design, Crossed Swords	110.00
Teapot, Figural Medallions, Rose Finial, Marked, Cobalt Blue, 8 In.	195.00
Tray, Handled, Floral, Impressed Mark, Signed, 15 X 11 In.	125.00
Vase, Floral, Crossed Swords, 7 In.	185.00

Mercury, or silvered, glass was first made in the 1850s. It lost favor for a while but became popular again about 1910. It looks like a piece of silver.

MERCURY GLASS, Candlestick, C.1910, 7 1/2 In.	17.50
Tieback, Curtain, Pair	40.00
Vase, Bulbous, Etched Grapevine Design	41.50
Vase, Etched, 3 In.	8.50

Mettlach, Germany, is a city where the Villeroy and Boch factories worked. Steins from the firm are known as Mettlach steins. They date from about 1842. PUG means painted under glaze.

METTLACH, Beaker, Girl Looking To Sea, Sitting On Stone Wall	60.00
Beaker, Man Playing Flute	65.00
Beaker, Woman Holds Peacock & Jug	65.00
Bowl, Green, Lettuce Leaves In Relief, Underplate, Open	120.00
Box, Stylized Hand-Painted Flowers, Brown & Yellow, 3 X 4 1/2 In.	55.00
Coaster, No.1032, Dwarf Holding Radish & Tankard Of Beer	95.00
Cup, Punch, Fruit Pattern	17.50
Jug, Earthenware, Brown, Peasants In Field, Pewter Mounts, 14 In.	175.00
Loving Cup, No.2170, Cavaliers, 3-Handled, 6 In.	*Illus* 100.00

Mug, Cream, John Gund Brewing Co. Advertising 50.00
Mug, Hire's Root Beer 95.00
Mug, Presentation, Egyptian Design, Whiting Mark, 14 Ounce 565.00
Mug, 1/4 Liter, St.Alice Hotel, Harrison Hot Springs, B.C. 55.00
Pitcher, Applied Leaves, Birch Handle, Marked, 8 1/2 In. 235.00
Pitcher, No.2947 .... 195.00
Planter, Panels Of Birds, Gold Trim, Oval, 8 3/4 X 3 5/8 X 4 In. 325.00
Plaque, Blue & White, Castle Scene, 12 In. 225.00
Plaque, Landscape Scene, Underglaze 125.00
Plaque, Mermaid & Oyster Shell, Dated 1898, Castle Mark, 17 1/4 In. 1250.00
Plaque, Mythological Men In Boat, No.2442, Dated 1799, 18 1/8 In. 1500.00
Plaque, No.1044/6123, Dark-Haired Girl, PUG, 19 In. 195.00
Plaque, No.2112, Dwarf On Nest Holding Wine, 16 In. 1500.00
Plaque, No.2113, Dwarf On Tree Branch Holding Mug, 16 In. 1295.00
Plaque, No.2443, Mythological Figures, 18 In. 1100.00
Plaque, No.2626, Cavalier At Table, Drinking From Tankard, 7 In. 289.00
Plaque, No.3051, Harbor, Ships, & House, Mercury Mark, 12 In.Diam. 125.00
Plaque, No.5058, Horses, River, Boathouse, PUG, Mercury Mark, 12 In. 125.00
Stein, No.24, 1/2 Liter, Man With Death, Hunting, Love, Mercury Mark 395.00
Stein, No.280, 1/2 Liter, Hand-Painted Crest, Street Scene 295.00
Stein, No.1028, 1/2 Liter, Girl, Man, & Grapes, Marked, 5 5/8 In. 225.00
Stein, No.1403, 1/2 Liter, Eight Bowlers 195.00
Stein, No.1786, 1/2 Liter, St.Florian Pouring Beer .... 425.00 To 600.00
Stein, No.1909/727, 1/2 Liter, Dwarfs Bowling 250.00
Stein, No.1909/993, 1/2 Liter, Comic Beer Hall Scene, PUG 290.00
Stein, No.1972, 1/4 Liter, Four Seasons 350.00
Stein, No.2001, 1/2 Liter, Doctor, Book 850.00
Stein, No.2001, 1/2 Liter, Engineer, Book 775.00
Stein, No.2057, 3/10 Liter, Six Beer-Drinking Revelers & Piper 500.00
Stein, No.2090, 1/2 Liter, Husband At Club, Wife With Broom 495.00
Stein, No.2092, 1/2 Liter, Man On Ladder Winding Clock, Men Watch 525.00
Stein, No.2179/961, 3/10 Liter, Prosit, PUG 145.00
Stein, No.2235, 1/2 Liter, Target, Girl With Beer 685.00
Stein, No.2255, 1 Liter, Wedding Scene, Brown, Black, Tan, White 825.00
Stein, No.2286, 3 Liter, Cavaliers On Inn Balcony, Castle, Heart 1095.00
Stein, No.2382, 1/2 Liter, Wine Cellar 695.00
Stein, No.2430, 3 Liter, Hunter In Blues & White, On Chair 1350.00
Stein, No.2441, 1/2 Liter, Dice Players, Music Box In Base 650.00
Stein, No.2501, 1/2 Liter, Outdoor Tavern Scene 345.00
Stein, No.2530, 1/2 Liter, Boar Hunt 875.00
Stein, No.2583, 1/2 Liter, Egyptian Design 565.00
Stein, No.2639, 1 Liter, Drinking Scene, Inlaid Lid 225.00
Stein, No.2692, 3 Liter, Musician, Beer Maid & Cavalier 1550.00
Stein, No.2794, 1/2 Liter, Rembrandt-Style Bust Portrait 325.00
Stein, No.2857, Blue Design, Marked 225.00
Stein, No.2900, 1/2 Liter, Cervececeria, Argentina, Dated '06 .... 150.00
Stein, No.2951, 1/2 Liter, Imperial Eagle, Cameo 490.00
Stein, No.2966, 1 Liter, Man With Stein, Tapestry 900.00
Stein, No.3200, 1/2 Liter, Castle On River, Music Box In Base 1500.00
Tile, Floral & Fruit Pattern, 3 In.Square, Pair 28.00

Mettlach, Loving Cup, No.2170, Cavaliers,
3-Handled, 6 In.

(See Page 381)

Tile, Pastoral Scene	75.00
Urn, Four Seasons, Etched, Marked, 13 In.	695.00
Vase, Blue Ground, Angular Design, Enamel Foliate, Elephant Handles	375.00
Vase, Cameo Figures, Blue Ground, Silver Trim, 9 In.	195.00
Vase, Cameo Figures, Silver Deposit, Blue, 9 In.	195.00
Vase, Children, Flowers, Brown, Rust, Marked, 6 In.	225.00
Vase, Etched Design, No.1874, Castle Mark, 8 In.	395.00
Vase, Four Panels Of Children At Play, Marked, 11 1/2 In.	600.00
Vase, No.1709, Strawberries & Leaves, Castle Mark, 12 1/2 In.	350.00
Vase, No.1710, Flowers & Birds, Castle Mark, 12 1/2 In.	350.00
Vase, No.1844, Florals, Gold Leaves, Pink Inside, Marked, 9 1/2 In.	395.00
Vase, No. 2505, Castle Mark, 12 1/2 In.	175.00
Vase, No. 2857, Raised Enamel & Gold Design, Marked, 8 1/4 In.	225.00
Vase, No. 2986, Art Deco Design, 13 1/2 In.	125.00

MICKEY MOUSE, see Disneyana

Milk glass was named for its milky-white color. It was first made in England during the 1700s. The height of its popularity in the United States was from 1870 to 1880. It is now correct to refer to some colored glass as blue milk glass, black milk glass, etc.

MILK GLASS, see also Cambridge; Cosmos

MILK GLASS, Ashtray, Heart, 4 3/4 In.	2.00
Banana Bowl, Footed, Oval, 12 In.	25.00
Banana Stand, Cut Out Pattern	30.00
Banana Stand, Openwork Base, Triple Split Stem, 11 In.	50.00
Basket, Hobnail, Ruffled & Crimped Edge, White, 8 In.	15.00
Berry Bowl, Leaf & Flower, Amber Flowers, 9 In.	55.00
Bottle, Barber	75.00
Bottle, Cologne, Stopper, Gourd Shaped, Floral Design, 7 In.	65.00
Bottle, Perfume, Figural, Oriental Figure, 5 In.	220.00
Bottle, Water, Trellis & Scroll	12.00
Bottle, World's Fair, 1939	10.00
Bowl, Grape & Cable, Crimped Sides, 9 1/2 In.	40.00
Bowl, Gyro, Covered, 4 3/4 In.	12.00
Bowl, Lacy Edge, Footed, 8 In.	55.00
Bowl, Mixing, Fruit Design, Set	9.75
Bowl, Scroll Pattern, Turquoise, 8 In.	20.00
Bowl, 5 Airplanes In Red On Sides, Wheaties Premium	35.00
Box, Fluted, Wooly Lamb Cover, Blue, 5 1/2 X 3 3/4 In.	22.00
Butter, Acorn Design, Covered	75.00
Butter, Roman Cross, Covered	40.00
Cake Plate, Cluster Of Grapes, 6 Plates	49.00
Cake Stand, Scalloped	20.00
Candleholder, Vertical Ribbed, Blue, Twisted Stem, 10 In., Pair	65.00
Candleholder, 6-Sided Base, Blue, 9 In., Pair	65.00
Candlestick, Chamber, Footed, Ring Handle, Design, Original Paint	20.00
Candlestick, Cornucopia	12.50
Candlestick, Crucifix, 10 In., Pair	70.00
Compote, Acorns & Leaves Pattern, Pink, 5 1/2 X 3 In.	8.00
Compote, Diamond Pattern, Pink	8.00
Compote, Dolphin & Shell, Westmoreland, 13 X 8 1/2 In.	25.00
Compote, Figural, Atlas	48.00
Compote, Grape, Covered, Footed, Opaline, 6 In.	30.00
Compote, Pedestal, Turquoise	16.00
Compote, Ribbed Edge, Ridged Base, Turquoise, 5 X 3 1/2 In.	14.50
Compote, Seashell Pattern, Footed, 6 In.	38.00
Cornucopia, Seashell Pattern, 3 In.	15.00
Creamer, Boat Shape, Impressed Roses, 5 3/4 X 4 1/2 In.	15.00
Creamer, Figural, Owl, Blue	35.00
Creamer, Grape & Cherry, Covered	16.00
Creamer, Owl	58.00
Creamer, Panel Wheat	45.00
Creamer, Paneled Flower & Atterbury Crossed Fern, Bail	35.00
Creamer, Swan	65.00

Cruet, Grapes, White, 5 In.	17.00
Cup & Saucer, Banded Raindrop	12.50
Cup, Punch, Child's, Wild Rose	20.00
Dish, Acorn Shape, Squirrel Finial, Covered, Blue	40.00
Dish, Admiral Dewey Cover, Oval	110.00
Dish, American Hen Cover	85.00
Dish, Battleship, 3 Guns, 2 Side Turrets, 8 In.	65.00
Dish, Black Chick Cover, White Basket Weave Ground	50.00
Dish, Candy, Grape & Leaf, Pink	8.50
Dish, Chick Emerging & 3 Small Chicks Cover, 7 In.	90.00
Dish, Chicken On Sleigh Cover, 4 1/2 X 5 1/2 In.	40.00
Dish, Chicken On Woven Nest Cover	15.00
Dish, Cow Cover, Blue	15.00
Dish, Dog Cover, Blue & White, 6 X 4 In.	60.00
Dish, Fish, Dated, 1872	15.00
Dish, Fox Cover, Glass Eyes, Blue	95.00
Dish, Hen Cover, British Lion Base	60.00
Dish, Horse Cover	140.00
Dish, Lion Cover, Amber Eyes, Dated 1889, 7 X 5 1/2 In.	150.00
Dish, Lion Cover, Dated 1889	145.00
Dish, Lion Cover, Rectangular	55.00
Dish, Oval, Grape & Leaf, Signed, 6 3/4 X 4 X 2 1/2 In.	7.50
Dish, Rooster On Nest Cover, Glass Eyes, 9 X 7 1/2 In.	100.00
Dish, Swan Cover, Closed Neck	38.00
Easter Egg, C.1875	62.00
Egg, Easter Greeting, Rabbit Head, Blue, 4 In.	30.00
Egg, Pontil, Victorian, Ribbon Scroll, Marked Easter	40.00
Eyecup	17.00
Eyecup, Marked On Bottom	9.00
Eyecup, Rose, Extra Large	21.00
Figurine, Dolphin, Westmoreland, 8 In., Pair	30.00
Fish Set, Dated 1872, Platter & 8 Plates, Fish Shape	295.00
Fish Set, Fish Shaped Platter, Patented 1872, 9 Piece	195.00
Goblet, Hobnail	10.00
Goblet, Mitered Bars	17.00
Guttate, Butter, Covered, White Opaque	80.00
Guttate, Creamer, Pink	60.00
Hat, Cowboy	25.00
Hat, Toothpick, Daisy & Button	12.00
Jar, Canning, Owl	30.00
Jar, Cheese, Metal Handled Holder, Covered	45.00
Jar, Cold Cream, Yardley, Art Deco Embossed Bee Knob, Hard Cover	4.00
Jar, Diamond Pattern, Covered, 12 In.	5.00
Jar, Dutch Children, Hexagonal Panels, Covered	18.00
Lamp, Christmas Tree, Miniature	165.00
Lamp, 1939 World's Fair, Metal Hemisphere On Top	30.00
Lunch Basket, Wicker Pattern, Raised Lid, Handle	29.00
Match Holder, Grape	12.00
Mug, Bird & Wheat, Pink, 3 1/4 In.Diam.	27.50
Mug, Bleeding Heart, 3 1/4 In.	55.00
Mug, Ceres Pattern, Lavender	28.00
Mug, Child's, Head Of Bull & Head Of Stag	34.00
Mug, Heron & Peacock, Child's	55.00
Mug, Monk's, Child's, Banded Rim, Small	22.00
Mustard, Bull's Head, Blue	145.00
Pitcher, Syrup, Scroll & Net	55.00
Pitcher, Water, Geometric, Applied Handle	185.00
Pitcher, Wild Iris, Bulbous, Pink, Yellow, Turquoise Design	145.00
Plate, Bust Of Columbus Center, 9 1/2 In.	26.00
Plate, Cat	15.00
Plate, Child's, Little Bopeep, 3-Section	20.00
Plate, Columbus, 1492-1892	15.00
Plate, Cupid & Psyche	15.00
Plate, Dated Memorial, John F.Kennedy, Backward C	45.00

Plate, Fish, Dated 1872 .... 15.00
Plate, Flags & Shields Border, Dated 1903 .... 14.00
Plate, Fleur-De-Lis Border, 7 1/2 In. 17.50
Plate, Indian Head, Beaded Loop 45.00
Plate, Keyhole Variant, 7 1/4 In. 15.00
Plate, Leaf Shape, Pierced Handle, Blue, 5 In. 10.00
Plate, No Easter Without Us, Chicken & Egg Design 30.00
Plate, Open Lattice Edge, 8 3/4 In., Pair 10.00
Plate, Puppies On Top, Squirrel On Branch In Center, 8 In. 68.00
Plate, Ruffled Edge, Grape & Leaf Design, Imperial, 8 1/2 In. 16.00
Plate, S Design Edge, Black 18.00
Plate, Three Owls, Dated 1908 .... 25.00
Plate, Triangular Leaf & Chain, 7 1/4 In. 22.00
Plate, Trumpet Vine, Open Lattice Edge, 10 1/2 In. 33.00
Plate, William Howard Taft 75.00
Plate, Yacht & Anchor, Colored Design, 7 1/4 In. 20.00
Platter, Retriever .... 95.00 To 100.00
Salt & Pepper, Farber Ware Holders 35.00
Salt & Pepper, G.E. Refrigerator, Pair .... 18.00 To 22.00
Salt & Pepper, Original Tin Tops, Blue 45.00
Salt & Pepper, Pansy 22.00
Salt & Pepper, St.Louis World's Fair, Metal Lids 35.00
Salt, Blackberry, Footed, 2 3/4 In. 24.00
Salt, Cactus, 3 3/4 In. 8.00
Saltshaker, Marbleized Pink, Fleur-De-Lis In Wreath 25.00
Saltshaker, Pansy Design, Original Top 18.00
Shoe, Tramp's 45.00
Smoke Bell, Cranberry Ruffled Edge, 7 1/2 In. 45.00
Smoke Bell, Ruffled, Flint, 8 In.Diam. 20.00
Spooner, Blackberry .... 48.00 To 75.00
Spooner, Ceres 22.00
Stein Set, Monk, Red Trim 165.00
Sugar & Creamer, Atterbury, Lace Edge 35.00
Sugar & Creamer, Diamond & Fan, Individual, 2 1/2 In. 22.00
Sugar Shaker, Netted Oak 60.00
Sugar Shaker, Sawtooth Band At Base 22.00
Sugar, Blackberry Pattern, Beading At Corners, Berry Finial 50.00
Sugar, Sawtooth Pattern, Acorn Finial On Lid 85.00
Sugar, Scroll Design, Domed Lid, Gold Trim, Oval, Blue 38.00
Sugar, Strawberry, Covered 65.00
Swan, 8 1/2 In. 95.00
Syrup, Alba 45.00
Syrup, Bulbous Base, Hand-Painted Ivy Lei, Brass Thumb Lift 75.00
Syrup, Hobnail 75.00
Syrup, Ribs Over Ribs, Blue, 7 1/2 In. 50.00
Syrup, Scroll & Net 45.00
Syrup, Strawberry Patch 85.00
Table Set, Diamond Panel, Blue, 4 Piece 245.00
Table Set, Swan Finials, 4 Piece 230.00
Toothpick, Daisy & Button, Hat Shape 12.00
Toothpick, Footed Palm Leaf 28.00
Toothpick, Hand Shape, Ruffled 25.00
Toothpick, Moss Rose 20.00
Toothpick, Shell And Seaweed, Decorated 45.00
Tray, Dresser, Rose Garland 14.00
Tray, Lady & Fan, 7 In. 45.00
Tray, Pin, Chrysanthemum Pattern, Fostoria 22.00
Tumbler, Beaded Rib, Gold Rim 12.00
Tumbler, Netted Oak, Enamel Design 38.00
Tumbler, Scroll, Blue 24.00
Tumbler, 1904 World's Fair 15.00
Vase, Applied Flower, Clear Stem, Rose Color, 6 1/2 In. 20.00
Vase, Beige Enamel Boy & Girl Rolling Hoops, 6 In. 55.00
Vase, Daisy & Button, Footed, 8 In. 25.00

Vase, Daisy Pattern, Black, 7 In.	15.00
Vase, Fan, Hobnail, Footed	15.00
Vase, Hand-Painted Indians, Brown Tones, 8 In.	40.00
Vase, Melon Rib, Crimped Top, Flowers, 8 1/2 In.	70.00
Vase, Raised Figure Design, Blue, Square, 4 In.	20.00
Water Set, Wild Iris, 5 Piece	275.00

Millefiori means, literally, a thousand flowers. It is a type of glasswork popular in paperweights. Many small flowerlike pieces of glass are grouped together to form a design.

MILLEFIORI, see also Paperweight

MILLEFIORI, Bottle, Stopper, 8 In.	75.00
Cruet, Clear Handle, Stopper, 7 1/2 In.	85.00
Vase, 8 In.	70.00

Minton china has been made in the Staffordshire region of England from 1793 to the present. The firm became part of the Royal Doulton Tableware Group in 1968, but the wares continued to be marked "Minton." Many marks have been used. The one shown dates from about 1873 to 1891, when the word "England" was added.

MINTON, Cup & Saucer, Floral Design, Gold Trim, Handled, Mark	38.00
Cup & Saucer, Fluted, Gold Trim, Flowers	30.00
Cup & Saucer, Green Band, Gold Design, Marked, Demitasse	10.00
Cup & Saucer, Green Band, Gold Foliage, Marked, Set Of 6	48.00
Cup & Saucer, Lacy Gold, Red Trim, Deep Saucer, C.1840	65.00
Cup & Saucer, Mustache, Blue Enamel Ground, Multicolored	110.00
Figurine, Little Jean	50.00
Jug, Pewter Hinged Top, Cherubs & Garland, Marked 1845, 11 1/4 In.	295.00
Plate, Beauchamp, 10 1/2 In.	20.00
Plate, Blue, Etched Gold Border, 6 1/2 In., Set Of 12	240.00
Plate, Cobalt Blue & Sterling Silver Border, Center Design, 9 In.	12.50
Plate, Different Centers, Botanicals, Gold Border, 8 1/2 In., Set Of 6	300.00
Plate, Fish, Artist Signed, 9 In.	50.00
Plate, Floral Border, Gold Edge, Blue, Orange, 10 In., Set Of 12	425.00
Plate, Fox Hunt Scene, 9 In.	50.00
Plate, Ivanhoe, 9 In.	86.00
Plate, Oyster, Shell & Seaweed	75.00
Plate, Platinum Monarch, 8 In.	6.00
Plate, Red Rose Design, 6 In.	25.00
Plate, Sardine & Scallop	75.00
Plate, Soup, Cobalt Blue Flange Rim, Gold Edge, Beaded, Marked	35.00
Platter, Deva Pattern, 12 X 15 In.	48.00
Platter, Well & Tree, White Ground, Basket Weave Band, 19 X 15 In.	50.00
Soup, Cobalt, White & Gold Beading, Set Of 6	135.00
Sugar & Creamer, Blue Willow, Blue Mark, Gold Trim	45.00

Minton, Vase, Fox After Grapes,
Majolica, 9 In., Pair

Tazza, Cupid Base, Blue & Coral 165.00
Teapot, Floral, White Ground 45.00
Tile, Arrowhead Shape, Mythological Boar Hunt Scene, 20 X 10 In. 165.00
Tile, Blue & White, Oriental Scene, 20 Children, Teacher, 6 X 6 In. 75.00
Tile, Old Blue State House, Boston, 1818, Marked, Framed 65.00
Tile, 5 Panel, Cattails & Dragonfly 250.00
Vase, Fox After Grapes, Majolica, 9 In., Pair ....*Illus* 400.00
Vase, Gold Insects, Blue Daises, Brown Ground, Signed, 7 In. 110.00
    MIRROR, see Furniture, Mirror

> Mocha ware is an English-made product that was sold in America during
> the early 1800s. It is a heavy pottery with pale coffee and cream
> coloring. Designs of blue, brown, green, orange, black, or white
> were added to the pottery.

MOCHA, Bowl, Brown & Green Multi Ring Design, England, C.1800, 7 1/4 In. 110.00
Bowl, Earthworm Design, Band On Rim, Brown & Orange, 10 3/4 In.Diam. 145.00
Bowl, Earthworm Design, Gray-Blue Band, Black Stripes, 5 3/4 X 3 In. 125.00
Bowl, Loops Of White, Blue, & Brown, Orange Tan, 6 3/8 In. 215.00
Bowl, Marbleized Design In Tan, Blue, & Brown, 7 3/8 X 3 1/4 In. 115.00
Mug, Brown Trees, Green Ground, Marked, 4 In. 195.00
Mug, White Wavy Lines On Gray Band, Leeds-Type Handle, 5 In. 150.00
Pitcher, Earthworm Design, Green Embossed Band, Stripes, 6 3/4 In. 205.00
Pitcher, Marbleized Design, Leeds-Type Handle, 7 In. 305.00
Pitcher, Seaweed Design 110.00
Pitcher, Seaweed Trees, Leeds-Type Handle, Embossed Bands, 8 1/8 In. 450.00
Saltshaker, Brown Seaweed Trees, White & Brown Stripes, 4 1/8 In. 155.00
Saltshaker, Earthworm Design In Blue, Brown, & White, 4 In. 125.00
Saltshaker, Feather Design, Ocher & White, Embossed Tooling, 3 3/4 In. 175.00
Saltshaker, Magenta Seaweed, White Band, Blue Stripes, 4 1/2 In. 185.00
Saltshaker, White & Brown Earthworm, Star Flower On Dome, 4 3/8 In. 45.00
Saltshaker, White & Brown Stripes, Orange & Tan, 4 3/8 In. 45.00
    MOLD, ICE CREAM, see Pewter, Mold, Ice Cream

MONMOUTH, Bowl, Matte Daffodils, Green Inside, Beige, 7 5/8 X 2 5/8 In. 9.00
Cookie Jar, Cork 16.00
Mug, Old Sleepy Eye, Marked 235.00
Pitcher, Horizontal Ribs, Tan, 5 1/2 In. 7.00
Vase, Handled, Blue Matte, 7 1/2 In., Pair 32.00
Vase, Matte Green, 8 In. 5.00
    MONT JOYE, see Mt.Joye

> William Moorcroft managed the art pottery department for James
> Mac Intyre & Company of England from 1898 to 1913. In 1913 he started
> his own company, Moorcroft Pottery, in Burslem, England. The earlier
> wares are similar to those made today, but color and marking will help
> indicate the age.

MOORCROFT, Bowl, Amaryllis, Cobalt, Marked, 4 1/2 In. 65.00
Bowl, Center Flower, Green Ground, 4 In.Diam. 35.00
Bowl, Grapevine, C.1920, 13 In. 150.00
Bowl, Orchid Design, Green Ground, Marked, 4 1/2 In. 40.00
Box, Floral Design On Lid, Cobalt Blue, 3 X 5 In. 50.00
Box, Green, Salmon Flowers, Covered, 6 In. 85.00
Cookie Jar, Roses & Insects, Beige & Brown, Marked, MacIntyre 85.00
Plate, Hibiscus, Cobalt Blue Ground, 4 1/2 In. 32.50
Plate, Orchid, Dark Green Ground, 4 1/2 In. 32.50
Plate, Yacht, 10 In. 75.00
Platter, Yacht, 15 In. 125.00
Teapot, Pink & Yellow Hibiscus, Blue Ground, Signed, 8 1/2 In. 250.00
Urn, Seaweed In The Breeze Pattern, Signed, 3 X 1 In. 295.00
Vase, Blue Base, Green Shading, Hibiscus, Leaves, Signed, 12 In. 175.00
Vase, Blue Ground, Peach & Grape Design, Paper Label, Marked, 6 In. 125.00
Vase, Brown & Orange Fruits & Ivy, Glazed, 4 In. 55.00
Vase, Bulbous, Blue-Green, Grape, Leaves Design, 9 In. 300.00

Vase, Cobalt Blue Pomegranate, Purple Grapes, 4 1/4 In. 150.00
Vase, Corset Shape, Yellow, White & Pink Bluebells, Marked, 5 In. 350.00
Vase, Crimson, Yellow Hibiscus, Green Leaves, Marked, 10 In. 200.00
Vase, Deep Blue, Red Pomegranates, Yellow Accents, Marked, 8 In. 40.00
Vase, Green Signature, C.1920, 4 In. 80.00
Vase, Iris Design, Gold, Red, Peach, Blue, & Green, 5 1/4 In. 85.00
Vase, Peach & Grape Design, Blue Ground, Marked, 8 In. 350.00
Vase, Peacock Feather, Yellow, Blue, & Green, Florian Ware, 10 In. 450.00
Vase, Pomegranates, Purple Grapes, Leaves, Cobalt Blue, 7 In. 145.00
Vase, White Ground, Blue Poppy, Fluted Top, 9 In. 325.00

MORAVIAN POTTERY, Tile, Grapes & Leaves, Blue, Square, 2 3/4 In. 10.00
Tile, Sculptured Fawn, Buff On Green, Square, 4 1/2 In. 25.00

MORGANTOWN, Goblet, Dancing Girl, Blue & Green, Set Of 8 .... 200.00
Sherbet, Dancing Girl, Set Of 5 .... 125.00
Wine, Dancing Girl, Blue & Green, Set Of 8 .... 200.00

*Moriage is used to identify Japanese pottery to which a raised overglaze
decoration has been added. This relief ornamentation may be elaborate.
The term applies to the style or technique.*

MORIAGE, Bottle, Barber, Red Roses 395.00
Bowl, Handled, Yellow Roses, 7 1/2 In. 40.00
Box, Puff, Pink Roses, Jeweled, 6 X 4 In. 120.00
Cake Plate, Yellow Roses, 10 1/2 In. 45.00
Chocolate Pot, Dragon, Mottled Ground, Nagoya Shofu Mark, Green 125.00
Chocolate Pot, Florals, Multicolored Enamels, 7 3/4 In. 190.00
Coffeepot, Allover Slip, Beading, Pastel, Footed, 9 In. 255.00
Cookie Jar, Central Medallion, Raised Enamel Design, 6 1/2 In. 150.00
Cookie Jar, Egyptian Design 190.00
Cracker Jar, Allover Beading & Enamels 220.00
Cracker Jar, Dragon, Covered 70.00
Creamer, Child's, Dragon, Covered 14.50
Cup & Saucer, Dragon 12.50
Cup & Saucer, Pink Beading 45.00
Ewer, Allover White Slip, Signed, Green Ground, 8 In. 185.00
Ewer, Multicolored Florals, Bulbous Base, Ribbed, Marked, 7 In. 148.00
Fernery, Melon-Ribbed, Flowers & Butterfly 125.00
Loving Cup, Allover Beading & Enamels, 3-Handled, 5 In. 240.00
Loving Cup, 3 Floral Reserves, Frosted, 3-Handled 125.00
Plate, Dragon, 8 In.Pair 20.00
Server, Shell Shape, Colored Design, Raised Rosette Center, 10 In. 145.00
Sugar & Creamer, Raised Floral Design, Covered, Lavender, Green 125.00
Sugar & Creamer, Yellow Roses 35.00
Tankard, Red Ground, Roses, Green Trim, 13 In. 290.00
Tea Caddy, Ivory & Aqua Beads, Band Of Violets 135.00
Tea Set, Blue-Eyed Dragon, Gray, 13 Piece 40.00
Tea Set, Dragons, Lighophane Maidens In Cup, Demitasse, 17 Piece 95.00
Tea Set, Pot, Sugar & Creamer, Pink Trailing Slip, Green Background 95.00
Vase, Birds Perched On Limb, Footed, Light Green, 9 1/4 In. 195.00
Vase, Dragon Design, Gray, 8 1/2 In. 175.00
Vase, Floral Design, Enameling, Double Handles, 10 In. 185.00
Vase, Floral, Allover Pattern, 5 1/2 In. 75.00
Vase, Florals, 4-Handled, 10 1/2 In. 250.00
Vase, Flowers, Beige Ground, Russet Beading, 1i 1/4 In. 269.00
Vase, Fuchsia & Green, 13 In. 95.00
Vase, Green & White Design, Rooster, Yellow Ground, 9 1/4 In. 225.00
Vase, Green Bisque, Rooster Decor, Flared Top, 9 3/8 X 3 3/4 In. 235.00
Vase, Green Ground, White Design, 7 1/2 In. 225.00
Vase, Hand-Painted Roses In Ovals, Aqua & Green, 8 In. 75.00
Vase, Hand-Painted Violets, Lacy Slipwork, 14 1/4 In. 295.00
Vase, Hand-Painted, Raised Floral, Handled, 5 1/2 In. 75.00
Vase, Panels Of Flowers, Green, 6 1/2 In. 95.00

Vase, Raised White Swan In Reeds, 9 In.	185.00
Vase, Red Ground, Yellow & Orchid Roses, Allover Green, 9 In.	260.00

Mosaic Tile Company of Zanesville, Ohio, was started by Karl Langenbeck and Herman Mueller in 1894. Many types of plain and ornamental tiles were made until 1959. The company closed in 1967.

MOSAIC TILE CO., Ashtray, Green	20.00
Figurine, Bear, Black, 10 1/4 X 5 3/4 In.	90.00
Figurine, German Shepherd, Lying Down, 10 1/2 X 6 In.	95.00
Grizzly Bear, 1912	150.00
Tile, General Pershing, Boxed	45.00
Tile, Large Black Bear	95.00
Tile, Stylized Leaves & Flowers, In Iron Trivet, 1954	12.00

Moser glass was made by Ludwig Moser und Sohne, a Bohemian glasshouse founded in 1857. Art Nouveau-type glassware and iridescent glassware were made. The firm is still working.

MOSER, Bottle, Cruet Shape, Gold & White Enamel, Signed, 6 1/2 In.	225.00
Bottle, Perfume, Enameled Florals, Jewels, Stopper, Signed, 4 3/4 In.	245.00
Bowl, Applied Acorns, Enameled Leaves, Gold Trim, Signed, 5 5/8 In.	1150.00
Bowl, Candy, Cranberry, Round, Gold Band, Marked, 5 In.	225.00
Bowl, Leaf Shaped, Gold Enameled Vines Overall, Pink Opaline, 10 In.	235.00
Bowl, Multicolored Leaves, Ruffled Foot, Boat Shape, Cranberry, 9 In.	395.00
Box, Amethyst, Hinged, Footed, Applied Salamander Design, 4 3/4 In.	595.00
Box, Cranberry, Gold & White Flowers, Ormolu Feet, 3 In.	120.00
Box, Dresser, Raised Enameling, Hinged Cover, Signed, 3 1/2 X 2 1/2 In.	195.00
Box, Leaves & Acorns, Enameled Bee On Lid, Signed, 3 X 1 3/4 In.	348.00
Box, Multicolored Acorns, Bee On Top Of Lid, Signed, 2 X 3 In.	275.00
Candleholder, Alexandrite, Signed, 4 1/4 In., Pair	90.00
Compote, Green To Clear, Flowers & Leaves, Footed, 5 X 3 In.	295.00
Cordial, Gold Trim, Clear Stem, Signed, Amethyst, Set Of 8	375.00
Cruet, Liqueur, Brass Holder, Green Mugs, Applied Berries, 5 Piece	495.00
Cup & Saucer, Enameled Flowers, Cranberry Windows, Gold Foliage	325.00
Cup & Saucer, Melon Shape, Gold, Enamel Design	65.00
Decanter, Clear Cut Glass, Grape & Leaves, Signed, 14 In.	135.00
Dish, Leaf Shaped, Cranberry Glass, Gold, 10 3/4 X 9 In.	425.00
Dish, Leaf Shaped, Gold & Cranberry Design, 10 3/4 X 9 In.Diam.	425.00
Goblet, Blue, Acorns & Flowers, Footed, 6 In.	95.00
Goblet, Butterflies On White Leaves, Amber, Set Of 4	140.00
Goblet, Gold Trim, Enamel, Cranberry, Signed, 7 In.	175.00
Goblet, Green To Crystal, Marked, Set Of 6	485.00
Liqueur Set, Allover Gold Leaves, Stopper, 6 Mugs, Cranberry, 8 1/2 In.	1250.00
Mug, Cranberry, Oak Leaves, Applied Acorns, Marked, 4 1/2 In.	450.00
Mug, Gold Design, Florals, Applied Handle, Signed, 4 3/4 In.	225.00
Perfume, Black, Gold Cut Design, Pedestal, Marked, 8 In.	215.00
Pitcher, Clear To Chartreuse, Flower Design, Pontil, 4 1/4 In.	100.00
Pitcher, Egyptian Designs, Signed, Cranberry, 9 1/2 In.	550.00
Plate, Home On The Range, Etched Buffalo, Signed, 9 1/2 In.	75.00
Tumbler, Liqueur, Enameled Oak Leaves, 2 Acorns, Amber, 2 1/8 In.	95.00
Vase, Alexandrite, Goblet Form, 9 In.	83.00
Vase, Applied Acorns, Oak Leaves, Signed, Orange, 2 1/2 X 4 In.	265.00
Vase, Blue Ruffled Top, Amethyst Pedestal, Gold Trim, Jewels, 15 In.	250.00
Vase, Clear Pedestal, Strawberry Diamond Cutting, Frosted, 8 In.	235.00
Vase, Clear To Cranberry, Gold Trim, 9 In.	260.00
Vase, Cobalt Blue, 6 X 6 In.	125.00
Vase, Cranberry, Floral Sprays, 4 In.	300.00
Vase, Cranberry, Floral, Gilt, 6 In.	185.00
Vase, Cut Flower, Leaves, & Buds On Angles Of Vase, 4 1/2 In.	125.00
Vase, Deer, Trees, Intaglio Cut, Marked, 8 In.	395.00
Vase, Diamond & Panel Cutting, Gold Fish, Signed, 8 1/4 In.	235.00
Vase, Enamel Birds & Flowers, Signed, Blue, 9 In.	350.00
Vase, Floral & Gilt, Cranberry, 6 In.	185.00
Vase, Flowers, 4 Alligators, Amethyst Ground, 5 In.	140.00

Vase, Gold Applied Acorns, Enameled Leaves, Signed, 4 1/4 In. 265.00
Vase, Gold Design, Green To Clear, 12 1/2 In., Pair 275.00
Vase, Lavender Cut To Clear Intaglio, Signed, 3 3/4 In. 350.00
Vase, Multicolored Grapes, Amber Rosette Feet, 5 3/4 In. 325.00
Vase, Rose, Band Of Warriors, 3 1/2 In. 100.00
Wine Set, Signed, Decanter & 6 Goblets, Blue & Gold 1380.00
Wine, Berry Prunts Applied To Wafer Below Bowl, Cranberry, 8 1/2 In. 125.00

*Moss rose china was made by many firms from 1808 to 1900. It refers
to any china decorated with the moss rose flower.*

MOSS ROSE, Butter Chip, Meakin, Ironstone, Set Of 6 .... 117.00
Shaving Mug, Meakin, Embossed, Ironstone 145.00
Soup, Flat 12.00
Spooner, Meakin, Ironstone 49.00
Tea Set, Tray, 16 1/2 X 12 1/2 In. 160.00
Vase, Brush, Drain, Shaw, Ironstone 97.00
Waste Receiver, Bamboo, Covered, Ironstone 330.00

*Mother-of-pearl glass, or pearl satin glass, was first made in the 1850s in
England and in Massachusetts. It was a special type of mold-blown satin
glass with air bubbles in the glass, giving it a pearlized color.
Mother-of-Pearl shell objects are listed under Pearl.*

**MOTHER-OF-PEARL, SATIN GLASS, see also Satin Glass; Smith
Brothers; Tiffany Glass; etc.**
MOTHER-OF-PEARL, Biscuit Jar, Silver Plated Top & Handle, Blue, 5 3/4 In. 475.00
Bottle, Perfume, Stopper, Diamond-Quilted, Blue Satin, 5 In. 350.00
Bottle, Scent, Diamond-Quilted, Blue, 1 3/4 X 3 3/4 In. 245.00
Cruet, Pink 75.00
Ewer, Herringbone, Apricot To White Satin, 10 1/2 In. 500.00
Ewer, Ruffled, Diamond-Quilted, Thorny Handle, Pink, 7 In. 225.00
Ewer, Tangerine To Pink, Zig Zag Design, Satin Glass, 9 In. 75.00
Jar, Sweetmeat, Diamond-Quilted, 5 1/8 X 3 1/8 In. 425.00
Jar, Sweetmeat, Flower & Acorn Pattern, Blue, 5 X 3 1/2 In. 650.00
Lamp, Table, Diamond-Quilted, Sectioned Shade, 14 3/4 In. 750.00
Pitcher, Diamond-Quilted, Lavender To Blue, 9 1/2 In. 250.00
Pitcher, Milk, Shell, Marked 65.00
Rose Bowl, Diamond-Quilted, 6-Crimp, 5 X 4 1/2 In. 285.00
Rose Bowl, Herringbone, White Lining, Pink, 3 1/2 X 3 In. 195.00
Rose Bowl, Rivulet Pattern, 8-Crimp Top, 4 1/4 X 2 5/8 In. 235.00
Rose Bowl, Vertical Pattern, Blue, 3 1/2 In. 118.00
Sugar & Creamer, Coin Spot, Rose To White Satin 550.00
Vase, Allover Leaf Pattern, White, 9 3/4 In. 395.00
Vase, Blue Satin, Herringbone, 5 1/2 In. 145.00
Vase, Blue Swirl, White Lining, Blue, 5 In., Pair 225.00
Vase, Blue, 8 In. 125.00
Vase, Diamond-Quilted, C.1885, Fuchsia, 8 1/4 In. 225.00
Vase, Diamond-Quilted, Rose, White Lining, 11 In. 265.00
Vase, Diamond-Quilted, Triangular Ruffled Top, 7 In. 195.00
Vase, Enameled Gold Design, Victorian, 10 In. 75.00
Vase, Herringbone, Thorny Handle, Pink, 9 In. 295.00
Vase, Moray, Satin, Pink, 13 In. 425.00
Vase, Rivulet Pattern, 4-Petal Shape, 5 1/4 In. 195.00
Vase, Rose Herringbone, Thorn Handle, 3-Petal Top, 6 3/4 In. 265.00
Vase, Rose Ribbon, Wafer Foot, Gold Prunus Design, 3 3/4 In. 345.00
Vase, Rose To Pink, Zig Zag Design, Satin Glass, 7 In. 80.00
Vase, Ruffled, White Lining, Peach, 5 3/4 In., Pair 298.00
Vase, Snowflake Pattern, Enameled, Pink Coralene, 4 3/8 In. 500.00
Vase, Trumpet, Gold To Purple 125.00
MOUSTACHE CUP, see Mustache Cup

Mont Joye is an enameled cameo glass made in the late nineteenth and the twentieth centuries by Saint-Hilaire Touvoir de Varraux and Co. of Pantin, France. This same company produced De Vez glass.

MT.JOYE, Bottle, Perfume, Etched, Decorated, Barrel Shaped, 3 1/2 X 2 1/2 In.	95.00
Vase, Amethyst, Carved Flowers, Textured Ground, 12 In.	350.00
Vase, Brown & Gold, Signed, 12 In.	150.00
Vase, Enameled Violets, Gold Leaves, Signed, 16 In., Pair	800.00
Vase, Enameled Violets, Gold Trim, Green, Signed, 11 1/2 In.	400.00
Vase, Gold Enamel Outlining Iris & Dragonfly, Green, 14 In.	200.00
Vase, Iris, Enameled, Pewter Top, 14 In., Pair	1400.00
Vase, Opaline, Enameled Cornflowers, 10 In.	250.00

Mt.Washington Glass was made at the Mt.Washington Glass Co. in New Bedford, Massachusetts. Many types of art glass were made there from 1850 to the 1890s.

MT.WASHINGTON, see also Burmese; Crown Milano

MT.WASHINGTON, Biscuit Barrel, Enameled Shasta Daisies, Vines, Signed	375.00
Biscuit Barrel, Pastel Design, Signed, 4 3/8 X 5 In.	495.00
Bowl, Burmese, Phantom Diamond-Quilted, 7 X 5 1/2 In.	750.00
Bowl, Finger, Underplate, Cream To Gold, 3 X 6 In.	350.00
Bowl, Peachblow, Tricornered, 5 Inches At Sides, 2 In.	985.00
Bowl, Phantom Diamond-Quilted, Berry Pontil, 7 X 5 1/2 In.	750.00
Box, White Shell, Lined, 4 In.Diam.	225.00
Bride's Bowl, Dragons & Flowers, White Ground, 8 1/4 In.Diam.	695.00
Castor, Pickle, Diamond-Quilted, Silver Plated Frame	375.00
Cookie Jar, Melon Ribbed, Pansy Sprays, Silver Plated Cover	275.00
Cracker Jar, Delft, Paneled Body, Scalloped Edge, Bail, Marked	395.00
Creamer, Melon Ribbed, Silver Plated Spout & Handle	160.00
Cruet, Inverted Thumbprint, Amber Stopper	245.00
Dish, Cheese, Strawberry Diamond Pattern, Covered, 8 X 10 In.	850.00
Dish, Sweetmeat, Melon Ribbed, Gold Outlined, Signed	375.00
Ewer, Burmese, Handled, 12 1/2 In.	750.00
Flute Cover, Hand-Painted, Tulips, 11 In.	30.00
Holder, Pansy, Toadstool Shape	275.00
Lamp, Kerosene, Cherubs On Shade, Lusterless White, 17 1/2 In.	750.00
Plate, Floral Design, Lusterless, 10 In.	25.00
Plate, Morning Flories, Lusterless, 10 In.	26.00
Plate, Pansies & Orange Blossoms, Lusterless White, 10 In.	95.00
Plate, Winter Scene, Opal Glass, Ruffled Paper Label	115.00
Plate, Winter Scene, Original Paper Label, 11 3/4 In.	150.00
Salt & Pepper, Cockle Shell, Pairpoint Holder	450.00
Salt & Pepper, Egg Shape, Florals, Acid Cut Ground	85.00
Saltshaker, Acorn, Enameled Flowers	75.00
Saltshaker, Burmese, Ribbed, Silver Plated Holder, Dated 1886	200.00
Saltshaker, Egg, Flat Side, Pewter Cap, Pink Floral	65.00
Saltshaker, Egg, Flat Side, Pewter Cap, 3 Shades Of Leaves	80.00
Saltshaker, Melon Shape	35.00 To 45.00
Saltshaker, Tomato, Blue, White, & Yellow	50.00
Saltshaker, Top, Fig Shaped, Fern Design, Red Dot Flowers	50.00
Saltshaker, White To Blue, Flowers, Melon Ribbed	35.00
Sugar & Creamer, Florals, Red Satin Glass	300.00
Sugar & Creamer, Mosaic Of Coral, Green, Blue, Red, 2 1/2 In.	1250.00
Sugar & Creamer, Red, Flower Design, Satin Glass	300.00
Sugar Shaker, Egg Shape, Ferns, White	285.00
Sugar Shaker, Ferns & Flowers, C.1879	200.00
Sugar Shaker, Tomato, Strawberries & Leaves	175.00
Tray, Thistles, Gold Enamel, Signed, 9 1/2 X 7 In.	1150.00
Vase, Acid Finish, Ruffled, Signed Pairpoint Holder, 10 In.	425.00

Vase, Lava, 5 3/4 In. 1350.00
Vase, Orchid Design, Gold, Scallop Top, 12 1/2 X 5 In. 345.00
Vase, Pair, Rose Interior, Triple Cased, Rigaree Drape, 12 In. 1200.00
Vase, Peachblow, Shaded Pink, 4 X 8 In. 1085.00
Vase, Shaded Pale Yellow To Pink, 13 In. 1150.00

Mud figures are small Chinese pottery figures made in the twentieth century. The figures usually represent workers, scholars, farmers, or merchants. Other pieces are trees, houses, and similar parts of the landscape. The figures have unglazed faces and hands but glazed clothing. They were originally made for fish tanks or planters.

MUD FIGURE, Country Woman, 4 In. 7.00
Fisherman With Poles, 5 1/2 In. 33.00
Fisherman, Sitting, 4 In. 28.00
Fisherman, 5 In. 35.00
Fisherman, 6 In. 40.00
Man With Bread, 4 1/2 In. 30.00
Man With Jug, 4 1/2 In. 30.00
Man, Sitting, 4 In. 28.00
Man, Standing, 1930s, 3 In. 28.00

Mulberry ware was made in the Staffordshire district in England from about 1850 to 1860. The dishes were decorated with a transfer design of a reddish brown, now called mulberry. Many of the patterns are similar to those used for flow blue and other Staffordshire transfer wares.

MULBERRY, Bone Dish, Tonquin 10.00
Bride's Bowl, Ruffled 85.00
Coffeepot, Pelew 160.00
Cup & Saucer, Genoa, Handled 35.00
Cup & Saucer, Ning Po, Handled 45.00
Cup & Saucer, Pelew 35.00
Cup Plate, Cypress 40.00
Cup, Handleless, Pekin Pattern, Wood, C.1835, Purple 8.00
Cup, Posset, Pelew, C.1840, Challinor 30.00
Dish, Vegetable, Canova Pattern, Romantic Scene, Mayer, C.1830 .... 85.00
Dish, Vegetable, Peruvian, 8-Sided, Covered, 8 In. 35.00
Dish, Vegetable, Venture Pattern, Interior Scene, C.1840, 9 1/2 In. 40.00
Plate, Corean, C.1850, Podmore & Walker, 9 3/4 In. 29.00
Plate, Dinner, Mingo Po 25.00
Plate, Jeddo, Adams, C.1840, 7 1/2 In. 16.00
Plate, Jeddo, Wm.Adams & Son, 9 1/4 In. 28.00
Plate, Longport, 10 1/2 In. 25.00
Plate, Ning Po, 9 1/2 In. 22.50
Plate, Pelew, E.Challinor, 7 1/2 In., Set Of 3 .... 48.00
Plate, Soup, Peru, Peter Holdcroft, 10 3/4 In. 32.00
Plate, Tivoli, Meigh, C.1840, Romantic Scenery, 9 In. 20.00
Plate, Tomb Of Absalom, 10 1/2 In. 25.00
Plate, University Of California, Dated 1932, 10 1/2 In. 20.00
Plate, Venus, 10 In. 30.00
Plate, Village Of Shalom, 10 1/2 In. 25.00
Plate, Washington Vase, 10 1/2 In. 37.00
Platter, Cyprus, Davenport, 18 In. 130.00
Platter, Jeddo, C.1845, 17 1/2 X 13 3/4 In. 150.00
Platter, Vincennes, Alcock, 10 1/2 X 8 In. 55.00
Platter, Vincennes, Alcock, 15 1/2 X 12 In. 125.00
Teapot, Jeddo 175.00

Muller Freres, French for Muller Brothers, made cameo and other art glass from the early 1900s to the late 1930s. Their factory was first located in Luneville and later moved to Croismaire, France.

MULLER FRERES, Vase, Cherubs Scene, Signed, Orange Satin Ground, 5 In. 1875.00

Vase, Elephant In Jungle Grass, Native, Fan Shape, 5 3/4 In. 400.00
Vase, Lake Scene, Handles, Signed, Green To Peach, 10 5/8 In. 2250.00
Vase, Mountain Scene, Signed, Mottled Gold & Blue, 9 3/4 In. 3500.00
Vase, Mountain Scene, Signed, Salmon Mottling, 6 X 9 3/8 In. 2500.00
Vase, Peonies, Signed, Gold Frosted Ground, 7 3/4 In. 1800.00
Vase, Red Carvings, Florals, White & Red Ground, Signed, 6 In. 650.00
Vase, Storks & House Scene, Signed, Gold Ground, 7 7/8 In. 1695.00
Vase, Tree Landscape, Signed, Gold Frosted Ground, 4 3/4 In. 650.00
Vase, Windmill Scene, Signed, Oval, Yellow Ground, 13 1/4 In. 1250.00
Vase, Yellow Roses, Maroon Leaves, Signed, Pink, 6 3/4 In. 1350.00
Vase, Yellow Roses, Maroon Leaves, Signed, Salmon, 7 1/4 In. 1800.00

MUNCIE, Pitcher, Matte Green Dripped Over Pink, 5 1/2 X 5 In. 20.00
Vase, Bud, Pink & Green, Marked, 8 1/2 In. 15.00
Vase, Corset Shape, Impressed Green Over Rust, 10 1/4 In. 38.00

MUSIC, Accordion, Scandalli, Case 90.00
Accordion, Sonora, Italian, 120 Bass, Case 150.00
Accordion, Steel Bronze Reeds, Original Box, Germany 70.00
Accordion, Tanzbar, Paper Roll, 3 Rolls 500.00
Accordion, Wurlitzer, 120 Bass, Case 100.00
Automaton, Bisque Head, Paperweight Eyes, Lorgnette, 18 In. 1750.00
Automaton, Conductor, Paperweight Eyes, Bisque Head, Arms Move, 20 In. 1540.00
Automaton, Cymbalist, Black Man, Head, Arms, & Feet Move, 19 In. 1600.00
Automaton, Flower Seller, Bisque Head, Turns Head, 17 In. 3100.00
Automaton, Gorilla, Fur-Covered, Plays Guitar, Mouth Moves, 18 In. 1750.00
Automaton, Marotte, French, Bisque, Glass Eyes, Twirls, 9 In. 330.00
Automaton, Singing Bird, Rectangular Box, 20th Century, 4 1/4 In. 1150.00
Automaton, Singing Bird, Simple Melody, 19th Century, Europe, 4 In. 4500.00
Band Organ, Limonair, Children's Carousel, 34 Key, 8 Books 6500.00
Banjo, Bega, 5 String, Case 900.00
Banjo, Hand-Painted Couple In Canoe, C.1920, Case, Bird's-Eye Maple 85.00
Banjo, Mardi Gras Type, Jewel-Eyed Head, Cymbals, Pole 5 1/2 Ft. 125.00
Banjo, Stella 75.00
Banjo, Stewart, Mother-Of-Pearl, Marquetry Work, 4 String 550.00
Banjo, Stewart, Wondertone, Early 1920s, Case 495.00
Banjo, Tenor, Case 150.00
Banjo, Waverly, Tenor 38.00
Bird In Cage, Pagoda Style, Tin & Brass 375.00
Box, Alexandra, 6 Sleeves, 6 Tunes Per Sleeve, 20 X 9 In. 1800.00
Box, Animated, Wax Baby Raises Head, Opens Eyes, Figure 11 In. 1450.00
Box, Bremond, Swiss, 8-Tune, Cylinder, 11 In. 3800.00
Box, Bremond, 8-Tune, Engraved Sterling Silver Tune Card, 20 In. 1500.00
Box, Bremond, 8-Tune, Pianoforte, Inlay Top, 25 X 6 In. 1600.00
Box, Bremond, 8-Tune, 21 X 7 X 6 In. 1250.00
Box, Church, Hand Cranked, Germany, Tin, 4 X 6 In. 125.00
Box, Ducommun Girod, C.1850, Hidden Drum & Bell Box, Fruitwood 4800.00
Box, Ducommun Girod, 12-Tune, 23 X 9 X 6 In. 1250.00
Box, Edison, Amberola III, With Opera Works 1700.00
Box, Expressive, Cylinder, Swiss, Walnut Case, 30 1/2 In. 1000.00
Box, Francois Nicole, Cylinder, Swiss, C.1830, Writing Surface, 30 In. 1650.00
Box, Harpe-Piccolo, 10-Tune, 23 X 6 In. 1400.00
Box, L'Epee, 6 Bells, 8-Tune, Gloral Inlay Top, 19 1/2 X 10 In. 1100.00
Box, L'Universelle, 6 Cylinders 800.00
Box, Manivelle, 4-Tune, Lithograph On Cover, 1922, 8 5/8 X 4 3/8 In. 450.00
Box, Mermod Freres, Cylinder, Swiss, Zither Attachment, Walnut, 23 In. 440.00
Box, Mermod Freres, 6-Tune, 16 Cylinders, 18 In. 6500.00
Box, Mermod Freres, 6-Tune, 20 X 6 1/2 In. 900.00
Box, Mermod Soprano Sublime, Operatic, 8-Tune, 2y X 8 In. 3400.00
Box, Mira Grand, 18 1/2 In.Disc, 31-Tune 5000.00
Box, Mira, Console, 24 Discs, 29 1/2 X 22 X 42 In. 6500.00
Box, Mira, Duplex Combs, 16 Discs, 27 X 20 X 13 In. 2700.00
Box, Mira, 12 In. Single Comb 1500.00
Box, Monopol, Double Comb, 12 Discs 1500.00

Box, Nickelodeon, Hexaphone 1325.00
Box, Nickelodeon, North Tonawanda Bab Organ, 46 Key 9000.00
Box, Nickelodeon, Seeburg-A 2455.00
Box, Nickelodeon, Street Mazzoletti 1500.00
Box, Nickelodeon, Welte Grand 1100.00
Box, Nicole Freres, Interchangeable Cylinder Box, Table, 31 X 8 In. 6000.00
Box, Nicole Freres, Pianoforte, Cylinder 2850.00
Box, Nicole Freres, Pianoforte, 6 Bells, 29 1/2 X 12 1/2 In. 3900.00
Box, Nicole Freres, 6-Tune, Keywind, Cylinder 11 In. 1400.00
Box, Nicole Freres, 123 Tooth, 8-Tune, C.1880, Inlaid Top & Front 1200.00
Box, Olympia, Coin-Operated, 20 Discs, 15 1/2 In. 2300.00
Box, Olympia, Double Comb, Mahogany Case, 15 1/2 In. .... 2700.00 To 2750.00
Box, Orchestral, 12-Tune, 6 Bells, Sphinx Head Beaters, 33 X 21 1/2 In. 4900.00
Box, Orphenion, French Walnut, 12 X 10 X 6 In. 750.00
Box, Otto & Sons, Capital Style, C Cuff, C.1893, Mahogany, 27 In. 4700.00
Box, Paillard, Carved Mahogany, Drawer, 3-Cylinder, 14 In. 2800.00
Box, Polyphon, Coin-Operated, 4 Discs, 36 In. 4500.00
Box, Polyphon, Disc, Coin-Operated, German, C.1900, Walnut, 89 In. 7150.00
Box, Polyphon, Disc, German, C.1895, Walnut, Inlaid Lid, 22 In. 1200.00
Box, Polyphon, German, Coin-Operated, Twenty 19 5/8 In.Discs 6000.00
Box, Polyphon, On Stand, Walnut Case, 12 Discs, C.1905, 43 In. 3300.00
Box, Polyphon, Walnut Case, 10 Discs, 15 1/2 In. 2495.00
Box, Quatour Expressive Mandolin, Cylinder, 17 X 3 1/4 In. 3800.00
Box, Regina, Automatic, Disc 27 In. 9000.00
Box, Regina, Base Cabinet, 10 Discs, Mahogany 5400.00
Box, Regina, Disc, Floor Model, Mahogany, 15 1/2 In. 4700.00
Box, Regina, Double Comb, Slides On Side For Records, 70 Discs 3600.00
Box, Regina, Dragon Front, Home Model, Mahogany, 27 In. 1050.00
Box, Regina, Folding Top, 15 Discs, Golden Oak, 27 In. 4750.00
Box, Regina, Hexaphone, 5-Cent Play, Lattice Front, Oak 6500.00
Box, Regina, Lion's Head, Mahogany Case, Twenty 15 1/2 In.Discs 3500.00
Box, Regina, Mahogany, Disc, 15 1/2 In. 2250.00
Box, Regina, Mahogany, 21 Discs, Serpentine Case, Cupola Top 6500.00
Box, Regina, Model UU, Double Comb, Mahogany 1975.00
Box, Regina, Model 25, Upright, Double Comb, 29 Records, 20 3/4 In.Disc 9000.00
Box, Regina, Model 31, 12 Disc Changer, Oak 8250.00
Box, Regina, No.33, Automatic Changer, Carved Dragons On Doors, 27 In. 8500.00
Box, Regina, Paradox, 2-Speed, 20 3/4 In. Discs 7900.00
Box, Regina, Serpentine, Table Model, Mahogany 5000.00
Box, Regina, Style 11, C.1898, Mahogany Case, Crank-Wound, 22 In. 2000.00
Box, Regina, Style 29, Disc, C.1904, Mahogany Case, 17 In. 950.00
Box, Regina, Style 35, Automatic Changer, Mahogany, 18 1/2 In. 8000.00
Box, Regina, Style 155, Double Comb, Oak Horn, Serpentine Cabinet 4500.00
Box, Regina, Style 240, Carved Dragon Heads .... 4000.00 To 4500.00
Box, Regina, Sublina, Upright, Coin-Operated, 6 Feet 3900.00
Box, Regina, Table Model, Coin-Operated, 15 1/2 In. 4000.00
Box, Regina, Upright, Single Play, 27 In. 5000.00
Box, Regina, Upright, 24 Discs, 24 In. X 13 In. X 5 Ft. 5 In. 3750.00
Box, Regina, 15 1/2 In. Double Comb 2500.00
Box, Regina, 20 3/4 In. Double Comb 3800.00
Box, Seeburg, Style E, Repeating Xylophone, Quartered Oak 2700.00
Box, Stella, Console, Carved Oak, 17 1/4 In.Disc .... 3300.00 To 3400.00
Box, Stella, Double Comb, Drawer, 14 Discs, 17 In. 1200.00
Box, Stella, Double Comb, 12 Discs, Mahogany, 15 1/2 In. 2250.00
Box, Stella, Floor Model, 17 1/4 In.Disc, Carved Oak 3300.00
Box, Swidd, 6-Tune, Tune Card, Lock With Key, 7 3/4 X 14 102 X 5 In. 650.00
Box, Swiss, C.1890, 8 Tune, Marquetry Walnut Case, 11 X 27 X 8 In. 1595.00
Box, Swiss, Inlaid Mahogany & Rosewood, Cylinder, 8-Tune, 18 In. 935.00
Box, Swiss, 6-Tune, Rosewood Case, 17 X 8 X 6 In. 940.00
Box, Swiss, 8-Tune, C.1895 .... 1200.00
Box, Symphonion, Base Cabinet, Coin-Operated, 24 Discs, 88 In. 7500.00
Box, Symphonion, Center Drive Capstan For Rotating Tree 300.00
Box, Symphonion, Disc, German, C.1905, Wind, Floral Design, 13 In. 475.00
Box, Symphonion, Double Comb, Disc 13 5/8 In. 1200.00

Box, Symphonion, Eroica, Disc, German, C.1900, Coin-Operated, 72 In. 7150.00
Box, Symphonion, Stand, Oak, Eleven 11 1/2 In.Discs 2850.00
Box, Symphonion, Table Model, Vertical Disc 2700.00
Box, Symphonion, Upright, Coin-Operated, Double Comb, 13 5/8 In. 2150.00
Box, Symphonion, 9 Discs, Duplex Combs, 19 1/2 X 15 X 11 In. 1750.00
Box, Universal, Interchangeable Cylinder, 6 Cylinders 925.00
Box, Voix Celeste, 4 Dancing Dolls, Coin-Operated, 36 In. 2000.00
Box, Wurlitzer, Model 1050 .... 4200.00
Bugle, Regulation U.S.Army, Brass 25.00
Calliope, Tangley, 43 Whistle, 2 Clark Rolls 3000.00
Castanets, Handle, Ebony, Pair 7.50
Changer, Record, Lincoln Engineering, Pneumatic 300.00
Clarinet, Le Blanc, French, Case 95.00
Clarinet, Otello, Italian, Ebony & Silver Trim, Case 75.00
Coat Rack, Carved Bear Playing Mandolin, Glass Eyes, 2-Tune, 13 In. 600.00
Dispenser, Cigar, 2 Tune, Open To Start, Close To Stop, Ebony Case 150.00
Drum, Child's, American Flag, Dated 1897 .... 125.00
Drum, World War I, Rainbow Division 75.00
Dulcimer, Hammer, Price Decal, Signed Joseph F.Stroehlein 600.00
Flute, Gemeinhardt, Solid Silver, MoS 750.00
Gramophone, Columbia, 1917, Oak Case, Crank, 10 Records, 15 X 15 In. 50.00
Gramophone, Victor R.C.A., Model S.F.G., Wooden Horn 600.00
Guitar, Estrada, 6 String, Case 100.00
Harmonica, Hohner, Alto Valve Harp, Boxed 18.00
Harmonica, Hohner, Echo, Boxed 18.00
Harmonica, Hohner, 4 Octave, Case 35.00
Harmonica, Hohner, 10 Hole, Marine Band 10.00
Harmonica, Hohner, 32 Hole, Sportsman, Germany 15.00
Harmonica, Rolmonica, 8 Music Rolls 100.00
Harmonica, Wien 12.50
Harp, Lyon & Healy, Single Action, C.1908, 5 Ft. 3000.00
Hexaphone, Regina, Coin-Operated, Original Sign 6200.00
Hurdy-Gurdy, 6-Tune, 5 Rolls, 2 Wheel Car 350.00
Mandolin Banjo, 30 Brackets, C.1900 .... 175.00
Mandolin, Inscribed Clifford, Warranted, America, C.1900 .... 300.00
Mandolin, Martin, Original Case 395.00
Melodeon, Top Folds Into Table, Pine, 44 X 22 X 31 In. 975.00
Melodeon, 1868, Stool, Rosewood 1050.00

A nickelodeon is a coin-operated piano or piano and other instrument
combination.

Nickelodeon, Cremona, 1905-10, Piano & Mandolin Attachment 3400.00
Nickelodeon, Engelhardt, A Roll, 44 Note, Oak, 20 X 40 X 58 In. 4200.00
Nickelodeon, Mira, Console, 29 1/2 X 22 X 42 In. 6000.00
Nickelodeon, National Electric Piano Co., 24 Flute Pipes, 56 X 61 In. 7500.00
Nickelodeon, Nelson-Wiggen, Art Glass, Piano, Mandolin, & Xylophone 4700.00
Nickelodeon, Seeburg, Model E 5700.00
Nickelodeon, Seeburg, Model G 1195.00
Nickelodeon, Seeburg, Model L, Art Glass, 10 Tune .... 4500.00 To 6000.00
Nickelodeon, Western Electric, Selectra, Model B .... 3000.00 To 7800.00
Orchestrion, Losche Jazzband, 7 1/2 Ft. 6800.00
Orchestrion, Street, Gavioli, 80 Key, Carved Facade 8500.00
Orchestrion, Western Electric, Derby Racehorse, Coin Operated, 1920s 7800.00
Organ, Aeolian, Grand Player, Rolls, Oak 2950.00
Organ, Aeolian, Model 1050 .... 2000.00
Organ, Aeolian, Six 46 Note Rolls, Ebony Case 1600.00
Organ, Amberola No.50 .... 375.00
Organ, Ariston, Crank, 17 Cardboard Discs 475.00
Organ, Band, BAB 8000.00
Organ, Band, Limonair, 34 Key, Child's Carousel, Music Books 6500.00
Organ, Barrel, Astor & Co., London, 18 Keys, 1860-70 .... 3200.00
Organ, Barrel, Hand Cranked, Wood Cylinder, 22 X 40 In. 300.00
Organ, Barrel, Monkey, Molinari, Original Tune Card, 15 X 9 17 In. 3650.00

Organ, Barrel, Monkey, 65 Pipes, 6 Automata Figures	6500.00
Organ, Bursens, Dance Hall, 10 Rolls	7500.00
Organ, Capenter, Pump, Church, Claw Feet Stool	850.00
Organ, Celestine, Paper Roll, 3 Rolls	425.00
Organ, Estey, Church, C.1904, 2 Manuals, Pedal Board	4200.00
Organ, Estey, Church, Reed, 2 Manuals, Full Pedal Board, 15 Stops	800.00
Organ, Estey, Church, 16 Stops, Sub-Bass, 1 Manual, Oak	3000.00
Organ, Estey, Parlor, Pump, Brass Candle Shelves, Mahogany, 4 Ft.	1000.00
Organ, Estey, Pump, Late 19th Century, Walnut, 47 1/2 X 65 In.	225.00
Organ, Gem, Cob, 20 Note Organette, 14 1/2 X 12 X 8 In.	450.00
Organ, Kimball, Reed Pump, 13 Stops, 1920, Walnut	1000.00
Organ, Limonaire, Fairground, 49 Key, Clarinet Pipes	9900.00
Organ, Link Style C, Pipes, Art Glass	8500.00
Organ, Miller, Pump, Carved Golden Oak Case	995.00
Organ, Multiphone, 24-Play	9800.00
Organ, Newman Bros., Pump, C.1900	500.00
Organ, North Tonawanda Bay, 46 Key	9000.00
Organ, Pipe, Aeolian Co., 1920s, Marie Antoinette Duo-Art	4900.00
Organ, Pipe, Hand, 31 X 20 X 45 In.	2500.00
Organ, Street, Carl Frei, 36 Pipe, Hand Cranked	7000.00
Organ, Street, Mazzoletti	1500.00
Organ, W.W.Putnam, C.1902	550.00
Organ, Wilcox & White, Pneumatic Symphony, Foot Pumped, Walnut	1900.00
Organette, Ariston, Twelve 13 In. Discs	650.00
Organette, Ariston, 24 Keys, 12 Cardboard Discs, 16 X 16 X 9 1/2 In.	350.00
Organette, Drawer, 11 Rolls, 34 X 22 X 47 In.	2600.00
Piano, Chickering, Ampico, Grand, Hand-Painted By Perille	5200.00
Piano, Chickering, Ampico, Model B, 1930, 5 Ft. 4 In.	7000.00 To 8500.00
Piano, Chickering, Decals Of Napoleon, Quarter Grand, 1840, 5 Ft. 8 In.	9000.00
Piano, Chickering, Upright, 1898, Red Mahogany	2500.00
Piano, Cremona, Player, Clear Glass Front	3400.00
Piano, Estey, Player, 94 Welte Rolls, Bench, Mahogany	5900.00
Piano, Farrand Cecilian, Push-Up Player	600.00
Piano, Farrand, Upright, 1928, Electric	1500.00
Piano, Fischer, Ampico, Model B, 1930, Mahogany, 5 Ft.	5000.00 To 6000.00
Piano, Fischer, Ampico, Upright, 1924, Decorative Case	6500.00
Piano, Fischer, Ampico, 1924, Decorative Case	6500.00
Piano, Haines Bros., Ampico, Grand, 1925, 5 Ft. 2 In.	2990.00
Piano, Haines Bros., Grand, Square, Rosewood, 1859	3200.00
Piano, Hallett & Davis, Grand, Flat Top, Square, 1870	3500.00
Piano, J.P.Hale, Grand, Square, C.1875, Stool, Hand-Carved Rosewood	1800.00
Piano, Kimball, Hand-Carved Front, Oak	2000.00
Piano, Knabe, Ampico, Upright, 1921	4300.00
Piano, Knabe, Ampico, 1919, Mahogany, 5 Ft. 8 In.	4200.00
Piano, Knabe, Ampico, 1922, 5 Ft. 2 In.	2750.00
Piano, Knabe, Grand, Square, 1880s	1500.00
Piano, Knabe, Upright, 1921	4300.00
Piano, Marshall & Wendell, Ampico, Baby Grand, 260 Rolls	7500.00
Piano, Mason & Hamlin, Player, 43 Red-Welte Rolls, 1912, Walnut	6500.00
Piano, Mathushek, Upright, 1891	2000.00
Piano, Maynard, Player, Automatic Rewind & Cut Off, Oak	2350.00
Piano, Seeburg, A-Roll, Art Glass, Keyboard Lanterns	4500.00
Piano, Stark, Player, 88 Note, Electrified, Mandolin & Tracker	4450.00
Piano, Steck, Duo-Art, Grand, 1919, 5 Ft. 2 In.	30000.00 To 5000.00
Piano, Steinway, Duo-Art, OR266996	9000.00
Piano, Steinway, Grand, 1865, Rosewood, 7 Ft. 2 In.	8000.00
Piano, Steinway, Model M, Grand, Mahogany, 5 Ft. 7 In.	8500.00
Piano, Twin Tractor, Electric	2175.00
Piano, Weber, Duo-Art, Grand	4500.00
Piano, Weber, Duo-Art, Upright	900.00
Piano, Welt-Mignon, 1930	2900.00
Piano, Wurlitzer, Style I, Coin-Operated	3800.00
Radio, Atwater Kent, Model 20, With Horn & Tubes	150.00
Rolls, Ampico, Set Of 96	400.00

Rolmonica, Blow & Crank, 2 Rolls 125.00
Saxophone, King, Key Of C, Case 95.00
Saxophone, Paramount, A Tenor, 1926, Case 555.00
Sheet, Bromo-Seltzer Advertising 8.50
Sheet, Casablanca, Bogart & Bergman 15.00
Sheet, Chicken Reel Song, 1911, Blacks Dancing On Cover 7.50
Sheet, Father Of Land We Love, Washington's 200th Anniversary, Cohan 5.00
Sheet, In My Merry Oldsmobile, 1915, Couple In Auto, 14 X 14 In. 6.00
Sheet, Jolson, Pre-1924, Set Of 3 .... 20.00
Sheet, Lucky Lindy 8.50
Sheet, Merry Brownies, 1902, Panels Of Palmer Cox Brownies 7.50
Sheet, September Morn, Black & White Illustration 10.00
Sheet, Shortnin' Bread, Black Lithograph 6.75
Sheet, Sing With Shirley Temple, Sam Fox, 1935 .... 25.00
Sheet, Sonny Boy, Jolson 5.00
Sheet, Spirit Of U.S.A., March, E.T.Paull, Spirit Of '76 Cover 12.50
Sheet, Walking Match, Ida Waugh 125.00
Sheet, Who's Afraid Of The Big Bad Wolf, Disney, 1933 .... 15.00
Stand, Boudoir, 20 Note Paper Strip, Ebony Finish 800.00
Ukulele, Lyon & Healy, Leather Case, Walnut 25.00
Violin, J.B.Vuillaume, Paris, C.1825 .... 7500.00
Violin, Karl Hofner, Spruce, Maple Back, Dated 1963, 13 In. 70.00

*Mustache cups were popular from 1850 to 1900. A ledge of china or silver
held the hair out of the liquid in the cup.*

MUSTACHE CUP, Aurora, Signed, Silver Plated, Large 32.00
Saucer, Gold Banding, White Porcelain 30.00
Saucer, Hand-Painted, Wine Bands, Rose & Buds, Marked 1847 .... 35.00
Saucer, Ivy & Red Berries, Gold Ivy Border 30.00
Saucer, Lighthouse Scene, Gold Trim, Eddystone, Germany 55.00
Saucer, Pink Roses, Gold Trim, Scalloped Footing .... 35.00 To 38.00
Saucer, Shell Fluted, Weimar Mark, Large 45.00
Think Of Me, Signed, Germany 25.00

*MZ Austria is a mark used by Moritz Zdekauer from about 1900. The
firm worked in the town of Alt-Rohlau, Austria.*

MZ AUSTRIA, Berry Bowl, Hand-Painted, Hapsburg China, Marked, 5 In., Set Of 6 .... 72.00
Bowl, Gold & Maroon Rim, 3 Size Roses, 10 1/2 In. 42.00
Bowl, Vegetable, Pink Florals, Foliate Finial, Handled, 10 X 4 In. 40.00
Chocolate Pot, Roses, 6-Sided 57.50
Chocolate Pot, White, Green, Pink, & White Flowers, Marked 175.00
Chocolate Set, White, Green, Floral, Gold Trim, Marked, 5 Piece 155.00
Cup & Saucer, Hand-Painted, Floral, Scalloped Saucer 16.00
Cup & Saucer, Witch On Broomstick, Witchcraft Symbols 25.00
Hair Receiver, Flora 22.00
Plate, Bird Of Paradise Scene, Gold Edge, Green, 7 1/2 In. 40.00

*Nailsea glass was made in the Bristol district in England from 1788 to
1873. Many pieces were made with loopings of colored glass as decorations.*

NAILSEA, Flask, Red On White Opaque, 6 1/4 In. 125.00
Flask, South Jersey 550.00
Lamp, Fairy, Clarke Base, Citron 195.00
Rolling Pin, Pink & White Looping 165.00
Vase, Clear Handles, Footed, 11 In., Pair 145.00

NAKARA

*Nakara is a trade name for a white glassware made around 1900 that was
decorated in pastel colors. It was made by the C.F. Monroe Company
of Meriden, Connecticut.*

NAKARA, Box, Bishop's Hat Shape, Hand-Painted Flowers, Apricot Ground, 6 In. 450.00

Box, Bishop's Hat Shape, Mirror In Cover, Enameled, Signed, 4 1/2 In.	285.00
Box, Dresser, Blue, Pink Clover Blossoms, Square, Ormolu Rim	135.00
Box, Dresser, Pink Clover Blossoms, Ormolu Rim, Open	135.00
Box, Green, Beige, Pink Florals, White Beading, 4 In.	385.00
Box, Hinged, Peach, Babies At Play, Signed, 4 In.	350.00
Box, Jewel, Enameled Flowers, Inisde Mirror, Signed, 4 In.Square	385.00
Box, Jewel, Floral, Brass Rim, 4 Footed, 5 1/2 X 3 1/2 In.	410.00
Box, Orchid Enameled Flowers, Hinged Cover, Signed	325.00
Box, Pink Enameled Flowers, 6-Sided, Blue Ground	295.00
Box, Salmon Trim, Pink Floral, Brass Ormolu, Hinged, 6 In.Diam.	195.00
Box, White & Brown Flowers, Lined, Signed, 6 In.Diam.	675.00
Jar, Rose Ground, Jeweled, Portrait Of Angles, 6 In.	565.00
Paperweight, Fleur-De-Lis, Gold Knob Handle, Octagonal	195.00
Tray, Pin, Ormolu Handles, Raised Dot Enamels, Florals, Blue Ground	175.00

Nanking china is a blue-and-white porcelain made in China for export during the eighteenth century.

NANKING, Dish, Continuous Spears & Posts, Blue & White, Oval, 7 In.	125.00
Tureen, Undertray	900.00

Napkin rings were popular from 1869 to about 1900. They were made of silver, porcelain, wood, and other materials. They are still being made today.

NAPKIN RING, Celluloid, Buster Brown's Tige	35.00
Century Of Progress, Sterling Silver	25.00
Cloisonne	25.00
Cloisonne, Two Dragons, Brass	35.00
Corset Waisted, Floral & Vining, Initialed	12.50
Embossed Band Of Childhood Designs, Gorham, 1 3/4 In.	250.00
Embossed Leaf Design, 2 Elves, Dog, & Dragon, Brass, 1 1/8 In.	15.00
Enameled, St.Louis 1904	38.00
Engraved Addie, Bird In Flight, C.1880, 1 1/8 In.	14.50
Engraved Floral Bouquets, Victorian, 1 1/2 In.	10.00
Figural, Angel, Head Down	129.00
Figural, Angels, Standing, Hold Ring, Silver Plated	95.00
Figural, Bear, Pushes Ring, With Bee, Palm Leaf Base	135.00
Figural, Bird & Bud Vase	150.00
Figural, Bird On Rectangular Base	85.00
Figural, Bird, Filigreed Base, Silver Plated ....*Illus*	70.00
Figural, Bird, Long Tail, Pearched On Stem, Leaf Base	85.00
Figural, Bird, Raised Wings, Nest With Eggs, Silver Plated	150.00
Figural, Boy On Horse, Kate Greenaway	195.00
Figural, Boy On Top Of Lacy Ring	85.00
Figural, Boy Painting Picture, Kate Greenaway	195.00
Figural, Boy Playing With Dog, Kate Greenaway	325.00
Figural, Boy Plays With Dog, Front Of Ring, Silver Plated	235.00
Figural, Boy With Cookie, Dog Begging, Kate Greenaway	155.00
Figural, Boy With Drumstick, Marked Pairpoint	189.00
Figural, Boy With Palette, Rectangular Base, Silver Plated	195.00
Figural, Boy With Schoolbook Under Arm, Marked Tufts	225.00
Figural, Bud, Simpson Hall Miller, Silver Plated ....*Illus*	80.00
Figural, Bulldog, Running, Ring On Back	85.00
Figural, Bulldog, Siting Next To Ring	225.00
Figural, Bust Of Child, Bud Vase, Sterling Silver	350.00
Figural, Butterflies, Hold Ring On Fan, Rogers Bros.	65.00
Figural, Butterfly & Reed Design, Sterling Silver, Anchor Mark	50.00
Figural, Cat Pulling Wheeled Car, Victorian, Silver Plated	250.00
Figural, Cherub Kneeling, Holds Vase On Head, Meriden	125.00
Figural, Cherub, Reed & Barton, Silver Plated ....*Illus*	140.00
Figural, Cherubs Sit On Dolphin With Paddle, Silver Plated	225.00
Figural, Cherubs Support Ring, Footed, Webster	85.00
Figural, Cherubs With Barrel On Shoulder	100.00
Figural, Cherubs, Simpson Hall Miller, Marked	33.50

Napkin Rings

Figural, Bird, Filigreed Base, Silver Plated

Figural, Bud, Simpson Hall Miller, Silver Plated

Figural, Cherub, Reed & Barton, Silver Plated

Figural, Greenaway, Rogers &
Smith, Silver Plated

Figural, Cherubs, Winged, Hold Ring, Oval Base, Meriden	115.00
Figural, Chick On Wishbone, Silver Plated, Derby, Birmingham, Ct.	68.00
Figural, Child, Astride Ring, Pedestal Base, Rogers Bros.	75.00
Figural, Chow Dog, Crawling Lizard	75.00
Figural, Clown, Standing	225.00
Figural, Cockatoos, Holding Ring, Footed Base, Pairpoint	150.00
Figural, Cow, Crouches Against Ring	225.00
Figural, Dog, Simpson Hall Miller	150.00
Figural, Eagle Each Side Of Ring, Silver Plated	75.00 To 115.00
Figural, Eagle, Spread Wings Each Side, Meriden Co.	45.00
Figural, Eagles, Spread Wings, Silver Plated, Roger Smith & Co.	55.00
Figural, Egyptian Figures Hold Ring, Vase Top, Silver Plated	125.00
Figural, Floral, Embossed Silver Plate, Middleton, Engraved	40.00
Figural, Fox Pulling A Cart With Ring, Wheels Revolve	199.00
Figural, Giraffe, Base	225.00
Figural, Girl, Pigtails Pushing Ring, William Rogers	125.00
Figural, Greenaway, Rogers & Smith, Silver Plated	*Illus* 55.00
Figural, Kewpie	95.00 To 125.00
Figural, Kitten Pulling Cart, Wheels Revolve	179.00
Figural, Knight, Babcock & Co., Silver Plated	*Illus* 35.00
Figural, Lily Pad Base, Flowers Vine, Silver Plated	75.00
Figural, Lily Pad With Frog & Fly, Silver Plated	135.00

NAPKIN RINGS

Figural, Open Salt,
Rogers Smith, Silver Plated

Figural, Knight, Babcock & Co.,
Silver Plated   *(See Page 399)*

Figural, Rabbits, Pairpoint Co.,
Silver Plated

Figural, Salt & Pepper, Derby
Silver, Silver Plated

Figural, Lion, Pulling Cart, Wheels Move	197.00
Figural, Oak Leaves & Branches Hold Barrel	60.00
Figural, Open Salt, Rogers Smith, Silver Plated .... *Illus*	55.00
Figural, Owls, 2 On Branch, 1 On Base	165.00
Figural, Parrot On Rectangle, Rogers Mfg. Co., No.284	45.00
Figural, Peacock, Strutting, Pedestal Base, Meriden	75.00
Figural, Rabbits, Pair	180.00
Figural, Rabbits, Pairpoint Co., Silver Plated .... *Illus*	105.00
Figural, Robin, On Limb & Branches	85.00
Figural, Salt & Pepper, Derby Silver, Silver Plated ....:	102.00
Figural, Salt & Pepper, Meriden Co., Silver Plated .... *Illus*	180.00
Figural, Scotty, Sterling Silver	32.00
Figural, Sphinx	165.00
Figural, Squirrel Eating Nut, Barbour Silver Co.	65.00

Ott & Brewer Tray, Shell-Shaped, Marked Belleek, C. 1890, 16 In.

Opalescent Glass Sugar, Double-Headed Eagles, C. 1830, Attributed To Providence Flint, 5½ In.

Silver Punch Bowl, Ball, Black & Co., New York, C. 1865, 12⅛ In.

Renaissance Revival Rosewood Cabinet, Thomas Godey, C. 1870, 48 In.

Side Chair, Sugar Maple,
Leather Upholstery, G.
Niardot, C. 1900, 36½ In.
(Top left)

Side Chair, Mahogany,
American, C. 1885, 38¾ In.
(Top right)

Center Table, Wicker,
Wakefield Reed Chair Co.,
C. 1880, 25 In.

Rosewood Cabinet, Mother-
of-Pearl, Brass, Copper &
Pewter, Herts Brothers,
C. 1885, 59½ In.

Side Chair, Maple, Mother-of-
Pearl Inlay, Herter Brothers,
C. 1881, 34½ In.

Side Chair, Gothic Revival, Oak,
American, C. 1857, 39 In.

Cabinet, Arts & Crafts, Ebonized Cherry,
Painted Panels, Art Worker's Guild,
1882, 52 In.

Silver Tea Set, Edward Lownes, Philadelphia, C. 1830, 4 Piece

Goblet and Silver Pitcher, Zalmon Bostwick, New York, C. 1845, Goblet: 7⅞ In., Pitcher: 11 In.

Silver Ewer, Classical Scenes, Bigelow Bros. & Kennard, Boston, Massachusetts, C. 1860, 14⅜ In.

Silver Tankard, Leaves & Berries, Gorham, C. 1900, 17 In.

Ottoman, Rosewood, Leather, Herter Brothers, C. 1882, 16½ In.

Mantel Clock, Bronze, Ceramic Tile, Marked J. & J. G. Low,
C. 1884, 12¼ In.

Figural, Squirrel On Leaf 95.00
Figural, Two Turtles, Ring On Back, Silver Plated 100.00
Floral & Bows, Herringbone Engraving 18.50
Floral, Engraved, Victorian, 1 5/8 In. 12.50
Ivory, Carved, Set Of 4 .... 75.00
Louisiana Purchase 15.00
Noritake, Man, Art Deco 40.00
Noritake, Woman, Art Deco 40.00
Open Florals & Olive In Script, 1 1/2 In. 15.00
Openwork Flowers On Oval Base, Ring Above 65.00
Petunia & Leafings, Engraved, Initialed H 12.50
Ribbed Edges, Plain Center, Silver Plated 9.00
Serrated Engravings, 1 1/8 In. 7.50
St.Louis World's Fair, 1904, Sterling Silver 19.50
Watchband Engraving, Plaque Open 10.00
Wooden, Transfer Of Summit Of Mt.Washington, N.H., C.1880 .... 15.00

*Nash glass was made in Corona, New York, by Arthur Nash and his sons
after 1919. He worked at the Webb factory in England and for the
Tiffany Glassworks in the United States.*

NASH, Candleholder, Vertical Green & Blue Stripes, 4 X 3 1/2 In. 75.00
Candy Dish, Amber, Footed, Marked, 4 In. 150.00
Pitcher, Cream, Green Matte, 4 In. 10.00
Vase, Chintz Pattern, Blue & Red, Bulbous, 9 In. 225.00
Vase, Chintz Pattern, Blue, Lime, Footed, Signed, 12 X 8 In. 375.00
Vase, Chintz Pattern, Marked, 6 In. 375.00
Vase, Chintz Pattern, Pedestal Foot, Signed, Aquamarine, 6 In.Diam. 375.00
Vase, Ribbed Lower Portion, Scalloped Top, Signed, Purple, 4 In. 185.00
Vase, Signed, Gold Iridescent, 5 In. 325.00

NAUTICAL, see also Scrimshaw
NAUTICAL, Ashtray, Costa Line, Metal 3.00
Ashtray, France Ocean Liner, Cobalt Blue 7.00
Ashtray, Holland America, China 8.00
Ashtray, Ship's Smokestack, North German Lloyd, 1970, Marked SPM 20.00
Ashtray, U.S. Line, Glass 8.00
Azimuth Circle, Boxed, Brass With Oak Case 35.00
Bell, Cast Iron Clapper, Brass, 5 X 5 1/4 In. 40.00
Bell, Ship's, Hanger Bracket, Brass, C.1870, 5 3/4 X 10 In. 135.00
Binnacle, Canister Case, Brass Chain, W.M.Welsh Mfg. Co. 110.00
Blinker, S.O.S. Blinker, Battleship Missouri 125.00
Boat, Tug, Ella M., Nautical, 2 In. 90.00
Bumper, Fender, Rope Construction, Steel Eyehook, 24 X 8 In. 15.00
Butter Chip, Clipper Line 6.00
Certificate, Lifejacket Instructions, 13 X 9 In. 10.00
Chronometer, Mahogany Box, John Bliss & Co., 1889, 7 X 7 In. 1045.00
Chronometer, Model 21, 3-Part Mahogany Box 1400.00
Chronometer, Model 22, 3-Part Mahogany Box 500.00
Clinometer, U.S.Navy, Bakelite Frame, Brass Pendulum, 1942, Mod.O 50.00
Coffeepot, Colombian Line 24.00
Coffeepot, N.Y. & C.M. Steamship Co. 48.00
Compass, Boxed, Brass, 8 In. 275.00
Compass, Gimbal, Liquid Filled 50.00
Compass, Gimbal, Wooden Box 25.00
Compass, Inscribed Dent Inventor, London, Wooden Box, Set Of 3 .... 880.00
Compass, Wall Bracket, Carrying Handle, World War I, Side Oil Lamp 225.00
Cover, Binnacle 95.00
Distance Meter, Felt-Lined Case, Signed, Patented, No.709, Marked 65.00
Dividers, Sailmaker's, Chamfered Legs, Brass Trim, C.1870, 18 In. 50.00
Drag Anchor, Cast Iron, 24 In. 12.50
Figurehead, Ship's, Bust Length, Woman Wearing Tiara, 28 In. 1100.00
Figurehead, The Captain's Wife, Green Dress, Flowing Shawl 990.00
Float, Glass, Rope Cover, Japanese Fishing Style, Round, 12 In. 20.00
Foghorn, Rotary, Bellows, Norwegian, C.1850, 14 1/2 X 8 In. 295.00

Fork, North German Lloyd 5.00
Gauge, For Henry Worthington Steamer, Pair 100.00
Gauge, Pressure, Amoskeag 420.00
Hatch Cover, Wooden, Steel Strapping, 30 X 29 In. 40.00
Knife, Dinner, Furness 8.00
Lamp, Mast, Galvanized & Brass, Kerosene, 4 1/2 X 5 X 11 1/2 In. 55.00
Lantern, Masthead, Clear Fresnel Lens 125.00
Lantern, Oil, Starboard & Port, Waffled Lens, Brass, 10 1/2 In., Pair 285.00
Lens, Enterprise, Fasteners, Brass 30.00
Life Ring, With Roping, Olympic Brook, Monrovia, Marked, 29 In. 30.00
Light, Man Overboard, Marked, Self-Igniting, Battery, 26 X 4 In. 30.00
Log, Ship's, Harpoon, C.1866, Brass, Walker & Sons, 19 In. 150.00
Model, Rigged Sloop Of War, Cannons, Case, 23 In.Long .... *Illus* 908.00
Model, Sailboat, Steel Rudder & Mast, Stand, 51 In. 125.00
Model, U.S.S.Constitution, C.1850, Rigged, 33 In. .... *Illus* 1210.00
Model, U.S.S.Mt.Vernon, Transport, 1906, Case, 50 In. .... *Illus* 1980.00
Model, Whaling Ship, C.1870 .... 395.00
Model, 3-Masted, Rigged Bark, U.S.Flag, Case, 32 In. .... *Illus* 605.00
Net, Cargo, All Rope Construction, 8 Ft.Square 30.00
Sailing Ship, Late 19th Century, Shadowbox, 33 X 22 In. 950.00
Sextant, Hezzanith, British, 1960s 650.00
Sign, Porcelain, Enamel, Drinking Water, Blue & White, 10 X 6 In. 5.00
Sign, Porcelain, Enamel, Red & White, No Smoking, 20 X 15 In. 12.00
Station Bill, Framed, Great Lakes Oil Tanker, Signed, 20 X 15 In. 12.00
Steam Gauge, Brass Instrument, Nickel Plate, Mahogany Case, Marked 125.00
Steam Gauge, Mahogany, Brass, Nickel Plate, Boxed, 1899, 9 X 7 X 5 In. 130.00
Taffrail Lug, 3 Porcelain Dial Meters, Brass, Marked E.Masseys 350.00
Tambourine, Italian Lines 6.00
Tea Set, Cunard Line, China, White, Gold 75.00
Telescope, Leather Bound, Brass, Extends To 16 1/2 In. 65.00
Telescope, One Draw, Brass With Leather Grip & Trim, 24 In. 175.00
Thermometer, Globe Shape, Green-Amber, Brass Fittings, S.S.Oceanic 25.00
Toothpick, Swedish-American 10.00
Wheel, Ship's, Wooden Spoke, Iron Hub, 60 In. Overall 400.00
Whistle, Brass, 5 In. 25.00

Nautical, Model, Rigged Sloop Of
War, Cannons, Case, 23 In.Long

Nautical, Model, U.S.S.Mt.Vernon,
Transport, 1906, Case, 50 In.

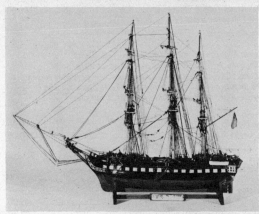

Nautical, Model, U.S.S.Constitution,
C.1850, Rigged, 33 In.

Nautical, Model, 3-Masted, Rigged
Bark, U.S.Flag, Case, 32 In.

NEEDLEWORK, see Textile, Picture; Textile, Sampler

Netsuke are small ivory, wood, metal, or porcelain pieces used as the button on the end of a cord holding a Japanese money pouch. The earliest date from the sixteenth century.

NETSUKE, Boxwood, Mushroom, Small Mushroom Extending To One Side	80.00
Ivory, Dragon, Coiled Tail, Signed, 2 In.	50.00
Ivory, Figure Supporting Large Bag Over Shoulders, Balancing	70.00
Ivory, Hannya, Woman Dressed Noh Costume, 20th Century, 2 5/8 In.	200.00
Ivory, Man Loading Basket On Water Buffalo, 2 In.	38.00
Ivory, Man Lying Over Crouched Tiger	90.00
Ivory, Man Mounting Horse	37.00
Ivory, Man Resting Across Water Buffalo	90.00
Ivory, Man Sawing Huge Log In Half, 2 In.	36.00
Ivory, Man Wearing Checkered Robe, Holding Tassel	65.00
Ivory, Man With Rats, Signed, 2 In.	1600.00
Ivory, Man Wrestling Pearl From Dragon	90.00
Ivory, Mice Playing In Rice Ball	90.00
Ivory, Monkey Riding Turtle, 2 In.	38.00
Ivory, Monkey, Sitting On Ball	95.00
Ivory, Revolving Face, Man Holds Up Hatchet, Signed, 2 In.	60.00
Ivory, Sage Recumbent On Sack, Triangular, 18th Century	90.00
Ivory, Samurai Carrying Large Bell, Signed	375.00
Ivory, Woman Feeding Kiwi, On Wicker Basket, 2 In.	40.00
Wood, Mask Of Okame, Smiling Face, Protruding Cheeks	145.00
Wood, Monk, Kneeling, Head Supported On Hands, Resting On Hibachi	150.00
Wood, Oni, Seated, Fierce Expression, Arm Resting On Raised Knee	80.00

Wood, Shishi, Paw Resting On Ball, Head Turned Sideways 80.00
Wood, Tiger, Seated, Head Turned Sideways, Inlaid Eyes 95.00
Wood, Woman 85.00

New Hall Porcelain Manufactory was started at Newhall, Shelton,
Staffordshire, England, in 1782. Simple decorated wares were made.
Between 1810 and 1825, the factory made a glassy bone porcelain sometimes
marked with the factory name. Do not confuse New Hall porcelain with
pieces made by the New Hall Pottery Company, Ltd., a twentieth-
century firm.

NEW HALL, Cup & Saucer, Orange Flowers 75.00
Teapot, Chinese Figures, Orange, Green, 8 In. 250.00

The New Martinsville Glass Manufacturing Company was established in
1901 in New Martinsville, West Virginia. It was bought and renamed
the Viking Glass Company in 1944 and is still producing fine glasswares.
NEW MARTINSVILLE, see also Peachblow
NEW MARTINSVILLE, Bookend, Horses, Rearing, 7 1/2 In., Pair 45.00
Bookend, Ship, Pair 45.00
Bookend, Starfish, Pair 70.00
Bottle, Perfume, Black Amethyst Stopper, Art Deco Design 12.00
Bowl, Fluting, Gold, Peachblow, 7 1/2 X 3 1/4 In. 110.00
Bowl, Moondrops, Pedestal, Green, 11 1/4 In.Diam. 22.50
Bowl, Peachblow, C.1901, Pink & White Exterior, 5 X 2 In. 385.00
Bowl, Peachblow, Gold Edge, 7 1/4 X 3 1/4 In. 145.00
Bride's Basket, Peachblow, Sunburst 43.00
Bride's Basket, Peachblow, 4 In.Diam. 155.00
Candleholder, Double, 2 Lower Baskets, Teardrop 12.50
Candlestick, Trindle, Pair 60.00
Console Set, Draped Roses, Crystal, Footed Bowl, Pair 65.00
Console Set, Flower & Wheat, Crystal, 3 Piece 60.00
Dish, Candy, Swan, Cobalt Neck 40.00
Figurine, Angelfish 45.00
Figurine, Baby Bear .... 30.00 To 45.00
Figurine, Dog, Police 75.00
Figurine, Elephant, 3 X 4 In. 38.00
Figurine, Janice, Swan, Ruby Neck, 11 In. 28.00
Figurine, Janice, Swan, 12 In. 52.00
Figurine, Mama Bear & 2 Baby Bears, Set .... 135.00 To 155.00
Figurine, Mama Bear, Clear, 4 1/2 In. 95.00
Figurine, Mother Hen, Crystal 35.00
Figurine, Rooster, Solid, 8 In. 48.50
Figurine, Seals With Ball, Crystal, 6 3/4 X 5 1/4 In., Pair 100.00
Figurine, Squirrel On Base, Pair .... 70.00 To 85.00
Figurine, Swan, Cobalt Blue Head & Neck, 12 In. 52.00
Figurine, Swan, Emerald, Crystal Neck, 7 1/2 In. 18.00
Figurine, Swan, Heart Shaped, Emerald 15.00
Figurine, Swan, Janice, Cobalt Head, 12 In. 52.00
Figurine, Swan, Ritz Blue Head & Neck 40.00
Figurine, Tiger, 8 X 6 1/2 In. 70.00
Figurine, Wolfhound 45.00
Pitcher, Oscar Pattern, 4 Tumblers, Amber 35.00

Newcomb Pottery was founded by Ellsworth and William Woodward at
Sophie Newcomb College, New Orleans, Louisiana, in 1896. The work
continued through the 1940s. Pieces of this art pottery are marked with
the letter N inside the letter C.

NEWCOMB, Bowl, Bulb, Inverted Tulip Top, Signed, 6 In. 375.00
Bowl, Green To Blue, Sticker, 3 X 2 In. 66.00
Bowl, Undecorated, Green & Blue, 3 X 2 In. 55.00
Plate, Crab Design, Teal Blue, Signed S.E.Wells, 9 In. 850.00
Vase, Bud, Geometric Floral, 6 1/2 In. 295.00

Vase, Crosshatching Top, Yellow & Green, Signed, 5 1/2 In. 275.00
Vase, Dark Green, Lavender, Rose, Bulbous, Dimpled, Marked, 4 In. 250.00
Vase, Dimpled, High Gloss, Green, Lavender, & Rose, 4 X 2 3/4 In. 220.00
Vase, Green Drip Glaze Over Red Clay, JM, FR, 7 In. 850.00
Vase, Pansies, Blue, Artist Signed, 4 In. 195.00
Vase, Pushed-In Dimples, Green Over Green, Marked, 4 X 2 3/4 In. 250.00
Vase, Ribbed, Purple, Blue, 3 1/2 In. 70.00
Vase, Snowdrops, Green Stems, Blue Ground, Signed, 6 3/4 In. 650.00
Vase, Spanish Moss, Scenic, Signed S.Irvine, 6 In. 575.00
Vase, White To Green, 3 1/2 In. 110.00

NILOAK

Niloak Pottery (Kaolin spelled backward) was made at the Hyten
Brothers Pottery in Benton, Arkansas, between 1909 and 1946.
Although the factory did make cast and molded wares, collectors
are most interested in the marbleized art pottery line.

NILOAK, Bowl, Red, Cream, Blue, Green, Swirl, 5 In. 22.00
Bowl, Swirl, 2 X 5 In. 40.00
Bowl, Swirl, 3 X 4 In. 40.00
Candlestick, Swirl, 8 1/4 In., Pair 145.00
Jar, Brown Swirl, Covered, Original Label, 4 In. 40.00
Lamp, Swirl, Signed, 21 In. 165.00
Pitcher, Brown Glazed, Paper Label, 4 In. 8.00
Pitcher, Cream, Pink, 5 In. 8.00
Pitcher, Dark Green, 7 In. 10.00
Pitcher, Powder Blue, Square, Flowers, Impressed Mark, 7 In. 18.00
Pitcher, Square Mouth, Molded Florals, Pink 12.50
Pitcher, White, 10 In. 110.00
Planter, Bear, Tan, Brown, 3 In. 15.00
Planter, Camel, Brown, 4 In. 15.00
Planter, Camel, Tan, 3 In. 15.00
Planter, Deer, Glazed, Off White 15.00
Planter, Duck, Pink, Blue, 5 In. 13.00
Planter, Elephant, White, Glazed, 7 In. 16.00
Planter, Fish, Brown, Glazed, 4 X 9 In. 22.00
Planter, Fox, Red, 4 In. 16.00
Planter, Holland Shoe, Pink, 2 1/4 X 5 In. 10.00
Planter, Kangaroo, White, 5 In. 15.00
Planter, Log, Multiholes, White, 7 In. 15.00
Planter, Parrot, Label 22.00
Planter, Parrot, White, 5 In. 16.00
Planter, Pelican, Tan, Brown, 5 In. 16.00
Planter, Policeman & Donkey, Blue, 5 In. 22.00
Planter, Rabbit, Light Green, 3 In. 10.00
Planter, Rabbit, White, 5 In. 15.00
Planter, Seal, Tan, 8 In. 15.00
Planter, Squirrel, Brown Glazed, 6 In. 15.00
Planter, Squirrel, Light Blue, 6 In. 15.00
Planter, Squirrel, White, 7 In. .... 9.00 To 22.00
Planter, Swallow, Green, 2 In. 8.00
Planter, Swallow, Pink, 2 In. 8.00
Planter, Swan, Blue, 8 In. 15.00
Planter, Swan, Light Brown, 3 In. 8.00
Planter, Swan, Pink, 8 In. 14.00
Plate, Swirl, 4 1/2 In. 40.00

Stein, Swirl Design 40.00
Vase, Blue, White, Red, & Brown, Speckled Interior, 4 1/2 In. 40.00
Vase, Bottle Shaped, 9 In. 40.00
Vase, Cornucopia, Light Pink, 3 In. 5.00
Vase, Cornucopia, Plum, 3 1/2 In. 6.50
Vase, Cylinder, Swirl, 8 In. 75.00
Vase, Ewer, Pink, Green, Wing & Star Design, Marked, 10 In. 28.00
Vase, Gloss Pink, 2-Handled, 5 1/2 In. 6.00
Vase, Mission Swirl, Blue, 5 1/4 X 3 3/8 In. 60.00
Vase, Swan, Blue 22.00
Vase, Swirl, Blue, Brown, & Tan, 9 1/2 In. 70.00
Vase, Swirl, Flared Rim, 8 In. 52.00
Vase, Swirl, 4 In. .... 33.00 To 38.00
Vase, Swirl, 4 1/2 In. .... 37.00 To 43.00
Vase, Swirl, 5 In. 40.00
Vase, Swirl, 5 1/4 In. .... 51.00 To 60.00
Vase, Swirl, 5 1/2 In. .... 35.00 To 47.00
Vase, Swirl, 6 In. 50.00
Vase, Swirl, 6 1/2 In. 50.00
Vase, Swirl, 9 1/2 In. 85.00
Vase, Swirl, 9 5/8 In. 110.00
Vase, Swirl, 10 In. 135.00
Vase, 5 Opening, Pink & Green, Signed, 7 1/2 In. 40.00

*Nippon-marked porcelain was made in Japan from 1891 to 1921.
"Nippon" is the Japanese word for "Japan."*

NIPPON, Ashtray, Dogs, Blownout 400.00
  Ashtray, Horsehead In Center 70.00
  Ashtray, House & Tree Scene, Tricornered, Marked 65.00
  Ashtray, Playing Cards, Blue Wreath 100.00
  Ashtray, Sailing Ships, Bisque 50.00
  Ashtray, Scenic, Rising Sun Mark, 3 1/2 In. 45.00
  Ashtray, Skull 145.00
  Ashtray, Swans, Crown Mark 75.00
  Basket, Allover Florals, Gold Rim, Green Wreath, 7 1/4 X 5 In. 45.00
  Basket, Forget-Me-Nots, Leaves, 7 X 5 X 3 1/2 In. 35.00
  Berry Set, Black Scenic, Gold Outlining, 6 Dishes 50.00
  Berry Set, Blue, Rose Design, 7 Piece 54.00
  Berry Set, Green & Red Floral, Blue Ground, Outline Gold 250.00
  Berry Set, Pink & Blue Flowers, White Beaded Center, Gold Trim 75.00
  Berry Set, Silhouette Pattern, Marked 125.00
  Berry Set, Swans, 7 Piece 175.00
  Bonbon, Pink Roses, Gold Trim, Handled 23.00
  Bottle, Cologne, Roses, Allover Gold, Blue Mark 65.00
  Bowl, Art Deco, 8-Sided, Handled, 7 3/4 In. 45.00
  Bowl, Basket Of Anemones, Handled, Green Wreath Mark, 11 1/4 In. .. 80.00
  Bowl, Beaded & Jeweled Rim, Florals, 4 Gold Feet, 7 1/2 X 5 1/2 In. .. 125.00
  Bowl, Blown-Out Acorns, Leaves, Footed, Brown & Green, 7 1/2 In. .. 125.00
  Bowl, Blown-Out Chestnuts, Jeweled Feet, Green Wreath Mark, 7 1/2 In. .. 120.00
  Bowl, Blue Painting Of Nile & Warship, Marked, 7 In. 65.00
  Bowl, Cherry Blossom Design, Pedestal, 9 In. 115.00
  Bowl, Cobalt & Gold Border, Handled, 10 In. 28.00
  Bowl, Floral, Gold Trim, Handled, 10 In. 47.50
  Bowl, Flowers, Raised Beading On Edge, Green Wreath Mark, 6 1/4 In. .. 35.00
  Bowl, Grape, Bluebirds & Blossoms, 7 In. 65.00
  Bowl, Green & Gold Border, Dainty Pink Flowers, 10 In. 75.00
  Bowl, Green & White, 3-Leaf Clover, Gold Beading, Marked, 7 In. 25.00
  Bowl, Green Ground, Blue Border, Pink Florals, 10 In. 135.00
  Bowl, Ice Cream, Scalloped, Roses, Gold Trim, Purple Mark, 5 1/2 In.Sq. .. 12.50
  Bowl, Marine Scene, Beading, Marked, 6 In. 70.00
  Bowl, Moriage, Pink Floral In & Out, Marked, 6 In. 60.00
  Bowl, Moriage, Rolled-In Top, Bisque Green Ground, 7 In. 75.00

Bowl, Pheasant Scene, Marked, 10 In.	45.00
Bowl, Pink & White Flowers, Handled, Marked, 8 1/2 In.	44.00
Bowl, Pink Flowers, Cobalt Blue Border, 9 In.	45.00
Bowl, Red & Pink Roses Interior, Gold Trim, Footed, Marked, 6 1/2 In.	65.00
Bowl, Red Roses, Green Leaves, Medallions, Gold Beading, 6 In.	95.00
Bowl, Red, Yellow Mums, Gold Trim, Oblong, 14 In.	165.00 To 450.00
Bowl, Scenic, Tree, Lake, House, Footed, 6 1/4 In.	45.00
Bowl, Scenic, Tree, Lake, House, Jeweled Handles, 7 1/4 In.	48.00
Bowl, Scenic, Water, Trees, Farm, Geometric Band, 9 In.	75.00
Bowl, Scenic, 3 Boats, Whitecapped Sea, Gold Handles, 10 1/2 In.	65.00
Bowl, Square, Pierced Handles, Hand-Painted, Green Wreath, M, 8 In.	95.00
Bowl, Trees With Cherry Bossoms, Lake, House, Handled, 6 In.	70.00
Bowl, Violets, Medallions, Gold Beading, Marked, 10 In.	115.00
Bowl, Violets, 3-Footed, 4 1/2 In.	25.00
Bowl, Walnut, Acorn, Peanut, & Leaves, 10 In.	85.00
Bowl, 3 Applied Peanuts, Jeweling, Tracing, Handled, 8 In.	115.00
Bowl, 3 Applied Walnuts Inside, Jeweling, Handled, 8 1/4 In.	125.00
Bowl, 8 Sided, Scene Of Capitol Building, Gold Trim, 7 In.	75.00
Box, Powder, Roses, Allover Gold Beads, 5 1/2 In.	150.00
Box, Trinket, Airplane, Triangular, Signed, Green M., 3 1/4 X 3 1/4 In.	145.00
Butter Chip, Seascape, Green Beaded Rim, Set Of 3	35.00
Butter, Scenic, Brown, Yellow, Green	88.00
Butter, White, Gold Band, Crown Mark	45.00
Cake Plate, Blue & Yellow Butterflies, Beige, 10 In.	55.00
Cake Plate, Bust Of Countess Potocka, Marked, 9 1/2 In.	125.00
Cake Plate, Desert Scene, Egyptian Symbols, Marked, 10 In.	229.00
Cake Plate, Floral Medallions, Gold Trim, 10 1/2 In.	45.00
Cake Plate, Gold Design On White, Open-Handled, 11 In.	38.00
Cake Plate, Scenic, Bridge, Stream, Jeweled, Satin Finish, 11 In.	125.00
Cake Plate, Scenic, Stick, Gold Trim, Jewel Stones, 8 In.	125.00
Cake Plate, Scenic, Trees, Boat, House, Gold Border, 10 1/2 In.	125.00
Cake Plate, 4 Scenic Medallions, Gold Design, Jeweled, 9 In.	115.00
Cake Set, Black Border, Orange Florals, Gold Beading, 7 Piece	110.00
Cake Set, Butterflies, Pink Band, Gold Trim, 7 Piece	110.00
Cake Set, Moriage, 7 Piece	80.00
Cake Set, Pink & Red Roses, Gold Beading, 7 Piece	125.00
Cake Set, Pink Band, Butterflies , Gold Trim, 7 Piece	110.00
Cake Set, Roses, 10 In. Platter, 6 Plates, 6 1/2 In.	35.00
Cake Set, White Heron, Powder Blue, 1 Large Plate, 6 Small	37.50
Candlestick, Wedgwood, Lavender, Pair	495.00
Candlestick, White & Cream Ground, Magenta & Green Bands, 5 In., Pr.	115.00
Candy, Landscape, Water, Ship, Open-Handled, 7 X 5 In.	50.00
Celery Set, Brown, Yellow Roses, Green Leaves, Gold Handles, 7 Piece	75.00
Celery Set, Pink Roses, Green Leaves, Gold Trim, 7 Piece	50.00
Celery Set, Rising Sun Mark, 7 Piece	39.00
Celery, Butterfly & Bird In Tree, M In Wreath, 8 1/2 In.	35.00
Celery, Gold Beading & Outline, Crown Mark, 12 1/4 In.	33.00
Celery, Roses, Gold Diamond Edge, Rising Sun Mark, 11 1/2 In.	32.00
Charger, Cobalt, Large Red & Pink Roses, Gold Trim, 13 In.	225.00
Charger, Cobalt, Red & Pink Roses, Gold Beading, 13 In.	225.00
Charger, Hand-Painted, Flower Panels, Gold Trim, 13 1/2 In.	185.00
Chocolate Cup & Saucer, Pink Flowers, White Ground, Red Mark	35.00
Chocolate Pot, Cobalt, Floral, Gold Beading, Roses, 9 1/2 In.	275.00
Chocolate Pot, Cobalt, Roses In Medallion, Gold Trim, Beading, 9 In.	150.00
Chocolate Pot, Cobalt, Roses In Medallion, Gold Trim, 9 1/4 In.	150.00
Chocolate Pot, Cobalt, Roses, Gold Beading, 9 1/2 In.	275.00
Chocolate Pot, Gaudy, Souvenir, Washington, D.C., Roses, Gold Trim	215.00
Chocolate Pot, Multicolored, Moriage, 7 3/4 In.	179.00
Chocolate Pot, Roses, Gaudy Cobalt, Gold Trim, 11 In.	145.00
Chocolate Pot, Scenic, Geishas, Blue Pagoda Mark, 10 In.	110.00
Chocolate Pot, Scroll Handle, Green Mark In Wreath, 10 In.	55.00
Chocolate Set, Cottage & Lake, Gold Rims, 6 Piece	375.00
Chocolate Set, Cottage Scene, 6 Piece	200.00
Chocolate Set, Flowers, Raised Jewels, Green Wreath Mark, 13 Piece	400.00

Chocolate Set, Gold Beading, Paneld Roses, Maple Leaf, 9 Piece 165.00
Chocolate Set, Gold Overlay & Beading, Spoke Wheel Mark, 9 Piece 195.00
Chocolate Set, Gold, Cobalt Blue, & Italian Blue, Green Wreath, 13 Pc. 280.00
Chocolate Set, Hand-Painted, Rose Design, Maple Leaf Mark, 10 Piece 225.00
Chocolate Set, Melon, Raised Gold Florals, Green Wreath Mark, 9 Piece 135.00
Chocolate Set, Orange Flowers, Pouring Guard, Marked, 9 Piece 135.00
Chocolate Set, Pink Flowers, Gold Beading, White, 7 Piece 150.00
Chocolate Set, Pink Rose Design, Green Wreath Mark, 9 Piece 135.00
Chocolate Set, River Scene, Yellow Ground, Marked, 7 Piece 295.00
Chocolate Set, Scenic, Gold Trim, 6 Cups 175.00
Chocolate Set, Seashore, Houses, Girl In Boat, 13 Piece 300.00
Chocolate Set, Violet Design, 6 Cups & Saucers 175.00
Chocolate Set, Violets, Gold Trim, Marked, 7 Piece 135.00
Chocolate Set, White Ground, Raised Gold Border, Marked, 5 Cups 169.00
Chocolate Set, White Ground, Raised Gold Flowers, Marked, 7 Piece 139.00
Chocolate Set, White, Raised Gold Floral, 4 Cups & Saucers, Marked 140.00
Chocolate Set, White, Roses, Rising Sun, 6 Piece 80.00
Chocolate Set, Woodland, 4 Cups & Saucers, Green Mark 450.00
Chocolate Set, Yellow Bands, Gold Floral, Leaves, 5 Piece 135.00
Cider Set, Grapes & Leaves, Pitcher, 5 1/2 In., 7 Piece 125.00
Coffeepot, Floral, Gold Trim, White Ground, 6 In. 65.00
Coffeepot, Floral, Gold Trim, White Ground, 9 In. 65.00
Coffeepot, Medallion Of Flowers, Gold On Yellow Ground, 8 In. 165.00
Compote, English Riding Scene, Marked 110.00
Compote, Floral Design, White Ground, Gold Rim, Green M Mark 30.00
Compote, Floral Panels, Black, Gold, White, 9 In. 45.00
Compote, Forest Scene, Gold Scrolls & Handles, Marked, 9 1/2 X 3 In. 130.00
Compote, Scenic, Pedestal, Gold Handles, Green Mark, 9 1/2 In.Diam. 75.00
Compote, Woodland Scene, No.769, 6 1/2 X 3 1/2 In. 155.00
Compote, Woodland Scene, 6 X 2 3/4 In. 165.00
Condiment Set, Bluebirds, Gold & White, Green Mark, 6 Piece 65.00
Condiment Set, Scenic, Round Tray, 5 Piece 125.00
Condiment Set, 4-Section, Center Well, Rose Swags, Maple Leaf Mark 45.00
Cookie Jar, Cobalt, Floral, Pink & Yellow Flowers, 7 In. 295.00
Cookie Jar, Dragon Pattern 135.00
Cookie Jar, Egyptian Gods 250.00
Cookie Jar, Floral, Gold Beading, 8 In. 125.00
Cookie Jar, Gold Beading, Flowers, 7 1/2 In. 275.00
Cookie Jar, Roses, Cream, White, & Cobalt Blue, Gold Trim 38.50
Cookie Jar, Underplate, Melon Rib, Beaded Tassels, Gold Trim 150.00
Corn Set, Open-Handled, Tray, 6 Corn Servers, Marked 350.00
Corn Set, Yellow & Brown, Master & 6 Plates, Marked 175.00
Cracker & Cheese, White Ground, Gold Scrolled Border, 9 In. 50.00
Cracker Jar, Cow Scene, Gold Beading, Blue Mark 225.00
Cracker Jar, Floral, Design In Gold, Matte Finish, 5 In. 275.00
Cracker Jar, Footed, Melon Ribbed, Celadon, Beading On Bottom, Covered 110.00
Cracker Jar, Gaudy Roses, Yellow Ground, 3-Handled, Marked 185.00
Cracker Jar, Geometric Design, Gold Trim, Marked 125.00
Cracker Jar, Light Green, Gold Beading, Maple Leaf Mark, 9 1/2 In. 159.00
Cracker Jar, Melon Shape, Cobalt, Gold Roses, 8 In. 235.00
Cracker Jar, Red & Pink Roses, Chartreuse & Yellow Ground, Marked 185.00
Cracker Jar, Ribbed, Raised Gold, Roses, Footed, 8 In. 125.00
Cracker Jar, White Ground, Floral, Footed, 7 In. 75.00
Creamer, Palm Trees, Sand, Sailboat Design 18.00
Creamer, Pink Flowers, Marked 17.00
Creamer, Seascape, Green Beaded Rim 15.00
Cruet, Seascape, Green Beaded Rim 85.00
Cup & Saucer, Cottage Scene 50.00
Cup & Saucer, Lilac Blossoms, Leaves, Hand-Painted, Green Mark 12.00
Cup & Saucer, Multifloral, Hand-Painted, Italian Green, Green Mark 14.00
Cup & Saucer, Mustache, Floral & Geometric, Rising Sun 60.00
Cup & Saucer, Nishiki Pattern, Green Mark 12.00
Cup & Saucer, Sailboat & Sunset, Beaded Trim, 6 Sets 150.00
Cup & Saucer, Scene, Gold Design, Medallion 20.00

Cup, Blue Floral, Gold Trim, Marked	3.00
Demitasse Set, Gold Dragon Decorated	275.00
Dish, Basket, Gold, Orange Floral, White Ground, Marked, 8 In.	62.00
Dish, Beaded, Gold Rose Medallion, White Ground, 5 In.	10.00
Dish, Berry, Roses, Green Rim, Scalloped, 5 In.	15.00
Dish, Black Bisque With Gold Overlay, Marked, 6 In.Square	110.00
Dish, Butterfly & Flowers, Footed, Marked, 6 1/2 In.	75.00
Dish, Cheese, Slant Top, Floral & Leaf Pattern, Rising Sun Mark	58.00
Dish, Cheese, Sloping, Pink Flowers & Leaves, Gold Trim, 7 1/2 X 5 In.	65.00
Dish, Club Shape, Desert Scene, Handled, Green Wreath Mark, 6 1/4 In.	32.00
Dish, Cottage Scene, Square, Mark, 7 In.	60.00
Dish, Cracker, 2 Tier	65.00
Dish, Floral, Oval, Gaudy, 9 1/4 In.	43.00
Dish, Gold Design, Floral, Green Wreath, Square, 7 1/4 In.	50.00
Dish, Indian Design, Handled, Oblong, Green Wreath, 8 X 3 3/4 In.	85.00
Dish, Olive, Boat Shape, Gold Flower On Outside Rim, Handles, Marked	36.00
Dish, Oval, Woodland Scene, 7 1/2 X 5 1/4 In.	135.00
Dish, Palm Tree, Open-Handled, Marked, 8 X 3 1/2 In.	85.00
Dish, Scenic, Fall Colors, Scrolled Edge, Oval, 8 In.	30.00
Dresser Box & Hair Receiver, Square, Footed	70.00
Dresser Set, Blue Forget-Me-Nots, Gold Trim, Marked, 3 Piece	75.00
Dresser Set, Floral Design, White, 4 Piece	55.00
Dresser Set, Gold & White, 4 Piece	100.00
Dresser Set, Pink Roses, Gold Trim, 5 Piece	175.00
Eggcup, Child's, Doll Face, Marked	65.00
Ewer, Cobalt Blue & Gold, Floral Trim, 10 1/2 In.	145.00
Ewer, Gaudy, Cobalt Blue, Gold Trim, 8 In.	195.00
Ewer, Green, Pink & Red Roses, Gold, Beading, Overlay, Marked, 7 In.	175.00
Ewer, Pale Green, Cherry Design, Green Mark, 7 In.	85.00
Ewer, Pink & Red Roses, Green Ground, Beading, 7 In.	175.00
Ewer, Red & Pink Roses, Green Leaves, Green Ground, 12 1/2 In.	250.00
Ewer, Red Roses, 8 In.	65.00
Ewer, Woman, Child Scene, Animal Footed, Moriage Trim, 7 1/4 In.	315.00
Fernery, Beaded Border, Floral Design, Green Wreath Mark, 10 In.	140.00
Fernery, Cobalt & Floral, Gaudy, 5 X 4 In.	125.00
Fernery, Etched Roses & Leaves, Gold Trim, Matte Brown, 7 1/2 In.	185.00
Fernery, Floral Design, Marigold, Cosmos Flowers, Marked, 10 In.	140.00
Fernery, Gold Feet, Gold Scalloped Rim, M In Wreath, 8 1/4 X 4 In.	179.00
Fernery, Gold Flowers & Beading, Marked, 5 1/2 X 3 1/2 In.	45.00
Fernery, Landscape On Sides, Enameled Jeweling, M In Wreath, 7 In.	135.00
Fernery, Large Roses, Lake, Trees, Satin Finish, 7 In.	98.00
Fernery, Moriage, Green, Red, Gooney Bird, 7 In.	160.00
Fernery, Pastel Roses, Gold Rim & Handles, Footed, 7 X 11 In.	165.00
Fernery, Roses On White, Cobalt Blue	150.00
Fernery, Roses, Lake, Trees, Satin Finish, 3 1/2 In.	96.00
Hair Receiver & Powder Box, Footed, Red, Green, Floral, 7 Mark	50.00
Hair Receiver, Allover Gold Beading, Roses	75.00
Hair Receiver, Allover Gold, Blue Mark	45.00
Hair Receiver, Blue Forget-Me-Nots, Gold Trim, Marked	75.00
Hair Receiver, Gold Herons, Pink Ground	38.00
Hair Receiver, Hand-Painted, Raised Gold, 3-Footed	48.00
Hair Receiver, Hunt Scene, Moriage Trim, 5 In.Diam.	125.00
Hair Receiver, Palm Tree, Matching Powder Bowl	55.00
Hair Receiver, Pink Roses, Green Lattice Work, Beading, 3 X 4 In.	30.00
Hair Receiver, Pink Roses, Green Latticework, Beading, 3 X 4 In.	30.00
Hair Receiver, Roses, Beading, 3 In.	18.00
Hairpin Holder, Flowered, Gold Scrolled Top, Marked, 2 1/2 In.	22.00
Hatpin Holder, Floral Design, Gold, 4 3/4 In.	35.00
Hatpin Holder, Floral, Rising Sun Mark	22.00
Hatpin Holder, Gold Chain Of Flowers, Marked	49.00
Hatpin Holder, Pink Flowers, White Ground, 6-Sided	35.00
Hatpin Holder, Violets, Cobalt Blue Trim	35.00
Hatpin Holder, White Ground, Pink & Green Floral Design, Marked	45.00
Hatpin Holder, Windmill Scene, White Ground, Beaded	65.00

Humidor, Blown-Out Horseheads, Horse Show, Tan & Brown, Marked, 7 In. 650.00
Humidor, Brown, 4 Scenic Panels, Palm Trees, Pyramids 400.00
Humidor, Florals, Lavender Ground, Hexagonal 165.00
Humidor, Flowers, Animals, Raised Beading, Medallions 175.00
Humidor, Man On Camel, Bisque, 18 X 7 In. 250.00
Humidor, Moriage & Floral, Marked, 6 X 5 1/2 In. 275.00
Humidor, Painted Ace Of Hearts, Pipe, Poker Chips, Green Mark 40.00
Humidor, Playing Card Design, Gray Bisque Trim, Marked, 4 In. 315.00
Humidor, Three Horses 550.00
Humidor, Tray, Bisque, Scenic 275.00
Humidor, 7 Fat White Geese Design, Marked 245.00
Inkwell, Tray, Sailboat Scene, 4 Piece 185.00
Jar, Potpourri, Pink Flowers, Blue Ground, Marked, 6 In. 75.00
Jar, Powder, Pink & Yellow Roses, Purple Border, Jewels, 3 3/4 In. 55.00
Jug, Flowers, Raised Leaves, Taupe, Marked 125.00
Jug, Raised Design, Multicolored, 7 1/2 In. 195.00
Jug, Syrup, Ship Scene, Pastels, Marked, Covered 110.00
Jug, Whiskey, Green, Moriage Trim, Scenic 150.00
Lazy Susan, Papier-Mache Box, Boat Trees, Water Scene 45.00
Lazy Susan, Sailboats, Lake, Palm Trees, Marked 120.00
Lemonade Set, Allover Orange Flowers, Marked E-OH, 7 Piece 225.00
Lemonade Set, Cobalt, Gold Trim, Brown Roses, Foliage, 7 Piece 275.00
Lemonade Set, Purple Violet Design, Gold Banded 160.00
Lemonade Set, Roses On Gold & Beige Ground, Marked, 6 Piece 185.00
Lemonade Set, Tree Scene, Green & Brown, White Ground 50.00
Luncheon Set, Child's, Lavender & White Floral 185.00
Match Holder, Scenic, Bisque Finish, Marked 65.00
Match Holder, Wall, Red & Pink Roses, Marked 45.00
Match Holder, White Heron, Powder Blue 37.50
Mayonnaise Set, Gold Design On White, Maple Leaf Mark, 3 Piece 18.00
Muffineer, Bisque Ground, Jeweled Band, 5 3/4 In. 75.00
Muffineer, Gold & Blue, Signed, 5 In. 68.00
Muffineer, Melon Shape, Enameled Flowers, 3 1/2 X 4 1/2 In. 50.00
Mug, Blown-Out Doll Face, Sun Mark, 3 In. 65.00
Mug, Red Flower, Water, Sailboat, Beaded Handle, Trim, 5 1/2 In. 170.00
Mug, Scotty, Scenic 30.00
Mug, Trees, Outdoors, Gold Beading, Leaf Marked 75.00
Mustard, Cobalt Blue, Yellow Florals, Spoon 40.00
Mustard, Covered, Noritake, Scenic 32.00
Mustard, Hand-Painted, Attached Underplate, Spoon 32.00
Mustard, Roses, Gold, Underplate 35.00
Mustard, Underplate, House, Trees, Gold Handles, Marked 22.00
Mustard, Yellow & Golden Florals, Blue Flow At Rim, Spoon, Covered 38.00
Napkin Ring, Scenic 50.00
Napkin Ring, Turquoise, Gold Beading, Medallions Of Roses 45.00
Nappy, Large Red & Pink Roses, Gold Ground, Handled 45.00
Nappy, Monoplane 135.00
Nappy, Moriage, Sailboat Scene, Mark 65.00
Nappy, Red & Pink Roses, Gold Ground, Handled 45.00
Nappy, Scene, Jeweled 23.00
Nappy, Violets, Handled, Green Wreath Mark 30.00
Nut Set, Black Beading, Gold Ground, 7 Piece 90.00
Nut Set, Gold Bead, Overlay On Black & White, E-Oh Mark 95.00
Nut Set, Hand-Painted Chestnuts, Footed, Green Wreath, 7 Piece 98.00
Nut Set, Oval, Pierced Handles, Nosegays On White Ground 75.00
Nut Set, Peanuts Inside Wicker Basket Design, 7 Piece 175.00
Nut Set, Raised Abstract Design, Set Of 4 .... 60.00
Pitcher, Cascading Berries, Gold Collar, Beaded, Green Wreath, 10 In. 150.00
Pitcher, Lime Green Base, Scene Border, Gold Beading, Marked, 5 In. 50.00
Pitcher, Milk, Flowers, Gold Banded Design Neck & Handle, 7 1/2 In. 115.00
Pitcher, Moriage Handle, Halloween Scene, 6 1/2 In. 185.00
Pitcher, Red Roses, Cobalt Neck, Gold Ground, Handled, Marked, 7 In. 149.00
Pitcher, Scenic, Gold Roses, Covered, 7 In. 139.00
Pitcher, Strawberries, Leaves, 2 Spouts, 4 In. 50.00

Planter, Blown-Out Indian Chief With Rifle, On Horse 1300.00
Plaque, Blown-Out Lion & Lioness, Green Mark In Wreath, 10 1/2 In. 675.00
Plaque, Blown-Out Squirrel & Nuts, 10 1/2 In. 450.00
Plaque, Charcoal Ground, Flowers & Grapes, Wicker Basket, 11 In. 477.00
Plaque, Country House Scene, Marked, 10 In. 215.00
Plaque, Dutch Children Scene, Border Gold, 10 In. 350.00
Plaque, Earth Ground, Basket Of Fruits, Nuts, Pierced, 11 In. 225.00
Plaque, Farmer Plowing Rice Field, Marked, 8 1/2 In. 65.00
Plaque, Florals, Grapes, Wicker Basket, 11 In. 365.00
Plaque, Hanging, Man On Camel, Green Mark, 10 In. 325.00
Plaque, House Scene, 8 In. 135.00
Plaque, Kingfisher Design, Wall Hung, 10 In. 175.00
Plaque, Man & Camel Scene, Gold Trim, 10 In. 295.00
Plaque, Owl In Sunset, Marked, 10 In. 125.00
Plaque, Palm Tree, Sea & Sand Scene, 9 In. 45.00
Plaque, Palms, Arabs, & Camels, Beading, 10 In. 50.00
Plaque, Primitive Scene, House, Tree Road, 7 3/4 In. 175.00
Plaque, Raised Blossom On Trees, Marked, 7 1/2 In. 50.00
Plaque, Raised Trees On Riverbank, No.908, 10 In. 155.00
Plaque, Sailboat Scene, Blue Maple Leaf, 9 In. 125.00
Plaque, Squirrel Eating Nuts In Forest, 10 1/2 In. 595.00
Plaque, Still Life, Fruits On Pedestal, Footed, Marked, 12 In. 250.00
Plaque, Sunset Colors, Forest Scene, Pierced, Marked, 10 In. 109.00
Plaque, Tree & Stream Scene, 9 In. 125.00
Plaque, Turquoise Palms, Pyramids, 10 1/2 In. 135.00
Plaque, Two Arabs On Camels, Enameled Rim, Blue Mark, 10 In. 285.00
Plaque, Water Scene, Ivy, Gold Leaves, Pierced, 10 In. 150.00
Plaque, Woodland Scene, Moriage, Greek Key Design 200.00
Plaque, Woodland Scene, 9 1/2 In. 135.00
Plate, Autumn Woods Scene, Open Handles, Green Wreath Mark, 9 1/2 In. 55.00
Plate, Blue Maple, Gold, Center Design, 10 In. 115.00
Plate, Chestnuts, 8 1/2 In. 45.00
Plate, Cobalt, Gold, Green, 11 1/2 In. 250.00
Plate, Dinner, White, Gold Border 20.00
Plate, Egyptian Scene, Open-Handled, 10 1/2 In. 55.00
Plate, Floral & Grapes, Wicker Basket, 11 In., Pair 450.00
Plate, Floral & Swan, Jeweled Gold Rim, 7 1/4 In. 20.00
Plate, Floral, Gold Trim, Mark, 10 In. 45.00
Plate, Girl, Horse, Green Wreath Mark, 10 In. 225.00
Plate, Gold With Gold Beading, Marked, 10 In. 115.00
Plate, Gold, Green, Ruby Border, Fruits & Berry, Marked, 10 In. 85.00
Plate, Gold, Orchids, Marked, 9 In. 80.00
Plate, Huddled Heron, Blue, 10 In. 8.00
Plate, Man & Boat Scene, 9 In. 175.00
Plate, Nile Scene, Gold Border, 9 In., Set Of 6 .... 350.00
Plate, Orange & Gold Floral, Gold Webbing, Marked, 9 3/4 In. 30.00
Plate, Orchids, Cobalt, Green, Gold, Scalloped, 11 1/4 In. 275.00
Plate, Pancake, Gold Beading, Pink Roses, Covered 125.00
Plate, Pink & Blue, Flowers, Green & Gold Trim, Marked, Set Of 5 .... 25.00
Plate, Pink Floral, Gold Around Scalloped Rim, Marked, 12 1/2 In. 185.00
Plate, Pink, Gold Roses, 8 1/2 In. 65.00
Plate, Pond Scene, White Swans, Gold Foliage, Marked, 10 In. 95.00
Plate, Portrait, Madam Potocka, Gold Ground, 10 1/2 In. .... 125.00 To 295.00
Plate, Raised Geometric Gold Deco, Cherubs, Clouds, Marked, 8 1/2 In. 125.00
Plate, River Scene, Green Wreath Mark, 8 1/2 In. 20.00
Plate, Roses, Gold Rim, RC Mark, 11 In. 75.00
Plate, Swan Handle, 10 1/2 In. 150.00
Plate, Swans, Raised & Molten Gold, Handled, 10 In. 165.00
Plate, Turquoise Ground, Florals, Bird On Branch, 9 1/2 In. 195.00
Plate, Woodland Scene, No.773, 6 1/4 In. 295.00
Punch Bowl, Large Grapes Inside & Out, Gold Feet, Marked, 11 X 6 In. 285.00
Punch Bowl, Yellow Roses, Gold Feet & Loop Handles, 12 X 7 In., 2 Pc. 350.00
Relish Set, Flowers & Jewels, Gold Beaded, 3 Piece 65.00
Relish, Pharaoh Heads Form Handles & Feet, Egyptian Symbols 185.00

Ring Tree, Figural, Hand, Green Mark, 2 X 3 1/2 In. 65.00
Ring Tree, Florals, Gold Beads 55.00
Salt & Pepper, Pink & Blue Flowers, Blue Mark, Pair 15.00
Salt & Pepper, Seascape, Green Beading 20.00
Salt & Pepper, White, Figures, Pink, Trees, Pagoda, Orange Trim, Marked 40.00
Salt & Pepper, White, Gold Rim, Pair 10.00
Salt Dip, Moriage, Round 45.00
Saltshaker, Huddled Heron, Blue 8.00
Sauce, Gaudy 9.50
Server, Pancake, Stylized Blue & Gold Design, Covered 125.00
Shaving Mug, Camel & Desert Scene, Signed 185.00
Shaving Mug, Scenic, Beaded Handle, Green M Wreath 40.00
Shaving Mug, Windmill 90.00
Shoe, Dutch, Scenic, Marked, 3 In. 125.00
Smoke Set, Art Deco Design, Humidor, Tray, Match Safe 275.00
Smoke Set, Match Holder, Cigar, Cigarette, Round Tray, 7 In. 435.00
Snack Set, Scenic, Gold Design .... 38.00 To 40.00
Stein, Arab Town, People, Flowing Robes, 7 In. 325.00
Stein, Horses, Marked, 5 1/2 In. 120.00
Stein, Japanese House Scene, Gold Trim, 7 In. 325.00
Stein, Scene Of House, Road, Trees, People, 7 In. 395.00
Sugar & Creamer, Apple Blossoms, Red Border, Covered 50.00
Sugar & Creamer, Butterflies, Gold Trim, Marked 52.00
Sugar & Creamer, Covered, White Heron, Powder Blue 35.00
Sugar & Creamer, Cream Ground, Tree With Roses, Art Deco Style 75.00
Sugar & Creamer, Floral 35.00
Sugar & Creamer, Gold Bands, Roses, Green Wreath 35.00
Sugar & Creamer, Hand-Painted Violets, Green Wreath 35.00
Sugar & Creamer, Hand-Painted, 3 Roses, Gold Trim & Beading, Marked 69.00
Sugar & Creamer, Lavender Mountains 37.00
Sugar & Creamer, Melon-Ribbed, Pink Roses, White Beading 45.00
Sugar & Creamer, Mill Scene, Blue & White 30.00
Sugar & Creamer, Mum Design, Blue & Green Banding, Gilt Beading 45.00
Sugar & Creamer, Painted Roses, Gold Trim, Green Mark 45.00
Sugar & Creamer, Palm, Signed 60.00
Sugar & Creamer, Red & Green Flowers, Gold Beading, Marked 35.00
Sugar & Creamer, Rose Bouquet Design, Enamel Beads, Marked 45.00
Sugar & Creamer, White Ground, Gold Pegasus, Marked 75.00
Sugar Shaker, Floral Design 45.00
Sugar Shaker, Gold Pastel Flowers, Gaudy, 5 1/2 In. 95.00
Sugar Shaker, Orange Roses, Black Leaves, Outlined In Gold, M Mark 38.00
Sugar Shaker, Rose Panels, Gold Scrolling, Dark Ground 65.00
Sugar Shaker, White Flowers, Gold Trim, Handled, Marked, 3 1/2 In. 35.00
Sugar, Floral, Covered, Rising Sun Mark 13.00
Sugar, Roses, Gold Trim, Brand Band, Covered, 3 1/4 In. 8.00
Syrup, Hand-Painted Floral, Design On Cover 19.00
Syrup, Peach Floral, Gold Trim & Beading, Blue Mark 25.00
Syrup, Peach Floral, Gold Trim, Black Mark, 3 3/4 In. 30.00
Syrup, Raised Gold Floral, Underplate, Covered 55.00
Tankard, Floral, Royal Nishiki, 12 1/2 In. 150.00
Tankard, Gold & Floral, Marked, 13 1/2 In. 265.00
Tankard, Lavender & Pink Asters, Indian Design, Gold Trim, 11 In. 175.00
Tea Set, Blue Ground, Hand-Painted Butterflies, Pedestal Cup, 8 Piece 185.00
Tea Set, Child's, Violets, Gold Trim, Blue Mark, 15 Piece 150.00
Tea Set, Cobalt, Gold, Roses, 3 Piece 195.00
Tea Set, Cottage, Meadow, & Trees, Green Wreath Mark, 21 Piece 225.00
Tea Set, Flying Goose, House On Lake, 23 Piece 195.00
Tea Set, Gold Trim, 17 Piece 475.00
Tea Set, Japanese Characters, Scroll Handles, Pedestaled, 3 Piece 350.00
Tea Set, Marked 47, Floral, Gold Trim, Cobalt Blue, 15 Piece 335.00
Tea Set, Orange & Green, Trees, Lake, Windmill, 11 Pieces 125.00
Tea Set, Red, Pink Roses, Gold Beading, 3 Piece 225.00
Tea Set, Scenic Design, Gold Trim, Marked, 3 Piece 200.00
Tea Set, White Ground, Swags Of Gold, 3 Piece 125.00

Tea Strainer & Underplate, Gold Trim, Beading, Multicolored Design 42.00
Tea Strainer, Thousand Faces, Signed 45.00
Tea Strainer, White Ground, Green Flowers, Marked 40.00
Teapot, Hand-Painted Violet & Leaves, Gold Trim 85.00
Teapot, Pink Roses, Gold Trim, Green Wreath Mark 60.00
Teapot, White Ground, Gold Overlay, Pedestaled 60.00
Teapot, White Heron, Powder Blue 45.00
Teapot, Woodland Scene, Marked 120.00
Tile, Tea, Scenic, Windmill & Cottage, 6 1/2 In. 35.00
Tobacco Jar, Applied Skull, Blue Mark 480.00
Tobacco Jar, Landscape, Green & Beige, Jewels, Medallions, Marked 525.00
Toothpick, Gold Floral, 3-Handled 70.00
Toothpick, Red Roses, Gold Trim 18.00
Toothpick, Sailboat Scene, 3 Green Handles, Marked 65.00
Toothpick, Stylized Flower Design, Gold Trim, 3-Handled 30.00
Tray, Blue & Gold, Roses, Marked, 13 1/2 In. 160.00
Tray, Enameled Flowers & Leaves, Green Wreath Mark, 3 1/2 In.Diam. 30.00
Tray, Floral, Rising Sun Mark, 8 X 5 3/4 In. 26.00
Tray, Hand-Painted, Horsehead, Indian, Green Wreath, 6 1/4 X 3 In. 165.00
Tray, Oval, River Scene, Cobalt Border, Green Wreath Mark, 12 In. 200.00
Tray, Playing Cards, Matches, Diamond Shaped, Green, 7 1/2 X 10 In. 95.00
Urn, Cobalt, Beading, Mums, Covered, 11 In. 450.00
Urn, Empress Portrait, Gold & Beading, 13 In. 450.00
Vase, Apple Blossoms, 8 In. 75.00
Vase, Arab Scene, Ribbon Handles, Gold Trim, 6 In., Pair 250.00
Vase, Autumn Leaves, Scenic Background, 7 1/4 In. 125.00
Vase, Basket Shape, Iris, Maple Leaf Mark, 9 In. 125.00
Vase, Basket, Roses, Green, 9 In. 195.00
Vase, Bird Design, Green, Pink To Lavender, 5 1/2 In. 275.00
Vase, Birds, Trees, Barn, Lake, Orange, Yellow, Brown, 5 In. 125.00
Vase, Black, Beaded & Jeweled, Gold Wreath Mark, 12 1/4 In. 150.00
Vase, Blackberries, Gold Beading, 8 In. 85.00
Vase, Blown-Out Leaf & Acorn Design, Signed, 7 In. 550.00
Vase, Blown-Out Oak Leaves, Signed, 10 In. 550.00
Vase, Blown-Out Roses, Enameled Collar, Signed, 11 In. 200.00
Vase, Blue Roses, Green Wreath Mark, 10 In. 165.00
Vase, Blue, Flowers, Yellow Panels, Marked, 9 In. 105.00
Vase, Bottle Shape, Rose Design, Gold On Collar, Marked, 9 In. 95.00
Vase, Cobalt & Floral, Pretzel Handled, Footed, Gold Beading, 12 In. 350.00
Vase, Cobalt & Jeweled Top, Red & Pink Roses, Marked, 5 1/2 In. 145.00
Vase, Cobalt Blue, Mums, Gold, Ornate Handles, Marked, 9 In. 80.00
Vase, Cobalt Blue, Raised Design, Handled, 8 In. 95.00
Vase, Cobalt, Medallion, 2 Swans, Lake, Gold Beads, 10 3/4 In. 395.00
Vase, Country Scene, Gold, Beading, 11 1/2 In. 350.00
Vase, Crimson Florals, Gold Handle & Base, 18 In. 450.00
Vase, Dogwood Flowers, Raised Gold Beading, Marked, 11 In. 189.00
Vase, Dragon, Molded Relief, 9 1/2 In. 300.00
Vase, Dragonfly, 2-Handled, 10 In. 45.00
Vase, Encrusted In Gold Dots, 12 In. 350.00
Vase, Floral, Blue Bands, Gold, Green Wreath Mark, 9 1/4 In. 125.00
Vase, Floral, Bulbous, 8 X 7 In. 95.00
Vase, Floral, Gold Outlined Leaves, Marked, Blue Ground, 12 1/2 In. 210.00
Vase, Floral, Gold, Brown, & Beige, 11 In. 95.00
Vase, Floral, Loving Cup Shape, Marked, 6 In. 35.00
Vase, Floral, Pink & Green Roses, Marked, 13 1/4 In. 265.00
Vase, Floral, Pink & Green, Loop Handles, Blue Mark, 7 1/2 In. 125.00
Vase, Floral, Pink, Gold Trim, Jewels, Bulbous, Marked, 3 In. 135.00
Vase, Floral, Red & Pink, Loop Handles, Marked, 9 In. 110.00
Vase, Floral, Red & White Roses, Handled, Marked, 12 In. 200.00
Vase, Floral, Stylized Flowers, Pink, Marked, 11 1/2 In. 150.00
Vase, Floral, Yellow, Indian Design, Jewels, Marked, 12 1/4 In. 180.00
Vase, Floral, 4-Sided, Gold Collar, Marked, 9 1/2 In. 170.00
Vase, Florals Outlined In Gold, Green Wreath Mark, 7 In. 55.00
Vase, Florals With Aqua Jewels, 8 3/4 In. 110.00

Vase, Florals, Gold & Bead Trim, Maple Leaf Mark, 8 1/2 In. 250.00
Vase, Florals, Gold Trim, Beaded, Pedestal, Maple Leaf Mark, 8 1/2 In. 250.00
Vase, Florals, Gold, Pastoral Scene, 11 3/4 In. 350.00
Vase, Flowers & Leaves, Gold Handles, Green Wreath, 9 1/2 In. 175.00
Vase, Forest Scene, Gold Beading, Signed, 11 1/2 In. 175.00
Vase, Fruit & Leaves, 10 In. 575.00
Vase, Gaudy, Raised Gold Beading, 2-Handled, Marked, 7 1/2 In. 200.00
Vase, Geese Flying Design, Moriage, 12 In. 240.00
Vase, Gold & Floral, Handled, 12 In. 175.00
Vase, Gold Base & Collar, Bisque Finish Roses, Marked, 11 In. 250.00
Vase, Gold Beaded Neck & Base, Floral, Black Wreath Mark, 10 1/2 In. 85.00
Vase, Gold Roses Design, Footed, Marked, 13 In. 395.00
Vase, Gold Scenic Design, 7 1/2 In. 225.00
Vase, Grapes & Leaves, Handled, 5 1/2 In. 48.00
Vase, Green Ground, Florals, Gold Bead, Marked, 9 In. 185.00
Vase, Green, Pink & Red Roses, Handled, Footed, 7 1/2 In. 150.00
Vase, Hand-Painted Cover, Fruits & Eagle On Limb, Marked, 12 1/2 In. 280.00
Vase, Hand-Painted, Red, Roses, Handled, Blue Leaf Mark, 7 1/2 In. 75.00
Vase, House & Water Scene, 6-Jewel, Handled, Marked, 6 1/2 In. 55.00
Vase, House Scene, Ribbon Handles, Gold Trim, 11 1/4 In. 240.00
Vase, Indian Head, Marked, 18 In., Pair 1200.00
Vase, Indian In Canoe, Ducks Around Rim, 9 In. 350.00
Vase, Japanese Woman, Yellow Ground, Flowers, Symbols, 14 In. 200.00
Vase, Jeweled, Florals, 9 In. 145.00
Vase, Kelly Green, Red Roses, Cream Ground, Marked, 5 1/2 In. 100.00
Vase, Lake Scene, Hourglass Shape, 3-Handled, 11 In. 180.00
Vase, Lake, Boat, Woodland Scene, 10 In. 225.00
Vase, Lavender Floral, Bisque Finish, 10 1/2 In. 185.00
Vase, Lilies On Water, 2-Handled, Marked, 10 In. 165.00
Vase, Medallions Of Roses, Ruffled, Magenta & Gold Ground, 7 3/4 In. 145.00
Vase, Moriage, Birds In Flight, Beading, 2-Handled, 11 In. 350.00
Vase, Moriage, Flowers, Pastel Bisque, 11 In. 395.00
Vase, Moriage, Flowers, 9 In. 250.00
Vase, Nile Scene, Gold Design, Marked, 8 In. 75.00
Vase, Orange & Yellow Floral, Gold Trim, Marked, 11 1/4 In. 210.00
Vase, Orchids, Gold Collar, Marked, 8 1/2 In. 165.00
Vase, Ornate Birds, Leaf, & Floral, White Base, Signed, 7 In. 95.00
Vase, Ovoid Shape, Floral, Gold Bead Handle, Maple Leaf Mark, 9 In. 185.00
Vase, Owl On Branch, Amber Eyes, Blue Leaf, 7 1/2 In. 119.00
Vase, Palm Trees, Sailboat, Gold Trim, Handles, 7 In. 50.00
Vase, Pastorial Scenic, 11 1/4 In. 325.00
Vase, Pillow Shape, Portrait, Gold Ground, 9 3/4 In. 350.00
Vase, Pink & Yellow Roses, Gold Trim, Marked, 12 In. 315.00
Vase, Portrait, Gold, Gold Beading, 9 1/4 In. 250.00
Vase, Purple Iris, Gold, Handled, Green Wreath, 7 In. 65.00
Vase, Queen Louise Portrait, Jeweled, Moriage Gold, 8 In. 295.00
Vase, Raised-Up Geese Flying Over Water, 12 In. 240.00
Vase, Red & Gold Flowers, Ivory Ground, 8 In. 125.00
Vase, Red & Pink Roses, Gold Beading, 9 In. 380.00
Vase, Red & Pink Roses, Gold Design, Jewels, 8 In. 195.00
Vase, Red & Pink Roses, Handled, Blue Maple Leaf Mark, 8 1/2 In. 80.00
Vase, Red Roses, Jewels, Gold Overlay, 8 1/2 In. 140.00
Vase, Red Roses, Kelly Green On Cream, Blue Mark, 5 1/4 In. 100.00
Vase, Rooster & Hen, 2-Handled, 12 In. 115.00
Vase, Roses, Gold Beaded Top & Base, M In Wreath, 10 1/2 In. 210.00
Vase, Roses, Gold Outlined, Ring Handle, Bisque, 9 X 12 In. 365.00
Vase, Roses, Gold Trim, Ring Handle, 12 In. 365.00
Vase, Roses, Gold, Pedestal, Handled, 5 1/2 In. 47.00
Vase, Roses, Red Ground, 9 In. 135.00
Vase, Rural Scene In Center, Gold Beading, 11 In. 350.00
Vase, Scene Of Rowboat At Shore, Gold Handles, Marked, 6 1/4 In. 58.00
Vase, Scenic & Floral Design, Handled, Green Wreath Mark, 8 In. 140.00
Vase, Scenic Design, Gold Handles, Signed, 11 In. 175.00
Vase, Scenic Insert, Gold Trim, Green Ground, Marked, 6 1/2 In., Pair 195.00

Vase, Scenic Panels, Tree, Stream, Gold Beading, Blue Ground, 5 In. 100.00
Vase, Scenic, Beaded Handles, Bisque, 5 1/2 In. 50.00
Vase, Scenic, Blue & Green, Yellow With Gold Trim, Marked, 9 In. 130.00
Vase, Scenic, Cottage, Lavender & Tan, Greek Key Design, Marked, 9 In. 110.00
Vase, Scenic, Gold Leafing, Birds, Water, Marked, 11 1/4 In. 140.00
Vase, Scenic, Handled, Blue Leaf Mark, 5 1/2 In. 75.00
Vase, Scenic, Hexagonal Shape, Ear Handles, Marked, 10 In., Pair 300.00
Vase, Scenic, Seahorse Handles, Green Wreath Mark, 10 1/2 In. 280.00
Vase, Scenic, Ships, Marked, 6 In. 40.00
Vase, Scenic, Tree, Stream, Gold Beading, Blue Ground, 5 1/4 In. 100.00
Vase, Scenic, Yellow Flowers, Enamel Trim, 10 1/2 In. 95.00
Vase, Scenic, 6 Square Medallions, Gold Trim, Marked, 9 In. 130.00
Vase, Spider Web In Gold, Pink & Gold Rim, Squatty, Marked, 7 1/2 In. 120.00
Vase, Stick, Stylized Floral, Art Deco, 11 In. 115.00
Vase, Tapestry & Moriage, 12 1/2 In. 600.00
Vase, Tapestry, Wisteria Flower Design, 9 In. 575.00
Vase, Violets, Lavender Ground, Scrolled Feet, Marked, 12 In. 75.00
Vase, White, Orchid Mums, 12 In. 375.00
Vase, Windmill Scene, Marked, 7 1/2 In. 75.00
Vase, Wisteria Design, Tapestry, Gold Banded Top, 9 1/2 In. 575.00
Vase, Woodland Scene With Handles, 6 In. 195.00
Vase, Woodland Scene, 5 1/4 In. 185.00
Vase, Yellow Roses, Tan & Brown Ground, Green Wreath Mark, 8 In. 65.00

*Nodders or nodding figures, or pagods, are porcelain figures with heads and
hands that are attached to wires. Any slight movement causes the parts to
move up and down. They were made in many countries during the eighteenth
and nineteenth centuries.*

NODDER, Alligator, Jaws Nod, Germany 55.00
    Bank, Black Boy Sitting Between 2 Oranges, Marked Florida, 6 In. 88.00
    Baseball Player, Hank Aaron, Original Box 18.00
    Baseball Player, Milwaukee Braves 25.00
    Black Girl, Sitting In Rocker, Nodding Head 145.00
    Black Girl, Sitting On Chair, Porcelain 125.00
    Black Man, Sitting Yoga Position, Coolie Hat .... 95.00 To 135.00
    Boy, Turban, China 125.00
    Clown, Sitting Position, Head & Legs Nod, Oriental 135.00
    Donkey, Head Nods, Celluloid 35.00
    Fat Man, Top Hat, Body & Head Nod 145.00
    Fishwife, Bisque 125.00
    Frog Family, Mother, Daughter, Son 75.00
    Girl At Piano, Man Singing, German, Porcelain 150.00
    Girl, Baby 125.00
    Girl, Seated, Bisque 125.00
    Indian With Fruit, China 125.00
    Man, Oriental, Sitting, Green, Pearl Luster, 7 In. .... 230.00 To 290.00
    Man, Oriental, White Beard, Leaning Over Strapped Bale, 4 1/2 In. 165.00
    Mandarin, Blue, Porcelain 125.00
    Oriental Girl & Boy, Chalkware, Pair 22.75
    Oriental Man & Lady, Pastel Robes, Gold Trim, 7 1/2 In., Pair 195.00
    Oriental Sage, Skullcap, Seated, Holds Dagger, Bisque Finish, 6 In. 130.00
    Salt & Pepper, Kangaroo, Mother & Baby 45.00
    Salt & Pepper, Monkey, Mother & Baby 45.00
    Tilda, Bisque 79.50

*Noritake-marked porcelain was made in Japan after 1904 by Nippon Toki
Kaisha.*

NORITAKE, Ashtray, Hand-Painted Scenic, 9 Cobalt Blue Jewels, 5 In. 48.00
    Ashtray, Individual Size, Green Mark In Wreath, Set Of 4 .... 22.00
    Ashtray, Orange Sunset, Cherry Blossom Mark, 4 1/2 X 2 1/4 In. 20.00

Berry Set, Purple Orchids, Green Leaves, Pods, Marked	60.00
Bowl, Azalea, 9 1/2 In.	80.00
Bowl, Fishing Scene, Hand-Painted, Silver Border, 9 1/2 In.	55.00
Bowl, Gold Floral, Ivory Panel, Allover Decor, 8 1/2 X 2 3/4 In.	28.00
Bowl, Nut, Figural Squirrel, Blown-Out Peanuts, 7 1/2 In.	65.00
Bowl, Outdoor Scene, Pierced Handle, 6 1/2 In.	20.00
Bowl, Trees, House, Water, Sunset, Marked, 6 In.	12.00
Bowl, Vegetable, Azalea, 9 1/2 X 7 1/2 In.	66.25
Bowl, Vegetable, Tree In Meadow, 9 1/4 In.	30.00
Bowl, Vegetable, Tree In Meadow, 10 1/2 In.	35.00
Bowl, Waste, Azalea	38.00
Bowl, Wild Rose & Plume Pattern, Ruffled, Signed, 8 3/4 In.	29.00
Bowl, Wood Scene Border, Gold, 8 1/2 In.	65.00
Butter Tub, Azalea, Liner	30.00
Butter Tub, Pierced Insert, Tree In Meadow	28.00
Butter, Azalea, Covered	60.00 To 80.00
Butter, Pontiac, Drain Trivet, Cover, 7 In.	30.00
Cake Plate, Azalea, 9 3/4 In.	35.00 To 42.00
Cake Plate, Flying Turkey, Pierced Handles, Blue, White, 9 3/4 In.	24.00
Cake Plate, Tree In Meadow, Pierced Handles	22.00 To 28.00
Cake Set, Imari, 7 Piece	95.00
Cake Set, Tree In Meadow, 7 Piece	50.00
Candlestick, Art Nouveau, 8 1/4 In., Pair	85.00
Casserole, Azalea, Covered	82.50
Celery, Azalea, 12 1/2 In.	45.00
Chocolate Pot, Samurai Scene, Flower Relief, Marked	68.00
Chocolate Pot, Scenic, Earth Colors, 9 In.	45.00
Chocolate Set, Florals, 7 Piece	125.00
Cigarette Holder, Pedestal, Golfer Scene	38.00
Condiment Set, Azalea, 6 Piece	47.50
Condiment Set, Tree In Meadow, 3 Piece	30.00
Cruet, Azalea	85.00 To 190.00
Cup & Saucer, Azalea	14.00 To 20.00
Cup & Saucer, Bouillon, Azalea	32.50
Cup & Saucer, Bouillon, Laureate	12.00
Cup & Saucer, Firenze	10.00
Cup & Saucer, Flying Turkey, C.1915, Blue & White	7.50
Cup & Saucer, Golden Butterfly, Mt. Fuji	12.50
Cup & Saucer, Tree In Meadow	12.00
Cup, Flying Turkey	8.00
Demitasse Set, Floral Banding, Blue	58.00
Demitasse Set, Tree In Meadow, 9 Piece	225.00 To 285.00
Dish, Candy, Apple Knob, Covered, Marked	30.00
Dish, Candy, Figural Apple Finial, Signed, Covered, 7 In.	32.00
Dish, Candy, Rosera, Green; Divided	45.00
Dish, Lemon, Azalea	14.00 To 18.00
Dish, Lemon, Tree In Meadow	14.00 To 15.00
Egg, Easter, Gold & Pink Flowers, 1980, Boxed	59.00
Fish Set, Marked, 9 Piece	75.00
Gravy Boat, Azalea	35.00 To 48.50
Gravy Boat, Eureka 9 1/2 In	18.00
Gravy Boat, Layalo	15.00
Honey Jar, Igloo Type, White, Raised Bees, Marked, 5 In.	18.00
Humidor, Orange, Black, Camel & Palm Tree	147.00
Humidor, Scenic Design	125.00
Jar, Jam, Azalea, Underplate	125.00
Jar, Jam, Tree In Meadow, Ladle, Figural Cherries On Lid	58.00
Jar, Mustard, Azalea	45.00
Jar, Mustard, Scenic, Swan, Covered	45.00
Jar, Tobacco, Henna Color, Wide Band Design, Clown Portrait	150.00
Mayonnaise Set, Azalea	39.00
Mayonnaise Set, Gold On White, Marked	18.00
Muffineer, Tree In Meadow, 6 1/2 In.	45.00

Napkin Ring, Rose Azalea	45.00
Nappy, Lemon Handled	18.00
Nut Set, Chestnuts Design, Green Mark In Wreath, 5 Piece	45.00
Pitcher, Milk, Azalea	75.00 To 100.00
Planter, Country Scene, Gold Footed, 5 1/2 X 6 1/2 X 3 1/2 In.	68.00
Plate, Azalea, 6 1/2 In.	6.00 To 7.50
Plate, Azalea, 7 1/2 In.	10.00
Plate, Azalea, 9 1/2 In.	18.00
Plate, Azalea, 10 In.	13.00
Plate, Hand-Painted Roses, Jeweled, Marked, Green Ground, 11 In.	135.00
Plate, Peach Border, Black Bands, Blue & White Flowers, 6 1/2 In.	6.00
Plate, Tree In Meadow, 6 1/2 In.	7.50
Plate, Tree In Meadow, 8 1/2 In.	12.00 To 20.00
Platter, Azalea, 11 1/2 In.	85.00
Platter, Eureka, 15 In.	24.00
Platter, Tree In Meadow, Oval, 12 In.	35.00
Punch Set, Scenic Design Of Swans, Raised Gold, Marked, 9 Piece	675.00
Relish, Azalea, Oval, 8 1/4 In.	27.00
Relish, Caltonia	20.00
Relish, Tree In Meadow, Divided	18.00
Salt & Pepper, Azalea, 3 1/2 In.	30.00
Salt & Pepper, Bulbous, 3 In.	8.50
Salt Cellar, Basket-Shaped, Handled, Blue Luster, Marked, Set Of 12	75.00
Sauce, Azalea, 5 1/4 In.	7.50
Soup, Dish, Azalea, 7 1/8 In.	16.00
Spoon Holder, Lay-Down Handle, White, Gold	30.00
Spooner, Azalea	67.50
Strainer, Tea, Florals	12.00
Sugar & Creamer, Azalea	38.00 To 75.00
Sugar & Creamer, Eureka	18.00
Sugar & Creamer, Gold-Leaf Raised Florals, Green Wreath Mark	22.50
Sugar Shaker & Creamer, Azalea	100.00
Sugar Shaker & Creamer, Tree In Meadow	55.00
Sugar Shaker, Tree In Meadow	35.00
Syrup, Azalea	33.00
Tea Set, Child's, White, Gold Trim, 21 Piece	85.00
Tea Set, Tree In Meadow	115.00 To 135.00
Tea Tile, Azalea	45.00 To 48.50
Teapot, Blue & Gold Design, Blue Wreath	14.00
Teapot, Blue & White, Black Lines, Oblong, 5 3/4 In.	12.00
Toothpick, Azalea	45.00
Tureen, Pontiac, Covered, 8 1/2 In.	30.00
Vase, Blackbirds, Yellow, 9 In., Pair	120.00
Vase, Bulbous, Scenic, Blue Ground, 4 1/2 X 6 1/2 In.	35.00
Vase, Handled, Orange Poppies, Black Ground, Gold Beading, 9 X 2 In	70.00
Vase, Orange, Gold Rim & Handle, Cottage At Lake, 5 1/2 In.	36.00
Vase, Scenic, Green M Mark, 10 3/4 In.	110.00
Vase, Scenic, 8 In.	40.00
Waffle Set, Tree In Meadow	45.00
Wall Pocket, Red Poppy, White & Blue Luster	18.00

The Norse Pottery Company started in Edgerton, Wisconsin, in 1903. In 1904 the company moved to Rockford, Illinois. The company made a black pottery which resembled early bronze relics of the Scandinavian countries. The firm went out of business in 1913.

NORSE, Bowl, Dragon Handle, 2 1/2 In.	80.00
Dish, Covered, Serpent Handles, 3 In.	80.00
Dish, High Stem, Incised Decoration, 8 In.	95.00
Vase, Black, Incised Decoration, 5 In.	85.00

The North Dakota School of Mines was established in 1892 at the University of North Dakota. Ceramics were made there for a short time.

NORTH DAKOTA SCHOOL OF MINES, Bowl, Pinecone, Signed, 9 In. 75.00
Dish, 3 In. 25.00
Grape Planter 95.00
Jar, Covered, Mauve Matte Glaze, 5 In. 40.00
Vase, Flat Side, Incised Floral Band, Pair 85.00
Vase, Green, 7 1/4 In. 100.00
Vase, Hand-Thrown, 1928, Blue Drip Glaze, 5 In. 70.00

Northwood Glass Company worked in Martins Ferry, Ohio, in the 1880s to about 1923. They marked some pieces with the underlined letter N. Many pieces of carnival glass were made by this company.
NORTHWOOD, see also Carnival Glass; Custard Glass; Goofus Glass; Pressed Glass

NORTHWOOD, Berry Set, Leaf Medallion, Cobalt Blue, 7 Piece 295.00
Berry Set, Leaf Medallion, Green, Northwood 350.00
Bowl, Blooms & Blossoms, Ruffled Edge, 7 1/4 In. 15.00
Bowl, Holly, Gold Trim, Emerald Green, 8 3/4 In. 80.00
Bowl, Ruffles & Rings With Daisy Band, 3 X 8 In. 30.00
Butter, Cherry & Thumbprint, Covered 75.00
Butter, Dogwood Pattern, Gold Trim, Covered 125.00
Card Receiver, Fluted Scrolls 25.00
Celery, Block, Blue, Opalescent 45.00
Creamer, Leaf Medallion, Green 55.00
Cruet, Stopper, Jackson, Vaseline 95.00
Cup, Punch, Cherry Thumbprint, Clear, 4 In. 60.00
Cup, Punch, Singing Bird, Clear 45.00
Dish, Pickle, Frosted Center, 2-Handled, Oval, 10 In. 37.50
Lamp, Peg, Ruffled Shade, Opaque & Turquoise Design, 14 In. 495.00
Pitcher, Water, Everglades, White Opalescent, Gold Trim 99.00
Pitcher, Water, Leaf Medallion, Amethyst 225.00
Pitcher, Water, Leaf Medallion, Cobalt Blue 265.00
Pitcher, Water, Scroll With Acanthus, Blue Opalescent 250.00
Plate, Grape, 6-Sided, 8 In. 45.00
Punch Set, Memphis, Clear, Signed, 9 Piece 165.00
Rose Bowl, Drapery, Pastel Blue 90.00
Spooner, Cherries, Green & Gold 55.00
Spooner, Daisy & Fern, Apple Blossom Mold, Cranberry 100.00
Spooner, Drapery, Gold Trim, Clear 40.00
Spooner, Geneva, Green 75.00
Spooner, Jewel & Flower, Gold & Ruby Stain, White Opalescent 70.00
Spooner, Peaches 55.00
Sugar Shaker, Blue Band 115.00
Sugar Shaker, Grapes & Leaves, Milk Glass, Original Top 35.00
Sugar Shaker, Parian Swirl, Green, Floral Design 110.00
Sugar, Cherry Thumbprint, Gold Trim, Clear 65.00
Sugar, Peaches, Covered 85.00
Sugar, Thumbprint 50.00
Syrup, Swirl, Cranberry 225.00
Table Set, Cruet, Salt, & Pepper, Tray, Sapphire Blue 125.00
Table Set, Maiden's Blush, Gold Trim, 4 Piece 185.00
Table Set, Thumbprint & Cable, Gold Trim, 4 Piece 295.00
Tumbler, Dahlia, Green 18.00
Tumbler, Everglades, White Opalescent, Gold 25.00
Tumbler, Inverted Rib, Enameled Flower Design, Frosted, Blue 20.00
Tumbler, Oriental Poppy, Blue, Set Of 4 .... 60.00
Tumbler, Poppy, Gold Trim, Green 18.00

Vase, Dark Green, Fluted, Marked, 10 In. 28.00
Vase, Ribbed, Fluted Top, Green, Gold, Iridescent, Marked, 10 In. 26.00
Vase, Silver Overlay Of Diamonds & Clubs, Cranberry, 8 1/2 In. 110.00
Water Set, Cherry & White, 4 Piece 135.00
Water Set, Open Rose, Red & Gold, 7 Piece 175.00
Water Set, Peach, Green, Signed, 5 Piece 225.00

*Nu-Art was a trademark registered by the Imperial Glass Co. of
Bellaire, Ohio, about 1920.*

NU-ART, Dish, Nude Lady Sitting On Edge, Pot Metal, 7 1/2 X 6 In. 75.00

NUTCRACKER, Alligator, Brass 85.00
  Blake, Platform, Patent 1859 .... 27.00
  Dog, Bronze, La Althoff Mfg. Co., Chicago 123.00
  Dog, Brown & Green, Porcelain 86.00
  Dog, Cast Iron 125.00
  Dog, Nickel-Plated Iron 33.00
  Eagle, Iron, 7 In. 35.00
  Fox Head, Pat. June 1920 .... 82.00
  Hand-Carved, Lady 10.00
  Legs, Brass .... 25.00 To 35.00
  Lion With Claw Foot, Iron, 6 In. 38.00
  Nude, Wooden 35.00
  Old Man With Nightcap, Wooden, 10 3/4 In. 35.00
  Perfection, Iron 17.00
  Rooster, Brass 20.00
  Santa, Wooden 95.00
  Screw Handle, Wooden .... 5.00 To 10.00
  Squirrel, Black 35.00
  St.Bernard, Cast Iron .... 40.00 To 45.00
  Table Clamp, 1915 .... 10.00

*Nymphenburg, a German porcelain factory, was established at
Neudeck-ob-der-Au in 1753 and moved to Nymphenburg in 1761. The company
is still in existence. Modern marks include a shield superseded by a star or
crown, and a crowned CT with a checkered shield.*

NYMPHENBURG, Figurine, Lady In Crinoline, 7 1/2 In. 275.00
  Plate, Green, Marked, 6 1/2 In. 40.00
  Plate, Green, Marked, 8 In. 85.00
  Plate, Green, Marked, 10 3/4 In. 130.00
  Plate, Pierced Rim, Gold Design, Beaded, Marked, 10 1/4 In. 18.00
  Soup, Cream, Brick Band Between Gold Bands 125.00
  Soup, Dish, Brick Band Between Gold Bands, 9 1/2 In. 100.00
  Tray, Basket, Open Trellis Border, Red, Gilt, C.1880 .... 135.00

*Occupied Japan is the mark used on pieces of pottery and porcelain made
during the American occupation of Japan after World War II, from 1945
to 1952. Collectors are now buying these pieces. The items were made for
export to the United States.*

OCCUPIED JAPAN, Ashtray, Bird On Branch, 4 1/4 In. 6.00
  Ashtray, Cherubs In Relief, Square, 4 1/2 In. 8.00
  Ashtray, Elephant, Brown 6.00
  Ashtray, Leaf, Green, Gold, Red, 3 3/4 In. 8.00
  Ashtray, North Carolina Map, 6 1/4 In. 8.00
  Ashtray, Orange Ceramic, Little Girl, Perched On Edge, 4 In. 12.50
  Ashtray, Who Left This Behind, Copper, Pants On Line 4.00
  Bottle, Cologne, Green, 4 In. 22.00
  Bowl, Green Inside, White Outside, Pink Orchid, 7 In. 10.00
  Box, Heart Shaped, Sailboat Design, Gold Trim, 2 3/4 In. 8.00
  Box, Pink, White, & Green, Gold Flowers, Country Scene, 3 In. 12.00
  Candleholder, Colonial Lady, 3 1/2 X 3 1/2 In. 15.00

Candleholder, Girl With Staff, Boy With Horn, 11 In., Pair 110.00
Candleholder, Man & Woman, Porcelain, Marked, Pair 42.50
Coffee Set, Demitasse, Cream, Yellow Flowers, Gold Trim 100.00
Condiment Set, Beehive, Bees, 4 Piece 22.00
Creamer, Figural, Cow 15.00
Cup & Saucer, Black, Blue, Mauve-Pink Orchid 60.00
Cup & Saucer, Blue Willow .... 12.00 To 25.00
Cup & Saucer, Cherry Fruit, Ivies, Blossoms, Multicolored 5.00
Cup & Saucer, Dragon, Set Of 5 .... 20.00
Cup & Saucer, Lovers In Country Scene, Blue, Gold Trim 11.00
Cup & Saucer, Red & Gold Floral Design 7.00
Cup, Child's, Blue Willow 6.00
Dish, Boat, Applied Roses, Gold Trim, Handled, 7 In. 12.00
Dish, Leaf, Oak, Ivies, 5 In. 4.00
Dish, Leaf, Scenic, Lakeside, Gold Trim 8.50
Dish, Rust, Reed Handle, Covered, 4 In. 8.00
Figurine, Angel, Seated, Book In Lap, Yellow Frock, 2 In. 7.00
Figurine, Ballerina, Lace Dress, Pair 25.00
Figurine, Bird, Tan Body, Red Head, Black Wings, 3 In. 9.00
Figurine, Boy & Girl, Standing Against Fence, Pair 75.00
Figurine, Boy Carrying Plate Of Fish & Pitcher 13.00
Figurine, Boy Fishing, Shelf Sitter, Bisque 15.00
Figurine, Boy Scout, Brown Hat, Yellow Collar, 4 In. 8.00
Figurine, Boy, Blue Top, Paint Can, Shelf Sitter, 4 In. 9.50
Figurine, Boy, Carrying A Bag Over Shoulder, 3 1/2 In. 10.00
Figurine, Boy, Dog, Boy Is Holding Staff, 3 1/2 In. 15.00
Figurine, Boy, Dog, Standing By Fence, 3 1/2 In. 17.50
Figurine, Boy, Duck, Boy Playing Flute, 3 In. .... 6.00 To 10.50
Figurine, Boy, Walking Stick, 3 In. 12.50
Figurine, Bride & Groom, 3 1/2 In. 15.00
Figurine, Bulldog, 4 X 3 In. 12.50
Figurine, Butler, Comic, Black Coat, Gold Tie, Palms Out 20.00
Figurine, Cherub, Plays Drum & Cymbals, 5 1/2 In. 20.00
Figurine, Clown, Yellow To Gold, Marked, 4 1/2 In. 12.00
Figurine, Colonial Boy & Girl, Arm In Arm, 2 1/2 X 3 In. 9.50
Figurine, Colonial Couple, Bisque, 8 In., Pair 28.00
Figurine, Colonial Couple, Standing, 2 1/2 X 3 In. 15.00
Figurine, Colonial Man, Hand-Painted, 6 In. 16.00
Figurine, Colonial Man, Playing Fiddle, 3 1/4 In. 7.50
Figurine, Colonial Man, Powdered Wig, 3 1/2 In. 7.00
Figurine, Colonial Man, 11 1/2 In. 22.00
Figurine, Colonial Woman, Bouquet, Bisque, 4 In. 17.50
Figurine, Colonial Woman, Standing, 3 In. 7.50
Figurine, Cowgirl, Black Shirt, Shelf Sitter, 3 1/2 In. 4.00
Figurine, Dalmatian, Lying Down, 3 X 2 In. 12.00
Figurine, Dog With Toothache, Bandage Around Jaw, 3 In. 9.00
Figurine, Dog, Bedside Planter, Green, White, Brown, 3 In. 10.50
Figurine, Dog, Poodle, White, Red Bow On Forehead, 3 In. 7.50
Figurine, Dog, Sitting Up, Green Bow At Neck, 2 1/2 In. 8.00
Figurine, Donald Duck, Red Cap, Blue Sailor Jacket, 3 In. 12.00
Figurine, Dutch Boy & Girl, 6 1/2 In., Pair 20.00
Figurine, Elf Riding A Snail, Pink, 2 1/2 X 4 In. 16.00
Figurine, Frog, Bisque, 3 1/2 In. 10.00
Figurine, Frog, Tan, Sits On Stump, Plays Concertina, 4 In. 9.00
Figurine, German Shepherd, Standing, Black, Brown, White 12.00
Figurine, Girl, Basket Of Flowers, Shelf Sitter, 3 1/2 In. 12.50
Figurine, Girl, Playing Banjo, Shelf Sitter, 4 1/2 In. 12.00
Figurine, Girl, Playing Mandolin, 3 1/2 In. 5.00
Figurine, Girl, Sitting On Fence, 4 1/4 In. 12.50
Figurine, Girl, With Roses, 3 1/2 In. 6.00
Figurine, Hobo, 4 In. 5.00
Figurine, Indian, Smoking Pipe, 4 1/4 In. 13.00
Figurine, Italian Man, Playing Accordion, 4 In. 15.00
Figurine, Man & Woman, On High-Back Chairs, 3 In. 16.00

Figurine, Man Leaning Against Bowl, 4 In. 145.00
Figurine, Mother, 2 Children, Porcelain 28.00
Figurine, Musician, 6 In. 15.00
Figurine, Oriental Boy, Brown Coolie Hat, Black Jacket, 4 In 11.00
Figurine, Oriental Girl, Pink Jacket, Aqua Trousers, 6 In. 10.00
Figurine, Oriental Girl, With Flowers, 4 In. 8.00
Figurine, Oriental Lady, Basket On Head, 8 In. 18.00
Figurine, Oriental Man With Lute, 9 In. 16.00
Figurine, Oriental Man, Seated, Tan Robe, Green Pants, 4 In. 12.00
Figurine, Peasant Lady, Carrying Yoke With Bucket, 3 1/4 In. 8.00
Figurine, Pig, Playing Tuba, 4 In. 8.00
Figurine, Rabbit, Beside Planter, 3 1/2 X 3 In. 11.50
Figurine, Reindeer, Porcelain 20.00
Figurine, Scotty Dog, Ceramic, 4 X 3 In. 12.00
Figurine, Seals, Mother & 2 Young, Gray & Brown, 3 3/4 In. 15.00
Figurine, Shepherdess, Rose Hat, Gray Bodice, 6 In. 18.00
Figurine, Skunk, Face Of Hitler, Tail In Air, Rising Sun Mark 25.00
Figurine, Uncle Sam, 8 In. 35.00
Figurine, Woman & Umbrella, 10 In. 20.00
Hand Warmer, Sterno, Pocket Size, 4 In. 8.00
Honey Pot, Covered 12.00
Incense Burner, Buddha, Black & Red, Pair 25.00
Incense Burner, Man, Seated, 3 1/2 In. 16.00
Lamp Base, Colonial Couple, 8 In. 15.00
Lamp, Colonial Couple, 10 1/2 In. 45.00
Lamp, Colonial Man, 7 1/2 In. 35.00
Lamp, Overall Design, 36 In. 125.00
Lighter, Cigarette, Mesh Cover 12.00
Match Holder, Wall, Bisque, Colonial Man, Woman, 7 X 4 1/2 In. 45.00
Mug, Comic Barrel, Cowboy Handle, 4 In. 16.00
Mug, Happy Hooligan, Smiling Face, Red Nose, 4 In. 22.00
Mug, Nude Lady Handle, 4 1/2 In. 37.50
Pitcher, Lion, Orange, Green, Yellow, Tail Handle, 5 In. 9.00
Planter, Baby Boot, Blue, Pierced For Hanging, 2 In. 4.00
Planter, Cherub, Bucket Of Grapes, 2 X 2 In. 10.00
Planter, Chest Of Drawers, 2 In. 4.00
Planter, Dog, Spotted, Pointed Nose, Tan, 3 In. 7.00
Planter, Duck, 5 3/4 In. 7.00
Planter, Dutch Couple, By Well, 3 1/4 In. 8.00
Planter, Gent & Donkey Cart, 3 X 3 In. 4.50
Planter, Giraffe, Small 10.00
Planter, Horse Pulling Wagon 7.00
Planter, Oriental Man, Basket Weave, Holds Fan, 4 X 3 In. 7.00
Planter, Rabbit Pulling Basket 14.00
Plate, Ambassador, Rose, 7 1/2 In. 10.50
Plate, Blue Willow, Crown Mark, 9 In. 12.00
Plate, Dragon, Green, Goldstone Ground, 19th Century, 7 3/4 In 385.00
Plate, Floral Center, Red & Gold Panels, 4 1/2 In. 3.50
Plate, Gold Castle, Floral Border, 10 In. 15.00
Salt & Pepper, Boy & Girl, Waist Up, Boy Plays Concertina 5.00
Salt & Pepper, Candle Shaped, With Tray 8.00
Salt & Pepper, Copper Luster, Red Flowers 3.00
Salt & Pepper, Dutch Boy & Girl, Seated, 2 1/2 In. 10.00
Salt & Pepper, Elsie The Cow & Calf, 4 1/2 In. 42.00
Salt & Pepper, George & Martha Washington 15.00
Salt & Pepper, Indians, Multicolored Headdress, 3 In. 11.00
Salt & Pepper, Mexican, Yellow Sombrero, 3 In. 9.00
Salt & Pepper, Nun, Black & White Habit 4.50
Salt & Pepper, Oriental Pair, Man With Flowers, Lady Fan 12.00
Salt & Pepper, Red Tomato, 4 1/2 X 2 1/2 In. 12.00
Salt & Pepper, Rooster & Hen, Sitting, Orange, Yellow, 2 In. 15.00
Salt & Pepper, Southern Belle Children, Big Bonnets, 3 In. 15.00
Salt & Pepper, Windmill 18.00
Stein, Tavern Scene, 6 In. 20.00

Sugar & Creamer, Swan Handle	25.00
Sugar & Creamer, White, Bold Trim, Covered, Marked	20.00
Tea Set, Aladdin, 14 Piece	80.00
Tea Set, Blue Luster Trim, Orange & Yellow Flowers, 15 Pc.	165.00
Tea Set, Child's, Blue Willow, 15 Piece	75.00
Tea Set, Gold Tracery Inside, Figures, SGK Mark, 14 Piece	125.00
Teapot, Blue Luster, Scenic	12.00
Teapot, Floral, Leaf, Gold Trim, Covered, 4 In.	8.50
Teapot, Hand-Painted Violets, Round, 5 1/2 In.	22.50
Teapot, Imari Colors, 7 In.	200.00
Toby Jug, Colonial Man, Cobalt Blue Coat, Black Trim, 3 In.	28.00
Toby Jug, Indian Chief, 2 1/2 In.	35.00
Toby Jug, Jailer, Napoleon Hat, 7 1/2 In.	22.00
Toby Jug, Lady, Colonial	14.00
Toby Jug, Man, Black Hat, Gray Hair, 2 In.	9.00
Toby Jug, Musketeer, Green Hat, Yellow Feather, Mustache	22.00
Toby Jug, Pirate, Brown Hat, Mask, 3 1/2 In.	14.00 To 15.00
Toby Jug, Woman, Red Blouse, Green Skirt, 2 1/2 In.	10.00
Toothpick, Boy With Knapsack, Girl With Cornucopia, 2 In.	9.00
Toothpick, Girl, Nude, Foot On Book, Luster Colors, 3 In.	10.00
Toothpick, Lady Concertina Player, Red Dress	4.50
Toothpick, Man, Seated, Holds Top Hat, Red Trim	6.00
Vase, Bud, Nude Cherub, Lying Down, Bottle Shaped	14.00
Vase, Bud, Squirrel & Flower, 2 3/4 In.	8.00
Vase, Holy Man, Yellow, Green, Gold Trim, 3 In.	6.50
Wall Pocket, Colonial Lady In Balcony, Pink Dress, 4 In.	12.00
Wall Pocket, Duck, Pair	18.00
Wall Pocket, Elephant, Full-Faced, Orange, Green, 7 In.	25.00
Wall Pocket, Girl & Flowers, Orange Dress, Green	8.00
Wall Pocket, Man, Holds Hat & Walking Stick, 7 In.	16.00
Wall Pocket, Oriental Girl Sitting On Corner, 5 3/4 In., Pr.	30.00
Water Set, White Opal, 7 Piece	225.00

G. E. OHR, BILOXI. *Ohr pottery was made by George E.Ohr in Biloxi, Mississippi, between 1883 and 1918. The pieces were made of very thin clay and were twisted, folded, and dented into odd, graceful shapes.*

OHR, Bowl, Green-Brown, Speckled, Flat Rim, Marked, 5 5/8 In.	210.00
Bowl, Thumb Push-Ins At Base, Gunmetal Iridescent, 4 1/2 X 3 In.	135.00
Bowl, White, Black, & Brown, Unglazed, 4 1/4 X 5 1/2 In.	95.00
Chamberstick, Black Handle, Marked, 4 1/2 In.	135.00
Cup, Black & Red, Horizonial Ribs, Marked, 3 X 3 In.	210.00
Cup, Seaweed Green Speckled, 2-Handled, Marked	210.00
Jug, 3 X 4 1/2 In.	200.00
Mug, Puzzle	300.00
Vase, Dark Brown Speckled, Mustard Ground, Pleated Rim, Marked, 5 In.	225.00
Vase, Gray, Red, Black, Black Inside, Impressed Stamp, 9 In.	210.00
Vase, Gunmetal Brown, Luster, Narrow Neck, Marked, 4 1/2 In.	175.00
Vase, Light Green, Dark Brown Ground, Marked, 3 5/8 X 4 3/8 In.	210.00
Vase, Mottled, Gritty Black & Red, 3 Horizontal Ribs, 3 X 3 In.	195.00
Vase, Pleated, Pinched, Dark Brown, 3 1/4 X 5 1/4 In.	200.00
Vase, Raspberry, Pinched Rim, Dimpled Belly, Marked, 3 1/2 In.	210.00
Vase, Tortured Rim, Pinched Neck, Signed, Black Spots, Green, 7 1/2 In.	950.00
Vase, Twisted Center Body, Signed, Black Semigloss, 6 X 4 In.	550.00

OLD IVORY 84 *Old ivory china was made in Silesia, Germany, at the end of the nineteenth century. It is often marked with a crown and the word "Silesia." The pattern numbers appear on the base of each piece.*

OLD IVORY, Berry Bowl, No.82	50.00
Bowl, Holly, 9 1/2 X 2 In.	58.00
Bowl, No.15, 10 In.	75.00
Bowl, Waste, No.16, 5 1/4 X 3 In.	70.00
Cake Plate, No.16, Pierced Handles, 10 In.	65.00 To 98.00
Cake Plate, No.16, Pierced Handles, 11 In.	125.00

Cake Platter, No.15, 11 In. 90.00
Cake Set, No.84, 7 Piece 200.00
Cake Set, No.200, Server, 10 1/2 In., 7 Piece 85.00
Celery, No.16, 11 3/4 In. .... 70.00 To 110.00
Celery, No.78, 9 3/8 In. 56.00
Chocolate Pot, No.28, Silesia 275.00
Chocolate Pot, Red & Yellow Roses, Handled 75.00
Creamer, No.16 .... 40.00
Creamer, No.84 .... 48.00
Cup & Saucer, No.10 .... 42.00
Cup & Saucer, No.15 .... 42.00 To 48.00
Cup & Saucer, No.16 .... 35.00 To 48.00
Cup & Saucer, No.84 .... 49.00
Cup & Saucer, No.166 .... 30.00
Cup, Chocolate, Thistle Pattern 70.00
Mustard, No.16 .... 50.00
Plate, Chop, No.16, 12 1/2 In. 125.00
Plate, No.15, 7 3/4 In. 30.00
Plate, No.16, 6 1/4 In. 24.00
Plate, No.16, 7 1/2 In. .... 22.00 To 30.00
Plate, No.84, 6 1/4 In. 28.00
Plate, No.84, 8 1/4 In. 35.00
Plate, No.200, 7 1/2 In. 38.00
Plate, Silesia, No.84, 9 1/4 In. 150.00
Relish, No.16, Oval, 6 3/4 In. 38.00
Relish, No.84, 6 1/2 In. 45.00
Salt & Pepper, No.84 .... 95.00
Saltshaker, No.75 .... 48.00
Sugar & Creamer, No.15 .... 110.00
Sugar & Creamer, No.16, Hand-Painted Roses, Covered .... 125.00 To 155.00
Sugar & Creamer, No.26, Covered 125.00
Sugar & Creamer, No.78, Covered 68.00
Sugar, No.15, Covered 45.00
Sugar, No.16, Covered 55.00
Toothpick, No.16 .... 85.00
Tray, No.15, Round, 12 3/4 In. 135.00
Tray, No.200, Handled, 8 1/2 In. 68.00
Tray, Pickle, No.16, Silesia, 8 1/4 X 5 In. 65.00
Trivet, No.16, Silesia, 6 1/4 In. 165.00
      OLD SLEEPY EYE, see Sleepy Eye

Onion, originally named "bulb pattern," is a white ware decorated with
cobalt blue or pink. Although it is commonly associated with Meissen, other
companies made the pattern in the late nineteenth and the twentieth centuries.

ONION, Board, Cheese, Meissen 40.00
      Bowl, Meissen, 4 1/4 In. 30.00
      Bowl, Shell, Deep, Meissen, 7 X 8 In. 145.00
      Butter, Meissen 125.00
      Compote, Openwork, Meissen, 9 In. 650.00
      Dish, Leaf Shaped, Handled, Meissen, 7 In., Pair 70.00
      Mustard, Matching Spoon, Blue & White 22.50
      Plate, Meissen, 7 1/2 In. 23.00
      Plate, Meissen, 9 3/4 In. 38.00
      Plate, Soup, Meissen, Crossed Swords, 9 1/2 In. 65.00
      Platter, Meissen 125.00
      Platter, Meissen, 19 In. 200.00
      Teapot, Hutschenreuther 68.00
      Teapot, Rose Finial, Meissen, 19th Century, 10 In. 185.00

Opalescent glass is translucent glass that has the bluish-white tones of the
opal gemstone. It is often found in pressed glassware made in Victorian
times. Some dealers use the terms opaline and opalescent for any of the
bluish-white translucent wares.

OPALESCENT, Basket, Hobnail, Handled, Pink, 10 1/2 In. 65.00
Basket, Hobnail, White & Clear, 6 In. 29.00
Berry Bowl, Alaska, White 25.00
Berry Bowl, Drape, Blue 25.00
Berry Bowl, Drape, Blue, Signed Northwood 25.00
Berry Bowl, Fluted Scroll, Vaseline .... 30.00 To 85.00
Berry Bowl, Fluted Scroll, Vaseline, Small 25.00
Berry Bowl, Hobnail, Square, Vaseline 22.00
Berry Bowl, Master, Alaska, Blue 75.00
Berry Bowl, Master, Fluted Scroll, Vaseline 85.00
Berry Bowl, Master, Regal, Northwood, Blue 95.00
Berry Bowl, Waterlily & Cattails, Ruffled, Amethyst 22.00
Berry Set, Scroll & Acanthus, Clear, 5 Piece 55.00
Bonbon, Fluted Scrolls, Canary, 7 1/2 In. 35.00
Bonbon, Fluted Scrolls, Footed, Sapphire Blue 35.00
Bottle, Barber, Daisy & Fern, Cranberry 125.00
Bottle, Barber, Daisy & Fern, Vaseline .... 75.00 To 95.00
Bottle, Barber, Hobnail, Pewter Top, Mauve 175.00
Bottle, Barber, Seaweed, Cranberry 140.00
Bottle, Barber, Stars & Stripes, C.1930, Cranberry 85.00
Bottle, Barber, Stars & Stripes, Clear 95.00
Bottle, Barber, Swirl, Cranberry 110.00
Bottle, Barber, Swirl, Cranberry, Square 135.00
Bottle, Cologne, Feather, White, 6 In. 40.00
Bottle, Perfume, Hobnail, Blue 25.00
Bottle, Scent, Ball-Shaped, Brass Cover, Chain, Blue 75.00
Bowl, Abalone, Green, 2-Handled 20.00
Bowl, Barbell, Ruffled, Blue, 6 1/2 In. 30.00
Bowl, Barbell, Ruffled, Clear, 8 1/2 In. 24.00
Bowl, Basket Weave, Double Lace Edge, Yellow, 4 3/4 In. 22.00
Bowl, Basket Weave, Open Edge, Green, 6 1/2 In. 19.00
Bowl, Beaded Stars, Ruffled, Blue 45.00
Bowl, Camphor, Painted Flowers, Footed, 8 In. 35.00
Bowl, Cane, Blue, 5 1/2 In. 19.50
Bowl, Cranberry, Crimped Ruffled Rim, Ribbed Base, 10 In. 45.00
Bowl, Fan With Beaded Oval Design, White, 9 In. 35.00
Bowl, Katy, Imperial, Green, 5 In. 15.00
Bowl, Pearl Flowers, Footed, Green, 7 1/2 In. 37.50
Bowl, Reflecting Diamonds, Blue, 9 In. 40.00
Bowl, Ruffled Ring, Green, 8 In. 26.00
Bowl, Scales, Peach, 9 1/2 In. 25.00
Bowl, Scroll With Acanthus, White, 5 1/2 In. 14.00
Bowl, Swirl, Silver Plated Holder, Blue, 10 In. 100.00
Bowl, Three Fruits, Ruffled, Blue, 9 In. 65.00
Bowl, Water Lily & Cattail, Green, 8 3/4 In. 35.00
Bowl, Wheel & Block, Blue, 10 In. 47.50
Butter Set, Alaska, Blue, 4 Piece 495.00
Butter, Everglades, Blue 350.00
Butter, Fluted Scroll, Covered, Vaseline 165.00
Butter, Frosted Leaf & Basket Weave, Clear 25.00
Butter, Jewel & Flower, Covered, Blue 95.00
Butter, Palm Beach, Vaseline 192.00
Butter, Regal, Covered, Northwood, Blue 195.00
Butter, Tokyo, Covered, Blue 250.00
Butter, Tokyo, Covered, Green .... 35.00 To 155.00
Butter, Wreath & Shell, Covered 28.00
Butter, Wreath & Shell, White 28.00
Cake Stand, Hobnail, Blue, 12 In. 55.00
Candlestick, Hobnail, Pink, 3 In., Pair 45.00
Carafe, Water, Reverse Swirl, Blue 45.00
Castor, Pickle, Daisy & Fern, Cranberry 250.00
Celery, Beatty Swirl, Blue 55.00
Celery, Beatty Swirl, White 35.00
Celery, Swirled Windows, Blue 80.00

Compote, Jelly, Maple Leaf, Green .... 35.00 To 45.00
Compote, Jelly, Regal, Blue 85.00
Compote, Jelly, Ribbed Spiral, Blue 38.00
Compote, Jelly, Swag Brackets, Blue 19.00
Compote, Jelly, Swag With Bracket, Green 72.50
Compote, Jelly, Tokyo, Sapphire Blue 35.00
Creamer, Alaska, Blue .... 45.00 To 70.00
Creamer, Alaska, Vaseline 50.00
Creamer, Beatty Rib, Clear 16.00
Creamer, Circled Scroll, Blue 75.00
Creamer, Circled Scroll, Green .... 65.00 To 85.00
Creamer, Everglades, Gold Trim, Blue 40.00
Creamer, Fluted Scroll, Vaseline 40.00
Creamer, Gonterman Swirl, Frosted Amber 100.00
Creamer, Intaglio, Blue .... 40.00 To 50.00
Creamer, Intaglio, White 25.00
Creamer, Jackson, Green 45.00
Creamer, Jeweled Heart, Blue .... 38.00 To 40.00
Creamer, Paneled Holly, Gold Trim, Signed, N, Clear To White 45.00
Creamer, Scroll With Acanthus, Vaseline 50.00
Creamer, Shell, White 30.00
Creamer, Swirl, Child's, Blue 50.00
Creamer, Tokyo, Blue 75.00
Creamer, Waterlily & Cattails, Blue 40.00
Cruet, Alaska, Original Stopper, White 68.00
Cruet, Argonaut Shell, Original Stopper, White 90.00
Cruet, Ball Stopper, Clear Handle, Base, & Pontil, Cranberry 43.00
Cruet, Chrysanthemum Sprig, Opaque Stopper, Blue 350.00
Cruet, Intaglio, Original Stopper, Blue 125.00
Cruet, Jackson, Yellow 75.00
Cruet, Jeweled Heart, Original Stopper, Green 195.50
Cruet, Paneled Sprig, Clear 50.00
Cruet, Regal, Original Stopper, White 68.00
Cruet, Toyko, Original Stopper, White 55.00
Cruet, Wild Bouquet, Blue 215.00
Decanter, Hobnail, Red, 10 In. 59.00
Dish, Blue, Footed, Turned-Up Sides, 8 1/2 In. 23.00
Dish, Candy, Beaded Panels, Pedestal, Blue 30.00
Dish, Candy, Jackson, White 10.00
Dish, Jelly, Scroll With Acanthus, Blue 35.00
Dish, Waterlily & Cattails, 2-Handled, White 15.00
Epergne, Jack-In-The-Pulpit, Vaseline, 9 1/2 In. 225.00
Epergne, 3-Horn, Diamond Lace, Blue, Large 145.00
Ewer, Ruby To White, Coin Spot Pattern, Clear Handle, 4 In. 25.00
Globe, Honeycomb, Quilted, Melon Rib, 16 X 10 In. 350.00
Hat, Swirl Stripe, Green, 6 X 9 In. 115.00
Jar, Jelly, Scroll With Acanthus, Blue 35.00
Lamp, Finger, Windows, Cranberry 255.00
Lamp, Snowflake, Blue, 7 1/2 In. 375.00
Mustard, Reverse Swirl, Original Cover, Vaseline 38.00
Nappy, Sea Spray, 3-Sided, Handled, Blue 37.50
Nappy, Swag & Brackets, Vaseline 35.00
Pitcher, Coin Dot, Cranberry, 9 1/2 In. 95.00
Pitcher, Coin Spot Pattern, Ruby To White, Clear Handle, 8 In. 150.00
Pitcher, Cranberry To Milky White, Coin Spot, Clear Handle, 9 In. 60.00
Pitcher, Cranberry, Clear Handle, Swirled Coin Spot, 5 In. 20.00
Pitcher, Daisy & Fern, 3-Spout, Blue, 8 1/2 In. 140.00
Pitcher, Intaglio, White, 8 1/4 In. 85.00
Pitcher, Lemonade, Daffodils, Hinged Guard, Pewter Cover, Vaseline 115.00
Pitcher, Milky Swirl To Cranberry To Clear, Handle, 8 In. 70.00
Pitcher, Water, Alaska, Northwood, Vaseline 350.00
Pitcher, Water, Apple Blossom, Enameled Green Collar, White 195.00
Pitcher, Water, Beatty Swirl, Blue 125.00
Pitcher, Water, Blue, Northwood 145.00

Pitcher, Water, Christmas, Blue 250.00
Pitcher, Water, Drapery, Northwood, Blue 175.00
Pitcher, Water, Fluted Scrolls, Blue 195.00
Pitcher, Water, Inverted Thistle, Green, Gold Trim 70.00
Pitcher, Water, Inverted Thumbprint, Amber Handle, Vaseline 79.00
Pitcher, Water, Jewel & Flower, Vaseline 400.00
Pitcher, Water, Poinsettia, Blue 155.00
Pitcher, Water, Reverse Swirl, Clear 110.00
Pitcher, Water, Reverse Swirl, White 85.00
Pitcher, Water, Seaweed, Blue 225.00
Pitcher, Water, Spiral Optic, Green 95.00
Pitcher, Water, Stars & Stripes, Clear 165.00
Pitcher, Water, Stripe, Burlington Mark, Ruffled, Vaseline 165.00
Pitcher, Water, Tokyo, Blue 375.00
Pitcher, Water, Tokyo, Green 125.00
Plate, Soup, Katy, Green 18.00
Plate, Spokes & Wheels, Blue, 9 In. 35.00
Rose Bowl, Butterscotch Beaded Cable, Aqua 225.00
Rose Bowl, Button Panels, Blue 45.00
Rose Bowl, Leaf & Beads, Scalloped Rim, Aqua 165.00
Rose Bowl, Pearl Flowers, Green 24.00
Rose Bowl, Wreath & Shell, Vaseline 65.00
Salt & Pepper, Hobnail, Blue, 3 1/2 In. 35.00
Salt, Master, Petal & Loop, Flint, Blue 25.00
Salt, Vaseline Applique Around Center, Silver Plated Holder 88.00
Saltshaker, Beatty Rib, Original Top, Blue 30.00
Saltshaker, Chrysanthemum, Blue 35.00
Saltshaker, Chrysanthemum, Clear 22.00
Saltshaker, Crisscross, Cranberry 110.00
Saltshaker, Fluted Scroll, Enamel Design, Gold Trim, Blue 45.00
Saltshaker, Jackson, Clear 25.00
Saltshaker, Periwinkle, Blue 20.00
Saltshaker, Reverse Swirl, Blue 25.00
Saltshaker, Ribbed Lattice, Original Lid, Cranberry 35.00
Saltshaker, Seaweed, Cranberry 50.00
Saltshaker, Vertical Stripe, Vaseline 38.00
Sauce, Beatty Rib, Clear 9.00
Sauce, Fluted Scrolls, Enameled, Vaseline 42.50
Saucer, Flute, Blue, 5 In. 10.00
Shade, Swirl, Ruffled Top, Clear, 5 In. 69.00
Shoe, Hobnail, Cat's Face, Blue 20.00
Slipper, Hobnail, Blue 15.00
Spittoon, Lady's, Thousand Eye 45.00
Spooner, Alaska, Blue 50.00
Spooner, Beatty Rib, Emerald Green 23.00
Spooner, Dolly Madison, Jefferson Glass Co., Blue 52.00
Spooner, Drapery, Gold Trim, Blue 55.00
Spooner, Drapery, White 45.00
Spooner, Fluted Scrolls, Blue 50.00
Spooner, Fluted Scrolls, Vaseline 45.00
Spooner, Fluted Scrolls, White 25.00
Spooner, Intaglio, Blue 45.00
Spooner, Intaglio, Vaseline 65.00
Spooner, Iris, Green .... 75.00 To 85.00
Spooner, Regal, Blue .... 60.00 To 65.00
Spooner, Wild Bouquet, Green 75.00
Spooner, Wreath & Shell, Clear 45.00
Spooner, Wreath & Shell, Vaseline 60.00
Sugar & Creamer, Alaska, Vaseline 185.00
Sugar Shaker, Beatty Rib, Blue .... 75.00 To 85.00
Sugar Shaker, Cone, Green 60.00
Sugar Shaker, Reverse Swirl, Blue 110.00
Sugar Shaker, Reverse Swirl, Cranberry 150.00
Sugar Shaker, Ribbed Lattice, Blue 70.00

Sugar Shaker, Twist Pattern, Blue	85.00
Sugar Shaker, 9-Panel Twist, Green	55.00
Sugar, Alaska, Vaseline	165.00
Sugar, Everglades, Covered, Blue	135.00
Sugar, Fluted Scroll, Open, Vaseline	25.00
Sugar, Tokyo, Blue	125.00
Syrup, Daisy & Fern, Blue	85.00
Syrup, Daisy & Fern, West Virginia Optic, Mold, Clear	55.00
Syrup, Fern, Blue	65.00
Syrup, Windows, Swirled, Blue	210.00
Syrup, Windows, Swirled, Bulbous, Clear	80.00
Table Set, Fluted Scrolls, Vaseline, 4 Piece	375.00
Table Set, Jackson Pattern, Northwood, Blue, 5 Piece	375.00
Table Set, Wreath & Shell, Blue, 4 Piece	495.00
Toothpick, Beatty Honeycomb, Blue	45.00 To 48.00
Toothpick, Beatty Ribbed, Clear	32.50
Toothpick, Diamond Spearhead, Green	55.00
Toothpick, Diamond Spearhead, Yellow	58.00
Toothpick, Gonterman Swirl, Amber Top, White	120.00
Toothpick, Iris With Meander, Blue	85.00
Toothpick, Iris With Meander, Clear	30.00 To 35.00
Toothpick, Iris With Meander, Gold Trim, Amethyst	45.00
Toothpick, Iris With Meander, Vaseline	55.00
Toothpick, Jeweled Heart, Apple Green	45.00
Toothpick, Ribbed Spiral, Vaseline	65.00
Toothpick, Spearpoint, Vaseline	60.00
Toothpick, Swirl, Blue	45.00
Toothpick, Wide Strip, Bulbous, Rigaree Rim, Enamel Florals, White	95.00
Toothpick, Wild Bouquet, Blue	85.00
Toothpick, Woman's Hand Shape, Scalloped Top, Blue	39.00
Tray, Card, Tokyo, On Stand, Blue	45.00
Tumbler, Apple Blossom, Blue Band, Cranberry	40.00
Tumbler, Beatty Swirl, White	25.00
Tumbler, Button & Braids, Blue	40.00
Tumbler, Circle Scroll, Clear	35.00
Tumbler, Croesus, Gold Trim, Green	40.00
Tumbler, Daisy & Fern, Cranberry	45.00
Tumbler, Fluted Scroll, Blue	45.00
Tumbler, Herringbone, Cranberry	75.00
Tumbler, Intaglio, Northwood, Crystal, Set Of 6	125.00
Tumbler, Inverted Thumbprint, Blue	30.00
Tumbler, Jeweled Heart, Blue	45.00
Tumbler, Oriental Poppy, Gold Trim, Green	20.00
Tumbler, Palm Beach, Vaseline	40.00
Tumbler, Paneled Holly, Gold Trim, Blue	30.00
Tumbler, Red Block, Ruby	25.00
Tumbler, Regal, Northwood, White	30.00
Tumbler, Ribbed Spiral, Blue	30.00
Tumbler, Swastika, Superimposed Diamonds & Clubs	85.00
Tumbler, Swirl, Blue	22.00
Tumbler, Swirl, Pink	30.00
Tumbler, Thumbprint, Blue	22.00
Tumbler, Vesta, Blue	30.00
Tumbler, Windows, Clear	25.00
Tumbler, Windows, Cranberry	35.00
Tumbler, Windows, Swirled, Blue	38.00
Tumbler, Windows, Swirled, Clear	28.00
Tumbler, Windows, Swirled, Cranberry	40.00
Tumbler, Windows, White	25.00
Tumbler, Wreath & Shell, Footed, Blue	75.00
Vase, Corn, Vaseline, 8 In.	50.00
Vase, Fan Shape, Blue, 6 In., Pair	49.00
Vase, Fan, Hobnail, Blue, 5 1/2 X 8 1/2 In.	35.00
Vase, Fan, Hobnail, Blue, 8 In.	25.00

Vase, Iris & Meander, Blue, 12 In.	60.00
Vase, Jack-In-The-Pulpit, Ruffled, Green, 6 1/4 In.	100.00
Vase, Jack-In-The-Pulpit, 3 Tree Trunk Knees, Green, 6 3/4 In.	56.00
Vase, Swirl, Applied Flowers, Green To Vaseline, 4 X 5 In.	95.00
Vase, Swirl, Ruby To White, 6 In.	20.00
Vase, Treebark, Blue, 11 In.	38.00
Vase, Treebark, Green, 11 In.	55.00
Vase, 3-Petal Top, Enameled Lilies Of The Valley, Blue, 5 1/2 In.	85.00
Water Set, Alaska, Vaseline	300.00
Water Set, Beehive, Cranberry, 9 Piece	400.00
Water Set, Buttons & Braids, Blue, 5 Piece	265.00
Water Set, Daisy & Fern, Cranberry, 7 Piece	285.00
Water Set, Flora, Green, 7 Piece	275.00
Water Set, Guttate, Gold Trim, Marked Burlington, White, 7 Piece	265.00
Water Set, Hobnail, Fenton, Cranberry, 9 Piece	275.00
Water Set, Poinsettia, Molded Tumblers, Blue, 7 Piece	375.00

Opaline, or opal glass, was made in white, green, and other colors. The glass had a matte surface and a lack of transparency. It was often gilded or painted. It was a popular mid-nineteenth-century European glassware.

OPALINE, Rose Bowl, Pale Green	75.00
Vase, Blue, Footed, Gold Enameled, 7 In.	69.00
Vase, Pink, Gold Decor, Enameled Flower, Flared Rim, 15 X 5 In.	75.00

OPERA GLASSES, Allover Turquoise Blue Enamel, Flowers & Festoons, French	125.00
Chevalier, Case	22.00
French, Blue Enamel, Inscribed Jaccard Jewellry Co., C.1900	80.00
French, Mother-Of-Pearl, Case	50.00
French, Mother-Of-Pearl, Le Clerc, Paris, C.1900	80.00
Mother-Of-Pearl, Leather Case	22.00

ORGAN, see Music, Organ

In August 1924 Little Orphan Annie was introduced through a comic strip written by Harold Gray. She has continued to be popular through comics, a broadway show, and movies.

ORPHAN ANNIE, Book, Published From 1929-32, Cupples & Leon Co., Set Of 9	125.00
Book, Song, 1938, 35 Pages	25.00
Cards, Rummy, Boxed	12.00
Cards, 1935, Boxed, Set Of 22	20.00
Circus Cutout, Cardboard, 1935, 32 Piece	55.00
Decoder, 1935	13.00
Decoder, 1936	17.00
Decoder, 1937	13.00 To 20.00
Decoder, 1938	12.00
Decoder, 1939	17.50
Decoder, 1940	20.00
Doll, Cloth, 3 Uncut Dresses, 1930s, 7 1/2 In.	65.00
Doll, Ideal	250.00
Figurine, Annie, Warbucks, & Sandy, Lead	10.00
Figurine, Bisque, Marked Japan	30.00
Mug, Ovaltine, Beetleware	15.00 To 25.00
Mug, Ovaltine, Ceramic	17.00 To 25.00
Mug, Ovaltine, Embossed Didja Ever Taste Anything So Good	30.00
Nodder, With Sandy, Bisque	125.00
Paper Doll, Daddy Warbucks	20.00
Pin, Membership, Secret Society, 1934	10.00
Radio, Designed Like Telephone, Picture On Dial, 1940s	275.00
Ring, Mystic Eye	24.00
Salt & Pepper, Annie & Sandy	26.00 To 32.00
Shaker, Ovaltine, Beetleware, 1936, Decal	45.00
Stove, Double Oven, Electric, Marx, 9 X 8 In.	55.00 To 75.00
Toy, Jack Set, 1930s	38.00

Toy, Sandy, Lever Action Tail, Tin	125.00
Watch, Annie & Sandy, Boxed	68.00
Watch, Sun, With Compass	35.00

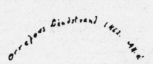

Orrefors Glassworks, located in the Swedish province of Smaaland, was established in 1916.

ORREFORS, Bottle, Perfume, Paperweight Base, Prism Cut Stopper, Clear, 6 In.	45.00
Bowl, Crystal, 4 People Skiing On Slopes, Marked	185.00
Paperweight, Cube, Air Bubble & Air Circle Pattern, 2 In.	20.00
Vase, Brown, Fish & Seaweed, 8 In.	575.00
Vase, Fishgraal, Signed Edward Hald, 8 1/2 In.	675.00
Vase, Green-Toned Interior, Swimming Fish, Seaweed, Marked, 5 In.	325.00
Vase, Intaglio Cut, Girl Holding Hem Of Nightie, 6 1/2 X 4 1/2 In.	250.00
Vase, Paperweight, Fish Swimming, Marked, 5 3/4 In.	285.00

Ott & Brewer Company operated the Etruria Pottery at Trenton, New Jersey, from 1863 to 1893. It was under the direction of William Bromley, Sr., from the Belleek factory at Belleek, Ireland, from 1883.

OTT & BREWER, Creamer, Pansies, Marked, 3 1/2 In.	225.00
Cup & Saucer, Tridacna Pattern, Gold Paste Leaves, Marked	225.00
Cup & Saucer, Tridacna, Pale Lavender Tint, Gilt Trim, Belleek	110.00
Ewer, Raised Gold Thistles, Cream Ground, 8 In.	675.00
Tumbler, Aqua Enamel, Fluted, 3 3/4 In.	225.00
Vase, Lily Shaped, Lavender Leaf, Gold Highlights	495.00

Owens Pottery was made in Zanesville, Ohio, from 1891 to 1928. The first art pottery was made after 1896. Utopian Ware, Cyrano, Navarre, Feroza, and Henri Deux were made. Pieces were usually marked with a form of the name Owens. About 1907 the firm began to make tile and gave up the art pottery wares.

OWENS, Ewer, Utopian, Aqua, Brown-Beige, Flowers, 9 1/2 In.	85.00
Ewer, Utopian, Pansies, Marked, 6 In.	185.00
Ewer, Utopian, Steele, 6 In.	168.00
Ewer, Utopian, 11 In.	165.00
Jar, Frogskin, Covered	60.00
Jardiniere, Lotus, Butterflies, 10 1/2 In.	190.00
Jardiniere, Slip-Painted Butterflies, Tan Ground, 10 1/2 In.	225.00
Jardiniere, Utopian, Matte, Pedestal	300.00 To 330.00
Jug, Utopian, Artist Signed, 5 3/4 In.	170.00
Lamp, Pansies, Glazed, 11 1/2 In.	200.00
Mug, Floral, Signed, 5 In.	75.00
Mug, Utopian, Berry, Signed	75.00
Mug, Utopian, Matte, 5 1/2 In.	40.00
Pitcher, Aqua, Verde, 3 1/2 In.	70.00
Pitcher, Water, Stork, 8 1/2 In.	565.00
Tankard, Cherries, 12 In.	275.00
Urn, Utopian, Vines & Berries, Footed, 7 X 7 In.	165.00
Vase, Aborigine, Green, 9 In.	60.00
Vase, Autumn-Colored Leaves, Signed, 7 1/2 In.	145.00
Vase, Feroza, 2-Handled, Black Metallic Luster, 6 X 5 In.	95.00
Vase, Pale Glaze, 1 1/2 X 2 1/2 In.	105.00
Vase, Pansies, Ovoid Shape, 5 In.	110.00
Vase, Pierced Neck, Marked, Aqua Verde, 6 3/4 X 5 1/4 In.	1169.00

Vase, Pillow, Flying Ducks, 4-Footed, 9 X 8 In. 600.00
Vase, Purple, Carnations, Cream Ground, Marked, 10 3/4 In. 360.00
Vase, Uralian, Twisted Shape, 4 1/2 In. 85.00
Vase, Utopian, Artist Signed, Square, 6 In. 155.00
Vase, Utopian, Artist Signed, 3-Footed, 3 1/4 In. 160.00
Vase, Utopian, Clover, 11 In. 165.00
Vase, Utopian, Flared Neck, Bottle Shape, Marked, 10 X 6 1/4 In. 145.00
Vase, Utopian, Orange Roses, Green Ivy, Brown Ground, 12 1/2 In. 150.00
Vase, Utopian, Signed Steele, 9 In. 165.00
Vase, Utopian, Signed, 6 In. 160.00
Vase, Utopian, Yellow, Orange Roses, Ivies, Stems, Marked, 10 1/2 In. 280.00
Vase, Utopian, Yellow, Orange, Brown Roses, Marked, 4 In. 90.00
Vase, Venetian, Paper Label, 10 X 3 1/2 In. 215.00
Vase, Verde, Bulbous, Pierced Neck, Handled, Marked, 6 3/4 X 5 1/4 In. 120.00
Vase, Yellow Pansies, 5 In. 110.00

*Paden City Glass Manufacturing Company was established in 1916 at
Paden City, West Virginia. It is best known for glasswares but also
produced a pottery line. The firm closed in 1951.*

PADEN CITY, Cake Plate, Crystal, Handled 35.00
    Dish, Candy, Crow's-Foot Pattern, 3-Part 40.00
    Figurine, Horse, Rearing, Clear, 7 1/2 In. 48.00
    Figurine, Pony, Standing 75.00
    Sugar & Creamer, Cupid, Etched 37.50

PAINTING, Oil On Panel, Eating Oysters, Man, Top Hat, Oysters, 46 X 31 In. 3000.00
    On Board, Sailing Ship At Sea, Signed R.Schmalzreid, 48 X 30 In. 300.00
    On Ivory, Josephine, Signed Du Pre, Frame, 3 1/2 In. .... *Illus* 175.00
    On Ivory, Lady In Pink Dress, Pearls, & Plume In Hair, Signed, 2 In. 130.00
    On Ivory, Lady, Draped Dress, Pearls, Signed, Oval, 3 1/4 X 2 1/2 In. 280.00
    On Ivory, Lady, Ivory & Ebony Frame, 1 3/4 X 2 In. .... *Illus* 70.00
    On Ivory, Lady, Signed Saint Aubin, 3 X 3 1/2 In. .... *Illus* 175.00
    On Ivory, Louis XV, Signed Gerard, 3 X 3 1/2 In. .... *Illus* 135.00
    On Ivory, Napoleon, Frame, Artist Initialed, 3 1/4 X 2 1/2 In. 280.00
    On Ivory, Portrait, French, Hand-Painted, 5 X 8 In. 125.00
    On Ivory, Princess Sophia, Done On Piano Key, 5 1/2 X 5 1/2 In. 325.00
    On Ivory, Taj Mahal, Teakwood Frame 165.00
    On Ivory, Wigged Gentleman, Silver Frame, 2 1/2 X 2 In. 200.00
    On Ivory, Woman With Fan, 17th-Century Costume, Signed, 5 1/2 In. 50.00
    On Ivory, Woman, Signed A.Hope, C.1800, 3 X 3 1/2 In. .... *Illus* 125.00
    On Porcelain, Lady With Gold Crown, Pearls, French Frame, 2 3/4 In. 135.00
    On Porcelain, Marie Antoinette, Signed, Framed, 3 1/4 X 2 1/2 In. 200.00
    On Porcelain, Roses, Hutchenreuther, 3 X 4 In. 60.00
    On Porcelain, St.Theresa, Metal Frame, Signed M.C. 70.00
    On Porcelain, Woman With Roses, 16 Diamonds At Top, C.1840 .... 395.00
    On Velvet, Basket Of Flowers With Bird, 11 X 15 In. 475.00
    On Velvet, Eagle With Arrows, American Flag, 29 X 38 In. 65.00
    On Velvet, Urn Of Flowers, Hummingbirds, Butterfly, 16 X 21 In. 535.00
    On Wood, Gentleman, Powdered Wig, Ruffled Collar, Oval, 15 In. 150.00
    On Wood, Pastoral Scene, Sheep, Dog, Puppies, Signed Nowey, 16 In. ... 750.00
    On Wood, Woman, Renaissance Costume, Framed, 10 X 12 In. 75.00
    Reverse On Glass, Bankers Indemnity Ins., Gold Letters, Eagle 175.00
    Reverse On Glass, Castle & Bridge, Framed, 14 1/2 X 18 In. 45.00
    Reverse On Glass, Diamonds, Black On Silver Ground, 36 X 7 In. 175.00
    Reverse On Glass, Ft.Dearborn, 1933 Chicago World's Fair 50.00
    Reverse On Glass, George & Martha Washington, Framed, 20 X 24 In. ... 550.00
    Reverse On Glass, J.J.Newberry, Gold Letters, Green, 45 X 12 In. 475.00
    Reverse On Glass, Sailboats, Scenic, Gold Frame, 5 X 7 In. 18.00
    Reverse On Glass, Scene In Venice 40.00
    Reverse On Glass, Young Napoleon 300.00
    Reverse On Glass, 1841 Security Insur. Of New Haven, 23 X 17 In. 150.00

Paintings, On Ivory

Josephine, Signed Du Pre, Frame, 3 1/2 In.

Louis XV, Signed Gerard, 3 X 3 1/2 In.

Ladies, Ivory & Ebony Frame, 1 3/4 X 2 In.; Signed A.Hope, C.1800, 3 X 3 1/2 In.;
Signed Saint Aubin, 3 X 3 1/2 In.

Pairpoint Corporation was a silver and glass firm founded in New Bedford, Massachusetts, in 1880. Although the company went through many reorganizations and name changes, it is still working.

PAIRPOINT, Biscuit Jar, Enamel Flower, Covered, Footed, 7 1/4 In.	325.00
Bottle, Cologne, Crystal, Blue	125.00
Bottle, Perfume, Stopper Inside Base, Pair	85.00
Bottle, Whiskey, Basket, Stopper, 12 In.	1250.00
Bottle, Whiskey, Old English, Stopper, 10 In.	1250.00
Bowl, Bell Fluted, Threaded Handle, Cobalt Blue, 13 X 10 In.	150.00
Bowl, Centerpiece, Engraved Bowl & Foot, Bubble Stem, 12 1/4 In.	175.00
Bowl, Etched Grape, Sterling Silver Footed Holder, 9 X 11 In.	225.00
Bowl, Jewel, Purple, Blue, Florals, Cream Ground, Marked, 6 X 4 In.	275.00
Bowl, Leaf Shaped, Acorn Design, Oval, 11 X 7 In.	85.00
Box, Dresser, Allover Florals, Silver Plated Collar, 6 1/4 In.	295.00
Box, Jewel, Allover Florals, Cream Ground, Signed, 6 1/4 X 4 In.	225.00
Box, Jewel, Viscaria, Opalescent Flowers, Covered	220.00
Box, Powder, Floral Enamel, Silver Plated Base, Signed, 6 In.	225.00
Box, Silver Plated, Lid Has Apple Blossoms, 6 X 3 In.	245.00
Cake Basket, Butterflies & Birds, Dated 1880, 10 X 7 In.	135.00

Cake Basket, Pierced Handle & Border, Oval, Dated 1901 .... 85.00
Candleholder, Blue Swirl, Bubble Base, 6 In., Pair 195.00
Candlestick, Aurora, Bulbous, Hollow Stem, 10 In., Pair 150.00
Candlestick, Etched Grape, Amethyst, 10 In., Pair 425.00
Candlestick, Etched Grape, Cobalt Blue, 12 In., Pair 295.00
Candlestick, Viscaria, Prisms, 9 In., Pair 295.00
Canister, Commemorative, 1870-1910, Brass, Rooster Finial 75.00
Castor, Pink, Satin Glass, Silver 210.00
Compote, Amber, Crystal Bubble Stem, 5 X 9 In. 52.00
Compote, Amethyst, Ball Stem, 7 X 8 In. 145.00
Compote, Amethyst, Bubble Ball 110.00
Compote, Bubble Ball, Green Connector 185.00
Compote, Clear, Amber Foot, 5 X 6 In. 95.00
Compote, Etched Grape, Green, 5 In. 45.00
Compote, Steeple Bubble Finial, Ruby Foot, Covered 115.00
Cracker Jar, Floral, Silver Plated Lid & Bail, Marked 250.00
Decanter, Vintage, Cobalt Blue, Footed, Stopper, Copper Wheel 165.00
Inkwell, Paperweight, Ruby Well, Bubble Bowl, 4 1/2 In. 275.00
Lamp, Berkeley Shade, Signed Base, 16 In. .... *Illus* 725.00
Lamp, Berkeley Shade, Signed G.Morley, 18 In. .... *Illus* 675.00
Lamp, Boudoir, Reverse Painted Base & Shade, Signed 725.00
Lamp, California Poppies, Red, Green, Marked 1400.00
Lamp, Carlisle Shade, Peacock & Floral Edge, 16 In. .... *Illus* 525.00
Lamp, Carlisle Shade, Signed, Green & Blue, 18 In. .... *Illus* 500.00
Lamp, Cased Glass, Copley Shade, Signed, 16 In. .... *Illus* 725.00
Lamp, Ceiling, Signed, Cream On Plum-Amber, 15 In. 1350.00
Lamp, Directoire Shade, Artist Signed J.Bariot .... *Illus* 800.00
Lamp, Directoire Shade, Onyx & Silver Base .... *Illus* 575.00
Lamp, Directoire Shade, Signed, 15 1/2 In. .... *Illus* 675.00
Lamp, Estelle Pattern, Silver Plated Trim .... *Illus* 1250.00
Lamp, Floral Paisley Shade, Bronze Base, 24 In. 2900.00
Lamp, Hurricane, Frosted Shade, Coralene Bluebirds, 19 In., Pair 1025.00
Lamp, Marlborough Shade, Floral Decor, Closed Top, Signed 2950.00
Lamp, Marlborough Shade, Yellow Ground, 14 In. .... *Illus* 1400.00
Lamp, Oriental Pheasant Shade, 8 1/2 In., Bronze Base, 15 In., 1910 .... 650.00
Lamp, Piano, Florals On 4 Sides, Signed 850.00
Lamp, Poppies On Lavender, 15 In. 525.00
Lamp, Puffy, Apple Tree, Tree Trunk Base, Signed, 12 In. 7500.00
Lamp, Puffy, California Poppies, Prisms, Signed, 12 X 15 In. 1000.00
Lamp, Puffy, Hummingbird, Yellow & Orange Mums, 21 In. 3990.00
Lamp, Puffy, Reverse Painted Shade, 23 X 14 In. 2250.00
Lamp, Reverse Painted Floral, Base & Shade Signed, 21 In. 1500.00
Lamp, Reverse Painted Octagonal Shade, Metal Base 750.00
Lamp, Reverse Painted Shade, Scenic, Signed, 17 In. 950.00
Lamp, Reverse Painted, Floral, Multicolored, 22 In. .... *Illus* 1750.00
Lamp, Reverse Painted, Octagonal Shaped Glass Insert 750.00
Lamp, Reverse Painted, Roses 1750.00
Lamp, Sailing Scene, Triple Dolphin Base 2800.00
Lamp, Shade, Acid Etched, White Metal Base, 16 X 8 In. 400.00
Lamp, Tri-Dolphin Bronze 185.00
Match Holder, Signed, Brass 30.00
Paperweight, Figural, Fish, Controlled Bubbles, Label, 7 In. 55.00
Paperweight, Swan 75.00
Pitcher, Blue, Enamel Floral, Yellow Ground, Marked 35.00
Pitcher, Claret, Nailhead Diamond Pattern, 2 Quart 285.00
Plate, Bread, Embossed Daily Bread, Marked, 13 X 15 3/4 In. 38.00
Shade, Exeter, 3-Light Neo Classical Base, Signed, 18 In. 1500.00
Shade, Hurricane, Birch Trees, Chipped Ice, Signed, 9 In., Pair 350.00
Shade, Jungle Bird, 3-Light Neo Classical Base, Signed, 18 In. 2200.00
Shade, Reverse Painted, Windmill & Moon, Closed Top, 8 In. 385.00
Sugar & Creamer, Repousse Fruit, Fluted Edge, Twig Handles 65.00
Urn, Vintage Grape, Amethyst, Covered, 14 In. 225.00
Vase, Amethyst, Trumpet Shaped, Etched Floral, 12 In. 250.00

Pairpoint, Lamps

Carlisle Shade, Peacock & Floral Edge, 16 In.

Carlisle Shade, Signed, Green & Blue, 18 In.

Berkeley Shade, Signed Base, 16 In.

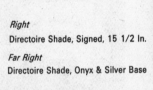

Right
Directoire Shade, Signed, 15 1/2 In.

Far Right
Directoire Shade, Onyx & Silver Base

Berkeley Shade, Signed G.Morley, 18 In.

Cased Glass, Copley Shade, Signed, 16 In.

Directoire Shade, Artist
Signed J.Bariot

Estelle Pattern,
Silver Plated Trim

(See Page 432)

Pairpoint, Lamps

Marlborough Shade,
Yellow Ground, 14 In.

Reverse Painted,
Floral, Multicolored, 22 In.

Vase, Blue, Clear Swirl, 12 In.	125.00 To 145.00
Vase, Cobalt Blue, Controlled Bubble Ball, 12 In.	85.00
Vase, Trumpet, Controlled Bubble Connector, Black, 16 In.	175.00
PAPER DOLL, Alice Fay, Merrill, 1942, Cut	38.00
Ann Southern, Saalfield, 1943, Cut	28.00
Ava Gardner, Whitman, 1949, Cut	23.00
Baby First Step, 1965, Uncut	10.00
Baby Patsy, 1934, Cut	25.00
Baby Sandy, Merrill, 1941, Cut	32.00
Baby Tender Love, 20 Outfits, Cut	10.00
Bear, Mama, Papa, Baby, 8 In.	10.00
Bette Davis, 1942, Cut	30.00
Betty Grable, Whitman, 1941, Cut	32.00
Betty, Carnation Ice Cream, 1950, Cardboard Punch-Out	2.50
Boots & Her Buddies, Merrill, 1943, Cut	20.00
Boots & Her Buddies, Uncut	26.00

Captain Marvel, 3 Flying Marvels, Dated 1945 .... 11.00
Carmen Miranda, 3 Dolls 35.00
Chatty Cathy, 1960, Uncut 10.00
Claudette Colbert, 1943, Cut 45.00
Deanna Durbin, Merrill, 1940, Cut 35.00
Debbie Reynolds, Whitman, 1957, Cut 16.00
Dinah Shore & George Montgomery, Whitman, 1959, Uncut 30.00
Dionne Quints, Merrill, 1940, Cut 55.00
Edith Tuck, Clothes, 4 Outfits & Hats, 1894, Original Box 65.00
Emilie, Let's Play House, Merrill, 1940, Cut 28.00
Esther Williams, Merrill, 1950, Cut 23.00
Gene Tierney, Whitman, 1947 .... 25.00
Gloria Jean, Saalfield, 1940, Cut 32.00
Greer Garson, Merrill, 1944, Cut 35.00
Jeanette Macdonald, Merrill, 1941, Cut .... 25.00 To 35.00
Joan Carroll, Saalfield, 1942, Cut 22.00
June Allyson, Whitman, 1950, Cut 22.00
Kewpies, Book & Kewpieville Stand-Ups, Uncut, 8 X 12 In. 17.50
Kis-Me-Gum, Cut Outs, Set Of 3 .... 17.00
Lana Turner, Whitman, 1945, Cut 25.00
Lettie Lane 15.00
Li'l Abner, Full Book 175.00
Li'l Abner, 1941, Cut 30.00
Liz Taylor, Whitman, 1949, Cut 23.00
Lucille Ball, Cut 15.00
Mary Martin, Saalfield, 1942, Cut 32.00
Mary Martin, 1952, Cut 45.00
Minnie Mouse, Saalfield, 1933, Cut 25.00
Mother Goose Village, 1935, Cardboard, Woman In Shoe, 13 X 14 In. 35.00
Patti Page, 1957 .... 30.00
Rita Hayworth, Merrill, 1942, Cut 35.00
Roy Rogers & Dale Evans, Whitman, 1950 .... 24.00
Royal Wedding, Charles & Diana, Color, Uncut 17.50
Shirley Temple, Saalfield, 1942, Cut 38.00
Snow White & The Seven Dwarfs, 1938, Cut, 17 1/2 X 24 In. 35.00
Sonja Henie, 1939, Cut 50.00
Spanish Costumes, 3 In., Set Of 2 .... 25.00
Sparkle Plenty, Uncut 12.00
Ziegfeld Girl, Cut 25.00

PAPER, Almanac, Burdock Blood Bitters, 1882 .... 12.00
Almanac, Burdock Blood Bitters, 1886 .... 12.00
Almanac, Diamond Dye, 1887 .... 12.00
Almanac, Dr. Pierce, 1880 .... 18.00
Almanac, Kate Greenaway, 1884, Illustrated, Miniature 50.00
Almanac, Kate Greenaway, 1887 .... 58.00
Almanac, Kate Greenaway, 1890, Illustrated, Miniature 50.00
Almanac, The Old Farmer's Almanac, 1859, Boston 5.00
Almanac, Uncle Sam's Almanac, 1833, Philadelphia 5.00
Book, Big Little Book, Apple Mary & Dennie's Lucky Apples 8.00
Book, Big Little Book, Big Chief Wahoo The Lost Pioneer 15.00
Book, Big Little Book, Blondie 12.00
Book, Big Little Book, Boris Karloff In The Lost Patrol 13.50
Book, Big Little Book, Bronc Peeler, The Lone Cowboy 10.00
Book, Big Little Book, Buck Jones In The Fighting Code 12.00
Book, Big Little Book, Dick Tracy Returns 19.00
Book, Big Little Book, Flash Gordon In The Water World Of Mongo 15.00
Book, Big Little Book, G-Men On The Trail 10.00
Book, Big Little Book, Hair Breadth Harry In Department Q.T. 13.50
Book, Big Little Book, Houdini's Book Of Magic, 1927 .... 45.00
Book, Big Little Book, In The Name Of The Law 10.50
Book, Big Little Book, International Spy, Dr.Doom Faces Death 12.00
Book, Big Little Book, Jackie Cooper, 1933 .... 10.00

Book, Big Little Book, Jane Arden, Vanished Princess	10.00
Book, Big Little Book, Ken Maynard, Gunwolves Of The Gila	17.00
Book, Big Little Book, Li'l Abner In New York, 1936	10.00
Book, Big Little Book, Little Miss Muffet	8.50
Book, Big Little Book, Oswald Rabbit Plays G-Man, Walter Lantz	22.50
Book, Big Little Book, Our Gang, 1934	10.00
Book, Big Little Book, Peggy Brown & Runaway Auto Trailer	9.50
Book, Big Little Book, Red Barry, Undercover Man	12.50
Book, Big Little Book, Roadrunner, 1968	4.00
Book, Big Little Book, Robinson Crusoe	12.00
Book, Big Little Book, Shooting Sheriffs	10.00
Book, Big Little Book, Skippy & Sooky, Jackie Cooper	12.50
Book, Big Little Book, Tailspin Tommy & The Lost Transport	12.50
Book, Big Little Book, Terry & The Pirates	10.00
Book, Big Little Book, The Spy	10.00
Book, Big Little Book, Tim McCoy, The Westerner	17.50
Book, Big Little Book, Tom Mix & His Circus On The Barbary Coast	16.00
Book, Big Little Book, Tom Mix, Terror Trail	15.00
Book, Big Little Book, Woody Woodpecker, 1967	4.00
Book, Big Little Book, Zip Saunders, Speedway King, 1939	10.00
PAPER, CALENDAR, see Calendar Paper	
Catalog, Albany Feed Store, Seeds, Tools, 1904, 4 Pages	3.00
Catalog, Lord & Taylor, Fall & Winter 1881, 144 Pages	5.00
Chart, Phrenological, 1873	20.00
Cigar Band, Buster Brown, 1920	1.00
Cigar Band, President Taft, 1920	1.50
Cookbook, Corn Starch Book Of Cooking, 1903	1.00
Cookbook, Pillsbury Bake-Off, 5th Bake-Off, 1954	5.00
Cookbook, Pillsbury Cookbook Of 1924	1.00
Cookbook, Seek No Further, Seneca Falls, 1886	4.00
Cookbook, Taste The Taste, Underwood Deviled Ham, 1909	3.00
Cookbook, Temperance, C.1888, 27 Pages, Wall Hung, 14 X 18 In.	50.00
Coupons, Ration, World War II, Block Of 20	295.00
Guide, New York World's Fair, 1964-65	6.00
Handbill, Galena Minstrel Troupe, Jan. 1886, 6 X 1 1/2 In.	6.00
Handbill, The Palace Of Varieties, London, July, 1900	15.00
Invitation, President & Mrs.Wilson, Reception At White House, 1914	20.00
Stock Certificate, Hestonville, Mantua, Fairmount Railroad, 1894, Brown	23.00

Paper, Stock Certificate, Standard Oil, 1880, 328 Shares

Stock Certificate, Quincy Mining Co. Of Michigan, 1854, Wood Block 42.50
Stock Certificate, Standard Oil, 1880, 328 Shares ....*Illus* 1450.00
Stock Certificate, Western Maryland Railway, 1940, 8 X 12 In. 4.00

PAPERWEIGHT, see also Baccarat, Paperweight
PAPERWEIGHT, Acme Brick, Miniature Brick Shape 10.00
Admiral Dewey, Square, C.1900, 3 1/4 X 1 In. 20.00
Art Glass, Controlled Clear Bubbles, Cranberry 35.00
Beaumont Carriage Co., Beaumont, Texas 11.50
Bohemian, Mushroom, Blue Overlay, Transparent, 2 9/16 In. 1800.00
Clichy, Canes, Floretts, Pink, Green, Signed Chequer, 2 In. 275.00
Clichy, Checkers, Barber Pole, Center Rose, 3 1/4 In. 1700.00
Clichy, Red & White Cane Basket, Purple Rose 1800.00
Fairbanks Scale, Nickel Over Brass 40.00
Figural, Alligator, Independent Stove Co., Cast Iron 15.00
Figural, Blacksmith, Hammer, & Anvil, Vulcan Rails Const.Co. 48.00
Figural, Fly, Brass Feelers, C.1880, Cast Iron, 2 1/2 X 4 1/2 In 75.00
Figural, Pig, Birmingham, Alabama, Iron 15.00
Figural, Red Lobster, Cast Iron 15.00
Figural, Stylized Flowers, Brass, 6 X 1 1/4 In. 15.00
Floral, Glass, Chain, Round 8.00
Flowers, High Glaze, Signed Rozanne 135.00
Frosted Lion, Oval, Signed Gillinder & Centennial 85.00
Frosted Lion, Round 55.00
Gillinder, Victoria Silhouette 425.00
Glass, Pearl In Clamshell, 5 X 5 In. 50.00
Hat, Shriner's, Metal, 2 1/2 In. 14.00
Hendrick Hudson, Steamship, Glass 10.00
Leather, Embossed Y, Circle Y Brand, Yokum, Texas 20.00
Main Building National Export Expo, Philadelphia 18.00
Marble, Gold Plated Plow, Marked John Deere 25.00
Millefiori, Bacchus, 3 1/2 In. 825.00
Millefiori, Blown, Multicolored Rods, C.1880, 2 3/4 X 4 1/4 In. 50.00
Millefiori, Canes Creating Flower, C.1880, 2 X 1 1/2 In. 50.00
Millefiori, Concentric, Yellow, Green, Blue, Pink, 3 In. 82.00
Millefiori, Facet, Jay Glass, 1 3/4 In. 35.00
Millefiori, Ring Tree, 4 In. 125.00
Missouri & Kansas Telephone Co. 50.00
Missouri State Life Ins. Co.1916, Building & Logo 14.00
National Lead Co., Pictures Dutch Boy, Lead 9.50
New England Poinsettia, Blue Flower, Leaves, 3 In. 165.00
New England, Blown Apple, Cookie Base, 3 In. 975.00
New England, Crown, 2 3/8 In. 625.00
New England, Millefiori, Running Hare & Moth Cane, 2 15/16 In. ... 650.00
Plymouth Rock, Legend Of Landing, Clear 55.00
Red, White, Blue, Poinsettia & Jasper, Blue Florete, 3 In. 30.00
Sandwich, Pink Dahlia, Clear Glass, Star-Cut Base, 2 3/4 In. 1150.00
Sandwich, Poinsettia On Basket, Light Blue & Pink, 2 3/4 In. 900.00
Sindel, Walter & Co., Clothiers, 841 Broadway, N.Y. 12.50
Smith Brother's Cough Drops, Cast Iron 70.00
St.Louis, Blue Dahlia On Basket, 2 3/4 In. 1500.00
St.Louis, Concentric, Pink Outer Staves, 2 5/8 In. 1525.00
St.Louis, Crown, Red & Green Twists, Blue Central Cane, 2 5/16 I .. 1400.00
St.Louis, Fruit, 2 7/8 In. 1350.00
St.Louis, Millefiori, 3 3/8 In. 285.00
St.Louis, Pink, Blue, Mauve, Jasper, 2 1/2 In. 110.00
St.Louis, Pope Pius IX, 1796-1878, Signed, 10 1/4 In. 425.00
Stuyvesant Insurance Co., Figural Stuyvesant In Cape, Iron 75.00
Union Glass, Brown, End Of Day Ground, White Flowers, 10 In. 85.00
Washington Life Insurance, Iron 40.00
Whitefriars, Concentric Circles Of Millefiori, Red Ground 138.00
Whitefriars, Millefiori, Dated 1848, Blue, Pink, Mauve, 4 In. ... 137.00
Whitefriars, Millefiori, Pink, White, Line, Dated 1843, 3 In. ... 165.00
Worcester Mutual Fire Ins. Co.1823-1923 Anniversary, Brass 29.00

Papier-mache is a decorative form made from paper mixed with glue, chalk, and other ingredients, then molded and baked. It becomes very hard and can be decorated. Boxes, trays, and furniture were made of papier-mache. Some of the early nineteenth-century pieces were decorated with mother-of-pearl.

PAPIER-MACHE, Bottle Cork, Cartoonlike Head, Moving Eyes 4.00
  Box, Jewelry, Mother-Of-Pearl Inlaid Cover, C.1860, 9 X 6 In. 150.00
  Box, Powder, Gowned Lady, French 54.00
  Case, Pince-Nez, Brass Hinged, Diamond Design On Top, 6 1/4 In. 12.50
  Decoy, Duck 95.00
  Egg, Lithograph Florals, C.1880, Cotton Chick Inside, 3 X 5 In. 12.50
  Figurine, Bird, String, Red Paint, 6 1/4 In., Pair 20.00
  Figurine, Dog & Cat, Seated, Pip Squeaks, Pair 450.00
  Figurine, Dutch Boy, Counter Display, 14 1/2 In. 85.00
  Figurine, Hen On Nest, Dated 1919 .... 65.00
  Figurine, Lady, Carrying Lamb, Pip Squeak 600.00
  Figurine, Parrot 12.00
  Figurine, Parrot, Polychrome 145.00
  Figurine, Rabbit 30.00
  Figurine, Santa Claus, 6 In. 45.00
  Santa Claus, Boot 90.00

PARAGON, Figurine, Lady Marilyn, 7 1/2 In. 200.00
  Figurine, Lady Sybil, Blonde Hair, Marked, 7 1/2 In. 195.00
      PARASOL, see Umbrella

Parian is a fine-grained, hard-paste porcelain named for the marble it resembles. It was first made in England in 1846 and gained in favor in the United States about 1860. Figures, tea sets, vases, and other items were made of Parian at many English and American factories.

PARIAN, Bowl, Blooming Roses, Crimped Edge, 8 1/2 In. 35.00
  Bust, Burns, Signed M.L. 20.00
  Bust, Grecian Woman, 4 1/2 In. 37.50
  Bust, Roman Youth, 3 1/2 In. 28.00
  Bust, Walter Scott, Signed J.& TB, 10 1/2 In. 90.00
  Dish, Goat's Heads, Laurels, Raised Pattern On Rim, 7 1/4 In. 28.00
  Figurine, Boar, Reclining, Dated 1904, Signed C.Valton, 10 1/2 In. 110.00
  Figurine, Boy Standing, Reading A Book, 12 In. 55.00
  Figurine, Draped Woman, Bare Bosom, Holding Mask, 14 In. 135.00
  Jug, White Embossed Soldiers Battling Turks, Alcock Mark, 5 3/4 In. 165.00
  Pitcher, Mythological Figures, 8 In. ....*Illus* 80.00

Parian, Pitcher, Mythological Figures, 8 In.

Vieux Paris, or Old Paris, is porcelain ware that is known to have been made in Paris in the eighteenth or early nineteenth century but has no identifying manufacturer's mark.

PARIS, Bowl, Molded Gold Leaves, Foliate Handles, Melon Finial, 12 In. 85.00
  Breakfast Set, Bray, 4 Piece 275.00
  Jar, Biscuit, Floral, Covered, Porcelain 125.00

Platter, Floral Design, Reticulated Sides, 9 3/4 In. 85.00
Urn, Cherubs, Gold & White Trim, Double Handle, C.1850 .... 400.00
Vase, Gilt Design, Flare Top, 9 1/2 In. 65.00
Vase, Portrait Of Lovers, Handled, Turquoise & Gold, 18 In. 250.00

> *Pate-de-verre is an ancient technique in which glass is made by blending and refining powdered glass of different colors into molds. The process was revived by French glassmakers, especially Galle, around the end of the nineteenth century.*

PATE-DE-VERRE, Base, Lamp, Multicolored, Signed G.Argy Rousseau, 9 In. 1395.00
Figurine, Dancer, Blue Shades, Signed A.Walter, 12 In. 5500.00
Tray, Egyptian Head Medallion, Buds On Rim, 6 1/4 X 3 1/2 In. 795.00

> *Pate-sur-pate means paste on paste. The design was made by painting layers of slip on the ceramic piece until a relief decoration was formed. The method was developed at the Sevres factory in France about 1850. It became even more famous at the English Minton factory about 1870.*

PATE-SUR-PATE, Box, Gold, Blue, White Ground, Covered, Deco, French, 5 In. 110.00
Dish, Sardine, Deep Brown, Signed, 4 1/2 X 5 1/2 In. 490.00

> *Paul Revere pottery was made at several locations in and around Boston between 1906 and 1942. The pottery was operated as a settlement-house type of program for teen-aged girls. Many pieces were signed "S.E.G." for Saturday Evening Girls. The firm concentrated on children's dishes and tiles. Decorations were outlined in black and filled with color.*

PAUL REVERE, Bowl, Blue, 6 In. 45.00
Cup & Saucer, Beige, Yellow, S.E.G., Set Of 3 .... *Illus* 225.00
Plate, Beige, Yellow, S.E.G., 8 1/2 In., 6 Piece .... *Illus* 425.00
Plate, Luncheon, Green & Sand, Set Of 6 .... 130.00
Tile, Tea, Beige, Yellow, Round, S.E.G., 5 1/2 In. .... *Illus* 110.00
Vase, Blue Matte, Unglazed Top 45.00
Vase, Dark Blue-Green, 6 1/2 In. 30.00
Vase, Landscape Band, Rose Ground, C.1930 .... *Illus* 225.00

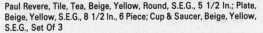

Paul Revere, Tile, Tea, Beige, Yellow, Round, S.E.G., 5 1/2 In.; Plate, Beige, Yellow, S.E.G., 8 1/2 In., 6 Piece; Cup & Saucer, Beige, Yellow, S.E.G., Set Of 3

Paul Revere, Vase, Landscape Band, Rose Ground, C.1930

> *Peachblow glass originated about 1883 at Hobbs, Brockunier and Company of Wheeling, West Virginia. It is a glass that shades from yellow to peach. It was lined in white. New England peachblow is a one-layer glass shading from red to white. Mt. Washington peachblow shades from pink to blue. Reproductions of peachblow have been made, but they are of poor quality and can be detected.*

PEACHBLOW, Bowl, New Martinsville, Sun Gold Pattern, Ruffled, 4 1/2 In. 115.00

Bride's Bowl, New Martinsville, Crimped, Melon Ribbed, 11 1/4 In. 200.00
Bride's Bowl, Wheeling, 12 In. 200.00
Creamer, Ribbed, World's Fair, 1893 .... 425.00
Creamer, Wheeling, Applied Anchor Loop Handle, 5 1/2 In. 695.00
Creamer, Wheeling, 4 In. 685.00
Cruet, Stopper 1250.00
Cruet, Wheeling, Amber Stopper, 7 1/4 In. 700.00
Cruet, Wheeling, Tepee, Amber Stopper 695.00
Cup, Punch, New England 300.00
Cup, Punch, New England, Alabaster Handle, World's Fair, 1903 .... 378.00
Darner, New England 275.00
Decanter, Reeded Lemon Handle, Egg-Shaped Stopper, 8 In. 175.00
Ewer, Enameled Flowers, English Victorian, Pair 175.00
Goblet, New England, 6 1/2 In. 295.00
PEACHBLOW, GUNDERSON, see Gunderson
Muffineer, Wheeling, 5 1/2 In.Tall 500.00
Pickle Castor, Butterfly & Flowers 350.00
Pickle Castor, New England, Footed Frame 375.00
Pitcher, Reeded Handle, Leaves, Mt.Washington, 1886, 5 1/2 In. 2500.00
Pitcher, Water, Applied Clear Handle & Leaf 695.00
Rose Bowl, 8 Crimp, Enameled Daisies, Yellow Stems & Buds 75.00
Sugar & Creamer, New England, Ribbed, White Handle 1150.00
Syrup, New England 775.00
Toothpick 25.00
Tumbler, Acid Finish 350.00
Tumbler, New England, Wild Rose Pattern 385.00
Tumbler, Yellow, Juice, Floral Engraved, Signed 50.00
Vase, Lily, Wild Rose Label, 8 In. 750.00
Vase, New England, Wild Rose Label, 8 In. 650.00
Vase, Stick, Wheeling 395.00
PEACHBLOW, WEBB, see Webb Peachblow

PEARL, Knife & Fork, Original Box, Set Of 6 .... 195.00
PEARL, OPERA GLASSES, see Opera Glasses

PEARLWARE, Bowl, C.1840, Blue, Ocher, Green, Yellow, Marked, 9 In. 550.00
Jug, Brown, Blue, Green, Ocher, C.1825, 7 In. 220.00
Plate, Napoleon, C.1800, 8 1/2 In. 350.00
Platter, Blue, Yellow, Floral, C.1830, 17 In. 715.00

Peking glass is a Chinese cameo glass of the eighteenth and nineteenth centuries.

PEKING GLASS, Bowl, Cameo, Flying Butterflies, Flowers, 8 In.Diam., Pair 390.00
Bowl, Flying Butterflies & Flowers, Blue & White, 8 In., Pair 385.00
Candlesticks & Vase, Metal Overlay, Flowers, Vase, 4 3/4 In. 220.00
Tea Caddy, Turquoise Ground, Pink Flowers, Vines, 4 X 6 In. 45.00
Vase, Honeycomb, Green Over White, 8 In. 175.00

Peloton glass is a European glass with small threads of colored glass rolled onto the surface of clear or colored glass. It is sometimes called spaghetti, or shredded coconut glass.

PELOTON, Dish, Sweetmeat, Silver Plated Rim, Hand, & Cover 585.00
Sugar, Covered, Underplate, Clear, 6 In. 125.00
Vase, Filaments Of Pink, Blue, & Yellow, 4 3/4 In. 485.00
Vase, Pink Lined, 2 3/4 In. 85.00
Vase, Ruffled Top, Ribbed Body, Lavender Pink, 5 In. 325.00

PEN, Ballpoint, Sheaffer, Sterling Silver, Boxed 25.00
Diamond, Fountain, 14K Gold Tip, Diamond 20.00
Eagle Glass Vial, Bright Nickel, Cartridge Style, 1898 .... 24.00
Eversharp, Green Marbleized, Gold Trim, Hangs On Chain, 1/2 X 4 1/2 In. 18.00
Holder, Figural, Alligator, White Painted Metal, Germany, 2 3/4 In. 8.00
John Hancock, Jade Green, Cartridge, 1926 .... 25.00

Liberty, Black, Full Size, Medium Point, 1926 .... 30.00
Midget Style, Black, Eyedropper, Boxed, 1915 .... 25.00
Parker, Big Red, Vacumatic Style, Fine Point, 1925 .... 70.00
Parker, Desk Set, Duofold, Burgundy & Black, Green Marble Base, 1932 .... 70.00
Parker, Duofold, Black, Fine Point, 1924 .... 60.00
Parker, Duofold, Lady's, Green 17.00
Parker, Duofold, Orange, Small 35.00
Parker, Duofold, Red 45.00
Parker, Nib Type, 14K Gold Band 40.00
Parker, Vacumatic, Gold Pearl, Fine Point, 1940 .... 35.00
Parker, 20, Lucky Curve, Eyedropper, 1917 .... 30.00
Parker, 31, Lucky Curve, Medium Point, 1924 .... 32.00
Ronson, Penciliter, Burgundy & Chrome, 1940s 16.00
Sears, Webster Skyrocket, Maroon, Pamphlet, Boxed 35.00
Sheaffer, Duofold, Lucky Curve Button Fill, Dated 1916, Yellow 75.00
Sheaffer, Lifetime, Black With Mother-Of-Pearl 35.00
Sheaffer, Lifetime, Red Pearl Stripe, 875, Fine Point, 1937 .... 35.00
Sheaffer, 14K Gold Filled Clip, Brown & Gold Stripe 12.00
Townsend, Lever Fill, Brown Marbleized, 14K Gold Trim 35.00
Wahl Eversharp, Gold Plated, Pencil Set, Swivel & Ribbon, Dated 40.00
Wahl Eversharp, Gold Seal Signature, Green & Red, Gold Foil 58.00
Waltham, Button Fill, Gold Trim, Black 12.00
Waterman 452 1/2, Sterling Silver, Medium Point, Hand Engraved, 1925 .... 35.00
Waterman 552 1/2, 14K Gold, Initialed, Fine Point, 1924 .... 450.00
Waterman, Allover Floral Engraving, Pump Type, Sterling Silver Case 55.00
Waterman, Eyedropper, Engraved Design, Fine Point, 1897 .... 85.00
Waterman, Penholder With Bronze Elephant Base 15.00
Wearever, Lever Fill, Green Marble 22.00

PENCIL, Box, Jackie Coogan, Tin 50.00
Eversharp, Lady's, Loop For Hanging, Gold Filled 35.00
Goodyear, Gold Plated, 4 Tires Floating In Water 35.00
Lead, Loop At Top, A.T. Co., Sterling Silver, 3 1/4 In. 30.00
Mechanical, Leaf Design, E.P. Co., N.Y., Chrome 12.00
Mechanical, Louisville Slugger Bats, Miniature 10.00
Mechanical, Peterson Oil Co., Marbleized Yellow Bakelite, 4 7/8 In. 6.00
Mechanical, Sterling Silver, Set Of 3 .... 31.00
Sharpener, Figural, Baker's Chocolates, Baker Girl, Cast Iron 37.50
Sharpener, Figural, Cowboy Wearing Hat & Bandana 39.00
Sharpener, Simplex, Student, Brass 9.00
Sharpener, Zeppelin 21.00
Sheaffer, Sterling Silver, 1918 .... 12.00
Top Loop Unscrews To Eraser & Lead, Green & Black Bakelite, 3 In. 4.00

PENNSBURY, Mug, Sweet Adeline 15.00
Sugar, Brown, 4 In. 10.00

Peters & Reed Pottery Company of Zanesville, Ohio, was founded by John D. Peters and Adam Reed in 1897. Chromal, Landsun, Montene, Pereco, and Persian are some of the art lines that were made until the company closed in 1920.

PETERS & REED, see also Zane
PETERS & REED, Bowl, Art Deco, C.1910, Low 30.00
Bowl, Geometric Relief, Pereco, Landsun, 3 3/4 X 2 3/4 In. 22.00
Bowl, Moss Aztec, 5 In. 20.00
Bowl, Pereco, Dark Blue, Berries & Ivys, Stems, 8 1/2 In. 55.00
Jardiniere, Grapes, Ferrell, 7 1/2 X 8 3/4 In. 78.00
Jardiniere, Grapes, 7 1/2 X 8 3/4 In. 78.00
Jardiniere, Green Lions' Heads On Beige, Fluted, 6 1/2 In. 70.00
Jardiniere, Moss Aztec, Grape Clusters, Ivys, Marked, 7 In. 75.00
Pitcher, Milk, Cavaliers, Brown 95.00
Pitcher, Sprigged-On Lion's Head, Brown Glaze, 4 X 5 In. 75.00
Planter, Stump, Moss Aztec, Pair 25.00

Tankard, Grape Design, Brown High Glaze, 17 In. 245.00
Vase, Applied Flowers, 3 In. 40.00
Vase, Applied Multicolored Flowers, Brown Ground, 5 In. 30.00
Vase, Applied Wreath, 6 In. 65.00
Vase, Brown, Flowers, 6-Sided, Pinched, 4 X 6 In. 75.00
Vase, Brown, Squatty, Applied Flower Swags, Handled, 5 In. 40.00
Vase, Brown, 3 Beige & Pink Applied Cavaliers, 5 In. 45.00
Vase, Glossy Brown, Outraised Lions' Heads, 6 In. 45.00
Vase, Iris, 15 In. 150.00
Vase, Landsun, Green, Blue, Flared, 5 X 5 In. 30.00
Vase, Landsun, Ivory, Brown, & Green, 4 In. 35.00
Vase, Landsun, Tan, Blue, Green, Flared, Bulbous, 5 In. 30.00
Vase, Molded Flowers, Green Glaze, Red Clay, 13 In. 65.00
Vase, Moss Aztec, Blackberry, 8 In. 18.00
Vase, Moss Aztec, Corset Shape, Iris Design, 15 In. 170.00
Vase, Moss Aztec, Sculptured Berries, 11 1/2 X 5 1/2 In. 65.00
Vase, Moss Aztec, Signed Ferrell, 8 In. 40.00
Vase, Pereco, Green, Corset Shape, Ivy Relief, Marked, 8 In. 30.00
Vase, Pinched, Floral Medallions, 4 X 6 In. 68.00
Vase, Trumpet, Applied Florals, 9 In. 55.00
Wall Pocket, Blue 30.00
Wall Pocket, Egyptian Ware, Profile 85.00
Wall Pocket, Fanned Triangles, Green, 7 3/4 In. 15.00
Wall Pocket, Leaves, Signed Ferrell 55.00
Wall Pocket, Moss Aztec, Berries & Ivy, Signed, 9 1/2 In. 60.00
Wall Pocket, Moss Aztec, Grapes & Vine, Signed Ferrell, 10 In. 30.00
    PETROUS REGOUT, see Maastricht

*Pewabic Pottery was founded by Mary Chase Perry Stratton in 1903
in Detroit, Michigan. Pewabic-type pottery is still being made.*

PEWABIC, Ashtray, Brown To Rust 125.00
    Vase, Flower, Gold Iridescent Ground, Round, Tapered Panel, 7 In. 300.00

*Pewter is a metal alloy of tin and lead. Some of the pewter made after
1840 has a slightly different composition and is called Britannia metal.*

PEWTER, Basin, John Townsend, Hammered Booge, London, 1750-60, 8 In.Diam. 260.00
    Basin, Marked, Split, 13 In. 15.00
    Basin, Richard Yates, London, C.1770, Engraved IH s, 9 IN. 195.00
    Basin, Samuel & Thomas Melville, C.1800, 8 1/8 In. 65.00
    Basin, Samuel Hamlin, Hartford & Providence, C.1767, 7 3/8 In. 550.00
    Beaker, Boardman & Hart, Incised Banding, Handled 350.00
    Beaker, Incised Paneling, Flaring Shape, C.1790, 3 3/4 In. 180.00
    Bottle, Hot Water, Ring Handle, Oval, 7 X 11 In. 15.00
    Box, Cigarette, Signed Max Reig, C.1825 .... 160.00
    Box, Desk, Inverted Bowl Feet, Marked John Heaney, 4 X 7 In. 100.00
    Box, Enamel On Copper, Hinged, Covered, 4 1/2 X 8 1/2 In. 40.00
    Box, Snuff, Stars & Flowers, Hinged, 1 X 1 1/2 In. 75.00
    Box, Tobacco, Engraved 1816, Covered, 4 3/4 In. 70.00
    Buttonhook, Figural, Lady's Leg & High-Button Shoe 20.00
    Cachepot, Reed & Barton, Footed, 4 1/2 X 5 In. 35.00
    Candlestick, Baluster Stem, Dome Base, 5 1/2 In., Set Of 4 .... 875.00
    Candlestick, Baluster Stem, High-Domed Base, Portugal, 7 In., Pair 550.00
    Candlestick, Baluster Stem, Molded Base, 1840-50, 8 In. 300.00
    Candlestick, Baluster Stem, 17th Century, 7 1/2 In., Pair 475.00
    Candlestick, C.1840, Push-Up, Pair 285.00
    Candlestick, Convex Base, Classical Figures, Germany, 17th Century 175.00
    Candlestick, Flaring Socket, Molded Crown Base, 4 1/2 In., Pair 200.00
    Candlestick, Long Socket, Turned Base, 6 In. 200.00
    Candlestick, Push-Up, 1867 .... 85.00
    Candlestick, Straight Sided, Bulbous Base, Portugal, 7 In., Pair 650.00
    Candlestick, Straight Stem, Domed Base, C.1830, 5 In. 110.00
    Candlestick, Urn-Shaped Baluster Stem, Domed Base, 5 5/8 In. 350.00

Candlestick, Urn-Shaped Stem, Crowned Base, Rolled Rim, 7 In., Pair 250.00
Candy, Scalloped, Sculptured Birds, Old English, 9 1/2 X 7 In. 30.00
Chamberstick, Embossed Poppies, Kayserzinn, 9 1/2 In. 125.00
Chamberstick, Marked Smith & Co., 4 3/8 In. 150.00
Charger, American, 15 In. 125.00
Charger, Marked, English, 13 1/2 In. 130.00
Charger, Tudor Rose, Raymond, 18 In. 425.00
Chocolate Pot, Stand, 1800s, English 250.00
Coffeepot, C.1824, Danforth, Scroll Handle, Wafer Design, 9 In. 100.00
Coffeepot, Hiram & Charles Yale, Lighthouse Shape 400.00
Coffeepot, Leonard, Reed, & Barton, Taunton, Ma., C.1835 .... 275.00
Coffeepot, Lighthouse, Cast Handle, Engraved Foliage, 12 1/2 In. 100.00
Coffeepot, Malden, Ma., High-Domed Cover, C.1835, 11 In. 200.00
Coffeepot, Marked Abram Brooksbank, Sheffield, 11 In. 118.00
Coffeepot, Roswell Gleason, Bulbous 500.00
Coffeepot, Roswell Gleason, Dorchester, Ma., C.1822, 4-Footed 375.00
Coffeepot, Wood Handle, Finial, Marked Vickers, 8 1/2 In. 125.00
Communion Set, Reed & Barton, 5 Piece 400.00
Dish, Ashbil Griswold, Meriden, Ct., C.1810, Marked, 13 1/8 In. 350.00
Dish, Benjamin & Joseph Harbeson, C.1800, 11 In. 300.00
Dish, Deep, Thomas Danforth II, C.1755, 13 In. 330.00
Dish, Jacob Whitmore, Middletown, 1780-90, Marked, 12 1/8 In.Diam. 300.00
Dish, Middletown, Ct., C.1785, Marked, 19 1/8 In. 175.00
Dish, Samuel Pierce, Massachusetts, Eagle Mark, 1800-1810, 12 1/8 In. 400.00
Dish, Thomas Badger, Boston, C.1790, 13 3/8 In. 200.00
Dish, Thomas Badger, Boston, Marked, 1790-1800, 13 3/8 In. 400.00
Flagon, Bifurcated Thumbpiece, Incised Mark, Scottish, C.1800, 8 In. 300.00
Flagon, Bulbous Thumbpiece, Hinged Lid, 9 1/2 In. 200.00
Flagon, Cobalt, Gray Body, Flowers, Bulbous, 15 In. 275.00
Flagon, Communion, Quart, T.D.Boardman & Co., Hartford, 1825-30, 8 In. 1150.00
Flagon, Cylindrical Form, Heart-Shaped Spout, Engraved, 10 In., Pair 550.00
Flagon, H.H.Graves, Middletown, Ct., C.1850 .... 500.00
Flagon, Heart & Tulip Engraving, 8 1/4 In. 65.00
Flagon, Sheldon & Feltman, Albany, N.Y., C.1847 .... 425.00
Flagon, Urn-Shaped Thumbpiece, Hinged Lid, 11 In. 225.00
Flagon, Waisted, Covered, R.W., English, 6 1/2 In. 115.00
Flask, Pewter Screw Cap, C.1900, Signed H.N.Jewitt & Co., England 25.00
Frame, Green Rib Feather Design, Art Glass Insert, Loetz 125.00
Inkstand, Disc Base, C.1850 .... 60.00
Inkwell, Ceramic Inset, 2 1/4 In. 30.00
Jar, Tobacco, Acorn Finial, Reeded Rim, Thomas Alderson, C.1790, 5 In. 150.00
Ladle, Turned Wooden Handle, 14 1/2 In. 35.00
Lamp, Capen And Molineux, Whale Oil, N.Y.C., C.1850, 10 1/4 In., Pair 475.00
Lamp, Fluid Burner, Brass Spout, Pewter Snuffer, 4 In. 75.00
Lamp, Gimbal, Whale Oil Burners, American, 4 In., Pair 870.00
Lamp, Petticoat, Fluid Burner, Brass Spout, 4 In. 55.00
Lamp, Saucer Base, Brass Collar, Tubular Wick, 9 3/4 In. 200.00
Lamp, Saucer Base, Marked R. Gleason, 4 1/2 In. 175.00
Lamp, Spark, Cylindrical Font, Small Saucer Base, 1840-50, 1 3/4 In. 100.00
Lavabo, Brass Spigot, 14 1/2 In. 175.00
Measure, Bellied, English, 2 5/8 In. 30.00
Measure, Bellied, Marked X & Crown, 3 In. 35.00
Measure, Engraved Beaker, James Yates, 1/2 Pint 70.00
Measure, Quart, Handled, English, Marked 92.00
Measure, Scottish, Excise Mark Of Crown, 1/4 Gill, 2 1/4 In. 20.00
Measure, Side Spout, Ear Handle, Quart, 6 1/2 In. 50.00
Measure, Signed A.James Yates, England, 1/2 Pint 60.00
Measure, Tankard, Ear Handle, Marked Beach, Chelsea, Quart 60.00
Measure, Tankard, English, 2 1/2 In. 25.00
Measure, Tankard, Marked C.B.C., Pint, 4 5/8 In. 30.00
Measure, Tankard, Marked Veitch, London, Pint, 4 1/2 In. 40.00
Measure, Tankard, Quart, 6 1/2 In. 100.00
Measure, Touchmark Crown, 1/2 Gill, 2 1/4 In. 25.00
Measure, Yates & Birch, C.1800, 1 Gill, 3 In. 40.00

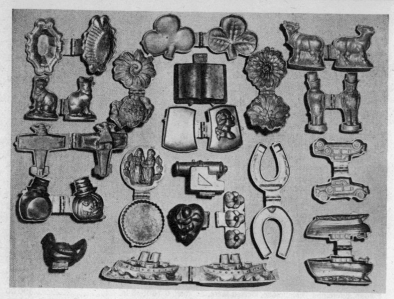

Pewter, Molds, Ice Cream

Mold, Candle, 18 Tubes, Pine Frame, Signed N.Y.	1200.00
Mold, Chocolate, Cross With Flowers, 9 In.	35.00
Mold, Chocolate, Lamp, 3, Sitting, 1 1/2 X 7 1/2 X 2 In.	45.00
Mold, Chocolate, Rabbit, 7 X 12 In.	50.00
Mold, Chocolate, Santa Claus, Hands Folded Into Sleeves, 7 In.	175.00
Mold, Chocolate, Seated Dogs	35.00
Mold, Chocolate, 4 Witches	65.00
Mold, Ice Cream, Airplane, E.& Co., N.Y., 5 In. .... *Illus*	65.00
Mold, Ice Cream, American Beauty Rose	32.00
Mold, Ice Cream, Banjo	36.00
Mold, Ice Cream, Basket, Oval	32.00
Mold, Ice Cream, Book, E.& Co., N.Y., 4 1/2 In. .... *Illus*	35.00
Mold, Ice Cream, Bride	36.00
Mold, Ice Cream, Cabbage, 3 1/2 In. .... *Illus*	35.00
Mold, Ice Cream, Cabin Cruiser, 5 1/2 In. .... *Illus*	50.00
Mold, Ice Cream, Candle & Candlestick	32.00
Mold, Ice Cream, Cannon, 4 1/4 In. .... *Illus*	30.00
Mold, Ice Cream, Car, E.& Co., N.Y., 4 3/4 In. .... *Illus*	55.00
Mold, Ice Cream, Card, Face, Jack Diamonds	32.00
Mold, Ice Cream, Card, Face, Jack Spades	32.00
Mold, Ice Cream, Card, Face, Queen Hearts	32.00
Mold, Ice Cream, Carnation, With Stem, 5-Point Leaf	32.00
Mold, Ice Cream, Cat, 3 1/2 In. .... *Illus*	70.00
Mold, Ice Cream, Chicken, 3 3/4 In. .... *Illus*	55.00
Mold, Ice Cream, Clover, E.& Co., N.Y., 5 In. .... *Illus*	50.00
Mold, Ice Cream, Cow, 4 1/2 In. .... *Illus*	100.00

Mold, Ice Cream, Cradle, Baby, 3 Piece 30.00
Mold, Ice Cream, Cross, Maltese 30.00
Mold, Ice Cream, Cupid 28.00
Mold, Ice Cream, Dahlia, 4 In. ....*Illus* 40.00
Mold, Ice Cream, Diamond 20.00
Mold, Ice Cream, Doves 32.00
Mold, Ice Cream, Ear Of Corn 28.00
Mold, Ice Cream, Elephant, Trunk Down, 3 3/4 X 3 In. 90.00
Mold, Ice Cream, Fan, Japanese, Flowers, Birds, Cattails 40.00
Mold, Ice Cream, Flower 30.00
Mold, Ice Cream, Football, 3 Piece 30.00
Mold, Ice Cream, G.Washington In Hatchet Head, 3 3/4 In ....*Illus* 50.00
Mold, Ice Cream, George Washington, Hatchet Shape, Profile, 3 In. 45.00
Mold, Ice Cream, Golfer, Female 36.00
Mold, Ice Cream, Grape, Bunch 30.00
Mold, Ice Cream, Groom 36.00
Mold, Ice Cream, Harp & Lady 70.00
Mold, Ice Cream, Hat, Ladies 30.00
Mold, Ice Cream, Heart 20.00
Mold, Ice Cream, Heart With Cupid, 3 In. ....*Illus* 75.00
Mold, Ice Cream, Heart, With Four-Leaf Clover 32.00
Mold, Ice Cream, Heart, With Hump 29.00
Mold, Ice Cream, Horseshoe, E.& Co., N.Y., 4 3/4 In. ....*Illus* 60.00
Mold, Ice Cream, Horseshoe, Good Luck 32.00
Mold, Ice Cream, Jack-O'-Lantern With Top Hat, 3 1/2 In ....*Illus* 55.00
Mold, Ice Cream, Kewpie Like Figures, Finger In Mouth, 9 X 6 1/2 In. 185.00
Mold, Ice Cream, Kiwanis Club Emblem 28.00
Mold, Ice Cream, Lamb 150.00
Mold, Ice Cream, Lily, Easter, 3 Piece 30.00
Mold, Ice Cream, Man & Woman In Disc, 3 3/4 In. ....*Illus* 55.00
Mold, Ice Cream, Man In Top Hat, E.& Co., N.Y., 5 In. ....*Illus* 45.00
Mold, Ice Cream, Masonic Emblem 25.00
Mold, Ice Cream, Masonic Emblem, Shrine 30.00
Mold, Ice Cream, New Orleans Airport 200.00
Mold, Ice Cream, Orange 15.00
Mold, Ice Cream, Passionflower Medallion 30.00
Mold, Ice Cream, Peach Half, With Stone 28.00
Mold, Ice Cream, Pears 20.00
Mold, Ice Cream, Poinsettia 34.00
Mold, Ice Cream, Puss 'n Boots, Marked E.& Co., 4 X 4 X 2 In. 90.00
Mold, Ice Cream, Ring, Engagement, With Diamond 28.00
Mold, Ice Cream, Santa, With Pack 34.00
Mold, Ice Cream, Scalloped Basket, 5 In. ....*Illus* 40.00
Mold, Ice Cream, Shamrock 30.00
Mold, Ice Cream, Skeletal Head & Crossbones, 3 3/4 X 1 3/4 In. 90.00
Mold, Ice Cream, Slipper 28.00
Mold, Ice Cream, Squash 175.00
Mold, Ice Cream, Steamer, E.& Co., , N.Y., 7 In. ....*Illus* 40.00
Mold, Ice Cream, Stork & Baby 32.00
Mold, Ice Cream, Strawberries 45.00
Mold, Ice Cream, Strawberry 19.00
Mold, Ice Cream, Turkey Roast .... 28.00 To 32.00
Mold, Ice Cream, Wedding Bell, With Cupid 32.00
Mold, Ice Cream, 3 Individual Pansies, 4 1/2 In. ....*Illus* 45.00
Mold, Meat, Register Mark, 1868, 1 1/2 Pint, 3 Piece 118.00
Muffineer, Urn-Shaped, Pedestal Base, Covered, C.1790, 5 1/2 In. 80.00
Mug, Bush & Walter, English, Handled, 1740-70 .... 350.00
Mug, Faucet, G.& J.Fenn, N.Y.C., C.1831 .... 150.00
Mug, Glass Bottom, Etched Dragon On Front, 5 In. 10.00
Mug, James Yates, English, 18th Century, Handled, 1 Quart 325.00
Pastry Tube, Plunger 40.00
Pitcher, Daniel Curtiss, Albany, N.Y., C.1822, 1 Gallon 750.00
Pitcher, Water, Cast Handle, 8 In. 65.00
Pitcher, Water, Wishbone Handle, Forbes, 6 In. 375.00

Pitcher, Water, 1835-60, Wishbone Handle, Flared Lip, 8 In. 120.00
Pitcher, Water, 7 3/4 In. 45.00
Pitcher, Windmill, England, 7 1/2 In. 55.00
Plate, American, Marked W, 8 In. 95.00
Plate, Art Nouveau, Kayserzinn, 10 1/2 In.Diam. 75.00
Plate, Ashbil Griswold, Meriden, Ct., C.1810, Marked, 7 3/4 In. 175.00
Plate, Boardman Group, Hartford, Ct., 1825-30, Marked, 8 7/8 In. 175.00
Plate, Burford & Green, London, 8 3/4 In. 95.00
Plate, Bush, London, C.1785, 8 In. 90.00
Plate, Continental, 19th Century, 9 In., Pair 190.00
Plate, David Melville, Newport, R.I., Marked, 1780-90, 8 1/8 In. 300.00
Plate, Edgar Curtis, London, C.1785, 8 In. 100.00
Plate, Frederick Basset, New York, C.1740, 15 In. 440.00
Plate, George Lightner, Baltimore, Md., C.1810, Marked, 7 In. 200.00
Plate, Gershom Jones, Providence, 1774-1809, 8 1/4 In. 375.00
Plate, Incised Line, Thomas Badger, C.1800, 13 3/8 In. 75.00
Plate, Knights In Armor, German, Signed & Numbered, Set Of 3, 9 In. . 300.00
Plate, Marked Townsend & Thomas Griffin, 7 5/8 In. 40.00
Plate, Nathaniel Austin, Boston, Marked, 1790-1800, 8 In. 150.00
Plate, Nathaniel Austin, Charlestown, Ma., 1763-1800, 8 5/8 In. 425.00
Plate, Raised Line Border, Crown & Medallion, Etain Bel Belge 45.00
Plate, Rose Touchmarks, Fein Zinn, German, 8 3/4 In. 40.00
Plate, Scalloped Rim Angel Of Justice, German, 9 1/4 In. 30.00
Plate, Soup, Angel Touchmarks, German, 9 In., Pair 85.00
Plate, Tankard, Marked James Dixon & Sons, 9 1/8 In. 30.00
Plate, Thomas Badger Jacobs, Rolled Rim, 18th Century, 8 3/8 In. 125.00
Plate, Thomas Badger, Boston, C.1800, Marked, 8 1/2 In.Diam. 200.00
Plate, Thomas Badger, Boston, Marked, C.1800, 7 3/4 In. 180.00
Plate, Thomas D.Boardman, Hartford, Ct., C.1805, 8 7/8 In. 250.00
Plate, Thomas D.Boardman, Hartford, Marked, 1810-20, 9 3/8 In. 250.00
Plate, Thomas S.Derby, Middletown, Ct., C.1812, 8 3/4 In. 1000.00
Plate, Townsend & Giffen, London, C.1777, 8 3/4 In. 95.00
Plate, W.Danforth, Middletown, Ct., C.1800, Marked, 7 7/8 In. 100.00
Plate, William Danforth, C.1800, 7 7/8 In. 150.00
Platter, Fish, Crab Among Water Lilies Rim, Kayserzinn, 10 X 20 In. .. 195.00
Porringer, Basin Type, Applied Heart Handle, 3 3/8 In. 110.00
Porringer, Crown Handle, Boston, C.1800, 5 3/8 In. 150.00
Porringer, Crown Handle, Marked SG, Boston, C.1800, 5 3/8 In. 250.00
Porringer, Domed Base, 18th Century, New England Handle, 4 1/8 In. . 125.00
Porringer, Flowered Handle, C.1780, 5 3/8 In. 120.00
Porringer, Flowered Handle, Rounded Body, Raised Bottom, 4 5/8 In. . 120.00
Porringer, Flowered Handle, Rounded Body, Straight Rim, 5 In. 175.00
Porringer, Heart & Crescent Handle, C.1800, 4 1/8 In. 200.00
Porringer, Heart And Crescent, American, 1800-25, 3 3/8 In.Diam. ... 170.00
Porringer, Old English Handle, American, 4 1/2 In. 200.00
Porringer, Pierced Scroll Handle, Castle, C.1678, 5 In. 300.00
Porringer, Thomas & Sherman Boardman, Flower Handle, 1820-30 ...... 525.00
Pot, Measure, Tankard, Engraved Shield, Chelsea 45.00
Punch Set, Bowl & 20 Cups 115.00
Salt, Footed, Engraved E.P. 1824, 3 1/4 In. 30.00
Salt, 3 Cabriole Legs, Pad Feet, Rolled Edge 35.00
Spoon, Medicine, 3 Inscribed Lines For Dosage, Apr. 10, '88 .... 65.00
Stein, Blue-Gray, Florals, Figures, German, Signed, 8 In. 45.00
Syrup, Hinged Cover, James Dixon & Son, 1799, 6 X 5 In. 249.00
Syrup, Thumbpress, Hinged Lid, 5 In. 40.00
Tankard, Bellied, German Angel Mark, 8 In., 2 Piece 40.00
Tankard, Fishtail Terminal, Domed, Scrolling Handle, 7 In. 522.00
Tankard, James Yates, C.1880, Pint 50.00
Tankard, Lidless, Crown Over X, Thomas Danforth, 6 In. 250.00
Tea Set, Embossed, Service For 6, Child's 68.00
Tea Set, Marked Insico, 5 Piece 125.00
Teapot, A.Porter, Southington, Ct., C.1830, 8 In. 195.00
Teapot, Cast Handle & Design, Marked Smith & Co., 8 In. 55.00

Teapot, Cast Handle & Finial, American, 6 3/4 In.	115.00
Teapot, Cast Handle & Finial, Marked Calder, 8 1/2 In.	135.00
Teapot, George Richardson	250.00
Teapot, Grape & Foliage, Finial	60.00
Teapot, I.Trask, Beverly, Ma., C.1807, Lighthouse Shape, 11 In.	695.00
Teapot, J.Danforth, Connecticut, C.1825, 6 1/2 In.	138.00
Teapot, Marked D & S	75.00
Teapot, Pear Shaped, Dome Lid, Faceted Spout, 6 1/4 In.	120.00
Teapot, Sellew & Co., Cincinnati	550.00
Teapot, Thomas D. & Sherman Boardman, 1810-30	375.00
Teapot, Wooden Handle & Finial, Floral Engraving, English, 8 In.	55.00
Teaspoon, Parker	25.00
Tray, Nouveau, Signed Kayserzinn, 8 1/2 In.	25.00
Tureen, Covered, Kayserzinn, Floral, Marked 4101, 12 In.	50.00
Urn, Applied Copper Squares, Wallace, 9 1/2 In.	20.00
Urn, Flagon Form, Cherub Feet, Brass Spigot, Lion Design, 20 In.	500.00
Vase, Bud, Liberty	88.00
Watch Holder, Birds, Ormolu, Birds, Base Circular, 7 X 5 1/2 In.	135.00
Wine Taster, C.1839, Floral Handle, Marked I.C.L. & Co.	140.00

Phoenix Bird, or Flying Phoenix, is the name given to a blue-and-white chinaware popular between 1900 and World War II. A variant is known as Flying Turkey. It is again being made.

PHOENIX BIRD, Berry Bowl, 5 1/2 In.	10.00 To 12.00
Bowl, Soup, 7 1/4 In.	22.50 To 35.00
Butter Chip, Set Of 4	25.00
Chocolate Set, Blue, White, Pot, Sugar, Creamer, 6 Cups & Saucers	125.00
Cup & Saucer, Demitasse	15.00
Eggcup	8.50 To 28.00
Marmalade, Open, Round	55.00
Match Holder, Wall Type	55.00
Mayonnaise Set, Flying Turkey, 3 Piece	95.00
Pitcher, Milk, Handled, 6 In.	70.00
Planter, 6 In.	2.50
Plate, Flying Turkey, Cobalt Blue, Nippon, 6 In.	4.50
Plate, 7 In.	7.00
Plate, 7 3/8 In.	3.00
Plate, 8 In.	7.00 To 12.00
Saucer	2.00
Sugar & Creamer, Bird, 5 1/2 In.	25.00
Sugar, Open	7.00
Teapot, Footed	35.00
Tureen, Soup, Signed, 5 X 8 In.	95.00

Phoenix Glass Company was founded in 1880 in Pennsylvania. The firm made commercial products such as lampshades, bottles, and glassware. Collectors today are interested in the sculptured glassware made by the company from the 1930s until the mid-1950s. The company is still working.

PHOENIX, Berry Bowl, Dancing Nudes, Frosted Mint Green	65.00
Bowl, Diving Girl, Gray Pearlized Finish, Label, 14 In.Long	195.00
Bowl, Lemons & Leaves, White Ground, Boat Shape, 8 In.	70.00
Bowl, Mermaid, 9 In.	165.00
Bowl, Nudes Swimming, Green To Clear, 14 In.	155.00
Box, Powder, Molded Floral, Milk Glass, Lavender, 7 X 4 1/2 In.	85.00
Box, Powder, Roses, Hummingbirds, Amethyst, 6 3/4 In.	125.00
Box, Powder, Violets & Leaves, Orchid Ground, Leaf Finial, 6 3/4 In.	88.00
Dish, Fruits, Pastel Luster, Covered, 7 1/4 X 5 In.	32.00
Flying Geese, Blue Ground, Pillow, 11 In.	125.00
Fruit Stand, Daffodil, Green, 11 In.Diam.	60.00
Lamp, Bellflowers, White & Turquoise, Pair	250.00
Lamp, Ferns & Foliage, Yellow Ground, Gold Trim, 11 In.	110.00
Lamp, Peony, White & Gold, 12 In.	140.00
Lamp, Raised Gold Trim, Brass Base, White, 29 In., Pair	200.00

Plate, Fruit, Pear Shaped, Green, 9 1/4 In. 9.00
Plate, Kumquats, Green, 8 1/4 In. 27.00
Plate, Kumquats, Yellow, 8 1/4 In. 27.00
Plate, Nudes, Frosted, 8 1/2 In. 40.00
Shaker, Window Box, Bluebirds, Brown Pinecones 160.00
Vase, Bird Of Paradise, Fan Shape, Tan, 6 1/2 In. 37.50
Vase, Birds, White, Green Ground, Pillow, 10 X 12 In. .... 95.00 To 125.00
Vase, Bluebells, Cream Ground, Marked, 7 In. 75.00
Vase, Bluebells, Light Blue, 7 In. 85.00
Vase, Bluebirds, 5 1/2 X 6 1/2 In. 95.00
Vase, Catalonian, Aqua, 11 3/4 In. 35.00
Vase, Chrysanthemum Flowers, Blue Ground, Spherical, 9 X 9 In. 110.00
Vase, Cosmos Pattern, Deco, Original Label 80.00
Vase, Dancing Women With Veils, Cranberry Flash, 9 In. 325.00
Vase, Dogwood, Yellow, Green, Brown, & White, 10 1/2 In. .... 155.00 To 160.00
Vase, Dragonflies, Green, 6 In. 37.50
Vase, Dragonfly & Leaves, Green, Pillow, 7 In. 85.00
Vase, Dragonfly Scene, 7 In. 75.00
Vase, Ferns & Leaves, Signed, Label, Blue, 7 3/4 In. .... 45.00 To 75.00
Vase, Ferns & Leaves, Sky Blue Ground, White, Marked, 7 3/4 In. 45.00
Vase, Floral Design, White Ground, 12 In. 190.00
Vase, Flowers, Blue, White, Pillow, 8 In. 65.00
Vase, Flowers, Custard, Satin Sculptured, Blue, 9 In. 75.00
Vase, Flying Geese, Brown Ground, Pillow, 11 In. 225.00
Vase, Frolicking Nudes, Cocoa Brown Ground, 11 1/2 In. 375.00
Vase, Geese, Blue Ground, Pillow Shape, 11 1/4 In. 198.00
Vase, Geese, White Frosted, Oval, 9 1/4 In. 95.00
Vase, Geese, White, Oval, Dark Blue, 9 1/2 In. 145.00
Vase, Grasshopper, Frosted Amber, 8 1/2 In. 60.00
Vase, Grasshoppers, Brown Grasses, White Ground, 7 In. 85.00
Vase, Leaf & Berries, Red, Clear, 9 1/2 In. 50.00
Vase, Leaves & Acorns, Sculpted On White Ground, 7 In. 99.50
Vase, Lovebirds, Yellow, Pastel Foliage, 6 In. 70.00
Vase, Madonna, White, Brown Ground, 10 In. 145.00
Vase, Peonies & Leaves, Custard, Green, 6 1/4 In. 37.50
Vase, Peonies, Multicolored, Custard Ground, Tapered, 12 1/2 In. 110.00
Vase, Peony, Leaves, Green, Bulbous, 10 X 8 1/4 In. 70.00
Vase, Pinecones & Florals, Blue Enamel, 7 In. 90.00
Vase, Pinecones, Blown-Out Design, Light Blue, 7 In. 95.00
Vase, Praying Mantis, Fan Shape, 4 1/2 X 8 In. 145.00
Vase, Praying Mantis, Label, Rose Beige, Pillow, 7 1/4 In. 155.00
Vase, Praying Mantis, Rose Beige, Pillow, Marked, 7 In. 155.00
Vase, Roses, White, Pink Ground, 10 In. 135.00
Vase, Roses, White, Rose Ground, 10 1/2 In. 110.00
Vase, Starflowers, Pink, 7 In. 95.00
Vase, Thistle, Frosted, 6 1/2 X 4 1/4 In. 35.00
Vase, Thistle, Frosted, 18 In. 525.00
Vase, Thistle, White, Blue, 5 In. 45.00
Vase, Three Flying Geese, Frosted White, Moon Shape, 10 X 12 In. 165.00
Vase, Tropical Birds, Ferns, White On White, 15 In. 145.00
Vase, Trumpet Vines, Blue, Green Leaves, 10 1/2 In. 95.00
Vase, Vines, Green Leaves, Custard, Blue, 10 In. 95.00
Vase, Wild Geese, Red, Signed, 9 1/4 In. 165.00
Vase, Wild Roses, Light Blue, 10 1/2 In. 115.00
Wild Roses, Dark Blue, Signed, 10 1/2 In. 125.00

The phonograph, invented by Thomas Edison in the 1880s, has been made by many firms. This section also includes other items associated with the phonograph.

PHONOGRAPH, Box, Needle, Victor, Dog Says His Master's Voice 18.50
Busy Bee, Purple Morning Glory Horn .... 350.00 To 395.00
Case, Needle, Victrola, Pictures Nipper, Tin 15.00
Cerola, Portable 195.00

Columbia, Model BC 1000.00
Columbia, Model BE, 1897, Horn, Golden Oak 425.00
Columbia, Model BN, Wooden Horn 950.00
Columbia, Serpentine, Mahogany Wooden Horn 1400.00
Duplex, Decals, Horn 1850.00
Edison, Amberola, Model DX 350.00
Edison, Amberola, Model 75, Floor Model 495.00
Edison, B-80, Belt Driven, 78 R.P.M. 350.00
Edison, Banner Home 275.00
Edison, Fireside, Model A-K 450.00
Edison, Gem, Morning Glory Horn, 2- & 4-Minute Attachment 400.00
Edison, Maroon Gem 1195.00
Edison, Model B, C.1906, Oak Case, Winding Handle, 13 In. 275.00
Edison, Opera, Oak 2500.00
Edison, Standard, Model D, Tulip Horn 450.00
Edison, Standard, Morning Glory Horn, 28 Cylinders 390.00
Edison, Triumph, 2- & 4-Minute Play 450.00
Edison, Triumph, 2- & 4-Minute Play, 100 Cylinders .... 975.00 To 995.00
Edison, 2-Minute Play 475.00
Figure, Dog, His Master's Voice, Large 800.00
Heywood Wakefield, Wicker 1750.00
Horn, Edison, Morning Glory .... 85.00 To 100.00
Horn, Linenoid, 26 3/4 In. 25.00
Horn, Morning Glory, Painted Roses 225.00
Horn, Swan Neck 40.00
Horn, Victor, Brass Bell, 20 1/2 X 29 In. 125.00

*A jukebox is a coin-operated disc phonograph. The machine offered a large
selection of recorded songs. The collectors refer to the 1939-50 period
as the "classic period" of jukeboxes. A few are still being made.*

Jukebox, Aireon, Plays 78 R.P.M. 650.00
Jukebox, Bing Crosby Junior 150.00
Jukebox, Capehart Orchestrope, C.1928 .... 2950.00
Jukebox, Capehart, Model 110, Coin-Operated Radio Phonograph ... 900.00
Jukebox, Chicago Bandbox 300.00
Jukebox, Mills, Paddle-Wheel Mechanism, C.1930, Walnut 1295.00
Jukebox, Mills, Zephyr 500.00
Jukebox, Nelson, Wiggins, Style, Xylophone 5500.00
Jukebox, Regina, Hexaphone, Model 103, 4-Minute Cylinder 5000.00
Jukebox, Reginaphone, Model 240, Case, Console .... 4700.00 To 5600.00
Jukebox, Rock Ola, Model 1426 .... 3500.00
Jukebox, Rock Ola, Model 1428 .... 800.00
Jukebox, Symphonion, Coin-Operated, Twenty 13 1/2 In.Discs, 28 In ... 2600.00
Jukebox, Symphonion, Double Comb, Coin-Operated, Upright 2450.00
Jukebox, Symphonion, Upright, Glass Door, 20 Discs, 28 In. 2600.00
Jukebox, Wurlitzer, Band, Model 105 .... 8000.00
Jukebox, Wurlitzer, Counter Model 71 .... 2750.00
Jukebox, Wurlitzer, Model 1015 .... 2450.00 To 4850.00
Jukebox, Wurlitzer, Model 1045, Bubbler 2250.00
Jukebox, Wurlitzer, Model 1050 .... 3995.00
Jukebox, Wurlitzer, Model 1080 .... 4000.00 To 5995.00
Jukebox, Wurlitzer, Model 1100 .... 1500.00 To 1600.00
Jukebox, Wurlitzer, Model 1450 .... 1450.00
Jukebox, Wurlitzer, Model 61, Metal Stand 1750.00
Jukebox, Wurlitzer, Model 616 .... 200.00
Jukebox, Wurlitzer, Model 616-A 275.00
Jukebox, Wurlitzer, Model 780 .... 4800.00
Jukebox, Wurlitzer, Model 800 .... 3200.00 To 3500.00
Jukebox, Wurlitzer, 1936 Simplex P12, 8 Play, Coin Slots 900.00
Kalamazoo Duplex, Victor Motor 1000.00
Needle, Tin, Victor, Nipper On Front 21.00
Orthrophonic Victrola, Model 1050, Albums 1250.00

Paperweight, Victor, Master's Voice	55.00
Record, Bill Haley & The Saddlemen, Green Tree Boogie, 78 R.P.M.	100.00
Record, Cylinder, Edison, Auction Sale Of Animal Store, 1902	6.50
Record, Cylinder, Edison, Black Theme, Let It Alone, 4-Minute Play	7.50
Record, Cylinder, Edison, Blue, Set Of 84	250.00
Record, Cylinder, Edison, Hebrew Vaudeville, 1902	6.50
Record, Cylinder, Edison, Uncle Josh & Sailor Stewart, Patent 190	6.50
Record, Edison, Cylinder, Pop Goes The Weasel, Children's	5.00
Record, Remington, Music To Shave By	11.00
Silvertone, Portable, Windup, Leather Case, 1930s	27.50
Standard, Model A, Outside Horn	650.00
Standard, Model X, Black Bell Horn	375.00
Standard, Rear-Mount Horn, Oak	600.00
Victor, Model II, Metal Horn	475.00
Victor, Model II, Wooden Horn	1100.00
Victor, Model III, Brass Bell Horn	650.00
Victor, Model III, Red Morning Glory Horn, Painted Flowers	550.00
Victor, Model MS, Disc, C.1905, Oak Corner Pillars, Horn, 25 In.	725.00
Victor, Model MS, Large Horn	1350.00
Victor, Model MS, Mahogany, Edison Black Crank	395.00
Victor, Model VI, Wooden Horn	2000.00
Victor, Model VI, 500 Records From 1899 To 1925, Wooden Horn	3000.00
Victor, Model VV-XXV, 1904, Oak	1500.00
Victor, School Model, Pleated Horn	2200.00
Victor, Schoolhouse, Oak Horn	1400.00
Victrola, Hinged-Top Portable, 1915, Golden Oak Case	175.00
Victrola, Stores & Includes 20 Albums, 1915, Mahogany	630.00
Zonophone, Concert Grand Disc	750.00

Albums were popular in Victorian times to hold the myriad pictures and cutouts favored by the collectors. All sorts of scrapbooks and albums can still be found.

PHOTOGRAPHY, Album, Brass Clasp, 29 Tintypes, 4 X 5 X 2 3/4 In.Thick	27.50
Album, Carte De Visite, Dated 1895	95.00
Album, Carte De Visite, Gold Lettering, Gilt Edged, 12 Pages	16.50
Ambrotype, Bearded Man, Waffled Medallion, 2 1/2 X 2 3/4 In.	10.00
Ambrotype, Boy In Chair Holding Toy Horn, 1/6 Plate	35.00
Ambrotype, Boy In Vest & Jacket, 1/6 Plate, 2 3/4 X 3 1/4 In.	25.00
Ambrotype, Civil War Band, 5 Union Soldiers With Instruments	750.00
Ambrotype, Civil War Soldier, Full Uniform, 1/3 Plate	100.00
Ambrotype, Civil War Union Sergeant, 1/6 Plate	37.50
Ambrotype, Gentleman, Edwardian Dress, 1/6 Plate, Plastic Case	75.00
Ambrotype, Head & Shoulders Of Lady, 1 7/8 X 2 1/8 In.	65.00
Ambrotype, Infant, 1/9 Plate, Cased	20.00
Ambrotype, Lady In Gilt Frame, Double-Sided, 3 1/4 X 3 3/4 In.	95.00
Ambrotype, Two Soldiers At Table, Officer & Corporal, 1/6 Plate	47.50
Ambrotype, Victorian House, Girls, 1/2 Plate, 4 1/4 X 5 1/2 In.	125.00
Ambrotype, Whately Express, 1850s, Framed, Whole Plate	900.00
Ambrotype, Woman & Two Girls, Case, 2 1/2 X 3 1/2 In.	45.00
Ambrotype, Woman, 50 Years Old, Gilt Frame, 2 X 2 1/2 In.	7.00
Cabinet Card, Family Poses With Hound Dog In Front	6.00
Cabinet Card, G.A.R. Bandsman Holding Horn	8.00
Cabinet Card, Pawnee Bill	55.00
Cabinet Card, Seminole Indians	55.00
Cabinet Card, Three Miners Swing Picks In Mouth Of Tunnel	6.00
Cabinet Card, Tom Thumb & Wife, With Third Midget	15.00
Cabinet Card, View Of 2-Masted Ship, Kodak, Circular	5.00
Cabinet Card, Young Boy Holds Stuffed Squirrel	6.00
Cabinet Card, Young Boy In Cap, In Wicker Chair, Playing Banjo	15.00
Cabinet Card, 2 Girls, One Holds Doll	6.00
Camera, Ansco Shurshot, Box	5.00
Camera, Argus, C3, Case, 35 M.M.	17.00
Camera, Argus, Single Lens, Reflex	25.00

Camera, Brownie Hawkeye	3.00
Camera, Brownie Junior	10.00
Camera, Brownie Kodak, 1905, Boxed	150.00
Camera, Brownie, Red Bellows	23.00
Camera, Cadet, Box Style, 2 1/2 X 3 1/2 X 4 1/2 In.	25.00
Camera, Gift Kodak, 1930, Original Art Deco Box	200.00
Camera, Graflex, Series D, Revolving Back	125.00
Camera, Herro-Flex, No.620, Herbert George Co., Chicago, Ill.	5.00
Camera, Kodak Autographic, Case, 1914	24.00
Camera, Kodak, Anastigmat 616, C.1935, Art Deco, Boxed	75.00
Camera, Kodak, Flash Bantam, Case	15.00
Camera, Kodak, No.2, Folding Cartridge, Ballbearing Shutter	12.00
Camera, Kodak, Pony, 35 M.M.	14.00
Camera, Kodak, Quick Focus	115.00
Camera, Kodak, Retina, Folding, Engraved Mar.'46, Paris	65.00
Camera, Kodak, Vest Pocket, 1905	20.00
Camera, Kodak, 3a Autographic, Portrait Lens, Box & Book	42.00
Camera, Minox BL, Spy	135.00
Camera, Putnam, 1890	125.00
Camera, Rainbow, Red	10.00
Camera, Rolleiflex	95.00
Camera, Scenex, Uses 828 Kodak Film, 2 X 2 X 3 1/2 In.	24.00
Camera, Sunart Photo Co., Red Bellows, Ball, & Hose, Case	250.00
Camera, Univex, C.1936	10.00
Camera, Vest Pocket, The C.M.C., Marked Japan, Case	10.00
Camera, Yashica, 35 M.M., Case	75.00
Carte De Visite, Abraham Lincoln, 1860s	85.00
Carte De Visite, Children, Aged 2 To 10 Years, Set Of 5	7.50
Carte De Visite, General George Custer, 1862	250.00
Carte De Visite, General Grand	15.00
Carte De Visite, John Wilkes Booth	65.00
Carte De Visite, Painting Of Governor John Longdon	6.50
Carte De Visite, Queen Victoria, 1860s	65.00
Carte De Visite, Sarah Bernhardt, 1880s	125.00
Carte De Visite, Thomas Edison, 1880s	85.00
Carte De Visite, Ute Indian Chief Piah, By William Jackson	225.00
Carte De Visite, Victorian Children, Set Of 6	11.50
Daguerreotype Case, Gutta-Percha, Angel Scattering Roses, 3 In.	48.00
Daguerreotype Case, Gutta-Percha, Bearded Man	55.00
Daguerreotype Case, Gutta-Percha, Black Man, Oval	55.00
Daguerreotype Case, Gutta-Percha, Bonneted Baby	65.00
Daguerreotype Case, Gutta-Percha, Bonneted Lady, 2 1/4 X 3 In.	45.00
Daguerreotype Case, Gutta-Percha, Boy Chasing Butterfly, Farm	55.00
Daguerreotype Case, Gutta-Percha, Civil War Soldier	35.00
Daguerreotype Case, Gutta-Percha, Dog, Woman, & Child	100.00
Daguerreotype Case, Gutta-Percha, Gents, Scissors In Pockets	65.00
Daguerreotype Case, Gutta-Percha, Huntress, 3 1/2 X 3 7/8 In.	85.00
Daguerreotype Case, Gutta-Percha, Lad, Oval Medallion	17.50
Daguerreotype Case, Gutta-Percha, Mother & Child, Both Sides	50.00
Daguerreotype Case, Gutta-Percha, Musicians	150.00
Daguerreotype Case, Gutta-Percha, The Musicians, Lyred Corners	110.00
Daguerreotype Case, Gutta-Percha, Woman On Horse, Dog	55.00
Daguerreotype Case, Gutta-Percha, Young Lady	24.50
Daguerreotype Case, Gutta-Percha, Young Lady, Curls	55.00
Daguerreotype Case, Gutta-Percha, Young Lady, Leaves	55.00
Daguerreotype, British Army Officer, 1840s, 1/9 Plate	150.00
Daguerreotype, Farmhouse, People, 1850, 1/4 Plate	175.00
Daguerreotype, Man In Stovepipe Hat, 1850, 16 Plate	100.00
Daguerreotype, Men Playing Checkers, 1855	250.00
Lamp, Darkroom, Kodak, 1920	45.00
Lamp, Red & Amber Glass	25.00
Lantern, Darkroom, C.1890, Tin	60.00
Lantern, Darkroom, Oil, Red Lens, Tin, 8 1/2 In.	22.50

Lantern, Darkroom, Tin, Oil, Red Glass, Red Paint, 8 In.	20.00
Magic Lantern Slide, American History, Civil War, 48	50.00
Magic Lantern Slide, American History, 70, 20 Color	70.00
Magic Lantern Slide, Best, Case	125.00
Magic Lantern Slide, Colored, 1 1/2 X 5 3/4 In., Set Of 23	25.00
Magic Lantern Slide, Egypt, Palestine, Africa, Black & White, 79	80.00
Magic Lantern Slide, Glass, Double Burner, Dovetailed Box	250.00
Magic Lantern Slide, History, Washington To Civil War, 51	60.00
Magic Lantern Slide, Kerosene Slide Projector, Complete	800.00
Magic Lantern Slide, Projector, Electric, Carrier, 10 X 23 In.	100.00
Magic Lantern Slide, Theater, 5	65.00
Magic Lantern Slide, Tin, Wood Box, Germany, 60	125.00
Magic Lantern Slide, Views Of Orient, C.1920, 7 Black & White	100.00
Photograph, Bolton Center Railroad Depot, Sepia, 4 X 5 In.	8.50
Photograph, Boy In Wicker Carriage, Sepia, C.1880	3.00
Photograph, Coal-Burning Steam Locomotive, C.1810, 4 X 5 In.	8.50
Photograph, F.D.R., Addressing 74th Congress, Matte, 14 X 25 In.	35.00
Photograph, Girl Making Confirmation, Sepia, 4 1/2 X 6 1/2 In.	3.50
Photograph, Horse-Drawn Sled, Sepia, C.1880, 6 X 8 1/4 In.	12.50
Photograph, Horse-Drawn Wagon, Sepia, C.1880, 7 1/2 X 6 1/2 In.	6.50
Photograph, Infant, Victorian Carriage, Sepia, 4 1/4 X 6 1/2 In.	18.50
Photograph, J.J.Corbett, Ankle-Length Tights, 4 1/4 X 6 1/2 In.	15.00
Photograph, Panorama Of Cape, Sepia, C.1890, 6 1/2 X 8 3/4 In.	3.50
Photograph, Putnam Machine Co., 1916, Crew, Sepia, 10 X 12 In.	4.50
Photograph, Rangeley Lake Views, Sepia, 5 1/4 X 8 1/2 In.	8.50
Photograph, The Proud Father, Sepia, 5 3/4 X 7 13/4	4.50
Photograph, Twin Seated On Victorian Chair, Sepia	4.00
Photograph, Wreck Of Freight Train Cars, 4 3/4 X 6 3/4 In.	8.50
Postcard, Viewer, Mirrored Lid, Storage Drawer	150.00
Projector, Firefighter Scenes, C.1930, Set Of 9	12.50
PHOTOGRAPHY, STEREO, see Stereo	
Tintype, Abraham Lincoln, Head & Shoulders, 2 1/2 X 4 In.	95.00
Tintype, Black Girl Child, Plaid Dress, 3 X 3 1/2 In.	55.00
Tintype, Bonneted Lady, Brass Mat, Frame, Leather Case	22.50
Tintype, Buffalo Bill Cody, 1890s	150.00
Tintype, Children In Unusual Costumes, Set Of 10	14.00
Tintype, Children, C.1880 Clothing, 2 1/2 X 4 In., Set Of 4	10.00
Tintype, Civil War Soldier With Rifle, Full Plate	85.00
Tintype, Civil War Soldier, Brass Mat	15.00
Tintype, Civil War, Rifle & Gear	140.00
Tintype, Family In Wagon, Building In Background	15.00
Tintype, Farm Scene, People, Horses, & Barn With Weather Vane	27.50
Tintype, Gentleman, Mustache & Muttonchops, 2 1/2 X 4 In.	16.50
Tintype, Jenny Lind, C.1860, Brass Frame, 1/2 In.Diam.	45.00
Tintype, John Wilkes Booth, 1865	275.00
Tintype, Little Boy, Leather Case, 2 1/2 X 2 3/4 In.	10.00
Tintype, Soldier In Dress Uniform, Civil War, 2 3/8 X 3 5/8 In.	45.00
Tintype, Union Sergeant In Uniform, Hardee Hat	22.00
Tintype, Union Soldier, Backdrop Of Cannons & Tents, Full Plate	47.50
Tintype, Victorian Girl With Doll, Stand-Up Frame	55.00
Tintype, Women, Children & Men, 1 X 3/4 In., Set Of 22	15.00
Tripod, Camera, Wooden	38.00
PIANO, see Music, Piano	

About 1880 the well-decorated home had a shawl on the piano. The bisque piano baby was designed to help hold the shawl in place. They range in size from 6 to 18 inches. Most of the figures were made in Germany.

PIANO BABY, Boy Sitting, Feet In Front, Hands Over Toes, 8 In.	300.00
Boy Sitting, Hands Over Toes, White Gown, 8 In.	300.00
Boy, Socks & Shorts, Holds Gray Dog, 8 1/2 In.	65.00
Crawling, Heubach Mark, 8 1/2 In.	300.00
Crawling, Intaglio Eyes, White Nightie, 5 In.	50.00
Crawling, 7 In.	65.00

Crawling, 8 In. 325.00
Laying On Back, Playing With Toes, 5 1/2 In. 185.00
Laying, Heubach Mark, 8 1/2 In. 300.00
Lying On Stomach, Bisque, 5 1/2 In. 85.00
Seated, Yellow Nightshirt, Flowers, 7 In. 85.00
Sitting Up, Hands Stretched Over Toes, Heubach, 8 In. 365.00

Pickard china was started in 1898 by Wilder Pickard. Hand-painted china was a featured product. The firm is still working in Antioch, Illinois.

PICKARD, Bonbon, Platinum Design, Ball Feet, Flaring Handle 47.00
Bowl, Dark Green, Gold Poppies, Marked, 9 1/2 In. 75.00
Bowl, Deserted Garden, 8-Sided, Signed, 2 1/2 In. 65.00
Bowl, Etched Flowers, Gold, 5 1/2 In. 20.00
Bowl, Fruit, Gold Border, Signed, 11 3/4 X 9 In. 215.00
Bowl, Fruit, Hand-Painted Medallion, Signed Voitral, 10 In. 145.00
Bowl, Fruit, Plums, Grapes, & Raspberries, Gold Daisies, Signed 150.00
Bowl, Hand-Painted Inside & Out, Pears & Plums, 14 X 7 1/2 In. 650.00
Bowl, Ivy Design, 9 3/4 In. 170.00
Bowl, Pansy Design, Gold Rim, Marked, 9 In. 210.00
Bowl, Poppies & Leaves, Gold Trim, Ruffled, 1905 Mark, 10 1/2 X 3 In. 175.00
Bowl, Poppies, Gold Handles, 8 In. 165.00
Bowl, Poppies, Gold Trim, Signed Hathaway, 1904, 9 1/2 In. 75.00
Bowl, Poppy, Artist Signed, 9 In. 95.00
Bowl, Rose Swags, Gold Outlined Medallion, 2 Gold Handles, 9 In. 195.00
Bowl, Rose, Poinsettia Design, Pearl Inside, 1903-10, Signed, 8 In. 285.00
Bowl, Roses, Gold Outlined Medallion & Handles, 1905 Mark, 9 In. 195.00
Bowl, Scenic, 2-Handled, Ball Feet, 5 1/2 In. 185.00
Bowl, Violets, Gold Band, Pearlized, Marked Ray, 7 1/2 In. 155.00
Bowl, Violets, Gold Trim, Marked, 10 In. 245.00
Bowl, Yellow & Maroon Ears Of Corn, Yellow Ground, Marked, 9 In. 125.00
Cake Plate, Floral Pattern, Allover Gold 50.00
Cake Plate, Flowers, Scalloped Gold, Signed, 11 In. 155.00
Cake Plate, Woodland Scene, Handled, Signed, 10 In. 295.00
Candlestick, Flowers, Gold Design, Signed Tolley, 7 1/4 In. 250.00
Candlestick, Green, Gold, 10 In. 32.00
Candlestick, Iridescent Ground, Red Flowers, Gold Trim, 7 In. 235.00
Celery, Floral Design, Gold Trim, Slit Handles, 11 X 5 1/4 In. 25.00
Chocolate Set, Pot, Sugar, & Creamer, Embossed Gold 255.00
Compote, Poppies & Daisies, Gold Feet, 1905 Mark, 6 X 4 1/2 In. 168.00
Creamer, Gold 20.00
Cup & Saucer, Floral, Gold Trim 30.00
Cup & Saucer, Garland 20.00
Dish, Canoe Shape, Flowers, Marked Efdon, 5 1/2 In. 65.00
Dish, Shell Shape, Gold Trim, White, 5 X 3 3/8 In. 38.00
Dish, Tapestry Finish, Pearlized, Pierced Handles, 4 X 7 In. 65.00
Dish, Tapestry Finish, Roses, Pearlized, Signed, 4 X 7 1/2 In. 65.00
Dresser Set, Leaf Mark, 3 Piece 150.00
Jug, Alexander, Hand-Painted, Signed, 1905-10, Large 225.00
Mug, Metallic Gold, Grape Design, 1898 .... 110.00
Mug, Tulips, Gold Handle, Signed, 5 1/4 In. 235.00
Nappy, Currants Design 95.00
Perfume & Stopper, Violets, C.1905, 6 1/2 In. 295.00
Pitcher, Art Deco Design, Signed, 5 3/4 In. 140.00
Pitcher, Art Nouveau, 24K Gold & Platinum, Signed, 24 In.Diam. 395.00
Pitcher, Aura Argenta, Silver Plated Rim, Gold Handle, 7 In. 235.00
Pitcher, Cider, Italian Garden, Challinor 450.00
Pitcher, Cider, Raised Flowers, Cream Ground, 6 In. 225.00
Pitcher, Foliage & Blossoms, Metal Bands, Signed, C.1912, 8 1/2 In. 285.00
Pitcher, Iris, Gold, Nouveau Style, Marked Lind, 3 1/4 In. 65.00
Pitcher, Iris, 1910, 13 In. 65.00
Pitcher, Lemonade, Forest Scene, Fruit, Signed, 6-Sided 260.00

Pitcher, Water, Gold Band & Handle 85.00
Plate, Apple Blossom Design, Gold Rim, Marked, 9 In 45.00
Plate, Castle In Woods, C.1919, Artist Signed, 9 In. 195.00
Plate, Challinor Scenic, 8 1/2 In. 225.00
Plate, Easter Lilies, Gold Trim On Rim, Marked, C.1905, 8 1/2 In. 85.00
Plate, Engraved Gold Band, 8 1/2 In., Set Of 10 .... 140.00
Plate, Famille Rose, Marked, 10 In. 25.00
Plate, Floral, Signed, 8 In. 40.00
Plate, Geometric Design, Raised Gold & Floral, Signed, 8 5/8 In. 135.00
Plate, Gold Edge, Cobalt Blue, 10 1/2 In., Set Of 8 .... 175.00
Plate, Harry S.Truman Portrait, 10 1/2 In. 100.00
Plate, Morning Glories, Scalloped Rim, Artist Signed, 8 1/2 In. 85.00
Plate, Scenic, Palm Trees, Marked, 8 1/2 In. 145.00
Plate, Scenic, Rawlins, Marked, 7 1/2 In. 125.00
Plate, Shaded Violets, Scalloped Gold Rim, Signed, 8 1/2 In. 85.00
Plate, Strawberries, Green, Orange Ground, Signed Gibson, 1905, 9 In. .. 95.00
Plate, Water Lily & Ribbons Design, Signed, 8 1/2 In. 75.00
Plate, Wild Roses, Gold-Banded, Signed, 1910, 8 3/4 In., Set Of 8 ...... 495.00
Platter, Basket Of Flowers, Gold Trim, 12 In. 55.00
Relish, Violets, Oval, Open-Handled, Marked Ralex, 9 In. 55.00
Rose Bowl, Christmas Red Poinsettias, Green Leaves, Marked, 8 In. 285.00
Salt & Pepper, Balustrade Shape, Footed, Allover Gold, 4 In. 22.00
Salt & Pepper, Gold 10.00
Salt & Pepper, Pink Rosebuds, Gold Scrolls, Bands & Top, 1905 Mark .. 35.00
Salt & Pepper, Plums, Grapes, & Strawberries, Artist Signed 85.00
Salt & Pepper, Urn Shape, Open-Handled, Allover Gold, 4 In. 35.00
Saltshaker, Lemon Tree Design 35.00
Server, Cheese & Cracker, 2 Tier, Allover Gold, Bottom, 9 1/4 In. 55.00
Stein, Gold Metallic, Grapes & Leaves, Gold Handle, C.189, , 7 In. 285.00
Sugar & Creamer, Art Deco Form, Hand-Painted, Signed, 1905 Mark 225.00
Sugar & Creamer, Art Deco, Gold Trim, High Handled 55.00
Sugar & Creamer, Covered, Art Deco, Signed 70.00
Sugar & Creamer, Debonair 25.00
Sugar & Creamer, Hand-Painted Poppies, Signed, 1905-10 Mark 235.00
Sugar & Creamer, Stylized Birds, Blue, Gold Trim, Signed 65.00
Sugar & Creamer, Violets, 1900, Marked 100.00
Sugar Shaker, Poppies, C.1910, Marked, 4 1/2 In. 235.00
Syrup, Covered, Artist Signed Miller 90.00
Tea Set, Encrusted Gold, Border Of Royal Blue, 3 Piece 345.00
Tea Set, Gold Leaf Handles, Hand-Painted Florals, Gold Band, 3 Piece .. 150.00
Tea Set, Turquoise & Black, Gold Trim, Tray, 11 1/2 In., 4 Piece 475.00
Tray, Bun, Poppy Design, Open-Handled, Signed, 12 X 5 1/2 In. 295.00
Vase, Etched Gold Roses, Flared Rim, 5 1/2 In. 35.00
Vase, Etched, Gold Signature, 11 In. 145.00
Vase, Gold Brocade Pattern, Band Of Roses, Signed, 1919, 7 In. 295.00
Vase, Gold Grapes, Vines, Gold Ground, 1905 Mark, 9 1/4 In. 205.00
Vase, Hand-Painted Florals & Leaves, Handled, Signed, 1910, 8 1/4 In. .. 190.00
Vase, Hand-Painted Florals, Handled, 1910 Mark, 8 1/4 In. 190.00
Vase, Harbor Scene, 1898-1904, Signed, 7 In. 250.00
Vase, Midnight Lake Scene, Turquoise Blue, Signed & Marked, 7 In. 335.00
Vase, Mums & Butterflies, Handled, Cream Ground, 1919 Mark, 8 1/2 In. .. 195.00
Vase, Palm Tree, Lake, 2-Handled, 7 In. 165.00
Vase, Palm Trees, Cream To Pink, C.1912, Marked, 8 3/4 In. 210.00
Vase, Scenic Design, Handled, 7 In. 176.00
Vase, Scenic, Summer Season, Signed, 8 In. 295.00
Vase, Sea Gull, Water, Gold Rim, Signed, 6 1/4 X 6 In. 365.00
Vase, Violets, Gold Leaves, Artist Kriesy, 1905-10 Mark, 6 1/2 In. 78.00
Vase, Wildwood Pattern, C.1912, Signed James, 8 1/4 In. 395.00
Wall Plaque, Edge Of Budlong Woods, Artist Signed, 12 In. 575.00
      PICTURE FRAME, see Furniture, Frame

      PICTURE, see also Painting; Print
PICTURE, Hair, Victorian, Oak Frame, 15 X 17 1/2 In. 100.00
  Hair, Victorian, Walnut Frame, 29 X 33 In. 165.00

Silhouette, Art Deco, Brass Frame, Blue Iridescent, 3 In.Diam. 22.00
Silhouette, Balding Gentleman, 19th-Century Dress, Rosewood Frame 302.00
Silhouette, Boy & Girl, Head & Shoulder, Framed, 7 X 9 In., Pair 35.00
Silhouette, Bust Of Man, Pasted-On Style, Maple Frame, Pair 220.00
Silhouette, Cut By Master Hankes With Scissors, Framed 85.00
Silhouette, Duke Of Wellington, 19th Century, Rosewood Frame 302.00
Silhouette, Gentleman, Signed Doyle 235.00
Silhouette, Girl On Swing, Man Pushing, Black On Silver, Framed 15.00
Silhouette, Profile, Man & Woman, Brass Frame, 4 1/2 X 4 In., Pair 150.00
     PIGEON BLOOD, see Cranberry Glass; Ruby Glass

PIGEON FORGE, Mug, Hemlock Tree Design, Matte Green, 4 1/4 In. 22.00

PINCUSHION DOLL, Arm To Waist, Black Hair, 3 3/4 In. 25.00
Art Deco, Nude, Blonde Marcel Wave, Germany, 8 In. 22.50
Attached To Whiskbroom, Low-Cut Pink Dress, Germany 25.00
Bisque Head, Germany, 17 In. 165.00
Bisque, Nippon 100.00
Blonde Hair With Beads, Blue Dress, Germany, 2 1/2 In. 24.00
Blonde Hair, Hands Clasped To Bosom, Germany, 3 3/4 In. 25.00
Blonde Hair, Pink Dress, 3 1/2 In. 12.00
Blonde Wig, On Cushion, Papier-Mache, Germany, 5 In. 60.00
Blonde, Blue Trim On Dress, Both Hands On Breast 28.00
Blue Bonnet, Shawl, Japan 10.00
Boebel Powder Base, Germany 250.00
Both Hands To Chest, Holding Fan, Japan, 2 In. 18.50
Brown Hair, Orange Ribbon, Strapless Gown, Japan, 3 3/4 In. 18.50
China, Elaborate Hairdo, Germany, Marked, 3 In. 25.00
Cloche Hat, Feather, Right Hand To Bosom, Japan, 2 3/4 In. 20.00
Closed Arms, Black Hair, Wire Skirt Frame, Dress, 3 In. 25.00
Colonial Lady, 11 In. 15.00
Deco Hairstyle, Crossed China Legs 30.00
Dutch Girl 75.00
Flapper, Black Hair, Red Brow Band, Germany, 4 1/4 In. 30.00
Flapper, Eyeshadow, Arms Away From Body, Germany, 4 1/2 In. 145.00
Flapper, Germany, Head Only, 3 1/4 In. 22.00
Flapper, Pink Hat, Dotted Yellow Blouse, Red Hair 18.50
Flapper, With Compact, 5 1/4 In. 145.00
Flexed Arms, Hands Behind Back, Pink Blouse, Germany, 2 In. 25.00
Folded Hands, Flapper, Germany, 3 In. 18.00
Full Figured, Gray Hair, Long Skirt, Japan, 3 1/2 In. 22.50
Gainsborough Lady, Rose In Hand, No.19117, 4 In. 75.00
Golden Haired, Arm & Hand Out From Body, 2 1/4 In. 30.00
Gray Hair, Blue Ribbon, Hand To Bosom, Germany, 4 In. 25.00
Gray Hair, Purple & Ivory Hat & Gown, Germany, 6 1/2 In. 80.00
Gray Hairdo, Both Hands Free, No.14753, 4 3/4 In. 145.00
Gray Molded Hairdo, Red Eyelines, Germany, Bisque, 4 In. 62.50
Lamp, Extended Arms, Original Clothing & Wig, 15 In. 95.00
Low-Cut Gown, Green Collar, Arms At Neck, Brown Hair, 3 In. 30.00
Marie Antoinette Hairdo, Blue Dress, Pink Rose, 3 1/2 In. 21.50
Marie Antoinette, Crown Mark, Goebel 170.00
Marie Antoinette, Hands Clasped To Bossom, 3 3/4 In. 25.00
Marked Schneider, 5 1/2 In. 88.00
Mohair Wig, Marked K.C., 1925 .... 28.00
Nude Lady, Holding Rose At Hair, No.12756, 5 In. 95.00
Queen Anne Type Ruffled Collar, Green Scarf, Germany, 4 In. 35.00
Queen Anne, Ruffled Bonnet & Collar, Germany, 4 In. 30.00
Spanish Dancer, Blue Comb, Arm To Head, Germany, 3 3/4 In. 25.00
Spanish Dancer, Comb In Hair, Germany 25.00
Spanish Dancer, Hair Comb, Gold Net, Germany, 3 In. 25.00
Spanish, Hat & Shawl 24.00
Strapless Green Gown, Comb In Hair, Japan, 3 3/4 In. 18.50
Victorian Lady, Gray Hair, Righ Hand To Breast, 2 1/4 In. 20.00
Victorian Lady, Molded Hair, Painted Features, 9 In. 25.00

PINK SLAG, see Slag, Pink
PINOCCHIO, see Disneyana, Doll

PIPE HOLDER, Country Store, Rosewood, Holds 12 Pipes 45.00
  Pompous Lady Top, Bare Bottom Underneath, Cast Iron 35.00

PIPE, Briar, The Brassnose, Figural, Head Of Goblin 7.50
  Carved Briar Horsehead, No Stem 15.00
  Czechoslovakian, C.1880 .... 250.00
  Dog Head, 2 1/2 In. 14.50
  Man's Head Bowl, 2 X 1 1/4 In. 10.00
     PIPE, MEERSCHAUM, see Meerschaum, Pipe
  Old Man Winter Bowl, White Body, Clay, Signed L.Fiolel A St.Omer, 5 In. 85.00
  Opium, Bamboo, Sculptured Sterling Silver Band, 22 In. 100.00
  Opium, Ivory Bowl, 2 1/4 In. 22.00
  Opium, Jade Bowl, Bamboo Stained, Bag Attached 45.00
  Opium, Sculptured Animals, Bamboo Stem, 22 In. 140.00
  Opium, Silver & Bamboo, Staghorn Case, C.1780 .... 1200.00
  Porcelain, Transfer Of Peasant Man & Woman, C.1890, Germany, 10 In. 12.50
  Reclining Deer, Ivory Stem, Bowl 3 In. 30.00
  Swiss Gentleman's Head, Bowl From Side Hat, 3 3/4 X 2 In. 75.00

Pirkenhammer is a porcelain manufactory started in 1802 by Friedrich Holke and J.G. List. It was located in Bohemia, now Brezova, Czechoslovakia.

PIRKENHAMMER, Butter, 3 Piece 45.00
  Plate, Cream Ground, Gold Gilding, Parrot, Perched, 8 In. 145.00

Pisgah pottery pieces that are marked "Pisgah Forest Pottery" were made in North Carolina from 1926 until the present. Vases, teapots, jugs, candlesticks, and many other items were made.

PISGAH FOREST, Bowl, Turquoise Outside, Pink Inside, 8 1/2 In. 28.00
  Pitcher, Water 35.00
  Pitcher, 1929, Pink Interior, Green, 4 1/2 In. 28.00
  Sugar & Creamer 36.00
  Teapot, Covered Wagon Scene, Jasper, Signed Stephen 550.00
  Vase, Bulbous, Signed, Plum 65.00
  Vase, Celadon Handled, 6 In. 12.00
  Vase, Corset Shape, Crackled Turquoise, Signed, 3 3/4 In. 42.00
  Vase, Crackled Turquoise, Lined, Handled, Dated 1941, 6 1/2 In. 52.00
  Vase, Crystalline, Brown 185.00
  Vase, Turquoise, Plum, Crackled, 8 X 5 In. 65.00
  Vase, 1929, Turquoise & Wine, 9 In. 40.00

Planters Nut and Chocolate Company was started in Wilkes-Barre, Pennsylvania, in 1906. The Mr. Peanut figure was adopted as a trademark in 1916. National advertising for Planters Peanuts started in 1918. The company was acquired by Standard Brands, Inc., in 1961. Some of the Mr. Peanut jars and other memorabilia have been reproduced.

PLANTERS PEANUTS, Ashtray, Ceramic .... 55.00 To 60.00
  Ashtray, Figural 65.00
  Badge, For Workers At Convention, Pin-On, Figural 15.00
  Bag, Burlap, Small 12.50
  Bank, Mr.Peanut, Plastic, Red, 8 1/2 In. .... 6.00 To 7.50
  Blotter, Peanut Shape 25.00
  Book, Coloring, American Heroes, 1935 .... 15.00
  Book, Coloring, Mr. Peanut & Fifty States 6.00
  Book, Coloring, Mr. Peanut & Smokey The Bear 6.00

Book, Happy Time Paint, Letter From Company	27.00
Book, Physical Fitness Guide With Mr. Peanut	4.00
Box, Original, Cardboard, Peanut Logo	32.50
Bracelet, Mr.Peanut	15.00
Candy Container, Plastic, Says Planters	6.50
Cart, Vendor	85.00
Chopper, Original Can, Dated 1938	10.00
Clock, Alarm, Boxed	55.00
Cocktail, Pick, Figural, Plastic	1.00
Container, Counter, Blue Hat, Plastic	18.00
Cookie Cutter, Figural, Plastic	35.00
Cruet, Ceramic, Pair	38.00
Dish, Lithograph, Tin, Boxed, Set Of 4	75.00
Dish, Nut, Tin, Lithograph, 6 In.Diam.	8.00
Doilies, Boxed, Set Of 4	8.50
Doll, Jointed, Wooden	100.00 To 120.00
Earrings	20.00
Fork, Silver Plated	24.00
Glass, Cocktail, Figural, Plastic	16.50
Jacket, Workers, Long Sleeve, Embroidered Mr. Peanut	65.00
Jar, Football	125.00
Jar, Leap Year, Peanut Man On Lid, 1940	42.50 To 45.00
Jar, Nut House, Embossed	125.00
Jar, Pennant	125.00
Jar, Square, Peanut Finial	25.00
Jar, Squirrel, Embossed	100.00
Jar, Streamline, Made In U.S.A.	45.00 To 47.00
Jar, 6-Sided, Peanut Finial Cover	65.00
Jar, 8-Sided, Embossed, Peanut Finial Lid	135.00
Knife, Barlow, 2 Blades	5.75
Knife, Figural, Metal	20.00
Knife, Gold Scoop, Silver Scoop, Fork, Set	110.00
Label, Valentine, Foil, Mr. Peanut Logo	5.50
Letter Opener, Figural, Metal, Says Planters	200.00
Light Switch, Figural, Glow In The Dark, Plastic	2.00
Lighter, Cigarette, Peanut Shape	30.00
Marble, Logo On Label, 1940s	7.00
Matchbook, Figural	40.00
Mirror, Pocket, Rectangular	4.00
Mr.Peanut, Wall Mounted, Papier-Mache, 5 Ft.	495.00
Nodder, Papier-Mache, Figural	65.00
Pencil, Mechanical, Celluloid	15.00
Pencil, Mr.Peanut Logo, Gold Color, Wooden	4.25
Pin, Lapel, Figural	2.00
Pocket Protector, Logo	2.50
Postcard, Showing Different Stores	4.00
Ring, Metal, Premium	7.00
Roaster, Peanut, Hi Hat, Silver-Colored Pot	75.00
Salad Set, Oil, Vinegar, Salt, Pepper, 4 Piece	50.00
Salt & Pepper, Tan & Black	12.00
Shaker, Salt & Pepper, Figural, Plastic, Red	8.00
Shaker, Salt & Pepper, Gold Color, Plastic, Giveaway	18.50
Shaker, Salt & Pepper, Plastic, Cork Bottom, Blue	8.00
Silverware, Baby's, Plastic, 3 Piece	12.50 To 15.00
Socks	7.50
Spoon, Nut	12.00
Spoon, Serving, Figural, Charlton Silver Plate	8.00
Spoon, Serving, Figural, Pierced Bowl, Silver Plated	6.00
Spoon, Silver Plate, Wm.Rodgers	9.00
Sticker, Store, Used On Bags	20.00
T-Shirt	7.50
Tin, C.1909, 10 Pound	75.00
Tin, Contains 5 Free Jumbo Bars, 10 Pound	85.00
Towel, Beach, Large	25.00

Toy, Walker, Figural, Plastic, Windup, Red	125.00
Toy, Walker, Figural, Windup, Black & Tan	165.00
Tray, Engine & Peanut Shaped Car, Plastic	125.00
Tray, Mr. Peanut	7.50
Wallpaper, Original Peanut Store, 2 1/2 X 3 In.	50.00

PLATE, see under special types such as ABC; Calendar

Plated amberina was patented June 15, 1886, by Edward D. Libbey and made by the New England Glass Works. It is similar to amberina, but is characterized by a cream-colored or chartreuse lining (never white) and small ridges or ribs on the outside.

PLATED AMBERINA, Vase, 8 In.	22.00

PLATED SILVER, see Silver Plate

Plique a jour is an enameling process. The enamel was laid between thin raised metal lines and heated. The finished piece has transparent enamel held between the thin metal wires.

PLIQUE A JOUR, Tea Strainer, Blue, Red, Silver Wire	85.00

POLITICAL, Ashtray, Lyndon Johnson, Ceramic, Portrait, 5 1/2 In.	5.00
Badge, Police, 1937 Inaugural	450.00
Badge, 1941 Inaugural	350.00
Bandana, Admiral Dewey	85.00
Bandana, Harrison, Morton	95.00
Bandana, Teddy Roosevelt 1912 Battle Flag, 22 X 24 In.	60.00
Banner, Al Smith, Framed	95.00
Bar Pin, G.A.R., Dated 3/7/92, Celluloid	15.00
Book Of Matches, Stick With Ike, 1955, Red, White, & Blue	4.00
Book, Inaugural, 1905, President Roosevelt, 28 Pages	37.50
Book, McGovern, The Man & His Beliefs, Paperback, 1972	5.00
Book, Roosevelt Bear Adventures	95.00
Bookmark, Franklin D.Roosevelt, Die Cut Metal	25.00
Bookmark, R.B.Hayes, W.A.Wheeler, Republican Candidates, Ohio, Silk	95.00
Bookmark, Wm.H.Taft, Flag, Image, & White House, Woven Silk, 7 In.	46.00
Button, Anderson In 1980, 3 In.	2.50
Button, Boost Hoover For President, Tin	10.00
Button, Campaign, William McKinley	15.00
Button, Capt.Hoover, Figural Elephant, Nickel Over Brass	8.00
Button, Carter For President, 1 1/4 In.	.50
Button, Clothing, 1789 Inaugural, George Washington	600.00
Button, Democrats & Republicans For Willkie, Celluloid, 1 In.	12.00
Button, Dewey, Bricker, Picture	20.00
Button, Eisenhower, In Uniform, Celluloid, 1 1/4 In.	14.00
Button, For President Warren G. Harding, Brown & White, Red Edge	6.50
Button, Gerald R. Ford, Blue & Gold, Marked The White House	25.00
Button, Harriman For Governor, Picture, Red & Blue	2.00
Button, Harry S.Truman, Inauguration, 1949, Celluloid, 1 3/4 In.	18.00
Button, Herbert Hoover, Image Of Hoover Facing Left, 1 In.	12.50
Button, I Like Ike	2.00
Button, I Like Ike Even Better, Red, White, & Blue	4.00
Button, I Used To Be A Republican, LBJ *Illus*	12.50
Button, John Anderson For President, 3 1/2 In.	2.50
Button, John F. Kennedy, Flasher Type, 2 1/2 In.	4.00
Button, Johnson-Humphrey, Flasher Type, 2 1/2 In.	3.00
Button, Landon, Knox, Elephant On Sunflower, 3/4 In.	4.00
Button, Let's Kick The Carters Out Of The White House, 3 1/2 In.	2.50
Button, McCarthy, 1 1/2 In.	1.50
Button, McClellan For President, 1864, Tin	200.00
Button, McGovern-Eagleton 72, Flasher Type, 2 1/2 In.	3.50
Button, McGovern-Eagleton, 1 In.	175.00
Button, McKinley	10.00
Button, Progressive Policies Become Law Under Wilson, 7/8 In.	20.00
Button, Reagan, Bush, 3 1/2 In.	2.50

Political, Button, I Used To Be
A Republican, LBJ

Button, Rockefeller For President, Blue & White	3.50
Button, Rockefeller, Image, Celluloid, 1 1/2 In.	10.00
Button, Ronald W. Reagan For President, 2 In.	1.50
Button, Roosevelt, Curley, & Hake, No.155, Shield	84.50
Button, Smith & Robinson, Red, White, & Blue	12.00
Button, Vote Adlai, Image, Flasher, 2 1/2 In.	18.00
Button, Vote Socialist Workers In 80, 3/4 In.	2.00
Button, W.J.Bryan, 9 Stars, Blue Ground, Red & White Stripes	13.50
Button, Wanted-Ronald Reagan For President, 3 In.	2.00
Button, Warren Harding, Picture	8.00
Button, William McKinley, Red, White, & Blue Flag Edge	20.00
Button, Willkie For President	6.00
Button, Willkie, Display Picture, 10 In.Diam.	70.00
Button, Wilson, Picture, 1 1/4 In.	28.00
Button, Wm.H.Taft, Image, Celluloid, 3/4 In.	18.00
Button, Wm.Howard Taft, New Hampshire Choice 1912, 7/8 In.	15.00
Button, Woodrow Wilson, The Man On The Job	18.50
Button, World War I, Ambulance, French Orphans League, 3/4 In.	4.00
Cane, Franklin Roosevelt, Figural Head, Century Of Progress	90.00
Cane, McKinley, Hobart, 1896	45.00 To 60.00
Clip, Name, Hoover, Blue & Gold, 1 X 1/4 In.	7.50
Clock, Metal, Uncle Sam & Franklin D. Roosevelt	140.00
Clock, Nixon As Superman, Wall, 1969	45.00
Clock, Spiro Agnew As Mickey Mouse, Wall, 1969	45.00
Coatrack, Admiral Dewey	125.00
Death Mask, Abraham Lincoln, Dated February 1886	100.00
Figurine, Lyndon Johnson, Rubber & Celluloid	15.00
Jar, McKinley, Protection & Prosperity, Pressed Glass, Covered	45.00
Jug, Harrison & Morton, Stoneware, C.1889, Brown	70.00
Jugate, Roosevelt, Fairbanks, 1 1/4 In.	25.00
Knife, Folding, Jimmy Carter, Mr.Peanut For President, 1976	15.00
Knife, Pocket, Carter, Mondale, 1980, 3 1/2 In.	3.50
License Plate, Boost Hoover For President, Tin	10.00
License Plate, Carter, 1977 Inaugural, Pair	10.00
License Plate, Reagan, 1981 Inaugural, Pair	14.00
License Plate, Wallace For President, Tin	15.00
Lithograph, Chester A. Arthur, Republican, Framed, 10 X 14 In.	85.00
Lithograph, General Eisenhower, 1944, Framed	35.00
Match Holder, Teddy Roosevelt, Porcelain, Bear Scene, 3 1/2 In.	55.00
Medal, Truman Inaugural	225.00
Medallion, Jugate, McKinley & Hobart, March 4, 1897	75.00
Mirror, Pocket, Engel For County Treasurer	10.00
Money, Anti-Dewey Campaign, 1944, Dollar Size	12.50
Mug, George Wallace, 1976 Campaign	4.00
Mug, Roosevelt's New Deal	10.00
Music, Sheet, We Want Willkie, 1940	5.00
Napkin, Alfred Landon, Image In Sunflower, Song Words	4.00
Paperweight, Embossed Harry S.Truman Medal, Marble, 1884-1972	40.00
Paperweight, Jimmy Carter, Boxed	8.50
Paperweight, McKinley, Commemorative, Canton, Ohio, 1907, Pewter	18.00

Pin, Alfred E.Smith, Raised Head & Shoulders, 3/4 In.	15.00
Pin, Franklin Roosevelt & Gardner, Brass	35.00
Pin, Republican Convention, Toledo, 1897	19.00
Pin, Willkie, Campaign, Elephant, Brass	10.00
Pin, 1932 Hoover, Embossed Head, Brass, 1 In.	12.50
Plate, Admiral Dewey, 5 1/2 In.	55.00
Plate, Bryan, 7 In.	14.00
Plate, Campaign, Our Choice 1908, William Howard Taft, Marked	45.00
Plate, J.F.Kennedy, Memorial, 9 In.	10.00
Plate, William Jennings Bryan, Photograph, Ceramic, 3 5/8 In.	45.00
Poem, If Al Smith Is Elected, Anti-Catholic, Irish, Italian	100.00
Postcard, Taft, Sherman	10.00
Poster, Harding & Coolidge, 11 X 17 In.	25.00
Poster, James Garfield, Commemorative, Dated 1881	12.00
Poster, Nixon's The One, 28 X 20 In.	45.00
Poster, Wallace Has It, Do You, 22 X 14 In.	15.00
Program, Inauguration Ball, 1885, 20 Pages	18.00
Ribbon, Funeral, Lincoln	125.00
Ribbon, I Saw Douglas, 1918	8.00
Ribbon, I Saw Lincoln, 1918	8.00
Ribbon, 1888 Republican Rally	6.00
Ring, Hoover, Embossed Figural Elephant, Silver Plated	35.00
Saucer, Portrait Of F.D.Roosevelt, 100th Birthday, 5 In.Diam.	12.50
Scorecard, 1940 Election, Roosevelt Vs. Willkie, Red, White, Blue	4.50
Stationery, Millard Fillmore For President, Profile, 2 In.	55.00
Stickpin, William Jennings Bryan	13.50
Stud, Lapel, Roosevelt & Honson, Gold Moose, Red, White, & Blue	22.50
Stud, Lapel, Wm.Jennings Bryan, Pewter, 7/8 In.	27.50
Thimble, Nixon's The One, Elect Nixon In 1968	1.50
Ticket, Democratic, Adams For Governor, C.1880, 4 X 10 In.	5.00
Tie Clasp, Kennedy, Flasher	3.50
Toby Jug, General Eisenhower, Marked Barrington, 7 1/4 In.	150.00
Token, Franklin D. Roosevelt, Onward America, 7/8 In.	8.00
Torch, Campaign Parade, Tin	85.00
Torch, Campaign, Gray Tin, 6 1/2 In.	15.00
Tray, Tip, Admiral Dewey	40.00
Tumbler, J.F.Kennedy Memorial	6.00
Tumbler, Wm.McKinley, Head & Shoulder, C.1896, 4 In.	40.00
Watch Fob, Bryan-Kern, Silver, Leather Strap, Eagle, Flag	22.50
Watch Fob, Taft, Brass, 1 In.Square	20.00
Watch Fob, Theodore Roosevelt, 1904	50.00
Watch Fob, Wilson, His Pen Mightier Than The Sword, Copper	58.00
Watch, Spiro Agnew	60.00
Yo-Yo, Jimmy Carter, 1980	2.00

Pomona glass is clear with a soft amber border decorated with pale blue or rose-colored flowers and leaves. The colors are very, very pale. The background of the glass is covered with a network of fine lines. It was made from 1885 to 1888 by the New England Glass Company.

POMONA, Bowl, Collared Rim & Foot, Amber Stained Rim, 8 1/2 In.	140.00
Bowl, Cornflower, Crimped Rim, 2nd Grind, 8 X 3 1/2 In.	295.00
Bowl, Cornflowers, 1st Grind, 5 In.	140.00
Compote, Swirl, Green, Signed, 7 In.	135.00
Cup, Punch, Amber Reserves At Middle, 1st Grind, Handled	150.00
Finger Bowl, Ruffled Top, 1st Grind, 5 In.Diam.	115.00
Finger Bowl, 2nd Grind	45.00
Pitcher, Enameled Floral, 2nd Grind, 4 In.	185.00
Pitcher, Water, Cornflower, Square Mouth, 2nd Grind, 7 1/4 In.	495.00
Tumbler, Cornflower, Quilted, 2nd Grind	75.00
Tumbler, Cornflower, Set Of 8	550.00
Tumbler, Cornflower, 2nd Grind	105.00
Tumbler, Diamond Optic, Scalloped, Amber Band, Top, 3 3/4 In.	95.00

Tumbler, Water, Cornflower, 3 3/4 In. 150.00
Vase, Floral Etching, 2nd Grind, Amber, 8 1/2 In. 160.00
    PONTYPOOL, see Tole
    POO WARE, see Banko

*Popeye was introduced to the Thimble Theater comic strip on January
17, 1929. The character became a favorite of readers. In 1932 an animated
cartoon featuring Popeye was made by Paramount Studios. The cartoon
series continued and became even more popular when the old movies were
used on television starting in the 1950s. The full-length movie with an actor
as Popeye was made in 1980.*

POPEYE, Ashtray Stand, Full Figural, Original Paint, 34 In. 165.00
  Bank, Dime, Boxed 40.00
  Bank, 1970 .... 15.00
  Big Little Book, Popeye & The Jeep 25.00
  Big Little Book, Popeye Deep Sea Mystery 25.00
  Big Little Book, Popeye In Quest Of Poopdeck Pappy 25.00
  Big Little Book, Popeye Seas The Sea 25.00
  Bubble Set, Original Box, 1936 .... 15.00
  Checkers 35.00
  Cookie Jar 110.00
  Crayon Box, Lithograph, Tin 25.00
  Doll, Carnival, 10 In. 125.00
  Doll, Ceramic, 1930s 90.00
  Figurine, Cast Iron 60.00
  Figurine, Chalkware, 16 In. 35.00
  Figurine, Enameled, Signed K.F.S., 1933, Chalkware 170.00
  Figurine, Olive Oyl, Wimpy, Iron, 3 1/2 In. 160.00
  Figurine, Pipe, Rubber, 1935, 6 In. 30.00
  Fountain Pen, Epenco 27.00
  Game, Ball Toss 20.00
  Game, Bingo, 1929, Tin 19.00
  Game, Darts, Original Card 20.00
  Game, Pipe Toss, Dated 1935, Boxed .... 32.00 To 45.00
  Game, Sling Darts, 1957 .... 30.00
  Game, The Juggler, Glass Top, Tin, 5 Balls, 3 X 5 In. 50.00
  Gameboard, Shipwreck, Lithography, 1933 .... 25.00
  Lamp, Dated 1934 .... 60.00
  Lamp, Dated 1935, Metal, 9 In. 115.00
  Lamp, Figural, Metal, 1935, 14 In. .... 95.00 To 145.00
  Lantern, Battery, Boxed 75.00
  Lantern, Lineman .... 95.00 To 135.00
  Marionette 22.00
  Mug, Ceramic .... 40.00 To 50.00
  Mug, Plastic 7.50
  Music Box, Pop-Up, 1961 .... 20.00
  Paint Book, 1937, Giant 25.00
  Pen & Pencil Set 55.00
  Pencil Case, Illustrated, 1929 .... 25.00
  Pencil, Mechanical, 10 In. 20.00
  Pencil, Sharpener 13.00
  Pipe, Ivory, Boxed 45.00
  Pipe, Kazoo 15.00
  Pocket Knife, Double Blade .... 24.00 To 35.00
  Printing Kit, Photo, 1958 .... 12.00
  Ring, Red Stone, 14K Gold 130.00
  Soap, Figure, 5 In. 40.00
  Stamp Set, The Printer, 13 Character Stamps, 1935, Boxed 28.00
  Toy, Arms Spin Round As Fighting, Holds Rod, Windup 60.00
  Toy, Barnacle Bill, Marx 100.00
  Toy, Blowing Bubbles, Linemar .... 325.00 To 450.00
  Toy, Bobbing Head, Linemar 200.00

Toy, Bubble Target, Durable Toy Co., Tin 115.00
Toy, Carrying Parrots In Cage, 8 1/2 In. 150.00
Toy, Dated 1929, King Features Syndicate, Wooden 45.00
Toy, Drives Airplane, 1940, Windup, King Features .... 350.00 To 375.00
Toy, Float, Rubber Boat 12.50
Toy, In Barrel, Walks, 1930s, Chein, Windup .... 175.00 To 250.00
Toy, Jack-In-The-Box 55.00
Toy, Juggler, With Olive Oyl, Linemar 800.00
Toy, On The Roof 350.00
Toy, Paint Set, Wimpy, Olive Oyl& Sweet Pea 18.00
Toy, Playing Basketball 375.00
Toy, Punching Bag 350.00
Toy, Rollerskater 325.00
Toy, Spinach Wagon, Original Figure, Hubley 295.00
Toy, Spinning Olive Oyl Overhead 400.00
Toy, Tank, Turnover 125.00
Toy, Tumbling 200.00
Toy, Unicycle 275.00
Watercolor Set, Tin 18.00

PORCELAIN, see also Copeland; Nippon; RS Prussia; etc.
PORCELAIN, Beaux A Verre, French, Foliate Monogram, 8 1/2 In., Pair 60.00
Box, Baby Carriage Form, Baby, Child, Doll, Germany, 6 In. 70.00
Box, Dresser, Covered, Portrait, Signed Prussia, 4 1/2 In. 60.00
Box, Figural, Colonial Maid, Yellow Gown, Germany, 4 1/4 In. 24.00
Bust, Napoleon, Oval, Portrait, Incised No.82, 3 1/2 In. 95.00
Candlestick, Blue, Pink Clustered Roses, Leaves, 5 In., Pair 45.00
Chocolate Pot, White Ground, Floral Relief, Germany, 4 1/4 In. 60.00
Compote, Figural, Tree Form, Flower, Vines, Courting Scene, 16 In. 550.00
Cup & Saucer, Russian, Blue & Gold Trim 55.00
Dish, Applied Roses, Leaves, Cupid Handle, Covered, 9 In. 70.00
Ewer, French, Gilt Mounted, Electrified, Cobalt Blue, 27 In., Pair 175.00
Ewer, Red Shades, Handled, Ball Shaped, French, 10 3/4 In. 85.00
Figurine, Bull, White, Brown, Germany, C.1870, Marked, 12 1/2 In. 375.00
Figurine, Cavalier, C.1900, Stands With Hat, Germany, 10 In. 90.00
Figurine, Dancing Couple, White, Marked & Dated, 1913, 13 In. 375.00
Figurine, Dancing Girl, Pink Net Skirt, Polychromed, 10 In. 100.00
Figurine, Dog, Setter, Standing, Gray & Off-White, 11 In. 45.00
Figurine, Girl, Dancing, Germany, 8 1/2 In. 30.00
Figurine, Girl, Goose, Umbrella, 1877, Blue Crown Mark, 5 1/4 In. 95.00
Figurine, Kwan Yin, Blue, White, Praying, Lotus Blossom, 7 1/2 In. 55.00
Figurine, Monk, Bisque, Germany, 5 In., Pair 150.00
Figurine, Musical Monkey, 4 In., Set Of 8 .... 395.00
Figurine, Putti With Harlequin, Leaning On Shell Bowl, 7 In. 225.00
Figurine, Reclining Girl With Basket, Casades, 9 X 9 In. 95.00
Figurine, Viking, Seated, Signed, 14 X 8 In. 675.00
Garden Seat, Elephant-Form, Yellow Lead Glazed, Chinese, 24 In. 275.00
Ginger Jar, Chinese, Covered, 8 1/4 In. 220.00
Holder, Cigarette, Figural, Bellboy Standing, Orange, 4 In. 22.00
Holder, String, Lovebirds 15.00
Jar, Foo Dog Finial, Blue & White, Large 135.00
Jar, Pomade, Car Scene, Mark Crown & Shield, 4 In. 25.00
Jar, Temple, Famille Rose Peonies, Green Scale Ground, 18 In., Pr. 600.00
Nativity Scene, Infant Joseph, Mary, 10 X 7 In. 30.00
Pitcher, Sprig Design, Helmet Shaped, 5 1/4 In. 150.00
Plaque, Grecian Woman, Seated, Ewer At Feet, Marked Traumera, 7 In. 400.00
Plaque, Gypsy Woman, Standing, Birch Tree, Marked 7 X 5 In. 550.00
Plaque, Portrait, French, Young Woman, 3 1/2 X 5 1/2 In. 40.00
Plaque, Venus, Seated, Pool, Flowers, Cupid, Signed Landgraf, 18 In. 2750.00
Plaque, Woman, Long Flowing Hair, White Gown, 3 X 2 In. 225.00
Plate, Blue, Red Foliage, 20th Century, Marked Fukagawa, 7 In. 100.00
Shoe, Black, Cat Climbing Up Back 30.00
Spittoon, Lady's, Hand-Painted, Gargoyle Spout, French 125.00
Spittoon, P.O.D. Stenciled On Front 25.00

Porcelain, Urn, Ornate Design, 3 Parts,
Schierholz Mark, 24 In.

Teapot, Figural, Terrier, Black & White, 7 In. 48.00
Teapot, Russian, Blue & Gold Trim 225.00
Teapot, Willow Pattern, Chi'en Lung, 5 3/4 In. 225.00
Urn, Ornate Design, 3 Parts, Schierholz Mark, 24 In. .... *Illus* 250.00
Vase, Bottle Form, Lotus Form Lip, Classical Design, 23 In., Pair 175.00
Vase, Chinese Sang De Boeuf, Bottle Form, 8 1/4 In. 300.00
Vase, Design, Square Shaped, Gilt Handles, Mandarin, 4 1/4 In., Pair 220.00
Vase, Iridescent Blue, Woman & Boat Scene, Blue Lagoon, 8 In. 95.00
Watering Can, Applied Purple Flowers, 3 1/2 In. 65.00
Wrist Rest, Oriental, Unrolled Scroll Form, 4 Figures, 3 1/4 In. 300.00

Postcards were first legally permitted in Austria on October 1, 1869.
The United States passed postal regulations allowing the card in 1873.
Most of the picture postcards collected today date after 1910.

POSTCARD, A Good Crop In Dixieland, Black Boys Hair Gets Cut, 1940 .... 2.00
Admiral Speery At Santa Barbara 3.00
Admiral Train's Funeral, 5 Views 12.50
Akron Lamp 3.50
Aspects Of Slave Days, Black People, Set Of 10 .... 6.00
Atlantic City, 1930s & 1940s, Set Of 7 .... 3.75
Babe Ruth, Set Of 6 .... 1.50
Black Boy Riding Turkey .... 3.00 To 4.00
Boston Rubber Shoe Co., 1910, Set Of 10 .... 37.00
Calendar, Turnback, 1914 .... 6.75
Cherry Smash, Advertising 100.00
Christmas, Hold To Light, Set Of 2 .... 12.00
Christmas, Set Of 20, Pre-1920 .... 15.00
Christmas, 1906, Embossed, 1 Cent Stamp 3.00
Cloverine Salve 3.50
Colorado, Set Of 10 .... 1.50
Columbian Exposition, Set Of 10 .... 150.00
Coney Island, Folder, 18 Views 10.00
Cracker Jack Bears, No.9 .... 20.00
Cupid, Easter .... 3.00 To 5.00
Cupid, Wedding Trip 3.00
Dopey, Walt Disney, Squeaker, 1961 .... 8.50
Dousman Street, Green Bay, Wis., 1915 .... 2.50
Easter, Bunnies & Chicks, German, Set Of 17 .... 20.00

Excursion Steamers, Detroit River, 1913	4.00
Faro	5.00
France, Souvenir, 1903-39, Set Of 50	15.00
Grand Pop Embarrassed, 1940s, Old Black Man With Daughter	1.50
Grandmother Cupid	5.00
Great White Fleet, Entering Golden Gate & Frisco Bay, Pair	6.00
Hershey Chocolate	8.00
Hudson Fulton Celebration, 1909, Set Of 4	28.00
Intercourse, Pa., Set Of 10	2.00
Jamestown Exposition, 1907	7.00
Jerusalem, Real Flowers, Set Of 6	16.00
Kelloggs	8.00
Knapp Shoes	8.00
Leather, Set Of 50	50.00
Leather, 1906	5.00
Leather, 1907	5.00
Lincoln County, Oregon, Covered Bridge, Set Of 7	1.00
Main Street, Erie, Buffalo, N.Y., 1907	3.50
Mars Attack, Complete Set	300.00
Mexican War, 1714, Battle & Camp Scenes, Set Of 63	400.00
Michigan National Guard, Ludington, 1907	3.00
Minnesota Centennial, 1858-1958, Set Of 12	5.00
Minstrel, Flag Scene, Liberty Society Minstrel Show, 1918	7.50
National Hotel, Washington, D.C., Penn. Ave.	3.50
Negro Melodies, Tuck	15.00
New Year, 1907, Ambossed, 1 Cent Stamp, Pair	5.00
New Year's Greetings, 1912	1.50
Ochs Brick & Tile	8.00
Old Black Joe, Elderly Man Sits On Steps Of Shack, 1940	2.00
Panama Canal, Pictures Construction, Set Of 25	40.00
Path Finder Radio	3.50
Pied Piper, Maxfield Parrish, Elongated	20.00
Polo Grounds, N.Y., Home Of N.Y. Giants	25.00
R.M.S.Empress Of Ireland, C.1910, Woven In Silk	25.00
Roosevelt Bears, No. 3	10.00
Roosevelt Bears, No.10	10.00
San Francisco Earthquake, 1906, Set Of 4	20.00
Santa Claus, Reading, 1920	1.50
Sinking Pere Marquette Car Ferry 18, Sept.1910	6.00
Solid Comfort, Old Black Smoking Pipe, 1940s	2.00
Spanish-American War, Associated Press Correspondent	4.00
Spanish-American War, Filipino Prisoners, 1899	5.00
Spanish-American War, Hotchkiss Quick-Firing Gun	5.00
Spanish-American War, 17th U.S.Infantry, 1899	4.00
St.Louis World's Fair, 1904, Set Of 4	22.50
State Capitals, Set	50.00
State Street Chicago, Turn-Of-The-Century Scene, 1906	3.50
Steamer Dewitt Clinton, Hudson River	4.00
Teddy Bear, Leather	5.00
Teddy Bear, Tuesday, Leather	5.00
The Speedwar, N.Y., 1902	1.00
The Three Bares, Comic, 3 Black Girls With Bare Bottoms, 1940s	2.00
U.S.S.Mississippi, In Dry Dock, 1922	5.00
U.S.Troops In Philippines, Watching Bow & Arrow Marksmanship	3.00
Underwood Typewriter	3.50
Valentine, Candy Heart In Waxed Paper	3.00
World War II, Black & White, Let Us Do Our Part For Victory	.75
World War II, Blackout Of The Rising Sun, Color, Comic	1.00
World War II, Captured Balloon, Black & White Photo, Zeppelin	1.00
World War II, Faces Of Hitler, Hirohito, & Mussolini On Bombs	.75
World War II, Our Armed Forces Work Together, Army & Navy	1.00
World War II, Soldier Kicking Hitler In Bottom, Comic, Color	1.50
World War II, Tagged For Tokyo, Pilot With Bomb, Color	1.00
4th Of July, 1905	5.00

4th Of July, 1908 .... 5.00
48 State Capitals, Illustration Card Co. 57.50

POSTER, Alice Soulie, 1926, Alice, Feather Fan, Signed, 46 X 63 In. 600.00
   Buffalo Bill, Famous Generals, 1887, 24 X 34 In. 400.00
   Cherry Chevalier, Cherry Brandy, Maurice Chevalier, 46 X 62 In. 250.00
   Chocolat Mexicain, Matador In Blue, Chocolate, Linen, 32 X 48 In. 110.00
   Circus, Achille Philion, Copyright 1899, Courier Co., 28 X 42 In. 195.00
   Dolly Davis Drinking Bonal, French, Linen, 46 X 62 In. 30.00
   Dutch, Nouveau, Signed Beethon, Oak Frame, 14 X 18 In. 140.00
   Federal Cartridge Corp., Hunting Scene, 1933, 20 1/2 X 26 1/2 In. 125.00
   Fudgicle, Boy Selling Newspaper, 1950s, 7 1/2 X 20 In. 4.50
   Hobart's, Best Show In The World, 1906, Circus, 41 X 27 In. 80.00
   Hobart's, Circus Arts, 1906, Acrobats, Linen, 41 X 26 In. 95.00
   Le Havre, Bogart, Film Festival, Linen, 29 X 46 In. 60.00
   Les Fetards, The Playboys, Operetta, Dancers, Linen, 23 23 X 31 In. 125.00
   Madame Lemays Antiseptic Vaginal Suppositories, 1913, 6 X 10 In. 7.00
   Montagnes De France, Mountains Of France, Linen, 23 X 38 In. 60.00
   Monte Carlo Beach, Watershed Pulled By Serpent, 47 X 31 In. 60.00
   Movie, Brother Martin, Servant Of Jesus, 27 X 41 In. 30.00
   Movie, Carroll Baker, Harlow, 1965, 14 X 22 In. 15.00
   Movie, Merrily We Live, Constance Bennett, Brian Aherne, 27 X 41 In. 15.00
   Movie, Swiss Family Robinson, C.1844, Cast Pictured, 27 X 41 In. 15.00
   Movie, Wm.S.Hart, Tumbleweeds, Silk Screened, 14 X 22 In. 8.50
   Northern Pacific R.R., Montana Roundup, 30 X 40 In. 45.00
   Portrait Of Esmeralda, Paris, 31 X 45 In. 25.00
   Remington Anniversary, 150th, 1966, 12 X 16 1/4 In. 15.00
   Remington Shotguns & Shells, Pictures Gun, Hanging, 23 X 29 1/2 In. 25.00
   Rice's Seeds, True Early Winnings Start, 22 X 28 In. 300.00
   Ringling Bros. World's Greatest Shows, Horses, Brothers, 18 X 24 In. 140.00
   Sarge LiPar, Creation DeChamprusay, 1940, 46 X 63 In. 50.00
   Savage, Stevens, & Fox Rifles & Shotguns, Bird Dogs, 22 X 27 In. 125.00
   Societe Generale, 1917, Mother, Child, Bed, Linen, 22 X 31 In. 30.00
   Sonny 5 Cent Sugar Cones, 4-Color, Pictures Boy, 8 X 19 In. 6.00
   Spirit Of America, World War I, Christy, 20 X 30 In. 100.00
   Travel, Furness Lines, 1930s, 25 X 17 In. 22.00
   Uniforms Of French Army, C.1918, Printed In English, 25 X 20 In. 17.50
   Veuve Amiot, Champagne, Couple Toasting, Linen, Signed, 45 X 61 In. 175.00
   Veuve Amiot, 1922, French Champagne Poster, Linen, 47 X 63 In. 100.00
   Vichy, 1895, City Of Vichy, Lady, Parasol, Linen, 35 X 51 In. 100.00

      POTLID, see also Pratt
POTLID, Charing Cross 75.00

      POTTERY, see also Buffalo Pottery; Staffordshire; Wedgwood; etc.
POTTERY, Ashtray, Security National Bank, New Jersey Porcelain Co., 1927 .... 9.00
   Biscuit Jar, Tapestry Finish, Marked Tunnecliffe, 6 1/2 In. 118.00
   Bowl, North State Pottery Co., Shaded Greens, 6 1/2 X 4 3/4 In. 42.00
   Mug, Child's, Canary Yellow, Brown Design, C.1830, 2 1/4 In., Pair 325.00
   Pitcher, Brown Leaves, Scroll Decor, New Geneva 485.00
   Sugar & Creamer, Child's, Ildefonso, Mark, 1 1/2 X 3 In. 225.00
   Tile, Country, Duty, Monor, Shield, Gray-Blue, 4 In.Square 20.00
   Tray, Flowers, Brass Rim & Feet, 15 1/2 In.Diam. 195.00
   Turk's Head Mold, Buff, Tan Glaze, Fluted, Side Handle, 9 1/2 In. 17.50
   Vase, Double Handles Form Wide Arc, Rainbow Pottery, 4 3/4 In. 50.00
   Vase, Metallic Glaze, Seldon Bybee, Brown Ground, 10 In. 30.00
   Vase, Pink Filigree On Cream, Gold Feet, Collins, 6 1/2 X 5 3/4 In. 120.00

POWDER FLASK, Black, Dead Game On Sides, 8 In. 95.00
   Black, Embossed Game, Marked, 8 In. 90.00
   Dixon & Sons, Hanging Game Scene, Brass 50.00
   Fluted Design, 8 In. 25.00
   Hunter, Gun, Dog, & Forest, Copper, 6 In. 55.00
   Hunting Scene, Brass & Copper 34.00

Shell Design, Brass 85.00
Shell Design, Brass Collar & Dispenser, Pewter, 4 1/4 In. 59.00

POWDER HORN, American Flag, Domestic Scenes, Marked John Rubie, 1793 .... 1050.00
Attached Shot Pouch & Leather Bag, 10 In. 200.00
Carved Design, Northwest Coast, 4 In. 700.00
Curved, Brass Chain, 15 In. 18.00

PRATT
FENTON

Pratt ware means two different things. It was an early Staffordshire pottery, cream colored with colored decorations, made by Felix Pratt during the late eighteenth century. There was also Pratt ware made with transfer designs during the mid-nineteenth century in Fenton, England.

PRATT, Cradle, Ocher, Blue, Brown, Ladies, Putti, Foliate Border, C.1790, 12 In. 450.00
Creamer, 2 Young Girls, Doll, Polychrome, Heart Frame 195.00
Figurine, Child, Standing, Holding Rooster, 4 3/4 In. 75.00
Figurine, Spring & Autumn, Pair 3450.00
Jar, Matador Design On Cover, Transfer 3000.00
Jar, Pomade, Blue Glaze, Boar Hunt Scene Transfer, 4 In. 22.00
Jar, Terra-Cotta, Shakespearean Transfer 25.00
Jug, Commemoration, Nelson, C.1815, 6 1/4 In. 125.00
Jug, The Wine Maker, Polychrome, Embossed Design, C.1820 .... 135.00
Jug, Toby, Brown Tricorn, Yellow Coat, Blue Pants, C.1800, 9 In. 330.00
Mustard, Boar Hunt Transfer, Blue 30.00
Pitcher, Floral, Leafy Border, Green, Brown, Gold, 4 3/4 .... 152.00
Pitcher, Floral, Leafy Border, 2 Girls, Blue, Green, 7 1/4 In. 325.00
Pitcher, George Washington On Horseback, Acorn Border, 6 In. 75.00
Pitcher, Gold, Cobalt, Green, Ovoid, 6 1/4 In. 190.00
Pitcher, Hunt Scene, Leafy Border, Green, Yellow, Blue, 6 In. 110.00
Pitcher, Man Smoking Pipe, Olive, Brown, Gold, C.1790, 4 7/8 In. 140.00
Pitcher, Peafowl, Iris, Green, Yellow, Blue, & Rust, 6 In. 100.00
Pitcher, Pink, Gold Trim, Classical Figures, 5 1/2 In. 110.00
Plaque, Venus, Arising From Sea, Seaweed, Flowers, 7 3/4 In. 850.00
Plaque, Wall, Sad Sailor's Farwell, Blue Jacket, Boat, Shore, 6 In. 675.00
Potlid, Scene Transfer, Dated 1845 .... 115.00
Stop, Mirror, Polychromed Boy Holding Bird's Nest, 4 1/8 In., Pair 100.00
Teapot, Several Scenes, C.1850, Blue Ground, Large 150.00
Teapot, 1850 Scenes, Blue Ground 185.00

Pressed glass was first made in the United States in the 1820s after the invention of pressed glass machines. Hundreds of patterns of pressed glass were made in complete table settings. Although the Boston and Sandwich Works was the most famous of the pressed glass factories, there were about sixteen other factories making pressed glass from 1830 to 1850, and still more from 1850 to 1900, when pressed glass reached its greatest popularity. It is now being widely reproduced.

PRESSED GLASS, Aberdeen, Goblet 20.00
Aberdeen, Tumbler, Footed 27.00
    ACANTHUS, see Ribbed Palm
    ACME, see Butterfly With Spray
Acorn, Compote, Covered, Footed, 8 In. 70.00
Acorn, Pitcher 165.00
Acorn, Sugar Shaker, C.1890, Blue 90.00
Acorn, Sugar Shaker, Emerald Green 65.00
Acorn, Syrup, Emerald Green 125.00
Actress, Bowl, 5 In.Diam. 25.00
Actress, Bread Plate .... 32.00 To 65.00
Actress, Bread Plate, Miss Neilson, Oval 95.00
Actress, Butter, Covered .... 25.00 To 55.00
Actress, Cake Stand 125.00
Actress, Celery 155.00
Actress, Celery, 7 In. 83.00
Actress, Compote, Frosted, Covered, 7 3/4 In. 75.00

Actress, Compote, Frosted, Covered, 12 X 7 In. 155.00
Actress, Dish, Cheese, Dromios, Covered .... 135.00 To 185.00
Actress, Dish, Pickle 38.00
Actress, Goblet 65.00
Actress, Jar, Jam, Covered 110.00
Actress, Sauce, Footed .... 10.00 To 15.00
Actress, Sauce, Frosted 16.00
Actress, Tumbler, Gold Enamel, Green Design 22.00
Admiral Dewey, Dish, Candy, Covered 60.00
Admiral Dewey, Pitcher, Water .... 50.00 To 75.00
Admiral Dewey, Pitcher, Water, 6 Tumblers 325.00
Adonis, Tumbler 20.00
Aegis, Spooner 12.00
Alabama, Creamer .... 18.00 To 32.50
Alabama, Dish, Relish 12.00
Alaska, Creamer, Blue Opalescent 65.00
Alaska, Creamer, Vaseline Opalescent 70.00
Alaska, Sauce, Green, 3 3/4 In. 17.00
Alaska, Shaker, Frosted & Gold, Pair 195.00
Alaska, Spooner, Blue Opalescent .... 65.00 To 95.00
Alaska, Sugar & Creamer 185.00
Alaska, Sugar, Covered, Green .... 60.00 To 68.00
Alaska, Sugar, Frosted & Gold, Covered 290.00
Almond Thumbprint, Compote 30.00
Almond Thumbprint, Creamer, Child's, 2 1/2 In. 25.00
Almond, Wine 14.50
Amazon, Butter, Covered, Etched 32.00
Amazon, Butter, Dome Lid, 5 1/4 In. 18.00
Amazon, Creamer, Footed 25.00
Amazon, Dish, Oval, Covered, Lion Finial, Handled, 7 X 4 In. 15.00
Amazon, Goblet 35.00
Amazon, Sugar, Covered 54.00
Amazon, Tumbler 20.00
  AMBERETTE, see Klondike
Anthemion, Pitcher, Water 36.00
Anthemion, Sugar, Covered .... 25.00 To 39.00
Apollo, Cruet, Clear Stopper, Pink 40.00
Apollo, Goblet, Frosted 28.00
Apollo, Sauce, Etched, Stemmed, Set Of 6 .... 89.00
Apollo, Spooner 35.00
Apollo, Sugar Shaker, Etched 65.00
Apollo, Sugar, Creamer, & Spooner, Etched 134.50
Apollo, Syrup, Etched 65.00
Apollo, Tray, Water 29.50
Apple Blossom, Sugar Shaker 57.00
Aquarium, Pitcher .... 140.00 To 180.00
Aquarium, Pitcher, Green 245.00
Arabesque, Goblet 27.50
Arabesque, Tumbler, Footed 26.00
Arched Fleur-De-Lis, Bowl, Sloped Sides, Square, 10 In. 20.00
Arched Fleur-De-Lis, Cruet, Stopper 26.00
Arched Fleur-De-Lis, Dish, Relish, 8 1/4 X 4 1/2 In. 10.00
Arched Forget-Me-Not Bands, Goblet 16.00
Arched Forget-Me-Not Bands, Spooner 18.00
Arched Grape, Goblet .... 25.00 To 27.00
Arched Leaf, Plate, 7 1/2 In. .... 25.00 To 28.00
Arched Ovals, Creamer, Green, 1908, 2 1/4 In. 20.00
Arched Ovals, Toothpick .... 10.00 To 20.00
Arched Ovals, Tumbler, Gold Trim 15.00
Arched Ovals, Wine 22.00
Arched Ovals, Wine, Cranberry Top 18.00
Argus, Champagne, Flint 52.00
Argus, Eggcup 24.00
Argus, Eggcup, Flint 25.00

Actress

Arched Fleur-De-Lis

Arched Grape

Arrow Sheaf, Tumbler 29.00
Arrowhead In Oval, Compote, Jelly, 5 X 5 In. 18.00
Art, Cruet, Original Stopper 75.00
Art, Spooner 35.00
Art, Sugar, Covered .... 30.00 To 35.00
Artichoke, Berry Bowl 30.00
Ashburton, Celery, Flint 55.00
Ashburton, Champagne, Flint .... 20.00 To 45.00
Ashburton, Claret, Flint, 4 1/2 In. 20.00
Ashburton, Eggcup, Barrel Shape 28.50
Ashburton, Eggcup, Double 145.00
Ashburton, Eggcup, Flared 28.50
Ashburton, Eggcup, Flint .... 25.00 To 32.00
Ashburton, Goblet, Flint .... 30.00 To 48.00
Ashburton, Wine .... 26.00 To 45.00
Ashburton, Wine, Flint .... 35.00 To 38.00
Ashman, Compote, Covered 57.50
Atlanta, Compote, Jelly, Square 54.00
Atlanta, Creamer 42.00
Atlanta, Dish, Relish, Fish Shape 36.00
Atlanta, Goblet 67.00
Atlanta, Saltshaker 45.00
Atlanta, Tumbler, Water, 1896 .... 55.00
Atlas, Creamer 12.50
Atlas, Creamer, Etched 22.50
Atlas, Goblet .... 18.00 To 33.00
Atlas, Sauce, Footed, 4 In. 12.50
Atlas, Tankard, 12 In. 45.00
Atlas, Toothpick 14.00
Atlas, Tumbler 30.00
Atlas, Wine 15.00
Aurora, Tray, Water 25.00
Aurora, Wine .... 15.00 To 22.00
Aurora, Wine, Etched 23.00
Austrian, Creamer .... 29.50 To 50.00
Austrian, Goblet 45.00
Austrian, Sugar, Covered 38.00
Austrian, Tumbler 25.00
Aztec, Plate, 6 1/2 In. 10.00

Baby Face, Compote, Open, 8 X 7 3/4 In. 58.00
Baby Face, Creamer 110.00
    BABY THUMBPRINT, see Dakota
    BALDER, see also Pennsylvania
Balder, Bowl, Gold Trim, 8 1/2 In. 24.50
Balder, Creamer 30.00
Balder, Creamer, Child's 19.50
Balder, Cup, Punch, Gold Rim 15.00
Balder, Glass, Juice 15.00
Balder, Goblet 20.00
Balder, Spooner 26.50
Balder, Sugar, Covered 35.00
Balder, Wine, Gold Rim 19.00
    BALKY MULE, see Currier & Ives
Ball & Bar, Creamer 19.00
Ball & Bar, Tumbler, Amber 20.00
Ball & Swirl, Compote, Footed 32.00
Ball & Swirl, Creamer 22.50
Ball & Swirl, Goblet, Etched 20.00
Ball & Swirl, Tankard 40.00
Balloon, Goblet 5.00
Baltimore Pear, Creamer 32.00
Baltimore Pear, Pitcher 20.00
Baltimore Pear, Sugar, Covered 48.00
    BAMBOO, see Broken Column
Banded Arch Panels, Mug, 2 5/8 In. 9.00
Banded Buckle, Spooner 26.00
Banded Buckle, Sugar & Creamer 80.00
Banded Buckle, Sugar, Covered 34.00
    BANDED FINE CUT, see Fine Cut Band
Banded Fleur-De-Lis, Salt & Pepper 32.50
Banded Fleur-De-Lis, Wine 18.00
Banded Kokomo, Wine 28.00
    BANDED PORTLAND, when flashed with pink, is sometimes called Maiden
    Blush
Banded Portland, Bottle, Water 75.00
Banded Portland, Celery 30.00
Banded Portland, Compote, Open 42.00
Banded Portland, Creamer, Large 35.00
Banded Portland, Cruet, Original Stopper 39.50
Banded Portland, Cup, Punch 18.00
Banded Portland, Dish, Gold Trim, Oval, 6 1/2 X 1 1/4 In. 16.00
Banded Portland, Dish, Relish 22.50
Banded Portland, Goblet .... 14.00 To 30.00
Banded Portland, Pitcher, Water, Child's, Gold Trim 22.00
Banded Portland, Toothpick 20.00
Banded Portland, Toothpick, Gold Trim .... 24.00 To 28.00
Banded Portland, Toothpick, Maiden's Blush 40.00
Banded Portland, Tumbler .... 23.00 To 30.00
Banded Portland, Vase, 6 1/4 In. 11.00
Banded Portland, Wine .... 22.00 To 35.00
    BANDED RAINDROP, see Candlewick
Banded Star, Celery 48.00
Banded Star, Creamer 40.00
Banded Stippled Star Flower, Goblet 15.00
    OTHER BANDED PATTERNS, see under name of basic pattern: e.g., Banded
    Honeycomb, see Honeycomb, Banded
    BAR & DIAMOND, see Kokomo
Barberry, Celery .... 18.00 To 23.00
Barberry, Compote, Covered, 7 1/2 X 9 In. 40.00
Barberry, Compote, Low Standard, Covered, 8 1/4 In. 42.00
Barberry, Creamer .... 20.00 To 30.00
Barberry, Eggcup 22.00
Barberry, Goblet .... 20.00 To 25.00

Barberry, Plate, 6 In. 18.50
Barberry, Spooner .... 20.00 To 26.50
Barberry, Syrup, Pewter Lid, Dated 130.00
Barberry, Tumbler, Footed .... 21.00 To 25.00
    BARLEY & OATS, see Wheat & Barley
    BARLEY & WHEAT, see Wheat & Barley
Barley, Bread Plate, 9 1/4 X 11 1/2 In. 35.00
Barley, Cake Stand 25.00
Barley, Goblet .... 22.00 To 27.00
Barley, Jar, Jam, Covered 25.00
Barley, Pitcher 35.00
Barley, Sauce, Footed 10.00
Barley, Spooner 8.00
Barley, Tumbler 20.00
Barred Forget-Me-Not, Creamer 35.00
Barred Forget-Me-Not, Spooner 20.00
Barred Hobnail, Goblet 21.00
    BARRED OVALS, see Banded Portland
Barred Star, Goblet 12.00
Barrel Ashburton, Goblet, Flint 35.00
Barrel Ashburton, Spooner 115.00
Barrel Excelsior, Goblet 42.50
    BARREL HONEYCOMB, see also Honeycomb
Barrel Honeycomb, Goblet, Flint 18.00
    BARRELED BLOCK, see Red Block
    BARTLETT PEAR, see Pear
Basket Weave, Goblet 18.00
Bead & Scroll, Creamer, Child's, Etched 35.00
Bead Swag, Sugar, Covered 25.00
Bead Swag, Toothpick 95.00
Beaded Acorn, Sauce, Medium 10.00
Beaded Band, Dish, Pickle 12.50
Beaded Band, Goblet 28.00
Beaded Band, Sugar, Covered 28.00
Beaded Band, Wine .... 16.50 To 22.00
    BEADED BULL'S-EYE & DRAPE, see Alabama
Beaded Dart Band, Goblet 19.00
Beaded Dewdrop, Banana Stand, Turned-Up Sides, 7 1/2 X 4 In. 75.00
Beaded Dewdrop, Compote, Tricornered Shape 45.00
Beaded Dewdrop, Pitcher, Milk 50.00
Beaded Dewdrop, Salt & Pepper 34.50
Beaded Dewdrop, Sugar Shaker 55.00
Beaded Dewdrop, Syrup 45.00
Beaded Dewdrop, Syrup, Spring Lid 55.00
Beaded Dewdrop, Wine 30.00
Beaded Diamond Band, Spooner 21.50
Beaded Ellipse, Butter, Covered 48.00
Beaded Ellipse, Pitcher, Water 32.50
Beaded Frog's-Eye, Goblet 24.00
Beaded Grape Medallion Banded, Goblet 28.50
Beaded Grape Medallion, Butter, Covered 40.00
Beaded Grape Medallion, Eggcup, Pattern In Base 22.50
Beaded Grape Medallion, Goblet .... 26.00 To 33.00
Beaded Grape Medallion, Sauce 5.00
Beaded Grape Medallion, Spooner .... 22.00 To 24.00
Beaded Grape, Butter, Covered, Green .... 75.00 To 125.00
Beaded Grape, Cake Stand, Green 75.00
Beaded Grape, Celery, Green 35.00
Beaded Grape, Creamer 52.00
Beaded Grape, Cruet, Original Stopper, Green .... 90.00 To 95.00
Beaded Grape, Pitcher, Water, Green 85.00
Beaded Grape, Sugar, Covered 55.00
Beaded Grape, Sugar, Gold Trim, Green 55.00
Beaded Grape, Toothpick, Green 55.00

Beaded Grape, Tumbler 15.00
Beaded Loop, Dish, Relish, 9 In. 10.00
Beaded Loop, Goblet .... 28.00 To 32.00
Beaded Loop, Pitcher, Milk .... 20.00 To 37.50
Beaded Loop, Saltshaker 45.00
Beaded Loop, Sauce 25.00
Beaded Loop, Sauce, Flat, 4 1/4 In. 5.00
Beaded Loop, Sugar, Covered, Ruby & Clear Bottom 38.00
Beaded Loop, Syrup, Spring Tin Top 35.00
Beaded Loop, Tumbler 15.00
  BEADED MEDALLION, see Beaded Mirror
Beaded Mirror, Goblet, Flint 22.00
Beaded Mirror, Sauce, Flat 6.00
Beaded Oval & Scroll, Creamer 16.00
Beaded Oval & Scroll, Goblet 42.00
Beaded Oval & Scroll, Sauce 12.00
Beaded Ovals In Sand, Butter, Covered, Gold Trim, Green 165.00
Beaded Ovals In Sand, Creamer, Green .... 45.00 To 65.00
Beaded Ovals In Sand, Sugar, Covered, Green 85.00
Beaded Panel, Celery 26.00
Beaded Rosette, Goblet 16.00
  BEADED STAR, see Shimmering Star
Beaded Swirl & Disc, Cup 4.00
Beaded Swirl & Disc, Pitcher, Water, Gold Trim 25.00
Beaded Swirl, Bottle, Cologne, Stopper 27.00
Beaded Swirl, Bowl, Master Berry, Gold Trim, Green 75.00
Beaded Swirl, Butter, Child's, Covered 22.00
Beaded Swirl, Butter, Covered, Green 50.00
Beaded Swirl, Butter, Gold Trim, Green, Covered 110.00
Beaded Swirl, Celery, Gold Trim, Green 45.00
Beaded Swirl, Creamer, Child's 18.00
Beaded Swirl, Sauce 12.00
Beaded Swirl, Tumbler, Gold Trim, Green 25.00
Beaded Tulip, Goblet, Odd Fellow 30.00
  BEARDED MAN, see Viking
Beatty Rib, Toothpick, Blue Opalescent 18.00
Beautiful Lady, Celery 11.00
Belcher Loop, Goblet 16.00
Bellaire, Cruet 31.50
Bellaire, Dish, Cheese, Covered 125.00
Bellaire, Salt & Pepper 41.50
Bellflower, Bowl, Coarse Rib, Footed, 8 In. .... 59.00 To 68.00
Bellflower, Bowl, Silver Plated Frame, Flint, 6 X 1 3/4 In. 75.00
Bellflower, Butter, Covered 75.00
Bellflower, Champagne, Flint 90.00
Bellflower, Compote 125.00
Bellflower, Cordial 100.00
Bellflower, Creamer, Flint 140.00
Bellflower, Decanter, Original Bellflower Stopper, Flint 150.00
Bellflower, Double Vine, Bread Plate 23.00
Bellflower, Eggcup, Flint 25.00
Bellflower, Eggcup, Rayed Base, Flint 42.00
Bellflower, Goblet .... 28.00 To 45.00
Bellflower, Goblet, Flint .... 30.00 To 35.00
Bellflower, Mug 20.00
Bellflower, Pitcher, Water, Flint 200.00
Bellflower, Salt, Master 40.00
Bellflower, Sauce, 5 In. 12.00
Bellflower, Spooner 35.00
Bellflower, Spooner, Double Vine, Flint 50.00
Bellflower, Spooner, Fine Rib, Banded 25.00
Bellflower, Spooner, Flint 35.00
Bellflower, Sugar, Covered, Flint 50.00
Bellflower, Sugar, Single Vine, Open, Flint 45.00

Bellflower, Syrup, Original Tin Top 550.00
Bellflower, Tumbler, Flint .... 75.00 To 110.00
Bellflower, Wine, Flint .... 75.00 To 95.00
Bellflower, Wine, Straight Side 52.00
    BELTED WORCESTER, see Worcester, Belted
    BENT BUCKLE, see New Hampshire
Berry Cluster, Creamer 31.50
Bethlehem Star, Compote, Covered, 4 1/2 In. .... 45.00 To 50.00
Bethlehem Star, Compote, Covered, 5 1/4 In. 45.00
Bethlehem Star, Creamer .... 18.00 To 35.00
Bethlehem Star, Pitcher, Water 43.50
Bethlehem Star, Sugar, Covered 42.00
Bethlehem Star, Toothpick 40.00
Bethlehem Star, Tumbler 35.00
Beveled Diagonal Block, Celery 20.00
Beveled Diamond & Star, Creamer 22.00
Beveled Diamond & Star, Cruet, Original Stopper 25.00
Beveled Diamond & Star, Sugar, Covered .... 31.50 To 32.50
Beveled Diamond & Star, Wine 14.00
    BIG BLOCK, see Henrietta
Bigler, Bowl, Flat Base, Flint, 8 1/2 In. 12.00
Bigler, Decanter, Bar Lip, Flint 25.00
Bigler, Goblet, Flint .... 30.00 To 35.00
Bird & Strawberry, Berry, Master, 3-Legged 40.00
Bird & Strawberry, Bowl, Footed, Oval, 9 1/2 In. 75.00
Bird & Strawberry, Bowl, Footed, 4 In. 25.00
Bird & Strawberry, Bowl, 5 In. 22.00
Bird & Strawberry, Bowl, 8 In. 45.00
Bird & Strawberry, Bowl, 10 In. .... 55.00 To 75.00
Bird & Strawberry, Butter, Covered 85.00
Bird & Strawberry, Cake Stand, 8 In. .... 35.00 To 55.00
Bird & Strawberry, Cake Stand, 8 3/4 In. 55.00
Bird & Strawberry, Cake Stand, 9 1/2 In. .... 50.00 To 65.00
Bird & Strawberry, Creamer, Gold Rim 135.00
Bird & Strawberry, Cup, Punch .... 18.00 To 35.00
Bird & Strawberry, Dish, Heart Shaped 35.00
Bird & Strawberry, Pitcher, Water .... 200.00 To 285.00
Bird & Strawberry, Tumbler .... 25.00 To 70.00
Bird & Strawberry, Water Set, Pink, Blue, & Clear, 7 Piece 295.00
    BIRD IN RING, see Butterfly & Fan
Birds At Fountain, Goblet .... 30.00 To 42.00
Birds In Swamp, Goblet 30.00
Bismarc Star, Goblet 13.00
Blackberry, Goblet .... 32.00 To 35.00
Bleeding Heart, Dish, Relish, Oval, 3 X 5 In. .... 30.00 To 35.00
Bleeding Heart, Goblet .... 22.00 To 38.50
Bleeding Heart, Mug, 3 1/4 In. 30.00
Bleeding Heart, Salt, Master .... 35.00 To 65.00
Bleeding Heart, Sauce 12.00
Bleeding Heart, Spooner 25.00
Bleeding Heart, Sugar 24.00
Block & Circle, Celery 27.50
Block & Circle, Goblet 19.00
Block & Circle, Sauce, Flat 9.00
Block & Circle, Wine 18.00
Block & Fan, Bowl, Ice 22.00
Block & Fan, Celery 15.00
Block & Fan, Cruet 34.00
Block & Fan, Cup, Punch 9.50
Block & Fan, Dish, Oblong 25.00
Block & Fan, Goblet 55.00
Block & Fan, Nappy, Handled 21.00
Block & Fan, Sauce, Footed, 4 In. 15.00

Block & Fan, Sauce, 5 In. .... 10.50 To 13.00
Block & Fan, Wine 42.00
      BLOCK & FINE CUT, see Fine Cut & Block
Block & Jewel, Goblet 22.00
      BLOCK & STAR, see Valencia Waffle
Block With Sawtooth Band, Wine 17.00
      BLOCK WITH STARS, see Hanover
Block, Compote, Covered, Flint, 12 X 8 In. 160.00
Block, Goblet, Blue 52.50
Block, Pitcher & 6 Tumblers, Gold 100.00
Block, Tumbler, Amber .... 22.00 To 25.00
      BLOCKADE, see Diamond Block with Fan
      BLOCKHOUSE, see Hanover
      BLUEBIRD, see Bird & Strawberry
Bohemian, Celery, 2-Handled, Green 190.00
Bouquet, Bowl, 9 In. 11.00
Bow Tie, Goblet .... 45.00 To 55.00
Bow Tie, Jar, Jam 52.00
Bow Tie, Salt, Master 65.00
Bow Tie, Salt, Master, Round 25.00
Bow Tie, Spooner 29.50
Bow Tie, Tumbler 45.00
Branched Tree, Pitcher, Water 58.00
Branched Tree, Water Set 65.00
Brazilian, Toothpick 30.00
Brazilian, Tumbler, Gold Trim 20.00
Brazilian, Tumbler, Gold Trim, Green 25.00
Brilliant, Goblet, Flint .... 45.00 To 65.00
Britannic, Compote, Open, 8 1/2 X 8 In. 35.00
Broken Column, Bowl, Master Berry 40.00
Broken Column, Cake Stand 85.00
Broken Column, Compote, Flared, 6 In. 55.00
Broken Column, Compote, Scalloped Rim, 7 1/4 X 5 In. 35.00
Broken Column, Compote, 6 In. 25.00
Broken Column, Cracker Jar 48.00
Broken Column, Creamer .... 25.00 To 32.50
Broken Column, Cruet, Original Stopper .... 45.00 To 89.00
Broken Column, Dish, Relish 20.00
Broken Column, Goblet 35.00
Broken Column, Plate, 4 7/8 In. 29.00
Broken Column, Syrup, Pewter Top, C.1884 .... 80.00
Brooklyn, Goblet, Flint 35.00
Brooklyn, Sauce 14.00
      BRYCE, see Ribbon Candy
Buckingham, Tumbler, Champagne 6.00
Buckingham, Wine 15.00
Buckle & Diamond, Sugar Shaker 30.00
Buckle & Star, Creamer .... 25.00 To 28.00
Buckle & Star, Dish, Oval, 7 1/4 In. 14.00
Buckle & Star, Goblet 28.00
Buckle & Star, Pitcher, Water, Applied Handle 100.00
Buckle & Star, Sauce, Footed .... 9.50 To 13.00
Buckle & Star, Spooner 24.50
Buckle & Star, Sugar, Covered 35.00
Buckle & Star, Wine 23.00
Buckle With Shield, Goblet 22.00
Buckle, Butter, Covered, Flint, 5 1/2 In. 68.00
Buckle, Goblet .... 20.00 To 59.00
Buckle, Goblet, Flint 45.00
Buckle, Spooner .... 18.00 To 25.00
Buckle, Wine 18.00
Budded Ivy, Goblet 15.00
Budded Ivy, Spooner .... 20.00 To 22.00

Bulging Loops, Toothpick, Green 75.00
Bull's-Eye & Buttons, Creamer, Green 75.00
Bull's-Eye & Buttons, Sugar, Green 65.00
Bull's-Eye & Daisy, Goblet, Gold Rim 35.00
Bull's-Eye & Daisy, Goblet, Green 27.00
Bull's-Eye & Daisy, Goblet, Pink Eyes, Gold Top 24.00
    BULL'S-EYE & FAN, see Daisies in Oval Panels
Bull's-Eye & Spearhead, Cruet 22.00
Bull's-Eye & Spearhead, Decanter, Stopper, 1/2 Pint 15.00
Bull's-Eye & Spearhead, Wine 24.00
    BULL'S-EYE BAND, see Reverse Torpedo
    BULL'S-EYE VARIANT, see Texas Bull's-Eye
Bull's-Eye With Diamond Point, Goblet .... 85.00 To 95.00
Bull's-Eye With Diamond Point, Wine, Flint 85.00
Bull's-Eye With Fleur-De-Lis, Celery, Flint 35.00
Bull's-Eye With Fleur-De-Lis, Compote, Scalloped 25.00
Bull's-Eye With Fleur-De-Lis, Goblet .... 70.00 To 75.00
Bull's-Eye, Bottle, Cologne, Original Stopper 60.00
Bull's-Eye, Celery, Flint .... 55.00 To 72.00
Bull's-Eye, Goblet 50.00
Bull's-Eye, Goblet, Amethyst, Knobby 22.50
Bull's-Eye, Goblet, Giant 75.00
Bull's-Eye, Goblet, Gold Trim, Amethyst 18.00
Bull's-Eye, Syrup, Honeycomb Neck 60.00
Bullet Emblem, Sugar, Covered 220.00
Bunker Hill, Bread Plate .... 65.00 To 80.00
Bunker Hill, Cup Plate 25.00
Butterfly & Fan, Celery 22.00
Butterfly & Fan, Platter 37.00
Butterfly & Fan, Sauce 6.00
Butterfly & Fan, Tumbler 14.00
Butterfly Ears, Mustard, Covered 24.00
Butterfly With Spray, Creamer 24.00
Button & Star Panel, Toothpick .... 18.00 To 20.00
Button Arches, Pitcher, Milk 65.00
Button Arches, Pitcher, Tankard, Banded 175.00
Button Arches, Toothpick, Gold Trim 18.00
Button Arches, Tumbler, Banded 40.00
Button Arches, Wine, Ruby Top 32.00
Button Band, Celery, Etched 30.00
Button Panel, Table Set, Child's, 4 Piece 225.00
Cabbage Leaf, Goblet 30.00
Cabbage Rose, Butter, Covered 40.00
Cabbage Rose, Celery .... 35.00 To 38.00
Cabbage Rose, Compote, Covered, 7 In. 55.00
Cabbage Rose, Compote, Covered, 8 In. 50.00
Cabbage Rose, Compote, 9 In. 35.00
Cabbage Rose, Dish, Relish, Teardrop Shaped 30.00
Cabbage Rose, Goblet .... 35.00 To 52.00
Cabbage Rose, Salt, Master 22.00
Cabbage Rose, Salt, Open 14.00
Cabbage Rose, Spooner 35.00
Cabbage Rose, Tumbler .... 40.00 To 45.00
Cabbage Rose, Wine .... 32.00 To 40.00
Cable, Eggcup, Flint 40.00
Cable, Goblet 60.00
Cable, Goblet, Flint .... 40.00 To 65.00
Cable, Salt, Master 25.00
Cable, Spooner .... 50.00 To 95.00
Cadmus, Creamer 16.00
    CALIFORNIA, see Beaded Grape
California, Sugar, Gold Trim, Green 55.00
Camel Caravan, Goblet 65.00
    CAMEO, see Ceres

Ashburton

Barberry

Beaded Grape

Bellflower

Bigler

Bleeding Heart

Broken Column

Buckle

Bull's-Eye

Bull's-Eye With Diamond Point

CANADIAN DRAPE, see Garfield Drape

Canadian, Butter, Covered	65.00
Canadian, Creamer	45.00 To 55.00
Canadian, Dish, Double Handled, 6 1/2 In.	25.00
Canadian, Goblet	45.00 To 65.00
Canadian, Pitcher, Milk	65.00 To 85.00
Canadian, Pitcher, Water	60.00 To 95.00
Canadian, Spooner	42.00
Canadian, Wine	38.00 To 46.50
Candlewick, Creamer	20.00

CANDY RIBBON, see Ribbon Candy

Cane & Rosette, Celery	29.00
Cane & Rosette, Champagne	20.00
Cane & Rosette, Sauce, Footed	25.00
Cane Column, Goblet	20.00
Cane Horseshoe, Pitcher, Water, Miniature	20.00
Cane, Goblet	16.00 To 20.00
Cane, Goblet, Green	20.00 To 58.00
Cane, Pitcher, Water	25.00 To 35.00
Cane, Pitcher, Water, Amber	45.00
Cane, Pitcher, Water, Blue	60.00
Cane, Plate, Toddy, Amber	14.00
Cane, Plate, Toddy, Green	14.00
Cane, Sauce, Footed	15.00
Cane, Tumbler, Blue	22.00 To 28.00
Cannonball, Butter, Covered, Round	65.00
Cannonball, Compote, Footed	35.00
Cannonball, Creamer	23.00
Cannonball, Creamer, Individual	24.00
Cape Cod, Goblet	35.00
Capitol Building, Goblet	25.00
Cardinal Bird, Creamer	33.00
Cardinal Bird, Goblet	27.00 To 35.00
Cardinal, Creamer	23.00
Cardinal, Goblet	32.00 To 34.50
Carnation, Pitcher, Water	65.00
Carolina, Compote, 9 1/4 In.	26.00
Carolina, Creamer	22.00
Cat's Eye & Block, Butter, Covered	49.50
Cat's Eye & Block, Goblet	32.00
Cat's Eye & Block, Sugar	37.50
Cathedral, Butter, Covered	40.00
Cathedral, Compote, Ruffled, Open, Amber	39.50 To 42.00
Cathedral, Cruet, Original Stopper, Amber	100.00
Cathedral, Goblet	27.00
Cathedral, Sauce, Footed, Amethyst	35.00
Cathedral, Spooner	22.00

Bull's-Eye & Daisy

Cable

Button Arches

Cabbage Rose

Cathedral

Canadian

Cardinal

Cathedral, Tumbler 25.00
Cathedral, Tumbler, Ruby Stained 50.00
Cathedral, Wine .... 25.00 To 30.00
Cathedral, Wine, Blue .... 50.00 To 55.00
Cattails & Fern, Goblet .... 22.00 To 24.50
Cavitt, Plate, 7 1/4 In. 10.00

CENTENNIAL, see also Liberty Bell; Washington Centennial

Centennial, Bread Plate
Centennial, Glass, Ale, 1776-1876 .... 65.00
Centennial, Glass, Ale, 1776-1876 .... 28.00
Centennial, Goblet, Pittsburgh 125.00
Centennial, Mug, 1776-1876 .... 60.00
Centennial, Platter, Marked, 13 In. 85.00
Centennial, Tray, Eagle 75.00
Ceres, Mug, Child's, Blue, 2 In. 20.00
Ceres, Mug, Purple 60.00
Ceres, Spooner 22.00
Chain & Shield, Creamer .... 14.00 To 27.00
Chain & Shield, Platter, Oval, 12 X 8 1/2 In. 25.00
Chain & Shield, Sauce, Flat 9.00

CHAIN WITH DIAMONDS, see Washington Centennial

Chain With Star, Cake Plate, Handled 27.00
Chain With Star, Creamer 23.50
Chain With Star, Dish, Relish 10.50
Chain With Star, Goblet .... 17.00 To 25.00
Chain, Creamer 16.00
Chain, Goblet 20.00
Chain, Sauce, Footed 8.00
Chain, Spooner 19.00
Champion, Toothpick 20.00
Champion, Toothpick, Gold Rim, Green 35.00
Champion, Wine 10.00
Chandelier, Butter, Covered 45.00
Chandelier, Cake Stand, 10 In. 95.00
Chandelier, Creamer, Etched 32.00
Chandelier, Goblet 65.00
Chandelier, Spooner 35.00
Charleston Flute, Goblet, Flint 16.00
Checkerboard, Wine 13.50
Cherry & Cable, Saucer, Gold Trim, Pink & Clear 10.00
Cherry & Fig, Sauce 8.00
Cherry With Thumbprint, Butter, Decorated 90.00
Cherry With Thumbprint, Creamer 25.00
Cherry With Thumbprint, Sugar & Creamer, Northwood .. 85.00
Cherry, Goblet .... 20.00 To 39.00
Cherry, Spooner 24.00
Chilson, Goblet, Flint 150.00
Chrysanthemum Leaf, Creamer, Gold Trim 35.00
Chrysanthemum Leaf, Toothpick .... 24.00 To 30.00
Chrysanthemum Sprig, Compote, Jelly 50.00

CHURCH WINDOWS, see Tulip Petals

Circle, Butter, Covered, Clear & Frosted 55.00
Classic Medallion, Bowl, Footed 25.00
Classic Medallion, Sugar & Creamer 25.00
Classic, Berry Bowl 75.00
Classic, Bowl, Footed, 6 1/2 In. 30.00
Classic, Butter, Covered, Clear & Frosted 195.00
Classic, Butter, Open Feet, Covered 150.00
Classic, Celery, Collared Base 155.00
Classic, Creamer, Open Feet 135.00
Classic, Goblet .... 175.00 To 185.00
Classic, Pitcher, Water 285.00
Classic, Pitcher, Water, Collared Base 285.00
Classic, Pitcher, Water, Open Feet 300.00
Classic, Plate, Cleveland Portrait, 10 In. 135.00

Ceres

Chain & Shield

Classic

Colorado

Colonial

Classic, Plate, Warrior, Clear & Frosted, Signed	110.00 To 145.00
Classic, Sauce, Collared Base, 5 In.	38.00
Classic, Sauce, Open Feet, 5 In.	40.00
Classic, Spooner	125.00
Classic, Sugar, Log Feet, Open	75.00
Classic, Sugar, Open Feet, Covered	155.00
Clear Block, Goblet	15.00
Clear Circle, Compote, Jelly	15.00
Clear Circle, Creamer	30.00
Clear Circle, Goblet	28.00
Clear Ribbon, Bread Plate, Motto, Rectangular	35.00
Clear Ribbon, Cake Stand, High Standard, 9 In.	38.00
Clear Ribbon, Goblet	29.00
Clear Ribbon, Jar, Jam, Covered	28.00
Clematis, Spooner	21.50
Clover & Daisy, Goblet	8.00 To 15.00
Coarse Rib, Goblet	10.00
Coarse Zig-Zag, Cake Stand	25.00
Coin & Dewdrop, Goblet	12.00
COIN SPOT, see Coin Spot Category	
Colonial Panel, Punch Bowl, 16 In.	45.00
Colonial, Goblet, Knob Stem	45.00
Colonial, Pitcher, 8 1/2 In.	65.00
Colonial, Sugar & Creamer	30.00
Colorado, Berry Set, Green, Crimped Top, 7 Piece	195.00

Colorado, Bowl, Green, Footed, 8 In.	60.00
Colorado, Bowl, Ruffled, Green, 7 1/2 In.	23.00
Colorado, Butter, Covered, Gold Trim, Green	115.00 To 140.00
Colorado, Butter, Covered, Green	85.00 To 129.50
Colorado, Butter, Dome Top	45.00
Colorado, Compote, Child's, Beaded Rim, 4 3/4 X 1 3/4 In.	20.00
Colorado, Compote, Green, Tricornered, 6 1/2 X 5 1/2 In.	70.00
Colorado, Compote, Green, 8 1/4 X 7 In.	90.00
Colorado, Compote, Open, Beaded Rim, Green, 8 1/2 X 7 1/2 In.	110.00
Colorado, Condiment Set, Green	295.00
Colorado, Creamer, Gold Trim, Green	70.00
Colorado, Creamer, Green	40.00 To 45.00
Colorado, Creamer, Souvenir, Ethel, 1927, Green	18.00
Colorado, Cup, Etched, My Girl, Handled, Green	20.00
Colorado, Cup, Punch, Footed	15.00
Colorado, Dish, Green, 7 In.	20.00
Colorado, Match Holder, Green	35.00
Colorado, Mug, Applied Handle, Green $ 18.50 To	20.00
Colorado, Mug, 1904, L.Weaver	35.00
Colorado, Nappy, Ruffled, Blue	49.50
Colorado, Pitcher, Water, Gold Trim, Green	250.00
Colorado, Sauce	15.00
Colorado, Sauce, Footed, Green	13.00
Colorado, Sauce, Gold Trim, Green	22.00
Colorado, Sugar & Creamer, Individual	65.00
Colorado, Sugar, Enameled 1898, Open, Ascalon Commandery	45.00
Colorado, Sugar, Green	20.00
Colorado, Sugar, Souvenir, Mary, Wheeling Fair, Open	19.00
Colorado, Table Set, Gold Trim, Green, 4 Piece	325.00
Colorado, Toothpick	40.00
Colorado, Toothpick, Footed, Gold Trim, Green	34.00
Colorado, Tray, Green	22.00
Colorado, Tumbler, Etched	35.00
Colorado, Tumbler, Gold Trim, Green	30.00
Colorado, Tumbler, Green	35.00
Colorado, Violet Bowl, Blue	64.50
Colorado, Wine	21.00
Colossus, Goblet	24.00
Columbia, Bread Plate, Amethyst	175.00
Columbia, Sugar, Covered, Yellow, Green Decoration, Roses	40.00
Columbia, Tumbler	12.50
Columbian Coin, Champagne, Gold Coins	22.00
Columbian Coin, Goblet, Gold Coins	50.00
Columbian Coin, Syrup, Frosted	125.00
Columbian Coin, Syrup, Frosted, Patent Date On Lid	160.00
Columbian Coin, Table Set, Gold Trim, 4 Piece	395.00
Columbian Coin, Toothpick	90.00
Comet, Goblet, Flint	60.00 To 80.00
Comet, Tumbler, Flint	110.00
COMPACT, see Snail	
Concaved Almond, Goblet	17.00
Constitution, Bread Plate	90.00
Continental, Bread Plate	58.00 To 65.00
Coral Gables, Goblet	14.00
Cord & Tassel, Cake Stand, 10 1/2 In.	50.00
Cord & Tassel, Goblet	25.00 To 32.00
Cord & Tassel, Mustard	24.00
Cord & Tassel, Salt & Pepper, Pink	45.00
Cord & Tassel, Spooner	23.00
Cord Drapery, Compote, Covered, 6 1/2 In.	40.00 To 70.00
Cord Drapery, Cup, Punch	10.00
Cord Drapery, Dish, Relish, Oval, 9 1/2 In.	20.00
Cord Drapery, Goblet	12.00
Cord Drapery, Saltshaker	45.00

Cord Rosette, Goblet	25.00
Cordova, Creamer	18.00
Cordova, Creamer, Green	18.00
Cordova, Inkwell	89.50
Cordova, Punch Set, Bowl & 6 Cups	85.00
Cordova, Saltshaker	29.50
Cordova, Sugar, Covered, Individual	54.50
Cordova, Toothpick	15.00
Coreopsis, Pitcher, Milk, Green Band	65.00
Coreopsis, Syrup	195.00
Cornell, Cruet	28.00
Cornucopia, Pitcher, Water	40.00
Cornucopia, Wine	15.00

COSMOS, see Cosmos Category

Cottage, Cake Stand, 9 In.	40.00
Cottage, Celery, Amber	30.00
Cottage, Compote, Covered, Footed, Large	65.00
Cottage, Compote, Open	19.00
Cottage, Creamer	25.00 To 28.00
Cottage, Cruet, Original Stopper	39.50
Cottage, Cup & Saucer	30.00 To 35.00
Cottage, Tray, Water, Large	35.00
Cottage, Tumbler	12.00

CRANE, see Stork

Crescent & Fan, Champagne	21.50
Crescent & Fan, Decanter	58.00
Crescent & Fan, Rose Bowl	19.50

CRISSCROSS, see Rexford

Croesus, Berry Bowl, Green	155.00 To 195.00
Croesus, Bowl, Fruit, Purple, Rocaille, Design, Footed, 8 In.	50.00
Croesus, Butter, Covered, Green	75.00 To 175.00
Croesus, Butter, Gold Trim, Covered	165.00 To 197.50
Croesus, Butter, Gold Trim, Green	135.00
Croesus, Butter, Purple, Rocaille, Design, 7 3/4 In.	130.00
Croesus, Creamer, Green, Individual	295.00
Croesus, Cruet, Green	85.00
Croesus, Dish, Relish, Gold Trim, Purple, Kidney Shape, 9 In.	30.00
Croesus, Pitcher	175.00
Croesus, Pitcher, Water, Green With Gold	100.00
Croesus, Pitcher, Water, Purple, Footed, Sawtooth Rim, 11 In.	40.00
Croesus, Salt & Pepper, Gold Trim, Purple	95.00
Croesus, Salt & Pepper, Green	48.00 To 120.00
Croesus, Saltshaker, Gold Trim, Green	65.00
Croesus, Spooner	45.00
Croesus, Spooner, Gold Trim, Green	65.00
Croesus, Sugar & Creamer, Gold Trim, Purple, Covered	100.00
Croesus, Sugar, Green	145.00
Croesus, Toothpick, Gold Trim	85.00
Croesus, Toothpick, Gold Trim, Purple, Scalloped, 2 3/4 In.	105.00
Croesus, Tumbler, Gold Trim, Purple	72.00 To 75.00
Croesus, Water Set, Gold Trim, Green, 6 Piece	325.00 To 350.00

CROSSBAR & FINE CUT, see Ashman

Crowfoot, Creamer	17.00 To 35.00
Crowfoot, Pitcher, Water	38.00
Crowfoot, Spooner	20.00
Crowfoot, Tumbler	20.00

CROWN JEWELS, see Chandelier; Queen's Necklace

Crusader Cross, Goblet	15.00
Crystal Queen, Creamer, Applied Handle	32.00
Crystal Wedding, Basket, Banana, 12 1/2 X 8 In.	75.00
Crystal Wedding, Butter, Covered	49.50
Crystal Wedding, Cake Stand	54.50
Crystal Wedding, Compote, Covered, Pair	120.00
Crystal Wedding, Compote, Covered, Square, 6 1/2 X 3 1/2 In.	36.00

Columbian Coin

Croesus

Cupid & Venus

Crystal Wedding, Sugar & Creamer, Covered, Amber	195.00
Crystal Wedding, Tumbler	22.00
CUBE & DIAMOND, see Milton	
CUBE & FAN, see Pineapple & Fan	
Cube, Pitcher, Water, 3 Tumblers	45.00
Cube, Tumbler	12.00
CUPID & PSYCHE, see Psyche & Cupid	
Cupid & Venus, Berry Bowl, Footed, 3 1/4 In.	10.00
Cupid & Venus, Bowl, Oval, 9 In.	28.00
Cupid & Venus, Bowl, 7 In.	15.00
Cupid & Venus, Bowl, 8 In.	15.00
Cupid & Venus, Bread Plate, Vaseline	60.00
Cupid & Venus, Bread Plate, 10 1/2 In.	28.00 To 42.00
Cupid & Venus, Butter, Covered	75.00
Cupid & Venus, Celery	36.00 To 52.00
Cupid & Venus, Champagne	95.00
Cupid & Venus, Compote, Covered	60.00
Cupid & Venus, Compote, Covered, Low	50.00
Cupid & Venus, Compote, 7 1/2 X 3 1/4 In.	21.00
Cupid & Venus, Creamer	45.00 To 50.00
Cupid & Venus, Dish, Pickle, 5 1/2 X 8 In.	18.00
Cupid & Venus, Goblet	50.00
Cupid & Venus, Jar, Jam, Covered	38.00
Cupid & Venus, Mug	27.50
Cupid & Venus, Pitcher, Milk	42.00 To 59.00
Cupid & Venus, Pitcher, Water	55.00 To 62.00
Cupid & Venus, Pitcher, 8 In.	65.00
Cupid & Venus, Plate, Amber, Handles, 10 In.	40.00 To 48.00
Cupid & Venus, Plate, 10 1/2 In.	40.00
Cupid & Venus, Sauce, Footed, 3 3/4 In.	8.00 To 10.00
Cupid & Venus, Sauce, 3 1/2 In.	10.00
Cupid & Venus, Sauce, 4 1/2 In.	10.00
Cupid & Venus, Spooner	40.00
Cupid & Venus, Wine	80.00
Curled Leaf, Butter, Covered	35.00
Currant, Goblet	22.00 To 26.00
Currant, Sugar, Open	22.00
Currier & Ives, Compote, Open	49.00
Currier & Ives, Dish, Boat Shape	20.00
Currier & Ives, Goblet	12.00 To 45.00
Currier & Ives, Pitcher, Milk	35.00 To 38.00
Currier & Ives, Saltshaker	45.00
Currier & Ives, Spooner, Blue	45.00
Currier & Ives, Sugar, Open, 3 1/2 In.	12.00
Currier & Ives, Syrup, Covered	43.00
Currier & Ives, Water Set, 5 Piece	145.00
Currier & Ives, Wine	15.00 To 17.50
Curtain Tieback, Goblet	14.00 To 22.00
Curtain Tieback, Sugar, Footed	17.50

Curtain, Spooner 22.00
Cut Log, Berry Bowl, Scalloped, Master, 8 1/2 In. .... 40.00 To 45.00
Cut Log, Carafe, Water 15.00
Cut Log, Celery 39.00
Cut Log, Compote, Candy 32.50
Cut Log, Compote, Covered, Finial, 7 3/4 In. 45.00
Cut Log, Compote, Jelly 32.00
Cut Log, Compote, Open, 10 In. 30.00
Cut Log, Compote, Scalloped Rim, 8 1/2 X 10 1/4 In. 75.00
Cut Log, Creamer .... 24.00 To 39.00
Cut Log, Creamer, 3 In. 14.00
Cut Log, Dish, Olive, 9 1/4 In. .... 18.50 To 22.50
Cut Log, Goblet .... 30.00 To 55.00
Cut Log, Mug .... 14.00 To 20.00
Cut Log, Nappy 18.50
Cut Log, Pitcher, Tankard, Water 48.00
Cut Log, Sauce, Footed 45.00
Cut Log, Spooner 38.00
Cut Log, Sugar, Covered 55.00
Cut Log, Tumbler 35.00
Cut Log, Wine .... 15.00 To 30.00
Czarina, Celery 14.00
Dahlia, Cake Stand, Amber 65.00
Dahlia, Champagne 55.00
Dahlia, Creamer .... 20.00 To 22.00
Dahlia, Creamer, 1870 .... 35.00
Dahlia, Goblet 30.00
Dahlia, Mug, Child's, Blue 40.00
Dahlia, Pitcher, Footed, 9 In. 15.00
Dahlia, Pitcher, Water .... 35.00 To 38.00
Dahlia, Sauce 5.00
Dahlia, Spooner 15.00
Daisies In Oval Panels, Bowl, 8 In. 19.50
Daisies In Oval Panels, Butter, Covered, Gold Trim, Green 75.00
Daisies In Oval Panels, Creamer 17.00
Daisies In Oval Panels, Creamer, Individual 16.00
Daisies In Oval Panels, Cruet 28.50
Daisies In Oval Panels, Dish, Relish, 9 X 5 3/4 In. 12.00
Daisies In Oval Panels, Goblet, Gold Trim 21.50
Daisies In Oval Panels, Lemonade, Handled 27.00
Daisies In Oval Panels, Pitcher, 5 Tall Cups, Gold Rims 105.00
Daisies In Oval Panels, Rose Bowl 26.00
Daisies In Oval Panels, Toothpick 18.00
Daisies In Oval Panels, Tray, Fan 18.00
Daisies In Oval Panels, Tumbler 25.00
Daisies In Oval Panels, Tumbler, Gold Trim 12.00
Daisies In Oval Panels, Wine, Gold Trim 20.00
Daisy & Button With Crossbar, Butter, Footed, Covered 35.00
Daisy & Button With Crossbar, Celery 22.00
Daisy & Button With Crossbar, Celery, Amber 35.00
Daisy & Button With Crossbar, Compote, 6 1/2 In. 25.00
Daisy & Button With Crossbar, Creamer, Amber 35.00
Daisy & Button With Crossbar, Creamer, Blue 40.00
Daisy & Button With Crossbar, Goblet, Amber 36.00
Daisy & Button With Crossbar, Pitcher, Water, Canary 69.00
Daisy & Button With Crossbar, Sugar & Creamer, Amber 39.00
Daisy & Button With Narcissus, Cruet, 1890s 35.00
      DAISY & BUTTON WITH OVAL PANELS, see also Hartley
Daisy & Button With Oval Panels, Dish, Relish, 6 3/4 In. 12.00
Daisy & Button With Thumbprint, Tumbler, Amber 28.00
Daisy & Button With V-Ornament, Dish 10.00
Daisy & Button With V-Ornament, Toothpick 18.00
Daisy & Button With V-Ornament, Tumbler 11.00
Daisy & Button, Bottle, Castor 10.00

Daisies In Oval Panels   Daisy & Button With Crossbar   Daisy & Button With Thumbprint

Daisy & Button, Bowl, Amber Panels, Silver Plated Holder 165.00
Daisy & Button, Bowl, Amber, Scalloped, 11 In. 65.00
Daisy & Button, Bowl, 7 1/2 X 5 In. 30.00
Daisy & Button, Celery 25.00
Daisy & Button, Compote, 9 1/2 X 9 In. 85.00
Daisy & Button, Goblet .... 16.00 To 32.50
Daisy & Button, Goblet, Amber .... 20.00 To 28.00
Daisy & Button, Hat, Clear, 3 1/2 X 2 1/2 In. 5.00
Daisy & Button, Hat, Green 10.00
Daisy & Button, Pitcher 30.00
Daisy & Button, Pitcher, Water, Bulbous, Handled, Canary, 8 In. 135.00
Daisy & Button, Plate, 7 In.Square 12.00
Daisy & Button, Salt Dip, Sleigh 10.00
Daisy & Button, Saltshaker, Corset Shape, Amber 25.00
Daisy & Button, Shoe, Amber, 5 3/4 In. 20.00
Daisy & Button, Slipper, Amber, 5 3/4 In. 10.00
Daisy & Button, Slipper, Blue, 5 3/4 In. 25.00
Daisy & Button, Slipper, 4 3/4 In. 12.00
Daisy & Button, Syrup, Thumbprint Panels, Amber 185.00
Daisy & Button, Toothpick, Barrel Shape, Amber 23.00
Daisy & Button, Toothpick, Hat Shape, 2 X 2 In. 10.00
Daisy & Button, Toothpick, Red Dots 45.00
Daisy & Button, Tray, Handled, 9 1/4 X 16 1/2 In. 45.00
Daisy & Button, Tumbler, Vaseline .... 25.00 To 28.00
Daisy & Fern, Pitcher, Yellow, Large 99.00
Dakota, Basket, Ruffled 165.00
Dakota, Butter, Covered .... 25.00 To 50.00
Dakota, Cake Stand, Etched, 10 In. .... 59,00 To 65.00
Dakota, Celery .... 15.00 To 43.00
Dakota, Celery, Etched .... 28.00 To 52.00
Dakota, Celery, Flat Bottom 32.00
Dakota, Compote, Covered, 10 1/2 In. 65.00
Dakota, Compote, Etched, Stemmed, 9 X 9 1/4 In. 137.50
Dakota, Compote, Jelly, Open, 5 X 5 In. 35.00
Dakota, Compote, Open, 6 3/8 In. 25.00
Dakota, Creamer .... 25.00 To 30.00
Dakota, Creamer, Etched Fern & Berry, Masonic, 1890 .... 32.00
Dakota, Cruet, Amberina, Reeded Handle, Clear Ball Stopper 125.00
Dakota, Goblet .... 10.00 To 20.00
Dakota, Goblet, Barrel Shape 11.00
Dakota, Goblet, Etched .... 28.00 To 42.00
Dakota, Goblet, Piecrust Edge 50.00
Dakota, Goblet, Ruby Flashed, Etched 75.00
Dakota, Sauce, Cobalt Blue 55.00
Dakota, Sauce, Flat, 4 1/4 In. 18.00

Dakota, Sauce, Footed, Etched	10.00
Dakota, Spooner	24.50
Dakota, Spooner, Etched	24.50 To 57.50
Dakota, Sugar, Covered, Etched	55.00 To 59.00
Dakota, Tankard, Etched	119.00
Dakota, Tray, Piecrust Rim, 10 1/4 In.Diam.	85.00
Dakota, Tumbler	25.00 To 36.00
Dakota, Tumbler, Etched	25.00 To 55.00
Dakota, Wine	18.50
Dakota, Wine, Etched	42.50
Deer & Doe With Lily-Of-The-Valley, Goblet	80.00
Deer & Doe, Platter, Green	75.00
Deer & Dog, Goblet	30.00
Deer & Dog, Goblet, U Shaped	70.00
Deer & Dog, Mug, Child's, 2 1/2 In.	30.00
Deer & Dog, Pitcher, Water	230.00 To 260.00
Deer & Dog, Spooner	30.00
Deer & Oak Tree, Pitcher	130.00 To 150.00
Deer & Oak Tree, Pitcher, Water	160.00
Deer & Pine Tree, Bread Plate	50.00 To 55.00
Deer & Pine Tree, Butter	45.00 To 75.00
Deer & Pine Tree, Compote	65.00
Deer & Pine Tree, Cup, Punch	45.00
Deer & Pine Tree, Goblet	25.00 To 35.00
Deer & Pine Tree, Mug	45.00
Deer & Pine Tree, Mug, Apple Green	90.00
Deer & Pine Tree, Pitcher, Water	90.00
Deer & Pine Tree, Sauce, Oblong	85.00
Deer & Pine Tree, Sauce, Set Of 4	126.00
Deer & Pine Tree, Spooner	64.00
Deer & Pine Tree, Spooner, C.1860, Sandwich Glass Co.	37.50
Deer & Pine Tree, Tray, Water	35.00 To 45.00
Deer Alert, Pitcher, Water	195.00 To 250.00
Delaware, Banana Boat, Green	60.00
Delaware, Banana Boat, Rose, Gold	75.00
Delaware, Berry Bowl, Green, Gold, 4 In.	20.00
Delaware, Berry Bowl, Master, Gold Trim, Green	40.00
Delaware, Bottoms-Up Set	50.00
Delaware, Bowl, Green, 10 In.	38.00
Delaware, Bowl, Pink & Gold, Oval, 10 1/2 In.	65.00
Delaware, Butter	100.00
Delaware, Butter, Covered, Green	70.00
Delaware, Butter, Gold Trim, Green	145.00
Delaware, Celery, Green	80.00
Delaware, Creamer	40.00
Delaware, Creamer, Green	40.00
Delaware, Cruet, Pink Flowers, Gold Trim, Original Stopper	250.00
Delaware, Cup, Gold	30.00
Delaware, Jar, Powder, Glass Jeweled Lid, Green With Gold	175.00
Delaware, Jug, Claret, Rose	140.00
Delaware, Pitcher, Water	49.00
Delaware, Pitcher, Water, Bulbous, Gold Trim, Gree	165.00 To 185.00
Delaware, Salt & Pepper, Green, Gold	90.00
Delaware, Sugar	65.00
Delaware, Sugar & Creamer, Gold Trim, Cranberry	115.00
Delaware, Tankard, Green	90.00
Delaware, Toothpick, Gold Trim, Green	65.00
Delaware, Toothpick, Gold Trim, Rose	110.00
Delaware, Tray, Pin	35.00
Delaware, Tumbler	18.00 To 22.00
Delaware, Tumbler, Gold On Flowers & Rim, Green	28.50 To 30.00
Delaware, Tumbler, Gold Trim, Rose	30.00
Delaware, Vase, Clear, Rose Flowers, Gold Trim, 9 1/2 In.	85.00
Delaware, Vase, Green, Gold Trim	60.00

Delaware, Water Set, Gold Trim, Cranberry, 5 Piece 265.00
Delaware, Water Set, Gold Trim, Green, 7 Piece 235.00
Delaware, Water Set, Green, 5 Piece 250.00
Dew & Raindrop, Bowl, 8 In. 38.00
Dew & Raindrop, Cup, Punch .... 7.00 To 25.00
Dew & Raindrop, Pitcher, Water 50.00
Dew & Raindrop, Wine, Set Of 5 .... 34.00
Dewberry, Sugar, Covered 15.00
Dewdrop & Feather, Plate, 7 In. 10.00
Dewdrop & Flowers, Shaker, Amber 32.00
Dewdrop Band, Goblet .... 12.00 To 25.00
Dewdrop Drapery, Goblet 15.00
Dewdrop In Points, Butter 10.00
Dewdrop In Points, Goblet 28.00
    DEWDROP WITH FLOWERS, see Quantico
Dewdrop With Sheaf Of Wheat, Bread Plate, Round, 11 In. 65.00
Dewdrop With Small Stars, Goblet 16.00
Dewdrop With Star, Dish, Cheese, Covered 175.00
Dewdrop With Star, Plate, 7 1/4 In. 7.50
Dewdrop With Star, Sugar, Covered 45.00
Dewdrop With Star, Tumbler 20.00
Dewdrop, Goblet, Amber 20.00
Dewdrop, Tumbler, Applied Handle, 3 1/4 In. 20.00
    DEWEY, see also Admiral Dewey
Dewey, Butter, Covered, Green 115.00
Dewey, Dish, Relish, Green 53.00
Dewey, Pitcher, Water .... 50.00 To 82.50
Dewey, Pitcher, Water, Cannonballs 75.00
Dewey, Sauce, Amber, 4 1/2 In. 22.00
Dewey, Sauce, Footed, Amber, 4 1/2 In. 25.00
Dewey, Tray, Serpentine Shape, Amber 30.00
Dewey, Tumbler .... 20.00 To 35.00
Diagonal Band & Fan, Goblet .... 16.00 To 28.00
Diagonal Band & Fan, Wine 18.00
Diagonal Band, Butter, Covered 30.00
Diagonal Band, Creamer 20.50
Diagonal Band, Goblet .... 15.00 To 28.00
Diagonal Band, Sauce, Footed 9.00
    DIAMOND, see Umbilicated Sawtooth
    DIAMOND & SUNBURST, see also Flattened Diamond & Sunburst
Diamond & Sunburst, Celery 18.00
Diamond & Sunburst, Goblet 20.00
Diamond & Sunburst, Spooner 22.00
Diamond & Sunburst, Tumbler 12.00
Diamond Band, Decanter 45.00
Diamond Block With Fan, Spooner 18.00
Diamond Cut With Leaf, Creamer 14.00
Diamond Cut With Leaf, Creamer, Blue 45.00
Diamond Cut With Leaf, Wine 23.00
    DIAMOND HORSESHOE, see Aurora
Diamond Medallion, Cake Stand, Gold Trim 55.00
Diamond Medallion, Celery 24.00
Diamond Medallion, Creamer .... 10.00 To 15.00
Diamond Medallion, Dish, Relish 8.00
Diamond Medallion, Goblet .... 18.00 To 25.00
Diamond Medallion, Plate, 10 In. 21.00
Diamond Medallion, Toothpick, Gold Trim 18.00
Diamond Peg, Toothpick, Souvenir, Overland, Kansas 45.00
    DIAMOND POINT DISCS, see Eyewinker
Diamond Point With Flutes, Wine, Blue 30.00
    DIAMOND POINT WITH PANELS, see Hinoto
Diamond Point, Bowl, Discs, 8 X 4 1/4 X 1 3/4 In. 22.00
Diamond Point, Champagne, Flint 60.00
Diamond Point, Compote, High Standard 60.00

Deer & Dog

Delaware

Diagonal Band

Diamond Cut With Leaf

Diamond Point

Diamond Thumbprint

Diamond Point, Creamer, Flint	90.00
Diamond Point, Eggcup, Flint	42.00 To 125.00
Diamond Point, Goblet	12.00 To 30.00
Diamond Point, Goblet, Flint	33.00 To 50.00
Diamond Point, Honey, Flint	12.00
Diamond Point, Pitcher, Buttermilk, Flint	18.00
Diamond Point, Spittoon	105.00
Diamond Point, Spooner, Flint	40.00
Diamond Point, Tumbler, Flint	45.00
Diamond Point, Vase, Openwork Rim, 4-Footed, Amber, 5 In.	15.00
Diamond Quilted, Creamer, Amethyst	45.00
Diamond Quilted, Goblet, Blue	35.00
Diamond Quilted, Mug, Handled, Blue	40.00
Diamond Quilted, Sauce, Amber, Footed, 5 1/2 In.	10.00
Diamond Quilted, Tumbler, Blue	25.00 To 40.00
Diamond Quilted, Wine	12.00
Diamond Quilted, Wine, Vaseline	30.00
Diamond Ridge, Toothpick	22.00
Diamond Splendor, Celery	16.00
Diamond Splendor, Goblet, Gold Trim	18.00
Diamond Sunburst, Cake Stand	20.00
Diamond Sunburst, Compote, Jelly	20.00
Diamond Sunburst, Goblet	14.00 To 25.00
Diamond Sunburst, Tumbler	35.00
Diamond Thumbprint, Champagne, Flint	225.00
Diamond Thumbprint, Compote, Scalloped Edge, Flint, 6 1/2 In.	80.00
Diamond Thumbprint, Creamer, Flint	125.00

Diamond Thumbprint, Spooner	75.00
Diamond Thumbprint, Tumbler	95.00
Diamond Thumbprint, Tumbler, Flint	75.00
Diamond Thumbprint, Wine, Flint	200.00 To 250.00
Dice & Block, Cruet, Original Stopper, Amber	75.00
Dickinson, Sauce	11.00
Dickinson, Spooner, Flint	20.00
Divided Block With Sunburst, Pitcher	125.00
Divided Diamonds, Eggcup, Flint	15.00
Divided Hearts, Goblet	45.00
Dogwood, Berry, Master	52.00
Dolphin, Compote, Jelly, Frosted	38.00
Dolphin, Spooner	80.00
Dolphin, Spooner, Etched Top	40.00
DORIC, see Feather	
Dot & Dash, Compote, Covered, 7 3/4 In.	50.00
Dot & Dash, Creamer	30.00
Dot & Dash, Spooner	30.00
Dot & Dash, Sugar, Covered	40.00
Double Arch, Compote	30.00
Double Beaded Band, Wine	16.00
Double Beetle Band, Wine, Blue	50.00
Double Donut, Creamer	18.00 To 19.00
Double Leaf & Dart, Goblet, Diamond Ornament	24.50
DOUBLE LOOP, see Double Loop & Dart	
Double Loop & Dart, Goblet	25.00
Double Loop & Dart, Wine	24.50
Double Panel Daisy & Button, Compote, Large	30.00
Double Ribbon, Saltshaker	12.00
Double Snail, Pitcher, Handle, Bulbous	125.00
DOUBLE VINE, see Bellflower, Double Vine	
Draped Fan, Wine	20.00
Draped Red Block, Tumbler	32.50
Drapery, Butter, Covered	26.00
Drapery, Creamer	29.00
Drapery, Eggcup	18.00
Drapery, Goblet	20.00 To 40.00
Drapery, Spooner	22.00 To 55.00
Drapery, Sugar	22.00
Drapery, Water Set, 7 Piece	85.00
Drum, Butter, Child's, Covered	100.00 To 125.00
Drum, Spooner, Child's	50.00
Drum, Sugar, Cannon Finial, Covered	68.00
Drum, Sugar, Child's, Covered	75.00
Duke, Goblet	14.00
Duncan Block, Goblet, Ruby	36.00
DYNAST, see Radiant	
Eagle, Mug	20.00
EARL, see Spirea Band	
Early Thumbprint, Spooner	58.00
Edgerton, Sauce, Flat	9.00
Egg In Sand, Goblet	25.00 To 32.50
Egg In Sand, Goblet, Amber	49.00 To 59.50
Egg In Sand, Spooner, Amber	55.00
Egg In Sand, Tray	12.50
Egg In Sand, Tumbler	36.50
Egyptian, Bread Plate, Large, Cleopatra Center	45.00
Egyptian, Butter, Covered	50.00 To 60.00
Egyptian, Celery	50.00 To 75.00
Egyptian, Compote, Covered, Sphinx On Base	180.00
Egyptian, Compote, Open, 8 In.Diam.	70.00
Egyptian, Creamer	29.00 To 35.00
Egyptian, Dish, Pickle	20.00 To 30.00

Dolpnin

Double Ribbon

Egg In Sand

Egyptian

Egyptian, Dish, Relish	22.00 To 30.00
Egyptian, Goblet	35.00 To 45.00
Egyptian, Pitcher, Water	150.00 To 230.00
Egyptian, Plate	75.00
Egyptian, Sauce	12.00 To 17.50
Egyptian, Spooner	30.00 To 35.00
Egyptian, Sugar	20.00 To 65.00
Electric, Salt & Pepper	29.50
Elk Medallion, Goblet	60.00
Elongated Honeycomb, Tumbler, Ale, Flint	65.00
Empress, Bowl, Ice Cream, Fluted, Gold Trim, Green, 8 1/2 In.	45.00
Empress, Creamer	30.00
Empress, Creamer, Green	120.00
Empress, Cup, Punch, Green, Gold	35.00
Empress, Pitcher, Water, Gold Trim	60.00
Empress, Pitcher, Water, Green	145.00
Empress, Sugar, Covered, Green, Gold	75.00
Empress, Sugar, Green	145.00
Empress, Toothpick, Green	120.00
ENGLISH HOBNAIL CROSS, see Klondike	
English Hobnail, Basket, Scalloped Rim, Handled, 5 1/2 In.	18.50
English Hobnail, Condiment Set, Child's, 3 Piece	35.00
English Hobnail, Creamer	15.00
Enigma, Cake Stand, 9 In.	37.50
Esther, Berry Set, Green, 7 Piece	85.00
Esther, Celery, Green	210.00
Esther, Creamer, Gold Trim, Emerald Green	145.00
Esther, Creamer, Green	125.00
Esther, Cruet, Green, Original Stopper	145.00 To 220.00
Esther, Pitcher, Water, Green	110.00
Esther, Salt & Pepper, Gold Trim, Green	45.00
Esther, Saltshaker, Green	55.00
Esther, Spooner, Gold Trim, Green	50.00 To 75.00
Esther, Spooner, Green	35.00 To 95.00
Esther, Sugar, Covered, Gold Trim, Emerald Green	90.00 To 110.00
Esther, Toothpick	25.00
Esther, Toothpick, Etched	35.00
Esther, Toothpick, Green	110.00
Esther, Water Set, Gold Trim, Emerald Green, 6 Piece	345.00
Esther, Wine	28.00

    ETCHED BAND, see Dakota
    ETCHED DAKOTA, see Dakota
    ETCHED FERN, see Ashman

ETCHED PATTERNS, see under main pattern: e.g., Etched Dakota, see Dakota

Eugenie, Bowl, Covered, Oval, Flint, 9 In. 95.00
Eureka, Platter 30.00
Eureka, Toothpick, National's 25.00
Excelsior With Maltese Cross, Goblet, Flint 55.00
Excelsior, Eggcup 31.50
Excelsior, Goblet, Barrel Shape 42.50
Excelsior, Pitcher, Water 325.00
Excelsior, Wine, Flint .... 35.00 To 50.00
Eyewinker, Butter, Covered 65.00
Eyewinker, Butter, Covered, Amber 115.00
Eyewinker, Celery 50.00
Eyewinker, Compote, Covered 85.00
Eyewinker, Compote, Jelly 21.50
Eyewinker, Goblet 20.00
Eyewinker, Nappy, Folded-Up Sides, Square, 7 1/4 In. 30.00
Eyewinker, Salt & Pepper 45.00
Eyewinker, Saltshaker, Original Top 18.00
Eyewinker, Sugar, Open 49.50
Eyewinker, Wine 18.00

FAGOT, see Vera

FAN, see also Butterfly & Fan

Fan & Bull's-Eye, Goblet 35.00
Fan & Feather, Creamer, Gold Trim, Green 65.00
Fan & Feather, Spooner, Green, Gold, Inverted 65.00
Fan With Crossbars, Pitcher, Water 69.50
Fan With Diamond, Goblet .... 20.00 To 21.00
Fan With Diamond, Spooner .... 18.00 To 19.00
Fancy Diamonds, Wine 12.00
Fancy Loop, Goblet 38.00
Fancy Loop, Toothpick 25.00
Fancy Loop, Tumbler, Green 40.00
Fancy Loop, Wine 25.00
Feather Band, Pitcher 20.00
Feather Duster, Compote, Jelly, Clear, 4 1/2 X 4 1/2 In. 8.00
Feather Duster, Water Set, Green, 8 Piece 125.00
Feather, Bowl, Oval, 7 In. 12.00
Feather, Butter, Covered .... 35.00 To 55.00
Feather, Butter, Covered, Green .... 33.00 To 60.00
Feather, Cake Stand 40.00
Feather, Champagne 50.00
Feather, Creamer 30.00
Feather, Cruet, Original Stopper 45.00
Feather, Dish, Relish, Oval 18.00
Feather, Eggcup 25.00
Feather, Goblet 46.50
Feather, Pitcher, Milk .... 30.00 To 50.00
Feather, Pitcher, Water .... 30.00 To 45.00
Feather, Plate, 9 1/4 In. .... 30.00 To 35.00
Feather, Salt & Pepper 32.50
Feather, Sauce, Flat 8.00
Feather, Spooner .... 18.00 To 26.00
Feather, Spooner, Green 75.00
Feather, Sugar, Covered .... 28.00 To 45.00
Feather, Toothpick 22.00
Feather, Tumbler, Footed, 4 In. 50.00
Feather, Tumbler, Footed, 5 In. 60.00
Feather, Vase, Spill 40.00
Feather, Whiskey, Handled 65.00
Feather, Wine 35.00
Feathers & Arches, Cracker Jar, Handles 45.00
Fern Burst, Goblet 15.00
Fern Whirl, Wine 12.00

Ferris Wheel, Sauce 4.00
FESTOON & GRAPE, see Grape & Festoon
Festoon, Cake Plate, Footed 38.00
Festoon, Creamer .... 22.00 To 25.00
Festoon, Pitcher 50.00
Festoon, Tray, Water, 10 In. .... 27.00 To 32.50
Festoon, Tumbler .... 20.00 To 22.00
Fickle Block, Cake Stand, 11 In. 28.00
Fickle Block, Compote, Scalloped, Pedestal, 8 X 5 1/2 In. 18.00
Fickle Block, Tray, Water 23.00
Fickle Block, Wine 15.00
File, Creamer, 5 1/4 In. 22.00
Fine Cut & Block, Berry Bowl, Blue 14.00
Fine Cut & Block, Compote, Jelly 18.00
Fine Cut & Block, Cordial, Clear With Blue 85.00
Fine Cut & Block, Creamer 33.00
Fine Cut & Block, Creamer, Blue & Clear 65.00
Fine Cut & Block, Eggcup 19.50
Fine Cut & Block, Pitcher, Clear, Yellow Blocks 67.00
Fine Cut & Block, Pitcher, Water, Blue & Clear 95.00
Fine Cut & Diamond, Goblet 19.00
Fine Cut & Panel, Compote, Amber 60.00
Fine Cut & Panel, Compote, Open, High Standard 32.00
Fine Cut & Panel, Goblet 16.00
Fine Cut & Panel, Wine 16.00
Fine Cut & Panel, Wine, Amber 28.00
Fine Cut & Panel, Wine, Blue 32.00
Fine Cut Band, Pitcher, Water, 1/2 Gallon 30.00
FINE CUT MEDALLION, see Austrian
Fine Cut, Celery, Canary, Handled, Footed 25.00
Fine Cut, Creamer 15.00
Fine Cut, Creamer, Blue 48.00
Fine Cut, Pitcher, Water, Blue 95.00
Fine Cut, Plate, Amber, 7 In. 25.00
Fine Cut, Spooner 20.00
Fine Cut, Tumbler 20.00
Fine Cut, Tumbler, Vaseline 30.00
Fine Cut, Wine, Green 22.00
Fine Rib With Cut Ovals, Celery 115.00
Fine Rib With Cut Ovals, Wine 95.00
Fine Rib, Eggcup, 3 Row Cut 125.00
Fine Rib, Goblet, Flint 45.00
Fine Rib, Sugar, Plain Band, Flint 35.00
Fine Rib, Wine, Flint 45.00
Fine Rib, Wine, 3 Row Cut 115.00
Fishscale, Berry Bowl 17.50
Fishscale, Butter, Covered 34.00
Fishscale, Cake Stand, 9 In. 22.00
Fishscale, Cake Stand, 11 In. 35.00
Fishscale, Celery 28.00
Fishscale, Compote, Jelly .... 9.00 To 16.50
Fishscale, Compote, Open 25.00
Fishscale, Goblet .... 15.00 To 26.00
Fishscale, Pitcher, Milk 30.00
Fishscale, Plate, 7 In. .... 15.00 To 17.50
Fishscale, Plate, 8 In.Diam. 24.00
Fishscale, Plate, 9 In.Square 27.00
Fishscale, Salt & Pepper 59.50
Fishscale, Sauce, Flat, 4 1/2 In. 5.50
Fishscale, Sauce, Square 5.00
Fishscale, Sauce, 4 1/2 In. 6.00
Fishscale, Tumbler 45.00
Flamingo Habitat, Celery 25.00
Flamingo Habitat, Goblet .... 40.00 To 55.00

FLAT DIAMOND & PANEL, see Lattice & Oval Panels

Flat Diamond, Cordial	16.00
Flattened Diamond & Sunburst, Butter, Child's	25.00
Flattened Diamond & Sunburst, Cup, Punch, Child's	7.00
Flattened Diamond & Sunburst, Punch Set, Child's, 5 Piece	55.00
Fleur-De-Lis & Drape, Goblet	17.00
Fleur-De-Lis & Drape, Goblet, Green	13.50
Fleur-De-Lis & Drape, Pitcher, Green	95.00
Fleur-De-Lis & Drape, Spooner	21.50
Fleur-De-Lis & Drape, Tumbler, Green	25.00 To 38.00
Fleur-De-Lis Tassel, Compote, Footed, Green, 4 7/8 X 5 1/4 In.	25.00
Fleur-De-Lis, Celery, Flint	55.00
Fleur-De-Lis, Cruet, Original Stopper	37.50
Fleur-De-Lis, Goblet	50.00
Fleur-De-Lis, Toothpick	18.00
Fleur-De-Lis, Wine	18.00
Fleur-De-Lis, Wine, Blue	85.00
Flora, Creamer, Gold Trim, Green	35.00
Flora, Cruet, Gold, 7 In.	50.00
Flora, Cruet, Green & Gold Enameled	85.00
Flora, Sugar, Covered	30.00
Flora, Tumbler, Green	10.00

FLORIDA, see Herringbone

Flower & Honeycomb, Spooner	18.00
Flower & Honeycomb, Sugar, Covered	28.00
Flower & Pleat, Sauce	10.50
Flower & Pleat, Sauce, Amber	6.00
Flower & Pleat, Sauce, Amber, Set Of 6	37.50
Flower Band, Sauce, Footed, 4 In.	10.00

FLOWER FLANGE, see Dewey

Flower Medallion, Tumbler, Gold & Pink Trim, Clear	18.00

FLOWER PANELED CANE, see Cane & Rosette

Flower Pot, Bowl	18.00
Flower Pot, Cake Stand, 7 In.	38.00
Flower Pot, Cake Stand, 10 In.	44.00
Flower Pot, Creamer	31.00
Flower Pot, Sauce, Footed	8.00
Flower Pot, Spooner, Amber	30.00 To 34.00
Flower With Cane, Pitcher, Tinted	45.00
Flute, Eggcup, 2-Way, Flint	12.50
Flute, Goblet	17.50
Flute, Goblet, Flint	25.00
Flute, Toothpick, Blue Enamel Flowers	18.00
Flute, Tumbler, 6 Panels, Cobalt Blue	100.00
Flute, Tumbler, 10 Panels, Amethyst	100.00
Fluted Scrolls, Butter, Covered	45.00
Fluted Scrolls, Butter, Covered, Blue Opalescent	135.00
Fluted Scrolls, Creamer	18.50
Fluted Scrolls, Sugar, Covered	75.00
Flying Birds, Berry Bowl	110.00
Flying Birds, Goblet	40.00

FLYING ROBIN, see Hummingbird

Flying Stork, Goblet	30.00
Forget-Me-Not In Scroll, Goblet	15.00 To 22.00

FORGET-ME-NOT IN SNOW, see Stippled Forget-Me-Not

Forget-Me-Not, Goblet, Scrolls, 1870	25.00
Forget-Me-Not, Saltshaker, Blue	28.00
Four Petal, Sugar & Creamer, Covered, Flint	135.00
Four Petal, Sugar, Covered	38.00
Fox & Crow, Pitcher, Water	175.00
Fox & Crow, Pitcher, Water, Blue	175.00
Fringed Drape, Cordial	16.00

FROSTED PATTERNS, see also under name of main pattern

Frosted Block, Creamer	18.00
Frosted Circle, Butter, Covered	45.00
Frosted Circle, Cake Stand, 9 1/2 In.	35.00 To 40.00
Frosted Circle, Compote, Covered, 9 In.	65.00
Frosted Circle, Compote, 7 X 6 In.	42.00
Frosted Circle, Creamer	45.00
Frosted Circle, Cruet, Original Stopper	18.00
Frosted Circle, Goblet	35.00
Frosted Circle, Saltshaker, Shrine	45.00
Frosted Circle, Spooner	35.00
Frosted Circle, Wine	35.00
FROSTED CRANE, see Frosted Stork	
Frosted Dog, Compote, Covered, Clear, 9 X 11 In.	140.00
Frosted Eagle, Bowl, Covered, 7 In.	195.00
Frosted Eagle, Butter, Covered	135.00 To 275.00
Frosted Eagle, Creamer	45.00
Frosted Eagle, Creamer, Footed	45.00
Frosted Eagle, Salt Dip, Individual	45.00
Frosted Eagle, Saltshaker	45.00
Frosted Eagle, Spooner	45.00
Frosted Eagle, Sugar, Covered	85.00 To 115.00
Frosted Eagle, Sugar, Covered, Etched	225.00
Frosted Foot, Compote, Etched	40.00
Frosted Fruits, Compote, Covered	35.00
Frosted Fruits, Pitcher, Water	69.00
Frosted Leaf, Eggcup	130.00
Frosted Leaf, Goblet, Flint	70.00 To 75.00
Frosted Leaf, Pitcher, Buttermilk	49.00
Frosted Leaf, Spooner	24.00
Frosted Leaf, Sugar, Open, Flint	49.00
Frosted Leaf, Wine	130.00
Frosted Lion, Berry Bowl, Miniature	45.00
Frosted Lion, Bread Plate, Give Us This Day Our Daily Bread	85.00
Frosted Lion, Celery	55.00
Frosted Lion, Compote, Covered	135.00
Frosted Lion, Compote, Lion Rampant, Covered, 4 X 7 In.	105.00
Frosted Lion, Compote, Open, Standard	90.00
Frosted Lion, Compote, Rampant Lion Lid, Frosted Collar, 9 In.	52.00
Frosted Lion, Creamer	40.00 To 60.00
Frosted Lion, Creamer, Collared Base	70.00
Frosted Lion, Dish, Cheese, Covered	300.00
Frosted Lion, Goblet	45.00 To 80.00
Frosted Lion, Jar, Jam	90.00
Frosted Lion, Jar, Jam, Rampant Lion Finial	55.00 To 70.00
Frosted Lion, Jar, Sweetmeat, Lion Finial	65.00
Frosted Lion, Platter, Oval	73.00
Frosted Lion, Sauce, Footed	12.50 To 18.00
Frosted Lion, Spooner	40.00
Frosted Lion, Spooner, Etched	75.00
Frosted Lion, Sugar, Open	80.00
Frosted Lion, Vase	75.00
Frosted Ribbon, Creamer	38.00
Frosted Ribbon, Pitcher	40.00
Frosted Ribbon, Spooner	38.00
Frosted Roman Key, Spooner, Ribbed	42.50
Frosted Roman Key, Tumbler	95.00
Frosted Stork, Sugar	50.00
Frosted Stork, Tray, Water	125.00
FROSTED WAFFLE, see Hidalgo	
Fruit Panels, Goblet	18.00 To 24.00
Fuchsia, Goblet	28.00 To 32.00
G.A.R., Mug	70.00
Gaelic, Dish, Heart Shaped, 6 1/2 In.	14.00

Gaelic, Goblet 20.00
Galloway, Bowl, Covered With Gold, 3 In. 14.00
Galloway, Cake Stand 50.00
Galloway, Creamer 20.00
Galloway, Cup, Punch, Set Of 10 .... 70.00
Galloway, Dish, Relish 35.00
Galloway, Goblet, Water, Gold, Set Of 6 .... 165.00
Galloway, Pitcher, 9 In. 45.00
Galloway, Salt, Master, 3 1/4 X 2 1/2 In. 18.00
Galloway, Sugar, Covered .... 30.00 To 43.00
Galloway, Syrup .... 27.00 To 35.00
Galloway, Toothpick .... 10.00 To 20.00
Galloway, Vase, Bud, 9 1/4 In. 10.00
Galloway, Vase, Long Stemmed 22.00
Garden Fruits, Compote, Covered, 8 In. 48.00
    GARDEN OF EDEN, see Lotus & Serpent
Garfield Drape, Bread Plate ....
Garfield Drape, Celery 40.00
Garfield Drape, Compote, Covered, 8 X 13 In. 75.00
Garfield Drape, Creamer .... 35.00 To 40.00
Garfield Drape, Goblet 30.00
Garfield Drape, Pitcher 35.00
Garfield Drape, Pitcher, Milk 50.00
Garfield Drape, Pitcher, Water 45.00
Garfield Drape, Spooner .... 25.00 To 29.00
Garfield Drape, Sugar, Open 12.00
Garfield Memorial, Bread, Plate, 11 In. .... 25.00 To 65.00
Garfield, Mug, Martyr's Memorial, 2 1/4 In. 65.00
Garfield, Plate, Star Shape, 6 In. 25.00
Geneva, Banana Boat, Gold Trim, Green, 7 1/2 X 11 1/4 In. ... 65.00
Geneva, Bowl, Oval, Green, 9 1/2 In. 35.00
Geneva, Salt & Pepper, Gold Trim, Original Tops, Green ... 75.00
Geneva, Spooner, Gold Trim, Green 35.00
Georgia Gem, Butter, Covered, Gold Trim, Green 75.00
Georgia Gem, Spooner, Emerald Green 50.00
Georgia Gem, Toothpick, Opaque, Pea Green, Souvenir ... 30.00
Georgia Gem, Tumbler, Gold Trim, Green 30.00
Georgia, Sauce 20.00
Georgia, Table Set, 4 Piece 200.00
Giant Baby Thumbprint, Compote, Low Standard, Flint ... 38.00
Giant Bull's-Eye, Cruet, Findlay 18.00
Giant Prism With Thumbprint Band, Champagne, Flint ... 65.00
Giant Prism, Goblet, Flint .... 68.00 To 75.00
Giant Sawtooth, Celery 24.00
Giant Sawtooth, Goblet 85.00
Giant Sawtooth, Tumbler 75.00
Girl With Fan, Goblet 31.00
Goat's Head, Spooner 65.00
Goat's Head, Sugar, Covered 100.00
    GOOD LUCK, see Horseshoe
Gooseberry, Goblet 20.00
Gooseberry, Spooner 23.00
Gothic Arch, Sugar, Covered, Flint 35.00
Gothic, Goblet .... 35.00 To 65.00
Gothic, Goblet, Findlay 24.00
Gothic, Goblet, Flint .... 55.00 To 60.00
Gothic, Wine, Flint 65.00
    GRACE, see Butterfly & Fan
Graduated Diamonds, Goblet 15.00
    GRAND, see Diamond Medallion
    GRAND ARMY OF THE REPUBLIC, see G.A.R.
Grant Memorial, Bread Plate 60.00
Grant, Bread Plate, Peace, Green 40.00

Grant, Plate, Square 20.00
    GRAPE, see also Beaded Grape; Beaded Grape Medallion; Magnet &
    Grape; Magnet & Grape With Frosted Leaf; Paneled Grape; Paneled
    Grape Band
Grape & Festoon With Shield, Goblet 20.00
Grape & Festoon With Shield, Mug .... 12.00 To 25.00
Grape & Festoon With Shield, Spooner 25.00
Grape & Festoon, Goblet .... 18.00 To 52.50
Grape & Festoon, Goblet, Stippled Leaf 25.00
Grape & Festoon, Pitcher 65.00
Grape & Festoon, Plate, 6 In. 22.50
Grape & Festoon, Sauce .... 9.00 To 10.00
Grape & Festoon, Spooner 25.00
Grape & Festoon, Spooner, Stippled Leaf Trim .... 26.50 To 36.50
Grape & Gothic Arches, Butter, Gold Trim, Green 90.00
Grape & Gothic Arches, Pitcher, Water, Gold Trim, Green 85.00
Grape & Gothic Arches, Pitcher, Water, Green & Gold, N Mark 85.00
Grape & Gothic Arches, Tumbler, Gold Trim, Green .... 25.00 To 28.00
Grape Band, Compote 29.00
Grape Band, Goblet .... 18.50 To 24.00
Grape Band, Saltshaker 14.00
Grape Band, Spooner 24.00
Grape Bunch, Eggcup 5.00
Grape Bunch, Sugar & Creamer 60.00
Grape Medallion, Sugar, Covered 45.00
Grape With Vine, Compote, Covered 60.00
Grape With Vine, Pitcher, Water 60.00
Grapes, Bread Plate 35.00
Grasshopper, Bowl, Footed, 7 In. 15.00
Grasshopper, Bowl, Footed, 8 1/2 In. 20.00
Grasshopper, Compote, Covered 50.00
Grasshopper, Creamer 22.50
Grasshopper, Pitcher, Water, 9 In. 28.50
Grasshopper, Salt, Master, Footed, Round 16.00
Grated Diamond & Sunburst, Toothpick 22.50
Greek Key, Spooner 25.00
Greenfield Swirl, Goblet, Amber .... 22.00 To 40.00
Grenade, Dish, Relish, 7 3/4 X 4 1/2 In. 8.00
Gridley, Pitcher 42.00
Gridley, Pitcher, Water, Battle Of Manila, May 1st, 1898 .... 115.00
Hairpin, Ale 25.00
Hairpin, Cordial 30.00
Hairpin, Decanter, Flint 55.00
Hairpin, Wine 24.00
Halley's Comet, Tumbler .... 16.00 To 28.00
    HAMILTON WITH CLEAR LEAF, see Hamilton with Leaf
Hamilton With Leaf, Sugar, Covered 75.00
Hamilton, Eggcup 34.00
Hamilton, Goblet .... 38.00 To 45.00
Hamilton, Goblet, Flint .... 30.00 To 40.00
Hamilton, Spooner, Flint 40.00
Hamilton, Tumbler, Water 75.00
Hamilton, Wine, Flint 50.00
    HAND, see Pennsylvania Hand
Hanover, Sugar, Covered 24.50
Harp, Butter, Covered 105.00
Harp, Cake Stand 20.00
Harp, Salt, Master 35.00
Hartley, Creamer 23.00
Hartley, Goblet, Amber 28.50
Hartley, Sauce, Footed, Blue 13.00
Hawaiian Lei, Compote, 8 In. 35.00
Hawaiian Lei, Saltshaker, Pair 15.00

Fine Rib With Cut Ovals

Frosted Eagle

Frosted Stork

Excelsior

Fruit Panels

Grape & Festoon

Garfield Drape

Grape & Festoon
With Shield

Hamilton

Harp

Hawaiian Lei, Tumbler 15.00
Hawaiian, Pineapple, Goblet .... 85.00 To 90.00
Heart Band, Creamer, Stained Ruby 30.00
Heart Band, Toothpick, Ruby Top 20.00
Heart Stem, Creamer 30.00
Heart Stem, Spooner 25.00
Heart With Thumbprint, Berry Bowl, Gold 40.00
Heart With Thumbprint, Bowl, Clear, 9 In. 30.00
Heart With Thumbprint, Bowl, Ruffled, 9 In. .... 28.00 To 30.00
Heart With Thumbprint, Bowl, Square, 7 X 3 1/2 In. 38.00
Heart With Thumbprint, Bowl, 9 In. 32.50
Heart With Thumbprint, Creamer, Emerald Green 35.00
Heart With Thumbprint, Creamer, Gold Top, Green 38.00
Heart With Thumbprint, Cruet 48.00
Heart With Thumbprint, Cup, Punch 12.50
Heart With Thumbprint, Cup, Punch, Gold Rim 22.00
Heart With Thumbprint, Goblet .... 38.00 To 55.00
Heart With Thumbprint, Jelly, Pewter Rim 18.00
Heart With Thumbprint, Nappy, Handled 24.00
Heart With Thumbprint, Plate, Gold Trim, 6 1/4 In. 30.00
Heart With Thumbprint, Plate, 11 1/2 In. 45.00
Heart With Thumbprint, Rose Bowl .... 32.00 To 49.00
Heart With Thumbprint, Rose Bowl, Miniature .... 15.00 To 25.00
Heart With Thumbprint, Sugar 18.00
Heart With Thumbprint, Sugar & Creamer 27.00
Heart With Thumbprint, Sugar, Double Handle, Green 35.00
Heart With Thumbprint, Sugar, Individual 18.00
Heart With Thumbprint, Tray, Card, Gold Edge .... 18.00 To 23.00
Heart With Thumbprint, Tumbler .... 25.00 To 32.00
Heart With Thumbprint, Tumbler, Gold Trim 35.00
Heart With Thumbprint, Tumbler, Gold, Footed 25.00
Heart With Thumbprint, Vase, Gold Trim, Clear, 6 In. 25.00
Heart With Thumbprint, Vase, 7 3/4 In. .... 32.00 To 44.00
Heart With Thumbprint, Vase, 9 1/4 In. .... 42.00 To 45.00
Heart With Thumbprint, Vase, 10 In. 40.00
Heart, Creamer, Pedestal 33.00
HEARTS OF LOCH LAVEN, see Shuttle
Heavy Gothic, Butter, Covered 35.00
Heavy Gothic, Compote, 5 1/2 In. 22.00
Heavy Gothic, Tumbler 20.00
HEAVY PANELED FINE CUT, see Paneled Diamond Cross
Henrietta, Syrup 45.00
Henrietta, Tumbler 12.00
Heron & Peacock, Mug 25.00
Heron & Peacock, Mug, Child's, Blue 45.00
Herringbone Band, Spooner .... 15.00 To 24.50
Herringbone, Banana Boat, Folded-Up Sides, Emerald Green 35.00
Herringbone, Bowl, Emerald Green, 9 In. .... 30.00 To 35.00
Herringbone, Butter, Covered, Emerald Green 44.00
Herringbone, Creamer 14.00
Herringbone, Goblet .... 18.00 To 20.00
Herringbone, Goblet, Emerald Green 35.00
Herringbone, Pitcher, Green 60.00
Herringbone, Pitcher, Milk, Green 50.00
Herringbone, Pitcher, Water, Emerald Green Herringbone Band 55.00
Herringbone, Pitcher, Water, Green 85.00
Herringbone, Sauce, Green .... 10.00 To 12.00
Herringbone, Table Set, Emerald Green 175.00
Herringbone, Tumbler, Green 25.00
Herringbone, Water Set, Emerald Green, 7 Piece 195.00
Herringbone, Wine, Emerald Green .... 45.00 To 55.00
Hexagon Block, Compote, Covered 50.00
Hickman, Bowl, 6 1/4 In. 10.00

Hickman, Bowl, 7 1/2 X 8 1/2 In. 8.50
Hickman, Compote, Jelly 16.00
Hickman, Creamer 9.00
Hickman, Creamer, Gold Trim 24.50
Hickman, Cup, Punch 48.00
Hickman, Dish, Olive 16.50
Hickman, Goblet 32.00
Hickman, Goblet, Green 36.50
Hickman, Pickle, 7 3/4 In. 7.00
Hickman, Pitcher 36.00
Hickman, Sugar, Covered 29.00
Hickman, Toothpick 45.00
Hidalgo, Goblet 16.00
Hidalgo, Sugar Shaker, Frosted 55.00
Hidalgo, Tumbler, Frosted 20.00
Hinoto, Celery, Fluted, Pair 195.00
Hinoto, Eggcup, Flint 22.00

HOBNAIL & BARS, see Barred Hobnail

Hobnail & Fan, Goblet .... 14.00 To 35.00
Hobnail Band, Spooner 18.00
Hobnail With Fan, Goblet .... 14.00 To 35.00
Hobnail With Thumbprint Base, Butter, Covered, Blue 75.00
Hobnail, Cake Stand, 10 In. 27.50
Hobnail, Creamer, Child's, Amber 20.00
Hobnail, Cruet, Stopper 25.00
Hobnail, Goblet .... 12.00 To 20.00
Hobnail, Mug, Handled 12.00
Hobnail, Pitcher, Child's, Blue, 3 1/2 In. 27.00
Hobnail, Sauce 4.00
Hobnail, Toothpick, Amber 30.00
Hobnail, Tumbler, Line Band 19.00
Hobnail, Tumbler, Ruby 38.50

HOLBROOK, see Pineapple & Fan

Holly Band, Celery 45.00
Holly Leaves, Goblet .... 15.00 To 20.00
Holly, Goblet 90.00
Holly, Tumbler 90.00

HONEYCOMB, see also Barrel Honeycomb

Honeycomb, Celery, Flint 25.00
Honeycomb, Compote, Open, 8 In. 20.00
Honeycomb, Compote, Scalloped Rim, Flint, 5 1/2 X 6 In. 55.00
Honeycomb, Compote, Wafer Connection, 9 X 7 In. 30.00
Honeycomb, Cordial 22.00
Honeycomb, Creamer, Flower Rim, Amber .... 31.50 To 34.50
Honeycomb, Decanter, Original Stopper, Quart 40.00
Honeycomb, Eggcup, Flint 17.00
Honeycomb, Goblet .... 12.00 To 25.00
Honeycomb, Spooner .... 12.00 To 16.50
Honeycomb, Spooner, Scalloped Rim, Flint 24.50
Honeycomb, Sugar, Flint 35.00
Hooks & Eyes, Goblet 15.00
Hops Band, Creamer 25.00
Hops Band, Goblet 22.00
Hops Band, Spooner 18.00
Hops Band, Sugar 19.00
Horn Of Plenty, Bottle, Sauce, Pewter Top 125.00
Horn Of Plenty, Butter Chip, Flint 18.00
Horn Of Plenty, Celery, Flint 165.00
Horn Of Plenty, Champagne, Flint 125.00
Horn Of Plenty, Compote, Low Standard, Open, 7 1/4 In. 70.00
Horn Of Plenty, Creamer, Small 200.00
Horn Of Plenty, Decanter, Flint, Original Stopper 210.00
Horn Of Plenty, Eggcup, Flint .... 35.00 To 40.00
Horn Of Plenty, Eggcup, Flint, Flared Rim 35.00

Horn Of Plenty, Goblet 65.00
Horn Of Plenty, Goblet, Flint .... 55.00 To 65.00
Horn Of Plenty, Sauce 15.00
Horn Of Plenty, Tumbler, Flint 90.00
Horn Of Plenty, Tumbler, Handled, Small 135.00
Horn Of Plenty, Wine, Flint .... 125.00 To 145.00
Horseheads Medallion, Celery 15.00
Horseheads Medallion, Spooner .... 35.00 To 45.00
Horsemint, Sauce, Gold Trim, 4 In. 8.00
Horsemint, Wine 12.00
Horseshoe, Bowl, 4 1/2 X 7 In. 15.00
Horseshoe, Bowl, 7 X 4 1/2 In. 15.00
Horseshoe, Bowl, 9 X 6 In. 15.00
Horseshoe, Bread Plate .... 33.00 To 60.00
Horseshoe, Cake Stand, 9 In. 30.00
Horseshoe, Butter, Covered 75.00
Horseshoe, Cake Stand, 10 In. 45.00
Horseshoe, Compote, Covered, Plain Stem, 12 In. 50.00
Horseshoe, Compote, Knob Stem, 9 In. 40.00
Horseshoe, Compote, 8 In. 20.00
Horseshoe, Creamer .... 25.00 To 29.00
Horseshoe, Dish, Relish .... 10.00 To 15.00
Horseshoe, Dish, Relish, 1880s 15.00
Horseshoe, Goblet .... 20.00 To 30.00
Horseshoe, Goblet, Knob Stem .... 27.00 To 40.00
Horseshoe, Jar, Jam, Covered 135.00
Horseshoe, Mug 50.00
Horseshoe, Pitcher, Water 75.00
Horseshoe, Plate, 6 In. 29.00
Horseshoe, Plate, 8 1/4 In. 42.00
Horseshoe, Salt, Master 125.00
Horseshoe, Sauce, Footed .... 7.00 To 13.50
Horseshoe, Spooner 30.00
Horseshoe, Sugar & Creamer, Knobbed 50.00
Horseshoe, Sugar, Knobbed 25.00
Horseshoe, Tray, Water 125.00
Horseshoe, Wine 115.00
Hotel Argus, Goblet 12.00
Huber, Compote, Flint, 7 1/2 In. 26.00
Huber, Eggcup, Flint 22.50
Huber, Wine, Flint 20.00
   HUCKLE, see Feather Duster
Hummingbird, Celery 35.00
Hummingbird, Creamer 33.00
Hummingbird, Goblet 34.50
Hummingbird, Pitcher, Amber 120.00
Hummingbird, Pitcher, Milk, Blue 90.00
Hummingbird, Pitcher, Water .... 70.00 To 100.00
Hummingbird, Waste Bowl, 5 1/2 X 2 In. 35.00
Hundred-Leaved Rose, Sauce, Flat, 4 1/4 In. 5.00
Hundred-Leaved Rose, Tumbler 15.00
   IDA, see Sheraton
   IDAHO, see Snail
Idyll, Condiment Set, Sapphire Blue, 5 Piece 350.00
Illinois, Berry, Square, 8 In. 35.00
Illinois, Creamer, Individual .... 17.50 To 20.00
Illinois, Pitcher, Green 180.00
Illinois, Pitcher, Water, Silver Plated Top 75.00
Illinois, Plate, Square, 7 In. 16.00
Illinois, Spooner 18.00
Illinois, Sugar, Covered 45.00
Illinois, Sugar, Flint, Individual 19.00
Illinois, Syrup, Original Pewter Lid 95.00
Illinois, Toothpick 22.00

Illinois, Vase, 6 In. 22.00
    INDIAN TREE, see Sprig
    INDIANA SWIRL, see Feather
Inominata, Creamer ....
Intaglio, Amethyst Glass, Creamer, Sterling Design Overlay 15.00
Interlocked Hearts, Cruet, Stopper 15.00
Inverted Fern, Butter, Covered 32.00
Inverted Fern, Champagne, Flint 85.00
Inverted Fern, Compote, 8 In. 120.00
Inverted Fern, Creamer, Flint 55.00
Inverted Fern, Eggcup 160.00
Inverted Fern, Goblet 25.00
Inverted Fern, Goblet, Flint 22.00
Inverted Fern, Sugar & Creamer, Flint .... 32.00 To 35.00
Inverted Fern, Sugar, Covered 55.00
Inverted Strawberry, Compote, Candy 75.00
Inverted Strawberry, Cup, Punch, Miniature 28.00
Inverted Strawberry, Pitcher, 8 In. 9.00
Inverted Strawberry, Toothpick 55.00
Inverted Strawberry, Water Set, Signed, 7 Piece 10.00
    INVERTED THISTLE, see Late Thistle 150.00
Inverted Thumbprint And Star, Goblet, Blue 54.50
Inverted Thumbprint, Cordial, Amber 25.00
Inverted Thumbprint, Goblet .... 10.00 To 16.00
Inverted Thumbprint, Goblet, Vaseline 39.00
Inverted Thumbprint, Syrup, Pewter Lid, Blue .... 95.00 To 110.00
Inverted Thumbprint, Syrup, Vaseline 35.00
Inverted Thumbprint, Toothpick, Light Green 40.00
Inverted Thumbprint, Tumbler, Enamel Design, Green 28.00
Inverted Thumbprint, Wine, Amber 30.00
Inverted Thumbprint, Wine, Blue 40.00
Ionia, Goblet .... 12.00 To 16.00
Iowa, Cup, Gold Rim 18.50
Iowa, Plate, Cat, Be Playful 75.00
Iowa, Plate, Dog, Be True 70.00
Iowa, Table Set, Clear With Pink, 4 Piece 235.00
Iowa, Toothpick .... 18.00 To 25.00
Iris With Meander, Pitcher, Water, Green 85.00
Iris With Meander, Toothpick, Amethyst 40.00
Iris, Bowl, Fruit, Large 15.00
Iris, Cruet, Etched, Stopper 27.00
Iris, Water Set, 5 Piece 65.00
Isis, Tumbler 8.00
Ivy In Snow, Cake Stand, 8 In. 20.00
Ivy In Snow, Celery, Gold Leaf 30.00
Ivy In Snow, Compote, Flint, 8 1/2 X 7 In. 37.50
Ivy In Snow, Pitcher, Water 39.00
Ivy In Snow, Sugar & Creamer, Gold Leaves 16.00
Ivy In Snow, Tumbler 20.00
Jacob's Coat, Sugar, Covered 35.00
Jacob's Coat, Sugar, Covered, Amber 65.00
Jacob's Ladder, Butter, Covered 42.00
Jacob's Ladder, Cake Stand, 9 1/2 In. 40.00
Jacob's Ladder, Celery .... 30.00 To 40.00
Jacob's Ladder, Compote, Open, 7 1/2 In. 30.00
Jacob's Ladder, Compote, Scalloped, 6 3/4 X 8 1/4 In. 30.00
Jacob's Ladder, Compote, Scalloped, 7 1/4 X 9 1/2 In. 45.00
Jacob's Ladder, Compote, 5 3/4 X 8 1/2 In. 30.00
Jacob's Ladder, Compote, 8 In. .... 34.50 To 38.00
Jacob's Ladder, Compote, 8 1/4 X 8 1/2 In. 30.00
Jacob's Ladder, Creamer .... 29.00 To 47.00
Jacob's Ladder, Dish, Oval, 7 3/4 X 5 1/2 In. 20.00
Jacob's Ladder, Dish, Relish .... 12.00 To 25.00

Jacob's Ladder, Goblet, 6 3/8 In., Pair 55.00
Jacob's Ladder, Pitcher, Water .... 85.00 To 150.00
Jacob's Ladder, Salt, Footed, 2 7/8 In. .... 20.00 To 23.00
Jacob's Ladder, Salt, Master .... 13.00 To 20.00
Jacob's Ladder, Sauce, Flat, 4 1/2 In. 10.00
Jacob's Ladder, Spooner 29.50
Jacob's Ladder, Sugar 24.00
Jacob's Ladder, Sugar & Creamer 60.00
Jacob's Ladder, Syrup, Pewter Lid 30.00
Jacob's Ladder, Table Set, 4 Piece 125.00
Jacob's Ladder, Wine .... 29.50 To 39.00
     JASPER, see Late Buckle
Jefferson Colonial, Toothpick, Green 25.00
Jefferson Optic, Table Set, White Enamel, Salmon, 4 Piece 165.00
Jefferson Optic, Water Set, Enamel Design, 4 Piece 195.00
Jenny Lind, Compote 65.00
Jenny Lind, Compote, Frosted Base 110.00
Jersey Swirl, Celery 45.00
Jersey Swirl, Goblet 22.00
Jersey Swirl, Tumbler, Amber 38.00
Jersey, Table Set, Clear, Etched, 4 Piece 149.00
Jersey, Table Set, Etched, 4 Piece 149.00
Jewel & Dewdrop, Bread Plate, Our Daily Bread, Oval 50.00
Jewel & Dewdrop, Cake Stand, 9 In. 55.00
Jewel & Dewdrop, Compote, 6 In. 40.00
Jewel & Dewdrop, Dish, Covered, 4 1/4 In. 40.00
Jewel & Dewdrop, Dish, Relish .... 20.00 To 35.00
Jewel & Dewdrop, Dish, Vegetable, 8 In. 40.00
Jewel & Dewdrop, Goblet 35.00
Jewel & Dewdrop, Jar, Jam 50.00
Jewel & Dewdrop, Mug, Child's 15.00
Jewel & Dewdrop, Mug, 3 1/4 In., Pair 22.00
Jewel & Dewdrop, Plate, 10 In. 24.00
Jewel & Dewdrop, Toothpick 30.00
Jewel & Dewdrop, Wine 45.00
     JEWEL & FESTOON, see Loop & Jewel
     JEWEL BAND, see Scalloped Tape
Jeweled Drapery, Goblet 12.00
Jeweled Heart, Berry Set, Opalescent, 9 Piece 135.00
Jeweled Heart, Bowl, 9 1/2 In.Square 14.00
Jeweled Heart, Creamer 17.50
Jeweled Heart, Plate, 6 1/2 In. 12.00
Jeweled Heart, Tumbler 10.00
Jeweled Heart, Tumbler, Blue 28.00
Jeweled Moon & Star, Carafe .... 35.00 To 40.00
Jeweled Moon & Star, Compote ' 52.00
Jeweled Moon & Star, Compote, Clear, 6 3/4 X 8 In. 80.00
     JOB'S TEARS, see Art
     JUBILEE, see Hickman
     KAMONI, see Pennsylvania
     KANSAS, see Jewel & Dewdrop
Kentucky, Cup, Punch, Green 13.00
Kentucky, Tumbler, Green .... 25.00 To 28.00
Kentucky, Wine, Green 40.00
Keystone Grape, Goblet .... 20.00 To 22.50
King's Crown, Bottle, Castor, Shaker Top 29.00
King's Crown, Butter, Covered 90.00
King's Crown, Celery .... 75.00 To 80.00
King's Crown, Compote, Covered 82.00
King's Crown, Compote, Gold Trim 28.00
King's Crown, Compote, 7 In. .... 32.00 To 35.00
King's Crown, Cup, Punch 11.50
King's Crown, Goblet 21.00

Hairpin

Jacob's Ladder

Holly Band

Hobnail

Jeweled Heart

Holly

Horn Of Plenty

Inverted Fern

Horseshoe

King's Crown, Goblet, Green Eyes, Gold Rim .... 14.00 To 21.00
King's Crown, Goblet, Souvenir, Columbia City, Ind. 30.00
King's Crown, Pitcher, Milk, Ruby, 8 In. .... 82.00 To 85.00
King's Crown, Pitcher, 8 1/2 In. .... 95.00 To 105.00
King's Crown, Salt, Master 35.00
King's Crown, Saltshaker 35.00
King's Crown, Spooner 60.00
King's Crown, Sugar 50.00
King's Crown, Sugar & Creamer, Individual 45.00
King's Crown, Toothpick .... 24.50 To 30.00
King's Crown, Tumbler 27.50
King's Crown, Wine .... 14.00 To 32.50
King's 500, Nappy, Handled, Cobalt Blue 15.00
King's 500, Tumbler, Cobalt Blue 30.00
Kitten, Plate 19.00
Klondike, Celery, Cross Flashing, 4 1/2 X 10 1/2 X 2 3/4 In. 195.00
Klondike, Creamer, Amber 74.50
Klondike, Salt & Pepper 89.50
Klondike, Salt & Pepper, Amber 135.00
Klondike, Spooner, Amber 175.00
Klondike, Sugar, Amber, Covered 245.00
Klondike, Tumbler, Amber & Frosted .... 140.00 To 150.00
Klondike, Vase, Trumpet, Amber & Frosted, 10 1/2 In. 245.00
Knight, Bowl, Blue 95.00
Knights Of Labor, Bread Plate, Blue 250.00
Knights Of Labor, Bread Plate, Vaseline 145.00
Knives & Forks, Goblet, Flint 20.00
Knobby Bull's-Eye, Goblet 18.50
Kokomo, Goblet, Clear 28.00
Krom, Champagne, Flint 49.00
Krom, Goblet 22.00
    LACE, see Drapery
Lacy Daisy, Berry Set, Child's, 7 Piece 68.00
Lacy Daisy, Creamer 23.00
Lacy Daisy, Sugar & Creamer 45.00
Lacy Dewdrop, Goblet 24.00
Lacy Dewdrop, Tumbler, Amber 27.00
Lacy Medallion, Salt & Pepper, Souvenir, Green 69.50
Lacy Medallion, Toothpick, Gold Trim 13.00
Lacy Medallion, Tumbler, Souvenir, Gold Trim, Green 20.00
    LACY SPIRAL, see Colossus
Ladder With Diamonds, Plate, 8 In. 13.00
Ladder With Diamonds, Toothpick .... 25.00 To 35.00
Ladder With Diamonds, Wine, Tarentum Glass .... 20.00 To 22.00
Last Supper, Bread Plate 50.00
Late Buckle, Sauce .... 5.00 To 8.00
Late Paneled Grape, Sauce, Flat 4.00
Late Sawtooth, Goblet 12.50
Late Thistle, Berry Set, Gold Trim, Green, 6 Piece 110.00
Late Thistle, Bowl, 8 1/2 In. 20.00
Late Thistle, Butter, Covered, Gold Trim, Green 85.00
Late Thistle, Butter, Covered, Green 135.00
Late Thistle, Creamer, Gold Trim, Green 40.00
Late Thistle, Pitcher, Water, Green With Gold .... 50.00 To 60.00
Late Thistle, Sugar, Covered, Gold Trim, Green 55.00
Late Thistle, Tumbler, Gold Trim, Green .... 25.00 To 28.00
Late Thistle, Tumbler, Green With Gold, Pair 25.00
Later Paneled Diamond Point, Goblet 15.00
Lattice & Oval Panels, Sugar 39.00
Lattice & Oval Panels, Tumbler, 3 3/4 In. 39.00
Lattice, Pitcher, 10 In. 40.00
Lattice, Sauce 9.00
Lattice, Wine 25.00
Leaf & Dart, Celery 30.00

Leaf & Dart, Eggcup 18.00
Leaf & Dart, Goblet .... 17.00 To 28.00
Leaf & Dart, Sugar, Covered .... 35.00 To 45.00
Leaf & Dart, Tumbler, Footed 24.00
Leaf & Flower, Berry, Master, Amber 82.50
Leaf & Flower, Creamer 25.00
Leaf & Flower, Pitcher, Tankard, Clear Handle, Amber Stain 110.00
Leaf & Flower, Sauce, Frosted 22.00
Leaf & Flower, Spooner, Amber Stain 45.00
Leaf & Flower, Spooner, Frosted 39.00
Leaf & Flower, Syrup, Original Lid 65.00
Leaf & Flower, Tumbler 20.00
Leaf & Flower, Tumbler, Frosted .... 15.00 To 56.00
Leaf Medallion, Creamer, Gold Trim, Green 60.00
Leaf Medallion, Creamer, Green, Gold 65.00
Leaf Medallion, Sauce, Blue 54.50
Leaf Medallion, Sugar & Creamer, Green 175.00
Leaf Medallion, Sugar, Creamer, & Spooner, Gold Trim, Green 260.00
Leaf Medallion, Sugar, Gold Trim, Covered 145.00
Leaf Medallion, Sugar, Gold Trim, Purple 25.00
Leaf Medallion, Sugar, Green, Gold 80.00
Leaf, Dish, Pickle 15.00
Leaf, Pitcher, Water, 2 Quart 45.00
Lee, Wine 175.00
Lee, Wine, Flint 100.00
LENS & STAR, see Star & Oval
Liberty Bell, Bell 22.50
Liberty Bell, Berry Bowl 60.00
Liberty Bell, Bread Plate .... 40.00 To 100.00
Liberty Bell, Butter, Covered .... 25.00 To 35.00
Liberty Bell, Creamer .... 95.00 To 100.00
Liberty Bell, Goblet .... 25.00 To 52.50
Liberty Bell, Mug 95.00
Liberty Bell, Pitcher 75.00
Liberty Bell, Plate 75.00
Liberty Bell, Sauce, Footed 25.00
Liberty Bell, Spooner .... 65.00 To 85.00
Liberty Bell, Sugar, Covered .... 110.00 To 125.00
Liberty Bell, Sugar, Open 50.00
Liberty, Jar, Apothecary, With Gold 135.00
Liberty, Wine .... 10.00 To 15.00
Lily Of The Valley, Creamer, Applied Handle 45.00
Lily Of The Valley, Eggcup 35.00
Lily Of The Valley, Goblet .... 35.00 To 40.00
Lily Of The Valley, Pitcher, Bulbous 125.00
Lily Of The Valley, Pitcher, Water 95.00
Lily Of The Valley, Tumbler, Footed 55.00
Lincoln Drape, Eggcup, Flint 40.00
Lincoln Drape, Sauce, Flat, Flint, Round 16.00
Lined Ribs, Goblet 18.00
LION, see also Frosted Lion
Lion In Jungle, Goblet, Etched 28.00
Lion, Butter, 2 Face Lion Finial, Covered 75.00
Lion, Celery .... 36.00 To 60.00
Lion, Creamer 35.00
Lion, Goblet 60.00
Lion, Platter, Oval 85.00
Lion, Spooner .... 48.00 To 53.00
Lion, Sugar, Covered 50.00
Lion's Head, Bowl, Serving, 5 X 8 In. 55.00
Lion's Head, Butter, Covered 55.00
Lion's Head, Cake Plate, Footed 95.00
Lion's Head, Dish, Jelly, Footed 38.00

Lion's Head, Dish, Relish, Oval	45.00
Lion's Head, Goblet	45.00
Lion's Head, Pitcher, Water	110.00
Lion's Head, Toothpick	35.00
LION'S LEG, see Alaska	
LIPPMAN, see Flat Diamond	
Little Lamb, Creamer, Child's	55.00
Locket On Chain, Cake Stand	185.00
Locket On Chain, Wine	110.00
Log & Star, Condiment Set, Amber	135.00
Log Cabin, Creamer	135.00
Log Cabin, Pitcher	310.00
Log Cabin, Spooner	95.00
Loganberry & Grape, Goblet	8.00
Long Maple Leaf, Creamer	21.00
LOOP, see also Seneca Loop; Yuma Loop	
Loop & Chain Band, Goblet	9.00
Loop & Dart With Diamond Ornament, Goblet	18.00
Loop & Dart With Diamond Ornament, Tumbler, Footed	26.00
Loop & Dart With Round Ornament, Eggcup	17.00
Loop & Dart With Round Ornament, Goblet, Buttermilk	40.00
Loop & Dart With Round Ornament, Tumbler, Footed	28.00
Loop & Dart With Round Ornament, Wine, Barrel Shape	35.00
Loop & Dart, Creamer, Applied Handle	45.00
Loop & Dart, Eggcup, Flint	22.00
Loop & Dart, Goblet	18.00 To 27.00
Loop & Dart, Spooner	22.00
Loop & Fisheye, Goblet	18.00 To 25.00
Loop & Jewel, Sugar, Covered	28.50
Loop & Pyramid, Goblet	19.00
Loop & Pyramid, Wine, Gold	16.50
Loop With Dewdrop, Goblet	15.00
Loop With Dewdrop, Goblet, Gold Rim	23.00
Loop With Dewdrop, Sugar, Covered	30.00
LOOP WITH STIPPLED PANELS, see Texas	
Loop, Goblet	14.00
Loop, Goblet, Flint	22.00
Loop, Spooner, Flint	30.00
LOOPS & DROPS, see New Jersey	
Loops & Ovals, Goblet, Flint	25.00
Lotus & Serpent, Sauce	20.00
Lotus, Dish, Relish, 7 X 4 1/2 In.	10.00
Louis XV, Berry, Green, Large	75.00
Louise, Sugar & Creamer, Covered	35.00
Louisiana, Pitcher, Milk	40.00
Magnet & Grape With American Shield, Goblet	175.00
Magnet & Grape With American Shield, Sugar, Frosted Leaf	285.00
Magnet & Grape With Frosted Leaf, Goblet	55.00 To 85.00
Magnet & Grape With Frosted Leaf, Goblet, Flint	40.00 To 55.00
Magnet & Grape With Frosted Leaf, Tumbler	135.00
Magnet & Grape With Stippled Leaf, Spooner	25.00
Magnet & Grape, Goblet	25.00 To 32.00
Magnet & Grape, Spooner	23.00
Magnet & Grape, Sugar, Covered	95.00
Magnolia, Pitcher, Water	55.00
MAIDEN BLUSH, see Banded Portland	
Maine, Berry Bowl, Master, Green	35.00 To 40.00
Maine, Butter, Covered	45.00
Maine, Cake Stand	35.00 To 53.00
Maine, Cake Stand, Green	50.00
Maine, Compote, Green, 8 In.	48.00 To 65.00
Maine, Compote, Jelly, Green	40.00 To 60.00
Maine, Syrup, Green	195.00

Klondike

Leaf & Dart

Liberty Bell

Loop & Fisheye

Lincoln Drape

Magnet & Grape With Stippled Leaf

Maine

Lion

Majestic, Cruet, Stopper		18.00
Man's Head, Spooner		35.00
Manhattan, Cracker Jar, Rose Flashed, Covered		60.00
Manhattan, Plate, Handled, 4 1/2 In.		7.50
Manhattan, Plate, Scalloped, Turned-Up Sides, Clear, 5 1/4 In.		10.00
Manhattan, Plate, 10 1/2 In.		24.00
Manhattan, Salt & Pepper		25.00
Manhattan, Sauce, Amber, 4 1/2 In., Pair		8.50

Manhattan, Sauce, 1 Handled, 4 1/4 In., Pair	8.00
Manhattan, Toothpick	28.00
Manting, Goblet	20.00
Manting, Goblet, Flint	28.50
Manting, Tumbler, Flint	40.00
Many Diamonds, Butter Chip	3.00
Maple Leaf, Band, Goblet	30.00 To 35.00
Maple Leaf, Bowl, Underplate, Footed, Canary	140.00
Maple Leaf, Platter, Oval, Yellow	75.00
Maple Leaf, Sugar, Gold Trim, Covered, Green	65.00
Marquisette, Celery	38.00 To 42.00
Marquisette, Goblet	24.00 To 28.00
Marquisette, Spooner	24.00 To 26.00
Martha's Tears, Goblet	15.00
Martha's Tears, Goblet, Amber	20.00 To 22.00
Martyrs, Mug	40.00 To 50.00
Maryland, Pitcher, Milk	35.00
Maryland, Tumbler	35.00
Mascotte, Celery, Etched	35.00
Mascotte, Etched, Sugar, Covered	38.00
Mascotte, Goblet, Canary	80.00
Mascotte, Goblet, Etched	32.50
Mascotte, Sauce, Footed	8.00
Mascotte, Spooner, Etched	28.00
Mascotte, Sugar, Covered	28.00 To 40.00
Mascotte, Sugar, Etched, Covered	45.00
Mascotte, Sugar, Open	17.00
Masonic, Pitcher, Silver Plated Pouring Lip	59.00
Massachusetts, Banana Bowl	55.00
Massachusetts, Bottle	50.00
Massachusetts, Bottle, Bar	45.00
Massachusetts, Bowl, Bulbous, Footed, 6 1/2 X 8 In.	75.00
Massachusetts, Cruet, 5 In.	68.00
Massachusetts, Decanter, Stopper	135.00
Massachusetts, Goblet	23.00 To 35.00
Massachusetts, Jug, Rum, Clear	75.00
Massachusetts, Mug, Gold Edge	18.00
Massachusetts, Sugar, Open	18.00
Massachusetts, Vase, Trumpet, Blue & Gold Trim, 6 1/2 In.	35.00
Massachusetts, Wine	30.00
McKinley Memorial, Bread Plate	20.00 To 25.00
McKinley, Mug	20.00 To 25.00
McKinley, Paperweight, Square	15.00
Medallion Sprig, Table Set, Green	350.00
Medallion, Creamer, Gold Trim, Green	65.00
Medallion, Creamer, Green	55.00
Medallion, Goblet, Amber	29.50
Medallion, Pitcher, Blue	90.00
Medallion, Spooner, Amber	20.00
Medallion, Spooner, Gold Trim, Green	60.00
Medallion, Spooner, Green	45.00
Medallion, Sugar, Covered, Gold Trim, Green	110.00
Medallion, Sugar, Covered, Green	60.00
Melrose, Celery	20.00
Melrose, Compote	18.00
Melrose, Compote, Jelly	14.50
Melrose, Sugar, Covered	32.00
Melton, Goblet	14.00
Memphis, Bowl, Green & Gold, 9 In.	35.00
Memphis, Bowl, Green, 9 In.	45.00
Memphis, Creamer, Gold Trim, Green	50.00
Memphis, Creamer, Green	30.00
Memphis, Cup, Punch	5.00

Memphis, Pitcher, Water 105.00
Memphis, Water Set, Gold Trim, Green, 7 Piece 255.00
Michigan, Berry Set, Gold & Pink Stain 110.00
Michigan, Bowl, Ruby, Oblong, 12 X 8 1/2 In. 65.00
Michigan, Celery, Pink Stain 58.00
Michigan, Creamer .... 17.00 To 27.00
Michigan, Creamer, Individual, Vaseline Stain, Enameled 18.00
Michigan, Creamer, Pink & Gold 50.00
Michigan, Cruet 35.00
Michigan, Cup, Punch 9.50
Michigan, Dish, Pickle 13.50
Michigan, Dish, Relish 16.50
Michigan, Goblet 40.00
Michigan, Pitcher, Beaded Silver Collar, 11 In. 150.00
Michigan, Pitcher, Tankard, Silver Rim 65.00
Michigan, Pitcher, Tankard, Water 48.00
Michigan, Pitcher, Water, Child's, Gold Trim 28.00
Michigan, Pitcher, Water, Gold Trim 120.00
Michigan, Saltshaker 45.00
Michigan, Spooner, Pink & Gold 50.00
Michigan, Spooner, Yellow Stain 40.00
Michigan, Sugar, Covered, Pink & Gold 80.00
Michigan, Sugar, Individual 22.00
Michigan, Toothpick, Hand-Painted Flower 35.00
Michigan, Tumbler .... 26.00 To 32.00
Michigan, Vase, 12 In. 28.00
Michigan, Water Set, Souvenir, Conneaut Lake, 5 Piece 235.00
Mikado Fan, Goblet 15.00
Milton, Goblet 15.00
Milton, Plate, 10 In. 20.00
Milton, Saltshaker, Original Top, Amber 18.00
Milton, Tankard 48.00
Minerva, Bread Plate .... 25.00 To 45.00
Minerva, Butter, Covered .... 45.00 To 60.00
Minerva, Cake Stand, 11 In. 145.00
Minerva, Dish, Pickle, Loves Request Is Pickles 20.00
Minerva, Dish, Relish 30.00
Minerva, Dish, Vegetable 20.00
Minerva, Goblet 68.00
Minerva, Sauce, Flat, 5 In. 20.00
Minerva, Sauce, Footed 15.00
Minnesota, Creamer 24.00
Minnesota, Goblet, Gold Trim 20.00
Minnesota, Toothpick .... 22.50 To 35.00
Minnesota, Toothpick, Gold Trim 18.00
Minnesota, Toothpick, 3-Handled 15.00
Mioton Pleat Band, Goblet, Flint 45.00
Mioton, Goblet, Red Top 28.00
Mirror & Loop, Eggcup, Flint 30.00
Mirror, Champagne, Flint 32.50
Missouri, Butter, Covered .... 32.50 To 55.00
Missouri, Cruet .... 25.00 To 29.50
Missouri, Pitcher, Milk $ 34.50 To 45.00
Missouri, Sugar, Covered, Green 55.00
Missouri, Wine, Green 35.00
Mitered Bars, Cake Stand, Amber 75.00
Mitered Bars, Tumbler 20.00
    MITERED DIAMOND POINT, see Mitered Bars
Mitered Diamond, Cake Stand, Amber, Square, 10 In. 85.00
Mitered Diamond, Condiment Set, Glass Stand, 5 Piece 65.00
Mitered Diamond, Salt & Pepper, Glass Stand 45.00
Mitered Diamond, Tumbler, Amber .... 25.00 To 26.00
Mitered Diamond, Tumbler, Blue 32.00

Mitered Diamond, Water Set, Blue, 6 Piece 175.00
Mitered Diamond, Wine, Amber 45.00
Mitered Prisms, Goblet .... 18.00 To 25.00
Monkey, Mug, Amethyst 75.00
Monkey, Spooner 85.00
Moon & Star, Celery .... 38.00 To 45.00
Moon & Star, Compote, Open, 6 1/2 In. 28.00
Moon & Star, Compote, 8 1/4 In. 42.00
Moon & Star, Creamer, Footed, Reeded Handle 66.00
Moon & Star, Dish, Relish 21.50
Moon & Star, Salt, Set Of 6 .... 50.00
Moon & Star, Tumbler 15.00
    MOON & STORK, see Ostrich Looking At The Moon
Mormon Temple, Bread Plate 325.00
Morning Glory, Eggcup 175.00
Morning Glory, Wine, Flint 150.00
Nail, Cake Stand, 9 In. 55.00
Nail, Pitcher, Water, Applied Handle 55.00
Nail, Tumbler, Ruby Stained 45.00
Nailhead, Cake Stand, 9 1/2 In. .... 18.00 To 30.00
Nailhead, Creamer 15.00
Nailhead, Creamer, Footed 35.00
Nailhead, Goblet 37.00
Nailhead, Plate, Square, 7 In. 15.00
Nailhead, Plate, 9 In. .... 12.00 To 14.00
Nailhead, Sugar, Creamer, & Spooner, Covered 75.00
Nailhead, Table Set, 4 Piece 95.00
Near Cut, Tumbler, Green 28.00
    NEBRASKA, see Bismarc Star
Nellie Bly, Tray 185.00
Nestor, Creamer, Gold Trim, Blue 28.00
Nestor, Wine, Enameled, Blue 25.00
Nestor, Wine, Enameled, Green 35.00
Nevada, Biscuit Jar 38.00
New England Centennial, Goblet 67.50
New England Flute, Goblet, Flint 20.00
New England Flute, Wine, Flint 20.00
New England Pineapple, Eggcup 42.00
New England Pineapple, Goblet 65.00
New England Pineapple, Goblet, Flint 35.00
New England Pineapple, Spooner, Flint 45.00
New England Pineapple, Sugar, Covered, Flint 95.00
New England Pineapple, Tumbler, Water 85.00
New England Pineapple, Vase, Spill 58.00
New England Pineapple, Wine 35.00
New England Pineapple, Wine, Flint 85.00
New England, Goblet, Windmill & Stork 60.00
New Hampshire, Cruet, Gold Trim 30.00
New Hampshire, Dish, Relish 12.00
New Hampshire, Goblet 22.00
New Hampshire, Mug, Pink Stain 45.00
New Hampshire, Spooner, Pink Stain 40.00
New Hampshire, Sugar, Open 18.00
New Hampshire, Sugar, Pink Stain 26.50
New Hampshire, Toothpick 25.00
New Hampshire, Tray, Pin, Souvenir, Green, Oval, 4 In. 30.00
New Hampshire, Tray, Pin, Souvenir, White Mountain, N.H., Oval 24.00
New Hampshire, Tumbler 17.00
New Hampshire, Wine 15.00
New Hampshire, Wine, Gold Trim .... 18.50 To 20.00
New Jersey, Bowl, 9 In. 18.00
New Jersey, Creamer, Gold Trim 30.00
New Jersey, Dish, Pickle 13.50

New Jersey, Goblet 28.00
New Jersey, Goblet, Gold Trim .... 25.00 To 32.50
New Jersey, Pitcher, Water 58.00
New Jersey, Pitcher, Water, Gold .... 57.00 To 58.00
New Jersey, Plate, 11 1/2 In. 30.00
New Jersey, Spooner 23.00
New Jersey, Sugar, Covered 25.00
New Jersey, Wine, Gold Trim 30.00
New York, Berry Bowl 14.50
Niagara Falls, Platter, 11 X 16 In. 125.00
Nicotiana, Goblet, Frosted 12.00
Nursery Rhymes, Bowl, Punch, Child's, 2 Cups 125.00
Nursery Rhymes, Butter, Child's, Covered 75.00
Nursery Rhymes, Creamer, Child's 52.00
Nursery Rhymes, Pitcher, Water, Child's 60.00
Nursery Rhymes, Plate, Child's, Little Bopeep 25.00
Nursery Rhymes, Spooner, Child's 52.00
Nursery Rhymes, Table Set, Child's, 4 Piece 175.00
O'Hara Diamond, Syrup, Original Lid 45.00
Oak Leaf Band, Tumbler 30.00
Oak Leaves, Goblet 22.00
Oak Leaves, Goblet, Gold Trim 19.00
Oaken Bucket, Creamer, 1880 .... 35.00
Oaken Bucket, Pitcher, Water .... 50.00 To 85.00
Oaken Bucket, Pitcher, Water, Blue 95.00
Oaken Bucket, Sugar, Amber 22.50
Oaken Bucket, Sugar, Covered .... 20.00 To 35.00
Oaken Bucket, Toothpick, Wooden Pail 40.00
    ONE HUNDRED ONE, see One-O-One
One-O-One, Creamer .... 30.00 To 38.50
One-O-One, Goblet 36.00
    ONE-THOUSAND EYE, see Thousand Eye
Open Plaid, Goblet 15.00
Open Rose, Eggcup .... 15.00 To 21.00
Open Rose, Goblet .... 16.00 To 27.00
Open Rose, Spooner 26.00
    OREGON, see also Beaded Loop
Oregon, Dish, Relish 20.00
Oregon, Tumbler, Ruby Stain 35.00
Oriental, Celery 35.00
Oriental, Sauce, Footed 8.00
    ORION, see Cathedral
Ostrich Looking At The Moon, Goblet 50.00
    OVAL LOOP, see Question Mark
Oval Miter, Goblet, Flint 30.00
Oval Miter, Salt, Footed, Flint 32.00
Oval Miter, Spooner 36.50
Oval Star, Butter, Child's, Covered 30.00
Oval Star, Creamer, Child's, 3 In. 20.00
Oval Star, Sugar, Child's 25.00
Oval Star, Table Set, Child's, 3 Piece 65.00
    OWL, see Bull's-Eye with Diamond Point
    OWL & FAN, see Parrot & Fan
Owl & Possum, Goblet 45.00
Paisley, Cup, Punch, Purple Eyes 9.50
Paisley, Pitcher 20.00
Paling, Goblet 12.00
Palm Beach, Butter, Vaseline, Opalescent 265.00
Palm Leaf Fan, Compote 15.00
Palm Leaf Fan, Sauce, Footed 8.00
Palm Leaf, Toothpick, Pink 60.00
Palm Stub, Goblet 19.00
Palmette, Compote, High Standard, Covered, 10 In. 75.00

Palmette, Goblet .... 32.50 To 35.00
Palmette, Salt, Master, Footed 20.00
Palmette, Spoon Holder 40.00
Panama, Nappy, Handled 10.00
Panel & Star, Saltshaker, Blue 55.00
Paneled Acorn Band, Creamer, Applied Handle 35.00
Paneled Acorn Band, Goblet 26.50
Paneled Cable, Syrup 60.00
Paneled Cane, Sugar & Creamer, Covered 40.00
Paneled Cherry, Creamer 42.00
Paneled Cherry, Pitcher, Water, Signed 80.00
Paneled Daisy, Celery 38.00
Paneled Daisy, Compote, Covered 42.00
Paneled Dewdrop, Bread Plate 40.00
Paneled Dewdrop, Creamer .... 18.50 To 45.00
Paneled Dewdrop, Goblet 16.00
Paneled Dewdrop, Tumbler 35.00
Paneled Diamond & Flowers, Goblet 20.00
Paneled Diamond Cross, Goblet 16.00
Paneled Diamond Point, Celery, 8 3/4 In. 67.50
Paneled Diamond Point, Goblet 28.00
     PANELED DOGWOOD, see Dogwood
Paneled Fern, Spooner, Flint 30.00
Paneled Flowers, Goblet 21.00
Paneled Forget-Me-Not, Compote, Open, 7 In. 22.00
Paneled Forget-Me-Not, Compote, Open, 7 1/2 In. 30.00
Paneled Forget-Me-Not, Dish, Relish .... 11.00 To 16.50
Paneled Forget-Me-Not, Goblet 30.00
Paneled Forget-Me-Not, Jar, Jam 48.00
Paneled Forget-Me-Not, Pitcher, Milk 45.00
Paneled Forget-Me-Not, Pitcher, Water 65.00
Paneled Forget-Me-Not, Wine 45.00
Paneled Forty-Four, Goblet 27.00
Paneled Grape Band, Goblet 24.00
Paneled Grape Band, Jar, Honey, 3 3/4 In. 7.50
Paneled Grape, Goblet .... 17.00 To 25.00
Paneled Grape, Pitcher 45.00
Paneled Grape, Pitcher, Water, Footed 65.00
Paneled Heather, Creamer, Footed 25.00
Paneled Heather, Goblet 24.00
Paneled Heather, Sugar, Covered, Gold Trim 23.00
Paneled Heather, Tumbler 12.50
Paneled Herringbone, Goblet 15.00
Paneled Herringbone, Tumbler, Green 10.00
Paneled Hexagons, Compote, Jelly, Blue 31.50
Paneled Hobnail, Goblet 30.00
Paneled Holly, Tumbler, Gold Trim, Green 35.00
Paneled Iris, Wine 16.50
Paneled Ivy, Goblet 29.00
Paneled Jewel, Goblet, Amber .... 30.00 To 35.00
Paneled Jewel, Wine, Amber .... 30.00 To 35.00
Paneled Jewels, Goblet .... 12.00 To 22.00
Paneled Julep, Goblet 25.00
Paneled Nightshade, Celery 38.00
Paneled Nightshade, Goblet .... 20.00 To 30.00
Paneled Ovals, Goblet, Flint .... 28.00 To 40.00
Paneled Palm, Wine 12.00
Paneled Sprig, Pitcher, 9 1/2 In. 40.00
     PANELED STAR & BUTTON, see Sedan
     PANELED STIPPLED BOWL, see Stippled Band
Paneled Stippled Scroll, Cruet 20.00
Paneled Strawberry, Berry Set, Gold, Red Berries, 6 Piece 110.00
Paneled Strawberry, Berry Set, Key Band, 6 Piece 125.00
Paneled Strawberry, Goblet 25.00

Paneled Strawberry, Pitcher	45.00
Paneled Strawberry, Tumbler	20.00
Paneled Sunflower, Goblet	18.00
Paneled Sunflower, Pitcher, Water	35.00
Paneled Thistle, Compote, Jelly	18.00
Paneled Thistle, Cruet, Facet Stopper	32.00
Paneled Thistle, Goblet	25.00
Paneled Thistle, Honey, Covered	30.00 To 60.00
Paneled Thistle, Honey, Square, Covered, Signed Bee	67.50
Paneled Thistle, Pitcher, Milk	55.00
Paneled Thistle, Pitcher, Water	45.00
Paneled Thistle, Rose Bowl	35.00
Paneled Thistle, Salt & Pepper	60.00
Paneled Thistle, Toothpick	20.00
Paneled Thumbprint, Toothpick, Gold Trim	15.00
Paneled Thumbprint, Tumbler	12.00
Pansy & Moss Rose, Creamer	17.00
Pansy, Toothpick, Green	38.00
Parrot & Fan, Goblet	25.00 To 41.50
Parrot, Goblet	42.00
Parrot, Wine	35.00
Pathfinder, Goblet	26.00
Pathfinder, Pitcher, Water, Gold Trim	35.00
Pathfinder, Wine	12.00
Pavonia, Goblet	12.00 To 25.00
Pavonia, Goblet, Etched	25.00 To 30.00
Pavonia, Pitcher, Water, Etched	55.00 To 75.00
Pavonia, Tray, Water, 12 1/4 In.Diam.	45.00
Pavonia, Tumbler	30.00
Pavonia, Tumbler, Ruby	25.00
Pavonia, Water Set, Maple Leaf Etching, 7 Piece	125.00 To 145.00
Pavonia, Wine	15.00
Pavonia, Wine, Etched	26.00 To 32.50
Peacock Feather, Bonbon, Footed	29.00
Peacock Feather, Celery	29.50
Peacock Feather, Creamer	24.00
Peacock Feather, Cruet	24.00
Peacock Feather, Cruet, Ball Shape Stopper, Pyramid Shape	28.00
Peacock Feather, Pitcher, Water	65.00
Peacock Feather, Sugar, Covered	38.00
Peacock Feather, Tumbler	35.00
PEACOCK'S EYE, see Peacock Feather	
Pear, Butter, Covered	45.00
Peek-A-Boo, Toothpick, Sapphire Blue	40.00
Peek-A-Boo, Toothpick, Tall	24.00
Peerless, Spooner	23.50
PENNSYLVANIA, see also Balder	
PENNSYLVANIA HAND, see also Pennsylvania	
Pennsylvania Hand, Celery	45.00
Pennsylvania, Butter, Covered	55.00
Pennsylvania, Cracker Jar, Covered	42.00
Pennsylvania, Creamer	19.00 To 27.50
Pennsylvania, Creamer, Individual	20.00 To 21.00
Pennsylvania, Cup, Punch	8.00 To 11.00
Pennsylvania, Dish, Pickle	14.00
Pennsylvania, Dish, Relish	14.00
Pennsylvania, Goblet	19.00 To 22.50
Pennsylvania, Goblet, Gold Trim	18.00 To 30.00
Pennsylvania, Sauce, 4 1/4 In., Set Of 8	40.00
Pennsylvania, Shot Glass, Green	35.00
Pennsylvania, Spooner	24.00 To 25.00
Pennsylvania, Sugar & Creamer, Gold Top	20.00
Pennsylvania, Syrup, Spring Lid	48.00

Paneled Nightshade

Moon & Star

New England Flute

Open Rose

New England Pineapple

Parrot & Fan

Ostrich Looking At The Moon

Paneled Forget-Me-Not

Pennsylvania, Tumbler .... 10.00 To 16.00
Pennsylvania, Tumbler, Gold Trim 18.50
Pennsylvania, Tumbler, Juice 12.00
Pennsylvania, Whiskey 12.50
Pennsylvania, Wine 18.00
Pennsylvania, Wine, Green .... 35.00 To 38.00
Petticoat, Table Set 325.00
Philadelphia Centennial, Goblet 36.00
Picket, Goblet .... 27.00 To 35.00
Picket, Spooner 26.50
Pigs In Corn, Goblet 175.00
    PILLAR & BULL'S-EYE, see Thistle
Pillar, Ale 32.00
Pillared Crystal, Goblet 20.00
Pillow Encircled, Celery 19.50
Pillow Encircled, Pitcher, 1890, 12 1/2 In. 40.00
Pillow Encircled, Spooner, Etched 28.50
Pillow Encircled, Tankard 40.00
    PINAFORE, see Actress
Pineapple & Fan, Bowl, 8 X 3 In. 25.00
Pineapple & Fan, Compote 29.00
Pineapple & Fan, Cruet 30.00
Pineapple & Fan, Cup, Punch 20.00
Pineapple & Fan, Sugar, Open 19.00
Pineapple & Fan, Tumbler 20.00
Pineapple & Fan, Vase, Trumpet, 9 In. 12.00
Pineapple, Bowl, Fruit, Blue, 12 In. 15.00
Pineapple, Salt & Pepper, 1 Pink, 1 Green 65.00
Pineapple, Saltshaker, Blue 65.00
Pineapple, Spooner 39.00
Pinwheel, Butter, Covered 32.00
Pinwheel, Dish, Candy 45.00
Pinwheel, Goblet 15.00
Pioneer, Saltshaker 38.00
Pittsburgh Fan, Goblet 12.00
Pittsburgh Flute, Wine, Flint 45.00
Pittsburgh Tree Of Life, Wine, Blue 35.00
Pittsburgh, Salt Dip, Individual 12.00
Pleasant To Labor For Those We Love, Bread Plate 35.00
Pleat & Panel, Bread Plate .... 30.00 To 35.00
Pleat & Panel, Celery 36.50
Pleat & Panel, Compote, Covered 35.00
Pleat & Panel, Creamer 28.00
Pleat & Panel, Goblet .... 17.00 To 22.00
Pleat & Panel, Pitcher, Water 55.00
Pleat & Panel, Spooner .... 22.00 To 26.50
Pleated Medallion, Cruet 20.00
Pleating, Spooner, Ruby Stain 24.00
Plume & Block, Celery 12.00
Plume & Block, Sauce, Footed 8.00
Plume, Bowl, Scalloped, 8 1/2 In. 12.00
Plume, Butter, Covered .... 47.50 To 79.00
Plume, Cake Stand .... 37.50 To 48.00
Plume, Cake Stand, 10 In. .... 50.00 To 54.00
Plume, Compote .... 37.50 To 52.00
Plume, Goblet .... 26.00 To 35.00
Plume, Sauce 8.00
Plume, Sauce, Acorn Base, Opalescent 115.00
Plume, Spooner 23.50
Plutec, Decanter & 6 Wines 95.00
Pointed Jewel, Goblet .... 17.00 To 38.00
    POINTED PANELED DAISY & BUTTON, see Queen
    POINTED THUMBPRINT, see Almond Thumbprint

Polar Bear, Bread Plate, Clear & Frosted 145.00
Polar Bear, Goblet .... 55.00 To 90.00
Polar Bear, Goblet, Frosted 75.00
Popcorn, Butter, Covered 55.00
Popcorn, Cake Stand, 11 In. 65.00
Popcorn, Goblet, Handled 50.00
Popcorn, Pitcher, Milk 75.00
Popcorn, Sugar, Covered 45.00
Popcorn, Wine 47.50
    PORTLAND WITH DIAMOND POINT BAND, see Galloway; Virginia
Portland, Creamer, Gold Trim, Individual .... 9.00 To 14.50
Portland, Cruet, Stopper 40.00
Portland, Goblet .... 18.00 To 31.00
Portland, Pitcher, Water, Child's 17.00
Portland, Salt & Pepper 26.00
Portland, Salt & Pepper, Gold Trim 35.00
Portland, Spooner 17.00
Portland, Sugar, Covered 35.00
Portland, Toothpick .... 16.00 To 22.00
Portland, Tumbler .... 18.00 To 20.00
Post, Celery, Frosted 29.00
Post, Goblet 42.00
    POTTED PLANT, see Flower Pot
Powder & Shot, Spooner .... 22.00 To 35.00
Powder & Shot, Sugar, Open, Flint 32.00
    PRAYER RUG, see Horseshoe
Pressed Diamond, Butter, Covered, Vaseline 90.00
Pressed Diamond, Cake Stand 30.00
Pressed Diamond, Compote, Scalloped, Open, 8 3/4 In. 35.00
Pressed Diamond, Creamer, Amber 45.00
Pressed Diamond, Pickle Castor, C.1850, 4 1/4 X 3 1/4 In. 32.50
Pressed Diamond, Saltshaker, Amber, Pair 30.00
Pressed Diamond, Spooner, Vaseline 45.00
Pressed Diamond, Sugar, Covered, Amber 55.00
Pressed Leaf With Chain, Goblet 15.00
Pressed Leaf, Goblet .... 15.00 To 22.50
Primrose, Celery 18.00
Primrose, Compote, Footed, 6 3/4 In. 25.00
Primrose, Creamer, Amber 29.00
Primrose, Dish, Pickle 18.00
Primrose, Pitcher, Milk, Amber 38.00
Primrose, Plate, Amber, 6 In. 16.50
Primrose, Plate, Amber, 7 In. 15.00
Primrose, Plate, Toddy, Blue 22.00
Primrose, Plate, Toddy, 4 1/2 In. 12.00
Primrose, Wine, Amber 34.00
Prince Albert, Pitcher, 8 1/2 In. 38.00
    PRINCESS FEATHER, see also Lacy Medallion
Princess Feather, Butter, Covered 50.00
Princess Feather, Celery 45.00
Princess Feather, Creamer 50.00
Princess Feather, Goblet .... 20.00 To 37.50
Princess Feather, Spooner .... 24.00 To 35.00
Princess Feather, Sugar, Covered 45.00
Printed Hobnail, Tumbler 18.00
Priscilla, Bowl, 9 3/4 X 2 1/8 In. 22.00
Priscilla, Butter, Covered 45.00
Priscilla, Cake Stand, 9 1/2 X 5 1/2 In. * 50.00 To 60.00
Priscilla, Cake Stand, 10 In. 45.00
Priscilla, Cake Stand, 11 X 6 1/2 In. 65.00
Priscilla, Compote, Covered, 9 X 6 In. .... 55.00 To 65.00
Priscilla, Compote, Flared, Open, 8 3/4 X 9 3/4 In. 60.00
Priscilla, Compote, Jelly, Covered .... 45.00 To 50.00

Priscilla, Compote, Open, High Standard, 8 1/2 In. 55.00
Priscilla, Compote, Straight, Open, 8 X 9 In. .... 32.00 To 40.00
Priscilla, Dish, Relish, Double, 7 1/4 X 4 7/8 In. 20.00
Priscilla, Dish, 2 1/2 X 10 5/8 In. 45.00
Priscilla, Dish, 9 1/8 In. .... 32.00 To 40.00
Priscilla, Donut Stand, 5 3/4 X 4 1/4 In. 45.00
Priscilla, Donut Stand, 9 X 5 3/4 In. .... 50.00 To 60.00
Priscilla, Goblet 24.00
Priscilla, Nappy, Handled 5.00
Priscilla, Pitcher 75.00
Priscilla, Plate, 10 3/4 In. 18.00
Priscilla, Table Set, 4 Piece 185.00
Prism & Broken Column, Bowl, Metal Rim, 8 X 3 In. 18.00
Prism & Clear Panels, Goblet 18.00
Prism & Clear Panels, Wine 14.00
Prism & Daisy Bar, Goblet, Blue 25.00
Prism & Diamond, Compote, Footed, Flint, 8 X 5 In. 48.00
Prism & Flattened Sawtooth, Bread Plate, Motto 55.00
Prism & Flute, Goblet 17.00
Prism & Flute, Goblet, Knob Stem 24.00
Prism & Flute, Wine, Large 16.00
Prism Column, Sauce 8.00
Prism With Diamond Points, Goblet 45.00
Prize, Cup, Punch 14.00
Psyche & Cupid, Celery 45.00
Psyche & Cupid, Creamer 25.00
Psyche & Cupid, Goblet 39.00
Psyche & Cupid, Pitcher, Water 67.50
Psyche & Cupid, Sugar 30.00
Quaker Lady, Goblet .... 20.00 To 22.00
Quantico, Sugar Shaker, Amber 32.50
       QUEEN ANNE, see Viking
Queen, Compote, Open, Low 32.00
Queen, Goblet .... 20.00 To 29.50
Queen, Goblet, Amber .... 29.50 To 32.00
Queen, Goblet, Green 39.00
Queen, Spooner, Amber 20.00
Queen's Necklace, Bottle, Perfume 36.00
Queen's Necklace, Vase, 8 3/4 In. 40.00
Question Mark, Celery 26.00
Racing Deer, Pitcher, Water 145.00
Radiant, Goblet 19.00
Radiant, Pitcher, Water 38.75
Rainbow, Decanter, Wine, Fitted Stopper 24.00
Raindrop, Saucer, Blue 10.00
Ramsay, Grape, Berry Bowl 30.00
Raspberry & Grape, Creamer 45.00
Ray, Creamer 22.00
Rayed Flower, Tumbler 12.00
Reardon, Goblet, Etched 18.00
       RECESSED OVALS WITH BLOCK BAND, see Recessed Ovals
Recessed Ovals, Goblet 18.00
Red Block, Goblet 48.00
Red Block, Spooner 38.00
Red Block, Spooner, Handled 35.00
Red Block, Wine 32.00
Reeding, Cordial 12.00
       REGAL, see Paneled Forget-Me-Not
Regal Block, Wine, Gold Trim .... 18.50 To 21.00
       REGENT, see Leaf Medallion
Regina, Wine 16.50
Reticulated Cord, Pitcher, Water, Amber 60.00
Reverse Torpedo, Berry Bowl 18.00

Reverse Torpedo, Butter, Covered, Square 92.00
Reverse Torpedo, Cake Stand, 10 In. .... 62.00 To 75.00
Reverse Torpedo, Compote, Ruffled Top 65.00
Reverse Torpedo, Compote, 8 1/2 In. .... 47.00 To 50.00
Reverse Torpedo, Compote, 10 X 6 1/2 In. 79.50
Reverse Torpedo, Saltshaker 45.00
Reverse Torpedo, Saltshaker, Original Lid 24.00
Reverse Torpedo, Sauce 21.50
Reverse Torpedo, Sugar, Covered 85.00
Reverse Torpedo, Tumbler .... 22.50 To 30.00
Reverse 44, Creamer, Gold Floral 20.00
Reverse 44, Cup, Punch, Silver Floral 60.00
Reverse 44, Dish, Relish, Silver Trim, 5 X 8 In. 25.00
Reverse 44, Iced Tea, Silver Rim 35.00
Reverse 44, Pitcher, Silver Rim 45.00
Reverse 44, Pitcher, Water 45.00
Reverse 44, Salt, Master, Signed 35.00
Reverse 44, Salt, Silver Plated Cover 20.00
Reverse 44, Sugar Basket 30.00
Reverse 44, Water Set, Pedestal Feet, 7 Piece 210.00
Reverse 44, Water Set, Ruby Pitcher, 5 Stemmed Goblets 185.00
Rexford, Goblet 14.00
Ribbed Acorn, Compote, Flint, Low, 8 In. 55.00
Ribbed Bands, Creamer 15.00
Ribbed Forget-Me-Not, Creamer, Individual 18.50
Ribbed Forget-Me-Not, Cup 20.00
Ribbed Forget-Me-Not, Mustard 15.00
Ribbed Grape, Creamer, Flint 120.00
Ribbed Grape, Spooner, Flint 29.50
Ribbed Ivy, Compote, High Standard, Rope Top, 7 1/2 In. 88.00
Ribbed Ivy, Compote, Scalloped Top, 8 In. 78.00
Ribbed Ivy, Eggcup, Flint 30.00
Ribbed Ivy, Goblet 40.00
Ribbed Ivy, Goblet, Flint 35.00
Ribbed Ivy, Spooner 45.00
Ribbed Ivy, Tumbler 75.00
Ribbed Ivy, Tumbler, Flint 75.00
Ribbed Ivy, Whiskey 68.00
Ribbed Ivy, Wine, Flint 90.00
Ribbed Ivy, Wine, Rayed Base, Flint 45.00
    RIBBED LEAF, see Bellflower
Ribbed Leaves, Mug, Child's 20.00
    RIBBED OPAL, see Beatty Rib
Ribbed Palm, Celery, Flint 55.00
Ribbed Palm, Creamer, Flint 110.00
Ribbed Palm, Eggcup 20.00
Ribbed Palm, Eggcup, Flint 28.00
Ribbed Palm, Goblet 38.00
Ribbed Palm, Goblet, Flint 35.00
Ribbed Palm, Plate 20.00
Ribbed Palm, Tumbler 110.00
Ribbed Palm, Wine 20.00
    RIBBED PINEAPPLE, see Prism & Flattened Sawtooth
Ribbon Candy, Bowl, 8 In. 22.50
Ribbon Candy, Butter, Footed, Covered 70.00
Ribbon Candy, Cake Stand, Child's, Green 45.00
Ribbon Candy, Compote, Covered, Footed, Bryce, 7 X 6 1/4 In. 35.00
Ribbon Candy, Creamer .... 18.00 To 21.50
Ribbon Candy, Goblet 25.00
Ribbon Candy, Plate, 10 1/2 In. 10.00
Ribbon Candy, Spooner .... 18.00 To 22.50
Ribbon Candy, Tumbler 20.00
Ribbon Candy, Wine 27.50

Ribbon, Butter, Covered, Square 26.50
Ribbon, Cake Stand, 8 1/2 In. 15.00
Ribbon, Cake Stand, 9 1/2 In. 22.00
Ribbon, Celery 24.50
Ribbon, Compote, Covered, 6 1/2 In. 30.00
Ribbon, Compote, Covered, 8 1/4 In. .... 40.00 To 50.00
Ribbon, Compote, Open, 7 In. 22.00
Ribbon, Goblet 28.00
Ribbon, Pitcher, Water, Quart 36.50
Ribbon, Spooner 30.00
Ribbon, Table Set, 4 Piece 110.00
Richmond, Pitcher, Water, Etched 25.00
Rising Sun, Goblet, Green 19.50
Roanoke Star, Pitcher, Water, 9 1/2 In. 48.00
Roanoke, Spooner 20.00
Robin Hood, Sugar, Covered 35.00
    ROCHELLE, see Princess Feather
Rock Of Ages, Bread Plate 60.00
Rock Of Ages, Bread Plate, Milk Glass Center 135.00
Rock Of Ages, Mug 130.00
Roman Key With Ribs, Goblet, Frosted 38.50
Roman Key, Compote, Opalescent, Flint, 4 1/4 In. 90.00
Roman Key, Creamer, Applied Handle 37.00
Roman Key, Creamer, Frosted, Flint 65.00
Roman Key, Goblet .... 32.00 To 50.00
Roman Key, Goblet, Flint 28.00
Roman Key, Goblet, Frosted, Flint 40.00
Roman Key, Mustard 24.00
Roman Key, Wine, Flint 55.00
Roman Rosette, Bread Plate 27.00
Roman Rosette, Compote, Jelly .... 12.00 To 28.00
Roman Rosette, Creamer .... 25.00 To 40.00
Roman Rosette, Pitcher, Milk 35.00
Roman Rosette, Pitcher, Milk, Footed 70.00
Roman Rosette, Plate, 7 1/2 In. 18.00
Roman Rosette, Sauce .... 6.00 To 9.00
Roman Rosette, Sauce, Opalescent 95.00
Roman Rosette, Spooner 22.00
Roman Rosette, Tumbler 55.00
Romeo, Goblet 17.00
Romeo, Spooner 16.00
Roosevelt Teddy Bears, Bread Plate, Clear & Frosted 95.00
Rooster, Creamer, Child's, Clear 95.00
Rope & Ribs, Butter, Covered, Blue 55.00
Rope & Thumbprint, Compote, Amber 35.00
Rope & Thumbprint, Syrup, Amber 90.00
Rope Bands, Cake Stand, 10 In. 24.00
Rope Bands, Sugar, Covered 28.00
Rope Bands, Wine 19.00
Rose Band, Wine 15.00
Rose In Snow, Bottle, Bitters, Original Stopper 55.00
Rose In Snow, Butter, Round 35.00
Rose In Snow, Cake Stand 80.00
Rose In Snow, Compote, Covered, 7 X 8 In. 60.00
Rose In Snow, Compote, Covered, 9 X 8 In. 45.00
Rose In Snow, Compote, 5 1/2 X 4 3/4 In. 20.00
Rose In Snow, Creamer .... 28.00 To 42.00
Rose In Snow, Creamer, Amethyst 45.00
Rose In Snow, Dish, Oval 16.00
Rose In Snow, Dish, Relish, 8 X 5 1/4 In. .... 20.00 To 22.50
Rose In Snow, Goblet .... 22.00 To 52.00
Rose In Snow, Goblet, Amber .... 30.00 To 50.00
Rose In Snow, Mug, In Fond Remembrance .... 15.00 To 16.00

Pennsylvania

Pleat & Panel

Pressed Leaf

Princess Feather

Primrose

Roman Rosette

Rose In Snow

Rose In Snow, Pitcher, Water .... 45.00 To 85.00
Rose In Snow, Plate, Handled, 9 1/2 In. .... 25.00 To 30.00
Rose In Snow, Plate, 5 In. 35.00
Rose In Snow, Plate, 7 In. 15.00
Rose In Snow, Plate, 9 1/2 In. 30.00
Rose In Snow, Sauce .... 5.00 To 10.00
Rose In Snow, Spooner .... 25.00 To 35.00
Rose In Snow, Sugar & Creamer, Open, Square 49.00
Rose In Snow, Sugar, Covered 45.00
Rose In Snow, Tumbler, Applied Handle 38.00
Rose Leaves, Goblet 18.00
Rose Of Sharon, Goblet 18.00
Rose Point Band, Bowl, Footed, 9 In. 16.00
Rose Point Band, Cake Stand, 9 In. 35.00
Rose Point Band, Creamer 16.00
Rose Point Band, Pitcher 45.00
Rose Point Band, Sugar, Covered, Footed, Small 25.00
Rose Point Band, Tumbler 19.00
Rose Point Band, Wine 20.00
Rose Point Band, Wine, Gold Trim, Purple Eyes 28.00
Rose Sprig, Celery 36.00
Rose Sprig, Goblet 26.00
Rose Sprig, Pitcher, Canary 65.00
Rose Sprig, Salt, Amber, Dated 35.00
Rose Sprig, Tumbler, Amber 27.00
Rose, Spooner 18.50
  ROSETTE MEDALLION, see Feather Duster
Rosette With Palms, Cake Stand, 9 1/4 In. 28.00
Rosette With Palms, Compote, Clear, Open, 8 1/4 X 6 In. 19.00
Rosette With Palms, Goblet .... 22.00 To 25.00
Rosette With Palms, Pitcher, Water 50.00
Rosette With Palms, Wine 18.00
Rosette With Pinwheels, Creamer 16.00
Rosette, Bread Plate 20.00
Rosette, Compote 16.00
Rosette, Compote, Jelly .... 12.00 To 14.50
Rosette, Compote, 9 In. 14.00
Rosette, Dish, Relish 13.50
Rosette, Goblet .... 18.50 To 27.00
Rosette, Pitcher 30.00
Rosette, Plate, Handles, 9 1/4 In. 15.00
Royal Ivy, Cruet, Frosted, Clear 98.00
Royal Ivy, Pickle Castor, Frosted 260.00
Royal Ivy, Rose Bowl, Frosted 135.00
Royal Ivy, Rose Bowl, Frosted, 5 X 4 In. 65.00
Royal Ivy, Saltshaker, Clear To Cranberry, Pair 65.00
Royal Ivy, Spooner, Cranberry, Northwood 100.00
Royal Ivy, Sugar, Covered, Frosted Cranberry To Clear 118.00
Royal Ivy, Syrup, Cranberry To Clear 265.00
Royal Ivy, Toothpick 55.00
Royal Ivy, Toothpick, Cranberry To Clear 65.00
Royal Ivy, Toothpick, Frosted Cranberry To Clear 110.00
Royal Lady, Creamer 25.00
Royal Oak, Butter, Frosted Cranberry To Clear, Covered 195.00
Royal Oak, Salt & Pepper, Original Tops, Frosted, Square Bases 135.00
Royal Oak, Sugar, Cranberry, Covered 100.00
Royal Oak, Toothpick, Cranberry To Clear 90.00
Royal, Wine 12.00
  RUBY ROSETTE, see Pillow Encircled
  RUBY THUMBPRINT, see also King's Crown
Ruby Thumbprint, Creamer, Individual 27.50
Ruffled Eye, Pitcher, Water, Green 95.00
S Repeat, Cruet, Clear Stopper, Amethyst 75.00

S Repeat, Cup, Punch, Gold Trim, Apple Green 18.00
S Repeat, Goblet, Apple Green 75.00
S Repeat, Saltshaker, Amethyst, Gold, Pair 35.00
S Repeat, Toothpick, Rayed Bottom 20.00
S Repeat, Tray, Condiment, Footed, Amethyst, Gold 30.00
S Repeat, Wine, Blue & Gold 35.00
SANDWICH LOOP, see Hairpin
Sandwich Plume, Bowl, 9 In. 35.00
Sandwich Star, Vase, Spill 40.00
Sawtooth & Star, Syrup 35.00
SAWTOOTH BAND, see Amazon
Sawtooth Circle, Salt, Master, Flint 24.00
SAWTOOTH WITH PANELS, see Hinoto
Sawtooth, Butter, Covered .... 42.00 To 80.00
Sawtooth, Butter, Covered, Child's 45.00
Sawtooth, Celery .... 25.00 To 82.00
Sawtooth, Celery, Knob Stem 42.00
Sawtooth, Compote, Covered, Flint, 14 X 9 In. 175.00
Sawtooth, Compote, Deep, 5 1/2 X 7 1/2 In. 38.00
Sawtooth, Compote, Flint, Covered, 8 In. 85.00
Sawtooth, Compote, Shallow, 6 3/4 X 10 In. 50.00
Sawtooth, Compote, 8 X 8 In. 35.00
Sawtooth, Creamer, Applied Handle, Bulbous, 6 1/2 In. 75.00
Sawtooth, Creamer, Molded Handle, 6 1/4 In. 25.00
Sawtooth, Eggcup 12.00
Sawtooth, Goblet, Knob Stem, 1870s 35.00
Sawtooth, Goblet, 5 5/8 In. 48.00
Sawtooth, Goblet, 6 3/8 In. 25.00
Sawtooth, Plate, Flint, 6 1/2 In. 18.00
Sawtooth, Salt & Pepper, Bulbous, Blue 30.00
Sawtooth, Salt, Master 15.00
Sawtooth, Spooner, Flint, Small 45.00
Sawtooth, Sugar, Child's .... 25.00 To 45.00
Sawtooth, Sugar, Covered 50.00
Sawtooth, Sugar, Covered, White, Flint, Opaque .... 25.00 To 45.00
Sawtooth, Sugar, Open, Flint 25.00
Sawtooth, Table Set, Child's, 4 Piece 100.00
Sawtooth, Vase, Spill 46.50
Sawtooth, Wine, Flint 30.00
Sawtooth, Wine, Knob Stem, 4 1/2 In. 18.00
Sawtoothed Honeycomb, Pitcher, Cider 39.50
Saxon, Goblet, Etched, Set Of 6 .... 79.50
Scalloped Diamond Point, Goblet 28.00
Scalloped Panel, Toothpick 35.00
Scalloped Tape, Bread Plate 35.00
Scalloped Tape, Dish, Relish 7.50
Scalloped Tape, Sauce .... 18.00 To 19.00
Scalloped Tape, Sauce, Footed 10.00
Scalloped Tape, Vase, Spill, 2-Row Double-Ringed Punty 60.00
Scalloped Tape, Wine .... 9.00 To 16.00
Scroll With Acanthus, Butter, Covered, Blue 95.00
Scroll With Acanthus, Compote, Blue Opalescent 25.00
Scroll With Cane Band, Cruet, Matching Stopper 25.00
Scroll With Cane Band, Toothpick 25.00
Scroll With Cane Band, Toothpick, Amber 45.00
Scroll With Flowers, Cake Plate, Handled 22.00
Scroll With Flowers, Creamer 40.00
Scroll With Flowers, Sauce, Footed 25.00
Scroll With Flowers, Sauce, 2-Handled 9.00
Scroll With Flowers, Spooner 24.00
Scroll With Flowers, Table Set, 4 Piece 115.00
Scroll With Flowers, Wine, Amber .... 35.00 To 40.00
Scroll, Goblet .... 18.00 To 23.00

Scroll, Sauce 18.00
Scroll, Spooner 20.00
Scroll, Wine 14.00
Sedan, Creamer 21.00
Sedan, Wine 18.00
Seed Pod, Celery, Gold Trim, Green 45.00
Seed Pod, Table Set, Green 385.00
Seed Pod, Vase, Green 145.00
Seneca Loop, Compote, Scalloped, Flint, 9 In. 24.00
Seneca Loop, Goblet, Flint 35.00
Seneca Loop, Spooner, Flint 28.00
Seneca Loop, Syrup, Applied Handle, Pewter Lid, Dated 1870 .... 95.00
Serrated Prism, Pitcher, Gold Flashing, 1880s 50.00
SHEAF & DIAMOND, see Fickle Block
Sheaf Of Wheat, Bread Plate, Oval 55.00
Sheaf Of Wheat, Decanter, Flutes & Panels, C.1830, 9 1/2 In. 195.00
Sheaf Of Wheat, Pitcher, Water 45.00
Shell & Jewel, Dish, Relish 15.00
Shell & Jewel, Pitcher .... 25.00 To 35.00
Shell & Jewel, Pitcher, Portland Glass, 1864-73 .... 65.00
Shell & Jewel, Pitcher, Water .... 30.00 To 32.00
Shell & Jewel, Pitcher, Water, Blue 95.00
Shell & Jewel, Tumbler .... 12.50 To 20.00
Shell & Jewel, Tumbler, Green 45.00
Shell & Jewel, Water Set, Amber, 7 Piece 250.00
Shell & Jewel, Water Set, 5 Piece 150.00
Shell & Tassel, Berry Bowl, Footed, Square, 4 In. 16.00
Shell & Tassel, Bowl, Footed, Oval, 12 In. 75.00
Shell & Tassel, Bowl, Oval, Amber, 9 In. 50.00
Shell & Tassel, Bowl, Oval, Amber, 10 In. 110.00
Shell & Tassel, Bowl, Oval, 10 In. 27.00
Shell & Tassel, Bowl, Oval, 11 1/2 In. .... 48.50 To 54.50
Shell & Tassel, Bowl, 12 X 6 1/2 In. .... 42.00 To 55.00
Shell & Tassel, Cake Stand 90.00
Shell & Tassel, Celery, Round 45.00
Shell & Tassel, Creamer, Square 55.00
Shell & Tassel, Goblet 35.00
Shell & Tassel, Pitcher, Water, Square 125.00
Shell & Tassel, Platter, Oval, 12 In. 58.00
Shell & Tassel, Sauce, Footed, Square 9.00
Shell & Tassel, Sugar, Open 25.00
Shell & Tassel, Tray, 11 3/4 X 8 1/4 In. 45.00
Shell, Sauce, Footed, Green Opalescent, 4 In. 25.00
Sheraton, Bread Tray, Blue 25.00
Sheraton, Celery, 8 In. 20.00
Sheraton, Compote, Covered, 8 In. 35.00
Sheraton, Compote, Open, Amber, 7 In. 25.00
Sheraton, Compote, 6 3/4 X 5 1/4 In. 20.00
Sheraton, Creamer .... 18.00 To 22.50
Sheraton, Creamer, Amber 32.00
Sheraton, Creamer, Blue 38.00
Sheraton, Dish, Pickle, Amber, 8 3/4 In. 16.00
Sheraton, Dish, Relish, Octagonal, Amber, 8 3/4 X 4 1/4 In. 18.00
Sheraton, Goblet 17.00
Sheraton, Pitcher, Milk, Amber 40.00
Sheraton, Pitcher, Milk, Handled 20.00
Sheraton, Pitcher, Water, 9 In. .... 28.00 To 39.50
Sheraton, Plate, Octagonal, 10 In. 20.00
Sheraton, Spooner 16.00
Sheraton, Sugar, Covered, Amber .... 42.00 To 45.00
Sheraton, Wine 15.00
Shields, Spooner .... 22.00 To 28.00
Shimmering Star, Tumbler 20.00

Royal

Rose Sprig

Sandwich Star

Sawtooth

Scroll With Flowers

Shell & Tassel

Short Loops, Goblet	22.00
SHORT TEASEL, see Teasel	
Shoshone, Bowl, Emerald Green, Square	18.00
Shoshone, Cruet, Original Stopper, Greeen	90.00
Shoshone, Toothpick	22.00
Shoshone, Tumbler, Amber	22.00
Shovel, Goblet	14.00
Shrine, Dish, Relish	14.50 To 36.00
Shrine, Goblet	19.00
Shrine, Pitcher, Water	35.00
Shrine, Spooner	15.00
Shuttle, Cup, Punch	7.00
Simple Scroll, Toothpick, Gold Trim	28.00
Single Rose, Salt & Pepper	35.00
Single Rose, Tumbler	19.00
Snail, Banana Stand, Large, Footed, Compact	165.00
Snail, Berry Bowl, Footed, Blue	45.00
Snail, Bowl, Low, 7 In.	22.50 To 28.00
Snail, Butter, Covered	85.00
Snail, Cake Stand, 10 In.	45.00
Snail, Celery	45.00
Snail, Celery, Etched	58.00 To 65.00
Snail, Creamer, Etched	18.00
Snail, Cup, Punch	35.00
Snail, Pitcher, 12 In.	90.00

Shrine

Snail, Rose Bowl, Large	39.00
Snail, Syrup	85.00
Snail, Syrup, Tin Cover	65.00
Snail, Tankard, 7 In.	155.00
Snow Band, Goblet	14.00
SPANISH AMERICAN, see Admiral Dewey	
SPANISH COIN, see Columbian Coin	
Spearpoint & Daisy Band, Goblet	12.00 To 17.00
Spearpoint Band, Creamer, Gold Trim	15.00
Spearpoint Band, Dish, Vegetable, Oval, Etched	10.00
Spearpoint With Daisy Band, Goblet	12.00
Spirea Band, Creamer, Amber	41.50 To 45.00
Spirea Band, Dish, Relish, Oval, Amber	14.00
Spirea Band, Goblet	16.00 To 20.00
Spirea Band, Goblet, Amber	25.00 To 32.50
Spirea Band, Goblet, Blue	30.00
Spirea Band, Pitcher, Blue	55.00
Spirea Band, Tray, Card, Gold Rim	14.00
Split Diamonds, Goblet	15.00
Sprig, Bowl, 9 1/2 In.	27.50
Sprig, Cake Stand, 8 In.	24.00
Sprig, Celery	32.00 To 45.00
Sprig, Compote, Low Pedestal	39.00
Sprig, Goblet	25.00
Sprig, Tumbler, Amber	20.00
Sprig, Wine	28.00 To 38.00
Square Daisy & Button, Goblet	23.00
Square Waffle, Goblet	25.00
Squirrel, Goblet	375.00
Squirrel, Pitcher, 2 Squirrels & Tree Branches, Water	175.00
Star & Circle, Plate, 6 In.	75.00
Star & Oval, Vase, Spill, Scrolled Figure, 6-Sided	58.00
Star & Palm, Goblet	15.00 To 16.00
STAR & PUNTY, see Moon & Star	
Star In Bull's-Eye, Bowl, 8 X 6 In.	12.00
Star In Bull's-Eye, Bowl, 8 1/2 X 6 3/4 In.	20.00
Star In Bull's-Eye, Compote, Open	35.00 To 45.00
Star In Bull's-Eye, Salt, Master	20.00
Star In Diamond, Cordial	15.00
Star In Diamond, Goblet, Amber	22.00
Star In Honeycomb, Wine	15.00
Star Of David, Tumbler	11.00
Star Rosetted, Bread Plate, Good Mother Makes A Happy Home	45.00
Star, Compote, Amber	40.00
Starlight, Syrup	38.50
Stars & Bars, Cruet Set	55.00
Stars & Bars, Cruet Set, Amber	120.00

Stars & Bars, Cruet Set, Blue 140.00
Stars & Bars, Goblet .... 17.00 To 26.00
Stars & Stripes, Cordial 9.00
Stars & Stripes, Finger Bowl, 4 1/2 In. 75.00
Stars & Stripes, Night-Light, Green 28.50
Stars & Stripes, Pitcher, Water 45.00
Stars & Stripes, Sauce, Flat 20.00
Stars & Stripes, Wine 22.00
   STATES, see The States
   STAYMAN, see Tidy
Stippled Band, Butter, Covered 27.00
Stippled Beaded Shield, Wine 25.00
Stippled Chain, Dish, Relish 13.00
Stippled Chain, Goblet .... 14.00 To 23.00
Stippled Chain, Sauce 8.00
Stippled Chain, Spooner .... 20.00 To 22.00
Stippled Cherry, Bowl, 8 In. 19.00
Stippled Cherry, Butter, Covered 35.00
Stippled Cherry, Water Set 55.00
   STIPPLED DAHLIA, see Dahlia
Stippled Daisy, Berry Bowl, Master 25.00
Stippled Daisy, Celery 12.50
Stippled Daisy, Compote, Open, 8 In. 28.00
Stippled Daisy, Sugar, Covered 23.00
Stippled Daisy, Tumbler .... 14.00 To 20.00
Stippled Diamond, Creamer, Child's 20.00
Stippled Double Loop, Tumbler 18.00
Stippled Double Loop, Wine 24.00
Stippled Fans, Bread Plate, Handled 22.00
Stippled Fleur-De-Lis, Water Set, Green, 5 Piece 140.00
Stippled Forget-Me-Not, Goblet 27.00
Stippled Forget-Me-Not, Pitcher, Milk .... 32.00 To 36.00
Stippled Fuchsia, Goblet 19.00
Stippled Grape & Festoon, Creamer 42.00
Stippled Grape & Festoon, Creamer, Clear Leaf 40.00
Stippled Grape & Festoon, Goblet 25.00
Stippled Grape & Festoon, Spooner 25.00
Stippled Grape & Festoon, Sugar 23.00
Stippled Ivy, Goblet 24.00
Stippled Ivy, Sugar 25.00
Stippled Maidenhair Fern, Goblet .... 19.00 To 21.00
Stippled Medallion, Eggcup, Pedestal, Flint 29.00
   STIPPLED PANELED FLOWER, see Maine
Stippled Peppers, Tumbler, Footed 28.00
Stippled Sandbur, Compote, Jelly 16.50
Stippled Sandbur, Spooner 12.00
   STIPPLED SCROLL, see Scroll
   STIPPLED STAR VARIANT, see Stippled Sandbur
Stippled Star Flower, Goblet .... 15.00 To 21.00
Stippled Star, Creamer, 1870 .... 46.00
Stippled Star, Spooner .... 22.00 To 24.00
   STORK LOOKING AT THE MOON, see Ostrich Looking At The Moon
Stork, Bread Plate 27.50
Stork, Bread Plate, Frosted 49.00
Stork, Creamer 45.00
Stork, Goblet 55.00
Straight Banded Worcester, Goblet, Flint 28.00
Strawberry & Currant, Goblet 32.00
Strawberry & Currant, Sauce 9.00
Strawberry, Berry Bowl 10.00
Strawberry, Creamer 48.00
Strawberry, Goblet 28.00
Strawberry, Pitcher, Water 37.00

Strawberry, Spooner 30.00
Strigil, Cake Stand, 10 In. 28.00
Strigil, Cruet, Stopper 24.00
Stylized Flower, Sugar, Covered 27.00
Sugar Pear, Goblet 17.00
Sunbeam, Champagne, Footed, Gold Trim, Green 12.00
Sunbeam, Toothpick, Green 30.00
Sunburst & Diamond, Sugar 45.00
Sunburst Medallion, Goblet 20.00
Sunburst, Pitcher, Flint 95.00
Sunburst, Pitcher, Water 35.00
Sunburst, Plate, 7 In. 15.00
Sunk Honeycomb, Celery, Pedestal, Flint, 10 In. 75.00
Sunk Honeycomb, Cruet 20.00
     SUNKEN BUTTONS, see Mitered Diamond
Sunken Diamond & Lattice, Pitcher 24.00
Sunken Primrose, Compote, Open 30.00
     SUNRISE, see Rising Sun
Sunset, Saltshaker, Blue 65.00
Swag With Bracket, Banana Stand 32.00
Swag With Bracket, Spooner, Green 55.00
Swan & Flowers, Plate, 2-Handled, 8 In. 25.00
Swan With Tree, Creamer 55.00
Swan, Compote, Covered, 8 X 12 In. 110.00
Swan, Creamer .... 35.00 To 55.00
Swan, Spooner .... 23.00 To 40.00
Swan, Sugar 35.00
Sweetheart, Table Set, Child's, 4 Piece 95.00
Swimming Swan, Pitcher, Water .... 150.00 To 185.00
Swimming Swan, Plate 35.00
Swirl & Cable, Creamer 30.00
Swirl, Cruet, Original Stopper 25.00
Swirl, Spittoon, Lady's, Blue 68.00
Swirl, Table Set, Child's, 4 Piece 87.50
Tackle Block, Goblet 25.00
Tacoma, Cruet 22.00
Tandem Bicycle, Celery, 12 In. 20.00
Tandem Bicycle, Goblet .... 15.00 To 30.00
     TAPE MEASURE, see Shields
Tapered Prisms, Goblet 20.00
Tappan, Table Set, Child's, 4 Piece 78.00
Teardrop & Tassel, Berry Set, Blue, 6 Piece 75.00
Teardrop & Tassel, Butter, Covered .... 50.00 To 65.00
Teardrop & Tassel, Creamer 45.00
Teardrop & Tassel, Dish, Relish, Green, 8 1/4 In. 30.00
Teardrop & Tassel, Pitcher, Water 65.00
Teardrop & Tassel, Sauce, Blue .... 16.00 To 25.00
Teardrop & Tassel, Sauce, Flat, 4 1/4 In. .... 9.00 To 12.00
Teardrop & Tassel, Tumbler 35.00
     TEARDROP & THUMBPRINT, see Teardrop
Teardrop Flower, Tumbler, Gold Trim, Blue 38.00
Teardrop, Compote 20.00
Teardrop, Creamer 39.00
Teardrop, Creamer, Large 14.00
Teardrop, Goblet 32.50
Teardrop, Tumbler, Blue 40.00
Teardrop, Wine 16.00
Teardrop, Wine, Etched 32.50
Teasel, Goblet 30.00
Teasel, Goblet, Flint 30.00
Teddy Roosevelt, Teddy Bear Plate, Clear & Frosted 100.00
Tennessee, Bowl, Vegetable, Oval 22.00
Tennessee, Compote, Open 38.00

Tennessee, Toothpick	68.00
Tepee, Toothpick	16.00 To 30.00
Texas Bull's-Eye, Goblet	15.00 To 30.00
Texas Star, Sugar	45.00
Texas Star, Toothpick	25.00
Texas, Creamer	17.50
Texas, Creamer, 1900	45.00
Texas, Creamer, 3 In.	30.00
Texas, Dish, Relish, 5 3/4 X 4 3/4 In.	22.00
Texas, Goblet	25.00 To 45.00
Texas, Sauce, Gold Trim, Footed, 4 3/4 In.	18.00
Texas, Sherbet, Footed	6.00
Texas, Spooner	35.00
Texas, Sugar	6.00
Texas, Sugar & Creamer, Individual	25.00 To 27.50
Texas, Toothpick	18.00
Texas, Toothpick, Gold Trim	30.00
Texas, Wine	40.00 To 45.00
The States, Butter, Covered	65.00
The States, Champagne	16.00
The States, Creamer, Gold Trim	24.50
The States, Dish, Relish, Green	28.00
The States, Goblet	22.50
The States, Goblet, Green	85.00
The States, Salt & Pepper	23.50
The States, Saltshaker	30.00
The States, Sugar & Creamer, Green, Small	80.00
The States, Tumbler, Green	55.00
The States, Wine	12.00 To 20.00
Thistle Shield, Goblet	29.00 To 30.00
Thistle, Compote, Ruffled Top, 6 1/2 In.	30.00
Thistle, Dish, Relish	22.00
Thistle, Goblet	22.00 To 44.00
Thistle, Goblet, Flint	50.00
Thistle, Pitcher, Milk	55.00
Thistle, Tumbler	20.00
Thistle, Tumbler, Footed	45.00
Thistle, Vase, 10 In.	950.00
Thousand Eye, Butter, Covered	45.00
Thousand Eye, Compote, Low Standard, Amber	69.00
Thousand Eye, Compote, Open, Apple Green	32.00
Thousand Eye, Compote, 3-Knob Stem, Apple Green	75.00
Thousand Eye, Compote, 3-Knob Stem, Blue, 8 1/2 In.	65.00
Thousand Eye, Cordial	18.00
Thousand Eye, Cruet, Original Stopper, Amber	65.00
Thousand Eye, Dish, Dessert, 8 In., Set Of 6	135.00
Thousand Eye, Goblet	30.00
Thousand Eye, Goblet, Clear	30.00
Thousand Eye, Goblet, Green	42.00
Thousand Eye, Goblet, Vaseline	42.00
Thousand Eye, Mug, Amber, Handled	49.00
Thousand Eye, Pitcher, Floral, Reed Handle, Amber	55.00
Thousand Eye, Pitcher, Water	72.50
Thousand Eye, Pitcher, Water, Scalloped Base	95.00
Thousand Eye, Plate, 8 In.	40.00
Thousand Eye, Plate, 10 In.	52.00
Thousand Eye, Spooner	20.00
Thousand Eye, Toothpick	28.00
Thousand Eye, Tumbler, Blue	22.00
Thousand Eye, Water Set, Oval Tray, 5 Tumblers, Apple Green	240.00
Three Face, Butter, Covered, Etched	150.00
Three Face, Cake Stand, 9 In.	75.00
Three Face, Celery	65.00 To 110.00

Three Face, Compote, Covered, 6 In. 115.00
Three Face, Compote, Covered, 8 In. 27.50
Three Face, Compote, Open, 9 In. 90.00
Three Face, Compote, 4 In. 60.00
Three Face, Goblet 55.00
Three Face, Salt & Pepper 70.00
Three Face, Saltshaker, Original Pewter Top 37.50
Three Face, Spooner .... 60.00 To 85.00
    THREE GRACES, see Three Face
Three Panel, Berry Bowl 45.00
Three Panel, Berry, Master, Blue 35.00
Three Panel, Bowl, Fruit, Blue, 10 3/4 X 4 In. 65.00
Three Panel, Bowl, Fruit, Vaseline, 10 X 4 In. 50.00
Three Panel, Celery, Amber 28.00
Three Panel, Compote, Footed, Amber, 10 In. 32.00
Three Panel, Compote, Footed, Sapphire Blue, 7 1/2 In. 45.00
Three Panel, Compote, Low 35.00
Three Panel, Creamer 22.00
Three Panel, Creamer, Blue 38.00
Three Panel, Creamer, Vaseline 40.00
Three Panel, Goblet 32.00
Three Panel, Goblet, Amber .... 32.00 To 37.00
Three Panel, Goblet, Blue 40.00
Three Panel, Goblet, Vaseline 35.00
Three Panel, Spooner 20.00
Three Panel, Spooner, Amber 20.00
Three Panel, Sugar, Covered 28.00
Three Panel, Sugar, Covered, Vaseline 68.00
Three Panel, Sugar, Vaseline 35.00
Three Presidents, Bread Plate .... 48.00 To 110.00
    THREE SISTERS, see Three Face
Thumbprint & Diamond, Eggcup, Rabbit On Side 17.50
Thumbprint & Diamond, Goblet 10.00
Thumbprint, Ale, Flint 45.00
Thumbprint, Goblet 52.00
Thumbprint, Goblet, Baluster Stem 52.00
Thumbprint, Pitcher, Amber, Square Mouth 60.00
Thumbprint, Spooner .... 48.50 To 58.00
Thumbprint, Sugar Shaker 26.00
Thumbprint, Toothpick, Ruby 35.00
Thumbprint, Wine, Flint 35.00
Tidy, Spooner 18.50
Tokyo, Sugar & Creamer, Covered, Gold Trim 70.00
Tong, Wine, Flint 45.00
Torpedo, Bowl, 7 In. 26.00
Torpedo, Bowl, 9 In. 28.00
Torpedo, Cake Stand, 9 In. 75.00
Torpedo, Cake Stand, 11 X 7 In. 75.00
Torpedo, Celery 45.00
Torpedo, Compote, Covered, 8 In. 75.00
Torpedo, Compote, Covered, 8 X 14 In. 125.00
Torpedo, Compote, Jelly, Covered 49.50
Torpedo, Compote, 8 In. 50.00
Torpedo, Creamer 38.00
Torpedo, Cup, Punch .... 19.00 To 30.00
Torpedo, Decanter, Stopper 60.00
Torpedo, Goblet .... 35.00 To 55.00
Torpedo, Jar, Jam, Metal Cover 45.00
Torpedo, Pitcher, Milk 75.00
Torpedo, Pitcher, Tankard, 10 1/2 In. 85.00
Torpedo, Pitcher, Water .... 55.00 To 135.00
Torpedo, Pitcher, Water, Applied Handle 85.00
Torpedo, Pitcher, Water, Tankard, Small 48.00

Torpedo, Pitcher, Water, 11 1/2 In. .... 110.00 To 125.00
Torpedo, Salt, Master 18.00
Torpedo, Sauce, Flat, 4 1/4 In. .... 18.00 To 20.00
Torpedo, Spooner 35.00
Torpedo, Sugar 28.00
Torpedo, Sugar, Covered 95.00
Torpedo, Syrup 50.00
Torpedo, Syrup, Original Lid 85.00
Torpedo, Tray, Water, Round, 10 In. 45.00
Torpedo, Tumbler .... 15.00 To 30.00
Transcontinental Railroad, Bread Plate 75.00
Tree Of Life With Hand, Pitcher, Milk 60.00
Tree Of Life, Butter Chip, Shell Shape 10.00
Tree Of Life, Celery, Flint 25.00
Tree Of Life, Celery, Frosted Band, Ball Base, 9 In. 40.00
Tree Of Life, Compote, Frosted Stem & Base, 6 X 4 In. 67.00
Tree Of Life, Compote, Frosted Stem & Base, 9 In. 70.00
Tree Of Life, Goblet, Portland 32.00
Tree Of Life, Goblet, Sandwich 32.50
Tree Of Life, Pitcher, Water .... 58.00 To 65.00
Tree Of Life, Portland, Compote, Footed, Signed, 8 1/2 In. 48.00
Tree Of Life, Portland, Compote, Signed, 8 1/2 In. 75.00
Tree Of Life, Portland, Sugar & Creamer, Metal Holder 90.00
Tree Of Life, Saltshaker 25.00
Tree Of Life, Spooner, Flint 35.00
Tree Of Life, Sugar, Covered .... 25.00 To 45.00
Tree Of Life, Tumbler, Footed 22.00
Triangular Prism, Goblet, Flint 22.00
Triple Thumbprints, Celery 20.00
Triple Triangle, Goblet, Ruby 40.00
Tulip & Honeycomb, Table Set, Child's, 4 Piece 95.00
Tulip Petals, Toothpick 26.00
Tulip With Sawtooth, Compote, Covered, Flint, 6 X 9 In. 120.00
Tulip With Sawtooth, Goblet .... 28.00 To 34.00
Tulip With Sawtooth, Goblet, Flint 48.00
Tulip With Sawtooth, Tumbler, Footed 35.00
Tulip With Sawtooth, Tumbler, Footed, Flint 34.00
Tulip, Celery, Flint 35.00
Tulip, Sugar, Green 25.00
Twin Teardrops, Celery 20.00
    TWINKLE STAR, see also Utah
Twinkle Star, Pitcher, Water 35.00
Two Band, Creamer .... 18.00 To 22.00
Two Band, Creamer, Child's 22.00
Two Band, Spooner .... 12.00 To 21.00
Two Panel, Berry Set, Amber, 5 Piece 65.00
Two Panel, Bowl, Oval, Blue 38.00
Two Panel, Bowl, Waste, Blue 31.00
Two Panel, Creamer, Amber 42.50
Two Panel, Goblet 25.00
Two Panel, Goblet, Amber 28.00
Two Panel, Goblet, Blue 22.00
Two Panel, Goblet, Sapphire Blue 55.00
Two Panel, Pitcher, Water, Amber 49.00
Two Panel, Salt 17.50
Two Panel, Salt, Blue 17.50
Two Panel, Salt, Individual, Green 10.00
Two Panel, Sauce 21.00
Two Panel, Tray, Blue 40.00
Two Panel, Tumbler, Amber .... 20.00 To 28.00
Two Panel, Tumbler, Blue 25.00
Two Panel, Water Set, Blue, 7 Piece 265.00
Two Panel, Wine, Amber 38.00

Two Panel, Wine, Blue	35.00
U.S.Coin, Compote, 11 1/2 In.	500.00
U.S.Coin, Sauce, Frosted	75.00
U.S.Coin, Spooner, Dollar	95.00
U.S.Rib, Butter, Covered, Gold Trim, Green	55.00
U.S.Rib, Creamer, Gold Trim, Emerald Green, Square	20.00
U.S.Rib, Toothpick, Gold Trim, Green	33.00
U.S.Thumbprint, Pitcher, Water	35.00
Umbilicated Sawtooth, Cake Stand	12.00
Umbilicated Sawtooth, Decanter	50.00
Umbilicated, Tumbler, Water	75.00
Utah, Compote, Covered	50.00
Valencia Waffle, Bread Plate, Amber	45.00
Valencia Waffle, Compote, Covered, Amber, 7 In.	75.00
Valencia Waffle, Goblet, Amber	35.00
Valencia Waffle, Pitcher, Amber	55.00
Vera, Bowl, Frosted, 5 In.	10.00
Vermont, Berry Set, Green, 6 Piece	50.00
Vermont, Berry, Master, Gold Trim, Green	18.00
Vermont, Creamer, Gold Trim	60.00
Vermont, Creamer, Gold Trim, Green	65.00
Vermont, Pitcher, Green, 4 In.	35.00
Vermont, Spooner	16.00
Vermont, Sugar, Green	65.00
Vermont, Toothpick, Gold Trim, Green	45.00 To 90.00
Vermont, Toothpick, Green	45.00
Vermont, Toothpick, Hand-Painted Flowers	55.00
Vermont, Tumbler, Gold Trim, Green	38.00 To 40.00
Victoria, Bowl, Waste, Frosted	30.00
Victoria, Tumbler, Ruby Stained	55.00
Viking, Butter	55.00
Viking, Compote, Covered	75.00
Viking, Creamer	21.50
Viking, Cup, Toddy	75.00
Viking, Eggcup	40.00
Viking, Pitcher, Water	75.00 To 80.00
Viking, Salt, Master	20.00
Viking, Sauce, Footed	8.00
Viking, Sugar, Covered	50.00
Vine & Beads, Table Set, Child's, 4 Piece	125.00
Virginia Dare, Bread Plate	48.00
VIRGINIA, see also Galloway	
Virginia, Decanter, Water	30.00
Virginia, Plate, 8 In.	12.00
Virginia, Saltshaker, Top	12.00
Virginia, Sugar, Covered	30.00
Waffle & Thumbprint, Goblet, Flint	55.00
Waffle & Thumbprint, Goblet, Knob Stem	40.00 To 55.00

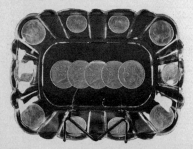

U.S. Coin Frosted

Viking

Squirrel

Strawberry

Three Face

Thistle

Tree Of Life

Thumbprint

Waffle & Thumbprint

Tulip With Sawtooth

Waffle & Thumbprint, Wine 55.00
Waffle & Thumbprint, Wine, Flint .... 45.00 To 50.00
Waffle, Butter, Covered, Flint 125.00
Waffle, Celery, Footed, Flint 35.00
Waffle, Creamer, Flint 155.00
Waffle, Eggcup, Flint 35.00
Warrior, Bread Plate, Signed 145.00
Warrior, Butter, Covered, Signed 195.00
    WASHBOARD, see Adonis
Washington Centennial, Berry Bowl, Small 12.00
Washington Centennial, Bread Plate, Frosted 135.00
Washington Centennial, Bread Plate, George .... 95.00 To 110.00
Washington Centennial, Bread Plate, Hall .... 95.00 To 105.00
Washington Centennial, Butter, Covered 50.00
Washington Centennial, Cake Stand, 8 1/4 In. 50.00
Washington Centennial, Celery 45.00
Washington Centennial, Compote, Covered, 7 X 10 1/2 In. 70.00
Washington Centennial, Compote, Covered, 8 1/4 X 12 In. 105.00
Washington Centennial, Compote, Open .... 25.00 To 38.00
Washington Centennial, Compote, Open, 8 1/4 X 7 1/2 In. 50.00
Washington Centennial, Creamer .... 70.00 To 75.00
Washington Centennial, Dish, Relish 47.00
Washington Centennial, Dish, Relish, Bear Paw Handles, Dated 35.00
Washington Centennial, Eggcup .... 45.00 To 50.00
Washington Centennial, Goblet .... 38.00 To 45.00
Washington Centennial, Pitcher, Water .... 85.00 To 95.00
Washington Centennial, Sauce 15.00
Washington Centennial, Spooner .... 30.00 To 45.00
Washington Centennial, Sugar, Open 25.00
Washington, Celery, Flint 85.00
Washington, Early, Goblet 95.00
Washington, Early, Tumbler 110.00
Washington, Goblet, Flint 72.00
    WATER LILY, see Rose Point Band
Waterford, Champagne, Flint, C.1840 .... 40.00
Waterford, Tobacco Jar, Thumbprint Edge, Covered 38.00
Way Colonial, Wine 37.50
Way's Currant, Goblet 22.00
Wedding Ring, Fruit Stand, Footed 75.00
Wedding Ring, Goblet 48.50
Wedding Ring, Water Set, 1880s, Square Pitcher, 7 Piece 250.00
Wedding Ring, Wine, Flint 50.00
Westmoreland, Carafe, Water 36.00
Westmoreland, Celery .... 14.50 To 26.00
Westmoreland, Cup, Punch 6.00
Westmoreland, Sugar, Covered .... 26.50 To 28.00
Westmoreland, Syrup 65.00
Westmoreland, Vase 15.00
Westward Ho, Bread Plate, C.1870 .... 125.00
Westward Ho, Butter, Covered .... 200.00 To 215.00
Westward Ho, Compote, Covered 75.00
Westward Ho, Compote, Indian Finial, 11 1/2 In. 135.00
Westward Ho, Compote, 5 In. 165.00
Westward Ho, Goblet .... 45.00 To 70.00
Westward Ho, Sauce, Footed, 4 In. .... 25.00 To 30.00
Wheat & Barley, Bowl, Covered 35.00
Wheat & Barley, Cake Plate, Handled, Blue, 11 In. 14.00
Wheat & Barley, Compote, Jelly, Blue 32.50
Wheat & Barley, Creamer, Amber 29.50
Wheat & Barley, Mug .... 45.00 To 68.00
Wheat & Barley, Pitcher, Water, Amber .... 62.00 To 140.00
Wheat & Barley, Salt & Pepper 20.00
Wheat & Barley, Sugar, Cube Square Stem, Covered 25.00

Wedding Ring

Washington Centennial

Wildflower

Westward Ho

Wheat & Barley, Tumbler, Amber	30.00
Whirligig, Butter, Child's, Covered	25.00
Whirligig, Creamer, Child's	25.00 To 45.00
Whirligig, Spooner, Child's, 2 1/4 In.	25.00
Whirligig, Spooner, 2-Handled, 6 In.	35.00
Whirligig, Sugar, Creamer, & Spooner, Child's	50.00
Whirligig, Table Set, Child's, 4 Piece	47.00 To 48.00
Whirligig, Toothpick	18.00 To 30.00
Whitton, Goblet	24.00
Wild Bouquet, Cruet, Blue Opalescent, Stopper	375.00
Wild Rose With Bowknot, Compote, Jelly, Footed	30.00
Wild Rose With Scrolling, Creamer, Green	50.00
Wildflower, Celery	33.00
Wildflower, Celery, Amber	45.00 To 55.00
Wildflower, Compote, Jelly, Covered, High Standard, 5 3/4 In.	35.00
Wildflower, Creamer	15.00
Wildflower, Goblet	25.00
Wildflower, Pitcher, Water	35.00
Wildflower, Plate, Blue	45.00
Wildflower, Platter, Oval, 13 In.	66.00
Wildflower, Saltshaker, Amber	24.00
Wildflower, Saltshaker, Blue	22.00
Wildflower, Saltshaker, Original Top, Blue	45.00
Wildflower, Sauce, Flat, Green	15.00
Wildflower, Spooner	15.00
Wildflower, Spooner, Amber	35.00
Wildflower, Spooner, Blue	30.00
Wildflower, Syrup, Amber, Dated July 15, 1984	185.00
Wildflower, Table Set, Amber, 4 Piece	135.00
Wildflower, Tray, Water, Oval, Amber	90.00

Wildflower, Tumbler .... 26.00 To 29.50
Wildflower, Tumbler, Amber .... 30.00 To 45.00
Wildflower, Tumbler, Blue .... 26.00 To 30.00
Wildflower, Tumbler, Green .... 30.00 To 35.00
Wildflower, Vase, Pink & Blue Matte, 6 1/2 In. 22.00
Willow Oak, Bowl, 7 In. 20.00
Willow Oak, Cake Stand, Amber 60.00
Willow Oak, Compote, Covered, 7 In. 14.00
Willow Oak, Compote, Covered, 10 In. 38.00
Willow Oak, Compote, Open, Amber, 7 1/2 In. 42.00
Willow Oak, Creamer .... 24.00 To 35.00
Willow Oak, Creamer, Blue 45.00
Willow Oak, Goblet 35.00
Willow Oak, Pitcher 75.00
Willow Oak, Pitcher, Milk 65.00
Willow Oak, Pitcher, Water, Deep Amber 85.20
Willow Oak, Plate, Amber, 9 In. 32.00
Willow Oak, Plate, 7 In. 27.50
Willow Oak, Plate, 9 In. 24.00
Willow Oak, Plate, 9 1/2 In. 24.00
Willow Oak, Sauce, Footed 9.00
Willow Oak, Tray, Water 25.00
Willow Oak, Tumbler 30.00
Windflower, Bowl, Oval, 5 1/2 X 8 In. 12.00
Windflower, Goblet 36.50
    WISCONSIN, see Beaded Dewdrop
Wishbone, Creamer .... 21.50 To 26.50
Wishbone, Wine 12.00
Wooden Pail, Creamer, Amethyst 95.00
Wooden Pail, Creamer, Child's 30.00
Wooden Pail, Pitcher, Water, Amber 85.00
Wooden Pail, Spooner, Child's, Blue 18.00
Worcester, Belted, Goblet, Flare Top, Flint 25.00
Worcester, Belted, Goblet, Flint 30.00
Wyoming, Cake Stand 70.00
Wyoming, Pitcher, Water .... 48.00 To 68.00
Wyoming, Pitcher, 9 In. 38.00
X-Ray, Berry Set, Gold Trim, Green, 7 Piece .... 145.00 To 165.00
X-Ray, Butter, Covered, Green 65.00
X-Ray, Pitcher, Green 65.00
X-Ray, Pitcher, Water, Gold Trim, Green 40.00
X-Ray, Sugar, Covered, Gold Trim, Green 36.00
X-Ray, Sugar, Covered, Green 55.00
X-Ray, Toothpick, Gold Trim, Green 60.00
X-Ray, Tumbler, Green 28.00
X-Ray, Water Set, Gold Trim, Green, 6 Piece 195.00
    YALE, see Crowfoot
Yoked Loop, Goblet, Flint .... 18.00 To 20.00
Yoked Loop, Shot Glass, Handled 40.00
Yoked Loop, Tumbler 45.00
York Herringbone, Wine, Etched Top 15.00
Yuma Loop, Goblet 14.00
Yuma Loop, Spooner 20.00
Yuma Loop, Tumbler, Footed 14.00
Zephyr, Syrup, Silver Plated Top, 3 1/2 In. 35.00
Zipper Slash, Berry Bowl, Frosted, Amber Stain, Etched 55.00
Zipper Slash, Toothpick 16.00
Zipper, Celery 18.50
Zipper, Cup, Punch 8.00
Zipper, Goblet .... 15.00 To 21.00
Zipper, Pitcher, Milk, Canary 55.00
Zipper, Spooner .... 18.50 To 24.50
Zipper, Sugar, Blue 30.00

100-LEAVED ROSE, see Hundred Leaved Rose
101, see One-O-One
1,000-EYE, see Thousand Eye

The size of the print is given, not the overall size with frame.
    PRINT, see also Poster; Store, Sign

PRINT, Armstrong, Live Wire	65.00
Baillie, Coronation Of The Virgin, Virgin, Christ, Angels	24.00
Baillie, The Sisters, Women With Parasol, Garden Wall	60.00
Baillie, The Young Mother, Girl Seated, Holding Dog	58.00
Bartlett, Ballston Springs, Oxen, People, Town Street	20.00
Bartlett, Barhydt's Lake, Saratoga	20.00
Bartlett, Caterskill Falls, From Below	18.00
Bartlett, Descent Into The Valley Of Wyoming, Pa.	20.00
Bartlett, Fairmount Gardens, Philadelphia	22.00
Bartlett, Indian Falls, Near Cold Spring, Deer, Lake, Falls	30.00
Bartlett, Sing Sing Prison And Tappan Sea	18.00
Bartlett, Tomb Of Kosciusko, Hudson River	18.00
Bartlett, Valley Of The Connecticut, Hunter Firing On Bird	30.00
Bartlett, Viaduct On Baltimore & Washington Railroad	30.00
Bartlett, Village Of Catskill, Couple, Sheep, Hills	20.00
Bartlett, Wilkesbarre, Canal Along River	20.00
Chandler, Skating In The Moonlight, Signed, Framed	185.00

    PRINT, CURRIER, see Currier
    PRINT, CURRIER & IVES, see Currier & Ives

Gutmann, Cherub & Butterfly At Lily Pool, Framed, 15 X 20 In.	35.00
Gutmann, Cupid, 9 3/4 X 13 In.	18.00
Haskell & Allen, A Brush For The Lead, 2 Racing Sleighs	600.00 To 900.00
Haskell & Allen, Fearnaught Stallions, Pulling Sleigh	895.00 To 950.00
Haskell & Allen, Kingtown, Steamer Approaches Town	85.00
Haskell & Allen, Little Charles, Bust Portrait Of Child & Cat	30.00
Haskell & Allen, Little Emma, Woman, Red Bow On Hat	56.00
Haskell & Allen, Martha, Reeded Walnut Frame, 11 X 15 In.	35.00
Haskell & Allen, Prize Fruit, Grapes, Pears, Apples	65.00
Haskell & Allen, Stag At Bay, Black & White	75.00
Haskell & Allen, The Riverside, Couple, Cattle, Home	75.00 To 85.00
Haskell & Allen, Warming For The Trot, 2 Horses Pulling Sleigh	875.00
Haskell & Allen, Yacht Dauntless, 18 X 22 In.	110.00
Icart, Dame Aux Camelia, Marked, 19 X 23 In.	650.00
Icart, Flamingo Dancer, Smoking Cigarette, Marked, 24 X 16 In.	500.00
Icart, Les Chatons, Pencil Signed, 22 X 25 In.	600.00
Icart, Les Hortensias, Marked, 27 X 24 In.	600.00
Icart, Seminude, Standing, Holding Candlestick, Signed, 21 X 17 In.	750.00

Japanese prints are listed as follows: Print, Japanese, name of artist,
title or description, type, and size. The following terms are used to denote
type: Tate-e is a vertical composition. Yoko-e is a horizontal composition.
The words Aiban, Chuban, Hosoban, Oban, and Koban denote size.
The sizes are 13 x 9 inches, 10 x 7 1/2 inches, 12 x 6 inches,
15 x 10 inches, and 7 x 4 inches respectively.

Japanese, Eishi, Courtesan Hanamurasaki Of Tamaya, Walking Robes	7500.00
Japanese, Eishi, Courtesan Segawa Of Matsubaya, With Kamuro & Shinzo	4200.00
Japanese, Eishi, Courtesans With The Attendants, Triptych	6500.00
Japanese, Eishi, Prince Genji Greeting A Princess	2800.00
Japanese, Eishi, Princess Sotoori	5500.00
Japanese, Eishi, The Courtesan Hanamurasaki	7500.00
Japanese, Eishi, The Courtesan Segawa	4200.00
Japanese, Eishi, Twelve Courtesans, Triptych	6500.00
Japanese, Harunobu, Hair Dressing, Parlour Views	3500.00
Japanese, Harunobu, Kioto Teahouse, Client & Waitress	6500.00
Japanese, Harunobu, Komachi Woodcutter	9500.00
Japanese, Harunobu, Lady Regarding Sleeping Boy	2200.00
Japanese, Hasui, Tokyo Street Scene	1600.00

Japanese, Hiroshige, Ohashi Bridge, Edo Series .... 480.00 To 6500.00
Japanese, Hiroshige, Ommayagashi Sumidagawa, Edo Series 1600.00
Japanese, Hiroshige, Shono, Tokaido Series .... 2600.00 To 4000.00
Japanese, Hokusai, Auezawa Manor From Fuji 6000.00
Japanese, Hokusai, Fuji Above Lightning, Fuji Series 7250.00
Japanese, Hokusai, Sumidagawa Sekiya 2100.00
Japanese, Hokusai, Tama River, Fuji Series 2200.00
Japanese, Hokusai, Umezawa Manor, Fuji Series, Woodblock 6000.00
Japanese, Jacoulet, Le Tresor, Coree, 15 1/2 X 20 In. .... *Illus* 250.00
Japanese, Jacoulet, Parisian Lady, 1934 .... *Illus* 3000.00
Japanese, Jacoulet, Vendeur De Masques, 15 1/2 X 20 In. .... *Illus* 225.00
Japanese, Kirifuri, Waterfall 1100.00
Japanese, Kokusai, Amida Waterfall 6000.00
Japanese, Koryusai, Courtesan Dressing Her Kamuro 3500.00
Japanese, Munakata, Rakan, Judaideshi Series, Dated 1959 .... 6000.00
Japanese, Nagasaki-E, Western Steam & Sail Ship 1700.00
Japanese, Onchi Kochiro, Woman Drying Her Hair 1600.00
Japanese, Shigenaga, Yoshiwara Revelers 8000.00
Japanese, Shinsui, Woman Applying Cosmetics To Her Neck 2000.00
Japanese, Toyokuni, Bijin & Man 2600.00
Japanese, Utamaro II, Two Women 1900.00
Japanese, Utamaro, Bijin & Her Kamora .... 4100.00 To 6000.00
Japanese, Utamaro, Bijin Conversing With The Penitent Oni 4000.00
Japanese, Utamaro, Courtesan 3500.00
Japanese, Utamaro, Courtesans Hinamatsu & Hinatori Of The Chojiya 8500.00
Japanese, Utamaro, Kisegawa Of The Matsubaya 8500.00
Japanese, Utamaro, Parody Of Chushingura, Act VII 2600.00
Japanese, Utamaro, Two Samurai 2000.00
Kellogg, Battle Of Bull's Run, Cannon, Infantry, July 186 .... 60.00 To 68.00
Kellogg, Battle Of Chattanooga, Union Troops Attack Confederates 60.00
Kellogg, Falls Of Niagara, From The Canada Side 100.00
Kellogg, Maj.Genl.George B.McClellan, 1/2 Length In Uniform 25.00
Kellogg, St.Patrick, The Apostle Of Ireland .... 25.00 To 28.00
Legros, Seminude Women, Pair 350.00
Nutting, Book Settle, 1909, Signed, Framed, 16 1/2 In. 70.00
Nutting, Decked As A Bride, Framed, 10 X 12 In. 30.00
Nutting, Garden Steps, Framed & Signed, 10 X 13 In. 38.00
Nutting, Her First At Home, Signed, 10 X 7 3/4 In. 90.00
Nutting, Lady In Hall, Framed, Miniature 50.00
Nutting, October On The River, Framed, 14 X 20 In. 48.00
Nutting, Spinet Corner, Framed, 13 X 10 3/4 In. 55.00
Nutting, Stepping-Stones At Bolton Abbey, Gilt Frame, 18 In. 75.00
Nutting, Still Life, Signed, Framed, 17 In. 80.00
Nutting, Very Satisfactory, Original Frame 40.00
Nutting, Warm Spring Day, Framed, 10 X 16 In. 40.00
Nutting, Woman Churning Butter, Framed, Signed 60.00
Parrish, Aladdin & Magic Bottle, 11 X 9 In. 50.00
Parrish, Circe's Palace 50.00
Parrish, Daybreak, Original Frame, 7 X 11 In. 35.00
Parrish, Daybreak, Original Frame, 9 X 14 In. 45.00
Parrish, Deck Fifty-Two Reveries, Playing Cards 115.00
Parrish, Garden Of Allah, Label, Framed, 18 X 30 In. 110.00
Parrish, Golden Hours, 1929, Framed, 16 X 24 In. 100.00
Parrish, In The Mountains 75.00
Parrish, Knave By Bridge 125.00
Parrish, Lampseller Of Baghdad, Original Period Frame, 14 1/2 X 19 In 230.00
Parrish, Lantern Bearers, Framed, 10 X 12 In. 75.00
Parrish, Lute Players, Original Frame, 12 X 18 In. 120.00
Parrish, Old King Cole 435.00
Parrish, Pied Piper 350.00
Parrish, Reveries, 11 1/2 X 15 In. 85.00
Parrish, Rubaiyat, Framed, 10 X 32 In. 210.00
Parrish, Spirit Of Transportation 450.00

Prints, Japanese, Jacoulet, Vendeur De Masques, 15 1/2 X 20 In.; Le Tresor, Coree, 15 1/2 X 20 In.; Parisian Lady, 1934

Parrish, Stars, Framed, 11 1/2 X 19 1/2 In.	235.00
Parrish, Swift's Premium Ham	75.00
Parrish, Twilight, 1937, Small	95.00
Parrish, Venetian Lamplighter, Small	85.00
Parrish, Where The Dinkey Bird Is Singing, Label & Frame	150.00
Parrish, Wild Geese	85.00 To 110.00
Rockwell, Art Critic, Autographed	300.00
Rockwell, Doctor & Doll, Signed	1800.00
Rockwell, Walking To Church, Autographed	300.00
Sarony, Major & Knapp, Camp Bates, Bird's-Eye View Of Camp	150.00
Sarony, Major & Knapp, Camp Oliver, Tents, Troops, Parade	150.00
Tait, American Field Sports, On A Point	300.00
Tait, Chickens, 5 Chicks, 2 With Bugs	85.00
Vincent, 2 Girls On Diving Board, 12 X 12 In.	65.00
Waugh, Walking Match	125.00
PURPLE SLAG, see Slag, Purple	
PURSE, Beaded, Carnival Glass, Purple	50.00
Beaded, Clutch, 1940	5.00
Beaded, Envelope Style, Black,, 1940s	15.00
Beaded, Navy Blue & Gold Design, Gold Frame, Long Chain	65.00
Beaded, Striped With Silver-Cream Material, Silver Plated Frame	40.00
Change, Abalone	16.00
Change, Beaded, Coral Color	3.00
Drawstring, Crocheted	5.00
Drawstring, Victorian, Beaded, Fringe	35.00
Evans Co., Rhinestone Encrusted, Lighter, Pillbox, Compact, 1938	175.00
Leather, Suede Lining, Mirror, Early 1900s	24.00
Mesh, Alumesh, Whiting & Davis	25.00
Mesh, Art Nouveau, Sterling Silver ....*Illus*	125.00
Mesh, Blue Teardrop Beads	22.00
Mesh, Child's, Metal	50.00
Mesh, Enameled, Art Deco	25.00
Mesh, Enameled, Embossed Frame, Fringe	18.00
Mesh, Enameled, Silver Plated, Art Deco Frame	32.00
Mesh, Geometric Design, Pointed Bottom Scallops, Brown	35.00
Mesh, German Silver, Chain, 7 X 5 1/2 In.	38.00
Mesh, Sapphires & Diamonds Set In Platinum, 14K Gold	9500.00
Mesh, Silver Plated Frame, Silver Strap Handle, 3 X 7 In.	40.00

(See Page 537)

Purse, Mesh, Art Nouveau, Sterling Silver

Mesh, Sterling Silver Top, English, 6 X 4 1/2 In.	135.00
Mesh, Whiting & Davis, Engraved Top, Chain Handle, 6 X 7 1/2 In.	35.00
Mesh, Whiting & Davis, Rhinestone Clip, 1930	10.00
Miser's, Silver Bead Design, 2-Ring Closure	35.00
Opera, Victorian, Blue Glass Overlapping Beads	31.00
Petit Point, Picnic Scene, Sterling Silver Frame, 5 X 5 1/2 In.	23.00
Pouch, Drawstring, Printed Cloth Lining, Tassel, 4 1/2 X 6 1/2 In.	22.50
Scenic Engraving, Child's, Silver Plated, Chain	25.00
Woven Wire, Chain Handle, 1900s	20.00

Quezal
Quezal glass was made from 1901 to 1920 by Martin Bach, Sr. He made iridescent glass of the same type as Tiffany.

QUEZAL, Compote, Feathered Underpart, Green Leaves, Snakeskin Foot, 5 1/2 In.	1450.00
Compote, Gold Iridescent, Signed, 8 In.	275.00
Compote, Tulip Shaped, 5 Leaf Design, Green, Gold, Marked, 4 In.	475.00
Dish, Nut, Gold, Signed, 3 X 1 1/2 In.	135.00
Globe, Green & Ivory, Feather Design, 6 1/4 In.	265.00
Salt Dip, Gold Aurene, Ribbed, Marked	115.00
Salt Dip, Golden Tones, Open, Marked, 2 3/4 In.	225.00
Shade, Allover Gold Threading, Gold Lined, Green & Gold, Signed, Pair	225.00
Shade, Calcite Exterior, Gold Threading, Hearts, Signed, Set Of 4	875.00
Shade, Flared Bottom, Paneled, Iridescent Gold, Signed, 4 X 4 In., Pair	150.00
Shade, Gold Aurene, Signed, Pair	250.00
Shade, Gold Hearts, Allover Gold Threads, Gold Lining, Pair	225.00
Shade, Gold Hook Feather, Gold Lining, Marked, 7 In.	185.00
Shade, Gold Ribbed, Signed, Pair	165.00
Shade, Gold Spider Webbing, Green, Gold Leaves, Pair	309.00
Shade, Green & Gold Heart, Allover Gold On Opal, Pair, Signed	225.00
Shade, Green Feathering, Signed, 5 In.	135.00
Shade, Green Pulled Feathers, Gold Outlined, Signed	160.00
Shade, King Tut, Gold, Signed, 6 1/2 In.	950.00
Shade, Lamp, Puffy, Green Feather Design, Calcite, Marked, 6 In.	120.00
Shade, Pulled Feathers, Gold Iridescent, Signed, 6 X 4 1/4 In., Pair	290.00
Shade, Ruffle Top, Gold & Blue Highlights, Signed, 2 1/4 In.	390.00
Shade, Silver Overlay Top, Iridescent Blue Green Base, 5 1/2 In.	1500.00
Shade, Spun Gold, Pulled Feather, Marked, 5 In.	150.00
Shade, Swirl Pattern, Bulbous, Gold On Opalescent, 2 5/8 In.	115.00
Vase, Aurene Gold, Signed, 8 In.	399.00
Vase, Bud, Orange, Gold Iridescent, Scalloped Top, Marked, 10 In.	250.00
Vase, Bulbous, Amber, Marked, 4 X 4 In.	200.00
Vase, Double Pulled Feather, Iridescent Gold Interior, 3 3/4 In.	950.00
Vase, Easter-Lily Shaped, Onion Form Base, Signed, 8 1/2 In.	450.00
Vase, Flower Form, Signed, Gold Iridescent, 12 In.	875.00
Vase, Gold & Brown Design, Yellow Ground, 8 In.	1200.00
Vase, Gold & Platinum Feathering, Shaded Green, Gold Edge, 8 In.	2250.00
Vase, Gold At Top Of Platinum Feathering, 5 1/2 In.	1250.00
Vase, Gold Feathers, Edged In Green, Yellow Cased, Signed, 3 1/2 In.	325.00
Vase, Gold Iridescent, Amphora Shape, Gold To Rose, Marked, 5 In.	475.00
Vase, Gold Iridescent, Dimpled, Long Neck, Marked, 6 In.	225.00
Vase, Gold With Rose Highlights, Silver Overlay, 7 In.	1500.00
Vase, Gold, Rose, & Blue, Signed, 8 In.	400.00

Quezal, Vase, Silver Overlay, 4 1/2 In.

Vase, Green To Ivory, Blue Base, Signed, 11 X 4 1/2 In. 2540.00
Vase, Interlocking Feathering In Gold & Platinum, 8 In. 1650.00
Vase, Jack-In-The-Pulpit, Gold Face, Marked, 9 In. 1200.00
Vase, Lily, Signed, 4 1/2 In. 395.00
Vase, Platinum & Gold Feathering, Green Ground, 7 1/4 In. 2500.00
Vase, Platinum & Gold Feathering, Touch Of White, 7 1/4 In. 1750.00
Vase, Platinum Feathers, Twisted White Neck, Signed, 5 In. 1450.00
Vase, Pulled Feather, Sweet Pea, Gold, Signed, 6 In. 1295.00
Vase, Pulled Green Feather, Gold Rim, Opalescent, Signed, 6 1/2 In. 1250.00
Vase, Round, Gold Iridescent, Marked, 6 1/4 In. 110.00
Vase, Silver Overlay, 4 1/2 In. .... *Illus* 1025.00
Vase, White Ground, Green Floral Design, Signed, 8 1/2 In. 650.00
Vase, Yellow, Gold, & Brown Design, 8 In. 1200.00

QUILT, Appliqued, Stylized Tulips, Green & Brown, Blue Ground .... *Illus* 350.00
Calico, Red, Yellow, Green, Tulips, Leaves, Stars, 72 X 72 In. 250.00
Child's, Pink, White, 56 X 59 In. 30.00
Log Cabin Squares, Star Center, Multicolored, 28 X 94 In. 95.00
Patchwork, Amish, Diamond In The Square, Wool, C.1900, 80 X 80 In. 1800.00
Patchwork, Applique, Bougainvillea, Fuchsia, White Floral, 78 X 90 In. 140.00
Patchwork, Applique, Eight Petal, Colored Border, 1910, 83 X 70 In. 95.00
Patchwork, Applique, Fish, Blue, White Ground, 80 X 80 In. 240.00
Patchwork, Applique, Floral Design, Red, Orange On White, 16 X 86 In. 95.00
Patchwork, Applique, Floral, Art Deco, 72 X 90 In. 450.00
Patchwork, Applique, Floral, Goldenrod, Orange, Green, White, 74 X 90 In. 185.00
Patchwork, Applique, Floral, Lime Green, White Ground, 78 X 88 In. 170.00
Patchwork, Applique, Flower Garland, Trapunto, Scalloped, 100 X 74 In. 550.00
Patchwork, Applique, Red, Yellow, & Green, White Ground, Double Size 2200.00
Patchwork, Applique, Star & Moon, Pennsylvania, Blue, 78 X 78 In. 950.00
Patchwork, Applique, Tulip, C.1900, 3/4 Size 250.00
Patchwork, Applique, 5 Floral Design, Green, Orange, Peach, 84 X 84 In. 155.00
Patchwork, Art Deco, Pink & White, 60 X 75 In. 80.00
Patchwork, Basket, Diamond Border, Orange & White, 72 X 72 In. 155.00
Patchwork, Baskets, Trapunto, Circular, 8 Hearts, Wreath, 80 X 96 In. 125.00
Patchwork, Beige, Red, Yellow, Rose Of Sharon, White Ground, 46 X 68 In. 385.00
Patchwork, Blue & White, Diamond Pattern, Crib .... 40.00 To 400.00
Patchwork, Butterfly, Crib 18.00
Patchwork, Calico, Black, Brown, Orange, Beige, Mammies, 1930, 88 X 80 In. 2200.00
Patchwork, Calico, Fan, Overstuffed, Cream Ground, 66 X 70 In. 65.00
Patchwork, Calico, Four Patch, Pink, 52 X 86 In. 60.00
Patchwork, Calico, Red, Green, Pinwheel, 88 X 84 In. 495.00
Patchwork, Calico, Red, White, Blue, Flying Geese & Stars, 64 X 76 In. 192.00

Patchwork, Calico, Red, Yellow, Green, Floral, Snowflake, 80 X 84 In.	495.00
Patchwork, Calico, Square & Diamond, Pink, Green, 64 X 76 In.	60.00
Patchwork, Castle Wall, Browns, Red, & Yellows, Youth, 52 X 80 In.	195.00
Patchwork, Chrysanthemum, 8 Panel, Blue & White, 66 X 96 In.	310.00
Patchwork, Cotton & Flannel, Gray, Reds, Yellow, 72 X 82 In.	65.00
Patchwork, Crazy, Feather Stitched, C.1900, Velvet, 62 X 62 In.	450.00
Patchwork, Crazy, Velvet, Feather Stitched, 66 X 88 In.	35.00
Patchwork, Crossword Puzzle, Pink, Navy, Blue, & White, 72 X 72 In.	340.00
Patchwork, Double Wedding Ring, Scalloped Border, 80 X 80 In.	425.00
Patchwork, Double Wedding Ring, White Ground, 84 X 104 In.	150.00
Patchwork, Dresden Plate, Velvet On Cotton	150.00
Patchwork, Dresden Plate, 80 X 90 In.	65.00
Patchwork, Drunkard's Path, Pink, Green, Rainbow Quilting, 82 X 82 In.	260.00
Patchwork, Duck's Foot In Mud, Multicolored, Peach Border, 21 X 75 In.	75.00
Patchwork, Embroidered, Baskets Of Flowers, 1929, 72 1/4 X 72 1/4 In.	250.00
Patchwork, Fan, New England, 19th Century, Green, 110 X 93 In.	55.00
Patchwork, Floral Ribbon, Flowers, New England, C.1820, 72 X 82 In.	300.00
Patchwork, Floral, Red Flowers, White Ground, 70 X 78 In.	85.00
Patchwork, Flower Basket, Calico, Blue & White, 82 X 110 In.	240.00
Patchwork, Flower Basket, Calico, Colonial, Red, White, 66 X 78 In.	55.00
Patchwork, Flowers In Circles, 72 X 90 In.	135.00
Patchwork, Flying Geese, C.1900, 72 X 74 In.	175.00
Patchwork, Four Patch, Alternating Squares & Patches, 64 X 72 In.	175.00
Patchwork, Four Patch, Diamond, White Ground, 92 X 98 In.	110.00
Patchwork, French Rose, Pink & Green Rosettes, White, 81 X 81 In.	110.00
Patchwork, Friendship, Dated 1849, Signed, Red On White, 72 X 82 In.	250.00
Patchwork, Geometric, Hand-Quilted, Blue & White, 68 X 85 In.	110.00
Patchwork, Grandmother's Flower Garden, Green, Calico, 80 X 96 In.	140.00
Patchwork, Grandmother's Flower Garden, 72 X 76 In.	135.00
Patchwork, Grape Basket, Pink, White Ground, Pink Trim, 80 X 90 In.	130.00
Patchwork, Green, Gray, Yellow, Red, Antique Cars, C.1930, 84 X 68 In.	690.00
Patchwork, Hand-Embroidered, C.1880, 58 X 66 1/2 In.	155.00
Patchwork, Hourglass, Alternating Red & White Patterns, 80 X 80 In.	265.00
Patchwork, Japanese Fans, Red & Blue, Black Ground, 79 X 79 In.	310.00
Patchwork, Kentucky Pinwheel, Mariner's Compass, White, 70 X 80 In.	225.00
Patchwork, Linsey-Woolsey, Green, Red Plaid, Stars, Diamonds, 7 X 7 Ft.	375.00
Patchwork, Linsey-Woolsey, Red, Blue, White, Plaid Center, 8 X 7 Ft.	300.00
Patchwork, Little Girl, Embroidered & Appliqued, Cotton, 72 X 86 In.	85.00
Patchwork, Log Cabin Barn Raising, Red, Yellows, & Blues, 74 X 78 In.	95.00
Patchwork, Log Cabin, Silk Taffeta, Polychrome Colors, 66 X 66 In.	230.00
Patchwork, Lone Star Ground, Hand-Stitched, 74 X 85 In.	135.00
Patchwork, Monkey Wrench, Stars, Wine & Navy Wrenches, 80 X 88 In.	380.00
Patchwork, Mosaic, Octagonal, White Floral Ground, 76 X 84 In.	160.00
Patchwork, Mosaic, Pieced, Green & White, 54 X 76 In.	55.00
Patchwork, Mosaic, Polychrome, Cotton, Scalloped Edge, 88 X 72 In.	110.00
Patchwork, Multicolored Stars, White Squares, 70 X 76 In.	125.00
Patchwork, Nine Patch, Black & White, Red Trim, 62 X 76 In.	85.00
Patchwork, Oak Leaf, Open Corners, White Ground, Double Size	375.00
Patchwork, Oak Leaf, Pink & Green, White Ground, 73 X 90 In.	210.00
Patchwork, Oak Leaf, Red, White Ground, Red Binding, 85 X 85 In.	130.00
Patchwork, Ocean Wave, Black & White, Calico, C.1860, 82 X 82 In.	425.00
Patchwork, Ohio Star, Green & Brown, White Ground	300.00
Patchwork, Orange Starburst, Double Size	1300.00
Patchwork, Overstuffed, Wool, Blue, Brown, Green, Pink, 74 X 82 In.	65.00
Patchwork, Pennsylvania, Red, White Ground, Floral, Crib	75.00
Patchwork, Pinwheel Design, Red & White *Illus*	350.00
Patchwork, Postage Stamp, Polychrome, Pink Border, 56 X 76 In.	65.00
Patchwork, Postage Stamp, Red, White, Blue, Pink Trim, 64 X 82 In.	110.00
Patchwork, Princess Feather, Presentation, A.Allens, 1883, 83 X 93 In.	1000.00
Patchwork, Roman Square, Taffeta, Dark Colors, 66 X 68 In.	130.00
Patchwork, Rosettes, Scalloped, Red, Lemon, Pink Dots, 81 X 83 In.	675.00
Patchwork, Snowflake, Scalloped Edge, 80 X 71 In.	125.00
Patchwork, Square Patch, Mustard & White, 64 X 86 In.	70.00

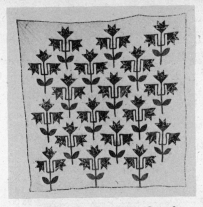

Quilt, Appliqued, Stylized Tulips, Green & Brown, Blue Ground   *(See Page 539)*

Quilt, Patchwork, Pinwheel Design, Red & White

Patchwork, Star Of Many Points, Red & White, 64 X 76 In. 200.00
Patchwork, Star Variation, Diamonds Of Star, Blue, 82 X 82 In. 380.00
Patchwork, Star Variation, 7-Point Star, 21 Triangles, 80 X 82 In. 170.00
Patchwork, Striped Silk Squares, American, 19th Century, 50 X 55 In. 25.00
Patchwork, Sunbonnet Baby, Floral Ground, Crib 40.00
Patchwork, Sunburst, Red Star, Surrounded By White & Blue, 84 X 84 In. 450.00
Patchwork, Sunflower Star, Zigzag Border, White, Blue, 102 X 102 In. 125.00
Patchwork, Tree Of Life, Multicolored, 79 X 89 In. 200.00
Patchwork, Trellis, Green Ground, 6 X 7 Ft. 150.00
Patchwork, White On White, Leaf, 83 X 83 In. 190.00
Patchwork, Yo-Yo, Outlined In White, 90 X 87 In. 125.00
Patchwork, 9 Applied Rabbits, Embroidered Outline, 1900, Crib 30.00
Star Design, Red, Blue, Brown, White, 70 X 88 In. 395.00
Trapunto, Pinwheel Center, Flowers, Pineapple, 82 X 86 In. 600.00

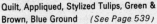

Tin-glazed, hand-painted pottery has been made in Quimper, France, since the late seventeenth century. The earliest firm, founded in 1685 by Jean Baptiste Bousquet, was known as HB Quimper. Aother firm, founded in 1772 by Francois Eloury, was known as Porquier. The third firm, founded by Guillaume Dumaine in 1778, was known as HR or Henriot Quimper. All three firms made similar wares decorated with designs of Breton peasants and sea and flower motifs. The Eloury "Porquier" and Dumaine "Henriot" firms merged in 1913. Bousquet "HB" merged with the others in 1968. The factory is now called Les Faenceries de Quimper.

QUIMPER, Bell, Figural, Bagpipe 85.00
Bowl, Peasant Girl, Blue Handles, White Ground, 6 In. 60.00
Bowl, Peasant Man, Dark Yellow Ground, 11 In. 95.00
Bowl, Peasant Woman, 2 1/2 In. 65.00
Bowl, Woman's Portrait, Signed, 9 7/8 In. 90.00
Box, Condiment, Covered, 2 1/2 In. 65.00
Candlestick, Horse, Floral Design, 8 1/2 X 6 In. 225.00
Coffeepot, Man & Woman, Signed 125.00
Compote, Peasant, Pedestal, Signed, 8 1/2 X 4 1/2 In. 75.00
Cruet, Crisscrossed Bottles 60.00
Cup & Saucer, Peasant, Green 25.50
Cup & Saucer, Wishbone Handle 22.50
Dish, 3-Part, Marked, 8 In. 170.00
Eggcup, Double, Henriot 19.50
Eggcup, Figural Chick 14.50
Figurine, Breton Flutists, S.Kervellak, 12 In. 400.00

Figurine, Le Grand Pere, S.Sevellac	375.00
Inkwell, Heart Shaped, Signed	165.00
Jug, 2-Sided, Marked, 7 1/2 In.	140.00
Knife Rest	47.00
Match Holder, Base, Small	62.00
Mustard, 2 Attached Open Salts, Peasant On Back, Signed	75.00
Napkin Ring, Signed Henriot, 2 1/2 In.	24.00
Pitcher, Bagpipe, Green, Brown, Blue Bow, Marked, 5 3/4 In.	130.00
Pitcher, Peasant Man, Hand-Painted, Signed, 5 1/2 In.	65.00
Pitcher, Peasant Man, Red & Blue Florals, White Ground, 6 In.	65.00
Pitcher, Peasant Man, Signed, 5 In.	45.00
Pitcher, Peasant Woman, Bulbous, Yellow Ground, 5 In.	45.00
Pitcher, Rooster, Flowers, & Leaves, 6 In.	20.00
Plate, Boy Surrounded By Floral Garland, Marked, 10 In.	40.00
Plate, French Sayings, 8 In.	60.00
Plate, Peasant Man & Woman, 10 1/2 In., Pair	105.00
Plate, Rooster, Blue Flowers, Yellow, Marked, 7 3/4 In.	75.00
Salt & Pepper, Peasant Man & Woman, Signed, 3 1/2 In., Pair	110.00
Salt & Pepper, Peasant Woman's Head, Marked	95.00
Salt, Fleur-De-Lis, Marked	68.00
Spoon Rest, Fish Shaped	34.00
Tea Set, Peasant, Yellow, 3 Piece	115.00
Tureen, Soup, Man & Flowers, Marked HB	225.00
Vase, Flowers, 15 In.	65.00
Vase, Peasant Woman, 7 3/4 In.	65.00
Wall Pocket, Man & Woman, Double	195.00

RADFORD
JASPER

Radford pottery was made by Alfred Radford in Broadway, Virginia, Tiffin and Zanesville, Ohio, and Clarksburg, West Virginia, from 1891 until 1912. Jasperware, Ruko, Thera, Radera, and Velvety Art Ware were made.

RADFORD, Vase, Bust Of Lincoln, Eagle, No.12, 17 In.	495.00
Vase, Lady, Grapes, No.58, 5 1/2 In.	150.00
Vase, Man With Spear, No.52, 6 In.	145.00

RADIO, Atwater Kent, Ei Speaker	135.00
Atwater Kent, Model 20, Horn & Battery Eliminator, Extra Tubes	275.00
Atwater Kent, Model 49	55.00
Atwater Kent, Model 60c, Kiel Cabinet, Table, 36 X 25 In.	325.00
Bullwinkle	25.00
Clock, Robot, Standing Robot, Silver, Black, Battery, 9 In.	75.00
Daven, Amplifier	30.00
Dayfan, Battery	70.00
Diemens, Nazi	125.00
Echophone, Cathedral Style, Electric	65.00 To 75.00
Echophone, 3 Tube	175.00
Fada, Console, Model 290	500.00
Fairbanks Morse, Model 6C, Battery Operated	18.00
Fairbanks Morse, Model 63, Shortwave, Electric, 13 X 9 1/2 X 17 In.	28.00
Grebe Syncrophase, 1925, Battery Operated	275.00
Hallicrafter, 4 Band	60.00
Hotel, Coin-Operated, Plays 2 Hours, Metal	45.00
Microphone, Floor Model, Brass	125.00
Night-Light, Star Explorer 2, Black & Silver, AM Band, 7 In.	45.00
Philco, Cathedral	100.00
Philco, Round Dome	50.00
Philco, Transitone, Portable	20.00 To 28.00
R.C.A., Model 28, With Loop	75.00
R.C.A., Radiola, Model 60, Peerless Beehive Speaker, Mahogany Veneer	160.00
R.C.A., Radiola, Model 812, Speaker	150.00
R.C.A., Radiola, Super-Heterodyne, Open Top, Headphones, Walnut, 14 In.	45.00
Robot, I-R-4-U Sing Along, Starroid, Black & Silver, 9 In.	50.00

Robot, Star Force Alien, Gor, Purple, Dial Eyes, 6 In. 35.00
Sanora, Upright, Battery Operated 95.00
Scott, No.23, Allwave 250.00
Silvertone, Art Deco, Bakelite, Marbleized 28.00
Space Robot, Silver, Dial & Knobs On Chest, Plastic, 8 In. 30.00
Sparton, Tabletop, Blue Mirror 1200.00
Splendid Deluxe, Battery 50.00
Station, Marx, Original Box 108.00
Steinite, Cathedral, Small 50.00
Washington, 3 Tube 375.00
Westinghouse, Jukebox Shape 45.00

RAILROAD, Ashtray, C.& O.R.R., G.Washington 75.00
Ashtray, Erie R.R., 100th Anniversary 10.00
Ashtray, Rock Island, Smoke Colored Glass, 4 1/2 In. 12.00
Bag, Security, Wabash R.R. 130.00
Bell, Crossing, 1909, Large .... 80.00 To 90.00
Bell, Steam Locomotive, Yoke & Cradle, Bronze 750.00
Blanket, Pullman 35.00
Blanket, Southern Pacific 40.00
Bowl, Harpers Ferry Scene, B.& O., Centennial, Blue, 9 In. 40.00
Bowl, Kitchen, N.Central, Metal, 15 In. 25.00
Bowl, Pennsy R.R., Open, Silver Plated 30.00
Box, First Aid, No.1751, N.Y.C., Hasp, Carry Bail, Tin, 8 1/2 X 2 In. 25.00
Bucket, Fire, Boston & Maine R.R., Collapsible, Canvas, Metal Frame 35.00
Button, Bay State Street Railway Trolley, 1915 .... 8.50
Button, Coat, Metal Clips, AMTRAK 2.00
Cabinet, Ticket, Roll Front, Walnut, 46 X 67 In. 625.00
Can, Boston & Maine R.R., Embossed Eagle, Bail Handle, 5 Gallon 30.00
Can, Drinking Water Filler, Boston & Maine R.R., Tin, 2 Gallon 18.00
Can, Kerosene, Daisy, 1881 .... 85.00
Can, Kerosene, N.Y.C., 1 Gallon 9.00
Can, Oil, Engine, A.T. & S.F.R.R. 95.00
Can, Spout Cap, Boston & Maine R.R., Iron Bail, 5 Gallon 30.00
Can, Watering, D.&h.R.R. 20.00
Car Seat, Reversing Back, Velvet Covered, Carved Oak .... 350.00 To 400.00
Carafe, Water, B.& O.R.R. 100.00
Card, Playing, Bangor Aroostook 14.00
Card, Playing, Chessie Cats 11.75
Card, Playing, Conrail 19.00
Card, Playing, Illinois Central Gulf 22.00
Card, Playing, Penn Central 18.00
Card, Playing, S.P. Line, Boxed 20.00
Cards, Playing, Chesapeake & Ohio R.R., Celluloid Box 18.00
Cards, Playing, Great Northern 13.00
Celery, Purple Laurel, P.R.R. 8.00
Chisel, Boston & Maine R.R., Cast Iron, 8 In. 7.50
Cocktail, N.Y.C. Logo, Stemmed 16.50
Coloring Book, Seaboard Coast Line, Tommy & Tess Take A Train Trip 3.00
Creamer, B. & O. R.R., Lamberton 60.00
Creamer, Nickel Plate R.R., Cobalt Blue & Silver Trim 18.00
Cup & Saucer, B. & O., Centennial 45.00
Cup & Saucer, Demitasse, B.& O., Lamberton, 1827-1927 .... 35.00 To 40.00
Cup & Saucer, Demitasse, Marked Lamberton 68.00
Cup & Saucer, Marked Lamberton 75.00
Cup & Saucer, S.P. R.R. 57.00
Cup & Saucer, Salt Lake Route 500.00
Cushion, Pullman, Straw Filled, Green Striped, 36 In. 12.00
Cuspidor, Pullman R.R., Brass 65.00
Desk, Folding, Conductor's 75.00
Eggcup, Milwaukee, Double 8.00
Fire Extinguisher, Embossed, C.& N.W.R.R., 17 1/2 In. 100.00
Fire Extinguisher, Glass, C. & N.W. R.R. 45.00

Globe, Dietz, Vesta, N.Y.C., Clear 15.00
Globe, Embossed, P.R.R. 20.00
Globe, Glass, C.& O. 20.00
Globe, N.Y.C., 1907, 10 In. 27.00
Globe, Raised Letters, Burlington, Tall 95.00
Globe, Red, Maine 32.00
Hat Rack, Pullman, 32 In. 30.00
Hat, Conductor's, Boston & Maine R.R. 33.00
Horn Whistle, 19th Century, England 45.00
Key, Pullman Berth, Brass 7.00
Key, Wabash R.R. 20.00
Kit, Brakeman's, Fitted Side For Torpedos, Flag, U.P. .... 20.00 To 30.00
Kit, First Aid, N.Y.C., Hasp & Bail, Tin, 8 1/2 X 4 1/2 In. 25.00
Lamp, Bracket, Fonts Embossed, Urbana, Ohio, 21 In. 75.00
Lamp, Caboose, P.R.R., Bracket 38.00
Lamp, Car Inspector's, Battery Operated, A.T. & S.F. R.R., Large 35.00
Lamp, Carbide, Oxweld 35.00
Lamp, Oil, Double-Sided, Bull's-Eye Lens, Dietz, 9 1/2 In. 35.00
Lamp, Switch, Red & Blue 125.00
Lantern, A. & W., Adams, S.P., Insert Fount, Tall Clear Globe 75.00
Lantern, A.& W., Kerosene, Dated 2-43, S.P., Clear Globe 30.00
Lantern, A.& W., Kerosene, R.I. R.R., Etched Globe, Clear 35.00
Lantern, A.& W., Kerosene, Steel Wick Guide, World War II, Clear 30.00
Lantern, A.T.& S.F. R.R., Hand 75.00
Lantern, Adlake, Kerosene, C. & O., Dome Top, Etched, Dated 4-49 .... 35.00
Lantern, Adlake, Kerosene, C.M.& St.P.& P., Red Etched Globe 30.00
Lantern, Adlake, Kerosene, C.M.& St.P.R.R., Etched Globe, 1913 .... 50.00
Lantern, Adlake, Kerosene, S.P., Dated 2-46, Clear Globe 30.00
Lantern, Adlake, Kerosene, Washington Terminal Co. 25.00
Lantern, Adlake, No.200, St.L.S.W., Clear Globe 75.00
Lantern, Adlake, No.250, C.B. & Q. R.R., Red Globe 40.00
Lantern, Adlake, No.250, D. & H. R.R., Clear Globe 40.00
Lantern, Adlake, No.250, Erie R.R., Ring Base, Red Etched Globe 40.00
Lantern, Adlake, No.250, Pere Marquette, Red Etched Globe 45.00
Lantern, Adlake, No.250, S.P., Red Globe 45.00
Lantern, Adlake, No.250, Seaboard, Red Globe 30.00
Lantern, Adlake, No.250, W.P. R.R., Clear Globe 50.00
Lantern, Adlake, Reliable, S.P., Clear Tall Globe 50.00
Lantern, Adlake, Reliable, S.P., Flat Top, Tall Clear Globe 65.00
Lantern, Adlake, Reliable, S.P., Red Tall Globe 55.00
Lantern, Aladdin, Caboose, Instructions For Adjusting 275.00
Lantern, Aladdin, Caboose, Wall Mount 45.00
Lantern, Aladdin, No.23, Caboose, Aluminum 16.00
Lantern, Armspear, 1925, G.N.R.R., Flat Verticals 40.00
Lantern, C. & E.I. R.R., Etched Globe, Marked Frame 45.00
Lantern, C.N.R., Clear Globe, 3 1/4 In. 35.00
Lantern, Central 55.00
Lantern, Dietz, Inspector, P.R.R. 47.00
Lantern, Dietz, Vesta, B.& M. R.R., Ring Base, Clear Globe 25.00
Lantern, Dressel, No.1144, B. & O. R.R., Red Globe 30.00
Lantern, Dressel, No.1144, C.M.& St.P. R.R., Gray Paint, Clear 35.00
Lantern, Dressel, No.1144, G.N., Gray Paint, Red Globe 30.00
Lantern, Dressel, No.1144, M.K.T. R.R., Clear Etched Globe 40.00
Lantern, Dressel, No.1144, S.P., Gray Paint, Amber Globe 30.00
Lantern, Hand, C.& N.W. R.R. 75.00
Lantern, Hand, Wabash R.R. 35.00
Lantern, Inspector's, Dietz Acme, Bail Handle, Black, 13 In. 50.00
Lantern, Inspector's, Globe Marked Prisco 45.00
Lantern, M.S.T.P.& P.R., Red Globe 47.50
Lantern, Maine Central R.R., Red Globe 32.00
Lantern, N.Y.C., Tall Globe 10.00
Lantern, Oil, C.P.R., Ruby Globe, Folding Handle, Globe 3 1/4 In. 75.00
Lantern, Oil, Caboose, Wall, Iron Frame, Tin Font, 21 In. 115.00

Lantern, P.R.R., Red Globe	30.00
Lantern, P.R.R., Tall Globe	40.00
Lantern, Pullman	425.00
Lantern, Ressel, Caboose, Amber Bull's-Eye Lens	50.00
Lantern, Ruby Globe, Marked N.Y. N.H. & H.	40.00
Lantern, Southern Pacific	30.00
Lantern, W. & W., Kerosene, D. & H. R.R., Dated 2-45, Clear Globe	30.00
Lantern, Wall, Caboose, Sheet Iron Frame, Wall Bracket, 21 In.	115.00
Light, Depot, Blue Metal Exterior	10.00
Light, Running, Marked Pyle National Co., Bull's-Eye Lens, Pair	225.00
Light, Steam Engine	900.00
Lock, A.& W.P. R.R., Yale	22.00
Lock, B.& O. R.R., Heart, 2 1/2 X 4 In.	45.00
Lock, Baggage Car, Brass	30.00
Lock, Boston & Maine, Attached Iron Rod, Sheet Iron	22.50
Lock, Caboose Door, Brass	30.00
Lock, G.N.R.R., Steel	10.00
Lock, Key, C.P.R., Mitchell, Brass	30.00
Lock, L & N, Brass	20.00
Lock, N.& W. Railway Co., 1957, 2 1/2 X 3 1/2 In.	50.00
Lock, Signal, N.K.P., Brass	18.00
Lock, Signal, R.I., Brass	15.00
Lock, Signal, Wabash, Flag On Side, Key	30.00
Lock, Southern Pacific, Embossed Rising Sun, Brass	75.00
Lock, Switch, Adlake, Marked S.P., Steel	20.00
Lock, Switch, Adlake, Sealake, Steel	10.00
Lock, Switch, Brass, Union Pacific	45.00
Lock, Switch, C.B.& Q. R.R., Steel	18.00
Lock, Switch, Embossed Union Pacific, Heart Shaped, Brass	37.50
Matchbook, Set Of 6, Chesapeake & Ohio Lines, Chessie The Cat	20.00
Matches, Erie R.R., 6 Pack	9.50
Menu, N.Y.Central R.R.	7.00
Mirror, Iron Mountain, Pocket	35.00
Monkey Wrench, C. & N.W.R.R., 18 In.	17.00
Paperweight, Penn Central R.R., Figural Metroliner Car	32.50
Pass, Civil War, Dated Jan. 1, 1861	45.00
Pitcher, Calumet, Pullman	67.00
Pitcher, Omaha Express, 1898, Blue Willow, Wedgwood	15.00
Plate, A.T. & S.F., California Poppy, 7 1/2 In.	16.00
Plate, B. & O. R.R., Thomas Viaduct, Blue, 7 In.	35.00
Plate, B.& O., Harpers Ferry	95.00
Plate, B.& O.R.R., Centennial Blue, 10 In.	40.00
Plate, G.N.R.R., Glacier, 8 In.	75.00
Plate, N.Y.C., DeWitt Clinton, 8 In.	30.00
Plate, S.P. R.R., Prairie Mountain, 9 1/2 In.	55.00 To 60.00
Platter, A.C.L., Flora Of South, Square	119.00
Platter, Union Pacific R.R., Blue Scroll Edge, 9 X 6 1/2 In.	22.00
Recipe Book, B.& O., Cartoon 31 Pages	20.00
Saucer, A.T.& S.F., California Poppy, 5 1/4 In.	6.00
Sign, Crossing, Cast Iron, Large	145.00
Sign, Warning, Explosive, Handle Carefully, C.1820, 11 X 14 In.	4.00
Signal, Rock Island, Brass	12.00
Soup, Dish, Feather River	27.50
Spittoon, Pullman, Brass	75.00
Step Stool, Pullman	135.00
Sugar, Amtrak, China	4.00
Sugar, Union Pacific, Covered, International Silver	30.00
Thermos, Pullman	70.00
Timetable, Michigan Central, 1881	40.00
Timetable, Missouri Pacific, 1901	15.00
Tongs, Silver Plated, P.R.R., 5 In.	20.00
Tongs, Sugar, N.Y. N.H. & H. R.R.	15.00
Torch, Boston & Maine R.R., Marked, Tin	27.50

Torch, Cone Shaped, Screw Top, C.1870, 12 1/2 In.	22.50
Trivet, A.C.L. R.R., Virginia, Metalcrafters	12.00
Trivet, Cast Iron, Seaboard Coast Line, Handled	10.00
Tumbler, Long Island R.R.	8.00
Tumbler, P.R.R., 4 1/2 In.	15.00
Uniform, Conductor's, Railroad Buttons	18.00
Whistle, Back-Up, L.P.R.R., Brass	65.00
Whistle, Back-Up, Peanut Type, Caboose, C.& O. R.R.	40.00
Whistle, Caboose, C.& O.R.R., Brass	45.00
Whistle, Caboose, Peanut Type, Brass	40.00
Whistle, Locomotive, Northeastern Lines, C.1880, Brass, 9 1/2 In.	125.00
Wrench, Adjustable, Boston & Maine R.R., Cast Iron, 13 In.	15.00
Wrench, Michigan Central, Bemis & Call, 12 In.	18.00
Wrench, N.Y.C., Pexto, 12 In.	18.00

RAINBOW, see Mother-of-Pearl; Satin Glass

RAZOR, Bone Handle	4.50
Hone, Diamond King, Case	10.00
Hone, In Embossed Tin Box	20.00
Ivory Handle, Mustache Trimmer	24.00
Keen Kutter, Dimmon's	25.00
Keen Kutter, Straight	30.00
Safety, Keen Kutter, Leatherette Box	30.00
Sharpener, Kriss Kross, Instructions, Boxed	25.00
Sharpener, Kriss Kross, Round Turnover	5.00
Straight, Challenge	20.00
Straight, Crown Razor Works, Germany, Black Handle	4.00
Straight, Embossed Nude On Celluloid Handle	30.00
Straight, Griffon Carbo Magnetic, Black Handle, Engraved Blade	4.00
Straight, J.A.Henckels, Twinworks, Solingen, Germany	30.00
Straight, Keen Kutter	20.00
Straight, Kropp, Hamburg, Black Handle	4.00
Straight, Non-XII, Sheffield, Ivory Celluloid, 9 3/8 In.	15.00
Straight, Scrimshaw Railroad Engines & Covered Bridge, Ivory Handle	45.00
Straight, Shumate, Austin, Texas	20.00
Straight, Wade & Butcher	8.50 To 15.00
Straight, Wilson & Hawks, Wooden Handle	4.00
Straight, Winchester, Original Box	35.00
Straightedge, Chocolate Rocky Road Case	12.00
Strop, Brandt's Automatic	8.00
Strop, Horsehide, 26 In.	12.00
Strop, Wall Hanging, Victorian, Silver Plated Top, Retractable Case	45.00
Taylor Sheffield, Celluloid Handle	25.00
Will & Finck, Box	25.00
Winchester, Safety, Original Blade	25.00

*Reamers, or juice squeezers, have been known since 1767, although
most of those collected today date from the twentieth century.*

REAMER, Bosson Chef, 1969, Signed	35.00
Clown, Green Body, White Ruffle, Porcelain, 5 X 4 3/8 In.	68.00
Clown, 5 In.	25.00
Clown, 7 In.	32.00
Juice, Vaseline Color	55.00
Lemon-Shaped Bottom, Leaf Spout, Handled, White Top, Germany	30.00
Lemon, Cast Iron	25.00 To 45.00
Lemon, Maple	35.00
Lemon, Pearl, Cast Iron	18.00
Lemon, Wooden	30.00 To 40.00
Milk Glass, Blue, Jeanette	50.00
Milk Glass, Blue, Sunkist	85.00
Milk Glass, Green	35.00
Milk Glass, Green, Sunkist	11.00
Milk Glass, Sunkist	5.00 To 10.00

Orange Blossom, China	40.00
Orange Juice, Clear, Extractor	12.00
Orange, Twisted	30.00
Painted Baby's Orange, Duck In Plaid Tuxedo, Frosted Glass, 2 Piece	125.00
Sunkist, Advertising	12.00 To 18.00
Sunkist, Clear, California Fruit Growers Exchange	25.00
Sunkist, Clear, Oranges & Lemons	22.00
Sunkist, Green Opaque	25.00
Sunkist, Marked Patent No.68764, Milk Glass	15.00
Sunkist, Pink	35.00

The Red Wing Pottery of Red Wing, Minnesota, was a firm started in 1878. It was not until the 1920s that art pottery was made. It closed in 1967. Rumrill pottery was made for George Rumrill by the Red Wing Pottery Company and other firms. It was sold in the 1930s.

RED WING, Ashtray, Burgundy	16.00
Ashtray, Maroon	25.00
Bean Pot, Cream & Brown, Finger Handle, Bail, Covered	79.00
Bowl, Bulb, Scenic, Castles, High-Glaze Interior, 6 In.	30.00
Bowl, Green & Brown Flowers, Leaves, 8 X 3 In.	65.00
Bowl, Spatter, Blue & Rust, Tan Ground, Rolled Rim, 7 In.	65.00
Bowl, Sponged Band, 7 In.	45.00
Bowl, Spongeware, 11 In.	135.00
Bowl, Tan, Green, 5 In.	20.00
Bowl, White, Ivies, Berries, Bows In Relief, 6 3/4 In.	9.00
Butter Jar, Advertising, Covered, 3 Pound	220.00
Butter Jar, Covered, 5 Pound	200.00
Butter, Bobwhite	5.50
Candleholder, White, 5 In.	7.00
Casserole, Bobwhite, Covered, Large	35.00
Casserole, Bobwhite, Covered, Medium	35.00
Casserole, Capistrano, Covered	45.00
Casserole, Grayline, 3 Pint	55.00
Casserole, Spatter, Signed	45.00
Casserole, St.Olof, Iowa, Sponged Band	100.00
Churn, Covered, 4 Gallon	40.00
Churn, Dated 1915, Handled, 2 Gallon	250.00
Churn, Marked, 3 Gallon	75.00
Cookie Jar, Barrel Shaped, Sponge Band Around Middle	80.00
Cookie Jar, Bobwhite	60.00
Cookie Jar, Cattail, Blue-Gray	95.00
Cookie Jar, Chef, Blue	30.00 To 39.00
Cookie Jar, Chef, Yellow	28.00 To 35.00
Cookie Jar, Dutch Girl, Blue	25.00 To 40.00
Cookie Jar, Dutch Girl, Yellow	28.00 To 30.00
Cookie Jar, Monk, Blue	25.00 To 28.00
Cookie Jar, Monk, Ivory	35.00
Cookie Jar, Monk, Yellow	24.00 To 35.00
Cooler, Water, 3 Gallon	245.00
Cooler, Water, 4 Gallon	245.00
Cornucopia, Antique White, 8 1/2 X 8 1/2 In.	10.00
Cornucopia, Gray & Pink, 7 1/2 In., Pair	25.00
Cornucopia, Gray, 11 In.	25.00
Cornucopia, Leaf Relief, Italian Green, 11 In.	25.00
Crock, Butter, Brown, 1 Pound	50.00
Crock, 2 Gallon	25.00
Crock, 20 Gallon	225.00
Feeder, Poultry, Domed Top, 2 Gallon	40.00
Figurine, Gopher	98.00 To 130.00
Figurine, High Button Shoe, Green	95.00
Figurine, High Button Shoe, Lavender, Marked, 6 In.	50.00
Figurine, Madonna, White Matte, 10 In.	15.00
Fruit Jar, Mason, Black, 1/2 Gallon	90.00

Fruit Jar, Mason, Blue, 1 Gallon 285.00
Fruit Jar, Mason, 1 Quart .... 95.00 To 135.00
Fruit Jar, Wax Sealer, Barrel Shaped, Brown, Signed, 2 Quart 35.00
Holder, Hor D'oeuvres, Bobwhite .... 35.00 To 45.00
Jar, Beater, Advertising, Juneau, Wis., Blue & White 50.00
Jar, Beater, Advertising, Mallard 75.00
Jar, Beater, Advertising, Rudd, Iowa 75.00
Jar, Beater, Advertising, Stewartville, Minn., Saffron 65.00
Jar, Beater, Advertising, Titonka, Iowa 75.00
Jar, Beater, Inside Advertising, Sponged Band 40.00
Jar, Beater, Parkersburg, Iowa, Signed 60.00
Jar, Butter, Sponged Band, Covered, Bail, 3 Pound 195.00
Jar, Pantry, Lid, 5 Pound 250.00
Jar, Perfection Self-Draining, Stand, 50 Gallon 400.00
Jar, Refrigerator, Blue & White 130.00
Jar, Spice, Set Of 5 .... 275.00
Jug, Union, 5 Gallon 185.00
Mug, Blue Decal 95.00
Pitcher, Advertising, Grayline, Large 145.00
Pitcher, Cattails, Fredman Bros., Collinsville, Ill., Blue & Gray 150.00
Pitcher, Cherries & Leaves, Advertising, Blue & White 175.00
Pitcher, Cherry Band, Centuria, Wis. Advertising 180.00
Pitcher, Grayline, Advertising 145.00
Pitcher, Sponged Band, Gray, Signed, 7 1/2 In. .... 125.00 To 145.00
Pitcher, Water, Bobwhite 35.00
Planter, Green Glaze, 4 X 8 In. 7.00
Planter, Reclining Deer, Lady Strumming Harp, Green, 14 In. 14.00
Plate, Bobwhite, Vegetable, Divided 35.00
Plate, Quail, 10 In. 40.00
Platter, Aqua, 12 X 7 1/4 In. 16.00
Platter, Green Glaze, 12 X 7 1/4 In. 16.00
Salt & Pepper, Bobwhite, Figural Birds 20.00
Sauce, Bobwhite 8.50
Server, Bobwhite 40.00
Server, Coffee, Green Waffle Weave, Covered, 12 3/4 In. 15.00
Sugar, Bobwhite, Covered 20.00
Teapot, Chicken, Figural, Yellow, 8 X 7 In. 25.00
Teapot, Lady, White 38.00
Vase, Basket, Pink, 10 In. 15.00
Vase, Blue, Deer In Relief, 8 In. 20.00
Vase, Bud, Turquoise, 7 In. 10.00
Vase, Bulbous, Ribbed & Flared Top, Relief Design, 6 1/4 In. 9.00
Vase, Fan, Blue Outside, Pink Inside, Footed, Scrolled, 7 1/2 In. 12.00
Vase, Gray & Brown Panels, 9 1/2 In. 45.00
Vase, Green, Outraised Flowers, Marked, 9 In. 10.00
Vase, Marked, Peach, 5 In. 5.00
Wall Pocket, Guitar Shape, Marked, Speckled Turquoise, 13 1/2 In. 18.00

Redware is a hard red stoneware that originated in the late 1600s and continues to be made. The term is also used to describe any common clay pottery that is reddish in color.

REDWARE, Bank, Frog, Coin Slit, Orange-Brown, White & Green Spots, 2 1/2 In. 220.00
Bowl, Cylindrical, Footed, Lead Glaze, 3 1/4 In. 260.00
Bowl, Milk, Yellow & Green Design, 12 1/2 In. 65.00
Bowl, Sloping Sides, Yellow Glaze Inside, 19 1/2 X 12 In. 250.00
Bowl, Spherical Body, 2 Applied Handles, Black, Cream Design, 5 In. ... 350.00
Bowl, Sugar, Hemispherical Shape, Covered, C.1760, 4 In. 300.00
Bowl, Yellow Glaze Inside, Oak Leaf Design, Signed Ana, 9 In. 165.00
Bust, Portrait, George III, Medals, Wiglet, Uniform, 7 In. 250.00
Charger, Dish Form, Peacock Design, Sweeping Tail, 13 In.Diam. 6325.00
Creamer, Rust, Marbleized Splotching, Squatty, 3 1/2 In. 195.00
Cup Plate, Sprig, Yellow, Notched Rim 385.00
Figurine, Bear, Reclining, Orange-Brown, Dark Brown Streaks, 3 In. 165.00

Redware, Figurine, Dog, Fetching, Virginia,
White & Black, 9 In.

Figurine, Bird, Chocolate Brown, Stipple, 2 1/2 In., Pair 550.00
Figurine, Bird, Reclining Dog, Cream Ground, Brown Glaze, 3 In. 330.00
Figurine, Cat, Seated, Orange, Dark Brown Spongings, 5 In. 525.00
Figurine, Cat, Standing, Long Tail, Leaf Border, Orange-Brown, 4 In. 1320.00
Figurine, Dog, Fetching, Virginia, White & Black, 9 In. .... *Illus* 1540.00
Figurine, Dog, Reclining, Lying In Front Of Basket Of Fruit, 4 In. 330.00
Figurine, Dog, Seated, Small Keg In Jaws, John Bell, 5 In. 1870.00
Figurine, Dog, Standing, Incised Fern, Dark Brown, 4 1/2 In. 330.00
Figurine, Dog, With Flowerpot, Poodle, Brown & White, Bell, 4 In. 375.00
Figurine, Ducks, 3 Ducks, Orange, Dark Brown, Rose, 2 In. 137.00
Figurine, Goose, Orange Head & Neck, Body White, Bell, 3 In. 495.00
Figurine, Horse, Elongated, Orange-Brown, Brown Drippings, 5 In. 440.00
Figurine, Lovebirds, Doves, Rose, Brown, & Yellow, 3 1/2 In., Pair 220.00
Figurine, Parrot, Mounted On Perch, Incised Wing, 6 1/2 In. 1045.00
Figurine, Rooster, Orange, Dark Brown Markings, 2 1/4 In. 192.00
Figurine, Rooster, Pink, White, Blue Glaze, 5 In., Pair 220.00
Figurine, Rooster, Stylized, Orange, Green, Breast Incised, 4 1/4 In. 137.00
Figurine, Squirrel, Seated, Holding Nut, John Bell, 5 In. 660.00
Figurine, Whippet, Forelegs Crossed, White Ground, Bell, 6 In. 715.00
Flask, Brown Glaze, Lip, 7 1/2 In. 40.00
Flask, Pig, Orange Brown Glaze, Dr. Shenfelder, With Cork, 4 X 9 In. 4400.00
Jar, Applied Strap Handle, Impressed Solomn Way, 14 In. 35.00
Jar, Clear Glaze, Brown Daubs, 5 3/8 In. 40.00
Jar, Clear Glaze, Brown Speckles, 8 In. 10.00
Jar, Mustard Glaze, Brown Spots, 8 In. 260.00
Jug, Black Glaze, Tooling, Strap Handle, 24 In. 20.00
Jug, Brown Pottery, Miniature 75.00
Jug, Handled, Brown Glaze, Ovoid, 13 3/4 In. 75.00
Jug, Slip Design, 8 In. 50.00
Mantel Ornament, Basket Of Fruits & Leaves, Green, Red, White, 11 In. 1100.00
Mold, Cake, Fluted, Mottled, Lead Glaze 50.00
Mold, Fish 95.00
Mold, Pudding, 8 1/2 In. 38.00
Mold, Turk's Head, 2 1/4 In. 45.00
Mug, Shaving, Brown Glaze, Strap Handle, 4 1/2 In. 45.00
Pan, Milk, Burnt Orange, Flared, 4 1/2 In. 45.00
Pan, Milk, Yellow, Orange, Brown Design, Yellow Wash, 2 1/2 In. 125.00
Pincushion, Lady's Shoe, Black & Gilt Design, 5 In.Long 38.00
Pitcher, Clear Glaze, Green Mottling, 8 3/4 In. 85.00
Pitcher, High Flared Rim, 19th Century, 8 1/4 In. 425.00
Pitcher, Ovoid Body, Strap Handle, Brown, Black Splashes, 6 In. 275.00
Pitcher, Ovoid Form, Strap Handle, Red-Orange Glaze, 14 In. 55.00
Pitcher, Slip Design, 9 In. 50.00
Plaque, Eagle, Spread Winged, Laurel Branches, Marked Neuman, 4 In. 500.00
Plate, Brown Glaze, Crimped Edge, 8 In. 80.00
Plate, Pie, Scalloped Bands, 2 In. 50.00
Plate, Pie, Slip Design, Inscribed Lemon Pie, 8 In. 70.00
Plate, Shallow, 1876 In Yellow Slip, 7 1/4 In. 110.00

Porringer, Lead Glaze, 3 In. 250.00
Pot, Tooled Strap Hinges, Black Glaze, 7 In. 5.00
Sander, Form Of Girl, Feathered Hat, Guitar, Braid, 5 In. 192.00
Sugar, Slip-Decorated, Early 1900s 175.00
Teapot, Tooled Lines, Brown Glaze, Strap Handle, Covered, 5 In. 50.00
Tray, Orange-Brown, Inscribed Cheap As Mud In Yellow Slip, 12 In. 3410.00
Vase, Orange, Olive Green, Elongated Neck, Handled, 9 In., Pair 495.00
Whistle, Bird, Incised Wing & Feather, Brown Glaze, 3 In. 358.00
Whistle, Fish, Reddish Brown, Yellow Slip, 4 3/4 In. 495.00
Whistle, June Bug, Applied Crawlers, Reddish Brown, 3 1/2 In. 175.00
Whistle, Man, Wearing Top Hat, 3 1/4 In. 110.00
Whistle, Peacock, Orange-Brown, Dark Brown Trim, 5 In. 1870.00
Whistle, Rooster, Upright, Bushy Tail, 4 3/4 In. 300.00
   REGOUT, see Maastricht
   REVERSE PAINTING, see Painting, Reverse on Glass

REVOLVER, Army, Colt, Model 1860 .... 350.00
 Hopkins Allen, XL, Nickled 50.00
 Percussion, Colt, Baby Dragoon, Wells Fargo 500.00

Richard was the mark used on acid-etched cameo glass vases, bowls, night-lights, and lamps in Lorraine, France, during the 1920s.

RICHARD, Goblet, Tree Landscape Frosted Bowl, Knobbed Stem, Signed, 7 3/4 In. 450.00
 Vase, Castle, Lake, & Trees, Orange & Black Ground, 10 In. 775.00
 Vase, Church & Mountains In Maroon, Signed, Red Ground, 8 3/4 In. 475.00
 Vase, Glass, Castle Scene, C.1850, Vitrified Enamel, 8 1/2 In. 145.00
 Vase, Glass, Hammered Out Ground, Footed, Signed, Blue, 12 In. 325.00
 Vase, House & Bridge Scene, Bomb Shape, Signed, Orange Ground, 8 In. 650.00
 Vase, Loie Fuller Doing Scarf Dance, Signed, Blue Ground, 9 7/8 In. 1100.00
 Vase, Scenic, Castle & Lake, Orange & Black, 10 In. 900.00

Ridgway pottery has been made in the Staffordshire district in England since 1808 by a series of companies with the name Ridgway. The transfer-design dinner sets are the most widely known product. They are still being made.

   RIDGWAY, see also Flow Blue
RIDGWAY, Bowl, Grecian, 7 In. 30.00
 Celery, Coaching Days, Walking Up The Hill, 13 1/2 X 5 1/4 In. 45.00
 Chamber Pot, Duck Head Handle, Vista 85.00
 Dish, Soup, Harpers Ferry, Blue, 9 In. 80.00
 Dish, Vegetable, Franklin Flying Kite, Open, 3 X 4 In. 135.00
 Mug, Coaching Days .... 35.00 To 45.00
 Mug, Copper, Handled, Rustic Seascape, 4 3/4 In. 22.00
 Mug, Handled, Scene, Royal Vista, 4 3/4 In. 22.00
 Pitcher, Coaching Days, Silver Rim & Handle, 7 In. 75.00
 Pitcher, Coaching Days, 5 3/4 In. 65.00
 Pitcher, Dark Brown Glaze, Light Brown Decorations, 8 1/2 In. 45.00
 Pitcher, Green, Knights On Horseback, 9 In. 75.00
 Pitcher, Molded Marsh Reeds, Dated Oct.1835, Gray Ground, 8 In. 53.00
 Pitcher, Pea Green, Rope Handle, C. 1835, Marked, 9 In. 75.00
 Pitcher, Water, Wilkes-Barre, Vale Of Wyoming, Blue 185.00
 Plaque, Coaching Days, Pierced, 12 In.Diam. 88.00
 Plate, Albion, Lavender, 10 In. 32.00
 Plate, Blue, Opaque, Granite China, Marked, 1834, 9 1/4 In., Set Of 10 .... 150.00
 Plate, Coaching Days, Paying Toll, Silver Luster Rim, 9 In. 35.00
 Plate, Coaching Days, 8 In. 28.00
 Plate, Franklin Flying Kite, 3 1/2 In. 70.00
 Plate, Lake George, Blue, 7 3/4 In. 60.00
 Plate, Pink & Yellow Floral, Green, 1834-54, Marked, 9 1/4 In. 14.00

Plate, Simlay, 9 1/2 In.	18.00
Plate, Tuscan Rose, Light Blue, 7 3/4 In.	22.00
Plate, View From Ruggles House, Hudson River, Blue, 10 In.	80.00
Platter, Wilkes-Barre, Vale Of Wyoming, Blue, 8 X 11 In.	175.00
Sugar & Creamer, Coaching Days	50.00
Tankard Set, Coaching Days, Signed, 6 Piece	225.00
Tankard, Holly Leaves & Berries, Gold Trim, C.1900, 9 In.	75.00
Tankard, Leaves & Berries, Gold Trim, C.1900	75.00
Tray, Franklin Flying Kite, 3 1/4 X 4 1/2 In.	95.00
Tray, Franklin Flying Kite, 4 X 5 1/2 In.	135.00
Tray, Mr.Pickwick At The Election, Silver Luster Rim, 12 1/2 In.	95.00
Tumbler, Coaching Days, 4 In.	35.00
Vase, Coaching Days, Marked, 10 In.	85.00

Riviera Ware was made by the Homer Laughlin Co. from 1938 to 1950.
Plates were square and cup handles were squared.

RIVIERA, Bowl, Serving, Mauve Blue, Square, 8 In.	4.00
Butter, Green, 1/4 Pound	25.00 To 32.00
Butter, Ivory, 1/4 Pound	35.00
Butter, Mauve Blue, 1/4 Pound	34.00 To 45.00
Butter, Yellow, 1/4 Pound	45.00
Casserole, Mauve Blue, Covered	23.00
Cup & Saucer, Green	5.00 To 10.00
Cup & Saucer, Old Ivory	6.00 To 7.50
Cup & Saucer, Red	5.00 To 10.00
Gravy Boat, Old Ivory	9.00
Gravy Boat, Red	6.00 To 9.00
Jug, Light Green, Covered, 8 In.	50.00
Pitcher, Juice, Mauve	65.00
Pitcher, Juice, Yellow	55.00
Plate, Green, 10 In.	5.00
Plate, Old Ivory, 9 In.	3.50
Platter, Red, Square, Well, Handled, 12 In.	10.00 To 12.00
Platter, Yellow, Square, Well, 13 In.	12.00 To 14.00
Shaker, Ivory, Pair	4.00
Sugar & Creamer, Green, Covered	5.50 To 15.00
Sugar, Light Green, Covered	6.00
Syrup, Red, Covered	27.50
Tea Set, Mauve Blue, 5 Piece	80.00 To 100.00
Tumbler, Ivory, 5 Ounce	6.00 To 11.50
Tumbler, Juice, Light Green	27.50

ROBERTSON, Vase, Crackled, 3 In.	60.00

Rockingham, in the United States, is a brown glazed pottery with a
tortoiseshell-like glaze. It was made from 1840 to 1900 by many American
potteries. Mottled brown Rockingham wares were first made in England at
the Rockingham factory. Other wares were also made by the English firm.

ROCKINGHAM, Bank, Piggy, Brown, Rust, & Cream, 4 X 6 In.	75.00
Bottle, Mermaid, Cork Stopper, 7 1/2 In.	118.00
Bowl, Mixing, Rib Pattern, 10 X 4 1/2 In.	85.00
Bowl, 4 1/2 In.	50.00
Bowl, 6 1/2 In.	27.00
Bowl, 7 1/2 X 3 1/4 In.	45.00
Box, Salt, Hanging, Peafowls On Lid, Animals Around Sides	130.00
Butter, Covered	50.00
Crock, Peafowl In Relief, Wall Hung, 6 1/4 In.	125.00
Cruet, Brown, 4 In., Pair	40.00
Cup, Custard	15.00

Cuspidor, Glazed, Ribbed Sides, 4 1/2 In. 40.00
Cuspidor, 13 1/2 In.Diam. 550.00
Figurine, Lion, Pair 1200.00
Flask, Book, Glazed, 6 In. 150.00
Inkwell, Embossed Foliage, 3 1/8 X 2 1/4 In. 30.00
Jug, Figural Form, 9 1/2 In. 70.00
Jug, Raised Characters, 2 Frogs Inside, 2-Handled, 6 1/2 X 12 In. 195.00
Jug, Whiskey, Crockery Stopper 250.00
Mug, Frog, Signed 135.00
Mug, Strap Handle 62.00
Pan, Milk, 13 1/2 In. 125.00
Pitcher, Anchors With Chains, Rope Handle 115.00
Pitcher, Apostle Cathedral, 8 1/2 In. 150.00
Pitcher, Batter, Handled, 7 In. 150.00
Pitcher, Blackberry Pattern, 6 In. 65.00
Pitcher, Brown, 12 1/2 In. 55.00
Pitcher, Horsehead Handle, Country House Scene, 7 In. 60.00
Pitcher, Vertical Panels, 9 3/4 In. 75.00
Pitcher, Yellow Glaze, Chocolate Sponging, 3 3/4 In. 115.00
Plate, Pie, 9 1/4 In. 40.00
Plate, Pie, 10 1/2 In. 65.00
Tea Set, Porcelain, Green & White, Floral Design, 5 Piece 135.00
Toby Pitcher, Taking Snuff, 9 In. 135.00
    ROGERS, see John Rogers

 Rookwood pottery was made in Cincinnati, Ohio, from 1880 to 1960. All of this art pottery is marked, most with the famous flame mark. The R is reversed and placed back to back with the letter P. Flames surround the letters.

ROOKWOOD, Ashtray, Advertising, Western Southern Insurance Co., 3 Piece 110.00
Ashtray, Baldwin Rodeo, Cincinnati, Large 40.00
Ashtray, Figural, Owl, Tan 95.00
Ashtray, Nude 50.00
Ashtray, Pink Poppy, 1929 .... 32.00
Ashtray, Rook, White, 1946 .... 85.00
Ashtray, Rook, Wings Extending Around Edge, Blue, 1916 .... 75.00
Bookend, Bird, Gray, Blue, Signed, Pair 390.00
Bookend, Blue-Gray, Pair 390.00
Bookend, Blue, McDonald, 1929, 5 X 5 In., Pair 195.00
Bookend, Elephant, High-Gloss Celadon, 1945, Pair .... 160.00 To 175.00
Bookend, Girl, Blue, Dated 1920, Pair 135.00
Bookend, Hound Dogs, Cream Gloss, Pair 110.00
Bookend, Owl, Blue Ground, 1911, 5 In., Pair 65.00
Bookend, Owl, White, 5 1/2 In., Pair 125.00
Bookend, Owls, Tan Glaze, Pair 85.00
Bookend, Pond Lily, White, Pair 95.00
Bowl, Batter, Oriental Flowers, Tangerine & White, 1884, 5 In. 225.00
Bowl, Border Of Cherry Tree Limbs, Blossoms, 1912, 5 In. 225.00
Bowl, Centerpiece, Female Dancers, Cream, Green Interior 90.00
Bowl, Cherry Blossom, 1888, 6 In. 250.00
Bowl, Gray, Blue, Pink Oriental Flowers, 1885, 5 In. 225.00
Bowl, Lotus, Flower Frog, 13 In. 135.00
Bowl, Orange Flowers, 1903, 8 In. 400.00
Bowl, Oriental Flowers, 1885, Italian Gray To Blue, 5 In. 225.00
Bowl, Pansy, Blossoms, 1892, 4 In. 245.00
Bowl, Pansy, High Glaze, 1893, 4 X 2 In. 200.00
Bowl, Pink Matte, 3 X 5 In. 50.00
Bowl, Pouring, Tangerine, White Oriental Flowers, 1884, 5 In. 225.00
Bowl, Salon, White Blossoms, Brown Leaves, 5 X 2 In. 285.00
Bowl, Stems & Buds In Relief, 1909, Footed, 3 1/4 X 6 In. 65.00
Bowl, Tripod, Gray Crackle, Custard Band, Flowers, 6 In. 200.00
Bowl, White Matte Outside, Green Glaze Inside, 1929, 10 1/2 In. 50.00

Box, Cigarette, Dalmatian, Hand-Painted, Blue, Signed, 6 X 4 X 2 In. 150.00
Box, Covered, No.2556, 4 X 3 In. 60.00
Candleholder, Shieldback, 1951, Green Over Rose, 7 1/2 In. 75.00
Candlestick, Dark Blue, 1920 .... 45.00
Candlestick, Dolphin, Ivory Matte, Twisted Stem, 11 In., Pair 200.00
Creamer, Standard, Glazed, No.655, 1897 .... 185.00
Decanter, Greek Key, Green Matte, Stopper 110.00
Dish, Columbia University, 1902, 7 1/2 In. 55.00
Ewer, Allover Fruit, 1900, 5 1/4 In. 425.00
Ewer, Brown, Yellow Floral, 1888, Artist Signed, 4 In. 395.00
Ewer, Flowers, 1900, 9 In. 575.00
Figurine, Penguin, Reba, Yellow, Black, White, 2 3/4 In. 55.00
Flower Frog, Flowers, Blue, 1927, 4 X 3 In. 80.00
Flower Frog, Nude, Frog At Her Foot, Green, 1923 .... 100.00
Flower Frog, Satyr & Turtle, 1921 .... 100.00
Flower Frog, Water Lily, 1919, Aqua 22.00
Ginger Jar, Pink, 3 1/2 In. 58.00
Inkwell, Sphinx Shaped, Blue, C.1909, 9 X 9 In. 300.00
Jar, Potpourri, Dragonflies & Spiders, 1883, 7 In. 1000.00
Jug, Carved Fern, Wandering Jew, Moss Green, 4 X 2 1/2 In. 265.00
Jug, Carved Fern, Wandering Jew, Sticker, 2 5/8 In. 290.00
Jug, Whiskey, Two Ears Of Corn, Amelia Sprague, 7 In. 500.00
Lamp, Oil, Brass Font, Mauve Matte, 1919, 15 In. .... 145.00 To 195.00
Matchbox, Gold Flower Form, 1921, 3 In. 60.00
Mug, Cornhusk, Green Matte, 1905 .... 195.00
Mug, Cornhusk, 1905, Matte Green 195.00
Mug, Geometric, Green To Rose, 4 1/4 In. 185.00
Paperweight, Dog, White, 1946, 3 1/2 X 5 In. 100.00
Paperweight, Elephant, Artist Signed 165.00
Paperweight, Lady, 1926, White 115.00
Paperweight, Nude, Crystalline, Blue 145.00
Paperweight, Owl, Black, 1924, 6 In. 70.00
Paperweight, Rabbit, White, 1954, 3 In. 80.00
Pitcher, Cherries, Brown, Signed, 1900, 5 1/2 In. 275.00
Pitcher, Clover, Butterfly Handle 125.00
Rose Bowl, Geometric Floral, Black, 1922, 5 In. 350.00
Sign, Dealer, 1946, High Glaze Tan 850.00
Sugar & Creamer, Autumn Leaf, Brown 600.00
Sugar & Creamer, Ship, Blue .... 68.00 To 85.00
Teapot, No.404, Maroon, Handled, 1906, 5 In. 125.00
Teapot, Poppy, Josephine Zettel, 1898, 5 In. 425.00
Teapot, Roses, Yellow, Cube Finial, 1908 .... 390.00 To 420.00
Tile, Crowned Frog, Footed, 4 X 4 In. 95.00
Tile, Floral Abstract, Vellum, Charles Todd, 1920, 11 1/2 In. 295.00
Tile, Rabbit, Seafoam Green, Matte, 3 1/2 X 3 1/2 In. 72.50
Tile, Scenic, Square, Marked, 6 In. 85.00
Tile, Tea, Crowned Frog, Footed, 4 X 4 In. 95.00
Tray, Figural, Bunch Of Grapes On Leaf, Green, 7 X 6 In. 85.00
Urn, Greek, Green, Blue Flowers, Signed, 1920 .... 205.00
Vase, Abstract Leaves, 1905, 5 In. 130.00
Vase, Art Deco, Blue, 1919, 8 In. 59.00
Vase, Art Deco, Scene Of Deer, Turquoise Interior, 7 1/2 In. 75.00
Vase, Blue Matte, 1909, 6 In. 65.00
Vase, Blue, 2-Handled, 5 X 5 1/2 In. 45.00
Vase, Brown Matte, 1907, 13 In. 200.00
Vase, Bud, Four Pansies, Lisabeth Lincoln, 1901, 6 1/2 In. 200.00
Vase, Butterflies, Cream Glaze, 4 In. 35.00
Vase, Cherry Design, 8 In. 450.00
Vase, Chinese Shape, Green, 1920, 6 In. 38.00
Vase, Clover & Leaves, Iris Glaze, C.Steinle, 1906, 4 1/2 In. 500.00
Vase, Clover, Yellow, 1901, 5 1/2 In. 350.00
Vase, Cylinder Shape, Pink To Gray, 1916, 6 In. 70.00
Vase, Cylinder, Deep Blue Glaze, 9 In. 85.00
Vase, Daisy, Yellow, 1905, 5 1/4 In. 350.00

Vase, Dark Blue Exterior, Yellow Interior, Handled, 15 In.	275.00
Vase, Decorative Band, Matte Pink, 1930, 5 1/2 In.	40.00
Vase, Dogwood Blossoms, Turquoise, 1919, 9 In.	400.00
Vase, Encircling Floral, Brown Vellum, 1916, 8 1/2 In.	395.00
Vase, Flared, Scrolls, Black Interior, Signed, 6 1/4 X 6 3/8 In.	225.00
Vase, Floral & Blackberries, Thorny Vines, Vellum, 1911, 11 In.	375.00
Vase, Floral Band At Top, Vellum, K.Van Horne, 1913, 6 In.	200.00
Vase, Floral Band, Blue & Lavender, Pink Matte, 1925, 6 In.	190.00
Vase, Floral, Dark Glaze, 1904, Signed, 7 In.	425.00
Vase, Floral, Vellum, Signed Carole Steinle, 1909, 6 1/2 In.	110.00
Vase, Flower, Brown, Gray, Molded, 6 1/4 In.	70.00
Vase, Flowers On Vine, Wax Matte, 1925, Rose Ground, 7 In.	150.00
Vase, Flowers, Red, Dark Green, 5 1/2 In.	170.00
Vase, Forest Scene, Blue, Green, Cream, C.1905, 9 In.	900.00
Vase, Gazelles Dancing, White, 1933, 7 1/2 In.	75.00
Vase, Geometric Design Around Top, Blue, 7 1/2 In.	42.00
Vase, Geometric Flowers, Aqua, 1922, 5 1/2 In.	75.00
Vase, Geometric Flowers, Dark Blue, 1925, 6 In.	350.00
Vase, Geometric Flowers, Pink, Vellum, 1920, 7 1/2 In.	225.00
Vase, Geometric Flowers, Pink, 1920, 7 1/2 In.	225.00
Vase, Geometric, Green Matte, 3-Handled, 6 In.	85.00
Vase, Gooseberry, Gourd Shaped, J.Zettel, 11 1/2 In.	395.00
Vase, Greek Key Around Base, Green, Swirling Rim, 5 3/4 In.	24.00
Vase, Green To Rose, Flared, Footed, 6 1/2 In.	40.00
Vase, Green, Red Floral Band, 5 1/2 In.	135.00
Vase, Incised, White To Gray, 1924, Reuben Menzel, 4 1/4 In.	100.00
Vase, Iris Glaze, Rothenbusch, 1903, 7 In.	595.00
Vase, Iris, Clover Flowers & Leaves, 1906, 4 In.	500.00
Vase, Iris, Floral, Glaze, 4 In.	475.00
Vase, Iris, Signed, C.Steinle, 1908, 6 1/4 In.	310.00
Vase, Iris, Thistle Flowers & Leaves, 1910, 8 In.	1200.00
Vase, Iris, Wax Matte, 7 In.	175.00
Vase, Iris, Yellow Roses, Green Ivy, Yellow Ground, 1904, 7 In.	550.00
Vase, Leaf & Nut, 1892, 10 1/4 In.	200.00
Vase, Leafy Branch, Tobacco Brown, 1891, 3 1/2 In.	130.00
Vase, Maple Leaves, Rothenbusch, 1901, 3 In.	250.00
Vase, Mirror Black, Urn Shaped, Handled, 10 In.	165.00
Vase, Molded Rooks, 6 1/2 In.	65.00
Vase, Narcissus Relief, Transparent High Gloss, 1944, 3 1/2 In.	65.00
Vase, Nat'l Conference Of Catholic Charities, Matte, 1934, 5 In.	175.00
Vase, Nude, White, 6 In.	40.00
Vase, Orange Flowers, Standard Glaze, 1903, 8 In.	400.00
Vase, Palm Fronds, Olive & Brown, Matt Daly, 1892, 30 In.	1000.00
Vase, Petal Form, Pink To Gray, 1919, 4 In.	20.00
Vase, Pink Matte, 1929, 4 1/2 In.	47.00
Vase, Poppies & Foliage, S.Tookey, 1900, 26 1/2 In.	3400.00
Vase, Red & Black, Pink, Glaze, 1930, 6 1/2 In.	200.00
Vase, Red Bell Design, Ivory, 1914, 9 1/2 In.	215.00
Vase, Rose, Molded, Matte, 1925, 5 1/2 In.	55.00
Vase, Rose, Red, Lavender, Blue, C.1904, Marked, 9 In.	750.00
Vase, Rose, 5 In.	39.00
Vase, Sailboat Scene, Rothenbusch, 8 In.	750.00
Vase, Scenic, Blue, Vellum, Rothenbusch, 1930, 12 1/4 In.	1500.00
Vase, Scenic, No.1667, Vellum, 11 In.	1500.00
Vase, Scenic, Vellum, Lorinda Epply, 1911, 6 1/2 In.	575.00
Vase, Scenic, Vellum, Rothenbusch, 8 In.	575.00
Vase, Sculptured Nude Figures, Turquoise, Signed, 1922, 5 In.	135.00
Vase, Sea Horse, Brown Glaze, 1915, 9 In.	69.00
Vase, Strawberries, Pink To Blue, 1926, 10 In.	350.00
Vase, Swirl, Aqua, 1922, 8 In.	25.00
Vase, Thistle & Leaves, 1910, 8 In.	1200.00
Vase, Tigereye, Blue & Cream, Mahogany Glaze, 3 In.	200.00
Vase, Turquoise Matte, 10 In.	79.00
Vase, Violet & Leaves, Lisabeth Lincoln, 1828, 5 1/2 In.	200.00

Vase, Winter Forest Scene, Vellum, 1907, 9 In.	625.00
Wall Pocket, Geometric, Tan Ground, 1926, 7 3/4 In.	55.00
RORSTRAND, Figurine, Dwarf, Kneeling, Horn Of Plenty On Back, Ivory, 8 In.	135.00
Figurine, Porcelain, Dwarf Kneeling, Horn Of Plenty, 8 In.	135.00

Rosaline glass is a rose-colored jade glass that was made by the Steuben Glass Works in Corning, New York.

ROSALINE, Alabaster Finial, Covered	295.00
Bobeche, Steuben, Pair	95.00
Bowl, Signed, 12 In.	625.00
Compote, With Alabaster Base, Stem, & Finial, 7 In.	590.00
Goblet, Threading, Twist Stem, Set Of 4	495.00

Rose bowls were popular during the 1880s. Rose petals were kept in the open bowl to add fragrance to a room. The glass bowls were made with crimped tops, which kept the petals inside. Many types of Victorian art glass were made into rose bowls.

ROSE BOWL, Jack-In-The-Pulpit Top, Camphor Feet, Flower Petals, 6 In.	95.00
Pink, White, & Yellow Swirl, Signed Grey, 5 X 5 1/2 In.	95.00
Rose Tapestry, Blue Mark	245.00

Rose Canton china is similar to Rose Medallion except no people are pictured in the decoration. It was made during the nineteenth and twentieth centuries in greens, pinks, and other colors.

ROSE CANTON, Cup & Saucer, Demitasse, Birds, Butterflies, Fruits, & Badgers	50.00
Plate, Flowers & Butterflies, Blue Scrolls On Back, 8 1/2 In.	75.00
Teapot, Birds, Butterflies & Roses, 1 1/2 Cup	120.00
Teapot, Birds, Flowers, Marked, 5 In.	125.00

Rose Medallion china was made in China during the nineteenth and twentieth centuries. It is a distinctive design picturing people, flowers, birds, and butterflies. They are colored in greens, pinks, and other colors.

ROSE MEDALLION, Ashtray, Leaf Shaped, Marked	25.00
Bottle, Water & Stand, Genre Scenes, Birds, Florals, 15 In.	700.00
Bowl, Bouillon, Original Stand & Lid, Set	325.00
Bowl, Green Wreath Mark, 8 1/4 X 7 1/2 In.	38.00
Bowl, Marked, 9 In.	75.00
Bowl, Oval, 11 X 9 X 2 In.	300.00
Bowl, Punch, Floral & Picture Panels, 13 In.	150.00
Bowl, Punch, Floral, 13 In.	150.00
Bowl, Rice, Covered, Marked, 4 1/2 In.	50.00
Bowl, Vegetable, Butterflies, Birds, & Flowers, Oval, 8 1/2 In.	150.00
Bowl, 7 1/2 In.	75.00
Box, Bats & Bird, Seated Mandarin, Lid, 7 1/4 X 2 1/2 In.	375.00
Brushpot, C.1800	200.00
Candlestick, Design, 7 1/2 In., Pair	700.00
Chamber Pot, Covered, Handled, 10 In.	600.00
Chamber Pot, Genre Scenes, Floral, Birds, Butterflies, 11 In.	225.00
Charger, Genre & Floral Design, 18 1/2 In. .... *Illus*	550.00
Charger, 13 1/2 In.	325.00
Chop Plate, Marked, 13 3/4 In.	125.00
Creamer, Bulbous, C.1800	195.00
Creamer, Helmet	80.00
Cup & Saucer	45.00 To 50.00
Cup & Saucer, Demitasse	50.00 To 55.00
Cup & Saucer, Demitasse, People Panels, 6 Sets	395.00
Cup & Saucer, Scene Of Gentlemen, Mark	34.00
Cup & Saucer, Wishbone Handle, 2 1/2 In.	75.00
Dish, Leaf, Lemon Peel Design, 7 1/2 In.	85.00
Dish, Rectangular, Marked, 9 1/2 In.	160.00
Dish, Serving, Floral Panels, Birds, Butterflies, 9 In.	225.00

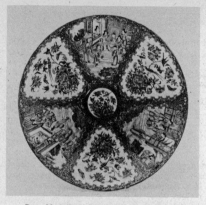

Rose Medallion, Charger, Genre & Floral
Design, 18 1/2 In. *(See Page 555)*

Rose Medallion, Garden Seat, Genre,
Floral, & Bird, 18 1/2 In.

Dish, Trefoil, Orange Peel Glaze, 7 1/2 In.	100.00
Dish, Vegetable, Oval, Covered	475.00
Garden Seat, Genre, Floral, & Bird, 18 1/2 In. .... *Illus*	2100.00
Gravy Boat	95.00
Jar, Covered, 3 1/2 X 2 1/2 In.	45.00
Jar, Marked, Covered, 2 1/4 In.	115.00
Jar, Pomade, Cylindrical, Man At Window On Lid, 2 1/2 In.	115.00
Plate, Birds, Flowers, & People, 13 In.	325.00
Plate, Butterflies, 8 1/2 In., Pair	90.00
Plate, Cutout Rim, People, Floral, & Birds, 7 1/4 In.	95.00
Plate, Dinner, 9 3/4 In.	30.00
Plate, Figures & Birds, 9 3/4 In.	34.00
Plate, Lobed, 8 1/2 In.	65.00
Plate, Mandarin, 6 In.	25.00
Plate, Marked, 6 In.	25.00
Plate, Marked, 8 1/2 In.	50.00
Plate, Marked, 10 In.	65.00
Plate, Octagonal, 8 1/2 In.	73.00
Plate, People Panels, Gold Trim, 8 In.	70.00
Plate, Up-Turned Rim, 8 X 2 In.	88.00
Plate, 7 In.	22.50
Plate, 8 1/2 In.	95.00
Plate, 8-Sided, 8 1/2 In.	65.00
Plate, 9 1/2 In.	55.00
Platter, C.1800, 11 X 8 1/2 In.	650.00
Platter, Orange Peel Back, 13 3/4 X 11 In.	300.00
Platter, Orange Peel, 13 X 16 In.	395.00
Platter, Oval, Marked, 18 1/4 In.	400.00
Platter, 12 X 10 In.	300.00
Platter, 13 X 16 In.	325.00
Punch Bowl, China, Genre Scene, 19th Century, 6 1/4 X 14 In.	550.00
Salt & Pepper, Marked	40.00
Sauce, Double Handled, 8 X 4 In.	75.00
Spoon, Rice, C.1820	50.00
Sugar & Creamer, Bulbous, Covered	275.00
Sugar & Creamer, Marked	125.00
Sugar & Creamer, People In Porch Scene, Flowers, 5 In.	275.00
Sugar, Crab Design, Double Twisted Handles	165.00
Sugar, Crossed Twig Handles, Raspberry Finial, Covered	145.00
Sugar, Twisted Handle, Medallion Lid, 5 In.	260.00
Tea Set, Insulated, 2 Handleless Cups, Fitted Into Basket	160.00

Tea Set, 2 Cups & Saucers, 7 Piece 245.00
Teacup, Figures & Birds, Marked 34.00
Teapot, Basket Handles, Covered 195.00
Teapot, Miniature, Covered, China, 18th Century, 4 3/4 In. 100.00
Teapot, Pear Shape 275.00
Teapot, Wicker Handle, Floral With Birds, 6 3/4 In. 110.00
Tray, Oval, Marked, 8 3/4 In. 65.00
Tureen, Covered, China, Oval, 19th Century, 11 X 15 In. 1950.00
Tureen, Flowers Inside, Nut Finial, Oblong 375.00
Tureen, Underplate, Covered, Twisted Handles 950.00
Vase, Foo Dog Each Side, 10 1/4 In. 185.00
Vegetable, Covered, 9 1/2 X 8 In. 325.00
    ROSE O'NEILL, see Kewpie

> *Rose Tapestry porcelain was made by the Royal Bayreuth factory of Germany during the late nineteenth century. The surface of the ware feels like cloth.*

ROSE TAPESTRY, Basket, Pink Roses, Signed, Royal Bayreuth 315.00
Berry Bowl Set, 3-Color Roses, 7 Piece 950.00
Berry Bowl, Royal Bayreuth, 10 3/4 In. 475.00
Biscuit Jar, Floret Pattern, Royal Bayreuth 195.00
Bowl, 4-Color Roses, Embossed Edge, Royal Bayreuth, 11 In. 625.00
Box, Pin, Colonial Scene, Blue Mark, Oval 145.00
Box, Powder, All Orange, Blue Mark 235.00
Box, Powder, Colonial Scene, Dome Shaped, Covered 155.00
Box, Powder, Orange, Covered 235.00
Box, Powder, Pink, Covered, Blue Mark 145.00
Cake Plate, 3-Color, Open Handle, Blue Mark 235.00
Chocolate Pot, Roses, 3-Color 1100.00
Clock, Daisy, Blue Mark 375.00
Creamer, Corset Shape, Blue Mark, 4 In. 195.00
Creamer, Lady With Horse, Blue Mark 125.00
Creamer, Multicolored Roses, Gold Rim & Handle, Blue Mark 180.00
Creamer, Pinched Nose, Pink, Blue Mark 125.00
Creamer, Tavern Scene, Blue Mark 125.00
Creamer, 3-Color, Squat, Blue Mark 125.00
Cup, Nut, Footed, Pink Roses In & Out, Red Mark 125.00
Dish, Cloverleaf, Orange, Blue Mark 175.00
Dish, Cloverleaf, Pink, Blue Mark 125.00
Dish, Colonial Scene, Maple Leaf Shape, Blue Mark 125.00
Hair Receiver, Pink, Blue Mark .... 135.00 To 215.00
Hair Receiver, Royal Bayreuth 125.00
Hair Receiver, Tricolor, Blue Mark, 4 In.Diam. 165.00
Pitcher, Don Quixote, Women Bathing, Blue Mark, 6 In. 475.00
Pitcher, Milk, Corset Shape, Pink, Blue Mark 165.00
Pitcher, Milk, Goat Scene, Blue Mark 110.00
Pitcher, Pinch Spout, Pink Roses, 4 X 3 1/2 In. 145.00
Pitcher, Pink Roses, Gold Handle, Pinched Nose, Marked, 4 1/2 In. 165.00
Pitcher, Tricolor Roses, Blue Mark, 7 1/2 In. 185.00
Planter, Yellow Rose 250.00
Plaque, Fishing Scene, Blue Mark 250.00
Plaque, Pink Roses, 9 1/2 In. 375.00
Plate, Pink Roses, Gold Rim, Blue Mark, 7 1/2 In. 175.00
Plate, Reticulated Handles, Gold Tracery, Blue Mark, 10 In. 450.00
Relish, Oval, Blue Mark, 8 In. 165.00
Sugar & Creamer, 3-Color Roses, Gilt Handles & Rim 175.00
Tea Set, Covered Teapot, 3-Color Roses, Cylindrical, 4 Piece 750.00
Tray, Dresser, Colonial Scene, Blue Mark 195.00
Tray, Dresser, Goat Scene, Blue Mark 150.00
Tray, Dresser, Violet, Blue Mark 195.00
Tumbler, Castle Scene, Blue Mark 125.00
Vase, Bud, Castle Scene, Blue Mark 125.00
Vase, Bud, Cavalier Scene, Bulbous, Blue Mark, 5 In. 150.00

Vase, Chrysanthemums, 5 1/2 X 12 In.	245.00
Vase, Cows, Meadows, & Mountain, Blue Mark, 4 1/4 In.	225.00
Vase, Goat Scene, Handled, Blue Mark, 8 In.	165.00
Vase, Pink & Yellow Roses, Marked, 4 1/4 In.	175.00
Vase, Polar Bears, Water, & Iceberg, Blue Mark, 4 1/4 In.	235.00
Vase, Silver, Bulbous, 7 In.	950.00

MARKE

Rosenthal porcelain was established in Selb, Bavaria, in 1880. The German factory still continues to make fine-quality tableware and figurines.

ROSENTHAL, Berry Set, Hydrangeas On White, Gold Trim, Signed Picourt, 6 Piece	75.00
Biscuit Jar, Victorian Maiden	70.00
Bowl, Dutch Girl & Swimming Ducks, 6 3/4 In.	38.00
Bowl, Gold & Blue, Open Handled, 10 X 2 1/2 In.	65.00
Bowl, Pink Ground, Strawberries, Leaves, Signed, 10 3/4 In.	75.00
Bowl, Raised Border, Gilt, Marked R.C. & Crown, 10 1/2 In.Diam.	75.00
Box, Collar, Swastika On Lid, White	25.00
Cake Plate, Mercury, Gold Design, Blue Ground, 10 In.	40.00
Cake Set, Selb, Bavaria, Rainbow Glaze, Signed, 6 Piece	75.00
Charger, Scenic, Delft Blue, Large	220.00
Chocolate Set, Blue Fan Flowers, Abstract Gilding, 14 Piece	225.00
Chocolate Set, White, Orange, Gold, Art Deco, Marked, 15 Piece	85.00
Cup & Saucer, Demitasse, Ivory, 6 Sets	100.00
Cup & Saucer, Maria Pattern, Silver Overlay	55.00
Cup, Cigarette, Sterling Silver Pedestal, Moss Rose Pattern	65.00
Dessert Set, Gold Rim, Raised Embossing, 6 Octagonal Plates, Bowl	100.00
Dish, Ronson Cigarette Lighter Insert, Ball Feet, 4 1/2 X 3 In.	12.00
Ewer, Pink Flowers, Green Foliage, Marked, 9 In.	45.00
Figurine, Bikini Girl, 13 In.	300.00
Figurine, Bulldog, French, Sitting, 3 X 4 In.	155.00
Figurine, Bulldog, French, 2 1/2 In.	40.00
Figurine, Chickadees On Branch, Artist Signed	95.00
Figurine, Dachshund, Frowning, Signed Kusper, Brown, 3 1/2 X 4 In.	75.00
Figurine, Dog, Doxie Sitting Up On Haunches, 7 In.	130.00
Figurine, Duck, 2 1/2 In.	35.00
Figurine, Irish Setter	225.00
Figurine, Kneeling Nude, Signed, 9 In.	150.00
Figurine, Mallard Duck & Mate, 5 1/2 X 2 7/8 In.	75.00
Figurine, Mallard Duck, 4 1/4 X 2 1/2 In.	60.00
Figurine, Nude Child Riding Green Grasshopper, 4 1/4 X 3 1/2 In.	115.00
Figurine, Orangutan, Sitting, Reading Page In Lap, 4 1/4 In.	145.00
Figurine, Pigeon, White, Fan-Tail, Marked, 6 X 6 In.	114.00
Figurine, Pouter Pigeon, Pair, Signed, H 1590	250.00
Figurine, Princess With Crowned Frog, No.7333, Signed, 11 In.	375.00
Figurine, Rabbits, Sitting Up Laughing, 4 Rabbits	315.00
Figurine, Russian Wolfhound, Lying Down, Black & White, 11 In.	155.00
Figurine, Scotty, White	95.00
Figurine, Squirrel, Ears & Tail Erect, Holds Walnut, Marked, 7 In.	160.00
Figurine, Terrier, Lying Down, 5 3/4 In.	125.00
Figurine, Terrier, Playing	75.00
Figurine, Turkoman, 7 1/2 In.	35.00
Figurine, Turtle, Swimming, Decorated, 2 1/2 X 1 In.	55.00
Figurine, Victorian Lady With Wolfhound, No.805A, Signed, 11 In.	395.00
Gravy Boat, Aida Pattern, Attached Underplate, Signed	30.00
Holder, Egg, Chickens Around Body, Green Trim	35.00
Jardiniere, Hand-Painted Leaf & Acorn Design, 7 In.	28.00
Mug, Deer, Winter Scene, Dragon Handle, 6 In.	45.00
Mug, Man Drinking, Dragon Handle	22.50
Mustard, Underplate, Pink Roses, Covered	65.00
Plate, Cameo, Mauve On Cream	12.00
Plate, Delft, 6 In.	25.00
Plate, Floral, 10 In.	125.00

Plate, Hand-Painted Six Medallions, 8 In. 22.00
Plate, Open Roses, Cobalt Blue Border, 10 In. 25.00
Plate, Portrait, Marked R.C. & Crown, 9 1/2 In. 65.00
Vase, Portrait, Cobalt, Victorian, Gold Scrolling, 11 1/4 In., Pair 400.00

Roseville
U.S.A.   *Roseville Pottery Co. was organized in Roseville, Ohio, in 1890.*
         Another plant was opened in Zanesville, Ohio, in 1898. Many types
         of pottery were made. The firm closed in 1954.

ROSEVILLE, Ashtray, Conical, Throw Ashes On Floor, Keep Me Clean 125.00
Ashtray, Creamware, Hotel Rogers, 3 In. 42.00
Ashtray, Florentine 50.00
Ashtray, Ming Tree, Blue 38.00
Ashtray, Snowberry, Green 23.50
Ashtray, Snowberry, Rose 30.00
Ashtray, Wincraft, Brown 35.00
Basket, Apple Blossom, Blue, 10 In. 55.00
Basket, Apple Blossom, Blue, 11 In. 77.00
Basket, Apple Blossom, Pink, 9 In. 50.00
Basket, Apple Blossom, Pink, 10 In. 60.00
Basket, Bittersweet, White, 6 In. 47.50
Basket, Bittersweet, White, 10 In. 77.50
Basket, Bleeding Heart, Pink, 10 In. 60.00
Basket, Bushberry, Blue, 8 In. 45.00
Basket, Bushberry, Green, 8 In. 48.00
Basket, Bushberry, Green, 12 In. 95.00
Basket, Bushberry, Rust, 6 1/2 In. 48.00
Basket, Columbine, Blue, 7 In. .... 55.00 To 57.50
Basket, Cosmos, Blue, 12 In. 155.00
Basket, Cosmos, Tan, 10 In. 85.00
Basket, Dahlrose, Brown, 5 1/2 In. 65.00
Basket, Florentine, Brown, 8 In. 57.50
Basket, Freesia, Blue, Handled 40.00
Basket, Freesia, Brown, 7 In. 50.00
Basket, Freesia, Tangerine, 10 In. 44.00
Basket, Fuchsia, Flower Frog, 10 In. 110.00
Basket, Gardenia, Green, 8 In. 50.00
Basket, Hanging, Apple Blossom, Blue 65.00
Basket, Hanging, Apple Blossom, Green 70.00
Basket, Hanging, Donatello, 1915, 6 1/4 X 5 In. 125.00
Basket, Hanging, Florentine, Marked, 9 1/2 X 5 1/2 In .... 75.00 To 125.00
Basket, Hanging, Freesia, Blue .... 45.00 To 65.00
Basket, Hanging, Ivory 52.00
Basket, Hanging, Jonquil 225.00
Basket, Hanging, Magnolia, Green 65.00
Basket, Hanging, Moss, Chains .... 100.00 To 140.00
Basket, Hanging, Mostique, Chains 60.00
Basket, Hanging, Peony, Coral 80.00
Basket, Hanging, Pine Cone, Brown 150.00
Basket, Hanging, Pine Cone, Gold 100.00
Basket, Hanging, Pine Cone, Green, 6 X 8 In. 120.00
Basket, Hanging, Silhouette, White 40.00
Basket, Hanging, Snowberry, Blue 85.00
Basket, Hanging, Vista, Chains 80.00
Basket, Hanging, Wincraft, Blue 65.00
Basket, Hanging, Zephyr Lily, Blue .... 55.00 To 65.00
Basket, Hanging, Zephyr Lily, Orange, Brown, & Yellow 88.00
Basket, Imperial II, 7 In. 195.00
Basket, Imperial, 12 1/2 In. 85.00
Basket, Magnolia, Blue, 7 In. 42.50
Basket, Magnolia, Green, 8 In. 50.00
Basket, Ming Tree, Aqua 100.00
Basket, Mock Orange, Yellow & Rust 45.00

Basket, Moderne, Cream, 6 In.	85.00
Basket, Morning Glory, White, 12 1/4 In.	295.00
Basket, Peony, Green, 12 In.	90.00
Basket, Pine Cone, Brown, 10 1/2 X 13 In.	290.00
Basket, Pine Cone, Green, 6 In.	45.00
Basket, Poppy, Handled, 9 In.	40.00
Basket, Rozane, Roses, Ivory Ground, Marked, 6 3/4 In.	120.00
Basket, Silhouette, Brown, 8 In.	45.00
Basket, Snowberry, Raised Pattern, Blue & Black Ground, 10 In.	80.00
Basket, Snowberry, White, Rose, Green, & Brown, 12 In.	85.50
Basket, Water Lily, Pink, 8 In.	30.00
Basket, White Rose, Green, 10 In.	65.00
Basket, Wincraft, Blue, 12 In.	54.00
Basket, Wincraft, Brown & Beige, 12 In.	47.00
Bookend, Bittersweet, Green, 4 X 5 In., Pair	77.50
Bookend, Clematis, Brown, Pair	50.00
Bookend, Magnolia, Brown, Pair	45.00
Bookend, Peony, Green	25.00
Bookend, Pine Cone, Brown, Pair	95.00 To 145.00
Bookend, Zephyr Lily, Blue	65.00
Bowl & Creamer, Child's, Sitting Rabbit, 4 In.	80.00
Bowl & Frog, Rosecraft, 2 1/2 X 6 In.	125.00
Bowl, Baneda, 7 3/4 In.	53.00
Bowl, Bleeding Heart, Green, Flat & Round, 6 In.	32.50
Bowl, Bleeding Heart, Green, 4 In.	19.00
Bowl, Bushberry, Green, 6 In.	18.00
Bowl, Bushberry, Rust & Green, 3 In.	15.00
Bowl, Carnelian I, Green, 8 In.	52.00
Bowl, Cherry Blossom, Green & Pink, 4 In.	97.50
Bowl, Clemana, Brown, 5 In.	77.50
Bowl, Clemana, Green, 11 X 4 In.	75.00
Bowl, Clematis, Green, Handled, 10 In.	35.00
Bowl, Columbine, Pink, 10 In.	25.00
Bowl, Console, Blackberry, 13 In.	125.00
Bowl, Console, Bushberry, Blue, 12 In.	40.00
Bowl, Console, Donatello, 10 In.	65.00
Bowl, Console, Freesia, Green, 14 In.	47.50
Bowl, Console, Fuchsia, Flower Frog, Brown, 8 In.	41.00
Bowl, Console, Mock Orange, Marked, 12 In.	65.00
Bowl, Console, Peony, Pink, 12 In.	45.00
Bowl, Console, Snowberry, Blue, 12 In.	38.00
Bowl, Console, Water Lily, Blue, 10 In.	34.00
Bowl, Console, Wisteria, Brown, 9 In.	75.00
Bowl, Corinthian, Flower Frog, 3 1/2 X 8 In.	57.50
Bowl, Corinthian, 8 In.	42.00
Bowl, Cremona, Green, 9 In.	47.00
Bowl, Dawn, Yellow, 6 In.	42.00
Bowl, Donatello, Flat, 8 In.	50.00
Bowl, Donatello, Marked, 5 X 5 In.	120.00
Bowl, Donatello, 5 In.	38.00
Bowl, Donatello, 7 In.	50.00 To 70.00
Bowl, Earlam, Tan, 4 In.	47.00
Bowl, Ferrella, Raspberry, 5 In.	225.00
Bowl, Florentine, 4 1/2 In.	23.00
Bowl, Foxglove, Blue, Handled, 14 In.	40.00
Bowl, Fuchsia, Green, Oval, 14 In.	95.00
Bowl, Fuchsia, Green, 4 In.	29.00
Bowl, Gardenia, 4 In.	12.50
Bowl, Imperial, 8 In.	35.00
Bowl, Imperial, 9 In.	40.00
Bowl, Ixia, Green, 4 In.	27.50
Bowl, Jonquil, Brown, Gold Paper Label, 8 In.	30.00
Bowl, Jonquil, 6 In.	46.00
Bowl, Laurel, Brown, 6 X 6 In.	60.00

Bowl, Magnolia, Blue, Handled, 3 In. 17.50
Bowl, Magnolia, Brown, 2 In. 25.00
Bowl, Magnolia, Green, 4 In. 29.00
Bowl, Mock Orange, Yellow & Green, 5 In. 30.00
Bowl, Mostique, 6 1/2 X 3 In. 20.00
Bowl, Mostique, 8 X 3 In. 25.00
Bowl, Pine Cone, Brown, 3 In. 25.00
Bowl, Pine Cone, Green, 11 X 5 In. 65.00
Bowl, Pine Cone, Green, 16 X 10 X 7 In. 140.00
Bowl, Rosecraft Vintage, 4-Footed, 5 1/2 In. 15.00
Bowl, Rosecraft, Black, 5 In. 45.00
Bowl, Rosecraft, Black, 6 In. 35.00
Bowl, Rosecraft, Blue, 6 In. 30.00
Bowl, Snowberry, 5 In. .... 35.00 To 40.00
Bowl, Snowberry, 6 In. 35.00
Bowl, Topeo, 8 1/4 In. 85.00
Bowl, Tourmaline, Blue, 8 In. 45.00
Bowl, Water Lily, Green, 4 In. 20.00
Bowl, White Rose, Brown Rose, Flower Frog, 10 In. 60.00
Bowl, With Frog, Florane, 8 1/2 In. 25.00
Box, Cigarette, Silhouette, Blue 48.00
Candleholder, Bittersweet, Green, 3 In. 52.50
Candleholder, Bittersweet, Yellow, 3 In. 52.50
Candleholder, Blackberry, 4 1/2 In. 125.00
Candleholder, Burmese, Black Female 55.00
Candleholder, Bushberry, Blue, 2 In., Pair 32.00
Candleholder, Carnelian, Blue 27.50
Candleholder, Cherry Blossom, Blue & Tan, Pair 150.00
Candleholder, Cosmos, Blue, 2 In., Pair 27.00
Candleholder, Cosmos, Green, 4 1/2 In. 25.00
Candleholder, Dahlrose, 3 1/2 In., Pair 57.00
Candleholder, Freesia, Blue 35.00
Candleholder, Freesia, Green, 4 1/2 In. .... 22.00 To 27.00
Candleholder, Fuchsia, Green, 5 In., Pair 95.00
Candleholder, Morning Glory, White, 5 In. 85.00
Candleholder, Panel, Brown 50.00
Candleholder, Pine Cone, Blue, 4 In., Pair 48.00
Candleholder, Rozane, Green, 3 In., Pair 22.00
Candleholder, Silhouette, Maroon, 3 In., Pair 30.00
Candleholder, Snowberry, 4 In., Pair 22.00
Candleholder, Sunflower, Pair 160.00
Candleholder, Water Lily, Pair 20.00
Candleholder, Zephyr Lily, Blue, 2 In., Pair 39.00
Candlestick, Donatello, 6 1/2 In,, Pair 75.00
Candlestick, Donatello, 8 In., Pair 170.00
Candlestick, Florentine, 8 1/2 In., Pair 85.00
Candlestick, Futura, Brown, Hexagonal 75.00
Candlestick, Panel, Brown, 8 In. 65.00
Candlestick, Panel, Green, 8 1/2 In., Pair 115.00
Candlestick, Snowberry, 6 In., Pair 45.00
Candlestick, Velmoss Scroll, 10 In., Pair 185.00
Cider Set, Bushberry, Blue, 5 Piece 325.00
Coffee Set, Wincraft, Bittersweet 175.00
Compote, Donatello, 5 3/4 In. 60.00
Compote, Florentine, 10 In. 55.00
Compote, Imperial, 6 1/4 In. 46.00
Conch, Foxglove, Brown, 6 In. 45.00
Conch, Rozane, Brown 45.00
Console Set, Dahlrose, 3 Piece 45.00
Console Set, Freesia, Bowl 16 In. 40.00
Console Set, Luffa, Bowl, 13 X 8 In. 150.00
Console Set, Panel, Brown, 3 Piece 175.00
Console Set, White Rose, Brown, 3 Piece 65.00
Console, Luster Pink, Footed, 10 In. 75.00

Console, Moderne, Blue	49.00
Console, Poppy, Green	35.00
Cookie Jar, Clematis, Brown, 8 In.	115.00 To 135.00
Cookie Jar, Freesia, Rust & Brown, Covered	150.00
Cookie Jar, Magnolia, Blue	135.00
Cookie Jar, Zephyr Lily, Blue	90.00
Cookie Jar, Zephyr Lily, Brown & Green	120.00
Cornucopia, Bittersweet, Gray	28.00
Cornucopia, Bittersweet, Yellow, 8 In.	52.50
Cornucopia, Foxglove, Blue, 6 In.	30.00
Cornucopia, Gardenia, Green, 6 In.	18.00
Cornucopia, Mostique, 12 X 6 1/4 In.	40.00
Cornucopia, Snowberry, Green, 6 In.	25.00
Cornucopia, White Rose, 8 In.	35.00
Cornucopia, Zephyr Lily, Brown, 8 In.	15.00
Creamer, Peony, Green	20.00
Creamer, Rabbit	35.00
Creamer, Rozane, Pedestal, 1917, 8 In.	210.00
Creamer, Thornapple, Pink & Green	40.00
Creamer, Wincraft, Yellow Flowers, Marked, Blue	25.00
Eggcup, Creamware, Chicks, Green, 4 In.	47.00
Ewer, Bleeding Heart, Blue, 6 In.	49.50
Ewer, Bushberry, Blue, 10 In., Pair	150.00
Ewer, Bushberry, Brown, 6 In., Pair	80.00
Ewer, Clematis, Green, 15 In.	155.00
Ewer, Clematis, 10 In.	45.00
Ewer, Cosmos, Tan, 10 In.	27.00
Ewer, Foxglove, Pink, 10 In.	60.00
Ewer, Freesia, Blue, 6 In.	40.00
Ewer, Iris, Pink, 10 In.	65.00
Ewer, Magnolia, Blue, 6 In.	32.50
Ewer, Pine Cone, Brown, 10 In.	85.00
Fernery, Windsor, Blue	150.00
Flower Frog, Clematis, Brown & Yellow	40.00
Flower Frog, Water Lily, Pink	12.50
Flower Frog, White Rose, Green	25.00
Flowerpot, Apple Blossom, Tray, Green	52.00
Flowerpot, Tuscany, Saucer	36.00
Jar, Corinthian, Pedestal, 29 In.	700.00
Jar, Futura, Pedestal, Brown, 28 In.	750.00
Jar, Strawberry, Mirror Black, 9 1/2 In.	25.00
Jardiniere, Apple Blossom, 5 1/4 X 8 In.	250.00
Jardiniere, Apple Blossom, 17 In.	150.00
Jardiniere, Artcraft, Brown, 10 In.	210.00
Jardiniere, Baneda, 7 In.	125.00
Jardiniere, Blackberry, 8 In.	225.00
Jardiniere, Blackberry, 10 X 7 In.	145.00 To 165.00
Jardiniere, Bleeding Heart, Blue, 3 In.	24.50
Jardiniere, Bleeding Heart, Green, 3 In.	24.50
Jardiniere, Bushberry, Blue, 3 In.	12.50
Jardiniere, Clematis, Green, 8 In.	350.00
Jardiniere, Columbine, Blue, 3 In.	24.00
Jardiniere, Columbine, Blue, 4 In.	42.00
Jardiniere, Columbine, Blue, 6 In.	52.00
Jardiniere, Columbine, Blue, 8 In.	95.00
Jardiniere, Corinthian, 9 X 12 In.	210.00
Jardiniere, Corinthian, 32 In.	650.00
Jardiniere, Cosmos, Tan, 3 In.	27.00
Jardiniere, Dahlrose, 6 In.	55.00
Jardiniere, Dogwood II, Pedestal, 28 1/2 In.	400.00
Jardiniere, Donatello, Pedestal, 27 In.	550.00
Jardiniere, Foxglove, Blue, Pedestal, 30 1/2 In.	675.00
Jardiniere, Foxglove, Blue, 3 In.	24.00
Jardiniere, Freesia, Blue, 6 In.	65.00 To 75.00

Jardiniere, Futura, Brown, 6 In.	85.00
Jardiniere, Futura, Brown, 28 In.	650.00
Jardiniere, Luffa, Green & Rust, Pedestal, 24 1/2 In.	650.00
Jardiniere, Magnolia, Green, Pedestal, 25 In.	275.00
Jardiniere, Mostique, Pedestal, 28 In.	300.00
Jardiniere, Normandy, 7 In.	135.00
Jardiniere, Pauleo, 19 In.	700.00
Jardiniere, Peony, Gold, Pedestal, 10 In.	750.00
Jardiniere, Peony, Green & Pink, Pedestal, 24 1/2 In.	450.00
Jardiniere, Persian, 8 In.	200.00
Jardiniere, Persian, 8-Color, 15 X 44 In.	325.00
Jardiniere, Primrose, Pedestal, Brown, 27 In.	350.00
Jardiniere, Rosecraft, Pedestal, 30 1/2 In.	425.00
Jardiniere, Sylvan, Stags, 15 In.	550.00
Jardiniere, White Rose, Blue, Pedestal	450.00
Jardiniere, White Rose, Pink, 8 In.	82.00
Jardiniere, Wisteria, Blue, Pedestal, 10 In.	1650.00
Jardiniere, Zephyr Lily, Green, 8 1/2 In.	70.00
Jug, Baneda, Green, 4 1/2 In.	65.00
Jug, Cherry Blossom, Brown, 4 In.	100.00
Jug, Cherry Blossom, Rose To Green, 8 In.	100.00
Jug, Monticello, Bulbous, Brown	125.00
Lamp, Cherry Blossom, Brown	175.00
Lamp, Cosmos, Cone Shaped, Handled, Wooden Base, 22 In.	95.00
Lamp, Freesia, 2-Handled, 17 In.	175.00
Lamp, Moderne, Shade, Tan, 11 In.	95.00
Lamp, Pauleo, Original Tiffany Fittings, 20 In.	400.00
Lemonade Set, Peony, Green, 7 Piece	300.00
Mug, Creamware, Dutch, Carrying Water, 5 In.	57.00
Mug, Creamware, Dutch, Unhooking Fish, 4 1/2 In.	37.00
Mug, Elk, 5 In.	75.00
Mug, Indian	110.00
Mug, Magnolia, Brown	45.00
Mug, Magnolia, Signed, Blue, 3 In.	60.00
Mug, Peony, Pink	45.00
Mug, Pine Cone, Green, 4 In.	50.00
Mug, Sunflower	22.00
Nappy, Snowberry, Handled, Green, Brown & White, 10 X 3 In.	58.00
Pitcher, Carnelian I, Green & Purple, 10 In.	85.00
Pitcher, Carnelian II, Turquoise, 15 In.	125.00
Pitcher, Child's, Chicks, 3 1/2 In.	35.00
Pitcher, Cider, Fuchsia, Brown	75.00
Pitcher, Cow	75.00
Pitcher, Freesia, Blue, 10 In.	58.00
Pitcher, Morning Glory, 15 In.	500.00
Pitcher, Pine Cone, Brown, 10 In.	150.00
Pitcher, Poppy, Green, 10 In.	45.00
Pitcher, Water, Rozane, 1917	125.00
Planter, Apple Blossom, Blue, 12 In.	57.00
Planter, Bitersweet, Green, 8 In.	25.00
Planter, Bittersweet, Yellow, 10 In.	47.50
Planter, Burmese, Black, 9 In.	60.00
Planter, Freesia, Window Box, Brown, 9 In.	30.00
Planter, Magnolia, 8 In.	30.00
Planter, Silhouette, Turquoise, 14 In.	35.00
Planter, Snowberry, 11 X 3 In.	30.00
Plate, Child's, Chicks, 8 1/4 In.	55.00
Plate, Child's, Dogs, 7 3/4 In.	45.00
Plate, Child's, Ducks, Green, 8 In.	67.00
Plate, Child's, Nursery Rhyme, 8 In.	97.00
Plate, Child's, Rabbits, Brown, 8 In.	67.00
Shell, Capri, Green, 10 In.	52.00
Spooner, Gardenia, Gray	28.00

Stein, Better Late Than Never 175.00
Strawberry Pot, Earlam 75.00
Strawberry Pot, Jonquil, 4-Spout, Ringed Top 125.00
Sugar & Creamer, Landscape, Blue Sailing Ship, White Ground 120.00
Sugar & Creamer, Mock Orange, Covered 65.00
Sugar, Landscape, Cream, 5 In. 77.00
Tankard, Dutch, 11 1/2 In. 230.00
Tankard, Elk, 11 1/2 In. 140.00
Tea Set, Clematis, Brown, 3 Piece .... 85.00 To 100.00
Tea Set, Snowberry, Rose 85.00
Tea Set, White Rose, 3 Piece 75.00
Tea Set, Wincraft, Blue .... 65.00 To 125.00
Teapot, Apple Blossom 70.00
Teapot, Clematis, Blue, 5 In. 68.00
Teapot, Foxglove, Green & White, Lavender Flowers 75.00
Teapot, Freesia, Green 67.50
Tray, Gardenia, Green, 15 In. 45.00
Tray, Pine Cone, Green, 2 X 5 In. 35.00
Tumbler, Conventional, 4 In. 62.00
Tumbler, Pine Cone, Green, Signed, 5 In. 55.00
Umbrella Stand, Vista 350.00
Urn, Baneda, Green, 10 In. 135.00
Urn, Baneda, Plum, 1933, 5 In. 42.00
Urn, Foxglove, Blue, 8 In. 40.00
Urn, Iris, Pink, 3 In. 19.00
Urn, Magnolia, Blue, Handled, 8 1/4 In. 55.00
Urn, Moss, Blue, 9 In. 60.00
Urn, Orian, Yellow, 12 In. 175.00
Urn, Silhouette, Nude, 10 In. .... 120.00 To 125.00
Urn, Snowberry, Green, 8 In. 34.00
Urn, Sunflower, 10 In. 80.00
Urn, Wisteria, Blue, 5 In. .... 60.00 To 75.00
Urn, Wisteria, Blue, 7 1/2 In. 75.00
Vase, Apple Blossom, Blue, 7 In. 30.00
Vase, Apple Blossom, Blue, 8 In. 47.00
Vase, Apple Blossom, Green, Cylindrical, 9 In. 25.00
Vase, Apple Blossom, Green, 6 In. 32.50
Vase, Apple Blossom, Green, 7 In. .... 32.50 To 39.00
Vase, Apple Blossom, Lion's Heads, Garlands, Blue, 18 In. 195.00
Vase, Apple Blossom, Pink, 2-Handled, 1 1/2 In. 38.00
Vase, Artwood, 8 In. 30.00
Vase, Baneda, Green, 4 1/2 In. 57.50
Vase, Baneda, Green, 5 1/4 In. 58.00
Vase, Baneda, Green, 6 In. .... 40.00 To 45.00
Vase, Baneda, Red, 6 In. 65.00
Vase, Bittersweet, Green, 12 In. 40.00
Vase, Bittersweet, White, Double Bud, 6 In. 47.50
Vase, Bittersweet, Yellow, 10 In. 27.50
Vase, Blackberry, 6 In. .... 115.00 To 145.00
Vase, Blackberry, 6 1/2 In. 80.00
Vase, Blackberry, 8 In. .... 110.00 To 235.00
Vase, Blackberry, 10 In. 295.00
Vase, Blackberry, 12 In. 135.00
Vase, Bleeding Heart, Blue, 6 In. 9.00
Vase, Bleeding Heart, Blue, 8 In. 30.00
Vase, Bleeding Heart, Green, 6 In. 12.50
Vase, Bleeding Heart, Green, 8 In. 18.00
Vase, Bleeding Heart, Green, 9 In. 22.50
Vase, Bud, Bushberry, Blue, Pair 70.00
Vase, Bud, Clematis, Green, 7 In. 32.50
Vase, Bud, Corinthian, Double, 7 1/2 X 4 1/2 In. .... 47.50 To 49.00
Vase, Bud, Dahlrose, Double, 6 In. 47.00
Vase, Bud, Dahlrose, 8 In. 35.00
Vase, Bud, Donatello 40.00

Vase, Bud, Rosecraft, Black, Double 85.00
Vase, Bud, Rosecraft, Blue 30.00
Vase, Bud, Rozane, Green, 6 In. 30.00
Vase, Bud, White Rose, Pink 25.00
Vase, Bushberry, Blue, Footed, 2-Handled, 9 X 7 In. 50.00
Vase, Bushberry, Blue, 18 In. 175.00
Vase, Bushberry, Brown, 4 In. 25.00
Vase, Bushberry, Green, 4 In. 12.50
Vase, Bushberry, Green, 9 In. 27.50
Vase, Bushberry, Open-Handled, 6 1/4 In. 12.50
Vase, Carnelian I, Green, 10 In. 65.00
Vase, Carnelian I, Pillow, Green, 6 In. 40.00
Vase, Carnelian II, Green, 8 In. 47.50
Vase, Carnelian II, 12 In. 60.00
Vase, Cherry Blossom, Blue, 8 In. 115.00
Vase, Cherry Blossom, Pink, 5 In. 110.00
Vase, Clemana, Brown, 6 In. 70.00
Vase, Clematis, Blue, 6 In. 30.00
Vase, Clematis, Brown & Yellow, 7 In. 38.00
Vase, Columbine, Brown, 8 In. 27.50
Vase, Columbine, Pink & Green, 14 In. 150.00
Vase, Columbine, Pink, 14 In. 95.00
Vase, Corinthian, 6 1/2 In. 55.00
Vase, Cosmos, 4 In. 25.00
Vase, Cremona, Green, 10 1/2 In. 83.00
Vase, Cremona, Pink, 5 In. 42.00
Vase, Cremona, Pink, 10 In. 50.00
Vase, Dahlrose, 6 In. 20.00
Vase, Dahlrose, 10 In. 80.00
Vase, Dawn, Pink, 8 In. 42.00
Vase, Dogwood, 6 In. 50.00
Vase, Dogwood, 14 1/2 In. 125.00
Vase, Donatello, Cylindrical, 4 1/2 X 10 In. 65.00
Vase, Donatello, 7 In. 55.00
Vase, Earlam, 5 1/2 In. 30.00
Vase, Falline, 8 In. 135.00
Vase, Fan, Zephyr, 6 1/4 In. 30.00
Vase, Fan, Zephyr, 6 3/4 In. 30.00
Vase, Ferrella, Brown, 5 In. 225.00
Vase, Ferrella, Brown, 9 In. 225.00
Vase, Ferrella, Red, 4 In. 115.00
Vase, Florane, Red, 8 In. 50.00
Vase, Florentine, Moss Green & Pink, 12 1/2 In. 95.00
Vase, Florentine, 8 1/2 In. 47.00
Vase, Foxglove, Blue, 7 1/2 In. 45.00
Vase, Foxglove, Blue, 8 In. 30.00
Vase, Foxglove, Blue, 18 In. 215.00
Vase, Foxglove, Green & Pink, 14 In. 85.00
Vase, Freesia, Brown, 10 In. 43.00
Vase, Freesia, Green, 9 1/4 In. 40.00
Vase, Freesia, Green, 10 In. 40.00
Vase, Freesia, Rust To Brown, Handled, 5 In. 55.00
Vase, Freesia, Rust To Dark Brown, Handled, 7 In. 48.50
Vase, Fuchsia, Brown, 6 In. 35.00
Vase, Fuchsia, White, 15 In. 195.00
Vase, Futura, 7 In. 65.00
Vase, Futura, 7 1/2 In. 75.00
Vase, Futura, 8 In. .... 85.00 To 150.00
Vase, Gardenia, Gray, 10 In. 42.00
Vase, Gardenia, Green, 10 In. 45.00
Vase, Gardenia, Green, 14 In. .... 90.00 To 95.00
Vase, Imperial I, 8 In. 60.00
Vase, Imperial I, 12 In. 105.00
Vase, Imperial II, 6 In. 110.00

Vase, Imperial, Double-Handled, 10 1/2 In.	68.00
Vase, Imperial, 8 In.	25.00
Vase, Iris, Brown, Gold Trim, 4 In.	36.00
Vase, Iris, Green To Pink, 5 In.	25.00
Vase, Ixia, Yellow, 6 In.	30.00
Vase, Jonquil, Double Handled, 3 In.	55.00
Vase, Jonquil, 4 In.	30.00 To 40.00
Vase, Jonquil, 8 In.	69.00 To 85.00
Vase, Jonquil, 9 1/2 In.	115.00
Vase, Laurel, Coral, 6 1/2 In.	50.00
Vase, Laurel, Green, 6 In.	45.00
Vase, Laurel, Yellow, 7 In.	50.00
Vase, Lotus, 10 In.	165.00
Vase, Luffa, Brown, 6 1/4 In.	65.00
Vase, Luffa, Brown, 8 In.	65.00
Vase, Luffa, Brown, 15 In.	250.00
Vase, Luffa, Orange, 6 1/4 X 6 3/4 In.	48.00
Vase, Magnolia, Blue, 5 X 7 In.	30.00
Vase, Magnolia, Blue, 6 X 9 In.	35.00 To 65.00
Vase, Magnolia, Green, 8 In.	35.00
Vase, Magnolia, Orange, 9 In.	43.00
Vase, Mock Orange, Pink, 10 In.	50.00
Vase, Mock Orange, Pink, 12 In.	68.00
Vase, Monticello, Blue & Green, 8 In.	85.00
Vase, Monticello, Blue & Green, 8 1/4 In.	85.00
Vase, Monticello, Blue, 7 In.	75.00
Vase, Monticello, Brown, Handled, 5 In.	68.00
Vase, Monticello, Green, 7 In.	85.00
Vase, Morning Glory, Green, 7 1/2 In.	110.00
Vase, Morning Glory, Green, 9 1/2 In.	250.00
Vase, Morning Glory, 15 In.	625.00
Vase, Moss, Blue, 6 In.	35.00
Vase, Mostique, 10 X 5 In.	35.00
Vase, Mostique, 12 X 6 1/4 In.	40.00
Vase, New Hampshire Vintage, 12 In.	200.00
Vase, Panel, Brown, 6 In.	60.00
Vase, Panel, Brown, 11 In.	225.00
Vase, Pauleo, Gold & Orange, 18 In.	850.00
Vase, Pauleo, Luster, Green, Gold Oily Appearance, 19 In.	800.00
Vase, Peony, Green, 2-Handled, 7 In.	35.00
Vase, Peony, Green, 2-Handled, 8 1/2 In.	60.00
Vase, Peony, Pink, 4 In.	18.00
Vase, Peony, Yellow, 6 In.	30.00
Vase, Pine Cone, Blue, Handled, Paper Label, 8 1/2 In.	25.00
Vase, Pine Cone, Blue, 7 In.	40.00
Vase, Pine Cone, Brown, 7 In.	45.00
Vase, Pine Cone, Brown, 10 In.	83.00 To 90.00
Vase, Pine Cone, Brown, 12 In.	75.00
Vase, Pine Cone, Green, 8 In.	55.00 To 65.00
Vase, Primrose, Pink, 6 In.	38.00
Vase, Rosecraft, Black, 7 In.	35.00
Vase, Rosecraft, Black, 10 In.	35.00
Vase, Rozane, Blue, 9 1/4 In.	35.00
Vase, Rozane, Hanging Leaves & Flowers, Artist Signed, 15 1/2 In.	225.00
Vase, Rozane, Orchid, 15 In.	125.00
Vase, Russco, 7 In.	50.00
Vase, Silhouette, Ming Red, 9 In.	25.00
Vase, Snowberry, 6 In.	18.00 To 28.00
Vase, Sunflower, 7 In.	70.00 To 125.00
Vase, Sunflower, 8 In.	75.00
Vase, Sunflower, 10 1/4 In.	155.00
Vase, Topeo, Green & Blue, 6 In.	75.00
Vase, Torpedo, Blue, 9 In.	115.00

Vase, Tourmaline, Aqua, 8 In.	35.00
Vase, Tourmaline, Blue, 8 In.	65.00
Vase, Tuscany, Pink, 5 In.	15.00 To 35.00
Vase, Tuscany, Pink, 6 In.	35.00
Vase, Tuscany, Pink, 8 In.	30.00
Vase, Velmoss II, Blue, 10 In.	60.00
Vase, Vista, 10 In.	85.00
Vase, Vista, 15 In.	250.00
Vase, Volpato, Ivory, 8 In.	55.00 To 58.00
Vase, Water Lily, Blue, Double Handled, 7 In.	12.00
Vase, Water Lily, Pink, 6 In.	35.00
Vase, White Rose, Beige, 8 1/4 In.	50.00
Vase, White Rose, Green, 6 In.	30.00
Vase, White Rose, Turquoise, 8 In.	43.00
Vase, Wincraft, Blue, 8 1/4 In.	40.00
Vase, Wincraft, Puma, Brown, 12 In.	150.00
Vase, Wincraft, Yellow, 10 In.	40.00
Vase, Wincraft, Yellow, 10 1/4 In.	40.00
Vase, Wisteria, Blue, 7 1/4 In.	85.00
Vase, Wisteria, Blue, 10 In.	120.00
Vase, Wincraft, Yellow 2-Handled, 10 In.	48.00
Vase, Zephyr, Green & Rust, 15 In.	140.00
Vase, Zephyr, Green, 12 3/8 In.	55.00
Vase, Zephyr, Multicolored, 10 1/2 In.	45.00
Wall Pocket, Apple Blossom, Blue	48.00
Wall Pocket, Apple Blossom, Pink	30.00 To 65.00
Wall Pocket, Bittersweet, Yellow, 7 In.	22.50
Wall Pocket, Burmese, Blue-Green	95.00
Wall Pocket, Burmese, Green, Pair	200.00
Wall Pocket, Carnelian I, 8 In.	47.50
Wall Pocket, Carnelian II, Blue-Green, 7 In.	55.00
Wall Pocket, Clematis, Green, 8 In.	42.00
Wall Pocket, Columbine	95.00
Wall Pocket, Corinthian	85.00
Wall Pocket, Cosmos, Tan, Double, 8 In.	52.00
Wall Pocket, Dahlrose	58.00
Wall Pocket, Donatello	45.00 To 95.00
Wall Pocket, Florane, 9 1/4 In.	95.00
Wall Pocket, Florentine, Brown, 9 1/2 In.	62.50
Wall Pocket, Florentine, 7 1/4 In.	55.00
Wall Pocket, Florentine, 8 1/2 In.	63.00
Wall Pocket, Florentine, 12 1/2 In.	65.00
Wall Pocket, Foxglove	48.00
Wall Pocket, Freesia, 9 In., Pair	60.00
Wall Pocket, Futura, 8 In.	100.00
Wall Pocket, Jonquil	150.00
Wall Pocket, Lotus, Blue	150.00
Wall Pocket, Luffa	150.00
Wall Pocket, Magnolia, Green	45.00
Wall Pocket, Mayfair, Tan	35.00
Wall Pocket, Panel, Brown, 9 1/2 In.	80.00 To 85.00
Wall Pocket, Peony, Green	45.00
Wall Pocket, Rosecraft Vintage	95.00
Wall Pocket, Silhouette	65.00
Wall Pocket, Snowberry, Blue	40.00
Wall Pocket, Snowberry, Pink	25.00

Rowland & Marsellus Company is a mark which appears on historical Staffordshire dating from the late nineteenth and early twentieth centuries. Rowland & Marsellus is believed to be the British Anchor Pottery Co. of Longton, England. Many American views were made.

ROWLAND & MARSELLUS, Plate, Denver, Rolled Edge, 10 1/2 In.   35.00

Plate, George Washington, 10 In.	65.00
Plate, Niagara Falls, Blue & White, 10 1/2 In.	35.00
Plate, Wellesley College, 10 1/2 In.	45.00

Roy Rogers was born in 1911 in Cincinnati, Ohio. In the 1930s he made a living as a singer and in 1935 his group started work at a Los Angles radio station. He appeared in his first movie in 1937. From 1952 to 1957 he made 101 television shows. Roy Rogers memorabilia is collected, including items from the Roy Rogers restaurants.

ROY ROGERS, Badge, Hideaway	25.00
Bank, Cast Iron	20.00
Book, Coloring, Oversized, 1950	20.00
Book, Little Big Book	10.00
Book, Raiders Of Sawtooth Ridge, 1946	10.00
Camera	15.00
Clock, Animated, Alarm, Roy & Trigger On Face	115.00 To 150.00
Clock, Ingraham, Animated	95.00
Creamer, Figural Head, Plastic	16.00
Cup, Figural Head, Plastic	4.50
Flashlight	20.00
Glass, Drinking, 1950, 6 In.	20.00
Guitar, Cardboard, 27 In.	35.00
Gun & Holster	30.00
Harmonica	5.00
Holster Set, Boxed, Leather	140.00
Holster, King Of Cowboys, Brown Leather	15.00
Horseshoe, Lucky, Black Rubber	18.00
Jeep, With Figures, Boxed	50.00
Lantern, Ranch, Original Box	35.00
Lariat, Glow In Dark	18.00
Lunch Box, Chuck Wagon, Dale Evans Pictured	6.00 To 12.00
Lunch Box, Thermos	9.00 To 16.00
Mug, Plastic	10.00
Outfit, Dale Evans Cowgirl, Complete, Gun & Holster, Boxed	33.00
Pin, Roy & Trigger, Yellow Ground, 1 3/4 In.	3.00
Plate, Roy & Trigger, Ceramic, 9 In.	18.00
Potholder	12.00
Ring, Branding Iron	20.00
Ship, 5 In.	30.00
Spurs, Boxed	35.00
Stickpin, Sheriff, 1953	9.00
T Shirts, Pair	15.00
Toy, Jeep, Nelly Belle, Marx	65.00
Toy, Stagecoach, Pulling 3 Tin Boxcars, 15 In.	28.00
Toy, Wagon Train, Marx	75.00
Watch, Signed, Pocket	50.00
Wristwatch, Dale Evans	45.00
Wristwatch, Ingersoll, 1930s	85.00

The Royal Bayreuth factory was founded in Tettau, Bavaria, in 1794. It has continued to modern times. The marks have changed through the years. A stylized crest, the name "Royal Bayreuth," and the word "Bavaria" appear in slightly different form from 1870 to about 1919. Later dishes include the words "U.S. Zone," the year of the issue, and do not have the word "Bavaria."

ROYAL BAYREUTH, see also Rose Tapestry; Sand Babies; Snow Babies; Sunbonnet Babies

ROYAL BAYREUTH, Ashtray, Chimpanzee Seated, Holds Vessel, Black-Gray, Signed	135.00
Ashtray, Clown, Mother-Of-Pearl, Blue Mark	135.00
Ashtray, Devil Arms Over Top, Legs Around Base	140.00
Ashtray, Eagle	325.00

Ashtray, Elk, Blue Mark 125.00
Ashtray, Goat Scene, Blue Mark 40.00
Ashtray, Mountain Goat, Blue Mark 125.00
Ashtray, Scene, Women Herding Sheep, Footed 100.00
Ashtray, Swan Scene, Swirled Handle, Marked .... 40.00 To 45.00
Ashtray, Triangular, Hunting Scene, Gold Trim 50.00
Ashtray, Turkey, Blue Mark 295.00
Bell, Nursery Rhyme, Blue Mark 150.00
Berry Set, Green, Portraits Of Ladies, 5 Piece 335.00
Bottle, Children's Scene, Silver Rim, 3 1/2 In. 50.00
Bowl, Fruit, Grape Design, Reticulated Rim, Signed, 10 1/2 In. 269.00
Bowl, Musicians, Scalloped, Scroll Feet, Blue Mark, 6 7/8 In. 110.00
Bowl, Nut, Almonds With Leaves, Master 55.00
Bowl, Poppy, Blue Mark, 6 In. 85.00
Bowl, Shepherd Girl With Geese, Blue Mark, 10 1/2 In. 165.00
Bowl, Violets, Marked, 4 1/2 X 3 1/2 In. 38.00
Box, Covered, Jack & Jill Design, Heart Shaped, Blue Mark 80.00
Box, Cuff Links, Scenic, Dogs Attacking Stag, Covered 45.00
Box, Dome Lid, 3-Color, 3 Gold Feet, Marked, 2 X 4 In. 225.00
Box, Pin, Little Miss Muffet, Oval, Blue Mark 75.00
Box, Powder, Flowers, Covered, Footed, Matte Finish 75.00
Box, Red Tomato Shape, Lidded, Marked, 2 1/2 X 3 In. 35.00
Box, Trinket, Club Shape, Scenic Cows, Holly Berries, 3 In. 85.00
Cake Plate, Desert Scene, Handled, 10 In. 195.00
Cake Plate, Jack Horner, Open-Handled, Blue Mark 145.00
Candleholder, Elks, Handled, Squatty, Low, Pair, Blue Mark 105.00
Candleholder, Goat, Handled, Blue Mark 75.00
Candleholder, Green, With Storks, Marked 90.00
Candleholder, Jack & Jill, Saucer 125.00
Candleholder, Little Boy Blue, Shieldback 185.00
Candleholder, Little Jack Horner, Gold, 4 1/4 In. 120.00
Candleholder, Moose & Dogs, Handled, Blue Mark 85.00
Candleholder, Pansy, Purple, Green Mark 195.00
Candleholder, Pearlized Pink & Gold Well, Poppy, Signed 385.00
Candleholder, Rose, Figural, Ring Handle, Marked 275.00
Candleholder, Sheep, Blue Mark 45.00
Candleholder, Stork, Green, Enamel Design, 4 In. 90.00
Candleholder, Storks, Green, Blue Mark 90.00
Candlestick, Goats, Woods, Brown, 6 In. 70.00
Celery, Lobster, Blue Mark 105.00
Celery, Pierced Handles, Rose Design, Gold, 12 1/2 In. 55.00
Celery, Shell, Satin, Marked 135.00
Celery, 3 Donkeys, Man, 10 In. 145.00
Child's Set, Nursery Rhyme, Sayings, 7 Piece 150.00
Cracker Jar, Red Poppy, Blue Mark 275.00
Cracker Jar, Tomato, Blue Mark 105.00
Creamer, Alligator, Blue Mark .... 135.00 To 195.00
Creamer, Apple, Blue Mark, 3 3/4 In. .... 65.00 To 80.00
Creamer, Arabs, Blue Mark, Squatty 48.00
Creamer, Bass 110.00
Creamer, Bird Of Paradise, Blue Mark 185.00
Creamer, Bopeep, Blue Mark 120.00
Creamer, Buffalo, Black, Blue Mark 145.00
Creamer, Bull, Black 130.00
Creamer, Bull, Black, Plympton N.S. On Horn 90.00
Creamer, Bull, Brown, 3 3/4 In. 165.00
Creamer, Bull, Gray, Tettau Mark .... 110.00 To 125.00
Creamer, Butterfly 165.00
Creamer, Card, Devil Handle, Bermuda On Side 75.00
Creamer, Cat, Black .... 115.00 To 145.00
Creamer, Cat, Gray 70.00
Creamer, Clown 165.00
Creamer, Coachman, Red Coat, Mark 155.00

Creamer, Conch, Blue Mark, 5 In. .... 45.00 To 75.00
Creamer, Corinthian, Yellow, Rust Lining, 3 3/4 In. 85.00
Creamer, Cow, Black 125.00
Creamer, Cow, Brown, Mottled, Blue Mark 175.00
Creamer, Cow, Tan 85.00
Creamer, Cows In Pasture 55.00
Creamer, Cows, Green, Pinched Spout, Marked, 3 1/2 In. 80.00
Creamer, Crow, Black, Blue Mark 65.00
Creamer, Crow, Black, Signed .... 98.00 To 130.00
Creamer, Dachshund, Blue Mark 145.00
Creamer, Devil & Card, Green Mark 75.00
Creamer, Devil & Cards, Blue Mark 95.00
Creamer, Duck, Blue Mark 120.00
Creamer, Eagle, Blue Tettau Mark 165.00
Creamer, Elk, Blue Mark, 4 In. .... 50.00 To 75.00
Creamer, Elk, Stirrup Cup, 4 1/2 In. .... 125.00 To 150.00
Creamer, Figural, Robin .... 125.00 To 165.00
Creamer, Fish, Blue Mark 165.00
Creamer, Flounder, Blue Mark 220.00
Creamer, Forest Scene, Pinched Spout, Brown, Orange, 4 In. 75.00
Creamer, French Poodle, Gray .... 165.00 To 187.00
Creamer, Frog, Green .... 135.00 To 150.00
Creamer, Frog, Red, Blue Mark 135.00
Creamer, Frogs & Bee, Blue Mark 95.00
Creamer, Girl With Basket, Blue Mark 325.00
Creamer, Girl With Dog, Blue Mark 65.00
Creamer, Goat's Head, Horns Form Handle, Blue Mark 180.00
Creamer, Grape, Yellow 70.00
Creamer, Greenaway Girl With Puppy, Blue Mark, 3 1/2 In. 80.00
Creamer, Ibex 95.00
Creamer, Jack & Jill, Blue Mark 65.00
Creamer, Jack & Jill, Corset Shape, Pinched Spout, Blue Mark 110.00
Creamer, Jack & The Beanstalk, Blue Mark, 5 In. 90.00
Creamer, Kangaroo, Blue Mark 350.00
Creamer, Lemon, Blue Mark .... 75.00 To 95.00
Creamer, Lettuce Leaf, Red Lobster Handle 25.00
Creamer, Little Jack Horner, Blue Mark 65.00
Creamer, Lobster, Blue Mark, 4 In. .... 58.00 To 75.00
Creamer, Man Of The Mountain, Blue Mark .... 65.00 To 95.00
Creamer, Melon, Blue Mark, 4 In. .... 135.00 To 145.00
Creamer, Milkmaid, Blue Mark 295.00
Creamer, Miss Muffet 120.00
Creamer, Moose .... 119.50 To 122.00
Creamer, Mountain Goat .... 145.00 To 155.00
Creamer, Mountain Goat, Blue Tettau Mark .... 160.00 To 175.00
Creamer, Musicians 69.00
Creamer, Oak Leaf 85.00
Creamer, Old Man Of The Mountain, Marked 65.00
Creamer, Orange 65.00
Creamer, Pansy 118.00
Creamer, Parakeet 195.00
Creamer, Parrot 155.00
Creamer, Peach, Blue Mark 165.00
Creamer, Pelican, Blue Mark 250.00
Creamer, Pig, Blue Mark 295.00
Creamer, Platypus, Blue Mark 350.00
Creamer, Polar Bears In Moonlight, 4 In. 135.00
Creamer, Poodle, Black B Mark 150.00
Creamer, Ram 165.00
Creamer, Red Poppy .... 45.00 To 60.00
Creamer, Red Poppy, Blue Mark 70.00
Creamer, Red Poppy, Marked 65.00
Creamer, Red Poppy, Signed 100.00

Creamer, Rooster, Blue Mark 165.00
Creamer, Seal, Blue Mark .... 115.00 To 230.00
Creamer, Sheep Grazing, Pinched Spout, Blue Mark, 4 In. 120.00
Creamer, Shell .... 60.00 To 95.00
Creamer, Shell, Coral Handle, Blue Mark 55.00
Creamer, Shell, Lobster Handle, Blue Mark 75.00
Creamer, Shell, Sea Horse Handle, Brown & Gray, 3 In. 45.00
Creamer, St.Bernard Dog Head, Blue Mark .... 145.00 To 195.00
Creamer, Strawberry 65.00
Creamer, Strawberry, Blue Mark 100.00
Creamer, Tomato .... 35.00 To 48.00
Creamer, Trees & Cows, Marked 70.00
Creamer, Trout 185.00
Creamer, Water Buffalo, Black & Red, Blue Mark 125.00
Creamer, Water Buffalo, Black, Blue Mark 90.00
Creamer, Water Buffalo, Gray, Blue Mark 110.00
Creamer, Watermelon, Blue Mark 110.00
Creamer, White Roses, Green Ground, Butterflies, Marked, 4 In. 35.00
Creamer, Yellow Chicks 75.00
Crow, Black 150.00
Cup & Saucer, Chocolate, Red Star 50.00
Cup & Saucer, Corinthian, Black, White Figures 22.00
Cup & Saucer, Purple, Marked 35.00
Cup & Saucer, Rose Tapestry, Blue Mark 125.00
Cup & Saucer, Rose, Pink, Blue Mark 165.00
Cup & Saucer, Scenic, Dutch Boy With Donkey, Marked 40.00
Cup & Saucer, Strawberry, Demitasse 45.00
Cup & Saucer, Uncle Wiggily 65.00
Cup, Loving, Arab Scene, 3-Handled, Blue Mark 60.00
Cup, Loving, Corinthian, 3-Handled, Marked, 3 In. 55.00
Cup, Loving, Jack & The Beanstalk, Blue Mark, 3 3/4 In. 110.00
Dish, Baby, Little Miss Muffet 110.00
Dish, Candy, Conch Shell, Blue Mark 45.00
Dish, Celery, Lobster, Marked 105.00
Dish, Child's, Jack & The Beanstalk 65.00
Dish, Leaf Handled, Florals, Blue Mark, 6 3/4 In. 28.00
Dish, Leaf, Iridescent, Blue Mark, 7 X 6 In. 85.00
Dish, Man, Turkey Design, 6 In. 22.00
Dish, Mint, Rose Tapestry, Blue Mark, 4 In. 50.00
Dish, Pin, Jack & Beanstalk 65.00
Dish, Pin, Rosebuds, 3 In. 125.00
Dish, Powder, Covered, Pansy 198.00
Dish, Shell, Opalescent, 4 X 4 In. 65.00
Dish, Tomato On Lettuce, Covered 60.00
Ewer, Roses, Gold Trim, Lavender Ground, Blue Mark, 4 5/8 In. 45.00
Hair Receiver, Goose Girl, 3 Gold Feet, Blue Mark 75.00
Hatpin Holder, Floral 185.00
Hatpin Holder, Hunter, Dog, 6 1/2 In. 235.00
Hatpin Holder, Mother-Of-Pearl, 8-Sided, Blue Mark 65.00
Hatpin Holder, Owl, Marked 325.00
Hatpin Holder, Oyster & Pearl 180.00
Hatpin Holder, Poppy, Blue Mark .... 225.00 To 265.00
Hatpin Holder, Rose Design, Blue Mark 65.00
Hatpin Holder, Underplate, Hunting Dogs, Elk In Water 150.00
Holder, Spoon, Roses, Handled, 6 X 3 In. 45.00
Humidor, Man Fishing In Boat, Blue Mark 150.00
Humidor, Man With Pope, Blue Mark 150.00
Humidor, Moose With Dogs, Blue Mark 150.00
Humidor, Pipe Rack, Sailboat River Motif, Signed, Blue Mark 269.00
Humidor, Tavern Scene, Blue Mark 150.00
Inkwell, Hunter, Beagles, & Pheasant, Blue Mark, 5 X 4 1/2 In. 125.00
Jar, Marmalade, Grape, Underplate, Marked 195.00
Jar, Marmalade, Pansy, Covered, 5 1/4 In. 75.00

Royal Bayreuth, Match Holder, Reclining
Clown, 3 In.

Match Holder, Clown, Red, Blue Mark 160.00
Match Holder, Devil & Cards .... 145.00 To 195.00
Match Holder, Fishing Scene, Hanging, Blue Mark 75.00
Match Holder, Green, Crane Scene, Hanging, Blue Mark 75.00
Match Holder, Green, Stork Design, Covered, Blue Mark 68.00
Match Holder, Hanging, Mountain Goat, Blue Mark 250.00
Match Holder, Horse Trainer 85.00
Match Holder, Reclining Clown, 3 In. .... *Illus* 100.00
Match Holder, White Poppy, Pearlized, Blue Mark 110.00
Mayonnaise Set, Poppy, Pearlized, Blue Mark 135.00
Mayonnaise, Shell, Green & Light Green, Lobster Handle, 5 In. 25.00
Mayonnaise, Shell, White & Pink, Lobster Handle, Marked, 6 In. 35.00
Men's Shoes, With Laces, Brown, Pair, 5 In. 150.00
Mug, Child's, Jack & Beanstalk, Blue Mark 95.00
Mug, Fox Hunt Scene, 3-Handled 55.00
Mug, Queen Victoria Jubilee, 1897 .... 50.00
Mug, Shaving, Elk, Scuttle, Marked 325.00
Mustard, Lobster, Covered, Spoon, Blue Mark .... 45.00 To 65.00
Mustard, Tomato, Covered .... 25.00 To 27.00
Mustard, Tomato, Covered, Blue Mark 40.00
Nappy, Gold, Yellow Flowers, Leaves, Marked 60.00
Nappy, Little Jack Horner, Signed, Blue 87.50
Nappy, Shell, Iridescent, Blue Mark 38.00
Nut Cup, White Poppy, Mark DePose 65.00
Nut Set, Almond, Marked, Set 195.00
Pig, Creamer, Blue Mark 295.00
Pincushion, Elk, Blue Mark 75.00
Pitcher, Apple, Blue Mark, 5 1/2 In. 195.00
Pitcher, Cavalier Design, Pinched Spout, Tapestry, 5 In. 375.00
Pitcher, Clown, Red, 4 1/2 In. 150.00
Pitcher, Clown, Yellow, 4 1/2 In. 210.00
Pitcher, Coachman, Marked, 5 In. 250.00
Pitcher, Conch Shell, Green Mark, 4 1/4 In. 55.00
Pitcher, Corinthian, Milk, Red Lining, Marked 85.00
Pitcher, Corset Shaped, 3-Color Roses, Gold Trim, 4 In. 225.00
Pitcher, Cows, Blue Mark, Pink & Green Ground, 6 1/2 In. 70.00
Pitcher, Devil & Cards, Marked, 5 In. 150.00
Pitcher, Devil & Cards, 7 In. .... 265.00 To 325.00
Pitcher, Duck, 4 1/2 In. 165.00
Pitcher, Dutch Children In Boat, Blue Mark 48.00
Pitcher, Eagle, Blue Mark, 6 1/2 In. 625.00
Pitcher, Elk, Blue Mark, 7 In. 225.00

Pitcher, Fisherman, Blue Mark, 5 1/4 In. 65.00
Pitcher, Frolicking Frogs & Bee, Maroon, Blue Mark, 3 1/4 In. 95.00
Pitcher, Gold Rose, Handled, 4 1/2 In. 100.00
Pitcher, Goose Girl, Marked, 5 In. 95.00
Pitcher, Hound, 8 1/2 In. 225.00
Pitcher, Hunt Scene, Green, 4 1/2 In. 145.00
Pitcher, Milk, Apple, Blue Mark 195.00
Pitcher, Milk, Devil & Cards, Blue Mark 200.00
Pitcher, Outdoor Scene, Waterfall, Cottage, Marked, 5 In. 275.00
Pitcher, Owl, Marked, 5 In. 295.00
Pitcher, Parrot, 4 3/4 In. 145.00
Pitcher, Pelican, Blue Mark, 6 1/2 In. 625.00
Pitcher, Poppy, Red, 4 1/2 In. 95.00
Pitcher, Robin, 7 1/2 In. 185.00
Pitcher, Shell With Lobster Handle, Marked 100.00
Pitcher, Shell, Coral Handle, 5 In. 60.00
Pitcher, St.Bernard Dog, 6 In. .... 195.00 To 225.00
Pitcher, Swan Scene, Pinched Spout, Marked, 6 In. 125.00
Planter, Corinthian, 2 Piece 65.00
Planter, Yellow Poppies, Leaves, Blue Mark 85.00
Plate, Barefoot Boy & 3 Donkeys, Blue Mark, 1i 1/2 In. 200.00
Plate, Bopeep, 6 1/4 In. 85.00
Plate, Boy Blue, 6 In. 85.00
Plate, Corinthian, 6 1/4 In. 25.00
Plate, Girl With Dog, Blue Mark, 8 In. 70.00
Plate, Girl With Geese, Blue Mark, 6 In. 67.50
Plate, Hunting Scene, Blue Mark, 8 In. 119.00
Plate, Hunting Scene, Blue Mark, 9 In. 110.00
Plate, Jack & Jill, 6 In. .... 45.00 To 75.00
Plate, Jack And The Beanstalk, Blue Mark, 7 In. 60.00
Plate, Little Boy Blue, 6 In. 42.00
Plate, Mountain Goat Scene, Open-Handled, Blue Mark, 10 In. 70.00
Plate, Oranges, Blossoms, Leaves, Twig Handles, 6 In. 20.00
Plate, Poppy, Mother-Of-Pearl, Blue Mark, Apricot Tint, 6 In. 40.00
Plate, Priscilla, 10 1/2 In. 16.00
Plate, Roses, Gold Design, Blue Mark, 5 3/4 In. 26.00
Plate, Wild Turkeys, Gold Scalloped Rim, Blue Mark, 8 3/4 In. 85.00
Relish, Lobster, Tail Handle, 6 1/2 In. 24.50
Relish, Roses, Blue Mark 45.00
Rooster, String Holder, Wall Hung, Blue Mark 135.00
Salt & Pepper, Chili Pepper 45.00
Salt & Pepper, Devils & Cards 70.00
Salt & Pepper, Grapes, Purple, Signed .... 110.00 To 125.00
Salt & Pepper, Oranges, Green Footed 30.00
Salt & Pepper, Tomato, Green Mark 65.00
Salt, Grape, Purple, Marked .... 35.00 To 50.00
Saucer, Jack And The Beanstalk, 5 1/4 In. 55.00
Saucer, Playing Card 45.00
Shoe, Man's, Cinnamon, Stitching, Eyelet 85.00
Shoe, Rose Tapestry, Marked 352.00
Shoe, Tan 70.00
Shoe, Woman's, High, Black 100.00
String Holder, Rooster, Blue Mark .... 185.00 To 265.00
Sugar & Creamer, Apple, Marked, Covered 210.00
Sugar & Creamer, Clown, Red, Mark 350.00
Sugar & Creamer, Corinthian 65.00
Sugar & Creamer, Floret 240.00
Sugar & Creamer, Grape, Purple, Blue Mark 125.00
Sugar & Creamer, Oak Leaf, Blue Mark 195.00
Sugar & Creamer, Poppy, Orange, Marked, 4 In. 200.00
Sugar & Creamer, Strawberry, Gold Twist Handle 175.00
Sugar & Creamer, Tomato, Blue Mark 75.00

Sugar, Apple, Underplate, Blue Mark	75.00
Sugar, Boy Blue	55.00
Sugar, Brittany Women	20.00
Sugar, Conch Shell, Covered, Blue Mark	45.00
Sugar, Grape, Purple	75.00
Sugar, Lobster, Covered, Blue Mark	35.00 To 60.00
Sugar, Poppy, Pearlized White	125.00
Sugar, Poppy, Red, Covered	95.00
Sugar, Tomato, Covered, Blue Mark	40.00 To 54.00
Tea Set, Miniature Flowers, 18 Piece	235.00
Tea Set, Poppy, Red, 3 Piece	275.00
Tea Set, Roses, Violets, Pansies, Gold Handle, Marked	250.00
Tea Strainer, Sunflower	235.00
Teacup & Saucer, Donkey & Boy	150.00
Teapot, Boy & Donkey, Blue Mark	125.00
Teapot, Cows In Stream, Lavender Shades, Green	140.00
Teapot, Man With Donkeys, 3 Cup	195.00
Teapot, Poppy, Red	175.00
Teapot, Tomato, Blue Mark	75.00 To 95.00
Toothpick, Boy & Donkey, 3-Footed, Blue Mark	65.00
Toothpick, Conch Shell, Blue Mark	75.00
Toothpick, Corinthian, Brown, Blue Mark	50.00 To 75.00
Toothpick, Elk, Blue Mark	110.00
Toothpick, Goose Girl	75.00
Toothpick, Hunt Scene, 2-Handled, Blue Mark	65.00
Toothpick, Murex Shell	25.00
Toothpick, Musician, 4-Handled, Blue Mark	65.00
Toothpick, Peacock Scene, Squatty, Blue Mark	55.00 To 65.00
Tray, Dresser, Ring Around The Rosie	175.00 To 195.00
Tray, Elk, Signed, 6 1/2 In.	100.00
Tray, Pin, Arab Scene, 6 1/2 In.	30.00
Vase, Bowl, Violets, Marked, 4 X 3 In.	38.00
Vase, Bulbous Shaped, Tavern Scene, Black Mark, 4 3/4 In.	99.50
Vase, Cattle In Pasture, Orange, 3-Handled, 5 In.	50.00
Vase, Corset Shape, Cows In Pasture, 7 In.	110.00
Vase, Cows In Forest, 5 1/2 In.	38.00
Vase, Dutch Boy & Girl, Bulbous, Blue Mark, 9 In.	110.00
Vase, Dutch Boy & Girl, Silver Rim, Green Mark, 3 1/2 In.	40.00
Vase, Dutch Boy & Goose, 5 1/2 In.	35.00
Vase, Dutch Children Scene, 5 1/4 In.	75.00
Vase, Dutch Girl Pulling Wagon, Blue Mark, 4 1/4 In.	48.00
Vase, Fruit Design, Signed, 9 In.	110.00
Vase, Goat Scene, Marked, 7 In.	110.00
Vase, Green & Brown Ground, Deer, Gold Trim, 12 In.	250.00
Vase, Green & Golds, Purple Iridescent, 8 1/2 X 5 1/4 In.	169.00
Vase, Horses, Farm Scene, 3-Handled, 3 1/4 In.	30.00
Vase, Hunt Scene, 3-Handled, Blue Mark, 3 In.	48.00
Vase, Lady With Horse, Blue Mark, 8 1/2 In.	55.00
Vase, Musicians, 2-Handled, Silver Rim, Marked, 3 1/4 In.	50.00
Vase, People In Garden, 2-Handled, Silver Rim, Green Mark	45.00
Vase, Polar Bear Scene, Blue Mark, 4 1/2 In.	60.00 To 125.00
Vase, Red Shading To Green, Grapes, 9 3/4 In.	79.00
Vase, Red, Mountain Goats, 7 In.	135.00
Vase, Roses, Gilt Butterflies, Blue Mark, Green Ground, 4 In.	35.00
Vase, Tavern Scene, Blue Mark, 11 In.	125.00
Vase, Three Cows In Center Band, 7 In.	250.00
Vase, White, Roses, Green Ground, Butterflies, Marked, 4 In.	35.00
Wall Pocket, Grape, Green, 9 In.	250.00
Wall Pocket, Grape, Purple	195.00
Wall Pocket, Green Leaf Design, Yellow Grape, Signed	265.00
Wall Pocket, Jester, Court, Hanging, Blue Mark, 9 In.	95.00
Wall Pocket, Peaches, Blue Mark	125.00

Royal Berlin, Vase, C.1800, Scenic
Medallions, Gold Trim, 18 In.

ROYAL BERLIN, see also KPM

ROYAL BERLIN, Figurine, Boy, Carrying Lamb On Shoulder, 4 1/4 In.	135.00
Vase, C.1800, Scenic Medallions, Gold Trim, 18 In. .... *Illus*	850.00

Royal Bonn is the nineteenth- and twentieth-century trade name for the Bonn China Manufactory established in 1755 at Bonn, Germany. A general line of porcelain dishes was made.

ROYAL BONN, see also Flow Blue

ROYAL BONN, Bowl, Florals, Oblong, 10 X 11 1/2 In.	40.00
Compote, Scenic Sailboats, 3 X 9 1/2 In.Diam.	80.00
Cookie Jar, Floral & Gilt, Marked	85.00
Ewer, 2 Bluebirds, Flowers, 10 In.	80.00
Pitcher, Gold & Cranberry, 6 1/4 In.	70.00
Plate, Interior Scene, Transfer Print, 6 In.	25.00
Tankard, Boy, Girl, Sled, Yellow Ground, Gold Trim, 12 In.	125.00
Urn, Green & Yellow Ground, Flowers, Tree Scene, Marked, 14 In.	250.00
Urn, Handled, Green Ground, Floral, Signed Roden, 14 1/2 In.	250.00
Vase, Bulbous, Red Roses, 4 In.	75.00
Vase, Cream Ground, Handled, Gold & Pink Floral Design, 9 In.	50.00
Vase, Farm Scene, Handled, White Ground, Signed Sticher, 12 1/4 In	195.00
Vase, Flower Design, Raised Gold, Marked, 11 In., Pair	325.00
Vase, Hand-Painted Design, Signed, Green, Gray, & Black, 8 X 8 In.	85.00
Vase, Hand-Painted Poppies, Raised Gold, 11 In.	150.00
Vase, Multicolored Flowers, Green Band, Gold Trim, Marked, 6 In.	95.00
Vase, Orchids, Raised Gold Trim, Handled, 7 1/2 In.	42.00
Vase, Portrait, 12 1/2 In.	225.00
Vase, Red Roses, Green, Handled, Bulbous, 4 In.	75.00
Vase, Rooster Scene, Green Ground, Signed Sticher, 6 1/4 In.	165.00
Vase, Tapestry, 8 1/2 In.	150.00
Vase, Yellow & Red Flowers, Brown To Green Ground, 14 In.	175.00

Royal Copenhagen porcelain and pottery have been made in Denmark since 1772. They are still being made. One of their most famous wares is the Christmas Plate Series.

ROYAL COPENHAGEN, Bowl, Blue, Open Lace, 7 1/2 In.	75.00

Coffeepot, Fluted, Snail Handle, Blue 9 3/4 In.	115.00
Figurine, Ballerina, No.4095, C.1905, 9 1/2 In.	935.00
Figurine, Bear, Cub On Back, Paws Raised, 2 X 4 In.	90.00
Figurine, Bear, Polar, Cub Lying On Back, 2 X 4 In.	145.00
Figurine, Cat, Siamese, Sitting, No.2851, 7 In.	115.00 To 145.00
Figurine, Dachshund Puppy, Chasing Tail, 4 1/2 In.	80.00
Figurine, Fox, Seated, Looking Up, No.946/437	150.00
Figurine, Frog, No.884	85.00
Figurine, German Shepherd, 7 3/4 In.	450.00
Figurine, Lovebirds, No.402	75.00 To 100.00
Figurine, Man With Scythe & Wheat, No.685, 10 In.	275.00
Figurine, Mermaid On Rock	325.00
Figurine, Mermaid On Stomach	125.00
Figurine, Mouse, 2 X 1 3/4 In.	38.00
Figurine, Squirrel, 3 In.	45.00
Figurine, Swallow, No.2374	40.00
Figurine, The Gossips, No.1319	675.00
Figurine, Tiger, 12 1/2 In.Long	500.00
Figurine, West Highland Terrier, 5 In.	70.00
Picture, Silhouettes, Christian IX & Family Members	245.00
Pitcher, Lacy Fluted, Mask Handle, 3 In.	35.00
Plate, Christian & Alexandrine, Silver Wedding, 1923	75.00
Plate, Christmas, 1812	125.00
Plate, Christmas, 1913	65.00
Plate, Christmas, 1914	110.00
Plate, Christmas, 1948	195.00
Plate, Christmas, 1960	88.00
Plate, Christmas, 1961	60.00
Plate, Christmas, 1964	125.00
Plate, Christmas, 1966	40.00 To 45.00
Plate, Christmas, 1968	15.00
Plate, Christmas, 1969	10.00 To 25.00
Plate, Commemorative, King & Queen Anniversary, C.1923	75.00
Server, Coffee, Blue Fluted, Snail On Handle, 9 3/4 In.	125.00
Server, Coffee, Snail On Handle, Fluted, 9 1/4 In.	115.00
Tea Set, Blue Fluted Half Lace Pattern, 3 Piece	295.00
Vase, Blue, White Flowers, 6 In.	40.00
Vase, Bottle, Scene Of Rosenborg Castle	75.00
Vase, Large Butterfly & Marsh Grass, H.542/235, 6 1/2 In.	50.00
Vase, Morning Glory Design, 2 1/2 In.	20.00

Royal Copley was produced by the Spaulding China Company of
Sebring, Ohio, from 1939 to 1960.

ROYAL COPLEY, Figurine, Cat	30.00
Figurine, Parrot, 8 In.	8.00
Planter, Duck, 8 In.	14.50
Planter, Dutch Boy, 7 In.	12.00
Planter, House	12.00
Planter, Kitten On Ball Of Yarn	15.00
Planter, Kitten On Stump	15.00
Vase, Daisies On Green, 8 In.	7.00
Wall Pocket, Hat Shaped	15.00

Royal Crown Derby Company, Ltd., was established in England in 1876.
ROYAL CROWN DERBY, see also Derby

ROYAL CROWN DERBY, Cup & Saucer, Demitasse, Gold Design, 6 Sets	145.00
Cup & Saucer, Imari Pattern	45.00 To 50.00
Plate, Flower & Leaf Design In Allover Gold, 9 In.	90.00
Plate, Hand-Painted, Ship, Pair, Signed W.E.J.Dean, 10 In.	335.00

Plate, 1882, Blue, Orange, & Gold, 8 In.	30.00
Vase, Bud, Floral Gold Design, Green, Signed, 7 In.	175.00
Vase, Cream Ground, Flowers, Gourd Shape, Jeweled, 10 In.	210.00

Royal Doulton was the name used on pottery made after 1902. Doulton and Company of England was founded in 1815. Their wares are still being made. For a more complete listing, see "Kovels' Illustrated Price Guide to Royal Doulton."

ROYAL DOULTON, Ash Pot, Auld Mac, A Mark	85.00
Ash Pot, Old Charley, A Mark	85.00 To 100.00
Ash Pot, Paddy, A Mark	85.00
Ashtray, Barleycorn	75.00
Ashtray, Coaching Days, Gypsy Caravan, 4 3/4 In.	22.00
Ashtray, Flambe, Country Scene, Noke, 4 1/2 In.	35.00
Ashtray, Kingsware, Forty Thieves, Miniature	300.00 To 350.00
Ashtray, Kingsware, Forty Thieves, Oversized	145.00
Ashtray, Major, Yellow	30.00 To 45.00
Bank, Bunny, Rabbit Holding Drum	60.00
Bank, Bunnykin, Pottery, Marked, 3 1/4 X 6 X 9 In.	125.00
Biscuit Jar, Coaching Days, Silver Plated Top, Rim	225.00
Bottle, Liqueur, Flambe, Floral & Leaf, Stopper, Signed	695.00
Bottle, Whiskey, Old Crow	90.00
Bottle, Zorro, Black, Red Sherry, 4 In.	35.00
Bottle, Zorro, Red Sherry, A Mark, 10 1/2 In.	50.00
Bowl, Bunnykins, 7 3/4 In.	30.00
Bowl, Cherry, Signed, 5 3/4 X 13 In.	550.00
Bowl, Coaching Days, Silver Plated Rim, 8 In.	85.00
Bowl, Fat Boy, Octagon, 9 In.	85.00
Bowl, Gaffers, Oval, 11 In.	95.00
Bowl, Gleaners, 6 In.	35.00
Bowl, Gleaners, 8 In.	45.00
Bowl, Gnomes, 8 In.	60.00
Bowl, I Be All The Way From Zummerset, Marked, 10 1/2 In.	88.00
Bowl, Ladies & Men Center, Scalloped, Marked, 7 3/4 In.	65.00
Bowl, May Day Children's Procession, 9 In.	50.00
Bowl, Old Peggotty, 9 1/2 In.	90.00
Bowl, Robert Burns, Scenes Outside, 7 1/2 In.	135.00
Bowl, Robin Hood & Friar Tuck, Marked, 7 3/4 In.	55.00
Bowl, Scenic With 3 Deer, 8 In.	65.00
Bowl, Sir Roger De Coverley, Scalloped, 8 X 11 In.	85.00
Bowl, Wooded Scene Silhouetted On Brown, 9 In.	125.00
Bust, Mr.Micawber	70.00
Bust, Pickwick	79.00
Bust, Sairey Gamp	70.00
Bust, Sam Weller	70.00 To 79.00
Bust, Sgt.Buz Fuz	79.00
Candleholder, Witches All Around, Brown Glaze, 2 1/4 In., Pair	165.00
Candlestick, Better Do It Than Wish It Done, 6 1/4 In.	37.50
Candlestick, Black Cat Watching Ladies, 6 1/2 In., Pair	125.00
Candlestick, Dutch Scene, 6 In.	125.00
Candlestick, Shakespeare, Better Do It Than Wish It, 6 In.	67.50
Candlestick, Yellow, Black Sailboat, Signed, 9 In.	125.00

Character jugs are modeled of the head and shoulders of the subject. They were made in four sizes: large, 5 1/4 to 7 inches; small, 3 1/4 to 4 inches; miniature, 2 1/4 to 2 1/2 inches; and tiny, 1 1/4 inches. Toby jugs depict a full seated figure.

Character Jug, 'ard Of 'earing, Large	675.00 To 1200.00
Character Jug, 'ard Of 'earing, Miniature	1100.00 To 1195.00
Character Jug, 'ard Of 'earing, Small	675.00
Character Jug, 'arriet, Large	175.00
Character Jug, 'arriet, Tiny	155.00 To 220.00

Character Jug, 'arry, A Mark, Large 175.00
Character Jug, 'arry, A Mark, Small 85.00
Character Jug, 'arry, A Mark, Tiny 150.00
Character Jug, 'arry, Large 125.00
Character Jug, 'arry, Tiny .... 200.00 To 210.00
Character Jug, Auld Mac, A Mark, Large 55.00
Character Jug, Auld Mac, A Mark, Miniature .... 32.50 To 40.00
Character Jug, Auld Mac, A Mark, Small 39.50
Character Jug, Auld Mac, Music, Large 375.00
Character Jug, Auld Mac, Tiny .... 200.00 To 250.00
Character Jug, Beefeater, A Mark, Miniature 25.00
Character Jug, Cap'n Cuttle, A Mark, Small .... 85.00 To 88.00
Character Jug, Captain Hook, Large 375.00
Character Jug, Captain Hook, Miniature 340.00
Character Jug, Captain Hook, Small .... 240.00 To 250.00
Character Jug, Cardinal, A Mark, Large 100.00
Character Jug, Cardinal, A Mark, Miniature 46.00
Character Jug, Cardinal, Large .... 118.00 To 150.00
Character Jug, Cardinal, Miniature 60.00
Character Jug, Cavalier, Large .... 135.00 To 140.00
Character Jug, Cavalier, Small 70.00
Character Jug, Dick Turpin, Gun Handle, Large 135.00
Character Jug, Dick Turpin, Gun Handle, Miniature 55.00
Character Jug, Dick Turpin, Gun Handle, Small 65.00
Character Jug, Dick Turpin, Horse Handle, Large 49.50
Character Jug, Dick Turpin, Horse Handle, Miniature 22.50
Character Jug, Dick Turpin, Horse Handle, Small 39.50
Character Jug, Dick Whittington, A Mark, Large 300.00
Character Jug, Dick Whittington, Large .... 385.00 To 400.00
Character Jug, Drake, Small .... 65.00 To 85.00
Character Jug, Falstaff, Small 37.50
Character Jug, Farmer John, A Mark, Small .... 55.00 To 90.00
Character Jug, Farmer John, Large 140.00
Character Jug, Fat Boy, Miniature .... 54.00 To 65.00
Character Jug, Fat Boy, Small 75.00
Character Jug, Fat Boy, Tiny .... 75.00 To 100.00
Character Jug, Field Marshal, Smuts, Large 1975.00
Character Jug, Fortune Teller, Large .... 265.00 To 375.00
Character Jug, Fortune Teller, Miniature 385.00
Character Jug, Fortune Teller, Small 290.00
Character Jug, Friar Tuck, A Mark, Large 300.00
Character Jug, Friar Tuck, Large 350.00
Character Jug, Gardener, Large 65.00
Character Jug, Gardener, Small 45.00
Character Jug, Gladiator, Large 550.00
Character Jug, Gladiator, Medium 325.00
Character Jug, Gladiator, Small .... 300.00 To 385.00
Character Jug, Gondolier, Large 500.00
Character Jug, Gondolier, Miniature 350.00
Character Jug, Granny, A Mark, Large 50.00
Character Jug, Gulliver, Large 550.00
Character Jug, Henry Morgan, Small 35.00
Character Jug, Jarge, Large 320.00
Character Jug, Jarge, Small .... 169.00 To 200.00
Character Jug, Jester, A Mark, Small 95.00
Character Jug, Jester, Marked, 3 1/8 In. 80.00
Character Jug, Jester, Small .... 80.00 To 90.00
Character Jug, John Barleycorn, Small 75.00
Character Jug, John Peel, A Mark, Large 245.00
Character Jug, John Peel, A Mark, Miniature 65.00
Character Jug, John Peel, Miniature 45.00
Character Jug, John Peel, Tiny 275.00
Character Jug, Johnny Appleseed, Large .... 239.00 To 270.00
Character Jug, Long John Silver, Small 65.00

Character Jug, Lord Nelson, Large 252.00
Character Jug, Mephistopheles, Large .... 2250.00 To 2500.00
Character Jug, Mephistopheles, Small 1000.00
Character Jug, Mikado, Large 400.00
Character Jug, Mikado, Miniature .... 265.00 To 335.00
Character Jug, Mikado, Small .... 285.00 To 375.00
Character Jug, Mine Host, Small 35.00
Character Jug, Mr.Micawber, A Mark, Miniature 55.00
Character Jug, Mr.Micawber, A Mark, Small 72.00
Character Jug, Mr.Micawber, Miniature .... 41.00 To 59.00
Character Jug, Mr.Micawber, Tiny .... 75.00 To 90.00
Character Jug, Mr.Pickwick, A Mark, Small 50.00
Character Jug, Mr.Pickwick, Miniature 59.00
Character Jug, Mr.Pickwick, Tiny 275.00
Character Jug, Old Charley, A Mark, Large .... 69.00 To 100.00
Character Jug, Old Charley, A Mark, Miniature .... 55.00 To 65.00
Character Jug, Old Charley, A Mark, Small .... 35.00 To 55.00
Character Jug, Old Charley, Music, Large 375.00
Character Jug, Old Charley, Tiny .... 65.00 To 100.00
Character Jug, Old King Cole, Large 250.00
Character Jug, Old King Cole, Small .... 95.00 To 110.00
Character Jug, Paddy, A Mark, Large 115.00
Character Jug, Paddy, A Mark, Miniature .... 40.00 To 46.00
Character Jug, Paddy, Large .... 125.00 To 145.00
Character Jug, Paddy, Miniature 49.50
Character Jug, Paddy, Tiny .... 60.00 To 110.00
Character Jug, Pied Piper, Large 49.50
Character Jug, Punch & Judy Man, Large 600.00
Character Jug, Punch & Judy, Man, Small .... 300.00 To 400.00
Character Jug, Regency Beau, Small 475.00
Character Jug, Sairey Gamp, A Mark, Small 39.50
Character Jug, Sairey Gamp, Miniature 22.50
Character Jug, Sairey Gamp, Small 25.00
Character Jug, Sam Johnson, A Mark, Small 165.00
Character Jug, Sam Johnson, Large 265.00
Character Jug, Sam Johnson, Small 175.00
Character Jug, Sam Weller, A Mark, Large 125.00
Character Jug, Sam Weller, A Mark, Small 75.00
Character Jug, Sam Weller, Large .... 145.00 To 160.00
Character Jug, Sam Weller, Tiny 110.00
Character Jug, Scaramouche, Large 500.00
Character Jug, Scaramouche, Miniature .... 375.00 To 400.00
Character Jug, Scaramouche, Small 400.00
Character Jug, Simple Simon, A Mark, Large 500.00
Character Jug, Simple Simon, Large .... 469.00 To 500.00
Character Jug, Smuggler, Small .... 30.00 To 39.50
Character Jug, St.George, Small 75.00
Character Jug, Tam O'Shanter, Large 85.00
Character Jug, Tam O'Shanter, Miniature 29.50
Character Jug, Tam O'Shanter, Small 39.50
Character Jug, Toby Philpots, Miniature 50.00
Character Jug, Tony Weller, A Mark, Miniature 35.00
Character Jug, Tony Weller, Large 140.00
Character Jug, Tony Weller, Small .... 45.00 To 55.00
Character Jug, Touchstone, A Mark, Large 185.00
Character Jug, Touchstone, Large .... 200.00 To 225.00
Character Jug, Town Crier, Large 135.00
Character Jug, Town Crier, Small 99.00
Character Jug, Ugly Duchess, Large 375.00
Character Jug, Ugly Duchess, Miniature 275.00
Character Jug, Ugly Duchess, Small .... 245.00 To 300.00
Character Jug, Uncle Tom Cobbleigh, Large 450.00
Character Jug, Vicar Of Bray, Large .... 169.00 To 210.00
Character Jug, Viking, Large .... 110.00 To 125.00

Character Jug, Viking, Miniature 107.00
Character Jug, Viking, Small 70.00
Character Jug, Yachtsman, Large 75.00
Charger, African, Lioness, 13 1/2 In. 85.00
Cheese Dish, Coaching Days, Covered 345.00
Cigarette & Match Holder, Art Deco, Green 20.00
Coffee Set, Reynard The Fox, Hand-Painted 238.00
Coffeepot, Old Leeds Spray 48.00
Cookie Jar, Coaching Days, Covered 225.00
Creamer, Coaching Days, Marked, 3 1/4 In. 45.00
Creamer, Gaffer 75.00
Creamer, Gaffer, 4 1/2 In. 80.00
Creamer, Hunting Scene 45.00
Creamer, Monk, Refectory Bell, Octagonal, Marked, 6 1/4 In. 125.00
Creamer, Monk, Tan Ground, Square, 7 1/4 X 3 5/8 In. 110.00
Cup & Saucer, Burleigh, Blue & White 9.00
Cup & Saucer, Coaching Days .... 35.00 To 40.00
Cup & Saucer, Demitasse, Clematis, Cream Ground 35.00
Cup & Saucer, Demitasse, Glamis Thistle 25.00
Cup & Saucer, Dickens Ware, Adam 35.00
Cup & Saucer, Don Quixote, Saucer 5 1/2 In. 75.00
Cup & Saucer, Jackdaw Of Rheims 55.00
Cup & Saucer, Mother Goose, Nursery Rhyme Series 22.00
Cup & Saucer, Mr.Micawber 65.00
Cup & Saucer, Norfolk, Harbor Scene, Blue & White 25.00
Cup & Saucer, Rose Medallion 45.00
Cup & Saucer, Sam Weller 55.00
Cup & Saucer, Under The Greenwood Tree, 2 3/4 X 6 In. 75.00
Cup, Loving, ElizabethII Coronation, 1953 .... 525.00
Demitasse Set, Fox, 7 Piece 450.00
Dessert Set, Coaching Days, 16 Piece 350.00
Dish, Child's, Bunnykins .... 50.00 To 75.00
Dish, Gaffer, Square, 4 In. 40.00
Dish, Pin, Winston Churchill Portrait, 4 In. 75.00
Dish, Soup, Lynn Pattern 13.00
Ewer, Cobalt & Tapestry, Marked, 7 3/4 In. 195.00
Ewer, Pansy, Pink Collar, Gold Handle, Signed, 7 In. 195.00
Fernery, Blue & Green, 7 X 4 In. 87.00
Figurine, A Gentleman From Williamsburg, HN .... 90.00 To 135.00
Figurine, A La Mode, HN 2544 .... 175.00 To 195.00
Figurine, A' Courting .... 495.00 To 550.00
Figurine, Abdullah, HN 2104 .... 560.00 To 675.00
Figurine, Adriene, Blue, HN 2304 .... 100.00 To 150.00
Figurine, Affection, HN 2236 .... 60.00
Figurine, Afternoon Tea, HN 1747 .... 179.00 To 210.00
Figurine, Airedale, HN 1024 .... 127.00
Figurine, Alexandra, HN 2398 .... 135.00 To 159.00
Figurine, Alsatian, HN 1115 .... 300.00
Figurine, Annabella, HN 1872 .... 525.00
Figurine, Annette, HN 1550 .... 325.00 To 350.00
Figurine, Apple Maid, HN 2160 .... 325.00 To 375.00
Figurine, At Ease, HN 2473 .... 135.00
Figurine, Autumn Breezes, Green, HN 1913 .... 175.00 To 250.00
Figurine, Autumn Breezes, HN 2147 .... 140.00
Figurine, Autumn Breezes, Pink, HN 1911 .... 179.00
Figurine, Babie, HN 1679 .... 74.00
Figurine, Bachelor, HN 2319 .... 195.00 To 225.00
Figurine, Ballad Seller, HN 2266 .... 250.00 To 295.00
Figurine, Ballerina, HN 2116 .... 210.00 To 325.00
Figurine, Balloon Seller, HN 583 .... 325.00
Figurine, Basket Weaver, HN 2245 .... 450.00
Figurine, Bather, HN 687 .... 675.00
Figurine, Bedtime Story, HN 2059 .... 140.00 To 155.00
Figurine, Beggar, HN 526 .... 495.00

Figurine, Beggar, HN 2175 .... 460.00 To 575.00
Figurine, Bell O' The Ball, HN 1977 .... 205.00 To 225.00
Figurine, Belle, HN 2340 .... 45.00
Figurine, Bernice, HN 2071 .... 795.00
Figurine, Bess, Red, HN 2002 .... 220.00 To 275.00
Figurine, Biddy-Penny-Farthing, HN 1843 .... 140.00
Figurine, Biddy, HN 1513 .... 150.00 To 200.00
Figurine, Blacksmith Of Williamsburg, HN 2240 .... 135.00
Figurine, Blithe Morning, HN 2021 .... 140.00 To 200.00
Figurine, Blithe Morning, Red, HN 2065 .... 150.00 To 200.00
Figurine, Bo Peep, HN 1811 .... 74.00
Figurine, Bon Appetite, HN 2444 .... 185.00 To 190.00
Figurine, Bonnie Lassie, HN 1626 .... 225.00 To 310.00
Figurine, Boudoir, HN 2542 .... 350.00
Figurine, Boy With Turban, HN 1212 .... 450.00
Figurine, Bride, HN 1600 .... 425.00
Figurine, Bride, HN 2166 .... 225.00
Figurine, Bride, HN 2873 .... 95.00
Figurine, Bridesmaid, HN 2148 .... 185.00 To 225.00
Figurine, Bridesmaid, HN 2196 .... 115.00
Figurine, Bridget, HN 2070 .... 275.00 To 295.00
Figurine, Brindle Bulldog, HN 1043 .... 135.00
Figurine, Broken Lance, HN 2041 .... 550.00 To 695.00
Figurine, Bulldog, Flambe, Signed, 2 3/4 In. 150.00
Figurine, Bunny, HN 2214 .... 100.00
Figurine, Buttercup, HN 2309 .... 90.00
Figurine, Calumet, HN 1689 .... 600.00
Figurine, Calumet, HN 2068 .... 650.00 To 700.00
Figurine, Camellia, HN 2222 .... 225.00 To 260.00
Figurine, Captain MacHeath, HN 464 .... 750.00
Figurine, Carmen, HN 2545 .... 225.00
Figurine, Carpet Seller, HN 1464 .... 210.00 To 300.00
Figurine, Cat, Flambe, Sitting, 5 In. .... 58.00 To 75.00
Figurine, Cat, Flambe, 12 In. 260.00
Figurine, Celeste, HN 2237 .... 200.00 To 225.00
Figurine, Cellist, HN 2226 .... 335.00 To 475.00
Figurine, Charmian, HN 1569 .... 700.00
Figurine, Chelsea Pair, HN 577 .... 495.00
Figurine, Chief, HN 2892 .... 115.00 To 135.00
Figurine, Child Of Williamsburg, HN 2154 .... 65.00
Figurine, Child Study, HN 603 .... 395.00
Figurine, Chitarrone, HN 2700 .... 725.00
Figurine, Chloe, HN 1476 .... 285.00
Figurine, Chloe, HN 1765 .... 240.00
Figurine, Chloe, M9 .... 215.00
Figurine, Christine, HN 1840 .... 740.00
Figurine, Christine, HN 2792 .... 195.00
Figurine, Christmas Morn, HN 1992 .... 110.00 To 125.00
Figurine, Christmas Time, HN 2110 .... 300.00 To 375.00
Figurine, Clarinda, HN 2724 .... 145.00 To 199.50
Figurine, Clarissa, HN 1525 .... 495.00
Figurine, Clarissa, HN 2345 .... 140.00
Figurine, Cleopatra & The Slave, HN 2868 .... 895.00 To 1095.00
Figurine, Clockmaker, HN 2279 .... 185.00 To 250.00
Figurine, Clown, HN 2890 .... 165.00 To 200.00
Figurine, Coachman, HN 2282 .... 450.00
Figurine, Cobbler .... 259.00 To 275.00
Figurine, Cobbler, HN 1705 .... 240.00
Figurine, Cobbler, HN 1706 .... 295.00
Figurine, Cockatoo, Rocky Base, Turquoise, 16 In. 200.00
Figurine, Cocker Pheasant, HN 1029 .... 100.00
Figurine, Cocker Spaniel & Pheasant, HN 1029 .... 100.00
Figurine, Cocker Spaniel & Pheasant, HN 1137 .... 225.00
Figurine, Cocker Spaniel, HN 1002 .... 198.00 To 250.00

Figurine, Cocker Spaniel, HN 1078	72.00
Figurine, Cocker Spaniel, HN 1186	235.00
Figurine, Cocker Spaniel, HN 1187, Copper Coat, 5 1/2 In.	83.00
Figurine, Collie, HN 1057	275.00
Figurine, Collinette, HN 1999	295.00 To 325.00
Figurine, Cookie, HN 2218	125.00
Figurine, Coppelia, HN 2115	650.00
Figurine, Curly Locks, HN 2049	250.00
Figurine, Cymbals, HN 2699	625.00 To 700.00
Figurine, Dachshund, HN 1140	152.00
Figurine, Daffy Down Dilly, HN 1712	250.00 To 350.00
Figurine, Dainty May, HN 1639	265.00 To 295.00
Figurine, Dainty May, HN 1656	265.00
Figurine, Dancing Years, HN 2235	250.00 To 325.00
Figurine, Daphne, HN 2268	145.00
Figurine, Darby, HN 2024	265.00 To 300.00
Figurine, Darling, HN 1319	110.00
Figurine, Darling, HN 1985	30.00
Figurine, Dawn, HN 1858	725.00 To 800.00
Figurine, Debutante, HN 2210	300.00
Figurine, Deidre, HN 2020	350.00
Figurine, Delicia, HN 1663	550.00
Figurine, Delight, HN 1772	170.00 To 200.00
Figurine, Delphine, HN 2136	250.00
Figurine, Denise, HN 2273	245.00
Figurine, Diana, HN 1986	90.00 To 135.00
Figurine, Dimity, HN 2169	300.00
Figurine, Dinky Do, HN 1678	60.00
Figurine, Doctor, HN 2858	140.00
Figurine, Dorcas, HN 1558	225.00 To 425.00
Figurine, Drake, Flambe, No. 137	60.00
Figurine, Dreamweaver, HN 2283	200.00
Figurine, Drummer Boy, HN 2679	246.00 To 310.00
Figurine, Duke Of Edinburgh, HN 2386	395.00 To 595.00
Figurine, Dulcie, HN 2305	119.00
Figurine, Dulcimer, HN 738	565.00 To 725.00
Figurine, Dulcinea, HN 1419	1200.00
Figurine, Easter Day, HN 1976	600.00
Figurine, Easter Day, HN 2039	250.00
Figurine, Eleanor Of Provence, HN 2009	700.00
Figurine, Elegance, HN 2264	125.00
Figurine, Elephant, Flambe, Signed, 4 1/2 In.	150.00
Figurine, Elfreda, HN 2078	510.00 To 645.00
Figurine, Eliza, HN 2543	175.00 To 195.00
Figurine, Embroidering, HN 2855	135.00
Figurine, Enchantment, HN 2178	90.00
Figurine, English Setter & Pheasant, HN 2529	235.00
Figurine, Ermine Coat, HN 1981	225.00 To 295.00
Figurine, Esmeralda, HN 2168	325.00
Figurine, Fair Maiden, HN 2211	60.00
Figurine, Family Album, HN 2321	325.00
Figurine, Farmer's Boy, HN 2520	700.00 To 775.00
Figurine, Farmer's Wife, HN 2069	469.00
Figurine, Fat Boy, HN 1893	300.00
Figurine, Favorite, HN 2249	110.00
Figurine, Fiddler, HN 2171	765.00
Figurine, Fiona, HN 1925	575.00
Figurine, Fiona, HN 2694	105.00 To 149.50
Figurine, First Steps, HN 2242	450.00
Figurine, First Waltz, HN 2862	150.00
Figurine, Fleurette, HN 1587	400.00
Figurine, Fortune Teller, HN 2159	395.00 To 475.00
Figurine, Fortune Teller, HN 3505	280.00

Figurine, Forty Winks, HN 1974 .... 180.00 To 225.00
Figurine, French Peasant, HN 2075 .... 375.00
Figurine, Friar Tuck, HN 2143 .... 400.00 To 425.00
Figurine, Gaffer, HN 2053 .... 310.00
Figurine, Gay Morning, HN 2135 .... 225.00 To 300.00
Figurine, Genevieve, HN 1962 .... 160.00 Ro 205.00
Figurine, Gentlewoman, HN 1632 .... 700.00
Figurine, Georgiana, HN 2093 .... 650.00 To 950.00
Figurine, Geraldine, HN 2348 .... 135.00 To 149.00
Figurine, Girl With Yellow Frock, HN 588 ....1100.00
Figurine, Giselle, HN 2139 .... 325.00
Figurine, Good King Wenceslas, HN 2118 .... 269.00 To 325.00
Figurine, Goody Two Shoes, HN 2037 .... 60.00 To 65.00
Figurine, Goody Two Shoes, M 81 .... 425.00
Figurine, Gossips, HN 2025 .... 295.00 To 395.00
Figurine, Grace, HN 2318 .... 100.00 To 139.50
Figurine, Grand Manner, HN 2723 .... 190.00 To 227.00
Figurine, Grandma, HN 2052 .... 295.00
Figurine, Granny's Shawl, HN 1647 .... 390.00
Figurine, Greyhound, HN 077 .... 198.00
Figurine, Griselda, HN 1993 .... 335.00 To 400.00
Figurine, Gypsy Dance, HN 2230 .... 245.00
Figurine, Harlequin, HN 2186 .... 180.00
Figurine, Harlequinade, HN 635 ....1200.00
Figurine, Heart To Heart, HN 2276 .... 300.00 To 310.00
Figurine, Henrietta Maria, HN 2005 .... 550.00 To 600.00
Figurine, Her Ladyship, HN 1977 .... 225.00 To 315.00
Figurine, Here A Little Child I Stand, HN 1546 .... 225.00
Figurine, Hermina, HN 1704 .... 850.00
Figurine, Hilary, HN 2335 .... 149.50
Figurine, Honey, HN 1909 .... 325.00 To 345.00
Figurine, Hornpipe, HN 2161 .... 650.00
Figurine, Huntsman, HN 2492 .... 125.00 To 140.00
Figurine, In The Stocks, HN 2163 .... 650.00 To 700.00
Figurine, Innocence, HN 2842 .... 85.00
Figurine, Invitation, HN 2170 .... 139.00
Figurine, Irene, HN 1621 .... 285.00 To 325.00
Figurine, Ivy, HN 1768 .... 75.00
Figurine, Jack, HN 2060 .... 150.00 To 170.00
Figurine, Janet, HN 1737 .... 285.00 To 300.00
Figurine, Janice, HN 2022 .... 285.00
Figurine, Jean, HN 1877 .... 275.00
Figurine, Jean, HN 2032 .... 265.00 To 300.00
Figurine, Jersey Milkmaid, HN 2057 .... 225.00 To 325.00
Figurine, Jill, HN 2061 .... 150.00
Figurine, Joan, HN 1422 .... 535.00
Figurine, Joan, HN 2023 .... 300.00
Figurine, Jolly Sailor, HN 2172 .... 560.00 To 625.00
Figurine, Jovial Monk, HN 2144 .... 175.00
Figurine, Judith, HN 2086 .... 275.00
Figurine, Karen, HN 1994 .... 350.00
Figurine, Kate Hardcastle, HN 1718 .... 425.00 Ro 535.00
Figurine, Kate Hardcastle, HN 1719 .... 575.00
Figurine, Kate Hardcastle, HN 1861 .... 475.00 To 500.00
Figurine, Katrina, HN 2327 .... 265.00 To 295.00
Figurine, King Charles, HN 404 .... 500.00 To 850.00
Figurine, Ko-Ko .... 385.00 To 450.00
Figurine, Kurdish Dancer, HN 2867 .... 525.00 To 750.00
Figurine, La Sylphide, HN 2138 .... 325.00 To 350.00
Figurine, Lady April, HN 1958 .... 325.00 To 350.00
Figurine, Lady Betty, HN 1967 .... 275.00 To 375.00
Figurine, Lady Charmian, HN 1948 .... 200.00
Figurine, Lady Charmian, HN 1949 .... 175.00 To 225.00

Figurine, Lady Fayre, HN 1557 .... 675.00
Figurine, Lady From Williamsburg, HN 2228 .... 135.00
Figurine, Lady Pamela, HN 2718 .... 125.00 To 159.50
Figurine, Lady With Rose, HN 48a 1900.00
Figurine, Lambing Time, HN 1890 .... 105.00 To 195.00
Figurine, Laurianne, HN 2719 .... 125.00
Figurine, Lavinia, HN1955 .... 90.00
Figurine, Leading Lady, HN 2269 .... 200.00
Figurine, Leisure Hour, HN 2055 .... 385.00 To 475.00
Figurine, Lights Out, HN 2262 .... 215.00
Figurine, Lilac Time, HN 2137 .... 275.00
Figurine, Lisa, HN 2310 .... 110.00
Figurine, Little Boy Blue, HN 2062 .... 150.00
Figurine, Little Bridesmaid, HN 1433 .... 125.00
Figurine, Little Bridesmaid, HN 1434 .... 95.00
Figurine, Little Lady Make Believe, HN 1870 .... 350.00
Figurine, Little Land, HN 67 .... 1750.00
Figurine, Little Mistress, HN 1449 .... 295.00
Figurine, London Cry, Strawberries, HN 749 .... 700.00
Figurine, Long John Silver, HN 2204 .... 450.00
Figurine, Loretta, HN 2337 .... 100.00 To 139.50
Figurine, Love Letter, HN 2149 .... 295.00
Figurine, Lucy Lockett, HN 524 .... 595.00 To 600.00
Figurine, Lunchtime, HN 2485 .... 155.00 To 184.50
Figurine, Make Believe, HN 2225 .... 60.00 To 80.00
Figurine, Mantilla, HN 2712 .... 285.00 To 325.00
Figurine, Margaret Of Anjou, HN 2012 .... 700.00
Figurine, Margaret, HN 1989 .... 250.00 To 300.00
Figurine, Margery, HN 1413 .... 395.00 To 400.00
Figurine, Marguerite, HN 1928 .... 265.00 To 310.00
Figurine, Marietta, HN 1341 .... 375.00
Figurine, Marjorie, HN 2788 .... 115.00
Figurine, Market Day, HN 1991 .... 325.00
Figurine, Mary Had A Little Lamb, HN 2048 .... 60.00 To 80.00
Figurine, Mary Jane, HN 1990 .... 475.00
Figurine, Mary Mary, HN 2044 .... 160.00
Figurine, Mask Seller, HN 1361 .... 250.00
Figurine, Masquerade, HN 600 .... 350.00
Figurine, Masquerade, HN 2251 .... 240.00 To 395.00
Figurine, Master, HN 2325 .... 80.00 To 115.00
Figurine, Matilda, HN 2011 .... 600.00
Figurine, Maureen, HN 1770 .... 170.00 To 255.00
Figurine, Maureen, M 84 .... 400.00
Figurine, Mayor, HN 2280 .... 425.00
Figurine, Maytime, HN 2113 .... 240.00 To 285.00
Figurine, Meditation, HN 2330 .... 140.00
Figurine, Melanie, HN 2271 .... 149.50
Figurine, Melody, HN 2202 .... 300.00
Figurine, Memories, HN 1855 .... 325.00
Figurine, Memories, HN 2030 .... 300.00
Figurine, Mendicant, HN 1365 .... 225.00
Figurine, Merely A Minor, HN 2567, Dapple Gray Horse 315.00
Figurine, Meriel, HN 1931 .... 965.00
Figurine, Mexican Dancer, HN 2866 .... 525.00 To 750.00
Figurine, Midinette, HN 2090 .... 255.00 To 295.00
Figurine, Midsummer Noon, HN 1899 .... 550.00
Figurine, Midsummer Noon, HN 2033 .... 395.00 To 675.00
Figurine, Milady, HN 1970 .... 700.00
Figurine, Milkman, HN 2057 .... 130.00
Figurine, Minuet, HN 2019 .... 235.00 To 295.00
Figurine, Miss Demure, HN 1402 .... 170.00
Figurine, Miss Muffet, HN 1936 .... 100.00 To 150.00
Figurine, Miss Muffet, HN 1937 .... 175.00 To 225.00

Figurine, Modern Piper, HN 756 .... 1395.00
Figurine, Monica, HN 1467 .... 50.00
Figurine, Mr.Micawber, HN 2097 .... 275.00 To 310.00
Figurine, Mr.Pickwick, HN 2099 .... 350.00
Figurine, Mrs.Fitzherbert, HN 2007 .... 725.00
Figurine, My Love, HN 2339 .... 140.00
Figurine, My Pretty Maid, HN 2064 .... 300.00
Figurine, Nell Gwynn, HN 1887 .... 475.00
Figurine, Newsboy, HN 2244 .... 495.00 To 625.00
Figurine, Nina, HN 2347 .... 165.00
Figurine, Ninette, HN 2379 .... 120.00
Figurine, Noelle, HN 2179 .... 350.00 To 375.00
Figurine, Nyala Antelope, HN 2664 .... 135.00 To 200.00
Figurine, Old Balloon Seller, HN 1315 .... 115.00 To 140.00
Figurine, Old King Cole, HN 2217 .... 695.00 To 700.00
Figurine, Old King, HN 2134 .... 350.00
Figurine, Old Lavender Seller, HN 1492 .... 625.00
Figurine, Old Meg, HN 2494 .... 250.00
Figurine, Olga, HN 2463 .... 179.00 To 200.00
Figurine, Omar Khayyam, HN 2247 .... 115.00
Figurine, Orange Lady, HN 1953 .... 175.00 To 225.00
Figurine, Orange Seller, HN 1325 .... 475.00
Figurine, Organ Grinder, HN 2173 .... 595.00
Figurine, Owd Willum, HN 2042 .... 200.00 To 235.00
Figurine, Paisley Shawl, HN 1460 .... 265.00
Figurine, Paisley Shawl, HN 1987 .... 235.00 To 275.00
Figurine, Paisley Shawl, HN 1988 .... 120.00 To 160.00
Figurine, Paisley Shawl, M 26 .... 300.00
Figurine, Pamela, HN 1469 .... 475.00
Figurine, Pantalettes, HN 1362 .... 300.00
Figurine, Pantalettes, M 16 .... 225.00
Figurine, Parisian, HN 2445 .... 135.00 To 150.00
Figurine, Parson's Daughter, HN 564 .... 350.00
Figurine, Patchwork Quilt, HN 1984 .... 285.00 To 350.00
Figurine, Patricia, HN 1414 .... 400.00
Figurine, Patricia, M28 .... 225.00
Figurine, Pecksniff, HN 2098 .... 325.00 To 350.00
Figurine, Peggy, HN 2038 .... 65.00
Figurine, Penny, HN 2338 .... 40.00
Figurine, Persian Cat, White, Seated, 5 In. 145.00
Figurine, Philippine Dancer, HN 671 .... 575.00
Figurine, Phyllis, HN 1420 .... 575.00
Figurine, Phyllis, HN 1486 .... 575.00
Figurine, Picnic, HN 2308 .... 60.00
Figurine, Pierrette, HN 644 .... 525.00
Figurine, Pierrette, HN 732 .... 925.00
Figurine, Polish Dancer, HN 2836 .... 595.00 To 615.00
Figurine, Polly Peachum, HN 549 .... 175.00
Figurine, Polly Peachum, HN 589 .... 350.00
Figurine, Pope John Paul II, HN 2888 .... 105.00
Figurine, Potter, HN 1518 .... 550.00
Figurine, Primroses, HN 1617 .... 650.00
Figurine, Prince Charles .... 410.00 To 675.00
Figurine, Prince Charles & Lady Diana, Pair 1500.00
Figurine, Professor, HN 2281 .... 115.00 To 164.50
Figurine, Proposal, HN 725 .... 210.00
Figurine, Punch And Judy Man, HN 2765 .... 165.00 To 200.00
Figurine, Puppetmaker, HN 2253 .... 450.00 To 475.00
Figurine, Rabbit, K 39 .... 35.00
Figurine, Rag Doll, HN 2142 .... 50.00
Figurine, Rendezvous, HN 2212 .... 300.00 To 375.00
Figurine, Repose, HN 2272 .... 165.00 To 175.00
Figurine, Rhapsody, HN 2267 .... 179.00

Figurine, Rhinoceros, Flambe, 19 In.	445.00
Figurine, River Boy, HN 2128	125.00
Figurine, Rocking Horse, HN 2072	1500.00
Figurine, Romance, HN 2430	145.00
Figurine, Rosamund, HN 1497	975.00
Figurine, Rose Medallion, Cup & Saucer, 6 In.	45.00
Figurine, Rose, HN 1368, Potted	75.00
Figurine, Roseanna, HN 1926	340.00 To 400.00
Figurine, Rosebud, HN 1580	150.00
Figurine, Rosebud, HN 1983	225.00 To 300.00
Figurine, Rosemary, HN 2091	295.00
Figurine, Royal Governor's Cook, HN 2233	135.00
Figurine, Ruth The Pirate Maid, HN 2900	385.00 To 435.00
Figurine, Sabbath Morn, HN 1982	195.00 To 280.00
Figurine, Sandra, HN 2275	85.00
Figurine, Schoolmarm, HN 2223	164.50
Figurine, Scottish Highland Dancer, HN 2436	575.00
Figurine, Scottish Terrier, K 10, Miniature	45.00
Figurine, Sea Harvest, HN 2257	175.00
Figurine, Seafarer, HN 2455	200.00
Figurine, Seashore, HN 2263	180.00 To 250.00
Figurine, Setter With Pheasant, HN 2529	350.00
Figurine, Setter, HN 1051	82.00
Figurine, She Loves Me Not, HN 2045	110.00
Figurine, Silks & Ribbons, HN 2017	75.00 To 100.00
Figurine, Silversmith Of Williamsburg, HN 220	90.00 To 135.00
Figurine, Simone, HN 2378	119.00 To 140.00
Figurine, Sir Walter Raleigh, HN 2015	560.00 To 650.00
Figurine, Skater, HN 2117	335.00 To 350.00
Figurine, Sleepyhead, HN 2114	680.00 To 850.00
Figurine, Sophie, HN 2833	50.00
Figurine, Southern Bell, HN 2229	100.00
Figurine, Spring Flower, HN 1945	600.00
Figurine, Spring Flowers, HN 1807	200.00 To 320.00
Figurine, Spring Morning, HN 1922	195.00
Figurine, St.George, HN 2051	295.00
Figurine, St.George, HN 2067	2500.00
Figurine, Stitch In Time, HN 2352	125.00 To 144.50
Figurine, Stop The Press, HN 2683	115.00 To 145.00
Figurine, Summer, HN 2086	340.00 To 390.00
Figurine, Sunday Best, HN 2206	165.00 To 200.00
Figurine, Sunday Morning, HN 2184	265.00
Figurine, Suzette, HN 2026	245.00 To 300.00
Figurine, Sweet And Fair, HN 1865	850.00
Figurine, Sweet And Twenty, HN 1298	225.00 To 240.00
Figurine, Sweet Anne, HN 1496	200.00
Figurine, Sweet Anne, M27	200.00 To 290.00
Figurine, Sweet April, HN 2215	300.00 To 400.00
Figurine, Sweet Seventeen, HN 2734	140.00
Figurine, Sweet Sixteen, HN 2231	225.00
Figurine, Symphony, HN 2287	350.00
Figurine, Teenager, HN 2203	235.00 To 280.00
Figurine, Tete-A-Tete, HN 798, Potted	1150.00
Figurine, Thanks Doc, HN 2731	135.00
Figurine, Thanksgiving, HN 2446	180.00
Figurine, This Little Pig, HN 1793	80.00
Figurine, Tiger On Rock, A Mark, HN 2639	1200.00
Figurine, Tinkle Bell, HN 1677	45.00
Figurine, Tony Weller, HN 684	950.00
Figurine, Tootles, HN 1680	45.00 To 65.00
Figurine, Top O' The Hill, HN 1834	68.00 To 225.00
Figurine, Top O' The Hill, HN 1849	135.00 To 175.00
Figurine, Town Crier, HN 2119	210.00 To 265.00
Figurine, Toymaker, HN 2250	360.00 To 450.00

Figurine, Uncle Ned, HN 2094	500.00
Figurine, Uriah Heep, HN 554	275.00
Figurine, Uriah Heep, HN 2101	310.00
Figurine, Vanessa, HN 1836	450.00
Figurine, Venetta, HN 2722	120.00 To 159.50
Figurine, Veronica, HN 1517	265.00 To 275.00
Figurine, Victoria, HN 2471	130.00
Figurine, Victorian Lady, HN 728	250.00
Figurine, Victorian Lady, HN 1452	350.00
Figurine, Vivienne, HN 2073	220.00 To 250.00
Figurine, Votes For Women, HN 2816	140.00 To 180.00
Figurine, Wardrobe Mistress, HN 2145	425.00 To 450.00
Figurine, Wayfarer, HN 2362	170.00
Figurine, Wee Willie Winkie, HN 2050	375.00
Figurine, Wendy, HN 2109	74.00
Figurine, West Indian Dancer, HN 2384	625.00
Figurine, Wigmaker Of Williamsburg, HN 2239	95.00 To 135.00
Figurine, Windflower, HN 2029	295.00 To 325.00
Figurine, Windflower, M 79	425.00
Figurine, Winter, HN 2088	350.00 To 395.00
Figurine, Wistful, HN 2396	168.00 To 210.00
Figurine, Wizard, HN 2877	115.00 To 165.00
Figurine, Wunsome, HN 2220	110.00
Figurine, Young Love, HN 2735	540.00
Figurine, Young Master, HN 2872	185.00
Figurine, Young Miss Nightingale, HN 2010	725.00
Flask, Mr.Micawber, 8 In.	200.00
Flask, Tony Weller, Kingsware, Dewars	225.00
Humidor, Applied Relief Toby Figures, Tan & Brown, 6 In.	90.00
Inkwell, Floral, Gray, Black, 10 In.	475.00
Jar, Tea, Coaching Days	265.00
Jardiniere, Farm & Country Scene, Cobalt & White, Marked	180.00
Jardiniere, Tan & Gold Flowers, Brown Tapestry, Marked, 9 In.	175.00
Jug, Columbian Exposition	250.00
Jug, Commemorative, Dickens Characters, 1936	750.00
Jug, Concord, Bayeux Tapestry, 6 In.	110.00
Jug, Regency Coach, Limited Edition, 10 3/4 In.	495.00
Lamp, Blue, Light Blue & Brown, 28 1/2 In.	490.00
Lamp, Old Balloon Seller	225.00
Lighter, Beefeater	95.00
Lighter, Long John Silver	37.50
Lighter, Poacher	95.00
Match Holder, Mr.Squeers, Scenic, 2 In.	95.00
Match Holder, Sam Weller, Dickens Ware, 3 In.	70.00
Match Holder, Welsh Ladies, Scenic, Square, 2 1/2 In.	95.00
Mug, Bunnykins, Barbara Vernon, 3 1/2 In.	20.00
Mug, Coaching Scenes, Marked	55.00
Mug, Dickens Ware, Incised Indian Chief, Spring Lid, Signed	450.00
Mug, Dickens Ware, Monk At Table	375.00
Mug, Kingsware, Man With Pipe, Drink Wisely, Signed, 5 In.	110.00
Mug, Peace, 1919	45.00
Mug, Retrievers, 3-Handled, Silver Rim, Artist Signed	650.00
Pitcher, Arabian Nights, 6 In.	295.00
Pitcher, Authors & Inns, Chaucer Ye Tabard, Marked, 7 1/2 In.	110.00
Pitcher, Better So Than Worse, 7 In.	115.00
Pitcher, Classical Figures, Blue & White, 8 In.	85.00
Pitcher, Coaching Days, 6 1/2 In.	135.00
Pitcher, Dickens Ware, Curiosity Shop, Square	150.00
Pitcher, Dickens Ware, Fagin, 7 In.	175.00
Pitcher, Dickens Ware, Mr.Pickwick, 6 1/2 In.	100.00
Pitcher, Flow Blue, Italian Country Scene, 6 1/4 In.	95.00
Pitcher, Gaffers, Marked, 5 In.	85.00
Pitcher, Geneva, Flow Blue, Marked, 5 1/2 In.	88.00
Pitcher, Gilt Design, Floral, Scroll Handle, 12 In.	200.00

Pitcher, Green With Pink Floral, Signed, 8 In.	70.00
Pitcher, Hunt Scene, 4 In.	70.00
Pitcher, Jack's The Boy For Play, 6 In.	95.00
Pitcher, Milk, Canterbury Pilgrims, Handle, 8 In.	125.00
Pitcher, Monk, 7 1/2 In.	250.00
Pitcher, Moorish Gate, Marked, 4 5/8 In.	85.00
Pitcher, Nelson Commemorative, With Silver Collar, 9 In.	200.00
Pitcher, Night Watchman, Signed, 8 In.	98.00
Pitcher, Norfolk, 7 In.	95.00
Pitcher, Parson Brown, 9 In.	200.00
Pitcher, Romeo, Rocket Shaped, C.1914, 4 1/2 In.	55.00
Pitcher, Rural Scene, Signed, 5 In.	54.00
Pitcher, Scene Of Queen Elizabeth & Retinue, 5 X 5 In.	58.00
Pitcher, St.Louis World's Fair, 1934, Dutch Scene, 2 1/2 In.	45.00
Pitcher, Stoneware, Blue & Green, Geometric Etching, 8 In.	95.00
Pitcher, Tan, Blue Flowers, Ribbed, Marked, 5 1/2 In.	70.00
Pitcher, Tan, Blue Flowers, Ribbed, Marked, 7 In.	95.00
Pitcher, Watchmen, Tankard Shape, 8 1/2 In.	120.00
Pitcher, Water, Jack's The Lad For Work, Signed Nokes	175.00
Pitcher, Ye Squire, Ye Passenger, 8 In.	119.00
Pitcher, Zunday Zmocks, Na In Hat, Marked, 7 In.	165.00
Plate, Admiral, 10 In.	55.00
Plate, All Fools Are Not Knaves, All Knaves Are Fools, 10 In.	42.00
Plate, Anne Hathaway's Cottage, 10 1/2 In.	25.00
Plate, Anne Page, 7 1/2 In.	47.50
Plate, Arrival Of The Unknown Princess, Marked, 10 3/8 In.	110.00
Plate, Cavalier, Blue & White, 10 In.	45.00
Plate, Character, Ye Squire, Ye Passenger, 10 1/4 In.	42.00
Plate, Dickens Ware, Blue & White, 10 In.	48.00
Plate, Doctor, 10 In.	55.00 To 60.00
Plate, Don Quixote & Sancho Panza, 10 In.	75.00
Plate, English Cottage Scene, 10 In.	62.00
Plate, Falconer, 10 In.	47.50 To 65.00
Plate, Fish, White Ground, Mackerel Center, Gold Border, Marked	165.00
Plate, Game, Cobalt, Birds, Pair, Signed Charles Hart, 9 1/2 In.	400.00
Plate, George V & Queen Mary Coronation, 7 In.	25.00
Plate, George V & Queen Mary Coronation, 8 In.	37.50
Plate, Gnomes & Toadstools, Worms, & Cobwebs, 8 1/2 In.	225.00
Plate, Harvest Scene, 10 1/4 In.	35.00
Plate, Hurtsmonceaux Castle, 10 In.	62.00
Plate, Itch Yer On Guvenor, Marked, 9 1/4 In.	175.00
Plate, Jackdaw Of Rheims, Marked, 10 1/4 In.	55.00
Plate, Jackdaw Of Rheims, Ruffled Edge, 9 1/2 In.	65.00
Plate, Jester, 10 In.	45.00 To 60.00
Plate, Knight On Horse, 10 In.	50.00
Plate, Mayor, 10 In.	50.00 To 55.00
Plate, Monk, Green & Tan, Signed Noke, 10 In.	45.00
Plate, Mr.Pickwick, Signed Noke, 10 1/2 In.	65.00
Plate, Muckrose Abbey, 10 1/2 In.	35.00
Plate, Old Moreton Hall, 10 In.	75.00
Plate, Old Mother Hubbard, 7 In.	35.00
Plate, Oriental Figures Among Ruins, 10 In.	62.00
Plate, Pan In Forest Setting, 10 In.	62.00
Plate, Parson, 10 In.	42.00 To 65.00
Plate, Ploughing Scene, 10 In.	62.00
Plate, Portia, Shakespeare Character Series, 8 In.	30.00
Plate, Robert Burns, 10 1/4 In.	50.00
Plate, Rustic England, 10 1/4 In.	35.00
Plate, Sam Weller, Raised Figures, 1938, 10 1/2 In.	80.00
Plate, Sir Roger De Coverly, 10 In.	70.00
Plate, Sir Toby Belch, 10 In.	50.00 To 65.00
Plate, Spanish Armada, 10 1/2 In.	40.00 To 50.00
Plate, Squire, 10 In.	40.00 To 65.00

Plate, Stratford Church, Shakespeare In Foreground, 8 In.	42.00
Plate, Tony Weller & Fat Boy In Low Relief, 10 3/4 In.	110.00
Plate, Under The Greenwood Tree, Scalloped, 10 3/8 In.	70.00
Plate, Valentine, 1978, Boxed	29.00
Plate, Wall, Jester & Falconer, 10 In., Pair	60.00
Plate, Washington Mansion, Mt.Vernon, Blue On White, 10 In.	48.00
Plate, Washington, D.C., George Bowman, 10 In.	30.00
Punch Set, Coaching Scene, 10 Piece	650.00
Saucer, Clover, 4 In.	4.00
Soup, Dish, Coaching Days, 7 1/2 In.	20.00
Sugar & Creamer, Coaching Days	145.00
Sugar, Norfolk, Covered	30.00
Sugar, Sam Weller, Rectangular Handled, 6 1/8 In.	50.00
Tankard, Eglinton Tournament, 6 1/2 In.	65.00
Tankard, Oliver	200.00
Tea Set, Canterbury Pilgrims, Marked	375.00
Tea Set, Kingsware, Old Woman Sipping Tea, 7 Piece	350.00
Teapot, Dutch Scene, Noke, 8 1/2 In.	275.00
Teapot, Floral, Hexagonal, Marked	38.00
Teapot, Windmill, Dutch Harbor Scene, Marked, 9 1/2 In.	300.00
Tile, Coaching Days, 6 1/2 In.Square	20.00
Tile, Tea, Tavern Scene, Lion & Shield Border, Marked, 7 In.	48.00
Tobacco Jar, Monks, 5 1/2 In.	230.00
Tobacco Jar, Windsor Castle	95.00
Toby Jug, Cliff Cornell, Blue, 5 1/2 In.	299.00
Toby Jug, Cliff Cornell, Blue, 9 In.	249.00
Toby Jug, Cliff Cornell, Brown, 9 In.	249.00
Toby Jug, Falstaff, 8 1/2 In.	52.50
Toby Jug, Happy John, 9 In.	52.50
Toby Jug, Huntsman, 7 1/2 In.	47.00
Toby Jug, Mr.Micawber, Marked A, 4 1/2 In.	180.00
Toby Jug, Old Charley, 5 1/2 In.	125.00
Toby Jug, Sir Winston Churchill, 4 In.	22.00
Toby Jug, Sir Winston Churchill, 5 1/2 In.	32.00
Toothpick, John Barleycorn, Large	95.00
Tray, Canterbury Pilgrims, 7 3/4 X 17 1/2 In.	125.00
Tray, Dickens Ware, Barnaby Rudge, 4 X 5 3/8 In.	40.00
Tray, Falconry, Handled, 18 In.	95.00
Tray, Old English Inns, Fighting Cocks, 4 X 6 In.	31.00
Tray, Under The Greenwood Tree, Marked, 5 X 11 In.	85.00
Trivet, Crusader	35.00
Tumbler, Jackdaw Of Rheims, 3 X 4 In.	125.00
Tumbler, Nursery Rhymes	110.00
Tureen, Victorian Scenes, Blue & White	95.00
Urn, Covered, Artist Elsie Simmance, Art Union	395.00
Vase, Babes In Woods, Dog In Front Of Little Girls, 5 In.	259.00
Vase, Babes In Woods, Handled, Gold Trim, 2 3/4 X 4 1/4 In.	250.00
Vase, Babes In Woods, Lady Picking Berries, 5 1/4 In.	235.00
Vase, Babes In Woods, Mother, 2 Girls, Dog Under Tree, 9 In.	325.00
Vase, Barnaby Rudge, Handled, Marked, 8 1/2 In.	165.00
Vase, Beige Tapestry, Gold Flowers, Rust Inside, Marked, 8 In.	270.00
Vase, Beige, Gold & Turquoise Flowers, Marked, 6 1/4 In.	100.00
Vase, Blue, Grape Festoons, Hanging Bunches, 6 In.	60.00
Vase, Brangwyn Ware, Art Nouveau, 12 In.	175.00
Vase, Brown Ground, Green & Blue Design, 7 1/2 In.	80.00
Vase, Coaching Days, Marked, 5 In.	85.00
Vase, Coaching Scene, C.1900, Porcelain, 7 1/2 In.	95.00
Vase, Dickens Ware, Barnaby Rudge, C.1905, 10 1/2 In.	250.00
Vase, Dickens Ware, Fagin, 2-Handled, 7 In.	118.00
Vase, Dickens Ware, Monk, Singing Monk, 10 1/2 In.	450.00
Vase, Dickens Ware, Sydney Carton, C.1905, 10 1/2 In.	250.00
Vase, Dickens Ware, Sydney Carton, Handled, 7 In.	135.00
Vase, Dickens Ware, Tony Weller, Square, 4 5/8 X 8 In.	165.00

Vase, Dutch Scene, Marked, 1 1/4 In., Pair	65.00
Vase, Elfred Jingle, Handled, Marked, 5 1/2 In.	95.00
Vase, Faience, 1879, 15 In.	240.00
Vase, Festoons Of Beads, Florals, Green-Gray Top, Marked, 12 In	90.00
Vase, Flambe, Art Deco Shaped, Deer Design, Signed Ock, 7 In.	175.00
Vase, Flambe, Bull Elk & Mate, 4 1/2 In.	175.00
Vase, Flambe, Countryside Scene, Barrel Shape, 5 In.	85.00
Vase, Flambe, Countryside Scene, 6 X 5 1/2 In.	200.00
Vase, Flambe, Deer, Marked, 7 In.	175.00
Vase, Flambe, Fish, Artist Signed FM, 8 1/2 In.	995.00
Vase, Flambe, Harbor Scene, Sailing Vessels, 8 X 5 In.	165.00
Vase, Flambe, Hunter With Rifle, Woodcut, 8 In.	225.00
Vase, Flambe, Pumpkin Shaped, 7 1/2 In.	525.00
Vase, Flambe, Scenic, 6 1/2 In.	62.00
Vase, Flambe, Scenic, 8 1/2 In.	280.00
Vase, Flambe, Veined Sung, Ovoid, 10 In.	235.00
Vase, Flambe, Woodcut, 9 X 8 In.	185.00
Vase, Floral Design, Slaters Patent, C.1900, 8 1/2 In., Pair	195.00
Vase, Friar Tuck Joins Robin Hood, 9 In.	125.00
Vase, Gaffers, 2-Handled, Marked, 5 1/4 In.	85.00
Vase, Goats, Gold Top Edge, Marked, 3 3/8 X 5 In.	65.00
Vase, Idle Thoughts, Lady, Fan, Fence, Marked, 7 3/4 In.	165.00
Vase, Incised Grape, Brangwyn Ware, 12 In.	350.00
Vase, Jackdaw Of Rheims, Handled, Marked, 5 1/4 In.	85.00
Vase, Jackdaw Of Rheims, Verse, Little Boys Singing, 6 In.	98.00
Vase, Morrisian, 9 1/2 In.	150.00
Vase, Mottled Blue & Brown, Raised Beading, Marked, 11 In.	125.00
Vase, Mr.Micawber, Dickens Ware, 2-Handled, 5 In.	85.00
Vase, Sheep & Sheep Dog, Signed Hannah Barlow, 11 In., Pair	1300.00
Vase, Sheep, Handled, Sunset Colors, Marked, 6 5/8 In.	95.00
Vase, Sheep, Pedestal Foot, Marked, 3 X 6 1/2 In.	145.00
Vase, Stylized Flowers Reserve, Green & Gray, 16 In., Pair	480.00
Vase, Sung, Peacock Feather Design, Ovoid Shape, 6 In.	375.00
Vase, Tan Tapestry Body, Chrysanthemums, Ivies, Marked, 12 In.	270.00
Vase, Tapestry, 11 In.	150.00
Vase, Urns Of Florals, Florals With Bows, Marked, 12 In.	95.00
Vase, Welsh Ladies, 3 1/4 In.	95.00
Vase, White & Turquoise, Gold Footed, 8 1/2 In.	180.00

Royal Dux is a porcelain made by Duxer Porzellanmanufaktur, a
factory established in 1860 in Dux, Bohemia (now Czechoslovakia). After
1918, "Bohemia" was no longer part of the mark. Reproductions are being
made.

ROYAL DUX, Bookend, Pierrot, Blue & White, C.1920, 9 1/2 In., Pair	325.00
Bowl, Girl On Side, Oval	590.00
Bowl, White, Gold Design, Women's Heads, Footed, Oval, 7 1/2 X 11 In	225.00
Bust, Woman, Bisque, Impressed Mark, 13 In.	550.00
Figurine, Bohemian Shepherdess, Toga & Turban, 14 3/4 In.	595.00
Figurine, Boy, Girl, Frog, 8 1/2 In.	475.00
Figurine, Dancer, Flute Player, Snake Charmer, Blue, White, Pink	250.00
Figurine, Donkey, Saddle & Eye Guard	315.00
Figurine, Donkey, 4-Color, 6 X 5 In.	300.00
Figurine, Elephant, Pink	35.00
Figurine, Girl Holding Hat, Skirt Blowing	125.00
Figurine, Girl, Seated, Ruffled, Skirt, Marked, 10 X 13 In.	185.00
Figurine, Lady In Blue Dress, 10 In.	150.00
Figurine, Maiden Milking White Cow	425.00
Figurine, Man & Woman, Pink Triangle Mark, 20 In., Pair	2000.00
Figurine, Man With Pheasant, 13 In.	335.00
Figurine, Parrot On Stand, 15 In.	110.00
Figurine, Peasant, Satin Finish, 11 1/4 X 4 In., Pair	595.00
Figurine, Princess, Seated, Gold Ruffled Dress, Marked, 10 In.	210.00

Figurine, Two Hounds, 8 X 10 In. 130.00
Figurine, Woman Playing Mandolin, 34 In. 1500.00
Figurine, Young Girl, Cobalt Blue Outfit, Gold Trim, 9 In., Pair 195.00
Planter, Boy In Boat With Fish, Signed, 10 X 7 In. 285.00
Shell, Beige & Gold, Signed & Numbered, 14 In. 695.00
Vase, Grapes, Handled, 15 In. 450.00
Vase, Oriental Figurine, Beige Satin, Triangle Mark, Pair, 7 1/2 In 275.00
Vase, Plums, Pink Triangle Mark, 11 In. 145.00

Royal Flemish glass was made during the late 1880s in New Bedford, Massachusetts, by the Mt.Washington Glass Works. It is a colored satin glass decorated in dark colors with gold designs.

ROYAL FLEMISH, Cracker Jar, Signed M.W. 1200.00
Ewer, Blue & Tan Panels, Center Crosses, Chrysanthemum, 12 In. 3500.00
Vase, Raised Gold Separating Panels, Signed, 6 In. 2250.00
Vase, Roman Coins In Body, Window Sefrions, Signed, 4 1/2 In. 2250.00
    ROYAL HAEGER, see Haeger
    ROYAL IVY, see Pressed Glass, Royal Ivy
    ROYAL OAK, see Pressed Glass, Royal Oak
    ROYAL RUDOLSTADT, see Rudolstadt

ROYAL SAXE, Bouillon, Saucer, Pedestal, Kauffmann Scene 95.00
Plate, Nude Classical Scene, 10 In., Pair 245.00
Urn, Beehive, Handled, Covered, Burgundy Ground, Gold Trim, 14 In. 275.00
Vase, Portrait, Gold Handle, 8 1/4 In. 95.00
Vase, Portrait, Green, Yellow, Marked, 9 In. 55.00

Royal Vienna was established in Vienna by Claude Innocentius du Paquier in 1719. The factory closed in 1865. Since then, various German and Austrian factories have reproduced Royal Vienna wares, complete with the original beehive mark.

    ROYAL VIENNA, see also Beehive
ROYAL VIENNA, Biscuit Jar, Scenic In Gold Scroll Circle, Signed Kauffmann 150.00
Biscuit Jar, Scenic, People, Marked 140.00
Bowl, Burgundy Ground, Grape Design, Portrait, Amorosa, 10 In. 485.00
Bowl, Epergne Ormolu, Detailed Griffin, 10 X 9 In. 250.00
Chocolate Pot, Yellow Violets, Gold, 12 In. 150.00
Dish, Undertray, Oval, Porcelain Covered, Green & Gold, 4 1/2 In 140.00
Ewer, Ladies, Cupids, Gold Trim, Red, Beehive Mark, 4 1/2 In., Pr. 425.00
Figurine, Boy With Vases On Both Sides, Wahliss, 6 X 7 In. 118.00
Figurine, Boy, Gray Onyx, Marked, 7 In. 350.00
Figurine, Boy, Porcelain Base, Beehive Mark, 7 In. 350.00
Jar, Powder, Gold Design, Cupid On Lid, Beehive Mark 35.00
Plate, Asters In Center, Gold Floral Border, Marked, 7 In. 50.00
Plate, C.1900, Green Luster, Gilt, Pair ...... *Illus* 2310.00
Plate, C.1900, Green Luster, Gilt, 9 1/2 In., Pair 5500.00
Plate, C.1900, Wagner Theme Gilt, Pair ...... *Illus* 1540.00
Plate, Chintz, Beehive, 8 1/2 In. 23.00
Plate, Classical Scene, Cobalt & Gold, Marked, 10 In. 125.00
Plate, Deco Young Lady, Filmy Gown, Dove On Arm, 9 1/2 In. 165.00
Plate, Maid On Bank Of River, Cherub In Lap, Signed, 8 1/2 In. 295.00
Plate, Maiden Playing An Instrument, Blue Mark, 12 In. 850.00
Plate, Maria Theresa, Wagner, 7 In. 365.00
Plate, Portrait, Gold Trim, Artist Signed, 8 1/2 In. 75.00
Plate, Woman, Gold Border, Signed Wagner 550.00
Plate, 19th Century, Blue, Gilt, 9 5/8 In., Pair ...... *Illus* 2750.00
Tea Set, Purple Violets, Yellow Ground, Gold Bands, 3 Piece 70.00
Teapot, Hand-Painted, Scene, 5 1/2 In. 195.00
Tray, Dresser, Roses, Gold Rim, Beehive Mark, 12 1/2 In. 65.00
Urn, Burgundy Ground, Gold Design, Signed Rosley, 35 In. 2500.00

(See Page 591)

Royal Vienna, Plates, *from left to right:* C.1900,
Green Luster, Gilt; C.1900, Wagner Theme, Gilt;
19th Century, Blue, Gilt, 9 5/8 In.

Urn, Paris & Helen, Covered, Gold Center, Marked, 8 1/4 In.	395.00
Vase, Cobalt Blue Ground, Portrait, Marked, 8 1/4 In.	500.00
Vase, Gold, Peonies, Applied Handle, 10 In.	85.00
Vase, Portrait, Green Iridescent Glaze, 4 7/8 In.	750.00
Vase, Portrait, Rose Luster, Gold Trim, Artist Signed, Pair	1500.00
Vase, Raised Gold Flowers, Bust Of Lady, Marked, 9 1/2 In.	275.00

*Royal Worcester porcelain was made in the later period of Worcester
pottery, which was originally established in 1751. The Royal Worcester
trade name has been used by Worcester Royal Porcelain Company, Ltd.,
of England since 1862. The company became Royal Worcester Spode in
1976.*

ROYAL WORCESTER, see also Worcester

ROYAL WORCESTER, Basket, Allegorical Scenes, Children, Horses, Green, 7 In.	195.00
Basket, Wicker Basket Pattern, Gold Trim, C.1903, 5 1/2 In.	90.00
Biscuit Jar, Floral, Raised Gold Leaves, Silver Plated Lid	295.00
Bowl, Bandstand Pattern, Chinese Scene, 5 1/2 In.	300.00
Bowl, Basket Weave, Oval, Handled, 1904, Marked, 7 X 9 In.	310.00
Bowl, Dessert, Multicolored Flowers, Crimped Edge, 6 In.	28.00
Bowl, Embossed Grape Leaves, Openwork Edge, C.1896, 9 In.	325.00
Bowl, Floral Center, Bird Of Paradise, Marked, C.1860, 10 In.	125.00
Bowl, Florals, Bird Of Paradise, Marked, 10 In.	125.00
Bowl, Peacock & Flowers, 10 1/2 In.	45.00
Bowl, Salad, Blue & White, Pinecone Pattern, 10 1/8 In.	900.00
Bowl, Salad, Dated 1891, 8 1/2 In.	225.00
Bowl, Stylized Flowers, Gold Stems, 1918 Purple Mark, 8 In.	75.00
Box, Cottage Loaf, Sterling Hinges, Marked, Dated 1900	195.00
Cachepot, Handled, Gold Design, Purple Mark, 5 X 3 In.	62.00
Candle Centerpiece, Cricklight, Figural, Gilded, 17 In.	1150.00
Candlesnuffer, French Cook	36.00
Candlesnuffer, Hush	41.00
Candlesnuffer, Japanese, Green Mark	160.00
Candlesnuffer, Monk	85.00
Candlesnuffer, Mr. Caudle	40.00
Candlesnuffer, Punch	45.00
Candlesnuffer, The Witch, Purple Mark	160.00
Candlesnuffer, Toddle	40.00
Candlesnuffer, Young Girl	40.00
Cocoa Pot, Bamboo Handle, Purple Mark, 7 1/4 In.	158.00
Cologne, White, Gold Trim, Double Wall, 7 In.	248.00
Compote, Kate Greenaway Girl Base, Top Oval Tray, C.1885	275.00
Cracker Jar, Florals & Gold, Signed & Numbered	125.00
Creamer, Cream Ground, Multicolored Flowers	195.00
Creamer, Robin On Branch, Dated 1880, 2 1/4 In.	55.00
Cup & Saucer, Daisies, Pink & Gold Trim, Demitasse	34.00
Cup & Saucer, Floral Design, Marked, Dated 1903	70.00
Cup & Saucer, Floral, Gold Rim, Demitasse	55.00

Cup & Saucer, Paneled, Gold Rim, Dated 1895, Demitasse 98.00
Cup & Saucer, Plate, Hand-Painted, Roses Design, C.1904 .... 78.00
Cup & Saucer, Roanoke, Demitasse 35.00
Cup & Saucer, Roses, Turquoise, Marked 25.00
Cup & Saucer, Sheep, Hand-Painted, Signed, Demitasse 350.00
Cup & Saucer, The Milkmaids, Grazing Cows, 2 5/8 In. 325.00
Cup, Loving, Yellow & Pink Roses, Leaves, 3-Handled, 2 In. 98.00
Demitasse Pot, Purple, Cream Ground, Floral, Marked 300.00
Dinnerware, Elysian Pattern, 45 Piece 250.00
Dish, Bird's Head & Wings Shaped Rim, Dated 1910, Signed 95.00
Dish, Serving, Blue & White Willow, Covered, 9 X 6 1/2 In. 98.00
Eggcup, Gold Edging, Dark Blue, 1938-43 Mark 20.00
Ewer, Beige Ground, Purple Violets, Birds, 5 1/2 In. 130.00
Ewer, Beige, Hand-Painted, Artist Signed, C.1895, 17 In. 1400.00
Ewer, Embossed Lion, Cherubs, & Dolphins, Dated 1894, 17 In. 1400.00
Ewer, Enameled Bird On Limb, Buds, Serpent Handle, 6 1/2 In. 65.00
Ewer, Flowers & Leaves, Gold Edge, C.1889, Marked, 10 1/2 In. 225.00
Ewer, Flowers, Salamander Handle, 1887 Mark, 9 In. 495.00
Ewer, Gold Salamander Handle, 1880 Mark, 11 1/2 In. 495.00
Ewer, Grotesque Stork, Dolphin Handle, 1886, 13 In. 1750.00
Ewer, Turquoise Ground, Gold Trim, Signed, 8 1/2 In. 295.00
Figurine, Babes In The Woods, No.3381 .... 115.00
Figurine, Bird, Hedge Sparrow 65.00
Figurine, Blue Kingfisher, Gold & White, 6 In. 95.00
Figurine, Bluebird, Matte Finish 50.00
Figurine, Boy & Dog, 1869, 10 X 5 1/2 X 8 1/4 In. 395.00
Figurine, Bringatree Indians, Pair 875.00
Figurine, Bullfinch, No.2662, On Stump, Marked, 6 In. 165.00
Figurine, Cairo Water Carrier, Male, 1888 Mark, 21 In. 590.00
Figurine, China 95.00
Figurine, First Dance, No.3629, Green 150.00
Figurine, First Dance, Purple 150.00
Figurine, Fox, Seated, 7 In. 95.00
Figurine, Goat Woman, 6 1/2 In. 90.00
Figurine, Grandmother's Dress, No.3081, Yellow 150.00
Figurine, Hedge Sparrow 50.00
Figurine, India 95.00
Figurine, January, Boy 135.00
Figurine, Joan, Blonde, Lavender Dress, Marked, 4 1/2 In. 165.00
Figurine, June, No.3450, Boy 150.00
Figurine, Lady With Cymbals, Marked, 11 1/8 In. 595.00
Figurine, March, 5 1/8 In. 75.00
Figurine, May, No.3455 .... 145.00
Figurine, Michael, Crawling Boy, Marked, 2 1/2 In. 125.00
Figurine, Mother Machree, No.2824 .... 295.00
Figurine, Nightingale 50.00
Figurine, Noel, C.1941, 6 3/4 In. 200.00
Figurine, November, 7 3/4 In. 135.00
Figurine, Only Me, Girl, Curling Toes, Yellow, 6 In. 225.00
Figurine, Oriental Child, Eating Rice, 2 1/2 In. 60.00
Figurine, Parakeet, Boy, Green 175.00
Figurine, Parakeet, Boy, Red 175.00
Figurine, Parakeet, Gold & White, Base, 6 In. 95.00
Figurine, Pheasant, Joseph Stinton, 5 In. 245.00
Figurine, Playmate, Dog & Girl, 7 In. 165.00
Figurine, Saturday's Child, Boy 175.00
Figurine, Scotland, Marked 95.00
Figurine, Spaniel, Springer 75.00
Figurine, Spring, Blonde Girl With Lamb, N.3012, 8 1/2 In. 180.00
Figurine, The Dandelion, No.3084 .... 135.00
Figurine, Thursday's Child, No.3522, Girl 175.00
Figurine, Tommy, Blonde-Haired Boy, Marked, 4 1/2 In. 165.00
Figurine, Tommy, No.2913, Pink 145.00

Figurine, Two Babies, Baby & Spotted Dog, Marked, 3 3/4 In.	225.00
Figurine, Two Babies, No.3150	135.00
Figurine, Wednesday's Child, 7 In.	120.00 To 135.00
Figurine, Woman, Dead Bird, Gold Tunic, 10 In.	475.00
Figurine, Yankee, Marked, 7 In.	269.00
Jar, Potpourri, Gold Outlined Flowers, 1917, Marked, 14 In.	1195.00
Jug, Chrysanthemums, Artist Signed, Dated 1889, 7 In.	215.00
Jug, Figural Stag Handle, C.1885, Green Mark, 8 1/2 In.	185.00
Jug, Milk, Sparrow Beak, Three Flowers Pattern, 5 In.	300.00
Jug, Sabrina, Blue, Gray, Green, Oak Leaves, C.1907	225.00
Jug, Tusk Shape, Ivory, Staghorn Handle, Marked, 8 In.	185.00
Lamp, Fairy, Triple, All Original, 10 1/2 X 19 In.	1500.00
Pitcher, Elephant Handle, Gold Trim, C.1885, Marked, 6 In.	185.00
Pitcher, Florals Design, Gold Handle, Dated 1899, 4 1/4 In.	175.00
Pitcher, Flowers, Flat Back, Gold Rim & Handle, 5 In.	75.00
Pitcher, Moss Rose, Footed, Yellow, Small	65.00
Pitcher, Multicolored Flowers, Gold Trim, Marked, 4 3/4 In.	165.00
Pitcher, Owl Design, Antler Shaped Handle, Marked, 7 In.	575.00
Pitcher, Pinchback, Yellow Glaze, Gold Handle & Trim, 5 In.	80.00
Pitcher, Tusk Shaped, Gold Scroll, Green Mark, 8 1/4 In.	158.00
Pitcher, White, 9 X 5 In.	95.00
Pitcher, Yellow, Moss Rose, Footed	65.00
Plate, Dinner, 1880, 11 In.	45.00
Plate, Flowers, Scalloped & Ribbed Rim, Purple Mark, 8 In.	75.00
Plate, Game, Medallion Snipes, Green Rim, Signed G.Johnson	145.00
Plate, Oyster, Gold Outlined, Quilted Ground, 1902 Mark	135.00
Plate, Purple Mark, 9 1/4 In.	30.00
Rose Bowl, Dragonfly & Burgundy Roses	120.00
Salt, Snail Shape	78.00
Sauceboat, Blue & White, Strap Handle, Diaper Border, 8 In.	110.00
Sugar & Creamer, Leaves, Green, Pink, Yellow	50.00
Sugar, Floral, Beige Ground, Leaf Handle, 4 3/4 In.	95.00
Sugar, Swirled Fluted, Blue Design, Marked, 5 1/2 In.	200.00
Teapot, Firs & Ferns, Gold Trim, Ribbed Body, Marked, 6 In.	285.00
Teapot, Ribbed Body, Gold Handle & Spout, Signed, 6 In.	285.00
Tray, Spoon, Mandarin, Rose, Pink Coat, 6 In.	600.00
Tureen, Elephant Handles	250.00
Urn, Roses, Leaves, Flying Fish Handles, Marked, 15 1/4 In.	1295.00
Vase, Bamboo Shape, Flowers, Bamboo Handle, 6 X 10 In.	110.00
Vase, Bamboo Shape, Green, 7 1/4 In.	350.00
Vase, Bud, Hand-Painted Violets, C.1890, Signed, 6 1/2 In.	98.00
Vase, Bud, Violets, Yellow Flowers, Marked, 6 In.	98.00
Vase, Cutout Hearts, 6 1/4 In.	160.00
Vase, Cylinder, Bamboo In Relief, Green Mark, 4 3/4 In.	65.00
Vase, Florals, Ring & Shell Ears, 1861-75 Mark, 4 1/4 In.	255.00
Vase, Gold Chrysanthemums, Red, Brown, Ivies, 6 1/2 In.	140.00
Vase, Gold Outlined Flowers, 1902 Mark, 8 3/4 In.	225.00
Vase, Hand-Painted Robin, Ivory Ground, 6 3/4 In.	345.00
Vase, Hand-Painted, Floral, Flower Sachet Shaped, 5 In.	128.00
Vase, Ivory, Gold Floral Design, Cattle, River, Castle, 8 In.	325.00
Vase, Nautical Scene, Blown-Out Flowers, Covered, 18 In., Pr.	1800.00
Vase, Pedestal, Handled, Nautical Scene, Signed, 18 In., Pair	1800.00
Vase, Sabrina Ware, Shades Of Blue, 12 In.	250.00
Vase, Spiral, White, Pink Highlights, Floral, 10 In.	635.00
Vase, Turquoise Ground, Gold Design, Marked, 4 In.	68.00
Wall Pocket, Orchid, Brown & Orange	499.00

 Roycroft products were made by the Roycrofter community of East Aurora, New York, in the late nineteenth and early twentieth centuries. The community was founded by Elbert Hubbard. The products included furniture, metalware, leatherwork, and jewelry.

ROYCROFT, Bookend, Arched, Pair 85.00

Roycroft, Lamp, Hammered Copper,
Mica Panels, 13 1/4 In.

Bookend, Art Nouveau, Pair	45.00
Bookend, Dome Shaped, Brown Patina, 3 1/2 X 4 In., Pair	45.00
Bookend, Floral Design, Pair	60.00
Bookend, Leather Insert, Brass, Pair	90.00
Bookend, Viking Ship, Pair	60.00
Calendar, Desk, Copper	48.00
Candlestick, Copper, Pair	45.00
Incense Burner	45.00
Inkwell, Cylindrical, Dome Covered, Brass	65.00
Inkwell, Hammered	85.00
Jar, Tan, Covered, Marked, 4 In.	25.00
Jug, Brown, 4 In.	15.00
Jug, Handled, 5 In.	28.00
Jug, Rose Color, 4 In.	35.00
Lamp, Hammered Copper, Mica Panels, 13 1/4 In. .... *Illus*	800.00
Letter Holder, Flower Design	40.00
Letter Opener, Copper, Hammered	38.00
Sconce, Wall, Single Candle, Copper	30.00
ROZANE, see Roseville	

*RRP is the mark used by the firm of Robinson-Ransbottom. The firm was
founded by the Ransbottom brothers in 1900 in Ironspot, Ohio. In 1920
they merged with the Robinson Clay Product Company of Akron, Ohio,
to become Robinson-Ransbottom. Pieces are often confused with those
of the Roseville Pottery. The factory is still working.*

RRP CO., Ashtray, Green, 1956, 100 Years	15.00
Bowl, Turquoise, Scalloped, Layered Exterior, 8 1/2 In.	9.00
Flowerpot, Attached Saucer, Vertical & Horizontal Ribs, 6 1/2 In.	6.00
Jardiniere, Brown Top, Green Bottom, 7 In.	15.00
Pitcher, Batter, Yellow, Kitchen Tools Design, 6 3/4 In.	12.00
Planter, Brown, 8 1/2 X 3 1/4 In.	5.00
Planter, Figural, Green & Yellow Bug, With Turtle Head, 7 In.	8.00
Planter, Figural, Yellow Bug, 7 X 3 1/2 X 2 1/4 In.	8.00
Planter, Figure Eight Swirled Scales, Marked, 8 1/2 X 3 1/4 In.	6.00
Vase, White, Acanthus Leaf Relief, Impressed, 10 In.	7.00

*The RS Germany mark was used on porcelain made at the factory of
Rheinhold Schlegelmilch from about 1910 to 1956 in Tillowitz, Germany.
It was sold decorated or undecorated.*

RS GERMANY, Ashtray, Floral 30.00
Ashtray, Poppies 20.00
Basket, Handled, Calla Lily, 7 X 4 1/4 In. 65.00
Basket, Irregular Scalloped Edge, Carnations, Handled, 7 X 4 In. 85.00
Berry Bowl, Green, White Roses, Marked 325.00
Berry Bowl, Pink & White Roses, Beaded Edge, 5 In. 12.00
Berry Set, White Flowers, Green Leaves, Gold Trim, 7 Piece 150.00
Bonbon, Dish, Purple Violets, 1 Pink Rosebud, Gilt Edge 28.00
Bowl, Blue & Lavender, Iris Design, Signed, 9 In. 67.50
Bowl, Cotton Plant, 8 1/2 In. 35.00
Bowl, Floral, Gold Leaves, Pedestal, 9 In. 30.00
Bowl, Floral, Pale Yellow Ground, 9 1/4 In. 25.00
Bowl, Game Birds, 8 In. 200.00
Bowl, Hand-Painted, Floral Design, Footed, Oval, Open-Handled, 7 In .. 26.00
Bowl, Hand-Painted, Floral Design, Round, Footed, 6 1/2 In. 22.00
Bowl, Hand-Painted, Round, Footed, Gold Rim, 6 1/2 In. 38.00
Bowl, Ladle, Footed, 9 1/2 In. 38.00
Bowl, Lilies, Gold Trim, Blue Mark, 10 X 8 1/2 In. 45.00
Bowl, Lilies, Gold Trim, 9 1/2 X 2 1/2 In. 38.00
Bowl, Mayonnaise, White Lilies, Brown Ground, Ladle 28.00
Bowl, Orange Lilies & Lilac Design, 10 In. 50.00
Bowl, Peach & Yellow Carnations, Gold Trim, 9 In. 25.00
Bowl, Rose & Gold Stars, 2-Handled, Square, Marked 35.00
Bowl, Roses On Rim, Red Mark, 10 1/2 In. 95.00
Bowl, White Lilies, Leaves, Brown Ground, 9 1/2 In. 38.00
Bowl, Wicker Basket Design, Orange, Red Roses, Green Ground, 9 In. .. 35.00
Box, Pin, White Porcelain, Germany, C.1880 .... 25.00
Box, Pink Poppies, Gold Trim, Domed Cover, 3-Footed, Round, 4 In. .. 65.00
Box, Powder, Calla Lily Design, Covered 31.00
Box, Powder, Floral Sides, Scenic Cover, Marked, 4 X 2 1/4 In. .. 97.00
Cake Plate, Cream & Gold Ground, Pink & Peach Roses, Marked .. 60.00
Cake Plate, Floral, Open-Handled, Marked, 10 In. ...... 40.00 To 42.00
Cake Plate, Floral, Tan & Green, Open-Handled, 8 In. 38.00
Cake Plate, Gardenias, 10 In. 45.00
Cake Plate, Lilacs, Open-Handled, 10 In. .... 47.00 To 55.00
Cake Plate, Pierced Handles, Floral Design, Gold Edging, 12 In. .. 35.00
Cake Plate, Poppy, 10 In. 45.00
Cake Plate, Roses, Open-Handled, Red Star Mark, 10 1/2 In. 148.00
Cake Plate, Yellow, White Roses, 12-Sided, 10 In. 45.00
Cake Set, Circles Of Roses, 7 Piece 160.00
Cake Set, Green, Brown Ground, Pierced Handle, 6 Plates, Blue Mark .. 110.00
Cake Set, Lily Design, Gold Trim, 8 Piece 85.00
Cake Set, Poinsettias, Gold Edge, Artist Signed, 7 Piece 175.00
Cake Set, Stylized Urn, Multicolored Flowers, Marked, 8 Piece .. 135.00
Cake Set, White Lilies, Leaves, Brown Ground, 7 Piece 95.00
Candy, Handles, Poppies 25.00
Celery, Pierced Handles, Floral Design, Gold Edging, 12 In. 35.00
Celery, Poppies, Gold Stem, Open-Handled, Green Mark, 12 1/2 In. .. 62.50
Cheese & Cracker, Tiered, Pink Sweetpeas, Gold Florals, 9 In. .. 55.00
Cheese Dish, Green, Hand-Painted Tulips 98.00
Chocolate Pot, Roses, Flowers Form Handle 65.00
Chocolate Pot, Single White Rose, Brown Leaves, Beige Ground .. 100.00
Chocolate Pot, White, Gold Design, Steeple Mark, 9 3/4 In. 85.00
Chocolate Set, Gold & Peach, Gold, 11 Piece 395.00
Chocolate Set, Poppies Inside & Out, Gold Bands, Marked, 10 Piece .. 325.00
Chocolate Set, White Lilies, Green Ground, 7 Piece 275.00
Compote, Floral, Pedestal, 5 X 3 In. 55.00
Cracker Dish, Lilies, Blue Mark 97.00
Cracker Jar, Covered, Shaded Greens, Rose Design 150.00
Cracker Jar, Covered, Surreal Dogwood Blossom, Pearlized Luster .. 95.00
Cracker Jar, Greens, Pink & White Roses, Covered 150.00
Cracker Jar, Hand-Painted Violets, Gold Trim, Cream, Blue Mark .. 90.00
Cracker Jar, Hydrangeas, Ear Handles 85.00

Cracker Jar, Roses	68.00
Cracker Jar, Surreal Dogwood Blossoms, Pearlized Luster, Marked	125.00
Creamer, Cobalt, Steeple Mark	24.00
Creamer, Floral, Gold Words Anti Cobden, 1914	35.00
Creamer, Scalloped Rim, Blossoms, Footed, White Luster, 3 1/4 In.	45.00
Cup & Saucer, Child's, Boy, Girl, & Bunny, Red Mark	10.00
Cup & Saucer, Floral, 5 1/2 In.	20.00
Cup, Mustache, Gold Edge, Roses All Around, Aqua Base	30.00
Dessert Set, Calla Lillies, Gold Border, Marked, 8 Piece	160.00
Dish, Boat Shaped, Tulips, Handled, 8 1/2 In.	25.00
Dish, Candy, Raspberries, Marked	35.00
Dish, Cheese & Cracker, Gold Tracings, Blue Band, 10 In.Diam.	60.00
Dish, Cheese & Cracker, 2-Tiered, Tulips, Blue Mark	120.00
Dish, Cracker & Cheese, Floral	45.00
Dish, Lilies, Pale Green, 9 X 4 3/4 In.	35.00
Dish, Pickle, Flowers	29.00
Dish, Poppy, Handled, Oval, 8 In.	29.00
Dresser Tray, Blown-Out Poppy, Multicolored Pansy Design	95.00
Gravy Boat & Underplate, Lilacs	50.00
Hair Receiver & Powder Box, Pink Roses, Scalloped Lids, Marked	115.00
Hair Receiver, Floral, Footed	47.00
Hair Receiver, Lily	40.00
Hair Receiver, Pastel, Entwined Stems, Green Mark	69.00
Hair Receiver, Pink Flowers, Signed, Light Green	55.00
Hatpin Holder, Floral, Signed	60.00
Hatpin Holder, Green, White & Yellow Flowers, Marked	32.00
Hatpin Holder, Hand-Painted Poppies, Green Mark, 4 3/4 In.	27.50
Hatpin Holder, Pink & White Roses, Soft Green Ground, Marked	68.00
Hatpin Holder, Roses	65.00
Hatpin Holder, Shaded Gray With Calla Lily	40.00
Hatpin Holder, Snow Scene, Blue Mark, Artist Signed	85.00
Jar, Powder, Gold Cherries, Pink & Yellow Roses, Covered	45.00
Jar, Rose, Double Lattice Ball Top, Florals, Covered, 6 In.	135.00
Letter Holder, Floral Design	65.00
Mug, Shaving, Floral	95.00
Mug, Shaving, Orange Poppy Design	70.00
Mustard , Covered, White Roses, Gold Trim	34.00
Mustard, Poppies, Marked Germany	21.00
Mustard, Red Roses, Hand-Painted	28.00
Mustard, White Roses	40.00
Nut Cup, Roses, Gold Trim, Footed, Set Of 5	45.00
Planter, Pale Green, Fuchsia Flowers, Footed, Marked	97.00
Plate, Blue Flowers, 8 In.	21.00
Plate, Blue Ground, Floral, Gold Leaves, Steeple Mark, 8 1/4 In.	57.00
Plate, Cake, Daffodil Design, 6 1/2 In., Set Of 4	42.00
Plate, Cherubs, Scalloped Gold Rim, Blue Mark, 7 1/4 In.	125.00
Plate, Floral, 6 In.	15.00
Plate, Flowers, Hand-Painted, Open Handles, 9 3/4 In.	28.00
Plate, Hand-Painted Poppies, Beaded Edging, Blue Mark, 5 In.	72.00
Plate, Hand-Painted, Green, Floral, Marked, 6 1/2 In., 5 Piece	50.00
Plate, Lily Of The Valley, 2-Handled, 10 In.	30.00
Plate, Man With Horse, 10 In.	285.00
Plate, Roses, Gold Center & Border, Green Mark, 8 In.	38.00
Plate, Sweet Peas, Roses, Blue Ground, 8 1/4 In.	45.00
Plate, White & Pink Bell Shaped Flowers, Marked, 8 In.	20.00
Relish, Boat Shaped, Poppy, Violets	23.00
Relish, Carnations, Gold Trim, Tillowitz, Handled	22.00
Relish, Icicle Mold, 8 In.	20.00
Relish, Multicolored Flowers, Ivory Ground, Marked	45.00
Relish, Shaded Roses	30.00
Relish, Swan Scene, Gold Trim, Handled, Marked, 8 1/2 In.	125.00
Sugar & Creamer, Iris	25.00
Sugar & Creamer, Mill Scene, Hand-Painted	90.00

Sugar & Creamer, Mums On Yellow, Green Mark 35.00
Sugar, Covered, Floral, Brown-Yellow Ground 18.50
Syrup & Underplate, Floral 35.00
Syrup & Underplate, Hydrangeas, Covered 78.00
Syrup, Bluebells, Gold Trim, Covered, Blue Mark, 3 1/2 In. 82.00
Syrup, Underliner, Lilies, Green Ground, Green Mark 68.00
Talcum Shaker, Floral, Gold Trim, Marked, 5 In. 69.00
Talcum Shaker, Pearlized 69.00
Tankard, Gold Wreaths At Bottom, Roses, White Ground, 6 3/4 In. 200.00
Teapot, Blue, White & Maroon Flowers, Gold Trim 45.00
Teapot, Gold, Octangular Shape Spout, 5 In. 45.00
Teapot, Maroon Flowers, Gold Trim, White Panels, Squatty 45.00
Toothpick, Embossed Flowers, Gold Trim, Footed 55.00
Toothpick, Floral Luster, 3-Handled 135.00
Tray, Bead, Iris, Blue & White, Gold Outline, Marked 125.00
Tray, Bread, Blue & White Petals, Gold Trim, Flowers, Marked 115.00
Tray, Pin, Hand-Painted, Blue Mark 35.00
Tray, Pink Roses, Single Handled 34.00
Tray, White Flowers, Yellow Center, Gold Design, Marked 95.00
Vase, Blue, Pink, Purple, Irises, Multicolored Ground, 12 In. 85.00
Vase, Bud, Hand-Painted Rose, 6 In. 24.00
Vase, Bulbous, Roses, White & Orange, 5 1/4 In. 35.00
Vase, Colonial Lady Scene, Green Mark, 4 X 2 X 3/4 In. 250.00
Vase, Gold Medallion & Portrait, Gold Scrolls, 5 1/4 In. 65.00
Vase, Lilies, Red Band, 8 In. 55.00
Vase, Orange Glaze, Basket Of Flowers, Marked, 5 In. 35.00

*The RS Poland (German) mark was used by the Rheinhold Schlegelmilch
factory at Tillowitz from about 1945 to 1956.*

RS POLAND, Dresser Set, Roses, Gold Trim, Tray, 9 X 12 3/4 In., 6 Piece 265.00
Vase, Chinese Pheasant Scene, 2-Handled, Red Mark, 3 3/4 In. 95.00
Vase, Ewer Shape, Roses, Brown Shading To White, 6 1/4 In. 160.00

*RS Prussia is a mark that appears on porcelain made at the factory of
Rheinhold Schlegelmilch from the late 1870s to 1914 in Tillowitz,
Germany, or on items made at the Erdmann Schlegelmilch factory in Suhl,
Germany, from about 1910 to 1956. It was sold decorated or undecorated.*

RS PRUSSIA, Basket, Floral, 3-Handled 400.00
Berry Bowl, Barnyard Scene, Marked 65.00
Berry Bowl, Floral Center, Gold-Braided Rim, Red Mark, 5 1/2 In. 135.00
Berry Bowl, Floral, Gold Beaded, Leaves At Rim, Marked, Set Of 4 .... 135.00
Berry Set, Floral, Red Mark, 7 Piece 290.00
Berry Set, Lilies, Blue Ground, Red Mark, 7 Piece 450.00
Berry Set, Mixed Flowers, Red Mark, Bowl, 10 In., 7 Piece 525.00
Berry Set, Pearlized, Yellow Rose, Scalloped, Marked, 7 Piece 225.00
Biscuit Jar, Floral, Red Mark 295.00
Biscuit Jar, Iris, Jeweled, 10 In. 295.00
Biscuit Jar, Light Green, Cream, Roses, Marked, 6 X 6 In. 225.00
Bonbon, Roses, Raised Gold Wheat, Cream & Green, Marked, 7 1/2 In 88.00
Bowl, Blown-Out Sides, Twisted Flutes, Roses, Red Mark, 6 3/4 In. 260.00
Bowl, Carnations, Blown Out, Roses, Marked, 8 In. 175.00
Bowl, Center Poppies, Floral Rim, Steeple Mark, 10 1/4 In. 100.00
Bowl, Cottage Scene, Sawtooth Mold, 10 In. 390.00
Bowl, Floral Center, Blown-Out Mold, Roses, Red Mark, 10 1/2 In. 175.00
Bowl, Floral, Blown-Out Leaves & Grapes, Marked, 11 In. 125.00
Bowl, Floral, Blown-Out Rim, Marked, 10 In. 185.00
Bowl, Floral, Red Mark, 11 In. 110.00
Bowl, Flowers Inside, Red Mark, 10 In. 225.00
Bowl, Fruit Design, Pierced Handle, 11 In. 275.00
Bowl, Gold Crimped Rim, Shading, 11 In. 185.00
Bowl, Gold Ribbon Scalloped, Rose Bouquets, Pink, Marked, 10 In. 169.00

Bowl, Green Leaf Rayed Out To Florals, Steeple Mark, 10 1/4 In.	200.00
Bowl, Green, White, Gold, Flowers, Signed, 10 1/2 In.	225.00
Bowl, Hand-Painted, Floral Design, Footed, Red Mark, 8 In.	125.00
Bowl, Iris Mold, Pink Roses, Yellow Ground, Red Mark, 10 1/2 In.	180.00
Bowl, Lilies, Red Mark, 11 In.	165.00
Bowl, Masted Schooner, Red Mark, Blue & Orange, 11 In.	585.00
Bowl, Mill Scene, Pastel Colors, Gold, 10 1/4 In.	425.00
Bowl, Mill Scene, Red Mark, 7 In.	295.00
Bowl, Nut & Acorn Mold, Red Mark, 10 In.	375.00
Bowl, Pastel Floral, Gold, Blown-Out Side, 10 1/2 In.	175.00
Bowl, Pearlized Finish, Orchid Border, Marked, 10 In.	265.00
Bowl, Pink & White Roses, Red Mark, 10 1/2 In.	195.00
Bowl, Pink Flowers, Gold Vertical Divider, Red Mark, 10 1/2 In.	300.00
Bowl, Pink Roses, Green Leaves, Marked, 10 In.	135.00
Bowl, Pink Roses, Leaves, Red Mark, 10 In.	135.00
Bowl, Pink, Red, & Lavender Flowers, Red Mark, 10 1/2 In.	200.00
Bowl, Point & Clover Mold, Floral, 11 In.	125.00
Bowl, Poppies In Center, Gold & Lavender Trim, 11 In.	240.00
Bowl, Poppies On Green, 10 In.	125.00
Bowl, Portrait, Lady & Man, 10 In.	535.00
Bowl, Purple Flowers, Blown-Out Rim, Marked, 10 3/4 In.	169.00
Bowl, Raised Circle, Iris Mold, Pink & White Roses, 10 In.	145.00
Bowl, Red & Yellow Rose Decor, Gold Scalloped Edge, Marked, 10 In.	125.00
Bowl, Red Cabbage, Blown Out, Wild Rose, 9 X 3 1/4 In.	600.00
Bowl, Rose Design, Scalloped, Red Mark, 10 In.	140.00
Bowl, Rose, Cover Lattice Ball, Signed, 6 In.	135.00
Bowl, Roses, Blown-Out Carnations, Marked, 8 In.	175.00
Bowl, Roses, Fluted, Marked, 10 In.	135.00
Bowl, Roses, Gold Trim, Yellow Ground, Marked, 11 In.	145.00
Bowl, Roses, Leaves, Gold Trim, Marked, 11 1/2 In.	225.00
Bowl, Roses, Leaves, Red Mark, 10 In.	135.00
Bowl, Roses, Poppies, & Daisies, Puffed Panels, Red Mark, 10 3/4 In	140.00
Bowl, Roses, Scalloped Green Rim, Red Mark, 9 In.	150.00
Bowl, Satin, Red & White Flowers, Red Mark, 10 In.	195.00
Bowl, Scalloped, Floral Pattern, Pastel, Gold Border	95.00
Bowl, Scalloped, Gold Trim, Puffed Panels, Red Mark, 10 3/4 In.	150.00
Bowl, Scalloped, Pink Roses, White Ground, 9 In.	105.00
Bowl, Schooner, Red Mark, 10 In.	750.00
Bowl, Shadow Flowers, Steeple Mark, 10 In.	100.00
Bowl, Stippled Floral, Blown-Out Dome Sections, Red Mark, 10 In.	170.00
Bowl, Sunflower Edge, Rose Center, Red Mark, 10 1/2 In.	275.00
Bowl, Swag & Tassel, Pine Trees & Swans, Red Mark, 9 1/4 In.	300.00
Bowl, White, Pink, Flowers, Orange Berries, Marked, 10 In.	165.00
Bowl, Wicker Basket Shape, Orange Roses, 10 1/2 In.	200.00
Bowl, Winter Season, Marked, 10 In.	950.00
Bowl, Yellow To Green, Roses & Leaves, Red Mark, 10 In.	425.00
Bowl, 5 Panel, Floral, Gold, Red Star Mark, 10 In.	195.00
Box, Powder, Pink & Yellow Iris, Gold Trim, Open-Handled, Marked	65.00
Butter, Blown-Out Petal Rim, Blossoms, Liner, Red Mark, Covered	285.00
Cake Plate, Band Of Roses, Red Mark, 10 In.	95.00
Cake Plate, Basket Of Flower, Marked, 11 In.	140.00
Cake Plate, Castle Scene, Orange, Yellow, Gold, Open-Handled, 10 In	175.00
Cake Plate, Fruit Design, Pears, Grapes, & Plums, Marked, 10 In.	225.00
Cake Plate, Gold Stenciled Design, Scalloped, Red Mark, 1/2 In.	175.00
Cake Plate, Laurel Chain, Hanging Basket Design, Marked, 10 In.	165.00
Cake Plate, Leaf Mold, Violet, Green, Cream, Marked Rm, 10 3/4 In.	135.00
Cake Plate, Lilies, Gold Leaves, Handled, Red Mark, 10 3/4 In.	125.00
Cake Plate, Open Roses, Gold Trim, Open-Handled, 11 1/2 In.	150.00
Cake Plate, Pierced Handles, Water Lilies, Red Mark, 10 1/4 In.	165.00
Cake Plate, Pink, Red Rose Sprays, Gold Trim, 11 In.	75.00
Cake Plate, Pink, Red, Roses, Gold Trim, 11 In.	75.00
Cake Plate, Red Rose Center, White Daisies, Green Border, 11 In.	125.00

Cake Plate, Roses, Daisies, & Leaves, Handled, Red Mark, 10 1/2 In. 150.00
Cake Plate, Water Lilies, Handled, Red Mark, 10 1/4 In. 155.00
Candy, Footed, Green Ground, Rose Design, Gold Overlay, 6 1/4 In. 70.00
Celery, Carnation Mold, Floral Center, Dark Green, Marked, 12 In. 210.00
Celery, Carnation, Pink Roses, Blue Ground, 12 In. 195.00
Celery, Roses, Satin Finish, Marked, 12 X 6 In. 140.00
Celery, Roses, 12 1/2 In. 50.00
Celery, Satin Finish, Roses, Red Mark, 12 X 6 In. 140.00
Celery, Turquoise, 12 In. 175.00
Chamberstick, Satin Finish, 5 X 2 In. 185.00
Chocolate Pot, Floral, Scroll Handle 95.00
Chocolate Pot, Flowers, Ball Feet, Green Ground, Red Mark 225.00
Chocolate Pot, Leaves & Gold, White Ground, Red Mark 147.00
Chocolate Pot, Roses, Shaded Ivory, Tan & Green Ground 275.00
Chocolate Pot, Swan Scene, Marked, 9 In. 349.00
Chocolate Set, Blown-Out Roses, Red Mark, 7 Piece 950.00
Chocolate Set, Floral, Red Mark, 6 Piece 650.00
Chocolate Set, Fruit Design, Stippled Floral, 8 Piece 2750.00
Chocolate Set, Gold Outlining, Ball-Footed, Red Mark, 13 Piece 975.00
Chocolate Set, Green Floral, 6 Cups & Saucers, Pot, Red Mark 1200.00
Chocolate Set, Ivy, 4 Cups & Saucers 225.00
Chocolate Set, Poppies, Daisies, Reflected In Water, Marked 875.00
Chocolate Set, Roses, Pearlized Finish, Marked, 4 Cups & Saucers 675.00
Chocolate Set, Swan Pattern, Red Star, Marked 295.00
Chocolate Set, White, Gold, & Green Floral, Marked 475.00
Cracker Jar, Beading & Jewels, Red Mark 345.00
Cracker Jar, Covered, Cream Ground, Carnation Design 190.00
Cracker Jar, Florals, Octagonal, Red Mark 235.00
Cracker Jar, Flowers & Leaves Stenciled, Green Ground, 7 1/2 In. 195.00
Cracker Jar, Melon Ribbed, Roses, Handled, 8 1/2 X 5 1/2 In. 225.00
Cracker Jar, Pink & Orchid, Satin Finish, 5 In. ....*Illus* 275.00
Cracker Jar, Raised Feathers Outlined In Gold, Red Mark 225.00
Cracker Jar, Red Roses, Red Mark 350.00
Cracker Jar, Surreal Flowers, Gold Enameling, Red Mark 295.00
Cracker Jar, White, Gilt Roses, Reflections In Water, Marked 225.00
Cracker Jar, Yellow & Pink Rose, Blue Ground, Red Mark 485.00
Creamer, Apricot Roses, Red Star Mark 94.00
Creamer, Castle Scene, Red Star Mark, 3 1/4 In. 250.00
Creamer, Madam LeBrun, Marked, 3 1/2 In. 350.00
Creamer, Melon Boy, Jeweled, Gold Trim, Marked, 5 In. 375.00
Creamer, Mill Scene, Footed, Green Ground .... 115.00 To 195.00
Creamer, Pink Rose Spray 47.00
Cup & Saucer, Apple Blossoms, Marked 38.00
Cup & Saucer, Calla Lily, Pearlized, Red Mark 79.00
Cup & Saucer, Floral Design, Red Marked Cup 38.00
Cup & Saucer, Flower Form, Tiffany Iridescent, Red Mark 109.00
Cup & Saucer, Ringneck Pheasant, Gold Trim, Demitasse 145.00
Cup & Saucer, Rose Design, Gold Trim, Red Mark 75.00
Cup & Saucer, Swan Design, Demitasse 40.00
Cup & Saucer, Village Scene 210.00

RS Prussia, Cracker Jar, Pink & Orchid,
Satin Finish, 5 In.

Demitasse Set, Beige & Gold Trim, White, Red Mark, 11 Piece 1200.00
Demitasse Set, Dogwood Pattern, Red Mark 850.00
Dish, Blooming Roses, White & Green Ground, 9 X 4 In. 44.00
Dish, Pink & White Roses, Scalloped, Pearlized, 7 1/2 In. 45.00
Dish, Roses, Gold Border, Handled, 6 1/2 In.Diam. 40.00
Dish, Vegetable, Scalloped Edge, Red Mark, 12 1/2 X 8 1/2 In. 240.00
Dresser Set, Icicle Mold, Box & Tray, Red Mark, 5 1/2 X 3 1/4 In. 395.00
Ewer, Watered Silk Finish, Red Mark, 7 In. 250.00
Fernery, Poppy Design, Satin, Red Star, 7 X 4 In. 100.00
Gravy Boat, Underplate, Hand-Painted, Handled, Red Mark 200.00
Gravy Boat, White Iris, Gold Trim, Underplate 145.00
Hair Receiver, Floral Design, Red Mark 52.00
Hair Receiver, Yellow Roses 32.00
Hatpin Holder, Floral Design, 4 1/2 In. 92.00
Hatpin Holder, Floral Design, 6-Sided, Red Mark 110.00
Hatpin Holder, Pale Blue, Gold, Roses, Marked 425.00
Hatpin Holder, Sheepherder, Marked 400.00
Hatpin Holder, Swan Scene, Beaded, Pearlized, Hexagonal 135.00
Jar, Powder, Pink Roses, Gold Trim, Dome Lid, Marked 35.00
Muffineer, Ruffled Skirt Base, Ribbed, Red Mark 140.00
Mug, Child's, Pink Flowers, Green Leaves, Marked .... 80.00 To 97.00
Mug, Lilies, White, Red Mark 120.00
Mug, Shaving, Soap Shelf, Allover Garland, Footed, Red Mark 285.00
Mustache Cup, Floral, Red Mark 95.00
Mustard, Semijeweled, Footed, Flower Finial 98.00
Pitcher, Milk, Swans & Castle, Bulbous, Red Mark 495.00
Pitcher, Water, Roses, Shadow Work Leaves, Red Mark 365.00
Planter, Scalloped, Florals 150.00
Plate, Beaded Edge, Tulips, Marked, 6 In. 35.00
Plate, Beige Ground, Rose Design, Gold, Open-Handled, 11 1/4 In. 150.00
Plate, Dessert, Sunflower, Gold Rim, Red Mark, 7 1/2 In. 150.00
Plate, Dice Player, Marked, 10 In. 950.00
Plate, Floral & Gold, Wreath Mark, 7 In. 22.50
Plate, Floral Border, Gold Stars On Ivory, Red Mark, 8 1/2 In. 125.00
Plate, Floral, 6 1/2 In. 35.00
Plate, Flowers & Gold Star Center, Ivory Ground, 8 1/2 In. 125.00
Plate, Flowers, Clover Mold, Marked, 10 1/2 In. 225.00
Plate, Flowers, Gold Trim, Red Mark, 6 1/2 In. 85.00
Plate, Gold Border, Pink Roses, Orange, Steeple Mark, 9 3/4 In. 150.00
Plate, Gold Medallions, Center Roses, Red Mark, 8 1/4 In. 95.00
Plate, Green, Lavender, Floral, Raised Gold, Iridescent, 11 1/2 In. 145.00
Plate, Iris, Blown Out, Cutout Handles, 11 In. 165.00
Plate, Ivory Ground, Jonquil Design, Gold, 11 1/4 In. 150.00
Plate, Masted Schooner, 11 In. 425.00
Plate, Masted Schooner, 6 In. 225.00
Plate, Melon Eater, Red Mark, 10 In. 850.00
Plate, Mill Scene, Pink, Iris, Satin, Red Mark, 9 1/2 In. 550.00
Plate, Mill Scene, 6 In. .... 50.00 To 145.00
Plate, Pearl Luster, Pink Roses, Crimped Border, Marked, 8 In. 135.00
Plate, Pearlized Jewels, Pink Roses, Blue Ground, Marked, 9 In. 125.00
Plate, Pink Flowers, Gold Stars, Ivory Tapestry, Marked, 8 In. 125.00
Plate, Plumed, Poppies, Gold Trim, 9 In. 90.00
Plate, Portrait, Le Brun, Floral Design, Lily Mold, 8 In. 440.00
Plate, Portrait, Pale Green, Pierced Handle, 11 In. 375.00
Plate, Portrait, Pierced Handle, Marked, Green Lusterware, 11 In. 375.00
Plate, Roses & Daisies, Marked, 8 1/2 In. 125.00
Plate, Scalloped & Beaded Rim, Roses, Red Mark, 8 1/4 In. 35.00
Plate, Spring, Beaded Edge, Roses, Red Mark, 8 7/8 In. 855.00
Plate, Swan Scene, Beaded Rim, 7 3/4 In. 279.00
Plate, Swans, Swimming, Marked, 9 In. 400.00
Plate, Triple Flower Forms, Green Ribbon, Red Mark, 11 In. 225.00
Plate, V Forms, Foral, Red Mark, 10 1/2 In. 190.00
Plate, White Flowers, Satinized, 7 1/2 In. 60.00

Plate, Winter, Beaded Edge, Roses, Red Mark, 8 7/8 In. 855.00
Platter, Carnation, Red Mark, 10 In. 380.00
Platter, Floral, Green, Gold, 10 1/2 In. 235.00
Platter, Floral, Violet, Floral Center, Greens, Marked, 10 In. 235.00
Platter, Lily Of The Valley, Red Mark, 11 In.Diam. 125.00
Relish, Rose Design, Gold, Opal Jeweled, Scalloped, 12 In. 140.00
Relish, Roses, Gold With Jewel Each Side, Handled, 10 3/4 In. 135.00
Shaker, Pearl Finish, Pierced Handles, Marked, 5 In. 85.00
Sugar & Creamer, Blown-Out Gaston, Blossoms, Red Mark 175.00
Sugar & Creamer, Blue, Green, Florals, Handled 32.00
Sugar & Creamer, Carnation, Blue Ground 100.00
Sugar & Creamer, Castle Scene, Red Mark 495.00
Sugar & Creamer, Cottage & Mill Design 650.00
Sugar & Creamer, Egg Mold, Pink Roses, Pedestal, Marked 210.00
Sugar & Creamer, Florals, Lavender Ground 250.00
Sugar & Creamer, Fuchsia, Green Border 89.00
Sugar & Creamer, Jeweled, Satin Finish, Marked 185.00
Sugar & Creamer, Lavender Ground, Floral, Gold Design, 5 In. 250.00
Sugar & Creamer, Mill Scene 550.00
Sugar & Creamer, Mums Design, Blown Base, Red Mark, Set 225.00
Sugar & Creamer, Pedestal, Satin Ground 169.00
Sugar & Creamer, Pink Roses, Square, Pedestal, Marked 235.00
Sugar & Creamer, Sunflower, Red Mark 185.00
Sugar Shaker, Full Figure Of Young Girl, Red Mark 350.00
Sugar, Barnyard Scene, Icicle Mold, Covered, Red Mark 350.00
Sugar, Carnation Pattern, Open, Marked 100.00
Sugar, Dogwood, Piecrust Edge, Gold, Covered, Red Mark .... 78.00 To 95.00
Sugar, Iris, Green 27.00
Sugar, Pink Florals, Pedestal, Red Star Mark 97.00
Sugar, Swans In Lake, Green Pearlized, Red Mark 115.00
Sugar, Swans, Cinnamon, Ecru, Blue, Covered, Red Mark 135.00
Sugar, Swans, Satin Finish, Red Mark 50.00
Syrup, Easter Lily Design, Covered, Marked 68.00
Syrup, Pearlized, Florals, Covered, Red Mark 42.00
Syrup, Purple, Yellow, Roses, Marked 195.00
Syrup, Underplate, Blown Drapery, Yellow & Purple Luster 185.00
Syrup, Underplate, Lily Design, Satin Finish, Marked, Covered 190.00
Syrup, Underplate, White Roses, Marked 35.00
Tankard, Floral, Orchid, Apricot, Pearlized, Red Mark, 11 1/2 In. 895.00
Tankard, Jewels, Molded Feet, Marked, 10 3/4 In. 550.00
Tankard, Mill Scene, Summer Season, Red Mark, 15 In. 3500.00
Tankard, Poppy, Red Mark, 11 1/2 In. 500.00
Tankard, Roses, Pierced Handle, Blown Out, 13 In. 750.00
Tea Set, Blown-Out Bodies, Florals, Green Ground, Gold Trim, 3 Pc. 360.00
Tea Set, Blown-Out Shapes, Melon Ribbed, Dogwood Blossoms, 3 Pc. 335.00
Tea Set, Child's, Shadow Flowers, 11 Piece 500.00
Tea Set, Floral, Gold Ground, 3 Piece 185.00
Tea Set, Melon Ribbed, Dogwood Blossoms, Red Mark, 3 Piece 335.00
Teapot, Florals, Scalloped Gold Rim, Double Handle, Red Mark 195.00
Teapot, Large Pink Roses, Green Ground, Gold Trim, Covered 80.00
Teapot, Pink Rose, Green Ground, Red Mark, 5 1/2 In. 225.00
Teapot, Pink Roses, Pearl Luster, Red Mark 295.00
Teapot, White, Green Ground, Orange Blossoms Design, Marked 125.00
Toothpick, Blown-Out Star Mark 75.00
Toothpick, Floral, 2-Handled, Footed 110.00
Toothpick, Icicle, Double Handle, Red Mark, 2 1/2 In. 125.00
Toothpick, Icicle, Pond Lilies Scene 205.00
Toothpick, Red Carnation, Red Mark 45.00
Tray, Blown-Out Iris, Gold Trim, Red Mark, 11 1/4 In.Diam. 270.00
Tray, Blue, Floral Design, Marked, 3 X 5 In. 40.00
Tray, Bun, Medallion Mold, Basket Of Roses, Red Mark, 14 In. 125.00
Tray, Bun, Open-Handled, Flowers Over Water, Red Mark, 13 3/4 In. 175.00
Tray, Celery, Mold, Carnation, Pearlized, 12 X 6 In. 235.00
Tray, Floral, Gold Trim, Red Mark, 11 1/2 X 7 1/2 In. 79.00

Tray, Flowers, Daisies, Red Mark, 11 3/4 X 7 3/4 In. 185.00
Tray, Flowers, 6 Circle Mold, Red Mark, 11 X 7 In. 185.00
Tray, Jewels Over Blue, Footed, Red Mark, 11 5/8 In. 150.00
Tray, Pearlized & Satin Finish, 11 X 7 In. 350.00
Tray, Portrait, Summer, Iris Mold, Round 800.00
Tray, Relish, Pink Roses, Lily Of The Valley, Marked 110.00
Tray, Relish, Red Ground, Portraits, Handled, Red Mark, 12 1/4 In. 400.00
Tray, Shepherd Scene, Red Mark, 7 X 11 3/4 In. 200.00
Tray, Snowbirds, Red Mark, 7 1/2 X 12 1/4 In. 1500.00
Vase, Ball Shape, Blue Flowers & Leaves, 6 1/2 X 19 In. 150.00
Vase, Blown-Out Swirls, Handled, 11 In. 135.00
Vase, Blue, Gold, Design, Pedestal, Red Mark, 9 In. 375.00
Vase, Diana The Huntress, Floral, 9 In. 850.00
Vase, Floral, Pearlized, Handled, Marked, 9 In. 275.00
Vase, Goddess Of The Sea, Gold Handles, Fluted, Marked, 8 1/2 In. 300.00
Vase, Green Ground, Gold Handles, Marked, 6 In. 185.00
Vase, Irregular Rim, Blue, Gold, & White, Steeple Mark, 5 1/2 In. 130.00
Vase, Lovers Scene, 2-Handled, 5 In. 190.00
Vase, Mill Scene, Bottle Shape, 4 In. 145.00
Vase, Mill Scene, Green Ground, Gold Trim, 3 3/4 In. 395.00
Vase, Old Man Of The Mountain, Bluebirds, 9 In. 650.00
Vase, Old Man Of The Mountain, Club Shape, Red Mark, 7 In. 395.00
Vase, Opalescent Jewels, Mother-Of-Pearl Finish, Red Mark, 8 In. 325.00
Vase, Pink & White, Cabbage Rose, Marked, 8 3/4 In. 195.00
Vase, Pink Tinged White Roses, Red Mark, Green, 6 In. 135.00
Vase, Poppy Design, Gold Handles, Red Mark, 9 In. 125.00
Vase, Sheepherder Scene, Handled, Red Mark, 9 1/2 In. 550.00
Vase, Winter Portrait, Skirted Base, Steeple Mark, 10 1/2 In. 155.00
Vase, Winter Season, Gold Handles & Trim, Red Mark, 9 In. 950.00
Vase, 2-Handled, Lovers Scene, 5 In. 190.00

The RS Silesia mark appears on porcelain made at Reinhold
Schlegelmilch's Tillowitz factory from about 1920 to the mid-1930s.

RS SILESIA, Plate, Floral, 10 In. 75.00

RS Suhl was a mark used by the Erdmann Schlegelmilch factory in Suhl,
Germany, from c. 1900 to the mid-1920s.

RS SUHL, Cake Set, White Roses, Hand-Painted, 7 Piece 65.00

The RS Tillowitz mark was used by the Rheinhold Schlegelmilch
factory at Tillowitz, near Silesia, from about 1920 to the mid-1930s.
Table services and ornamental pieces were made.

RS TILLOWITZ, Berry Bowl, Floral, 6 Nappies 79.00
Bowl, Blue, Bird On Blossom Branch, Open-Handled, 3 1/2 In. 125.00
Bowl, Pastel Florals, Gold Roses & Rim, 9 7/8 In. 87.50
Cake Plate, White Lilacs, Blue Ground, Handled, 9 1/4 In. 48.00
Creamer, Floral, Artist Signed 39.00
Cup & Saucer, Floral Design, Star & Wreath Mark, Plate 8 In. 20.00
Plate, Dinner, Cream, Pink Pond Lilies, 10 In., Set Of 8 .... 125.00
Vase, Basket Of Flowers & Ribbons, Signed, 5 1/2 In. 35.00

Rubena Verde is a Victorian glassware that was shaded from red to green.
It was first made by Hobbs, Brockunier and Company of Wheeling,
West Virginia, about 1890.

RUBENA VERDE, Cracker Jar, Crackle Glass 85.00
Creamer, Vaseline Handle & Feet, Fluted Top, 4 7/8 In. 95.00
Shade, Shell Pattern, Ruffled, 5 X 9 X 9 In. 395.00
Tumbler, High Relief Enamel, 5 In. 65.00
Tumbler, Water, Inverted Thumbprint, 3 3/4 In. 50.00

Vase, Bud, Spiral Applique, Petal Feet, Green, 8 In. 85.00
Vase, Cylinder, Enameled Design Of Florals, Ruffled, 12 1/4 In. 195.00

Rubena is a glassware that shades from red to clear. It was first made by
George Duncan and Sons of Pittsburgh, Pennsylvania, about 1885.

RUBENA, see also Pressed Glass, Royal Ivy; Pressed Glass, Royal
    Oak

RUBENA, Basket, Blown-Out Ribs, Flower Medallions, Thorn Handle, Square 90.00
    Bottle, Perfume, With Atomizer, 9 In. 40.00
    Castor, Pickle, Original Holder 395.00
    Celery, Threaded, Northwood 135.00
    Creamer, Clear Handled, Medallion 150.00
    Cup, Punch, Set Of 9 .... 80.00
    Dish, Jam, Ruffled, Silver Plated Stand 90.00
    Epergne, Center Trumpet, 2 Side Bowls 375.00
    Mustard, Silver Plated Holder, 3 1/2 In. 85.00
    Pitcher, Applied Handle, Ground Pontil, 8 In. 118.00
    Pitcher, Bulbous, Cranberry To Clear, 8 1/2 In. 165.00
    Pitcher, Inverted Thumbprint, Applied Twisted Rope Handle, 8 In. 250.00
    Pitcher, Melon Ribbed, Clear Reed Handle, Overshot, 6 X 3 3/4 In. 125.00
    Spooner, Silver Plated Frame 195.00
    Sugar & Creamer, Thumbprint, Silver Plated Frames 395.00
    Sugar Shaker, Medallion Sprig 165.00
    Syrup, Threaded 205.00
    Toothpick, Optic 45.00
    Tumbler, Crane & Leaves, 3 3/4 In. 50.00
    Tumbler, Water, Reversed Inverted Thumbprint, 4 In. 40.00
    Vase, Bulbous Base, Floral Design, Flaring Rim, 10 In. 95.00
    Vase, Celery, Crisscross Frosted, Opal, Satin Finish 245.00
    Vase, Enameled Flowers, Outlined In Gold, Crimped, 9 3/4 In., Pair 265.00
    Vase, Fuchsia, Cranberry To Vaseline, 9 In., Pair 195.00

Ruby glass is a dark red color. It was a Victorian and twentieth-century
ware. The name means many different types of red glass.

RUBY GLASS, see also Cranberry Glass; Pressed Glass; Souvenir

RUBY GLASS, Banana Stand, Royal Crystal Pattern 150.00
    Berry Bowl, Thumbprint, Boat Shape 28.00
    Berry Set, Button Arches With Frost Band, 5 Piece 55.00
    Berry Set, Cherry & Scale, 7 Piece 295.00
    Berry Set, Flower & Pleat, 5 Piece .... 85.00 To 90.00
    Berry Set, Thumbprint, Boat Shape, 6 Piece 195.00
    Bowl, Beaded Ivy, 4 In. 14.00
    Box, Jewel, Hinged Top, Ormolu Feet, Brass Rings, Floral, 6 1/8 In. 245.00
    Butter, Beaded Drape, Covered 95.00
    Butter, Beveled Diamond, Covered 120.00
    Butter, Block & Honeycomb, Covered 119.00
    Butter, Block & Star, Covered 110.00
    Butter, Fleur-De-Lis, Gold Trim, Covered 75.00
    Butter, Floria, Gold Trim, Covered 75.00
    Butter, Honeycomb 85.00
    Butter, Loop & Block, Covered 85.00
    Butter, Pioneer's Victoria, Covered 104.00
    Butter, Prize Pattern, Covered 65.00
    Butter, Red Block, Covered 85.00
    Butter, Royal Crystal, Clear Base 89.50
    Butter, Thumbprint, Covered 135.00
    Butter, York Herringbone, Covered 95.00
    Carafe, Tacoma 125.00
    Celery, Block & Lattice 65.00
    Celery, Millard 35.00
    Celery, Nail 65.00
    Celery, The Prize 89.50
    Chamber Pot, Souvenir, Niagara Falls 14.00

Claret, Thumbprint 45.00
Compote, Button & Arches 32.00
Compote, Jelly, Eureka, National 35.00
Condiment Set, Thumbprint, 4 Bottles 350.00
Creamer, Button & Arches, 4 1/4 In. 30.00
Creamer, Colorado, Souvenir, Soldier's Home 35.00
Creamer, Grape & Gothic Arch 40.00
Creamer, King's Crown 22.50
Creamer, King's Crown Pattern, Hot Springs, 1892 .... 18.00
Creamer, Nail .... 60.00 To 65.00
Creamer, New Hampshire 70.00
Creamer, Oregon 45.00
Creamer, Plume, Etched 50.00
Creamer, Red Block .... 60.00 To 70.00
Creamer, Ruby Thumbprint, Souvenir, Indianapolis 49.00
Creamer, Sunk Honeycomb, World's Fair 1890 .... 67.00
Creamer, Thousand Islands, 1904 .... 16.50
Creamer, Thumbprint 55.00
Creamer, Triple Triangle 45.00
Creamer, Wedding 85.00
Creamer, Winona 45.00
Cruet, Beaded Swirl With Discs, Original Stopper 95.00
Cruet, Block & Lattice, Stopper .... 95.00 To 110.00
Cruet, Eureka 160.00
Cruet, Sunk Honeycomb, Etched, Original Stopper 135.00
Cup & Saucer, Thumbprint Pattern 68.00
Cup, Punch, Scroll, Cane Band 22.00
Decanter, Liquor, Double Red Block 175.00
Goblet, Block & Lattice 42.00
Goblet, Bull's-Eye 24.00
Goblet, Button & Arches, Souvenir 27.00
Goblet, Dartband 25.00
Goblet, Loop & Block .... 35.00 To 38.00
Goblet, Paneled Diamonds 25.00
Goblet, Red Block .... 25.00 To 40.00
Goblet, Thumbprint 35.00
Goblet, Thumbprint, Etched 45.00
Goblet, Truncated Cube 30.00
Goblet, Yoked Loop 25.00
Inkwell, Paneled Design, Hinged Faceted Top, 4 1/4 In. 650.00
Jar, Powder, Winged Scroll 45.00
Mug, Button & Arches, Frosted Band, 1903 .... 50.00
Mug, Child's, Drum & Eagle, Gold Trim, Souvenir, York, Pa. 20.00
Mug, Heart Pattern, Frosted Band 10.00
Mug, Triple Triangle, World's Fair, 1893 .... 18.00
Pitcher, Button Arches, Frosted Band With Gold Trim 135.00
Pitcher, Milk, Art 145.00
Pitcher, Milk, Hobnail 59.00
Pitcher, Stars & Pinwheels, Cut Crystal, Overlay 125.00
Pitcher, Sunk Primrose 119.00
Pitcher, Tilt, Round 20.00
Pitcher, Water, Block & Honeycomb 107.00
Pitcher, Water, Mario 135.00
Pitcher, Water, Red Block 125.00
Pitcher, Water, Roanoke .... 95.00 To 120.00
Pitcher, Water, Sheaf & Block, Footed 60.00
Pitcher, Water, Spearpoint Band, Frosted Band, Bulbous 115.00
Pitcher, Water, Star Of Bethlehem 175.00
Pitcher, Water, Sunk Honeycomb 130.00
Relish, Barred Oval, 10 1/2 X 5 In. 60.00
Salt & Pepper, Flat Diamond Box 70.00
Salt & Pepper, Thumbprint, Original Lids 75.00
Sauce, Blocked Thumbprint Band, Souvenir, Sedan, Kansas 22.50

Sauce, Honeycomb Pattern, Set Of 4	32.00
Sauce, Thumbprint, Boat Shape	24.50
Saucer, Berry, Daisy & Button With Red Dots, 4 1/2 In., Square	20.00
Shoe, Daisy & Button	110.00
Shot Glass, Stratton, Maine	12.00
Slipper, High-Heel, 5 In.	32.50
Spooner, Oregon	52.00
Spooner, Pavonia	50.00
Spooner, Radiant Daisy & Button	45.00
Spooner, Red Block	64.00
Spooner, Shoshone	40.00
Spooner, Spearpoint Band, Gold Trim, Frosted Band	50.00
Spooner, Star In Square	40.00
Spooner, Thumbprint	48.00
Spooner, Wedding, Crystal	75.00
Spooner, York Herringbone	45.00 To 55.00
Sugar Shaker, Block & Star	25.00
Sugar, Arched Ovals, Souvenir, Open, 1917, 2 1/4 In.	18.00
Sugar, Grape & Gothic Arch, Covered	55.00
Sugar, Loop & Block, Covered	60.00
Sugar, New Hampshire, Individual	35.00
Sugar, Red Block	81.00
Sugar, Sunk Honeycomb, Covered	55.00
Sugar, Triple Triangle, Covered	60.00
Sugar, Wedding	95.00
Syrup, Block	120.00
Syrup, Button Arches	160.00
Syrup, Sunk Honeycomb	125.00
Syrup, Torpedo, Original Lid	145.00
Syrup, Zipper Border, Etched	110.00
Table Set, Frost Crystal, Gold Trim, 4 Piece	195.00
Table Set, Red Block, 4 Piece	215.00 To 235.00
Table Set, Royal Crystal, 4 Piece	255.00 To 265.00
Table Set, Seed Pod, 4 Piece	385.00
Table Set, Triple Triangle, 4 Piece	200.00
Toothpick, Buttons & Arches	27.00
Toothpick, Daisy Button, V Ornament	16.00
Toothpick, Diamond Peg, E.E.Hucke, 1907	27.50
Toothpick, Inverted Thumbprint, Bulbous	65.00
Toothpick, Shamrock, Souvenir, Providence, R.I.	30.00
Toothpick, Stars & Stripes Commemorative	16.00
Toothpick, Swirl, Scalloped, Ruby Flashed	38.00
Toothpick, Thumbprint	35.00
Toothpick, Zanesville, Chautauqua Lake	25.00
Toothpick, Zipper Slash	35.00
Tray, Wine, Aurora	85.00
Tumbler, Arched Ovals, Souvenir, 1906, 3 7/8 In.	20.00
Tumbler, Baby Thumbprint, Etched Atlantic City, 1897, Edgar	35.00
Tumbler, Beaded Thumbprint Block, Inscribed, Annie, Atlantic City	35.00
Tumbler, Block & Star	30.00
Tumbler, Button & Arches	24.00 To 26.00
Tumbler, Button Arches, Inscribed 1898	35.00
Tumbler, Colorado, Souvenir, Pan American, 1901	32.00
Tumbler, Crystal Wedding	58.00
Tumbler, Daisy, Footed, Gold Trim	35.00
Tumbler, Double Red Block	50.00
Tumbler, Duncan Block	38.00
Tumbler, Fleur-De-Lis, Gold Trim	40.00
Tumbler, Georgian, 4 1/4 In., Set Of 4	36.00
Tumbler, Hand-Painted Ivory Lilies & Leaves	50.00
Tumbler, Hidalgo	35.00
Tumbler, Petaled Dogwood, Gold Flowers	40.00
Tumbler, Pillow Encircled	15.00
Tumbler, Red Block	25.00 To 35.00

Ruby Glass, Vase, Cornucopia, Gilt Bronze Mounted, 9 3/4 In., Pair

Tumbler, Roanoke	30.00
Tumbler, Sunk Honeycomb	30.00
Tumbler, Tacoma	32.00
Tumbler, Thumbprint, Etched	40.00
Tumbler, Torpedo	35.00
Tumbler, Truncated Cube	28.00
Vase, Basse-Taille Dimpling, Birds, Bamboo, & Leaves, 4 3/4 In.	115.00
Vase, Basse-Taille Work Of Birds, Bamboo, & Leaves, 7 1/2 In.	140.00
Vase, Block, Large	12.00
Vase, Cornucopia, Gilt Bronze Mounted, 9 3/4 In., Pair	*Illus* 935.00
Vase, Globe Shape, Ruffled, 1/ 1/4 X 1/ 1/4 In.	95.00
Vase, Hoover Pattern, Beaded Top, 9 In.	32.50
Vase, Jack-In-The-Pulpit, 10 X 9 In.	110.00
Wastebowl, Pavonia, Etched	114.50
Water Set, Checkerboard, Gold Trim, 5 Piece	215.00
Water Set, Hexagon Block, 7 Piece	245.00 To 255.00
Water Set, Pavonia, Etched, 5 Piece	245.00
Water Set, Serrated Block, Gold Trim, 5 Piece	235.00
Water Set, Thumbprint, Bulbous, 6 Piece	150.00
Wine Set, Sunk Honeycomb, Decanter & 5 Wines	245.00
Wine, Button Arches, Equinunk, Pa.	22.00
Wine, Dakota	50.00
Wine, Diamond Horseshoe	30.00
Wine, Overlay To Clear, Set Of 5	20.00
Wine, Red Block	25.00 To 35.00
Wine, Sawtooth, G.E.H., 1906	25.00
Wine, Teardrop	30.00
Wine, Thumbprint	28.00 To 35.00
Wine, Truncated Cube	35.00
Wine, Zipper Slash, E.L.Richey, Sept.22, 1904	25.00
Witch's Ball, 3 1/4 In.Diam.	30.00

Rudolstadt was a faience factory in the Thuringia region of Germany from 1720 to about 1791. In 1854, Ernst Bohne began working in the area. From about 1887 to 1918, The New York and Rudolstadt Pottery made decorated porcelain marked with the RW and crown familiar to collectors. This porcelain was imported by Lewis Straus and Sons of New York, which later became Nathan Straus and Sons. The word "Royal" was included in their import mark. Collectors often call it "Royal Rudolstadt." Late nineteenth- and early twentieth-century pieces are most commonly found today.

RUDOLSTADT, see also Kewpie

RUDOLSTADT, Bowl, Gold Scallops, Clusters Of Roses, Marked, 9 3/4 In. 85.00
Bowl, Hand-Painted, Rose, Grape Design, Gold Rim, 9 In. 48.00
Bowl, Mill Scene, Gold Trim, Signed, 11 In. 100.00
Bowl, Multicolored Flowers, 9 In. 40.00
Bowl, Pink & White Roses, Signed F.Kahn, 9 1/4 In. 40.00
Bust, Lady, Gown, 10 In. 550.00
Cake Plate, Orange Poppies, Yellow, Purple Flowers, Marked 40.00
Cake Set, Yellow Roses, Green Ground, 5 Piece 110.00
Creamer, Pink Roses, Gold Trim, Marked, 4 1/2 In. 85.00
Cup, Red Trim 15.00
Ewer, Cream Body, Florals, Gilded Handle 59.00
Mayonnaise Set, Roses, Pink, Green, & Yellow, Marked, 3 Piece 65.00
Plate, Florals, Gold Trim, 7 1/2 In. 10.00
Plate, Grape & Leaves, Gold Border 9.00
Plate, Leaf Shape, White & Gold, 6 In. 30.00
Plate, Portrait, George Washington, Gold Border, 8 In. 50.00
Plate, Roses & Holly, Gold Edge, 7 1/2 In. 35.00
Plate, Yellow Roses, Holly Berries, Marked, 10 1/4 In. 75.00
Rose Bowl, Underplate, Lavender Flowers, Signed, 6 1/4 In. 225.00
Sugar & Creamer, Pink Roses, Squatty, 1913 .... 25.00
Tea Set, Child's, Happifats, 23 Piece 300.00
Tray, Dresser, Floral Border, Gold Trim, Handled, 12 In. 85.00
Vase, Cobalt, Floral Enameling, 6 In. 165.00
Vase, Dolphin Handle, Openwork, Beige, 13 In. 150.00
Vase, Floral, 2-Handled, 19th Century Mark, 8 In. 45.00
Vase, Ivory, Flowers, Ornate Gold Handles, 7 In. 50.00

RUG, Appliqued & Embroidered, Brown Wool, Leaves, Flowers, Hearth 1000.00
Baluchi, Trellis Design, White Blossom Motif, 2 Ft.9 In.X 4 Ft.10 In. 325.00
Bergama, Dark Blue, Red, Ivory Border, Peach, Yellow, 2 X 3 Ft. 425.00
Beshir Torba, Red, Floral, Navy, Brown, Fringe, 4 X 2 Ft. 425.00
Bijar, Blue Field, Herati Design, Yellow Border, 4 X 6 Ft. 325.00
Bijar, Blue, Trellis Design, Lions, Ivory Border, 5 X 6 Ft. 4000.00
Bokhara Hatchli, Cross Design, Camel Field, 4 X 5 Ft. 400.00
Bokhara, Cream Ground, Guls, 6 Ft.5 In. X 9 Ft. 850.00
Bokhara, Cream, Geometric Border, 7 X 9 Ft. 700.00
Bokhara, Red Field, 5 X 7 Ft. 400.00
Bokhara, Red Field, 7 Guls, 4 X 5 Ft. 450.00
Bokhara, 7 Gulls, Beige Field, 3 Ft. 2 In. X 5 Ft. 325.00
Braided & Hooked, Geometric, Log Cabin, 5 X 4 In. 170.00
Braided, Oval, 30 X 45 In. 25.00
Caucasian, Blue Ground, Geometric Design, Ivory Border, 3 X 5 Ft. 475.00
Caucasian, Flat Woven, 1 Ft. 11 In. X 5 Ft. 2100.00
Caucasian, 3 Medallions, Geometric Forms, C.1900, 56 X 37 1/2 In. 600.00
Chinese, Animal Figures, Ivory Borders, 8 X 10 Ft. 1100.00
Chinese, Blue Field, Heron, Florals, 7 X 3 Ft. 90.00
Chinese, Tan Field, Border Of Fans, 4 X 2 Ft. 55.00
Chinese, 11 Mortals, Ivory Ground, 6 X 4 Ft. 2100.00
Daghestan, Prayer, White, Floral, Red, 3 X 4 Ft. 2800.00
Embroidered, Red Basket, Buff Flowers, Black, 5 X 2 Ft. 5750.00
Ersari, Rows Of Guls, Red Field, Navy & Red Edge, 8 X 11 Ft. 650.00
Ferahan, Herati Design In Ivory, Navy, 10 1/2 X 19 1/2 Ft. 1500.00
Ferahan, Indigo, Ivory, Salmon, 11 Ft. 9 In X 20 Ft. 6 In. 7700.00
Hamadan, Camel Field, Ivory, Heanna, 3 Ft. 2 In. X 7 Ft. 50.00
Hamadan, Medallion Center, Animal Form Edges, 3 Ft. 3 In. X 5 Ft. 8 In. 40.00
Hamadan, Medallion, Navy Field, Ivory Edges, 6 Ft. 6 In. X 6 Ft. 5 In. 275.00
Hamadan, Prayer 695.00
Hamadan, Red & Cream, 20 X 30 In. 50.00
Hamadan, Repeating Floral Design, 3 1/2 X 10 1/2 Ft. 525.00
Hamadan, Runner, Coral Pink, Blue, 3 Ft. 5 In. X 8 Ft. 60.00
Hamadan, Scatter, 6 Ft. X 3 Ft. 8 In. 50.00
Hamadan, 9 Ft. 2 In. X 11 Ft. 6 In. 400.00
Hand-Loomed, Amana Colonies, Multicolored, 14 X 11 Ft. 425.00

Rug, Hooked, American, Late
19th Century, 31 X 62 In.

Rug, Hooked, Cherry Sprigs & Leaf
Borders, 10 Ft. 8 In.

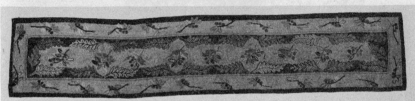

Hand-Loomed, Amana Colonies, Red & Black, 25 X 15 Ft. 800.00
Heriz, Blue Field, Herati Design, Ivory Turle, 6 X 14 In. 725.00
Heriz, Blue Medallion, Red Field, Ivory Corner, 10 X 12 Ft. 2800.00
Heriz, Red Field, Blue Border, Flower Heads, 8 X 11 Ft. 1850.00
Heriz, Red Field, Blue Medallions, Pink Corner, 11 X 8 Ft. 1100.00
Heriz, 8 Ft. 9 In. X 11 Ft. 1800.00
Heriz, 12 Ft. 3 In. X 8 Ft. 3 In. 1300.00
Hooked Checkerboard, Black Edged Squares, C.1880, 18 X 36 In. 50.00
Hooked, American, Brown, Beige, Rose, Green, Marbleized Pattern, 51 X 94 In 1320.00
Hooked, American, Late 19th Century, 31 X 62 In. .... *Illus* 375.00
Hooked, Art Deco Pattern, Oval, 27 X 40 In. 35.00
Hooked, Basket Of Mixed Florals, New England, C.1900, 16 1/2 X 32 In. 75.00
Hooked, Bird Nestled In Flowers, New England, 19 In.Diam. 40.00
Hooked, Black Scotty Dog, On Green Grass, Beige Ground, 24 X 36 In. 175.00
Hooked, Burlap, Flower-Filled 8-Point Star Motif, 6 Ft.1 In. X 9 Ft. 500.00
Hooked, Cherry Sprigs & Leaf Borders, 10 Ft. 8 In. .... *Illus* 350.00
Hooked, Floral Wreaths, New England, C.1920, Octagonals, 20 X 45 In. 60.00
Hooked, Floral, Electric Blue Ground, Green Design, 2 X 6 Ft. 325.00
Hooked, Floral, Green-Black Field, Red, Blue, Yellow, 2 Ft. 8 In X 4 Ft. 50.00
Hooked, Floral, Tan Field, Red & Blue Flowers, 2 Ft. 11 In. X 5 Ft. 100.00
Hooked, Geometric & Floral, Rose, Brown, Green, 53 X 60 In. .... *Illus* 375.00
Hooked, Graphic Geometric, Oak Leaf Pattern, 65 X 33 In. 100.00
Hooked, Greenfeld, Newfoundland, Dogsled Scene, 20th Century, 26 X 40 In. 325.00
Hooked, Horse, Oak Leaf Corners, 28 X 51 In. 225.00
Hooked, House, 30 X 42 In. 350.00
Hooked, Maine Moose, Red House, Mountains, C.1900, Wool, 17 X 34 In. 225.00
Hooked, Maple Sugaring Scene, New England, Wool, 17 X 34 In. 250.00
Hooked, Maple Sugaring Scene, Wool, 11 X 14 1/2 In. 110.00
Hooked, Oriental Pattern, Reds, Green, Yellow, & Black, C.1885, 48 X 28 In. 155.00
Hooked, Red Flower, Gray-Green Ground, Black Band, 1 X 3 Ft. 80.00
Hooked, Stylized Floral Spray, C.1830, 29 1/2 X 37 In. 850.00
Hooked, Wool, Green, Brown, & Beige, 5 X 6 Ft. 60.00
Hooked, Wreath Of Flowers, Wool & Mixed, C.1920, Oval, 19 X 35 1/2 In. 60.00
Indian, Airbrush Sea Blue Field, 8 Ft. 9 In. X 12 Ft. 6 In. 605.00
Indo Sarduk, 10 Ft. X 8 Ft. 5 In. 1400.00

Rug, Hooked, Geometric & Floral,
Rose, Brown, Green, 53 X 60 In.
(See Page 609)

Rug, Khamseh, 36 X 204 In.

Indo-Aubusson, Floral, Cream Field, 6 X 6 Ft.	....	200.00
Indo-Savonnerie, Floral Medallion, Blue, 12 1/4 X 14 Ft.	....	3000.00
Indo-Savonnerie, Ivory Medallion, Blue, 12 1/4 X 14 Ft.	....	2900.00
Joshagan, Red, Teal Medallion, Diamonds, Ivory, 7 X 10 Ft.	....	440.00
Karabagh, Blue Field, Pink & Orange Diamonds, 19 Ft.	....	600.00
Karastan, Oriental Design, Magenta Ground, Wool, 1930s, 8 X 12 In.	....	550.00
Karastan, Oriental Design, Magenta Ground, Wool, 8 X 12 In.	....	550.00
Kazak, Blue Field, Geometric, Stars, 5 X 3 Ft.	....	100.00
Kazak, Caucasus, 4 Ft. 5 In. X 7 Ft. 2 In.	....	3080.00
Kazak, Cloud Band, Red Field, Ivory Border, 4 X 9 Ft.	....	125.00
Kazak, Red Field, Blue & Green, Medallions, 4 X 6 Ft.	....	500.00
Kazak, Red, White Medallion, Ivory Border, 6 X 5 Ft.	....	1800.00
Kazak, Scatter, Geometric & Animal Motif, C.1900, 106 X 72 In.	....	1700.00
Kerman, Crimson Field, Floral Center, 5 X 3 Ft.	....	200.00
Keshan, Blue Ground, Floral Sprays, Dogtooth Design, 6 X 4 Ft.	....	2600.00
Keshan, Figures On Horse, Persian Sign Border, 5 X 8 Ft.	....	9500.00
Keshan, Prayer Design, Rose Ground, Tree Of Life, 4 X 2 Ft.	....	2000.00
Keshan, Red Ground, Floral, 5 Floral Borders, 9 X 18 Ft.	....	5000.00
Khamseh, 36 X 204 In.	.... *Illus*	850.00
Kilim, Scatter, 4 Ft. 7 In. X 3 Ft. 1 In.	....	60.00
Kilim, 5 Ft. 6 In. X 8 Ft. 2 In.	....	1700.00
Kirman, Central Medallion, Floral Edges, 16 X 13 Ft. 8 In.	....	4200.00
Kirman, Central Rose Medallion, Green Field, 2 Ft. X 4 Ft. 9 In.	....	300.00
Kirman, Medallion, Raspberry, 5 Ft. 10 In. X 8 Ft. 10 In.	....	950.00
Kirman, Overall Palmettes, Rose Field, 11 Ft. 4 In. X 18 Ft.	....	650.00
Kuba, Brown, Black, Trellis Design, Ivory Border, 3 X 4 Ft.	....	950.00

Kurdish, Polychrome Rosette, Navy Field, 3 Ft. X 9 Ft. 3 In. 325.00
Mahal, 12 1/2 X 9 1/2 Ft. 1200.00
Malager, 8 Ft. 2 In. X 4 Ft. 6 In. 450.00
Marasali, Blue, Animals, Horse, Star Border, 4 X 5 Ft. 6800.00
Mina Khani, Brown, Diamonds, Red Border, 3 X 6 Ft. 325.00
Mosul, Cherry, Floral, Green, Pink, Ivory, 6 Ft. X 10 In. 195.00
Oriental, Aubusson, Beige Field, Scroll Design, Floral Border, 10 X 16 Ft 800.00
Oriental, Azerbajian, Red, Floral, Leaf Border, 5 X 14 Ft. 3900.00
Prayer, Cream, Mosque Lamp, 2 Ft. 5 In. X 4 Ft. 125.00
Prayer, Turkish, 42 In. X 66 In. 140.00
Qasvin, Floral Design, Ivory Field, Pink, Brown, 8 X 12 Ft. 600.00
Qasvin, Tomato Red, Blue Medallion, Ivory Trim, 13 X 9 Ft. 2750.00
Qum, Prayer, Wool & Silk, 5 X 7 Ft. 2000.00
Sabino, Box, Bonbonniere Pattern, Covered, 2 1/2 X 2 In. 90.00
Sarouk, Blue Ground, Floral, Red Border, Ivory Guards, 2 X 6 Ft. 100.00
Sarouk, Blue Ground, Red, Ivory Floral, Border Stripes, 6 Ft. 2000.00
Sarouk, Ivory, Blue, Peach, Floral, Pink Border, 6 X 4 Ft. 1300.00
Sarouk, Red Ground, Floral Sprays, 9 X 12 Ft. 1700.00
Sarouk, Red Ground, Florals, Shah Abbas Design, 10 X 13 Ft. 3750.00
Sarouk, Tan, Blue Center, Pink-Red Corners, 3 X 4 Ft. 350.00
Sarouk, 4 Ft. 10 In. X 3 Ft. 4 In. 125.00
Sarouk, 5 Ft. X 3 Ft. 3 In. 1000.00
Sarouk, 9 X 12 Ft. 300.00
Senneh, Dark Blue Ground, Herati Design, 3 Ft. 10 In. X 6 Ft. 280.00
Serab, Blue Anchored Medallion, Rust Field, 3 Ft. 3 In. X 6 Ft. 350.00
Serapi, Red Field, Floral Design, Blue, Ivory, 11 X 12 Ft. 4100.00
Shirvan, Blue, Afshan Design, Ivory Border, 4 X 7 Ft. 2300.00
Shirvan, Blue, Diamond Medallion, Red Ends, 4 X 3 Ft. 250.00
Shirvan, Keyhole Garden Design, Ivory Border, 10 X 2 Ft. 1550.00
Shirvan, 5 Ft. 10 In. X 3 Ft. 10 In. 750.00
Soumak, 9 Ft. X 6 Ft. 8 In. 75.00
Sparta, Blue, Classical Design, Maroon Border, 10 X 13 Ft. 450.00
Table, Tree Of Life, Burlap, 14 X 20 In. 155.00
Tabriz, Blue, Herati Design, Red Turtle Border, 8 X 11 Ft. 3700.00
Tabriz, Ivory, Tree, Bird, Ivory Border, 4 X 6 Ft. 2000.00
Tabriz, Romania, Cream Field, 14 X 9 Ft. 1400.00
Tabriz, Tree Of Life, Woman, Animals, Portraits, 6 X 4 Ft. 7500.00
Tabriz, 7 X 9 Ft. 400.00
Tekke Bokhara, 6 Ft. 4 In. X 9 Ft. 6 In. 1300.00
Tekke Bokhara, 43 X 68 1/2 In. .... 525.00|
Turkoman, Red Field, Arrowhead Design, Multicolored, 5 X 2 Ft. 350.00
Turkoman, Woven Central Panel, Mafrash Grid, 3 Ft. 2 In. X 3 Ft. 4 In. 150.00
Turkoman, 45 X 38 In. 500.00
7 Guls, Wine Field, Geometric, 4 X 6 Ft. 350.00

RumRill *Rumrill Pottery was designed by George Rumrill of Little Rock,
Arkansas. From 1930 to 1933, it was produced by the Red Wing
Pottery of Red Wing, Minnesota. In 1938, production was transferred
to the Shawnee Pottery in Zanesville, Ohio.*

RUMRILL, Pitcher, Blue, 11 1/2 In. 25.00
  Pitcher, Water, Green 14.00
  Vase, Bud, Mottled Blue, 7 In. 25.00
  Vase, Green To Lavender, 6 In. 22.00

*Ruskin Pottery was established in 1898 at West Smethwick,
Birmingham, England. The factory worked until 1935.*

RUSKIN, Saltshaker, Blue, 2 1/2 In. 40.00
  Vase, Red, Blue, Mottled Glaze, 12 In. 125.00

Russel Wright designed dinnerwares in modern shapes for four companies. Iroquois China Company, Harker China Company, Steubenville Pottery, and Justin Therod and Sons made dishes marked Russel Wright. The Steubenville wares, first made in 1938, are the most common today.

RUSSEL WRIGHT, Butter, Charcoal Lid, Pink Bottom	30.00
Butter, Iroquois, Covered, Brown	40.00
Butter, Iroquois, Covered, White	50.00
Casserole, Divided, Covered, White, 10 In.	27.00
Celery, Gray	20.00
Coffeepot, Seafoam	35.00
Cordial, American Modern	15.00
Creamer, Blue	8.00
Gravy Boat, Underplate, Gray	15.00
Gravy, Coral	15.00
Mug, Iroquois, Blue	15.00
Mug, Nutmeg	15.00
Pitcher, Coral	35.00
Plate, Bread & Butter, Coral, Pair	3.00
Platter, Coral	15.00
Platter, Oval, Chartreuse, 11 In.	8.00
Relish, American Modern, Green	27.50
Sugar & Creamer, Chutney	9.00
Tumbler, Juice, American Modern	15.00

Sabino glass was made in the 1920s and 1930s in Paris, France. Founded by Marius-Ernest Sabino, the firm was noted for Art Deco lamps, vases, nudes, figures, and animals in clear, colored, and opalescent glass. Production stopped during World War II but resumed in the 1960s with manufacture of nudes and small opalescent glass animals. The new pieces are a slightly different color and can be recognized.

SABINO FRANCE

SABINO, Blotter, Rocker, American & French Crossed Flags, 6 X 3 In.	275.00
Bottle, Cologne, Petalia Design, Original Stopper, 5 1/2 In.	145.00
Plate, Sailing Ships, Dated 1912, Signed C.Harris, 8 1/2 In.	225.00
Vase, Ball-Footed, Frosted, Signed, 9 X 10 In.	385.00

Salopian ware was made by the Caughley factory of England during the eighteenth century. The early pieces were in blue and white with some colored decorations. Another ware called "Salopian" today is elaborate color-transfer decorated tablewares made during the late nineteenth century.

SALOPIAN, see also Caughley

SALOPIAN, Cup & Saucer, Turquoise Border, Scene	85.00
Plate, Scenic, 7 1/8 In.	300.00

SALT & PEPPER, see Pressed Glass; Porcelain; etc.

Salt glaze is a hard, shiny glaze that was developed for pottery during the eighteenth century. It is still being made.

SALT GLAZE, Box, Salt, Wall Hung, Cream & Blue, Good Luck Embossed, 6 X 4 In.	85.00
Butter, Dragonfly & Flower, Lid & Bail, Blue & White	185.00
Churn, Large Wing, Covered, 6 Gallon	120.00
Coffeepot, Acorn Finial, Metal Base, Swirl, Blue & White	575.00
Creamer, Polychrome Floral Design, 3 1/8 In.	90.00
Creamer, Sgraffito Floral Design, Cobalt, 3 1/4 In.	80.00
Crock, Butter, Sunflowers, Blue	52.50
Crock, Incised Mark, 4 Gallon	235.00
Cup, Custard, Fish Scale	115.00
Dish, Soap, Cutout Corners, Blue & White, 3 1/2 X 4 3/4 In.	145.00
Dish, Soap, Flower Cluster At Edge, Green & White	45.00
Flowerpot, Mistletoe & Basket Weave, Inside Glazed, 4 X 5 In.	30.00
Jug, Cobalt Blue Leaf, 5 Gallon	125.00
Jug, Heiser, Buffalo, N.Y., Cobalt Blue Print, 2 Gallon	150.00
Mug, Beer, Rochester Brewing Co.	50.00

Mug, Flying Bird, Blue & White 185.00
Pitcher, Classical Figures, Pewter Tilt-Top Cover, Green, 6 In. 50.00
Pitcher, Jones & Walley, Dated 1842, The Gypsy, 9 3/4 In. 175.00
Pitcher, Pewter Cover, C.1850 .... 75.00
Pitcher, Relief Figures Of Sleeping Children, Beige, 6 In. 85.00
Pitcher, Tan, Gypsy, Dated 1843 .... 155.00
Syrup, Pewter Top 35.00
Teapot, Birds Flying Among Bamboo, Caned Handle, White, 7 In. 135.00
Vase, Bud, Blue & White, 10 1/4 In. 145.00
      SAMPLER, see Textile, Sampler

Samson and Company, a French firm specializing in the reproduction of collectible wares of many countries and periods, was founded in Paris in the early nineteenth century. Chelsea, Meissen, Famille Verte, and Oriental Lowestoft are some of the wares that have been reproduced by the company. The company uses a variety of marks to distinguish its reproductions. It is still in operation.

SAMSON, Cup & Saucer, Pseudo-Dr.Wall Worcester, Blue & White 75.00
Ewer, Pseudo-Chinese Export, Blue, Gold, Red, 10 In., Pair 650.00
Vase, Pseudo-Sevres, Scalloped, Floral Spray, 19th Century, 9 1/2 In. 200.00

Sand Babies were used as decorations on a line of children's dishes made by the Royal Bayreuth China Company. The children are playing at the seaside. Collectors use the names "Sand Babies" and "Beach Babies" interchangeably.

SAND BABIES, Bowl, Cereal, Water & Beach, Marked, 5 3/4 In. 65.00
Creamer, Blue Mark 65.00
Planter 95.00
Plate, Blue Mark, 9 In. 84.50
Plate, 7 1/2 In. 100.00
Tray, Dresser, Blue Mark 165.00
Wall Pocket, Triangular Shape 150.00

Sandwich glass is any one of the myriad types of glass made by the Boston and Sandwich Glass Works in Sandwich, Massachusetts, between 1825 and 1888. It is often very difficult to be sure whether a piece was really made at the Sandwich factory because so many types were made there and similar pieces were made at other glass factories.
      SANDWICH GLASS, see also Pressed Glass, etc.
SANDWICH GLASS, Bottle, Barber, Enamel Design, Gilt, Amethyst, 8 1/2 In. 85.00
Bottle, Cologne, Blue, Gold Overlay, Clear, 7 In. 135.00
Bottle, Cologne, Bulbous Base, 8-Sided, Amethyst, 3 3/4 In. 45.00
Bottle, Cologne, Ground Glass Stopper, Flashed Ruby, 5 3/4 In 52.00
Bottle, Cologne, Purse, Bluish-Purple, 4 3/4 In. 80.00
Bottle, Cologne, Purse, Down-Folded Lip, Cobalt Blue, 6 1/2 In 120.00
Bottle, Cologne, Purse, Fiery Opalescent 65.00
Bottle, Cologne, Purse, Infolded Lip, Ice Blue 85.00
Bottle, Cologne, Purse, Rolled Lip, Amethyst, 6 5/16 In. 80.00
Bottle, Cologne, Purse, Tooled Lip, Emerald Green, 4 3/4 In. 140.00
Bottle, Cologne, Purse, White Swirls, Pewter Stopper, Amethyst 50.00
Bottle, Cologne, Waisted, 8-Sided, Blue With Amber, 4 3/4 In. 220.00
Bottle, Cologne, Waisted, 8-Sided, Emerald Green, 4 3/4 In. 220.00
Bottle, Cologne, Waisted, 8-Sided, Lip, Cobalt, 4 1/8 In. 120.00
Bottle, Cologne, Waisted, 8-Sided, Purplish-Blue, 4 3/4 In. 220.00
Bottle, Cologne, Waisted, 8-Sided, Tooled Lip, Green, 4 1/8 In. 180.00
Bottle, Perfume, Bull's-Eye & Ellipse, Green, 5 1/4 In. 325.00
Bottle, Sauce, Tooled Lip, Edge Design, Amethyst, 6 1/2 In. 120.00
Bowl, Flint, Octagonal, 7 3/4 X 1 1/2 In. 65.00
Bowl, Geometric Pattern, Folded Rim, 5 1/4 In. 165.00
Bowl, Heart Pattern, C.1830, 6 7/8 In. 85.00
Bowl, Oak Leaf Pattern, Beaded Border, 7 1/4 X 1 1/2 In. 85.00
Bowl, Oak Leaf Pattern, 6 1/2 X 1 1/5 In. .... 55.00 To 65.00

Bowl, Oak Leaf Pattern, 10 3/8 In. 280.00
Bowl, Oak Leaf, Clear Border, 6 5/8 In. 55.00
Butter, Indiana, Covered, Crystal 70.00
Butter, Star Pattern, Covered, Electric Blue 1000.00
Candelabrum, Daisy & Button, Bobeches & Prisms, 1 Light 45.00
Candlestick, Canary, 2 In. 135.00
Candlestick, Petal & Loop, Canary, 7 In., Pair 185.00
Candlestick, Petal & Loop, Clear, 6 3/4 In., Pair 45.00
Candlestick, Scroll Standard, Lacy Peacock Eye Top, Pair 850.00
Candlestick, Wafer, Clear, 8 In. 35.00
Celery, Holly, Footed 75.00
Celery, Loop, 1835-45, 9 3/4 In. 125.00
Celery, Waffle, 9 In. 75.00
Coaster, Harp, Clear, Set Of 8 .... 20.00
Compote, Honeycomb, Etched Garlands, Flint, 7 1/4 X 6 3/4 In. 58.00
Compote, Horn Of Plenty, 7 In. 185.00
Compote, Horn Of Plenty, 8 1/2 In. 245.00
Compote, Lacy, 3 5/16 In. 70.00
Compote, Overshot Clear, Crackle Glass, 4 X 6 In. 45.00
Compote, Overshot Pedestal, 4 1/2 X 6 In. 35.00
Compote, Petal & Loop, Flint, 10 1/2 X 7 In. 290.00
Compote, Prism With Diamonds, Open, Flint, 8 1/4 X 6 1/4 In. 55.00
Creamer, Red & Gold Snake Around Body, Forms Handle, Flint 110.00
Creamer, Three Mold, Cobalt Blue 425.00
Darner, Blue Opaque, Blown, 4 3/4 In. 185.00
Decanter, Cape Cod Pattern, Original Stopper 160.00
Decanter, Shell & Rib Pattern, Stopper 175.00
Decanter, Teardrop Pattern, Mushroom Stopper, 10 1/4 In., Pr. 575.00
Dish, Oak Leaf Pattern, 5 1/4 In. 52.00
Dish, Vegetable, Peacock Eye Pattern, Oblong, Large 150.00
Dish, Wavy Lines On Edges, Footed, Oblong, 7 1/4 In. 145.00
Dish, Wavy Sides & Ends, Florals, Footed, Oblong, 6 1/4 In. 125.00
Eggcup, Bellflower 10.00
Eggcup, Cable 45.00
Ewer, Flower Design, Clear Thorn Handle, 10 1/2 In. 650.00
Goblet, Bellflower Pattern, Flint 32.50
Jar, Pomade, White Bear Form 475.00

SANDWICH GLASS, LAMP, see Lamp

Pipe Whimsey, White Loopings, Clear, 15 In. 325.00
Plate, Beehive Pattern, Octagonal, 9 1/2 In. 195.00
Plate, Cabled Edge & Acorn Variant, 5 In. 95.00
Plate, Horn Of Plenty, 6 In. 80.00
Plate, Lacy Floral, 8 In., Set Of 5 .... 100.00
Plate, Peacock Eye & Thistle, 8 In. 95.00
Plate, Thistle & Beehive, Octagonal, 9 1/4 In. 115.00
Plate, Waffle & Lacy, 5 In. 105.00
Rose Bowl, Peachblow 97.50
Salt & Pepper, Blue, Christmas 175.00
Salt & Pepper, Christmas, Agitator On Salt, Honey Amber 110.00
Salt, Pedestal, 6-Sided, Amethyst, 2 7/8 X 1 3/4 In. 165.00
Salt, Sawtooth, Covered 60.00
Salt, 6-Sided, Canary, 2 7/8 X 1 3/4 In. 165.00
Saltshaker, Christmas, Dated Pewter Lid & Agitator, Amber 85.00
Sauce, Lacy, 4 1/2 In. 48.00
Sauce, Two-Paneled Diamond Pattern, 3 7/8 In., Pair 10.00
Spill, Grapevine Pattern 48.00
Spill, Horn Of Plenty, 4 5/8 In. 82.00
Spill, Lyre Pattern, 3 1/8 X 4 11/16 In. 85.00
Sugar & Spooner, Single Vine Ivy, Pedestal, 5 1/2 In. 65.00
Sugar, Gothic Pattern, Covered, Pair 350.00
Tieback, Ruby, 3 In.Diam. 25.00
Tumbler, Diamond-Quilted, C.1820 .... 65.00
Vase, Blue, Floral Design, Thorn Handle, Reeded Feet, 10 In. 425.00

Vase, Clear, Overshot, Melon Ribbed, Scalloped, 8 1/2 In.	225.00
Vase, Tulip, Octagonal Foot, 9 5/8 In.	125.00
Whiskey Taster, Single Vine Ivy	52.00
Wine, Ashburton, Flint	42.00

Utzschneider and Company, a porcelain factory, made ceramics in Sarreguemines from 1770. Transfer-printed wares and mojolica were made in the nineteenth century.

SARREGUEMINES, see also Kate Greenaway

SARREGUEMINES, Character Jug, Rosy Cheeks, Nose, & Mouth, Marked, 5 1/4 In.	65.00
Character Jug, The Scotsman, Majolica, Mark, 7 1/2 X 4 1/2 In.	75.00
Dish, Candy, Copper Luster, Covered, Signed, 6 1/2 X 5 1/2 In.	95.00
Hot Plate, Persian Moss, Flow Blue, Utzschneider	65.00
Plate, Napoleon, 7 1/2 In.	25.00
Plate, Oyster, Gray, Peach, White	60.00
Plate, Rabbits	15.00
Plate, 3 Running Rabbits, Thistles, & Verse, Green, 8 In.	35.00

Satin glass is a late nineteenth-century art glass. It has a dull finish that is caused by a hydrofluoric acid vapor treatment. Satin glass was made in many colors and sometimes had applied decorations.

SATIN GLASS, Basket, Bride's, Milk Glass, Blue, 5 Applied Clear Feet, 9 In.	85.00
Basket, Diamond-Quilted, Camphor Handle, Blue, 7 In.	65.00
Biscuit Jar, Floret, Silver Plated Rim, Top, & Handle, 7 In.	235.00
Bottle, Cologne, Diamond-Quilted, Bird & Flower, Stopper, 6 In.	375.00
Bottle, Scent, Prunus Blossoms, Sterling Silver Screw, 2 1/2 In.	325.00
Bowl, Black, 3 1/2 X 7 In.	25.00
Bowl, Bride's, Blue, Silver Plated Holder, 7 X 7 In.	195.00
Bowl, Turned-Down Pleated Ruffles, Enameled Flowers, 9 1/4 In.	225.00
Bride's Basket, Silver Plated Holder, Pierced Dish, 12 1/4 In.	145.00
Bride's Bowl, Enameled Wheat Ears & Florals, 11 1/8 In.Diam.	295.00
Candlestick, Blue Rim, Baluster Turnings, 8 In.	20.00
Compote, Frosted Rim, Silver Plated Foot, Rose, 6 3/4 In.	135.00
Condiment Set, Floret Pattern, Blue	150.00
Condiment Set, Quilted Pattern, Pink ....*Illus*	65.00
Cracker Jar, Yellow, White Florals, Brown Leaves, 9 1/2 In.	195.00
Creamer, Coreopsis, White Enamel Design	150.00
Cruet, Enameled Carnations & Forget-Me-Nots, Stopper	45.00
Easter Egg, Allover Design	20.00
Ewer, Apricot, White Lining, Cream & Pale Lavender Flowers, 8 In	132.00
Ewer, Coin Spot Design, Rose & Blue On Milk Glass, 10 In.	375.00
Ewer, Flattened Oval Shape, Flowers & Scrolls, Yellow, 9 In.	145.00
Ewer, Melon Ribbed, Blue, White Lining, Ruffled Top, Handled, 9 In	128.00
Ewer, Melon Ribbed, Cream Lining, Pedestal Foot, Enameled, 9 In.	95.00
Ewer, Pink, Floral Design, Twisted Handle, 9 3/4 In., Pair	195.00
Ewer, Thorn Handle, Mellon Sections, Birds & Flowers, 12 1/4 In.	245.00
Figurine, Madonna, 10 In.	30.00
Finger Bowl, Diamond-Quilted, Mother-Of-Pearl, Ruffle, 4 1/2 In.	195.00

Satin Glass, Condiment Set, Quilted Pattern, Pink

Hatpin Holder, Mushroom Shape, Floral Pattern, 3 In. 70.00
Jar, Sweetmeat, Diamond-Quilted, Silver Plated Top, 5 1/2 In. 275.00
Lamp, Fairy, Rose Pink, Milk Ground, Blue, 4 X 4 In. 75.00
Lamp, Oil, Beaded Drape, Pink 250.00
Pitcher, Brown Swirl Design, Yellow Over Milk Glass, 8 In. 70.00
Pitcher, Diamond-Quilted, Rose, White Lining, 3 1/4 X 3 In. 245.00
Pitcher, Green Ground, Pink, Yellow, Florals, 8 1/2 In. 115.00
Pitcher, Rainbow, 10 1/2 In. 625.00
Pitcher, Raindrop Pattern, Bulbous, Frosted Handle, 8 1/2 In. 255.00
Pitcher, Rose Lining, Clear Outside, Thorn Handle, Hobnail, 8 In. 145.00
Pitcher, Rose, Quilted Cushion Design, Clear Handle, 7 In. 80.00
Pitcher, Thorn Handle, Fluted Spout, C.1885, Blue, 8 3/4 In. 135.00
Pitcher, Water, Floret, Frosted Handle, 6 1/4 X 7 1/4 In. 198.00
Pitcher, Water, Opalescent Stripes, Blue 125.00
Pitcher, Water, Wild Iris, Blue 165.00
Rose Bowl, Applique Flower, 8-Crimped, Pink & White, 4 In. 110.00
Rose Bowl, Blue, 3 In. 50.00
Rose Bowl, Crimped, Rose To White, 6 1/2 In. 155.00
Rose Bowl, Diamond-Quilted, Crystal Applique, Striped, 4 In. 1050.00
Rose Bowl, Diamond-Quilted, 3 Feet, 5 X 6 In. 75.00
Rose Bowl, Egg Shape, White Lining, Petal Feet, Blue, 6 1/4 In. 145.00
Rose Bowl, Pale Yellow To Deeper Yellow, Ruffled Edge, 4 In. 55.00
Rose Bowl, Shell & Seaweed Pattern, 8-Crimped, 4 5/8 In. 150.00
Rose Bowl, White Lining, Crimped, Petal Feet, Rose, 5 1/4 In. 145.00
Shade, Lion's Head, Ball Shape, Red 225.00
Shade, Red, Artichoke, Signed 375.00
Sugar Shaker, Cone Pattern, Nickel Plated Top, 3 1/2 In. 75.00
Sugar Shaker, Melon Ribbed, Enameled 30.00
Syrup, Shell & Seaweed, Pink 495.00
Tumbler, Coralene Design 22.00
Tumbler, Diamond-Quilted, Mother-Of-Pearl, Rose, 3 3/4 In. 110.00
Tumbler, Floret Pattern, Pink, 3 3/4 In. 110.00
Vase, Apricot To Red, 10 In. 250.00
Vase, Apricot, 6 In. 125.00
Vase, Black, Daffodils, Bark Pattern, Bulbous, Flared Rim 35.00
Vase, Blue, Bottle Shape, Diamond-Quilted, 10 In. 195.00
Vase, Blue, Herringbone, 7 1/2 In. 149.00
Vase, Blue, Mother-Of-Pearl, 13 In. 310.00
Vase, Bud, Green, Bulbous Bottom, Enameled Rose, 8 In. 14.00
Vase, Bud, Green, Enameled Rose & Ivys, 8 In. 14.00
Vase, Bud, Woodland Scene, 8 In. 90.00
Vase, Clear To Cranberry, Frosted, Crimped Top, 8 1/2 In. 28.00
Vase, Cornucopia, Blue On Pink, Zigzag Design, 10 In. 100.00
Vase, Cranberry, 9 In. 150.00
Vase, Diamond-Quilted, Cut Velvet Ruffled Top, 6 3/4 In. 195.00
Vase, Diamond-Quilted, Ormolu Base, Rose To Pink, 5 1/2 In. 155.00
Vase, Diamond, Velvet Overlay, Rose, 7 1/2 In. 195.00
Vase, Double Gourd Shape, Blue To Turquoise, 3 In. 210.00
Vase, Frosted Clear, Cranberry Crimped Top, 8 1/4 In. 28.00
Vase, Herringbone, Yellow To White, 7 1/4 In. 150.00
Vase, Honeycomb, Butterscotch, 8 1/2 In. 85.00
Vase, Lime Green Over White Inside, 3 3/4 X 8 3/4 In. 175.00
Vase, Mother-Of-Pearl, Diamond-Quilted, 6 1/8 In. 950.00
Vase, Mother-Of-Pearl, Rose Red Ribbon, 5 3/8 X 4 3/4 In. 495.00
Vase, Mother-Of-Pearl, Rose Shading, 4 7/8 X 11 1/4 In. 275.00
Vase, Pastel Floral Design, Footed, 10 1/4 X 3 1/2 In., Pair 195.00
Vase, Peach Overlay, Frosted Handle, Enameled Daisies, 9 1/2 In. 98.00
Vase, Peach Shading To Apricot, Inverted Drape Pattern, 9 In. 245.00
Vase, Pink Shades, White Interior, Birds, Coralene, 6 1/2 In. 350.00
Vase, Pink, Diamond-Quilted, 5 In. 30.00
Vase, Polka Dot Pattern, Pinched Sides, 4 1/2 In. 215.00
Vase, Rose Design, Rose To White Core, 8 1/4 In. 90.00
Vase, Rose To White, Clover Design, 11 In., Pair 250.00
Vase, Ruffled, Mother-Of-Pearl, Peach, 9 In. 235.00

Vase, Stick, White, Enamel Blue & Green, 8 In.	65.00
Vase, Tangerine To Pink, Milk Glass Core, 5 In.	25.00
Vase, Trumpet, Black, 10 In.	25.00
Vase, White To Apricot, Thorn Handles, 5 X 5 In.	75.00
Vase, Woman, Pink, White Lining, Blue Dress, 1/ 1/2 In.	325.00
Wall Pocket, Black, 9 In.	20.00
SATIN GLASS, WEBB, see Webb	

Satsuma is a Japanese pottery with a distinctive creamy beige crackled glaze. Most of the pieces were decorated with blue, red, green, orange, or gold. Almost all the Satsuma found today was made after 1860. Japanese faces are often a part of the decorative scheme.

SATSUMA, Ashtray, Cigarette Holder, Elephant, Brown	49.00
Ashtray, Plum Blossom Mark, 4 1/2 In.	10.00
Bowl, Flower & Girls Design, 6 In.	150.00
Bowl, Sugar, Tea Gatherers Design, C.1865, 4 In.	425.00
Box, Covered, Bamboo Finial, Floral, C.1900, 5 In.	205.00
Box, Melon Ribbed, Butterflies Inside, C.1865, 5 In.	180.00
Brushpot, Kinkazan Design, Water Plants	100.00
Buckle, Silver Gilt Back, Ladies With Parasol, Marked	275.00
Chamberstick, Gold	49.00
Coffeepot, Encrusted Gold & Enamel, Sages, Cobalt Blue, 10 3/4 In.	175.00
Cookie Jar, Immortals On Brown	60.00
Cup & Saucer	20.00
Dish, Four Sages Picnic, 5 1/2 In.	450.00
Ewer, Chrysanthemums, Scrolls, Jewels, Bulbous, 11 1/4 In.	125.00
Figurine, Quan Yen, Lady With Basket Of Fish, 14 In.	175.00
Ginger Jar, Melon Ribbed, Gold & Enamel Mums, C.1890, 8 3/4 In.	170.00
Holder, Stickpin, Attached Saucer, Gold	65.00
Incense Burner, Shishi Design, C.1860, 4 In.	165.00
Incense Burner, Winged Tortoise Design, 4 In.	195.00
Jar, Dog Design, Heart Shaped Panels, Children, 6 1/2 In.	105.00
Jar, Lion's Head Handles, Flower Design, Diaper Pattern, 5 In.	375.00
Jar, Warriors, Lion Finial & Handles, Rectangular, 16 In.	350.00
Koro, Bud Design, Gold Trim, Diaper Pattern, 3 Feet, Marked, 3 In.	150.00
Koro, Warriors & Scholars, 3 1/2 In.Diam.	425.00
Lamp, Elephant, Brown	50.00
Luncheon Set, C.1855, 14 Piece	250.00
Mustard, Diaper Design, Covered, Twin Handle	29.00
Pail, Water, Nobles & Scholars, Gold Trim, 9 In.	110.00
Pitcher, Kinkazan, Flowers, Bamboo-Shaped Handle, Signed, 4 In.	65.00
Plate, Mountains, Pheasants, Black Border, Gold Flowers, 7 In.	80.00
Plate, Scroll-Shaped Reserve, Floral & Bird, 19th Century, 10 In.	110.00
Rose Jar, Bird, Floral Motif, Gold, Polychrome, 19th Century, 5 1/2 In	500.00
Rose Jar, One Thousand Flower Design, 10 In.	375.00
Saki Set, Whistling Bottle, Dragon Motif, 6 Lithophane Cups	75.00
Sugar & Creamer, Multifloral Pattern, Covered, Creamer 3 3/4 In.	350.00
Tea Caddy, Green To Beige, Foliage, Covered, 4 1/2 In.	90.00
Tea Set, Royal Blue Ground, Blue, White, Pink Florals, 6 Cups	195.00
Tea Set, Wisteria, 21 Piece	250.00
Teapot, Black Ground, Landscape Design, 3 X 7 In.	55.00
Teapot, Dragon Scale, C.1900, 5 1/2 In.	145.00
Teapot, Elephant, 10 X 7 In.	115.00
Teapot, Figures, Gold Halos, Marked, 7 In.	90.00
Teapot, Floral Design, Dragon Handle, Marked, 5 1/2 In.	95.00
Teapot, Flower Shape, Leaf Handle, C.1870, 2 1/2 In.	200.00
Teapot, Melon Ribbed, Dragon Handle & Spout, 8 1/2 In.	45.00
Teapot, Serpent, Head Spout, Tall Handle, 6 In.	65.00
Teapot, Shape Of Flower, Leaf Handle, C.1870.2 1/4 In.	200.00
Teapot, 2 Figures & Leaf Fronds, Orange & Gold, Crackle, 2 1/8 In.	135.00
Vase, Acting Scene, Man & Woman, Costumes, 11 In.	95.00
Vase, Awata, Large Lilies, 7 X 14 In., Pair	200.00
Vase, Bearded Man In Hopping Position, Oriental Writing, 3 1/2 In.	128.00

Vase, Bird & Floral Pattern, Gray-Blue, 19th Century, 9 3/4 In. 525.00
Vase, Birds & Flowers, Outlined In Gold, 10 1/8 In. 495.00
Vase, Black Ground, Gold Scene, 5 In. 60.00
Vase, Bud, People On Summer Day, Lake, Diaper Pattern, 6 In. 425.00
Vase, Cartouches, Figures & Scenic, Pink Ground, 3 1/2 In. 495.00
Vase, Chrysanthemums, Scrolls, Florals, 14 In., Pair 450.00
Vase, Cross In Circle Design, Haloed Seated Men, 1 3/4 X 1 In. 64.00
Vase, Diaper Design At Neck, 3 Seated Sages, Signed, C.1890, 15 In. 395.00
Vase, Enameled Flowers & Birds In Flight, Blue Beading, 13 In. 250.00
Vase, Enameled Flowers, Orange, 12 In. 85.00
Vase, Enameled, Panel Scene, Signed, 11 1/4 In. 250.00
Vase, Figural Foo Dogs On Top, Florals, 15 1/2 In. 175.00
Vase, Figures In Medallions, Angled Shoulders, 19th Century, 8 In. 275.00
Vase, Florals, Dolphin, C.1860, Blue Imperial Mark, 4 In. 245.00
Vase, Flowers & Leaves, Lion-Dog Handles, Covered, 13 In. 260.00
Vase, Flowers & Pheasants Outlined In Gold, Marked, 4 X 7 1/4 In. 325.00
Vase, Geisha & Children, Blue & Gold Flowers, Signed, 2 3/8 In. 130.00
Vase, Geisha With Child, Flowers On Reverse, Blue & Gold, 2 5/8 In. 120.00
Vase, Geishas & Flowers, 12 In. 100.00
Vase, Geometric Ground, Figural Design, Bulbous, 2 3/4 In. 80.00
Vase, Gilt Polychrome Panels, Men & Woman, 19th Century, 5 7/8 In. 475.00
Vase, Gold & Enameled Florals, Figural Elephant Handles, 12 In. 215.00
Vase, Gold Flowers, Panel Scenes Of Geishas, Signed, 10 In. 125.00
Vase, Grape Moriage Design, 15 In. 180.00
Vase, Haloed Arhats & Kwannon, Taisho Period, 15 1/2 In. 350.00
Vase, Heart Shaped, Flowers, Birds, Animal Head, Ears, 5 In. 320.00
Vase, Kinkazan, Foliage, Signed, 4 1/4 In. 80.00
Vase, Man & Phoenix Design, C.1915, 7 1/2 In. 170.00
Vase, Moriage Design, Horsehead Handles, C.1875, 9 In., Pair 1400.00
Vase, Ovoid Body, Overall Jeweling & Enameling, Scenes, 16 In. 250.00
Vase, People, Cranes, Gold Border, Marked, 2 In. 255.00
Vase, Pink & Orange Lilies, Twisted Handle, 14 In., Pair 175.00
Vase, Raised Florals, Leaves, Butterflies, Crackle Ground, 4 1/2 In. 225.00
Vase, Rakan & Kannon, Golds, C.1910, 12 In. 200.00
Vase, Rust Orange Grape, Lattice Design, 12 In. 235.00
Vase, Sage Design, C.1860, 5 In. 450.00
Vase, Scene Of Geisha, Mountains, & Trees, Blue & Gold, 2 1/2 In. 110.00
Vase, Stylized Clouds, Geometric Designs, 8 In. 250.00
Vase, Taisho, Birds & Flowers, Yellow & Orange, 7 In., Pair 125.00
Vase, Temple, 2 Bird-Form Handles, Red Ground, 31 In. 250.00
Vase, Turtle Diaper Pattern, Children & Flowers, C.1885, 4 In. 225.00
Vase, Warlords Pattern, Marked, 4 3/4 In. 200.00
Vase, 7 Immortals & Dragon, Predominantly Gold, 3 In. 175.00
Wall Pocket, Warlords 30.00

SCALE, Apothecary, Countertop, Franklin, Porcelain Tops, Cast Iron, 15 1/4 In. 135.00
Apothecary, Henry Troemner, Marble Top 195.00
Balance, Gram, Porcelain Tops 45.00
Balance, Mahogany Case, Marked Germany, 11 X 18 In. 125.00
Balance, Spring, Chas.Forschner, I.D.Plaque, Nickel Over Brass, 16 In. 45.00
Barrel, Stimpsone 175.00
Beam, Weights, 320 Pounds 67.50
Brass Scale Pan, Pedestal Base, Brass, 21 3/4 X 12 1/4 X 7 1/2 In. 125.00
Buffalo Hide, H.Buker & Co. 75.00
Butter, Wooden 275.00
Candy Store, Counter Style, Weights To 5 Pounds 85.00
Cenco, Aluminum Pans, Brass Weights, Attached Wooden Holder 35.00
Cenco, Double Pan, Brass, Gram Weights 25.00
Chatillons Improved Spring Balance, N.Y., Up To 50 Pounds, 13 In. 22.50
Computing Scale Co., Dayton, Ohio, Patent Date 1898 .... 400.00
Computing, Dated 1894, Brown Marble & Brass 285.00
Counter Platform, Howe, Brass Measure Bar 50.00
De Grave & Co., London, C.1900, 2 Pans, C.1900, 39 In. 220.00

Drugstore, Brass & Nickel Plated	195.00
Egg, Toledo	16.00
Fan, Glass Tray, Beveled Glass Panels	225.00
Fortune, Watling	95.00
Fortune, Weight, & Date, Peerless Weighing & Vending, 1930, 64 In.	750.00
Gold & Silver, Voland & Sons, Glass Case, Weights, Wooden Box	295.00
Grain, Fairbanks, Brass	355.00
Grain, Winchester, With Bucket, Brass	165.00
Hanging, Chatillons, Brass, Weights To 100 Pounds	26.00
Hanging, Escelsior Improved Spring Balance, Brass Front, Metal	22.00
Hanging, Hanson, Iron Body, Brass Face, 2 1/2 X 1 3/4 X 17 In.	28.00
Hide, Trading Post, Brass Face, Iron Halo, Hooks, & Rings, 10 1/2 In.	125.00
Hide, Trading Post, Half Moon Shaped Face, Hooks, Brass, 10 In.	125.00
Howe, Brass Bar, Chicken Foot Base, Weights, Cast Iron	65.00
Howe, Counter, Platform, Brass Arms & Scoops, Original Paint, Weights	80.00
Ivory Architect 2 Ft., 4 Fold, German Silver, Arch Joint	300.00
Letter, Leather Case, Small	7.50
Map, Boxwood, 1 1/2 X 6 In.	33.00
Map, Ivory, 1 3/8 X 6 In.	36.00
Map, Solid Brass, Beveled Edges, 1 3/4 X 6 In.	110.00
Meat, Red & Gold, Iron, Porcelain Tray, C.1905, 27 In.	375.00
Medical, Balance, Green Velvet Lined Case, Weights, 1850-60	45.00
Milk, Spring Balance, Chatillon, Brass, 60 Pound, 11 X 4 1/2 In.	45.00
Peerless Weighing & Vending Corp., 1930, Fortune, Weight, & Date	750.00
Pharmacy, Brass Pans, Marble, Oak	85.00
Pocket, Balance, Brass Front, Germany	12.00
Post Office, Weights, Steel	85.00
Postage, John Chatillon, 1914	20.00
Postage, Liberty, No.2	11.00
Postage, Lithograph, Dated 1903, Pelouze Mfg.Co., Calibrated To 3 Cent	30.00
Postage, Tin & Celluloid, 1904	20.00
Sidewalk, National, C.1891, Claw Feet	950.00
Simplex, Double Brass Pan, Cast Iron, Marked	80.00
Spring Balance, Cylindrical, Brass, 50 Pounds, 14 1/2 In.	25.00
Spring Scale, Round Base, Brass, Dated 1878, 10 In.	65.00
Spring, Brass Oval Scoop, 1 & 2 Pound Weights, Cast Iron, 18 1/2 In.	150.00
Steelyard, 70 Whitmore	27.00
Toledo, Barrel, Beveled Glass	175.00
Torsion Balance Co., Glass Enclosed, Rectangular Case	100.00
Tradesman's, Counter, Brass Pan, Calibrated Arm, 2 Weights, Cast Iron	185.00
Watling, Floor, 1930, Takes Pennies	125.00
Watling, Lollipop, 1 Cent	600.00 To 775.00
Watling, Profit Sharing, Sidewalk, Wooden Cabinet, Penny Drop, 6 Ft.	850.00
Weight & Fortune, Watling, Porcelain, Patent 1915	325.00
Weight On Card, Picture Of Movie Star, Fortune, & Date, 1 Cent, 64 In.	795.00

Schafer & Vater, makers of small ceramic items, are best known for their amusing figurals. The factory was located in Volkstedt, Germany, from 1890 to 1962.

SCHAFER & VATER, Hatpin Holder, Chinaman Seated	175.00
Nodder, Boy With Tongue Wagging	85.00
Pitcher, Boy With Open Umbrella, 4 In.	120.00
Pitcher, Chinese Woman, Stork, 5 1/4 In.	115.00
Pitcher, Devil With Wings, 3 In.	95.00
Pitcher, Fairy Godmother, 4 In.	100.00
Pitcher, Girl With Basket, 4 In.	85.00
Pitcher, Housekeeper With Keys, 3 1/2 In.	95.00
Pitcher, Indian In Full Headdress, 5 In.	160.00
Pitcher, Minstrel With Mandolin, 3 In.	95.00
Pitcher, Monkey Dressed As Man, 6 In.	110.00

Pitcher, Mother Goose, 4 In.	160.00
Pitcher, Oriental Man, Monkey, 5 In.	145.00
Pitcher, Oriental Woman, Flying Stork, 5 In.	145.00
Pitcher, Standing Bear, Coat & Muff, 5 In.	150.00
Sugar & Creamer, Jasperware	80.00

Schneider

Schneider Glassworks was founded in 1903 at Epinay-sur-Seine, France, by Charles and Ernest Schneider. Art glass was made between 1903 and 1930. The company still produces clear crystal glass.

SCHNEIDER, Compote, Signed, 7 1/2 X 10 In.	350.00
Compote, White, Orange, Yellow, 4 X 17 In.	115.00
Dresser Set, Red & Multicolored, Frosted Stopper, 3 Piece	125.00
Pitcher, Pink, Original Paper Label, Signed, 6 1/4 In.	295.00
Vase, Blown-Out Glass, Art Deco Metal Holder, Signed, 6 In.	225.00
Vase, Blue, Black, Clear Glass, Wrought-Iron Base, 1925, 5 1/2 In.	275.00
Vase, Flared, Design, Red Rim, White, Rust, 7 3/4 In.	95.00
Vase, Orange & Purple, Shaded, Signed, 6 In.	375.00
Vase, Orange, Puple, Art Deco, Marked, 6 In.	295.00
Vase, Purple, Orange, & White, Art Deco Metal Matrix, Signed, 6 In.	325.00
Vase, Purple, Orange, White, Floral Design, Marked, 6 In.	325.00

Scrimshaw is bone or ivory or whale's teeth carved by sailors and others for entertainment during the sailing-ship days. Some scrimshaw was carved as early as 1800.

     SCRIMSHAW, see also Nautical

SCRIMSHAW, Busk, Decorated, Stars, Pinwheels, Floral Motif, C.1800, 12 1/2 In.	125.00
Clothespin, Whalebone	68.00
Cribbage Board, Oak Mounted, Paw Feet, 24 In.	50.00
Fossil Tooth, Ship, Clouds, & Gulls, 2 1/4 In.	50.00
Needle, Ivory	15.00
Sewing Kit, Sailor's, Open End Thimble, Shark Shape, 4 Piece	195.00
Shoe Horn, Ivory, Alaska	50.00
Thimble, Ivory, Ship & Flowers	15.00
Thimble, Ship & Flowers	15.00
Tusk, The Ship Abigail, Motto, Free Trade & Liberty, 20 In.	3200.00
Tusk, 2 Sides, Silver Capped, 11 X 1 3/4 In.	300.00
Watch Holder, Women, Temple Flying Flag, Whalebone, 8 X 11 In.	2640.00
Whale's Tooth, Captain Lecturing Cabin Boy, 4 In.	80.00
Whale's Tooth, Ship & Water, 5 In.	205.00
Whale's Tooth, Walrus, Oak Base, 4 1/2 In.	120.00
Whale's Tooth, 1 Large Ship, 2 Small Ones, 3 1/4 In.	99.00
Whale's Tooth, 3 Seals, Marked, 3 1/2 In.	140.00
1 Tooth, Ship, Clouds, & Gulls, Walnut Base, 2 1/4 In.	50.00

SEBASTIAN MINIATURES, Clown	175.00 To 225.00
Covered Bridge	75.00 To 95.00
Dia-Mel Fat Man, 1963	1000.00
Family Sing	150.00 To 200.00
First House	125.00 To 150.00
Henry Wadsworth Longfellow, 1965	300.00
Jell-O Whale, 1954	325.00
Lexington Minuteman	250.00 To 325.00
Menotomy Indian, 1949	325.00
Phoebe	125.00 To 175.00
Romeo, 1947	250.00
Santa, 1980	40.00 To 50.00
Shaker Man & Lady, 1938	250.00 To 300.00
St.Joan, Square Base, 1952	300.00
The Thinker, 1949	280.00
Uncle Sam In Orbit	275.00 To 325.00

     SEG, see Paul Revere Pottery

Sevres porcelain has been made in Sevres, France, since 1769. Many copies of the famous ware have been made. The name originally referred to the works of the Royal Porcelain factory. The name now includes any of the wares made in the town of Sevres, France.

SEVRES, Biscuit Jar, Gold Trim, Purple & Clambroth Ground, Signed	450.00
Bowl, Punch, Cartouches, Lovers In Garden, Blue, Bronze Stand, 8 In.	750.00
Box, Patch, Hinged Top, Scene, 2 1/2 In.	85.00
Burner, Pastille, Pink & White Kiosk, Gold Trim, 8 1/4 In.	250.00
Chandelier, 12 Lights, Flowers & Cherubs, Turquoise & Gilt Bronze	325.00
Clock & Vases, Louis XVI Style, Gilt Bronze, Inset Jewels, 3 Piece	9500.00
Cup & Saucer, Chateau Fontainebleau, Animals, Vines, Demitasse, 6 Sets	250.00
Cup, Armorial, Roses, Crest Design, Gilt, 5 1/2 In.	275.00
Figurine, Bulldog, Artist Signed, White Bisque, Dated 1921, 5 In.	90.00
Jardiniere, Turquoise, Ormolu Mounted, 3 Scenes, 14 1/2 In.	625.00
Plate, Chateau Des Tuileries, Gold Scrolls, C.1846, 9 1/2 In.	215.00
Plate, Chateau St.Cloud, Gold Tracery, Signed, 9 1/2 In.	150.00
Plate, Courtesan, C.1863, 9 1/2 In.	100.00
Plate, Louis Philippe Crested, Marked, 1846, 8 3/4 In., Set Of 6	175.00
Plate, Napoleon On Horseback, Green & Gilded Edge, 9 1/2 In.	110.00
Plate, Oyster, Floral, C.1836, 8 In.	65.00
Plate, Portrait, Young Girl, Scalloped Blue Edge, Signed, 9 1/2 In.	155.00
Plate, Service, Louis Napoleon's Emblem, Marked N With Crown	150.00
Urn, Free-Standing Flower Form, Handled, 19 In.	125.00
Urn, Girl & Boy, With Scene On Other Side, Signed, 10 1/4 In.	350.00
Urn, Mounted On Empire Style Gilt Bronze, 14 In.	3750.00
Urn, Napoleonic Scene, Bronze-Mounted, 19th Century, 12 In., Pair	3500.00
Urn, Raised Bird & Basket Design, Scroll Handles, Marked, 19 In.	900.00
Vase, Art Deco, Peacock Eye Drip Glaze, 11 In.	175.00
Vase, Bronze Gourd Shape, Modele Sevres, 19th Century, 5 3/4 In.	175.00

Sewer tile figures were made by workers in the sewer tile factories in the Ohio area during the late nineteenth and early twentieth centuries.

SEWER TILE, Bookends, Indian Head	60.00
Doorstop, Dog, Sitting Position, Molded, 11 In.	175.00

SEWING, Ball, Darning, Flat Bottom, Black	6.00
Basket, Child's, Top Handle, Wicker, Oval, 5 1/2 X 2 1/2 In.	12.00
Basket, One Thousand Skeins D.M.S.Floss, Picnic Style, Large	175.00
Basket, Scalloped Top, Board Base, Cretonne Lining, Wicker, 8 In.Diam.	12.00
Basket, Set Of Implements, Lined, 7 X 7 In.	40.00
Bird, Brass, Spring Strap Off, Patented February 15, 1853	58.00
Bird, Double Pad, Brass	45.00
Bird, Patented 1858, Embossed Brass	110.00
Bird, Silver Plate, Dated 1853	115.00
Bird, Table Clamp, Embossed Feathers & Florals, Silver, Brass	85.00
Book, Needle, Army & Navy, Vintage Cruiser & Plane On Cover	4.00
Box, Knitting, Moire Grosgrain Cover, Rope Handle, C.1935, 7 5/8 In.	25.00
Box, Lift Tray, 6 Sections, Lock, Walnut, 7 3/4 X 11 1/4 In.	35.00
Box, Lift-Off Top Holds 20 Spools, Pincushion Top, Oak, 12 X 3 In.	55.00
Box, Pin, Pincushion Top, Mirror Under Cover, Japan, 2 1/2 X 1 1/2 In.	6.50
Box, Pine Hill, N.Y., J. & P.Coats Crochet & Darning, 3 X 3 1/2 In.	39.00
Box, Spool, Coffee Grinder Shape, Top Pincushion, Maple	30.00
Box, Spool, Dome Top, Fitted Interior, Wooden, 4 1/4 X 2 1/2 In.	25.00
Box, Spool, Pinwheel-Carved, Dated 1711, 3 X 3 1/2 In.	325.00
Box, Thread, Loch Tummel, Queen's View, Clark Label	55.00
Box, Walnut, Maple & Cherry, Drawers, 8 Ivory Eyelets, 5 X 7 In.	60.00
Box, 5 Spool Holders, Pincushion, Thimble Holder, & Thimble, Walnut	45.00
Cabinet, Merrick, Mirrored Sides, 1897	575.00
Caddy, Maple, 2 Tier Spools, Finial, Turned Feet, 8 1/8 In.	50.00
Caddy, Pine, Sliding Tambour Doors, Spindles, 2 Drawers, 4 X 9 X 12 In	120.00
Case, Needle, Accept My Best Wishes, Barrel Shape, Boxwood	30.00
Case, Needle, Black & Green, Tin	20.00
Case, Needle, Fish, Ivory	95.00

Case, Needle, Leatherette, C.1900, Advertising, 5 X 2 1/2 In. 5.00
Case, Needle, Opens At Both Ends, Carved Horn 55.00
Case, Needle, Pigskin Color, 1900, 5 X 2 1/4 In. 5.00
Case, Needle, Sterling 35.00
Darner, Glove, Wooden 8.00
Darning Egg, Amber Glass, Knob Handle 35.00
Darning Egg, Glass 45.00
Darning Egg, Handled, 6 In., 1 Piece .... 6.50 To 16.00
Darning Egg, Shawnee 35.00
Darning Egg, Sterling Silver Handle .... 20.00 To 30.00
Hook, Crocket, Bone Handled 3.50
Kit, Calvert Whiskey Advertising 10.00
Kit, Darning, Elsie The Cow, Borden's 6.00
Kit, Thimble Signed Calvert Whiskey, Enameled, Yellow, 1 3/4 In. 12.00
Kit, Wooden Shoe, Velvet Cushion, Blue & Green Dots 12.00
Kit, Wooden Shoe, Velvet Pincushion, Marked Heidelberg, 2 1/2 In. 6.00
Kit, Yellow Enameled, Calvert Whiskey, 1 3/4 In. 12.00
Machine, Elias Howe, Treadle, Patent 1871 .... 50.00
Machine, National, Belvidere, Ill., C.1880, Eagle Medallion, Clamp Type 65.00
Machine, Treadle, Patent Date 1862 .... 350.00
Machine, Wilcox & Gibb, Treadle, Gooseneck Head, 1880s 195.00
Mold, Thimble, Used By Silversmith, Brass, Size 5 .... 30.00
Needle, Crochet, Celluloid, Ivory Color, 5 1/2 In. 3.00

SEWING, PINCUSHION DOLL, see Pincushion Doll category

Pincushion, Beaded Victorian, Velvet, Scalloped Floral, 7 1/2 In. 25.00
Pincushion, Cat, Germany, 8 3/4 In. 125.00
Pincushion, Chair Shape, Velvet Trim, 3 X 5 In. 6.50
Pincushion, Elephant, Sterling 85.00
Pincushion, Embroidered Velvet, Braid Trim, Victorian, 13 X 7 In. 12.00
Pincushion, Form Of Leg & Boot, 12 1/2 In. 36.00
Pincushion, Hanging, Beaded Bird In Flight, Dated 1913 .... 45.00
Pincushion, Heart Shaped, Indian Beaded, 1895, 5 X 4 In. 35.00
Pincushion, Man's Shoe, McKinley Monument, Buffalo, N.Y., Velvet 18.00
Pincushion, Metal & Velvet, Lady's Shoe Shape, Gold Finish Metal 18.00
Pincushion, Oxford, Metal, Japan 10.00
Pincushion, Rabbit 12.00
Pincushion, Tomato Shape, 3 Babies Climbing Sides, Silk 18.00
Scissors, Buttonhole, With Rouletted Marker, Marked Butterick 22.50
Shears, Mother-Of-Pearl Handle, 2 Blades, E.Wisthof Solingen 25.00
Shears, Tailor's, Brass Joining, 1859, 14 In. 55.00
Shears, Tailor's, Left Hand, 15 In. 60.00
Shuttle, Ivory 15.00
Shuttle, Tatting, Ivory 4.50
Shuttle, Tatting, Sterling Silver 18.00
Sleeve Iron, Grand Union Tea Co., 1897 .... 35.00
Tape Measure, Aunt Jemima 2.00
Tape Measure, B. & M.Station, Winnisquam, N.H., Celluloid 18.00
Tape Measure, Bear, Celluloid 30.00
Tape Measure, Beehive, Windup, C.1860 .... 220.00
Tape Measure, Butterfly, Celluloid 45.00
Tape Measure, Celluloid 45.00
Tape Measure, Champagne Bottle In Cooler, Windup 165.00
Tape Measure, Chick With Worm In Mouth 195.00
Tape Measure, Clockworks 65.00
Tape Measure, Coronation Coach, Red Windows 35.00
Tape Measure, Dog, Black Fur Tail Pulls Out, 2 X 3 In. 26.00
Tape Measure, Egg, With Fly Pull, Tin 330.00
Tape Measure, Flask, Sterling 30.00
Tape Measure, Frigidaire 25.00
Tape Measure, General Electric Refrigerators 18.00
Tape Measure, Gutta-Percha, Patented 1870 .... 36.00
Tape Measure, Hoover Vacuum Cleaner, Figural 15.00
Tape Measure, Illinois Surgical Supply Co. 26.00

Tape Measure, Kangaroo With Baby In Pouch, C.1880, Windup	275.00
Tape Measure, Man's Work Shoe, 3 Feet In One Shoe, Brass	45.00
Tape Measure, Money, Brass, Windup	250.00
Tape Measure, National Casket Co., Picture Of Girl	28.00
Tape Measure, Retractable, Mr.Peanut, Boxed	3.50
Tape Measure, Shoe, Three Feet In One Shoe	35.00
Tape Measure, Silk Floss Mattresses, Boston, Celluloid	23.00
Tape Measure, Squirrel, Celluloid	35.00
Tape Measure, Teakettle, Brass	65.00
Tape Measure, Tenison Saddlery, Dallas, Texas, Celluloid	18.00
Tape Measure, Turtle, Sterling	75.00
Tape Measure, Walnut, Celluloid	40.00
Tape Measure, Wheel Barrow With Rabbit, Windup, C.1880	185.00
Thimble Holder, Acorn, Wooden	45.00
Thimble Holder, Figural, Doll, Celluloid, German	38.00
Thimble Holder, Pierced, Sterling Silver	85.00
Thimble, Kewpie, Metal, Marked	25.00
Thimble, Luzianne Coffee	7.00
Thimble, Sterling Silver, Floral At Base, Size 8	25.00
Thimble, Sterling Silver, Size 12	35.00
Thimble, Sterling Silver, Wide Floral Band, Size 11	30.00
Thimble, Sterling Silver, Wide Paneled Band, Size 11	19.00
Thimble, Sterling, Leaf & Circle, Wide Band, Size 9, Anchor Mark	28.00
Thimble, Sterling, Leaf Design, Anchor Mark	25.00
Thimble, Sterling, Scroll Design, Beaded Edge, Wide Band	22.00
Thimble, Sterling, Size 10, Engraved Mamma	35.00
Thimble, Sterling, Wide Paneled Band, Size 11	20.00
Thimble, Sterling, 1933 World's Fair	30.00
Thread, Brook's, Lockstitch & Chainstitch Machines, 4 X 1 3/4 In.	14.50

Shaker-produced items are characterized by simplicity, functionalism, and orderliness. There were many Shaker communities in America from the eighteenth century to the present day.

SHAKER, Basket, Mending Inside, Pocket, Wrapped Rim, Base 7 1/2 In., 3 In.High	45.00
Basket, Palm Leaf Design, Kentucky, 6-Sided, 6 3/4 In.	35.00
Basket, Reed, Double Hinged Lid, 13 X 10 In.	120.00
Basket, Reed, Woven, 7 X 11 In.	60.00
Basket, Sewing, Satin Lining, Green, Splint, 3 1/2 X 2 1/2 In.	60.00
Basket, Sewing, Tufted Satin Lining, Fitted, Ash Splint, 5 X 4 In.	65.00
Basket, Spint With Flaring Sides, Bentwood Handles, Yellow, 5 In.	150.00
Basket, Splint, Oval Interior, 2-Arched Handles, Square, 10 In.	95.00
Basket, Straw, Pink Ribbon Woven In, Floral Design On Lid, 9 In.	20.00
Basket, Straw, Pink Ribbon Woven, Oval, 5 X 7 In.	20.00
Basket, Straw, Woven, Red Ribbon Trim, Silk Panel, 4 1/2 X 10 In.	35.00
Basket, Woven Reed, Double Hinged Lid, Handled, 10 X 14 In.	55.00
Beater, Carpet, Wooden, Gray, Handled, 40 1/4 In.	80.00
Bonnet, Summer, White Cotton	65.00
Book, Music, Mt. Lebanon, C.1870, Songs & Hymns, 250 Pages	75.00
Bottle, Hair Restorer	22.00
Box, Bentwood, Brown, 2 In.	140.00
Box, Bentwood, Finger Construction, Red, Dated 1920, 3 In.	185.00
Box, Bentwood, Wooden Handle, Green Stain, 5 1/4 In.	100.00
Box, Finger Construction, Copper Tacks, Blue, 5 3/4 In.	475.00
Box, Finger Construction, Round, 1 7/8 In.	55.00
Box, Gray-Blue, Copper Tacks, 3-Finger, Oval, 8 X 11 In.	575.00
Box, Knife, Bentwood, Oak Base, Wooden Grip, 8 X 13 X 4 In.	125.00
Box, Lid, Oval, Natural Finish, Iron, Copper Tacks, 4 3/4 X 6 3/8 In.	95.00
Box, Oval, Massachusetts, 4 1/2 X 3 1/2 X 1 3/4 In.	185.00
Box, Oval, Robin's Egg Blue, 3 1/2 X 5 1/4 In.	175.00
Box, Oval, 3-Finger Construction, 7 3/8 X 9 7/8 In.	165.00
Box, Round, Massachusetts, 4 X 2 In.	185.00
Box, Sewing, Curly Maple, 1 Drawer, 2 Tier, Pincushion, 6 X 8 In.	200.00
Box, Sewing, 3-Finger Construction, Blue Lining, Pincushion, 7 In.	200.00

Box, Straw, Hinged Lid, 6 X 6 In.Square 30.00
Box, Wooden, Dark Green, Covered, 4-Finger, Oval, 9 7/8 In. 500.00
Box, 3-Finger, Deep Green, Copper Tacks, Oval, 11 In. 525.00
Box, 3-Finger, Oval, Dark Green, 8 3/8 X 11 In. 375.00
Box, 3-Finger, Oval, Red Cherry Stain, Covered, 11 3/8 In. 1150.00
Broom, Horsehair, Turned Maple Handle 50.00
Brush, Black & Gray Bristles, Turned Handle, 10 In. 30.00
Brush, Black Horsehair Bristles, Signed Adams, 11 In. 45.00
Brush, Clothes, Wooden Teeth 85.00
Brush, Corner, Horsehair, Maple Handle, 11 In. 50.00
Brush, Curved Handle, Eyelet Hand Up, Horsehair Bristles, 6 In. 65.00
Brush, Hearth, Curvy Black Handle, Concentric Lines, 7 1/2 In. 80.00
Brush, Honey Maple, Turned & Dyed, Lavender Bristles, 8 In. 75.00
Brush, Horsehair Bristles, Black Enameled, 8 In. 40.00
Brush, Maple Handle, Blonde Pig Bristles, 8 In. 90.00
Brush, Utility, 10 In. 40.00
Bucket, Maple Sugar, Red Paint, Signed N.F., White Interior 75.00
Bucket, Sap, Metal Band, Impressed N.E.Shakers, Lavender, 9 In. 55.00
Carrier, Ember, Envelope Corner, T-Shaped Handle, Brass Pull, 18 In. 180.00
Cloak, Dorothy, Light Beige, Hood, Wide Cape Collar, 20th Century 200.00
Clothes Hanger, Pine, 15 In. 60.00
Comb, Each Side Has Row Of Teeth, Regular & Fine, 2 3/4 X 4 In. 85.00
Comb, Scalp, Maple, Massaging The Scalp, 2 In. 50.00
Darner & Needle Holder, Maple, Mushroom Shaped End, 3 In. 45.00
Darner, Ball & Socket, 2 3/4 In. .... 60.00 To 120.00
Darner, Removable Handle, Needle Storage, Wooden Design, 2 3/4 In. 40.00
Darner, Sock, Maple, Removable Needle Holder, 6 In. 70.00
Dipper, Gray, Tin, Tubular Handle, 7 In. 65.00
Dipper, Tin, 43 In. 195.00
Dispenser, Powder, Butternut, 4 Holes On Top, 6 In. 80.00
Drainer, Cheese, 25 1/4 X 8 1/4 In. 45.00
Dryer, Glove, Child's, Maple, Marked C, 12 1/8 In. 110.00
Fan, Lady's, Splint, Blue, Red, Yellow, 9 X 10 In. 40.00
SHAKER, FURNITURE, see Furniture
Herb Crusher 48.00
Holder, Spool, Pincushion, Sabbathday Lake, 7 Spool Spindles, 5 In. 110.00
Holder, String, Inlaid Treen, Maple, Brass Port, 4 3/8 In. 75.00
Measure, Bentwood, Turned Handle, 7 1/4 In. 150.00
Measure, Round, Red Paint, 6 In. 65.00
Mirror, Hand, Maple Frame, Marked No. 10, 4 X 6 In. 40.00
Mirror, Hand, Maple, Mother-Of-Pearl Inlay, 11 1/2 In. 100.00
Mirror, Hand, Oval, Maple, 10 In. 90.00
Mirror, Travel, Folding, Walnut, 1 Magnifying, 1 Regular, C.1810 .... 75.00
Napkin Ring, Mosaic Effect, Corset Waist Sabbathday Lake, 1 In. 70.00
Pamphlet, United Inheritance, Canterbury, C.1870, 14 Pages 10.00
Pegboard, Rack, Pine & Maple, Red Stain, 12 X 16 In. 425.00
Pie Lifter, Wooden Handle, 18 In. 30.00
Pin Roll, Thimble Container, Leather Lined, C.1900, 7 1/2 In. 50.00
Pincushion, Set In Sweet Grass Woven Basket, C.1900, 3 1/4 X 2 In. 40.00
Pincushion, Split Poplar Trim, 4 In. 75.00
Pincushion, Sweet Grass, Tufted Green Velvet, 3 1/2 In. 35.00
Pincushion, Turned Stem, 5 3/4 In. 25.00
Pincushion, Velvet, Poplar Wood, Sabbathday Lake, 2 In. 40.00
Reel, Cherry Hub, Maple Spokes, 20 In. 45.00
Rolling Pin, Double, 20 1/4 In. 195.00
Scoop, Apple Butter, Pine, 12 In.Long 150.00
Sewing Caddy, 2 Tier, Wooden, Red & Mustard Wash, Spired Corner, 7 In. 95.00
Sewing Kit, Leather, Name Imprint, Alice Chase 45.00
Sieve, Finger Construction, Original Woven Horsehair, 9 X 12 In. 575.00
Sled, Child's, Red Paint, Square Nails, 16 X 5 In. 85.00
Strainer, Applesauce, Tin, No.2, Dark Gray, 6 X 6 1/2 In. 90.00
Stretcher, Glove, Pair, 15 In. 275.00
Textile, Bonnet, Quilted Teal Silk, Iridescent, Cotton Lining, 15 In. 45.00

Tongs, Stove, Iron, Shaker Design, C.1870, 15 In.	45.00
Tool, Basket Making, Brass Teeth, Maple, 7 X 1 In.	45.00
Tray, Cutlery, Divided	127.50
Tray, Wooden, Green, 3 3/4 X 5 In.	150.00

Shaving mugs were popular from 1860 to 1900. Many types were made, including occupational mugs featuring pictures of the man's job. There were scuttle mugs, silver plated mugs, glass-lined mugs, and others.

SHAVING MUG, Compliments Alsobrook Liquor Co., Chattanooga	16.00
Figural, Swan, White & Gold	48.50
Flared Top, Rose & Gilt Design	25.00
Floral Design	75.00
Floral Spray, Blue & Pink Ground	22.00
Fraternal, Flags, Name In Gold, Signed	48.00
Gold Lettering & Borders, Flowers, A.Kern Barber Supply, Bottom	28.00
Gold Trace, Flowers, Lavender Luster	14.00
Hand-Painted Daisies, Gold Outlined, C.1890, Gold Handle	7.50
Hand-Painted Pansies, Limoges, Signed & Dated	30.00
Hand-Painted Pink Roses, Gold Trim, Germany	24.00
Horsehead, Signed Germany	22.00
Hunt Scene, Bulbous, Soap Compartment, Green, Gold, & Red	50.00
Lilies Of The Valley, Gold Rim	25.00
Milk Glass Insert, Quadruple Plated, Mirrored Case	75.00
Name, William Ferris	42.50
Occupational, Bar Scene With Workman, Gold Name	250.00
Occupational, Bartender, Men In Bar, Name In Gold	125.00
Occupational, Cowboy	68.00
Occupational, Gay 90s Singer, Stovepipe Hat, Green	75.00
Occupational, Harp & Shamrock Scene, Gold Name	160.00
Occupational, Horse & Driver, Name Worn, Germany	78.00
Occupational, Pheasant Scene, Gold Name	150.00
Occupational, Storekeeper Selling Cigars To Man With Cane	225.00
Occupational, Telephone, Gold Trim	135.00
Occupational, Top Hat, Cleaning & Blocking Hats	95.00
Peacock Feathers	47.00
Pink & Gilt Floral Spray, Flared Pink Top	25.00
Pink Flowers, Gilt Leaves, Pink Top Band, White	22.00
Roses, Out-Curving Top & Bottom, Handled	25.00
Soap Rest, Moss Rose, Brown Leaves	24.00
Tin, Handled, Rectangular Brush Pocket, 4 1/2 In.	40.00
White Flower Spray, Blue & Pink Ground	25.00

Shawnee USA

Shawnee pottery was made in Zanesville, Ohio, from 1935 until 1961. Shawnee also produced pottery for George Rumrill during the late 1930s.

SHAWNEE, Bank, Dotted Pig	12.00
Bank, Mugsey Dog	20.00
Basket, Green, Purple Berries	12.00
Bowl, Corn King	12.00
Bowl, Corn Queen, 8 In.	14.00
Butter, Corn King, Oval, Covered	35.00
Butter, Covered, Little Red Riding Hood	110.00
Casserole, Corn King	18.00 To 45.00
Casserole, Corn King, Individual	35.00
Cookie Jar, Clown With Seal	45.00
Cookie Jar, Corn King	65.00
Cookie Jar, Dutch Boy	24.00 To 39.00
Cookie Jar, Dutch Girl	25.00
Cookie Jar, Dutch Girl, Gold Trim	35.00
Cookie Jar, Elephant, Dumbo	45.00
Cookie Jar, Farmer Pig, Green Handkerchief	28.00

Cookie Jar, Farmer Pig, Red Bandanna 40.00
Cookie Jar, Lady Pig 40.00
Cookie Jar, Mugsey .... 40.00 To 45.00
Cookie Jar, Puss 'n Boots .... 28.50 To 45.00
Cookie Jar, Rabbit 28.00
Cookie Jar, Reclining Clown 55.00
Cookie Jar, Sailor Boy 35.00
Cookie Jar, Schoolhouse 20.00
Cookie Jar, Smiley Pig, Red Bandanna, Flowers 35.00
Cookie Jar, Winking Owl 50.00
Cookie Jar, Winnie Pig .... 30.00 To 45.00
Creamer, Cat .... 11.00 To 12.50
Creamer, Corn King .... 12.00 To 14.00
Creamer, Duck 7.50
Creamer, Elephant 7.50
Creamer, Pig, Gold Trim 35.00
Creamer, Pig, Yellow 15.00
Creamer, Puss 'n Boots .... 8.00 To 25.00
Dish, ABC, Little Red Riding Hood 75.00
Dish, Corn Holder 5.00
Holder, Sucker, Chief Watta Pop 130.00
Jug, Water, Child's, Smiley Pig, 2 Quart 32.00
Mug, Corn King 20.00
Mug, Mugsey Dog 65.00
Pitcher, Bo Peep, Gold, Flowers 30.00
Pitcher, Chick, Marked 10.00
Pitcher, Child's, Puss n' Boots 22.00
Pitcher, Elephant .... 10.00 To 15.00
Pitcher, Figural, Rooster 25.00
Pitcher, Little Boy Blue 35.00
Pitcher, Milk, Bopeep .... 20.00 To 26.00
Pitcher, Milk, Corn King .... 15.00 To 28.50
Pitcher, Milk, Goldilocks, 8 In. .... 30.00 To 32.00
Pitcher, Milk, Smiley Pig 15.00
Pitcher, Puss 'n Boots .... 12.00 To 18.00
Pitcher, Smiley Pig .... 30.00 To 35.00
Pitcher, Smiley Pig, Small 17.50
Planter, Bookends, Buddha 28.00
Planter, Bridge Over Pool 5.00
Planter, Colonial Girl 9.00
Planter, Covered Wagon .... 8.00 To 15.00
Planter, Deer, Brown & Green, Gold Trim, 6 X 6 In. 15.00
Planter, Doe & Fawn .... 9.00 To 13.50
Planter, Dutch Boy & Girl 15.00
Planter, Globe 10.00
Planter, Gristmill 9.00
Planter, Long Seashell, Blue, 6 In. 8.00
Planter, Polynesian Lady 12.00
Planter, Pup In Shoe 6.00
Planter, Squirrel 5.00
Planter, Touche Line, Green 4.00
Planter, Touring Car 6.50
Planter, Wishing Well, Blue 12.50
Planter, Wishing Well, Green 12.50
Planter, Wishing Well, Yellow 12.50
Platter, Corn King 20.00
Salt & Pepper, Alpine Boy & Girl 10.50
Salt & Pepper, Bopeep 11.00
Salt & Pepper, Corn King .... 8.00 To 17.00
Salt & Pepper, Corn Queen, 5 1/2 In. .... 13.00 To 30.00
Salt & Pepper, Dutch Boy & Girl, Gold Overglaze, 4 3/4 In. 10.00
Salt & Pepper, Dutch Boy & Girl, Large 20.00

Salt & Pepper, Elephant 10.00
Salt & Pepper, Farmer Pig 14.00
Salt & Pepper, Farmer, Large 20.00
Salt & Pepper, Figural, Flowerpot, 3 1/2 In. 7.00
Salt & Pepper, Figural, Smiling Pigs, Rehoboth, Del. 22.00
Salt & Pepper, Flowers In Pot, Pink, Blue, Yellow 10.00
Salt & Pepper, Mugsey .... 17.00 To 24.00
Salt & Pepper, Owl .... 9.00 To 12.50
Salt & Pepper, Puss 'n Boots .... 6.00 To 16.00
Salt & Pepper, Sleeping Ducks, Shawnee Label 10.00
Salt & Pepper, Swiss Boy & Girl 15.00
Salt & Pepper, Winnie Pig .... 7.00 To 15.00
Sugar & Creamer, Corn King, Covered .... 20.00 To 23.00
Sugar & Creamer, Corn Queen 30.00
Sugar & Creamer, Corn, Covered 20.00
Sugar Shaker, Dutch Boy, 6 In. 6.00
Sugar, Corn King, Covered .... 9.00 To 24.00
Teapot, Corn King .... 35.00 To 45.00
Teapot, Granny Ann .... 28.00 To 38.00
Teapot, Granny Ann, Lilac Apron, Green Trim 40.00
Teapot, Hearts & Flowers 38.00
Teapot, Rosebud, Gold Trim 75.00
Teapot, Tom Tom The Piper's Son .... 20.00 To 38.00
Vase, Bow Knot Pattern, Kelly Green 10.00
Vase, Bud, Dark Green, Black Stripes, Marked, 11 In. 12.00
Vase, Bud, Green, White, 9 In. 10.00
Vase, Diamond-Quilted, Gray, 10 In. 12.00
Wall Pocket, Little Jack Horner 15.00

SHEARWATER, Pitcher, Bronze Burnish, Marked, 5 1/2 In. 55.00
    SHEFFIELD, see Silver-English; Silver Plate

> *Shirley Temple dishes, blue glassware, and any other souvenir-type objects*
> *with her name and picture are now collected. Cobalt blue glassware*
> *decorated with Shirley Temple's picture was made by the Hazel Atlas*
> *Glass Company from 1934 to 1942.*

SHIRLEY TEMPLE, Album, Song, No.2 .... 35.00
Album, Song, Sing Along With Shirley, 1935 .... 55.00
Book, At Play, 1935 .... 25.00
Book, Christmas 85.00
Book, Christmas, 1937 .... 45.00
Book, Dimples 24.00
Book, Little Princess 65.00
Book, Little Star 50.00
Book, Pictorial, Heidi, 1937 .... 30.00
Bowl, Cereal, Cobalt .... 30.00 To 45.00
Buggy, Doll .... 375.00 To 650.00
Cereal Set, Mug, Pitcher, & Bowl 65.00
Cereal Set, 3 Piece 115.00
Creamer .... 22.00 To 40.00
Dishes, Pink, Boxed 115.00
Doll, Baby, Marked, 20 In. 550.00
Doll, Chalk 45.00
Doll, Composition Head & Body, Flirty Eyes, Dressed, 25 In. 475.00
Doll, Composition, Baby Take A Bow, Blue & White, 22 In. 850.00
Doll, Composition, Flirty Eyes, 18 In. 300.00
Doll, Composition, 27 In. 550.00
Doll, Flirty Eyes, Original Tagged Dress, 27 In. 795.00
Doll, Hair Net, Red Shoes, 1973 .... 50.00
Doll, Horse, Electric, Store Display, Late 1930s, 26 In. 650.00
Doll, Madame Alexander, Flirty Eye, Original Dress, 19 In. 175.00
Doll, Madame Alexander, Original Dress, 12 In. 75.00
Doll, Madame Alexander, 13 In. 325.00

Doll, Original Box, 1957, 12 In.	150.00
Doll, Original Tagged Dress, 15 In.	150.00
Doll, Pink Party Tagged Dress, Signed Head, 16 In.	800.00
Doll, Red Sailor Suit, 36 In.	825.00
Figurine, Sailor Suit, Marbleware, 5 In.	13.00
Game, Jigsaw Puzzle, Large	20.00
Mirror, Celluloid, Marked, 1936	30.00
Mug, Blue	44.00 To 58.00
Mug, Portrait, Yellow	12.00
Music, Sheet, Poor Little Rich Girl	15.00
Music, Sheet, Rebecca Of Sunnybrook Farm	15.00
Music, Sheet, Stowaway	20.00
Paper Doll & Clothes	20.00
Paper Doll, Pinback Picture, Green Background, 1 1/4 In.	2.50
Paper Doll, Uncut, Boxed, 1976	8.00
Pin, The World's Darling	22.50
Pitcher, Cobalt	20.00 To 40.00
Pitcher, Picture & Signature	50.00
Playing Cards, Fan Club, Coors	150.00
Poster, Young People, 27 X 41 In.	35.00
Saltshaker	25.00
Teacup, Glass, Cobalt Blue	750.00
Wristwatch, Little Colonel On Face, 1960 Issue	25.00

SILHOUETTE, see Picture, Silhouette

Silver deposit glass was made during the late nineteenth and early twentieth centuries. Solid sterling silver was applied to the glass by a chemical method so that a cutout design of silver metal appeared against a clear or colored glass. It is sometimes called silver overlay.

SILVER DEPOSIT, Liquor Set, Decanter, 4 Glasses, Green	65.00
Mustard Jar, Krystol, Signed, 4 In.	40.00
Pitcher, Tankard, Art Nouveau, Floral Design, 7 In.	155.00
Sherbet, Art Nouveau Design, Set Of 6	23.50
Sugar & Creamer, Brown Porcelain, Art Nouveau	165.00
Sugar & Creamer, Heisey Mark, 2 In.	40.00
Sugar & Creamer, Poppy Design, Footed	17.00
Syrup, Silver Top, 5 1/2 In.	60.00
Vase, Gold Aurene, 7 In.	475.00
Vase, Green, 6 In.	56.00
Vase, Jack-In-The-Pulpit, 6 In.	30.00

Silver plate is not solid silver. It is a ware made of metal such as nickel or copper, then covered with a thin coating of silver. The letters EPNS are often found on American and English silver plated wares. Sheffield silver is a type of silver plate.

SILVER PLATE, Basket, Cake, Lacy Openwork, Swing Dial, Webster	35.00
Basket, Cake, Oval, Gadrooned Border, Sheffield, 14 In.	200.00
Basket, Circular Double Handle, Scrolls & Leaves, 6 X 7 In.	75.00
Basket, Footed, Engraved, Marked Tufts, 9 1/2 X 3 1/2 In.	50.00
Basket, Fox & Grape Figures On Sides, 12 X 13 In.	35.00
Basket, Openwork Sides & Ends, Footed, Handled, 8 1/2 X 2 In.	12.00
Bottle, Wine, Floral Scrolls & Leaves, Wooden Base	30.00
Bowl, Punch, Flowers, Foliage, 12 Cups & Ladle, 16 In.Diam.	475.00
Bowl, Vegetable, Rosemary Pattern, Covered	40.00
Box, Collar Button, 3 Ball Feet, Button Finial On Cover, Poole	28.00
Box, Stamp, Embossed Design On Hinged Lid, 1 1/8 X 1 1/8 In.	35.00
Box, Stamp, Figural Horsehead With Hames, Reed & Barton	95.00
Box, Stamp, Ship & Waves In Relief On Cover	40.00
Bride's Basket, Art Glass Bowl, Hartford Silver Plate Co.	35.00
Butter Knife, Art Deco Design, Wm. Rogers	4.00
Butter, Cow Design, Meriden	30.00
Butter, Dome Topped, Footed, Swan Design, Marked Meriden	60.00
Butter, Knife Holder, Scroll Handles, Glass Insert, Meriden	45.00

Cake Basket, Double Bail, Floral Center, Marked Tufts, Boston	50.00
Candlesnuffer, Tray	125.00
Candlestick, Matthew Boulton, Sheffield, Pair	1200.00
Candlestick, Sailing Ship & Globe Of World, Pair	50.00
Candlestick, Snuffer, Pair, Georgian, Sheffield	84.00
Cigar Cutter & Match Holder, Ring-Handled, Saucer Base, 6 In.	45.00
Coffeepot, Side Handle, Albert Pick & Co., 10 In.	15.00
Compote, Leaf & Berry Design, Oaks Horse Show, 1939, 8 1/2 In.	30.00
Cup, Child's, Little Boy Blue Design, Wm. Rogers	35.00
Cuspidor, Texture Design, Meriden, 7 1/2 X 4 1/4 In.	110.00
Cutter, Cigar, El Roi-Tan Perfect Cigars, Dated 1913, 2 1/2 In.	15.00
Cutter, Cigar, R.R.Johnstone, Milwaukee, 2 Blades, Pocket	18.00
Dish, Brownie Decor, Marked Royal Baby Plate, U.S.A.	55.00
Dish, Cheese, Mouse On Cover, Band Of Birds, Berries, & Floral	58.00
Dish, Repousse Bunches Of Grapes, Homan, Oval, 7 X 1 1/2 In.	20.00
Dish, Serving, Art Nouveau, Applied Floral Center, Derby, 14 In.	35.00
Figurine, Flamingos, 5 1/2 In., Pair	18.00
Flask, Art Nouveau Raised Design, Cap Inverts, Extends	50.00
Fork, Pickle, Flower Design, Niagara Falls Co., 1877	6.00
Hairbrush, Woman In Relief	20.00
Holder, Watch, Scrolls, Pedestal, Footed	48.00
Holder, 2 Pink Cased Glass Dishes, Enameled, Tufts, 10 1/4 In.	75.00
Ice Bucket, Handle Control Cover, 12 X 8 In.	49.00
Knife Rest, Cherubs At Each End, Roger Smith & Co., 3 1/2 In.	30.00
Knife Rest, Figural, Bears	45.00
Knife Rest, Figural, Boars	45.00
Knife Rest, Figural, Foxes	35.00
Mirror, Art Nouveau, Raised Roses, Beveled Glass, Hand	20.00
Mirror, Hand, Victorian, Rose Florals, Wallace Bros., 9 1/2 In.	20.00
Mustache Cup & Saucer, Bright Cut, Gold Wash Interior, Tufts	110.00
Name Plate, Coffin, 1880s, 6 In., Pair	15.00
SILVER PLATE, NAPKIN RING, see Napkin Ring	
Pitcher, Eskimos, Walrus, Bear, Meriden, 13 In.	75.00
Pitcher, Floral Pedestal Feet & Handle, Ice Lip, Bulbous	75.00
Pitcher, Fred Harvey, 3 1/2 In.	35.00
Plate, Serving, Painted Flowers, Octagonal Gold Edge	135.00
Razor, Floral Embossed, King Gillette, Case	25.00
Salad Set, Gorham, Dorflinger Cut Glass Handles	395.00
Shears, Grape, Kings Pattern	48.00
Spoon Warmer, Melon-Ribbed Nautilus, Sheffield, England	150.00
Spoon Warmer, Shell Shape, C.1890, English Hallmarks	95.00
SILVER PLATE, SPOON, SOUVENIR, see Souvenir, Spoon, Silver Plate	
Spooner, Swallow Finial, Squirrel Handle, Wm.Rogers, C.1894	85.00
Stand, Cruet, Foliate Handle & Border, Sheffield, C.1840	170.00
Strainer, Tea, Figural, Chick, Sheffield	45.00
Sugar Shell & Butter Knife, Assyrian Pattern, Rogers, Set	12.00
Sugar, Engraved Flowers & Leaves, Scrolled Handles, Victor	35.00
Tea & Coffee Service, C.1900, Wallace Bros., 5 Piece	225.00
Tea Set, Engraved Flowers, 3 Piece	40.00
Tea Tray, Pierced Foliate Border, Leaf Clad Handle, 28 In.	90.00
Teapot, Art Deco, Black Bakelite Handle & Finial, Wilcox, 2 Cup	15.00
Thimble, Crest With Lion & Crown, 5 1/4 In., Set Of 4	40.00
Tongs, Sugar, Tulip Ends, Holmes & Edwards	10.00
SILVER PLATE, TOOTHPICK, see Toothpick	
Tray, Card, Etched Leaf Design, Reed & Barton, 7 In.Diam.	15.00
Tray, Card, Footed, Handled, Design, Reed & Barton, 8 In.	45.00
Tray, Card, Round, Fan Shape, Engraved, Leaf Design	50.00
Tray, Flowers, Shellwork, Loop Handle, Gadrooned Rim, 26 In.	220.00
Tray, Rope Design Handle, 2 Tier	40.00
Tray, Tea, Gadrooned Rim, Foliate Handles, 31 In.	60.00
Tray, Tea, Oblong, Canted Corners, 20 In.	75.00
Tray, Wm.Rogers Co., 10 X 3 1/2 In.	1.50
Trivet, Baumamtlegent, Large	38.00
Tureen, Raised Lion's Face, Handled, C.1870, Hoof Feet	95.00

American silver was usually marked with the name or initials of the silver-smith or silver company. The word "sterling" was not in general use until about 1860.

SILVER-AMERICAN, see also Tiffany Silver; Silver-Sterling

SILVER-AMERICAN, Basket, Cake, Bates & Co., C.1880, 12 1/2 In.	550.00
Bowl, Circular, Foliate Border, Gorham, 8 In.	75.00
Bowl, Fruit, Circular, Everted Rim, Foliate, 9 In.	110.00
Bowl, Gorham, Handled, 2 1/4 In.Diam., Set Of 5	100.00
Bowl, Melon Shape, Footed, C.L.Boehme, C.1799, 3 3/4 In.	1050.00
Box, Stamp, Rectangular Hinged Lid, 2 Fleur-De-Lis	22.50
Brush, He Loves Me, Unger	90.00
Butter, Presentation, Wood & Hughes, Covered, 12 X 7 1/2 In.	1250.00
Candlesnuffer, Gorham	25.00
Case, Card, Engraved Bird, Gorham, 4 1/2 X 2 1/2 In.	95.00
Case, Cigarette, Embossed Cupid Design, Unger Brothers	300.00
Compote, Pedestal, Repousse Rim, S.Kirk & Son, 6 1/4 In.	90.00
Creamer, Melon Shape, Footed, C.L.Boehme, C.1799, 4 7/8 In.	1100.00
Creamer, Pear Shape, Floral Design, W.Brown, C.1835, 6 In.	325.00
Cruet Set, Acanthus Foliage, J & I Cox, C.1825, 10 In.	1540.00
Cup, Baby, Engraved Allover With Activities, Blackinton	125.00
Cup, Baby, Half Heart-Shaped Hollow Handle, Lunt, 1 3/4 In.	30.00
Cup, Beaded Top & Bottom, M.W.Galt & Bro., C.1840, 3 1/2 In.	250.00
Cup, Demitasse, Twisted Handle, G.A.R.1894, Pittsburg	20.00
Cup, Julep, P.L.Krider, Philadelphia, 3 5/8 In.	375.00
Cup, Reeded & Beaded Band Top & Bottom, J.Conning, 3 In.	495.00
Dish, Candy, Pedestal, Repousse Rim, Kirk & Son, 4 1/4 In.	135.00
Dish, Candy, Whiting, C.1890, 8 7/8 X 5 1/4 In.	75.00
Dish, Entree, Covered, C.1875, Gorham, 11 In.	675.00
Dresser Set, Warwick Pattern, International, 3 Piece	135.00
Fish Slice, D.B.Brower, Albany, C.1850, Coin, 12 1/2 In.	125.00
Fish Slice, Engraved Fish & Ferns, J.Conning, 11 1/8 In.	595.00
Flask, Smoking Woman, Unger Brothers, 6 1/4 In.	750.00
Fork, Asparagus, Lancaster Rose Pattern, Gorham, 9 1/4 In.	160.00
Fork, Beaded Edge, Wm.Carrington, C.1850, 8 In.	45.00
Fork, Cottage Pattern, Hyde & Goodrich, C.1829, Set Of 12	750.00
Fork, Dessert, Fiddle Tipped, Foster & Purple, C.1844	145.00
Fork, Fiddle Thread Shell, R.& A.Campbell, C.1835, 7 1/4 In.	85.00
Fork, Fiddle Thread, Engraved ETC, A.Knapp	70.00
Fork, Fiddle Thread, Hayden & Whilden, 7 3/4 In.	75.00
Fork, Fiddle Thread, Horton & Rikeman, C.1850, 6 7/8 In.	85.00
Fork, Fiddle Tipped, C.Gennet, Jr., Coin, 7 1/4 In., Set Of 6	375.00
Fork, King's Pattern, A.G.Medley, C.1832, 6 7/8 In.	40.00
Fork, Meat, Shell Design, Patented 1893	60.00
Fork, Olive, S.Wilmot, C.1850, 6 7/8 In.	65.00
Fork, Pickle, Douvanine Pattern, Unger Bros.	45.00
Goblet, Lincoln & Reed, C.1835, Negro Head On Side	550.00
Goblet, Tulip-Shaped Bowl, Pedestal, Fisher, 4 3/4 In.	42.50
Goblet, 272 Pattern, Bell-Shaped Body, Gorham, 6 1/2 In.	95.00
Gravy Boat & Tray, J.E.Caldwell, Boat, 7 1/4 In.Long	480.00
Holder, Blotter, Beaded Scroll, Gorham, Set Of 4	32.00
Holder, Sugar Cube, Grill Work Sides, Weston Co., 6 In.	60.00
Holder, Thermometer, Marked Unger Bros., Embossed	90.00
Knife, Butter, Fiddle Tipped, A.T.& F.A.Leslie, C.1850	125.00
Knife, Butter, Fiddle Tipped, Engraved Brooks, J.Conning	145.00
Knife, Butter, Hollow Handle, Traugott Leinbach, C.1855	225.00
Knife, Butter, Scalloped Blade, Kitts & Werne, C.1865	60.00
Knife, Butter, Twisted Handle, T.Leinbach, 6 3/4 In.	270.00
Knife, Fish, Ivory Handle, Hallmarked, 7 1/4 In.	30.00
Knife, Fruit, Floral Design, Frederick Marquand, C.1820	85.00
Ladle, Gravy, J.Conning, Mobile, C.1850, 7 1/4 In.	275.00
Ladle, Mustard, Farrington & Hunnewell, Boston, 5 1/2 In.	35.00
Ladle, Mustard, Fiddle, Day & Maussenet, C.1842, 5 1/2 In.	125.00
Ladle, Mustard, Fiddle, Gale & Hayden, C.1840	55.00

Ladle, Mustard, Fiddle, S.Justis, C.1818, 4 3/4 In. 135.00
Ladle, Mustard, Joseph Draper, 1826-56, Flared End, 5 5/8 In. 125.00
Ladle, Mustard, Pinched Fiddle, Gabriel Duvall Clark, C.1830 .... 55.00
Ladle, Mustard, Sheaf Of Wheat, J.Eyland, C.1819 .... 20.00
Ladle, Sauce, Fiddle Tipped, Jennings & Ames, C.1840, 6 In. 40.00
Ladle, Sauce, Humboldt Pattern, Wood & Hughes, C.1845 .... 75.00
Ladle, Sauce, Shell Handle, Stodder & Frobisher, C.1816 .... 72.50
Ladle, Soup, Coffin End, John Pearson, C.1802, 15 In. 795.00
Ladle, Soup, Engraved Handle, J.Conning, 13 3/4 In. 445.00
Ladle, Soup, Fiddle Tipped, Anthony Rasch, 12 In. 650.00
Ladle, Soup, Fiddle Tipped, S.D.Choate, C.1841, 13 3/8 In. 375.00
Ladle, Soup, Fiddle, C.1830, Franklin Richmond 137.00
Ladle, Soup, Flared Handle, R.E.Smith, 1821-49, 12 1/2 In. 395.00
Ladle, Soup, Josephine, W.Pearce & Co., C.1831, 13 3/8 In. 375.00
Ladle, Soup, Old English Pattern, Myer Myers, C.1780, 14 In. 4950.00
Ladle, Toddy, Crest, Wood Handle, J. Blowers, C.1730, 14 In. 275.00
Ladle, Tostrup, 1853, Gold Washed Bowl 75.00
Locket, Spring-Loaded Sections, Webster, Chain, 2 X 1 In. 65.00
Lunch Box, Handmade, Cartier, 4 1/2 X 4 1/2 In. 235.00
Mug, Kirk Baby, Embossed Flowers & Ferns, 3 In. 245.00
Mug, Knurled Handle, Acanthus Thumbpiece, 1888 Gorham, 3 In. 165.00
Mug, Presentation, Acanthus & Scroll Handle, 8 Ounce 475.00
Mustard, Grillwork Base, Cobalt Blue Liner, Reed & Barton 65.00
Napkin Ring, Basket Weave Engraving, Willie, 1/2 In. 15.00
Pie Server, Louis XV Pattern, Whiting, 9 1/4 In. 80.00
Pin, Diana, Unger, 1 1/2 In. 85.00
Pin, Nouveau Woman, Chain, Unger 48.00
Pitcher, Water, Adolphe Himmel, New Orleans, C.1853, Coin 2750.00
Pitcher, Water, Vase Shape, Gorham & Co., C.1860, 10 In. 770.00
Plate, Chop, Cinderella Pattern, Gorham, 14 In. 325.00
Plate, Wallace, 6 1/8 In., Set Of 12 .... 1320.00
Porringer, Bombe Sides, Keyhole Handle, C.1775, 5 In. 412.00
Porringer, Child's, Whiting, Dixie Monogram 95.00
Porringer, Standing Rim, Flowered Handle, 4 7/8 In. 890.00
Porringer, William Smith Pelletreau, C.1815, 5 1/4 In. 900.00
Purse, Dance, 4 Compartments, Calendar, Early 1900s 195.00
Rattle, Figurine, Girl, Gorham Co., 4 1/2 In. .... *Illus* 418.00
Rattle, Figurine, Jester, Gorham Co., 4 3/4 In. .... *Illus* 495.00
Riding Crop, Horsehead Handle, Tiffany & Co., C.1880 .... 467.00
Salt Dip, Shreve & Co., San Francisco, Spoon, Set 35.00
Salt Spoon, E.F.Miller, Providence, R.I., C.1830, 3 7/8 In. 15.00
Salt Spoon, King Pattern, Marquand, Charleston & New York 65.00
Salt Spoon, Low, Ball & Co., Boston, C.1840 .... 22.50
Salt Spoon, Shell Bowl, Willard & Hawley, 1844-51, 3 3/4 In. 25.00
Saltshaker, Form Of African Head, Shiebler & Co., 2 3/4 In. 300.00
Shoehorn, Monogram On Handle Back, Shiefler & Co. 27.50
Skewer, Imperial Queen, Whiting, 9 1/4 In. 27.50
Spectacles, Octagonal Shape, Peter Mood, C.1820 .... 195.00
Spoon, A.A.Mead, Montpelier, Vt., C.1840, 6 1/4 In. 30.00
Spoon, Berry, Griffin On Handle, C.1890, J.R.Reed & Co. 85.00
Spoon, Chrysanthemum Pattern, Gorham, 9 In. 160.00
Spoon, Dessert, Fiddle Thread, D.B.Nichols, C.1820, 7 In. 110.00
Spoon, Dessert, Fiddle Tipped, H.P.Buckley, C.1850 .... 60.00
Spoon, Dessert, Fiddle Tipped, Harding & Co., C.1840 .... 24.00
Spoon, Dessert, Fiddle Tipped, L.W.Welles, C.1841 .... 25.00
Spoon, Dessert, Fiddle Tipped, Mitchell & Tyler, 7 3/8 In. 55.00
Spoon, Dessert, Fiddle, F.W.Burwell, C.1846, 7 In. 55.00
Spoon, Dessert, Fiddle, Geo.W.Webb & Co., C.1865, 7 1/4 In. 35.00
Spoon, Dessert, Fiddle, George W.Riggs, C.1820, 6 7/8 In. 95.00
Spoon, Dessert, Fiddle, Mitchell & Whitney, C.1830 .... 25.00
Spoon, Dessert, Fiddle, T.Nowlan, C.1840 .... 85.00
Spoon, Dessert, Fiddle, W.M.Savage, 7 In. 75.00
Spoon, Dessert, Flared Handle, C.1840, S.Kirk, 7 1/8 In. 35.00

Spoon, Dessert, Hayden, J., Columbus, Ga., C.1840, 7 In. 65.00
Spoon, Dessert, J. & I.Cox, New York, C.1830, 7 In. 55.00
Spoon, Dessert, J.Draper, Wilmington, Del., 7 1/4 In. 95.00
Spoon, Dessert, Joseph Foster, Boston, 7 3/4 In. 55.00
Spoon, Dessert, King's Pattern, S.Wilmot, 6 7/8 In. 95.00
Spoon, Dessert, Oval End, A.Osthoff, C.1809, 7 1/8 In. 40.00
Spoon, Dessert, Pinched Fiddle, J.Kneffly, C.1820, 7 3/8 In. 50.00
Spoon, Dessert, Wm.McDougall, Jr., Meredith, N.H., C.1825 .... 35.00
Spoon, Dognose, Rattail Bowl, John Edwards, C.1713, 7 In. 990.00
Spoon, Egg, Fiddle, W.M.Savage, 5 In. 75.00
Spoon, Fiddle Handle, Pitman, 9 In. 32.00
Spoon, G.C.Munsell, Northampton, Mass., C.1835, 5 3/4 In. 18.00
Spoon, Honey, Fiddleback Handle, M.D.C. Touchmark 22.50
Spoon, Kimball & Gould, C Initial, 7 1/4 In. 20.00
Spoon, Moore & Hibbard, C.1815, 6 In. 15.00
Spoon, Mustard, Flared Handle, S.F.Hobbs, C.1859, 5 5/8 In. 65.00
Spoon, Old Colonial, Towle, Set Of 6 .... 100.00
Spoon, Pink Quartz At Twist Handle End 15.00
Spoon, Salt, Bright Cut, Standish Barry, C.1795, 3 7/8 In. 65.00
Spoon, Salt, Fins, G.Gaither, C.1821, 3 7/8 In. 65.00
Spoon, Salt, Oval End, Littleton Holland, C.1800 .... 60.00
Spoon, Salt, Scalloped Bowl, Twist Handle, Star Mark, Coin 14.00
Spoon, Salt, Shell Bowl, Drummond, Marked 10.15 .... 30.00
Spoon, Tea Caddy, Marie Antoinette, Gorham, 3 3/4 In. 45.00
Strainer, Tea, Webster Co., Cutout Handle, Ribbed Bowl 65.00
Strainer, Teapot Shape, Durgin 90.00
Strainer, Watrous, Double-Handled 40.00
Sugar & Creamer, Baluster Form, Classical Design, 7 In. 325.00
Sugar & Creamer, Oval, Loop Handles, C.1790, 4 1/2 In. 248.00
Sugar & Creamer, Vase Form, Samuel Kirk & Sons, 8 In. 990.00
Sugar & Creamer, Vase Shaped, Hearts, Bogert, 9 In. 600.00
Sugar Shell, Farrington & Hunnell, Coin 30.00
Sugar Shell, Fiddle, Philip B.Sadtler, C.1840, 6 5/8 In. 45.00
Sugar Shell, Prince Albert, Rikeman, 6 3/8 In. 110.00
Sugar Shovel, Gale & Hayden, Charleston & New York 75.00
Sugar Tongs, Claw Ends, Geo.B.Morrill & Co., 5 1/4 In. 30.00
Sugar Tongs, M.Taber & Co., Providence, R.I., 5 3/4 In. 60.00
Tablespoon, A.Carlile, Philadelphia, 1780-94, Coin, 8 1/8 In. 125.00
Tablespoon, Bright Cut, A.Stowell, Coin 25.00
Tablespoon, C.Davison, N.Y. & Norwich, Ct., 9 In. 45.00
Tablespoon, Davis Palmer & Co., Boston, 1841, Set Of 4 .... 100.00
Tablespoon, Dunbar & Story, Worcester, Mass., 9 In. 35.00
Tablespoon, F.Hart, Norwich, Ct., C.1800, 9 1/4 In. 70.00
Tablespoon, Fiddle Shell, Josiah Penfield, C.1800, 9 In. 145.00
Tablespoon, Fiddle Thread, Louis Muh, 8 1/2 In. 65.00
Tablespoon, Fiddle Tipped Back, R.Mathews, Fins, 8 7/8 In. 75.00
Tablespoon, Fiddle Tipped, Clark, Rackett, C.1740, 8 1/4 In. 80.00
Tablespoon, Fiddle Tipped, F.A.Brahe, C.1845, 8 1/4 In. 120.00
Tablespoon, Fiddle Tipped, Greenwood & Bros., 8 3/4 In. 55.00
Tablespoon, Fiddle Tipped, Henry Hudson, C.1841, 8 3/4 In. 55.00
Tablespoon, Fiddle Tipped, J.Conning, 8 3/4 In. 125.00
Tablespoon, Fiddle Tipped, J.Kilienthal, C.1853, 8 5/8 In. 55.00
Tablespoon, Fiddle, A.E.Warner, C.1830, 9 In. 55.00
Tablespoon, Fiddle, A.Knapp, Mobile, C.1826, 8 In. 75.00
Tablespoon, Fiddle, A.O.Fairchild, C.1839, 9 1/8 In. 90.00
Tablespoon, Fiddle, B.Lord, Large Fins, 8 3/8 In. 100.00
Tablespoon, Fiddle, Clark, Rackett & Co., 8 1/4 In. 125.00
Tablespoon, Fiddle, Eagle Mark, 1824-27, S.Kirk, 8 3/4 In. 75.00
Tablespoon, Fiddle, Gale & Hayden 50.00
Tablespoon, Fiddle, H.I.Pepper, Wilmington, C.1825, 9 In. 70.00
Tablespoon, Fiddle, Jacob Walter, C.1800, Fins, 8 3/4 In. 55.00
Tablespoon, Fiddle, John Lynch, C.1825 .... 65.00
Tablespoon, Fiddle, John M.Sehorn, C.1842, 8 1/2 In. 155.00

Tablespoon, Fiddle, Joseph Bishop, C.1816, 8 3/8 In. 210.00
Tablespoon, Fiddle, R.H.L.Villard, C.1833, 8 5/8 In. 85.00
Tablespoon, Fiddle, Robert Keyworth, C.1830, 8 3/4 In. 75.00
Tablespoon, Fiddle, Thomas Boyle Campbell, C.1825, 9 1/8 In. 145.00
Tablespoon, Fiddle, W.A.Williams, C.1820, 8 3/4 In. 145.00
Tablespoon, Fiddle, W.M.Savage, 1813, 8 5/8 In. 85.00
Tablespoon, Hand-Engraved On Back, A.B.Touchmark 50.00
Tablespoon, Hazen, Troy, N.Y., C.1810, 8 7/8 In. 45.00
Tablespoon, J.A.& S.S.Virgin, C.1834, 8 3/4 In. 135.00
Tablespoon, J.H.Clark, N.Y., C.1812, Coin 45.00
Tablespoon, J.Howell, Philadelphia, C.1802, 9 5/8 In. 85.00
Tablespoon, Joseph Hill, Portsmouth, N.H., C.1800, 9 In. 55.00
Tablespoon, L. Kimball & Co., 7 In. 20.00
Tablespoon, Medallion, Coin 65.00
Tablespoon, Olive, E.A.Tyler, C.1838, 8 1/4 In. 65.00
Tablespoon, Oval End, Gilbert Bigger, C.1795, 9 1/4 In. 65.00
Tablespoon, Oval End, Philip B.Sadtler, C.1815, 8 3/4 In. 95.00
Tablespoon, Palmer & Batchelder, Boston, C.1815, Coin 45.00
Tablespoon, Pinched Fiddle, C.Asman, C.1863, 8 5/8 In. 50.00
Tablespoon, Pinched Fiddle, Moses Bensinger, C.1865, Coin 58.00
Tablespoon, Pointed End, Johnson & Reat, C.1805, 8 5/8 In. 145.00
Tablespoon, R.R.Conn, Fitchburg, Mass., C.1850, 8 4/8 In. 25.00
Tablespoon, Sheaf Of Wheat, Moses Eastman, C.1826, 8 3/4 In. 165.00
Tablespoon, W.Moulton, Fiddleback, C.1772, Pair 50.00
Tea Caddy, Marie Antoinette, C.1890, Gorham, 3 3/4 In. 45.00
Tea Infuser, Teapot Shape 40.00
Tea Service, C.1870, Gorham, Kettle, 12 1/2 In., 6 Piece 3600.00
Tea Service, Ivory Handles, Georg Jensen 1500.00
Tea Set, Gorham, C.1860 .... *Illus* 715.00
Tea Set, Vintage Pattern, C.1850, C.Bard & Son, 6 Piece 6400.00
Tea Strainer, Beaded Rim, Wire Handles, Whiting, 4 In. 37.50
Tea Strainer, Fits Over Cup, Handled, Webster, 5 1/2 In. 65.00
Teapot, Inverted Pear Form, Thomas Hummersley, C.1760, 6 In. 9350.00
Teapot, Queeen Anne Pattern, Gorham, 4 In. 160.00
Teaspoon, Beaded Edge, J.M.Freeman, 6 1/8 In., Set Of 4 .... 50.00
Teaspoon, Bradberry, Newburyport, Ma., 1815, Coin 20.00
Teaspoon, Bright Cut, Andrew McBride, C.1910, 5 5/8 In. 185.00
Teaspoon, E.Smith, Brookfield, Conn., C.1775, Coffin Handle 12.50
Teaspoon, E.Tarbell, Coffin End, C.1830, Initialed, Coin 12.00
Teaspoon, Ebenezer Smith, Brookfield, Conn., 1785, Set Of 6 .... 100.00
Teaspoon, F.Curtis, C.1845, Coffin End, Coin 12.50
Teaspoon, Farrington & Hunnewell, Boston, 1830, Set Of 6 .... 100.00
Teaspoon, Farrington & Hunnewell, Coffin End, C.1830 .... 20.00

Silver-American, Tea Set, Gorham, C.1860

Teaspoon, Fiddle Thread, Louis Muh, C.1823, 5 3/4 In.	40.00
Teaspoon, Fiddle Tipped, Henry Hudson, 5 3/4 In.	25.00
Teaspoon, Fiddle Tipped, J.P.Barnes, C.1848	30.00
Teaspoon, Fiddle Tipped, T.J., Egear, 6 In.	18.00
Teaspoon, Fiddle Tipped, Thomas Gowdey, C.1825, 5 3/4 In.	65.00
Teaspoon, Fiddle Tipped, Wm.H.Thompson, C.1849, 5 7/8 In.	55.00
Teaspoon, Fiddle, Benjamin Lord, C.1796, 5 5/8 In.	55.00
Teaspoon, Fiddle, C.K.Wentworth & Co., C.1847, 5 5/8 In.	55.00
Teaspoon, Fiddle, D.S.Smith, C.1831, 5 3/8 In.	65.00
Teaspoon, Fiddle, F.& H.Clark, C.1830, Fin, 6 In.	65.00
Teaspoon, Fiddle, Initials, A.Knapp, 5 7/8 In.	40.00
Teaspoon, Fiddle, J.A.& S.S.Virgin, 5 7/8 In.	70.00
Teaspoon, Fiddle, Joseph Wharfe, C.1804, Fins	50.00
Teaspoon, Fiddle, Otis Childs, C.1836, Design, 6 In.	65.00
Teaspoon, Fiddle, S.I.Lea, C.1814, 5 5/8 In.	38.00
Teaspoon, Fiddle, T.J.Megear, C.1830, 5 5/8 In.	45.00
Teaspoon, Fiddle, Thomas Trotter, C.1840, 5 5/8 In.	45.00
Teaspoon, Fiddle, W.M.Savage, 1813, 6 In.	45.00
Teaspoon, Fiddle, Wm.& A.Cooper, C.1838, 5 3/4 In.	30.00
Teaspoon, Fiddleback, C.Kendall, C.1780, Coin	12.00
Teaspoon, Fiddleback, Ebed Whiton, Boston, 1826, Coun	15.00
Teaspoon, Fiddleback, P.Stevens, Coin, Pair	40.00
Teaspoon, Fiddleback, W.McGrew, Script Initial	20.00
Teaspoon, Flared Handle, F.H.Clark & Co., C.1840, 5 7/8 In.	55.00
Teaspoon, Flared Handle, J.Haydon, C.1840, 6 In.	35.00
Teaspoon, Flared Shoulder, Lincoln & Reed, C.1835, 5 3/4 In.	12.00
Teaspoon, Flared Shoulder, Simmons & Walter, C.1830	15.00
Teaspoon, Gothic Design, Gale & Hayden	45.00
Teaspoon, Gurney Bros., Coin	15.00
Teaspoon, H.J.Pepper, Delaware Coin, Set Of 12	450.00
Teaspoon, Hutchinson & Connel, Coffin End, Coin	20.00
Teaspoon, I.Hall, Concord, N.H., C.1781, Script Name	12.50
Teaspoon, J.B.Dumoutet, Philadelphia, Trenton, & Charleston	125.00
Teaspoon, J.B.Jones & Co., Boston, 1813, Fiddleback	12.00
Teaspoon, J.Church, Hartford, Ct., C.1840, 5 7/8 In.	18.00
Teaspoon, J.Draper, Wilmington, Del., 5 3/4 In.	75.00
Teaspoon, J.J.Low & Co., Coin	20.00
Teaspoon, J.J.Stowell, Fiddleback, Coin	20.00
Teaspoon, J.Mott, Schenectady, C.1790, 5 7/8 In.	45.00
Teaspoon, Joseph Carpenter, Norwich, Ct., C.1770, 5 3/8 In.	95.00
Teaspoon, King's Pattern, F.Marquand, 5 3/4 In.	45.00
Teaspoon, Littleton & Dunn, Boston, Fiddleback, Coin	12.50
Teaspoon, N.Harding, Silversmith From Boston, C.1830	20.00
Teaspoon, Oval End, C.A.Burnett, 5 3/4 In.	60.00
Teaspoon, Palmer & Batchelder, Boston, 1815, Set Of 6	100.00
Teaspoon, Pinched Fiddle Tipped, T.G.Calvert, C.1840	35.00
Teaspoon, Pointed End, Ezekiel Burr, Coin	30.00
Teaspoon, Pointed End, Marcus Merriman	30.00
Teaspoon, Pointed End, Rufus Farnam	30.00
Teaspoon, R.R.Conn, Ditchburg, Mass., C.1850, 6 In.	15.00
Teaspoon, Reverse Tipped, J.A.Coles, C.1841, 5 7/8 In.	15.00
Teaspoon, S. & H.Gerould, Coffin End, Coin	50.00
Teaspoon, S.T.Crosby, Boston, 1850, Initialed, Coin	12.00
Teaspoon, Serrated, Thomas S.Spear, C.1850, 6 1/8 In.	68.00
Teaspoon, Smith & Chamberlain, Salem, Mass., C.1830, Coin	15.00
Teaspoon, Stowell, Baltimore, C.1855, Coffin End	15.00
Teaspoon, T.Dunlap, Coffin End, Signed	20.00
Teaspoon, T.Eltonhead, Baltimore, Md., 6 1/8 In.	25.00
Teaspoon, W.Moulton, C.1814, Newburyport, Mass., Coffin End	20.00
Teaspoon, Wm. McDougal, Meredith, N.H., C.1825, Coin	14.50
Teaspoon, Wm.Stinson, N.Y., 1813, Coffin End, Coin	12.50
Tomato Server, Adams Pattern, Whiting	30.00
Tongs, Bright Cut, William Needels, C.1798, 5 3/8 In.	275.00

Tongs, Fiddle Body, Zalmon Bostwick, C.1845, 6 1/4 In. 75.00
Tongs, Queen Anne, Plain Pattern, Claw End, Dominick & Haff 20.00
Tongs, Sugar, Egyptian Pattern, Georg Jensen 70.00
Tongs, Sugar, Fiddle, Joseph Draper, 6 In. 220.00
Tray, Pin, Art Nouveau, Gorham,-7 X 3 1/2 In. 62.00
Tray, Signed Black, Starr, & Frost, 18 In. 700.00
Tray, Tea, Oval, Integral Handles, Gorham, 22 In. 600.00
Urn, Cigarette, Bulbous Lower Body, Amston Co., 3 1/4 In. 32.50
Urn, Cigarette, Gadrooned Rim, Pedestal, Hamilton, 2 7/8 In. 23.50
Vase, Repousse, Jenkins & Jenkins, C.1890, 7 1/2 In. 180.00
Vase, Tapering Pierced Form, Gorham, 9 In. 110.00
Vase, Trumpet Shape, Scrolls, C.1890, Gorham, 18 In. 350.00
Vinaigrette, Monogram, T.Simpson & Son, 1819, 1 1/2 X 1 In. 195.00

SILVER-AUSTRIAN, Box, Floral & Landscape Scenes, 2 3/4 In. 350.00
Box, Jewel, Lion Feet, Floral Design, Filigree, 4 In. 900.00
Centerpiece, Art Nouveau, C.1900, 14 1/4 In. .... *Illus* 1100.00

Silver-Austrian, Centerpiece, Art Nouveau,
C.1900, 14 1/4 In.

SILVER-CAMBODIAN, Bowl, Embossed Figures, 7 1/2 X 5 In. 800.00

SILVER-CANADIAN, Box, Ring, Velvet Lined, Marked Birk 50.00

SILVER-CHINESE, Candleholder, Elephant Trunk Top Of Holder, 7 1/2 In., Pair 1160.00
Mug, Chinese Martial Games, Leeching, C.1860, 5 In. 660.00
Pitcher, Truncated Base, Engraved Scene, C.1890, 6 X 7 In. 275.00
Shaker, Cocktail, Raised Dragon Design, 10 Silver Goblets 795.00
Tablespoon, Characters On Backs, Chased Designs, Set Of 11 .... 395.00

SILVER-CONTINENTAL, Bowl, Mermaid Base, 6 1/4'X 6 3/4 In. 380.00
Box, Hinged Cover, Finial, Footed, Marked, 4 1/2 In. 270.00
Case, Cigarette, Enamel Horses On Blue Ground, 3 In. 185.00
Cup, Handleless, Blue & Green Cabochon Stones, 5 1/2 In. 65.00
Decanter, Cupid Stopper, Ruby Glass, 12 1/2 In. 600.00
Decanter, Etched Crystal Insert, 10 3/4 In. 225.00
Miniature House, Lovebird Design, 2 1/2 In., 3 Piece 450.00
Miniature, Tea Service, Pot, 1 1/2 In., 4 Piece 550.00
Salt & Pepper, Bird Form, 2 3/4 In. 400.00
Smoking Set, Contemporary Design, 2 In Ashtray & Urn 110.00
Snuffbox, Oval, Repousse, Cherubs, Marked JW, 2 In. 25.00

SILVER-DANISH, Bottle Opener, Georg Jensen, Monogram 35.00
Bowl, Footed, Large 175.00
Knife, Serving, Acorn Pattern, Georg Jensen, 9 In. 95.00
Pin, Bar, Georg Jensen 75.00
Pin, Double Leaf, Georg Jensen 35.00
Salt, Spoon, & Pepper, Mushroom Shape, Blue Enamel 40.00
Spoon, Curl In Handle 50.00
Spoon, Tea Caddy, Acorn Pattern, Georg Jensen, 4 In. 45.00

SILVER-DUTCH, Bowl, Scene Of Children & Goat, 2-Handled, Late 1800s 325.00
Box, Bear Form, Garnet Eyes, 2 1/2 In. 750.00
Box, Groups & Profile Medallions, Elliptical, 8 1/2 In. 220.00
Box, Sugar, Dock & Harbor Scenes, 4-Sided, Small 325.00
Goblet, Brandy, Pedestal, Hallmark City Of Zwolle, 4 1/2 In. 225.00
Pillbox, Allover Embossing, Gold Wash Interior 50.00

SILVER-EGYPTIAN, Chamberstick, Cairo, 1916, Dolphin Handle, 4 In. 65.00

English silver is marked with a series of four or five small hallmarks.
The standing lion mark is the most commonly seen sterling quality mark.

SILVER-ENGLISH, Basket, Sugar, Boat Form, Samuel Massey, C.1790, 3 In. 300.00
Basket, Sweetmeat, Grape Design, C.1770 .... 375.00
Beaker, George III, Engraved, Henry Chawner, 1788, 5 3/8 In. 577.00
Bowl, Hammered Design On Lid, Drew & Sons, 1908, 6 3/4 In. 65.00
Brandy Warmer, Coat Of Arms Handle, 1812-13, 7 In. 75.00
Brandy Warmer, 1901, Ball Feet, Ivory Handle, 2 1/2 X 2 In. 125.00
Buttonhook, 11 In. 24.00
Cake Basket, Neoclassical, Oval, Single Handle, 16 X 19 In. 600.00
Cann, Bulbous, Double Scroll Handle, C.1781, 3 1/4 In. 160.00
Card Case, Leather Case, Birmingham, 1851, 2 1/2 X 3 1/2 In. 95.00
Caster, Pear Form, Paneled, J.Delmester, 1763, 4 3/4 In. 137.00
Centerpiece, George III, John Edington, C.1875, 10 1/4 In. 880.00
Coaster, Wine, Stylized Rim, 19th Century, 6 1/8 In., Pair 70.00
Creamer, George III, Bright-Cut Girdle, 3 3/4 In. 137.00
Creamer, George III, Floral Festoons, 1810, 4 In. 137.00
Creamer, Pear Shape, Scroll Handle, Hester Bateman, 5 In. 100.00
Cruet Set, George III, Smith, Tate, & Co., 1810, 5 3/4 In. 55.00
Cruet Set, George III, 5 Bottles, Wooden Base, 8 1/2 In. 330.00
Cruet Set, Rebecca Emes & E.Barnard, 1911, 5 3/4 In. 275.00
Cup, Caudle, Marked, 1707, 2 7/8 In. 440.00
Cup, Caudle, Nathaniel Lock, 1707, 4 1/8 In. 715.00
Cup, Caudle, Timothy Ley, 1711, 3 1/4 In. 632.00
Cup, Demitasse, George Angell, C.1868, Scroll Handle 65.00
Cup, Wine, Commonwealth, 1958, Marked, 6 5/8 In. 4400.00
Fish Slice, King's Pattern, William Eaton, 12 7/8 In. 247.00
Fish Slice, Wm. Fley & Wm. Fern, C.1819, 11 1/8 In. 275.00
Frame, Photograph, Seal Of The U.S., H & Co., Ltd., 18 In. 440.00
Funnel, Wine, George III, Detachable Rim, Marked, 5 1/4 In. 220.00
Funnel, Wine, P.& Q.& W.Bateman, 1802, 5 1/4 In. 412.00
Infuser, Egg Shape, 3 In. 160.00
Inkstand, Gadrooned Border, 2 Pen Recesses, 1894 .... 190.00
Jug, Ale, George III, William Eaton, 1815, 7 1/4 In. 2200.00
Knife, Fruit, Pocket, Leather Case 60.00
Ladle, Soup, George III, W.Eley & W.Fearn, 1802, 12 3/4 In. 275.00
Ladle, Soup, Old English, P.& A.Bateman, 1793, 13 1/8 In. 275.00
Ladle, Soup, Queen's Pattern, Marked D.D., Oval Bowl, 13 In. 275.00
Ladle, Wine, Gadroon Border, Claret, H.Bateman, C.1780 .... 110.00
Marrow Scoop, T.Chawner, 1774, 8 3/4 In. 265.00
Pitcher, Wine, Trumpet Shape, C.1831, Reily & Storer, 12 In. 1700.00

Silver-English, Rattles, 9 Bells, C.1885, 4 1/2 In.;
5 Bells, Ivory Handle, C.1871, 3 3/4 In.

Rattle, 5 Bells, Ivory Handle, C.1871, 3 3/4 In. .... *Illus*	308.00
Rattle, 9 Bells, C.1885, 4 1/2 In. .... *Illus*	330.00
Salt Cellar, Beaded Rim, Robert Hennell, 1774, 3 1/4 In., Pair	550.00
Salt Cellar, George III, Corded Rim, 1779, 2 1/2 In., Pair	302.00
Salver, George II, Shell & Scroll, Marked, 1738, 10 1/2 In.	770.00
Sauceboat, Waved Rim, T.Meriton, 1801, Hoof Feet, 6 1/8 In.	330.00
Scoop, Cheese, Solid Ivory Handle, Longon, 1843, 9 In.	120.00
Scoop, Marrow, George III, T.Wallis II, 1789, 8 1/2 In.	165.00
Server, W.Eley & W.Fearn, 1807, Shovel Shape, 8 5/8 In., Pair	770.00
Shaving Set, George III, 1817, 1817, Marked, 2 Piece	467.00
Spoon, Berry, Fiddle Pattern, E.& F.& W.Chawner, 1816, Pair	137.00
Spoon, Dessert, Hanoverian Pattern, Stephen Adams, Set Of 3	137.00
Spoon, Dessert, P.& A.Bateman	45.00
Spoon, Salt, Fiddle Handle, J.Stone, Exeter, 1844, 4 In.	21.00
Spoon, Salt, Fiddle Handle, London, 1842, 4 3/8 In.	25.00
Spoon, Stuffing, Benjamin Smith, 1838, 12 In.	115.00
Spoon, Stuffing, Molded Drop, T.Danial, 1801, 12 In.	175.00
Spoon, Stuffing, Peter & William Bateman, 1809, 11 In.	145.00
Spoon, Stuffing, Thomas Dexter, 1822	145.00
Spoon, Stuffing, Wm.Elliot, 1829	140.00
Spoon, Tea Caddy, Engraved Bowl & Handle, Birmingham, 1834	155.00
Strainer, Wine, 1910, 5 Ounce	150.00
Sugar, George III, Basket Form, B.M.Mark, 1790	302.00
Sugar, Husk Rim, Pedestal, P.& A.& William Bateman, 4 3/4 In.	110.00
Tankard, Charles F.Kendler, 1738, 8 1/4 In.	2200.00
Tankard, Engraved Armorials, C.1674, 5 3/4 In.	3300.00
Tea Caddy, Oval, Beaded Edge, C.1909, 3 3/8 In.	70.00
Tea Service, C.F.Hancock, 1868, Gilt Interior, 4 Piece	4250.00
Tea Set, Queen Anne Pattern, Teapot 3 1/2 In., 3 Piece	320.00
Teapot & Stand, Oval Form, J.Emes, 1769, Marked, 6 3/4 In.	990.00
Teapot, James Young, 1779, 4 7/8 In.	412.00
Teapot, Oval, Beaded, C.Hougham, 1791, 6 3/4 In.	825.00
Tongs, Fiddle Pattern, D.McDonald, 1819, 6 In.	72.50
Tongs, Fiddle Pattern, Jos & Albert Savory, 1838, 5 In.	48.00
Tongs, Fiddle Pattern, T. Barker, 1823, 5 3/4 In.	42.50
Tongs, Sugar, H.Bateman, C.1775, 5 1/2 In., Pair	137.00
Tray, Tea, Wood Base, Sheffield	90.00
Vinaigrette, Gilt Filigree Grill, J.Taylor, 1905, 1 1/8 In.	275.00
Vinaigrette, Oval, J.Willmore, 1910, 1 In.	165.00
Vinaigrette, Quiver Shaped, Hinged, C.1874, 4 5/8 In.	400.00
Waiter, Molded Border, R.Burcombe, 1731, 5 5/8 In.	632.00

Silver, Rattles, American, Figurine, Jester, Gorham Co., 4 3/4 In.; American, Figurine, Girl, Gorham Co., 4 1/2 In.; French, Lady With Child, Bone Handle, 6 In.; French, Lady's Head, 4 Bells, 5 In.

(See Page 631)

Warming Stand, George III, S. & J.Crespell, 1744, Marked 990.00
Watch Hutch, Cross-Grained Ivory, 1883, 2 X 4 In. 270.00
Wine Strainer, Bowl Form, Reeded Band, Chesterman, 1790 .... 120.00

SILVER-FRENCH, Bowl, Silver & Silver Gilt, Covered, Jean Puiforcat, 78 Ounce 3250.00
Bowl, Silver & Silver Gilt, Jean Puiforcat, 24 Troy Ounce 4000.00
Box, Raised, Chased, Paris, 18th Century, 1 3/8 X 2 7/8 In. 180.00
Coffee & Tea Set, Overall Chasing Of Flowers, C.1870, 5 Piece 2400.00
Compact, Enameled Garden Scene, Marked 800, 6 In.Square 250.00
Dessert Forks & Teaspoon, C.1835, 5 Of Each, 10 Piece 350.00
Rattle, Figurine, Jester, Bone Handle, 5 3/4 In. 550.00
Rattle, Figurine, Puccinello, 5 1/4 In. Illus 858.00
Rattle, Lady With Child, Bone Handle, 6 In. .... *Illus* 495.00
Rattle, Lady's Head, 4 Bells, 5 In. .... *Illus* 495.00
Tongs, Sugar, Shell Tips, Hallmarked, 4 In. 45.00

SILVER-GERMAN, Candelabra, 6 Light, C.1900, Gilt, 23 1/4 In., Pair .... *Illus* 3520.00
Case, Cigarette, U.S.Zone, Germany 195.00
Chatelaine, Art Nouveau, Coin Holder, Ivory Leaves 195.00
Chatelaine, Art Nouveau, Ivory Leaves, Coin 185.00
Snuffbox, Letters JA Incised On Bottom 50.00
Tea Set, Paneled Bodies, Pineapple Finials, C.1884, 4 Piece 525.00
Triptych, Holy Water Font, Holy Family In Center, 6 In. 110.00

SILVER-HOLLAND, Box, Shoe Shaped, Buckled, Floral Design, 5 1/8 In. 225.00
Urn, Hot Water, Swan Design, Gadrooned Neck, Paw Feet, 14 In. 450.00

SILVER-ISRAELI, Seder Set, Hebrew Characters, Tray, 7 1/2 In. 1000.00

Silver-German, Candelabra, 6 Light, C.1900, Gilt, 23 1/4 In., Pair

Silver-Italian, Centerpiece, Agmas, Overall 19 3/4 In.

SILVER-ITALIAN, Centerpiece, Agmas, Overall 19 3/4 In. .... *Illus* 2640.00

SILVER-JAPANESE, Box, Drum Shaped, Wood Grain Pattern, 3 1/4 In. 160.00
   Humidor, Camphorwood Lined, 6 X 3 5/8 X 2 3/4 In. 800.00
   Salt & Pepper, Closed Carriages With Turning Wheels 145.00

SILVER-MEXICAN, Bottle, Snuff, Silver Spoon, 1 1/4 In. 20.00
   Bracelet, Cabochon Cut Onyx Ovals In Silver, Claw Mounts 22.00
   Cordials, Inverted Bell Shape, C.1940, 4 In., 6 Piece 90.00
   Earrings, Ball Design On Circles, Screw Type, 1 3/4 In. 12.00
   Pendant, Sterling Silver & Black Design, 1 3/4 In.Diam. 15.00
   Wine, Style Of Jensen, Set Of 12 .... 1840.00

SILVER-NORWAY, Spoon, Stuffing, Laurentzen Drammen, 1855, 14 In. 235.00

SILVER-PERUVIAN, Coffee & Tea Set 1400.00

 *Russian silver is marked with the Cyrillic or Russian alphabet. The numbers 84, 88, or 91 indicate the content of solid silver pieces. Russian silver may be higher or lower than sterling standard. Other marks indicate maker, assayer, or city of manufacture.*

SILVER-RUSSIAN, Bell Push, Jade Platform, Faberge, C.1910, 2 1/2 In. 250.00
   Candlestick, Turned & Crossed Stem, Marked OC, 1891, 15 In. 500.00
   Cigarette Case, Imperial Eagle, Floral Design, 4 In. 425.00
   Cross, Baptismal 120.00
   Salt, Gold Bowl, Clear Liner, Spoon, Signed 100.00
   Tea Ball, Chain 48.00
   Tongs, Moscow, Fiddle Body, Pear Shaped, 84 Mark, 6 In. 145.00
   Tumbler, Plique A Jour, Gilt, Blue Enamel, Marked, 3 1/8 In. 800.00

SILVER-SCOTCH, Ladle, Soup, George III, Marked R.G., 1801, 13 1/2 In. 220.00
   Spoon, Dessert, W.P. Mark, 1798, Shell Pattern, Set Of 6 .... 220.00
   Tea Set, Fluted Oval Form, W.P.Dunningham, 1800, 3 Piece 825.00

SILVER-SIAM, Case, Needle, Repousse Deities & Birds, Marked, 3 X 3/4 In. 155.00

Sterling silver is made with 925 parts of silver out of 1, 000 parts of metal. The word "sterling" is a quality guarantee used in the United Sates after about 1860.

SILVER-STERLING, see also Silver-American; Silver-English; etc.

SILVER-STERLING, Art Nouveau, Marked	45.00
Badge, Deputy Sheriff, Monterey County	150.00
Bank, Chest Form, Inscribed May 17th 1900, 3 X 2 X 2 In.	80.00
Basket, Sugar, Cobalt Blue Glass Liner	72.00
Basket, Trumpet Shape, 1775, Marked, 13 In.	600.00
Bell, 4 In.	40.00
Bottle, Teardrop Shape, Vines Design, Signed, 2 1/2 In.	50.00
Bowl, Fruit, Repousse Rim, Signed Harris & Schafer	200.00
Box, Filigree, 4 X 3 In.	50.00
Box, Jewel, Lappet Border, Velvet Interior, 5 X 3 In.	60.00
Box, Stamp, Canceled Stamp Design, Dated 1890, 1 In.Diam.	35.00
Box, Venus On Shell, 1 1/4 In.	40.00
Brush, Man's Hair, Art Nouveau, Monogram WFM, Pair	40.00
Brush, Table, Art Nouveau	65.00
Butter, Presentation, Southern Regatta, Biloxi, 1870	950.00
Buttonhook	21.00
Buttonhook, Art Nouveau, Monogram	12.00
Buttonhook, Embossed Handle, Dated 1894, 10 1/4 In.	25.00
Buttonhook, Glove	8.50
Case, Calling Card, Victorian, Chain, Marked	65.00
Case, Card, Basket Of Flowers, 3 1/2 In.	40.00
Case, Cigarette, 14K Inlay, 3 X 3 1/2 In.	35.00
Charm, Rocking Chair, Rococo Style, Cupids, 2 1/2 In.	75.00
Clip, Bib, 2 Figural Bunnies Attached To Chain, 6 In.	35.00
Clippers, Nail	35.00
Clips, Bib, 2 Figural Bunnies Attached To Chain, 6 In.	35.00
Coaster, Wood Base, 1 1/2 In., Set Of 12	100.00
Compote, Pedestal, Lily Of The Valley, White, 9 1/2 In.	350.00
Cup, Bouillon, Lenox Liner, Set Of 14	560.00
Darner, Glove, Floral Design, 4 1/2 In.	25.00
Dispenser, Coin, Form Of Watch Case	35.00
Dresser Set, Nouveau Design, 4 Piece	60.00
Flask, Pocket, 19 1/2 Ounce	90.00
Flask, 3 1/2 In.	60.00
Frame, Engraved, Oval Opening, 3 1/2 X 2 1/2 In.	55.00
Frame, 4 X 6 In.	15.00
Funnel, Perfume, Letters BL Form Handle	25.00
Gramophone, Floral, Cherubs At Corners, Pierced, 4 X 2 In.	935.00
Holder, Cigar, Engraved, Marked Silver 950	25.00
Holder, Cigarette, Top Hat	25.00
Infuser, Tea, Hepplewhite Pattern	40.00
Inkwell, Art Nouveau, 3 7/8 X 3 In.	280.00
Inkwell, Flower Design, Lift-Off Top, 3 In.	110.00
Jar, Powder, Repousse Cherubs & Roses, Gorham	175.00
Label, Bottle, Gin, With Chain	20.00
Ladle, Gravy, Bamboo Design Handle, Faceted Bowl, 6 In.	50.00
Locket, Perfume, Heart Shaped, Ornate Silver Necklace	235.00
Locket, Perfume, Round, Pierced Front, Back, Velvet	160.00
Match Holder, Grape Branches, Open Pocket, Wall, Iron	25.00
Match Holder, Hunting Scene, Iron	50.00
Match Holder, Parker, Dated 1870, Wall, Iron	45.00
Match Holder, Scalloped, 19th Century, Pine, Wall, 7 X 11 In.	65.00
Match Safe, Floral & Geometric Both Sides	48.00
Match Safe, Lobed Top & Bottom, Scrollwork, 2 3/8 In.	50.00
Match Safe, Scroll Border, C.1890, Gorham, 2 3/4 In.	45.00
Match Safe, Scroll Border, Hunting Scene, C.1880, 2 1/2 In.	125.00
Mug, Baby's, Embossed Bunny, Embossed Handle	45.00
Mug, Presentation, Allover Repousse, Loring Andrews Co.	1250.00
Paper Clip, Ornate	40.00

Silver-Sterling, Tea Set, Marked Peru, 5 Piece

Perfume, Long Stopper, Flower Design, Crown Top, 2 In.	59.00
Pillbox, 1 1/8 X 1 1/2 X 3/8 In.	25.00
Pin, Cinderella's Coach	25.00
Pitcher, Water, Wide Mouth, Fisher, 7 In.	275.00
Porringer, Hansel, Sloan, & Co., Bottom Dated 1867, 4 In.	150.00
Purse, Coin Holder & Money Clip, 4 X 2 1/2 In.	45.00
Salt & Pepper, Rickshaw Shape	65.00
Scoop, Cheese, Initial P On Back, 7 In.	25.00
Sealer, Wax, Hollow Handle, 3 3/4 In.	24.00
Shears, Grape, & Leaves In Relief, Marked, 7 In.	80.00
Spoon, California Scene On Handle, Oranges	40.00
Spoon, Ice Cream Sipper, Set Of 6, Box	75.00
SILVER-STERLING, SPOON, SOUVENIR, see Souvenir, Spoon, Sterling Silver	
Stamp Roll Holder, Udall & Ballou, 4 1/8 X 1 7/8 In.	36.00
Strainer, Tea, Underbowl	45.00
Stretcher, Glove, Ornate Art Nouveau Handles, Flowers	30.00
Sugar & Creamer, Scalloped Fluted Pattern, Creamer, 5 In.	160.00
Syrup, Floral Thumb Lift, Acorn Finial, Marked, 5 1/2 In.	90.00
Tea Ball, Basket Weave In Repousse	113.00
Tea Ball, Simons, Chain	55.00
Tea Set, Marked Peru, 5 Piece *Illus*	900.00
Thimble, Mother's, Gold Band, Boxed	75.00
Thimble, Wide Band, Willage Scene, Marked	100.00
Tongs, Claw Arms, George Foster, Coin	32.00
Tray, Bread, Art Nouveau, Monogrammed, 12 In.	220.00
Tray, Bread, Heavy Repousse, Gorham, 15 X 7 1/4 In.	250.00
Tray, Pin, Lady's	16.00
Tray, Set Of 12, Fluted Rims, 3 1/2 In.Diam.	200.00
Tray, Shell, 14 X 8 1/2 In.	190.00
Vase, 4 Stemmed Tulips, Emerald Green Baluster, 12 In.	795.00
Vinaigrette, Vermeil Interior, 1 In.'	50.00
Watch Holder	280.00
Yo-Yo	85.00
SILVER, SHEFFIELD, see Silver Plate; Silver-English	

Sinclaire cut glass was made by H.P.Sinclaire and Company of Corning, New York, between 1905 and 1929. Pieces were made of crystal as well as amber, blue, green, or ruby. Only a small percentage of Sinclaire glass is marked.

SINCLAIRE, Bowl, Bengal, Marked, 9 1/2 X 7 X 3 1/2	380.00
Bowl, Console, Canary Band, Medallions, Etched Ladies, Top 12 In.	140.00
Bowl, Console, Etched, Amber, 11 In.	40.00
Candlestick, Intaglio Cut Grapes & Leaves, Signed, Amber, 11 In.	175.00
Tray, Woodland Scene, Moose Wading In River, Acorn Border, 14 In.	1500.00
Tumbler, Queen's Pattern, Signed	75.00
Vase, Carnation Pattern, Signed, 5 X 12 In.	245.00
Vase, Fan, Footed, Amber, Floral Engraving, Signed, 8 1/2 In.	55.00
Vase, Sterling Silver & Blue Enamel Band At Top, Signed, 5 In.	200.00
Vase, Tulip, Intaglio Cut, Signed, 10 In.	350.00

Slag glass is streaked with several colors. There were many types made from about 1880. Pink slag was an American Victorian product of unknown origin. Purple and blue slag were made in American and English factories. Red slag is a very late Victorian product. Other colors are known, but are of less importance to the collector.

SLAG, Blue, Pitcher, Bulbous, Gold Handle & Trim, 5 In.	45.00
Blue, Spooner, Bird	16.00
Blue, Vase, Pedestal, Molded Flowers & Geometric Design, 8 In.	75.00
SLAG, CARAMEL, see Chocolate Glass	
Green, Chick & Egg, Easter, 7 In.	27.50
Pink, Cake Stand, Scalloped Edge, Top Design, 13 X 4 1/2 In.	100.00
Pink, Salt & Pepper, Inverted Fan & Feather, Original Tops	150.00
Pink, Toothpick, Inverted Fan & Feather	35.00
Pink, Tumbler	175.00
Purple, Bell, Hobnail, Fenton, 5 1/2 In.	10.00
Purple, Bowl, Footed, 4 1/2 X 3 3/4 In.	66.00
Purple, Bowl, Inverted Fan & Feather, Footed, 4 1/2 X 2 1/2 In.	325.00
Purple, Bowl, Pleated, 8 1/2 In.	80.00
Purple, Bowl, Stylized Ivys, Scalloped, Serrated Rim, Footed, 4 In.	70.00
Purple, Bowl, Threaded, 6 X 4 1/4 In.	65.00
Purple, Butter, Covered	10.50
Purple, Candlestick, Dolphin Heads	135.00
Purple, Celery, Pedestal Foot, Embossed Fleur-De-Lis, English, 7 3/4 In.	65.00
Purple, Chalice, Maple Leaf	55.00
Purple, Creamer, Fish, Open Mouth, Signed	85.00
Purple, Dish, Soap	30.00
Purple, Lamb On Nest, 5 X 5 In.	65.00
Purple, Match Holder, Dolphin Heads	65.00
Purple, Shoe, Baby	30.00
Purple, Slipper & Kitten, Hobnail	8.50
Purple, Spooner, Flower & Panel	65.00
Purple, Spooner, Scroll & Acanthus	45.00
Purple, Toothpick Holder, Fan Shaped	18.00
Purple, Tumbler, English Mark	30.00 To 33.00
Purple, Tumbler, Marked 1/2 Pint	38.00
Purple, Vase, Cluster Grape, Northwood, 1905	95.00
Purple, Vase, Ruffled & Fluted Rim, 11 In.	125.00
Purple, Vase, Serpent Handles, Footed, Covered, 7 1/2 In.	40.00
Red, Bowl, Fenton, C.1930, 8 1/2 In.	50.00
Red, Butter, Sawtooth Pattern, Covered	13.50
Red, Console Set, 3 Piece	225.00
Red, Console Set, 4 Piece	195.00
Red, Toothpick, Cherries	8.75

Sleepy Eye pottery was made to be given away with the flour products of the Sleepy Eye Milling Co., Sleepy Eye, Minnesota, from about 1893 to 1952. It is a heavy stoneware with blue decorations, usually the famous profile of an Indian.

SLEEPY EYE, Bowl, Salt, Blue On Gray Stoneware	265.00 To 325.00
Crock, Butter, Blue On Gray Stoneware	450.00 To 750.00
Label, Centennial, Barrelhead	35.00
Label, Chief Sleepy Eye	12.00
Mug, Blue On White, 4 1/2 In.	120.00 To 150.00
Mug, Blue On White, 4 3/4 In.	225.00
Mug, 1980 Cedar Rapids Convention	65.00
Pitcher, Blue On Cream, 1 Quart	250.00
Pitcher, Blue On White, Blue Lip, 1 Quart	250.00
Pitcher, Blue On White, Blue Rim, 1 Gallon	250.00
Pitcher, Blue On White, Blue Rim, 1 Pint	175.00
Pitcher, Blue On White, Set Of 5	750.00
Pitcher, Blue On White, 1/2 Gallon	185.00 To 325.00
Pitcher, 1/2 Pint	125.00 To 175.00

Sack, Flour, Black & White 200.00
Spoon, Indian Head, Silver Plate 75.00
Stein, Blue On Gray Stoneware 325.00
Stein, Brown, 8 1/2 In. 450.00
Stein, Tan & Brown 1500.00
Vase, Black On Yellow, 8 1/2 In. 560.00
Vase, Cattails & Dragonflies, Brown On White, 8 1/2 In. 200.00
Vase, Cattails & Indian, Blue On White, 8 1/2 In. 250.00
Vase, Indian Head, Blue On Gray Stoneware 225.00

Slip is a thin mixture of clay and water, about the consistency of sour cream, that is applied to the pottery for decoration.

SLIPWARE, Bowl, Mixing, Flared Sides, Wavy Line On Rim, Green Wash, 11 1/2 In. 130.00
Plate, Decorated, Deep, Crimped Rim, 19th Century, 9 3/4 In. 225.00
Plate, Molded Deep Body, Pie Crimped Edge, 19th Century, 8 In. 200.00
     SLOT MACHINE, see Coin-Operated Machine

Smith Bros. Co.

Smith Brothers glass was made after 1878. The owners had worked for the Mt. Washington Glass Company in New Bedford, Massachusetts, for seven years before going into their own shop.

SMITH BROTHERS, Bowl, Allover Gold Acorns, Satin Ground, Signed, 9 In. 320.00
Bowl, White Flower, Leaves, Gold Tracing, Marked, 9 In. 450.00
Bowl, White Flowers, Green Leaves, Marked, 9 In. 500.00
Cracker Jar, Barrel Shape, Multicolored Pansies, Signed, 7 In 295.00
Cracker Jar, Silver Lid, Enameled Flowers, Cream, 8 In. 225.00
Lamp, Heron & Cattails 220.00
Mustard, Winter Scene 55.00
Plate, Santa Maria, 6 1/2 In. 95.00
Salt, Cabin, Glossy 45.00
Salt, Lay Down, Columbia 1890, Souvenir 65.00
Salt, Lay-Down Egg 55.00
Salt, White, Melon Ribbed, Blossoms, Gold Beaded, Signed 125.00
Sugar & Creamer, Mt. Washington, Melon Ribbed, Jeweled, Lion 485.00
Sugar & Creamer, Pansy Design, Covered, Signed 135.00
Vase, Hand-Painted Chrysanthemums, White To Tan, 9 3/4 In. 165.00
Vase, Melon Ribbed, White, Floral, Autumn Colors, Marked, 2 In. 150.00

Snow Babies, made from bisque and spattered with glitter sand, were first manufactured in 1864 by Hertwig and Company in Thuringia. Other German and Japanese companies copied the Hertwig designs. Originally, Snow Babies were made of candy and used as Christmas decorations. There are also Snow Babies tablewares made by Royal Bayreuth.

SNOW BABIES, Box, 4 X 4 In. .... 135.00 To 150.00
Chocolate Pot, Demitasse .... 195.00 To 225.00
Creamer, Blue Mark 85.00
Doll, Seated, Pink Snowsuit, Jointed Arms, Windup, 5 3/4 In. 16.00
Figurine, Lying On Tummy, 1 1/4 In. 37.50
Figurine, Reclining, Outstretched Arms, 2 1/2 X 1 1/2 In. 55.00
Figurine, Sitting With Outstretched Hands, 1 3/4 In., Pair 47.50
Figurine, Sliding Down Wall, Double, Bisque 95.00
Figurine, 3 Blonde Girls, On Sled, Snowsuits, Bisque 245.00
Inkwell 95.00
Pitcher, Milk, Blue Mark 125.00
Plate 120.00
Plate, Girl & Dog, 6 1/4 In. 75.00
Sitting, 1 In. 35.00
     SNUFF BOTTLE, see Bottle, Snuff

SNUFFBOX, Bone, Hinged Lid, Oval, 19th Century 65.00
Hinged Cover, Brown Japanning, Oval, Tin, 2 1/2 X 1 In. 10.00

Musical, 3 Tune, Oriental Scene On Lid, 4 1/4 X 1 1/2 In.	225.00
Pine, Hand-Hewn, Rectangular, Slide Cover	40.00
W.E.Garrett & Sons, Scotch, Embossed Lid, Tin, 2 1/4 X 1 3/4 In.	4.00
Wooden, Leather Shoe, 4 1/2 In.	7170.00

Soapstone is a mineral that was used for foot warmers or griddles because of its heat-retaining properties. Soapstone was carved in many countries in the nineteenth and twentieth centuries.

SOAPSTONE, Bookend, Urn With Flowers, Fruits, Rust & Tan, 4 X 5 In., Pair	12.00
Figurine, Egret, Dark Brown, 3 1/2 In.	28.00
Figurine, Hound Dog, Lying Position	65.00
Figurine, Man, Holding A Vessel, Painted Eyes & Lips, 5 1/2 In.	40.00
Figurine, Manchurian Gentleman, Brown, 8 In.	89.00
Figurine, Rooster	9.00
Figurine, Stallion, Black, 6 X 5 In.	55.00
Foot Warmer, Wire Bail Handle, 11 Pounds, 6 X 9 In.	25.00
Incense Burner, Black, C.1860, 10 In.	275.00
Inkwell, Curved Shoulders, C.1790, Square, 1 3/4 X 1 1/2 In.	45.00
Inkwell, Marked R.S., 1 1/2 In.	30.00
Monkey, Group Of Three	12.00
Planter, Leaf Design, Pierced, 6 X 4 In.	24.00
Pot, Paint, Artist's, Large	35.00
Seal, Foo Dog, 6 1/4 In.	78.00
Toothpick, Monkeys	35.00
Vase, Brown, Flowers, Ivies, Fruit, 4 X 5 In.	22.00
Vase, Carved Florals, Red Tone, 6 In., Pair	80.00
Vase, Double, Flowers, Leaves, & Fruit, Brown, 4 X 5 In.	22.00
Vase, Figure Standing Under Tree, Cranes, Flowers, 3 In.	650.00
Warming Stone, New Hampshire, C.1860, 4 3/4 X 1 1/2 In.	12.50
4 Vases, Flowers, Leaves, 2 Squirrels, 6 X 7 In.	75.00

SOFT PASTE, Coffeepot, Matte Floral Design, Gold Trim, Handled	60.00
Compote, Covered, 8 In.	60.00
Cup & Saucer, Chariot With Driver, Pink, Demitasse	24.00
Plate, Polychrome Floral Border, The Serious Boy, 5 In.	135.00
Plate, Rose Design, Blue Flowers, Green Leaves, 10 1/4 In.	45.00
Teapot, Floral Design, 12 In.	450.00
Toby Mug, Colonial Gentleman Seated, Gray, Black, & Red, 5 In.	85.00

SOUVENIR, Cup & Saucer, Crown Ducal, New Orleans, Miniature, 2 1/2 In.	18.00
Cup, Custard Glass, Minnesota State Fair, 1902, Green	37.50
Fork, Sterling Silver, Washington, D.C., 6 In.	30.00
Goblet, Pittsburg Centennial	65.00
Mug, Bayette, Idaho, Custard Glass, 2 1/4 In.	20.00
Mug, Custard Glass, Baraboo, Wisc.	45.00
Mug, Dwight, Ill., Custard Glass, 2 1/2 In.	35.00
Mug, Salem, S.D., Custard Glass	25.00
Patchbox, Atlantic City, Ivory Ground, Rose Design, Footed, Germany	20.00
Pitcher, Marlboro, N.H., Custard Glass, Small	15.00
Plate, Longfellow House, Portland, Maine, 10 In.	1.25
Plate, Los Angeles, 1906, 6 In.	35.00
Plate, Mason, Los Angeles, May, 1906, 7 In.	17.50
Plate, Panama California Exposition, 1915, 9 In.	25.00
Salt & Pepper, Bullet Shape, Statue Of Liberty, 3 1/2 In.	4.50
Saltshaker, Milk Glass, Columbian Exposition 1893, Orange & Blue	40.00
Spoon, Niagara Falls, Canada, Enameled Maple Leaf, Brass, 4 1/8 In.	14.50
Spoon, Silver Plate, California, Wm.Rogers & Son	5.00
Spoon, Silver Plate, Canada, Figural Indian's Head, 4 3/4 In.	10.00
Spoon, Silver Plate, Chicago World's Fair, Dirigold	5.00
Spoon, Silver Plate, Chicago, 1934 World's Fair	7.00
Spoon, Silver Plate, Connecticut, Enameled Flag, 3 1/2 In.	10.00
Spoon, Silver Plate, Connecticut, Wm.Rogers & Son	5.00
Spoon, Silver Plate, Douglas Fairbanks	5.00

Spoon, Silver Plate, Elephant Head, Figural, Good Luck On Stem	15.00
Spoon, Silver Plate, Engraved Boston, Mass., Embossed Bean Pot	10.00
Spoon, Silver Plate, Fijui, Embossed Grass House, 4 1/4 In.	10.00
Spoon, Silver Plate, George Washington, 1889, Bust, Eagle Handle	12.50
Spoon, Silver Plate, Gloria Swanson	5.00
Spoon, Silver Plate, Grand Bahama, Figural Pirate & Ship	10.00
Spoon, Silver Plate, Hero Of Manila, Flagship Olympia, 4 1/4 In.	22.00
Spoon, Silver Plate, Illinois	5.00
Spoon, Silver Plate, Indiana, Map Shield, Flag, 4 1/4 In.	10.00
Spoon, Silver Plate, La Sagrada Familia Barcelona, Holland	10.00
Spoon, Silver Plate, Las Vegas, Enameled Crest, Dog, 5 1/2 In.	10.00
Spoon, Silver Plate, Mae Murray	5.00
Spoon, Silver Plate, Maine, Pine Tree, Enameled Shield, 4 1/4 In.	10.00
Spoon, Silver Plate, Maine, Wm.Rogers & Son	5.00
Spoon, Silver Plate, Mary Pickford	8.50
Spoon, Silver Plate, Maryland, Enameled Shield, Map, 3 1/4 In.	10.00
Spoon, Silver Plate, Massachusetts, Wm.Rogers & Son	5.00
Spoon, Silver Plate, Michigan, Mackinac Bridge, Enameled Shield	10.00
Spoon, Silver Plate, Mississippi, Enameled Shield, Paddle-Wheeler	10.00
Spoon, Silver Plate, New Hampshire, Granite State, Gold Seal	10.00
Spoon, Silver Plate, New Jersey, Wm.Rogers & Son	5.00
Spoon, Silver Plate, New York, Wm.Rogers	5.00
Spoon, Silver Plate, Niagara Falls, Enameled Crest, 4 1/4 In.	10.00
Spoon, Silver Plate, Oriental Man Holding World, Figural, 4 3/4 In.	10.00
Spoon, Silver Plate, Pennsylvania, Sword Over Felled Lion, 4 In.	10.00
Spoon, Silver Plate, Puss 'n Boots	12.00
Spoon, Silver Plate, Queen Victoria, 1837-97, Ship In Bowl	22.50
Spoon, Silver Plate, Ramon Navarro	5.00
Spoon, Silver Plate, Rhode Island, Shield & Rooster, 4 3/4 In.	10.00
Spoon, Silver Plate, St.Augustine, Enamel Orange, Newell	35.00
Spoon, Silver Plate, State Of New York, Wm.M.Rogers, 5 In.	3.00
Spoon, Silver Plate, U.S.Capitol, Washington, D.C., Shield, 3 3/8 In.	10.00
Spoon, Silver Plate, Vermont	9.50
Spoon, Silver Plate, Vermont, Wm.Rogers & Son	5.00
Spoon, Silver Plate, Victor Herbert, Demitasse	7.00
Spoon, Silver Plate, Virginia, Enameled State Seal, 4 1/2 In.	10.00
Spoon, Silver Plate, Wisconsin, Enameled Shield, Indian Profile	10.00
Spoon, Silver Plate, 1890 World's Fair	12.50
Spoon, Silver Plate, 1904, St.Louis, Jefferson, 4 1/2 In.	22.00
Spoon, Sterling Silver, Alaska Yukon Exposition, 1908	30.00
Spoon, Sterling Silver, Alvarado Hotel, Albuquerque, N.M.	22.00
Spoon, Sterling Silver, Arkansas Traveler	30.00
Spoon, Sterling Silver, Baltimore, Embossed Turtle & Oysters	37.00
Spoon, Sterling Silver, Bathhouse Row, Hot Springs	30.00
Spoon, Sterling Silver, Bear, Boulder, Colorado ....*Illus*	45.00
Spoon, Sterling Silver, Bear, San Francisco ....*Illus*	55.00
Spoon, Sterling Silver, Belize	24.00
Spoon, Sterling Silver, Berlin Brandenburgertor, Figural Gate	10.00
Spoon, Sterling Silver, Birth Record, 1907, Stork	15.00
Spoon, Sterling Silver, Bolivar, N.Y., Scene In Bowl, Initial	25.00
Spoon, Sterling Silver, Bridgehampton, 1856-1956, Bridge In Bowl	12.00
Spoon, Sterling Silver, Brooklyn Bridge, Scene, Scroll Stem	35.00
Spoon, Sterling Silver, Buffalo, N.Y., Open Flowered Handle	25.00
Spoon, Sterling Silver, Bunker Hill, Boston, Mass.	15.00
Spoon, Sterling Silver, California	20.00
Spoon, Sterling Silver, Carnegie Library, Pittsburgh, Pa.	22.00
Spoon, Sterling Silver, Cathedral, Panama	22.00
Spoon, Sterling Silver, Cedar Falls, Iowa	35.00
Spoon, Sterling Silver, Chicago Public Library	15.00
Spoon, Sterling Silver, Chicago Seal, Rushville Cutout	17.00
Spoon, Sterling Silver, Chicago World's Fair, 1933	9.00
Spoon, Sterling Silver, Chicago, Enameled Wolf's Point In Bowl	25.00
Spoon, Sterling Silver, Chicago, 1893 Exposition, Demitasse	22.50
Spoon, Sterling Silver, Chilton, Wisc., Name In Bowl, Roses Handle	25.00

Spoon, Sterling Silver, Chilton, Wisconsin, High School In Bowl 25.00
Spoon, Sterling Silver, Cincinnati, Full Figure, Demitasse 35.00
Spoon, Sterling Silver, Cincinnati, Ohio, Suspension Bridge 25.00
Spoon, Sterling Silver, Cleveland, Etched In Bowl, Initial B 20.00
Spoon, Sterling Silver, Cliff House, San Francisco 22.00
Spoon, Sterling Silver, Colorado, Cowboy Roping Steer Bowl 35.00
Spoon, Sterling Silver, Colorado, Miner On Front, Indian On Back 35.00
Spoon, Sterling Silver, Cornell University Library 15.00
Spoon, Sterling Silver, Cornwall, Engraved, 3 1/2 In. 16.50
Spoon, Sterling Silver, Corpus Christi, Texas 15.00
Spoon, Sterling Silver, Council Bluff, Engraved Bowl, Demitasse 20.00
Spoon, Sterling Silver, Denver Building In Bowl, Indian Chief 17.00
Spoon, Sterling Silver, Denver, Colorado, 1901 .... *Illus* 38.00
Spoon, Sterling Silver, Denver, Gold Wash Bowl, Demitasse 6.50
Spoon, Sterling Silver, Digby, Nova Scotia, Enameled Leaves 25.00
Spoon, Sterling Silver, Donkey, Tucson, Arizona .... *Illus* 20.00
Spoon, Sterling Silver, Ellsworth College, Flowers 26.00
Spoon, Sterling Silver, Escanaba, Michigan 15.00
Spoon, Sterling Silver, Fort George, Canada, Enameled Crest 9.50
Spoon, Sterling Silver, Fort Mackinac, Mackinac Island 15.00
Spoon, Sterling Silver, Fulton, Ill., High School In Bowl 35.00
Spoon, Sterling Silver, Galena, Ill., Openwork On Handle, Name 20.00
Spoon, Sterling Silver, Golden State, Scene In Bowl, Poppy Handle 25.00
Spoon, Sterling Silver, Grand Canyon, Arizona .... *Illus* 49.00
Spoon, Sterling Silver, Guilford, Ill., Printed In Bowl 20.00
Spoon, Sterling Silver, Hartford, Leaves, Acorns, & Heart At Top 37.00
Spoon, Sterling Silver, Helena, Mont., State Building, Emblem Handle 27.50
Spoon, Sterling Silver, Houston, Tx., Post Office, Courthouse 35.00
Spoon, Sterling Silver, Hudson, N.Y., New Courthouse In Bowl 25.00
Spoon, Sterling Silver, Indian Chief, Seattle 20.00
Spoon, Sterling Silver, Indian, Gardiner, Montana .... *Illus* 95.00
Spoon, Sterling Silver, Jackson, Wy., Cowboy On Handle 25.00
Spoon, Sterling Silver, Jeannette, Engraved In Bowl, Plain Handle 20.00
Spoon, Sterling Silver, Juneau, Alaska, Scene In Bowl .... *Illus* 40.00
Spoon, Sterling Silver, Kansas City, Cupid, 1889 .... 18.00
Spoon, Sterling Silver, Kansas, Former & State Seal 35.00
Spoon, Sterling Silver, Kearney Opera House, Picture In Bowl 21.00
Spoon, Sterling Silver, Knights Of Pythias Bldg., Indianapolis 22.00
Spoon, Sterling Silver, Las Vegas 12.00
Spoon, Sterling Silver, Lincoln, Nebraska 15.00
Spoon, Sterling Silver, Long Beach, Calif., Auditorium In Bowl 30.00
Spoon, Sterling Silver, Los Angeles In Bowl, 1896, Wallace 12.00
Spoon, Sterling Silver, Los Angeles, California 12.00
Spoon, Sterling Silver, Los Animas, Colorado 12.00
Spoon, Sterling Silver, Mackinac Island, Michigan 15.00
Spoon, Sterling Silver, Manitou, Colorado, Train 30.00
Spoon, Sterling Silver, Mendon, Missouri 15.00
Spoon, Sterling Silver, Mexico, Gaucho Playing Guitar, Sugar Shell 10.00
Spoon, Sterling Silver, Miami, Florida, Alligator 15.00
Spoon, Sterling Silver, Michigan, Medallion On Handle, 4 1/2 In. 15.00
Spoon, Sterling Silver, Milwaukee, Wisc., Group Of Buildings 25.00
Spoon, Sterling Silver, Miner, Fairbanks, Alaska .... *Illus* 100.00
Spoon, Sterling Silver, Minneapolis, Minn., Teamster On Handle 25.00
Spoon, Sterling Silver, Minnehaha Falls, Minneapolis, Minn. 15.00
Spoon, Sterling Silver, Minnesota 22.00
Spoon, Sterling Silver, Mobile, Alabama, Pienville Square 28.00
Spoon, Sterling Silver, Mt.Ranier 18.00
Spoon, Sterling Silver, Music Hall, Cincinnati, Ohio 22.00
Spoon, Sterling Silver, Nan, Engraved In Bowl, Dated 1911 .... 15.00
Spoon, Sterling Silver, National Park, Waterfall, Demitasse 10.00
Spoon, Sterling Silver, Neptune, Full Figure, Demitasse 50.00
Spoon, Sterling Silver, New Orleans, Nude Handle 45.00
Spoon, Sterling Silver, New York, Embossed Front & Back 28.00
Spoon, Sterling Silver, Niagara Falls, Canada, Made In Holland 10.00

Sterling Silver, Souvenir, Spoons, *from left to right:* Miner, Fairbanks, Alaska; Scene In Bowl, Juneau, Alaska; Grand Canyon, Arizona; Donkey, Tucson, Arizona; Bear, Boulder, Colorado; Portland Mine, Colorado; 1901, Denver, Colorado; Post Office, Oakland, California; Bear, San Francisco, California; Indian, Gardiner, Montana

Spoon, Sterling Silver, Niagara Falls, New York	15.00
Spoon, Sterling Silver, O.E.S.Lodge, Emblem Printed On Handle	20.00
Spoon, Sterling Silver, Oberammer Oalu, Theater Building, Austria	10.00
Spoon, Sterling Silver, Old Church, Jamestown, Va.	25.00
Spoon, Sterling Silver, Old Courthouse, Charleston, Ill.	15.00
Spoon, Sterling Silver, Old Kentucky Home, Louisville	22.00
Spoon, Sterling Silver, Oregon, Beaver State, Enameled Seal	14.50
Spoon, Sterling Silver, Pan Am, 1901	18.50
Spoon, Sterling Silver, Peoples Church, Head Of Man On Handle	35.00
Spoon, Sterling Silver, Pierce, S.Dak., State Capital, Indian	25.00
Spoon, Sterling Silver, Pikes Peak, Colo., Summit, Train & Track	25.00
Spoon, Sterling Silver, Pittsfield, Mass., Longfellow House	25.00
Spoon, Sterling Silver, Portland Mine, Colorado ....*Illus*	65.00
Spoon, Sterling Silver, Portland, Maine, Engraved In Bowl, 4 In.	12.50
Spoon, Sterling Silver, Portland, Or., Man's Head On Handle	25.00
Spoon, Sterling Silver, Post Office, Oakland, Calif. ....*Illus*	35.00
Spoon, Sterling Silver, Pratt, Kansas, Greer Eating House Bowl	25.00
Spoon, Sterling Silver, Prison, Waupun, Wisconsin	22.00
Spoon, Sterling Silver, Pugent Sound, Washington, Fish Handle	22.00
Spoon, Sterling Silver, Racine, Wisc., Etched In Bowl, Scrolls	20.00
Spoon, Sterling Silver, Randolph, Nebraska, Engraved In Bowl	15.00
Spoon, Sterling Silver, Riverfront, Detroit	15.00
Spoon, Sterling Silver, Rochester, N.Y., Enameled, Demitasse	35.00
Spoon, Sterling Silver, Rockies, Dubuque, Delta Kappa Gamme, 10 In.	20.00
Spoon, Sterling Silver, Salem Witch, House Of 7 Gables On Stem	45.00
Spoon, Sterling Silver, Salem Witch, Orange	150.00
Spoon, Sterling Silver, Salt Lake, Pavilion Building, Open Handle	25.00
Spoon, Sterling Silver, San Francisco	18.00
Spoon, Sterling Silver, San Gabriel Mission, California	22.00
Spoon, Sterling Silver, Santa Fe, Fort Pictured On Handle	25.00
Spoon, Sterling Silver, Santa Fe, New Mexico	15.00
Spoon, Sterling Silver, Saratoga, Florals On Shank	25.00
Spoon, Sterling Silver, Savanna, Ill., Engraved In Bowl, Emblem	25.00
Spoon, Sterling Silver, Scales Round, Etched In Bowl	20.00
Spoon, Sterling Silver, Seattle, Washington, Mt.Rainier On Handle	25.00
Spoon, Sterling Silver, Silverton, Colorado, 1874, Cabin & Mountain	35.00
Spoon, Sterling Silver, Sioux City, In Bowl, Flowered Handle	25.00
Spoon, Sterling Silver, Snoavalmie Falls, Picture In Bowl	21.00
Spoon, Sterling Silver, Soldiers & Sailors Monument, Indianapolis	22.00
Spoon, Sterling Silver, Spokane, Washington, Bridge In Bowl, Scroll	25.00
Spoon, Sterling Silver, Springfield, Mo., State Emblem, Demitasse	25.00
Spoon, Sterling Silver, St. Louis, Mo., Union Station In Bowl	25.00

Spoon, Sterling Silver, St.Louis, 1904, Cascade Garden Pictured 30.00
Spoon, Sterling Silver, St.Paul, Minn., Etched In Bowl 20.00
Spoon, Sterling Silver, State Capital, Columbus, Ohio 15.00
Spoon, Sterling Silver, Suffolk County Whaling Museum, Whale 10.00
Spoon, Sterling Silver, Summit Of Pike's Peak, Colorado 15.00
Spoon, Sterling Silver, Superior, Engraved In Bowl, Flowered Handle 20.00
Spoon, Sterling Silver, Temple, Salt Lake City, Picture In Bowl 21.00
Spoon, Sterling Silver, Thousand Island House, N.Y. 25.00
Spoon, Sterling Silver, Toronto, Colored Emblem, Demitasse 15.00
Spoon, Sterling Silver, U.S.N., Openwork Anchor Handle, Demitasse 15.00
Spoon, Sterling Silver, Victor, Colorado, 4 1/4 In. 35.00
Spoon, Sterling Silver, Victorian Rosary & Crucifix 20.00
Spoon, Sterling Silver, Wapello, Iowa 45.00
Spoon, Sterling Silver, Washington State, Rhododendron Handle 35.00
Spoon, Sterling Silver, Washington's Mansion, Mt.Vernon, Vt. 15.00
Spoon, Sterling Silver, Wisconsin, State Spoon, Emblem On Handle 25.00
Spoon, Sterling Silver, World's Fair, 1939, Empire State Building 20.00
Spoon, Sterling Silver, Wyoming, Shield Handle, Cowboy On Bronco 10.00
Spoon, Sterling Silver, Yellowstone Park, Cutout Pinecones 17.00
Toothpick, Benton Harbor, Michigan, Custard Glass, 2 1/2 In. 25.00
Toothpick, Colorado, Green & Gold 25.00
Toothpick, Compliments, A.N.Marks, Kansas City, Mo., Custard Glass 27.50
Tumbler, Crystal, N.D., Schoolhouse Scene, Custard Glass, 2 1/4 In. 35.00
Tumbler, Ferd Lukes, Protovin, Iowa, Green, Custard Glass, 3 1/2 In. 35.00
Tumbler, Ruby, Jacksonville, Florida, 1912 .... 24.00
Vase, Barton, N.D., Custard Glass 45.00
Vase, Dow City, Footed, Custard Glass, 6 In. 40.00
Vase, Pluto Springs, French Lick, In., Footed, Custard Glass, 6 In. 40.00
Wine, McIntosh, Minn., Custard Glass 60.00

Spangle glass is multicolored glass made from odds and ends of colored glass
rods. It includes metallic flakes of mica covered with gold, silver, nickel, or
copper. Spangle glass is usually cased with a thin layer of clear glass over
the multicolored layer.

SPANGLE GLASS, see also Vasa Murrhina
SPANGLE GLASS, Vase, Green, Art Nouveau Design, 12 In. 95.00

SPANISH AMERICAN WAR, Buckle, Belt, Brass 17.50
    Canteen 18.00
    Knapsack, Medical 20.00
    Newspaper, 1889, Uncle Sam Dressed As Soldier 22.50

Spanish lace is a Victorian glass pattern that seems to have white lace on
a colored background. Blue, yellow, cranberry, and clear glass was made with
this distinctive white pattern. It was made in England and the United
States after 1885.

SPANISH LACE, Bride's Basket, Blue Opalescent 40.00
    Finger Bowl, Vaseline 25.00
    Rose Bowl, Opalescent Yellow 40.00
    Rose Bowl, Yellow Opalescent, 4 In. 45.00
    Sugar Shaker, Cranberry Opalescent 135.00
    Tumbler, Opalescent Blue 32.00
    Vase, 6 X 4 In. 55.00
    Water Set, Cranberry Opalescent, 5 Piece 375.00

Spatter glass is a multicolored glass made from many small pieces of
different colored glass. It is sometimes called End-Of-Day glass.

SPATTER GLASS, Basket, Brown, Pink, Pinecone Mold, Thorn Handle, 8 In. 215.00
    Basket, Multicolored, Flower Design, Clear Handle 78.00

Berry Set, 8 Piece 115.00
Bottle, Cologne, Threaded, Stopper, 2 3/4 X 6 3/4 In. 110.00
Bowl, Multicolored, 6 In. 69.00
Candlestick, Ruffled Base, Green Aventurine, 5 1/4 In. 65.00
Carafe, Purple, Yellow, Twist Neck, Blown Stopper, 10 In. 40.00
Creamer, Leaves, Cranberry, Mica Flakes, Northwood 150.00
Decanter, 3 Applied Rings, Mushroom Stopper, Acorn Engraving 70.00
Jar, Crystal Shell Trim, White Lining, Maroon, 5 1/2 In. 75.00
Light Shade, 6 1/2 In. 30.00
Light Shade, 8 In. 35.00
Pitcher, Inverted Thumbprint, Clear Handle, Maroon, 8 In. 110.00
Pitcher, Inverted Thumbrpint, C.1885, Vaseline, 6 1/4 In. 89.50
Pitcher, Ruffled, White Lining, Handle, 7 In. 68.00
Pitcher, Tricornered, Clear Handle, Polished Pontil, 8 In. 125.00
Ring Tree, Scroll Design, Yellow, 2 1/4 X 2 1/4 In. 35.00
Rose Bowl, Crimped Rim, Pink & White, 5 In. 30.00
Salt, Crystal Loop Feet, Green Aventurine, 2 1/4 In. 45.00
Saltshaker, Swirl, Ruby & White 30.00
Shoe, Crystal Rigaree & Leaf Applied, White Lining, 5 1/4 In. 60.00
Sugar Shaker, Cranberry 65.00
Sugar Shaker, Leaves, Cranberry, Mica Flakes 110.00
Sugar Shaker, Ribbed Pillar, Cranberry 85.00
Tumbler, Inverted Thumprint, Pink & White, Set Of 4 .... 60.00
Tumbler, Red To Opaque, 4 In. 15.00
Vase, Green, Pink, 6 X 4 In. 69.00
Vase, Jack-In-The-Pulpit, Ruffled, Green, 5 1/4 In. 65.00
Vase, New England, 3 Rings At Neck, 11 In. 225.00
Vase, Opaque, Clear Handles And Neck, 4 1/2 In. 10.00
Vase, Rigaree Trim, Clear Hobnail Outside, 9 In. 85.00
Wine, Inverted Thumbprint, Green, 4 3/4 In. 45.00

Spatterware is a creamware or soft-paste dinnerware decorated with spatter designs. The earliest pieces were made during the late eighteenth century, but most of the wares found today were made from 1800 to 1850. Spatterware dishes were made in the Staffordshire district of England for sale in America.

SPATTERWARE, see also Spongeware
SPATTERWARE, Bowl, Dark Blue, Reddish-Brown On Gray Ground, 4 1/4 In. 59.00
Bowl, General Store, West Union, Iowa, Red, Blue, & Cream, 7 In. 55.00
Bowl, Mixing, White Glaze, Blue, Tan, 7 5/8 In. 32.50
Bowl, Vegetable, Blue & Brown, Oval, 9 X 7 In. 75.00
Cup & Saucer, Blue & White, Large Coffee 75.00
Cup & Saucer, Handleless, Red & Green 65.00
Cup Plate, Peafowl, Red Rim, Red Feathers, Blue Body, 4 1/4 In. 250.00
Jar, Beater, Blue 75.00
Jug, Milk, Platter, Rainbow, C.1840, Marked 880.00
Jug, Peafowl, C.1840, 8 In. 357.00
Pitcher & Bowl, Open Rose 1895.00
Pitcher, Octagonal, Blue, 12 In. 375.00
Plate, Bull's-Eye Pattern, Red & White, 10 1/2 In. 165.00
Plate, Peafowl, C.1840, 7 1/4 In., Pair 385.00
Platter, Castle, C.1840, Marked, 15 1/2 In. 1100.00
Sugar & Creamer, Covered 110.00
Tea Set, Child's, Peafowl, 14 Piece 800.00
Teabowl & Saucer, Rooster, C.1840, Marked, PR 825.00
Teabowl & Saucer, Schoolhouse, C.1840, Pair 770.00
Teabowl & Saucer, Star, C.1840, Marked, PR 385.00

Spelter is a synonym for a zinc alloy. Figurines, candlesticks, and other pieces were made of spelter and given a bronze or painted finish.

SPELTER, Figurine, Seated Boy With Thorn, Bronzed Finish, 8 In. 65.00
Urn, Art Nouveau Handles, Bronzed Finish, 8 In. 55.00

Spode pottery, porcelain, and bone china were made by the Stoke-on-Trent factory of England founded by Josiah Spode about 1770. The firm became Copeland and Garrett from 1833 to 1847, then W.T.Copeland or W.T.Copeland and Sons until 1976. It then became Royal Worcester Spode. The word "Spode" appears on many pieces made by the Copeland factory. Most collectors include all the wares under the more familiar name of Spode.

SPODE, see also Copeland

SPODE, Bridal Rose, 6 In.	6.00
Butter, Wickerdale	8.00
Coffeepot, Royal Windsor Pattern, White With Green	95.00
Cup & Saucer, Bridal Rose	18.00
Cup & Saucer, Buttercup, Demitasse	16.00
Cup & Saucer, Cowslip, Demitasse	20.00
Cup & Saucer, Fairy Dell, Demitasse	16.00
Cup & Saucer, Patrician, Green	7.50
Cup & Saucer, Stylized Oriental Birds & Dragons, Crossed Swords	40.00
Cup & Saucer, Wickerdale	22.00
Cup & Saucer, Wickerdale, Demitasse	16.00
Demitasse Pot, Blue Tower	75.00
Paperweight, Owl & Cat, Signed	45.00
Plate, Bridal Rose, 6 In.	8.00
Plate, Bridal Rose, 7 In.	12.00
Plate, Chelsea Garden, 9 In.	29.00
Plate, Exotic Bird Center, Green Border, 8 In.	40.00
Plate, Service, Jared Coffin House, Nantucket Island	250.00
Plate, Wickerdale, 7 3/4 In.	17.00
Plate, Wickerdale, 9 In.	22.00
Soup, Flat, Bridal Rose	20.00
Sugar & Creamer, Romney	45.00
Teapot, Covered, Bridal Rose	55.00
Vegetable, Oval, Wickerdale	35.00

Spongeware is very similar to spatterware in appearance. The designs were applied to the ware by daubing the color. Many dealers do not differentiate between the two wares and use the names interchangeably.

SPONGEWARE, Beanpot, Blue & White	250.00
Bowl, Bail & Cover, 10 1/2 In.	80.00
Bowl, Batter, Bail Handle, Blue & White, 6 In.Diam.	250.00
Bowl, Batter, Blue & White, 9 In.Diam.	250.00
Bowl, Blue Mottling Over Cream, 9 1/4 X 3 1/4 In.	135.00
Bowl, Blue On Yellow, 11 X 3 1/2 In.	80.00
Bowl, Brown & Yellow, 12 In.	32.00
Bowl, Green, Brown, & Off-White, 9 In.	35.00
Bowl, Mixing, Blue, 11 1/2 In.	95.00
Bowl, Mixing, Brown & Yellow, Concentric Lines Rim, 9 In.	60.00
Bowl, Mixing, Rust, Blue, 8 In.	48.00
Bowl, Oval, Brown & Yellow, 11 In.	70.00
Bowl, Vertical Ribbed Sides, 9 In.	55.00
Bowl, West Union, Iowa, 7 1/2 In.	45.00
Butter Crock, Blue-Gray, Handled	75.00
Butter Crock, Green, Yellow, Brown, Ribbed, Covered, 4 1/2 In.	50.00
Butter Crock, Wild Flower	125.00
Butter, Covered, Blue	40.00
Canister, Desert Scene, Camel & Rider, Blue	65.00
Casserole, Covered, Blue & Rust	56.00
Chamber Pot, Blue, 4 3/4 X 9 1/4 In.	125.00
Chop Plate, Blue & White, 10 1/4 In.	150.00
Cooler, Water, Birch Leaves, Churn Type, Covered	270.00
Cooler, Water, Blue & White, 2 Gallon	495.00
Cooler, Water, Wing, Covered, 5 Gallon	275.00
Creamer, Cobalt On Cream, Grape Sprays Body, 3 In.	45.00
Cup & Saucer	125.00

Cup & Saucer, Handleless, Red Flowers, Blue Sponged Florets 35.00
Cup, Custard, C.1870, Blue, Set Of 6 .... 310.00
Cup, Wine, Blue, French Saying In Bottom 24.00
Cuspidor, Blue & White, 7 1/2 X 5 In. 90.00
Custard, Brown On Yellow 9.00
Dish, Soap, Blue & White .... 80.00 To 195.00
Ice Bucket, Lid & Bail, Blue & White 210.00
Jardiniere, Blue & White, 7 In. 80.00
Jug, Blue & Cream, 1 Gallon 95.00
Jug, Blue & Gray, Grandmother's Maple Syrup, Embossed 325.00
Jug, Green, Blue, & Cream, 1 Gallon 225.00
Jug, Pink, 3 1/2 In. 22.00
Pitcher & Basin, Buff Ground, Green & Brown Bands, 7 In. 410.00
Pitcher & Bowl, Blue & White 495.00
Pitcher, Blue & Rust, 9 1/4 In. 85.00
Pitcher, Blue & White, 8 3/4 In. 80.00
Pitcher, Blue On White, Embossed Leaf, 5 In. 75.00
Pitcher, Blue, Brown, Floral Embossed Design, 9 1/4 In. 65.00
Pitcher, Blue, White, 9 In 135.00
Pitcher, Brown & Yellow, Bulbous, 7 In. 60.00
Pitcher, Central Food Market, 6 In. 32.00
Pitcher, Columbia, Lady With Shield, 9 In. 450.00
Pitcher, Cosmos, 9 In. 235.00
Pitcher, Cream & Green, 9 In. 95.00
Pitcher, Diamond Design, Blue & White, 9 In. 135.00
Pitcher, First Convention, Blue & White, 9 In. 65.00
Pitcher, Fish, 9 In. 500.00
Pitcher, Good Luck, 6 1/2 In. 35.00
Pitcher, Green & Yellow, 6 In. 45.00
Pitcher, Green, Avenue Of Trees, 6 In. 50.00
Pitcher, Rust & Blue, 7 3/4 In. 65.00
Pitcher, Solid Rim, 9 In. 210.00
Pitcher, Spatter, Blue & White, Blue Embossed Design, 9 In. 85.00
Pitcher, Spatter, Green & White, Blue Rim & Base, 6 1/2 In. 45.00
Pitcher, Water, Signed Burford Bros., Blue & White, 9 In. 195.00
Planter, Hanging, Blue & White 225.00
Plate, Blue & Green, 6 1/4 In. 28.00
Roaster, Meat, Covered 275.00
Spittoon, Blue & White, 8 In.Diam. .... 70.00 To 165.00
Spittoon, Blue, 8 In. 75.00
Spittoon, Corset Waisted, Blue & White, 4 1/4 X 4 3/4 In. 135.00
Spittoon, Earthworm Pattern, Blue & White, Blue Band 80.00
Spittoon, Green & White 65.00
Sugar, Covered, Blue & Yellow 85.00
Umbrella Stand 400.00

ST.LOUIS, Bottle, Scent, Bust Of Napoleon, Sulfide, Signed, C.1830, 3 1/4 In. 450.00
Bottle, Scent, Sulfide, Bust Of William Of Orange, Signed, 3 1/4 In. 425.00
Decanter, Cranberry Overlay, Diamond Cut, Signed, 11 In. 475.00
Decanter, Paperweight, Signed, 10 In., Pair 495.00
Vase, Acid Cut Florals, Green Ground, Marked, Light Green, 12 In. 225.00

> *Staffordshire is a district in England where pottery and porcelain have been made since the 1700s. Thousands of types of pottery and porcelain have been made in the hundreds of factories that worked in the area. Some of the most famous factories have been listed separately. See Royal Doulton; Royal Worcester; Spode; Wedgwood; and others.*

STAFFORDSHIRE, see also Flow Blue; Mulberry
STAFFORDSHIRE, Bowl, Light Blue Design, English Countryside, 5 1/4 In. 95.00
Bowl, Scenes Of The Dove, Mulberry Edge, 1802-28, 6 1/2 In. 75.00
Box, Cherry Tooth Paste, Patronized By Queen, 4 In. 35.00
Breakfast Set, Chicken, Eggcups Inside, 7 In., 2 Piece 595.00
Bust, Alexander I Of Russia, C.1800, 10 3/4 In. .... *Illus* 260.00

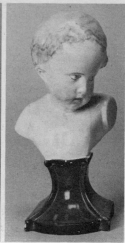

Staffordshire, Bust, Alexander I Of Russia, C.1800, 10 3/4 In.

(See Page 651)

Staffordshire, Bust, Napoleon, C.1810, 10 1/4 In.

Staffordshire, Bust, Young Boy, Enoch Wood, C.1790, 9 1/4 In.

Bust, Napoleon, C.1810, 10 1/4 In.	*Illus*	240.00
Bust, Young Boy, Enoch Wood, C.1790, 9 1/4 In.	*Illus*	220.00
Charger, Lobed Rice Molded Rim, 1750-60, 17 In.		165.00
Coffeepot, Bosphorus Pattern, C.1850, Jamieson & Co.		85.00
Coffeepot, Lafayette At The Tomb Of Franklin, Marked, 11 In.		1210.00
Creamer, Cow, Brown, Black, Seated Figure, C.1820, 6 In.		412.00
Creamer, Cow, Ocher & Brown, Green Base, Marked, 5 1/4 In.		1075.00
Creamer, Cow, 7 1/2 In.		137.00
Cup & Saucer, Garden Scenery, Pink, Handleless		24.00
Cup & Saucer, Garlands Of Pink Roses, Handled		25.00
Cup & Saucer, Garlands Of Pink Roses, Handleless		22.50
Cup & Saucer, Girl & Animals, Marked, Brown Tones		35.00
Cup & Saucer, Handleless, Floral		22.00
Cup & Saucer, Handleless, Floral, Green		25.00
Cup & Saucer, Handleless, Isola Belle, Blue, 4 Sets		110.00
Cup & Saucer, Handleless, Seasons, Pink		45.00
Cup & Saucer, Handleless, Sower, Pink		45.00
Cup & Saucer, New Orleans, Black		85.00
Cup & Saucer, Old Britain Castles, Pink & White, 1792		28.00
Cup Plate, Asiatic Planter, Green		35.00
Cup Plate, Corinth, Light Blue		28.00
Dish, Floral Basket Design, Underglaze Blue, Marked, 5 In.		115.00
Dish, Fruit, Garlands Of Husks, C.1790, 7 In., Pair		350.00
Dish, Hen Cover, Bisque Top, Basket Weave Base, 7 1/2 In.		495.00
Dish, Hen Cover, Bisque Top, Green Base, 9 1/2 X 8 1/4 In.		295.00
Dish, Hen On Nest Cover, Terra-Cotta Basket Weave Base, 7 In.		200.00
Dish, Sheltered Peasants, Rectangular, 9 X 12 In.		165.00
Dish, Soup, Harpers Ferry, Light Blue, 9 In.		80.00
Dish, Soup, Suspension Bridge, Wood, 10 1/4 In.		32.00
Figurine, Actor, Costume, Resting By Tree, 7 1/2 In.		90.00
Figurine, Actor, Liston As Sam Swipes, C.1824, 6 In.		95.00
Figurine, Amelia Bloomer, C.1851, 8 In.		30.00
Figurine, British Lion & Napoleon III, Pair	*Illus*	180.00
Figurine, Dog, Black & White, 5 In.		45.00

Figurine, Dog, Dalmatian, Sits, Blue Base, 6 In. 120.00
Figurine, Dog, Luster Highlights, White, 13 1/2 In. 175.00
Figurine, Dog, Mid-19th Century, 9 1/2 In., Pair .... *Illus* 380.00
Figurine, Dog, Pointer, Black, White, Grassy Mound, Marked, 3 In. 450.00
Figurine, Dog, Whippet, Seated Near Tree, Signed, 8 In. 75.00
Figurine, Dog, White, Black Trim, 4 In., Pair 99.50
Figurine, Eagle On Rock, Flexing Wings, 7 1/2 In., Pair 200.00
Figurine, Elijah & Raven, C.1830 .... 750.00
Figurine, Girl & Lamb, 6 X 5 In. 79.00
Figurine, Girl, Seated On Stump, Dog, 6 1/2 In. 70.00
Figurine, Girl, Seated, Holding Puppy, Yellow, Red, Black, 3 In. 60.00
Figurine, Girl, Seated, Holds Basket Of Fruit, 3 3/4 In. 50.00
Figurine, Girl, Wearing Long Robe, Large Doll, 4 In. 50.00
Figurine, Goat, Brown, White, Oval Green Base, 2 In. 23.00
Figurine, Goat, Shaggy Coat, Gray, Rocky Mound, Marked, 8 In. 950.00
Figurine, Grecian & Daughter, C.1830 .... 1450.00
Figurine, Highlander, Gun, Pointer, Flatback, 15 In. 130.00
Figurine, Horse, Red-Brown Coat, Black Highlight, 8 In. 165.00
Figurine, Jules Perrot & Wife, Polychrome Colors, 7 5/8 In. 90.00
Figurine, Lion, Paw On Ball, Black Mane, Red Tongue, 5 In. 1760.00
Figurine, Lions, Couchant, Fawn & Ocher, Marked, 4 3/4 In., Pr. 1350.00
Figurine, Lord Wolsley On Horseback, 14 In. 85.00
Figurine, Maid, Holding Bouquet, Creamware, Marked, 4 1/4 In. 500.00
Figurine, Man & Woman Seated, Reads Book, Plays Violin, 4 In. 100.00
Figurine, Man, Holding Flask, Blue-Green, 4 3/4 In. 100.00
Figurine, Parson & Clerk, C.1790 .... 850.00
Figurine, Poodles, Seated, 4 1/2 In., Pair 125.00
Figurine, Prince Of Wales, Prince Alfred, 10 In., Pair 200.00
Figurine, Pug, Curled Tail, Fawn, Black Muzzle, 3 1/2 In. 450.00
Figurine, Queen Victoria & Prince Albert, Pair .... *Illus* 240.00
Figurine, Ram, Standing On Grassy Knoll, Lamb, 7 3/4 In. 85.00
Figurine, Sankey & Moody, C.1873, Pair 850.00
Figurine, Sleeping Beauty, 2 3/4 In. 20.00
Figurine, Spaniel, Seated, Gold Luster Spots 110.00
Figurine, The Hunter, C.1860 .... 265.00
Figurine, The Poacher, 13 In. 175.00
Figurine, Tithe Pig Group, Farmer, Wife, Marked, 7 In. 1800.00
Figurine, Vase, 2 Figures Against Tree Trunk, Polychrome 35.00
Figurine, Victoria, Multicolored, C.1900, 11 1/2 In. 110.00
Figurine, Woman With Lamb, 7 1/2 In. 75.00
Figurine, Zebra, C.1865, Pair 350.00
Figurine, 2 Hunters, Bows, Deer, Clock, 9 1/2 In. 45.00
Footbath, Blue & White, Loop Handle, Landscape, 10 1/4 In. 278.00
Holder, Posy, Figural, 2 Seated Poodles, Marked 30.00
Holder, Quill, Figural, Woman 45.00
Inkwell, Pear, Flower Stopper, 3 In. 55.00

Staffordshire, Figurines, British Lion & Napoleon III, Pair; Dog, Mid-19th Century, 9 1/2 In., Pair

Jar, Cracker, Bamboo Handle, Homeland Series, Africa, Signed 37.50
Jug, Commemorative, Bust Of Lafayette, Cornwallis, 4 In. 195.00
Jug, Commemorative, General Jackson, Yellow & Copper, 7 In. 825.00
Jug, Earthenware, C.1815, Red, Green, Brown, 5 In. 495.00
Jug, Yellow Ground, Copper Luster, Printed Design, 7 In. 40.00
Ladle, Sauce, Medium Blue Design, Building, 6 1/2 In. 105.00
Match Holder, Full-Bodied Chicken & Fox, Pedestal 75.00
Mug, Black Transfer Cornucopia With Tan Luster, 3 In. 50.00
Mug, Child's, George Black Transfer, Floral & Geometric 65.00
Mug, Child's, Green & White 45.00
Mug, Child's, This Is The House That Jack Built, Creamware 65.00
Mug, Child's, Whaling Scene Transfer, Blue & White 55.00
Mug, Pink Luster, House, Trees, Pond, Cattle, Quart 68.00
Pitcher, Water, Wilkes-Barre, Vale Of Wyoming, Blue 185.00
Pitcher, Wild Rose Design, 10 In. 175.00
Plate, Adelaids's Bower, C.1840, 10 1/2 In. 35.00
Plate, America & Independence, 15 States Border 275.00
Plate, Archery, Blue, 6 In. 15.00
Plate, Aurora Pattern, Purple, 7 1/5 In. 18.00
Plate, Black, Swiss, 9 1/4 In. 18.00
Plate, Boston Hospital, Stevenson, Dark Blue, 9 In. 365.00
Plate, Brown Border, Purple Center, 8 1/2 In. 28.00
Plate, Brown Willow, 8 1/2 In. 18.00
Plate, City Hall, Lowell, Ma., Marked, 10 In. 20.00
Plate, Clews, Landing Of Lafayette, Blue & White, 10 In. 350.00
Plate, Columbia University, Blue & White, 9 3/4 In. 9.50
Plate, Commemorative, Hoover Dam, 10 In. 25.00
Plate, Commodore McDonough's Victory, Wood, Blue, 7 1/2 In. 165.00
Plate, Commodore McDonough's Victory, Wood, 6 1/2 In. 285.00
Plate, Corinthia Pattern, Cast Le Scene, Pink, 8 1/2 In. 28.00
Plate, Crusaders, Blue & White, Marked, 10 In. 28.00
Plate, Faneuil Hall, Boston, From The Harbor, Marked, 10 In. 25.00
Plate, Fishermans Island, Lago Maggiore, 9 1/4 In. 45.00
Plate, For To Fish He Doth Incline, 5 1/4 In. 85.00
Plate, Franklin Flying Kite, 2 1/2 In. 70.00
Plate, Fruits & Flowers, Dark Blue, 8 In., Set Of 6 .... 225.00
Plate, Hanover Lodge, Regent's Park, 9 1/4 In. 40.00

Staffordshire, Figurine, Queen
Victoria & Prince Albert, Pair

(See Page 653)

Plate, Harry Baiting Is His Line, 5 1/4 In.	85.00
Plate, Hartford, Connecticut, Black, 10 In.	90.00
Plate, Hartford, Connecticut, Pink, 10 In.	90.00
Plate, Home Of Washington, Mt. Vernon, Marked, 10 In.	20.00
Plate, Ivanhoe Pattern, Blue & White, 7 3/4 In.	12.00
Plate, Lake George, Light Blue, 7 3/4 In.	65.00
Plate, Landing Of The Pilgrims, British Anchor, 10 In.	25.00
Plate, Lewis & Clark Expo, Rolled Edge, 1905, 10 In.	90.00
Plate, Marine Hospital, Ky., Blue, 8 1/2 In.	350.00
Plate, Millennium, Black, 10 1/4 In.	54.00
Plate, Pine Orchard House, Catskills, Wood, Blue, 10 In.	275.00
Plate, Pomerania, Lavender, 10 1/4 In.	26.00
Plate, Promenade A Quatre-Walking, 5 1/4 In.	85.00
Plate, States, Blue, 8 In., Pair	700.00
Plate, Temple, Elephant With Howdha, Blue & White, 6 5/8 In.	40.00
Plate, Temple, Elephant, People, Blue & White, 6 5/8 In.	45.00
Plate, Texas Campaign, Green, 7 1/2 In.	38.00
Plate, The Baltimore & Ohio Railroad, 9 1/4 In.	375.00
Plate, The Boston Massacre, 1770, 10 In.	20.00
Plate, Tuscan Rose, C.1820, 9 In.	10.00
Plate, Union Line Steamship, Blue, 9 1/2 In.	350.00
Plate, View From Ruggles House, Hudson River, 10 In.	80.00
Plate, View Of Upper Ferry Bridge Over Schuylkill, 8 3/4 In.	300.00
Plate, Vue De Chateau, Ermonoville, Incised Wood, 10 In.	95.00
Plate, Washington Crossing The Delaware, 1776, Marked, 10 In.	30.00
Plate, Washington's Prayer At Valley Forge, 1777, 10 In.	30.00
Plate, Wild Rose, Blue & White, 9 In.	22.00
Plate, William Penn's Treaty With The Indians, 10 In.	20.00
Plate, 5 Branch Fruit, Diaper Scalloped, C.1750, 9 In.	385.00
Platter, American Marine, Brown, Marked, 15 In.	42.00
Platter, Chinese Jar, T.Green, Royal Blue, 8-Sided, 20 X 16 In.	65.00
Platter, Country Scenes, Wood & Son, 9 X 11 In.	75.00
Platter, Dr. Syntax, C.1828, Dark Blue Border, Marked, 11 In.	220.00
Platter, Dublin, Custonhouse, Well-N-Tree, 15 X 19 In.	700.00
Platter, Erith On Thames, Shell Border, Wood, 13 In.	450.00
Platter, Falls Of Niagara, Pink, 20 In.	425.00
Platter, Fruits On Table, Birds, Dark Blue, 11 In.	150.00
Platter, Highbury Cottage, London, Adams, 9 X 1 11 1/2 In.	225.00
Platter, Isola Belle, Light Blue, 20 In.	95.00
Platter, Limehouse Dock, London, Dark Blue, 14 3/4 In.	295.00
Platter, Newburgh, Black, 16 In.	265.00
Platter, Oriental Scenery, J.Hall & Sons, 14 1/2 X 11 1/2 In.	115.00
Platter, St.George Chapel, Dark Blue, 15 In.	295.00
Platter, Well & Tree, C.1830, Maritime Scene, 16 In.	200.00
Platter, Wilkes-Barre, Vale Of Wyoming, 8 X 11 In.	175.00
Pot, Pepper, White, Brown Design, Flowers, Leaves, 4 1/2 In.	65.00
Salt & Pepper, Toby Men, Red, Blue, & Yellow	125.00
Saltshaker, Figural, Bobby, 6 In.	118.00
Sugar & Creamer, Buff-Colored Leaves	24.00
Sugar, Scenic, C.1840, Dark Blue	95.00
Sugar, Spring Design, 5 1/4 In.	25.00
Sugar, Washington Scroll In Hand, Wood, Covered	450.00
Tea Set, Child's, Brown Transfer Child & Cats, 17 Piece	45.00
Tea Set, Child's, Brown, Flowers, 6 Cups & Saucers	175.00
Teapot, Gold Castle On Lid & Sides, Gold Spout & Handle	35.00
Teapot, Lavender Transfer Of Lady, Child, & Dog, 9 1/2 In.	135.00
Teapot, Palestine, Purple	135.00

STAFFORDSHIRE, TOBY JUG, see Toby Jug

Toby Pitcher, Spaniel, 10 In.	90.00
Toothpick, Figural, Kate Greenaway	45.00
Tub, Foot, Brown Design, Fisherman & Harbor, 8 In.	100.00
Tureen, Soup, Child's, Cover, Underplate, & Ladle, 6 Soups	130.00
Vase, Blue & White Portrait, Landscape Scene, C.1870, 12 In.	125.00
Vase, Flair, 6 X 6 In.	60.00

Vase, Japan Pattern, Blue, Red, Green, Copper, 16 In., Pair 2860.00
Vase, Stump, Crane With Frog, 5 1/2 In. 15.00

The Stangl Pottery was organized in 1929, succeeding the Fulper Pottery Company. Stangl porcelain birds are popular collectibles.

STANGL, Ashtray, Duck In Flight, Gray, 11 X 8 In. 15.00
Ashtray, Hand-Painted, Black & Gold 5.00
Ashtray, Mallard, Silver Deposit Trim, 6 In. 15.00
Ashtray, Mallard, Silver Deposit Trim, 8 In. 20.00
Bird, Allen Hummingbird, No.3634 .... 45.00 To 50.00
Bird, Bird Of Paradise, No.3408 .... 60.00 To 95.00
Bird, Black-Throated Warbler, No.3814 .... 42.00
Bird, Blue Jay With Peanut, No.3715 .... 345.00
Bird, Blue-Headed Virec, No.3448 .... 48.00
Bird, Bluebird, No.3276S .... 48.00 To 55.00
Bird, Bluebirds, No.3276D 125.00
Bird, Brewer's Blackbird, No.3591 .... 60.00
Bird, Broadtail Hummingbird, No.3626 .... 70.00
Bird, Brown-Backed Chickadees, No.3581, Marked 165.00
Bird, Canary, No.3746 .... 52.50
Bird, Canary, No.3747 .... 52.50
Bird, Cardinal, Gray, No.3596 .... 42.00
Bird, Cardinal, No.3444, Dark Pink .... 38.00 To 65.00
Bird, Cerulean Warbler, No.3456 .... 43.00
Bird, Chickadees, Group, No.3581 .... 130.00
Bird, Cockatoo, No.3405D, 10 1/2 In. 55.00
Bird, Cockatoo, No.3405S .... 39.00 To 55.00
Bird, Cockatoo, No.3580, Medium, Marked 135.00
Bird, Cockatoo, No.3580, 9 In. 60.00
Bird, Cockatoo, No.3584, 6 In. 48.00
Bird, Cockatoo, Signed Jacobs, 11 3/4 In. .... 190.00 To 225.00
Bird, Cockatoo, 3580, 9 In. 60.00
Bird, Cockatoos, No.3405D, Deep Pink .... 70.00 To 75.00
Bird, Evening Grosbeak, No.3813, Marked 120.00
Bird, Flying Duck, No.3443, 11 X 9 In., Pair .... 275.00 To 350.00
Bird, Hummingbirds, No.3599D, 10 1/2 X 8 In. .... 220.00 To 240.00
Bird, Indigo Bunting, No.3589 .... 38.00 To 55.00
Bird, Kentucky Warbler, No.3598 .... 39.00 To 55.00
Bird, Key West Quail, No.3454 .... 275.00 To 250.00
Bird, Kingfisher, No.3406 .... 48.00
Bird, Kingfisher, No.3406D 135.00
Bird, Lovebird, No.3400 .... 45.00 To 65.00
Bird, Nuthatch, No.3593 .... 45.00
Bird, Oriole, No.3402S .... 42.00 To 50.00
Bird, Orioles, No.3402D, 5 1/2 In. .... 85.00 To 95.00
Bird, Owl, No.3407 .... 55.00
Bird, Painted Bunting, No.3452, Marked 95.00
Bird, Paradise, No.3408 .... 56.50
Bird, Parakeet, No.3582D, Blue 120.00
Bird, Parakeet, No.3582D, Green 120.00
Bird, Parrot, Eating Worm, No.3449 .... 110.00 To 135.00
Bird, Parula Warbler, No.3583 .... 38.00 To 55.00
Bird, Red-Breasted Nuthatch, No.3851 .... 36.50
Bird, Redstarts, No.3490D .... 120.00 To 165.00
Bird, Rieffers Hummingbird, No.3628 .... 125.00
Bird, Rivoli Hummingbird, No.3627 .... 125.00
Bird, Rufous Hummingbird, No.3585 .... 45.00 To 50.00
Bird, Titmouse, No.3592 .... 45.00
Bird, Warbler, No.3447, Signed E.M.F. 25.00
Bird, Wilson Warbler, No.3597, 4 X 3 In. .... 35.00 To 40.00
Bird, Wren, No.3401 .... 38.00 To 45.00
Bird, Wren, No.3401D, Marked 95.00

Bird, Wrens, No.3401D .... 65.00 To 70.00
Bird, Wrens, On Branch, No.3581, 3 Birds 35.00
Bird, Yellow Warbler, No.3400 .... 55.00
Bird, Yellow Warbler, No.3447 .... 50.00
Bowl, Terra Rose, Blue, 4 In. 10.00
Bowl, Tropical Ware, No.2028 .... 25.00
Box, Cigarette, Flying Mallard, Silver Deposit, Covered, 5 1/2 In. 20.00
Candleholder, White Calla Lily, Blue Leaf, 6 In., Pair 16.00
Creamer, Thistle, White Outside, Brown Inside, 2 1/2 In. 5.00
Cup, Golden Harvest 3.00
Dish, Caribbean, 3-Section 15.00
Figurine, Dog 150.00
Figurine, Mother & 3 Yellow Chicks, On Branch 95.00
Horsehead, Vase, Green & Pink 100.00
Jug, Tilt, Yellow, Ice Lip, Swirl Design 28.00
Mug, Caricature F.D. Roosevelt 45.00
Planter, Figural, Female Head, Blue On Cream, Marked, 6 1/2 In. 18.00
Planter, 2-Handled, Beige Outside, Green Inside, 4 1/4 In.Square 5.00
Plate, Bittersweet, 8 1/4 In. 4.00
Plate, Dogwood, White, Pierced For Hanging, 6 In. 3.50
Plate, Golden Blossom, 8 In. 5.00
Plate, Magnolia, 8 In. 5.00
Plate, Starflower, 10 In. 5.00
Salt & Pepper, Rooster & Hen, No.3285, 3286 .... 55.00
Server, Tidbit, Thistle, Brass Center Handle, 10 In. 14.00
Sugar, Bluebell & Daisy, White Over Red, Covered 8.00
Vase, Blossom, 4 X 4 1/2 In. 15.00
Vase, Fuchsia, Handled, 7 In. 15.00
Vase, Granada, Gold, 5 1/2 In. 10.00
Vase, Orange, Brown, Gold, Handled, Paper Label, 3 X 4 In. 12.00
Vase, Pale Blue To Yellow, Reeded, Scalloped, 8 In. 13.00
Vase, Satin White, Scroll Leaf, 9 In. 20.00
Vase, Scrolled, Modified Cornucopia, Blue, 7 1/2 In. 15.00
Vase, Terra Rose, Blue & Gray, 3 In. 15.00
Vase, White, 4 Overlapping Ivys Form, 11 In. 12.00
Wall Pocket, Nautilus Shell, Yellow, 8 X 5 1/2 In. 12.00

Star Holly is a milk glass type of glass made by the Imperial Glass Company of Bellaire, Ohio, in 1957. The pieces were made to look like Wedgwood jasperware. White holly leaves appear against colored borders of blue, green, or rust. It is marked on the bottom of every piece.

STAR HOLLY, Plate, Blue, 6 In. 50.00

Steins have been used for over 500 years. They have been made of ivory, porcelain, stoneware, faience, silver, pewter, wood, or glass in sizes up to nine gallons. Although some were made by Meissen, Capo-di-Monte, and other famous factories, most were made in Germany. The words "Geschutz" or "Musterschutz" on a stein are the German for patented or registered design, not company names.

STEIN, Bowling Ball, Beige & Brown, Marked, Musterschutz 350.00
Bowling, Beige, Brown, Musterschutz, Hash Mark 350.00
Budman Beer 40.00
Card Players, No.280, Pewter Lid & Thumbpiece, 1/2 Liter 165.00
Character, No.726, 1/2 Liter, German 195.00
Devil Forms Finial, Pewter, 16 In. 275.00
Figural, Bowling Pin Shape, German Wording At Base, 9 In. 175.00
Glass, Enameled Design, Flat Pewter Top, Thumb Latch, Germany 85.00
Hotel Touraine 799, 1/2 Liter, Pewter Thumb Lift & Cover, Advertising 225.00
Landscapes, Lithophane Base, 5 3/4 In. 80.00
Lithographic Scene, Domed Cover, Thumb Rest, 1/2 Liter 37.00
    STEIN, METTLACH, see Mettlach, Stein

Musicians & Peasants, Dwarf Finial, Pottery, Gray, 7 3/4 In.	195.00
Radish, Bismark	350.00
Regimental, Lithophane Of Nude, 1901, Johann Berger, Griffin Handle	175.00
Seated Ram, Musterschutz	475.00
Tree Trunk Shape, Embossed Acorns, Twig Finial, German, 10 1/8 In.	195.00

Stereo cards that were made for stereopticon viewers became popular after 1840. Two almost identical pictures were mounted on a stiff cardboard backing so that, when viewed through a stereoscope, a three-dimensional picture could be seen.

STEREO, Card, Black Boy Eating Watermelon, Set Of 4	25.00
Card, Centennial Exhibit Of 1876 Philadelphia, Ship In Foreground	6.00
Card, Centennial Exhibition, Wilson & Adams, Set Of 24	60.00
Card, Children Paying Honor To Old Glory, Set Of 4	18.00
Card, Duck Hunting, Litho Color, 1898, Set Of 28	30.00
Card, First Date, Marriage, Child, Set Of 25	30.00
Card, Life Of Christ, Color Lithograph, Set Of 29	25.00
Card, Manhattan, Set Of 25	28.00
Card, Naval Life, Battleships, 1906, Set Of 24	40.00
Card, Ruins Of Fire In Boston, November 1872, Dilburn	6.00
Card, Scenery On The Lehigh Valley R.R., Set Of 4	15.00
Card, Texas Jack	125.00
Card, Trouble Ahead, Keystone View Co.1902	6.50
Card, Windsor Hotel, Montreal, Parks Photo Studio	3.00

Stereoscopes, or stereopticons, were used for viewing stereo cards. The hand viewer was invented by Oliver Wendell Holmes, although more complicated table models were used before his was placed in production in 1859.

STEREOSCOPE, All Wood, Walnut, 50 Cards, C.1870	525.00
Embossed Deer Medallion, Brushed Aluminum	40.00
Eye Hood, Walnut	25.00
Ica, Focusing Lenses, 45 X 107 Mm	88.00
Keystone World Tour, Book, Adjustable Viewer, Stand	500.00
Keystone, Box Of Trip Around The World Cards	75.00
The Perfescope, Dated 1895	35.00 To 45.00
Titled World War Through Stereoscope, 300 Cards	325.00
STERLING SILVER, see Silver-Sterling	

Steuben glass was made at the Steuben Glass Works of Corning, New York. The factory, founded by Frederick Carder and T.C.Hawkes, Sr., was purchased by the Corning Glass Company. They continued to make glass called "Steuben." Many types of art glass were made at Steuben. The firm is still producing glass of exceptional quality.

STEUBEN, Ashtray, Flat, 2 Teardrop Blob Rests, Marked, 8 1/2 In.	160.00
Atomizer, Gold Aurene, Blue Highlights	350.00
Bottle, Cologne, Cintra, Pink	850.00
Bottle, Cologne, Green Stopper, C.1930, Signed, 5 & 5 1/2 In., Pair	250.00
Bottle, Cologne, Threaded Stopper, Signed, Flemish Blue, 5 1/2 In.	140.00
Bottle, Perfume, Ribbed Body, Steeple Top, Green	60.00
Bowl & Underplate, Amethyst, Marked	55.00
Bowl, Aurene, Calcite, 10 X 2 In.	125.00
Bowl, Black Applied Threads, Signed, Bristol Yellow, 5 X 2 In.	35.00
Bowl, Calcite, Gold Interior, Pink, 10 X 2 1/4 In.	475.00
Bowl, Calcite, Silver Plated Holder	85.00
Bowl, Centerpiece, Green Jade, Alabaster Pedestal, Signed, 10 In.	110.00
Bowl, Centerpiece, Turned-Over Rim, Signed, Green, 11 1/2 In.	75.00
Bowl, Cintra, Pink, 5 In.	750.00
Bowl, Clear, Diamond-Quilted, Green Threading, Marked, 6 In.	70.00
Bowl, Cluthra, Lime Ground, Oval, Signed, 2 In.	350.00
Bowl, Diamond-Quilted, Green Threading, 2-Handled, Marked, 4 In.	75.00

Bowl, Inverted Bell Form, Round Foot, Scroll Handles, Marked, 5 In.	150.00
Bowl, Inverted Bell, Applied Handle, Marked, 4 In., Pair	150.00
Bowl, Ivorene, 4 3/4 In.	45.00
Bowl, Lotus, Oriental, Green Crystal, Marked, 3 In.	135.00
Bowl, Moss Agate, Turned-Down Rim, 9 1/2 In.	150.00
Bowl, Turned-Down Rim, Amethyst, Signed, 2 1/2 X 13 In.	75.00
Bowl, Underplate, Green Crystal, Marked, 4 1/2 In.	35.00
Bowl, Verre De Soie, 5 5/8 In.	22.00
Bowl, Verre De Sole, 10 In.	95.00
Box, Ormolu Banding, Blue Jade, Oval, 6 1/4 X 3 1/2 In.	195.00
Box, Pagoda Shaped Cover, Gold Puff, Signed, 6 X 4 1/2 In.	550.00
Candleholder, Gold Iridescent, Marked, 10 In.	335.00
Candleholder, Green Jade, Alabaster Prunts, Signed, 4 In.	85.00
Candlestick, Citron Green, Teardrop Stem, 11 In., Pair	75.00
Candlestick, Engraved Wafer, Floral Design, Signed, 7 In., Pair	395.00
Candlestick, Gold, Tulip Top, Signed, 12 In., Pair	1950.00
Candlestick, Green Jade, Signed, 4 In.	85.00
Candlestick, Green, Twisted Bowl & Base, Marked, 10 In.	98.00
Candlestick, Jade Wih Alabaster, 10 In., Pair	650.00
Candlestick, Signed, French Blue, 4 In.	45.00
Candlestick, Verre De Soie, Twisted Stem, 10 In.	157.50
Centerpiece Set, Ivorene, Fan Shape, Pedestal, Marked, 13 In.	450.00
Chandelier, 5-Light, Green Feather Shades, Brass, 22 X 36 In.	1500.00
Cocktail, Cone-Shaped Bowl, Teardrop Stem, Signed, Clear, Set Of 12	950.00
Cocktail, Green, Bubbles, Threaded, Signed, 2 3/4 In.	25.00
Compote, Blue, 7 1/2 In.	195.00
Compote, Calcite, Tall Stem, Wide Top, 8 In.	750.00
Compote, Celeste Blue, Ribbed, Folded Edge, Signed, 2 1/2 X 6 In.	85.00
Compote, Citron Green, Bubble Glass Knob, Teardrop Stem, 8 In.	65.00
Compote, Flaring Rim, Swirl Feet, Marked, 6 1/2 In.	350.00
Compote, Green Jade, Fluted Edge, Disc Stem, Signed, 5 X 7 In.	145.00
Compote, Green, Ribbed, Scalloped Top, Footed, Signed, 2 X 8 In.	70.00
Compote, Jade & Alabaster, Footed, Signed, 4 In.	450.00
Compote, Jade & Alabaster Pedestal, Low, Signed, 8 1/2 X 2 In.	135.00
Compote, Nile Green, Random Bubbles	75.00
Compote, Set, Stemmed, Black, Pink, Blue, Green, Daisies, Roses, 5 1/2 In	60.00
Compote, Vintage Pattern, Clear Air Twist Stem, 5 1/2 X 6 1/2 In.	325.00
Console Set, Ivorene, Footed, Signed, Bowl, 14 X 6 In., 3 Piece	695.00
Console Set, Lotus-Leaf Shape, Ivorene, Signed, Bowl, 14 In.Diam.	750.00
Cordial, Pedestal, Light Green, Signed, 2 3/4 In., Set Of 6	65.00
Cordial, Ruby Swirl, Clear Wafer Foot, Cerise	30.00
Cordial, Teardrop, Set Of 6	80.00
Cornucopia, Fluted Top, Ribbed, Square Base, Signed, 6 1/2 In.	95.00
Cruet, Engraved Floral, Stopper, Signed Hawkes, 7 1/2 In.	125.00
Cup, Green, Reeded, Bubbles, Signed, 2 3/4 In.	45.00
Cup, Punch, Signed, Aurene	275.00
Dish, Candy, Jade & Alabaster, Signed, 8 X 4 In.	325.00
Dish, Rampant Lion Holding Ax, Marked, 3 3/4 In.	45.00
Dresser Set, Green Threading, Faceted Stopper, Signed, 4 Piece	275.00
Figurine, Blowfish, Signed, 7 In.Wide	395.00
Figurine, Dolphin, Clear, 6 In.	125.00
Figurine, Gazelle, Clear	275.00
Figurine, Penguin, Blue, Script Signed, 5 In.	150.00
Figurine, Pineapple, Internal Air Twist, Signed, 7 In.	295.00
Figurine, Rooster, Crystal, 10 1/4 In.	450.00
Finger Bowl, Underplate, Bristol Yellow, Vintage, Signed	165.00
Goblet, Double Teardrop	75.00
Goblet, French Blue, Marked	210.00
Goblet, Ribbed Side, Signed, Amber, 3/4 In., Set Of 4	220.00
Goblet, Ribbed, Bristol Yellow Stem, Aqua, Signed, 6 In.	45.00
Goblet, Ruby Red, Ball Stem, Marked, 6 In.	65.00
Goblet, Ruby Top Border, Marked, 10 In.	150.00
Goblet, Stemmed, Signed, Bristol Yellow, 6 In.	55.00

Goblet, Stemmed, Signed, Gold & Ruby Red, 6 In. 65.00
Lamp, Jade, Oriental 1150.00
Luminor, Art Deco, Made & Signed By Frederick Carder, 1920s 2800.00
Mug, Topaz, Cerise Blue Handle, 2 1/2 In. 85.00
Paperweight, White Flowers, Red Swirl 125.00
Perfume, Cut & Floral, Etched Top, Winged Stopper 98.00
Perfume, Jade & White Opalescent, 6 In. 175.00
Perfume, Scrolled Heart Stopper, Marked, 4 1/2 In. 310.00
Pitcher, Clear, Green Handle, Marked, 5 In. 75.00
Pitcher, Green Jade, Applied Handle, Marked, 6 1/2 In. 150.00
Pitcher, Jade Spiral, Handle, 9 3/4 In. 150.00
Pitcher, Lemonade, Swirl, Green, Handled, Fleur-De-Lis Mark, 5 3/4 In. 95.00
Pitcher, Verre De Soie, Dimpled 85.00
Plate, Aurene, Calcite, 6 1/4 In. 50.00
Plate, Bristol, Yellow, Black Reeding, 8 1/2 In. 35.00
Plate, Copper Wheel Engraved Design, Green, 8 1/2 In. 22.00
Plate, Fish, 6 1/2 In. 450.00
Plate, Gold, Calcite, 6 In. 65.00
Plate, Green Jade To Alabaster, Acid Cut, 7 1/2 In. 95.00
Plate, Jade, 8 3/4 In., Set Of 8 .... 195.00
Plate, Signed, Block Letters, Dark Green, 8 1/2 In., Set Of 7 .... 275.00
Plate, Swirled Pattern, Fleur-De-Lis Mark, Ruby, 6 In., Set Of 5 .... 85.00
Salt, Rosa 95.00
Shade, Aurene, Calcite Interior .... 110.00 To 135.00
Shade, Bell Shape, White Feather, Signed, Gold Iridescent, 6 In. 175.00
Shade, Brown Aurene, Applied Platinum & Gold Border, 4 In. 350.00
Shade, Cased Acid Cut Back, Amber, Pair 225.00
Shade, Diamond-Quilted, Gold Iridescent, Crystal Feather 150.00
Shade, Gold Aurene, White Opalescent Feathers, Signed, 6 In. 68.00
Shade, Gold Drape On Calcite 150.00
Shade, Gold Drape, Bulbous, Flared, Pair 155.00
Shade, Gold Iridescent, Signed, 6 In. 85.00
Shade, Ribbed, Gold Bands, Signed 110.00
Shade, White, Pull Feather, Gold Aurene, Gold Lined 140.00
Sherbet & Underplate, Aurene On Calcite .... 170.00 To 245.00
Sherbet & Underplate, Clear, Bristol Yellow Stem, Marked, Set 55.00
Sherbet, Optic Rib, Signed, Pomona Green, 3 1/2 In. 20.00
Smoker Set, Intaglio Heraldic Lion, Unicorns, Marked 200.00
Tazza, Clear Blue, Spiral Threading, 7 X 8 In. 110.00
Tumbler, Applied Reeding, Flared Top, Signed, Flemish Blue, 3 In. 35.00
Tumbler, Footed, Amethyst, 5 In. 32.00
Tumbler, Jade Spiral, Alabaster Handles, 5 1/2 In. 40.00
Tumbler, Lemonade, Swirled Green, Alabaster Handle, Marked, 5 1/2 In. 95.00
Urn, Ivorene, Signed, 8 In. 225.00
Vase, Applied Pulled Lily Pads, Ovoid, Amethyst, 6 1/2 In. 95.00
Vase, Aquamarine, 11 In. 425.00
Vase, Barrel Shape, Floral Design, Blue, 5 X 4 In., Pair 450.00
Vase, Blue, Ribbed, Signed, 7 X 7 In. 115.00
Vase, Clear, Controlled Bubbles, Marked, 5 1/2 In. 65.00
Vase, Cluthra, Strawberry Ground, 9 X 11 In. 750.00
Vase, Cone Shape, Signed, Green On White, 12 In. 950.00
Vase, Controlled Bubbles, Signed, Bristol Yellow, 5 X 7 In. 95.00
Vase, Copper Wheel Engraved, 10 In. 235.00
Vase, Cornucopia, Footed, Green, 8 In. 125.00
Vase, Cornucopia, Ivorene, Pedestal, Ruffled Top, Signed, 6 1/2 In. 250.00
Vase, Cranberry Threading, Clear, Marked, 7 X 7 In. 127.00
Vase, Crystal, Applied Heart Shaped Handle, 10 In. 85.00
Vase, Crystal, Black, Trumpet Form, Marked, 17 In. 950.00
Vase, Crystal, Flared Rim, Marked, 6 In. 68.00
Vase, Crystal, Heart Shaped Handles, 10 1/2 X 5 In. 85.00
Vase, Diagonal Swirl, Amethyst, 7 In. 110.00
Vase, Diagonal Swirl, Emerald Green, 7 In. 110.00
Vase, Eggcup Shape, 2 Spined Spears Around Base, Marked, 6 In. 260.00
Vase, Fan Shaped, Optic Ribbed, Green, Signed, 8 In. 100.00

Vase, Fan, Amber-Green, Marked, 8 1/2 In. 180.00
Vase, Fan, Amber, Crisscross Pattern, Signed, 8 In. 225.00
Vase, Fan, Transparent Green, Marked, 7 1/4 In. 120.00
Vase, Green Jade, Alabaster Foot, Signed, 5 In. 160.00
Vase, Green Jade, Alabaster Handles, 12 In. 500.00
Vase, Green, Applied Threads Top, 6 X 8 In. 105.00
Vase, Green, Pomona, Green, Topaz Foot, 10 In. 115.00
Vase, Green, Ribbed Fan, Ball Stem, Marked, 8 In. 75.00
Vase, Green, Ribbed, Pedestal Base, Signed, 8 In. 55.00
Vase, Grotesque Pattern, Clear, Signed, 9 In. 125.00
Vase, Inverted Teardrop Form, Diagonal Swirl, Amethyst, 7 In. 150.00
Vase, Inverted Teardrop Form, Green, 7 In. 115.00
Vase, Ivorene, Fluted Top, Donut Base, Signed, 4 1/2 In. 135.00
Vase, Ivory Ribbed, Flared Top, Signed, 5 1/2 In. 125.00
Vase, Jack-In-The-Pulpit, Ivorene, Script Signed, 12 In. 995.00
Vase, Leaf & Vine Design, 22 Millefiori, Turquoise, 12 In. 3950.00
Vase, Marlene Design, Signed, Rosaline To Alabaster, 7 In. 875.00
Vase, Millefiori, Gold Aurene, Leaf & Vine Design, Signed, 12 In. 2950.00
Vase, Optic Pattern, Turned-Under Rim, Marina Blue, 16 In. 295.00
Vase, Optic Rib, Rolled Rim & Foot, Amethyst, 6 In. 30.00
Vase, Ovoid Shape, Allover Air Traps, Applied Lily Pads, 6 1/2 In. 70.00
Vase, Pomona Green Paneled, Topaz Domed Foot, Signed, 10 1/4 In. 115.00
Vase, Pussy Willow Pattern, Signed, Black On Alabaster, 6 In. 1775.00
Vase, Reeding Upper Section Of Body, Green, 6 In. 75.00
Vase, Rosaline On Alabaster Foot, Signed, 7 In. 395.00
Vase, Rosaline Over Alabaster, C.1920, 6 X 7 3/4 In. 2850.00
Vase, Ruffled Top, Ivory, Signed, 8 In. 175.00
Vase, Rustic Pattern, Signed, French Blue, 6 In. 185.00
Vase, Stick, Rosaline & Alabaster, 8 1/2 In. 125.00
Vase, Stick, Verre De Soie, Floral, Garlands, 8 In. 60.00
Vase, Swirl, Green Jade, Signed, 6 1/2 In. 175.00
Vase, Swirled, Verre De Soie, 7 In. 165.00
Vase, Threading On Top, Bubbly, Clear, 7 3/4 In. 50.00
Vase, Triple Thorn, Blue, Gold Ground, Marked, 6 1/4 In. 300.00
Vase, Trumpet Shape, Flared, 6 Rolled Swirls, Marked, 7 In. 265.00
Vase, Trumpet Shape, 4 Scroll Feet, Marked, 12 In. 365.00
Vase, Wisteria, Applied Handles, 10 1/2 In. 350.00
Vase, 3 Prong Tree Stump, Blue, Signed, 6 1/4 In. 550.00
Wine, Funnel Shape, Double Teardrop Stem, Crystal, Signed 35.00
Wine, Green Jade, Twisted Stem, Alabaster, 7 1/4 In. 95.00
Wine, Twisted Alabaster Stem, Signed, Green Jade, 7 1/4 In. 95.00

*Stevengraphs are woven pictures made like ribbons. They were manufactured
by Thomas Stevens of Coventry, England, and became popular in 1862.*

STEVENGRAPH, Bookmark, Christmas 85.00
Bookmark, Full Cry 200.00
Bookmark, Happy May Thy Birthday Be, Tasseled, Signed 75.00
Bookmark, Philadelphia Centennial, Washington Portrait, Poem 95.00
Bookmark, The Finish 150.00
Full Cry 150.00

*Stevens & Williams of Stourbridge, England, made many types of glass,
including layered, etched, cameo, and art glass, between the 1830s and
1930s. Some pieces are signed "S and W."*

STEVENS & WILLIAMS, Bottle, Cologne, Intaglio, Silver Collar, 8 X 3 In. 195.00
Bottle, Cologne, Intaglio, Silver Top, Green, 9 3/4 In. 195.00
Bottle, Cologne, Swirl, Crystal, Silver Collar, 9 In. 165.00
Bowl, Bride's, Burnt Orange, Blue Acorns, Marked, 11 In. 250.00
Bowl, Connected Diamonds, Pink Lining, Handled, 11 In. 750.00
Bowl, Swirls, Petal Feet, Gold Rigaree Edge, 7 3/4 In. 95.00
Dish, Jam, Rubena, Ornate Stand 98.00
Jar, Ribbed, Silver Plated Top, Rim, & Handle, 4 1/4 In. 125.00
Lamp, Fairy, Ruffled Base, Clarke Insert, Pink, 5 3/8 In. 550.00

Pitcher, Cut Back Flowers, Rayed Foot, Orange, 9 3/4 In. 475.00
Rose Bowl, Cream Satin Lining, 3 1/4 X 4 3/8 In. 195.00
Rose Bowl, Yellow, Applied Floral Design 125.00
Vase, Alabaster Stem & Base, Footed, Signed, 6 In. 135.00
Vase, Amber Bellflower, Applique Overlay, 11 1/4 In. 295.00
Vase, Amber Leaves, White Flowers, Signed, 6 In. 165.00
Vase, Applied Flowers & Leaves, Amber Rim, Signed, 6 In. 225.00
Vase, Applied Trailing Lily Pads, Footed, Label 125.00
Vase, Aqua Lining, Mother-Of-Pearl Swirls, 16 3/4 In. 1195.00
Vase, Branch & Leaves, Applied Pears, Rose, 6 5/8 In. 365.00
Vase, Chain Design Bottom, White Flowers, Label, 15 In. 5250.00
Vase, Gold, Tomato Color, Clear Handles, 6 1/2 In. 130.00
Vase, Jack-In-The-Pulpit, Swirls Around Stem, 13 In. 195.00
Vase, Mother-Of-Pearl, Blue, Amber, & Gold, 15 In. 1150.00
Vase, Pink & White, Striped, Ruffled Top, 9 In. 140.00
Vase, Silveria, Signed, S&W, 4 5/8 In. Tall 1250.00
Vase, Swirled Fan, Ruffled Feet, Blue, 4 1/4 X 6 In. 165.00
Vase, White Flowers, Top & Bottom Border, Label, 15 In. 6500.00
Wine, Alabaster Stem & Foot, Blue, 6 1/4 In. 35.00
Wine, Alabaster Stem & Foot, Green, 6 1/4 In. 35.00
Wine, Alabaster Stem & Foot, Yellow, 6 1/4 In. 35.00

> *Henry William Stiegel started his first factory in Pennsylvania in
> 1763. He remained in business until 1774. Glassware in the Stiegel style
> has been made by many factories. The wares are made in clear or colored
> glass and are decorated in various styles.*

STIEGEL TYPE, Basket Of Flowers, 5 1/2 In. 125.00
Flask, Diamond Pattern, Clear 135.00
Flip, Potted Tulip, Fronds & Swirls, 18th Century, 6 In. 100.00
Tumbler, Flip, Peafowl, 7 1/2 In. 135.00
Tumbler, George III, Ship, 19th Century, 1/2 Pint, Pair 40.00

> *Stoneware is a coarse, glazed, and fired potter's ware that is used to make
> crocks, jugs, etc.*

STONEWARE, Bean Pot, Blue Banded 65.00
Bean Pot, Brown & Beige, Handled, 1 Quart 16.50
Bean Pot, Chocolate Brown Top, Cream Bottom, 1 Quart 18.50
Bean Pot, Shaded Blue 95.00
Bean Pot, Whites Utica, Dated Spirt Of '76 Centennial 300.00
Bean Pot, Wild Flower 150.00
Bedpan, Tortoiseshell, Brown On Cream, C.1850 .... 75.00
Berry Bowl, Flying Bird, Blue & White 65.00
Bottle, Chocolate Brown, Lip Flange, 10 In., 1 Quart 35.00
Bottle, Chocolate Brown, Rope Handle, 10 In. 35.00
Bottle, Ginger Beer, R.M.Bird & Co., Stratford-On-Avon, Brown 15.00
Bottle, Ginger Beer, Yellow & Tan, Marked Portobello 15.00
Bottle, Gray, Blob Top, 10 In., 1 Quart .... 22.50 To 25.00
Bottle, Gray, Incised Blue Name, Blob Top, 9 3/4 In. 35.00
Bottle, Ink, Beige, Cone Shaped, Concave Base, 2 X 2 3/4 In. 18.50
Bottle, Ink, Curved Pouring Lip, Cream Glazed, 6 1/4 In. 20.00
Bottle, Ink, Master, Cream, Pouring Lip, 6 In. 20.00
Bottle, Ink, Seal On Top, Brown 18.00
Bottle, Wine, Handled, 11 In. 12.00
Bowl, Advertising, Burdette, Iowa, Blue & Gray 50.00
Bowl, Blue Band, Set Of 4 .... 140.00
Bowl, Blue Inside & Out, 9 In. 30.00
Bowl, Blue Over Cream, 9 X 3 In. 135.00
Bowl, Brown & Yellow, Concentric Lines To Rim, C.1870, 9 In. 60.00
Bowl, Chocolate Brown, Bail Handle, Footed, C.1880, 10 In. 45.00
Bowl, Chocolate Brown, Bail Handle, Tab Feet, C.1886, 8 In. 25.00
Bowl, Chocolate Brown, Holed Ears, Bail Handle, Tab Feet, 8 In. 25.00
Bowl, Daisy, Blue & Gray, 9 In. 65.00
Bowl, Diamond Point, Blue & White, 8 In. 45.00

Bowl, F.C.Pope, 8 1/2 In. 85.00
Bowl, F.C.Pope, 9 In. 85.00
Bowl, Good Luck, Blue & White, Covered, 8 1/2 X 5 3/4 In. 65.00
Bowl, Mixing, Brown, Bail Swing Handle, C.1880, 8 X 4 In. 22.50
Bowl, Mixing, Chocolate Brown, 4 Section Base, Semi-Foot, 10 In. 40.00
Bowl, Mixing, Yellow, Chocolate Brown, 9 X 4 In. 35.00
Bowl, Mixing, Yellow, Cream Bands, C.1880, 8 In. 35.00
Bowl, Wedding Band, 6 1/2 In. 10.00
Bowl, Wedding Band, 7 1/4 In. 45.00
Bowl, Wedding Ring, Blue & White, 8 1/2 In. 65.00
Bowl, Wedding Ring, Blue-Gray, 7 3/4 In. 30.00
Bowl, Wedding Ring, Nested Set Of 3 .... 175.00
Bowl, Wedding Ring, Yellow & Green, 6 1/2 In. 30.00
Box, Salt, Blue-Gray, Leaf, Scroll, Flowers, Round, 6 In. 110.00
Box, Salt, Hanging, Lidded, U.S.Shield & Eagle, Blue & Gray 165.00
Butter Churn, Blue Design, 4 Gallon 310.00
Butter, Apricot, Covered, Blue & White 170.00
Butter, Blue & Gray, Bail & Lid 65.00
Butter, Butterfly, Blue & White 55.00
Butter, Daisy & Waffle, Covered .... 50.00 To 85.00
Butter, Daisy, Blue & White .... 60.00 To 110.00
Butter, Good Luck, Covered 85.00
Butter, Indian Good Luck Sign, Covered 79.00
Butter, Peacock, Blue & White 250.00
Butter, Rose & Waffle, Blue & White 49.00
Butter, Scroll, Covered 100.00
Butter, Wild Flower, Blue & White 55.00
Canister, Barrel, Wild Flower 75.00
Canister, Bean & Tea, Wild Flower 65.00
Canister, Coffee, Basket Weave 195.00
Canister, Dutch Boy & Girl In Country, 6 1/2 X 3 1/2 In. 95.00
Canister, Farina, Wild Flower, Barrel Shape 75.00
Canister, Prunes, Wildflower 75.00
Canister, Sugar, Basket Weave 195.00
Canister, Tea, Snowflake, Original Lid 140.00
Casserole, Daisy, Blue & White 69.00
Casserole, Guernsey Earthenware, Covered, 8 1/4 In. 20.00
Chamber Pot, Basket Weave, Flowers, Blue & White 135.00
Chamber Pot, Rose, Fish Scale, Small 45.00
Churn, Blue House, Witmore Havana 1100.00
Churn, Blue Squiggle Design, Marked Lyons, N.Y., 6 Gallon 235.00
Churn, Cobalt, Floral Design, 17 1/2 In., 6 Gallon 95.00
Churn, Dazey No.20, 1922 .... 30.00
Churn, Dotted Blue Design, A.K.Ballard, 4 Gallon 295.00
Churn, Fantail Bird, Blue, Whites Utica, 6 Gallon .... Illus 950.00
Churn, Peacock, Cobalt Blue, J.& E.Norton, 17 3/4 In. .... Illus 2350.00
Churn, 1 Flower, Cobalt Blue, 19 1/2 In., 6 Gallon 85.00
Cistern, Dr.Bond's Patent Regulating Filter, Spigot, 22 In. 330.00
Colander, Brown, Coggle Line Design, 9 1/2 X 5 In. 110.00
Cookie Jar, Blue & Brown Waist, Earred Handle, Covered, 8 In. 165.00
Cookie Jar, Blue & White .... 150.00 To 165.00
Cooler, Ice Water, Blue & White, 3 Gallon 100.00
Cooler, Rebecah At The Well, Western Stoneware Co., Blue & White 350.00
Cooler, Water, Blue Bands, Cover, Spigot, Gray Ground, 2 Gallon 65.00
Cooler, Water, Blue Design Middle, Banded Rings, 3 Gallon 395.00
Cooler, Water, Cobalt Blue Peony, Pewter Faucet, 4 Gallon 160.00
Cracker Jar, Flying Bird, Blue & White 350.00
Creamer, Arc & Leaf, Blue & White 65.00
Creamer, Brown, Yellow Base, Raised Leaf Design, 5 In. 40.00
Creamer, Chain Links, Blue 45.00
Crock, Ballard Vale, 7 1/4 In. 85.00
Crock, Beehive & Floral, Hubbell & Chesebro, Geddes, N.Y., 3 Gal. 195.00
Crock, Bird In Flight, Cobalt Robin, Brown Interior, 1 Gallon 375.00
Crock, Bird Silhouettes, Blue, J.C.Waelde, 11 1/4 In. .... Illus 1500.00

Stoneware, Churn, Peacock, Cobalt Blue, J.& E.Norton, 17 3/4 In.; Umbrella Stand, Crossed Birds & Floral, 22 In.; Churn, Fantail Bird, Blue, Whites Utica, 6 Gallon *(See Pages 663, 669)*

Crock, Blue & Gray, Initials A.H., 3 Gallon 175.00
Crock, Blue Fern & Dotted Antenna, 2 Gallon 85.00
Crock, Blue Flower, Evert Bissett, Old Bridge, N.J., Ovoid, 1 Gal. 98.00
Crock, Blue Leaf Design, Stamped White's, Utica, Eared, 7 1/2 In. 135.00
Crock, Blue Oak Leaf, Stamped E. & L.P.Norton, 1858-81, 7 In. 125.00
Crock, Blue Stencil Flower, 1 Gallon 22.00
Crock, Blue, Swirls, Eared Handle, 3 Gallon 65.00
Crock, Brown Interior, Wide Mouth, Gray Exterior, 9 In. 30.00
Crock, Brown, Incised Rings, Wide Mouth, 6 X 3 In. 25.00
Crock, Brushed Cobalt Blue Floral Design, 11 1/2 In. 40.00
Crock, Brushed Cobalt Design, Floral, 12 In., 4 Gallon 55.00
Crock, Cobalt Blue Design, Levin's 167-169 S.Broad St., 5 Gallon 145.00
Crock, Cobalt Blue Design, Open Handles, 6 In. 35.00
Crock, Cobalt Blue Leaf Design, 3 1/2 In., 2 Gallon 90.00
Crock, Cobalt Blue Lines, Brown Interior, E.S. & B., 7 In. 115.00
Crock, Cobalt Blue, Swirls, Eared Handles, 5 X 5 In., 3 Gallon 65.00
Crock, Cobalt Bluebird, Incised Lines, 2 Gallon 325.00
Crock, Copenhagen's Snuff, Beige, Brown Interior, 6 In. 75.00
Crock, Cottage Cheese, Daum Dairy, Blue & White, Large 50.00
Crock, Cream & Brown, Covered, 7 1/2 In. 25.00
Crock, Cream & Chocolate Brown, 1 Gallon 25.00
Crock, Cream & Dark Brown, Flat Wooden Cover, 7 In. 25.00
Crock, Dark Gray, Blue Plume, Marked Heinechen & Co., 10 In. 95.00

Stoneware, Crock, Bird Silhouettes, Blue, J.C.Waelde, 11 1/4 In.; Jug, Tree, Fence, & House, Blue, J.& E.Norton, 2 Gallon; Crock, Dog, Blue, N.Y. Stoneware Co., 11 1/2 In. *(See Pages 663, 667)*

Crock, Design On 2 Sides, Double Handles, Cobalt Blue, 8 In. 175.00
Crock, Design, Ovoid, 1800s, 1 1/2 Gallon 100.00
Crock, Dog, Blue, N.Y. Stoneware Co., 11 1/2 In. .... *Illus* 700.00
Crock, Double Flower & Leaves, Blue & Gray, Wide Mouth, 3 Gallon 168.00
Crock, Double Flower Design, Stamped Cortland, Gray, 7 1/4 In. 160.00
Crock, Double Leaf Pattern, Somerset Potter Works, 1 Gallon 87.00
Crock, Eared Handles, Blue Flowers, J.Weaver, 3 Gallon 175.00
Crock, Flower & Squiggly Leaves, L.& B.B.Chace, 3 Gallon 150.00
Crock, Flower Design, Cobalt Blue, 13 3/4 In., 6 Gallon 60.00
Crock, Flower, Cobalt Blue, 11 1/2 In. 45.00
Crock, Gray, Brown Interior, Wide Mouth, 6 X 9 In. 30.00
Crock, Gray, Brown, Wide Mouth, 6 3/4 In., 1 Gallon 30.00
Crock, Gray, Chocolate Brown Interior, 1 Pint 12.50
Crock, Gray, Eared Handles, Incised Lines, 1 Gallon 30.00
Crock, Gray, Incised Ring, Eared Handles, 3 Gallon 65.00
Crock, Hamilton & Jones, Greensboro, Pa., 4 Gallon 125.00
Crock, Incised Rings, Brown Interior, C.1830, 1 Gallon 125.00
Crock, Marked Jas.Benjamin, 10 Gallon 95.00
Crock, Marked Ottman Bros. & Co., Fort Edward, N.Y., 3 Gallon 350.00
Crock, Monmouth, Cobalt Blue Tulips, 2 Gallon 30.00
Crock, Number 2 & Squiggles In Blue, 2 Gallon 95.00
Crock, Orchid-Style Flower, N.A.White & Co., 3 Gallon 160.00
Crock, Pickle, Wire & Wooden Handle, Covered 25.00
Crock, Salt, Apricot, Wooden Cover 85.00
Crock, Salt, Butterfly, Wooden Cover, Blue & White 165.00
Crock, Salt, Dental's, Ackley, Iowa, Blue & Gray 65.00
Crock, Snooty Bird, Cobalt Blue Bird, Beak In Air, 6 In. 325.00
Crock, Stylized Leaf Design, 3 Gallon 85.00
Crock, Tulip Design, 4 Gallon 140.00
Crock, Wavy Lines, Brushed Cobalt, 11 In., 3 Gallon 40.00
Crock, West Troy, Bird Design, 2 Gallon 125.00
Crock, Western, Tulip Design, 2 Gallon 35.00
Crock, Whites-Utica, Bird On Branch, 3 Gallon 235.00
Crock, Wings, Geddes, N.Y., 2 Gallon 150.00
Crock, 3-Winged Insect, Geddes, N.Y., 1883-87, Gray, 2 Gallon 190.00
Cup, Bowtie, Blue & White 45.00
Cup, Custard, Blue On Cream, Raised Swirling, 2 1/4 In. 40.00
Cup, Custard, Brown & Yellow, 2 1/2 In. 18.50
Cup, Custard, Brown To Tan, Rolled Rim, Embossed England, 3 In. 8.50
Cup, Custard, Chocolate Brown & White, Set Of 3 .... 15.00
Cup, Custard, Yellow, Cream Interior 10.00
Cuspidor, Bowtie .... 89.00 To 90.00
Cuspidor, Chocolate Brown, Incised Vertical Lines 35.00
Cuspidor, Chocolate Brown, Vertical & Horizontal Incised Lines 35.00
Cuspidor, Tulip, Blue & White 79.00
Dish, Soap, Beaded Rose, Blue & White 80.00
Dish, Soap, Bowtie, Round 60.00
Dish, Soap, Lion's Head Design, Utica, Blue & Gray 135.00
Dish, Soap, Readed Rose 39.00
Dish, Soap, Rose Pattern, Covered, Pink 110.00
Egg, Black Inside, Star, Indentations, E.Brinkman, 3 3/4 In. 48.00
Feeder & Waterer, Chicken, Bell Shaped, Cream, 7 In., Pair 30.00
Feeder, Chicken, Brown, 10 In. 18.50
Feeder, Chicken, Cobalt Blue Design 115.00
Feeder, Chicken, Grain Bags Over Back, Park & Pollard Co., 1910 .... 115.00
Feeder, Chicken, Knob Top, Mother, Father, & Baby Chicks, Blue 45.00
Feeder, Chicken, Park & Pollard Co., Boston, 1913, 10 1/2 In. 125.00
Figurine, Spaniel, Albany Slip 150.00
Flask, Book Form, Smoky Blue Glaze, Coming Through The Rye, 5 In. 135.00
Flask, Cobalt, Circular Body, Scrolls, 6 1/2 X 3 In. 95.00
Flask, Gray Salt Glaze, 8 1/4 In. 15.00
Flask, Tan Salt Glaze, Lip, 8 1/2 In. 25.00
Flowerpot, Attached Saucer, Gray Glaze, 5 X 6 In. 60.00
Flowerpot, Basket Weave, Blue & Gray 75.00

Foot Warmer, Henderson	150.00
Foot Warmer, Logan, Blue & White	5.00
Holder, Toothbrush, Beaded Rose, Blue & White	99.00
Holder, Toothbrush, Blue & White, Fish Scale & Wild Rose	45.00
Holder, Toothbrush, Rose Pattern, Pink	75.00
Holder, Toothpick, Swan, Blue & White	45.00
Inkwell, Brown, Tan Glaze, Applied Vintage, 2 7/8 X 2 1/8 In.	20.00
Inkwell, Dark Glaze, Center Spout, Tooled Lines, 3 In.	30.00
Inkwell, Schoolhouse, Tan, 2 X 2 In.	15.00
Inkwell, Schoolhouse, Thick Collar, C.1870, 2 X 2 1/8 In.	14.50
Inkwell, Shape Of Sleeping Youth, 5 1/2 X 4 In.	75.00
Jar, Abstract Flower Ends In Arrow, Ovoid, 1 1/2 Gallon	120.00
Jar, Abstract Flower, Ovoid, Gray Glaze, 1 1/2 Gallon	125.00
Jar, Abstract Flower, Pennsylvania, Brown Glaze, 12 In.	125.00
Jar, Alexander Conrad, New Geneva, Pa., Stencil, C.1782, 1 Gallon	120.00
Jar, Batter, Pig Snouted, Brown, Bail Handle, Pour Spout, 8 In.	55.00
Jar, Beater, Blue Spatter	75.00
Jar, Beige, 16 In.	35.00
Jar, Brushed Floral Design, Cobalt, 11 In.	85.00
Jar, Cortland, Floral Design, 10 3/4 In.	125.00
Jar, Cream, Squatty, Cork, 4 In.	10.00
Jar, D.Goodale, 1818-30, Ear Handles, Incised Rings, 14 In.	165.00
Jar, Flower In Cobalt Blue, 13 In., 6 Gallon	55.00
Jar, Fruit, Weir	25.00
Jar, Fruit, 3 Horizontal Blue Bands, Gray Glaze, 8 1/2 In.	75.00
Jar, H.Wilson, Tie Top, 2 Gallon	85.00
Jar, Impressed Solomon Bell, 8 1/2 In.	40.00
Jar, Jam, Beige, Covered, Iron Neck Wire, 1 Gallon	25.00
Jar, Jam, Beige, Iron Neck, Wire Locking Device, Covered, 1 Gallon	25.00
Jar, Light Tan, Incised Rings, C.1860, 1 Gallon	45.00
Jar, Pantry, Cover, 5 Pound	250.00
Jar, R.F.Reppert, Greensboro, Pa., Blue Stencil, Gray, 2 Gallon	145.00
Jar, Storage, Black Flint Enamel, Covered, 7 In., 1 Gallon	45.00
Jar, Storage, Brown Interior, Gray Exterior, Signed Kendall, 2 Gal.	125.00
Jar, Storage, Brown Interior, Gray Out, Signed Kendall, 2 Gallon	125.00
Jar, Storage, Ear Handles, Brown Interior, Gray Out, 2 Gallon	125.00
Jar, Storage, Ear Handles, Chocolate Brown, C.1850, 2 Gallon	125.00
Jar, Storage, Gray, Incised Neckline, C.1870, 1/2 Gallon	20.00
Jar, Tan Glaze, Incised Ring, C.1860, 1 Gallon	35.00
Jar, 3-Petal Design, Covered, Gray Glaze, 10 1/2 In.	110.00
Jardiniere, Incised Letters, Brown Glaze, Signed, Cowden, C.1860	110.00
Jardiniere, Monmouth, Ill., Indian Design, Tan & Brown, 6 1/2 In.	28.00
Jug, Advertising, Urbana, Ia., Marked Minnesota Stoneware Co.	125.00
Jug, Batter, Blue Flower, Signed F.H.Cowden, Harrisburg, Tin Lid	375.00
Jug, Batter, Bluebird	430.00
Jug, Beehive Shape, Saloon, Brooklyn, Ill., Brown & Cream, Pint	75.00
Jug, Beige, Amber, Incised Lines, C.1820, 2 Gallon	165.00
Jug, Beige, Applied Handle, Incised Lettering, C.1860, 1 Gal.	60.00
Jug, Beige, Charlestown, Applied Handle, C.1840, 1 Gallon	100.00
Jug, Beige, Incised Goodwin-Webster, C.1810, 1 Gallon	165.00
Jug, Bird Sitting On Branch, Charlestown, Gray Glaze, 14 1/2 In.	240.00
Jug, Bird, J.& E.Norton, 2 Gallon	525.00
Jug, Blue Floral Design, 9 In., Pair	210.00
Jug, Blue Flower & Leaf, Binghamton, N.Y., Blue & Gray, Gallon	138.00
Jug, Blue Flowers, N.A.White & Son, Utica, N.Y., 5 Gallon	250.00
Jug, Brown & White, 2 Gallon	18.00
Jug, Brown Glaze, Albany, Ovoid, 7 1/2 In.	35.00
Jug, Brown Glaze, 17 3/4 In.	110.00
Jug, Brown, Applied Handle, Pour Spout, Wooden Stopper, 1 Gallon	30.00
Jug, Burger Jr., Rochester, N.Y., 2 Gallon	55.00
Jug, Chocolate Brown, Applied Handle, 1 Quart	22.50
Jug, Cider, Dated 1882	32.50
Jug, Cobalt Blue Bird, Whites Utica, N.Y., 3 Gallon	250.00

Jug, Cobalt Blue Flower, J.Burger, Rochester, N.Y., 2 Gallon	135.00
Jug, Cobalt Blue Foliage Design, 15 1/2 In.	105.00
Jug, Cobalt Blue Slip, Ovoid, C.1840, 2 Gallon	175.00
Jug, Cobalt Blue, Robin Perched On Branch, Handled, 2 Gallon	325.00
Jug, Dark Gray, Concentric Lines, Charlestown, C.1800, 1 Gallon	165.00
Jug, Double Handled, Blue Floral, 19th Century, 21 In., 5 Gallon	25.00
Jug, Drunken Tilt, Dark Gray, C.1850, 1 Gallon	125.00
Jug, E.Swasey & Co., Portland, Me., Brown Glaze, Pour Neck, 1/2 Gal.	40.00
Jug, Eagle Saloon, H.W.Loesch, 1 Quart	60.00
Jug, Floral Design, Cobalt Blue, 16 In., 3 Gallon	70.00
Jug, Floral Design, Gray Ground, 5 1/2 X 3 1/2 In.	250.00
Jug, Flower, Julius Norton, 2 Gallon	85.00
Jug, Goodwin & Webster, C.1820, Handled, 1 Gallon	95.00
Jug, Gray, Beige, Applied Handle, Thick Lip, 1/2 Gallon	22.50
Jug, Gray, Beige, Goodwin & Webster, C.1820, 1 Gallon	150.00
Jug, Gray, Blue Design, Tilt Neck, C.1840, 1 Gallon	150.00
Jug, Gray, Incised Lines, C.1830, 15 In.	130.00
Jug, Gray, Tipsy Collar, Fat Waist, 1 Gallon	100.00
Jug, Haxtun & Co., Fort Edward, N.Y., Cobalt Blue Flowers, 1 Gallon	158.00
Jug, Hayner, Dayton, Ohio, Blue Underglaze, 1 Gallon	35.00
Jug, Impressed Label Hart Fulton, Cobalt Blue, 13 In.	125.00
Jug, Impressed Label, Cobalt Blue, 11 3/4 In.	35.00
Jug, Insect Design, Roberts, Binghamton, N.Y., C.1848, 2 Gallon	250.00
Jug, J.Norton & Co., Bennington, Vt., I.Trask, 2 Gallon	375.00
Jug, James Benjamin, Stoneware Depot, Cincinnati, Ohio, 2 Gallon	85.00
Jug, Liquor, Blue Design, 14 In.	80.00
Jug, Little Brown, Chocolate Brown, Incised Lines, 1/2 Gallon	25.00
Jug, Marked Peoria Pottery, 1/2 Gallon	65.00
Jug, Medium & Light Tan, Strap Bands, Marked, 13 In.	75.00
Jug, Nichols & Boynton, Stylized Cobalt Blue Design, 1 Gallon	145.00
Jug, Oak Leaf, Incised Blue Letters, Gray Glaze, 1 Gallon	125.00
Jug, Orange, Gray, Blue Lettering, Frank H. Lampson, 1/2 Gal.	60.00
Jug, Polly, Cobalt Blue, 11 In.	195.00
Jug, Reddish-Brown, Lyman & Clark, 1840, 1 Gallon	140.00
Jug, Signed Cowden & Wilcox, Harrisburg, Pa., Free Hand Tulip, Gal.	195.00
Jug, Tree, Fence, & House, Blue, J.& E.Norton, 2 Gallon *Illus*	950.00
Jug, Vinegar, Hughes, Monogram, 1 Gallon	55.00
Jug, Whiskey, Canteen Shape, The Fleischmann Co., 9 1/4 In.	115.00
Mold, Pudding, Chocolate Brown, Fluted, C.1870, 4 1/2 In.	85.00
Mortar, Mulling, Blue Band, 6 3/4 In.	15.00
Mug, Cattail, Blue & White	85.00
Mug, Flying Bird	180.00
Mug, Kansas City Chapter Sons Of The Revolution	40.00
Mug, Lash's Root Beer	32.00
Mug, Monk, Flemish Gray & Blue	100.00
Mug, Rose Pattern, Pink	85.00
Mug, Souvenir Of Concord, Gold Rim, Florals, Beige, Red	6.00
Mug, Sun Drug Co.	37.50
Mug, The First Drink, Cow & Calf, Brown	30.00
Pail, Butter, Wild Flower, Blue & White, Pour Lip, 5 In.	100.00
Pan, Milk, Mustard, C.1870, 11 X 3 In.	75.00
Pitcher & Bowl, Wild Flower	295.00
Pitcher, Advertising, Curlicue Curls, Flowing Curls Design, 7 In.	45.00
Pitcher, Banded Scroll, Blue & White	135.00
Pitcher, Basket Weave, Blue & White	95.00 To 145.00
Pitcher, Batter, Chocolate Brown, Lapped Rim, C.1870	85.00
Pitcher, Batter, Chocolate Brown, Pinched Spout, 1870	75.00 To 85.00
Pitcher, Batter, Chocolate, Pinched Spout, Incised Rings, 8 In.	75.00
Pitcher, Batter, Pinched Spout, C.1870, Brown Glaze, 2 Quart	85.00
Pitcher, Beer, Bavarian Alpine, Gray & Blue	400.00
Pitcher, Beer, Tavern Scene	210.00
Pitcher, Beige-Yellow Glaze, Flowers On Side, Barrel Rings, 5 In.	40.00
Pitcher, Beige, Pouring Lip, Concentric Lines, C.1800, 13 In.	125.00

Pitcher, Blue Bowtie, Red Roses 100.00
Pitcher, Bluebird Design, Blue & White 175.00
Pitcher, Boy, Girl, & Dog, Stenciled 150.00
Pitcher, Butterfly 225.00
Pitcher, Butterscotch & Brown, Black Dots, 8 In. 70.00
Pitcher, Carnation, Brown 85.00
Pitcher, Castle, Brown .... 30.00 To 65.00
Pitcher, Cattails, Blue & White, 7 In. .... 95.00 To 135.00
Pitcher, Cherries & Leaves, Blue & White 150.00
Pitcher, Colonial Boy & Girl, Brown 40.00
Pitcher, Columns, Blue & White 95.00
Pitcher, Cosmos, Blue & White .... 65.00 To 90.00
Pitcher, Cow Pattern, Green & Yellow, 10 In. 85.00
Pitcher, Cow, Blue & White .... 125.00 To 175.00
Pitcher, Cow, Cream & Green, 8 In. 115.00
Pitcher, Cow, Yellow & Green, 6 In. 85.00
Pitcher, Cows, Brown 55.00
Pitcher, Cows, Cream & Green, 8 In. 150.00
Pitcher, Cream, Blue, Chain Links 65.00
Pitcher, Dainty Fruit Pattern, Blue & White, 8 In. 110.00
Pitcher, Daisy 95.00
Pitcher, Deer & Fawn, Blue & White .... 85.00 To 165.00
Pitcher, Doe & Fawn, Blue & White 185.00
Pitcher, Dutch Boy & Girl Kissing, Blue & White .... 85.00 To 115.00
Pitcher, Dutch Boy, Girl & Dog, Squatty, Blue & White 150.00
Pitcher, Dutch Farm Scene, Blue & White 150.00
Pitcher, Embossed Water Lilies, Green 25.00
Pitcher, Fish Scale & Roses, Blue & White, 9 In. 70.00
Pitcher, Fish Scales, Cobalt Blue & Gray, 9 In. 150.00
Pitcher, Flemish Figures, Blue & White 225.00
Pitcher, Flying Bird, Blue & White 325.00
Pitcher, Good Luck, Brown .... 55.00 To 65.00
Pitcher, Good Luck, Swastika, Blue & White 175.00
Pitcher, Grape, Blue & White, Large 110.00
Pitcher, Grape, Blue & White, Small 165.00
Pitcher, Grape, Brown 75.00
Pitcher, Grape, Green, 8 In. 55.00
Pitcher, Grape, Raised Star On Bottom, Brown 65.00
Pitcher, Grapes & Leaves, Brown 45.00
Pitcher, Grapes In Relief, Waffle Ground, Blue & Gray, 9 In. 115.00
Pitcher, Grapes, Brown 30.00
Pitcher, Hunting Scene, Blue & White 250.00
Pitcher, Indian 250.00
Pitcher, Indian Boy & Girl, Blue & White 295.00
Pitcher, Indian Head, Blue & Gray, 8 1/4 In. 75.00
Pitcher, Indian Head, Blue & White .... 99.00 To 250.00
Pitcher, Kissing Dutchman, Blue & White 50.00
Pitcher, Leaping Deer .... 195.00 To 215.00
Pitcher, Leaping Deer, Brown 45.00
Pitcher, Lovebird, Blue & White .... 175.00 To 265.00
Pitcher, Lovebird, Brown 85.00
Pitcher, Merry Christmas, Blue & Gray, 7 In. 175.00
Pitcher, Merry Christmas, H.E.Morrison, Grundy Center, Iowa, 8 In. 150.00
Pitcher, Merry Christmas, Ornate Design, Blue & Gray, 7 In. 175.00
Pitcher, Milk, Bowtie 90.00
Pitcher, Milk, Butterscotch, Pour Spout, Applied Handle, 8 In. 70.00
Pitcher, Milk, Cream Glaze, Handled, Finger Notched, 10 In. 45.00
Pitcher, Milk, Dark Brown, Pinched Spout, Incised Rings, 7 In. 50.00
Pitcher, Milk, Dark Brown, Pinched Spout, 7 In., 1/2 Gallon 50.00
Pitcher, Mustard & Brown, Centaur, Half Man, Half Horse, 8 In. 85.00
Pitcher, Pearl, Padmore Walker & Co., A Washington Scene, 12 In. 125.00
Pitcher, Poinsettia, Blue & Gray, 7 In. 145.00
Pitcher, Portrait, Bust Of Bearded Man, Steins, 8 In. 90.00
Pitcher, Raised Grapes On Waffle Ground, 9 In. 110.00

Pitcher, Reed Marsh & Cattails, Dated 1835, 10 In.	65.00
Pitcher, Rose & Fish Scale, Blue & White	75.00 To 150.00
Pitcher, Rose & Trellis, Blue & Off-White	60.00
Pitcher, Rose & Trellis, Blue & White	75.00
Pitcher, Running Deer, Blue & White	225.00
Pitcher, Scroll, Blue & White	75.00
Pitcher, Scroll, Blue & White, Extra Large	175.00
Pitcher, Square Dance	85.00
Pitcher, Swan, Blue & White	265.00
Pitcher, Trees	95.00
Pitcher, Trellis & Rose	90.00
Pitcher, Tulip, Blue & White	99.00 To 135.00
Pitcher, Wild Rose, Blue & White, Small	95.00
Pitcher, Windmill & Bush	60.00 To 80.00
Pitcher, Windmill & Bush, Blue & White	65.00 To 95.00
Pitcher, Windmill & Bush, Blue & White, 6 1/2 In.	115.00 To 175.00
Pitcher, Windmill, Blue & White	135.00
Pitcher, Windmill, Brown	80.00
Pitcher, Windmill, Bush, Blue & White	80.00
Pitcher, Yellow & Green, Cows, 3-Sided	65.00
Plate, Child's, Puff Puff, Colored Train, 8 In.	75.00
Plate, Pie, Deep Dish, Brown, C.1880, 9 1/2 In.	30.00
Plate, Pie, Deep Dish, Chocolate Brown, C.1880, 9 In.	30.00
Plate, Pie, Star, Blue & White	95.00
Plate, Pie, Yellow	24.00
Pot, Boston Baked Beans, Blue & White	295.00
Poultry Fountain, Chocolate Brown, Bell Shaped, 7 X 8 In.	22.50
Rolling Pin, Wild Flowers, Small	135.00
Salt, Apricot, Wooden Lid	95.00
Salt, Blue & White, Butterfly	80.00
Salt, Butterfly, Blue & White	80.00 To 125.00
Salt, Butterfly, Covered, Blue & White	110.00
Salt, Diamond Point, Open	45.00
Salt, Eagle, Blue & White	210.00
Salt, Peacock, Blue & White, Covered	275.00
Salt, Sponge, Blue & White	175.00
Salt, Wild Flower, Blue & White	85.00
Soap Dish, Beaded Rose, Blue & White	39.00
Soap Dish, Cat's Head	130.00
Spittoon, Daisy & Vine, Blue & White	59.00
Spittoon, Rose Trellis, Blue & White	50.00
Spittoon, Solid Blue	35.00
Stein, Beer, Incised Bands, Handled, Gray, 4 3/4 In., Pair	100.00
Stein, Golfer, Blue & White	125.00
Teapot, Blue & White, Swirl	375.00
Teapot, Egyptian Relief	85.00
Tenderizer, Meat, Wild Flower	250.00
Toothbrush Holder, Rose	125.00
Toothpick, Swan, Blue & White	39.00 To 55.00
Tumbler, Bluebird	200.00
Umbrella Stand, Crossed Birds & Floral, 22 In.	*Illus* 500.00
Urn, Side Handles, Redware, 13 1/2 In.	85.00
Water Set, Basket Weave & Flower, Green, 6 Piece	175.00
Waterer, Chicken, Dome Topped, Pull Design, 8 X 13 In.	20.00

Store items include any of the fixtures and products found in an old general
store. Many of these collectibles advertised products offered for sale.

STORE, see also Card; Coffee Grinder; Planters Peanut; Scale; Tool

STORE, Ashtray, Armstrong Rubber Tire	15.00
Ashtray, Barba Rossa Beer	10.00
Ashtray, Camel Cigarettes, Tin	3.50
Ashtray, Firestone, Tire Shape, 5 1/4 In.	15.00
Ashtray, Ford Motors, 1939 World's Fair, Glass	10.00

Ashtray, Glenmore Whiskey 7.50
Ashtray, Grand Army Of The Republic, 1861-65, Cleveland, 1901, 5 In. 4.00
Ashtray, Green River Whiskey, C.1900 .... 15.00
Ashtray, Iron Fireman, Man Shoveling Coal, Cast Iron & Tin 27.50
Ashtray, Johnny Walker 10.00
Ashtray, Merrie England, Glass Co. 8.00
Ashtray, Michelin, Figural, Man 12.00
Ashtray, Mild C Ale 13.50
Ashtray, Noxzema, Cobalt Blue 15.00
Ashtray, Odd Fellows, Glass, 7 In. 4.00
Ashtray, Pabst Blue Ribbon Beer, Copper 8.00
Ashtray, Remington Rand, Brass 12.00
Ashtray, Seagram's 7 .... 3.50
Ashtray, Sikorsky's Jolly Green Giant Heliocopter, 7 In. 12.00
Ashtray, Super Chief, The Mohawk Rubber Co., 6 In. 20.00
Bag, Chewing Tobacco, 1920s, Scott, Dillen Co., Shows Peach, 3 X 5 In. .... .75
Bag, Chewing Tobacco, 1920s, Union Workman, 3 X 5 In. .... .75
Bag, Cigar, Solace, Havana, Litho, Lady On Front, 1892, 3 X 5 1/2 In. 1.25
Bag, George Washington Tobacco, Pocket 10.00
Bank, Red Circle Coffee 10.00
Banner, Dandruff Cure & Sponge Catarrh Remedy, Oilcloth, 2 X 3 Ft. 32.50
Barrel, Root Beer, Claw Feet, Brass Spigot, Porcelain Knob, Oak 125.00
Bayer Aspirin, Glass, Metal Cap, 2 1/2 In. 4.00
Beach Cap, Advertising, Nexo Chewing Gum 30.00
Beer Scraper, Budweiser 22.00
Beer Scraper, Kent Ale 18.00
Beer Scraper, Northwestern Bottle Co. 10.00
Bin, Black Hawk Coffee & Spice Co., Lithograph, 32 X 20 In. 180.00
Bin, Closset & Devers Coffee, Pull-Up Lid, Metal, 22 X 27 1/2 In. 125.00
Bin, Curved Front, Lift Cover, Painted Black, 13 X 14 X 19 In. 28.00
Bin, Diamond Coffees, Counter, Rolltop Lid, Tin, 19 X 20 X 13 In. 55.00
Bin, Grain, 3-Section, Painted Design, 54 X 25 In. 150.00
Bin, Millar Coffee, 15 1/2 X 17 1/2 X 24 In. 135.00
Bin, White Swan Coffee, Tin, 19 X 13 X 13 In. 135.00
Birdcage, Old Crow Whiskey, Crown Inside, Metal 35.00
Blotter, Kelly Springfield Tires, 1920s Girl, Lotta Miles 10.00
     STORE, BOTTLE, see Bottle
Bottle Carrier, Tin, Pepsi-Cola 4.00
Bottle Protector, Coca-Cola, No Drip, Patented 1933, Paper 1.00
Bottle Stopper, Cast Iron, Hires 7.00
Bowl, Red Slag, Citizens Mutual Trust 1924, Black Stand 65.00
Bowl, Uneeda Biscuits Cereal, Boy In Yellow Raincoat, Vitreous China 23.00
     STORE, BOX, see also Box
Box, Arm & Hammer Baking Powder 25.00
Box, Baker's Chocolate, Dovetail-Jointed 17.00
Box, Butter, Sleepy Eye, Minn., Indian, 1958, 1 Pound 12.50
Box, Climax Golden Twins 18.00
Box, Conkey's Worm Tablets, Chicken On Front 10.00
Box, Deed, Advertising Zeno Chewing Gum, Key, Tin 28.00
Box, Display, Chicklets, Glass Top, Green Leaves & Seals 30.00
Box, Display, Sen Sen Chewing Gum, Book Shape, 1906 .... 20.00
Box, Display, Totum Union Made Cigars, Boston, Mass., Counter Top, 7 In. 3.00
Box, John Deere, Tin 10.00
Box, Soap, Bear Cleaner 10.00
Box, Sweet Mist Chewing Tobacco, Lithograph, 10 X 7 In. 45.00
Box, Washing Powder, Gold Dust, 1940, 4 X 6 X 1 1/4 In. 60.00
Broadside, Dr. Leisure's Warranted Horse Remedies 22.00
Bucket, Folding, Canvas, The Planet Co. 250.00
Bucket, Luevs Lard, Tin 20.00
Bucket, Sugar, Heinz Mincemeat Label, Wooden, Covered 195.00
Cabinet, Barker's Razors, Counter Top, 2 Shelves, Walnut 65.00
Cabinet, Boye Sewing Needles, Counter Top, Tin Compartments 85.00
Cabinet, Century Fountain Pen, Oak & Glass, Small 60.00
Cabinet, Coate's Tatting Yarn 90.00

Cabinet, Diamond Dye, Cycle Of Life 695.00
Cabinet, Diamond Dye, Sliding Doors, Solid Cherry 185.00
Cabinet, Diamond Dye, The Baby 375.00
Cabinet, Diamond Dye, The Governess 625.00
Cabinet, Diamond Dye, Wood Grained Tin 34.00
Cabinet, Hamilton Watch, 2 Tier, Glass Top, Walnut, 6 X 6 X 6 In. 20.00
Cabinet, Hanford's Balsam Of Myrrh, Glass Front, Key, Oak 175.00
Cabinet, Hohner's Harmonica, Fold-Out, 3 Shelves, Wooden 95.00
Cabinet, Humphrey's Medicine, Lists Remedies, C.1850, 11 In. 55.00
Cabinet, Ingersoll Watch, 10 X 12 In. 45.00
Cabinet, Ingersoll, Glass Front, With 9 Watches 175.00
Cabinet, J.P.Coats, Tin & Glass 30.00
Cabinet, Kaywoodie Pipes, 12 Pipes, Glass Front, Maple 28.00
Cabinet, Kiwi Boot Polish, Revolving, Bird Figure On Top 35.00
Cabinet, Leonard Silk, 22 Drawers 875.00
Cabinet, Mazda, Tin 125.00
Cabinet, Needle Case, Turn Knob To Select, Tin 65.00
Cabinet, Paris Garters 75.00
Cabinet, Parker Pen, Marble Base 350.00
Cabinet, Phonograph Cylinder, Oak, 6 Rows Of Shelves, 48 In. 725.00
Cabinet, Putnam Dye, American Revolution Picture, 11 X 16 In. 95.00
Cabinet, Putnam Dye, 32 Compartments, Tin, 19 X 15 X 6 In. 48.00
Cabinet, Ribbon, Ash 325.00
Cabinet, Ribbon, Patented 1883, Erie, Pa. 950.00
Cabinet, Rit Dye, Wooden 30.00
Cabinet, Spool, John Clark, 3-Drawer 265.00
Cabinet, Spool, Merrick, Patent, 1897, Mirrored Sides 575.00
Cabinet, Spool, Round 500.00
Cabinet, Spool, Williamatic, 4-Drawer 350.00
Cabinet, Spool, 15-Drawer, Walnut, 38 X 25 X 17 In. 695.00
Cabinet, Thread, Corticelli, 8-Drawer, Oak, 21 1/2 X 26 1/2 In. 375.00
Cabinet, Waterman's Fountain Pens, Slant Shelves, 16 X 17 In. 125.00
Cake Spoon, Bottle Opener, Slotted, Brer Rabbit Syrup, Patented 1914 .... 7.50
Cake Tin, Calumet Baking Powder, Slide Lever On Bottom, 10 In. 4.00
Cake Tin, Py-O-My Dutch Apple, 8 3/4 In. 3.00
Can, After Glow Coffee, 4 Pound 28.00
Can, Baking Powder, Clabber Girl, C.1940, 10 Ounce 6.00
Can, Molasses, Clear, Syrup Pitcher, Tin Plated Top, Aug.22, 1915 .... 10.00
Can, Oil, Mobil, Gargoyle, Logo, 1/2 Gallon 8.00
Canister, Buffalo Bill Cut Plug 225.00
Canister, Cavalier Tobacco 150.00
Canister, Green River Tobacco, Cardboard 115.00
Canister, Hiawatha Tobacco, 2 X 8 In. 175.00
Canister, Humpty Dumpty, Round 50.00
Canister, Jolly Popcorn, Tin, 50 Pound 18.00
Canister, Just Suits Tobacco 85.00
Canister, Old Colony 125.00
Canister, Seal Of North Carolina 65.00
Canister, Sweet Burley Tobacco, Tin 70.00
Canister, Sweet Mist Chewing Tobacco, Lithograph, 10 1/2 In. 65.00
Canister, Tuxedo Tobacco, Oval Top 200.00
Canister, Uncle Daniel Tobacco 95.00
Card, Phonograph Needles, Champion, 1938, 12 X 1 1/2 In. 24.00
Carrier, Butter, Stenciled Artic Butter Box, Slate Lined, Wooden 195.00
Chair, Advertising, Piedmont Cigarette, Porcelain Insert In Back 175.00
Changer, Coin, Victorian, Dated 1883, Wood & Cast Iron 1000.00
Cigarette Box, Figure Of Johnny, Philip Morris, Covered 210.00
Clip, Money, Phillips 66 .... 23.00
Clip, Money, Schenley Is The Name, Rectangular, Enameled 6.50
Coaster, Commemorating U.S.Postal Service, China & Metal, 4 1/2 In. 12.00
Coaster, Falls City Laeger Beer, Made It Famous, Red & Blue, 4 In. 7.50
Coaster, Falstaff Beer, Logo Shaped 3.00
Coaster, Ye Tavern Brew, Lafayette Brewery, Inc., 4 In. 8.50
Compact, Powder, Advertising Photographer, 1910 .... 20.00

Counter, Seed, Oak 895.00
Crock, Imperial Cube Cut, Ironstone 38.00
Cup, Phillips Milk Of Magnesia, Crystal Handled 4.00
Cutter & Lighter, Cigar, Chancellor, Cast Iron 275.00
Cutter, Cigar, Barry Lyndon 140.00
Cutter, Cigar, Brighton No.3, Cast Iron 45.00
Cutter, Cigar, Circular Rotating Blade, Pocket, Tin Frame 10.00
Cutter, Cigar, Climax Plug 50.00
Cutter, Cigar, Counter, Reverse Painted Glass, Cast Iron 125.00
Cutter, Cigar, Czarina, Windup 150.00
Cutter, Cigar, Florde Melba 100.00
Cutter, Cigar, Harvester, Mechanical, Glass 195.00
Cutter, Cigar, John Finzer & Bros., Louisville, Ky., Cast Iron 48.00
Cutter, Cigar, Krusiuss Bros., Germany, 10K Gold, Pocket, 1 3/4 In. 30.00
Cutter, Cigar, Mechanical, Footed, Table Model, Cast Iron 125.00
Cutter, Cigar, Oak Base, Cast-Iron Handle, 15 In. 35.00
Cutter, Cigar, Plug Tobacco, Cast Iron 35.00
Cutter, Cigar, Roitan Advertising, Pocket 20.00
Cutter, Cigar, Scissors Type, Pocket, Brass 18.00
Cutter, Cigar, Scissors Type, Pocket, Nickel Plated 18.00
Cutter, Cigar, Slide Type, Advertising Liquor Store, Dated 1902, Pocket .. 10.00
Cutter, Cigar, Solingen Advertising, Mother-Of-Pearl Trim 25.00
Cutter, Cigar, Star 50.00
Cutter, Cigar, Tobacco, Brown's Mule 45.00
Cutter, Cigar, Tobacco, Rex, Counter Top 24.00
Cutter, Cigar, Tobacco, Rotary, Germany 35.00
Cutter, Cigar, Tobacco, Spearhead 100.00
Cutter, Cigar, Triangle A 160.00
Cutter, Cigar, Venable 50.00
Cutter, Cigar, Waste Drawer, Strike, Sterling Silver, C.1903, 3 3/4 In. 395.00
Dish, Soup, Moxie, 8 In. 50.00
Dispenser, Candy, Raisin, & Peanut, Little Abner, Verdar Bar 400.00
Dispenser, Ceramic Fowlers Root Beer Syrup 550.00
Dispenser, Cigarette Paper, Right Cut Chewing Tobacco 24.00
Dispenser, Cigarette Paper, Wall, Zigzag 25.00
Dispenser, Cigarette, Lager Man, Wooden, 21 X 12 1/2 X 4 In. 48.00
Dispenser, Cigarolla Cigarettes, Cast Iron 35.00
Dispenser, Dixie Cup, Glass 15.00
Dispenser, Gum, Jaw Teaser, 1 Cent 20.00
Dispenser, Hand Lotion, 1 Cent 250.00
Dispenser, Hires Root Beer, Hourglass, Ceramic .... 245.00 To 295.00
Dispenser, Hot Bouillon, Armors Vigoral, 5 Cups, Copper Tank 375.00
Dispenser, Little Boy Blue Bluing, Shows Botte 95.00
Dispenser, Malt, Hamilton 20.00
Dispenser, Match, Diamond 125.00
Dispenser, Match, Kool Cigarettes, Tin 17.00
Dispenser, Match, The Scup 275.00
Dispenser, Mission Orange Syrup 235.00
Dispenser, Nesbit Orange Drink, Green & White Clambroth, 1/2 Gallon .. 85.00
Dispenser, Orange Crush 275.00
Dispenser, Orange, Mission, Pink Crackle Glass 60.00
Dispenser, Syrup, Ice Cream Parlor, C.1870, Copper, 7 In. 85.00
Dispenser, Tape, Ornate, Nickel Plated 60.00
Dispenser, Ward's Lime Crush Syrup 575.00
Dispenser, Ward's Orange Syrup 475.00
Dispenser, Watta Pop Sucker 75.00
Door Push, Caldwell's Syrup Pepsin, Porcelain 85.00
Door Push, Camel, Winston 15.00
Door Push, Colonial Is Good Bread, White Letters, Blue 20.00
Fan, Desk, Polar Cub, Fluted Base, Cast Iron 55.00
Figurine, Green River Whiskey, Whiskey Without Regrets 55.00
Figurine, Lady, Bear Brand Wool 145.00
Figurine, Philip Morris, Johnny, 44 In. 62.00
Figurine, Whitehorse Whiskey, Horse 100.00

Flashlight, Eveready, Silver Plated, Case, Dated 1912, 2 X 2 In. 26.00
Flashlight, Hand-Operated Generator 75.00
Flashlight, Winchester, 1926, Chrome Over Brass 28.00
Flashlight, Winchester, 3 Cell 15.00
Flue Cover, Black Mammy Fortune-Teller 50.00
Flue Cover, Painted Scene, Tin, Pair 7.00
Flue Cover, Pink Roses 40.00
Flue Cover, Red Riding Hood & Wolf 50.00
Fork, Davis Baking Powder, Cocomalt, White & Blue, Wooden Handle 7.00
Fork, Silver Plate, Campbell Kid Boy 12.00
Holder, Ice Cream Cone, 4-Section, Glass, Metal Lid, 12 In. 175.00
Holder, Lollipop, Bulldog 40.00
Holder, Pad, Lone Star Cement, White Metal 25.00
Holder, Straw, Drugstore, Soda Fountain 75.00
Humidor, Tuxedo Tobacco, Glass, Lid & Labels 35.00
Ice Bucket, Electric, Miller's High Life 35.00
Ice Pick, Gainesville Ice Company, Save Food Flavor 3.50
Ice Pick, Glendora Coal 5.00
Jar, Chicos Spanish Peanuts, Curtiss, Makers Of Baby Ruth, Counter 450.00
Jar, Dutch Master Cigars, Covered, Blue & White 6.00
Jar, Dutch Master Cigars, Green & White 6.00
Jar, Horlick's Malted Milk, Tin Lid, Marked, Set Of 3 .... 97.50
Jar, Kis Me Gum 85.00
Jar, Lance Cookies, Tin Cover, 8-Sided, 14 In. 15.00
Jar, Larkin Cold Cream, Floral Design, Signed Larkin Co., Buffalo, N.Y. 32.50
Jar, McLaughlin's Manor House Coffee, Label, Glass, Metal Cover 6.50
Jar, Mumbo Peanut Butter 5.00
Jar, Necco Candy, Counter 28.00
Jar, Ramon's Pills, Embossed, Clear Glass 32.50
Jar, Richard Hudnut, N.Y., Cold Cream, Tin Cover, 1/4 Pint 1.50
Jar, Shepheard's Cigarettes, Green Glass, Brass Lid 55.00
Jar, Squirrel Brand Salted Peanuts 55.00
Jar, Zatek Chocolate 525.00
Jug, Bovax Consomme Special, Monk Smelling Flowers 40.00
Jug, Sheffield Buick & Tile, Brown, 2 In. 30.00
Juicer, Soda Fountain, National Super Juicer, Patented, 1934-35 .... 20.00
Keg, Beer, Piel's, Metal Elves On Side, 6 X 8 X 5 In. 7.50
Key Chain & Knife, Advertising, John 8 Scotch Whiskey 5.00
Knife & File, Folding, Mastercraft Printers, Glen Cove, N.Y. 6.00
Knife, Fork, & Spoon, Mr.Peanut, Silver Plated, Original Package 50.00
Knife, Palette, Swans Down Cake Flour, Makes Better Cakes 8.50
Label, Apple Crate, A-Plus, Bathing Beauty, Script, 9 1/2 X 11 In. 3.00
Label, Barrel, Silver Spring Brewery, Chromolitho, C.1910, 16 In.Diam. 16.50
Label, Bottle, Jonathan P.Hall & Co., Genuine Spice Bitters, 8 In. 7.50
Label, Broom, Litho, Ocean Liner, Atlantic, 1915, 3 1/2 X 6 In. .... .50
Label, Broom, Litho, 1915, Hudson River Steamboat .... .50
Label, Broom, Litho, 1915, Little Miss, Lady Sweeping .... .50
Label, Can, Hamburgh Peas, Fairy, Chromolitho, 1905, 4 X 11 In. 3.00
Label, Cigar Box, Portraits Of Mark Twain & Tom Sawyer, 1920s 3.00
Label, Cigar, Cigarettes, Tiger Racing Through Jungle, 2 X 5 1/2 In. 20.00
Label, Cigar, Judge Best, Judge With Long White Beard, 6 X 9 In. 14.00
Label, Cigar, Pug, Dog's Head, 4 X 4 In. 5.00
Label, Crock, Buffalo Ammonia, Buffalo Pictured, C.1910, 3 1/2 X 5 In. 2.00
Label, Dixie Boy Fruit, Waverly, Florida, Black Boy Biting Grapefruit 3.00
Label, Lemon Crate, Cub, Bear Cub Eating Lemons, 9 X 12 In. 4.00
Label, Orange Crate, Bronco, Cowboy On Horse, 10 X 11 In. 7.50
Label, Orange Crate, Mariposa, Flowers, Black Ground, 10 X 11 In. 9.50
Label, Orange Crate, Unicorn, Calico Unicorn, 10 X 11 In. 12.50
Label, Pickle Barrel, Heinz, Red, White, Green, 1930s, 11 In.Diam. 6.00
Label, Tobacco Barrel, Nosegay, Lady, Lithographed, 1870, 7 X 13 In. 12.00
Ladle, Sweet Clover Condensed Milk .... 9.50 To 14.00
Light & Cutter, Cigar, Chancellor 275.00
Lighter, Cigar Lighter Mfg., Advertising On 4 Sides, 1928 .... 645.00
Lighter, Cigar, Bottle Shape, Kem Co. 14.00

Lighter, Cigar, Figural, Woman's Face, C.1920, Lights At Mouth, Pewter 285.00
Lighter, Cigar, Jamestic, 1920, Original Box 20.00
Lighter, Cigar, Midland Jump Spark, Model 2 .... 310.00 To 550.00
Lighter, Cigar, Parker, Battery Operated, Art Deco Statue, 1930s 17.50
Lighter, Cigar, Stickney's 200.00
Lighter, Cigarett, Bird, Figural, Tabletop 15.00
Lighter, Cigarette, Ball Shape, Crystal, 2 1/2 In. 15.00
Lighter, Cigarette, Brown Scotty Dog, Enamel Cover, 3 X 2 1/4 In. 15.00
Lighter, Cigarette, Bust Of Man In Armor, Chrome, 3 In. 16.50
Lighter, Cigarette, Camden Beer 15.00
Lighter, Cigarette, Camel, Unused, Boxed 8.00
Lighter, Cigarette, Chesterfield, Figural, Pack Of Cigarettes 10.00
Lighter, Cigarette, Evans, Brass 6.00
Lighter, Cigarette, Fish, Dry Cleaning, Red Fish Shaped Lettering 10.00
Lighter, Cigarette, Mack Bulldog Emblem 15.00
Lighter, Cigarette, Penguin, Figural, Kools, 10 In. 90.00
Lighter, Cigarette, Queen Anne, Ronson 18.00
Lighter, Cigarette, Ronson, Crown, Table 16.00
Lighter, Cigarette, Starlite Musical, Mother-Of-Pearl Front, Metal 25.00
Lighter, Cigarette, Zippo, From General Maxwell Taylor 14.00
Lighter, Dayton Pump Co., Cast Iron 565.00
Lighter, Lopez Grande Spark, Cigar 125.00
Lighter, Midland Cigar 425.00
Lighter, Pipe, Nimrod Sportsman, Duck Caller Shape 15.00
Lunch Box, Black Dixie Kid 100.00
Lunch Box, Bonanza 7.50
Lunch Box, Brotherhood Tobacco 125.00
Lunch Box, Central Union Tobacco, Regular 35.00
Lunch Box, Central Union Tobacco, Tall 85.00
Lunch Box, Child's, Circus Scene 40.00
Lunch Box, Dan Patch 35.00
Lunch Box, Dixie Kid Tobacco, Black 325.00
Lunch Box, Dixie Queen Tobacco 55.00
Lunch Box, Fashion 80.00
Lunch Box, George Washington Tobacco .... 35.00 To 42.00
Lunch Box, Gold Shore Tobacco 125.00
Lunch Box, Gunsmoke 9.00
Lunch Box, Joe Palooka 35.00
Lunch Box, Just Suits Tobacco 45.00
Lunch Box, King Koal Tobacco 75.00
Lunch Box, Lost In Space, Thermos 18.00
Lunch Box, Mayo's 23.00
Lunch Box, Patterson's Seal Cut Plug .... 25.00 To 30.00
Lunch Box, Pedro 38.00
Lunch Box, Penny Post Tobacco 225.00
Lunch Box, Red Tiger Tobacco 15.00
Lunch Box, Redicut Tobacco 85.00
Lunch Box, Star Trek, Thermos, 1968 .... 35.00
Lunch Box, Tiger Tobacco 48.00
Lunch Box, Tom Corbett, Space Cadet, Thermos, Dated 1952 .... 12.00
Lunch Box, U.S. Marines Tobacco 16.00
Lunch Box, U.S.Marine Cut Plug 90.00
Lunch Box, Union Leader Cut Plug Tobacco, Poinsettias .... 25.00 To 40.00
Lunch Box, Wild Fruit Tobacco, 4 X 6 In. 35.00
Lunch Box, Wonder Woman 18.00
Lunch Pail, Behrens, Double Compartment, Cup In Cover 15.00
Lunch Pail, Dixie Kid 295.00
Lunch Pail, Hungry Man's, Gray, Tin, 5 Segments, Cup, C.1880, 6 X 9 In. 45.00
Lunch Pail, Just Suits Plug Tobacco 30.00
Lunch Pail, Napheys Lard, Dated 1776-1876, Philadelphia 35.00
Lunch Pail, Plowboy 45.00
Match Holder, Ideal Family Flour, Tin 22.00
Match Holder, Juicy Fruit Gum, Tin 75.00
Matchbox, Reliable Zephyr Flour, Blue & Gold 25.00

Measure, Druggist's, Pour Spout, 15 In. 25.00
Measure, Grain, Cast-Iron Handle, 15 In. 35.00

Pocket mirrors range in size from 1 1/2 to 5 inches in diameter. Most of these mirrors were given away as free advertising gifts.

Mirror, A.T.Cook Seed Specialist, Hyde Park, Writing & Pansy, Pocket 38.50
Mirror, Angelus Marshmallow, Pocket .... 15.00 To 22.50
Mirror, Ballard's Obelisk Edible Bran, Red & Blue Lettering, Pocket 23.50
Mirror, Bell Roasted Coffee, Bell, Celluloid, Pocket, 1 1/2 In. 20.00
Mirror, Bingaman & Co., Jewelers, Flowing-Haired Lady, Oval, Pocket 28.50
Mirror, Borden's Condensed Eagle Brand Milk, Can, Pocket 35.00
Mirror, Boston Herald, The Sunday Herald, Newsboy, Pocket 43.50
Mirror, Ceresota Flour, Happy New Year, Pocket 26.00
Mirror, Ceresota Flour, Pocket 30.00
Mirror, Columbia Tool Steel Co., Clarite, American Shield, Pocket 12.50
Mirror, Columbian Exposition, Head Of Columbus, Pocket 38.00
Mirror, Dr.Forbes, Pocket 20.00
Mirror, Duffy's Pure Malt Whiskey, Celluloid, Pocket .... 10.00 To 35.00
Mirror, Dutch Java Coffee, Kissing Couple, Celluloid Rim, Pocket 24.50
Mirror, Frank Street Hatter, Illinois, Pocket 24.00
Mirror, Frear & Co., Troy, N.Y., Pocket 18.00
Mirror, Fun House, C.1930, 36 X 71 In. 275.00
Mirror, Gets-It Removes Corns, Callouses, Oval, On Stand, Plated, Tin 95.00
Mirror, Hall's Chocolates, Pocket, 4 In. 20.00
Mirror, Herrmann Prestidigitator, 1876, Brass, Pocket 50.00
Mirror, Hershey Co., Beveled Glass, Pocket 44.00
Mirror, Hires, Pocket 235.00
Mirror, Horlick's Malted Milk, Maiden & Cow, Pocket 29.00
Mirror, Kaufman Bros.Family Liquor Store, Beer Keg Shape, Pocket 22.00
Mirror, Kleinert's Dress Shields, Beautiful Lady, Pocket 25.00
Mirror, Life Insurance Of Virginia, Pyramid Picture, Pocket 22.00
Mirror, Mascot Tobacco, Pocket 30.00
Mirror, Meet Me At Osborns, Kansas City, Ice Cream, Pocket 20.00
Mirror, Mennen Talc, Lithograph Of Talc Tin, Pocket 38.00
Mirror, Mill Garden, Kansas City, Missouri, Pictured Mill, Pocket 20.00
Mirror, Monarch Visible, Typewriter, Pocket 37.00
Mirror, Mortons Salt, Girl With Umbrella, Pocket 22.00
Mirror, Nature's Remedies, Pocket 20.00
Mirror, Niagara Falls, Oval, Pocket 10.00
Mirror, Old Reliable Coffee, Always Good, Old Man & Box, Pocket 26.00
Mirror, Pacific Shoe, Peru, Ill., Pocket 14.00
Mirror, Peoples National Bank, Tyler, Texas, 1892-1942, Pocket 22.00
Mirror, Polar Bear Flour, Bear, Celluloid, Swivel Handle, Pocket 30.00
Mirror, Princess Cox Stoves, Art Nouveau, Pocket 50.00
Mirror, Prudential Insurance Co., 1940s, Pocket 5.00
Mirror, Pullman Automobiles, Picture, Pocket 100.00
Mirror, R.C.A. Nipper & Gramophone, Pocket 3.00
Mirror, Red Seal Lye, Philadelphia, Pocket 22.50
Mirror, Regina Mills Corset, Framed, Lady, Corset, 12 X 14 In. 48.00
Mirror, Robin Hood Flour, Pocket 20.00
Mirror, Schrand Undergarments, Pocket 24.00
Mirror, Socony Motor Gasoline, Pocket 30.00
Mirror, St.Louis Plume Co., Cleaner Of Ostrich Goods, Pocket 13.50
Mirror, St.Louis World's Fair, 1904, Liberal Arts Building, Celluloid 21.00
Mirror, Star Soap, Schutz & Co., Zanesville, Ohio, Pocket 12.50
Mirror, Starrett Tools, Scribe, Caliper, Gold Lettering, Pocket 18.50
Mirror, Stoddar Gilbert & Co., Smoke The Green 10-Cent Cigar, Pocket 38.50
Mirror, West Coast Shoe Co, , Pocket 12.50
Mirror, Whirlpool Washer, Pocket 17.50
Mirror, White Cat Union Suits, Smiling White Cat, Celluloid, Pocket 30.00
Mirror, White House Coffee, Pocket 24.00
Mirror, Wm. Albrecht's Bottling Co., Pocket 30.00
Mirror, Wonder Woman, Figural, 1976, 7 1/2 In. 15.00

Mirror, Woodmen Circle, 1900, Pocket 15.00
Mortar & Pestle, Ironstone, Coors 15.00
Mug, Blatz Man, Beer Can Body, Holds Beer Mug In Hand 25.00
Mug, Lash's Root Beer, Blue Stripes, White Ground 35.00
Mug, Richardson's Root Beer, Beaded 17.00
Opener & Spoon, Anderson Peanut Co., Inc., Andalusia, Ala. 10.00
Opener, Box, Kipp Cigar Co., 1897 .... 15.00
Opener, Schlitz Beer, Wooden, 3 1/2 In. 15.00
Pail, After Glow Coffee, 4 Pound .... 25.00 To 35.00
Pail, Berry, Black Forest, 1911 .... 6.00
Pail, Blanke's Defy Coffee 22.50
Pail, Buffalo Brand Peanut Butter 40.00
Pail, Buffalo Peanut Butter, Covered, 1 Pound 55.00
Pail, Butternut Coffee, Bail Handle, Paper Label, 15 Pound 20.00
Pail, Butternut, No.10, Tin 18.00
Pail, Candy, Cardboard, 30 Pound 16.00
Pail, Candy, T'was The Night Before Xmas, Deco, Tin 35.00
Pail, Coffee, Nashes, Decal On Side, Tin 25.00
Pail, Cream Dove Shortening, 3 Pound 20.00
Pail, Essex Fruit Jelly, 11 3/4 X 11 In. 12.00
Pail, Gold Flake Peanut Butter 45.00
Pail, Jackie Coogan Candy 60.00
Pail, Jackie Coogan Peanut Butter 200.00
Pail, Jackie Coogan Salted Peanuts 100.00
Pail, Just Soap, Lidded, 1930-40, Orange & Black, 6 In. 12.00
Pail, Lard, Frosty Morn Meats, Bail, Lid, Blue, 8 Pound, 8 X 7 1/2 In. 30.00
Pail, Mac Laren Peanut Butter 85.00
Pail, Nigger Hair Tobacco, Covered .... 80.00 To 100.00
Pail, Old Partner's 100.00
Pail, Ontario Peanut Butter 15.00
Pail, Peter Pan Peanut Butter, Sample 28.00
Pail, Peter Rabbit Peanut Butter 100.00
Pail, Pickanniny Peanut Butter 100.00
Pail, Red & White Peanut Butter 45.00
Pail, Sears, Roebuck Combination Coffee, Tin 30.00
Pail, Shedd's Peanut Butter, Elves 9.00
Pail, Shedd's Peanut Butter, 5 Pound 5.00
Pail, Snowflake Axle Grease, Boston, Mass., Label, Tin, 1 Pint 3.00
Pail, Sultana Peanut Butter, Blue .... 25.00 To 35.00
Pail, Sultana Peanut Butter, Children, Atlantic & Pacific Tea Co. 30.00
Pail, Sultana Peanut Butter, Girl Offering Sandwich To Boy, 1 Pound 12.00
Pail, Sunny Boy Peanut Butter, 16 Ounce 40.00
Pail, Swift's Jewel Shortening, 4 Pound .... 3.00 To 4.00
Pail, Swift's Peanut Butter, Tin, 5 Pound 2.50
Pail, Swift's Silverleaf Lard, Covered, 4 Pound 4.00
Pail, Teddie Peanut Butter 65.00
Pail, Teenie Weenie Peanut Butter 150.00
Pail, Toyland Peanut Butter .... 65.00 To 75.00
Pail, Veribest Peanut Butter 55.00
Pail, Wizard Of Oz Peanut Butter, Yellow & Red, Cartoon .... 40.00 To 55.00
Paint Stirrer, Felton Sibley & Co., Wood, 12 In. 8.00
Pan, Rolled Edge, Morton Old Kentucky Recipe Bread, 5 X 9 In. 4.00
Paperweight, Broski Brothers Fence Company, Glass 12.00
Paperweight, Romanoff Cavier, Russia, Figural, Cast Iron, 5 1/2 In. 25.00
Pitcher, Calvert's, Imported Passport Scotch Emblem, Green, 8 1/2 In. .. 18.00
Pitcher, Henderson's Wild Cherry Beverage 20.00
Pitcher, Passport Scotch 10.00
Pitcher, Schlitz Beer, Red Logo, 2 Quart 15.00
Plaque, Green River Whiskey, Metal, 24 In. 137.50
Plate, Calendar, Kane, 1914 .... 32.00
Plate, Fred Krug Brewing Co. 50th Anniversary, 1859-1909 .... 90.00
Plate, Lorillard Tobacco, Night Of Stars In Chicago 22.00
Poster, Rices Seed, Man Lifting Head Of Cabbage, C.1890, 22 X 28 In. .. 125.00

Poster, Seagram's Kentucky Distillery, 1937 Cars, Color, 15 X 34 In. 10.00
Rack, Baby Ruth Gum 130.00
Rack, Broom, Cast Iron, Holds 24 Brooms 60.00
Rack, Display, Hohner Harmonicas, On Turnstile Base, Mahogany, 36 In. 125.00
Rack, Postcard, Twisted Wire, Displays 90 Cards, 20 X 30 In. 25.00
Register, Account, McCasky, Glass Lift-Top, 1899, Three Oak Panels 95.00
Roller, Cigarette, Brown & Williamson 18.00
Ruler, Metal, Wonder Bread Helps Build Strong Bodies, 12 In. 3.00
Ruler, Queen City Brewing, Seasons Greetings, Tin, 12 In. 3.00
Sack, Ceresota Flour, Pair 12.00
Sack, Red Comb Poultry Feed 12.00
Sack, Sprat Flour, Sprat Doll To Cut & Stuff, 48 Pound 40.00
Salt & Pepper Shaker, Sealtest, Figural Milk Bottles 18.00
Salt & Pepper, Borden's Milk 15.00
Salt & Pepper, Campbell Soup Kids, Plastic 17.00
Salt & Pepper, Coors, Pottery, 4 In. 19.50
Salt & Pepper, Esslinger's Beer, Amber Bottles, Bellboy 10.00
Salt & Pepper, Esslinger's, Beer Bottle Shape 20.00
Salt & Pepper, Esso, Gas Pumps, Original Box 15.00
Salt & Pepper, G.E.Refrigerator Shape, Milk Glass 15.00
Salt & Pepper, Goetz Country Club Pilsener Beer, Metal Caps 20.00
Salt & Pepper, Metz Jubilee Beer, Metal Caps 50.00
Salt & Pepper, Pepsi-Cola 25.00
Salt & Pepper, Prager Beer 12.50
Salt & Pepper, R.C.A. 20.00
Salt & Pepper, Royal Pilsener Beer, Stoneware, With Verse 28.50
Salt & Pepper, Schlitz Beer 10.00
Salt & Pepper, Shell Oil 6.00
Salt & Pepper, Sunshine Bakers 15.00
Salt & Pepper, Tappan Stoves 25.00
Scale, Candy, Counter Top, Brass Pan, C.1915, 13 X 4 X 9 In. 125.00
Scale, Fairbanks, Black Iron, Bass Pan, Measure Bar, C.1859 .... 50.00
Scoop, Candy, Copper Hang-Up Loop, Brass, 9 X 6 In. 50.00
Scoop, Dark Gray, Tubular Handle, Tin, 2 Pound, 11 1/2 In. 20.00
Scoop, Flour, Wood 70.00
Scoop, Gilcrest Ice Cream, No.31 .... 20.00
Scoop, Grain, Ice, Aluminum, Wearever, Marked, NSF, Holds 2 Pound 20.00
Scoop, Grocery, Aluminum, Medium, Marked Wagner, Sidney, Ohio 12.00
Scoop, Ice Cream, Brass 18.00
Scoop, Ice Cream, Cone Shaped, Tin .... 22.00 To 24.00
Scoop, Ice Cream, Hamilton Beach 20.00
Scoop, Ice Cream, Sealtest, Aluminum, Spoon Type 6.00
Screwdriver, Drink Coca-Cola, Pocket, 4 1/2 In. 1.00
Shoehorn, Shinola, 1907, Pictures Brushes, Can, & Polisher, Tin 35.00
Shot Glass, Jack Daniels Old No.7 .... 1.00
Showcase, Howard Cutlery, 3 Revolving Shelves, Mahogany, 26 1/2 In. 650.00
Sign, A-1 Beer, Black Bart, Barber Chair, Cardboard, 38 X 25 In. 125.00
Sign, AC Spark Plugs, Embossed, Tin, 1920s, 12 X 9 In. 30.00
Sign, Anheuser Busch Ginger Ale, 1920s, Porcelain, 12 X 20 In. 65.00
Sign, Anheuser Busch, Custers Last Fight, Paper, 46 X 36 In. 95.00
Sign, Arm & Hammer Soda, Emblem, Black & Gold, Cardboard, 16 X 12 In. 24.50
Sign, Ashland Whiskey, Hunter, Lodge, Tin, Framed, 1900, 24 X 20 In. 750.00
Sign, Aunt Jemima On A Swing, Chromolithograph, Tin, 17 In. 40.00
Sign, Auto-Lite Spark Plugs, Tin, 11 X 23 In. 25.00
Sign, Babbitt's Soap, Tom Sawyer Catching Fish, 1892, 27 X 14 In. 150.00
Sign, Barbershop, Porcelain, 12 X 24 In. 40.00
Sign, Barbershop, Vigorator Foaming Hair Tonic, Tin, 5 X 9 In. 35.00
Sign, Bartholomay, Nude Riding Wings, Board, 1900, 26 X 36 In. 475.00
Sign, Bayer Aspirin, Tin, 1920's, 15 X 18 In. 30.00
Sign, Beech Nut Bacon, Fold-Out, C.1915, Cardboard, 35 1/2 X 25 1/2 In 275.00
Sign, Beech Nut Gum, Cardboard, 10 X 21 In. 40.00
Sign, Beech Nut Mints, Cardboard, 10 X 21 In. 35.00
Sign, Beer, Horse Man O' War, 1930, Tin, 23 X 17 In. 110.00

Sign, Beer, Wine & Iron, Great Restorative Tonic, 20 X 36 In. 150.00
Sign, Bell System Underground Cable, Porcelain, 2 X 7 In. 15.00
Sign, Bell Telephone, Porcelain, 11 X 11 In. 18.00
Sign, Best Paint Sold, Porcelain, 14 X 20 In. 22.00
Sign, Bloch Bros. Mail Pouch, Tin, 22 1/2 X 21 1/2 In. 175.00
Sign, Blue Ribbon Bourbon, Wagon Pulled By Oxen, Canvas, 38 X 28 In. 350.00
Sign, Bluff City Brewing Co., Corner, Milk Glass, 18 In.Diam. 295.00
Sign, Boyscout Butternut Bread, Cardboard, 1950s, 5 1/2 X 16 1/2 In. 4.00
Sign, Briar Pipe, Man Smoking, Poster, 1910, 31 X 23 In. 195.00
Sign, Brown Shoe Co., Lithograph, Gold Leaf Frame, 15 X 29 In. 325.00
Sign, Brownies, Root Beer, Oak Barrel, Original, 25 In. 225.00
Sign, Buckshoe & Tiger Stripe Tobacco, 1895, 28 X 14 In. 275.00
Sign, Budweiser, Man, Lady, Beer Fondue, Round, 16 In. 275.00
Sign, Bull Durham, Lady, Tree, Bull, Tin, 37 X 27 In. 550.00
Sign, Bull's-Eye Beer, Red, White, Blue, Porcelain, Square, 18 In. 99.00
Sign, Bung Hammer, Sylvan Grove Rye, Wood, 21 In. 60.00
Sign, Bus Stop, Porcelain, 5 X 16 In. 28.00
Sign, Camel Cigarettes, Porcelain, 12 X 32 In. 15.00
Sign, Cardboard, Butternut Bread, Girl With Bread, 7 X 10 In. 5.50
Sign, Carhartt Overalls, Embossed, Tin, 1920s, 10 X 24 In. 25.00
Sign, Carstairs Whiskey, Mellow As A Sunny Morning, 1947, 19 X 12 In. 5.00
Sign, Carter's Ink, Kittens Playing Baseball, Framed, 13 X 11 In. 35.00
Sign, Caution, Keep Aisles Clear, Metal, Dated 1916, 9 X 13 In. 12.00
Sign, Centlivre Brewing Co., Factory, Pre-Prohibition, 27 X 40 In. 325.00
Sign, Champale, Champagne Glass Blinks, Electric, 12 X 5 In. 20.00
Sign, Cherry Blossoms, A Blooming Good Drink, Tin, 19 X 10 In. 75.00
Sign, Chesterfield Cigarettes, Tin, 17 3/4 X 13 3/4 In. 55.00
Sign, Chesterfield, Lady With Carton, 1940s, Cardboard, 24 X 24 In. 35.00
Sign, Chew Walla Walla Gum, It Aids Digestion, Metal, 9 X 19 In. 65.00
Sign, Chief Paint, Indian Chief In Full Color, 1940s, Tin, 12 X 28 In. 12.00
Sign, Clark's O.N.T., Girl, Doll, & Cats, 1880s, 20 X 15 1/2 In. 250.00
Sign, Clayton Whiskey, Hunters Drinking, Framed Paper, 20 X 30 In. 220.00
Sign, Coca-Cola, Policeman, Metal, Iron Base, 5 In. 325.00
Sign, Coke Bottle, Porcelain, 15 In. 45.00
Sign, Coke, Round, Yellow, Red, Green, Sold Here, 20 In. 99.00
Sign, Cole's Peruvian Wild Cherry Bitters, Porcelain, 16 X 6 In. 225.00
Sign, Columbia Batteries, 1910, Red Devil, Spaceman, Metal, 1910, 2 1/2 I 275.00
Sign, Columbian Beer, Tennessee Brewing, Tin, 10 X 13 In. 40.00
Sign, Continental Fire Ins., Co., Soldier & Gun, Metal, 20 X 30 In. 395.00
Sign, Continental Typewriter Co., Porcelain, Blue & White, 18 X 24 In. 75.00
Sign, Copenhagen Castle Beer, Bottle, King, Tin, 10 X 12 In. 30.00
Sign, Corset, Mechanical, Girl In Corset, 24 X 36 In. 600.00
Sign, Country Store, Howe Scale, Gold Over Black, Wooden, 40 X 13 In. 155.00
Sign, Cream Of Wheat, Stand-Up, 34 X 23 In. 125.00
Sign, Crown Quality Ice Cream, Crown, Tin, 18 X 23 In. 75.00
Sign, Crown Quality Ice Cream, Tin, 20 X 25 In. 75.00
Sign, Cupples Cord, Rhino Inside Auto Tire, Tin, 1920, 20 X 28 In. 250.00
Sign, Dad's Root Beer, 12 X 9 In. 15.00
Sign, Dalley's Pain Extractor, Elk, Dated 1889, 32 X 16 In. 350.00
Sign, Dam-I-Ana Invigorator, Nude Lady & Man, 1900, 24 X 3 In. 475.00
Sign, Danderine, Cardboard, Woman Pictured, 24 X 34 In. 60.00
Sign, Delaval, 5 Scenes, Women Of Various Countries, Paper, 21 X 30 In. 575.00
Sign, Delivery, Wooden, 63 X 19 1/2 In. 190.00
Sign, Dixon's Pencils, Horter Print, 1923, Paper, 15 X 20 In. 24.00
Sign, Dolly Dingle Chocolate Dairy Drink, Cardboard, 9 X 11 In. 17.50
Sign, Don Murano Cigars, Girl, Pink Dress, Tin, Round, 19 In. 325.00
Sign, Dr.Jayne's Expectorant & Tonic, Lithograph, 14 X 28 In. 375.00
Sign, Drink Cherry Julep, White Lettering, Red, Tin, 7 X 20 In. 18.50
Sign, Drink Grape Ola, Grapes & Bottle, 12 X 35 In. 65.00
Sign, Drink Piff's, Embossed, Tin, 1940s, 15 X 30 In. 25.00
Sign, Drink Sun Spot, Bottled Sunshine, Double-Sided, Metal, 15 1/4 In. 30.00
Sign, Drugs, Leaded Glass, Milk Glass Letters, Blue Ground, 72 X 22 In. 950.00
Sign, Dub-L-Valu, 5 Cents For 2 Glasses, Metal, 11 X 27 In. 45.00
Sign, Duke's Mixture, Solidiers, Spanish, Paper, 1899, 32 X 22 In. 395.00

Sign, Duluth Imperial Flour, Black Cook, Bread, Tin, 1910, 18 X 25 In. 750.00
Sign, Dunlop Motorcycle Tires, Metal, 28 X 33 In. 100.00
Sign, Dutch Cleaners, Porcelain, 22 X 32 In. 195.00
Sign, Early Times Whiskey, Distillery In Relief, Plaster, 23 X 27 In. 350.00
Sign, Early Times Whiskey, 3-D, Distillery Scene, 23 X 29 In. 300.00
Sign, Eastside Beer, Celluloid, 1930s, 21 X 9 In. 35.00
Sign, Eat Bread Made With Fleischman's Yeast, Tin, 3 1/4 X 8 3/4 In. 48.00
Sign, Ehlermann, Founder, Beer Plant, Workers, Tin, 26 X 18 In. 650.00
Sign, Eight Ball, Heres Your Cue, Bottle, Tin, 9 In.Diam. 20.00
Sign, Elgin Watch, Father Time, Paper, 1910, 16 X 22 In. 175.00
Sign, Elgin Watch, Tom Sawyer, Holding Watch, Wood, 16 X 23 In. 375.00
Sign, Emilia Garcia, Trifold Standee, 31 X 44 In. 125.00
Sign, Eveready Shaving Brush, Man Shaving, 1940s, 3 1/4 X 10 1/2 In. 4.00
Sign, Falstaff, Sir Falstaff, Drinking, Tin, 1910, 30 X 20 In. 650.00
Sign, Fatima Cigarettes, Harem Girl, Pack, Tin, 37 X 27 In. 850.00
Sign, Figure, Philip Morris, Johnny, 44 In. 75.00
Sign, Finch's Detroit Special Overalls, Pig Lithograph, Tin, 9 X 6 In. 50.00
Sign, Franklin Gardens Dance Hall, Embossed, Tin, 1930s, 10 X 24 In. 25.00
Sign, Friedman Shoes, Eagle Over Shield, Tin, 19 3/4 X 13 3/4 In. 45.00
Sign, Gast Beer, St.Louis, Metal, 21 1/2 X 9 3/4 In. 22.00
Sign, Gold Dust, Twins Scrubbin Tub, Dated 1921, 28 X 17 In. 80.00
Sign, Golden Girl Cola, Tin, 23 X 15 In. 45.00
Sign, Golden's Blue Ribbon Cigar, Metal, Blue & Yellow, 3 X 12 In. 10.00
Sign, Goodyear Tires, Winged Foot, Enamel, 66 X 24 In. 150.00
Sign, Grand Prize Beer, 1943, Texas Capital, Cardboard, 41 X 29 In. 85.00
Sign, Grape Nuts, Girl, St.Bernard, Tin, 1905, 20 X 31 In. .... 650.00 To 950.00
Sign, Grape-Nuts, Standee, Dizzy Dean, 22 X 30 In. 250.00
Sign, Harvard Rye, Graduates, Drinking, Tin, Wood Frame, 29 X 22 In. 450.00
Sign, Helmar Cigarettes, Brunette, Large Hat, Paper, 33 X 43 In. 275.00
Sign, Hires Root Beer, Stand-Up, 1892, Die Cut, Framed 60.00
Sign, Holihan's Beer, Wooden, 9 X 13 In. 20.00
Sign, Honest Scrap Tobacco, Dog & Cat Fight, Wooden Frame, 30 X 23 In. 495.00
Sign, Hoster Brewery, Factory, Wagon, Tin, 39 X 30 In. 550.00
Sign, Hoyts Cologne, Color Lithograph, C.1890, Metal, 20 X 28 In. 300.00
Sign, Hump Hairpins, Giant Hairpin, Camel, Tin, 16 X 14 In. 150.00
Sign, I.W.Harper, Auto, People, Just Married, Canvas, 33 X 44 In. 650.00
Sign, I.W.Harper, Here's To Happy Days, 1908, On Glass, 22 X 28 In. 600.00
Sign, Ice, Window, Cardboard 4.00
Sign, J.& P.Coats, Man, Woman, Eastlake Frame, C.1883, Paper, 30 X 27 In. 375.00
Sign, Jetter Brewery, Elk Bellowing, Bottle, Tin, 33 X 24 In. 650.00
Sign, Jordan Brewery, Cardboard, 11 X 14 In. 10.00
Sign, K-Lunch, Reverse Painted, Abalone, Silver Letters, 21 X 10 In. 325.00
Sign, Kato Beer, Glass With Eagle, 15 1/2 In. 125.00
Sign, Keen Kutter, Tin, 9 3/4 X 27 3/4 In. .... 20.00 To 25.00
Sign, Kodak, Printing On Top, Film & Box On Bottom, Enamel, 12 X 18 In. 285.00
Sign, Korbel Sec, Champagne, Girl, Grapes, Self-Framed, Tin, 13 X 19 In. 175.00
Sign, Labatte's, With Sea Horse, Electric, 12 X 6 In. 25.00
Sign, Lash's Bitters, Victorian Woman, Horse, Wood, 14 X 21 In. 395.00
Sign, Lemon, Lime, Bottle Shape, Tin, 1940, 28 In. 35.00
Sign, Lion Packing, For Steam Engines & Pumps, Cardboard, 9 X 10 In. 46.20
Sign, London Life Cigarettes, Man, Tux, Girl, Paper, 1935, 34 X 18 In. 225.00
Sign, Mail Pouch, Porcelain, Smoke Chew, 3 X 12 In. 30.00
Sign, Manhattan Shirts, Father's Day, Girl & Package, Cardboard, 20 In. 25.00
Sign, Marathon Brewery, Glass, 4 X 8 In. 8.00
Sign, Mass.Tourist Court Assn., Map, 2-Sided, Porcelain, 18 X 28 In. 110.00
Sign, Mayo's Plug, Rooster & Plugs, Yellow Ground, 19 X 29 In. 225.00
Sign, McIntyre's Ice Cream, Fruit On Plates, Night Scene, Streetcar 32.00
Sign, Mcvities Cracker, Family Feeding Parrot, 1920, 14 X 19 In. 80.00
Sign, Mikado Pencils, Our Gang Stars, 1930, 20 X 10 In. 75.00
Sign, Miller High Life Beer, Reverse On Glass, Signed, 24 X 10 In. 175.00
Sign, Miller High Life, Girl In Moon, Tin, 24 In.Diam. 325.00
Sign, Mobil Flying Red Horse, Porcelain, 92 X 68 In. 200.00
Sign, Mobil Gas, Shield Shape, Flying Horse, Porcelain, 12 X 12 In. 40.00
Sign, Mobil Oil Gargoyle, Round, Porcelain, 23 In. 75.00

Sign, Morton Salt, 2-Sided, Tin, 28 X 10 In. 28.00
Sign, Mountain Whiskey, Mountain Girl, Moonshine, Poster, 24 X 20 In. 175.00
Sign, Mule Hide, Embossed, Tin, 1930s, 10 X 32 In. 35.00
Sign, Munsingwear, Cardboard, Woman Pictured, 24 X 36 In. 85.00
Sign, N.Y. Bell Telephone, 2-Sided, Old Style Bell, 11 X 12 In. 75.00
Sign, Naegelli Sons, Imported Pilsener, Barmaid, Steins, Tin, 17 X 21 In 350.00
Sign, Nappanee Dutch Kitchenet, Girl Lithograph, Tin, 17 1/2 X 7 In. 45.00
Sign, National Fire Ins.Hartford, Brass, Woman With Flag, 16 X 28 In. 275.00
Sign, National Park Bank, N.Y., Tin, Self-Framed, 24 X 36 In. 300.00
Sign, Natural Cigarettes, Arab, Rifle, Horse, Poster, 26 X 18 In. 275.00
Sign, Nehi, Curb Service, Embossed, Tin, 19 1/2 X 27 1/2 In. 20.00
Sign, Nehi, Curb Service, 18 X 26 In. 28.00
Sign, Niagara Fire Insurance, Reverse On Glass, 24 X 12 In. 575.00
Sign, Nichol 5-Cent Kila, Tin, 10 X 14 In. 27.00
Sign, Nifty Fruit Beverage, Topless Girl, 6 1/2 X 4 3/4 In. 25.00
Sign, No Parking, Parking 30 Minutes, Metal, 13 X 18 In. 10.00
Sign, Oconto, Football Player, 3-D, Paperboard, 1930, 22 X 29 In. 95.00
Sign, OFC Bourbon, Hunters, Log, Drinking, Paper, 1900, 31 X 22 In. 495.00
Sign, Old Dutch Cleanser, Porcelain, 22 X 32 In. 130.00
Sign, Old English Cut Tobacco, Giant Pocket Tin, 1915, 14 X 2i In. 15.00
Sign, Old English, Englishman, Fireplace, Dog, 1900, 31 X 24 In. 225.00
Sign, Old Forester Whiskey, Bottle Shape, Cardboard, 29 In. 6.00
Sign, Old Jed Clayton Whiskey, Black Man, Whiskey, 20 X 30 In. 220.00
Sign, Oliver Plow, Signed, Framed, 34 X 25 In. 395.00
Sign, Opera Light Cigarettes, Dated 1892, Cardboard, 10 X 14 In. 48.50
Sign, Our Own Hardware, Oval, Tin, Blue & White, 13 1/2 X 19 In. 35.00
Sign, Pablo, Girl With Drink, Sandwich, Pabst Brewing, 9 X 13 In. 30.00
Sign, Pabst Brewing, Man, Bottle, Brewery, 1900, Tin, 36 X 48 In. 450.00
Sign, Pabst, Bottle, Sandwich, Dated 1924, Self-Framed, 9 X 13 In. 80.00
Sign, Palmer Cox Brownie, Lithograph, 1918, 60 X 21 In. 265.00
Sign, Pan Burn's Chocolate, Candy, 10 X 7 1/2 In. 35.00
Sign, Paul Jones Co., Negro Woman, Huge Watermelon, Child, 21 X 14 In. 650.00
Sign, Pennzoil, Round, Double Sided, Porcelain, 24 In. 65.00
Sign, Pepsi-Cola, 1910, Tin, 3 X 12 In. 100.00
Sign, Pepsi-Cola, 5 Cents, Bottle Shape, 29 In. 75.00
Sign, Phillip Morris, Gold Ground, Bellboy, Tin, 28 X 14 In. 32.00
Sign, Piedmont Cigarettes, Porcelain, 12 1/2 X 12 1/2 In. 60.00
Sign, Potosi Brewery, Metal, 7 X 11 In. 12.00
Sign, Pump, Flying A Ethyl Gasoline, Curved Glass, 12 X 12 In. 50.00
Sign, Pump, Gas, Richfield Ethyl, Glass Panel, 12 X 4 In. 25.00
Sign, Pump, Indian Gasoline, Glass Panel, 12 X 4 In. 10.00
Sign, Pure Oil, Metal, Round, Be Sure With Pure, 41 In. 100.00
Sign, Putnam Dyes, Redcoats On Horses, Tin, 14 X 19 In. .... 75.00 To 98.00
Sign, Quail Cigar, Cardboard, Pictures Quail, 1920s, 3 X 14 In. 4.00
Sign, R & G Corsets, Mechanical, Woman, Corset, Moves, 24 X 36 In. 600.00
Sign, R.C.Cola, 2-Sided, 10 X 17 In. 30.00
Sign, Railway Express, Diamond Shaped, Porcelain, 4 In. 125.00
Sign, Rapid Kool, Tin, 1940s, 10 X 24 In. 20.00
Sign, Red Rock Cola, Tin, 39 X 22 In. 45.00
Sign, Republic Tire, Eagle, Tire, Framed, 36 X 24 In. 195.00
Sign, Republic Tire, Old Man, Buggy, Horse, Paper, 34 X 24 In. 375.00
Sign, Reverse On Glass, Dr.Jaynes, Child's Face 250.00
Sign, Robert Smith Ale, Tiger's Head, Tin, 1900, Oval, 24 In. 850.00
Sign, Round Oak Stoves, Doe Wah Jack, Paper Under Glass, 29 X 14 In. 200.00
Sign, Royal Insurance, Reverse On Glass, 27 X 21 In. 350.00
Sign, Saloon, Don't Spit On The Floor, 6 X 9 In. 20.00
Sign, San Diego Quality Beer, Electric, C.1930, Metal & Glass, 15 In. 95.00
Sign, San Felice Cigars, Woman Hugging Man, Paper, 18 X 24 In. 215.00
Sign, Satin Skin Cream, Lithograph, 1903, 28 X 43 In. 100.00
Sign, Satin Skin Powder, Framed, Trolley Card 65.00
Sign, Schlitz, Cone Top Can, Tin, 1930s, 11 X 15 In. 100.00
Sign, Schlitz, Electric Glass Window, Hemisphere Logo, 22 X 30 In. 75.00
Sign, Schlitz, Electric, 12 X 20 In. 20.00
Sign, Schlitz, Servant Girl, Gentleman, Cardboard, 20 X 24 In. 20.00

Piano, Hallet, Davis & Co., Boston, Ebonized Cherry, Gilt, C. 1870, 95 In.

Etagere, Rosewood, Mirrored Backboard, American, 1850–1857, 7½ Ft.

Garden Bench, Cast-Iron, John McLean, New York, C. 1860, Green, 30¼ In.

Fireplace Mantel, Ebonized Wood, Marble Surround, Cast-Iron Grate, American, C. 1850, 51 In.

Armchair, Ebonized Cherry,
American, C. 1865, 38 In.

Armchair, American, Ebony,
Marquetry, C. 1875,
38¾ In.

Table, Sugar Maple,
G. Niardot, C. 1900,
29⅜ In.

Silver Dish, Van Sant & Co., Philadelphia, 10 In.

Tiffany & Co. Teapot, Cast
Iron & Silver, Wood Handle,
C. 1905, 6 In.

Tall Clock, Gustave Herter,
Walnut, Lion's Mask,
1857–1865, 70¾ In.

Tiffany Silver Vase, Amphora-Shaped,
Marked, C. 1891, 18 In.

Sideboard, Oak, Gustav Stickley,
C. 1910, 48¾ In.

Armchair, Reclining, Morris, Oak,
Theodore Hofstatter, Jr., 1881,
40½ In.

Glass Vase, Ruby-Stained, Etching of Capitol Building, Washington, D.C., C. 1850, 20½ In.

Lamp, Argand, Bronze, Cut Crystal, Messenger & Sons, London, C. 1825, 25¾ In., Pair

Armchair, Oak, Burns & Brother,
New York, C. 1857, 62¾ In.

Runner, Wool, Geometric, Rose Border,
C. 1910, 209 In. x 38¼ In.

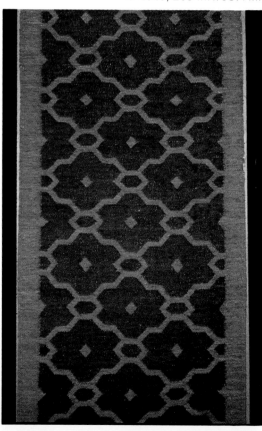

Sign, Schmidt's Beer, Die Cut, Bottle Shape, 5 1/2 X 16 1/2 In. 2.50
Sign, Schmidt's City Club, Tin, 13 1/2 X 39 In. 60.00
Sign, Shamrock Sunkist Valencia Oranges, 1920, 8 1/2 X 9 1/2 In. 2.00
Sign, Smoke Victory 5 **Cigars, Double Sided, 4 X 7 In.** 4.00
Sign, Southern Agriculturist, Embossed, Tin, 1920s, 7 X 10 In. 15.00
Sign, Star Tobacco, Porcelain, 12 X 24 In. 70.00
Sign, Star Tobacco, We Sell, Porcelain, Blue, White, 8 X 18 In. 50.00
Sign, Stroh's, Electric, 12 X 14 In. 15.00
Sign, Studio, Vocal & Instrumental Music, Porcelain, 9 X 23 In. 85.00
Sign, Sunoco Dynafuel, Diamond Shaped Inserts, 15 In.Diam., Pair 175.00
Sign, Sweetheart Soap Baby, Life-Size, Basket, Motorized, Boxed 300.00
Sign, Telephone, Bells On Each Side, Porcelain, 4 X 18 In. 55.00
Sign, Telephone, White, Blue, Porcelain, Pay Station, 12 X 16 In. 110.00
Sign, Tennessee, Brewing Co., Columbia Beer, Tin, 9 1/2 X 13 1/2 In. 90.00
Sign, Texaco Gas, Porcelain, 12 X 18 In. 15.00
Sign, Texas & Southwestern Cattle Raisers, Porcelain, 10 X 20 In. 95.00
Sign, The Bradley Shoe, Lithograph Shoe, Tin, 19 X 7 In. 37.50
Sign, Threshermen & Farmers Insurance, Metal, 8 X 15 In. 23.00
Sign, Toonerville Town, Cardboard Cutouts, 1920, 17 X 10 In. 75.00
Sign, Trade, Fish, Sheet Iron, 33 X 12 In. 495.00
Sign, Tuborg Bread, Wood, Cast Iron Brackets, 6 In. 100.00
Sign, Tubular Cream Separator, Tin, 24 X 5 In. 45.00
Sign, U.S.Fur Co., Black Hunter Surprised By Skunk, 26 1/2 X 20 In. 475.00
Sign, U.S.Royal Cord Tires, Die Cut, Double Faced, 32 In.Diam. 225.00
Sign, Velvet Pipe Tobacco, Porcelain, 12 X 39 In. 25.00
Sign, Velvet Tobacco, Pocket Tin, C.1920, Porcelain, 48 X 12 In. 150.00
Sign, Viceroy Cigarettes, Smoother, Dated 1954, Tin, 16 1/2 X 28 In. 65.00
Sign, Virginia Slim, You've Come A Long Way Baby, Tin, 9 X 13 3/4 In. 7.50
Sign, We Use DeLaval Cream Separator, Tin, 12 X 16 In. 25.00
Sign, We Use Sharples Cream Separator, Porcelain, 11 X 18 In. 110.00
Sign, Weidemann's, Old Man, Pipe, Mug, Poster, 1900, 20 X 16 In. 250.00
Sign, Welch's, Grapes & Vines, 12 X 12 In. 20.00
Sign, Wermer Brewery, German Party, Beer, 1915, 30 X 22 In. 30.00
Sign, Western Union, Double, Porcelain, 30 X 18 In. 90.00
Sign, Whippet Willy's Knight, 24 X 35 In. 350.00
Sign, Winchester, Western Sportsman's Fame Guide, Tin, 23 X 28 In. 77.50
Sign, Wiss Shear & Cutlery, Picture Of Shears, Metal, 12 X 23 In. 55.00
Sign, Woco, Pep King Of Motor Fuel, Porcelain, 30 X 60 In. 225.00
Sign, Wrigely's Gum, Pack, Girl, C.1920, Tin, 13 X 6 In. 125.00
Sign, Wrigley's Gum, Tin, Picture Pack & Elf, 13 1/2 X 6 1/2 In. 125.00
Sign, Yankee Girl Scrap Tobacco, 1930s, Embossed Tin, 5 X 20 In. 60.00
Sign, Yankee Girl, Cardboard, 1920s, 8 X 11 1/2 In. 8.00
Sign, Yuengling's Beer, Eagle, Pre-Prohibition, Tin, 13 X 7 In. 125.00
Sign, Yuengling's, Eagle, Reverse Painting, Glass, Oval, 20 In. 1500.00
Sign, Ziegler's Beer, Tin, 8 1/2 X 11 In. 32.00
Silk, Cigarette, Zira, Bathing Beauty, Signed Harrison King 8.00
Slate, Lap, Child's, Attached Chalk Box, Patent 1877 .... 75.00
Slate, School, Slate Pencil, Wooden Frame, 7 1/2 X 9 3/4 In. 15.00
Slate, School, 1-Piece Bent Hickory Border, 7 X 10 In. 36.00
Slate, Writing, Child's, 2-Sided 18.00
Slicer, Enterprise, Store, Decals, Dated, 1881 .... 65.00
Spoon, Cream Top, Dated 1924, Tin 12.50
Spoon, Huckleberry Hound 9.00
Spoon, Measuring, Schilling 6.00
Spreader, Butter, Steel, Bats Grease, Business Is Ingreasing 4.00
Stand, Gum, Teaberry, Clear 25.00
Stand, Gum, Teaberry, Vaseline .... 22.00 To 40.00
Stand, Teaberry Gum, Double-Footed, Amber Glass 49.00
Statue, Pair, Buster Brown, Boy & Girl, Tige On Base, 27 In. 145.00
Statue, Pfeiffer Beer 30.00
Stickpin, Star Brand Shoes 20.00
Strainer, Tea, Advertising, Quick Action Range, Marshalltown, Tin 7.50
String Holder, Art Deco, Girl Ice Skating, Iron, 3 1/2 X 7 In. 105.00
String Holder, Beehive Shape, Cast Iron 20.00

String Holder, Counter, Beehive, Iron	45.00
String Holder, Gypsy Kettle Advertising, Use Jaxon Soap, Iron	130.00
String Holder, Iron, Pyramid	20.00
String Holder, Red Goose	575.00
Sugar & Creamer, Lipton Tea, Yellow	14.00
Teapot, McCormick Tea, Purple, Porcelain	15.00
STORE, THERMOMETER, see Thermometer	
Thermos, Tom Corbett	15.00

Tin cans or canisters were first used commercially in the United States in 1819. Today the word "tin" is used by collectors for many types of containers, including food tins, biscuit boxes, roly poly tobacco tins, gunpowder cans, talcum powder sprinkle-top cans, cigarette flat fifty tins and more. We also list beer cans; store, bin; and store, cans.

Tin, Aladdin Electric Lamp, 13 1/2 In.	17.50
Tin, American Sunrise Lard, Indians Pictured, 25 Pound	38.00
Tin, Angelus Marshmallow, 5 Pound	30.00
Tin, Araban Coffee	25.00
Tin, Atco Cigarettes, Floral Cover, Silvertone, Pocket, 3 In.	10.00
Tin, Athlete Smoking Mixture, Canada	55.00
Tin, Bagdad Tobacco, Pocket	60.00 To 75.00
Tin, Baker's Chocolate Cocoa, Paper Label	22.50
Tin, Banknote Cigar, Square	20.00
Tin, Bee Brand Insect Powder, Picture Of Bee	6.00
Tin, Belfast Cut Plug, 4 X 6 In.	14.00
Tin, Best Family Biscuit	57.00
Tin, Bickmore Horse Powder	6.00
Tin, Big Ben Tobacco, Pocket	18.00
Tin, Biscuit Box, Huntley & Palmer, Elizabeth & Philip	21.00
Tin, Biscuit Box, Scotsman In Full Dress On Lid, 10 X 5 X 1 In.	10.00
Tin, Black & White, Tobacco, Tall, Pocket	30.00
Tin, Black Beauty Axle Grease, 1 Pound	10.00
Tin, Black Cat Cigarettes, Pocket	10.00
Tin, Blackston's Tasty Lax	10.00
Tin, Blanke's Coffee, Happy Thoughts, Trunk Shaped	45.00
Tin, Blue Boar Tobacco	30.00
Tin, Blue Boy Cherry, 30 Pound	35.00
Tin, Blue Label Tobacco, Flat Pocket	45.00
Tin, Bond Street Tobacco, Pocket	10.00
Tin, Box Mixture, Tobacco, Covered, 6 X 3 X 5 In.	10.00
Tin, Boye, Needle Case, Contains Needles & Shuttles	48.00 To 85.00
Tin, Brown's Coffee, 15 In.	34.00
Tin, Buckingham Tobacco, Pocket	28.00
Tin, Buckingham Tobacco, Trial Size	85.00
Tin, Bugley's Red Belt, Tobacco, Pocket	24.00
Tin, Bunnies Peanuts, Salted, 10 Pound	175.00
Tin, Bunte Candy, 5 Pound	13.00
Tin, Bunte Marshmallow, Boy Pictured, Large	175.00
Tin, Cake Box Mixture Tobacco, Lid, 6 1/2 X 3 3/4 X 5 In.	10.00
Tin, California Nugget Tobacco, Flat Pocket	55.00
Tin, California Perfume Co., Face Powder	20.00
Tin, Calumet Baking Powder	10.00
Tin, Calumet, Indian, Orange Paper Label, 1 Pound	20.00
Tin, Camel Cigarettes, Round 100s	25.00
Tin, Camel Vulcanizing Patches, Picture Of Camel, C.1946	15.00
Tin, Campbell Coffee	10.00
Tin, Campbell Coffee, Desert Scene, 4 Pound	50.00
Tin, Campfire Marshmallows, 5 Pound	20.00
Tin, Candy, Currier & Ives Lithograph, Men Cutting Ice Blocks	15.00
Tin, Carlton Club Tobacco	40.00
Tin, Carnation Malted Milk, 10 Pound	22.00
Tin, Carsten's Lard	15.00
Tin, Cavalier Cigarettes, Oval 100s	4.00
Tin, Cavalier 100 King Size Cigarettes, Man & Sword, 5 In.	6.00

Tin, Central Union Cut Plug, Round	30.00
Tin, Charles Pretzels	20.00
Tin, Chase & Sanborn's Coffee, 3 Pound	95.00
Tin, Chase & Sanborn's Teas Are Also Delicious, Round, 4 1/4 X 5 In.	7.50
Tin, Chesterfield Cigarettes, Flat 50s	7.00
Tin, Cinco Cigars, 8 X 5 X 1 In.	18.00
Tin, Cixco Netters Little Cigars, 5 1/4 X 3 3/4 In.	17.00
Tin, Class Cigars	18.00
Tin, Coach & Four Tobacco, Pocket	25.00
Tin, Corylopsis Talc	30.00
Tin, Cotton Centennial Exposition, New Orleans, 1884	15.00
Tin, Country Club Coffee, 1 Pound	38.00
Tin, Crescent Cracker, Tin, 7 1/2 X 8 1/2 In.	20.00
Tin, Crest Prophylactics, 2 1/2 X 1 3/4 In.	6.00
Tin, Culture Tobacco, Pocket	25.00
Tin, Daintee Soda Biscuit, White House, Lithograph, 7 1/2 X 7 1/2 In.	22.00
Tin, Dainty Cake Flour	18.00
Tin, Dan Patch Tobacco, Horse & Carriage Scene	35.00
Tin, Darmody's Fine Confections, Gold Letters, Round, 12 1/2 X 13 In.	25.00
Tin, Dayton Brand Peanuts, Old Plane Pictured, 7 3/4 X 10 1/4 In.	75.00
Tin, Dentogen Tooth Powder, Pure Food & Drug, 1906	14.00
Tin, Dill's Best Cut Plug, Pocket	8.00
Tin, Donniford Tobacco, Pocket	40.00
Tin, Dr.Johnson's Educator Crackers	30.00
Tin, Dr.Morses Indian Root Pills	10.00
Tin, Dr.Moses Cough Drops, 1880s	85.00
Tin, Du Maurier Cigarettes, 3 1/2 X 3 In.	7.00
Tin, Dubonnet Deluxe Cigars	15.00
Tin, Dupont Gunpowder	15.00 To 25.00
Tin, Dupont Super Fine Gunpowder, 1 Pound	10.00
Tin, Eckart Packing Co., Lard, 3 Pound	10.00
Tin, Ed Dalli Invincible Cigars	15.00
Tin, Edgemont Crackers	12.00
Tin, Edgewater Tobacco, Pocket	10.00
Tin, Edgewood Plug Tobacco, Pocket, 3 1/4 In.	5.00
Tin, Edgeworth, 1936, Pocket	15.00
Tin, Edgeworth, Tobacco	2.00
Tin, Edward's Coffee, No.2	8.00
Tin, El Roi Tan Cigars, 5 X 3 1/2 In.	2.00 To 10.00
Tin, Erzinger's Tobacco	28.00
Tin, Esko Anti-Freeze	18.00
Tin, Eureka Harness Oil	10.00
Tin, Evans Coffee, Round	90.00
Tin, Evans Coffee, Square	180.00
Tin, Ex-Lax Figs	16.00
Tin, Fatima Cigarettes, Flat	18.00
Tin, Fine Fairy Soda Crackers	24.00
Tin, Floressence Viollette Talcum, Floral Design	8.00
Tin, Forest & Stream, Duck, Pocket	10.00
Tin, Forest & Stream, Picture Of Fisherman, Pocket	50.00 To 100.00
Tin, Four Roses, Tobacco, Pocket	65.00
Tin, Fry's Pure Coca Extract, Round, 2 1/2 X 4 1/2 In.	8.00
Tin, Gays Laurel Coffee, Dome Top, Brown, Gold Lettering, C.1870, 4 In.	55.00
Tin, Genuine Louisiana Perique, Man, 3 X 1 1/2 X 2 In.	25.00
Tin, Glendora Coffee, Sample	22.00
Tin, Gold Bond Tobacco, Pocket	90.00 To 95.00
Tin, Gold Medal Tobacco, Flat Pocket	150.00
Tin, Golden Rule Tea, 5 Pound	20.00
Tin, Golden Siva Tea, Lithographed Elephants & Indians	20.00
Tin, Golden Twins, Tobacco, 5 X 5 In.	7.00
Tin, Golden Wedding Coffee	5.00
Tin, Golden Wedding Coffee, 3 Pound	22.50
Tin, Gordon's Potato Chips, 2 Pound	28.00
Tin, Granulated 54 Tobacco, Pocket, Tall	75.00

Tin, Griffith, Mayor & Co., Smoking Tobacco 28.00
Tin, Half & Half Tobacco 6.00
Tin, Half & Half, Dated 1930, Small 19.00
Tin, Handsome Dan, Stoddard Tob, Co., Bulldog, 3 X 2 X 1 In. 45.00
Tin, Heberling's Medicated Ointment, Red, White, & Blue, 3 1/2 In. 6.00
Tin, Henna, Coloring For Gray Hair, Lady On Lid, 1922 .... 25.00
Tin, Hershey's Cocoa 18.00
Tin, Hi Plane, Single Engine Plane, Pocket 30.00
Tin, High Brown Face Powder, Pictures Black Girl 12.50
Tin, Hill's Bros. Coffee, Man Drinking, 1/2 Pound 10.00
Tin, Honest Labor, Tobacco, Pocket 25.00
Tin, Honey Boy Clover Honey 25.00
Tin, Hot Spur Tobacco, 3 1/2 X 4 1/2 In. 35.00
Tin, Idle Hour, Hourglass & Wings, Pocket, Flat 45.00
Tin, Imperial Ginger, 5 X 5 X 1 In. 10.00
Tin, In-B-Tween, Cigarettes, 1924 .... 20.00
Tin, Instant Postum 11.00
Tin, Jack Sprat Marshmallows, Lithograph Of Jack, Round 24.00
Tin, Jack Sprat Peanut Butter, 10 Pound 85.00
Tin, Jap Rose, Talcum 20.00
Tin, Jumbo Popcorn, Elephant Picture, 10 Pound 30.00
Tin, Kentucky Club, Jockey On Horse, Pocket 10.00
Tin, Kibbes Salted Jumbo Peanuts, Blue, Red, & Yellow, Round, 10 Pound 50.00
Tin, King's Herald Cigars 750.00
Tin, Kipling Cut Plug, Flat, Pocket 40.00
Tin, Klein's Japanese Cough Drops 16.00
Tin, Kugler Chocolates, German Candy, People Horses, 10 X 4 In. 15.00
Tin, La Fendrich Cigars, Man, Gold Metal, 5 X 4 X 1 In. 22.00
Tin, La Palina Cigars, Lady, Pocket, Flat 20.00
Tin, Laflin & Rand Gunpowder 28.00
Tin, Lipton Coffee 20.00
Tin, Lipton Tea Bags 16.00
Tin, Lipton Tea, Lithograph Of Black Tea Pickers, 8 X 5 In., 3 Pound 48.00
Tin, Little Buster Popcorn, Elf Popping Corn 8.00
Tin, Log Cabin Syrup, Express Office Picture 45.00
Tin, Log Cabin Syrup, Large 30.00
Tin, Log Cabin, Sryup, Stockade School 65.00
Tin, Loose-Wiles Biscuits, Statue Of Liberty, Octagonal 20.00
Tin, Loose-Wiles Biscuits, World War II Battleships 25.00
Tin, Loose-Wiles Biscuits, 8-Sided, Bail Handle, Yellow & Green 25.00
Tin, Lord Salisbury Turkish Cigarettes, Flat 100s, 9 X 6 In. 8.00
Tin, Lord Salisbury Turkish Cigarettes, 7 X 5 In. 7.00
Tin, Love's Harmonicas, Musician, Harmonica, King & Queen, 5 X 4 In. 30.00
Tin, Lucky Strike Cigarettes, Flat 8.00
Tin, Lucky Strike Cigarettes, Flat 50s .... 7.00 To 15.00
Tin, Lucky Strike Cigarettes, Round 100s 25.00
Tin, Lucky Strike Cut Plug, Pocket .... 8.00 To 10.00
Tin, Lucky Strike Cut Plug, 4 X 2 X 3 In. 15.00
Tin, Lucky Strike Cut Plug, 4 1/2 X 2 3/4 In. 10.00
Tin, Luzianne Coffee, 3 Pound 20.00
Tin, Master Workman, Tobacco, Pocket 45.00
Tin, Matchless Coffee 22.00
Tin, Mayfair Tea, Tri Cornered 27.50
Tin, Mayo's Cut Plug Tobacco, Pocket 35.00
Tin, Mayo's Sliced Tobacco, Flat Pocket 40.00
Tin, Mayo's Tobacco, 6 X 4 In. 50.00
Tin, McCormick Tea, Black On Orange, Stencils 22.00
Tin, McGill Mixture, Tobacco, Pocket 25.00
Tin, McKesson's Aspirin, Contents Of 12 Tablets, Cello Wrapped 2.00
Tin, Melachrino Cigarettes, Flat 50s 12.00
Tin, Melrose Marshmallow, Round, 10 In. 14.00
Tin, Mennen's Sen Yang Talcum, Duck Flying 25.00
Tin, Mini Naphey's Lard, Dated 1876 .... 22.50

Tin, Model Tobacco, Pocket	8.00
Tin, Model Tobacco, Red, Mountaineer Smoking Pipe	45.00
Tin, Monarch Tea, 1 Pound	15.00
Tin, Morning Glow Coffee	22.00
Tin, Morning Sip Coffee	15.00
Tin, Mother's Joy Coffee	12.00
Tin, Mountain Pure Honey	18.00
Tin, Mrs.Tucker's Shortening	25.00
Tin, Mussers Potato Chips, 1 Pound	15.00
Tin, Nancee Coffee, Lid, 1 Pound	4.00
Tin, National Mills Mustard, Stag With Full Rack Of Antlers	55.00
Tin, New Schultze Gunpowder	75.00
Tin, Niles & Moser Cigars, Pocket	12.00
Tin, North Star Cigarettes, Flat	225.00
Tin, Nutine Candles, Knight Picture	95.00
Tin, Oceanic Cut Plug Tobacco	40.00
Tin, Old Brier American Tobacco Co., 5 X 4 In.	4.50
Tin, Old Colony Java Mocha, Tan, Lithograph	20.00
Tin, Old English Tobacco, Pocket	3.50
Tin, Old English, Curve Cut, Pocket, 3 In.	4.00
Tin, Old Fireside Tea, 1/2 Pound	32.00
Tin, Old Grand Dad, Pocket, 4 1/4 In.	4.00
Tin, Old Rip Tobacco, Pocket	4.00
Tin, Omar Cigarettes, Flat 50s	10.00
Tin, Palmy Days, Tobacco, Pocket	110.00
Tin, Pat Hand Tobacco, Pocket	65.00 To 95.00
Tin, Patterson's Tuxedo, Pocket	5.00
Tin, Peacock Blue Ink	28.00
Tin, Peak Coffee, 1936, Mountain Scene	20.00
Tin, Peter's Shoe, Baseball Hat, Peter Weatherbird Picture	22.50
Tin, Phillip Morris, Cigarettes, Round	20.00
Tin, Picadilly Little Cigars	16.00
Tin, Piper Heidsieck Chewing Tobacco	25.00
Tin, Piso's Tooth Powder, Floral	12.00
Tin, Players Navy Cut Cigarette	27.50
Tin, Popper's Ace Cigars, World War II Graphics	37.50
Tin, Pride Of Virginia Tobacco, Lady, Pocket, Flat	20.00 To 30.00
Tin, Prince Albert Tobacco, Barlow Knife Ad On Back, Red, Pocket	3.00
Tin, Prince Albert Tobacco, Covered, Round, Patent 1907	12.00 To 17.00
Tin, Prize Winner Cigars, Pocket	20.00
Tin, Queen Anne Peanuts, Picture Of Lady, 10 Pound	59.00 To 65.00
Tin, Raptco Wafers, Embossed Leaf, Pocket, Flat	25.00
Tin, Rawleigh's Talcum, Nursery Rhyme Characters	35.00
Tin, Rawleigh's Talcum, Nursery Scenes	30.00
Tin, Rawleigh's, Salve	15.00
Tin, Red Jacket Tobacco, Pocket	12.00
Tin, Reed's Butterscotch Wafers, 20 Pound	18.00
Tin, Repeater Plug Cut Tobacco	30.00
Tin, Revelation Tobacco, Pocket	8.00
Tin, Revelation Tobacco, Trial Size	24.00
Tin, Revelation Tobacco, 1/2 Size	7.00
Tin, Richelieu Tea, Orientals On Sides	18.00
Tin, Riley's Creamy Toffee	43.00
Tin, Rip Van Winkle Biscuit	35.00
Tin, Road Boss Motor Oil, Picture Of Farm, Truck	28.00
Tin, Robin Hood Gunpowder	95.00
Tin, Roly Poly, Dutchmen	425.00
Tin, Roly Poly, Mammy, Mayo's Tobacco	600.00
Tin, Roly Poly, Man From Scotland Yard, Mayo's	595.00
Tin, Roly Poly, Storekeeper	325.00
Tin, Schrafft's Candy, Metal, Gold Color	16.00
Tin, Schwan's Ice Cream, 2 1/2 Gallon	20.00
Tin, Schwepp's, Cake, 2 Shelves, Tin, Illustration Outside	35.00

Tin, Sea Gull Baking Powder, Baltimore, 1897 .... 15.00
Tin, Seidlitz Powders, 12 Dose Size 4.00
Tin, Sensible Sliced Plug Tobacco, 4 X 5 In. 8.00
Tin, Shaker, Soap 10.00
Tin, Sharp's Toffee, Dated, 7 X 10 In. 12.50
Tin, Shedds Peanut Butter, Circus Scene, Covered, 5 Pound 3.00
Tin, Silver Streak Tobacco, Mail Coach, Pocket, 6 In. 5.00
Tin, Sir Walter Raleigh Smoking Tobacco 125.00
Tin, Sir Walter Raleigh Tobacco, Pry Top 18.00
Tin, Sir Walter Raleigh, Pocket 10.00
Tin, Sir Walter Raleigh, Round Knob-Bed Lid 12.00
Tin, Songster Needles, Bird, 1 X 1 1/4 X 1/4 In. 25.00
Tin, St.Leger Tobacco, Pocket 6.00
Tin, Stollwerck Cocoa, 6-Sided 27.50
Tin, Straight Portage Cigars, 5 Cent, Lithograph, 8 1/2 X 5 1/2 In. 15.00
Tin, Striktape Aerial, Deco Girl, Has The Aerial 38.00
Tin, Sunset Trail Cigar King 135.00
Tin, Superior Tropical Peanuts, 10 Pound 70.00
Tin, Swee-Touch-Nee Tea, Trunk Shaped 30.00
Tin, Sweet Burley, Red 75.00
Tin, Sweet Cuba Tobacco, Pocket 100.00
Tin, Sweet Mist Chewing Tobacco 45.00
Tin, Sweet Mist, Children At Fountain 105.00
Tin, Sweet Mist, Cylinder 185.00
Tin, Sweetheart Talcum, Lady, Box 27.00
Tin, Tak-A-Lax Chocolate, Girl On Cover, 1920s, 2 1/4 X 3 3/4 In. 9.00
Tin, Three Feathers Tobacco, Pocket 150.00
Tin, Tiger Tobacco, Pocket, 6 X 8 In. 25.00
Tin, Tiger Tobacco, Red, 5 Pound 67.00
Tin, Toffee, Souvenir 1937 Coronation, George & Elizabeth 20.00
Tin, Tom Moore Cigars 20.00
Tin, Tortoise Shell Tobacco 125.00
Tin, Toyland Peanut Butter 65.00
Tin, Tuxedo Tobacco, Man In Tuxedo, Pocket .... 10.00 To 12.00
Tin, Tuxedo Tobacco, Man Wearing Hat, Pocket 20.00
Tin, Twin Oaks, Pocket 35.00
Tin, Uncle Sam Tobacco, Pocket 30.00
Tin, Uneeda Bakers Butter Wafers, 12 Ounce 18.00
Tin, Union Leader Cut Plug, Pocket 25.00
Tin, Union Leader Tobacco, Pocket .... 6.00 To 8.00
Tin, V-All-No Dinner 5.00
Tin, Van Baar's Cigarillos 12.00
Tin, Vantine Kutch Sandalwood, Talcum, Caravan Scene 22.50
Tin, Velvet Cigarettes 5.00
Tin, Velvet Tobacco, Gold Shields On Side, C.1920, Pocket .... 2.50 To 3.00
Tin, Velvet Tobacco, Short & Squat 12.00
Tin, Vermont Maple Syrup .... 15.00 To 20.00
Tin, Webster Cigars, Picture Of Daniel Webster, 5 X 3 X 1 1/2 In. 25.00
Tin, Webster Claro Cigars 35.00
Tin, White Cross Adhesive Bandages, Flip Top, 1940s 6.00
Tin, White House Coffee, White House, Paper Label, 1 Pound 20.00
Tin, White Label Five Cent Cigars, 10 X 14 In. 55.00
Tin, Yale Mixture, Marburg Bros., 3 X 2 X 1 In. 20.00
Tin, Yucatan Gum 45.00
Tobacco Tag, Mayo's, Tag Shows Rooster, Tin .... .50
Top, Spinner, Poll Parrot Shoes 10.00
Tray, Artic Ice Cream, Polar Bear 250.00
Tray, Ballentine Beer & Ale, Blue, 12 In. 3.50
Tray, Banner Bazaar Store, Dayton, O, Girl, Tin, 18 1/2 X 15 1/4 In. 250.00
Tray, Beer, Arrow, Gambrinus Rex, Drinking Orgy, American Can Co. 65.00
Tray, Berreteaga Liquor, Round, Spanish Writing, 1865, 6 In. 27.50
Tray, Bevo Non-Alcoholic Beverage, Anheuser Busch 85.00
Tray, Brownie's Ice Cream, Advertising 125.00

Tray, Budweiser, Hunters, Dog, Shadow From Fire, 13 X 10 In.	77.00
Tray, Budweiser, Internal Revenue Tax Bottle	42.00
Tray, Budweiser, Robert Lee Sidewheeler, Dock, Workers, 1914	88.00
Tray, Budweiser, St.Louis Levee Scene, 1914	85.00
Tray, Bull Brand Feeds, Yellow, Red, Black, White, Bull, 4 X 6 In.	60.00
Tray, Butte, Montana, Centennial	1200.00
Tray, Celebrated Dill's Best, Pipe, Tin Of Tobacco, Girl	70.00
Tray, Chero-Cola, Bottle Pictured	95.00
Tray, Christian Feigenspan Brewing Co., Newark, N.J., Woman	75.00
Tray, Dr Pepper, Roses, C.1905, 9 In.	130.00
Tray, Eagle, Theorem Design, Tin	95.00
Tray, Ehrets, New Yorker Beer & Ale	35.00
Tray, Emmerling Brewing Co., Johnstown, Pa., 1913, Man, Woman, German	335.00
Tray, Enterprises Beer, 1905	250.00
Tray, Golden State Beer, Men Drinking At Table, Pre-Prohibition	215.00
Tray, Golden West Factory	110.00
Tray, Goldenrod, Brewery Scene, Old Cars & Trucks	135.00
Tray, Gunther's Beer, 1934	40.00
Tray, Hamm's Preferred Stock, Brewery Scene, Black, Red On White	28.00
Tray, Hanley, White	24.00
Tray, Hull Beer	14.00
Tray, Iroquois Beer, Seal Of United Steelworkers Of America	30.00
Tray, Jacob Ruppert Beer, Ale, 1938, Oval, Filled Beer Steins	45.00
Tray, Jax Beer, Alamo Scene	25.00
Tray, Jax Beer, Cowboy On Horse, 10 X 13 In.	85.00
Tray, Lassen, Seattle, Co. Men, Pre-Prohibition	150.00
Tray, Lawrence Welk, Auto, Letter From Welk, 1956	40.00
Tray, Lawrence Welk, Champagne Music Makers, 9 X 13 3/4 In.	27.50
Tray, Lemp Beer, Old Man Drinking, Pre-Prohibition, 16 In.	155.00
Tray, Lily Beer, 6 1/2 X 4 1/2 In.	25.00
Tray, Maier's Brewery, Lady With Large Hat	60.00
Tray, McSorley's Cream Stock Ale, 4 Men, Innkeeper, 1936	45.00
Tray, Miller High Life Beer, Girl In Moon, Oval	45.00 To 60.00
Tray, Miller, Girl On Moon, Oval	95.00
Tray, National Beer, Cowboy & Horse	325.00
Tray, National Brewing Co., Cowboy	200.00
Tray, Nu-Grape Soda	55.00
Tray, Nu-Grape, Blonde Holding Bottle, 1920s, 10 1/2 X 13 1/4 In.	95.00
Tray, Old Pepper Whiskey	85.00
Tray, Olympia Beer, Horseshoe Over Waterfalls, Pre-Prohibition, 17 In.	265.00
Tray, Orange Julep, Girl With Umbrella	135.00
Tray, Ortlielers Lager Beer & Ale, Girl Holding Glass	45.00
Tray, Pepsi-Cola, Children Singing	15.00
Tray, Pickwick Ale, Man On Chair	25.00
Tray, Portrait Of Woman, 1890s, 16 1/2 In.	28.00
Tray, R.& H. Beer	75.00
Tray, R.C.A.	65.00
Tray, Rainier Beer, Girl On Bear, Pre-Prohibition	200.00
Tray, Rainier, Evelyn Nesbitt, C.1903	350.00
Tray, Rainier, Rabbit & Dove, 1915	350.00
Tray, Reno, Fredicksburg & Welland, Oval, 16 In.	200.00
Tray, Royal Bohemian Beer	15.00
Tray, Ruhstaller's Beer, Dover	200.00
Tray, Ruhstaller's Beer, Lady With Dove	100.00
Tray, Ruhstaller's Pan Pacific	250.00
Tray, San Diego Consolidated Brewery, Eagle	275.00
Tray, Schaefer, 1842, America's Oldest Lager Beer, 12 In.	3.75
Tray, Scheidt's Ram's Head Ale, Valley Forge	23.00
Tray, Schmidt City Club	15.00
Tray, Springfield Beer, Chrome Plated, Button Edge, 12 In.	500.00
Tray, St.Louis Lemp Beer, C.1909	225.00
Tray, St.Louis, Bud Beer, Levee Scene	82.50
Tray, Stockleys	15.00

Tray, Stroh's Bohemian, Bottles, Glasses, Food, Multi Colored 145.00
Tray, Tip, Allpax 20.00
Tray, Tip, Ben Franklin 20.00
Tray, Tip, Carnation Milk 17.50
Tray, Tip, Cortez Cigars 40.00
Tray, Tip, Cottolene, With Ad Booklet 55.00
Tray, Tip, DeLaval, Lady With Cream Separator 95.00
Tray, Tip, DeLaval, With Separator 55.00
Tray, Tip, Dixie Queen Tobacco 22.50
Tray, Tip, El Arabe Cigars 50.00
Tray, Tip, Harkert Cigar Co., Davenport, Iowa 45.00
Tray, Tip, Heath & Milligan Paints, 2 Girls & Dog, Round 20.00
Tray, Tip, Hebburn House Coal, Eagle 25.00
Tray, Tip, Hupfel Brewery, Embossed Trademark 50.00
Tray, Tip, Hyroler Whiskey 48.00
Tray, Tip, I Just Love Moxie, Don't You, Beach Co., Coshocton, Ohio 115.00
Tray, Tip, Jenny Aero Gasoline 58.00
Tray, Tip, Lily, Rock Island Brewing Co. 45.00
Tray, Tip, Marylyn Monroe, Nude 25.00
Tray, Tip, Mascot Crushed Cut Tobacco 12.00
Tray, Tip, Mathie Red Ribbon Beer, Oval 75.00
Tray, Tip, Miller Beer, Ducks 7.00
Tray, Tip, Miller High Life, Maid On Moon 4.50
Tray, Tip, Moxie, Floral 100.00
Tray, Tip, Moxie, Girl Drinking Moxie 75.00
Tray, Tip, Moxie, I Just Love Moxie, Don't You 155.00
Tray, Tip, Moxie, Lettering Only .... 55.00 To 125.00
Tray, Tip, National Beer, Cowboy & Horse 125.00
Tray, Tip, Oertel Brew, Cream Beer, Lady With Dove, 5 In. 75.00
Tray, Tip, Old Angus Scotch Whiskey 25.00
Tray, Tip, Owatonna Flour 12.00
Tray, Tip, Pepsi-Cola 750.00
Tray, Tip, Prudential Insurance 35.00
Tray, Tip, Quick Meal Range, Oval 30.00
Tray, Tip, Rockford Watch Co. 37.50
Tray, Tip, Rockford Watches, Lady Sitting On Grass, Rectangle 65.00
Tray, Tip, Rockford Watches, South Fork, Pa., Victorian Lady 40.00
Tray, Tip, Ruppert's Beer, Hans Flato Scene, 1 Cent 45.00
Tray, Tip, Ruppert's Beer, Hans Flato Scene, 2 Cent 45.00
Tray, Tip, Salem Witch 9.00
Tray, Tip, Schenley Whiskey .... 15.00 To 22.50
Tray, Tip, Schweppe's, Blue Willow 40.00
Tray, Tip, Stollwerck Chocolate & Cocoa 35.00
Tray, Tip, Sullivans 7-20-4 Cigar 24.00
Tray, Tip, Surburg High Grade Cigars 28.00
Tray, Tip, Teddy G Riding Giraffe, 12 Bears Line Border, 1906 .... 45.00
Tray, Tip, Tennent's Beer, Blue China 20.00
Tray, Tip, Terre Haute Brewing Co. 110.00
Tray, Tip, Trojan Girl Cigars, Galena, Ill. 65.00
Tray, Topper Beer 7.00
Tray, V.Loewer Gambrinus Brewery, Pre-Prohibition 150.00
Tray, Wacker, Birks Beer, Chicago 35.00
Tray, Weinhard's Beer, Portland, Oreg., Eagle, Pre-Prohibition 150.00
Tray, White Swan Flour, Red Ribbon Border, Oval, 16 1/2 X 13 1/2 In. 85.00
Tray, Zipp's Cherri-O 220.00
Trimmer, Cigar, Clause Fremont 10.00
Trimmer, Cigar, Osmond Cigars, Dated 1913 .... 15.00
Trimmer, Cigar, Pure Food Gelatin 10.00
Tumbler, Blatz, Enameled 7.00
Tumbler, Brooklyn Dodgers, Dem Bums 6.00
Tumbler, Moxie 20.00
Wastebasket, Massilon Wire Basket Co., Daisy, Red Tin Bottom, 1914 .... 22.00
Whiskey, Crystal, Hayner 1866, Dayton, Ohio, Usa 18.00

Whistle, Advertising, Weatherbird Shoes 2.50
Whistle, Peter's Weatherbird Shoes, Tin 5.00

STOVE, Camp, Penny Foot, 7 1/4 In. 400.00
  Charter Oak, Parlor 245.00
  Cook, Wood Burning, Warming Ovens, Reservoir, Trivets, Cast Iron 550.00
  Copper Clad Brand, Hot Water Reservoir, Cast Iron, 4 1/2 X 5 Ft. 1450.00
  Garland, No.46, Mica Windows, Nickel Trim 2100.00
  Gas, Silver Paint, Marked Daisy, 2 Burners & Hood, 4 1/4 In. 22.00
  Glendale, Wood Or Kerosene, Patent 1922, Cast Iron 1000.00
  Jewell, Wood, No.618, Oak 395.00
  Kalamazoo, Cook, 1927, Beige 475.00
  No.16, Wood, Round, Oak 295.00
  Parlor, Enamel, Blue 295.00
  Portuguese, Hand Pump, Camp, C.1900, 8 X 8 In. 45.00
  Quick Meal Brand, Gas 375.00
  Radiant, Parlor, Model 24, Black & Silver, Patent 1889, Ceramic Faces ... 1450.00
  Riverside, Parlor, No.35, Hard Coal 3400.00
  Stewart, Oak 950.00
  Two Burner, Griswold 75.00
     STRAWBERRY, see Soft Paste

STRETCH GLASS, Basket, Gray, 10 1/2 In. 110.00
  Basket, White, 10 1/4 In. 110.00
  Bottle, Pink, Square, Enameled Dutch Boy & Girl 38.00
  Bowl, Blue, Tree-Bark Foot, 9 1/2 In. 25.00
  Bowl, Blue, 6 In. 8.00
  Bowl, Crimped, Purple, 11 In. 68.00
  Bowl, Cupped, Green, 8 In. 30.00
  Bowl, Dark Collar Base, Signed D, Turquoise, 9 1/2 In. 50.00
  Bowl, Dolphin Handles, Pedestal, Green, 9 X 6 In. 75.00
  Bowl, Gray, Paneled, 8 1/4 In. 25.00
  Bowl, Green, Flared, 9 1/2 In. 25.00
  Bowl, Orange Rainbow, 12 In. 36.00
  Bowl, Polished Bottom, Red, 7 X 1 1/2 In. 88.00
  Bowl, Punch, Blue, Flared, Collar Bottom, 11 3/4 X 5 1/2 In. 50.00
  Bowl, Purple, Flared, Collar Bottom, 9 1/4 In. 34.00
  Bowl, Scalloped, Pink, 6 1/4 X 3 1/2 In. 30.00
  Bowl, White, Fenton, 12 In. 40.00
  Bowl, White, Flared, Fluted Panels, 10 1/4 In. 32.00
  Candlestick, Blue, Fenton, 8 1/2 In., Pair 50.00
  Candlestick, Blue, 1 3/4 In. 18.00
  Candlestick, Colonial, Olive, 8 1/2 In., Pair 55.00
  Candlestick, Colonial, White, 10 1/2 In., Pair 225.00
  Candlestick, Green, 9 In., Pair 45.00
  Candy Container, Covered, Amethyst 40.00
  Cologne, Stopper, Iridescent, Stemmed 25.00
  Compote, Blue, 8 In. 35.00
  Compote, Candy, White, Ribbed, 5 X 5 In. 17.00
  Compote, Footed, Iridescent Vaseline, 7 1/4 X 3 1/4 In. 22.00
  Compote, Imperial, Teal, 7 3/4 X 4 1/2 In. 48.00
  Compote, Purple, Stemmed, 7 X 6 In. 55.00
  Compote, Raised Paneled Body, Blue, 6 1/4 X 3 1/2 In. 18.00
  Compote, Scalloped Top, Blue-Gray, Imperial, 8 1/2 In. 57.00
  Compote, Teal, Imperial, 7 1/2 X 7 1/2 In. 65.00
  Dessert Set, Vaseline, 7 Piece 145.00
  Dish, Candy, Covered, Sapphire Blue, 8 In. 35.00
  Plate, Blue, 12 Panel, 11 In. 35.00
  Plate, Chop, Wide Panel Back, Amberina, 11 In. 95.00
  Plate, Pedestal, Blue Iridescent, 8 In.Diam. 45.00
  Plate, Smoke Violet, 8 In. 12.00
  Plate, White & Iridescent, 8 In. 7.00
  Plate, White & Iridescent, 8 1/2 In. 8.00

Rose Bowl, Pink, Footed, Melon Ribbed, Scalloped, 5 In. 32.00
Rose Bowl, Ruffled Top, Footed, Fenton, 9 In. 32.00
Salver, Green, Footed, 6 1/2 In. 35.00
Sherbet, Aqua 15.00
Sherbet, Red, Footed, Ribbed, 3 3/8 In. 50.00
Tumble-Up, Blue 40.00
Vase, Black Glass Base, Red, 8 In. 95.00
Vase, Fan Shape, Dolphin Handled, Pink 65.00
Vase, Fan, Blue, Dolphin Handled, Fenton, 5 In. 50.00
Vase, Fan, Green, Ribbed, 5 1/2 In. 25.00
Vase, Green, Tube, 10 In. 35.00
Vase, Peacock Colors, 9 1/4 In. 60.00
Vase, Pink, 6 X 6 In. 25.00
Vase, Red, Burned-In Rim, Signed Imperial, 8 1/2 In. 175.00
Vase, Red, 10 In. 145.00
Vase, Rubigold, 7 In. 25.00
Vase, Scalloped Top, Imperial Cross Mark, 5 X 5 In. 58.50

Sunbonnet Babies were first introduced in 1902 in the "Sunbonnet Babies Primer." The stories were by Eulalie Osgood Grover, illustrated by Bertha Corbett. The children's faces were completely hidden by the sunbonnets, and had been pictured in black and white before this time. The color pictures in the book were immediately successful. The Royal Bayreuth China Company made a full line of children's dishes decorated with the Sunbonnet Babies.

SUNBONNET BABIES, Album, Dated 1893, Celluloid & Velvet 55.00
Box, Pin, Little Miss Muffet, Oval, Blue Mark 75.00
Cake Plate, Jack Horner, Open-Handled, Blue Mark 145.00
Candleholder, Cape Cod, Babies, Fishing, Signed 275.00
Candlestick, Cleaning, Sweeping, Blue Mark, 4 1/4 In., Pair 185.00
Chocolate Pot, Mopping, Washing Window, Marked, 7 In. 250.00
Creamer, Cleaning 125.00
Creamer, Fishing, Royal Bayreuth, Blue Mark 150.00
Creamer, Girl With Dog, Blue Mark 65.00
Creamer, Jack & Jill, Blue Mark 65.00
Creamer, Little Jack Horner, Blue Mark 65.00
Creamer, Mending 150.00
Creamer, Washing, Pinched Spout 175.00
Cup & Saucer, Cleaning, Child's, Blue Mark 135.00
Cup & Saucer, Cup Washing, Saucer Mending, Marked 160.00
Cup & Saucer, Sweeping, Demitasse, Blue Mark 245.00
Dish, Club, Little Jack Horner, Blue Mark 65.00
Doorstop, Gold Floral Dress, Green Base, 6 In. 75.00
Figurine, Cast Iron, 6 1/2 In. 65.00
Hatpin Holder, Babies Fishing, Royal Bayreuth, Blue Mark 425.00
Jug, Jack & The Beanstalk, Blue Mark, Miniature 75.00
Mug, Jack & The Beanstalk, Child's, Blue Mark 95.00
Mush Set, Blue Mark 260.00
Needle Case, Figural, Green Felt, Green Ribbon, 4 In. 8.00
Pitcher, Blue, Babies Cleaning, 2 3/4 In. 160.00
Pitcher, Fishing, Royal Bayreuth, 4 1/2 In. 165.00
Pitcher, Mending, Royal Bayreuth, 4 1/2 In. 185.00
Pitcher, Milk, Babies Washing, Marked, 4 In. 165.00
Pitcher, Milk, Blue Mark, Large 225.00
Plaque, Walking, Carrying Books, C.1910, Brass, 4 X 8 In. 17.50
Plate, Babies Fishing 150.00
Plate, Cleaning, Royal Bayreuth, 6 1/8 In. 65.00
Plate, Feeding Ducks, Gold Lettered, Souvenir, 6 3/4 In. 95.00
Plate, Feeding, Boy In Overalls, 7 In. 89.50
Plate, Girl With Dog, Blue Mark, 8 In. 70.00
Plate, Ironing, Blue Mark, 7 1/2 In. 185.00
Plate, Kiss & Make Up, 6 In. 40.00
Plate, Washing, 7 1/2 In. 125.00

Plate, 2 Babies Fishing, Marked, 6 In. 125.00
Print, Baby Carrying Shovel, Sand Pail, Shells, 9 X 12 In. 35.00
Print, March, Baby Wearing Ermine Stole, 6 X 8 In. 40.00
Print, The Good Old Summertime, Framed 20.00
Quilt Top, Multicolored, 48 Squares 40.00
Quilt, 45 X 55 In. 35.00
Rattle, Celluloid 20.00
Sugar & Creamer, Squatty, Blue Mark 250.00
Sugar & Creamer, 2 Babies Mending & 2 Hanging Clothes 250.00
Teapot, 2 Babies Sweeping, Marked, 5 In. 250.00
Tray, Babies Washing & Hanging Clothes, Open-Handled 175.00
Vase, Cleaning, Scalloped, 5 In. 250.00
Vase, Dutch Boy & Girl, Bulbous, Blue Mark, 9 In. 110.00
Vase, Ironing, Flared, 4 1/2 In. 225.00
Wall Pocket, Hanging, Court Jester, 9 In. 95.00

Sunderland luster is a name given to a characteristic pink luster made by
Leeds, Newcastle, and other English firms during the nineteenth century.
The luster glaze is metallic and glossy and sometimes appears to have
bubbles as a decoration.

SUNDERLAND, Cup & Saucer, Cloud Pattern, Copper Luster Bands 65.00
Cup & Saucer, Cloud Pattern, Pink Luster 45.00
Jug, Pink Luster, Brown, Buildings, C.1820, 8 In. 110.00
Jug, Purple-Pink Luster, C.1820, British Ships, 8 In. 192.00
Pitcher, Masonic, Pink Luster, Bulbous, 2 Ladies, 8 In. 250.00
Pitcher, Masonic, Poems, Symbols, C.1900, Pink Luster, 8 1/2 In. 250.00
Plaque, Chinoiserie Scene, Pink Border, 8 1/2 In., Pair 130.00

SUPERMAN, Book, Coloring, 1940, Large 48.00
Clock, Alarm, Animated, 1940 .... 650.00
Figurine, Chalkware 60.00
Film & Viewer 15.00
Goggles, Swim, Senior, Boxed 12.00
Gun, Krypto Ray & 1 Film 85.00
Lunch Box, Tin, 1967 .... 10.00 To 18.00
Paint Set, Boxed 70.00
Ring, Crusader's 75.00
Rocket Gun, 2 Extra Rockers 85.00
Spoon 3.00
Toy, Paint By Numbers, Boxed 18.00
Toy, Tank, Marx 95.00
Turnover Tank, Battery, Linemar .... 275.00 To 300.00

SWORD, Bayonet & Sheath, British, World War II 6.95
Bayonet & Sheath, Japanese, World War II 32.95
Bayonet, Brass Handle, C.1880 .... 30.00
Bayonet, Leather Scabbard, Stamped Quebec, 1907 .... 35.00
Cutlass, Ship's Anti-Boarding, Pair 70.00
Dagger & Scabbard, Japanese Samurai, 18 In. 95.00
Dagger, Bone Hilt, Arabian, 13 In. 35.00
Dagger, Crescent Shape, Inlaid Hilt & Scabbard, 22 In. 65.00
Dagger, Luftwaffe, 1937 .... 250.00
Dagger, Wire Inlay, Crescent Shape 45.00
Dirk & Scabbard, Nael, Sign Of Nicholas II On Blade, 14 1/2 In. 160.00
Ivory Handle, Etched Blade, C.1910 .... 75.00
Japanese Samurai, No.179, Signed Yadoh Teruhide 450.00
Mori, Carved Demon Head Hilt, 28 In. 50.00
N.C.O., Civil War, Dated 1861 .... 75.00
Naval Officer's, Regulation, U.S., Sharkskin Grips 55.00
Persian, Large, D-Guard, 23 In. 65.00
Persian, 23 In. 40.00
Rooster Hilt, Stamped U.S.& N.C. 285.00
Saber, U.S.Artillery, 1840 .... 125.00

Scabbard, Etched Blade, India, 39 In.	75.00
Scabbard, Japanese Samurai, 29 In.	135.00
Scabbard, U.S.Calvary, 1860	175.00
U.S. Marines, Officer's, Regulation, Ivory Grips	40.00
1840, U.S.Artillery, Ames Mfg.	90.00

Syracuse is a trademark used by the Onondaga Pottery of Syracuse, New York. The firm was established in 1871. It is still working.

SYRACUSE, Luncheon Set, Clover Pattern, 89 Piece	575.00
Plate, Dinner, Selma	3.00

    TANKARD, see Stein
    TAPESTRY, PORCELAIN, see Rose Tapestry

TEA CADDY, Apple Form, Applewood, 5 In.	600.00
Blue Flowers & Gilt, Dresden	75.00
Brown, Yellow, Orange, Green, C.1870, 4 1/2 X 9 3/4 In.	35.00
Cobalt Blue & White Porcelain, 6 In.	125.00
Crest With Flying Horse, Oriental, Samson Logo, C.1875, 5 In.	135.00
Deutsche Blumen & Gold Design, Square, Dresden, 5 1/2 In.	115.00
George III, Shaped Top With Handle, Mahogany, 9 X 5 X 5 In.	100.00
Red Apple, Pennsylvania, Yellow, Green, & Red, 4 1/4 In.	345.00
Regency, Hinged Closure, Central Cut Bowl, Mahogany, 6 In.	120.00
Sterling, Ivory Pineapple Finial, 2 X 3 X 3 In	100.00
Tin, Gray, C.1890, 4 X 8 In.	14.50
Troubadour Scene, Hinged Lid, Barbour Bros., 3 3/4 X 3 1/2 In.	65.00
Zebra Wood, Ivory Inlay, Ball Feet, Embossed Lion's Head Handle	85.00

TEA LEAF IRONSTONE, Bacon Rasher	45.00
Bone Dish, Set Of 4	220.00
Bowl & Pitcher, J & E Mayer	300.00
Butter Chip	9.00 To 10.00
Butter, Shaw, Covered	120.00
Cake Plate, Open-Handled, Wedgwood, 10 In.	48.00
Cake Plate, 6-Sided	95.00
Casserole, Covered, Meakin, 10 1/2 X 6 In.	98.00
Coffeepot, Meakin	180.00
Copper, Chocolate Set, 9 Piece	400.00
Creamer, Burgess, 6 In.	100.00
Creamer, Shaw, 5 In	150.00
Creamer, Shaw, 6 In.	165.00
Cup & Saucer	50.00
Cup & Saucer, Handleless, Set Of 4	245.00
Dish, Soup, Shallow, Meakin, 9 In.	20.00
Dish, Vegetable, Mellor, Taylor, Covered	85.00
Dish, Vegetable, Shaw, Covered	120.00
Dish, Vegetable, Wedgwood, Covered	90.00
Gravy Boat & Tray, Luster, Meakin	35.00
Gravy Boat, Underplate	28.00
Mug, Shaw	65.00
Pitcher, Meakin, Square, 7 In.	50.00
Pitcher, Swan, 6 In.	55.00
Plate, Meakin, 9 In.	14.00
Plate, Powell & Bishop, Green, 8 In.	25.00
Plate, Square, 6 In.	45.00
Plate, 6 1/2 In.	10.00
Plate, 7 3/4 In., Set Of 8	40.00
Plate, 9 In.	10.00
Plate, 9 1/2 In.	35.00
Plate, 10 In.	18.00 To 24.00
Platter, Luster, 14 In.	35.00
Platter, Meakin, 12 X 8 1/2 In.	38.50
Platter, Meakin, 14 X 10 In.	37.00
Platter, Oval, 11 In.	12.50

Platter, Oval, 11 1/2 In. 14.00
Platter, Oval, 16 In. 35.00
Relish, Wedgwood, Open-Handled, 8 In. 45.00
Teapot .... 135.00 To 175.00
Teapot, Burgess, 9 1/2 In. 95.00
Teapot, Domed Cover, 10 In. 72.50

 Teco pottery is the art pottery line made by the Terra Cotta Tile
Works of Terra Cotta, Illinois. The company was founded by William
D.Gates in 1881. The Teco line was first made in 1902 and continued
into the 1920s. It included over 500 designs, made in a variety of colors,
shapes, and glazes.

TECO, Bowl, Flat, 4-Footed, 10 X 2 1/2 In. 165.00
  Candleholder 110.00
  Pitcher, Green, 9 In. 110.00
  Pitcher, Tigereye, Marked, 4 In. 350.00
  Vase, Ball Shape, Rolled, Rim, Green, 3 In. 55.00
  Vase, Matte Green, 5 In. 40.00
  Vase, 2 Fluted Handles, Signed, Avocado Green, 7 In. 225.00
  Vase, 4-Sided Form, 4 Perforated Handles, Signed, Green, 8 1/2 X 5 In. 295.00
  Wall Pocket, Green 195.00

TELEPHONE, American Bell Telephone Co., Hanging, 3 Coin Pay Box 425.00
  Booth, Mahogany 350.00
  Booth, Raised Panels Inside & Out, 1920, Oak 700.00
  Calugraph, Timer For Long-Distance Calls, C.1910 .... 135.00
  Candlestick, A.T. & T., 1913, Oak Box 275.00
  Candlestick, Kellogg 65.00
  Coin Slot 525.00
  Cranker, Oakwall, 1913, 21 In. 135.00
  Depot, Railroad 150.00
  Double Box, Crank 575.00
  Ericsson, Crank Type Cradle 125.00
  Kellogg, Candlestick, Scissor Holder 95.00
  Long Case, Wall, Replacement Receiver & Transmitter 100.00
  Magneto, Wooden Case 85.00
  Monarch, Fiddleback, Wall, Oak 235.00
  Railroad, Wall, Oak 125.00
  Stick, Western Electric Co., Patent 1904, Brass 130.00
  Switchboard, 1930s 350.00
  Tapered Shaft, Brass Shaft 290.00
  Wall, Copper 300.00
  Wall, Cradle Phone Attached, Crank & Bell Switch 85.00
  Wall, Crank, 1913, Oak, 21 In. 135.00
  Western Electric Co., Stick, Patent 1904, Brass 130.00
  Western Electric, Desk, Oak Bell Box, Bakelite, Crank Handle 55.00
  Western Electric, Ringer Box, Wall, Brass Bells, Oak, 8 X 11 In. 45.00
  Western Electric, Wall, Magneto, Oak 225.00

Teplitz refers to art pottery manufactured by a number of companies in the
Teplitz-Turn area of Bohemia during the late nineteenth and early
twentieth centuries. The Amphora Porcelain Works and the Alexandra
Works were two of these companies.

TEPLITZ, Basket, Flowered Medallion, Enameled Jewels, Turquoise Handle 68.00
  Bowl, Console, Yellow Rose Design, 4 Legs, Crown Mark 100.00
  Candlestick, Figural, Praying Mantis, Handled, Artist Signed, 11 In. 195.00
  Ewer, Boy & Duck, Stellmacher 65.00
  Figurine, Bird, Brown, 9 1/2 In. 195.00
  Jug, Boy & Dog, 3-Handled 60.00
  Pitcher, Comical Cat, Gray Spots, Black Tail, Red Ribbon, 10 1/2 In. 145.00
  Vase, Art Nouveau, Face Of Beautiful Woman, Mounted For Lamp, 13 In. 275.00

Vase, Art Nouveau, Gold Speckled, Cobalt Blue Ground, 9 3/4 In. 400.00
Vase, Butterfly, 7 In. 350.00
Vase, Children Scene, Sculptured, 13 In. 425.00
Vase, Dragonflies & Jewels, 18 In. 450.00
Vase, Figural, Mushroom, 8 In. 250.00
Vase, Floral Design, Handled, 6 3/4 In. 85.00
Vase, Girls, Face, Jeweled Headdress, Long Hair, 11 In. 325.00
Vase, Grapes, Berries, Beige Ground, 6 In., Pair 85.00
Vase, Gray, Lily Pad Design, Nude, Art Nouveau, Crown Mark, 9 In. 250.00
Vase, Handled, Fern In Relief, 7 In. 50.00
Vase, Indian Design, Blue, Gold, 2-Handled, 5 3/4 In. 120.00
Vase, Pillow Shape, Blue, Cherries, Leaves, White Ground, 4 In. 80.00
Vase, Portrait Medallion Center, Jewels, 6 In. 95.00
Vase, Silver Over Pottery, Signed Amphora, 8 In. 495.00
Vase, 4-Handled, Enameled Leaves, Golden Poppies, Amphora 225.00

TERRA-COTTA, Basket, Fruit, Pomegranates, Apples, & Grapes, 11 1/2 In. 50.00
Box, Dragon Around Lid, Stippling, Covered, 5 X 2 In. 25.00
Coffeepot, Long Spout, Enameled 1395.00
Figurine, Dog, Glass Eyes, Cigar In Mouth, 1920s, Advertising 225.00
Figurine, Gypsy Man With Fiddle, Woman, Tambourine, 16 In., Pair 255.00
Jar, Dragon Design, Covered, 6 1/2 In. 50.00
Teapot, Branch Handle, Bamboo Spout, Seal Mark, 6 X 8 In. 45.00
Teapot, Raised Dragons 40.00
Vase, Dragons, 6 In. 25.00
Vase, Enameled Flowers, Covered, 7 1/2 In. 36.00
Vase, Oriental Design, 8 In. 65.00
Vase, Oriental, Flying Dragon Design, 5 In. 15.00
Vase, Raised Dragons, Unglazed, 7 1/4 In. 40.00

Textile includes all types of table linens and household linens such as coverlets, fabrics, etc.

TEXTILE, Apron, Cutwork Flowers, Padded Satin Embroidery, Sheer Linen 30.00
Apron, Embroidered Souvenir Of France, White Silk 12.00
Apron, Mother Hubbard Flour, Worth The Difference, Coverall 12.00
Baby Shoes, Brown Leather, High Button 35.00
Baby Shoes, White Kid, High Button 35.00
Bag, Burlap, Kellogg's Hominy Feed 3.00
Bag, Mesh, Enameled, Ivory, Gold Chain & Frame 40.00
Bag, Mesh, Whiting Davis, Deco Colored Design 65.00
Banner, Lion Face Girl, Sideshow, Signed Snap Syatt, 7 X 8 Ft. 795.00
Banner, Sideshow, Sword Swallower, Canvas, 7 X 9 Ft. 895.00
Bathing Suit, Knit, Pink, 1930 .... 10.00
Bed Jacket, Crepe Lesere, Ribbon Through Lace 15.00
Bed Jacket, Embroidered Pink Roses, White Gauze 40.00
Bedspread & Sham, Candlewick, Knotted Fringe, Muslin, 71 X 82 In. 125.00
Bedspread, Battenburg Lace Center, Pillow Sham, 66 X 88 In. 165.00
Bedspread, Central Pattern, Vegetable Dyed, Cotton, 74 X 92 In. 35.00
Bedspread, Crocheted Diamonds, Yellow, 96 X 66 In. 50.00
Bedspread, Crocheted Popcorn Stitch, Pink Flowers, 9 X 9 1/2 Ft. 195.00
Bedspread, Crocheted, Hand-Knotted Fringe On 2 Sides, 90 X 100 In. 225.00
Bedspread, Crocheted, Linen, 74 X 59 In. 65.00
Bedspread, Crocheted, Popcorn Diamond 75.00
Bedspread, Crocheted, Star Design, 3 In. Fringe, Off-White, Double 175.00
Bedspread, Crocheted, 80 X 80 In. 135.00
Bedspread, Ecru Color, Violin Design Center, Full 175.00
Bedspread, Embroidered On Linen, Crocheted Insets, 90 X 84 In. 40.00
Bedspread, Floral Inserts At Center & Corners, Net, 73 X 110 In. 100.00
Bedspread, Hand-Woven, Crocheted, White, 90 X 72 In. 75.00
Bedspread, Jumping Jacks, Ducks, Ruffled Top, 64 X 72 In. 22.00
Bedspread, Marseilles, Allover Design, 80 X 108 In. 125.00
Bedspread, Marseilles, White, Double Size 45.00
Bedspread, Marseilles, Woven For Four-Poster Bed 35.00

Bedspread, Old King Cole Pattern Woven In, Crib Size	50.00
Bedspread, Pineapple Pattern, Crocheted, Liner, Ecru, 100 X 98 In.	160.00
Bedspread, Popcorn Star Pattern, White, 39 X 104 In.	95.00
Bedspread, Queen Anne Pattern, Crocheted, Cotton, 138 X 108 In.	145.00
Bedspread, Scalloped Edges, Embroidered Old Woman In Shoe, Crib	20.00
Bedspread, Southern Belle, Embroidered, Muslin, 74 X 88 In.	35.00
Bedspread, Split Stitch Embroidered Over Net, 88 X 102 In.	125.00
Bedspread, Star Pattern, Scalloped Edge, Fringe, Large	100.00
Bedspread, Teddy Bear Pattern, Crib, 69 X 49 In.	38.00
Bellpull, Needlework, Signed Klara Vogel, Natural Dyes, C.1833	210.00
Blanket, Horse, Milford, N.Y., S.S.Harrison Flour & Feed	100.00
Blanket, Mexican, Wool, Eagle Holding Snake, Blue, White, Black	25.00
Blanket, Mexican, Wool, Multicolored, Figures, 48 X 78 In.	25.00
Blanket, Mexican, Wool, Stripes Of Gray, Blue, White, 87 X 51 In.	30.00
Blanket, Wool, Coach, Horsehead Design, 3 X 5 In.	45.00
Blouse, Cotton, Lace High Neck, Button Back	55.00
Blouse, Crepe, De Chine, Beaded, Navy	60.00
Blouse, High Neck, Lace	65.00
Blouse, Lace & Tucks, White Batiste	40.00
Bolster Cover, Cross-Stitched Red Design, Ecru Linen, 23 X 44 In.	25.00
Bonnet, Baby, Victorian, Handmade Lace	12.00
Bonnet, Baby's, Hand Crocheted	8.00
Bonnet, Child's, Blue Flowers, 1900s	5.00
Bonnet, Child's, Linen & Pique, Blue Lined, Rickrack Trim	6.50
Bonnet, Hand-Sewn, Black Silk Covered With Lace, C.1850	20.00
Bonnet, Mourning, 1860s	30.00
Bonnet, Quilted Chambray, Lace Trim, White On Blue, C.1900	24.00
Bustle, Canvas Waist Strap & Buckle, Woven Wire	40.00
Camisole, Crocheted Yokes	12.00
Camisole, Pink Silk & Lace	22.50
Camisole, Silk Ribbons, Ivory Cotton	42.00
Camisole, White, C.1900	20.00
Cap & Apron, Maid's, Embroidered White Lace Edging, Black Ribbon	7.50
Cap, Beanie, Space Charms	15.00
Cap, Night, Lady's, Lace & Bow Trim, Crocheted, Blue, C.1890	20.00
Cap, Sleeping, Lady's, Tatted, Rose	17.00
Cap, Touring, Crocheted, White	5.00
Cape, Beading, Lace Ruffles, Embroidered Flowers, Black	17.50
Cape, Black Gabardine, Black Lace Shoulders, 1890s	25.00
Cape, Black, Red Silk Lining	50.00
Cape, Evening, Asymmetrical Bottom Flounce, 1920s	125.00
Cape, Evening, Braid Trim, Long	75.00
Cape, Flowers On Net, Snap At Neck, Black Lace	22.50
Cape, Monkey Fur Trim At Collar & Front, Velvet, C.1860	47.00
Cape, Red, Wool, Double Collar, Black Fur Fringe	300.00
Cape, Touring, Lady's, Hook & Eye Front, Black Lining, Black Plush	20.00
Capelet, Silk, Victorian, Mint Green, Lined, Bone Buttons	15.00
Cardigan, Cashmere, Tan, Pringle Of Scotland	25.00
Centerpiece, Brussels Lace, Cream Linen, Oval, 7 X 12 In.	25.00
Centerpiece, Maltese-Type Lace Border, Linen, 28 In.Diam.	25.00
Centerpiece, Venice-Style Lace, Drawnwork, Linen, Square, 19 1/2 In.	20.00
Chair Back, Cluny-Type Lace, 9 X 15 In., Pair	10.00
Chair Seat, Needlepoint, 17 In.	12.00
Chair Set, Pineapple Pattern, Crocheted	23.00
Chemise, Crepe De Chine	10.00
Christening Dress, Petticoat, Eyelet, C.1900, 42 In.	95.00
Christening Outfit, Lace & Ribbons, Batiste, 3 Piece	65.00
Coaster, Battenburg Trim, Round, Set Of 6	20.00
Coaster, Bobbin Lace Edge, Linen, 5 1/2 In.Diam.	3.50
Coaster, Cocktail, Fits Over Glass Bottom, Linen, Set Of 12	15.00
Coaster, Filet On Net, Snowflake Design Border	7.50
Coaster, Rose Design Filet, Knotted Net, 5 In.Diam., Set Of 4	10.00
Coaster, Silk Embroidery, Net, Scalloped Border, 4 1/2 In., Set Of 6	12.50
Coat & Vest, Swallowtail, Black	45.00

Coat, Broadtail Fur Collar, Black Silk, Size 12 .... 35.00
Coat, Christening, Infant, Ribbed Cotton, Lace Trimmed Collar 18.00
Coat, Evening, Velvet Buttons From Neck To Waist, Crushed Velvet 65.00
Coat, Lady's, Twisted Mink Collar, Black Wool, Size 20 .... 65.00
Coat, Man's, Horsehair, Brown, Quilted Lining, Wooden, Bottons 130.00
Coat, Wolf Manchurian Collar, 1940s 200.00
Collar, Beaded, Black Lace 12.00
Collar, Closes With Crochet Button, Pink Crocheted, 2 1/2 In.Wide 4.00
Comforter, Hand-Tied, 4 1/2 In.Squares, Flannel Back, Wool, 74 In.Sq. 55.00
Cover, Bolster, Shirred Lace Inserts, Ruffled End, 17 In., Pair 35.00
       TEXTILE, COVERLET, see Coverlet
Cowboy Suit, Prairie Ranger, Gun, Mask, & Holster, Boxed 15.00
Curtain, Ecru, Pair 10.00
Doily, Battenburg, Linen, Handmade, 16 In.Diam. 10.00
Doily, Battenburg, 7 In.Diam. 10.00
Doily, Bobbin Lace Edge, Linen, 14 X 16 In. ° 6.00
Doily, Bobbin Lace Edge, Rounded Corners, Linen, 13 X 17 In. 10.00
Doily, Brussels Lace, Oval, 4 X 6 In. 7.50
Doily, Center Medallion, Ring Of Medallions, Tatted, 8 1/2 In. 7.50
Doily, Cluny-Type Lace, Oval, Off-White, 9 1/2 X 15 In. .... 5.00 To 7.50
Doily, Eyelet, Flower Basket At Ends, 9 1/2 X 13 In. 5.00
Doily, Four Cutwork Designs, Bobbin Lace Center, Oval, 20 In. 15.00
Doily, Hairpin Lace Circles Around Center Linen, 8 In.Diam. 7.50
Doily, Hairpin Lace, Center Crocheted Flower, 24 In.Diam. 12.50
Doily, Hairpin Lace, 5 In.Diam. 3.50
Doily, Linen Center, Crocheted Border, Scalloped, 18 In.Diam. 6.00
Doily, Linen Center, Crocheted Diamond Design, Oval, 16 X 19 In. 12.50
Doily, Linen Center, Open Triangle Pattern, 13 1/2 In.Diam. 6.00
Doily, Medallion Surrounded By 8 Small Medallions, 14 1/2 In.Diam. 7.50
Doily, Needle Lace Inserts, Lace Border, Linen, 11 1/2 X 18 In. 12.50
Doily, Needle Lace Medallions, 6 3/4 In.Diam. 5.00
Doily, Ring Of Flowers & Leaves Of Padded Satin Stitch, 21 1/2 In. 15.00
Doily, Scalloped Satin Stitch Edge, Linen, Teacup Size, Set Of 12 .... 35.00
Doily, Tatted Medallion Border, Linen Center, 13 X 22 In. 12.50
Dress, Allover Black Beaded 20.00
Dress, Ankle Length, Cape Collar, Flowered Chiffon, 1930s 75.00
Dress, Baby's, Tucks & Lace, White 25.00
Dress, Beaded, Gold Silk, 1920s 75.00
Dress, Black Layer Of Lace Over Tea Rose Satin, Size 10 .... 40.00
Dress, Black, Cotton, Floral Lace, High Collar, Long Sleeves 30.00
Dress, Black, Silk Crepe De Chine, Pink Rose Print, 22 In.Waist 95.00
Dress, Bodice, Pink Silk & Lace 20.00
Dress, Boned Bodice, Silk, 2 Piece 20.00
Dress, Brown Calico, 1860s 100.00
Dress, Brown Silk Satin, Chemise, Beaded, 1920s 50.00
Dress, Bustle, 1880s 150.00
Dress, Christening, White 35.00
Dress, Cocktail, Black, Draped Front, Silk, Print, 1950s 30.00
Dress, Cotton, White, Lace Insets, C.1900 .... 55.00
Dress, Crepe, Black, Mauve Bodice, Palm Tree Design, 1940s 40.00
Dress, Crepe, Silver Gilt Lace, Embroidery, Crystal Beads, 1920 .... 75.00
Dress, Day, Blue, Plum, Teal, White, Square Neck, Silk, Belted 20.00
Dress, Dotted Swiss, Circular Lace Insets, Waist 24 In. 140.00
Dress, Edwardian, Lace Trim, White Lawn, Size 8 .... 90.00
Dress, Evening, Beading & Lace, Ivory Silk 50.00
Dress, Evening, Black Lace, Silk Underslip, V Front & Back, 1930s 40.00
Dress, Evening, Sequins, Belt, Satin, White, 1940s 20.00
Dress, Evening, Sequins, Jets, Satin & Lace 28.00
Dress, Evening, Velvet, Brown, Sash, Draped Neckline, 1930s 40.00
Dress, Eyelet, 23 In.Waist 140.00
Dress, Fitted Bodice, Black Lace Shawl, Silk & Lace, C.1890 .... 125.00
Dress, Flapper, Beaded 165.00
Dress, Flapper, Black, 1920s 30.00
Dress, Flapper, Green Crushed Silk Velvet 50.00

Dress, Flapper, Yellow Chiffon 18.00
Dress, Floral Embroidery, Lace Insets, 23 In.Waist 145.00
Dress, High Lace Neck, Silk Pongee, 1890-1900, 24 In.Waist 125.00
Dress, India Style, Embroidery, Pink Gauze, 1900-15, 24 In.Waist 110.00
Dress, Mennonite 45.00
Dress, Middle Neckline, Rickrack Edging, Linen, 1920s 30.00
Dress, Navy, Gabardine, Braid Trim, Piping, Long Sleeves 75.00
Dress, Party, Flesh Lace, Bias Cut, Sheer, V Front, Jacket, 1920s 30.00
Dress, Red & White Silk Print 8.00
Dress, Silk, Brown, Striped, 1 Piece, C.1860 .... 45.00
Dress, Silk, Cream, Floor Length, Beige Lace, Green Waistband 30.00
Dress, Silver Sequins, Brown Crepe, 1940s 12.00
Dress, Slip, Satin, Purple, World War I 40.00
Dress, Tan Lace At Neck, Long Sleeves, Blue Chiffon, 1920s 35.00
Dress, Victorian, Black Silk, Black Lace High Collar 45.00
Dress, Victorian, Gray Dots, White Sheer Fabric, Long Sleeves 65.00
Dress, Victorian, Lace Trim, White Cotton 50.00
Dress, Victorian, Ruffled Flounce, Lace Trim, Crepe, Size 16 .... 45.00
Dress, Wedding, Bustle, Leaf Print Calico, 1880s, 2 Piece 85.00
Dress, Wedding, Ivory Crepe, Sleeveless, Bolero Jacket, 1930s 45.00
Dress, Wedding, Ivory Embroidered Net, Silk Satin, 1913 .... 40.00
Dress, Wedding, Shaped Bodice, Leg-O'-Mutton Sleeves, Train, Satin 75.00
Dress, White Lawn, Lace Trim, Spider Web Insertions 85.00
Dress, White, Black Pinstripe, Linen, White Collar, 24 In.Waist 90.00
Duster, Hand-Embroidered, Linen, 1910 .... 15.00
Embroidered Picture, Spring, Winter, 19th Century, 6 X 5 In., Pair 220.00
Embroidery, Chinese, Silk, Pheasant Siting On Branch, C.1900 .... 120.00
Embroidery, Crewel, Floral, Scroll, Red & Blue, 31 X 19 In. 120.00
Ensemble, Lady's, Waist, Skirt With Bustle, & Jacket, Flowered 150.00
Flag, U.S., 48 Stars, Cotton Bunting, Embroidered Stars, 4 X 6 Ft. 8.00
Flag, United States, 1890-96, 44 Stars, 18 X 8 Ft. 125.00
Flag, 15 Stars, 9 Stripes 1950.00
Gloves, Lady's, Crocheted, White 9.00
Gloves, Men's, Sleigh, Horsehair 45.00
Gloves, No Fingers, Long Black Lace 8.00
Gown, Baby, Handworked Tucking, Embroidery, & Tatting, C.1900 .... 18.00
Gown, Black, Lace, Blue Underdress, Late 1800s 40.00
Gown, Bridal, Peau De Soie, Satin, 1940s 45.00
Gown, Dressing, Embroidered With Piping, Handmade, Cotton, 1880 .... 95.00
Gown, Dressing, Lady's, Embroidered Lace Colar, Kimona Sleeves 45.00
Gown, Evening, Beige Satin, 1940s 60.00
Gown, Evening, Harlequin Effect, Crepe-Backed Satin, Rose 35.00
Gown, Taffeta Slip, Matching Jacket, Lace, Periwinkle Blue 48.00
Gown, Wedding, Beaded Trim, Train, Underslip, Off-White, 1920s 65.00
Gown, Wedding, Raw Silk Bows, Bustle, Silk Taffeta 165.00
Greeting, Happy New Year, Punched Paper, Embroidered, Walnut Frame 65.00
Hand Towel, Tatted Edge, White Linen, 14 1/4 X 26 In. 7.50
Handkerchief, Chicago Fair, Silk, 1933 .... 12.00
Handkerchief, Child's, Satin Stitched, Fireman, 1920s 6.50
Handkerchief, Remember Me, Military Eagle, Silk, Set Of 4 .... 9.00
Handkerchief, World War II, Flags, Silk 5.00
Hat, Conductor's, Boston & Maine 27.50
Hat, High, Felt, Man's, Tied With String, Daniel Messinger, 6 In. 250.00
Hat, Stovepipe, Sheared Beaver, C.1860, 7 In. 60.00
Hat, Wide Brimmed, Black Velvet, Ostrich Plumes 55.00
Holder, Thimble, Tatted & Crocheted, Satin Bows, Beige, 11 In. 22.00
Jabot, Edges With Filet Lace, Tulle 6.00
Jacket, Bolero, Cutwork & Embroidered On Linen, Puffed Sleeves 40.00
Jacket, Deco, White Lining, Black Velvet 28.00
Jacket, Red, Military, Military Buttons, C.1870 .... 80.00
Kimono, Chinese, Silk Brocade, Turquoise, Gold, Gray, Orange, 1930s 40.00
Kimono, Frog Closures, Teal Blue Silk, Navy Silk Lined 125.00
Kimono, Hand-Painted, Japanese 60.00
Kimono, Red Flowered 60.00

Kimono, With Obi, Lined, Silk	175.00
Knickers, Lady's, Elastic At Bottom, Black Wool, 1920s	45.00
Lace, Honiton-Type, Handmade, Per Yard	5.00
Mat, Cluny-Type Lace, White, 10 X 16 In.	6.00
Mat, Ispahan, Inscription, Green Field, Arabic, Koran, 3 X 2 Ft.	200.00
Mat, Needle Lace Flowers Joined By Picots, 12 1/2 X 11 1/2 In.	20.00
Mat, Prayer, Persian, Cotton, Trellis Design, Blue, 3 X 4 Ft.	50.00
Memorial, Silk, Embroidered, Edward Hopper, 1840, Framed	165.00
Memorial, Silk, Embroidered, Scenic, Woman, 1823, 20 X 23 In.	1100.00
Mitts, Ruffle Trim, Lace, Natural Color	18.00
Needlework, White Bearded Man, Biblical Attire, Doves, 18 X 20 In.	200.00
Nightgown, Child's, White Cotton, 1885	20.00
Nightgown, Crochet Inserts On Front, Linen, Long	40.00
Nightgown, Hand-Embroidered, Draw Neck, Short Sleeves, Muslin	20.00
Nightgown, Homespun	20.00
Nightgown, Pale Yellow, Cap Sleeve, Lace Trim, Shirring Front, 1930s	15.00
Nightgown, Victorian, Long, Openwork Eyelet Ruffle, White	25.00
Obi, Brocade Patterns & Flowers, Buff Ground, Silk, Pair	145.00
Overalls, Scratch Matches On My Breeches, Patch Pockets	12.00
Panel, Linen, Dodecanse Island, Orange, Green, Leaves, 93 In.	300.00
Panel, Soumak, Geometric Design, Red, Indigo, Yellow, Brown, 3 X 2 Ft.	200.00
Pantalettes, Lace Flounced Legs, Lawn	15.00
Pantaloons, Lace Trim, Cotton	8.50 To 20.00
Panties, Black, Sheer, Ruffled, Bottom, Lace Trim, 1930s	15.00
Panties, Lace Trim, 1930s	12.00
Petticoat, Baby's, Lace Trim, White, 18 In.	12.00
Petticoat, Bustle Back, Lace Trimmed, Size 8	55.00
Petticoat, Bustle, Handmade Eyelet Ruffle	55.00
Petticoat, Eyelet Drawstring, Cotton	45.00
Petticoat, Eyelet Flounce, Long	18.00
Petticoat, Lace Edged Flounce, Muslin, 24 In.Waist	15.00
Petticoat, Silk, Ivory, Train, Ruffle, 1890	40.00
Petticoat, Victorian, Flannel, Size 10	10.00
Petticoat, White, 1895	15.00
Picture, Alice In Wonderland, Embroidered, Silk, 9 3/4 X 13 In.	145.00
Picture, Chinese Figures, Embroidered, Painted, Silk, 4 1/2 In., Pr.	330.00
Picture, Needlepoint, Amish Figures, Early 1800s, Framed	47.00
Picture, Needlepoint, Christ's Head, Framed, 10 X 12 In.	60.00
Picture, Needlework, Lady Holding Mirror, Dated 1814, 19 X 13 In.	175.00
Picture, Woven In Silk, Jeanne D'Arc, Neyret Freres, 8 1/2 X 13 In.	175.00
Pillow Sham, Sweet Violets	18.00
Pillow Top, Handmade Bobbin Lace Edge, Linen, 9 1/2 In.Square	6.00
Pillow Top, Lace Ruffle, Net & Lace, Dark Tan, 14 X 22 In.	10.00
Pillow, Embroidered, Gems Of Blue Bring Thoughts Of You	12.50
Pillow, Quilted Silk, Hessian Soldier, Indian Maiden, 23 X 23 In.	475.00
Pillow, Uzbekistan, Lavender, Green, Pink, Maroon, Yellow, 2 X 2 Ft.	100.00
Pillow, Victorian Net Lace, Pink Liner, Ecru, 11 X 15 In.	35.00
Pillowcase, Baby, Brussels-Type Lace Inserts In Corner, Linen	10.00
Pillowcase, Baby, Diamonds Of Drawnwork, Handkerchief Linen	12.50
Pillowcase, Baby, Scalloped Satin Stitch Edge, Flowers & Dots	7.50
Pillowcase, Counted Red Cross Stitch, Geometric Design, 15 X 22 In.	12.00
Pillowcase, Crazy Quilt Design, Velvet, 18 X 18 In.	22.00
Pillowcase, Cream Colored Linen, 20 X 32 In., Pair	25.00
Pillowcase, Edge Cut In Points, Crocheted, Linen, 22 X 34 In., Pair	15.00
Pillowcase, Hand-Embroidered, 4 Piece	20.00
Pillowcase, Needle Lace Worked Border, Silk, Apricot, Pair	30.00
Pillowcase, Scalloped, Satin Stitch Dot On Each Scallop, Linen, Pair	12.50
Pillowcase, Souvenir Of The Great War, Allied Flags, Embroidered	14.50
Pillowcase, Tatted Border, White Cotton, 20 X 32 In.	7.50
Place Mat, Drawnwork Border, Fleur-De-Lis & Flowers, Set Of 6	65.00
Place Mat, Geometric Design, Linen, 12 1/4 X 16 1/4 In., Set Of 12	30.00
Portrait, Embroidered, Ship, Full Sail, Port, Framed, 22 X 26 In.	270.00
Purse, Beaded, Cobalt, Carnival, Cross Design, Handled, 6 X 9 In.	45.00
Purse, Brown Velvet, Ornate Brass Frame, Lavender Glass Jewels	85.00

Purse, Mesh, German Silver, Silver Drops, 7 X 5 1/2 In. 38.00
Purse, Mesh, Gold Plated, Floral Design, Blue Stone, Braided Handle 30.00
Purse, Mesh, Orange, Beige, Yellow, Enameled Frame 38.00
Purse, Mesh, Silver, Chain Handle, German, 7 X 5 1/2 In. 38.00
Purse, Wicker 25.00
   TEXTILE, QUILT, see Quilt
Rainboots, High Button, Canvas Rubber, Size 7 .... 45.00
Ribbon, Burlington Industries, Silk, Rayon, & Tinsel, 1940s, 8 Yds. 3.75
Ribbon, Mourning, Jefferson Davis, Picture 85.00
Robe, Child's, Flannel Lined, Yellow Embroidery 16.00
Robe, Lap, Center Tiger, Glass Eyes, Red Roses, Mohair, 60 X 45 In. 75.00
Robe, Lap, Horsehair 75.00
Robe, Lap, Sleigh, Pictures Of Bears, Wool 45.00
Robe, Silk, China, C.1900, 4-Toed Dragons, Clouds, Water, 55 In. 70.00
   TEXTILE, RUG, see Rug
Runner, Battenburg, 6 Linen Diamonds, Drawnwork, 16 X 54 In. 55.00
Runner, Border Of Brussels Lace, Hemstitched Divided, 15 X 24 In. 25.00
Runner, Cluny-Type Lace, Handmade, Tan, 38 In. 25.00
Runner, Corner Filet Roses, White Linen, Monogrammed, 34 In. 17.50
Runner, Crocheted Edge, 84 In. 38.00
Runner, Cutwork Corners, Filet Drawnwork Sides, Linen, 16 X 52 In. 25.00
Runner, Deco Embroidered Corners, Fringed, Linen, 16 X 28 In. 7.50
Runner, Double Row Drawnwork, Needle Lace Corners, 18 X 23 In. 35.00
Runner, Double Row Of Tatting, Linen, 17 1/2 X 35 In. 17.50
Runner, Drawnwork At Corners, Grass Cloth, Sprays, 15 X 50 In. 15.00
Runner, Drawnwork Border, Fleur-De-Lis & Flowers, 16 X 50 In. 35.00
Runner, Drawnwork Flowers, Padded Satin Flowers, 16 1/2 X 51 In. 45.00
Runner, Eyelet Butterflies At Ends, Linen, 52 In. 9.00
Runner, Filet Crochet Ends, 40 In. 25.00
Runner, Filet Flowers & Scrolls, Tied Net, 12 X 18 In. 12.50
Runner, Filet Geometric Designs, White Lace, 12 1/2 X 42 1/2 In. 12.50
Runner, Flower Medallions, Diamonds, Cluny-Type Lace, 19 X 75 In. 45.00
Runner, Flowers In Zig Zag Border, Knotted Lace, Tan, 15 X 40 In. 15.00
Runner, Hand-Crocheted Border, Tasseled Points, 22 X 76 In. 25.00
Runner, Handmade Bobbin Lace Edge, Rounded Corners, 15 X 20 In. 7.50
Runner, Hardanger Embroidered & Cutwork Corners, 17 X 32 In. 15.00
Runner, Inserts Of Lace Boys, Girls, Cutwork, Linen, 21 1/2 X 55 In. 125.00
Runner, Isparta, Navy & Fuchsia Medallions, 3 Ft. X 22 Ft. 10 In. 450.00
Runner, Knotted Lace, Facing Dragons In Center, 10 X 19 In. 12.50
Runner, Lace Sides, No Seams, Battenburg, 26 X 82 In. 100.00
Runner, Lilihan, Overall Floral Sprays, 5 Ft. 8 In. X 8 Ft. 5 In. 400.00
Runner, Scalloped, Lacy Crochet, Linen, 18 X 50 In. 20.00
Runner, Turkish, Medallions, Ivory & Green Edge, 4 X 10 Ft. 300.00
Runner, White Embroidery, Cutwork Corners, 17 1/2 X 54 In. 10.00
Runner, 4 Different Borders, Maltese-Type Lace, 15 X 31 In. 3.00

*Samplers were made in America from the early 1700s. The best examples were
made from 1790 to 1840. Long, narrow samplers are usually older than square
ones. Early samplers just had stitching or alphabets. The later examples
had numerals, borders, and pictorial decorations. Those with mottoes are mid-
Victorian.*

Sampler, Alphabet, Acorns, Strawberries, 1832, 20 X 21 In. 175.00
Sampler, Alphabet, Geometric, Floral, 21 X 12 In. 150.00
Sampler, Alphabet, Hearts, & Birds, Signed, Dated 1789, 17 1/4 In.Sq. 950.00
Sampler, Alphabet, Numbers, Birds, Flowers, Framed, 16 X 7 In. 225.00
Sampler, Alphabet, Numbers, Brown, Blue, Gold, Dated 1735, 14 In. 315.00
Sampler, Alphabet, Numbers, Plants, Dated 1818, 14 1/4 X 14 In. 275.00
Sampler, Amanda Jacobs, Dated 1800, Verse, 12 X 12 In. 165.00
Sampler, America In 19th Century, Lucy Packson Keys, 17 X 7 In. 170.00
Sampler, Blue, Green, Pink, Alphabets, Vines, Birds, 1812, 19 X 15 In. 2530.00
Sampler, Building, Flowers, Trees, Birds, 1829, 20 X 23 In. 350.00
Sampler, Come Ye Sinners, Poor, & Needy, Dated 1886, Walnut Frame 50.00
Sampler, Cottage, Garden, Well Bucket, C.1900, 15 X 20 In. 300.00
Sampler, Farm Scene, Man, Lady, House, Sheep, 18th Century, 17 X 23 In. 1100.00

Sampler, Flowers, Birds, Chair, Yellow, Blue, Red, 1805, 23 X 23 In. 150.00
Sampler, God Bless Our Home, Flowery, Framed, 13 X 17 In. 35.00
Sampler, Home Sweet Home, Blue On White, Framed, 11 X 13 In. 25.00
Sampler, Home Sweet Home, Gold Lined Oak Frame, 19 X 23 In. 45.00
Sampler, How Dear To My Heart, Childhood Scenes, 6 X 12 In. 26.00
Sampler, Maria Woodnough 1835, Beige, Brown, Verse, 21 X 17 In. 495.00
Sampler, Mary Ann Somerby, Dated 1829, 13 X 10 In. 250.00
Sampler, No Place Like Home, Cross-Stitch, Trees, Garden, 11 X 14 In. 30.00
Sampler, Red, Blue, Brown, Green, Brick House, Trees, 1822, 19 X 13 In. 469.00
Sampler, Roses, Eagles, & 26 Star Flag, Worsted Silk, 19 X 21 In. 65.00
Sampler, Signed Charlotte B.Andrews, 8 Years Old, 8 X 18 In. 135.00
Sampler, Warm Friendship Like Setting Sun, 13 X 16 In. 35.00
Sampler, Who Has A Friend, Linen, Man, Lady, C.1920, 11 X 14 In. 30.00
Scarf, Crocheted, Mantel, Diamond Design, Tassels, 18 X 58 In. 52.00
Scarf, Dresser, Battenburg Lace, 16 X 46 In. 95.00
Scarf, Flower Design, Gold Flowers On Edge, Dark Rose Silk, 28 In. 10.00
Scarf, Piano, Fringe, White Silk, 96 X 17 In. 125.00
Scarf, Piano, Hand-Embroidered, Fringe, Black Silk, 47 X 50 In. 200.00
Scarf, Piano, Roses In Silk Thread, Reversible, Knotted Fringe 165.00
Scarf, Shelf, Crystal Beaded, Red Wool, Late 1800s 35.00
Scarf, Silk, Chinese, Magenta, Floral, Sea Creatures, 22 X 63 In. 25.00
Scroll, Landscape, 17th Century, Chinese, 2 X 6 1/2 Ft. 1200.00
Sham, Pillow, Drawnwork, Embroidered Flowers, 30 X 31 In. 35.00
Sham, Pink, Good Morning, Good Night, Morning Glories 25.00
Shawl, Black & White Flowers, Silk Blend 60.00
Shawl, Black Silk, Victorian, 26 X 80 In. 20.00
Shawl, Embroidered Pink & Rose Flowers, Silk 125.00
Shawl, Embroidered, Chinese, White On White, 65 In.Square 48.00
Shawl, Embroidered, 17 In.Fringe, Silk, 52 In.Square 75.00
Shawl, Green Silk, Victorian, Fringed, 48 In.Square 25.00
Shawl, Hand-Embroidered Pink & Red Flowers, Chiffon 25.00
Shawl, Hand-Embroidered Roses, Silk, Black, Large 105.00
Shawl, Hand-Embroidered White Floral On White Silk, Chinese, Large 280.00
Shawl, Mourning, Black, Small 5.00
Shawl, Mourning, Black, Victorian 10.00
Shawl, Piano, 17 In.Fringe, 50 X 50 In. 75.00
Shawl, Silk Thread Roses, Victorian, Fringe, Silk, 50 In.Square 160.00
Shawl, Silk, Green, Pink Embroidery, Fringed, 46 X 46 In. 75.00
Shawl, Silk, Ivory, Ivory Embroidery, Fringe, 52 X 52 In. 65.00
Shawl, Spanish, Off-White Silk, Silk Fringe, 46 In.Square 50.00
Shawl, Wool Challis Paisley, 5 Ft. Square 47.50
Sheet & Cases, Tatted Medallions At Edge, Row Of Half Medallions 85.00
Sheet, Appliqued Animals, Crib Size 15.00
Sheet, Hemstitched, Monogram M, Linen, 72 X 128 In. 30.00
Sheet, Hemstitched, Monogrammed In Diamond, Linen, 88 X 116 In. 45.00
Sheet, Homespun Linen, Amish, Center Seam, Small Monogram 70.00
Sheet, 2 Roses Hemstitched Top, Cutwork Circles, 60 X 81 In., Pr. 50.00
Shirt, Men's, Collar Band, 1920s, Set Of 6 .... 65.00
Shoe, Batting, Black, White Laces, C.1890s, Pair 25.00
Shoe, High Button, Black, Leather, Pair 25.00
Shoe, High Lace, Black Patent, Child's, Size M, Pair 35.00
Shoe, Spike Heel, Black Velvet, Black Satin Ribbon, Size M, Pair 12.00
Shoe, White, Lid Leather, High Lace, French Heel, Size 6, Pair 55.00
Skirt, Cotton Twill, Long 15.00
Skirt, Pleated, Train Back, Gray & White, 28 In.Waist 28.00
Skirt, Victorian, Black 20.00
Slip, Baby's, Flowers Embroidered At Neck, White Batiste, 13 In. 7.00
Smock, Child's, Smocking At Back Neckline, Sailor Collar, Silk 65.00
Spats, Cranberry 8.50
Spats, Taupe 8.50
Stumpwork, With Embroidery, Christ With Mary, Framed, 15 X 14 In. 225.00
Suit, Beige, Navy, Rust Embroidered, 3 Piece 75.00
Suit, Gabardine, Mint Green, Straight Skirt, Padded Sleeve, 1940s 30.00
Suit, Golf, White, Linen, Knee-Length Jacket, Golf Hat, 25 In. Waist 165.00

Suit, Gym, Wellesey College, Navy Blue Serge, 1923, Size 14 .... 25.00
Suit, Hunting, Man's, Wool, 1920s 40.00
Suit, Lady's, Sequins & Beads On Jacket, Fitted Waist, Gray, 1940s 70.00
Suit, Lady's, Victorian, Brown & Black, Size 14, 2 Piece 75.00
Suit, Skirt, Jacket, & Blouse, Cotton, Lace Trim, 23 In. Waist 160.00
Sweater, Beaded, Black, Schiaparelli Paris, White Seed Beads 30.00
Sweater, Beaded, Jet Floral Design, Cardigan 15.00
Tablecloth, Bands With Circles & Scrolls, Irish Linen, 64 X 108 In. 110.00
Tablecloth, Battenburg Lace, 36 In.Square 75.00
Tablecloth, Battenburg, Banquet Size 350.00
Tablecloth, Battenburg, 54 In. 130.00
Tablecloth, Bridge, Madeira, 4 Napkins 45.00
Tablecloth, Centered Eyelet Linen, Battenburg Lace, Handmade, 29 In. 50.00
Tablecloth, Christmas, Poinsettias, White Ground, 56 X 72 In. 12.00
Tablecloth, Chrysanthemums, Irish Linen Damask, 68 X 84 In. 65.00
Tablecloth, Cluny Lace Border & Insert, 72 In.Diam. 125.00
Tablecloth, Corner Inserts Of Bobbin Lace, Linen, 64 X 37 In. 12.00
Tablecloth, Cotton Circles With Crocheted Joinings, 58 X 76 In. 24.00
Tablecloth, Crocheted Corners, Damask, 6 Napkins, 62 X 86 In. 35.00
Tablecloth, Crocheted, Lacy Border, Ivory, 16 X 45 In. 85.00
Tablecloth, Crocheted, Pinwheel & Spider Web, White, 45 X 82 In. 125.00
Tablecloth, Crocheted, White, Pinwheel & Spider Web Design, 8i In. 145.00
Tablecloth, Crocheted, 52 X 52 In. 100.00
Tablecloth, Cross-Stitched Leaves, Gold Flowers, White, 52 X 60 In. 17.50
Tablecloth, Cross-Stitched Roses & Scrolls, Linen, 50 In.Square 20.00
Tablecloth, Cut & Crocheted Edges, Linen, 4 X 7 Ft. 22.00
Tablecloth, Cutwork, Peasant Men & Women, Swedish, 36 X 36 In. 60.00
Tablecloth, Dots & Scrolls, Irish Linen Damask, 88 X 110 In. 125.00
Tablecloth, Dots Form 5 Point Star Center, Scalloped, 33 In.Diam. 25.00
Tablecloth, Drawnwork Damask, Pink, 40 X 67 In. 30.00
Tablecloth, Drawnwork Squares, Embroidered Flowers, 35 X 33 In. 50.00
Tablecloth, Drawnwork, 5 Rows Each Side, Linen, 29 X 30 In. 35.00
Tablecloth, Edge Band Of Silk Thread Flowers, Linen, 45 X 55 In. 25.00
Tablecloth, Embroidered Asters, Appliqued Poppies, 34 X 46 In. 20.00
Tablecloth, Embroidered Flowers, French Knots, Crocheted Rim, 42 In. 85.00
Tablecloth, Embroidered Silk Thread Roses, 24 In.Diam. 25.00
Tablecloth, Embroidered, Drawnwork, 10 Napkins, 64 X 52 In. 225.00
Tablecloth, Eyelet Garland At Crocheted Border, Linen, 48 In.Diam. 25.00
Tablecloth, Ferns, Flowers, Irish Linen Damask, 67 X 118 In. 125.00
Tablecloth, Filet Crocheted, 44 X 44 In. 22.00
Tablecloth, Flower Design, Cotton Damask, 60 X 102 In. 45.00
Tablecloth, French Knot Flowers, Blue Outline, White, 34 In.Square 15.00
Tablecloth, Grape Pattern, Battenburg, Pre-1920, 70 In.Square 175.00
Tablecloth, Grapes & Leaves, Irish Linen Damask, 68 X 86 In. 85.00
Tablecloth, Green Geometric Pattern, Textured White, 51 X 47 In. 35.00
Tablecloth, Gros Point De Venice, 12 Napkins, 68 X 120 In. 1250.00
Tablecloth, Hand-Tatted, White, 70 X 90 In. 350.00
Tablecloth, Handmade, Beige Lace & Linen, 80 X 120 In. 275.00
Tablecloth, Handmade, Lace Border, Roses & Leaves, 31 In.Diam. 35.00
Tablecloth, Hemstitched 1 1/2 Inch Hem, Linen Damask, 64 X 100 In. 80.00
Tablecloth, Lace Worked On Linen Center, Battenburg, 66 In.Square 125.00
Tablecloth, Lacy Crocheted Border, 27 In.Diam. 85.00
Tablecloth, Linen, Cluny Lace Border, Embroidered, 25 In. 52.00
Tablecloth, Linen, Cutwork, Peasant Motif, 36 In. Square 45.00
Tablecloth, Morning Glories, Vines, Embroidered, Linen, 53 X 52 In. 25.00
Tablecloth, Multicolored, Hand-Crocheted, 48 X 58 In. 25.00
Tablecloth, North Carolina Governor's Mansion, Lace, 16 Ft.Long 650.00
Tablecloth, Opening Flowers For Inserting Napkins, Bridge Size 10.00
Tablecloth, Petticoat Border, Scalloped, Crocheted, 92 In.Diam. 15.00
Tablecloth, Quaker Lace, Off-White, 55 X 70 In. 52.50
Tablecloth, Ring Center, Irish Linen Damask, 68 X 70 In. 45.00
Tablecloth, Roses, Irish Linen Damask, 62 X 92 In. 45.00
Tablecloth, Scalloped Edge, 8 Napkins, White Linen, 80 In.Diam. 60.00
Tablecloth, Scroll & Flower Design, Center Medallion, 74 X 86 In. 75.00

Tablecloth, Shamrocks, Irish Linen Damask, 70 X 88 In. 85.00
Tablecloth, Unbleached Cotton, 58 X 66 In. 215.00
Tablecloth, White Damask, Matching Napkins, 72 X 92 In. 60.00
Tablecloth, 5 Bands Of Drawnwork, Linen, White, 28 X 30 In. 25.00
Tapestry, Camels, Donkeys, & Arabs, Belgian, 19 X 39 In. 20.00
Tapestry, Courtiers & Ladies, Belgium, 5 Ft. 60.00
Tapestry, Flemish, 17th Century, Ladies, Grecian, Trees, 70 X 54 In. 1300.00
Tapestry, French, 18th Century, Figures, Scenic, 10 X 12 Ft. 1400.00
Tapestry, Garden Scene, 10 People, 1 Lion, Trees, 6 X 88 Ft. 500.00
Tapestry, Military, Life Of Constantine, Blue, Brown, 113 X 91 In. 2600.00
Tapestry, Pharaoh & Court Scene, Egyptian, 17 X 54 In. 100.00
Tapestry, Rumanian, C.1930, 6 X 7 Ft. 4500.00
Tapestry, Wall Hung, Full Figures, Dancing, Moon, River, 50 X 70 In. 85.00
Tea Cozy, Filet Teapot, Cups, & Spoons, Crocheted, 12 X 18 In. 12.50
Teddy, Silk, Peach, Lace Trim, Cutout Sides, 1930s 30.00
Towel, Embroidered & Drawnwork, White Linen, 13 X 21 In. 6.00
Towel, Hand, Battenburg Trim, Pastel Linen 5.00
Towel, Hand, Monogram, JRN, Linen 3.00
Towel, Inserts Of Filet Crochet Flowers, Huck-Type, 27 X 36 1/2 In. 10.00
Towel, Monogram In Diamond, Hemstitched, Irish Linen, 25 X 42 In. 7.50
Towel, Tatted At Ends, White Linen, 14 1/2 X 25 In. 7.00
Towel, Turkish, Wedding, Castles, Flowers, 18 X 41 In. Pair 190.00
Toweling, Cream, Yellow Stripe On Sides, Linen, 3 Yards 6.00
Toweling, Roses, Bird's-Eye Linen, 4 Yards 10.00
Traycloth, Single Row Of Tatting Edge, Linen, 10 X 16 1/2 In. 6.00
Uniform, Policeman's, New Hampshire, Complete, Billy Stick, 22 In. 395.00
Uniform, WAVE, World War II, Complete 45.00
Wall Hanging, Crewel, Cranberry, Green, Blue, 64 X 108 In. 120.00
Wrap, Crocheted, Long Sleeves, White 28.00

THERMOMETER-Barometer, Maple Case Stick, 1860, 38 In. 1200.00
Bilt Rite, Embossed Sole & Heel 95.00
Biltrite, Sole & Heel, Shoemaker, 6 X 13 In. 95.00
Braums Town Talk Bread, 38 In. 45.00
Calumet, Kewpie Pictured, Wooden 85.00
Camel Cigarettes, Tin, 6 X 14 In. 24.00
Carstairs, Join The Carstairs Crown, 12 In.Diam. 25.00
Carstairs, 12 In.Diam. 25.00
Chesterfield, More Than Ever, They Satisfy.6 X 13 In. 25.00
Chicago World's Fair, 1933-34, Cast Iron 8.00
Columbus Citizen Newspaper, Tin, 6 X 24 In. 27.00
Dairy, Wooden Case 15.00
Dr. Legears Prescriptions For Livestock, Poultry, Dogs 95.00
Dr. W.H. Longs Vegetable Prairie Flower For The Blood 55.00
Dr.Legears, Yellow, 13 1/2 In. 10.00
Dr.Pepper Good For Life, Bottle, Clock 65.00
Dr.Pepper, 10-2-4 Cap, 12 In. 25.00
Electric Lustre Starch, Box With Lady, Wooden 110.00
Electric Lustre Starch, Wood, 21 In. 85.00
Ex-Lax, Porcelain, Large 95.00
Ex-Lax, Prescriptions, Drug, Toilet Articles, Porcelain 135.00
Fatima Cigarettes, Pack, Veiled Lady, 1913, Porcelain, 8 X 26 In. 150.00
Fatima Cigarettes, Porcelain 275.00
Figural, Black Boy, Pressed Wood 16.50
Goodyear, Yellow & Blue 40.00
Happy Jim Chewing Tobacco, Enamel On Tin 45.00
Hawthorne Coal, The Choice Of Buyers, 36 In. 90.00
Hires Root Beer, Figural, Tin, 8 X 28 1/2 In. 38.00
Jests, Large 95.00
Kentucky Club, Horse & Ride, Pipe In Ashtray 75.00
King Edward Cigar, Round, 19 In. 45.00
Kool Cigarettes 20.00
Mail Pouch Chewing Tobacco, Tin, 36 In. 50.00

Mail Pouch Tobacco, Porcelain, 6 Ft. 250.00
Marlboro, Phillip Morris, Both Packs, 6 X 12 In. 20.00
Moxie, Soda Clerk Pointing, 13 X 26 In. 135.00
Orange Crush, Tin, 18 In. 19.50
Orange Crush, 28 In. 45.00
Pepsi-Cola, Blown-Out Cap, Yellow, 27 X 7 In. 38.00
Pepsi-Cola, Girl With Straw 175.00
Pepsi-Cola, Pepsi Please, Clocklike Dial, Square, Tin 15.00
Pepsi-Cola, 7 X 28 In. 22.00
Peter's Shoes, Porcelain, 39 In. 75.00
Prestone Anti-Freeze, Red, White, & Blue, Canada, Round 85.00
Prestone Anti-Freeze, Your Safe, Porcelain, 36 In. 55.00
Prestone Anti-Freeze, 8 X 27 In. 25.00
Ramon's, Shows Little Doctor & Pills, Tin 75.00
RC Cola, 6 X 12 In. 15.00
Rochester Brewing, Round 95.00
Root Beer, Figural, Tin, 28 X 8 In. 38.00
Ships, Mercury, Copper Case, Etched Metal Face, Signed, 14 In. 20.00
Squirt, Bottle, Embossed Tin, 7 X 12 In. 30.00
Squirt, Embossed Tin 35.00
Standard Rochester Brewing Co., Glass Over Tin, 12 In.Diam. 85.00
Sun Crest Orange, 3-D Bottle Shape 30.00
Tennessee Stove Works, Wooden, 36 In. 75.00
Tums For The Tummy, 4 1/2 X 9 1/2 In. 20.00
U.S.S. American Fence & Posts, Porcelain, 18 1/2 X 6 In. 63.50
Universal Batteries, Since 1899, Blue & White, Large 125.00
Winston Cigarettes, Tin, 5 3/4 X 13 1/2 In. 8.00

Louis C. Tiffany Furnaces Inc. Favrile   *Louis C. Tiffany*

*Tiffany glass was made by Louis Comfort Tiffany, the American glass
designer who worked from about 1879 to 1933. His work included iridescent
glass, Art Nouveau styles of design, and original contemporary styles.
He was also noted for his stained glass windows, his unusual lamps, bronze
work, pottery, and silver.*

TIFFANY GLASS, Blue, Iridescent, 4 X 5 In. 875.00
Bonbon, Favrile, Red Highlights, Marked, 4 1/2 In. 150.00
Bonbon, Ruffled, Gold, 4 1/2 In. 195.00
Bottle, Gold Iridescent, Squatty, Pinched Sides, Marked, 3 In. 160.00
Bowl & Underplate, Finger, Gold Favrile, Ascot Pattern, Signed 250.00
Bowl, Black Center, Rolled Rim, Signed, Peacock Blue, 7 In. 375.00
Bowl, Bonbon, Signed, 2 X 4 1/4 In. 235.00
Bowl, Favrile, Gold Iridescent, Signed, 2 1/4 X 4 In. 225.00
Bowl, Flower, Lily Pads, Vines, Holder, Signed, 11 1/2 In. 1250.00
Bowl, Folded Rim, Gold Iridescent, Signed, 2 X 6 In. 375.00
Bowl, Fruit, Blue, Marked, 6 1/2 X 3 In. 185.00
Bowl, Gold Iridescent, Signed, 6 X 2 In. 350.00
Bowl, Gold Iridescent, Swirl Panel, Scalloped, Marked, 3 In. 450.00
Bowl, Gold, Dimpled Edge, Rainbow, Signed, 7 In. 795.00
Bowl, Gold, Handkerchief Ruffled, Signed, 6 In. 350.00
Bowl, Intaglio Carved Leaf Pattern, Signed, 7 X 2 1/2 In. 425.00
Bowl, Nut, Ribbed, Gold & Blue To Purple, Marked, 6 In. 300.00
Bowl, Nut, Ribbed, Gold With Purple, Signed, 6 In. 300.00
Bowl, Pastel Stretch Rim, Signed, 8 X 3 1/2 In. 125.00
Bowl, Peacock Blue, Flat, Marked, 5 In. 495.00
Bowl, Raised Ribs, Gold Iridescent, Marked, 8 In. 325.00
Bowl, Swirl, Blue, 2 3/4 X 7 In. 890.00
Brandy Snifter, Gold, Lily Pad Design, Signed, 3 3/4 In. 295.00
Candlestick, Gold, Marked, 4 In. 600.00
Champagne, Manhattan Pattern, C.1910, Signed, 7 In. 325.00

Compote, Diamond-Quilted, Signed, 8 X 4 In. 550.00
Compote, Diamond-Quilted, 6 X 3 1/4 In. 550.00
Compote, Gold & Lavender, Signed, 4 1/4 In. ....*Illus* 300.00
Compote, Gold Iridescent, Violet Highlights, Marked, 3 X 6 In. 400.00
Compote, Pink, Opalescent Optic Laurel Leaves, 5 3/4 In. 525.00
Compote, Scalloped Rim, Signed L.C.T., Gold, 6 In. ....*Illus* 275.00
Compote, Stretch Glass Rim, Footed, Gold, 8 X 3 1/2 In. 425.00
Compote, Yellow, Opalescent Strips, Signed, 2 X 5 In. 325.00
Cordial, Gold Stem, Signed, 4 1/2 In. 175.00
Cordial, Tulip Shaped-Top, Long Stem, Signed, 4 1/2 In. 165.00
Cordial, Tulip Shaped, Gold, Marked, 4 1/2 In. 165.00
Cup, Punch, Applied Lily-Pad Design, Signed, 2 1/4 In. 275.00
Cup, Punch, Pedestal, Clear, Bubble, Green Pulls, Marked, 3 In. 125.00
Decanter, Gold, Stopper, Signed ....*Illus* 700.00
Decanter, Stopper, Gold Iridescent, Round, Signed, 8 In. 525.00
Dish, Mint, Favrile, Iridescent, Blue, 1 1/2 X 5 In. 295.00
Dish, Mint, Pastel Yellow, Teardrop In Glass, Marked, 7 In. 150.00
Dish, Nut, Favrile, Silver-Blue Highlights, 2 X 3 In. 125.00
Dish, Nut, Gold, Signed, 4 In. ....*Illus* 135.00
Dish, Nut, Iridescent, Everted Lip, Marked, 1 1/4 X 2 1/4 In. 90.00
Dish, Nut, Purple, Blue, Opal Exterior, Signed, 3 1/4 In. 225.00
Dish, Nut, Ribbed, Iridescent, Signed, 1 1/4 X 4 In. 140.00
Dish, Serving, Footed, Favrile, Gold Iridescent, Signed, 2 X 4 In. 350.00
Dish, Serving, Footed, Gold, Violet, Blue, Signed, 8 In. X 2 In. 350.00
Finger Bowl & Underplate, Pig Tails, Signed, 4 1/4 In. 350.00
Finger Bowl & Underplate, Raised Punts, Red, Signed, 6 In. 400.00
Finger Bowl & Underplate, 4 1/2 In. & 6 1/2 In., Signed 900.00
Frog, Verre De Soie, 2 Tier, Marked 80.00
Ginger Jar, Grape & Leaf Engraved Design, Covered, 8 In. 1200.00
Goblet, Favrile, Amber, Marked, 4 3/8 In. 100.00
Goblet, Favrile, Amber, Marked, 5 3/4 In. 120.00
Goblet, Pink Bowl, Green Stem & Base, Signed, 8 In. 465.00
Goblet, Vintage Pattern, Intaglio Leaves, Signed, 6 1/2 In. 750.00
Green, Pulled Feather, Gold Ground, Ruffled, Marked, 6 In. 475.00
Jar, Ginger, Grape & Leaf, Signed, 8 In. 1200.00
Lamp, Arabian, Cone Shade, Bronze Base, Signed, 14 In. 1450.00
Night-Light, Favrile, Gold Shade, Signed, 16 1/2 In. 950.00
Night-Light, Favrile, Red & Green Design Shade, 17 1/2 In. 1300.00
Pitcher, Gold Iridescent, Applied Handle, Marked, 2 1/2 In. 325.00
Pitcher, Gold Iridescent, Loop Handle, Marked, 5 1/4 In. 325.00
Plate, Spears Of Opalescent Feathering, Signed, 11 In. 450.00
Rose Bowl, Leaves & Vines, Gold, Signed, 2 1/2 In. 775.00
Rose Bowl, Paneled Body, Stand-Up Collar, Marked, 1 3/4 In. 350.00
Salt, Favrile, Iridescent, Flat Bottom, Ruffled Edge, Signed 235.00
Salt, Flared Outward, Gold, Signed, 3 In. 150.00
Salt, Open, Pale Green, Paneled Body, Flared Top, 1 X 2 In. 125.00
Salt, Paperweight Body, Ribbed, Curled Feet, Signed, 1 3/4 In. 275.00
Salt, Ruffled, Gold Iridescent, Signed, 2 1/2 In. 150.00
Salt, Ruffled, Sapphire Blue, Signed, 3 In. 325.00
Salt, Shell & Floral Pattern, Marked, 2 In. 55.00
Salt, Thorn, Light Blue, Marked 225.00
Salt, 4 Feet, Pot Shape, Signed, 3 In. 195.00
Saltshaker, Gold Iridescent, Rainbow Colors, Signed 135.00
Scarab, Blue Iridescent, Signed, 3/4 In.Long 75.00
Seal, Iridescent, Triangular Body, 1 3/4 In. High 295.00
Shade, Green Body, Iridescent Silver Border, Opal Bottom 435.00
Shade, Green Crystal Cased, Lily, Marked 350.00
Shade, Green Feather, Gold Edge, Signed 250.00
Shade, Lily, Signed, Green Iridescent 295.00
Shade, Linenfold, Ruffled Border, 12 Panels, Signed, 19 1/2 In. 1650.00
Shade, Optic Diamond, Gold & Blue Highlights, Marked 135.00
Shade, Red & Orange Poppy, Signed, 20 In.Diam. 4500.00
Sherbet, Intaglio Cut, Leaf & Berry Border, Signed, 3 1/2 In. 210.00

Tiffany Glass, Compote, Gold & Lavender, Signed, 4 1/4 In.; Dish, Nut, Gold, Signed, 4 In.; Decanter, Gold, Stopper, Signed; Vase, Favrile, Blue, No.3523U, 8 In.

Sherbet, Vintage Pattern, Intaglio Cut Grapes, Signed	295.00
Sherry, Gold, Curving Stem, Signed, 4 In., Pair	165.00
Shot, Applied Threads At Middle, Signed, 1 3/4 In.	135.00
Shot, Gold, Twisted Pig Tails, Signed, 1 3/4 In. High	225.00
Shot, Threaded, Signed	135.00
Tazza, Signed, Gold & Blue	1250.00
Tile, Cypriote, Bronze Mounted, Signed, 4 In.Square	225.00
Tile, Daisy Pattern, Signed, 4 X 4 In.	75.00
Tile, Marbleized Green & Brown, Red Medallions, 3 In.Square	65.00
Tile, Raided Four Leaf Clover, 3 X 3 In.	50.00
Tile, Red, Yellow Mottling, 4 X 4 In.	55.00
Toothpick, Aurene, Signed	235.00
Toothpick, Orange, Gold Aurene, Marked & Numbered	138.00
Tray, Cocktail, Engraved With Names, Sterling, 15 In.	350.00
Tumbler, Dimpled, Iridescent Rainbow Highlights, 3 In.	145.00
Tumbler, Olive Iridescent, Lily Pad Design, Signed, 4 1/4 In.	285.00
Tumbler, Pale Green, Feather Design, Marked, 4 1/2 In.	95.00
Tumbler, Platinum Bands & Swirls, Marked, 3 In.	225.00
Vase, Alternating Blue & Speckled Blue, Signed, 6 1/2 In.	750.00
Vase, Beehive Shape, Gold & Pink, Signed, 1 3/4 In.	240.00
Vase, Beehive Shape, Gold Favrile, Pink, Marked, 2 In.	195.00
Vase, Blue Iridescent, Ribbed, Signed, 4 1/2 In.	750.00
Vase, Blue Iridescent, Round Bottom, 6 1/2 X 3 1/2 In.	550.00
Vase, Bronze, Raised Ribs, Signed & Numbered, 7 X 5 In.	250.00
Vase, Brown Feather Pulls, Artichoke Base, Signed, 14 1/4 In.	1100.00
Vase, Bud, Flared, Pulled Green, Signed, 8 In.	395.00
Vase, Bud, Gold Ribbed, Signed & Numbered, Label, 8 1/2 In.	590.00
Vase, Bud, Green Flames, Bronze Base, Signed, 16 In.	465.00
Vase, Bud, Pulled Shades Of Green, Flared Top, Signed, 8 In.	395.00
Vase, Bulb Form, Green, Violet, Gold, Blue Highlights, 4 In.	195.00
Vase, Bulbous, Leaves & Vines, Millefiori, Signed, 4 In.	1500.00
Vase, Dark Green Leaves, Blue Border, Marked, 1 1/2 In.	500.00
Vase, Favrile Intaglio, Green Leaves, 7 1/2 In. High	2500.00
Vase, Favrile, Blue Iridescent, Rounded, 6 1/2 In.	550.00
Vase, Favrile, Blue, No.3523U, 8 In. ....*Illus*	700.00
Vase, Favrile, Gold, Green Lotus Leaves, 4 1/2 In. ....*Illus*	700.00
Vase, Favrile, Intaglio-Carved, Gold, Signed, 10 In.	2500.00
Vase, Favrile, Ribbed, Gold Iridescent, Signed, 4 In.	400.00
Vase, Flat Brim, Pedestal Base, Signed, Gold, 6 In.	750.00
Vase, Flower Form, Gold Interior, Signed, 7 1/4 X 5 1/2 In.	825.00
Vase, Flower Form, Iridescent Green, Signed, 12 1/2 In.	800.00
Vase, Flower Form, Pedestal Foot, Ribbed Body, 11 1/2 In.	250.00

Tiffany, Compotes, Scalloped Rim, Signed L.C.T.,
Gold, 6 In; Bronze Pedestal, Gold Dore,
Signed, 12 X 10 In.
(See Pages 704, 708)

Tiffany Glass, Vase, Favrile,
Gold, Green Lotus Leaves,
4 1/2 In.
(See Page 705)

Tiffany, Candlestick, Green Glass
Design, Bronze, Signed, 15 In.

Vase, Flower Form, Striated Pale Green, Signed, 11 1/2 In. 2000.00
Vase, Gold Iridescent, Decorated, Signed, 2 1/2 In. 350.00
Vase, Gold Iridescent, Round Body, Signed, 4 1/2 In. 300.00
Vase, Gold Iridescent, Signed, 1 3/4 In. 325.00
Vase, Gold Iridescent, White & Green Design, Signed, 6 In. 1150.00
Vase, Gold, Bulbous, Iridescent, Signed, 3 In. 275.00
Vase, Gold, Green Feathers, 5 Deep Ruffles, Signed, 3 1/2 In. 575.00
Vase, Gold, 3 Tier Shape, Purple Highlights, Marked, 2 In. 275.00
Vase, Green Feathering, 1919, Numbered, 14 1/4 In. 1775.00
Vase, Green To Purple, Signed, 9 In. 550.00
Vase, Heart Shaped Leaves On Vines, Squatty, Signed, 6 In. 550.00
Vase, Iridescent Amber, Signed, 8 1/2 In. 750.00
Vase, Iridescent Gold, Green Leaves, 9 In. X 4 1/2 In. 1600.00
Vase, Iridescent, Signed, 3 1/2 In. 250.00
Vase, Jack-In-The-Pulpit, Allover Feathering, 8 X 16 In. 1250.00
Vase, Miniature, Stand-Out Ears, 2 1/2 X 3 In. 250.00
Vase, Onion Shaped, White Ground, Leaves Design, Signed, 15 In. 1350.00
Vase, Opalescent White, 2-Handled, Marked, 2 3/4 In. 285.00
Vase, Pedestal Foot, Gold Iridescent, Marked, L.C.T., 4 3/4 In. 320.00
Vase, Pedestal Foot, 6-Sided Body, Signed, 7 1/2 In. 385.00
Vase, Phantom Stripes, Signed, Ginger Brown, 10 In. 3200.00
Vase, Pink Iridescent, Signed, 5 1/2 X 8 In. 350.00

Vase, Pond Lilies, Purple & Gold, Bulbous, Marked, 9 In. 1500.00
Vase, Puffed Protrusions At Shoulder, Scalloped, Signed, 3 In. 285.00
Vase, Pulled Leaf, Silvered Bronze, Signed, 14 In. 775.00
Vase, Purple Highlights, 3 Tier, Gold, Signed, Numbered, 2 In. 275.00
Vase, Red Ground, Green Feathers, Signed, 8 In. 850.00
Vase, Red, Peacock Design, Spider Web Inside, Signed, 2 1/2 In. 2500.00
Vase, Ribbed, Fluted Top, Signed, Blue, 3 X 4 1/2 In. 875.00
Vase, Ribbed, Gold Iridescent With Violet, 4 X 2 1/4 In. 400.00
Vase, Scalloped, Ribbed Upper Section, Signed, 11 1/4 In. 275.00
Vase, Square Top, Ribbed Sides, Signed, 2 1/2 In. 325.00
Vase, Trumpet Shape, Pedestal, Stretched Edge, Signed, 6 In. 335.00
Vase, White & Gold, Feather Design, Pedestal, Marked, 8 In. 425.00
Vase, White Top Outlined In Green, Signed, Gold, 5 X 3 1/2 In. 1150.00
Vase, White Zig Zag, Shell Design, Marked, 5 1/2 In. 575.00
Vase, 2 Handles Pulled From Blue Body, Signed, 1 3/4 In. 325.00
Wine, Aqua Bowl, Yellow Stem & Foot, 1920, 4 1/4 In. 275.00
Wine, Aqua, Yellow Stem & Font, C.1920, 4 1/4 In. 275.00
Wine, Gold, Hollow Stem, Marked, 3 1/2 In. 225.00

TIFFANY GOLD, Salt, Footed, Set Of 6, Original Box 1500.00

TIFFANY POTTERY, Box, Relief Leaves & Fernery, Covered, Signed, 6 In.Diam. 360.00
   Vase, Brown Tones, Glazed, Signed, 5 1/2 X 9 In. 475.00

TIFFANY SILVER, Basket, Openwork, Handle, 8 3/8 X 3 1/2 In. 240.00
   Bottle, Perfume, Screw Top, Dauber, Signed, 1 3/4 In. 75.00
   Bowl, Pierced Border, Monogrammed, 9 In.Diam. 560.00
   Box, Gold Wash Interior, Scrolled Monogram, 1 3/4 X 3/4 In. 48.00
   Box, Stamp, Turtle, Gold Wash Over Sterling 115.00
   Cake Stand, Reticulated 375.00
   Coaster, Wine Bottle, Grapes & Vinings, Marked, 3 In. 18.50
   Compote, Repousse, 62 Troy Ounce 3250.00
   Dish, Candy, Leaf Shape, Ball Feet, Twig Handle, 6 X 4 In. 150.00
   Dish, Nut, Footed, Pierced, Monogrammed 32.00
   Dresser Set, 6 Piece 285.00
   Fish Set, Spoon & Fork, Saratoga Pattern, 2 Piece 480.00
   Holder, Napkin, Shell Shape, Pedestal, Signed 60.00
   Lamp, Spirit, Pierced Handles, Covered, 2 7/8 X 2 3/4 In. 175.00
   Letter Opener & Bookmark, Repousse Flowers 35.00
   Letter Opener, Shears In Case 225.00
   Match Safe, Portrait Of Seated Woman With Scales, Justice 110.00
   Pie Server, C.1850, 8 7/8 In. 170.00
   Pin, Winged Lion, Marked 90.00
   Rattle, Dumbbell Shape 60.00
   Server, Cracker, Olympian Pattern, 1878 .... 285.00
   Server, Pie, Leaf & Flower Pattern, Pierced, 10 1/2 In. 275.00
   Spoon, Baby, Mother Goose On Handle, Humpty Dumpty In Bowl 95.00
   Spoon, Demitasse, Vermeil Bowl, Dated 1899, Set Of 12 .... 225.00
   Spoon, Florals & Vines On Front & Back Of Handle, Pat.1872 .... 50.00
   Spoon, Nut, Pierced Floral Bowl, Marked, 4 1/2 In. 48.00
   Spoon, Serving, Beekman Pattern, 9 1/2 In. 160.00
   Spoon, Serving, Strawberry Pattern, 9 1/2 In. 220.00
   Stretcher, Glove, 4 1/2 Ounce 110.00
   Sugar, Grillwork Basket, Ruby Liner, C.1907, 3 1/4 In. 135.00
   Tray, Bread, Oval, Sterling Silver, Plain, Wide, High Rim, 12 In. 175.00
   Tureen, Soup, Lion's Head Handles, Greek Key Design, C.1854 .... 2200.00
   Vase, Reticulated, Cranberry Liner, C.1902, 8 In. 295.00

TIFFANY, Ashtray & Match Safe, Combination, Glass, Pine Needle, Signed, 5 In. 225.00
   Ashtray, Gold Dore, Rest At Each Side, 3 X 4 In., Signed 135.00
   Ashtray, Humidor, Bronze, 2 Cigarette Rests, Marked, 9 In. 325.00
   Ashtray, Raised Line Design, Gold Dore, Signed, 4 X 3 In. 135.00
   Blotter End, Indian Pattern, Marked, 12 X 2 In., Set 150.00
   Blotter End, Long, Pine Needle, Signed, 19 X 2 1/4 In., Pair 200.00

Blotter, Hand, Pine Needle Design, Marked, 6 X 3 In. 150.00
Blotter, Hand, Venetian, Marked, 5 1/2 X 2 1/4 In. 175.00
Blotter, Hand, Zodiac, Gold Dore, Decorated, Signed 110.00
Bookend, Abalone, Leaf Design, Signed, 5 1/2 In., Pair 495.00
Bookend, American Indian Pattenn, Signed, 6 X 4 1/2 In., Pair 400.00
Bookend, Figure Of Woman Buddha, Bronze, Marked, 6 In., Pair 350.00
Bowl, Circular Paneled Shape, Hammered Finish, Marked, 15 In. 1500.00
Bowl, Cream, Leaves & Fernery, Marked, 3 X 6 In. 495.00
Bowl, Marine Design, Signed, 8 X 4 In. 225.00
Box, Bronze, Abalone, Gold Dore, Signed, 1 1/4 X 5 1/2 X 3 1/2 In. 350.00
Box, Bronze, Venetian, 14K Gold Plate, Signed, 2 1/4 X 5 1/2 In. 450.00
Box, Cigarette, Venetian Pattern, Cedar Lined, Marked, 5 In. 385.00
Box, Ornate, Gold Dore Finish, Chinese, Signed, 8 1/2 X 4 In. 550.00
Box, Oval, Gold Dore, Adam, Signed, 4 X 3 In. 225.00
Box, Radiating Lines, Linear Pattern, Hinged, Marked, 4 X 2 In. 260.00
Box, Stamp, Abalone Pattern 135.00
Box, Stamp, Bronze, Zodiac Design, Hinged, Marked 135.00
Box, Stamp, Openwork Over Caramel Slag, Marked, 3 X 4 3/4 In. 135.00
Box, Stamp, Pine Needle, 3-Compartment Tray, Signed, 4 X 2 1/4 In. 250.00
Box, Stamp, Zodiac, Gold Dore, Hinged, Signed, 3 3/4 X 1 3/4 In. 195.00
Box, Venetian, 14K Gold Plate, Signed, 5 1/2 X 4 In. 450.00
Calendar, Flip, Zodiac, Bronze 195.00
Candelabra, 6-Branch, Gold Dore, Signed, 15 In. 1800.00
Candlestick, Glass & Bronze, 3 Ball Feet, Marked, 8 1/2 In. 450.00
Candlestick, Green Glass Design, Bronze, Signed, 15 In. ....*Illus* 750.00
Candlestick, Medallion On Base, Green Patina, Marked, 8 In. 285.00
Candlestick, 3 Ball-Feet, Glass & Bronze, Signed, 9 In. 850.00
Chalice, Hand-Cut Star On Top, Marked, 9 1/4 In. 625.00
Chalice, Wine, Engineers Club, Bronze, Marked, Dated 1907 .... 110.00
Charger, Abalone Edge, Signed, Bronze, 14 In.Diam. 175.00
Clock, Desk, Angelus Model, Brass Frame, 15 Jewel, 5 1/2 In. 45.00
Compote, Bronze Pedestal, Gold Dore, Signed, 12 X 10 In. ....*Illus* 1250.00
Compote, Gold Dore Finish, Geometric Design, Bronze, Marked, 6 In. 150.00
Cover, Note Pad, Zodiac Pattern, Bronze, Marked 145.00

Tiffany, Lamp, Bronze, Blue-Green
Feather, Signed

Tiffany, Inkwell, Bronze, Favrile Glass Insert, 11 1/2 In.

Desk Set, Abalone Pattern, 4 Piece	1425.00
Desk Set, Blue Enamel On Gold Dore, Marked, 6 Piece	550.00
Desk Set, Chinese Pattern, Covered Inkwell, Each Piece Signed	995.00
Desk Set, Zodiac Pattern, Signed & Numbered, 5 Piece	595.00
Dish, Bronze, Abstract Raised Border, Signed, 9 In.	85.00
Figurine, Boston Terrier, Signed, Bronze, 2 In.Long	225.00
File, Bill, Zodiac Pattern, Signed	145.00
Frame, Adams, Bronze, Signed & Numbered, 9 X 12 In.	400.00
Frame, Bronze, Glass, Easel Style, Grapevine, Signed, 9 1/2 X 8 In.	550.00
Frame, Calendar, Zodiac	20.00
Frame, Full Size, Geometric Design, Bronze, Signed, 9 1/2 X 12 In.	350.00
Frame, Grapevine, Bronze, 12 X 14 In.	485.00
Frame, Zodiac, Easel Style, Dore Finish, Marked, 8 X 7 In.	250.00
Holder, Letter, 2 Compartment, Venetian Pattern, Marked, 6 In.	300.00
Holder, Pad, Chain Link & Mink Design, Marked, 7 X 4 In.	250.00
Holder, Pad, Pine Needle Design, Marked, 7 3/4 X 4 3/4 In.	275.00
Humidor, Pine Needle Pattern, Signed, 6 1/2 In.	375.00
Inkstand, Bookmark Pattern, Bronze, Octagon Shape, Marked, 4 In.	299.00
Inkstand, Grapevine, Bronze, Signed	319.00
Inkstand, Grapevine, Green Glass, Bronze, Marked, 4 In. .... 295.00 To	319.00
Inkstand, Octagon Shape, Marked & Numbered, 4 1/2 In.	299.00
Inkwell, Adam, Gold Dore, Oval, Signed, 2 1/2 X 4 In.	250.00
Inkwell, American Indian, Bronze, Signed, 4 1/2 In.	340.00
Inkwell, Bronze, Favrile Glass Insert, 11 1/2 In. .... *Illus*	900.00
Inkwell, Chinese Pattern, Hinged Cover, Tapered, Signed, 4 In.	400.00
Inkwell, Double, Chinese Pattern, Signed, Brown & Green Patina	450.00
Inkwell, Nautical, Dolphin Feet, Signed	575.00
Inkwell, Triangular Body, Paw Feet, Beaded, Signed	500.00
Inkwell, Venetian, Double, Covered Chest	550.00
Inkwell, Zodiac, Bronze, Signed Dore .... 95.00 To	125.00
Jar, Glue, Pine Needle, Covered, Urn Shaped, Brush Cover, Signed, 3 In.	225.00
Lamp, Arabian, Green & Gold, Bronze Base, Signed, 14 In.	1500.00
Lamp, Bronze Shade & Platform Bottom, Etched, Signed, 15 In.	550.00
Lamp, Bronze, Blue-Green Feather, Signed .... *Illus*	1750.00
Lamp, Bronze, Lily Pad Feet, Signed, Shade, 9 3/4 In.	1500.00
Lamp, Candlestick Base, Gold Iridescent, Marked, L.C.T., 5 1/2 In.	140.00
Lamp, Candlestick, Apricot Satin Glass Dome, Signed, 4 Piece	1295.00
Lamp, Candlestick, Blue Iridescent, Footed, Pair, Signed, 15 In.	450.00
Lamp, Candlestick, Blue Iridescent, Original, 14 In.	2650.00
Lamp, Candlestick, Domed Apricot Shade, Filigree, Signed, 3 Piece	1250.00
Lamp, Candlestick, Gold, Spiral Rib Vase, Marked, 15 In.	850.00
Lamp, Candlestick, Green, Gold, Feather, Bronze Base, 1900	1250.00
Lamp, Candlestick, Spiral Ribbed, Ruffled Shade, Signed, 14 1/2 In.	850.00
Lamp, Dark Patina Finish, Amber Wire-Mesh Shade, 9 3/4 In.	150.00
Lamp, Desk, Brass, Fluted Foot, Balance Ball, Quezal Shade, 17 In.	650.00
Lamp, Desk, Bronze, Turtleback, 15 In. .... *Illus*	2100.00
Lamp, Desk, Favrile Decorated Shade, Bell Shaped, Signed Base & Shad	1200.00
Lamp, Desk, Gold Dore Finish, Bronze Shade, Signed, 11 1/2 In.	550.00
Lamp, Desk, Indian, Enamel Trim On Bronze Base, Signed, 17 1/2 In.	2600.00
Lamp, Desk, Panel, Dichroic Glass, Orange Glow, Marked, 21 In.	3000.00
Lamp, Desk, Quezal Shade, Bronze, Urn-Style Body, 14 In. High	1500.00

Tiffany, Lamp, Desk, Bronze,
Turtleback, 15 In.
(see Page 709)

Lamp, Desk, Student, Favrile Shade, 7 In., 19 1/2 In. High 2500.00
Lamp, Desk, Urn-Style Body, Damascene Shade, Deep Blue, 14 In. 2200.00
Lamp, Double-Arm, Bell-Shaped Light, Bronze Base, Signed, 20 In. 1800.00
Lamp, Fabrique, Amber Glass, Bronze Base, Signed, 20 In. 4000.00
Lamp, Fabrique, 10 Panel, Slender Stick Body, Bronze, 20 In. 400.00
Lamp, Floor, Adjustable, Wave Design Shade, Signed 1750.00
Lamp, Gold Shade, 3-Light Blossom, C.1900, Signed, Bronze, 16 1/2 In. 2600.00
Lamp, Ivy Leaf, Hanging Chain, Bronze Base, Signed, 22 In. 4200.00
Lamp, Leaded Geometric Shade, Green & White, 23 In. 6500.00
Lamp, Lemon Leaf, Dichroic Glass, Green To Orange, Signed, 18 In. 5500.00
Lamp, Lemon Leaf, Striated & Mottled, Bronze Base, Signed, 25 In. 7500.00
Lamp, Linenfold, Amber Glass, Dore Base, 10 X 17 In. 1750.00
Lamp, Paperweight, Hole For Vase, 7 In. 1800.00
Lamp, Paperweight, Vase, Shape, Orange Silk Shade, Signed, 20 In. 1795.00
Lamp, Pomegranate Shade, Bronze Base, Signed, 23 In. 3300.00
Lamp, Pomegranate Shade, Cast Bronze Base, Signed, 23 In. 3300.00
Lamp, Student, Double Post, Decorated, Numbered 3500.00
Lamp, Urn-Style Body, 14 In.Diam. Shade, 24 In. 4000.00
Lamp, Zodiac Pattern, Numbered 2000.00
Lamp, Zodiac, Bronze Base, Signed, 9 1/4 X 13 1/3 In. 700.00
Lamp, 3-Branch Lily, Gold Iridescent Shades, Signed, 12 1/2 In. 3000.00
Lamp, 3-Branch Lily, Red Shades, Gold Dore, Adjustable, Signed 4500.00
Letter Holder, Grapevine Pattern, Bronze & Glass, Signed, 5 1/2 In. 295.00
Letter Opener, Adam, Curved Handle, Signed, 10 In. 165.00
Letter Opener, American Indian Pattern, Bronze 70.00
Letter Opener, American Indian Pattern, Signed, 10 1/4 In. 165.00
Letter Opener, Pine Needle, Bronze 125.00
Letter Opener, Venetian Pattern, Signed, 10 1/4 In. 165.00
Letter Opener, Zodiac, Pattern On Half Of Opener, 8 In. 75.00
Letter Opener, 9th Century Pattern, Gold Dore, 10 1/4 In. 165.00
Letter Rack, Louis XVI Pattern, With Calendar Frame 395.00
Letter Rack, Nautical, 2-Section, Border Waves, Signed, 11 X 7 In. 600.00
Letter Rack, 3-Tier, Zodiac, Gold Dore, Signed, 8 X 12 In. 350.00
Lighter, Zodiac, Jug Form, Cover, Signed, 3 X 2 1/2 In. 350.00
Magnifying Glass, Bookmark, Enamel Symbol, Signed 275.00
Magnifying Glass, Grapevine, Amber Slag Glass, Signed 325.00
Magnifying Glass, Indian, Gold Dore Finish, Signed 275.00
Match Holder, Square Enameled Base 300.00
Match Safe, Bronze & Abalone, Gold Dore, Signed, 2 1/2 X 4 1/4 In. 125.00
Match Safe, Gold Dore, Signed, 2 1/4 X 1 1/4 In. 65.00

Mirror, Chivalry, Parts Of Armors, Bronze, Signed, 10 X 12 In. 550.00
Note Pad Holder, Zodiac, Hinged, Signed, 7 1/2 X 4 1/2 In. 125.00
Paper Clip, Graduate Pattern, Signed 95.00
Paper Clip, Indian Pattern, Raised Indian Mask, Marked 150.00
Paper Clip, Pine Needle, Glass Top, Signed, 2 1/2 X 3 3/4 In. 225.00
Paperweight, Figural, Dog Head, Signed, 3 1/2 X 2 1/4 In. 450.00
Paperweight, Figural, Tiger, Signed, 5 X 1 1/2 X 1 1/2 In. 375.00
Paperweight, Lion, Marked, 1 3/4 In.High 250.00
Paperweight, Lioness, Marked, 1 3/4 In.High 250.00
Paperweight, Pine Needle, Knob Handle, Glass, Signed, 3 1/2 In. 325.00
Paperweight, Plaque, Favrile, Gold, Signed, Numbered, 12 3/4 In. 1500.00
Pen Brush, Graduate Pattern, Signed, 2 X 2 1/2 In.Square 75.00
Pen Holder, Gold Dore Finish, Red & Black Pattern, Bronze, Marked 250.00
Pen Tray, Graduate, 4 Ball Feet, Signed, 9 X 2 1/2 In. 95.00
Pen Tray, Nautical, Seashell Form, Signed, 10 X 3 In. 250.00
Pen Tray, Zodiac, Gold Dore, Signed, 9 1/2 X 3 In. 110.00
Pitcher, Gold Iridescent, Applied Handle, Marked, 2 1/2 In. 325.00
Pitcher, Gold Iridescent, Loop Handle, Marked, 5 1/4 In. 325.00
Planter, Gold Dore, Original Insert, Bronze 375.00
Plate, Greek Key Edge, Signed, Bronze, 9 In.Diam. 80.00
Platter, Bronze, Footed, Gold Dore Finish, Marked, 9 In. 110.00
Platter, Gold Dore, Deep Center Well, Signed, 1 1/4 X 9 In. 95.00
Platter, Recess Center, Gold Dore Finish, Signed, 9 In. 95.00
Rack, Book, Adjustable, Bronze, Glass, Engraved, Signed, 5 1/2 X 6 In. 650.00
Rack, Letter, 3-Tier, Glass, Metal, Etched, Signed, 8 X 12 1/2 In. 600.00
Scale, Letter, Bronze & Glass, Gold Dore Finish, Marked 225.00
Scissor, Bronze & Steel, Line Design, Marked & Numbered 165.00
Sconce, Damascene Design Shade, Brass, Pair 1200.00
Sealer, Envelope, Cylinder, Perforated Top, Marked, 2 In. 35.00
Shade, Damascene, Favrile, Green Ground, Blue Swirls, Marked 375.00
Stand, Smoke, Wave Pattern, Bronze, Marked, 29 In. 550.00
Tray, Card, Gold Dore Finish, Etched Leaf & Berry Pattern, 7 In. 110.00
Tray, Indian Pattern, 2 Compartment, Scroll Design, Marked, 11 In. 125.00
Tray, Pen, Pine Needle Design, Ball Feet, Bronze, Marked, 8 In. 150.00
Tray, Pink, Dore Finish, Geometric Border, Bronze, Marked, 6 X 2 In. 95.00
Tray, Serving, Geometric Border, Gold Dore, Signed, 10 In. 225.00
Tray, Serving, Jeweled, Red, Gold Dore, Allover Pattern, Signed, 9 In. 200.00
Tray, Serving, Raised Border Design, Dore Finish, Round, 12 In. 175.00
Tray, Venetian, 2 Compartment, Marked, 10 X 3 1/2 In. 150.00
Vase, Bud, Bronze Holder, Green Feathers On Gold, Marked, 12 In. 450.00
Vase, Bud, Favrile, 2-Piece, Blue, Bronze Holder, 15 1/2 In. 650.00
Vase, Bud, Green Feather, Gold Ground, Bronze Base, Signed, 12 In. 425.00
Vase, Bud, Green Leaf Design, Bronze Base, Marked, 16 In. 425.00
Wine, Gold, Curved Stem, Signed, 3 X 4 In., Pair 165.00

*The Tiffin Glass Company of Tiffin, Ohio, was a subsidiary of the
United States Glass Co. of Pittsburgh, Pennsylvania. In 1892,
after several changes in management, the factory closed in 1980. Black
satin glass, made by the company between 1923 and 1926, is very popular
among collectors. Other types were also made.*

TIFFIN, Basket, Openwork Handle, 3 X 8 In. 240.00
  Champagne, Ramblin Rose 8.50
  Champagne, Rose Marie Pattern 15.00
  Cocktail Shaker, 4 Goblets, Clear, Floral Etched, 14 In. 40.00
  Dish, Candy, Black Amethyst, Covered, 7 X 6 In. 135.00
  Goblet, Cherokee Rose, 8 In. 12.00
  Goblet, Rose Marie Pattern 15.00
  Plate, Persian Pheasant, 8 In. 6.00
  Sherbet, Cherokee Rose 17.00
  Sherbet, Fuchsia 13.00
  Tumbler, Iced Tea, Cherokee Rose 22.00
  Tumbler, Iced Tea, Fuchsia 15.00
  Tumbler, Juice, Cherokee Rose 17.00

Tumbler, Water, Cherokee Rose 22.00
Vase, Bud, Cherokee Rose, 8 In. 22.00
Vase, Dahlia, Quilted, Black Amethyst, 11 1/4 In. 50.00
Vase, Floral Pattern, Black Satin Glass, Amethyst, 5 1/2 In. 32.50
Vase, Poppy Design, Amethyst Satin, 9 In. 85.00
Wine, Cherokee Rose 10.00
Wine, Fuchsia 17.00
Wine, Rose Marie Pattern 15.00

TILE, see also listing by company name
TILE, Art Nouveau, Gold Leaf, Pastel Colors 125.00
Batchelder, Man & Lion, 5 X 5 In. 85.00
Bird Dog, Green High Gloss, U.S.E.T., 6 X 6 In., Pair 150.00
Calendar, 1926, Coolidge Homestead, Wedgwood 55.00
Hamilton Portrait, Greek Woman, 6 X 6 In. 60.00
Minton, Hancock House, Boston 30.00
Monk, Brown & White, Framed, Artist Signed, 6 X 6 In., Pair 160.00
Norse, Broad, 8 In. 175.00
Owens, Utopian, Artist Signed, 6 In. 155.00
Tea, Floral & Gold, Bavarian Germany 16.00
Tea, Scene Of Hunting Dog, Germany 27.50
Tea, Transfer, St.Paul's School, Concord, N.H., Pink Luster, 5 1/2 In.Sq. 15.00
Window, Cobalt, Signed, 4 1/4 In., Square 9.00
Winged Cherub, Birds & Squirrel, Blue, 1883, Signed Low, 6 In. Square 75.00
Winton-Stoke On Trent, Churchyard 30.00

TIN, see also Store; Tole
TIN, Bin, Spice, Pie Wedge Shaped, Dome Covered, 8 X 6 In. 35.00
Bowl, Gray, Tinker-Made, Pour Lip, 8 In. 13.00
Box, Candle, Wall, Cylindrical, 10 In. 200.00
Box, Dome Topped, Hinged & Hasped, Wire Loop, 1 7/8 X 2 7/8 X 1 3/4 In. 20.00
Box, Stamp, 3 Curved Base Compartments, Hinged Lid, 4 X 6 X 2 In. 8.50
Box, Tinder, With Candleholder, 2 X 4 In. 220.00
Box, Tinder, With Candleholder, 4 1/4 In. 65.00
Bucket, Cream, Wire Bail Handle, Skirted Base, 9 X 7 In. 29.00
Cage, Squirrel, Doors & Windows, Wood Bottom, 25 X 16 X 10 In. 375.00
Can, Kerosene, Shaker, 9 1/2 In. 15.00
Can, Milk, Gray, Domed Cover, Lift Loop, 1/2 Gallon 22.50
Can, Water, Handle, Large 39.50
Candle Box, Green, Arched Back, Rectangular Box, C.1830, 7 1/2 In. 65.00
Candlestick, Cylindrical Shaft, Trefoil Handled, 9 1/2 In. 125.00
Candlestick, Deep Saucer Base 20.00
Candlestick, Hog Scraper, Marked, 18th Century, 7 In., Set Of 4 .... 250.00
Candlestick, Medial Drip Pan, Pear Shaped Base, White, 4 3/4 In. 40.00
Candlestick, Saucer Base, Cone Shaped Extinguisher, 7 1/4 In. 175.00
Canteen, Horseshoe Shaped, Wire Bail, 9 3/4 In. 15.00
Canteen, Lock-Lapped Hoops, 18th Century, Green Paint, 6 1/4 X 4 In. 350.00
Chamberstick, Brass Cap, Straight Side, 19th Century, 5 1/4 In. 60.00
Chamberstick, Deep Saucer Base, American Country Tin Ware, 5 In. 95.00
Chamberstick, Ring Handle, 2 1/2 In., Pair 14.00
Chandelier, Turned Central Drop, 5 Curved Arms, With Wood, 22 In. 750.00
Chandelier, 16-Light, Crimped Drip Plate, Scrolled Supports, 4 Ft. 800.00
Coffeepot, Block Shape, 9 1/2 In. 15.00
Coffeepot, Shaker, 8 In. 50.00
Coffeepot, The Young American, Dated 1859 .... 65.00
Coffeepot, Wooden Handle, 8 1/4 In. 35.00
Cookie Cutter, Lion & Parrot, 3 X 4 In. 10.00
Cup, Drinking, Folding, Ships On Top 1.50
Cup, Farmer's, Gray, Strap Handle, C.1900, 4 3/4 In. 5.00
Dipper, C.1860, 1/2 Gallon 15.00
Dipper, Camp, Round Up Time, Gray, Hang-Up Loop, C.1870, 7 In. 22.50
Dipper, Gray, 12 In., 1/2 Gallon 20.00
Dish, Food Warmer, Gray, Domed, Lift Loop, 9 X 11 In. 65.00
Egg Poacher, Patent, 1885 .... 50.00

Foot Warmer, Graduated Holes, Soapstone Lid 35.00
Funnel, Canning Jar, Gray, Strap Handle, 3 In. 5.00
Gunpowder, Cone Top, 2 Jigger Measure, Strap Handle, C.1860, 24 In. 25.00
Hog Scraper, C.1857 .... 60.00
Lamp, Conical Weighted Base, 3 Burners, Brass Sleeve, Snuffer, 13 In. 150.00
Lamp, Glass, Original Yellow Paint, 7 1/2 In. 175.00
Lamp, Saucer Base, Open Cylindrical Font, 6 1/2 In. 65.00
Lantern, Candle, Onion, Clear Glass, 11 In. 425.00
Lantern, Candle, Paul Revere Type, Punched, 14 In. 65.00
Lantern, Candle, Ribbed Top, Curved Body, Glass Door, 12 In. 125.00
Lantern, Clear Glass Globe, Oil, 11 In. 50.00
Lantern, Glass Door, Impressed Lines, 15 1/4 In. 100.00
Lantern, Handled, Pierced Smoke Vent, Arched, 18th Century, 17 3/4 In. 450.00
Lantern, Jack-O'-Lantern, Candle 100.00
Lantern, Skater's, 7 In. 45.00
Lantern, Wooden Frame, Glass Panels, Pierced Base, 13 In. 425.00
Lunch Bucket, 2 Inserts, Tin Cup, Wire Bail, Wooden Handle, 7 In. 30.00
Match Holder, Shelf, Hook, Kettle Shape, 4 X 3 1/2 In. 8.00
Match Safe, Pocket, Embossed German Writing 13.00
Measure, Cup Shaped, Gray, Strap Handle, Finger Grip, 1/2 Gallon 22.50
Measure, Strap Handles, Concentric Circles, C.1870, Quart 10.00
Mold, Candle, Rectangular, Double Handle, 16 Candles, 10 In. 275.00
Mold, Candle, 4 Tube, Handled 30.00
Mold, Candle, 4 Tube, Round Base & Top, 10 3/4 In. 70.00
Mold, Candle, 6 Tube, Black, 10 3/4 In. 30.00
Mold, Candle, 6 Tube, Strap Handle, C.1860, 10 1/4 In. 60.00
Mold, Candle, 8 Tube, Handled 45.00
Mold, Candle, 12 Tube, Double Handle, 2 X 6 In. 95.00
Mold, Candle, 24 Tube, Handled 175.00
Muffin Ring, Hungry Man's, Dark Gray, 3 1/2 X 2 In. 3.00
Pail, Milk, Gray, Flat Cover, Strap Handle, Gray, C.1870, 1 Gallon 35.00
Pail, Milk, Gray, Tin, Swing Handle, 2 Quart 30.00
Pail, Milk, Swinging Bail Handle, Gray, 4 Quart 30.00
Pail, Tin With Brass Handle, Take It Out, 1890 Label, 2 X 2 In. 35.00
Pan, Milk, Gray, C.1860, 9 In. 13.00
Pan, Milk, Nub Feet, C.1890, 11 In. 15.00
Pattern, Quilting Eagle, Flat, 8 X 13 In. 85.00
Plate, Girl Holding Jug Scene, Border, 10 In. 23.00
Salt, Weighted Base 1.00
Sconce, Arched Crimped Reflector, Semicircular Drip Pan, 13 In. 150.00
Sconce, Circular Reflector, Backplate, Incised, 9 3/4 In. 1000.00
Sconce, Oval, Bowed Reflectors, American, Late 19th Century, 9 In., Pair 375.00
Sconce, Wall, Arched Crimped Reflectors, Drip Pan, 9 In., Pair 250.00
Sconce, Wall, Broad Round Arch Reflector, 18th Century, 12 1/2 In., Pair 275.00
Sconce, Wall, Candle, Crimped, Crest, 9 1/2 In., Pair 200.00
Sconce, Wall, Cylindrical Reflector, Incised Lines, Single Socket, 11 In. 250.00
Sconce, Wall, Fan Shaped, Single Socket, American, 19th Century, 10 In. 130.00
Sconce, Wall, Fluted Arch Top, Single Socket, American, 8 In., Pair 120.00
Sconce, Wall, Oval Back, Fluted Edge, 19th Century, American, 15 In. 325.00
Sconce, Wall, Oval Backboard, Fluted Border, 19th Century, 15 In. 275.00
Sconce, Wall, Oval Fluted Reflector, Single Socket, 19th Century, 17 In. 300.00
Sconce, Wall, Oval, Crimped Edge Reflector, Single Socket, 11 In., Pair 500.00
Sconce, Wall, Painted, Bracket Mount, 19th Century, New England, 5 X 7 In. .. 375.00
Sconce, Wall, Rectangular Form, Fluted Top, 19th Century, 10 In., Pair 325.00
Scoop, Embossed Mason's, Gray, Holds 1 Pound, Wall Hung 5.00
Skimmer, Milk, Lapped Seams, Button Feet, Gray, 14 X 3 In. 20.00
Spill Holder, 9 3/4 In. 35.00
Strainer, Loop To Hang Screen, 8 In. 3.00
Torch, Campaign, Cylindrical Foot, Tin Frame, 8 In. 25.00
Toy Dishes, Tray & Kettle, Ohio Art, 21 Piece 50.00
Warmer, Toddy, Gray, Used In Pub, 3 Segment, Handled, 5 1/2 In. 85.00

TOBACCO JAR, Bison Top, Pressed Glass 95.00

Black Boy, Bisque	65.00
Black Boy, Turban	55.00
Black Man Smoking Pipe, Covered, Gold Collar, Bisque, 4 1/2 In.	88.00
Boy's Head, Beret, Bowtie, 5 1/4 In.	70.00
Bulldog, German Sailor's Cap	70.00
Indian Chief, Bust, Staffordshire	85.00
Maiden's Head, Barrel Shape, Art Deco	62.50
Mandarin, Papier-Mache	68.00
Mariner Head, Stocking Hat, Cigar In Mouth	110.00
Monk, Brown Hood	42.00
Moroccan, Head, Dark Skin	40.00
Old Fisherman, Covered, Bisque	58.00
Owl, Porcelain, Marked Austria	95.00
Winston Churchill, Cigar In Mouth	38.00

Toby jugs have been made since the seventeenth century.

TOBY JUG, see also Royal Doulton, Toby Jug

TOBY JUG, Admiral Nelson, Staffordshire, C.1830, 11 In.	375.00
Figural, King Of Clubs, White, Gold Trim, Staffordshire, 9 In.	135.00
King of Clubs, White Ground, Staffordshire, 9 In.	145.00

*Tole is painted tin. It is sometimes called japanned ware, pontypool, or
toleware. Most nineteenth-century tole is painted with an orange-red or
black background and multicolored decorations.*

TOLE, see also Tin

TOLE, Bowl, Floral On Black, 5 In.	9.00
Box, Cake, Japanning, Hinged, C.1890, 3 X 13 X 10 In.	30.00
Box, Candle, 2 Hanging Arms, Black, Brown-Red Splashes, 17 In.	400.00
Box, Cash, Bold Stenciled, 4 3/4 X 3 X 7 1/4 In.	12.00
Box, Deed, Brown Japanning, Floral Design, Red, Yellow, Green, 9 In.	125.00
Box, Document, Dome Lid, Ezepopper, 9 X 4 1/2 X 3 1/2 In.	85.00
Box, Eagle Design, Small	195.00
Box, Hat, Carrying Handle, Hinged Lid, Oval, Grained Finish, 7 X 11 In.	65.00
Box, Match, Red, 4 3/4 In.	25.00
Box, Oval, Hinged Lid, Hasp, Oak Graining, 11 1/2 X 15 1/2 X 10 1/2 In.	20.00
Box, Spice, Stenciled, Brass Handle, Black, Gold Design, C.1880, 4 X 9 In.	35.00
Canister, Coffee, Embossed Roses, Square	12.00
Coffeepot, Lighthouse, Decorated, Domed Cover, 19th Century, 10 In.	350.00
Coffeepot, Wrigglesware, Conical, Eagle & Flag, 10 In.	5170.00
Jar, Boudoir, Pontypool, Gold Over Black, Handled, C.1870, 14 1/2 In.	200.00
Lamp, Black, Pewter Burner, Tin	295.00
Lamp, Original Paint, Tan, Whale Oil Font, Tin	295.00
Lantern, Clear Globe, Blue Japanning, Ring Handle, 15 In.	100.00
Lantern, Glass, Trianular, Red, 9 In.	1200.00
Lunch Box, Flowers, Dots, Squiggly Lines, 19th Century, 8 In.	1400.00
Megaphone, Painted, Metal	35.00
Pitcher, Hand-Painted, Gold & Black, Folding Handle, C.1873, 13 1/2 In.	175.00
Pitcher, Syrup, Japanned Design, Gilt Stenciling, Hinged Lid	36.00
Pitcher, Water, Red & White, Roses, 12 In.	40.00
Planter, Glazed, 4 Arcaded Reserves, Labors Of Hercules, 8 1/4 In.	70.00
Sander, Ink, Dish Top & Bottom, Yellow Brushstrokes	215.00
Sconce, Electric, Flame Bulb, 8 In.	39.00
Sconce, Wall, 2 Candle Sockets, Crimped Back, 7 In.	225.00
Snuffbox, Japanned, C.1860, 1 1/2 In.	10.00
Sugar Shaker, Side Handle, Japanned Design, 3 1/2 In.	20.00
Tea Caddy, Domed Lid, 2 Compartments, Black, Orange, Gold, 4 In.	35.00
Tray, Basket Of Fruit, 19th Century, 12 In.Long	65.00
Tray, Bun, Elliptical Form, Cut Out Handle, 19th Century, 13 1/4 In.	90.00
Tray, Candlesnuffer, Black Crosshatch Design, Gold Lines	22.50
Tray, Candlesnuffer, Red, Cream, & Black Striping, C.1840, 4 X 9 In.	50.00
Tray, Painted Flowers, Oblong	35.00
Tray, Red, Yellow, & Green, 10-Sided, Center Seamed	155.00

TOM MIX, Book, Coloring, Whitman Publisher, 1935	125.00
Book, Terror Trail, Big Little Book, 1934	10.00
Buckle, Belt, Championship	35.00
Catalog, Ralston, New Premium, 1939	10.50
Compass & Magnifier, Glow In The Dark	30.00
Decoder, Six-Gun	32.00 To 45.00
Game, Card, Wildcat	45.00
Game, Safety Race, Advertising, 1929, Folds, 12 1/2 In.Square	8.00
Good Luck Spinner, Silver & Red Wheat Cereal, Ralston	25.00
Gun, Wood, 1936	65.00
Kerchief	25.00
Knife, Straight Shooter, Ralston, Pocket	35.00
Make Up Kit, 1st Issue, Original Unmarked Box	55.00
Pamphlet, Straight Shooters	12.00
Periscope	35.00
Phone Set, Secret	35.00
Pocketknife & Badge, C.1939, Ralston, Gun, 3 In.	29.00
Ring, Checkerboard	17.00 To 25.00
Ring, Magnet	35.00
Ring, Signature	22.00
Ring, Straight Shooters	35.00
Signal Set, Postal Telegraph, Mailing Carton	35.00
Spinner, Good Luck	25.00
Telegraph Set, Electric, Red	45.00
Telephone Set, Secret	50.00
Telescope	20.00
Watch, Sun	35.00

TOOL, see also Iron; Kitchen; Store; Tin; Wooden

TOOL, A-Level, All Wooden, Oak, 13 1/2 In. X 27 In.	135.00
Adze, Bowl, Wrought-Iron, 3 1/2 In. Blade	75.00
Adze, Cooper's	10.00 To 30.00
Adze, Keen Kutter, Original Handle, Signed	35.00
Angle Square, Disston, Wood & Brass	8.00
Anvil, Jeweler's, Brass, Ends Point, 4 1/2 In.	20.00
Anvil, Jeweler's, Flat Steel Base, 7 In.	35.00
Anvil, Jeweler's, Nickel Plated Over Brass, 3 1/2 In.	8.00
Auger Bits, James Swan, Brass Bit, Set Of 13	79.00
Auger, Nut, Bell System	6.00
Auger, Post Hole, Keen Kutter	16.00
Ax, Barlow	18.00
Ax, Double Bit, Keen Kutter	30.00 To 50.00
Ax, Goosewing	225.00
Ax, Hand, Early Wrought, 6 In. Blade, 13 In.Long	70.00
Ax, Hand, Winchester	50.00
Ax, Ice, Gifford	23.00
Ax, Pennsylvania Broad, Knife-Edge, Straight Handle, Signed	39.00
Ax, Pennslvania Goosewing, Bucks Co., Pa., 14 1/2 In.Blade	225.00
Ax, Winchester, Hand	38.00
Beater, Rug, Wicker	20.00
Beater, Rug, Wooden Handle, Wire	9.00
Bee Smoker, Bellows, 9 1/2 X 5 X 9 1/2 In.	12.50
Bench Stop, Dainty, Small, 4 In.	22.00
Bevel Square, Carpenter's, Brass & Walnut Handle, Marked, 8 3/4 In.	7.00
Bit, Keen Kutter, Wooden	6.00
Bitstock, Wooden, Copper Plate On End Of Chuck, Without Pad, 15 In.	350.00
Bitstock, Wooden, Wing-Nut Tightener, 14 In. Overall	320.00
Blade, Sawmill, 14 To 24 In., Set Of 7	100.00
Bleeder, 3 Blade, Brass Handle	55.00
Blowers, Blacksmith's, Hand-Cranked, Stand	95.00
Bootmaker Last, Brass Fitting	125.00
Bottle Opener, Milk, Advertising, White Lily, Wooden Handle	10.00
Box, Machinist, Oak	95.00

Box, Watchmaker's, Magnifying Lens Bottom, Tin-Sided, 4 X 2 In. 55.00
Brace & Bit, Brass Trim, Wooden 185.00
Brace, Iron With Solid Brass Head, Unique Piece, 10 1/2 In. Long 95.00
Brace, Screwdriver, Iron With Brass Head, Overall 11 In. 49.00
Brace, Sheffield, Brass Plates, Beech, Deluxe Model, Ebony Head 200.00
Broadax, Keen Kutter 50.00
Broadax, Parker, 12 In. 42.00
Broom, C.1830, Birch Splint, 11 In. 50.00
Calculator, Fuller, Mahogany, Brass Bars, Ivoroid Finish, 17 In. High 225.00
Calipers, Dancing Master, 4 1/2 In. 45.00
Calipers, Double, Wrought, Nice Small Size, 12 In. Long 80.00
Calipers, Log, Brass Fittings, Iron Jaws, R.D. Haselton 140.00
Calipers, Steel, Closed 13 1/4 X 27 In. 165.00
Calipers, Thickness, Elias Howe Co., Marked In 64ths, 9 In. Long 15.00
Capper, Beer, Cast Iron 15.00
Catcher, Pig, Fulcrum Pincers, Ringlets To Feed Twine, C.1850, Iron 25.00
Chain, Surveyor's, Complete With 3 Pins & Brass Increment Tags 65.00
Chain, Trammel, No.861 .... 225.00
Chasing, Pair, 16 Threads Per Inch 50.00
Chest, Machinist's, Locking Front, 7 Drawers, Key, Oak 95.00
Chisel, Carving, Fish Tail, Z-Z-Border 20.00
Chisel, Cold, Keen Kutter 6.00
Chisel, Wood, Winchester, 1 3/4 In. 25.00
Clamp, Saw Sharpening, Mortised Construction 32.00
Claw Hammer, Keen Kutter 15.00
Cleaning Rod, Shotgun, Wood, Brass Fittings 5.00
Cleaver, Bell System 14.00
Clipper, Keen Kutter, Fingernail, Signed 5.75
Clipper, Legs, Solid Brass, 5 1/2 In. Long 85.00
Comb, Flax, Iron, Stamped Tooling & Initials, 13 X 10 In. 45.00
Comb, Wool, 3-Inch Iron Teeth Set In Bone, Wooden Handle 30.00
Compass, Surveyor's, E.A.Kutz, N.Y., C.1840, Walnut Case 585.00
Cork Press, Apothecary, Presses 3 Sizes, C.1870, Cast Iron, 10 1/2 In. 70.00
Corn Shucker, Wooden, 47 In. 40.00
Croze, Cooper's 42.00
Cutter, Buttonhole, Adjustable, Fleur-De-Lis Design, Brass & Steel 12.00
Cutter, Glass, Keen Kutter 6.00
Cutter, Tobacco, Brass Gear, 1880s, Marked, Cast Iron, 12 X 6 X 7 3/4 In. 195.00
Detonator, E.I.Dupont Power Co., T Type Plunger, 1800s, Boxed 125.00
Die, Horse Collar Making, Set Of 176 .... 500.00
Digger, Post Hole, Keen Kutter 15.00
Divider, Mahogany Finish, Iron Tops, 33 In. 95.00
Divider, Wooden, Mahogany Finish, Iron Tips, 33 In. High 95.00
Drawing, Victor W.S. Jones, London, Fish Skin Container 35.00
Drawshave, Curled Handle, Large 18.00
Drawshave, Double, Straight, & Curved, Dated 1866 .... 20.00
Drill Bit, Keen Kutter 4.00
Drill, All-Brass Framed Eggbeater, Signed, J.B.towner, 11 In. 175.00
Drill, Iron Eggbeater, Brass Handle, Signed, Jcarter, 12 In. 80.00
Drill, Rusby Patent Extension, Newark, N.J. 45.00
Drill, Screw, Goodell Pratt Co., Greenfield, Mass., Steel, 10 In. 20.00
Dynamite Blasting Machine, Dovetailed Wooden Case, Atlas 75.00
Emory Stone, Original Pine Box, 1800s, 10 X 3 In. 18.00
File, Keen Kutter .... 6.00 To 8.00
Flashlight, Dated December 7, 1912, Silver Case 18.00
Flashlight, Winchester 8.50
Flax Wheel, C.1830 .... 325.00
Fleam, 3-Blade, Brass 55.00
Float, Planemaker's, Graduated Teeth, Overall 13 1/2 In. 69.00
Flyswatter, Daisy, Tin 15.00
Forceps, Glassblower's, Wrought-Iron, 21 In. 50.00
Fork, Hay, 3-Tine, Trilevel Doweling, Wooden, 59 In. 145.00
Fork, Hay, 3-Tine, Wooden .... 37.50 To 50.00
Froe, Cooper's Curved, 10 In. 85.00

Gauge, Clapboard, All Wood, Stepped-Style, 8 In. Wide 65.00
Gauge, Cooper's Stave, Width Markings Inscribed 17.00
Gauge, Marking, Round Bar, Adjustable Fence 5.00
Gauge, Steam, Ashton Valve Co., Boston, Brass Rim, 7 In. 25.00
Grain Cradle, 4 Wooden Tines, Handle, Iron Blade, 10 X 4 1/2 X 8 In. 150.00
Graining, Marked China Mel Grainer No.4, 1911, Mushroom Handle, 3 In. 22.50
Greaser, Tinner's Spouting, 5 In. Spouting 45.00
Hammer, Ball Peen, Claw, Keen Kutter 15.00
Hammer, Claw, Keen Kutter 15.00
Hammer, Cobbler's, Winchester 7.00
Hammer, Double Claw, Proper 2-Piece Head 165.00
Hammer, Embossed, Head Of Lady On Both Sides, 7 In. 58.00
Hammer, Goat's Head, Bronze, Horns Form Pulling Claw, 8 In. 60.00
Hammer, Log Marking 55.00
Hatchet, Bell Telephone 18.00
Hatchet, Congo, 15 1/2 In. 65.00
Hatchet, Hand-Forged Iron Spikes, Maple Plank, C.1860, 6 1/2 X 20 In. 25.00
Hatchet, Keen Kutter .... 10.00 To 30.00
Hatchet, Lathing, Keen Kutter 20.00
Hatchet, Marked Vaughn & Bushnell 20.00
Hatchet, Winchester .... 25.00 To 37.50
Hay Knife, Connecticut Style, 2-Handled 10.00
Head Bit, Upright, Thumbscrew 200.00
Head Bit, 3 Upright Sweep, 18th Century 350.00
Head Bit, 4 Upright Open Top, Spring Loaded Chuck 250.00
Hog Catcher, Iron 12.00
Holder, Whetstone, Belt Clip, Wooden, 1 Piece 75.00
Holder, Yarn, Cast Iron, 1860s 85.00
Hook, Barn, Hoisting, Hand-Forged Iron, 5 In. 4.50
Hook, Cant, Used In Sawmills, Small, 24 In. Long 39.00
Hoop Driver, Cooper's, Paddle Shape, Cherry, 3 1/2 X 8 In. 10.00
Horse Collar Manufacturing Instrument With Collar, 1849 .... 275.00
Horse, Saw Sharpening, Metal Clamp, Slideaway Tray, Pine 150.00
Husking Hook, Leather 4.00
Hydrometer, U.S.Customhouse, Boxed 15.00
Ice Pick, Cast Iron 12.00
Inflator, Balloon, Accordion Bellows, Cast Iron Foot Rest & Pedal 60.00
Iron, Branding, Cabinet Maker's, G.Humphrey, Cast Iron, 7 X 11 In. 25.00
Iron, Branding, Hawaiian, Registered 23.00
Iron, Branding, Initial R 20.00
Iron, Branding, J.C.Marble & Co. 40.00
Iron, Burning, Burn Holes In Horse Manes, 19 In. 10.00
Jack, Harness, Wooden 12.00
Jarvis, Wheelwright's, Dark Beech Brass Sole & Top Plates, 12 In. 79.00
Jointer Fence, Stanley, No.386 .... 15.00
Knife, Cooper's Curved Chamfer, 14 In. 39.00
Knife, Hay, Step-On 12.00
Knife, Tanner's Of Currier's, 20 In. Long 15.00
Knocker, Snow, Hand-Forged Iron, Wooden Haft, 8 1/2 In. 30.00
Ladder, Folding, Lamp-Lighter's, 10 Ft. 160.00
Ladle, Foundry, Rattail Handle, Forged Iron 25.00
Lamp, Warming, Chicken Coop, Kerosene 18.00
Lathe, Treadle Operated, Old Blue Paint 70.00
Level, Acme, Cast Iron, 24 In. 15.00
Level, American Level Mfg. Co., E.Detroit, Mi., Wooden, 12 In. 30.00
Level, Brass Fittings, Mahogany, J.W.Harmon, Boston, Mass., 30 In. 39.00
Level, Carpenter's, Brass At Each End & Top, Hardwood, 29 In. 13.00
Level, Carpenter's, Patent 1896, Cherry & Brass, 28 In. 15.00
Level, Carpenter's, Stanley, Brass End & Top, 24 1/4 In. 13.00
Level, Davis Level & Tool Co., Brass Center, Dated 1867, 22 1/2 In. 125.00
Level, Davis Springfield, 1867, Wooden, Brass & Bronze Trim 48.00
Level, Keen Kutter, Wooden 20.00
Level, Masonry, Brass Bound, 48 In. 20.00
Level, Political, Mahogany, Brass Trim, J&G.H.Walker, N.Y. 185.00

Level, Spirit, Rosewood With Solid Brass Top & Tips, 10 In. Long 45.00
Level, Stanley, No.30, Brass Nameplate & Fittings 40.00
Level, Stanley, No.36, Iron, 18 In. 22.50
Level, Stanley, No.98, Brass Bound 55.00
Level, Stanley, No.102, 12 In. 28.00
Level, Wood, Keen Kutter 20.00
Log Dog, Jointed, Wrought, 18 In. Long 20.00
Loom, Table, Columbia, Maple, Original Label 195.00
Machine, Candy, Hand Crank, 4 Sets Of Brass Molds 325.00
Machine, Ribbon Candy, Wooden Cogs, Cast Iron Bracket, 24 In. 100.00
Machine, Rope Making 75.00
Mallet, Bung, Maple Burl 28.00
Mallet, Carpenter's 18.00
Maul, Stone Cutter's 48.00
Maul, Stonecutter's 48.00
Mold, Iron, For Making Lead Sinkers 22.00
Mold, Lead, Cigar Wrapper, Wooden 20.00
Multiplane, Stanley 55, Cutters 250.00
Nail Bar, Curved Shape, 13 In. 5.00
Needle, Tapestry, 14K Gold, Velvet Pouch 45.00
Niddy Noddy 30.00
Opener, Box, Remington, Inscribed Morton's Salt, Wooden Handles 45.00
Opener, Crate, Advertising, Red J Chewing Tobacco 12.50
Opener, Watch, Ivory Handle, 5 In. 10.00
Ox Yoke, Pine & Wrought-Iron 125.00
Pick, Hoof, Wrought, Small, 6 In. Long 30.00
Pick, Hoof, Wrought, 5 In.Long 25.00
Pickax, Hand-Forged 16.00
Plane, Bailey, No.6 .... 15.00
Plane, Bench, Winchester 125.00
Plane, Block, Scioto, 1860s, 8 In. 7.00
Plane, Boxwood Thumb, 1 5/8 In, X 6 6/4 In. 140.00
Plane, Cooper's, D.B.Barton 80.00
Plane, Floor, Custom Made, Overall 46 In. 95.00
Plane, H.S.B. & Co., No.3 .... 22.00
Plane, Iron Chariot, Mahogany, Turtle Back Wedge, 2 X 5 In. 175.00
Plane, Jointer, Wooden, 22 In. 7.00
Plane, Keen Kutter 33.00
Plane, Low Angle Miter, Cast Bronze, Chisel Blade, 9 1/2 In. 125.00
Plane, Molding & Beading, Stanley, No.45, Blade Set, Boxed 100.00
Plane, Molding, Stanley & Heart, No.143 .... 60.00
Plane, Panel Raising, 5 1/4 In. X 14 In. 195.00
Plane, Plow & Beading, Stanley, No.45, Oak Dovetailed Box 175.00
Plane, Plow, Kimberly & Sons, Patent No.2848 .... 325.00
Plane, Plow, Signed J.Creagh 50.00
Plane, Plow, Wedge Arm, Beech, Depth Gauge 12.00
Plane, Pump Log, 15 In. Long 65.00
Plane, Sargent Hercules, 1927 .... 32.00
Plane, Smoothing, Keen Kutter, No.3 .... 30.00
Plane, Stanley, No.2 .... 110.00
Plane, Stanley, No.3 .... 33.00
Plane, Stanley, No.4C 33.00
Plane, Stanley, No.27, 1893-1899 .... 40.00
Plane, Stanley, No.40 .... 30.00
Plane, Stanley, No.45, 15 Cutters 65.00
Plane, Stanley, No.48, Tongue & Groove 50.00
Plane, Stanley, No.49 .... 12.00
Plane, Stanley, No.55, Complete With Cutters 250.00
Plane, Stanley, No.55, 60 Blades 100.00
Plane, Stanley, No.78 .... 25.00
Plane, Stanley, No.98 .... 30.00
Plane, Sterns, No.6, Original Box 8.00
Plane, Violinmaker's Extended Handle, 3/8 In. Blade, 13 In. Long 125.00
Plane, Winchester, 14 In. 40.00

Plane, Wood, Auburn, 16 In. 17.00
Planter, Corn, Hand 15.00
Planter, Corn, Tin, Primitive, 22 In. 20.00
Pliers, Fence, Keen Kutter 8.00
Pliers, Winchester 12.50
Plow, Rosewood, Boxwood Screws And Nuts, Brass Trim 595.00
Plum, Carpenter's, Brass 30.00
Plumb Bob, Diamond Edge 9.00
Plumb Bob, Take-Up Reel 63.00
Plunger, Clothes, Little Champion Washer, 1891, Signed Brass Plate 45.00
Plunger, Clothes, Little Champion Washer, 1897 .... 40.00
Pole, Lamplighter's, Octagonal, Walnut 65.00
Powderer, Glove, Shaker 195.00
Press, Cork, Whitehall, Tatum, Cast Iron 27.50
Protractor, Drafting, Thin Brass, 4 In. 8.00
Puller, Staplekeen Kutter 25.00
Pump, Tire, Brass 30.00
Pump, Vinegar Barrel, Wooden 35.00
Rake, Blueberry, 40 Tines, Tin, Original Gray Paint, 12 1/4 X 4 In. 35.00
Rasp, Wood, Kenn Kutter, 16 In. 6.00
Reamer, Bung, Cooper's, Tapered Reamer, Auger Top, 13 In. 5.00
Ring Dog, For Logging 4.00
Roller, Cigarette, V Master Deluxe 12.00
Rolling Block, Cigar Maker's, Cutter & Gauge, Wooden, 13 X 13 In. 25.00
Rope Maker, Cast Iron 25.00
Router, Carriage Maker's, Brass 65.00
Router, Hand, Stanley, No.5, 1884 .... 39.00
Rule, Brass Parallel With Protractor, Bliss, N.Y., 18 In. 100.00
Rule, Caliper, One Side Ivory, Other Side Solid Brass, 6 In. 135.00
Rule, Caliper, Stanley, No.36 .... 25.00
Rule, Folding, Stanley, No.61, Wood & Brass .... 6.00 To 20.00
Rule, Folding, Stanley, No.62, Brass Bound 6.50
Rule, Folding, Stanley, No.68 .... 10.00
Rule, German Silver Bound, Ivory 135.00
Rule, Interlox, No.106, Inside And Outside Measuring 20.00
Rule, Ivory 125.00
Rule, Keen Kutter, 2-Folding, K680 .... 12.50
Rule, Lufkin, No.171, Folding, Brass Ends & Slide, 6 In. 15.00
Rule, Lufkin, No.1206, Folding, Aluminum, 6 Ft. 25.00
Rule, Measuring Wine Barrels, Calibrated All Sides, Maple, 17 In. 35.00
Rule, Parallel Rolling, Shelton & Osborn Mfg. Coy's., 14 In. 39.00
Rule, Parallel, Ebony & Brass, 6 In. 30.00
Rule, Parallel, Ebony & Brass, 12 In. 35.00
Rule, Slide, 1/2 In. Thick, 2 In. Wide, 24 In. Long 49.00
Rule, 4-Fold, Ivory, Bound 85.00
Ruler, Folding, Brass Center & End, 24 In. 8.00
Ruler, Folding, Stanley, Brass Joint & End, 24 In. 8.00
Sander, Desk Pounce, Turned Cherry 65.00
Saw Set, Keen Kutter, Nickel Plated 32.00
Saw, Brass-Backed, Amathieson & Son, 14 In. Blade 42.00
Saw, Brass-Backed, Fine Teeth, 8 In. Blade 35.00
Saw, Coping, Keen Kutter 10.00
Sawbuck Table, Oak Base, Pine Top, 22 1/2 X 29 1/2 In. 200.00
Scoop, Ice Cream, Wooden Handle, Brass 28.00
Scope, Hand, Fruitwood, 5 In. 49.00
Scope, Surveyor's, 1920s 75.00
Scraper, Roller, Stanley, Patent Feb. 4, 1896 .... 43.00
Screwdriver, Bit, Keen Kutter 3.00
Screwdriver, Forked, For Saw Handle Screws 30.00
Screwdriver, Watchmaker's, Ivory Handle, Overall 4 1/2 In. 30.00
Screwdriver, Winchester 18.00
Screwdriver, Winchester, 2 In. 25.00
Sector, Boxwood, 6 In. 60.00
Sector, Brass, Folding, 6 In. Long 250.00

Sharpener, Crosscut Saw 11.00
Shave, Miniature Bronze, 4 In. Long, Flat 1 In. Cut 42.00
Shave, Spoon, Concave 1 1/4 In., 6 1/2 In. Long 62.00
Shave, Stair Rail, Boxwood, 11 1/2 In. 125.00
Shears, Glassblower's, Wrought-Iron, 15 In. 45.00
Sheller, Corn, Metal Teeth, 18th Century, Red Handled 220.00
Shoe Last, Cobbler's, Wrought, Turned Wooden Base, 30 In. High 32.00
Sieve, Winnowing, Splint Bottom, 18th Century, 24 In.Diam. 260.00
Sizer, Seed, Rudy Patrick Seed Co., Leather Case, Brass 15.00
Skimmer, Maple Sugar, Bellows Falls, Vt., Hand-Punched, 32 1/2 In. 175.00
Skimmer, Tallow, Pierced, Wooden, 24 In. 110.00
Slick, 4 1/2 In. 49.00
Smoothing Board, Maple, Arched Pine Handle, 1825, 25 1/2 In. 220.00
Smoothing Board, Open D Handle, Wooden, 28 1/2 In. 150.00
Spokeshave, Brass 65.00
Square, Bevel, Stanley, Wood & Brass 14.00
Square, Brass, Decorative Engraving, 4 1/4 In. X 4 1/4 In. 32.00
Square, Carpenter's, Brass & Walnut Handle, 7 1/2 In. 6.00
Square, Framing, Keen Kutter 18.00
Square, Wooden & Metal, Brass Corner & Edge 15.00
Stake, Wooden, Tinsmith's, Flat, Mortised & Pinned, 2 1/2 X 10 In. 5.00
Stencil Set, Brass 38.00
Stencil, Barrelhead, Marked Dixie, 0-9 Numbers, Brass, 14 In.Diam. 40.00
Stencil, Cut Out, G.X.W., Brass, 3 1/2 X 6 In. 9.00
Stencil, Genery Stevens & Sons, Worcester, Mass., Brass, 10 X 4 In. 14.00
Stencil, Geo. Nye & Son, Springfield, Mass., Brass, 10 1/2 X 4 In. 14.00
Stencil, Old English L, Brass, Hand-Up Hole, 5 X 3/4 In. 20.00
Stick, Scrubbing, 1 Piece Corrugated Wood, 29 In. 150.00
Stirrer, Maple Syrup, 1 Piece Maple, 32 In. 235.00
Stone, Sharpening, Winchester 20.00
Stretcher, Carpet, Patent 1884 .... 15.00
Stretcher, Fence, Richards-Wilcox, C.1880 .... 35.00
Stretcher, Glove, Scissors Type, Celluloid 9.00
Stretcher, Sock, Size 10, 34 In. 26.00
Swift, Hancock, Shaker 150.00
Swift, Yarn, Plank Base 35.00
Tack Hammer, Puller, Ruler, & Screwdriver, Combination, 1862 ..... 14.00
Telescope, Surveyor's, W. & L.E.Gurley, Troy, N.Y., Box 250.00
Telescope, 4 Sections, Folding, Brass 50.00
Template, Sash Miter, Brass Ends, Beech 20.00
Tester, Hay, Straight Handle 20.00
Threader, Wire, Wooden Handle 4.00
Tobacco Spear, Steel, Fits On Tobacco Lath, 9 In. 3.00
Tongs, Glassblower's, All Wood With Leathr Padding, 30 In. Long 85.00
Tongs, Ice, Butler Ice Co., 14 In. 12.00
Tongs, Ice, Straatsburg 21.00
Tongs, Logging, Open 26 In. 55.00
Traveler, Wheelwright's, Wrought, 6 In. Wheel, 13 In. Overall 49.00
Trencher, Tab Handles, Oval Dish, Hand-Hewn, Pine, 4 X 14 X 24 In. 260.00
Trowel, Mason's, Unusual Etching, Leaf And Dancing Man 75.00
Tub, Dowling, Cooper's 45.00
Vise, Bench, 2 In.Jaws, Small 150.00
Wagon Jack, Conestoga, Dated 1846 .... 130.00
Wash Stick, Clothespin Ended, Hickory, 38 In. 35.00
Washboard, Double-Sided Lingerie, Columbus, Red Picture, 8 1/2 X 18 In. 15.00
Washing Machine, Dated 1883 .... 145.00
Washing Machine, Maytag, Gas Engine, 1926 .... 275.00
Weaner, Calf, Daisy, Cast Iron 15.00
Wedge, Granite Quarry, Hand-Forged, 96 Piece 25.00
Wheel Drivers, Wool 18.00
Winder, Yarn, Darrel Type, Dated 1843 .... 265.00
Winder, Yarn, Dated 1781 .... 170.00
Winder, Yarn, Windsor Turings, Gray-Blue Paint 170.00
Workbench, Drawer Area, Tools, Oak, 36 X 45 In. 650.00

Workbench, Maple Butcher Block Top, Cherry Base 230.00
Wrench, Adjustable Alligator, Nilson-Waters, Castleton, N.D., 7 In. 14.00
Wrench, Adjustable Buggy Nut Wrench, Nov. 2, 1880, 8 In. 15.00
Wrench, Adjustable Buggy Nut Wrench, Wing Nut Adjustment, 8 In. 20.00
Wrench, Adjustable Iron, Loop Handle, Jan.1876, 12 In. 12.00
Wrench, Adjustable Knurled Screw Handle, Overall 7 1/2 In. 20.00
Wrench, Adjustable Sliding Wedge Type, 7 In. 12.00
Wrench, Adjustable, Brass Adjustment Screw, 6 In. 32.00
Wrench, Aluminum, Pipe, Schick, 24 In. 25.00
Wrench, Ax-Nut, Bell System 13.00
Wrench, Bicycle, Pressed Steel, Center Adjust, 5 In. 5.00
Wrench, Bicycle, Side Adjust, Barnes Tool Co., 5 In. 4.00
Wrench, Chain Pipe, Riesenberg's Universal, 6 In. 17.00
Wrench, Cochran-Speed Nut, May 2, 1916, 8 In. 12.00
Wrench, Convertible Angle Pipe, 2-Way Adjustable Trimo, June 18, 1889 .... 25.00
Wrench, Craftsman, Pipe 20.00
Wrench, Crescent, Ampco Bronze, W-71, 8 In. 23.00
Wrench, Crescent, Smith, 8 In. 20.00
Wrench, Cresco Pivoting Jaw Pipe, Oakmont, Pa., 10 In. 12.00
Wrench, Double Adjustable Socket, Orchard Park, N.Y., 8 In. 20.00
Wrench, Evergrip Pipe, 14 In. 25.00
Wrench, Farm Implement, 5 Sizes Openings, 8 In. 10.00
Wrench, Gas Pipe Pliers With Pulling Claw, Jamestown, N.Y., 9-8-1903 .... 5.00
Wrench, Gear Type, Craft Tool Co., Conneaut, Ohio, Nov.1907, 12 In. 25.00
Wrench, Girard, Iron Handle, 8 In. 6.00
Wrench, Grip, Bottom Pivot, B.Matteson, 6 1/2 In. 12.00
Wrench, Heller Bros.Masterench, Pat.7-5-27, 10 In. 9.00
Wrench, International Harvester, No.788, 8 In. 6.00
Wrench, Joar, Unique Pivot Adjustment, 7 In. 12.00
Wrench, Keen Kutter, Marked 10.00
Wrench, Large Open End, 2 1/2 In. Bolt, 16 In. Long 8.00
Wrench, Miniature Pocket, Side Adjustment, Screwdriver On End, 3 In. 10.00
Wrench, Monkey MH, Loop Handle, 8 In. 10.00
Wrench, Monkey, Iron Handle, Wrench Co., Meadville, Pa., 10 In. 8.00
Wrench, Monkey, Iron Loop Handle, Center Adjust, 4 In. 6.00
Wrench, Monkey, Iron Screw Handle, Clows Boss Wrench, 12 In. 50.00
Wrench, Monkey, Quick Adjust, Iron Handle, Wright-Tacoma, Wash., 8 In. 25.00
Wrench, Monkey, Wood Handle, Bemis & Call, 8 In. 8.00
Wrench, Monkey, Wooden, Pat.1880 .... 10.00
Wrench, Neverslip, Closed Alligator Type, 9 In. 10.00
Wrench, Pexto, Monkey, Iron Handle, 10 In. 7.00
Wrench, Pipe Cutter, E.V.Cousineau, Holyoke, Mass., 12 In. 50.00
Wrench, Pipe Tong, Jarecki Mfg., Co., Erie, Pa., 1879, 12 In. 14.00
Wrench, Pipe, Stillson Type, Pexto, Wood Handle, 6 In. 7.00
Wrench, Pocket Wrench, Tokyo Takag, 4 1/2 In. 8.00
Wrench, Pocket, Billings & Spencer, Hartford, Conn., Sept.29'96, 4 In. 8.00
Wrench, Pocket, Flat Center Adjust, Bullings & Spencer, 1879, 4 In. 8.00
Wrench, Pocket, Screwdriver In Handle, W. Dicks, Nov.11, 1893, 5 In. 10.00
Wrench, Quick Adjustable Pipe, Hinged Jaw, G.W.Neman, 10 In. 18.00
Wrench, Quick Opening, Iron Handle, Athol, Mass., 6 In. 10.00
Wrench, Quick, Adjustable Thumb Grip, Notched Slide, Loop Handle, 9 In. 25.00
Wrench, Rogers-Printz, Warren Pa., Sliding Wedge, June 9, 1908, 10 In. 25.00
Wrench, Sliding Wedge, Adjustable, Providence, RI., 9 In. 15.00
Wrench, Spiral Feed Pipe, H & E, March 27, 1923, 14 In. 50.00
Wrench, Strap, Warnock, Worcester, Mass., 6-5-1900, 12 In. 10.00
Wrench, Trimo, Pat., 12-19-11, 10 In. 12.00
Wrench, Universal Grip Double Alligator, Screw Taps, 8 In. 8.00
Wrench, Victor Pipe, Quick Adjust, 8-25-03 .... 25.00
Wrench, Wood Handle, American Beauty, 8 In. 10.00
Wringer Washer, Copper Bottom 110.00
Yarn Winder, Turned Post, Geared Counter, Wheel, 24 In. 205.00

*Toothpick holders are sometimes called toothpicks by collectors. The
variously shaped containers made to hold the small wooden toothpicks*

are of glass, china, or metal. Most of the toothpicks are Victorian.
TOOTHPICK, see also other categories such as Bisque; Slag; etc.

TOOTHPICK, Alabama, Crystal	22.00
Amberina, Square Top, Diamond-Quilted, 2 3/8 In.	175.00
Arched Ovals, Ruby	18.00
Argonaut Shell, Custard	275.00
Austrian, Canary, Smooth Rim	70.00
Banded Portland, Cranberry Flash	42.00
Bead Swag, Cranberry Flash, Souvenir	38.00
Bead Swag, White Opal, Gold Decoration	75.00
Beatty Honeycomb, Blue Opal	45.00
Beatty Ribbed, Blue Opal	35.00
Beatty Ribbed, Clear Opal	30.00
Beveled Star, Green	65.00
Bird & Basket, Frosted	25.00
Bird In Stump, Amber	45.00
Blazing Cornucopia, Clear	20.00
Box In Box, Green With Gold	40.00
Bulging Loops, Blue	55.00
Bulging Loops, Pink Cased, Rim Polished	45.00
Bundle Of Sticks, Blue	27.50
Button Panel, Clear, With Gold	25.00
Carnation, Clear With Gold	50.00
Cat, Christmas Design, Figural, Pot Metal	40.00
Champion, Green With Gold	40.00
Chicken & Basket, Glass	40.00
Colorado, Green With Gold, Souvenir	32.50
Coney Island, Ruby Glass	20.00
Croesus, Green With Gold	75.00
Daisy & Button, Hat, Canary, 1 3/4 In.	20.00
Daisy & Button, Ruby Flashed Top	45.00
Diamond Ridge, Clear	22.50
Diamond Spearhead, Green Opal	48.00
Diamond Spearhead, Vaseline Opal	55.00
Dog With Bone By Basket, Tufts Co.	125.00
Dog With Top Hat, Figural, Blue Glass, 3 3/8 X 2 1/4 In.	58.00
Domino, Clear	25.00
Double Dahlia, Lens, Color Stained Flowers	40.00
Empress, Green With Gold	125.00
Esther, Green With Gold	75.00
Eureka National, Ruby Flashed	65.00
Fan Button & Diamond, Amber	18.00
Flattened Diamond & Sunburst	16.00
Fleur-De-Lis, Figural, Crystal	16.00
Floral, Blue, Gold, Porcelain, Austria	13.00
Florette, Blue Shiny	55.00
Florette, Pink Satin	85.00
Flower & Pleat, Amber Stain	38.00
Frog Pulling Snail Shell, Lily Pad	3.00
Geneva, Chocolate	400.00
Hobnail Opalescent, Footed	22.50
Horsehead Medallion, Clear	45.00
Idyll, Green	85.00
Iowa, Rose Deco	55.00
Iris Meander, Amethyst With Gold	45.00
Iris Meander, Blue Opal	85.00
Iris Meander, Blue With Gold	48.00
Iris Meander, Vaseline Opal	60.00
Jefferson's Colonial, Green With Gold	40.00
Klondike, Amberette	325.00
Lacy Medallion, Green & Gold	20.00
Lacy Medallion, Green, Souvenir Rochester, Minn.	18.00
Ladders, Clear With Gold	45.00

Minnesota, Clear 25.00
Nester, Amethyst 75.00
Nester, Blue 65.00
Nevada, Clear Decoration 35.00
New Hampshire, Clear With Gold 20.00
Nursery Tales, Clear 45.00
Overall Hobnail, Blue Opal 42.00
Overall Hobnail, White Opal 28.00
Palm Leaf, Pink Opaque 65.00
Pansy, Pink Cased 55.00
Pennsylvania, Tumbler Toothpick, Green With Gold 35.00
Pineapple And Fan, Green With Gold 125.00
Plain Scalloped Panel, Green With Gold 24.00
Porcupine 85.00
Scalloped Swirl, Export Exposition 1899, Ruby & Clear 28.00
Seated Girl, Book & Cat, Figural, Germany, Bisque, 4 3/4 In. 38.00
Souvenir, Chester, Pa., Green 28.00
Sprig Paneled, Clear Opal 38.00
Sunbeam, Blue With Gold 65.00
Swirl Opal, Reverse Blue Spatter Satin 80.00
Texas, Clear With Gold 55.00
Three Dolphin Match, Amber 65.00
Thumbprint, Red Top 22.00
Vermont, Green, Gold 38.00
Ward's Regal, Green With Gold 28.00
Wild Rose With Bowknot, Frosted 45.00
X-Ray, Green With Gold 45.00

Torquay Terra-cotta Company was a pottery working in Hele Cross,
England, from 1875 to 1909. Pieces are marked with the word "Torquay."

TORQUAY, Biscuit Barrel, Covered, Handled, Ruby, Silver Rim 175.00
  Chamberstick, Miniature, Pair 35.00
  Creamer, Large 33.00
  Creamer, Marked England, 2 1/2 In. 18.00
  Cup & Saucer, Watcombe .... 28.00 To 35.00
  Cup, Watcombe 28.00
  Eggcup, Watcombe 30.00
  Figurine, Cockerel 35.00
  Pot, Hot Water, Covered, Watcombe, 7 In. 55.00
  Pot, Stick Handled, Lid, Spoon Opening, 3 3/4 X 3 3/4 In. 45.00
  Rack, Toast 35.00
  Shaker, Salt & Pepper 26.00
  Sugar, England, 1 7/8 X 3 1/2 In. 18.00

Tortoiseshell glass was made during the 1800s and after by the Sandwich
Glass Works of Massachusetts and some firms in Germany. Tortoiseshell
glass has been reproduced.

TORTOISESHELL GLASS, Tumbler, Water, 3 5/8 In. 70.00

TORTOISESHELL, Back Comb, Flat Top, Round, 10 In. 6.00
  Box, Carved Seated Figures, Fenced Garden, Covered, 4 1/4 In. 165.00
  Box, Georgian, Silver-Mounted, 18th Century, 2 X 3 3/4 In. 275.00
  Box, Pique & Mother-Of-Pearl Border, Lid, 2 1/2 X 5 1/2 In. 375.00

TOY, Acrobat, Man, Windup, Celluloid 250.00
  Air Devil, Windup, Tin, Strauss 275.00
  Air Terminal Baggage Truck, Tin, Windup, 6 1/2 In. 60.00
  Aircraft Carrier Set, Hubley 125.00
  Airplane, Aqua, Windup, Chein, Pontoons, Tin ....
  Airplane, Aqua, Windup, Pontoons, Tin, Chein 50.00
  Airplane, Army Scout, Steel Craft 75.00
  Airplane, DC-7C, Milti Action, Boxed 300.00

Airplane, Eastern, Friction, Hadson	25.00
Airplane, Girard, Tin, 1920	125.00
Airplane, Looping, Pilot, Yellow Helmet, Tin, Windup, 7 1/2 In.	65.00
Airplane, Lucky Boy, Iron, 4 In. Wingspan	58.00
Airplane, Roll-Over, Windup	50.00
Airplane, Transport, 4-Motored, Wooden Wheels, Blue, Metal, 10 In.	40.00
Airplane, Windup, Strauss, 1920	110.00
Airplane, World War II, Cooney Bird, Motored, Metal, Red, 9 In.	40.00
Airport, City, Lights, Battery, Tin & Steel, Marx	50.00
Alligator, Glass Eyes, Schoenhut	375.00
Alligator, Steiff	75.00
Amos & Andy, Mechanical, Tricky Taxi	400.00
Animated, Woman At Spinning Wheel	75.00
Ape Man, Outer Space, Space Suit, Walks, Head Swivels, Battery, 10 In.	40.00
Apollo Super Space Capsule, Battery, Boxed	38.00
Aquaplane, Windup, Tin, Chein, Boxed	65.00
Arabian Harness Racer, West Germany, Boxed	65.00
Astronaut, Rotate-O-Matic, Red & Blue Feet, Chrome, Walks, Metal, 12 In.	55.00
Auto Race, Windup, Jeannette, Boxed	125.00
Auto, A.C.Williams Roadster, Top Up, Arcade, 5 In.	65.00
Auto, Convertible, 2 Passenger, 1920s, Metal Wheels	55.00
Auto, Coupe, Hubley, Cast Iron, 6 In.	60.00
Auto, Coupe, Sun Rubber, Green	4.00
Auto, Ford, Tootsietoy, Black Metal	8.00
Auto, Model T Ford, Lever Action, Tin	37.50
Auto, Mr.Mercury, Schucco, Boxed	26.00
Auto, Open Touring, German, Tin, Fly Wheel Auto, Hess, 4 X 3 In.	385.00
Autogyro, Tootsietoy	45.00
Automobile, Coupe, Fin Tailed, Green, Tootsietoy, Iron, 6 In.	65.00
Babar, In The Classroom, Gray Elephant With Baton, Red Base, Windup	50.00
Baby Tractor, Mechanical, Tin, Animated Toy, 1916	65.00
Baby, Crawling, Celluloid, Mechanical, Boxed, Irwin Corp., 6 In.	25.00
Band, Merry Makers, Box	650.00
Bank, Bob's Big Boy Doll	7.00
Bank, L'il Abner, Directions & Box	210.00 To 225.00
Barn, Opens At Back, 4 Sheep, 10 X 6 X 4 1/2 In.	70.00
Bartender, Charley Weaver, Battery Operated, Boxed	65.00
Baseball Catcher, Celluloid, Windup, Boxed	75.00
Baseball Game, Tudor Tru Action, Metal Board, Boxed, 15 X 26 In.	25.00
Basket, Bunny Rabbit, Easter, Molded Cardboard, Winking, 8 In.	15.00
Basketball Game, Set Shot, Marx, Boxed	25.00
Bassinette, Doll's, Wicker, Wheeled, Bentwood Handles, 19 In.	100.00
Batmobile, Battery Operated	45.00
Bean Bag, Raggedy Ann	20.00
TOY, BEAR, see also Teddy Bear	
Bear, Barney, Drummer, Eyes Light, Head Moves, Walks, 11 In.	65.00
Bear, Book Reading, Flips Pages, Windup, Japan	75.00
Bear, Bubble Blowing, Plush Covered, Windup, Japan, 8 In.	30.00
Bear, Circus, Performing, Windup, Martin, Tin, 8 In.	135.00
Bear, Fishing, Rosko, Battery Operated, Blue Overalls, With Pond, 10 In.	33.00
Bear, Fur Covered Papier-Mache, Growls, 8 1/2 In. *Illus*	400.00
Bear, Glass Eyes, Schoenhut	325.00
Bear, Golfer, Windup, Boxed	115.00
Bear, Happy Drummer, Battery Operated, Boxed	60.00
Bear, Knitting, Chein	30.00
Bear, On Candy Wagon, Tin, Windup	300.00
Bear, On Wheels, Fur Covered, Papier-Mache	170.00
Bear, On Wheels, Muzzled, 12 X 6 In.	165.00
Bear, Original Felt Costume, Schucco, Tin, Windup, 4 1/8 In.	95.00
Bear, Pandy Fishing, Battery Operated	195.00
Bear, Papa, Smoking, Battery Operated	35.00
Bear, Papa, Walking, Smoking, Rubber Nose, Tin Eyes, Remote Control, Amico	80.00
Bear, Pewter Button, Steiff, 12 In.	195.00

Bear, Plaid Jacket, Cleaning Glasses, Tin 45.00
Bear, Reading Book, Plush, Japan 50.00
Bear, Reading With Pipe, Sitting On Tree Stump 45.00
Bear, Riding, Steiff 230.00
Bear, Smoking, In Rocker, Plush, Battery, Tin, Japan, 8 In. 25.00
Bear, Tumbles, Battery Operated, Boxed 40.00
Bear, Walking, Windup 20.00
Beater, Rotary, Marked Wooden Handles, 7 In. 10.00
Bed, Doll, Empire, Mahogany, Orange Design, C.1870, 23 X 14 In. 135.00
Bed, Doll, Folding, Tin, 1920s, 12 In. 40.00
Bed, Doll, Green, Roses, Carved Headboard, 1920s, 13 X 24 X 16 In. 30.00
Bed, Doll, High Sides, Dowel Sides, 1930s, 12 1/2 X 19 X 15 In. 10.00
Bed, Doll, Slatted Bottom, Pine, C.1900, 10 X 17 In. 60.00
Bed, Doll, Tester, Wooden, American, 19th Century, 15 X 17 In. 100.00
Bed, Doll, Wire Ends, Folds Flat, Straw Mattress, Crocheted Pillows 35.00
Beetle, Red Lithograph Top, Spots, Windup, Tin, 3 3/4 In. 5.00
Bell Ringer, Wild Mule Jack, Figure Rides Jackrabbit, Cast Iron 450.00
       TOY, BICYCLE, see Bicycle
Binocular, Tom Corbett 25.00
Biplane, Tippco, Germany 370.00
Bird, Canary, Singing, Windup, W.Germany, Box 85.00
Bird, Hopping, Tin, Germany 15.00
Bird, In Cage, Musical, Windup 12.50
Bird, Pecking, Tin, Lindstrom 10.00
Bird, Walking & Pecking, Windup, Tin, Dated 1927 .... 25.00
Black Man, Red Cap, Pushing Wheelbarrow, Top, Strauss, Windup 40.00
Black Men, Dancing, Clockwork, 1890s, American Mechanical Toy Co. 850.00
Blackboard, Stand-Up, Alphabet & Counting Beads 37.50
Blacksmith, Village, Hand-Painted, Plinth Base, England, Lead, 3 In. 8.00
Blimp, Akron, Steel Craft 70.00
Blimp, Sky Ranger, Tin 40.00
Blocks, A.B.C., Bliss, Original Box 230.00
Blocks, A.B.C., Horsman, 1880s, Original Box 55.00
Blocks, Building, Bliss, Boxed 225.00
Blocks, Nesting, McLaughlin, 1880s 125.00
Blocks, Picture, Fairy Story, Cardboard, Sam Gabriel & Sons, C.1939 .... 35.00
Blocks, Stacking, 1920s, Child & Bear Design 45.00
Blocks, Wooden, 1940s, Boxed, Baseball, Lithographed Box 65.00
Blondie & Dagwood Jalopy Car, Tin, Windup, Marx 1600.00
Blushing Willie, Battery, Boxed 32.50
Boat, German, Flywheel Drive, Tin, Brass, Warship, 10 In. 75.00
Boat, Lithographed, Oregon, Tin 180.00
Boat, Live Steam, 2 Cylinders, Bowman, 28 In. 700.00
Boat, Speed, Battery, Lights 22.00
Boat, Steam Powered, Weeden, Horizontal Boiler, Tin, 15 1/2 In.Long 155.00
Boat, Water Witch, Steam, Brass Boiler, Tin, 14 1/2 In. 185.00
Bobbin Express, Pull Toy, DeLuxe Education 12.00
Boiler, High Pressure, Stuart, Copper Tank, Metal Base, 11 3/4 In.Long 155.00
Boxer, Plush Coat, Glass Eyes, Stuffed, 8 1/2 In. 20.00
Boy On Tricycle, Celluloid & Tin, Windup, Japan, Boxed 37.50
Boy On Turtle, Lehman 55.00
Boy, Drummer, Let The Boy Play, While You Swing & Sway, Key Wind, Marx 225.00
Boy, Tyrolean, Ceramic Stein, Felt Costume, Tin, Windup, 5 1/4 In. 95.00
Brain The Bear & His Ballplaying Act, 5 Actions, 1 Ball 180.00
Bridge, Bascule, Lionel, No.131, Boxed 350.00
Bubble Blowing Monkey, Battery 65.00
Buffalo, Schoenhut 175.00
Bug, Walk, Wings Flap, 6 Legs, Tin, Windup, Japan 60.00
Bug, Windup, Tin, Marx, 1968 .... 18.00
Building Blocks, The Practical Architect No.18, Germany, Richter 700.00
Bull, Stuffed, Wooden Horns & Legs, Metal Nose Ring, 5 In. 180.00
Bulldog, Schoenhut 400.00
Bulldog, Ugly, Straw Stuffed, Honey Velvet Coat, Bell, 5 In. 60.00

Bulldozer, Hopper, Wooden Wheels, Delta Detroit Corp., 20 In.	40.00
Bunny, Easter, White, Pink Eyes & Ears, C.1910	75.00
Burro, Wooden, Leather Ears, Painted Eyes, Schoenhut, 7 In.	225.00
Bus, Arcade, Cast Iron, Green, 4 3/4 In.	45.00
Bus, Century Of Progress, Chicago, 1933, Arcade, Cast Iron	125.00
Bus, Double-Decker, Coast-To-Coast, Windup, 1930s	175.00
Bus, Double-Decker, Interstate, 1920s, Windup, Strauss	350.00
Bus, Double-Decker, Kenton, Cast Iron, 6 1/2 In.	350.00
Bus, Double-Decker, Lipton's Tea, Horse-Drawn, Lesney	65.00
Bus, Double-Decker, Red & Yellow, Rocket & Teddy Bear Design, 8 In.	45.00
Bus, Double-Decker, With Driver, 1920s, Windup, Germany	325.00
Bus, Greyhound Lines, Century Of Progress, Arcade, Iron, 10 3/4 In.	125.00
Bus, Greyhound Lines, Sightseeing, Chicago World's Fair, 1933, Cast Iron	65.00
Bus, Greyhound, Tootsietoy, 6 In.	10.00
Bus, School, Hubley, Cast Iron, 9 In.	18.00
Bus, Transamerica, Tootsietoy	75.00
Bus, Twin Coach, Iron, Metal Wheels, C.1910, 5 In.	50.00
Busy Bridge, Tin, Windup, Marx, 23 1/2 X 8 1/2 In.	400.00
Busy Secretary, Battery Operated, Linemar, Boxed	45.00
Butterfly, Friction Drive, Wings Move Up & Down, Metal, 5 In.	5.00
Cab, Driver, Orange & Black, Arcade, Cast Iron, 9 1/4 In.Long	300.00
Cab, With Horse, Driver, Passenger, Iron, 15 3/4 In.	210.00
Cab, Yellow, Rubber Tires, Driver, Arcade, Cast Iron, 9 In.	450.00
Cab, Yellow, Tin, Windup, Bing, 8 1/2 In.	690.00
Cab, Yellow, Tin, Windup, Strauss	355.00
Cab, Yellow, With Driver, Rubber Tires, Cast Iron, 9 In.	450.00
Cabinet, Glass Doors, 2 Drawers, Shelves, Mahogany, 7 1/2 X 9 1/2 In.	107.00
Cabinet, Kitchen, Hoosier Style, 4 Doors, Shelf, Boxed, 11 X 16 In.	35.00
Camel, One Hump, Schoenhut	175.00
Camel, Steiff, 1950s, 6 In.	50.00
Camel, Walking, Windup	195.00
Camera, Howdy Doody, Sun-Ray	18.00
Camera, Komic, 5 Panels Of Comic Strips, 1930s	80.00
Cannon, Big Band, Carbide, No.6f, Original Box & Catalog	60.00
Cannon, Black & Red Paint, Cast Iron	37.50
Cannon, Marlin, Original Box	75.00
Cannon, Nickel Plated Barrel, Cast Iron, 4 1/4 In.	5.00
Cannon, Red Dot, Shoots Wooden Balls, Plastic Tires, 14 In.	15.00
Cannon, Red Wheels, Shoots Blue Balls, Tin, 14 In.	20.00
Cannon, Shoots Wooden Balls, Tin	20.00
Cannon, Spring Loaded, Black Paint, Gold Japanning, Tin, 8 3/4 In.	10.00
Cape Canaveral Playset, Marx	110.00
Cappy, The Baggage Porter, Cragston, Boxed	135.00
Car Carrier, With 3 Austins, A.C. Williams, Cast Iron	390.00
Car, Brinks Armored, Plastic, Rubber Tires, Coin Deposit, Battery, 7 In.	30.00
Car, Bubble Blowing, Boil-Over, Battery, Boxed	55.00
Car, Buick, Friction, 1950s, Boxed, Large	275.00
Car, Carrier, Hubley, 1939, Cast Iron, 10 In.	235.00
Car, Carrier, Tootsietoy, Metal Wheels	145.00
Car, Charlie McCarthy Car, Tin, Windup, Marx	400.00
Car, Coo Coo Crazy, With Driver, Windup, Marx	195.00
Car, Corgi, Mercedes-Benz, 230 SE	8.00
Car, Crash, Rubber Tires, Hubley, Cast Iron, 4 3/4 In.	65.00
Car, Crazy, Charlie McCarthy, Boxed	400.00
Car, Crazy, Mortimer Snerd, Lithographed Tin, Marx	210.00
Car, Dagwood	325.00
Car, Dick Tracy, Square, Windup, Emergency Light, Marx	35.00
Car, Edsel, Yellow Cab, Original Box, Japan	20.00
Car, Ferrari, Lighographed Tin, Plastic, Battery Operated, Japan, 11 In.	110.00
Car, Fire Chief, Model A, 2 Men, Crazy Action	18.00
Car, Ford Sedan, Spring Motor, Metal, Wynadotte, 1937, 10 In.	40.00
Car, Ford, Model A, German, Windup, Tin, Driver, C.1930	85.00
Car, Ford, Retractable Skyliner, 1958, Tin, Boxed	75.00
Car, Ford, Skyliner, Retractable, Boxed, Tin	65.00

Car, Ford, 1947, Ft.Leavenworth Logos, Pot Metal, 3 In. 65.00
Car, G-Man Pursuit, Tin, Windup, Marx, Boxed 290.00
Car, Grand Pa, Rosko, Red & Gold Litho, Battery Operated, 9 In.Long 25.00
Car, House Trailer, Towing, LaSalle, 25 In. 110.00
Car, Hudson Opera Coupe, Metal, Wynadotte, Battery Headlight, Mid 1930s 45.00
Car, Jaguar, Doepke, Xk120 Roadster 300.00
Car, Model T Sedan, Battery Operated, Japan, Tin, 9 In. 45.00
Car, Model T Sedan, Blonde Local, Tin, Windup, Marx, 1930s, 8 In. 85.00
Car, Model T, Arcade, Cast Iron, 3 1/2 X 4 In. 90.00
Car, Packard Hawk, Lithographed Tin & Plastic, Battery Operated, Schuco 260.00
Car, Passenger, Railroad, Marked New York, Philadelphia, Iron, 17 In. 165.00
Car, Pedal, Pioneer, Wire Wheels 625.00
Car, Police, Battery Operated, Marx 25.00
Car, Police, Siren, Windup, Marx, Boxed 85.00
Car, Racing, Midget, Driver, Color Lithograph, Balloon Wheels, 7 In. 55.00
Car, Racing, Windup, Marx, Tin, 5 In. 37.50
Car, Railroad, Wooden, Paper Covered, Pull, Black Diamond, C.1870, 11 In. 165.00
Car, Rolls Royce, Headlights, Horn, Lady Takes Picture With Camera 38.00
Car, Sedan, Arcade, Cast Iron, 6 1/2 In. 75.00
Car, Sedan, Ford, Driver, Arcade, Cast Iron, 6 3/8 In. 245.00
Car, Sedan, Graham, Burgundy, Cor-Cor, 19 1/2 In. 375.00
Car, Sedan, Wolverine, Spring Motor, 1940s, 12 In. 40.00
Car, Shark Racer, Battery Operated, Remco 50.00
Car, Solido, Panhard-Levassor 1925, Gold & Black, In Display Container 10.00
Car, Studebaker, Windup, Army Cannon Swivels & Shoots, 1936, 15 In. 85.30
Car, T-Bird, Remote Control, 1963, 11 In. 125.00
Car, Thunderbird, Lithographed Tin, Friction, Korean, 8 In. 22.00
Car, Touring, Electric Lights, Fischer, 8 In. 1325.00
Car, Touring, G.& K.Gundka, 1920s, Germany 365.00
Car, Touring, German, 10 In. 1150.00
Car, Touring, Open, Red, Tin, Windup, Bing, 9 1/4 In. 1120.00
Car, Touring, Red Paint, C.1920's, Iron, 6 1/2 In. 185.00
Car, Touring, Red Paint, 1920s, Iron, 6 1/2 In. 185.00
Car, Universe, Beeping Sound, Blue, Green, Red, Battery, Tin, 10 In. 50.00
Car, Volkswagen, Battery Operated, Tin, 10 In. 20.00
Car, Whoopee Car, Windup, Tin, Marx 250.00
Carousel, 4 Horses, Riders, Windup, Tin, 8 1/2 X 14 5/8 In. 1150.00
Carousel, 6 Chair, Plink Plunk, Windup, Hand-Painted 495.00
Carriage, Doll, Basket Cradle On Wooden Wheels, Half-Doll 390.00
Carriage, Doll, Celluloid, Acme, Movable Parts, 2 1/2 X 1 1/2 In. 18.00
Carriage, Doll, Fold-Up Mechanically 37.50
Carriage, Doll, Painted Scene Of Children Playing, Tin, 4 1/4 X 5 In. 18.00
Carriage, Doll, Wicker .... 95.00 To 125.00
Carriage, Doll, Wooden Wheels, Metal Hood, Painted Wood, 4 1/2 X 4 In. 18.00
Cart, Doll, White Wheels, Wire Handle, Blue Metal, 3 X 5 In.Long 18.00
Cart, Fenders, John Deere, 28 In. 49.50
Cart, Oxen, Cast Iron, 5 In. 55.00
Cart, Pulled By Chinese Man, 1910, Windup, Carter Toy Co. 195.00
Cash Register, Animated, Fisher Price, Wooden 95.00
Cash Register, Gold Stenciling, Black Tin, Square, 1800, 3 1/2 In. 24.00
Cash Register, Happi Time, Our Own Trademark 15.00
Cash Register, Linemar, Metal 15.00
Cash Register, Tom Thumb, Boxed .... 15.00 To 35.00
Cat, Black, With Ball, Tin, Chein 20.00
Cat, Chases Ball In Circles, Celluloid, Windup, Occupied Japan 50.00
Cat, Knitting, Boxed 50.00
Cat, Mohair, Black & White, Jointed, Long Tail, 11 In. 225.00
Cat, Roll-Over, Mars, Original Box 48.00
Cat, Sassy, Moves Backward, Tail Wags, Gray, Black Spots, C.1930, 5 In. 90.00
Cat, Tin, Leather Ears, Wooden Ball, Tin Wheels, Mechanics Tail 45.00
Caterpillar, Windup, Marx, Boxed 65.00
Cement Mixer, Kenton Jaeger, Cast Iron, 6 1/2 In. 195.00
Cement Roller, Hubley, Cast Iron 95.00
Chariot, Circus, Separate Female Driver, Pulled By 3 Horses, Cast Iron 450.00

Charleston Trio, Black Man Dances, Other Plays Fiddle, 1921, Windup, Marx 395.00
Charlie Chaplin Bicycle, String Toy, Jointed, C.1920 .... 360.00
Charlie Chimp, The Hula Expert, Windup 30.00
Charlie, The Drumming Clown, Boxed 150.00
Cheery Cook, Windup, Celluloid, Japan 25.00
Chemistry Set, Chemcraft No.2, 1927 .... 60.00
Cherry Cook, Celluloid, Windup, Boxed 25.00
Chest, Doll's, Curved Front Drawers, Walnut, 12 1/4 X 9 1/4 In. 165.00
Chick, Chein, Tin, Windup, 4 1/2 In. 20.00
Chicken, Flapping Wings, Tin, Japan 10.00
Chicken, Pushes Her Chicks In Carriage, Battery, Tin 22.00
Chicken, Steiff 75.00
Chimpanzee, Bubble Blowing, Battery Operated 50.00
Chimpanzee, Bug-Eyed, Metal Face, Plastic Hands, Mouth Opens, Chatters 30.00
Chimpanzee, Dancing, Battery Operated 75.00
Chinamen, Walking, Flywheel Toy, Lehmann 615.00
Chipper The Chipmunk, Runs Around, Plastic Treadmill, Chein, 19 In. 50.00
Circus Wagon, Overland, White Bear, Box 225.00
Circus, Humpty Dumpty, Schoenhut, 14 Piece 495.00
Circus, Tent & Animals, Lithographed, German, C.1900, Boxed 95.00
Clock, Musical, Hickory Dicory, Boxed, Mattel, Movable Hands 15.00
Clothes Hanger, Doll's, Wireware, Green & Blue, 6 X 3 In. Set Of 3 .... 15.00
Clown & Mouse, Windup, Schuco 125.00
Clown With Violin, Felt Costume, Schuco, Tin, Windup, 4 1/8 In. 65.00
Clown, Animated, String Pull, Wooden, 12 1/2 In. 160.00
Clown, Battery Operated, Lippo Sonar, Original Box 22.00
Clown, Billy Ding Jr., Wooden 10.00
Clown, Bimbo 95.00
Clown, Cloth Suit, Crashes Cymbals, Hand-Painted, 1900, Windup 550.00
Clown, Dancing With Dog On Turntable, Windup, 1920s 275.00
Clown, Dandy, Windup, Boxed 115.00
Clown, Holds Billboard & Tips Hat, Windup 35.00
Clown, Jumping Rope, Windup 25.00
Clown, Lippo, Battery, Boxed 22.00
Clown, Magic Man, Boxed 185.00
Clown, Musical, Polychrome Paint, Rolly Dolly Toys, Germany, 12 In. 125.00
Clown, On Donkey, Windup, Celluloid 48.00
Clown, On Weighted Ball, Figure Upright When Rolled, C.1910, Tin, 8 In. 155.00
Clown, Pinky, Battery, Boxed 135.00
Clown, Roly Poly, Musical, Papier-Mache, 10 In. 85.00
Clown, Somersaults, Windup, Celluloid 20.00
Clown, Tumbling, Pull, Wood & Tin 55.00
Clown, Walking In Barrel, Windup, J.Chein, Tin, 7 1/2 In. 50.00
Clown, 3-Wheel Lever Driven Cart, C.1910, Germany, Tin, 8 3/4 In. 200.00
Coach, Buddy L, Steel 375.00
Coach, Steering Wheel, Side Mount Tires, Original Decals, Buddy L, Steel 375.00
Coach, Train, P.R.R., Narcissa No.44, Cast Iron, 11 In. 85.00
Coach, 8 Horses, Made In England, Cast Lead, 12 1/4 X 2 1/2 In. 25.00
Coal Loader, Marble Operated Toy, Wolverine, Boxed, 10 1/2 In. 25.00
Cock-A-Doodle Doo Rooster, Battery 75.00
Coffee Grinder, Free Standing, Double Wheel, Arcade, 4 In. 85.00
Commode, Doll's, Wooden, Towel Bar, Candle Shelves, Doors, 15 In. 60.00
Coney Island Playland Part, Ring Toss, Marble Bowling, Dart, Boxed 15.00
Coney Island Ride, Technofix, Boxed 85.00
Construction Co. Derrick, Wyandotte 55.00
Cookstove, Crescent, Cast Iron 100.00
Cop On Motorcycle, Blue Paint, Iron, 5 In. 65.00
Corner Grocery Store, Tin Display, Nabisco Miniatures, Awning 95.00
Couch, Fainting, 1960s, 23 In.Long 57.00
Coupe, Arcade, C.1930, Iron 60.00
Coupe, Convertible, Graham, Tootsietoy 35.00
Coupe, Model A, Arcade, 4 In. 50.00
Coupe, Mortimer Snerd & Charlie McCarthy, Windup Marx, Boxed 1700.00
Cow, Brown, Papier-Mache Body, Wooden Legs, Pull, C.1890, 5 In. 65.00

Cow, Glass Eyes, Straw Stuffed, Mohair Cover, 14 In. 70.00
Cow, Nodder, Glass Eyes, Leather & Fur Covered, Papier-Mache, 10 In.Long 285.00
Cow, Pull, Moo Working 420.00
Cowboy, Horse, Celluloid, Windup, Occupied Japan 95.00
Cowboy, On Donkey, Celluloid 20.00
Cowboy, Twirls Lasso On Horse, 1930s, Windup, Original Box, Germany 195.00
Cradle, Doll, Bonnet, Handmade, Original Paint, Pine 65.00
Cradle, Doll, Handmade, 36 X 21 In. 120.00
Cradle, Doll, Mattress, Wicker, 26 In. 40.00
Cradle, Doll, Square Nails, Old Brown Paint, 15 X 21 1/2 In.Long 20.00
Cradle, Doll, Twisted Metal, 1800s, 24 In. 45.00
Cradle, Raggedy Ann, Mattress, 21 X 16 In. 45.00
Cradle, Square Nails, Brass, Screws, Footboard, Pine, 15 In.Long 25.00
Crane Truck, Magnetic, Steel, Original Paint, Marx, 15 In. 28.00
Crapshooter, Battery, Gragstan, Boxed 30.00
Crash Car, 3 Wheel Motorcycle, Iron, Red, Hubley, 4 1/2 In. 48.00
Crater Cruncher, Micronaut, Motorized, Bull Dozer, Spaceman, 4 In. 35.00
Crazy Car, Charlie McCarthy, Windup, Tin 325.00
Crazy Car, Man, Dog, & Briefcase, Windup, 1920s, Marx 195.00
Crocodile, Windup, Tin 125.00
Cruiser, Battle, Micronaut, Remote Control, Interchangeable 45.00
Cruiser, Galactic, Micronaut, Twinsoft Missile, Multiple Action 25.00
Cyclist, Motor, Germany, Penny Toy, Tin, 3 5/8 In.Long 95.00
Dagwood Solo Flight, Tin, Windup, Boxed, Marx 500.00
Dancer, Ballroom, Windup, Original Paint, Germany, Tin, 4 3/4 In. 120.00
Dancing Couple, Celluloid, Occupied Japan 25.00
Dandy The Happy Drumming Pup, Alps, Boxed 140.00
Daniel Boone Kit, Canteen, Powder, 2 Piece 35.00
Daredevil, Black Man Drives Cart Pulled By Zebra, Windup, Lehmann 350.00
Dart Board, Sambo 60.00
Diesel, Road Roller, Hubley, 10 In. 30.00
Dishes, Tan With Bird, Japan, Doll Size, 12 Piece 15.00
Ditcher, Buckeye, Kenton, Cast Iron, 9 1/2 In. 500.00
Dog On Tin Platform, Pull, Hustler Toy Corp., Wooden 22.50
Dog, Brown, Barking Mouth, Carved, Wooden, C.1930, 7 X 4 In. 100.00
Dog, Chow, White, Fur Covered, C.1900, 8 1/2 X 6 1/2 In. 45.00
Dog, Dog House, Windup, 5 1/2 In. 35.00
Dog, Fuzzy, Tail Spins, He Hops, Windup 18.00
Dog, Gold Paint, Pull, Iron Platform & Wheels, 3 1/2 X 2 1/4 In. 125.00
Dog, Iron Wheels, 11 In. 250.00
Dog, On Wheels, Mohair 45.00
Dog, Pewter Button, Cast Iron Wheels, Steiff, 10 In. 175.00
Dog, Poodle, White, Jointed, 8 In. 35.00
Dog, Runner, Squeeze Toy, Occupied Japan, 3 In. 2.00
Dog, Scotty, Walking, Tin, Marx 45.00
Dog, Sniffy, Battery, Boxed 55.00
Dog, Spitz, White Fur, Glass Eyes, Red Ears, 3 X 3 In. 35.00
       TOY, DOLL, see also Doll
Doll, Nursing Set, Boxed 10.00
Dollhouse, Candlestick, Brass, 1 5/8 In., Pair 15.00
Dollhouse, Folding, McLaughlin's, Boxed 200.00
Dollhouse, Lithographed, 2 Rooms, Bliss Type 245.00
Dollhouse, Open Back, Hinged Front, Decal, Schoenhut, Large 375.00
Dollhouse, Table, Tub, & Washboard, Cast Iron, Table 4 In.Long, 3 Piece 25.00
Dollhouse, 2-Story, Dormer Roof, Dated 1927, Tootsietoy 475.00
Dollhouse, 2-Story, Marx, Boxed, No.4031 .... 85.00
Dollhouse, 6 Rooms, Glassed-In Sunroom, Side Porch, 36 X 22 In. 250.00
Donald Duck, Drummer 175.00
Donald Duck, Walker 125.00
Donkey Cart & Driver, Windup, Marx, 1930s 85.00
Donkey Cart, Driver, Lehmann, Tin, Windup, 6 In. 225.00
Donkey, Bobbing, Celluloid, Germany, 2 1/2 In. 12.00
Donkey, Cart With Clown, Windup, Tin, Germany, 7 1/2 In. 275.00
Donkey, Pull, Penny Toy, Tin, 3 1/4 In. 20.00

Donkey, Schoenhut 55.00
Donkey, Stubborn, Lehmann 165.00
Dresser, Porcelain Knobs, 5 Drawers, 19th Century, Oak, 17 X 14 1/2 In. 125.00
Drum Band, Hand-Painted Figures, Lead, Brown Uniform, 2 In. 4 Piece 100.00
Drum Major, Wolverine, No.27, Windup, Tin 135.00
Drum, Circus, Chein, Tin 12.00
Drummer Boy, Marx 60.00
Drummer, Black Man, Windup, Schuco 125.00
Drummer, George The Drummer Boy, Marx 80.00
Drummer, Rabbit Clown, Windup, Large 65.00
Drummer, Windup, Tin, Chein 40.00
Drunkard, With Bottle & Cup, Cloth Costume, Tin, Windup, 7 3/4 In. 205.00
Duck, Mechanical, Windup, Japan, Tin 38.00
Duck, Movable Feet & Wings, Windup, Germany 30.00
Duck, Squeaker, Stuffed, Felt, Pull, Tin Wheels, Wooden Beak, C.1870, 5 In. 175.00
Duck, Windup, German, Tin 20.00
Dump Truck, Buddy L, Pressed Steel, Rubber Tires, 1930s, 22 1/2 In. 165.00
Dump Truck, Driver, Dumps By Itself, 1910, Windup, French 650.00
Dump Truck, International, Driver, 1925, Arcade, Cast Iron, 10 1/2 In. 395.00
Dump Truck, Mack, Tin, Windup, Marx, No.550, 13 1/2 In. 140.00
Dump Truck, Sand & Gravel, Red & White, Buddy L, 13 In. 20.00
Dump Truck, Snub Nose, Wooden Tires, 16 X 6 In. 30.00
Earth Hauler, Euclid, Doepke Model 60.00
Egg, Celluloid Chick, Tin, Windup, Japan, 3 1/2 In. 55.00
Egg, Rolling, Pull, Boxed 15.00
Elephant, Jumbo, Bubble Blowing, Battery Operated 85.00
Elephant, Jumbo, Felt Blanket, Glass Eyes, Wheels, Steiff, C.1920, 35 In. 625.00
Elephant, On Wheels, Merrythought Toys, Straw Filled, Mohair, 23 X 14 In. 200.00
Engine, Vertical, Sheet Metal Boiler, Nickel Plated Fittings, 8 1/2 In. 65.00
Erector Set, Gilbert Beginner's, Original Box 15.00
Erector Set, Gilbert, Metal, Case 22.00
Erector Set, Gilbert, Wooden Box .... 35.00 To 40.00
Erector Set, No.6 1/2 .... 87.50
Erector Set, No.7 1/2, Gilbert, Book, Boxed 75.00
Erector Set, No.10 1/2 .... 118.00
Erector, Rocket Launcher, Manual 1929 .... 50.00
Fan, Doll's, Wooden Handle, Hand-Painted Paper, Birds, Florals, 6 In. 5.00
Farmer, Peasant, Blue Pants, Green Shirt, English, C.1920, 3 In. 5.00
Felix The Cat, Walking Stick Toy, Tin, 7 1/2 In. 75.00
Felix, Windup, 1920s, Germany 195.00
Felix, Wood Jointed, String, Dated June 23, 1925 .... 45.00
Ferris Wheel, Disneyland 225.00
Ferris Wheel, Lithograph Pickwick Children, Hand Crank, 1920s, Tin 85.00
Ferris Wheel, Mechanical, Hercules 80.00
Ferris Wheel, Mechanical, The Giant Ride 65.00
Ferris Wheel, Mickey Mouse, Chein 135.00
Ferris Wheel, Windup, Chein 115.00
Ferris Wheel, 4 Animals, Bell, Tin, Windup 75.00
Fire Chief, Metal, T.Cohn, Metal 40.00
Fire Engine & Pumper, Iron, Hubley, 12 In. 75.00
Fire Engine, Corgi 1143, Aerial Rescue, Red, Telescoping Ladder, 5 Men 12.50
Fire Engine, Dayton, Friction 185.00
Fire Engine, Fire Patrol, Kenton, Cast Iron, 7 In. 125.00
Fire Engine, Gold Wheels, Red, Hubley, Cast Iron, 6 1/2 In. 132.00
Fire Engine, Kingsbury, Tin, Windup, Red, Yellow Ladder, 24 In.Long 150.00
Fire Engine, Ladder Raises, Fisher Price 12.00
Fire Engine, Lights, Bell, Smoke, Battery Operated, 12 X 7 1/4 In. 60.00
Fire Engine, Original Wooden Tires, Hubley, Cast Iron, 4 3/4 In. 55.00
Fire Engine, Pumper, Iron, Hubley, 12 In. 75.00
Fire Engine, Pumper, Motor Driven, Kenton, Cast Iron, 8 1/2 In. 150.00
Fire Engine, Red, Hook & Ladder, Gilt Scroll, Buddy L, 26 In. 60.00
Fire Pumper, 2 Horses & Driver, C.1880, Cast Iron, 18 In.Long 275.00
Fire Pumper, 3 Horses, Pumper, Eagle Design, Driver, Iron, C.1880, 21 In. 475.00
Fire Truck, Buddy L, Plastic Tires 20.00

Fire Truck, Firemen, Removable Ladders, Schieble, Friction, Tin, 20 In. 375.00
Fire Truck, Hook & Ladder, Red Paint, Iron, 5 3/8 In. 40.00
Fire Truck, Ladder Wagon, Rubber Tires, Arcade, Cast Iron, 15 3/4 In.Long 115.00
Fire Truck, Pumper, With Driver, 1920s, Cast Iron, 9 1/2 In. 175.00
Fire Truck, Tonka, Hose Reel Pumper, C.1954, Red, Threaded Pump, 17 In. 32.00
Fire Truck, Wyandotte, Cast Iron 45.00
Fire Wagon, Horses, Men, Ladder, Partial Paint, Cast Iron, Late 1880s 300.00
Fireman, Climbing Ladder, Marx 130.00
Fireman, Climbing, Tin, Battery, Boxed 127.50
Flash Strato Wagon, Wyandotte, 9 1/2 In. 55.00
Flintstone Bedrock Band 85.00
Flintstone On Dino, Marx, Tin 132.50
Flutter Birds, Battery, Boxed 85.00
Flying Saucer 55.00
Ford Assembly Kit, Motorized With Remote Control, Original Box, Ideal 20.00
Ford, Roadster, 1934, Arcade, 5 In. 250.00
Frankenstein, Blushing, Battery Operated, Boxed .... 90.00 To 130.00
Fred Flintstone, On Dino, Battery 147.50
Frog On Park Bench, Metal 20.00
Frog, Schuco 45.00
Frontier Express, Boxed, England 60.00
Furniture, Chair, Doll's, Bent Bamboo, 6 3/4 In., Pair 25.00
Furniture, Chair, Dollhouse, Ice Cream Parlor, Wireware, 3 3/4 In. 5.00
Furniture, Dollhouse, Baby Carriage, Wooden Wheels, Blue & Red Metal 25.00
Furniture, Dollhouse, Bathtub, Tootsietoy 14.00
Furniture, Dollhouse, Bed, Mesh Springs, C.1900, Cast Iron, 15 X 20 In. 175.00
Furniture, Dollhouse, Bedroom Set, Tootsietoy, Metal, Pink, 5 Piece 25.00
Furniture, Dollhouse, Bedroom, Skipper 55.00
Furniture, Dollhouse, Candlestick, Brass, 1 In., Pair 4.50
Furniture, Dollhouse, Candlestick, Brass, 1 5/8 In., Pair 15.00
Furniture, Dollhouse, Candlestick, Brass, 2 In., Pair 15.00
Furniture, Dollhouse, Canister Set, China, Marked, Germany, 15 Piece 85.30
Furniture, Dollhouse, Carriage, Acme 3.00
Furniture, Dollhouse, Carriage, Pictured Boy & Girl, Tin, 5 1/4 In. 28.00
Furniture, Dollhouse, Church, Keystone, Wooden 55.00
Furniture, Dollhouse, Cupboard, Hoosier, White Metal 49.00
Furniture, Dollhouse, Cupboard, Step Back 140.00
Furniture, Dollhouse, Dining Room, Metal, Tootsietoy, 8 Piece 75.00
Furniture, Dollhouse, Dresser, Sleigh Front, Walnut, 12 In. 125.00
Furniture, Dollhouse, Fainting Couch 35.00
Furniture, Dollhouse, Fireplace, Pressed Brass & Tin 18.00
Furniture, Dollhouse, Hamper, Wicker 4.00
Furniture, Dollhouse, Kitchen, Wooden, 5 Piece 15.00
Furniture, Dollhouse, Ladder, Ironing Board, & Carpet Sweeper, Cast Iron 30.00
Furniture, Dollhouse, Lamp, Blue Glass Shade, Brass, 2 1/2 In. 12.00
Furniture, Dollhouse, Love Seat, Curved Arms & Back, 1 1/2 X 1 1/2 In. 20.00
Furniture, Dollhouse, Piano, Barbie 65.00
Furniture, Dollhouse, Piano, Grand, Hard Plastic 5.00
Furniture, Dollhouse, Rocker, Woven Seat, Dark Wood, 4 1/2 In. 15.00
Furniture, Dollhouse, Rug, Hooked, Winter Scene Of House, 4 X 3 In. 45.00
Furniture, Dollhouse, Rug, Lavender & Pink Silk, Braided, 15 X 17 1/2 In. 14.00
Furniture, Dollhouse, Rug, Oriental, 3 X 5 In. 4.00
Furniture, Dollhouse, Sewing Machine 6.00
Furniture, Dollhouse, Stove, Electric 6.00
Furniture, Dollhouse, Table, Card, Renewal 4.00
Furniture, Dollhouse, Table, Deco, Wood & Steel 3.00
Furniture, Dollhouse, Table, Empire, Original Red, Hand-Dovetailed 150.00
Furniture, Dollhouse, Table, Openwork Top, Metal, 2 1/2 X 2 1/8 In. 20.00
Furniture, Dollhouse, Table, Victorian, Marble Top, Oval, 4 1/8 X 3 In. 35.00
Furniture, Dollhouse, Telephone, Upright, Removable Receiver, Metal, Red 22.00
Furniture, Dollhouse, Toilet, Tootsietoy 15.00
Furniture, Dollhouse, Vacuum, Upright 3.00
Furniture, Dollhouse, Victorian Bedroom, Ornate Stenciling, Wood 180.00
Furniture, Dollhouse, Washer, Wringer 10.00

Furniture, Dollhouse, Washtub, Washboard, Red Enamel, 9 1/4 In.Diam.	37.50
Furniture, Table, Drop Leaf, Walnut, Doll's, Piecrust Edge, 5 X 9 In.	150.00
Furniutre, Table, Drop Leaf, Walnut, Child's, Trestle Legs, C.1880, 16 In.	135.00
G.I.Joe & His Jouncing Jeep, Tin, Windup, Unique Art, 6 1/2 In.	65.00
G.I.Joe & The K-9 Pups, Windup, Tin, Boxed, Unique Art	175.00
Gallery, Shooting, Circus & Carnival, Key Wind, Ohio Art, Tin	55.00
TOY, GAME, see Game	
Garage, Automatic, Battery	45.00
Garage, 2 Cars, Penny Toy, Germany, Tin, 2 1/2 In.	37.50
Girl, Bounding Ball, Windup	85.00
Glider, Space, Warrior Ship, Silver & Blue, Metal, 4 In.	25.00
Glider, Tab, Space Roto-Uro, Warrior Robot, Yellow, Green, Red, 8 In.	35.00
Goat, Pulling Wagon, Iron	195.00
Goat, Wooden, Painted Eyes, Black Leather Ears, Schoenhut, 8 In.	220.00
Goose, Pecking, Unique Art, 10 In.	25.00
Goose, Pull, Nodding Head, Penny Toy, Tin, 3 In.	95.00
Gorilla, Lithographed Tin, Plush Exterior, Windup, Japan, 8 In.	375.00
Graf Zeppelin, 1930s, Balsa & Tissue, 15 In.	26.00
Grandpa Rocking In Chair, Bib Overalls, Cigar Lights, 8 In.	75.00 To 95.00
Grasshopper, Movable Legs, Runs On Wheels, 1920s, Hubley, Iron, 10 In.	550.00
Greyhound Bus, 1933 Chicago Century Of Progress, Arcade, Cast Iron	115.00
Guitar, Occupied Japan, Tin Body, Wooden Handle, Blue & Red, 15 In.	12.50
Gun, Aeromatic, Jokel Co., Sheet Metal, 6 In.	5.00
Gun, Atomic, Bulbous, See-Thru Red Lucite, Sparkling, Tin, 9 X 4 In.	25.00
Gun, Auto-Magic Picture, Film, Projector, Dated 1938, Boxed	35.00
Gun, B-B, Red Ryder, Iron Cocking Lever	22.00
Gun, Cap Pistol, Big Chief, Stevens, Boxed	20.00
Gun, Cap Pistol, Bigger Bang	45.00
Gun, Cap Pistol, Billy The Kid, Stevens, Boxed	20.00
Gun, Cap Pistol, Bulldog	20.00
Gun, Cap Pistol, Dick, Metal	10.00
Gun, Cap Pistol, Echo, Single Shot, 4 1/2 In.	10.00 To 15.00
Gun, Cap, Big Smoky	85.00
Gun, Cap, Chinese Must Go, Animated, Original Green Label, Boxed	1200.00
Gun, Cap, Circle H	22.50
Gun, Cap, Cowboy Brand, Cast Iron	25.00
Gun, Cap, Dandy Shooter, Hubley	25.00
Gun, Cap, Doc	32.50
Gun, Cap, Frontier Smoker, Smokes, Product Engineering Co.	30.00
Gun, Cap, Hubley, Animated, Action Activities Barrel	52.00
Gun, Cap, Invincible	35.00
Gun, Cap, Kilgore Eagle	15.00
Gun, Cap, Kilgore Ranger	30.00
Gun, Cap, Little Boy's Head On Top End Of Handle, Cast Iron	85.00
Gun, Cap, National	27.50
Gun, Cap, Padlock Shape, Hubley, Nickel Plated, 4 1/2 In.	35.00
Gun, Cap, Pirate	37.50
Gun, Cap, Red Ranger, Wyandotte, Boxed	20.00
Gun, Cap, Scout	32.00
Gun, Cap, Scout, Dated June 17, 1890, Iron, 7 In.	15.00
Gun, Cap, Spy	25.00
Gun, Cap, Stallion 38	20.00
Gun, Cap, Stallion, Circle N	3.00
Gun, Cap, Stevens, 6 Shot, Cast Iron	70.00
Gun, Cap, Super, Yellow, 9 1/2 In.	15.00
Gun, Cap, Texas, Single Shot, 5 1/2 In.	4.00
Gun, Cap, Volunteer, 1873	75.00
Gun, Clicker, Red Ranger	12.00
in, Clicker, 6-Shooter, Red & Black, Red Ryder, Metal, 10 In.	15.00
n, Cork Shooter, Salo, Embossed Handle, Tin, 4 1/2 In.	15.00
, Electric Singal Ray, Remco, Battery	20.00
G-Man, Automatic Repeater	25.00
Gattling, On Wooden Tripod Legs, Sheet Metal, 9 In.	10.00
one Eagle Automatic Repeater	25.00

Pig, Spins, Ears Flop, Tin, Windup, German 60.00
Pig, Steiff, 4 In. 35.00
Pig, Windup, Tin, Litho, Ears Flop, Wiggles 65.00
Piggy, Windup, Marx, C.1940 .... 30.00
Pinball Game, Gold Star, Lindstrom 25.00
Pinocchio, Acrobat 135.00
Pinocchio, Plays London Bridge, Battery, Boxed 85.00
Pinocchio, Walker 175.00
Play-A-Sax 40.00
Playland Scooter 45.00
Plink Plunk Tune, Penny Toy, Germany, Telefon, All Attachments 475.00
Pluto, In Top Hat 175.00
Policeman, On Motorcycle, Sidecar, Windup, Yellow, Blue, 8 In. 45.00
Policeman, On Motorcycle, White Wheels, Blue Paint, Cast Iron 85.00
Polly Dolly, Dutch, Head Turns, Schoenhut, 15 In. 255.00
Polly Dolly, Musical Punch, Original Polychrome, 12 In. 155.00
Pony, Riding, Steiff 235.00
Poodle, Original White Paint, Wooden, Schoenhut, 7 In. 85.00
Poodle, Walking, Battery Operated .... 20.00 To 50.00
Pool Player, Hand-Painted, 12 In. 375.00
Pool Player, 1910, Windup, Germany 250.00
Pool Player, 1930s, Windup, Boxed 110.00
Poosh-M-Up, Pinball, Triple Play, Wooden Frame, 23 In. 40.00
Popgun, Single Barrel, Wyandotte, Boxed 15.00
Porter, With Trunk, Windup, Tin, Germany, 3 1/2 In. 25.00
Pot & Pan Set, Aluminum, Boxed, 8 Piece 35.00
Power Plant, Boiler, Pressure Gauge, 25V Generator, Germany, 14 1/2 In. 500.00
Powerful Katrinka, Jimmy, & Wheelbarrow 1000.00
Printing Press, Tin, Windup, Marx, Boxed, 10 X 5 In. 45.00
Professor Ludwig Von Drake, Tin, Windup, 6 In. 100.00
Projector, Keystone .... 25.00 To 28.00
Pumper, Fire Truck, Germany, C.1910, Tin, Windup, 5 1/2 In. 115.00
Pumper, Steam, Fire Engine, Red, White, Gold, Black, C.1893, 21 In. 30.00
Pumper, 3 Horses, Cast Iron, 10 1/2 In.Long 45.00
Punch & Policeman, Push-Pull Action, Penny Toy, Tin, 2 7/8 X 2 3/4 In. 85.00
Pup, Buttons, Battery, Boxed 200.00
Puppet, Alligator, Steiff 12.00
Puppet, Captain Hook, Felt Clothes 45.00
Puppet, Foxy, Steiff 35.00
Puppet, Hand, Bulldog, Original Label Bully, Steiff, Glass Eyes, 10 In. 20.00
Puppet, Hand, Howdy Doody & Gang, Set Of 5 .... 60.00
Puppet, Hand, Man With Beard, Steiff Label, Red Hat 35.00
Puzzle, Blocks, Child's Scenes, Wooden Box 165.00
Puzzle, Wood, Paper, Farm Animals, Reversible, 1901 .... 24.00
Queen Buzzy Bee, Pull, Fisher Price, 6 In. 10.00
Rabbit Pulling Chicks, Carrot Sled, Tin, Celluloid, Boxed 35.00
Rabbit, Busy Housekeeper, Boxed, Battery 95.00
Rabbit, Hopping, Tin, U.S. Zone Germany, 3 In. 45.00
Rabbit, Windup, Lindstrom 40.00
Rabbit, Windup, Tin, Chein, C.1940 .... 30.00
Rabbit, Windup, 5 1/2 In. 15.00
Rabbit, Wooden Pull, Advertising Jenny Wren Flour 18.00
Raccoon, Racy, Steiff, 8 In. 40.00
Racehorse, With Sulky & Driver, Wolverine, Windup, Plastic 20.00
Racer, Cast Iron & Metal, 7 1/2 In. 20.00
Racer, Hubley, Cast Iron, 5 1/2 In. 50.00
Racer, Jet, Friction, Tin, 10 In. 25.00
Racer, Lead Driver, Hubley, 7 In. 24.00
Racer, Metal, Dubigo Metal Products, Boxed, 10 1/2 In. 25.00
Racer, Mystery, Silver, Red Cockpit, Aluminum, 9 In. 22.50
Racer, Red, Gold Trim, Original Driver & Paint, Dayton, 7 In. 125.00
Racer, Rocket, Spaceship, Pilot, Vinyl Head, Sounds, Tin, Boxed, 8 In. 35.00

Racer, Warp, Space Racing Car, Motorized, Spaceman, 4 In. 35.00
Racing Scull, Wheels, Animated, Penny Toy, Germany, 2 Man, 6 1/2 In.Long 105.00
Range Rider, Sparkler, Marx, Boxed 115.00
Range Rider, Tin, Windup, Boxed 225.00
Range, Modern Miss Magic Glow, Electric, 12 Utensils, Lights, 12 In. 20.00
Rattle, 1910, Celluloid 7.00
Ray Gun, Captain Video, Luma-Glo Card, Secret Message, Premium, 3 In. 30.00
Record Player, Battery, 4 Two-Sided Records, Carnival Model 111 .... 15.00
Refrigerator, Tin & Glass, 20 Accessories Inside, Revolving Shelves 60.00
Rex The Answer Hound, West Germany, Boxed 35.00
Rider, Man Gets On & Off Motorcycle, Windup, Arnold Co. 350.00
Rifle, Dart, Daisy, C.1950, Boxed 20.00
Rifle, Scout, 250 Shot, Hubley, Metal 75.00
Ring-A-Ling Circus, 3 Animals, 1 Clown, Marx, Tin, Windup, 7 1/2 In. 130.00
Road Grader, Adams 50.00
Road Grader, Hubley, Cast Iron 8.00
Road Race Set, Sky Diver Jump, Marx Girard, Boxed 120.00
Road Roller, Army, Metal, Hubley, 10 In. 25.00
Road Roller, Hubley, Die Cast 75.00
Roadster, Wood Body, Iron Wheels & Motor, D.P. Clark & Co., 7 In. 110.00
Robby The Robot, Lithographed Tin, Battery Operated, Japan, 13 1/2 In. 1100.00
Robin, Windup, Germany, Tin 32.50
Robot, Battery Operated, Black Plastic, 11 1/2 In. 40.00
Robot, Battery Operated, Speaks Spanish, Original Box 25.00
Robot, Blue Body, Red Arms, Chrome Chest, Windup, Ray Gun, Plastic, 6 In. 25.00
Robot, Commander, Force, Micronaut, Fighting Fists, Missiles, 8 In. 35.00
Robot, Dog, Daggit, Battlestar Galactica Mascot, Vinyl, 3 In. 10.00
Robot, Egg Shaped, Radar Head, Windup, Wheels, Tin, Plastic, 3 In. 15.00
Robot, Fighter, Bandai, Defender Of Justice, Turns, Runs, Plastic, 15 In. 50.00
Robot, G-Force, Vinyl Head, Helmet, Visor, Cape, Walks, Tin, 9 In. 60.00
Robot, Jupiter, Walks & Sparkles, Windup, Tin & Plastic, 7 In. 60.00
Robot, Laughing, Blue, Red Face, Bumps, Battery, Plastic, 10 In. 50.00
Robot, Mars King, Battery, Tin, Boxed 230.00
Robot, Moon Explorer, Human Face, Stop, Go, Doors On Chest, Plastic, 11 In 35.00
Robot, Mouse, Rolls Along, Swings Arms, See Through Chest, Plastic, 10 In. 45.00
Robot, Plantet, Sparks In Chest, Throat, Face As It Walks, 9 In. 75.00
Robot, Qonto, Walks, Flashing Eyes, White, Blue, Red, Battery, 12 In. 50.00
Robot, Robert, Ideal, Boxed .... 225.00 To 300.00
Robot, Rotating, Shoots Gun, Walks, Black & Silver, Plastic, 9 In. 45.00
Robot, Roto, Striped Bowtie, Gun, Walks, Body Rotates 360 Degrees, 9 In. 85.00
Robot, Space Commander, Smile, Recessed Face, Fires Missiles, 11 In. 50.00
Robot, Sparky, Tin, Windup, Boxed, 7 In. 75.00
Robot, Star Fighter, Walks, Shoots, Gun Lights, Black, Chrome, 10 In. 50.00
Robot, Targetron, Electronic, Beeps, Lights Flash, Plastic, 7 In. 50.00
Robot, Vakkity Yob, Redheaded, Silver Tooth, Horseshoe Ring, 12 In. 85.00
Robot, Warrior, Acroyear, Disk Hands, Dagger & Crossbow, 4 In. 25.00
Robot, Warrior, Galaxy, White & Orange, Storm Trooper Head, 11 In. 40.00
Rocket Ride, Chein 110.00
Rocket, Nasa Space Twins, Cap-Firing, Plastic & Metal, 7 In. 25.00
Rocket, Retractable Nose Cone, Friction, Tin, Boxed, 12 In. 25.00
Rocket, Space, Solar-X No.7, Elevates & Lowers, Battery, 15 1/2 In. 150.00
Rocket, Sr-7 Nike, Nose Cone Hits, Automatically Stands, Tin, 7 In. 35.00
Rocking Horse, Carved Head, C.1870, Original Orange-Red Paint 425.00
Rocking Horse, Signed T.Pearson, Dated 1817 .... 125.00
Rocking Horse, Spring, Advertising, Simplex Flexi Shoes For Children 90.00
Rocking Horse, Tom Mix & Tony 250.00
Roller Coaster, Chein, Windup, 19 In. .... 60.00 To 125.00
Roller Coaster, 2 Cars, Chein, Mechanical, Boxed, 19 X 8 In. 90.00
Roller Skates, Deluxe, Harris Hardware, N.Y.C., Leather Straps, Key 12.50
Roller Skates, Winchester .... 25.00 To 40.00
Rooster In Cage, Squeak Toy 85.00
Rooster, Battery, Boxed 60.00
Rooster, Cock A Doodle Doo, Battery, Boxed 75.00
Rooster, Fed By Boy, From Pan, 1910, Windup, Japan 265.00

Rooster, Marx, Battery Operated 125.00
Rooster, Pecking, Felt Tail, Tin, Kohle, Germany 15.00
Royal Circus, 4 Wagons, Hubley, Small Size 800.00
Sadiron, Removable Handle 28.00
Sand Pail, Chein Train, Decorated With Children & Train 3.50
Sand Pail, Mary Had A Little Lamb, Color Litho, Chein, 5 X 5 In. 8.50
Sand, Cart & Hopper, Sandy Cindy, Wolverine Supply & Co., Tin, 14 3/4 In. 30.00
Sand, Sifter, 1920s, Tin 6.00
Santa Claus, Bell Ringer, Battery 45.00
Santa Claus, Chein, Tin, Windup, 6 In. 95.00
Santa Claus, Chein, Windup 225.00
Santa Claus, In Sled, 2 Reindeers, Tin, Windup 45.00
Santa Claus, On Helicopter, Battery Operator, Boxed 35.00
Santa Claus, On Scooter, Battery Operated, M-T Co., Boxed 65.00
Santa Claus, Plush Coat, Plaster Head, Battery, Tin, 9 In. 40.00
Santa Claus, Rings Bell, Eyes Light Up, Batteries, 12 1/2 In. 45.00
Santa Claus, Rings Bell, Waves, Windup, Tin, Japan, Boxed 75.00
Santa Claus, Rings Bells, Celluloid Face, Windup 20.00
Santa Claus, Swings Bell, Rocks Back & Forth, Windup, 10 In. 32.00
Santa Claus, Windup, Chein 135.00
Saucer, Ufo Gyro, Sparkling Engine, Climbs, Spins, Rolls, Plastic, 4 In. 15.00
Sax-O-Fun, Spike Jones 12.00
Scale, Counter, Tradesman's, Indicator, C.1930, 2 1/2 X 3 1/4 In. 15.00
Scissors, Sewing, Steel & Brass, Marked Germany, 2 3/4 In. 12.50
Scooter, Space, Battery, Boxed 95.00
Scotty, Windup, Marx, Boxed 30.00
Scurpy Pup, Battery 75.00
Seal With Ball, Ball Turns, Friction, Tin, Lehmann, 3 In. 35.00
Searcher, Star, Micronaut, 6-Wheeled, 6 Toys In 1, Mego Corp. 45.00
Service Station, Sunny Side, Marx, 1920s 135.00
Sewing Machine, American Girls 40.00
Sewing Machine, Battery, L.J.N., Foot Pedal, Drawers 25.00
Sewing Machine, Betsy Ross, Child's, Green Enameled Metal, 6 In. 35.00
Sewing Machine, Case, Blue Paint, Eagle Design, 6 X 8 In. 35.00
Sewing Machine, Casige, Germany, British Zone 22.00
Sewing Machine, Hand Crank, German, Cast Iron 28.00
Sewing Machine, Singer, Accessories, Cast Iron, 1930s 65.00
Sewing Machine, Singer, Battery Operated 150.00
Sewing Machine, Singer, Centennial 35.00
Sewing Machine, Singer, Model 20, Boxed 55.00
Ship, Space Patrol, Delta Bird 7, Red, Yellow, Green, Battery, 8 In. 35.00
Shoeshine Joe, Battery, Boxed 115.00
Shooting Gallery, Key Wind, Circus & Carnival, Ohio Art, Tin 50.00
Shooting Gallery, Plastic Pistols, Windup Ducks, 14 X 11 In. 75.00
Shovel, Power, P & H Vindex 375.00
Shovel, Steam, Red Paint, Iron, 4 5/8 In. 40.00
Sink, Running Water, Little S.O.S. Box, Wolverine 15.30
Sled, Champion, Dated 1881 .... 40.00
Sled, Curved Runners, Wooden, 25 X 9 1/2 In. 95.00
Sled, Curved-Up Scroll Runners, Bentwood Understructure, Pine 225.00
Sled, Doll's, Tole Flowers On Wood, Curved Iron Runners, C.1885, 18 In. 225.00
Sled, Ice, 3 Runner, Cannonball, Bar Handle, C.1910, 48 In. 125.00
Sled, Photon, Airplane Shaped, Motorized, Torque Motor, 4 In. 25.00
Sled, Red Racer, Wood Runners, Hand Holes, Oak, 30 In. 35.00
Sled, Stenciled Top, Wooden Runners, 9 1/2 X 34 In.Long 25.00
Sled, 3 Slat Top, Red Racer, Hand Holes, Oak, 30 In. 55.00
Sleigh, Animal Drawn, Red Paint, Leather Harness, C.1870, 8 X 17 In. ... 275.00
Sleigh, Child's, Hand-Painted Country Scenes, Russian 950.00
Sleigh, Child's, Red, Silver Handle, Wooden Runners, 40 X 34 In. 120.00
Sleigh, Doll, Straw-Stuffed Horse On Iron Wheels 350.00
Snookums, Their Only Child, Windup, Tin, Hand-Painted 500.00
Snoopy, Makes Noise When Nose Pulled, 13 X 4 In. 22.00
Snowman, Magic, Battery Operated 115.00
Soldier, Britains, Fife & Drum Corps, Hand-Painted, Lead, 7 Piece 165.00

Soldier, Britains, Marching Band, Hand-Painted, Lead, 5 Piece	125.00
Soldier, Chein, Tin, Windup, 6 1/4 In.	30.00
Soldier, Colonial, Attached To White Oxen, Sheep, Dog, Lead, 2 In., Set	35.00
Soldier, Fife Player, World War I, Hand-Painted, Lead, 2 5/8 In.	12.50
Soldier, Officer At Attention, World War II, Lead, 3 In.	3.00
Soldier, Officer On Black Horse, 4 Foot Troopers, C.1890, Lead, 3 In.	60.00
Soldier, Orderly Shining Pair Ob Boots, Lead, 1 7/8 In.	17.50
Soldier, U.S.Army, Cast Helmet, Hand-Painted, Lead, 3 3/4 In.	15.00
Soldier, With Flag, Bell Pull Toy, Polychrome Paint, Cast Iron, 6 1/4 In.	50.00
Soldier, With Rifle, Crawls, Hand-Painted, Windup, 1915	650.00
Soldier, World War I, Spiked Helmeted German Officer, 2 In.	4.00
Soldiers & Cannon, Red & Black Cannon, Wooden, 6 Piece	95.00
Space Dart Target, Metal, 1950s	42.00
Space Patrol R-10, Space Vehicle, Battery Operated, Japan, 12 1/2 In.	140.00
Space Vehicle, Tin Man, Sparking Action, Rubber Wheels, 8 In.	12.00
Spaceman, Moon McDare, Cloth Jumpsuit, Vinyl, Gilbert, 12 In.	30.00
Spaceman, Pete, Walks, Gun, Space Outfit, Battery, Tin, 5 In.	30.00
Spaceman, Pharoid, Fits Into Egyptian Time Chamber, 3 In.	25.00
Spaceman, Smoking, Battery Operated, Linemar, 12 In.	1100.00
Spaceship, Apollo, 3 Astronauts, Flashing Cone, Battery, Tin.9 In.	150.00
Spaceship, Buck Rogers, 4 People In Window, Marked 1927	75.00
Spaceship, Flying, Pilot, Lucite Bubble, Friction, Siren Sound, 5 In.	30.00
Spaceship, Mystery, Spins On Axis, Moon Base, Rocket Launcher, 7 In.	150.00
Spaceship, Saucer Shaped, Chrome, Battery, Plastic, American Flag	30.00
Spaceship, XZ-7, Astronaut, Bubble Cockpit, Friction, Tin, 7 X 3 In.	35.00
Speedboat, Lindstrom, Windup, Tin, Boxed	20.00
Speedboat, With Driver, 1930, Cast Iron, 5 1/2 In.	125.00
Spic & Span, Hams What Am, Windup, Drummer, Dancer, Marx	310.00
Spinner, Good Luck, Ralston	50.00
Square Shooter, Marx, Boxed	35.00
Squirt Gun, Cowboy On Handle, 3 1/4 X 2 1/4 X 2 1/4 In.	4.00
Squirt Gun, Wyandotte, Metal, Boxed	35.00
Stagecoach, Cloth Top, 2 Horses, Driver, Original Box, Iron, 15 In.	150.00
Stallion, Galactic, Micronaut, Oberon, White, Magno Power, Boxed	30.00
Stamp Set, Brownie, Original Pamphlet	50.00
Star Trek, Communicator, Blue, Enterprise Emblem, Beeper, 5 In.	35.00
Station Wagon, Cadillac, 1941, Tin	35.00
Station Wagon, Master, Windup, Metal	35.00
Station, Train, American Flyer, Tin, Plastic, Gray, Green, Red, White	68.00
Station, Train, Schoenhut	400.00
Steam Engine, Blue Paint, Marked Hero, Buffalo Toy Works, 4 3/4 In.	25.00
Steam Engine, Horizontal Brass Boiler, Weeden, Black Trim, 7 In.Long	55.00
Steam Shovel, Structo	26.00
Steam Shovel, Wooden Wheels, Moving Parts, Delta Detroit Corp.	40.00
Steamroller, Huber, Cast Iron, 4 1/2 In.	50.00
Steamroller, Hubley, Boxed	12.00
Stove, American, Pots & Pans, Cast Iron, 8 1/2 In.	150.00
Stove, Charm, Cast Iron	85.00
Stove, Cook, Pans, Venus, Cast Iron, 8 X 5 In.	75.00
Stove, Electric, Heat Gauge, Ivory & Green, Kingston Products, 10 X 9 In.	35.00
Stove, Empire, 2 Burners, Oven, Electric	175.00
Stove, Gas, Eagle, Patent 1896.4 1/2 In.	32.50
Stove, Little Chef, Electric, 13 1/4 X 7 X 10 1/2 In.	95.00
Stove, Parking, Metal Pot & Pan, Lid Stamped West Germany	32.00
Stove, Salesman's Sample, Utensils, Cast Iron	2600.00
Stove, Star, Cast Iron	38.00
Stove, Tot, Cast Iron	68.00
Stove, Venus, Iron, 3 Pots, 8 X 5 In.	80.00
Straight Shooter, Ralston, Makeup Container	20.00
Straw Man, Wizard Of Oz, Original Felt Costume, Straw, Tin, Windup, 6 In.	200.00
Streetcar, Orange, Red Roof, Friction, C.1906, D.P.Clark & Co., 13 In.	55.00
Stroller, Doll, C.1900, Wicker	340.00
Stutz, 1915, Front-End Crank Windup	250.00
Submarine, Diving, Orange & Green, Wolverine, 13 In.	20.00 To 65.00

Submarine, Revolving Guns, Tootsietoy 14.00
Submarine, Wolverine, Diving, Tin, Blue & White, 13 In. 40.00
Super Space Capsule, Metal, 1960 .... 95.00
Surrey, Blue, White Horse, Red Surrey, Yellow Fringe, Iron, 13 In. 25.00
Surrey, Fringe On Top, Child's Or Doll's, Victorian, Original 650.00
Surrey, Fringed Cloth Top, 2 Horses, Driver, Passenger, Iron, 11 In. 50.00
Surrey, Horse Drawn, Fringed Top, Crammer Toys, C.1906, 13 1/2 In. 75.00
Sweeper, Bissell's Little Daisy, Oak .... 45.00 To 60.00
Sweeper, Carpet, Handi-Aid, Tin, 6 Wooden Wheels, Red & Black 8.00
Swing, Doll, Original Paint, Gilt Trim, 18 1/2 In. 37.50
Swing, Doll, Wooden Platform, Swing Each Side 87.50
Table, Croquet Set, Victorian, Boxed 35.00
Table, Doll, Button Footed, Pine, C.1860, Red Paint, 7 In. 150.00
Table, Sewing, Child's, Pine, Ruler Insert, Trestle Legs, 9 3/4 In. 35.00
Tank, Planet Patrol, Marx, Windup, Tin 125.00
Tank, Roll Over, Casper, Linemar 85.00
Tank, Space Patrol, Mars, Blue, Brown, Red, Cannon Fires, Rex, 10 In. ... 65.00
Tank, Space, Gearshifts, Flashing Lights, Siren Sound, Battery, 10 In. 50.00
Tank, Space, M-18, Astronaut, Yellow Suit, Radar Scope, Tin, 8 In. 150.00
Tank, Sparking, Windup, Tin, 1939, Chein, Boxed 75.00
Tank, Windup, Movable Turret, Marx, 1930s, 10 In. 50.00
Tank, Windup, PomPom Cannon, 1950s, 10 In. 45.00
Target Game, Trophy Hunt, 2 Rubber Band Guns, Boxed, Cadaco 29.00
Taxi, De La Marne, 1907 Model Renault, Rami, France, Red & Black, Yellow 7.00
Taxi, Green & Black, Arcade, 8 In. 295.00
Taxi, Meter At Front Window, Rubber Tires, Tin, Yellow, 4 In. 10.00
Taxi, Yellow Taxi On Door, France, Lead With Tin Rook, 2 1/4 In. 45.00
Tea Set, Figural Strawberry Shape, Bisque, Japan, Boxed, Doll Size 40.00
Tea Set, Gold Flowers, Blue Bands, German, C.1900, 15 Piece 68.00
Tea Set, Ideal, Plastic 10.00
Tea Set, Little Hostess, Plastic, Original Napkins, Boxed 10.00
Tea Set, Ohio Art, 1937, 60 Piece 300.00
Tea Set, Roses, Daisies, China, Japan, 11 Piece 25.00
Tea Set, 22 Piece, Original Box, Doll Size 35.00
Teahouse, Chase & Sanborn, Paper 18.00
Teddy Bear, Beige Mohair, Button Ear, Button Eyes, Jointed, 1903, Steiff .. 500.00
Teddy Bear, Beige Mohair, Glass Eyes, Straw Stuffed, Steiff, 14 In. 325.00
Teddy Bear, Bellhop, Jointed, Blue Pants, Red Shirt, 14 1/2 In. 295.00
Teddy Bear, Black Mohair, Electric Eye, Lights Up, 10 In. 215.00
Teddy Bear, Brown Plush Cover, Black Eyes, Wired Legs, 6 In. 110.00
Teddy Bear, Electric Eye, Jointed Head & Arms, Black, 23 In. 300.00
Teddy Bear, Fully Jointed, Cream, 14 In. 195.00
Teddy Bear, Glass Eyes, Beige, 16 In. 175.00
Teddy Bear, Glass Eyes, On All Fours, Mohair, Brown, 10 X 16 In. 300.00
Teddy Bear, Gold Mohair, Jointed, Button Eyes, Squeaker, C.1903, 16 In. .. 650.00
Teddy Bear, Gold Mohair, 3-Wheel Scooter, Red Beret, Schuco, 5 In. ... 225.00
Teddy Bear, Gold Muzzle, Wool, Yellow, Jointed, Big Feet, 11 In. 180.00
Teddy Bear, Growls, Fully Jointed, 1940s, 22 In. 225.00
Teddy Bear, Humpback, Gold Mohair, Straw Filled, Jointed, 17 In. 250.00
Teddy Bear, Humpback, 13 In. 210.00
Teddy Bear, Jointed Except Neck, Long Hair, Yellow, 9 1/2 In. 95.00
Teddy Bear, Jointed, Big Feet, Long Nose, Steiff, Gold, Mohair, 5 1/2 In. .. 210.00
Teddy Bear, Jointed, Button Eyes, Brown Stitching, Steiff, 17 In. 600.00
Teddy Bear, Jointed, C.1820, 16 In. 250.00
Teddy Bear, Jointed, Glass Eyes, Working Music Box, Cinnamon, 13 In. .. 255.00
Teddy Bear, Jointed, Growler, Hermann Tag, C.1920, Gold Mohair, 18 In. .. 250.00
Teddy Bear, Jointed, Ideal, 1905 .... 350.00
Teddy Bear, Jointed, Mohair, Steiff, 10 1/2 In. 26.00
Teddy Bear, Jointed, Mohair, Steiff, 13 1/2 In. 38.00
Teddy Bear, Jointed, Mohair, Steiff, 20 In. 92.00
Teddy Bear, Jointed, Stitched Claws, Steiff, Beige Mohair, 14 In. 325.00
Teddy Bear, Jointed, Straw Stuffed, Blue, 13 In. 135.00
Teddy Bear, Jointed, Triangular Face, Squeaker, Mohair, Ideal, 1903, 16 In. .. 650.00
Teddy Bear, Jointed, White, 30 In. 195.00

Teddy Bear, Jointed, Wooden, 5 In.	22.00
Teddy Bear, Jointed, Yellow, 22 In.	225.00
Teddy Bear, Kathe Kruse, Brown, 12 1/2 In.	25.00
Teddy Bear, Killiken, Mohair, Bisque Head, Oriental, Good Luck, 12 In.	600.00
Teddy Bear, Long-Armed, Original Condition, 12 In.	350.00
Teddy Bear, Metal Nose, 1900, 12 In.	95.00
Teddy Bear, Mohair, Black, Electric Eye, Jointed Arms, Battery, 10 In.	215.00
Teddy Bear, Mohair, Jointed Button Eyes, Bride & Groom, 2 1/2 In., Pair	270.00
Teddy Bear, Musical, Brahms' Lullaby, Mohair, Cinnamon Color, 13 In.	225.00
Teddy Bear, On All Fours, Mohair, Glass Eyes, Wood Shavings Stuffing	300.00
Teddy Bear, On Iron Wheels, Steiff, 12 In.	400.00
Teddy Bear, On Wheels, Growls, Steiff, 30 X 20 In.	1250.00
Teddy Bear, On Wheels, Hump & Growler, Pull	475.00
Teddy Bear, On Wheels, Mohair, Glass Eyes, Leather Collar, 3 1/2 X 5 In.	165.00
Teddy Bear, On Wheels, Young Bear, Steiff, Tan, Growler, 10 1/2 X 16 In.	400.00
Teddy Bear, Pale Yellow Wool, Gold Muzzle, Glass Eyes, Jointed, 11 In.	180.00
Teddy Bear, Squeaker, C.1930, Cinnamon, 21 In.	225.00
Teddy Bear, Steiff, No Button, 10 In.	325.00
Teddy Bear, Steiff, 27 In.	395.00
Teddy Bear, Swivel Straw Hump, Short Arms, 2-Toned Gold & Brown	125.00
Teddy Bear, Tail Turns Head, Music Box, C.1940, Steiff, 16 In.	250.00
Teddy Bear, Teddy Bear, Mohair, Beige, Jointed, Steiff, 1903-1907, 15 In.	500.00
Teddy Bear, White Mohair, Body Is Velvet Pants, Nora Wellings, 9 1/2 In.	125.00
Teddy Bear, Yellow Mohair, Curved Arms, Jointed, 24 In.	250.00
Teddy Bear, Young Bear, On Wheels, Steiff, Mohair, 16 1/2 In.	350.00
Teddy Bear, Zotty Growler, Fully Jointed, Steiff, 15 In.	150.00
Teddy Bear, Zotty, Jointed With Button, Mohair, Steiff, 8 1/2 In.	150.00
Teddy Bear, 1980, Steiff	250.00
Teddy, The Boxing Bear, Battery, Boxed	130.00
Teddy, The Drummer, Battery Operated	25.00
Teeter-Totter, Children On Sides, Windup	48.00
Telephone, Metal, Mechanical, Rings	12.00
Telescope, Spaceship, Pilot, Star, Planet, Tin, 4 1/2 In.	20.00
Terrier, Black & White, Squeak	36.00
Their Only Child, Windup, From George McManus Comic Strip, Tin	450.00
Thermos, Barbie, Dated 1962	6.00
Threshing Machine, McCormick Deering, Arcade, Iron	350.00
Tiger, Steiff, 6 1/2 In.	1500.00
Tinker, Wooden, C.1915, Boxed	20.00
Tiny Teddy, Bear Plays Xylophone, Pull, Wooden, 6 X 7 In.	20.00
Toaster, Figural Face, Tin	50.00
Tom & Dick Railroad Handcar, Rubber Track, Japan	65.00
Tony The Tiger, Celluloid Head, Rubber Wheels, Tin, Marx, 6 In.	13.00
Tony The Tiger, Plush Covering, Celluloid Head, Tin, Windup, 8 In.	35.00
Tools, Young American, Display Box, Robinson & Co., Boxed	15.00
Toonerville Trolley	575.00
Tootsietoy, 53 Ford, Hi-Lift	25.00
Top Tap Man, With Wheelbarrow, Windup, Tin, Original Blue Label	475.00
Top, Germany	30.00
Top, Musical, Japan, Tin	5.00
Top, Spinning, Gyroscopic, Halo & Pivot, Brass Tipped, 3 3/4 In.	15.00
Top, Spinning, Snowflakes, Stars, Galaxy Pattern, 5 X 5 In.	10.00
Top, Wooden, Hyler Chocolate	4.00
Toy Shop, Figures, Accessories, Leaded & Stained Glass, C.1970, 23 In.	90.00
Tractor & Double Van Trailer, Consolidated Freightways, Friction	135.00
Tractor, Allis Chalmers, Auburn Rubber, 1946	35.00
Tractor, Allis Chalmers, Orange, White Rear Tires, Arcade, 5 In.	75.00
Tractor, Avery, Cast Iron	275.00
Tractor, Buddy L, Open Top, Original Paint, C.1920s, 15 In.	250.00
Tractor, Cat, Nickel Wheels, 3 In.	27.50
Tractor, Champion, Cast Iron	40.00
Tractor, Fordson, Arcade, Iron, 5 3/4 In.	80.00
Tractor, Hubley, Cast Iron	18.50
Tractor, Iron Wheels, Huber, Original Green Paint, Cast Iron, 5 In.	40.00

Tractor, Kingsbury, Cast Iron	165.00
Tractor, No Man, Fordson, Arcade, 6 In.	85.00
Tractor, Pulling Wagon, Arcade, Cast Iron	85.00
Tractor, Steam, Huber, Cast Iron	325.00
Tractor, Steam, With Flywheel, Weeden, 9 1/4 In.Long	105.00
Tractor, Windup, Rubber Wheels, Metal Man, Woodhaven Metal, 11 In.	85.00
Tractor, Windup, Tin, Rubber Track, Marx	40.00
Tractor, With Man, 1940s, Graham, Bradley, Rubber, 4 In.	22.00
Trailer, Freight Carrier, Buddy L	65.00
Trailer, Hauls Logs, Timber King, Strauss, 1920, 18 In.	137.00
Trailer, Linemar, Tin, Blue, 9 In.	22.50
Train Set, Batman & Robin	20.00
Train Set, Lionel, No.229, Engine & 3 Freight Cars, 1939	125.00
Train Set, The Mountain Climber, Marx, Tin, Windup, 4 1/4 In.	55.00
Train Set, 3 Cars, Tracks, Haffner, Metal	85.00
Train Set, 229 Engine, 3 Freight Cars, C.1939, Lionel	125.00
Train Station, Auburn Rubber	85.00
Train, Black, Steel, 4 Tin Cars, Brown, Red & Yellow, 32 In.	40.00
Train, Boxcar, McCoy, Standard Guage, Red, White, & Blue, Santa Monica	60.00
Train, Caboose, Tin, Marx	7.00
Train, Car, Lionel-Converse, Electric, Steel, Wood, Cast Iron	Illus 2000.00
Train, Coal Car, Tin, Marx	5.00
Train, Day Coach, Lionel, No.29, Painted Pressed Steel, Pair	Illus 650.00
Train, Engine, & Tender, Germany, Penny Toy, Tin, 5 1/2 In.Long	45.00
Train, Engine, & Tender, Lionel, 1970s, No.8141	25.00
Train, Engine, Air, Compressed, Flywheel, Nickel Plated, 5 3/8 In.	45.00
Train, Engine, Clockwork, 2-Speed, Track Trip, Tin, Marklin	Illus 1700.00
Train, Engine, Electric Fired, Empco, Nickel Plated Boiler, 8 In.Long	45.00
Train, Engine, Key Wind, Cast Iron, 7 In.	30.00
Train, Engine, Steam, Jensen, Style 76, Horizontal Dry Fuel Boiler	25.00
Train, Engine, Steam, Upright Boiler, Pressure Gauge, Whistle, 15 3/4 In.	125.00
Train, Engine, Traction, Spring Driven, Redstron, Marked	235.00
Train, Engine, Upright Engine No.1, Weeden, Brass, 9 1/2 In.	185.00
Train, Engine, 1 Cylinder Hot Air Uniflo, 2 Flywheels, 1930, 6 In.Long	75.00
Train, Hafner Overland Flyer, Sunshine Special	125.00
Train, Locomotive & Tender, Friction, Old Red & Green Paint, Metal	50.00
Train, Locomotive 3027, Marklin, HO Gauge, Heavy Goods, 2-10-0, Black	105.00
Train, Locomotive, Integral Tender, Steam, German, Brass	Illus 650.00
Train, Locomotive, Ives, Painted Cast Iron, Tin Roof	Illus 750.00
Train, Locomotive, Pulls-All, Black, Red, Tin, C.1820, Stenciling, 8 1/2 In.	110.00
Train, Locomotive, Sante Fe, Double Diesel, 1950s, Marx	35.00
Train, Locomotive, Silver Mountain, Engineer Bobs Head, Battery, 16 In.	25.00
Train, Locomotive, Sparkling, Marx, Boxed	50.00
Train, Locomotive, Tender, Lionel, Steel, Wood, Cast Iron	Illus 550.00
Train, Locomotive, Tender, Live Steam, Water Pump, Tin	Illus 3900.00
Train, Locomotive, Tender, 1902, Clockwork, Tin	Illus 775.00
Train, Locomotive, With Tender, Live Steam, Marklin	Illus 1100.00
Train, Mechanicraft Ltd., Variable Speed, Multicolored, Tin, 16 In.	45.00
Train, Mountain Climber, Sparkling, Oval, 3 In.	190.00
Train, N.Y.Central, Lionel, Standard Gauge, No.33	235.00
Train, Rapid Transit Open Streetcar, Lionel	Illus 800.00
Train, Slinky, Pulltoy, Boxed	14.00
Train, Steamweeden, 2 Cylinders, Tin Cars, Brass, Engine, 7 3/4 In., 3 Pc.	300.00
Train, Tootsietoy, Metal, 3 Piece	15.00
Train, Tower, Floodlight, American Flyer, Red, Gray, Silver, Green, 12 In.	28.00
Train, United Scale Models, HO Gauge, Saouhern Railway Pacific, 4-6-2	265.00
Train, Windup, Arnold, Tin	75.00
Train, Windup, Tracks, 3 Tin Cars, Boxed, Marx	25.00
Train, Zephyr, Tootsietoy	12.00
Train, 6-Car, Hornby	95.00
Trick Seal, Celluloid, Mechanical, Boxed, Japan	23.00
Trick Taxi, Marx, Box	40.00
Tricky Trike Clown Scooter, Tin	65.00
Tricycle, Bell Ringer, 1900, Cast Iron & Metal, 8 In.	475.00

(See Pages 724, 733, 736, 743)

Toy, Bear, Fur Covered Papier-Mache, Growls,
8 1/2 In.

Toy, Train, Car, Lionel-Converse, Electric, Steel,
Wood, Cast Iron

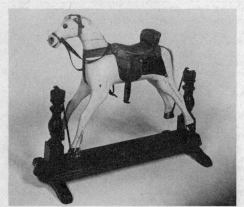

Toy, Hobbyhorse, Wooden, 19th Century

Toy, Noah's Ark, Carved, Painted People, Animals, 26 X 16 In.

Toy, Train, Day Coach, Lionel, No.29, Painted Pressed Steel, Pair

Toy, Train, Engine, Clockwork, 2-Speed,
Track Trip, Tin, Marklin

Toy, Train, Locomotive, Integral Tender,
Steam, German, Brass

Toy, Train, Locomotive, Ives,
Painted Cast Iron, Tin Roof

Toy, Train, Locomotive, Tender,
Lionel, Steel, Wood, Cast Iron

Toy, Train, Locomotive, Tender, Live Steam, Water Pump, Tin

Toy, Train, Locomotive, Tender, 1902,
Clockwork, Tin

(See Page 743)

Toy, Train, Locomotive, With Tend
Live Steam, Marklin

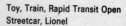

Toy, Train, Rapid Transit Open
Streetcar, Lionel

Trolley, Broadway, Chein, Windup	45.00
Trolley, Funny Andy, Street Railway No.622, Wooden Wheels, 13 In.	125.00
Trolley, Marked Broadway-270, Electrical Rod, Chein, 8 1/2 In.	65.00
Trolley, Open Air, Blue, Yellow, City Hall Park, Converse, 16 In.	185.00
Trolley, Tinkling, Battery, Boxed	75.00
Trolley, Toonerville, Painted, Cast Metal	250.00 To 365.00
Trolley, Toonerville, Windup, Tin	450.00
Truck, Army Transport, Buddy L, 19 In.	40.00
Truck, Army, Canvas Top, Hubley, 12 In.	28.00
Truck, Artic Ice Cream, 1925, Kilgore, Cast Iron, 6 1/2 In.	295.00
Truck, Auto Transport, Marx	65.00
Truck, Bell Telephone, Ladder, Hoist, & Shovel, Tag, Cast Iron	850.00
Truck, Borden's Milk, White Rubber Tires, Cast Iron	850.00
Truck, Buddy L, Dump, Child Steering, C.1930s, 22 In.	140.00
Truck, Cass, Rubber Tires, Metal Axle, Wooden Handle, 1930s, Boxed	95.00
Truck, Circus, Lion Jumps For Lion Tamer, Windup	350.00
Truck, Coal, Orange, Black Fenders, License Plates, Sturditoy, 25 In.	725.00
Truck, Coke, Metal Craft, Cast Iron, 11 In.	95.00
Truck, Concrete, Matchbox	10.00
Truck, Contractor's, Apple Green, Red Fenders, C.1915, Dayton, 11 In.	165.00
Truck, Crane, Electromagnetic Battery Operated, Marx, 1940s, 18 In.	60.00
Truck, Dairy, Lumar, 6 1/2 In.	22.50
Truck, Delivery, Blue & Gray Staked, C.1938, Buddy L, Steel, 22 In.	165.00
Truck, Dump, A-Frame, Rope Wench Hoist, Buddy L, Steel, 24 In.	125.00
Truck, Dump, Boycraft, 1929, 24 In.	95.00
Truck, Dump, Bump 'n Go, Tin, Japan	55.00
Truck, Dump, Chain Crank, Original Paint, Buddy L, Steel, 24 In.	135.00
Truck, Dump, Driver, Arcade, Cast Iron, 11 In.	375.00
Truck, Dump, Metal, Wynadotte, 1936, 14 In.	65.00
Truck, Dump, Roadster, Blue, Orange Bed, Red Roof, Schieble, 18 In.	135.00
Truck, Dump, Rubber Tires, 1940, Cast Iron, 7 1/4 In.	195.00
Truck, Dump, Snub Nosed, Wooden Tires, 16 X 6 In.	30.00
Truck, Dump, Steel Wheels, Rubber Tires, Steelcraft, 26 In.	150.00
Truck, Dump, Tootsietoy, 5 1/8 In.	18.00
Truck, Express, Spoke Wheels, Buddy L, Steel, 24 In.	185.00
Truck, Fire Pumper, White Rubber Tires, Red, 5 1/2 In.	50.00
Truck, Fire, Bells, Lights, Ladder, White Wall Tires, Structo, Metal	225.00
Truck, Fire, Extension Ladder, Rossomyne, Goodyear Tires, 28 In.	65.00

Truck, Fire, Friction, Tin & Cast Iron, 15 In. 595.00
Truck, Fire, Men Cast Into Sides, Balloon Tires, Arcade, 13 In. 395.00
Truck, Fire, Red, Ladder, Tootsietoy 10.00
Truck, Fire, Ride'm, Buddy L, Siren 225.00
Truck, Fire, 2 Ladders, Iron, Kenton, 11 1/2 In. 175.00
Truck, Fire, 3 Firemen, Sparks Fly Out, Tipp & Co., Tin, Windup, 8 In. 145.00
Truck, Gasoline, Champion, 1930, Cast Iron, 8 In. 275.00
Truck, Gasoline, Tank, Blue Paint, Iron, 5 1/8 In. 55.00
Truck, Giant Construction Co., Wyandotte, 18 1/2 In. 30.00
Truck, Heinz, Metalcraft 95.00
Truck, Ice, Metal, Wynadotte, 1930s, 11 In. 35.00
Truck, Jaeger Cement Mixer, Mechanical, Kenton, 1930, Cast Iron, 9 In. 650.00
Truck, Ladder, Driver, 3 Ladders, Red Paint, Tin, 19 1/2 In. 150.00
Truck, Ladder, Red, Orange Wheels, Friction Motor, Schieble, 20 In. 145.00
Truck, Ladder, White, Red & Green Trim, Ladder, Driver, Republic, 21 In. 75.00
Truck, Log, Die Cast, Hubley, Boxed, 19 In. 35.00
Truck, Mack Bulldog, Rack Body, 4 3/4 In. 65.00
Truck, Mack Ice, Arcade, 8 In. 295.00
Truck, Mack, Black & Red, Yellow Wheels, Marked Arcade, Iron, 5 In. 125.00
Truck, Milk, Universal Dairy, 1920, Wooden 125.00
Truck, Model T, Cab, Stake Body, Driver, Cast Iron, 9 In. 375.00
Truck, Model T, Stake Body, Arcade, 6 3/4 In. 125.00
Truck, Oil, Tootsietoy, 3 In. 10.00
Truck, Railway Express, Tootsietoy 75.00
Truck, Searchlight, Metal, Wynadotte, Battery Operated, 10 In. 65.00
Truck, Service, Inner City Delivery, Marx, 18 In. 15.00
Truck, Sinclair Gasoline, Green, Decals, Wyandotte, 18 In. 110.00
Truck, Sit-N-Ride, Buddy L 30.00
Truck, Tank, Buddy L, 1920s, Steel 625.00
Truck, Tank, Tootsietoy, 3 In. 5.00
Truck, Timber, Wood, Yellow & Black, Buddy L, Steel 145.00
Truck, Tipper, Matchbox 10.00
Truck, Towing, Pot Metal, 3 In. 7.50
Truck, Water, Tank Line, Brass Spigot, Pull Cord, Buddy L, Steel, 24 In. 625.00
Truck, Wrecker, With Crane, 1940, Cast Iron, 8 In. 150.00
Truck, 10-Wheeler, All American Toy Co., 19 X 7 X 8 In. 275.00
Trunk, Camelback 55.00
Trunk, Doll, Brass Banding, Wallpaper Interior, Tray, Tin, 10 X 6 1/2 In. 35.00
Trunk, Doll, Brass Handles, Hinges, & Lock, Humped, 12 X 5 In. 38.00
Trunk, Doll, Flat Top, Clasps & Lock, 5 1/2 X 9 3/4 X 4 In. 15.00
Trunk, Doll, Inside Tray, 16 X 9 X 7 In. 42.00
Trunk, Doll, Leather Handles, 3 Drawers, Original Labels, 11 X 6 1/2 In. 75.00
Trunk, Doll, Wallpaper Lined, Red Slat Top, Metal Banding, 12 X 7 In. 40.00
Trunk, Steamer, Doll's, C.1930, Labels, 8 X 14 In. 18.00
Tug Boat, Friction, Penny Toy, Yellow Paint, Japanning, Tin, 6 3/4 In.Long 70.00
Tumbling Monkey, Marx, Tin, Windup, 5 In. 40.00
Tunnel, Lincoln, Windup, Tin, Unique Art Co. 125.00
Tunnel, Tin, Litho, Farm Scene, Hills, Houses, Marx, 8 X 10 X 7 In. 20.00
Turkey, Strutting, Tin, Windup, 5 In. 60.00
Turtle, Windup, Tin 30.00
T V, Flash Gordon, Turning Knobs, 3 Boxed Films, Plastic, 2 X 3 In. 20.00
Typewriter, American Flyer, Boxed 45.00
Typewriter, Clown Trademark 4.00
Typewriter, Dial, Junior, Moving Carriage, Marx, 7 3/4 X 11 X 7 In. 35.00
Typewriter, Dial, Moving Carriage, Marx, 5 3/4 X 11 X 6 In. 35.00
Typewriter, Junior Dial, Marx, Metal 25.00
Typewriter, Marx Junior Dial 22.00
Typewriter, Simplex, Boxed .... 10.00 To 35.00
Typewriter, Simplex, 1907 .... 15.00
Typewriter, Tom Thumb, Boxed 15.00
Union Station, Marx, Boxed 95.00
Vacuum Cleaner, Painted Eagle, Tin, 1911 .... 65.00
Vehicle, Space, Tin Man, Sparking Action, Rubber Wheels, Tin, 8 1/2 In. 12.00

Wagon, Circus, Tiger Face Decal, Iron Driver, Dayton, 14 In. 95.00
Wagon, Doll, Go-Getter, Red, 15 In.Long 52.00
Wagon, Dump, 2-Horse, White Horse, Iron, C.1890, 16 In. 25.00
Wagon, Express, Drawn By Goat, Iron, 8 In. 120.00
Wagon, Farm Kenton, Iron, 14 1/2 In. 100.00
Wagon, Fire Hose, 2 Horses, Iron, 20 1/2 In. 135.00
Wagon, Hook & Ladder, Horses, Drivers, Ladders, Cast Iron, 16 1/2 In.Long 105.00
Wagon, Hook & Ladder, 3 Horses, Driver, Bucket, Cast Iron, 22 1/2 In.Long 150.00
Wagon, Hook & Ladder, 3 Horses, 2 Driver, Iron, 22 1/4 In. 90.00
Wagon, Hook & Ladder, 3 Horses, 2 Drivers, Ladders, Cast Iron, 21 In. 150.00
Wagon, Horse-Drawn, Borden Milk, Cast Iron 160.00
Wagon, Ice, Horse, Original Old Paint, 3 3/4 X 8 1/2 In. 95.00
Wagon, Kenton Bakery, Pulled By Horse, 1910, Cast Iron, 13 In. 450.00
Wagon, Ladder, Horse-Drawn, Cast Iron, 9 1/2 In. 75.00
Wagon, Ladder, 2 Horses, Driver, Iron, 19 1/2 In. 85.00
Wagon, Milk, Tin, Windup, Marx .... 85.00 To 95.00
Wagon, Milk, Toyland, Marx 85.00
Wagon, Sand & Gravel, Horse-Drawn, Driver, Cast Iron, 10 1/2 In. 75.00
Wagon, With Mouse, Bronze, 3 1/2 In. 20.00
Wagon, Wooden, 15 X 4 In. 7.00
Wagon, 2 Oxen, Back Driver, Original Paint, Iron, 15 3/4 In. 365.00
Walker, Harold Lloyd, Rolls Eyes, Marx 250.00
Warship, Sparkling, Tin, Windup, Marx, Boxed, 14 1/2 In. 125.00
Washboard, Daisy, 7 X 15 In. 15.00
Washboard, Zinc Scrubber, Daisey, 15 X 7 In. 24.00
Washer, Glass Tub, Marked C.G.Wood Co., Girard, Pa., 13 In. 35.00
Washing Machine, Maytag Wringer, Cast Iron 85.00
Washing Machine, Sunny Suzy, Hand Wringer, Metal, 9 X 7 In. 40.00
Washing Machine, Wringer, Maytag 195.00
Washtub & Board, Tin, 8 1/4 In 12.00
Washtub, Scrubboard, Tin, Red, 6 3/4 In. 25.00
Wheelbarrow, Homemade, Wood & Tin, U.S., 30 In. 45.00
Whistle, Jack Webb, Dragnet 5.00
Whistle, Squirrel Spins In Cage, French, Penny Toy 95.00
Whistle, Steam, Brass, Buckeye, 3-Tone, 8 In. 55.00
Whistle, Steam, Koweles Improved Whistle, Brass, 11 3/4 In. 55.00
Whistle, Steam, 1-Tone, Buckeye Brass Works, Dayton, Ohio, 12 1/2 In. 65.00
Whistle, Steam, 3-Tone, Crosby, Boston, Patent 1877, Brass, 9 In. 65.00
Whistle, With Dog, Spinning On Calliope, Penny Toy, Tin, 4 1/8 In.Long 60.00
Whoopee Car, Cowboy Drives Crazy Car, 1930s, Windup, Marx 195.00
Wild West Bucking Bronco, Windup, Lehmann, Patent 1903, Tin, 6 1/2 In. 200.00
Windmill, Cardboard, Wooden Wheels, Pull Toy, 11 X 15 In. 25.00
Windmill, Farm, Arcade, Cast Iron, 24 In. 125.00
Wonder Cyclist, Marx, 1920 .... 175.00 To 195.00
Wrecker, Arcade, Cast Iron, 4 In. 45.00
Wrecker, Buddy L, 21 In. 100.00
Wrecker, Graham, Tootsietoy 35.00
Wrecker, Scale Model, Rubber Tires, Richmond, Boxed, 12 In. 38.00
Wrecker, Workabel Winch, Red Paint, Iron, 6 3/4 In. 40.00
Wringer, Lovell Mfg. Co., Erie, Pa. 75.00
Zebra, Leather Ears, Windup, Made In China 25.00
Zebra, Steiff 75.00
Zeppelin, Hindenburg, Tippco, Germany 460.00
Zeppelin, Lehmann, 7 1/2 In. 250.00
Zeppelin, Los Angeles, Cast Iron, 11 In. 495.00
Zeppelin, Makes Noise, Moves In Circle, Whistle, E.C.Depose, France, 1900 .... 175.00
Zeppelin, Marx 95.00

Tramp art is a form of folk art made since the Civil War. It is
usually made from chip-carved cigar boxes.

TRAMP ART, Box, Hinged Lid, 12 1/2 X 9 1/2 X 7 1/2 In. 60.00
Box, Notched & Grooved, Leather, Hinge, C.1880, 6 X 9 In. 50.00
Box, Painted White & Brown Stain, 10 X 7 1/2 In. 8.50

Box, Pyramidal, Brass Nails, Leather Hinged Cover, 9 1/2 X 9 In. 55.00
Box, Terraced Pyramidal Layers, Hinged Cover, C.1880, 9 X 4 In. 50.00
Cupboard, Corner, C.1915, Lion, Fan, Design, 7 Ft. 2310.00
Dresser, Dollhouse Size 145.00
Frame, Crown Of Thorns 35.00
Frame, Picture, Double 57.50
Frame, 6 1/2 X 9 In. 35.00
Wall Pocket & Shelf 65.00
Washstick, Handcarved 25.00

TRAP, Bear, Newhouse, Kenwood Pans, No.5 .... 325.00
Bear, Newhouse, Kenwood Pans, No.50 .... 425.00
Bear, Yukon Territory, No.15, Teeth 315.00
Eel, Basket, Maryland Coast 95.00
Fly, Wooden Removable Base, Harper's Patent 2875, Balloon Flytrap 85.00
Mouse, Catch-Em-Alive, 1904 .... 48.50
Mouse, Delusion, 1876 .... 45.00
Mouse, McGill Metal, Illinois, Steel 15.00
Mouse, McGill, Round 4.50
Mouse, Wireware, Bail Handle, 6 X 6 X 11 In. 18.50
Rat, Sure Catch, Wooden 15.00

Trivets are now used to hold hot dishes. Most trivets of the late
nineteenth and early twentieth centuries were made to hold hot irons. Iron
or brass reproductions are being made of many of the old styles.

TRIVET, B & D, Lacy, 3-Footed, 4 X 6 In. 12.50
Basket, Fruit, & Flowers, Brass 35.00
Brass & Iron, 11 1/2 In. 195.00
Brass, Footed, 3 1/2 In. 8.00
Brass, Ornate, Iron Feet, Wood Handle 25.00
Child's, Cathedral, 5 7/8 In. 50.00
Child's, Divided Heart, Cathedral, Footed, Iron, 1 X 5 In. 40.00
Child's, Lacy, Iron, 2 1/8 X 3 In. 22.50
Child's, Oval & Double Pointed, Scroll Center, 2 X 3 In. 22.50
Child's, The Daisy, 17-Petaled Flower Center, Footed, 2 X 4 In. 35.00
Child's, 3-Sided Diamond, Oval, Lacy, Iron, 1 1/2 X 2 1/2 In. 30.00
Circles & Cutout, Paw-Footed, 6 In. 8.50
Circles & Diamond Stamped Out, 5 In. 18.50
Cleveland Foundry Co., 6-Pointed Star & Fan, 4 X 6 In. 22.50
Colebrookdale Iron Co., Order Of Cincinnati 55.00
Colebrookdale Iron Co., Pottstown, Pa. 40.00
Colebrookdale, 3-Footed, Iron, 4 X 6 In. 15.00
Concentric Heart Shaped, 3-Footed, Penny Feet 800.00
Double Point, I Want U Comfort, Strause Gas Co., Footed, 4 X 7 In. 30.00
Double Point, Lacy, 3-Footed, Iron, 2 X 5 In. 30.00
Economy, Syracuse, N.Y., Letter E, 3-Footed, 4 X 6 In. 16.50
Enterprise Mfg. Co., 2 Holes 10.00
Fleur-De-Lis Design, 2 1/2 X 6 1/2 In. 30.00
Fork Rest, Twisted Detail, Iron, 24 In. 25.00
Four Radiating Scrolls, 4-Footed, Loop End, Iron, 29 In. 120.00
George Washington, Cast Iron 105.00
God Bless Our Home, Horseshoe, Dated 1892 .... 55.00
Griswold, 8 In. 18.00
Heart & Hand, Interlocking Circle Handle, Brass 52.00
Heart Shaped, Notced Handle, 3 Legs, Iron, 18th Century 90.00
Heart, Cathedral, Iron, Loop Handle, 3-Footed, 3 X 8 In. 12.50
Heart, Peacock Feathered Interior, 3-Footed 22.50
Iron, Tin, & Asbestos 4.00
Lacy Heart, Iron, 3 3/4 In. 10.00
M In Circle, 4-Sided, 4-Footed, Iron, 3 1/2 In. 12.50
Maltese Crown, Footed, Cast Iron 12.00
Mickey Mouse 85.00

Ober, Chagrin Falls, Ohio, Embossed, Circles, Within Circles, 4 In. 25.00
Portland Stove Foundry, Pierced Maine Map, 9 1/2 X 7 1/2 In. 38.00
Railing On Sides, 4-Footed, Iron, 2 1/2 X 3 1/2 In. 25.00
Reversed Swastika, Indian Good Luck Sign, Iron, Footed, 4 X 4 In. 30.00
Sailing Galleon, Cutout, Turned Feet, Brass, 6 X 3 1/2 In. 18.50
Scalloped & Holed, Embossed S & Co., 6 1/8 In. 25.00
Scenic Design With Deers 95.00
Star, Stovepipe Lacy, Openwork Design, 6 5/8 In. 35.00
Swastika, Sadiron 8.00
Tree Of Life, Loop Handle, Iron, 4 1/2 X 10 In. 12.50
Uneedit Gas, Rosenbaum Factory, Scrolls, Figural Center, 4 X 7 In. 25.00
Urn, Cleveland Ferrosteel, Lacy Iron, 5 X 6 In. 22.50
Victorian, Christmas Tree, Brass, 4 X 8 In. 45.00
W Peerless, Double Pointed, Shield Center, Footed, 7 X 4 In. 25.00
W Royal, Iron 12.50
Wire, Footed, 7 X 9 In. 14.00
Wireware, Marked Acme Mfg. Co., Germany, Dark Gray, 13 X 5 In. 5.00
Witt, Nashville, Tenn., Openwork, 3-Footed, C.1912, 4 X 5 In. 30.00
6 Paws & 9 Hearts, Lacy, Iron, 5 1/4 In. 25.00
8 Arrows, 3-Footed, Iron, 5 1/4 X 5 1/4 In. 20.00

TRUNK, Child's, Embossed Leather, Stud Trim, Lock Dated 1877, 18 X 11 In. 80.00
Flame Stitch, Dome Top, Green, Red, Gold, Wallpaper Inside, 10 In. 950.00
Leather Covered, Brass Nailhead Design, Wallpaper Interior 85.00
Lift-Out Tray, England, Leather & Brass Mounted Camphorwood, 21 In. 275.00
Scene Of Ladies In Garden, Pigskin Covered, Chinese, 15 X 17 In. 150.00
Tudor, Painted Floral Patterns & Madonna, 1842 ....1100.00
Wrought-Iron Handles, 19th Century, Oak 225.00

*The Tuthill Cut Glass Company of Middletown, New York, worked
from 1902 to 1923.*

TUTHILL, Bowl, Hobstars, Sawtooth Scalloped Rim, Signed, 8 X 3 1/2 In. 150.00
Creamer, Flower Design, Hobstar Border, Marked 65.00
Nappy, Hobstars, Intaglio, Signed 85.00
Nappy, Scalloped, Hobs & Crosshatching, Signed, 7 In. 125.00
Sherbet Set, Draped Floral, Etched, Signed, 2 Piece 75.00
Tazza, Primrose, Turned-Down Rim 475.00
Tumbler, Rosemere, Signed 60.00

TYPEWRITER, Blickensderfer, No.5 .... 250.00
Blickensderfer, No.9 .... 200.00
Oliver, No.3 .... 45.00
Oliver, 1903 .... 25.00

UMBRELLA, Doll, Parasol, Etched Handle, Beige Silk, 18 In. 75.00
Doll, Parasol, Ivory Handle, Tassel Sheath, Black Silk, 13 In. 85.00
Doll, Parasol, Plaid, 10 In. 50.00
Evening, 200 Rhinestones, Curved Handle, Black 20.00
Handle, Gold-Filled, Mother-Of-Pearl, 11 In. 50.00
Parasol, Child's, Victorian 10.00
Parasol, Chinese, Bamboo & Paper, 1920 .... 30.00
Parasol, Victorian, Brass Tipped 25.00
Repousse Handle, Ritter & Sullivan, Baltimore, Silk 175.00

 *Union Porcelain Works was established at Greenpoint, New York, in
1848 by Charles Cartlidge. The company went through a series of
ownership changes and finally closed in the early 1900s.*

UNION PORCELAIN WORKS, Oyster Plate .... 70.00 To 95.00
Pitcher, Turquoise, Gold, 12 In. 225.00

Val St Lambert

Val St.Lambert Cristalleries of Belgium was founded by Messieurs Kemlin and Lelievre in 1825. The company is still in operation.

VAL ST.LAMBERT, Cup, 3 3/4 X 2 1/2 In.	25.00
Decanter, Cameo, Violets & Leaves, Frosted Ground, 9 1/2 In.	610.00
Plate, Crystal, Signed, 12 In.	45.00
Rose Bowl, Bats & Castles, Signed, Gray & Black, 6 In.	450.00
Vase, Bats & Castles, Pewter Collar, Signed, 6 In.	595.00
Vase, Cameo Glass, Polar Bear, Marked, 10 X 10 1/2 In.	1400.00
Vase, Cranberry Cut To Clear, 9 In.	135.00 To 150.00
VALENTINE, see Card, Valentine	

Vallerysthal

Vallerysthal Glassworks was founded in 1836 in Lorraine, France. In 1854 the firm became Klenglin et Cie. It made table and decorative glass, opaline, cameo, and art glass. The firm is still working.

VALLERYSTHAL, Eggcup, Chicken Pedestal, Signed	23.00
Jam Jar, Blue, Grapes, Marked, Covered	35.00
Plate, Thistle Pattern, Green, Signed, 6 In.	70.00

Van Briggle Pottery was made by Artus Van Briggle in Colorado Springs, Colorado, after 1901. Van Briggle had been a decorator at the Rookwood Pottery of Cincinnati, Ohio. He died in 1904. His wares were original and had modeled relief decorations with a soft, dull glaze. It is still being made.

VAN BRIGGLE, Ashtray, Deep Rose, Large	35.00
Ashtray, Hat, Blue-Green, Colorado Springs, 2 X 3 In.	20.00
Ashtray, Hopi Maiden	75.00
Ashtray, Mountains, Pikes Peak, Turquoise	70.00
Birdhouse, Blue, 2 X 3 In.	24.00
Bookend, Owl, Blue, 1920, Pair	80.00 To 100.00
Bookend, Peacock, Pair	90.00
Bookend, Polar Bear, Turquoise & Green, Pair	125.00
Bookend, Squirrel, 7 1/4 In., Pair	87.50
Bowl & Flower Frog, Molded Dragonflies, Matte, 2 1/2 In.	85.00
Bowl, Flower Frog, Frog Design, Blue, 8 In.	50.00
Bowl, Flowers, Raspberry, Raised Design, 3 1/2 In.	40.00
Bowl, Ming, 3 In.	35.00
Bowl, Persian Rose, Art Deco, 6 In.	25.00
Bowl, Pinecone, Shaded Blue & Cream Ground, 5 X 6 In.	50.00
Bowl, Shell, Turquoise, 12 In.	37.00
Bowl, Tobacco Brown, Marked, 6 In.	15.00
Bowl, Tulip, Frog, Turquoise, 6 In.	24.00
Bowl, Tulip, Turquoise, 8 In.	30.00
Candleholder, Brown, 4 In.	22.00
Candleholder, Dark Green, Marked & Dated 1914, 5 In., Pair	150.00
Candleholder, Persian Rose, Double, Signed & Dated, Pair	65.00
Candlestick, Blue, 9 In., Pair	35.00
Conch Shell, Persian Rose, 4 X 12 In.	45.00
Ewer, Red, 8 3/4 In.	24.00
Figurine, Dog, Turquoise	60.00
Figurine, Donkey, Turquoise	60.00
Figurine, Elephant, Turquoise	60.00
Figurine, Indian Girl Grinding Corn, White	85.00
Figurine, Rabbit, Ming, Turquoise	45.00
Figurine, Rabbit, 4 1/2 In.	40.00
Inkwell, Green & Tan, Covered, 3 1/2 X 2 1/2 In.	27.00

Lamp, Boudoir, Figurine Base, Paper Shade, 16 1/4 In., Pair	235.00
Lamp, Butterfly, Original Shade, Turquoise, 24 In.	135.00
Lamp, Grapes & Leaves, 12 In.	145.00
Lamp, Persian Rose, Draped Nude, 18 In.	250.00
Lamp, Swirl Base, Butterfly Shade, 1935 Era, Turquoise, 10 In.	260.00
Mug, Buff Clay, Unglazed, 4 3/4 In.	175.00
Night-Light, Owl, Blue	175.00
Paperweight, Hat Shaped	40.00
Paperweight, Indian, Persian Rose	65.00
Pitcher, Ming, VI Mark, 3 3/4 In.	90.00
Pitcher, Rose, 1930, 10 1/2 In.	20.00
Planter, Conch Shell, Maroon Glaze, 13 In.	65.00
Planter, Turquoise, Blue, Raised Floral, 1930, 5 X 4 In.	30.00
Plaque, Little Star, Indian, Red, 5 1/2 In.	85.00
Shade, Molded Borders, Custard Color Inside, Brown, 6 In.	225.00
Teapot, Persian Rose, Starfish Shaped, Reed Handled, Marked	90.00
Vase, Aqua, 4 In.	12.00
Vase, Bud, Purple	15.00
Vase, Butterfly, Martha Patton, 1922-29, 3 In.	90.00
Vase, Craig Brown, 4 1/2 In.	70.00
Vase, Deep Pink, Amethyst Striping, Marked, 5 In.	30.00
Vase, Dragonfly, Blue With Brown, 6 1/2 In.	225.00
Vase, Dragonfly, Persian Rose, 10 1/2 In.	48.00
Vase, Embossed, Blue Matte, 3 1/2 In.	20.00
Vase, Floral Relief, Red, C.1930, 5 In.	20.00
Vase, Floral, Turquoise & Blue, 7 1/2 In.	40.00
Vase, Floral, Turquoise, 5 3/4 In.	35.00
Vase, Flower Design, Persian Rose, 7 1/2 In.	69.00
Vase, Heart Shaped, Leaves Around Rim, Turquoise, 3 3/4 In.	120.00
Vase, Leaf, Maroon, 4 In.	37.00
Vase, Leaves & Stems, Aqua, Marked, 7 In.	40.00
Vase, Maroon, 1917, 7 1/2 In.	85.00
Vase, Ming Tree, Handled, 8 1/2 In.	50.00
Vase, Molded Tulips, Blue, Signed, 1920, 4 1/2 X 8 In.	75.00
Vase, Mostique, Hourglass Shaped, Marked, 10 In.	18.00
Vase, Persian Rose, Flowers & Ivys, 9 1/2 In.	70.00
Vase, Persian Rose, Stylized Flowers, 7 1/2 In.	69.00
Vase, Persian Rose, 1917, 6 In.	55.00
Vase, Persian Rose, 3-Faced Indian, 11 In.	125.00
Vase, Plum, Leaves, Marked, 4 1/2 In.	36.00
Vase, Reclining Nude On Side, Turquoise, 12 In.	175.00
Vase, Robin's Egg Blue, 1913, 9 In.	85.00
Vase, Rose, Turquoise, Raised Leaves, 8 In.	55.00
Vase, Tan & Green, C.1920, 4 In.	30.00
Vase, Tulip, Blue-Green, 3 1/2 In.	25.00
Vase, Turquoise, Bulbous, 6 In.	55.00
Vase, Turquoise, 5 1/2 In.	25.00
Vase, White Matte, Incised Band Of Leaves, Marked, 17 In.	300.00
Wall Pocket, Molded Flower, Turquoise	35.00
Wall Pocket, Mountain Craig	45.00
Wall Pocket, Turquoise	50.00

*Vasa Murrhina is the name of a glassware made by the Vasa Murrhina
Art Glass Company of Sandwich, Massachusetts, about 1884. The
glassware was transparent and was embedded with small pieces of colored
glass and metallic flakes. Some of the pieces were cased. The same type of
glass was made in England. Collectors often confuse Vasa Murrhina glass
with aventurine, spatter, or spangle glass. There is much confusion about
what actually was made by the Vasa Murrhina factory.*

VASA MURRHINA, see also Spangle Glass

VASA MURRHINA, Basket, Clear Ruffled Rim, Thorn Handle, Spangled, Small	65.00
Basket, Ruffled, Clear Twisted Thorn Handle, Green, 6 1/4 In.	145.00
Rose Bowl, Pink & White Splotches, Mica Flakes	82.00

Spooner, Leaf Mold, Cranberry Spatter 138.00
Syrup, Leaf Mold, Original Lid, Cranberry 165.00
Vase, Cased Ruffle Top, Gold Mica Flecking, 8 1/2 In., Pair 640.00
Vase, Crystal Applique On Sides, Mica Flakes, 9 3/8 In., Pair 225.00
Vase, Fan, Green With Blue 75.00
Vase, Jack-In-The-Pulpit, Oxblood Mottling, 8 1/8 In. 110.00
Vase, Melon Sectioned, Mica Flaking, Scalloped, 5 7/8 In. 85.00
Vase, No.6458, Autumn Orange, 4 In. 65.00
Vase, Peach, Silver Mica, 8 In. 65.00

*Vaseline glass is a greenish yellow glassware resembling petroleum jelly.
Some vaseline glass is still being made in old and new styles. Pressed
glass of the 1870s was often made of vaseline-colored glass. The old glass
was made with uranium, but the reproductions are being colored in a different
way. See Pressed Glass for more information about patterns that were also
made of vaseline-colored glass.*

VASELINE GLASS, Berry Set, Wreathed Shell, 4 Piece 85.00
Bonbon, Wreathed Shell .... 25.00 To 35.00
Bottle, Perfume, Swirl & Diamond, Cut Glass Stopper, 6 In. 45.00
Bowl, Ribbed Spiral, 7 In. 36.00
Butter Chip, Tree Of Life 25.00
Butter, Pressed Diamond, Covered .... 85.00 To 90.00
Butter, Wreathed Shell, Covered .... 110.00 To 155.00
Candlestick, Hexagonal Base, Top & Stem 6-Sided, 6 In., Pair 68.00
Canoe, Daisy & Button 45.00
Compote, Belmont 500 .... 160.00
Compote, Zipper, Egg Shaped 30.00
Creamer, Oaken Bucket .... 35.00 To 45.00
Creamer, Three Panel 35.00
Creamer, Wreathed Shell .... 65.00 To 135.00
Cruet, Daisy & Button 45.00
Cruet, Hobnail, Stopper 150.00
Dish, Candy, Center Post, Underside Florals, 5 In. 45.00
Figure, Danse De Luminere, Frosted, Nude, 8 1/4 In. 95.00
Goblet, Champagne, Daisy & Button 45.00
Jar, Jam, Thumbprint, Covered 48.00
Jar, Jam, Two Panel, Covered 75.00
Jar, Powder, Raised Flowers Around Center, Covered 40.00
Match Holder, Ribbed Hat 12.00
Mug, Dewey, Footed 50.00
Pitcher, Cranberry Striped, Handled, Wafer Foot, 3 5/8 In. 125.00
Plate, Cane, 4 1/4 In. 20.00
Plate, Chop, Twisted Optic, 13 1/2 In. 45.00
Plate, Twisted Optic, 7 In. 15.00
Plate, Twisted Optic, 8 1/2 In. 15.00
Spittoon, Lady's, Wreathed Shell 65.00
Spooner, Maple Leaf 30.00
Spooner, Pressed Diamond .... 38.00 To 45.00
Spooner, Wreathed Shell 45.00
Sugar & Creamer, Cherry Trim 31.50
Sugar, Medallion, Covered 55.00
Sugar, Oaken Bucket, Covered 65.00
Sugar, Petticoat, Covered 75.00
Sugar, Rope & Thumbprint, Covered 40.00
Sugar, Wreathed Shell, Covered 135.00
Syrup, Coin Dot, Hinged Tin Cover, 4 X 7 In. 95.00
Syrup, Inverted Thumbprint 35.00
Toothpick, Columbia 50.00
Toothpick, Gold Band 50.00
Top Hat, Daisy & Button 30.00
Tray, Condiment, Dewey 23.50
Tumbler, Diamond-Quilted 25.00
Tumbler, Finecut & Panel 38.00

Tumbler, Pressed Diamond	25.00
Vase, Fan, Cobalt Blue Ribbing	85.00
Vase, Jack-In-The-Pulpit, Diamond-Quilted, 7 1/8 In.	95.00
Vase, Jack-In-The-Pulpit, Opalescent, 8 In.	50.00
Water Set, Art Deco, Ice Lip, Opalescent Handle, 7 Piece	155.00
Wine, Paneled Jewel	55.00
Wine, Paneled Long Jewel	45.00

Venetian glass has been made near Venice, Italy, from the thirteenth to the twentieth century. Thin colored glass with applied decoration is favored, although many other types have been made.

VENETIAN GLASS, Bottle, Perfume, Gold Design & Portrait Medallion, 8 In.	300.00
Candlestick, Dolphin, Applied Gold Dust, 16 In., Pair	395.00
Decanter, Liqueur, Cranberry & Lace, 13 In.	125.00
Goblet, Champagne, Cranberry, Clear Dolphin Stem	40.00

Verlys

Verlys glass was made in France after 1931. It was made in the United States from 1935 to 1951. The glass is either blown or molded. The American glass is signed with a diamond-point-scratched name, but the French pieces are marked with a molded signature.

VERLYS, Ashtray, Lovebirds, Marked, 4 X 3 In.	45.00
Ashtray, Swallows, 4 1/2 X 3 1/2 In.	65.00
Bowl, Angelfish Swimming Amid Seaweed, Boat Shaped, 9 1/2 In.	110.00
Bowl, Birds & Honeybees, Opalescent, 11 1/2 In.	200.00
Bowl, Fish, Poisson, Opalescent, Lug Handle, 19 1/2 In.	349.00
Bowl, Goldfish, Tail Handle, Signed, 19 1/2 In.	349.00
Bowl, Hummingbirds & Fish, Satin Crystal, Marked, 13 In.	95.00
Bowl, Kingfisher Birds & Bees, Signed, 12 In.	140.00
Bowl, Orchid, 14 In.	127.50
Bowl, Pinecone, Sapphire Blue, Footed, Signed, 6 In.	95.00
Bowl, Pink, 1/2 Inch Ribbed Rim, 15 In.	145.00
Bowl, Thistle, Frosted, 8 1/2 In.	55.00
Bowl, Water Lilies, 13 In.	165.00
Dish, Classical Woman, Cupid, Deep Ruby, Oblong, 2 X 2 1/2 In.	55.00
Dish, Duck, Frosted Signature	55.00
Tray, Deco, Marked, 11 X 5 1/2 In.	65.00
Tray, Duck, Crystal	35.00
Vase, Fan, Dove, Crystal, 12 1/2 In.	225.00
Vase, Oriental Figure & Flowers, Frosted, Signed, 9 1/2 In.	285.00

VERNON KILNS, Bowl, Brown-Eyed Susan, 9 In.	8.00
Creamer, Modern California, Pistachio	7.00
Cup & Saucer, Modern California, Azure	7.00 To 8.50
Pitcher, Gingham, 1 Quart	10.00
Plate, Early California, Green, 10 1/2 In.	3.00
Plate, Hawaiian Coral, 10 In.	3.00
Plate, Hawaiian Flowers, 10 In.	10.00
Plate, Mayflower, 9 1/2 In.	3.50
Plate, State Scene, Augusta, Maine, 10 1/2 In.	12.00
Punch Bowl, Homespun, Cup Shaped	65.00
Salt & Pepper, Organdie	5.00
Saucer, Early California, Blue	2.00
Saucer, Gingham	3.00
Sugar, Organdie, Covered	5.00

Verre de soie glass was first made by Frederick Carder at the Steuben Glass Works from about 1905 to 1930. It is an iridescent glass of soft white or very, very pale green. The name means glass of silk, and it does resemble silk. Other factories have made verre de soie, and some of the English examples were made of different colors. Verre de soie is an art glass and is not related to the iridescent, pressed white Carnival glass mistakenly called by its name.

VERRE DE SOIE, see also Steuben

VERRE DE SOIE, Basket, Polished Pontil, Steuben, 10 1/2 In.	115.00
Berry Bowl, Underplate, Bowl, 4 3/4 X 2 1/2 In.	95.00
Bowl, Classic, 4 X 1 3/4 In.	65.00
Bowl, Crimped, 4 X 3 1/2 In.	60.00
Chandelier, Steuben	1250.00
Compote, Floral & Leaf Garlands, Hawkes, 7 X 5 In.	195.00
Compote, Ribbed, 6 X 2 1/4 In.	65.00
Ewer, Embedded Ivory On Beige, Enameled Florals, 8 In.	650.00
Saltshaker, Footed, 2 1/2 X 1 1/2 In.	42.00
Sherbet, Underplate	295.00
Vase, Ribbed, Scalloped Rim, 4 In.	45.00
Vase, Signed Cordey, 6 In.	90.00

Vienna Art plates were round metal serving trays produced around the turn of the century. The designs, copied from Royal Vienna porcelain plates, usually featured a portrait of a woman encircled by a wide, ornate border. Many were used as advertising or promotional items and were produced in Coshocton, Ohio, by J.F. Meeks Tuscarora Advertising Co. and H.D. Beach's Standard Advertising Co.

VIENNA ART, see also Coca-Cola

VIENNA ART, Plate, Anheuser-Busch, 1905	90.00
Plate, Barbee Whiskey, 1905	295.00
Plate, Coca-Cola, 1905	290.00
Plate, Dr.Pepper	165.00
Plate, Jamestown, Tin	45.00
Plate, Knights Of Columbus, 1905	100.00
Plate, Western Coca-Cola Bottling Co., Chicago, Ill.	105.00

VIENNA, see Beehive; Royal Vienna

The Villeroy & Boch Pottery of Mettlach, Germany, was founded in 1841. The firm made many types of pottery, including the famous Mettlach steins.

VILLEROY & BOCH, see also Mettlach

VILLEROY & BOCH, Bowl Set, White Ground, Blue Decor, Saxony Mark, 5, 6, 7, 8 In.	100.00
Cake Set, Napoleonic People, Square, 8 Piece	75.00
Eggcup & Saucer, Tulip	18.00
Pitcher, Geometric Pattern, Green, Rust, Cream, 8 In.	50.00
Plaque, Deers In Woodland, Blue, White, 12 In.	125.00
Plaque, Scenic, Delft Blue	65.00
Plate, Delft-Look, Signed, 10 1/2 In.	65.00
Platter, Blue Onion, Oval, 17 In.	100.00
Platter, Tulip, Covered	35.00
Sugar & Creamer, Wildlife Scene	22.50
Tureen, Underplate, Kaiser, Monuments, Marked, Finial, 15 In.	800.00
Vase, Front Figures, Pierced Handles, Gray, Marked, 10 In.	135.00
Vase, Raised Cathedral Design, Hexagon Shaped, 4 1/2 In.	40.00

VOLKMAR
Corona N.Y.

Volkmar pottery was made by Charles Volkmar of New York from 1879 to about 1911. He was associated with several firms, including the Volkmar Ceramic Company, Volkmar and Cory, and Charles Volkmar and Son.

VOLKMAR, Mug, Chrysanthemums, Brown Luster Ground, 7 1/4 In.	195.00
Pitcher, Green, Marked, 9 1/4 In.	165.00

Volkstadt was a soft-paste porcelain manufactory started in 1760 by Georg Heinrich Macheleid at Volkstadt, Thuringia. Volkstadt-Rudolstadt was a porcelain factory started at Volkstadt-Rudolstadt by Beyer and Bock in 1890.

VOLKSTADT, Bowl, Fruit, Five Cherubs Hold Bowl, Applied Fruit, 17 X 8 In. 550.00
  Figurine, Prometheus, Baroque Scroll Base, C.1880, 9 3/4 In. 175.00
  Figurine, 2 Ladies, Gold Dresses, Basket Of Flowers, 7 In. 145.00
    WALLACE NUTTING, see Print, Nutting

*Frederick Walrath was a potter who worked in Rochester, New York,
New York City, and at the Newcomb Pottery in New Orleans,
Louisiana. He died in 1920.*

WALRATH, Bowl, Seated Nude, Jug On Shoulder, Green, 10 1/2 In. 750.00
  WALT DISNEY, see Disneyana
  WALTER, see A. Walter

*Warwick china was made in Wheeling, West Virginia, in a pottery factory
working from 1887 to 1951.*

WARWICK, Bowl, Purple Flowers, Gold Ground, Footed, 8 In. 44.00
  Fernery, Deep Brown, Quince Berries & Foliage, Footed 55.00
  Gravy Boat, Currants & Leaves, Gold Trim 45.00
  Jar, Cracker, Beechnut, Brown Ground, Mark 85.00
  Mug, B.P.O.E., Elk, IOGA 9.00
  Mug, Monk Dressed In Red, IOGA .... 40.00 To 45.00
  Mug, Monk Smelling Flowers, Brown 45.00
  Pitcher, Floral, Cream Ground, 7 3/4 In. 35.00
  Pitcher, Portrait Of Old Man, Strumming Guitar, IOGA, 13 1/2 In. 225.00
  Platter, Dainty Blue Flower, Gold Scrolled Handles 10.00
  Tankard Set, B.P.O.E., Elks, Signed, 10 1/2 In., 1o Piece 385.00
  Tankard, Elk, IOGA, 15 In. 110.00
  Vase, Female Portrait, Gold Trim, IOGA, 22 In. 195.00
  Vase, Female Portrait, Handled, IOGA, Gold Trim, 11 In. 195.00
  Vase, Girl In Filmy Dress, 10 1/2 In. 145.00
  Vase, Gypsy Lady, Twig Handles, 10 In. 110.00
  Vase, Horn Of Plenty, 9 In. 45.00
  Vase, Hunting Dogs In Field, Marked, 12 In. 295.00
  Vase, Lady Of The Night, Twig Handles, IOGA, 10 In. 225.00
  Vase, Lady With Orchid In Hair, Twig Handles, IOGA 125.00
  Vase, Pillow, Portrait, Brown Ground, 9 In. 120.00
  Vase, Poppies, Brown & Cream, 12 In. 38.00

*Watch fobs were worn on watch chains. They were popular during Victorian
times and after.*

WATCH FOB, Adams Machinery, Man Mowing On Hillside 40.00
  Akron, Ohio, 1939 .... 12.50
  Allis Chalmers Caterpillar 10.00
  America Land Co. 25.00
  American Bantam Assoc., Embossed Bantam Chickens 30.00
  Anderson Tailors, Chicago 25.00
  Armour Meats 35.00
  Athletic Cut Clothes, J.Jolsech, Celluloid On Leather 37.50
  B.P.O.E. Elks 15.00
  Babe Ruth Scorekeeper .... 45.00 To 65.00
  Bank Of Ensley, Alabama, Embossed Bank, Brass 25.00
  Bar, 14K White & Yellow Gold Chain 200.00
  Battle-Ax Shoes, Richmond, Va., Embossed High Top Shoes 34.50
  Best Of Luck, Davis Bros., Clothing, Valdosta, Ga. 35.00
  Case Threshing Machine Co., Eagle On Globe, Strap 45.00
  Cat 60 .... 40.00
  Cedar Rapids, Ia. 10.00
  Chew Bulldog Twist, Red Dog On Celluloid 43.50
  Columbia Machine & Stopper Co., N.Y. & Philadelphia, Figural 27.50
  Columbian Fair, Keystone 25.00

Crossed Baseball Bats, Porcelain Baseball Between	27.50
Davy Crockett, Rubber, Mold	20.00
Dixon, Ill., Centennial, Lincoln On Front, Ford Tri Motor On Back	32.50
DuPont Envelope With Quail	25.00
E.C.Simmons Keen Kutter Cutlery, Enameled Shield, Obverse Name	54.50
Euclid Tractor, Figural Tractor, Brass	15.00
Excelsior Auto Cycle	75.00
Fairplay, Patriotic Figure Of Lady, Shield, Brass, 1 X 1 3/4 In.	10.00
Gibson Girl, Leather Back	22.50
Gold Mesh, 5 In.	12.00
Goodman Liquor Co., Ft.Worth, Texas	22.50
Granite City, Ill., Ruby Glass Hatchet	15.00
Great Seal Of New York, 14K Gold Plated Brass	25.00
Harold Lloyd, Dated 1950	15.00
Hire's, Brass	35.00
Hughes Tool Tri Cone Rock Bit	98.00
Huttig Satin Brand Mill Work, 2 Soldiers, Shield Obverse	28.50
Independent Stove Co., Iron Elephant	35.00
International Harvester Co., Embossed 2 Worlds & Cornstalks	60.00
J.J.Case Threshing Machines	35.00
John Deere, Embossed Brass Deer, Original Strap & Pearl Buckle	95.00
John Deere, Porcelain, Red, White, & Blue	90.00
K. Of C.	20.00
Kellogg Corn Flakes	20.00
Kellogg Telephone	70.00
Kraemer Pathfinder Compass, Cedarsburg, Wis., Indian Bust, Brass	43.50
Lady's Head, Tear From Eye, 13 Star Edge, Brass	30.00
Lion Buggy Co., Embossed Lion's Head, With Chain	85.00
Livestock Remedy Co., Hog, Sheep, & Rooster, Celluloid	58.50
Maryland State Fireman's Assn., 1931	25.00
Milwaukee Railroad, Bronze	10.00
Mohawk Trail, Relief Elk Standing On Rock, F.O.B., Copper	15.00
Monarch Insurance, Joseph Cannon	30.00
Monogrammed C.A.C., Gold Filled	35.00
Oklahoma Indian Territory Bankers Assn., 1907, Plated Brass	48.50
Order Of Railroad Conductors, Embossed Train, Redcap	45.00
Peerless Road Roller	20.00
Perkasie, Pa., 1929	15.00
Pointer Stoves & Ranges, Embossed Dog, Brass	43.50
Poll Parrott Shoes, Reverse, Star Brand Shoes, Celluloid	44.50
Post Toasties, Shaped Like Box	28.00
R.O.J., 1946, Billiken On Front	28.00
Revolving Locket, Lapis One Side, Carnelian On Other, 14K Gold	217.00
Rock Island, 70th Anniversary	25.00
San Francisco 1915, Panama-Pacific Exposition, Brass & Porcelain	45.00
Seal Of U.S.	16.00
Sharples Cream Separators	22.00
Smith Oil & Gas Separator, Tulsa, Okla., Plated Brass	34.50
Speier & Simon Clothiers, Lincoln, Nebr.	15.00
State Seal Of Illinois	22.00
Stitch In Time	12.00
Tacoma High School & Stadium	10.00
Texas Pharmaceutical Assn. Ft.Worth, 1910, Panther Pictured	22.50
Tractor, Fordson	60.00
W.S.Tyler Co., Cleveland, Ohio, Brass	40.00
Weather Bird Shoes	30.00
William H. Taft Campaign, Die-Cut Head Of Taft, Black Enamel	55.00
Winchester Envelope, Hunting Scene	20.00
Woven, 14K White Gold Chain, 3/4 Bar	125.00
Yellow Gold Filled Chain, 2 Blade Knife	30.00
WATCH, American Watch Co., Sterling Silver Hunting Case, 11J	195.00
American Watch Co., Waltham, Mass., Hairlined Dial, 15J	245.00
American Watch Co., Wm. Ellery, Fogg's Patent, 15J	115.00

Babe Ruth, Signed, Wristwatch 45.00
Ball, Engraved Back, Marked Case, 19 Jewel, Yellow Gold Filled 219.00
Ben J.Gaunt & Sons, Open Face, 7 Jewel, Silver Case, Key Wind 300.00
Benrus, Gold Numerals & Hands, 10K Gold Filled, 17 Jewel 65.00
Bulova, Gold Letters & Hands, 10K Gold Filled, Open Face, 17 Jewel 85.00
Bulova, Ring, C.1930, 15K White Gold 125.00
Bunn, Pocket, Santa Fe Special, Railroad 195.00
Bunn, Santa Fe Special, Railroad, Pocket 195.00
Bunn, 6 Position, 17 Jewel, Open Face, Coin Silver Case 175.00
Bunn, 6 Position, 21 Jewel, Gold Filled Case 175.00
Burlington Special, Pocket, Hunter Case, 19 Jewel 125.00
Burlington, Montgomery Dial, Yellow Gold Filled, 21 Jewel 139.00
Burlington, Pocket, 21 Jewel 100.00
C.H.Meylan, Pocket, 21 Jewel, Timer, 14K Yellow Gold 1200.00
Carrington Thomas, South Carolina, 18K Gold, Picture In Cover 1200.00
Chadwick, Simcoe, Ont., Screw-Back Case, 15J 135.00
E.Howard, Hinged Case, 15K Gold, Coles Escapement, 15 Jewel 1350.00
E.Howard, Hunter, Engraved Scene Inside, Dated 1890, 14K Gold 1500.00
Elgin, Arabic Dial, Gold Filled, 1900 .... 77.50
Elgin, B.W.Raymond, Double-Sunk Dial, 20 Year, 19 Jewel 225.00
Elgin, B.W.Raymond, 10K Gold Filled, 21 Jewel 175.00
Elgin, Father Time, Double Sunk, 21 Jewel, 20 Year, Open Face 200.00
Elgin, Father Time, Pocket, Up & Down Indicator, Yellow Gold Filled 900.00
Elgin, G.M.Wheeler, 25 Year, Hunting Case, 17 Jewel 110.00
Elgin, Gold Embossed Metal, 25 Year, Open Face, 17 Jewel 50.00
Elgin, Hunting Case, Fahys No.1, Roman Numbers, 7 Jewel, Fancy Hands 250.00
Elgin, Hunting Case, Porcelain Dial, Pocket, C.1907 .... 100.00
Elgin, Hunting, Case, Roman Numbers, 14K, 7 Jewel 375.00
Elgin, Lady's, Platinum Case, 32 Diamonds, 17 Jewel, Wristwatch 275.00
Elgin, Lady's, 14K Gold Case & Bracelet, 23 Jewel 475.00
Elgin, Pendant, Lady's, Hunting Case, 14K, 11 Jewel, Roman Numbers 475.00
Elgin, Pocket, Green Enamel Front & Back, Hunting Case 175.00
Elgin, Pocket, Hunting Case, Coin Silver, Arabic Numbers, 7 Jewel 95.00
Elgin, Pocket, Hunting Case, 7 Rose Cut Diamonds In Star & Crescent 150.00
Elgin, Pocket, Model 18s, Hunting Case, Coin Silver 135.00
Elgin, Pocket, 11 Jewel, Silverode Case, C.1908, Dial Double Sunk 40.00
Elgin, Pocket, 14K Gold Hunting Case, Porcelain Dial, C.1902 .... 300.00
Elgin, Railroad, Veritas 295.00
Elgin, Single-Sunk Dial, 1910, Gold Filled 82.50
Elgin, Stop, Black Face, White Hands, Open Face, 15 Jewel 175.00
Elgin, Wheeler Model, Pocket 59.00
English, T.Dent, Crest Hunting Case, Egg Shaped, 17 Jewel 535.00
Equity, Pocket, 15 Jewel, 20 Year Case, C.1908 .... 65.00
Excelsior, Pocket, Hunting Case, Gold Filled, C.1896 .... 65.00
F.Cumbert, Pendant, 20 Year, Hinged Cover, 11 Jewel 110.00
Girard, Peregerux, 10K Gold Filled, Award Watch 100.00
Gruen, Veri-Thin, 10K Gold Filled, 17 Jewel, Wristwatch 75.00
Haas Nevex, Art Deco, Onyx & Diamonds, C.1925 .... *Illus* 1600.00
Hamden Dueber, Pocket, No.307, 14K White Gold Case 200.00
Hamilton, Lady's, 8 Diamonds, 14K White Gold, Steel Band, Wristwatch 85.00
Hamilton, No.22, Chronometer, Box & Gimbals 450.00
Hamilton, No.910, Swing-Out Case, 20 Year, 17 Jewel 95.00
Hamilton, No.917, 14K Gold, 1935 Chevrolet Award, 17 Jewel 275.00
Hamilton, No.934, Pocket, 17 Jewel 140.00
Hamilton, No.940, Swing-Out Case, 25 Year, 21 Jewel 175.00
Hamilton, No.944, Open Face, Yellow Gold Filled, 19 Jewel 200.00
Hamilton, No.950b, 23 Jewel 400.00
Hamilton, No.974, Gold Filled Face, 17 Jewel .... 100.00 To 150.00
Hamilton, No.992, Pocket, 21 Jewel, Case .... 100.00 To 120.00
Hamilton, No.4992, White Dial, Sweep Second Hand, Nickel, 22 Jewel 750.00
Hamilton, No.9928, Gold Filled, 1920s 125.00
Hamilton, Pocket, Bar Bow, No.992E, Railroad 190.00
Hamilton, Pocket, Gold Filled, 17 Jewel, C.1901 .... 100.00
Hamilton, Pocket, No.946, Railroad 375.00

Hamilton, Pocket, 21 Jewel, C.1905 .... 125.00
Hamilton, Presentation, Open Face, 14K, 1935 100 Car Club Chevy 275.00
Hamilton, Radium Dial, Rectangular, 14K Gold Filled, Wristwatch 100.00
Hamilton, Railroad, No.992-B, 21 Jewel .... 200.00 To 225.00
Hampden, Hancock Model, 21 Jewel 110.00
Hampden, Lady's, Closed Case, 15 Jewel, Design On Case, Wristwatch 185.00
Hampden, Pocket, Hunting Case, Porcelain Dial, 17K Gold 175.00
Hampden, Pocket, John Dueber Special, 17 Jewel .... 79.00 To 95.00
Hampden, Railroad, No.104, 23 Jewel 295.00
Helbros, Railroad, Embossed Diesel, Open Face, 17 Jewel 55.00
Howard, Swing-Out Case, Montgomery Dial, 19 Jewel 295.00
Howard, Swing-Out Case, 14K Gold, 17 Jewel 375.00
Hyde Pack, Pocket, 17 Jewel, Open Face, Gold Case 95.00
Illinois, Bunn Special, Bunn Case, Metal Dial, 21 Jewel 140.00
Illinois, Bunn Special, 20 Year, Double Roller, 24 Jewel 850.00
Illinois, Bunn Special, 24 Rubies, Open Face, 24 Jewel 695.00
Illinois, Currier, Transition Movement, 11 Jewel 225.00
Illinois, Elite, Luminous Metal Dial, 10 Year, 19 Jewel 90.00
Illinois, Federal, 14K Gold Filled, 17 Jewel 125.00
Illinois, Gold Letters & Hands, 18K Gold Filled, 21 Jewel 175.00
Illinois, Hunting Case, Fahys No.1, Negley Watch Co., 15 Jewel 275.00
Illinois, Hunting Case, M.J.Pekor Co., 7 Jewel, Roman Numbers 175.00
Illinois, Negley, Extra, Chicago, 15 Jewel 350.00
Illinois, Nickeloid Case, Locomotive On Base, 17 Jewel 95.00
Illinois, Plymouth, Marked, 15 Jewel 85.00
Illinois, Pocket, Art Deco, Enameled, 18K Gold, 21 Jewel 600.00
Illinois, Sangamo Special, 19 Jewel .... 500.00 To 550.00
Illinois, Sangamo, 23 Jewel, Yellow Gold Filled 325.00
Ingersoll, Yankee, Radiolite 35.00
John Stevenson, Pittsburgh, Pa., Jeweled, 19th Century, 1 5/8 In. 95.00
Jules Jurgenson, 14K White Gold, Diamonds, Lid, Wristwatch 2995.00
Keystone, Silver Plated Hinged Cover, Dustproof, 15 Jewel 285.00
Knickerbocker, Blue Numbers & Locomotive, Steel Case, Train On Back 175.00
LaCloche, Lady's, 14K Yellow Gold, 17 Jewel, Wristwatch 277.00
Li'l Abner, Animated Flag, 1951, Wristwatch .... 95.00 To 175.00
Ligne, Open Face, Monogrammed, Plain Polished Case, 18K, 18 Jewel 815.00
Longines, Lady's, Framed In Diamonds, 15K Gold, Wristwatch 2500.00
Longines, Presentation Chronometer, Wood Case, Dial 3 In. 600.00
Manistee, Pocket, Gold Filled Hunting Case 265.00
Merano, Lady's, 30 Diamonds & Rubies Trim, 14K Gold .... *Illus* 500.00
Molde, Pocket, Hunting Case, Blue Enameling, Pinset, C.1883 .... 100.00
Movado, Lady's, 37 Diamonds, 18K Gold Band, Wristwatch 1200.00
Movado, Repeater, Hunter Case, Lever Set, Porcelain Dial, 38 Jewel 7000.00
National Watch Co., W.H.Ferry, Silver Hunting Case, 15 Jewel 160.00
Non-Magnetic Watch Co., Yellow Gold Filled, Nickel 150.00
Omega, Lady's, Geometric Face, 14K Gold On Sterling .... *Illus* 450.00
Omega, Model 7576160, Beige & Gold Hands & Numerals, Open Face 225.00
Patek Philippe, Lady's, 15K Yellow Gold, 18 Jewel, Wristwatch 1200.00
Pocket, Bunn Railroad, 24 Jewel 595.00
Pocket, Bunn Special Railroad, Bunn Case 225.00
Rockford, Dial With Red Outer Track, 2-Tone Movement, 15 Jewel 172.00
Rockford, Hunting Case, Engine Turned With Plain Shield, 15 Jewel 225.00
Rockford, 24 Jewel, Gold Filled, J.Boss Case 1200.00
Rodania, Lady's, 17 Jewel, 18K Gold, 15K Gold Strap, Wristwatch 900.00
Rolex, Explorer Chronometer, Black Face, Wristwatch 200.00
Rolex, Oyster, Perpetual Date, Man's, 18K Gold, Wristwatch 4200.00
Rolex, Oyster, Sterling Silver Band, Wristwatch 200.00
Roosevelt, Animated Helmsmen, Key Wind 135.00
Seth Thomas, Open Face, 10K Gold, 15 Jewel 110.00
South Bend, No.219, Pocket, 19 Jewel 90.00
South Bend, No.227, 20 Year, Open Face, 21 Jewel 175.00
Swiss, Gigandel For Blind, Braille, Hunting Case, Nickel, 17 Jewel 85.00
Swiss, Hebrew Symbols For Numbers, Pocket 125.00
Vacheron Constantin, 18K Gold, Pocket 475.00

Waltham, Appleton Tracy, 14K Gold, Open Face, 15 Jewel	750.00
Waltham, Cavalier, 20 Year Gold Case, 1 In.Diam.	95.00
Waltham, Colonial Premier, 14K White Gold, Open Face, 21 Jewel	225.00
Waltham, Deuber Special, Hunting Case, 7 Jewel	175.00
Waltham, Hunting Case, Porcelain Dial, 14K Gold, Pocket	275.00
Waltham, Lady's, Hunting Case, Enamel Dial, 14K Gold, Signed	275.00
Waltham, Maximus, Hunting, 21 Jewel, Yellow Gold Filled	400.00
Waltham, Maximus, 21 Jewel, Yellow Gold Filled	225.00
Waltham, No.1884, 5-Minute Repeater, Yellow Gold Hunting Case	3500.00
Waltham, P.S.Bartlett, 25 Year, Open Face, 17 Jewel	195.00
Waltham, Premier, 21 Jewel, Pocket	85.00
Waltham, Vanguard, Up & Down, Lossier Hairspring, White Gold	385.00
Waltham, Vanguard, 23 Jewel	165.00
Westclox, Pocket, Ben, Nickel	35.00

*Waterford-type glass resembles the famous glass made in the Waterford
Glass Works in Ireland. It is a clear glass that was often cut for
decoration. Modern glass is still being made in Waterford, Ireland.*

WATERFORD, Cordial, Applied Blown Handle	15.00
Decanter, Handled	400.00
Decanter, Triple Neck Ring, C.1810, Pint	140.00
Lamp, Gone With The Wind Type, 14 1/2 In.	350.00
Mustard, Covered, Signed	45.00
Salt & Pepper, Alana	90.00
Sherbet, Kylemore	20.00

*Wave Crest glass is a white glassware manufactured by the Pairpoint
Manufacturing Company of New Bedford, Massachusetts, and some French
factories. It was then decorated by the C.F.Monroe Company of
Meriden, Connecticut. The glass was painted in pastel colors and decorated
with flowers. The name Wave Crest was used after 1898.*

WAVE CREST, Basket, Candy, Blue Ground, Floral Panels, Marked, 5 In.	400.00
Biscuit Jar, Barrel Shaped, Pink To Rose Flowers, 9 In.	265.00
Biscuit Jar, Blown-Out Dogwood Sprays, Brass Collar, Lid, 11 In.	225.00
Biscuit Jar, Brown & Blue Florals, Beige, 11 In.	295.00
Biscuit Jar, Egg Crate, Silver Plated Bail & Cover, 10 In.	300.00
Biscuit Jar, Embossed, Square, Signed, CFM, 10 In.	325.00
Biscuit Jar, Floral Design, Puffy, Beading, 9 1/4 In.	325.00
Biscuit Jar, Floral, Signed Cover, C.F.Monroe, Blue, 10 1/2 In.	280.00
Biscuit Jar, Pink Flowers, Silver Over Brass Top, Marked, 8 In.	290.00
Biscuit Jar, Puffy, Egg Crate, Brass Rim, Marked, 8 In.	240.00
Biscuit Jar, Silver Over Brass, Puffy, Marked, 8 In.	260.00
Biscuit Jar, White To Yellow, Floral, Covered Marked, 10 In.	375.00
Bottle, Perfume, Diamond Shaped	110.00
Bowl, Dresser, Russet, 5 1/2 In.	145.00
Bowl, Dresser, Swirl, Lavender, 4 In.	150.00
Bowl, Pin, Open, Red, Yellow, Flowers, Pink Lining, Marked	90.00
Box, Banner Mark, 7 In.	550.00
Box, Baroque Shell, Pink Flowers, Blue Cartouche, 7 X 3 In.	525.00
Box, Blue & Coral Flowers, Marked, 7 In.	569.00
Box, Blue Ground, Orange Flowers, Round, Marked, 7 In.	650.00
Box, Cigar, Pink, White, Cigars Written In Gold, 6 In.	449.00
Box, Clover, Satin Lining, Hinged, Signed, 6 3/4 X 4 In.	750.00
Box, Corner Medallions, Lavender Lines, Footed, 5 X 7 In.	625.00
Box, Dancing Swans On Cover, 7 X 4 In.	790.00
Box, Dark Blue, White Floral, Silk Lining, 7 In.	525.00
Box, Dresser, Baroque Shell, Lined, Signed, 7 1/2 In.	625.00
Box, Dresser, Scenic, Mountains, Signed, 4 In.	250.00
Box, Egg Crate Shaped, Enameled, Footed, Signed, 5 1/4 X 6 In.	425.00
Box, Egg Crate, Brass Mountings, Florals, Hinged, 5 1/2 X 6 In.	400.00
Box, Embossed Shell, Covered, Banner Mark, 2 3/4 X 3 1/4 In.	225.00
Box, Enameled Flowers, Cherubs, Hinged Cover, 8 X 4 In.	575.00

Wave Crest, Boxes, Enameled Mums; Enameled Roses

Box, Enameled Flowers, Hinged Cover, Signed, 8 X 5 1/2 In.	300.00
Box, Enameled Mums .... *Illus*	225.00
Box, Enameled Roses .... *Illus*	225.00
Box, Floral, Blue & White, Marked, 4 X 4 In.	275.00
Box, Florals & Gold Dots, Ivory, 7 In.	595.00
Box, Flowers, Cream, 4 1/2 In.	175.00
Box, Flowers, Embossed Swirls Allover, Banner Mark, 7 1/4 In.	545.00
Box, Flowers, Hinged, Square, 5 X 8 In.	300.00
Box, Flowers, Pink, Lid Embossed, Marked, Round, 7 In.	460.00
Box, Flowers, Pink, Swirl, 5 1/2 In.	245.00
Box, Flowers, White & Blue, Covered, 3 X 3 In.	165.00
Box, Handkerchief, Helmschmeid Swirl, 5 X 6 In.	650.00
Box, Handkerchief, Shasta Daisies, Pink Ground, Signed, 5 X 6 In.	395.00
Box, Jewel, Large Flowers, Scroll Embossing, Signed, 5 1/2 In.	325.00
Box, Jewel, Puffy, Hinged Lid, White Beading, Lined, 7 X 7 In.	425.00
Box, Jewel, Shell, Enameled Floral, Lid, Banner Mark	225.00
Box, Jewel, Swirl Mold, White Beading, Hinged Lid, 7 X 4 In.	375.00
Box, Jewel, Swirl, Ormolu Collar, 3 In.	135.00
Box, Little Girl On Top, Hinged, Marked	275.00
Box, Pin, Daisies, Blue, Hinged	150.00
Box, Pin, Ormolu Rim, Signed, Oval, 4 X 3 In.	140.00
Box, Pin, Ormolu Rim, Signed, 4 X 3 1/4 X 1 1/2 In.	140.00
Box, Pin, Violets, 3 In.Square	145.00
Box, Powder, Daisies, Swirl, Covered, 5 1/4 In.	175.00
Box, Powder, Red Banner Mark, 3 In.	200.00
Box, Raised Enameled Forget-Me-Nots, 7 X 7 X 7 In.	750.00
Box, Shades Of Pink To Blue, Swirled, Marked, 5 X 3 In.	350.00
Box, Swirl, Enameled Flowers, 7 1/2 X 6 1/2 In.	375.00
Box, Swirl, Light Gray, Lily Of The Valley, 2 X 5 In.	85.00
Box, Trinket, Brass Rim, Floral Design, 4 In.	75.00
Box, White Spray, White Ormolu Rim, Hinged, Cover, 3 X 2 In.	200.00
Cookie Jar, Floral, Silver Handle, 9 In.	195.00
Cracker Jar, Embossed Rococo, Black, Green, Marked	400.00
Cracker Jar, Floral, Baroque Scrolls, Pink, Marked	165.00
Cracker Jar, Floral, Beige, Brown, & Blue, Signed	325.00
Cracker Jar, Floral, Blue, Marked, 1/ 1/2 In.	279.00
Cracker Jar, Floral, Cream To Yellow Ground, Covered	145.00
Cracker Jar, Light Blue	265.00
Cracker Jar, Ovoid Shape, Silver Plated Rim, Covered, Floral	150.00
Cracker Jar, Puffy Egg Crate, Florals, Blue & Brown	275.00
Creamer, Enameled Flowers, Raised Ribs, Scrolls, Handled	95.00
Dish, Brass Rim, Flowers, Raised Scrolls, Marked, 3 In.	75.00
Dish, Dresser, Enameled, Embossed, Handled, Oval, Signed, 4 X 3 In.	110.00
Dish, Pin, Brass Collar, Silver Handles, Signed, 4 In.	98.00
Dish, Pin, Ormolu Rim & Handles, Open, 4 1/2 X 2 In.	105.00
Fernery, Square, Brass Insert, Red Mark, 7 In.	225.00
Fernery, Yellow, Beige, & Brown Floral Design, White Ground, 8 In.	200.00
Holder, Card, Red Banner Mark, 4 1/2 X 2 1/2 In.	290.00

Holder, Pin, Brass Collar, Floral Design, Signed 95.00
Holder, Whiskbroom, Marked 575.00
Jar, Powder, Hinged, Swirl, Signed 250.00
Jar, Vanity, Swirl Pattern, Silver Plate, Cover, Pair 50.00
Jewel, Ormolu, Floral, Gold Dust, 6 1/2 X 6 In. 350.00
Lamp, Oil, Base, Rook & Flint Chimney, Lemon & White, 6 1/2 In. 350.00
Paperweight 375.00
Salt, Pink, Helmschmeid 125.00
Saltshaker, Enameled Flowers 75.00
Sugar & Creamer, Blue, White, Pink Flowers, Silver, Swirl 325.00
Sugar & Creamer, Helm Swirl, Blue, White Cast, Pink Flowers 325.00
Tray, Bonbon, Ribbed Corners, 4 Medallions, Red Banner Mark, Blue 165.00
Tray, Open, Brass Rim, Handled, Pink Banner Mark, 6 In.Square 225.00
Tray, Pin, Blue Flowers, Footed, 4 X 2 1/2 In. 135.00
Tray, Pin, Double Shell, Embossed Rococo, Banner Mark, 3 In. 139.00
Tray, Pin, Silver Handles, Signed 90.00
Tray, Trinket, Helmschmeid Swirl, Original Lining 145.00
Tray, Trinket, Open, Pink Banner, Hand-Painted, 3 In. 80.00
Vase, Blue Ground, Floral Design, Marked, 9 1/2 In. 550.00
Vase, Green, Portraits, 12 In. 250.00
Vase, Olive Green Ground, White Shells, Covered, Marked, 14 In. 595.00
Vase, Pink & White, Beading, Pair 350.00
Vase, Urn Shaped, Floral Design, Brass Footed, Ormolu, 11 In., Pair 225.00
     WEAPON, see Gun; Sword

WEATHER VANE, Cow, Arrow, 22 In. 65.00
Deer, Jumping, Full Body, Iron Head, Copper Body, 28 X 24 In. 750.00
Dog, Hunting, Nose & Tail Extended, Copper, 23 X 31 In. 520.00
Eagle, American, Standing, Copper Ball, Brass Arrow 400.00
Eagle, Spread, C.1870, Iron, Mounted On Ball, 32 In .... 300.00 To 900.00
Fish, Wooden, Salmon & White, 20 In. 95.00
Fox Running, Wooden, Old Red Paint 1000.00
Horse, Black, Sheet Copper, Lacy Iron Arrow, C.1890 .... 160.00
Horse, Copper, Lacy Iron Arrow, Black, 24 X 10 1/2 In. 145.00
Horse, Full Bodied, Trotting, Copper, 23 X 37 In. 425.00
Horse, Harris & Co., Cast Zinc Head, 27 1/2 In. .... *Illus* 700.00
Horse, Mounted On Arrow, Tin, 10 1/2 In. 80.00
Horse, Sheet Iron, 25 X 22 In. 395.00
Indian, Sheet Metal, Red, Black, & White 140.00
Locomotive, Cast Iron 200.00
Pig, Attached Lightning Rod 110.00
Rooster, Full Bodied, Metal 650.00
Rooster, Full Bodied, Plumed Tail, Copper, 26 X 27 In. 412.00
Rooster, Gold Painted Copper, 54 In. 250.00
Rooster, Sheet Iron, 19th Century 595.00
Rooster, Wooden, Red, Black, & White Paint 1045.00
Trotting Horse, Directionals, C.1860, 31 X 15 In. .... *Illus* 675.00

Weather Vane, Horse, Harris & Co., Cast
Zinc Head, 27 1/2 In.

Weather Vane, Trotting Horse,
Directionals, C.1860, 31 X 15 In.

Webb glass was made by Thomas Webb & Sons of Stourbridge, England. Many types of art and cameo glass were made by them during the Victorian era. The factory is still producing glass.

WEBB BURMESE, Lamp, Fairy, Ruffled Base, Clarke Insert, Marked, 5 5/8 In. 650.00
Lamp, Fairy, Ruffled Pedestal Base, Cup, 11 5/6 In. 2000.00
Lamp, Fairy, Tapestry Pottery Base, Paneled, Marked, 6 1/4 In. 750.00
Rose Bowl, 8 Crimp, Salmon Pink, 5 Petal Flowers, 2 3/4 In. 365.00
Toothpick, Acorns & Oak Leaves, 2 3/4 In. 325.00
Vase, Egg Shape, Yellow Feet, 2 1/2 X 3 1/2 In. 265.00
Vase, Flower Petal-Shaped, 3 1/2 X 3 In. 225.00
Vase, Folded-Over Star Shaped Top, Signed, 3 1/2 In. 225.00
Vase, Gourd Shaped, Signed, 11 3/4 In. 1050.00
Vase, Leaves & Berries, Squashed-In Front, Salmon, 3 1/4 In. 335.00
Vase, Leaves & Red Berries, Salmon Pink, Signed, 4 1/4 In. 395.00
Vase, Petal Top, Squatty, Leaves & Berries, Signed, 2 7/8 In. 425.00
Vase, Pinecones & Needles, Signed, 3 3/4 In. 450.00
Vase, Red Berries, Signed, 3 3/4 In. 450.00
Vase, Ruffled, Pedestal Foot, 3 X 4 1/4 In. 225.00
Vase, 5-Petal Flower Design, Yellow Handles, Signed, 5 In. 750.00

WEBB PEACHBLOW, Bottle, Scent, Enameled Florals, Sterling Silver Dome, 4 In. 750.00
Bottle, Scent, Gold Prunus & Butterfly Design, 4 3/4 In. 495.00
Bowl, Finger, Tricornered, Scalloped Top, 3 1/4 In. 195.00
Bowl, Gold Prunus Design, Cream Lining, 3 7/8 X 2 1/2 In. 395.00
Cup, Punch 175.00
Jar, Gold Prunus, Branches, Cream Lining, Covered, 4 1/2 In. 650.00
Jar, Sweetmeat, Prunus, Silver Plated Top, Handle, 4 5/8 In. 495.00
Lamp, Fairy, Pottery Base Marked Clarke, 4 X 5 In. 495.00
Vase, Egg Shaped, White Lining, 12 In. 150.00
Vase, Enameled, Signed, 14 In., Pair 1400.00
Vase, Gold & Silver Bird, Flowers, Marked, 9 3/4 In. 695.00
Vase, Gold Daisies, Dragonfly, Cream Lining, 6 7/8 In. 695.00
Vase, Gold Flowers & 2 Dragonflies, Gold Handles, 7 1/2 In. 395.00
Vase, Gold Flowers With Bee, Propeller Mark, 6 1/2 In. 450.00
Vase, Gold Prunus Design, Butterfly & Bee, 7 3/4 In., Pair 1250.00
Vase, Gold Prunus, Off-White Lining, 4 1/4 X 11 3/4 In. 995.00
Vase, Rigaree Neck, Berries & Loop Feet, 5 3/4 In. 525.00

WEBB, Bottle, Perfume, Blue Satin, Ball Shaped Body, White Leaves, 3 In. 875.00
Bottle, Perfume, Cameo, Red Ground, Flower, Sterling Top, 7 1/4 In. 1500.00
Bottle, Perfume, Flowers & Leaves, 3-Color, Frosted Beige, 5 In. 2750.00
Bottle, Perfume, Leaves & Flowers, Butterfly On Back, Amber, 4 In. 1400.00
Bottle, Perfume, White Flowers, Blue Ground, Lay Down, 4 In. 645.00
Bowl, Finger, Blue Diamond-Quilted, Cream Lining, Crimp Top, 9 In. 195.00
Bowl, Finger, Deep Gold, Ruffled, Cream Lining, 2 7/8 In. 125.00
Bowl, Flowers & Butterflies, Pearlized Underside, Salmon, Signed 490.00
Bowl, Prunus Blossoms, Butterfly On Back, Footed, 6 Crimp, 4 In.Diam. 295.00
Bride's Bowl, Tricornered, Blue Inside, Pewter Base, Signed, 9 1/2 In. 375.00
Candleholder, Crystal, Bubbles, Marked 95.00
Carafe, Water, Red To Rose, Gold Base, 7 7/8 In. 595.00
Case, Cameo, Daisy, Crimson Ground, Signed, 5 1/4 In. 1250.00
Chalice, Stylized Floral & Geometric Design, Signed, 2 1/4 In. 395.00
Compote, Shrimp, Flowers, Leaves, & Bands, Clear Foot, Blue, 5 3/4 In. 225.00
Cup & Saucer, Demitasse, Signed 95.00
Ewer, Mother-Of-Pearl, Rose Herringbone, Tree Bark Handle, Signed 385.00
Ewer, Rose Herringbone, Amber Tree Bark Handle, Signed 395.00
Jar, Red Ground, Morning Glory On Vine, Silver Cover, 6 In. 675.00
Jar, Sweetmeat, Dimpled Side, Gold Flowers & Foliage, 5 In.Square 195.00
Lamp, Delft Pattern, Signed, 14 In. 495.00
Lamp, Fairy, Ruffled Base, Marked Clarke, Insert Cup, 4 3/4 In. 450.00
Lamp, Fairy, Tapestry Tunnecliffe Base, Gold Trim, 5 3/8 In. 650.00
Lamp, Oil, Raspberry Ground, Floral Base, Shade, Cameo, 9 1/2 In. 1775.00
Perfume, Cameo, Ivory, Screw-On Sterling Top, 3 1/2 In. 695.00

Perfume, Sterling Top, Crystal Stopper, Hallmarked, 1900, 2 1/2 In.	675.00
Pitcher, Water, Bird & Floral Design, Aqua	275.00
Pitcher, Water, Leaf & Flower Design, Signed, Pink	250.00
Rose Bowl, Cameo Carved Flowers & A Bird In Flight, 3 In.	875.00
Rose Bowl, Diamond-Quilted, Cream Lining, 9 Crimp, Amberina, 7 In.	1495.00
Rose Bowl, Diamond-Quilted, Mother-Of-Pearl, 8 Crimp, Brown, 3 In.	350.00
Rose Bowl, Open, 8 Turned-In Petals, Signed, 2 1/4 X 2 7/8 In.	285.00
Rose Bowl, Turquoise, White Flowers, Butterflies, Marked, 2 X 3 In.	1295.00
Salt, Florals & Leaves, Citron Ground, Sterling Silver Frame, 1 1/2 In.	395.00
Spittoon, Crystal Drops, Amethyst Center, 8 In.	125.00
Tumbler, Satin Mother-Of-Pearl Pink, Square Top	185.00
Vase, Applied Crystal Leaves, Berry Prunts, Pair	875.00
Vase, Blue Satin, Ribbed, 7 In.	150.00
Vase, Bronze, Gold Trim, Butterflies, 6 1/2 In.	400.00
Vase, Bulbous, Yellow, Floral Design, Enameled, Signed, 8 X 4 In.	135.00
Vase, Butterfly On Back, Carved All Around, Signed, 3-Color, 6 1/4 In.	2750.00
Vase, Cameo, Gold To Green, White Cased, Butterfly Design, 7 1/2 In.	2175.00
Vase, Carved Florals, Top White Band, Leaves On Back, Blue, 10 3/4 In.	2250.00
Vase, Columbine Decoration, Signed, 3 1/2 In.	385.00
Vase, Coralene, Pearl, Floral Design, Pair, Signed, 6 1/2 In.	1800.00
Vase, Cut Roses Over Royal Blue, Signed, 9 X 9 In.	3500.00
Vase, Daisylike Flowers In White, Signed, Crimson Ground, 5 1/4 In.	975.00
Vase, Diamond-Quilted, Mother-Of-Pearl, Stick, Brown, 7 1/4 In.	295.00
Vase, Diamond-Quilted, Pink To Raspberry, 7 In.	225.00
Vase, Diamond-Quilted, White To Blue, Marked, 5 3/8 In.	175.00
Vase, Egg Shape, 8 Crimp Top, Clear Pedestal, Opaque, 3 1/2 In.	125.00
Vase, Fish Scale, Creamy Beige Ground, Berries, Marked, 5 In.	195.00
Vase, Floral With Bird, Butterfly & Spider, Signed, Citron, 8 In.	1200.00
Vase, Green Iridescent, Round, Double Rolled Rim, 7 In.	125.00
Vase, Herringbone Pattern, Ormolu Base, Signed, Shaded Pink, 6 1/2 In.	165.00
Vase, Hummingbird, Red To Pink, Gold Design, 10 1/4 In.	495.00
Vase, Ivory, Gold Flowers, Dragonflies, Maroon Trim, 5 In., Pair	230.00
Vase, Opaque Bands, Flowers, & Leaves, Olive Green, 3 5/8 In.	850.00
Vase, Opaque White Carved Florals, Cut Crocus Front, 5 5/8 In.	1500.00
Vase, Opaque Wild Roses, Buds, & Vines, Signed, Red Ground, 8 3/4 In.	2500.00
Vase, Overall Floral & Geometric Design, Enameled, Pink, 10 1/2 In.	235.00
Vase, Petit Point, Cream Ground, Blue, Red, Green, Yellow, 4 In.	110.00
Vase, Prunus Blossoms, Enameled, Rose To Pink To White, 10 1/2 In.	240.00
Vase, Seaweed Pattern, 2 Lug-Type Handles, Rigaree Top, 6 In.	485.00
Vase, Stick, Gold & Silver Floral, Maroon Cases, 7 1/2 In.	110.00
Vase, White Morning Glories, C.1900, Yellow Ground, 4 1/2 In.	850.00
Vase, 8-Sided Top, Leaves & Scrolls, Signed, Simulated Ivory, 7 7/8 In.	1800.00

WEDGWOOD

Wedgwood pottery has been made at the famous Wedgwood factory in England since 1759. A large variety of wares has been made, including the well-known jasperware, basalt, creamware, and even a limited amount of porcelain.

WEDGWOOD, Ashtray, Blue & White 3 1/2 In.	5.00
Ashtray, Club Shape, Blue, Marked	45.00
Basket, Willow, Grape & Vines, Yellow & White, 3 In., Pair	100.00
Bidet, Creamware, C.1830, Mahogany Case	1750.00
Biscuit Jar, Blue & White, Silver Plated Top, 6 In.	325.00
Biscuit Jar, Blue, Jasperware, Classical Figures, 6 1/2 In.	190.00
Biscuit Jar, Classical Figures, Silver Plated Base, Feet & Handle	225.00
Biscuit Jar, Dark Blue, Silver Plated Rim, Handle, & Lid	140.00
Biscuit Jar, Jasperware, Acorn & Leaves, Blue	95.00
Biscuit Jar, Jasperware, Lady Figures, Blue & White, Marked, 6 In.	145.00
Biscuit Jar, Jasperware, Silver Plated Bail & Top, Blue & White	450.00
Biscuit Jar, Jasperware, Silver Plated Top, Rim, & Handle, 6 1/2 In.	145.00
Biscuit Jar, Jasperware, Tricolor, Marked, 4 3/4 X 6 1/2 In.	395.00
Biscuit Jar, Ladies & Cupid, Silver Plated Top & Bail, 6 3/4 In.	145.00

Biscuit Jar, Washington & Lafayette Medallions, Green, Marked 325.00
Boat, Trinket, Medusa Head Handles, Gilded, 10 1/2 In.Long 750.00
Bonbon, Jasperware, Tricolor, Silver Plated Lid & Handle 1200.00
Bottle, Barber, Basalt, Bronze & Gold, 10 1/2 In. 1795.00
Bottle, Barber, Blue & White Jasperware, Covered, 10 1/2 In. 575.00
Bowl, Basalt, Dancing Hours, Black, 8 In. 600.00
Bowl, Basalt, Engine Turned, 8 3/4 In. 85.00
Bowl, Black Basalt, Flaring Sides, Footed, 19th Century, 10 1/4 In. 35.00
Bowl, Blue Trim, 6 X 4 In. 250.00
Bowl, Boat Race, 13 In. 175.00
Bowl, Butterfly Luster, Green, Orange, Gold Border, 4 In. 295.00
Bowl, Butterfly Luster, Octagonal, Brown, Gold Design, Marked, 4 In. 165.00
Bowl, Butterfly Luster, Orange & White Interior, Signed, 7 1/2 In. 525.00
Bowl, Butterfly Luster, Orange Exterior, Blue Interior, 6 1/2 In. 350.00
Bowl, Butterfly Luster, Oriental Design Edge, Marked, 7 1/8 In. 375.00
Bowl, Dark Blue, Flying Fish, Orange Inside, Signed, 2 3/4 In. 160.00
Bowl, Dragon Luster, Dragons Outlined In Gold, Octagonal, 5 1/8 In. 165.00
Bowl, Dragon Luster, Gold Symbols, Dragon Inside, Marked, 2 3/8 In. 80.00
Bowl, Dragon Luster, Green, Marked, 3 1/4 In. 210.00
Bowl, Fairyland Luster, Blue, Orange Inside, Hummingbirds, 9 In. 425.00
Bowl, Fairyland Luster, Butterfly, 13 In. 975.00
Bowl, Fairyland Luster, Gold Stars, Luster Ground, Marked, 4 3/4 In. 695.00
Bowl, Fairyland Luster, Hummingbird, 4 In. 265.00
Bowl, Fairyland Luster, Inner Garden Of Paradise, Marked, 8 In. 2000.00
Bowl, Gilt Fish, Mother-Of-Pearl Inside, Green, Marked, 2 1/2 In. 118.00
Bowl, Gilt Ornaments & Butterflies, Aqua Inside, Footed, 5 In.Diam. 165.00
Bowl, Gilt Ornaments, Multicolored Butterfly Inside, 5 In.Diam. 148.00
Bowl, Majolica, C.1865, Impressed Mark, 10 In.Diam. 175.00
Bowl, Orange Luster Interior, Flying Hummingbirds Inside, 3 In. 185.00
Box, Blue, White Design, Grecian Figures, Covered, Marked 150.00
Box, Covered, White Jasperware, Yellow, WW Mark, 3 1/2 In. 375.00
Box, Jasperware, Grecian Figures, Covered, 4 In.Diam. 485.00
Box, Jasperware, Heart Shaped, Covered, 5 In. 48.00
Box, Trinket, Crimsonware, Covered, 4 In. 100.00
Box, Turquoise, Figures On Cover, Marked, 5 1/2 In. 300.00
Box, Yellow & White, Classical Figures, Covered, Marked, 3 In. 375.00
Bust, Dwight D. Eisenhower, 8 1/2 In. 100.00
Bust, Franklin D.Roosevelt, 1943, Signed, 8 In. 115.00
Bust, George Washington, Basalt, 14 In. 1200.00
Bust, Mercury, Basalt, Signed, 18 1/2 In. 875.00
Bust, Shakespeare, Basalt, 12 In. 1100.00
Bust, Venus, Black, Basalt, Marked, 14 3/8 X 7 5/8 In. 895.00
Cake Server, Embossed Turquoise Flowers, Pedestal, 9 In. 40.00
Candlestick, Black & White, 5 1/2 In., Pair 275.00
Candlestick, Capri, Rosso Antico, Cutout Bases, 6 In., Pair 495.00
Candlestick, Ceres, White & Blue, 11 In. 400.00
Candlestick, Jasperware, Black & White, 5 1/2 In., Pair 275.00
Candlestick, Jasperware, Trees & Figures, 6 1/2 In., Pair 150.00
Candlestick, Rosso Antico, Capri Design, Marked, 6 In., Pair 495.00
Charger, Hanging, Ferrara, Blue & White, 16 In. 110.00
Clock, Mantel, Green & White, 6 X 4 1/2 In. 475.00
Coffeepot, Glazed Interior, Acanthus On Spout & Handle, 10 3/4 In. 475.00
Compote, Blue Luster, Fruit Design, Marked, 9 1/2 In. 235.00
Compote, Majolica, Cobalt Blue Center, Green Leaf Pattern, 9 In. 165.00
Condiment Set, Jasperware, Lady Figures, Marked, 5 3/4 In. 195.00
Cookie Jar, Jasperware, Bun Feet, Green 145.00
Creamer, Basalt, Raised Figures, 2 1/2 In. 50.00
Creamer, Basalt, Relief, C.1880, Pair 80.00
Creamer, Blue Willow Pattern 38.00
Creamer, Caneware, C.1860, 3 X 3 In. 95.00
Creamer, Commemorate King George & Queen Elizabeth To Canada 150.00
Creamer, Copper Luster, Brown Ground 65.00
Creamer, Drabware 100.00

Creamer, Jasperware, Dark Blue, 2 1/2 In. 45.00
Cup & Saucer, Black Basalt 65.00
Cup & Saucer, Blue, Hand-Painted, Fruit, Pair, Signed A.Holland 625.00
Cup & Saucer, Canada 18.00
Cup & Saucer, Cobalt Blue & White 125.00
Cup & Saucer, Fairyland Luster, Gold Trim, Demitasse, Set Of 6 .... 195.00
Cup & Saucer, Forget-Me-Not 18.00
Cup & Saucer, Harvard Building, Demitasse 12.00
Cup & Saucer, Jasperware, Can Shape, Black & White 1495.00
Cup & Saucer, Jasperware, Classical Figures, Blue & White 1000.00
Cup & Saucer, Jasperware, Figures, White Edges, Blue & White 175.00
Cup & Saucer, Jasperware, Swag & Lilac Medallions, Blue & White 1595.00
Cup & Saucer, Lady Templeton, Blue & White, 1790 .... 1390.00
Cup & Saucer, Lovelace 18.00
Cup & Saucer, Patrician, Gold Trim 12.00
Cup & Saucer, Prairie Flowers 36.00
Cup & Saucer, Primrose 18.00
Cup & Saucer, Rose Garland 16.00
Cup & Saucer, Royal Albert 18.00
Cup & Saucer, Strawberry Fruit 20.00
Cup & Saucer, Tea Rose 18.00
Cup & Saucer, White Figures, Dark Blue, Jasperware 130.00
Cup & Saucer, White Figures, Marked 126.00
Cup On Oval Plate, Shelley Bridal Rose 40.00
Cup, Chocolate, Dice Pattern, Green Ground, Covered, 4 In. 2100.00
Cup, Handleless, Geese, Hummingbirds, Luster, Blue & Orange 165.00
Cup, Peach Melba, Hummingbird Luster, Mottled Blue, 4 1/4 In. 275.00
Cup, Peach Melba, Leapfrogging Elves, Marked, 4 1/4 In. 795.00
Dessert Set, Strawberry, Platter 14 In., 11 Piece 375.00
Dish, Blue, Bust Of Churchill, White Ground, 4 1/2 In. 16.00
Dish, Cheese, Cobalt Blue, Covered, Made In England, 9 In.Diam. 350.00
Dish, Fern Frond, Caneware, C.1810, 13 X 7 In. 125.00
Dish, Heart Shaped, Jasperware, Cobalt, Hanley Coat Of Arms, 4 3/4 I 65.00
Dish, Pie, Biscuitware, Liner, 10 X 8 X 6 In. 265.00
Dish, Pie, Caneware, C.1803, 12 In.Long, 3 Piece 1190.00
Dish, Pie, Caneware, C.1805, 8 In.Diam. 675.00
Dish, Pierced Border, Creamware, Impressed, C.1830 .... 95.00
Dish, Vegetable, Newport, Oval, 10 3/8 In. 15.00
Figurine, Bird, Glass Eyes, Marked, 4 1/2 In. 575.00
Figurine, Black Basalt Tiger & Buck, 7 1/2 X 3 1/4 X 12 1/2 In. 575.00
Figurine, Boy, Turquoise, WW Mark, Impressed Pearl, 5 1/2 In. 300.00
Figurine, Lion, Basalt, 6 X 3 In. 600.00
Figurine, Snail, Signed, Crystal Glass, 3 1/2 X 9 1/2 X 5 1/2 In. 75.00
Flower Frog, Egret, Basalt, Black, 7 1/2 In. 650.00
Flower Holder, Jasperware, Pierced Lift-Off Lid, 5 3/4 In. 350.00
Flower Holder, Raised Flowers & Leaves, Pierced, Marked, 5 1/2 In. 295.00
Footbath, C.1840, White Stoneware, 18 In. 590.00
Heels, Jasperware, Ladies, Blue & White 295.00
Holder, Ring, Black & White 225.00
Incense Burner, Mesh Lid Supported By Dolphin, Blue & White 1395.00
Jar, Sweetmeat, Bail Handle, Silver Plated Cover, 3 3/4 X 3 1/2 In. 300.00
Jardiniere, Lion's Heads, Mythological Figures, Signed, 4 In. 165.00
Jardiniere, Ribbed Base, Keith Murray, Cream Color, 6 In. 175.00
Jug, Ale, Cambridge, 5 In. 150.00
Jug, Egyptian Terra-Cotta & Black, C.1805, 5 In.Wide 350.00
Jug, Milk, Olive, 1930, 5 1/2 In. 165.00
Jug, Milk, Trefoil Spout, Dark Blue, 5 1/4 X 6 1/2 In. 275.00
Jug, Molasses, Dark Blue Classical Figures, C.1870, 7 In. 65.00
Jug, Old Saying Design, Tan, Turquoise, C.1865, 7 In. 190.00
Jug, Orange Shape, Crimson, 3 1/2 In. 325.00
Jug, Saying Printed, Tan, Turquoise, Blue, Brown, 7 In. 190.00
Jug, The Egyptian, 1854 Date, Terra-Cotta & Black, 7 1/2 In. 595.00
Lamp, Basalt, 19th Century, 8 1/2 In. 1850.00
Lamp, Queensware, Peach, Floral Band 75.00

Muffineer, Blue, White Trees, Flowers, 5 1/4 In. 95.00
Mug, Blue Willow, 3 3/4 In. 35.00
Mug, Keith Murray, Green, Yellow, Blue-Gray, 4 3/4 In. 55.00
Pitcher, Basket Weave Sides, 4 X 4 In. 115.00
Pitcher, Blue & White, Incised 1953, 6 In. 75.00
Pitcher, Classical Figures, Rope Handle, Cobalt Blue, 4 In. 120.00
Pitcher, Cobalt Blue & White, 5 1/4 In. 125.00
Pitcher, Commemorative Of Queen Elizabeth I, 8 In. 250.00
Pitcher, Crimson Rope Handle, 4 3/4 In. 495.00
Pitcher, Dark Blue, White Figures, Leaves, Marked, 4 1/2 In. 110.00
Pitcher, Ferrara Pattern, Pedestal Base, Marked, 8 1/2 In. 88.00
Pitcher, Ferrara, White Ground, Purple Scene, Silver Trim, 4 1/2 In. 55.00
Pitcher, Hound Handle, Silver Overlay, 4 In. 30.00
Pitcher, Hunt, Fox Handle, 8 X 8 In. 75.00
Pitcher, Jasperware, Blue, White Figures, Rope Handle, 7 1/2 In. 200.00
Pitcher, Jasperware, Blue, 6 1/2 In. 85.00
Pitcher, Jasperware, Raised Figures, Blue & White, 5 1/2 In. 125.00
Pitcher, Jasperware, Squatty, Dark Blue, 4 In. 75.00
Pitcher, Jasperware, White Figures, Grape & Vine Border, 4 3/4 In. 100.00
Pitcher, Jug Form, Cobalt Blue & White, 5 In. 125.00
Pitcher, Milk, Blue & White Figures, Rope Handle, 6 1/2 In. 135.00
Pitcher, Milk, Jasperware, Dark Blue 75.00
Pitcher, Oriental Style, Cobalt Blue, Turquoise, & Pink 125.00
Pitcher, Silver Resist Of Hunting Scenes, Handled, 7 In. 95.00
Pitcher, Terra-Cotta, Bulbous, 5 3/8 In. 285.00
Pitcher, Water, Silver Overall Cream, Hunt Scene 95.00
Planter, Bulb, Figural Hedgehog, C.1800, Sky Blue 750.00
Plaque, Female Figures, Green, White, Marked, 6 In., Pair 360.00
Plaque, Jasperware, Bacchanalian Boys, C.1810, 9 3/4 X 4 3/4 In. 395.00
Plaque, Jasperware, C.1850, Mahogany Frame, 10 1/2 X 8 1/2 In., Pair 435.00
Plaque, Jasperware, Erotic, Framed, Blue, 5 1/2 X 7 9 16 In. 400.00
Plaque, Jasperware, Goddess & Cupid, 7 In. 65.00
Plaque, Napoleon, Blue & White, Framed, C.1820, 8 1/2 In. 575.00
Plate, August, Polychrome, 10 In. 150.00
Plate, Battle Of Tippecanoe, Etruria, Blue, 9 In. 26.00
Plate, Boys On Bridge, Pixie In Boat, Marked, 10 5/8 In. 1800.00
Plate, California, Blue, Marked, 8 1/2 In. 35.00
Plate, Christmas, 1969, Boxed 280.00
Plate, Christmas, 1970 .... 18.00
Plate, Christmas, 1976, Jasperware, Boxed 28.00
Plate, Christmas, 1979, Queensware, Child's 25.00
Plate, Clare Leighton, Ice Cutting 50.00
Plate, Commonwealth Ave., Boston, C.1882, Brown & Cream, 8 In. 55.00
Plate, Cupid, Blue, 9 In. 70.00
Plate, Embossed Grapes On Rim, Ivory, 9 In. 18.00
Plate, Ferrara Pattern, Marked, 9 3/8 In. 35.00
Plate, Ferrara, 9 1/4 In. 25.00
Plate, Friar Tuck Entertains Black Knight, 10 In. 50.00
Plate, Hedge Rose, 10 In. 10.00
Plate, Ivanhoe, Blue .... 37.50 To 45.00
Plate, Ivory, Grapes, Leaves Band, Marked, 9 In. 20.00
Plate, January, Polychrome, 10 In. 150.00
Plate, Longfellow's House, 9 In. 40.00
Plate, Majolica, Bird Motif, Signed, 8 1/2 In. 70.00
Plate, Majolica, Hexagonal, 9 1/2 In. 195.00
Plate, Maldon, Mass. 35.00
Plate, Melon & Grapefruit, Fleur-De-Lis Center, Off-White, 8 In. 120.00
Plate, Melon, Cream, Gold Design, Scalloped, 8 1/2 In. 120.00
Plate, Mercersburg Academy, Blue, White, 10 3/4 In. 20.00
Plate, Month Of January, 2 Girls In Center, 10 1/2 In. 135.00
Plate, Month, January, Flow Blue, 10 In. 125.00
Plate, Monticello, Pink On White, 8 In. 25.00
Plate, Moorish Castle, 9 In. 60.00
Plate, Mother's Day, 1972 .... 20.00

Plate, Patrician, 10 In.	7.00
Plate, Queensware, Raised Rim Design, 8 1/2 In.	12.00
Plate, Red Riding Hood, Dead Wolf & Hunter, Marked, 10 3/8 In.	125.00
Plate, Royal Blue, Spiral Rim, Blue Floral Center, 10 In.	5.00
Plate, September, Polychrome, 10 In.	150.00
Plate, Stratford, 8 In.	8.00
Plate, The White House, Etruria	35.00
Plate, Theodore Roosevelt, 9 In.	48.00
Plate, Twigware, 1790	150.00
Plate, Washington Crossing The Delaware, Blue, White	45.00
Plate, Washington, D.C., Black & White, 10 In.	20.00
Platter, Newport, Scalloped, 14 1/4 In.	20.00
Pot, Bough, Jasperware, Lilac & White, Impressed, C.1825, 4 7/16 In.	375.00
Pot, Posy, Dated 1958, Terra-Cotta, 3 3/4 In.	135.00
Rack, Toast, Blue, Creamware	225.00
Ring Tree, Cobalt, White, Letter Dated D	95.00
Salt, Jasperware, Green	65.00
Server, Walnut Design, Jeweled & Enameled Handle, 10 1/2 In.	185.00
Smoke Set, Jasperware, Green, 4 Piece	85.00
Snail, Figural, Marked, Crystal, 3 X 5 In.	75.00
Spittoon, Woodland, Pink & White	85.00
Sugar & Creamer, Blue & White	125.00
Sugar Bowl, Blue, Festoons, Fruits, Ram's Head, Marked	1750.00
Sugar, Basalt, Classical Figures, Covered	95.00
Sugar, Jasperware, Black	100.00
Sugar, Jasperware, Light Blue, Medium Blue Handles	90.00
Sugar, Jasperware, White Figures, Covered, Marked, 3 1/8 In.	395.00
Sugar, Rosso Antico, 12 In. *Illus*	220.00
Tankard, Jasperware, Classical Figures, Rope Handle, 8 In.	75.00
Tankard, Panels, Crazed White Glaze, Keith Murray	85.00
Tea Set, Black Jasperware, Yellow, England, 3 Piece	1200.00
Tea Set, Blue & White, 3 Piece	795.00
Teapot, Basalt, Classical Figures	125.00
Teapot, Basalt, Crested Rim, Incised Etruria England, Oval, 8 3/4 In	125.00
Teapot, Basalt, Melon Shape, Marked, 5 X 8 In.	145.00
Teapot, Blue & White, Raised Figures, Trees, Marked	145.00
Teapot, Capriware, Rosso Antico Ground, Curved Handle, C.1865	200.00
Teapot, Cauliflower Mold, Floret Spout, C.1765, 5 In.	1800.00
Teapot, Cobalt Blue & White, 8 1/2 In.	300.00
Teapot, Ferrara, Blue Transfer	50.00
Teapot, Jasperware, Beige & Blue, 1850	225.00
Teapot, Jasperware, Black	45.00
Teapot, Jasperware, Lady Figures, Blue & White, Marked, 4 1/8 In.	145.00
Teapot, Mayflower, 1871	185.00
Teapot, Strawberry Fruit, Etruria	32.00
Teapot, Terra-Cotta, C.1820	290.00
Teapot, Widow's Design, Basalt, 4 3/4 In.	95.00
Tile, Calendar, C.1865, Pink, 6 In.Square	75.00
Tile, Calendar, 1905, Locomotives	55.00
Tile, Calendar, 1906	55.00
Tile, Calendar, 1908	38.00
Tile, Calendar, 1908, Harvard Medical School	48.00
Tile, Calendar, 1911, U.S.Constitution & U.S.Florida	30.00
Tile, Calendar, 1916	38.00
Tile, January, Blue & White, 6 In.	75.00
Tile, Washington Station, Boston, Sepia, 6 In.Square	45.00
Toothpick, Jasperware, Black	32.00
Tray, Dresser, Jasperware, Classical Ladies, 7 1/2 X 10 1/2 In.	145.00
Tray, Lilac, 1960, 9 1/2 X 7 In.	145.00
Tray, Pink Jasperware, C.1875, 2 X 4 1/4 In.	79.00
Tray, White Ground, Chariot, Horses, Blue, Marked, 6 X 3 In.	26.00
Trinket Boat, Gilded Basalt, Medusa Head Handles, 10 In.	750.00
Tureen, Creamware, Hand-Painted Design, Attached Tray, Covered	250.00

Wedgwood, Sugar, Rosso Antico, 12 In.

Wedgwood, Vase, Jasperware, 1976, Marked,
Yellow, White, 4 1/2 In.

Urn, Basalt, C.1820, Covered, 7 1/2 In.	350.00
Urn, Blue, Ladies Dancing Around, Marked, 12 In.	425.00
Urn, Covered, Black & White Jasperware, 2-Handled, Mark, 10 In.	695.00
Urn, Creamware, Agate Design, C.1790, 9 1/4 In., Pair	2900.00
Urn, Creamware, Charlotte, Pistol Grip, Covered, C.1820, 10 3/4 In.	850.00
Urn, Jasperware, Tricolor, Jasper Medallion	795.00
Vase, Basalt, 6 3/4 In. ....*Illus*	605.00
Vase, Black & White, Silver Rim, 1875	250.00
Vase, Black, Basalt, Handle Base Masques, Florals, Marked, 5 1/4 In.	375.00
Vase, Black, Basalt, Trumpet, Vine Design, 11 In.	450.00
Vase, Blue Jasper, Portland, C.1800, 11 In.	425.00
Vase, Blue, White, Spill, C.1925, 1 1/2 In., Pair	195.00
Vase, Brown, 7 1/2 In.	300.00
Vase, Bud, Black, Basalt, Capri, Marked, 3 1/2 In.	350.00
Vase, Bud, Cobalt Blue & White, 5 In.	125.00
Vase, Bud, Seasons, Yellow & Black, 4 1/2 In.	350.00
Vase, Butterfly Luster, Footed, Gold Outlining, 8 1/2 In.	495.00
Vase, Dark Blue & White, Applied Putti, 4 Seasons, Marked, 5 In.	225.00
Vase, Dark Blue, Jasperware, Portland, England, Mark, 6 1/2 In.	475.00
Vase, Dragon Luster, Flared, Pedestal Foot, Inside Luster, 8 3/4 In.	495.00
Vase, Dragon Luster, Pedestal, Dragons Inside, Marked, 5 3/8 In.	325.00
Vase, Dragon Luster, Trumpet Shape, Blue, 8 In.	345.00
Vase, Dragon Luster, Trumpet, Blue, Gold Dragons, Marked, 8 In.	395.00
Vase, Engine Turned Brown Stoneware, Keith Murray, 7 1/2 In.	300.00
Vase, Fairyland Luster, Butterfly, 11 In.	550.00
Vase, Fairyland Luster, Firbolgs, Black Pixies, 8 1/2 In.	1250.00
Vase, Fairyland Luster, Imps On Bridge, Flame Ground, 11 In.	2500.00
Vase, Fairyland Luster, Rainbow, Marked, 3 5/8 X 8 3/4 In.	1995.00
Vase, Ferrara Pattern, Marked, Blue, 9 In.	65.00
Vase, Gilt Butterflies, Mottled Blue Inside, Mottled Orange, 9 In.	295.00
Vase, Gold Flowers, Creamware, C.1880, 14 In.	165.00
Vase, Green, Women In Toga, Cherubs, Trees, Marked, 4 In.	35.00
Vase, Hummingbird, Luster, 6 In.	125.00
Vase, Jasperware, Blue, 5 In.	58.00
Vase, Jasperware, Classical Figures, 4 In.	45.00
Vase, Jasperware, Figures At Top, Tricolor, Marked, 3 3/4 In.	495.00
Vase, Jasperware, 1976, Marked, Yellow, White, 4 1/2 In. ....*Illus*	20.00
Vase, Mottled Brown Glaze Top, Rust Matte, 11 In.	100.00
Vase, Muses, Acanthus Design, Urn Shaped, Handled, Covered, 11 In.	850.00
Vase, Rosso Antico, 5 1/2 In.Diam. ....*Illus*	220.00
Vase, Trumpet, Dragon Luster, Pearl Luster Inside, 8 In.	395.00
Vase, White Jasperware, Blue, 4 Putti, 4 Seasons, 5 In., Pair	225.00
Vase, White, Roses, 8 1/2 In.	325.00

Wedgwood, Vase, Rosso Antico, 5 1/2 In.Diam.

Wedgwood, Vase, Basalt, 6 3/4 In.

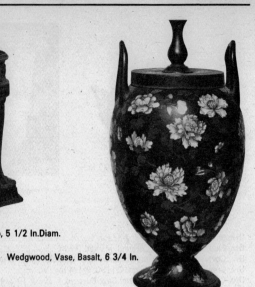

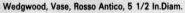

Weller pottery was first made in 1873 in Fultonham, Ohio. The firm moved to Zanesville, Ohio, in 1882. Art wares were first made in 1893. Hundreds of lines of pottery were made, including Louwelsa, Eocean, Dickens, and Sicardo, before the pottery closed in 1948.

WELLER, Ashtray, Woodcraft	50.00
Basket, Cameo, Blue, Original Hanger, 7 In., Pair	70.00
Basket, Hanging, Souevo, Chains, 11 In.	100.00
Basket, Malvern, 8 In.	30.00
Basket, Silvertone, 13 In.	165.00
Basket, Warwick, Rustic, Green, Twisted Handles, 6 3/4 In.	50.00
Basket, Woodrose, Rectangular, Tan Ground, Small Flower, 3 1/4 X 8 In.	30.00
Bowl, Ardsley, 12 1/2 X 2 In.	50.00
Bowl, Barcelona, 9 X 2 In.	75.00
Bowl, Breton, Green, 4 In.	45.00
Bowl, Burntwood, 3 X 7 In.	22.00
Bowl, Cameo, Blue, 7 In.	25.00
Bowl, Classic, Ivory Underplate, 11 1/2 In.	95.00
Bowl, Claywood, Floral, 3 1/2 In.	15.00
Bowl, Claywood, 4 In.	65.00
Bowl, Console, Coppertone, Flower Frog, 10 1/2 In.	150.00 To 175.00
Bowl, Console, Wild Rose, Tan, 18 X 6 In.	35.00
Bowl, Coppertone, Flower Frog	95.00
Bowl, Coppertone, Frog Sitting On End, Marked, 6 1/2 X 9 3/4 X 4 In.	125.00
Bowl, Copra, Flat Handles, Pansies, 9 1/2 In.	125.00
Bowl, Cornish, Handled, Rust Ground, Embossed Berry & Leaf, 9 In.	30.00
Bowl, Evergreen, Moire Glaze, Flower Frog, 13 In.	39.00
Bowl, Fairfield, Cherubs, Earthtones, 4 1/2 In.	65.00 To 75.00
Bowl, Flemish, Water Lily, 3 1/2 In.	50.00
Bowl, Forest, Earth Coloring, 2 7/8 X 5 1/4 In.	40.00
Bowl, Greenbriar, 9 3/4 In.	135.00
Bowl, Knifewood, Ivory	30.00
Bowl, Loru, Green, 11 X 7 In.	55.00
Bowl, Malvern, Boat Shape, Flower Frog	75.00
Bowl, Moss & Scroll, 9 X 3 In.	45.00
Bowl, Tutone, Green, 5 X 9 In.	35.00
Bowl, Water Lily, Blue, Flower Frog	125.00

Bowl, Woodcraft, Flemish, 7 In. 48.00
Bowl, Woodcraft, Squirrels On Side, 10 In. 125.00
Bowl, Xenia, 4 1/2 X 9 In. 275.00
Candleholder, Coppertone, 3 In., Pair 39.00
Candleholder, Malvern, Pair 45.00
Candleholder, Pumila, Green & Yellow, Lily Pad Form, 2 X 4 1/2 In., Pr 35.00
Candleholder, Wild Rose, Pink, Pair 12.00
Chalice, Floral Panels, Vertical Ribs, Matte Green, 10 1/4 In. 75.00
Console Set, Cameo Design, Tan, White Flowers 45.00
Console Set, Coppertone, 10 X 2 In. .... 150.00 To 155.00
Console Set, Lavonia, 6 Piece 65.00
Console Set, Malvern, Flower Frog, Oval, 3 Piece 95.00
Console Set, Silvertone, Flower Frog, 4 Piece 135.00
Cookie Jar, Mammy, 11 In. 395.00
Creamer, Lido, Yellow, 6 In. 24.00
Creamer, Mammy 120.00
Creamer, Zona, Apple 20.00
Cruet, Opaque Green, Glass, Original Stopper, 6 1/2 In. 35.00
Dish, Feeding, Creamware, Rabbit, Bird & Tree 30.00
Dish, Nut, Elberta, 3 In. 25.00
Dish, Zona, Child's 55.00
Ewer, Gloria, Brown, 9 In. 50.00
Ewer, Louwelsa, Flowers, Signed Virginia Adams, 10 In. 250.00
Ewer, Louwelsa, Half Circle Seal, Signed, 10 In. 185.00
Figurine, Bluebird, 3 In. Wingspan 50.00
Figurine, Bumblebee, 2 In. Wingspan 55.00
Figurine, Butterfly, Grayish Pink, 3 In. Wingspan 62.50
Figurine, Dragonfly, Comical, 3 In. Wingspan 60.00
Figurine, Muskota, Fishing Boy, Seated On Rock, With Bucket, 7 In. 150.00
Figurine, Muskota, Graceful Nude On Rock, 8 In. 125.00
Figurine, Muskota, Nude With Swan At Her Feet, 7 In. 135.00
Figurine, Red Bird, Tan, 2 1/4 In. 50.00
Flower Boat, Florenzo, 9 1/2 X 3 In. 30.00
Flower Frog, Boy Carrying Goose 65.00
Flower Frog, Coppertone, With Lily Bud 55.00
Flower Frog, Girl With Duck, Hobart 95.00
Flower Frog, Nude Boy, 7 In. 55.00
Flower Frog, Sitting Inside Pond Lily On A Leaf & Rock 70.00
Flower Frog, Turtle 30.00
Flower Frog, Yellow Lily Pad, 4 1/2 In. 125.00
Flower Holder, Figural, Crab, Green & Brown, 6 In. 15.00
Hanger, Cameo, Tan 60.00
Humidor, Dickens Ware, Tobacco, Embossed Figures, 3rd Line, Marked 725.00
Jar, Brown, Amber, Green, Yellow, 6 X 7 In. 60.00
Jar, Tobacco, Bird Dogs, Ducks, Marked, 6 1/2 In. 215.00
Jardiniere, Ardsley, 10 X 10 1/2 In. 110.00
Jardiniere, Art Nouveau, Water Lily Design, Brown & Greens 225.00
Jardiniere, Brown, Green, Claw Feet, Pedestal 225.00
Jardiniere, Copra, Cone Shape, 8 X 9 In. 125.00
Jardiniere, Copra, Jonquil Design, 8 In. 85.00
Jardiniere, Eocean, 11 1/2 In. 240.00
Jardiniere, Evergreen 25.00
Jardiniere, Evergreen, 13 1/2 X 10 In. 58.00
Jardiniere, Fairfield 60.00
Jardiniere, Flemish, Cream Background, Pedestal, 26 1/2 In., Set 295.00
Jardiniere, Floral, Signed CAD Wilbur 235.00
Jardiniere, Forest, 4 In. 40.00
Jardiniere, Forest, 7 In. 50.00
Jardiniere, Forrest, Pedestal, 40 In. 1800.00
Jardiniere, Hudson, Floral, Pink Matte Base, Gray Top, 9 In. 375.00
Jardiniere, Ivory, Daises On Cream & Brown, Pedestal, 31 1/2 In. 650.00
Jardiniere, Ivory, 7 1/2 In. 30.00
Jardiniere, Knifewood, Pheasants, 8 1/2 X 10 In. 120.00
Jardiniere, Knifewood, Robins In Trees, 6 X 6 In. 110.00

Jardiniere, Lavonia, 6 In. 22.50
Jardiniere, Louwelsa, Artist Signed, 10 X 13 In. 200.00
Jardiniere, Louwelsa, Floral .... 140.00 To 165.00
Jardiniere, Louwelsa, Tulip Design, Signed, 8 In. 95.00
Jardiniere, Louwelsa, 12 1/2 In. 300.00
Jardiniere, Luxor, Pedestal, 30 1/2 In. 350.00
Jardiniere, Marvo, Green, 7 In. 65.00
Jardiniere, Nile, 6 1/2 X 15 In. 150.00
Jardiniere, Water Lily Design, Brown & Green, Art Nouveau 225.00
Jug, Aurelian, Cherry Design, Signed, 9 In. 250.00
Jug, Gooseberries & Florals, Handled, Cork, Metal Stopper, 10 1/4 In. 375.00
Jug, Honey, Dickens Ware, Portrait Of Monk, 2nd Line, 6 In. 525.00
Jug, Louwelsa, Brown, Cherries, 6 In. 145.00
Jug, Louwelsa, Cherries, 6 In. 88.00
Juvenile Set, Zona, Molded Rabbit & Bird In Color, Cream Background 115.00
Lamp Base, Dickens Ware, Footed, Pansies, Green, 1st Line, 5 X 11 In. 300.00
Lamp Base, Frosted, 7 1/4 In. 125.00
Lamp, Arcola, 10 In. 100.00
Lamp, Banquet, Dickens Ware, Signed AC800, 1st Line, 32 In. 370.00
Lamp, Bronze Ware, 11 1/2 In. 165.00
Lamp, Burntwood 75.00
Lamp, Frosted Matte, 8 In. 100.00
Lamp, Roma, Glass Shade, 10 In. 60.00
Lamp, Woodcraft, Original Shade, Pair 285.00
Letter Holder, Turada, 4-Footed, Lacy Swirls, Blue, 4 1/2 X 3 In. ... 325.00
Loving Cup, Etched Matte, Orange Flowers, 6 1/2 In. 350.00
Mug, Claywood, Jester And Owl, 4 1/4 X 3 In. 55.00
Mug, Dickens Ware, Full Headdress Indian Portrait, 2nd Line 695.00
Mug, Dickens Ware, Monk Scene, 2nd Line 395.00
Mug, Eocean, Artist Signed, Gray To Raspberry Design, 6 1/2 In. ... 85.00
Mug, Eocean, Red Rose, 5 In. 120.00
Mug, Etna, Blues & Grays 75.00
Mug, Louwelsa, Cherries 118.00
Pitcher, Batter, Fleron, 10 1/2 In. 65.00
Pitcher, Child's, Zona, Duck 125.00
Pitcher, Coppertone, Fish, Handled 100.00
Pitcher, Lido, Yellow & Cream, 6 In. 24.00
Pitcher, Louwelsa, 5 In. 110.00
Pitcher, Marvo, Green, 8 In. .... 98.00 To 100.00
Pitcher, Zona, Apples 55.00
Pitcher, Zona, Dancing Duck, White & Green, High Glaze, 8 In. ... 100.00
Pitcher, Zona, Kingfisher & Cattails, Green Glazed, 8 In. 100.00
Pitcher, Zona, Kingfisher, 2 Panels, Kingfisher & Tree, 8 X 8 In. ... 150.00
Pitcher, Zona, Peaches 22.50
Pitcher, Zona, Waddling Duck, Green & White 85.00
Planter, Auroro, 8 3/8 In. 195.00
Planter, Bonito, 10 In. 155.00
Planter, Cactus, Ducks, Yellow, 5 In. .... 62.00 To 68.00
Planter, Cloudburst, 5 In. 85.00
Planter, Evergreen, Pelican, 5 1/2 In. 50.00
Planter, Figural, Patricia, Duck, Light Green, 2 1/2 In. 25.00
Planter, Hanging, Evergreen, Chain .... 25.00 To 28.00
Planter, Roma, Octagonal, Cream Background, 5 1/4 X 4 1/2 In. ... 35.00
Planter, Roma, 6 1/2 In. 25.00
Planter, Softone, Oval, Pink, 3-Footed, 10 In. 15.00
Planter, Warwick, Shell Lid, 2-Handled, Marked 25.00
Planter, Woodcraft, 3 Foxes, Oblong, 6 X 7 In. 100.00
Plaque, Grant 50.00
Plaque, Lincoln, 1904 .... 75.00
Plaque, McKinley, Marked 50.00
Plaque, Souvenir, World's Fair, St.Louis, 1904, 5 In.Diam. 75.00
Platter, Zona, 12 In. 35.00
Sign, Dealer, Weller Pottery 395.00
Spittoon, Claywood 85.00

Strawberry Pot, Greora 39.00
Tankard, Aurelian, Strawberries & Leaves, Signed J.T.Herald, 12 In. 495.00
Tankard, Louwelsa, Portrait, Indian, 12 In. 2000.00
Tea Set, Zona, 3 Piece 75.00
Tea Set, Zona, 15 Piece 250.00
Teapot, Claywood, 4 1/4 In. 30.00
Tile, Art, Dutch Boy Feeding Goose With Windmill, Glaze, 6 In. 175.00
Tobacco Jar, Turk, Dickens Ware, 2nd Line 500.00
Tub, Basket Weave, Roses, Flemish 30.00
Tub, Flemish, 9 1/2 X 5 1/2 In. 50.00
Umbrella Stand, Bedford Matt, Marked 160.00
Umbrella Stand, Cameo Jewel, 24 In. 400.00
Umbrella Stand, Flemish Blue Relief, Ivory, 22 In. 195.00
Umbrella Stand, Floral Rim, Cobalt Blue & Yellow, Signed, 21 In. 225.00
Umbrella Stand, Ivory, Flemish Design, 22 In. 195.00
Umbrella Stand, Orris, 19 X 10 In. 175.00
Urn, Hudson, Blue Matte With Dogwoods, Artist Signed, 14 In. 750.00
Vase, Ardsley, 11 1/2 In. 70.00
Vase, Art Nouveau, 17 1/2 In. 285.00
Vase, Auroro, Light Blue & White, High Glaze, Daisy, 4 3/4 X 3 1/4 In. 425.00
Vase, Baldin, Blue, 11 1/4 X 8 1/2 In. 130.00
Vase, Baldin, Twig Handle, Green-Brown, 9 3/4 X 9 1/2 In., Pair 150.00
Vase, Barcelona, 8 In. 50.00
Vase, Barcelona, 9 1/2 In. 75.00
Vase, Bedford, Glossy, 8 In. .... 55.00 To 60.00
Vase, Blue Drapery, 8 In. 15.00
Vase, Blue Ware, Grecian Lady, Grapes, 10 1/2 In. 95.00
Vase, Blue, Drapery, 6 1/2 In., Pair 75.00
Vase, Bonito, Handled, 5 In. 35.00
Vase, Bonito, Handled, 7 In. 65.00
Vase, Bonito, 6 In. 75.00
Vase, Bonito, 11 In. .... 85.00 To 138.00
Vase, Bouquet, Matte Blue, 4 1/2 In. 35.00
Vase, Breton, Green, 6 In. 30.00
Vase, Bud, Coppertone, Frog Climbing Reeds, Signed, 9 In. 125.00
Vase, Bud, Double, Marvo Pattern, Green, 4 1/2 In. 37.00
Vase, Bud, Double, Roma, 8 1/2 In. 30.00
Vase, Bud, Double, Woodcraft 30.00
Vase, Bud, Hunter, Swirling Peacock Feathers, Heart Center, Blue, 10 In. 135.00
Vase, Bud, Jap Birdimal, Stylized Feathers, Signed, 6 X 3 In. 175.00
Vase, Bud, LaSa, 6 In. 95.00
Vase, Bud, Louwelsa, Daffodil 11.00
Vase, Bud, Luxor, 7 1/2 In. 20.00
Vase, Bud, Woodcraft, Green, 11 In. 45.00
Vase, Bud, Woodcraft, 10 In. .... 25.00 To 55.00
Vase, Burntwood, Assyrian, 9 3/4 X 4 1/4 In. 85.00
Vase, Burntwood, Floral Design, 9 In. 95.00
Vase, Burntwood, 6 In. 40.00
Vase, Camelot, Tan & White, 4 1/2 In. 280.00
Vase, Cameo, Blue, 13 In. 25.00
Vase, Cameo, Pink & White, Double Handle, 7 In. 25.00
Vase, Chase, Blue, 5 In. 85.00
Vase, Chengtu, Marked, 9 In. 40.00
Vase, Chengtu, 3 1/2 In. 40.00
Vase, Claywood, Grapes, 10 1/4 In. 78.00
Vase, Claywood, Panels Of Flowers, 3 1/2 X 2 1/2 In. 30.00
Vase, Cloudburst, 10 In. 58.00
Vase, Coppertone, Figural Frog, 9 In. 75.00
Vase, Coppertone, Green With Copper-Black Overtones, 6 X 4 3/4 In. 45.00
Vase, Copra, Hand-Painted, 8 In. 115.00
Vase, Cornish, Blue, 10 In. 50.00
Vase, Cornucopia, Elberta, 6 In., Pair 52.00
Vase, Crystalline, 10 In. 70.00
Vase, Darsie, Turquoise, 7 1/2 In. 20.00

Vase, Dickens Ware, Cylindrical, Woman With Bouquet, 2nd Line, 12 In.	325.00
Vase, Dickens Ware, Domley & Sons Scene, 9 In.	650.00
Vase, Dickens Ware, Little Bopeep, Hourglass Shape, 2nd Line, 10 In.	975.00
Vase, Dickens Ware, Tricornered, Greenish Blue, 2nd Line, 6 1/2 In.	325.00
Vase, Double, Ardsley, 9 1/2 In.	55.00
Vase, Double, Sydonia, Blue, 9 1/2 In.	70.00
Vase, Etched Matte, 6 1/2 In.	95.00
Vase, Etna, Morning Glory, 5 In.	85.00 To 100.00
Vase, Etna, Pink Carnations, Gray Ground, 6 In.	135.00
Vase, Etna, Rose Design, 10 In.	125.00
Vase, Fan, Woodcraft, 5 In.	35.00
Vase, Flemish, Brown, 14 In.	125.00
Vase, Flemish, 9 1/2 In.	89.00
Vase, Flemish, 10 In.	50.00
Vase, Fleron, Labels, 4 1/2 In.	35.00
Vase, Floral, Marked, Aqua, 5 1/2 In.	18.00
Vase, Florenzo, Footed, 7 1/4 X 5 3/4 In.	50.00
Vase, Florenzo, 8 In.	35.00
Vase, Forest, 8 In.	55.00 To 75.00
Vase, Forest, 10 In.	65.00
Vase, Forest, 11 3/4 X 6 In.	110.00
Vase, Frosted Matte, Green Streaks, 9 3/4 In.	148.00
Vase, Frosted Matte, 6 3/4 X 3 1/2 In.	135.00
Vase, Golden Glow, Bulbous, Deco Design, Handled, 9 In.	45.00
Vase, Golden Glow, Double Handle, 11 In.	60.00
Vase, Greenbriar, 7 1/2 In.	40.00
Vase, Hudson, Design, Blue, 10 In.	55.00
Vase, Hudson, Gray Background, Iris, Signed H.Weller, 11 1/4 In.	185.00
Vase, Hudson, Handles From Base To Top, Cream To Blue, 10 In.	275.00
Vase, Hudson, Purple To Blue, Signed England, 8 In.	175.00
Vase, Hudson, Slip Berries, White, Pink, Blue, Green, 9 3/4 X 3 1/2 In.	175.00
Vase, Ivory, Clinton, 10 In.	25.00
Vase, Kenova, Horizontal Marbelizing, Green-Brown, 11 1/2 X 10 1/4 In.	225.00
Vase, Klyro, Footed, 6 1/2 X 6 1/4 In.	45.00
Vase, Lamar, 11 1/2 In.	175.00
Vase, LaSa, Gold, 4 1/2 In.	150.00
Vase, LaSa, Iridescent, Marked Weller LaSa In Glaze, 6 1/4 In.	175.00
Vase, LaSa, Marked, 16 In.	500.00
Vase, LaSa, Mountains & Trees, Rising Sun, 9 1/2 In.	200.00
Vase, LaSa, Pine Scene, Mountains, 6 In.	55.00
Vase, Louella, 7 1/2 In.	75.00
Vase, Louwelsa, Artist Signed, 9 1/2 In.	165.00
Vase, Louwelsa, Berries, 9 1/2 In.	135.00
Vase, Louwelsa, Dark Leaves & Flowers, Blue, 10 1/2 In.	675.00
Vase, Louwelsa, Marked, 10 In.	175.00
Vase, Louwelsa, Poppy Design, Pinched Top, Circled Mark, 8 1/2 In.	105.00
Vase, Louwelsa, Tulips & Leaves, Brown Ground, Signed, 10 In.	250.00
Vase, Louwelsa, Twisted Shape, Blackberries Design, 14 1/2 In.	550.00
Vase, Louwelsa, Yellow Roses On Front, Signed H.Mitchell, 13 1/2 In.	275.00
Vase, Malvern, Bulbous Base, Bud & Leaves, Signed, 7 In.	30.00
Vase, Malvern, 5 1/2 In.	25.00 To 28.00
Vase, Manhattan, Embossed Leaves, 7 1/2 In.	42.00
Vase, Manhattan, 10 1/2 In.	25.00
Vase, Marbleized, Brown & Ivory, 6 1/4 In.	100.00
Vase, Marvo, Green, 7 In.	59.00
Vase, Muskota, Single Dog, 5 1/2 In.	235.00
Vase, Nile, Green Drip Glaze, 8 In.	70.00
Vase, Nile, 8 In.	75.00
Vase, Paragon, Dark Red, 7 In.	25.00
Vase, Pillow, Jap Birdimal Type, 2-Sided Decor, Signed, 5 X 5 1/2 In.	275.00
Vase, Roba, 3 Twig Feet, Brown, 9 In.	50.00
Vase, Roma, Column, 8 In.	25.00
Vase, Roma, Paneled, 10 In.	75.00
Vase, Rosemont, Bird & Floral Branches, Block Letters, Black, 10 In.	120.00

Vase, Rudlor, Green, 7 In. 20.00
Vase, Rudlor, Yellow, 6 1/4 X 4 In. 25.00
Vase, Sabrinian, Blue, Sea Horse Handles, 10 In. 50.00
Vase, Seneca, Blue, 7 In. 15.00
Vase, Seneca, Yellow, 6 X 6 1/4 In. 30.00
Vase, Sicardo, Green, 5 1/2 In. 310.00
Vase, Sicardo, Iridescent, Gold To Green To Blue, 5 In. 300.00
Vase, Silvertone, Lilies, 15 1/2 In. 225.00
Vase, Silvertone, Marked, 7 1/2 In. .... 50.00 To 90.00
Vase, Silvertone, Twisted Arms, 12 In. 175.00
Vase, Softone, Yellow, Paper Label, 8 In. 90.00
Vase, Souevo, Black Design, Ivory Background, 5 1/2 X 5 1/2 In. 75.00
Vase, Souevo, 8 1/2 In. .... 75.00 To 100.00
Vase, Turkis, 8 In. 85.00
Vase, Velva, Blue, 6 In. 40.00
Vase, Velva, Green, 10 In. 65.00
Vase, Velva, 8 In. 25.00
Vase, Wild Rose, Handled, Pink, 12 3/4 In. 39.00
Vase, Wild Rose, Pedestal, Brown, 21 In. 65.00
Vase, Wild Rose, 6 1/2 In. .... 12.00 To 15.00
Vase, Wild Rose, 11 In. 27.00
Vase, Woodcraft, 3 Foxes, 5 1/2 X 7 In. 175.00
Vase, Woodcraft, 6 1/2 In. 38.00
Vase, Xenia, Blue-Gray Matte Background, Stylized Rose, 7 3/4 In. 225.00
Vase, 5 Hole, Alvin, Tree Trunk, 8 3/4 In. 40.00
Wall Pocket, Euclid, Roses, Black 45.00
Wall Pocket, Fairfield, 10 In. 50.00
Wall Pocket, Lavonia 60.00
Wall Pocket, Louwelsa, Brown Tones, 4 1/2 X 5 1/2 In. 85.00
Wall Pocket, Orris 50.00
Wall Pocket, Pearl, 7 3/4 In. .... 50.00 To 55.00
Wall Pocket, Roba, Brown & Yellow, 10 In. 40.00
Wall Pocket, Roma, Dupont Motif, 10 In. 70.00
Wall Pocket, Roma, 8 In. .... 18.00 To 25.00
Wall Pocket, Roma, 10 In. 63.00
Wall Pocket, Woodcraft, Owl, Brown, Green Ground .... 50.00 To 110.00
Wall Pocket, Woodcraft, Plums 65.00
Wall Pocket, Woodcraft, Squirrel .... 75.00 To 125.00
Wall Pocket, Woodrose, Marked, 5 3/4 In. .... 45.00 To 58.00

WHIELDON, Dish, Serving, Clouded Ware, Covered, 8 1/2 In. 50.00
Plate, Chop, Brown Sponged Design, Round, 12 3/8 In. 325.00
Teapot, Little Fenton, Brown, Yellow, Green, Spherical Shape, 5 In. 160.00

Willets Manufacturing Company of Trenton, New Jersey, worked from 1879. The company made Belleek in the late 1880s and 1890s in shapes similar to those used by the Irish Belleek factory. They stopped working about 1912.

WILLETS, Bottle, Cologne, Green, Enamel Decor, Brass Cap, Art Glass, 2 3/4 In. 32.00
Bowl, Gold Scroll Feet, Floral Design, Marked, 6 In. 85.00
Bowl, Ruffled Top, Roses, Gold Handles, Pink Interior, 7 1/2 In. 150.00
Bowl, Violet, Hand-Painted Violets Inside & Out, Gold Edge 99.50
Box, Hand-Painted Woman On Cover, Allover Gold, 4 1/2 In. 550.00
Chalice, Silver Overlay, Pink, 10 In. 185.00
Compote, Sterling Silver Overlay, Scalloped Rim, 3 3/4 X 3 1/2 In. 185.00
Creamer, Leaves & Flowers, Mask Spout, Dragon Handle, Serpent Mark 325.00
Cup & Saucer, Gold Trim, Monogrammed 65.00
Cup & Saucer, Old Barracks In Trenton, Brown Tones 35.00
Cup & Saucer, Red Mark, Iridescent 100.00
Cup, Bouillon, Raised Gold Design, Crimped, Underplate, Twig Handles 185.00
Cup, Chocolate, Fish Handle 60.00
Cup, Loving, Hand-Painted Ladies, Gold Beaded Cartouches, 5 In. 350.00

Cup, Punch, Footed, Sterling Silver Overlay, Pink	125.00
Hair Receiver & Powder Box, Ivory Ware, Signed, 4 In.Diam.	45.00
Hatpin Holder, Elk Design	70.00
Mug, Blackberries & Florals	65.00
Mug, Girl	155.00
Mug, Hand-Painted, Brown Mark, 7 In.	95.00
Mug, Leaf Trim, White, 4 1/2 In., Pair	90.00
Mug, Oriental Girl	95.00
Mug, Princeton University Tiger & Shield	95.00
Salt, Pedestal, Gold Raised Garland, Blue Enameled Jewels	12.00
Tea Set, Hand-Painted Flowers, 3 Piece	175.00
Vase, Hand-Painted Florals, Dark Green Ground, 7 In.Diam.	235.00
Vase, Hand-Painted, Floral, Gray Ground, 14 In.	200.00
Vase, Japanese Women, 15 In.	375.00

WILLOW, see Blue Willow

WINDOW, Beveled, Art Deco, 2 Ft.Square	225.00
Beveled, Colored, Swirl Pattern, 5 1/2 Ft.Wide	850.00
Beveled, Cut Glass Jewels, 58 In.Long	1800.00
Beveled, Victorian, 86 In., Pair	1900.00
Etched, Dog, Country Scene, 23 1/4 X 27 3/4 In.	250.00

WOOD CARVING, Angel, Gessoed, Gilt, C.1700, Portugal, 13 In., Pair	350.00
Benevolent Mandarin, Rosewood, Gold Detail, 30 In.	600.00
Bird, Pheasant, Woodpecker, On Tree Trunk, C.1900, 17 In.	770.00
Blackamoor, Polychrome, Venetian, 28 In.	150.00
Bloodhound, Victorian, 7 1/2 In.	25.00
Bookend, Alpine Couple With Barrel, 4 1/2 In., Pair	12.00
Boy, Black, Holding Watermelon, Painted, 5 1/2 In.	40.00
Buddha, Burmese, Gilt Wood, 17 In.	350.00
Bust, Man, Kneeling In Prayer, Oak, 63 In.	150.00
Bust, Man, Pedestal, 5 3/4 In.	800.00
Christ At The Pillar, Spanish, 11 1/4 In.	650.00
Horse, Black, 6 1/2 In.	60.00
Horse, Painted Red, Leather Fittings, 7 3/4 In., Pair	800.00
Horse, Pine, 13 In.	275.00
Horse, Yellowish Brown, C.1910, 9 In.	200.00
Indian Head, Primitive, 34 In.	68.00
Jesus, Painted, Spanish, 1800-20, 23 1/2 In.	550.00
Madonna, Italian, Renaissance, 30 X 30 In.	250.00
Mangling Board, Horse-Shaped Handle, Initials G.L.V., 1820	495.00
Martyrdom Of Saint Sebastian, 57 In.	2000.00
Mask, African	150.00
Medusa, Carved For Circus Wagon, 19th Century	1800.00
Peasant Man & Woman, Polychrome, 8 In., Pair	30.00
Plaque, Virgin & Child, Gilding, 20 X 27 In.	650.00
Putti, Polychrome, Italian, 18th Century	225.00
Rooster, Red Comb & Wattle, Standing On Mound, 5 In.	250.00
Saint Anne, Socle Base, Polychrome, 9 1/2 In.	200.00
St. George & The Dragon, Slaying Him With Lance, 19 In.	753.00
Troubadour, Seated, Cloaked Figure, Holding Horn, 24 In.	300.00
Virgin, Continental, 24 In.	275.00

Wood was used for many containers and tools used in the early home. Small wooden pieces are called "treenware" in England, but the term "woodenware" is more common in the United States.

WOODEN, see also Kitchen; Store; Tool

WOODEN, Barrel, Carved, Form Of Small Barrel, 6 In.	90.00
Barrel, Cider, 12 Bentwood Rings, 14 X 19 3/4 In.	75.00
Barrel, Grain, Hollowed-Out Log, New England, 30 In.	300.00
Barrel, Incised Line Design, 4 In.	45.00
Bootjack, Pine, Hole To Hang, 4 X 19 In.	15.00
Bowl, Burl Maple, 9 1/2 X 5 In.	175.00
Bowl, Burl, Circular, Molded Rim, Turned, American, C.1800, 15 In.	475.00

Bowl, Burl, Footed, 3 1/8 In. 105.00
Bowl, Burl, Protruding Lip, Footed, Pine Figure, 3 3/8 In. 475.00
Bowl, Burl, Protruding Rim & Foot, 8 In. 350.00
Bowl, Burl, Round, Rectangular Handle, 18th Century, 11 1/2 In. 450.00
Bowl, Burl, Stained Red, 2 X 5 In. 225.00
Bowl, Burl, Turned, 4 1/4 In. 260.00
Bowl, Burl, 19th Century, Turned Rim Handles, 19 X 7 In. 575.00
Bowl, Chopping, Hollowed Block Of Chestnut, 3 3/4 In. 140.00
Bowl, Chopping, Rectangular Form, 19th Century, American, 29 In. 160.00
Bowl, Chopping, Rectangular, Shallow, 18th Century, 22 In. 175.00
Bowl, Covered, 5 X 5 1/2 In. 1150.00
Bowl, Cylindrical, Blue, 18 In. 275.00
Bowl, Dough, Hand-Hewn, Oak, 18 In. 45.00
Bowl, Footed, Shallow, White Paint, 18th Century, 2 3/4 In. 125.00
Bowl, Footed, White Paint, 18th Century, 4 3/4 In. 175.00
Bowl, Incised Line Design, Flat Fitted Cover, 8 X 6 In. 70.00
Bowl, Incised Line Design, Footed Base, 3 1/8 X 1 3/4 In. 200.00
Bowl, Incised Line Design, Turned, Shallow Lip, 3 1/2 In. 45.00
Bowl, Maple, 3 1/4 X 1 1/2 In. 65.00
Bowl, Maple, 17 1/2 X 5 1/2 In. 70.00
Bowl, Oval, Molded Rim, 9 In. 30.00
Bowl, Painted White, 18th Century, 3 X 3 In. 100.00
Bowl, Pine, Interlocking Dovetail, Molded Lip, Red Paint, 3 3/8 In. 350.00
Bowl, Rectangular, Brown Stain, 19th Century, American, 10 In. 180.00
Bowl, Red Paint, Shallow, 18th Century, 6 In., Pair 110.00
Bowl, Round, Bird's-Eye Maple, 11 In. 60.00
Bowl, Spherical Body, Yellow, Knob Finial, Fitted Cover, 7 In. 600.00
Bucket, Lapped Loops, Blue, 2 1/4 In. 230.00
Bucket, Shoeshine, Shoe Handle, Covered, 1930s 12.00
Bucket, Staved, Blue & White, Swing Handle, 4 1/4 In. 450.00
Bucket, Staved, Metal Bands, Yellow, 9 1/2 In. 95.00
Bucket, Straight Sides, Bail Handle, Flat Cover, 8 1/2 In. 500.00
Bucket, Well, Iron Hoops, C.1840, Pine 38.00
Canteen, Pine, Round, Pewter Mouthpiece, 9 3/4 In. 120.00
Chalice, Chip Carved, Letters, 5 3/4 In. 5.00
Chalice, Domed Molded Base, 6 1/2 In. 100.00
Charger, Wide Rim, 18th Century, 10 1/2 In. 950.00
Cup, Burl, Handled, Tapered Sides, Handle Forms Horse's Head, 3 In. 325.00
Cup, Maple, 1 Piece, Old Red Finish, 3 In. 55.00
Cup, Red, Straight-Sided, 2 3/4 In. 150.00
Dish, Chestnut, Flat Rim, Deep Bottom, 15 In. 1100.00
Firkin, Blue-Gray, Tapered Sides, Copper Tack, 2 3/4 In. 150.00
Firkin, Finger Laps, Covered, Dark Green, 12 In. 35.00
Firkin, Sugar, Pivot Pegs, Copper Nails, Covered, 14 1/2 X 14 1/2 In. 125.00
Foot Warmer, Pierced Tin Heart Design, Wooden Post, Handled 150.00
Frame, Drying, 2 Bars, Upright Posts, Shoe Feet, Blue-Green, 12 In. 230.00
Holder, Spice, 4-Part, Threaded Top Lid, 7 1/4 In. 85.00
Hourglass, Blown Glass, Oak & Maple, New England, 18th Century 400.00
Jar, Lift Notches At Side, Covered, 5 1/4 X 4 In. 12.50
Keg, Oyster, Staves, Locked Laps, 7 X 4 In. 100.00
Keg, Rum, Interlocking Hoops, Painted Gray, 10 In. 50.00
Keg, Rum, Painted Blue, Turned, 18th Century, 5 1/2 In. 80.00
Keg, Rum, Staved, Green, Locked Laps, 5 In. 250.00
Keg, Rum, Staved, Locked Laps, 6 1/4 In. 210.00
Keg, Rum, Turned, Barrel Shaped, Incised Lines, Red Paint, 8 In. 90.00
Keg, Rum, Turned, Barrel Shaped, Incised Lines, Red Stain, 6 1/4 In. 110.00
Keg, Rum, Turned, Incised Lines, Hanging Hole, 3 1/2 In. 80.00
Mail Rack, 35 Pigeonholes, Bloomingdale, N.Y., 20 1/2 X 36 3/4 In. 68.00
Mold, Cigar, German, 8 X 22 In. 25.00
Mold, Cigar, Patent 1875 .... 40.00
Mold, Cigar, 2 Sections, 5 X 11 X 2 In., 2 Piece 30.00
Mold, Cigar, 10 Molds, 2 Sections, 5 X 13 In. 10.00
Mold, Cigar, 19th Century, German, 4 1/4 X 24 In. 45.00
Mortar & Pestle, Honey Color, Mushroom Knob, Pedestal, 9 In. 80.00

Mortar & Pestle, Walnut, C.1870, 5 1/2 X 6 7/8 In. 125.00
Mortar & Pestle, Walnut, 7 1/4 In. 125.00
Napkin Ring, Black, Old Pepperseass, C.1880 .... 15.00
Plaque, United States Shield, Scrolling Leafage, 15 X 79 In. 1210.00
Plaque, Virgin & Child, Gilding, 20 X 27 In. 650.00
Plate, Narrow, Molded Flat Rim, 7 7/8 In. 60.00
Plate, Shallow, Molded Rim, Turned, 8 5/8 In. 90.00
Plate, Turned, Deep, Smooth Rim, 11 In. 125.00
Plate, Turned, Molded Rim, New England, 8 3/4 In. 100.00
Platter, Maple, Flat Rim, Sharp Shoulder, 18th Century, 14 In. 900.00
Porringer, Cup Shaped, Maple, 18th Century, 4 1/2 In. 200.00
Porringer, Scroll-End Handle, 5 5/8 In. 145.00
Rack, Pipe, Pine, English, Scalloped Base, Crest, 12 X 12 In. 375.00
Rack, Spoon, Domed Top, Green, 16 In. 475.00
Rack, Spoon, Hanging, Pine, 18th Century, 26 1/4 X 11 3/4 In. 950.00
Rack, Spoon, Pine, Sawtooth Crest, Open Compartment, 21 X 11 In. 200.00
Rack, Towel, Painted, Pine, 3 Vertical Slats, 18th Century, 37 1/2 In. 120.00
Rack, Towel, Pine, Shoe Feet, 23 X 32 In. 140.00
Salt, Master, Concentric Rings, Covered, C.1840, 3 In. 85.00
Shaker, Powder, Glove, 1860, Sculptured Maple, 6 In. 85.00
Smoothing Board, Medallion Of Casino De Sebastian, 10 1/2 In. 20.00
Tankard, Hickory Hoops, 9 In. 325.00
Tankard, Painted Red, Interlocking Laps, Covered, 9 1/4 In. 925.00
Trencher, Deep Finger Slots, C.1900, Oval, 11 X 21 In. 150.00
Trencher, Pine, Natural Finish, 6 X 16 In. 130.00
Trough, American, Rectangular Form, 19th Century, 30 In. 83.00
Tumbler, Covered, Straight Tapering Sides, Red Paint, 4 1/4 In. 175.00
Wheel Barrow, Red Paint, Flowers 265.00
Yoke, Pine, Training, 31 In. 65.00
Yoke, Shoulder, Carries 2 Pails, 39 In. Long 33.00

Worcester porcelains were made in Worcester, England, from 1751. The
firm went through many name changes and eventually, in 1862, became the
Royal Porcelain Company. Collectors often refer to Dr. Wall, Barr,
Flight, and other names that indicate time periods and artists at the factory.

WORCESTER, see also Royal Worcester

WORCESTER, Basket, Desert, Flowers, Pink, Red, Purple, C.1770, 9 In. 1350.00
Basket, Desert, Lady, Man Kissing Hand, C.1770, 5 In. 1050.00
Bowl, Blue & White, Landscape, Pavilions, C.1765, 8 In. 137.00
Bowl, Blue, Three Flowers, Pattern, C.1775, 6 1/4 In. 250.00
Bowl, Gilt Trim, Outer Sculptured Leaves, 7 1/2 In. 145.00
Bowl, Grainger, Reticulated Cover, Pedestal Base, 6 1/4 X 3 In. 275.00
Cologne, Creamy White, Gold Trim, 7 In. 265.00
Cookie Jar, Raised Design Of Hops & Leaves, Beige Ground 145.00
Pitcher, Bird, Dr.Wall, Exotic, 8 In. 300.00
Stand, Pinecone Pattern, Oval, C.1770, 10 In. 192.00
Sugar, Cobalt, Gold, White Ground, Swirled Rib, C.1785 .... 175.00
Tankard, Bell Shape, King Of Prussia, C.1757, 4 3/4 In. 750.00
Teabowl & Saucer, Blue Crescent, C.1785 .... 195.00
Teapot, Black, Oriental Landscape, C.1755, 4 In. 165.00
Teapot, Melon, Raised Leaf Design, 1891 Mark 195.00
Tureen, Blue & White, Blossoms, Fruit, C.1770, 8 In. 165.00
Vase, Bud, Flowers, Ivory Ground, 6 1/2 In. 80.00
Vase, Bud, Hand-Painted, Orchid Panels, Green, Hadley, 3 1/2 In. 175.00

WORLD WAR I, Bag, Survival, Aviator's, Canvas, Shoulder Strap 30.00
Box, Ammunition, Wooden 20.00
Bucket, Water, Horse, Canvas 15.00
Canteen, U.S.Army, Canvas Cover, Dated 1903 .... 20.00
Handkerchief, Embroidered Flags, Anchors, Souvenir, Silk, Set 7.50
Hat, Officer's Campaign, Felt, Gold Cord, Knot & Tassel 30.00
Helmet, German Officer's, Brass Eagle & Spike 125.00
Money Belt, Leather 8.00
Pin, Award, Army & Navy, Sterling Silver, Enameled Stripes 6.50

Uniform, Tunic, Insignia, Pants, Leggins, Pack .... 80.00 To 82.50
Whistle, U.S.Army, Regulation, Brass, 15 In.Chain 16.50

WORLD WAR II, Arm Band, Police, Military, Nazi, White Strips, Swastika 35.00
Badge, Nazi Panzer Tank Assault, Bronze 35.00
Banner, Hitler Youth, 8 In. 135.00
Button, Mechanical, Tin, Uncle Sam Hanging Hitler 30.00
Case, Cigarette, Embossed Hitler & Mussolini, Dated 1937 .... 150.00
Currency, Concentration Camp, Theresienstadt 50.00
Dagger, Nazi, SA, Scabbard 145.00
Dagger, Officer's, Nazi, Black Handle 135.00
Dagger, Storm Trooper's 97.00
Drum, Pictures Soldier With Bayonet, Military Action 22.00
Flag, Car, Hitler's Emblem 350.00
Gas Mask, British, Case 9.95
Hat, Australian, Felt 35.00
Hat, U.S.A.F. Chief Staff 148.00
Hat, U.S.Navy Stitched In Gold, Ribbon Band, Size 7 1/8 .... 12.00
Helmet, Italian, Liner 8.00
Helmet, Japanese, Liner 15.00
Helmet, Pilot, Leather 50.00
Knife, British Commando 45.00
Knife, Combat, Japanese Paratrooper 85.00
Knife, Nazi Paratrooper's, Nickel Fittings 145.00
Lantern, Kerosene, Military Blackout 27.00
Pennant, Tank, Nazi, Panzer, Black, Red, White, Swastika, 29 In. 125.00
Periscope, Foxhole 17.50
Plaque, Nazi, Hitler, Swastika On Tie, Bronze 65.00
Postcard, Hitler, Stamp 3.50
Poster, Recruiting, Columbia Calls, C.1916, 30 X 40 In. 195.00
Saddlebags, Bridle, & Straps, German, Waffen Mark 175.00
Whistle, Chain, Army, Brass 12.00

WORLD'S FAIR, Ashtray, 1939, Trylon & Perisphere, Silver Plate 16.00
Ashtray, 1933, Century Of Progress, Copper 5.00
Ashtray, 1933, Chicago, Chrysler, Boxed 10.00
Ashtray, 1933, Embossed Who Serves Progress-General Motors 38.00
Ashtray, 1939, Ford Motors, Glass 10.00
Ashtray, 1939, New York, Brass 12.00
Ashtray, 1939, Trylon & Perisphere, Porcelain, 5 In. 7.50
Bookends, Soldier, Celluloid & Brass, 1939, 7 In. 375.00
Bookmark, 1939, Official Designs, New York, Cardboard 18.00
Bottle, Water, 1933, Chicago, Art Deco, Clear Glass 12.00
Bowl, 1940, New York, Glass 25.00
Brochure, 1934, Greyhound Bus Co., Chicago, Fold-Out, Photos 10.00
Cards, Playing, 1933, Chicago 18.00
Cover, Pillow, 1939, New York, Fair Scenes, Felt 24.00
Guide, 1964-65 .... 8.00
Handkerchief, 1933, Chicago, Silk 10.00
Inkwell, 1904, St.Louis, Ten-Legged Metal Crab 75.00
Jar, Powder, 1893, Building On Lid, Satin Glass, 5 In. 150.00
Key Chain, 1935 .... 5.00
Key Holder, 1933, Chicago 6.50
Key, 1933, Figural, Key To A Century Of Progress 30.00
Knife, 1962, Seattle 7.50
Mug, 1893, Child's, Silver Plate 15.00
Mug, 1904, Granite 25.00
Mug, 1933, Coffee, World's Fair Advertising 38.00
Paperweight, 1939, Trylon & Perisphere, 4 1/2 In. 12.00
Pen, 1939, 14K Gold Point, Orange & Blue 30.00
Pin, 1939, Trylon & Perisphere, New York, Brass 12.00
Plate, 1893, Chicago, Pink & White, Gold, 10 3/4 In. 65.00
Plate, 1933, Buckingham Fountain, 4 1/2 In. 25.00
Plate, 1939, George Washington Standing, Blue, White, 11 In. 30.00

Plate, 1939, The American Potter, Blue, 7 In. 14.00
Saucer, 1964, New York 1.10
Spooner, 1893, Ruby Thumbprint 60.00
Teapot, 1939 .... 35.00
Teaspoon, 1939, Sterling Silver, Empire State Building 24.00
Teaspoon, 1939, Trylon & Perisphere, Silver Plate, Set Of 9 .... 75.00
Tumbler, 1904, Glass, Embossed 15.00
Tumbler, 1939, Trylon & Perisphere, Orange, Red Enamel 5.00

YELLOWWARE, Bowl, Band Of Brown Slip Dots, 2 Applied Handles, 3 1/2 In. 650.00
Bowl, Bands Of Brown Slip Dots, 2-Handled, 3 X 5 In. 1950.00
Bowl, Beige, White & Aqua Stripes, Gold-N-Bake Ovenware, 12 In. 28.00
Bowl, Blue Band, 8 In. 35.00
Bowl, Cream, White Bands, 5 In. 10.00
Bowl, Mixing, Beige, Brown & White Stripes, 11 3/4 In. 24.00
Bowl, Mixing, Beige, Brown, White Stripes, 8 In. 15.00
Bowl, Mixing, Blue Band, 8 1/4 In. 25.00
Bowl, Mixing, Blue Stripes, 7 In. 16.00
Bowl, Mixing, Blue Trim, 8 In. 11.00
Bowl, Mixing, Brown Bands, 9 In. 19.00
Bowl, Mixing, Brown Rings, C.1880, 9 X 4 In. 35.00
Bowl, Mixing, Pink Bands, C.1890, 8 In., Set Of 3 .... 75.00
Bowl, Mixing, Tan, Embossed Pattern, 12 X 6 1/4 In. 25.00
Bowl, Mixing, Triple 1/4 In. White Band, 6 1/4 In., Pair 35.00
Bowl, Mixing, Tulips, Ovenware, Beige, 6 1/2 X 4 1/3 In. 10.00
Bowl, Mixing, 2 Cream Bands, 2 Brown Border Bands, 8 In. 35.00
Bowl, Pudding, C.1870, 8 3/4 X 2 1/2 In. 50.00
Box, Money, Bank In Form Of Jug, Brown Dots, England, 6 In. 750.00
Charger, Brown Combed Slip Design, Notched Rim, 11 In. 650.00
Charger, Brown Combed Slip Design, Notched Rim, 13 1/2 In. 1300.00
Creamer, Bands Of Brown Slip Dots, Bulbous, 2 3/4 In. 700.00
Cup, Custard, Cream Glaze 10.00
Dish, Bake, Brown Dots, Domed Cover, Knob Finial, 5 X 7 In. 3900.00
Dish, Loaf, Brown Combed Design, Oblong, Notched Rim, 11 In. 2600.00
Dish, Loaf, Deep Brown Slip Design, Yellow Glaze, Oblong, 10 In. 1750.00
Dish, Loaf, Notched Rim, Rectangular, Deep, 11 X 13 In. 2500.00
Flask, Embossed Man, Pipe, 7 1/2 In. 110.00
Jar, Beater, Foremost Dairies 30.00
Jar, Brown Dots, Applied Strap Handle, Footed, 5 1/4 In. 1000.00
Jar, Brown Slip Dots, Applied Handle, Footed Base, 5 1/2 In. 900.00
Jar, Mustard, Brown Glaze, Applied Handles, 3 In. 12.00
Jug, Bands Of Brown Slip Dots, Ovoid, Flared, 2 1/4 In. 350.00
Mold, Corn Bread 40.00
Mold, Food, Bunch Of Grapes, Paneled Sides 25.00
Mold, Food, Sheaf Of Wheat, Paneled Sides 25.00
Mug, Band Of Brown Slip Dots, Applied Handle, 3 In. 200.00
Mug, Bands Of Brown Slip Dots, Footed, 3 3/4 In. 600.00
Mug, Brown Dot Band On Lip, Marbleized Comb Design, 3 1/8 In. 1550.00
Mug, Brown Slip Dots, Applied Handle, Flared Rim, 2 5/8 In. 500.00
Mug, Random Brown Slip Dot Design, Strap Handle, 3 1/8 In. 550.00
Pan, Milk, Mustard, C.1870, 11 X 3 1/4 In. 75.00
Pitcher, Brown Design, Spots, Spherical, Footed, Handled, 7 In. 2600.00
Pitcher, Brown Slip On Rim, Applied Strap Handle, 3 3/4 In. 350.00
Pitcher, Embossed W.A. Garry, 4 1/2 In. 55.00
Pitcher, Milk, Brown Slip Dots On Base, Strap Handle, 5 In. 850.00
Plate, Brown Combed Design, Notched Rim, Deep, Round, 11 In. 1300.00
Plate, Brown Combed Slip Design, Notched, 8 In. 125.00
Plate, Combed Brown Slip Design, Round, Notched Rim, 9 3/4 In. 350.00
Plate, Pie, Deep Dish, C.1870, 10 In. 45.00
Plate, Yellow Glaze, Molded Deep, Plain Rim, 9 In. 50.00
Porringer, Brown Slip Band On Rim, Applied Handle, 2 1/4 In. 225.00
Porringer, Brown Slip Dot Design, Footed, Applied Handle, 3 In. 700.00
Porringer, Brown Slip Dots, Flaring Rim, Applied Handle, 4 In. 850.00
Porringer, Brown Slip Dots, Strap Handles, 3 1/4 In. 600.00

Pot, Brown Diamonds On Collar, Ovoid, Strap Handles, 5 In. 2300.00
Pot, Brown Dot, 2 Applied Strap Handles, 4 3/4 In. 1450.00
Pot, Brown Spot Design, Spherical Body, Strap Handle, 4 3/4 In. 225.00
Pot, Cream, Brown Slip Design, Applied Strap Handle, 3 3/4 In. 600.00
Pot, Marbleized Design, Applied Strap Handle, 5 1/2 In. 1900.00
Rolling Pin, 8 1/4 In. 60.00

ZANE WARE

Zane pottery was founded in 1921 by Adam Reed and Harry McClelland in South Zanesville, Ohio. It was sold in 1941.

ZANE, see also Peters & Reed
ZANE, Basket, Hanger, Moss Aztec 25.00
Bowl, Blue & Brown, Impressed, 8 1/4 X 2 1/2 In. 16.00
Vase, Blue Matte, 5 In. 10.00

LA MORO

The Zanesville Art Pottery was founded in 1900 by David Schmidt in Zanesville, Ohio. The firm made faience, umbrella stands, jardinieres, and pedestals. It worked until 1962.

ZANESVILLE, Bowl, Green, Fluted Rim, 6 1/2 In. 25.00
Candlestick 45.00
Vase, Brown Glazed, Flowers, Signed La Moro, 10 1/2 In. 75.00

ZSOLNAY

Zsolnay pottery was made in Hungary after 1862, and was characterized by Persian, Art Nouveau, or Hungarian motifs. A series of new Zsolnay figurines with green-gold luster finish is available in many shops today.

ZSOLNAY, Bowl, Fan Shaped, Chrysanthemums, Cobalt Ground, Marked, 9 In. 325.00
Bowl, Reticulated, Blue Mark, Blue, Yellow, & Gold, Oval, 7 In. 125.00
Ewer, Burgundy, Green Gilt, Scrolls, Marked, 12 In. 160.00
Ewer, Flowers, Gold Beading, 7 1/4 In. 265.00
Ewer, Pink, Griffin Handle, Green Ground, Multicolored Florals, 9 In. 275.00
Ewer, Pink, Griffin Handle, Olive Green Ground, 6 1/2 In. 350.00
Figurine, Bear, Polar, Gold, Green, Iridescent, 5 In. .... 80.00 To 165.00
Figurine, Girl, Sitting, Holding Basket, Blue, Gold, Green 85.00
Figurine, Little Girl With Flagon 150.00
Holder, Ring, Gold Iridescent 65.00
Pitcher, Ladies In Full Relief, Iridescent Green 75.00
Pitcher, Woman Figural, Hungarian 500.00
Rose Bowl, Melon Shape, Golds, Glazed, Marked, 5 In. 145.00
Vase, Art Nouveau Design, Iridescent, 4 1/2 In. 150.00
Vase, Art Nouveau, Reticulated, 9 In. 595.00
Vase, Bulbous, Ribbed, Blue Luster, 6 In. 85.00
Vase, Cobalt Blue, Gold, Reticulated, Marked, 6 1/2 In. 350.00
Vase, Iridescent, Blue, 3-Footed, 3-Handled, 8 In. 200.00

INDEX

CLOCK, 118–29; Coca–Cola, 133; cut glass, 158; Czechoslovakia, 161; Disneyana, 188; Kewpie, 323; Lalique, 343; musical, toy, 728; political, 459; Tiffany, 708; Wedgwood, 765. See also Alarm clock

CLOISONNE, 129–31

Clothes, 694–702

Clothes brush: Lone Ranger, 363; Shaker, 624

Clothes hanger: doll, 728; Shaker, 624

Clothes plunger, 719

Clothes press, 251

Clothespin, scrimshaw, 620

CLUTHRA, 131. See also Steuben

Coal hod, fireplace, 221

Coal oil lamp, 346

Coal scuttle, brass, 52

COALPORT, 131–32. See also Indian Tree

Coaster, 671; aluminum, 4; black amethyst, 36; brass, 52; Coca–Cola, 133; Depression glass, 171, 174; fabric, 695; Mettlach, 381; Sandwich glass, 614; silver, 636, 640; wine bottle, Tiffany silver, 707

Coat, 695–96

Coat rack, 251, 395

COBALT BLUE, 132. See also specific makers and articles

COCA–COLA, 132–34; bottle protector, store, 670; Halloween witch doll, 286; plate, 755; screwdriver, 677; sign, store, 678

Cocktail: Cambridge, 69, 70; Fostoria, 229, 232; Heisey, 293, 297; Planters Peanuts, 457; railroad, 543; Steuben, 659

Cocktail pick, Planters Peanuts, 457

Cocktail pitcher, Cambridge, 68

Cocktail set, chrome, 116

Cocktail shaker: Cambridge, 68, 70; chrome, 116; cut glass, 160; Hawkes, 290; Heisey, 294, 297; silver, 635; Tiffin, 711

Cocktail tray, Tiffany glass, 705

Cocoa: ladle, graniteware, 280; pot, Royal Worcester, 592

Coffee boiler, graniteware, 278

Coffee canister, tole, 714

Coffee dispenser, graniteware, 280

COFFEE GRINDER, 134; Autumn Leaf, 12; Delft, 166; toy, 728

Coffee mill, 326

Coffee pail, 676

Coffee percolator, 4, 281

Coffee roaster, 326, 336

Coffee server, 326; Red Wing, 548; Royal Copenhagen, 576

Coffee set: Belleek, 30; chrome, 116; Limoges, 358; Roseville, 561; Royal Doulton, 580

Coffee table, 265

Coffee tin, 682–86

Coffeepot: brass, 52; Copeland Spode, 139; cut glass, 158; Czechoslovakia, 161; Fiesta, 217; graniteware, 279; Hall, 285; Haviland, 288–89; ironstone, 313; Lenox, 354; Limoges, 358; McCoy, 376; moriage, 388; mulberry, 392; Nippon, 408; pewter, 443; Quimper, 541; Royal Copenhagen, 576; Royal Doulton, 580; Russel Wright, 612; salt glaze, 612; Satsuma, 617; ship's, 401; silver plate, 629; soft paste, 644; Staffordshire, 652; tea leaf ironstone, 692; terra–cotta, 694; tin, 712; tole, 714; Wedgwood, 765

Coin changer, 671; brass, 52; Coca–Cola, 133; coin–operated, 135

Coin dispenser, silver, 640

COIN–OPERATED MACHINE, 135–38; Coca–Cola, 133; music box, 394, 395

COIN SPOT, 135

Colander, 326; brass, 52; graniteware, 279

Cold cream jar: milk glass, 384; store, 673

Collar box, Rosenthal, 558

Collar stud box, 48

Collection box, 240

COLLECTOR PLATE, 138–39. See also Bing & Grondahl; Christmas plate; Royal Copenhagen

Cologne bottle, 43; Aurene, 10; Baccarat, 13; Beehive, 28; carnival glass, 89; cosmos, 142; cranberry glass, 144; custard glass, 154; cut glass, 158; Daum Nancy, 162; Duncan & Miller, 211; Hawkes, 289, 291; Lalique, 343; milk glass, 383; Nippon, 406; Occupied Japan, 419; opalescent, 424; Pairpoint, 431; Sabino, 612; Sandwich glass, 613; satin glass, 615; spatter glass, 649; Steuben, 658; Stevens & Williams, 661; Willets, 775; Worcester, 778

Coloring book: Beatles, 28; Disneyana, 188; Howdy Doody, 300; Planters Peanuts, 456; railroad, 543; Roy Rogers, 568; Superman, 691

Coloring set, Snow White, 188

Columbian Exposition (Chicago World's Fair, 1892–1893): bank, 25; jug, Royal Doulton, 587; mirror, 675; postcard, 463; saltshaker, 644; spoon, 645

Column, architectural, 7

Comb: flax, 716; Shaker, 624; wool, 716

Comforter, 696

COMIC ART, 139

COMMEMORATIVE, 139. See also Coronation; Political

Commemorative plate: Royal Copenhagen, 576; Staffordshire, 654

Commode, 251

Communion set, pewter, 443

Compass: brass, 52; Dick Tracy, 187; Flash Gordon, 222; marine, 401; Tom Mix, 715

Condiment bowl, custard glass, 156

Condiment box, Quimper, 541

Condiment dish, Jackfield, 316

Condiment set: Aunt Jemima, 36; Ceramic Art Co., 107; Chinese export, 109; cut glass, 158; flow blue, 223; Goebel, 277; Nippon, 408; Noritake, 416; Occupied Japan, 420; ruby glass, 605; satin glass, 615; Wedgwood, 765

Confection box, Kewpie, 323

Confederate: canteen, 116. See also Civil War

Console, 251

Console bowl: black amethyst, 36; Cambridge, 67, 69, 71; Cowan, 143; crackle glass, 144; Depression glass, 168, 174, 176, 182; Fostoria, 230–32; Fulper, 234; Heisey, 297; Hull, 301; McCoy, 376; Roseville, 560; Sinclaire, 641; Teplitz, 693; Weller, 770

Console set. See specific makers and materials

Console table, 265

Cookbook, 436; Jell–O, Kewpie, 323; Mazola, 324

Cookie cutter, 326–27; Mickey Mouse, 188; Planters Peanuts, 457; tin, 712

Cookie press, 336

Cookie roller, 336

Cooler: Coca–Cola, 133. See also Water cooler; Wine cooler

Cooper's tools. See Tool

COORS, 139

COPELAND, 140

COPELAND SPODE, 139–40. See also Flow blue

COPPER, 140

CORALENE, 141

CORDEY, 141

Cordial. See specific makers and materials

Cordial dispenser, chrome, 116

Cork press, 716, 719

CORKSCREW, 141, 326

Corn bread mold, yellowware; 780

Corn planter, 719

Corn popper, fireplace, 221

Corn set, Nippon, 408

Corn shucker, 716

Corn stick pan, 335

Cornucopia (horn of plenty): Abingdon, 2; Camark, 67; Duncan & Miller, 211; Frankoma, 233; Gunderson, 285; Heisey, 298; Hull, 301–2; milk glass, 383; Red Wing, 547; Roseville, 562; Steuben, 659

CORONATION, 142. See also Commemorative

COSMOS, 142

Costume: Charlie McCarthy, 108; Dick Tracy, 187; Roy Rogers, 568

Counter, store, 672

Coupe, Galle, 272

Court house figure, 8

COVERLET, 142–43

COWAN, 143–44

Cowboy suit, 696

Cracker dish: cheese and, see Cheese and cracker; Nippon, 409; RS Germany, 596

CRACKER JACK, 144

Cracker jar. See specific makers and materials

CRACKLE GLASS, 144–46

Cradle, 251; doll, 729

Cradle board, Indian, 309–10

CRANBERRY GLASS, 144–46

Crate opener, 718

Crayon box: Mickey Mouse, 188; Popeye, 461

Cream bowl, yellowware, 780

Cream bucket, tin, 712

Cream can, graniteware, 279

Cream ladle, 329

Cream pail, 335; graniteware, 280

Cream pitcher: graniteware, 281; Hall, 286; Lefton, 353; Nash, 401

Cream skimmer, 338

Cream strainer, 340

Creamer. See specific makers and materials

CREAMWARE, 146

Credenza, 251

Creel, 221

Crib, 251

Cribbage board, 273; Coca–Cola, 133; scrimshaw, 620

Cribbage box, 48

Cricket cage: brass, 51; ivory, 314

Cricket stool, 264

Crock: Bennington, 33; Fulper, 235; label, 673; Red Wing, 547; salt glaze, 612; stoneware, 663–65; store, 672. See also specific types

Crocket hook, 622

Croquet set, 274

Cross: gold, 318; silver, 639. See also Crucifix

CROWN DERBY, 146

CROWN MILANO, 147

Opium pipe, 456
Opium spoon, ivory, 316
Orange reamer, 547
Orchestrion, 395
Organ, 395–96
Organ stool, 264
Organette, 396
ORPHAN ANNIE, 428–29; doll, 201. See also Little Orphan Annie
ORREFORS, 429
OTT & BREWER, 429
Outhouse crescent, iron, 311
Ovaltine mug, Orphan Annie, 428
Ovaltine shaker, Orphan Annie, 361, 428
OWENS, 429
Ox yoke, 718
Oyster opener, 335
Oyster cocktail: Fostoria, 229–32; Heisey, 294, 297
Oyster keg, 777
Oyster plate: Haviland, 289; Limoges, 359; Minton, 386; Royal Worcester, 594; Sarreguemines, 621

Pad holder, 673; black, 38; Tiffany, 709
PADEN CITY, 430
Padlock: brass, 54; iron, 313
Pagods. See Nodder
Pail: brass, 54. See also Bucket
Paint pot, soapstone, 644
Paint set: Donald Duck, 190; Superman, 691
Paint stirrer, store, 676
PAINTING, 430. See also Picture
PAIRPOINT, 431–34
Pamphlet: Shaker, 624; Tom Mix, 715
Pan: copper, 140. See also specific materials and types
Pan American Exposition, clock, 119
Pancake dish, Limoges, 358–59
Pancake pitcher, KTK, 342
Pantalettes, 698
Panties, 698
Pantry box, 49, 324
Pantry jar, Red Wing, 548
PAPER, 435–37. See also specific types of paper products
Paper clip: Art Nouveau, 10; brass, 54; iron, 313; silver, 641; Tiffany, 711
PAPER DOLL, 434–35; black, 38; Charlie Chaplin, 108; Dionne Quintuplets, 187; Shirley Temple, 628
Paper towel holder, Aunt Jemima, 38
PAPERWEIGHT, 437. See also specific makers and materials
PAPIER-MACHE, 438
Parasol, 750
Parcheesi board, 273
PARIAN, 438
PARIS, 438–39
Parlor set, 258
Parlor table, 267
Partner's desk, 254
Pastry blender, 324, 325
Pastry jigger, 335
Pastry tube, pewter, 445
Pastry whip, 335
Patch, Girl Scout, 276
Patch box: cranberry glass, 145; cut glass, 157; Mary Gregory, 372
PATE-DE-VERRE, 439
PATE-SUR-PATE, 439
PAUL REVERE, 439
PEACHBLOW, 439–40. See also Gunderson; Webb
Peanut butter pail, store, 676
Peanut vending machine, 136
PEARL, 440
PEARLWARE, 440
Pedestal, 258
Peel, oven, 335
Peeler, 335–36
Pegboard, Shaker, 624
PEKING GLASS, 440
PELOTON, 440
PEN, 440–41; Popeye, 461
Pen box, 49; lacquer, 342
Pen brush, Tiffany, 711
Pen holder, 440; Tiffany, 711
Pen tray, Tiffany, 711
PENCIL, 441; Coca-Cola, 133; mechanical, 441; mechanical, chrome, 116; mechanical, Mickey Mouse, 190; mechanical, Planters Peanuts, 457; Planters Peanuts, 457; Popeye, 461;
Pencil box, 49; Charlie Chaplin, 108; Hopalong Cassidy, 300; Lone Ranger, 363
Pencil sharpener, Coca-Cola, 133
Pendant, 319; Indian, 310; silver, 639
Penknife: Girl Scout, 276. See also Pocket knife
Pennant: Captain Marvel, 79; World War II, 779
PENNSBURY, 441
Penny-arcade machine. See Coin-operated machine
Pepsi-Cola: bank, 18, 22; salt and pepper, 677; sign, store, 680; thermometer, 703; tip tray, 688; tray, 687

Perfume: atomizer, see Atomizer; bottle, see specific makers and materials
Perfume lamp, 350, 352; Fulper, 235
Periscope: Tom Mix, 715; World War II, 779
PETERS & REED, 441–42
Petticoat, 698
Pew, church, 258
PEWABIC, 442
PEWTER, 442–47
Pharmacy: scale, 619. See also Apothecary; Drugstore
PHOENIX, 447–48
PHOENIX BIRD, 447
PHONOGRAPH, 448–50; toy, 736, 738
PHOTOGRAPHY, 450–52. See also Camera
Phrenological chart, 436
Piano, 396; child's, 258; rolls, 396; toy, 736
Piano bench, 240
Piano lamp, 350
Piano stool, 264
PICKARD, 453–54; Christmas plate, 138
Pickax, 718
PICKLE CASTOR, 106; Cosmos, 142; Fenton, 215; Mt. Washington, 391; opalescent, 424; peachblow, 440; Rubena, 604
Pickle dish: cut glass, 158; Fostoria, 232; Haviland, 289; Northwood, 418; RS Germany, 597
Pickle fork, 328; silver plate, 629
Pickle ladle, 329
Picnic basket, 26
PICTURE, 454–55; Art Deco, 9; needlepoint, 698; Queen Elizabeth II coronation, 142. See also Painting
Pie bird, 38, 336
Pie crimper, 326
Pie dish: graniteware, 280; Wedgwood, 766
Pie holder, 329
Pie lifter, 329; Shaker, 624
Pie plate, 336; Bennington, 34; graniteware, 281; Hall, 286; redware, 549; Rockingham, 552; stoneware, 669; Tiffany silver, 707; yellowware, 780
Pie rack, 336
Pie safe, 258–59
Pie server, silver, 631, 707
Pig catcher, 716
PIGEON FORGE, 455
Piggy bank, 22–23
Pill box, 49; Indian, 310; Mary Gregory, 372; silver, 641
Pill jar, cut glass, 159
Pill roller, 380
Pillow, 698; Beatles, 28; sham, 698, 700; top, 698
Pillow cover: King George VI, 139; New York World's Fair (1939), 779
Pillowcase, 698; Charles Lindbergh, 361
Pin: award, World War I, 778; Batman, 27; Beatles, 28; Boy Scout, 50; Captain Midnight, 80; Cracker Jack, 144; Hopalong Cassidy, 300; horse blanket, 54; jewelry, 320; Lindbergh, 361; Masonic, 374; mourning, gutta-percha, 285; New York World's Fair (1939), 779; Orphan Annie, 428; Planters Peanuts, 457; political, 460; Roy Rogers, 568; Shirley Temple, 628; silver, 631, 636, 641; Tiffany silver, 707. See also specific types and materials
Pin bowl, Wave Crest, 760
Pin box, 621; Rose Tapestry, 556, 557; Royal Bayreuth, 569; RS Germany, 596; Sunbonnet Babies, 690; Wave Crest, 761
Pin dish: ES Germany, 213; ES Prussia, 213; Royal Bayreuth, 571; Royal Doulton, 580
Pin holder: Coca-Cola, 133; Wave Crest, 762
Pin roll, Shaker, 624
Pin tray: brass, 55; Buffalo Pottery, 63; carnival glass, 100; custard glass, 153, 156; Lalique, 344; milk glass, 385; Nakara, 398; silver, 635, 641; Wave Crest, 762
Pinback, Beatles, 28
Pinball game, 273, 737
Pinball machine, 136
Pince-nez, 276; case, papier-mache, 438
Pincushion, 622; black, 38; Indian, 310; luster, 365; redware, 549; Shaker, 624
PINCUSHION DOLL, 455
Pinocchio, 187–90; animation cel, 7; bank, 23; Christmas tree light bulb, 112; toy, 737; Valentine card, 81
PIPE, 456; Indian, 310; meerschaum, 380; Popeye, 461
Pipe box, 241
PIPE HOLDER, 456; Delft, 166; iron, 312
Pipe lighter, 674
Pipe rack, wooden, 778
Pipe tongs, iron, 313
PIRKENHAMMER, 456
PISGAH FOREST, 456
Pistol, 284. See also Gun; Revolver
Pistol, toy: Buck Rogers, 61; Dick Tracy, 187. See also Gun, toy
Pitcher. See specific makers, materials, and types
Place mat, 698
Placecard holder: Disneyana, 190; Limoges, 359
Plane (carpentry), 718–19

Roulette table, 268
ROWLAND & MARSELLUS, 567-68
ROY ROGERS, 568; lobby card, 81; paper doll, 435
ROYAL BAYREUTH, 568-74; collector plate, 139
ROYAL BERLIN, 575. See also KPM
ROYAL BONN, 575
ROYAL COPENHAGEN, 575-76
ROYAL COPLEY, 576
ROYAL CROWN DERBY, 576-77. See also Crown Derby;
  Derby
ROYAL DOULTON, 577-90. See also Doulton
ROYAL DUX, 590-91
ROYAL FLEMISH, 591
ROYAL SAXE, 591
ROYAL VIENNA, 591-92
ROYAL WORCESTER, 592-94
ROYCROFT, 594-95
Rozane. See Roseville
RRP CO., 595
RS GERMANY, 596-98
RS POLAND, 598
RS PRUSSIA, 598-603
RS SILESIA, 603
RS SUHL, 603
RS TILLOWITZ, 603
RUBENA, 604
RUBENA VERDE, 603-4
RUBY GLASS, 604-7
RUDOLSTADT, 607-8
RUG, 608-11; Indian, 310; Mickey Mouse, 191
Rug beater, 324, 715
Rule, 719
Ruler, 719; Coca-Cola, 133
Rum keg, 777
RUMRILL, 611
Runner, 699
Rushlight, 350; holder, copper, 140
RUSKIN, 611
RUSSEL WRIGHT, 612
Ruth, Babe: watch, 758; watch fob, 756

Saber, 691
SABINO, 612
Saddle bags, World War II, 779
Sadiron, 313, 337
Safety pin, 321
Sake bottle, Imari, 307
Sake cup, cloisonne, 129
Sake set: Dragonware, 209; Satsuma, 617
Salad bowl: cut glass, 157; Duncan & Miller, 211;
  Fiesta, 217; Royal Worcester, 592
Salad plate: Belleek, 32; Fenton, 215
Salad set: Planters Peanuts, 457; silver plate, 629
Salon set, 259
SALOPIAN, 612
Salt box, 49; Rockingham, 551; salt glaze, 612; stone-
  ware, 663
Salt dip: Haviland, 289; Nippon, 412; Quezal, 538;
  silver, 631
SALT GLAZE, 612-13
Salt spoon, silver, 631, 632, 636, 637
Saltshaker. See specific makers and materials
Salver, silver, 637
Samovar: brass, 54; copper, 140
Sampler, 699-700
SAMSON, 613
SAND BABIES, 613
Sand pail, Disneyana, 190
Sander, 719
Sandwich dish, Belleek, 31
SANDWICH GLASS, 613-15. See also specific objects
Sandwich plate: Belleek, 32; Cambridge, 69; Depression
  glass, 171; Duncan & Miller, 210; Heisey, 298
Sandwich server: Blue Willow, 40; Depression glass,
  176, 180
Santa Claus: bank, 23-24; boot, papier-mache, 438;
  candy container, 76-77; Christmas tree ornament,
  112; doll, 203, 204; postcard, 464; toy, 739
Sardine box: Limoges, 358; majolica, 367
Sardine dish, majolica, 367
SARREGUEMINES, 615
SATIN GLASS, 615-17
SATSUMA, 617-18
Sauce bottle, sandwich glass, 613
Saucepan: fireplace, 221; graniteware, 281-82
Sausage grinder, 329
Saw, 719
Sawbuck table, 719
Saxophone, 397
Scabbard, 692
SCALE, 618-19; candy, 677; coin-operated, 136; egg,
  337; Tiffany, 711; toy, 739
Scalpel, 380
Scarab, Tiffany glass, 704
Scarf, 700; Admiral Dewey, commemorative, 139;
  Beatles, 28; Elvis Presley, 212; Lone Ranger, 363

Scent bottle: cameo glass, 71; Capo-di-Monte, 79; clambroth, 117; cut glass, 157; mother-of-pearl, 390;

opalescent, 424; satin glass, 615; St. Louis, 651;
  Webb peachblow, 763
SCHAFER & VATER, 619-20
SCHNEIDER, 620
School bell, 29
School bus, horse-drawn, 104
School clock, 119, 122, 124, 128
School desk, 254
School map, 369
School phonograph, 450
School slate, 681
Schoolmaster's desk, 254
Scissors: barber, 25; buttonhole, 622; sewing, 739;
  Tiffany, 711
Scoop, 337-38; brass, 54; tin, 713. See also specific
  types
Scope, surveyor's, 719
Scorecard, election, 469
Scouring box, 49
Screen, 259; fireplace, 221
Screwdriver, 719; Coca-Cola, 133, 677
SCRIMSHAW, 620
Seal, Tiffany glass, 704
Searchlight, fire truck, 220
Seat: ferris wheel, 104; garden, Chinese export, 110;
  garden, porcelain, 462; garden, Rose Medallion, 556;
  hall, 256
SEBASTIAN MINIATURES, 620
Secretary, 259-60
Sector, 719
Seder set, silver, 638
Seed box, 49
Seed packet, Disneyana, 191
Seeder, raisin, 338
SEG. See Paul Revere
Seltzer bottle, 45
Server, 260. See also Salver; and specific types
Serving dish: Canton, 79. See also specific types
Serving table, 268
Settee, 260-61
Settle, 262
SEVRES, 621
SEWER TILE, 621
SEWING, 621-23
Sewing basket, 26, 621; Indian, 309; Shaker, 623
Sewing bird, 621
Sewing box, Shaker, 623
Sewing caddy, 621; Shaker, 624
Sewing kit, 622; scrimshaw, 620; Shaker, 624

Sewing machine, 622; toy, 739
Sewing stand, 262
Sewing table, 268
Sextant, 402
SHAKER, 623-25. See also under Furniture; and specific
  categories of objects
Sharpener: knife, 53, 329, 338; saw, 720
Sharpening stone, 720
Shaving mirror, 258; brass, 54; celluloid, 107
SHAVING MUG, 625; graniteware, 282; ironstone, 314;
  luster, 366; moss rose, 390; Nippon, 412; redware,
  549; RS Germany, 597; RS Prussia, 601
Shaving set: celluloid, 107; silver, 637
Shaving stand, 262
Shawl, 700
SHAWNEE, 625-27
Shears: glassblower's, 720; tailor's, 622. See also
  Scissors
Sheep bell, 29
Sheet, 700
Sheet music, 397; Boy Scout, 50; Elvis Presley, 212;
  Mickey Mouse, 191; Shirley Temple, 628; We Want
  Willkie, 459
Shelf, 8, 262; Cordey, 141; majolica, 368
Sherbet. See specific makers and materials
Ship. See Nautical
Shoe chest, 250
Shoe last, 720
Shoe polish box, Howdy Doody, 300
Shoehorn: brass, 54; celluloid, 107; ivory, 316;
  scrimshaw, 620; Shinola, 677; silver, 631
Shoes, 700; baby, 694
Shoeshine box, 49
Shoeshine stand, 54
Shooting gallery, 739; figures, folk art, 228; game, 274
Shot glass: Coca-Cola, 133; Jack Daniels, 677; Lenox,
  355; ruby glass, 606; Tiffany glass, 705
Shotgun, 285; cleaning rod, 716
Shovel, fireplace, 221
Shrimp cocktail, Cambridge, 70
Shrimp dish, Crown Derby, 146
Shuttle, tatting, 622
Sideboard, 262
Sidelight, auto, 11
Sieve: horsehair, 338; winnowing, 720
Sifter, 338
Sign: Coca-Cola, 133; Frankoma, 234; railroad, 545;
  Rookwood, 553; store, 677-81; Weller pottery, 772
Signal, railroad, 545